STATUTORY

INSTRUMENTS

1976

PART I

(in two Sections)

SECTION 1

Published by Authority

LONDON
HER MAJESTY'S STATIONERY OFFICE
1976

PRINTED AND PUBLISHED BY HER MAJESTY'S STATIONERY OFFICE

To be purchased from

49 High Holborn, LONDON, WC1V 6HB

13a Castle Street, EDINBURGH, EH2 3AR   41 The Hayes, CARDIFF, CF1 1JW

Brazennose Street, MANCHESTER, M60 8AS   Southey House, Wine Street, BRISTOL, BS1 2BQ

258 Broad Street, BIRMINGHAM, B1 2HE   80 Chichester Street, BELFAST, BT1 4JY

or through booksellers

1976

Price for the two Sections: £26.50 net

PRINTED IN ENGLAND

ISBN 0 11 840149 1*

Contents of the Volume

PART I
Section 1

Section 2

PART II

PART III

Preface

Scope and arrangement of the Annual Volume

1. The Annual Volume gives the full text of the statutory instruments (**a**) registered in the year 1976 which were classified as general, and gives particulars of those which were classified as local (**b**). Certain other instruments are contained in the Appendix (as to which see paragraph 3 below).

2. The general instruments are arranged according to their S.I. numbers (**c**), that is to say, in the order of their registration as statutory instruments. The volume is published in three Parts, containing the instruments registered between 1st January and 30th April, 1st May and 31st August, and 1st September and 31st December respectively.

Contents of the Annual Volume

3. **Parts I and II.** At the beginning of each of these Parts is a list of the instruments whose text is contained in that Part, showing their S.I. numbers and titles. The list is followed by the text of the statutory instruments registered in the relevant period and an **Appendix of certain Instruments not registered as Statutory Instruments** issued in that period. This Appendix includes Orders in Council issued under the royal prerogative or otherwise outside the definition of a statutory instrument, Royal Proclamations which are of a legislative nature, and Letters Patent and Royal Instructions which relate to the constitutions etc. of overseas territories.

At the end of each Part is a Table showing the modifications to legislation and an Index. Each Table gives particulars of those Acts and instruments which have been affected by instruments in the Part or Parts. The Index and Table in Part II is cumulative, covering both Parts.

4. **Part III.** At the beginning is a list of the instruments in Part III followed by the text of those instruments.

At the end of Part III are the features which are required by regulation 10 of the Statutory Instruments Regulations 1947 to be included in the Annual Volume of Statutory Instruments. They cover the instruments in all three Parts. In the order in which they occur in the Volume, they are as follows:—

The **Classified List of Local Instruments** gives particulars, including the S.I. numbers, of all local statutory instruments registered in the statutory instrument series of the year to which the Annual Volume relates. They are grouped in classes according to their subject-matter.

The **Tables.** Table A gives particulars of the Acts of Parliament and Table B

(**a**) As to Orders in Council made under s. 1(3) of the Northern Ireland (Temporary Provisions) Act 1972 (c. 22), and para. 1 of sch. 1 to the Northern Ireland Act 1974, (c.28), see para. 4A below.

(**b**) *See* Statutory Instruments Regulations 1947 (S.I. 1948/1 (Rev. XXI, p. 498: 1948 I, p. 4002)), reg. 4 of which provides that S.I. which are in the nature of public general Acts of Parliament shall be classified as general and those which are in the nature of local and personal or private Acts shall be classified as local.

(**c**) Reg. 3 of the Statutory Instruments Regulations 1947 provides for instruments to be numbered in a separate series for each calendar year. Certain instruments bear also a subsidiary number—

C.   Commencement Orders (bringing an Act or part of an Act into operation).

L.   Instruments relating to fees or procedure in courts in England or Wales.

N.I.   Orders in Council made under s. 1(3) of the Northern Ireland (Temporary Provisions) Act 1972, and para. 1 of sch. 1 to the Northern Ireland Act 1974.

S.   Instruments made by a Scottish rule-making authority and applying to Scotland only.

particulars of statutory and other instruments, the operation of which was affected by the instruments appearing in the Volume. They include the information as to amendments, repeals, revocations, etc., already given in tables of Modifications to Legislation in Parts I and II and corresponding information with respect to the instruments in Part III. In addition, Table B gives particulars of general instruments whose operation was affected expressly by Public General Acts of the year in question, or which ceased to operate through becoming spent during that year as a result of legislation of the year.

The **Numerical and Issue List** gives particulars of all statutory instruments which were printed and put on sale by the Queen's Printer of Acts of Parliament under the provisions of the Statutory Instruments Act 1946 (**a**) during the year, with, in each case, the date of first issue by Her Majesty's Stationery Office.

The **Index** is cumulative, covering all three Parts of the Volume.

4A. **Northern Ireland.** Orders in Council under section 1(3) of the Northern Ireland (Temporary Provisions) Act 1972 (**b**) are excluded pursuant to the Statutory Instruments (Amendment) Regulations 1972 (**c**); Orders in Council made under paragraph 1 of schedule 1 to the Northern Ireland Act 1974 (**d**) are excluded pursuant to sub-paragraph (8) of that paragraph. All such Orders in Council are included in the annual volumes of Northern Ireland Statutes. Particulars are given in the Numerical and Issue List in Part III of this volume.

Definition of a statutory instrument

5. To determine whether or not any instrument is required to be a statutory instrument, reference must be made to section 1 of the Statutory Instruments Act 1946, regulation 2 of the Statutory Instruments Regulations 1947, and article 1 of the Statutory Instruments (Confirmatory Powers) Order 1947 (**e**).

The definition of what constitutes a statutory instrument, as respects instruments made under Acts passed before the commencement (1st January 1948) of the 1946 Act, is governed by definitions contained in the Rules Publication Act 1893 (**f**) (which was repealed and replaced by the 1946 Act); as respects those made under Acts passed after the commencement of the 1946 Act, the document is a statutory instrument if it is an Order in Council or if it is made by a Minister of the Crown and the Act provides that the power is to be exercisable by statutory instrument.

Citation

6. For the purposes of citation, statutory instruments are given a title. In addition, all statutory instruments may be identified by the year and number. The first instrument in Part I of this Volume would, by this method, be cited as " S.I. 1976/1". When a statutory instrument is referred to in another statutory instrument, a lettered footnote is provided in the latter, giving the identification of the first instrument as above, and also its Part and page reference in the Annual Volume. The footnote reference for the same instrument would therefore be "S.I. 1976/1 (1976 I, p. 1)".

(**a**) 1946 c. 36. (**b**) 1972 c. 22. (**c**) S.I. 1972/1205 (1972 II, p. 3571).
(**d**) 1974 c. 28. (**e**) S.I. 1948/2 (Rev. XXI, p. 504: 1948 I, p. 4008). (**f**) 1893 c. 66.

If the text of the instrument is set out in the third edition (published 1949–1952) of *Statutory Rules and Orders and Statutory Instruments, Revised,* the footnote references give the volume reference in that edition as well as the page reference in the Annual Volume (see for example footnote (e), page vi). If a footnote contains the references of a number of instruments, they may in certain circumstances be run together, so as to give all the instrument numbers together and all the volume references together, e.g. "S.R. & O. 1946/157; S.I. 1948/1073, 1961/1942 (1946 II, p. 26; 1948 II, p. 13; 1961 III, p. 2650)".

Production in Court

7. Under section 2 of the Documentary Evidence Act 1868 (**a**), read with section 2 of the Documentary Evidence Act 1882 (**b**), *prima facie* evidence of any proclamation, order or regulation made by certain rule-making authorities may be given in courts of justice by production of a copy purporting to be printed by the Government Printer or under the superintendence or authority of Her Majesty's Stationery Office. The Act of 1868 has since been extended by numerous Acts (**c**) to rules, etc., made thereunder by other rule-making authorities. The copies of proclamations, orders, regulations, etc., made by the authorities referred to above, as printed in these volumes, may therefore be produced as *prima facie* evidence.

Information on statutory instruments

8. The *Index to Government Orders* contains, under subject headings, summaries of all powers to make subordinate legislation conferred by statute on Her Majesty in Council, the Privy Council, government departments and certain other public bodies. Below each summary appear particulars of any general instruments, made in exercise of the power, which were in force at the date of publication of the *Index*. Details are also given of certain instruments made under prerogative powers. The work contains also a Table of Statutes showing the subject headings under which references to particular sections of enabling Acts appear. The *Index* is published every two or three years by H.M.S.O.

9. Information as to whether any instrument is still in operation, or whether anything has happened to it since it was made, can be obtained from the *Table of Government Orders*. This Table lists general statutory rules and orders and statutory instruments in numerical order, and gives the history of those which have been affected (i.e. revoked, amended, etc.) by subsequent legislation, whether statute or subordinate legislation, identifying the Act or instrument in question. Where any instrument has been amended, the Table gives particulars of the article, section, rule, etc., affected. A user who is interested in one particular provision only of the earlier instrument can thus ascertain whether or not he need consult the text of the amending enactment. The *Table of Government Orders* is published annually by H.M.S.O. and is cumulative. A Noter-Up is issued once or twice yearly.

Authority for Publication

10. The Annual Volumes of Statutory Instruments are published in pursuance of regulation 10 of the Statutory Instruments Regulations 1947 and are prepared

---

under the direction of the Statute Law Committee. Any suggestion or communication relating to their contents should be addressed to the Editor, Statutory Publications Office, 12 Buckingham Gate, London SW1E 6LJ.

Abbreviations

Addnl. Instructions	... ...	Additional Instructions.
A.S....	...	Act of Sederunt.
am., amdg, amdt....	...	amended, amending, amendment.
appx.	...	appendix.
art(s).	...	article(s).
authy.	...	authority.
bd(s).	...	board(s).
c.	...	chapter(s).
cl(s).	...	clause(s).
Cmd., Cmnd.	...	Command Paper.
Commn.	...	Commission.
cont.	...	continued.
ct(s).	...	court(s).
ctee.	...	committee.
E.	...	England.
exc.	...	except, excepted.
excl.	...	excluded.
expl.	...	explained.
ext.	...	extended, extension.
G.B.	...	Great Britain.
gen.	...	generally.
govt.	...	government.
H.C.	...	House of Commons Paper.
H.M.	...	Her Majesty, Her Majesty's.
I.	...	Ireland.
incl.	...	included, including.
instrt.	...	instrument.
Is.	...	Island(s), Isle(s).
L.P....	...	Letters Patent.
Min(s).	...	Minister(s).
misc.	...	miscellaneous.
mod., mod(s).	...	modified, modification(s).
N.	...	North.
N.I.	...	Northern Ireland.
No.	...	number.
O.	...	Order(s).
O. in C., O. of C....	...	Order(s) in Council, Order(s) of Council.
p., pp.	...	page(s).
para(s).	...	paragraph(s).
prerog.	...	prerogative.
prosp.	...	prospectively.
prov.	...	provisional, proviso.
provn(s).	...	provision(s).
pt.	...	part.
r.	...	repealed, revoked.
R.C.	...	Rules of the Court of Session.
R. Instructions ...	...	Royal Instructions.
R. Warrant	...	Royal Warrant.
reg(s).	...	regulation(s).
restr.	...	restricted.
retrosp.	...	retrospectively.
Rev.	...	Statutory Rules and Orders and Statutory Instruments Revised (Third Edition, 1948).
Rev. 1903	...	Statutory Rules and Orders (Second Revised Edition, 1903).
revn.	...	revocation.
S.	...	Scotland.
s., ss.	...	section(s).
S.I.	...	Statutory Instrument(s).
S.R. & O.	...	Statutory Rule(s) and Order(s).
sch(s).	...	schedule(s).
Secy.	...	Secretary.
susp.	...	suspended.

temp.	...	...	...	...	temporarily, temporary.
transfd.	...	...	...	...	transferred.
Treas.	...	...	...	...	Treasury.
U.K.	...	...	...	...	United Kingdom of Great Britain and Northern Ireland.
vol. ...	...	...	...	...	volume.
W. ...	...	...	...	...	Wales.

Statutory Instruments in Part I

xi

OTHER INSTRUMENTS IN PART I

STATUTORY INSTRUMENTS

1976 No. 1

SOCIAL SECURITY

The Social Security (Contributions, Re-rating) Consequential Amendment Regulations 1976

Made - - - -	*2nd January* 1976
Laid before Parliament	*14th January* 1976
Coming into Operation	*6th April* 1976

The Secretary of State for Social Services, in exercise of the powers conferred upon her by section 129 of, and paragraph 4(*a*) of Schedule 1 to, the Social Security Act 1975(**a**) and of all other powers enabling her in that behalf, hereby makes the following regulations which are made for the purpose of making provision consequential on, and contain only provisions in consequence of, the Social Security (Contributions, Re-rating) Order 1975(**b**).

Citation, interpretation and commencement

1. These regulations, which may be cited as the Social Security (Contributions, Re-rating) Consequential Amendment Regulations 1976, shall be read as one with the Social Security (Contributions) Regulations 1975(**c**) (hereinafter referred to as "the principal regulations") and shall come into operation on 6th April 1976.

Amendment of regulations 1(2) *and* 77 *of the principal regulations*

2. In regulations 1(2) and 77 of the principal regulations (interpretation) there shall in each of those regulations be inserted at the appropriate point the following definition—

' "The Re-rating Order 1975" means the Social Security (Contributions, Re-rating) Order 1975'.

Amendment of regulation 88 *of the principal regulations*

3. In regulation 88 of the principal regulations (special transitional provisions)—

(*a*) at the beginning of paragraph (2) there shall be inserted the words "Subject to the provisions of the next succeeding regulation,";

(*b*) in paragraph 3(*b*) (ii) after the words "the second of those two periods" there shall be inserted the words "and the payment of earnings is made before 6th April 1976".

(**a**) 1975 c. 14.
(**c**) S.I. 1975/492 (1975 I, p. 1516).

(**b**) S.I. 1975/1829 (1975 III, p. 6901).

Insertion of regulation 88A in the principal regulations

4. After regulation 88 of the principal regulations there shall be inserted the following regulation—

"*Transitional provisions consequent upon the Re-rating Order* 1975

88A. As respects any payment of earnings made on or after 6th April 1976 (the date on which the Re-rating Order 1975 comes into operation) to or for the benefit of a mariner for his employment as such during the voyage period, the provisions of the Re-rating Order 1975 shall not apply in the cases and to the extent specified in the next two succeeding paragraphs and in those cases the contributions payable shall be calculated as if the Re-rating Order 1975 had not been made: —

(*a*) in the case of employment during a voyage period which begins before 6th March 1976 and ends before 6th May 1976, to the extent of the whole of the earnings for that employment;

(*b*) in the case of employment during a voyage period which begins before 6th March 1976 and ends on or after 6th May 1976, to the extent of so much of the earnings as relates to that part of the employment which occurs before 6th April 1976."

Amendment of regulation 89 of the principal regulations

5. In regulation 89(*c*) of the principal regulations (modification in relation to share fishermen of Part I of the Act and so much of Part IV thereof as relates to contributions) for "£3·01" there shall be substituted "£3·21".

Substitution for Schedules 1, 4 and 6 to the principal regulations

6. For Schedules 1, 4 and 6 to the principal regulations (weekly and monthly scales of contributions under the Act at the standard rate and reduced rate and at the respective rates appropriate for mariners and members of the forces) there shall respectively be substituted the Schedules set out in Schedules A, B and C to these regulations.

Barbara Castle,

Secretary of State for Social Services.

2nd January 1976.

SCHEDULE A   Regulation 6
Substitution for Schedule 1 to the principal regulations

Schedule 1   Regulation 7
CONTRIBUTIONS UNDER THE ACT

PART I
WEEKLY SCALE

Column 1	Column 2	Column 3	Column 4
Payments of Earnings	Primary Contributions at Standard Rate	Primary Contributions at Reduced Rate	Secondary Contributions
£	£	£	£
13·00	0·76	0·26	1·16
13·50	0·79	0·27	1·20
14·00	0·82	0·28	1·25
14·50	0·85	0·29	1·29
15·00	0·88	0·30	1·33
15·50	0·91	0·31	1·38
16·00	0·93	0·32	1·42
16·50	0·96	0·33	1·47
17·00	0·99	0·34	1·51
17·50	1·02	0·35	1·55
18·00	1·05	0·36	1·60
18·50	1·08	0·37	1·64
19·00	1·11	0·38	1·68
19·50	1·14	0·39	1·73
20·00	1·16	0·40	1·77
20·50	1·19	0·41	1·82
21·00	1·22	0·42	1·86
21·50	1·25	0·43	1·90
22·00	1·28	0·44	1·95
22·50	1·31	0·45	1·99
23·00	1·34	0·46	2·03
23·50	1·37	0·47	2·08
24·00	1·39	0·48	2·12
24·50	1·42	0·49	2·17
25·00	1·45	0·50	2·21
25·50	1·48	0·51	2·25
26·00	1·51	0·52	2·30
26·50	1·54	0·53	2·34
27·00	1·57	0·54	2·38
27·50	1·60	0·55	2·43
28·00	1·62	0·56	2·47
28·50	1·65	0·57	2·52
29·00	1·68	0·58	2·56
29·50	1·71	0·59	2·60
30·00	1·74	0·60	2·65
30·50	1·77	0·61	2·69
31·00	1·80	0·62	2·73
31·50	1·83	0·63	2·78
32·00	1·85	0·64	2·82
32·50	1·88	0·65	2·87
33·00	1·91	0·66	2·91
33·50	1·94	0·67	2·95

PART I (*contd.*)

Column 1	Column 2	Column 3	Column 4
Payments of Earnings	Primary Contributions at Standard Rate	Primary Contributions at Reduced Rate	Secondary Contributions
£	£	£	£
34·00	1·97	0·68	3·00
34·50	2·00	0·69	3·04
35·00	2·03	0·70	3·08
35·50	2·06	0·71	3·13
36·00	2·08	0·72	3·17
36·50	2·11	0·73	3·22
37·00	2·14	0·74	3·26
37·50	2·17	0·75	3·30
38·00	2·20	0·76	3·35
38·50	2·23	0·77	3·39
39·00	2·26	0·78	3·43
39·50	2·29	0·79	3·48
40·00	2·31	0·80	3·52
40·50	2·34	0·81	3·57
41·00	2·37	0·82	3·61
41·50	2·40	0·83	3·65
42·00	2·43	0·84	3·70
42·50	2·46	0·85	3·74
43·00	2·49	0·86	3·78
43·50	2·52	0·87	3·83
44·00	2·54	0·88	3·87
44·50	2·57	0·89	3·92
45·00	2·60	0·90	3·96
45·50	2·63	0·91	4·00
46·00	2·66	0·92	4·05
46·50	2·69	0·93	4·09
47·00	2·72	0·94	4·13
47·50	2·75	0·95	4·18
48·00	2·77	0·96	4·22
48·50	2·80	0·97	4·27
49·00	2·83	0·98	4·31
49·50	2·86	0·99	4·35
50·00	2·89	1·00	4·40
50·50	2·92	1·01	4·44
51·00	2·95	1·02	4·48
51·50	2·98	1·03	4·53
52·00	3·00	1·04	4·57
52·50	3·03	1·05	4·62
53·00	3·06	1·06	4·66
53·50	3·09	1·07	4·70
54·00	3·12	1·08	4·75
54·50	3·15	1·09	4·79
55·00	3·18	1·10	4·83
55·50	3·21	1·11	4·88
56·00	3·23	1·12	4·92
56·50	3·26	1·13	4·97
57·00	3·29	1·14	5·01
57·50	3·32	1·15	5·05
58·00	3·35	1·16	5·10
58·50	3·38	1·17	5·14

PART I (contd.)

Column 1	Column 2	Column 3	Column 4
Payments of Earnings	Primary Contributions at Standard Rate	Primary Contributions at Reduced Rate	Secondary Contributions
£	£	£	£
59·00	3·41	1·18	5·18
59·50	3·44	1·19	5·23
60·00	3·46	1·20	5·27
60·50	3·49	1·21	5·32
61·00	3·52	1·22	5·36
61·50	3·55	1·23	5·40
62·00	3·58	1·24	5·45
62·50	3·61	1·25	5·49
63·00	3·64	1·26	5·53
63·50	3·67	1·27	5·58
64·00	3·69	1·28	5·62
64·50	3·72	1·29	5·67
65·00	3·75	1·30	5·71
65·50	3·78	1·31	5·75
66·00	3·81	1·32	5·80
66·50	3·84	1·33	5·84
67·00	3·87	1·34	5·88
67·50	3·90	1.35	5·93
68·00	3·92	1·36	5·97
68·50	3·95	1·37	6·02
69·00	3·98	1·38	6·06
69·50	4·01	1·39	6·10
70·00	4·04	1·40	6·15
70·50	4·07	1·41	6·19
71·00	4·10	1·42	6·23
71·50	4·13	1·43	6·28
72·00	4·15	1·44	6·32
72·50	4·18	1·45	6·37
73·00	4·21	1·46	6·41
73·50	4·24	1·47	6·45
74·00	4·27	1·48	6·50
74·50	4·30	1·49	6·54
75·00	4·33	1·50	6·58
75·50	4·36	1·51	6·63
76·00	4·38	1·52	6·67
76·50	4·41	1·53	6·72
77·00	4·44	1·54	6·76
77·50	4·47	1·55	6·80
78·00	4·50	1·56	6·85
78·50	4·53	1·57	6·89
79·00	4·56	1·58	6·93
79·50	4·59	1·59	6·98
80·00	4·61	1·60	7·02
80·50	4·64	1·61	7·07
81·00	4·67	1·62	7·11
81·50	4·70	1·63	7·15
82·00	4·73	1·64	7·20
82·50	4·76	1·65	7·24
83·00	4·79	1·66	7·28
83·50	4·82	1·67	7·33

PART I (contd.)

Column 1	Column 2	Column 3	Column 4
Payments of Earnings	Primary Contributions at Standard Rate	Primary Contributions at Reduced Rate	Secondary Contributions
£	£	£	£
84·00	4·84	1·68	7·37
84·50	4·87	1·69	7·42
85·00	4·90	1·70	7·46
85·50	4·93	1·71	7·50
86·00	4·96	1·72	7·55
86·50	4·99	1·73	7·59
87·00	5·02	1·74	7·63
87·50	5·05	1·75	7·68
88·00	5·07	1·76	7·72
88·50	5·10	1·77	7·77
89·00	5·13	1·78	7·81
89·50	5·16	1·79	7·85
90·00	5·19	1·80	7·90
90·50	5·22	1·81	7·94
91·00	5·25	1·82	7·98
91·50	5·28	1·83	8·03
92·00	5·30	1·84	8·07
92·50	5·33	1·85	8·12
93·00	5·36	1·86	8·16
93·50	5·39	1·87	8·20
94·00	5·42	1·88	8·25
94·50	5·45	1·89	8·29
95·00 or more	5·46	1·90	8·31

PART II

MONTHLY SCALE

Column 1	Column 2	Column 3	Column 4
Payments of Earnings	Primary Contributions at Standard Rate	Primary Contributions at Reduced Rate	Secondary Contributions
£	£	£	£
56·33	3·29	1·14	5·00
58·00	3·39	1·18	5·16
60·00	3·51	1·22	5·34
62·00	3·62	1·26	5·51
64·00	3·74	1·30	5·69
66·00	3·85	1·34	5·86
68·00	3·97	1·38	6·04
70·00	4·08	1·42	6·21
72·00	4·20	1·46	6·39
74·00	4·31	1·50	6·56
76·00	4·43	1·54	6·74
78·00	4·54	1·58	6·91
80·00	4·66	1·62	7·09
82·00	4·77	1·66	7·26
84·00	4·89	1·70	7·44
86·00	5·00	1·74	7·61
88·00	5·12	1·78	7·79
90·00	5·23	1·82	7·96
92·00	5·35	1·86	8·14
94·00	5·46	1·90	8·31
96·00	5·58	1·94	8·49
98·00	5·69	1·98	8·66
100·00	5·81	2·02	8·84
102·00	5·92	2·06	9·01
104·00	6·04	2·10	9·19
106·00	6·15	2·14	9·36
108·00	6·27	2·18	9·54
110·00	6·38	2·22	9·71
112·00	6·50	2·26	9·89
114·00	6·61	2·30	10·06
116·00	6·73	2·34	10·24
118·00	6·84	2·38	10·41
120·00	6·96	2·42	10·59
122·00	7·07	2·46	10·76
124·00	7·19	2·50	10·94
126·00	7·30	2·54	11·11
128·00	7·42	2·58	11·29
130·00	7·53	2·62	11·46
132·00	7·65	2·66	11·64
134·00	7·76	2·70	11·81
136·00	7·88	2·74	11·99
138·00	7·99	2·78	12·16
140·00	8·11	2·82	12·34
142·00	8·22	2·86	12·51
144·00	8·34	2·90	12·69
146·00	8·45	2·94	12·86
148·00	8·57	2·98	13·04

PART II (contd.)

Column 1	Column 2	Column 3	Column 4
Payments of Earnings	Primary Contributions at Standard Rate	Primary Contributions at Reduced Rate	Secondary Contributions
£	£	£	£
150·00	8·68	3·02	13·21
152·00	8·80	3·06	13·39
154·00	8·91	3·10	13·56
156·00	9·03	3·14	13·74
158·00	9·14	3·18	13·91
160·00	9·26	3·22	14·09
162·00	9·37	3·26	14·26
164·00	9·49	3·30	14·44
166·00	9·60	3·34	14·61
168·00	9·72	3·38	14·79
170·00	9·83	3·42	14·96
172·00	9·95	3·46	15·14
174·00	10·06	3·50	15·31
176·00	10·18	3·54	15·49
178·00	10·29	3·58	15·66
180·00	10·41	3·62	15·84
182·00	10·52	3·66	16·01
184·00	10·64	3·70	16·19
186·00	10·75	3·74	16·36
188·00	10·87	3·78	16·54
190·00	10·98	3·82	16·71
192·00	11·10	3·86	16·89
194·00	11·21	3·90	17·06
196·00	11·33	3·94	17·24
198·00	11·44	3·98	17·41
200·00	11·56	4·02	17·59
202·00	11·67	4·06	17·76
204·00	11·79	4·10	17·94
206·00	11·90	4·14	18·11
208·00	12·02	4·18	18·29
210·00	12·13	4·22	18·46
212·00	12·25	4·26	18·64
214·00	12·36	4·30	18·81
216·00	12·48	4·34	18·99
218·00	12·59	4·38	19·16
220·00	12·71	4·42	19·34
222·00	12·82	4·46	19·51
224·00	12·94	4·50	19·69
226·00	13·05	4·54	19·86
228·00	13·17	4·58	20·04
230·00	13·28	4·62	20·21
232·00	13·40	4·66	20·39
234·00	13·51	4·70	20·56
236·00	13·63	4·74	20·74
238·00	13·74	4·78	20·91
240·00	13·86	4·82	21·09
242·00	13·97	4·86	21·26
244·00	14·09	4·90	21·44
246·00	14·20	4·94	21·61
248·00	14·32	4·98	21·79

PART II (*contd.*)

Column 1	Column 2	Column 3	Column 4
Payments of Earnings	Primary Contributions at Standard Rate	Primary Contributions at Reduced Rate	Secondary Contributions
£	£	£	£
250·00	14·43	5·02	21·96
252·00	14·55	5·06	22·14
254·00	14·66	5·10	22·31
256·00	14·78	5·14	22·49
258·00	14·89	5·18	22·66
260·00	15·01	5·22	22·84
262·00	15·12	5·26	23·01
264·00	15·24	5·30	23·19
266·00	15·35	5·34	23·36
268·00	15·47	5·38	23·54
270·00	15·58	5·42	23·71
272·00	15·70	5·46	23·89
274·00	15·81	5·50	24·06
276·00	15·93	5·54	24·24
278·00	16·04	5·58	24·41
280·00	16·16	5·62	24·59
282·00	16·27	5·66	24·76
284·00	16·39	5·70	24·94
286·00	16·50	5·74	25·11
288·00	16·62	5·78	25·29
290·00	16·73	5·82	25·46
292·00	16·85	5·86	25·64
294·00	16·96	5·90	25·81
296·00	17·08	5·94	25·99
298·00	17·19	5·98	26·16
300·00	17·31	6·02	26·34
302·00	17·42	6·06	26·51
304·00	17·54	6·10	26·69
306·00	17·65	6·14	26·86
308·00	17·77	6·18	27·04
310·00	17·88	6·22	27·21
312·00	18·00	6·26	27·39
314·00	18·11	6·30	27·56
316·00	18·23	6·34	27·74
318·00	18·34	6·38	27·91
320·00	18·46	6·42	28·09
322·00	18·57	6·46	28·26
324·00	18·69	6·50	28·44
326·00	18·80	6·54	28·61
328·00	18·92	6·58	28·79
330·00	19·03	6·62	28·96
332·00	19·15	6·66	29·14
334·00	19·26	6·70	29·31
336·00	19·38	6·74	29·49
338·00	19·49	6·78	29·66
340·00	19·61	6·82	29·84
342·00	19·72	6·86	30·01
344·00	19·84	6·90	30·19
346·00	19·95	6·94	30·36
348·00	20·07	6·98	30·54

PART II (contd.)

Column 1	Column 2	Column 3	Column 4
Payments of Earnings	Primary Contributions at Standard Rate	Primary Contributions at Reduced Rate	Secondary Contributions
£	£	£	£
350·00	20·18	7·02	30·71
352·00	20·30	7·06	30·89
354·00	20·41	7·10	31·06
356·00	20·53	7·14	31·24
358·00	20·64	7·18	31·41
360·00	20·76	7·22	31·59
362·00	20·87	7·26	31·76
364·00	20·99	7·30	31·94
366·00	21·10	7·34	32·11
368·00	21·22	7·38	32·29
370·00	21·33	7·42	32·46
372·00	21·45	7·46	32·64
374·00	21·56	7·50	32·81
376·00	21·68	7·54	32·99
378·00	21·79	7·58	33·16
380·00	21·91	7·62	33·34
382·00	22·02	7·66	33·51
384·00	22·14	7·70	33·69
386·00	22·25	7·74	33·86
388·00	22·37	7·78	34·04
390·00	22·48	7·82	34·21
392·00	22·60	7·86	34·39
394·00	22·71	7·90	34·56
396·00	22·83	7·94	34·74
398·00	22·94	7·98	34·91
400·00	23·06	8·02	35·09
402·00	23·17	8·06	35·26
404·00	23·29	8·10	35·44
406·00	23·40	8·14	35·61
408·00	23·52	8·18	35·79
410·00	23·62	8·22	35·95
411·67 or more	23·67	8·23	36·02

SCHEDULE B Regulation 6
Substitution for Schedule 4 to the principal regulations

Schedule 4 Regulation 82(2)

SECONDARY CONTRIBUTIONS UNDER THE ACT AT RATES
REDUCED IN ACCORDANCE WITH REGULATION 80

PART I

WEEKLY SCALE

Column 1	Column 2	Column 3	Column 4
Payments of Earnings	Secondary Contributions at rate reduced in accordance with regulation 80(1)(a)	Secondary Contributions at rate reduced in accordance with regulation 80(1)(b)	Secondary Contributions at rate reduced in accordance with regulation 80(1)(a) and (b)
£	£	£	£
13·00	1·13	1·07	1·04
13·50	1·18	1·11	1·08
14·00	1·22	1·15	1·12
14·50	1·26	1·19	1·16
15·00	1·30	1·23	1·20
15·50	1·35	1·27	1·24
16·00	1·39	1·31	1·28
16·50	1·43	1·35	1·31
17·00	1·47	1·39	1·35
17·50	1·52	1·43	1·39
18·00	1·56	1·47	1·43
18·50	1·60	1·51	1·47
19·00	1·65	1·55	1·51
19·50	1·69	1·59	1·55
20·00	1·73	1·63	1·59
20·50	1·77	1·67	1·63
21·00	1·82	1·71	1·67
21.50	1·86	1·75	1·71
22·00	1·90	1·79	1·75
22·50	1·95	1·83	1·79
23·00	1·99	1·87	1·83
23·50	2·03	1·91	1·86
24·00	2·07	1·95	1·90
24·50	2·12	1·99	1·94
25·00	2·16	2·03	1·98
25·50	2·20	2·07	2·02
26·00	2·24	2·11	2·06
26·50	2·29	2·15	2·10
27·00	2·33	2·19	2·14
27·50	2·37	2·23	2·18
28·00	2·42	2·27	2·22
28·50	2·46	2·31	2·26
29·00	2·50	2·35	2·30
29·50	2·54	2·39	2·34
30·00	2·59	2·44	2·37
30·50	2·63	2·48	2·41
31·00	2·67	2·52	2·45

PART 1 (*contd.*)

Column 1	Column 2	Column 3	Column 4
Payments of Earnings	Secondary Contributions at rate reduced in accordance with regulation 80(1)(*a*)	Secondary Contributions at rate reduced in accordance with regulation 80(1)(*b*)	Secondary Contributions at rate reduced in accordance with regulation 80(1)(*a*) and (*b*)
£	£	£	£
31·50	2·71	2·56	2·49
32·00	2·76	2·60	2·53
32·50	2·80	2·64	2·57
33·00	2·84	2·68	2·61
33·50	2·89	2·72	2·65
34·00	2·93	2·76	2·69
34·50	2·97	2·80	2·73
35·00	3·01	2·84	2·77
35·50	3·06	2·88	2·81
36·00	3·10	2·92	2·85
36·50	3·14	2·96	2·88
37·00	3·18	3·00	2·92
37·50	3·23	3·04	2·96
38·00	3·27	3·08	3·00
38·50	3·31	3·12	3·04
39·00	3·36	3·16	3·08
39·50	3·40	3·20	3·12
40·00	3·44	3·24	3·16
40·50	3·48	3·28	3·20
41·00	3·53	3·32	3·24
41·50	3·57	3·36	3·28
42·00	3·61	3·40	3·32
42·50	3·66	3·44	3·36
43·00	3·70	3·48	3·40
43·50	3·74	3·52	3·43
44·00	3·78	3·56	3·47
44·50	3·83	3·60	3·51
45·00	3·87	3·64	3·55
45·50	3·91	3·68	3·59
46·00	3·95	3·72	3·63
46·50	4·00	3·76	3·67
47·00	4·04	3·80	3·71
47·50	4·08	3·84	3·75
48·00	4·13	3·88	3·79
48·50	4·17	3·92	3·83
49·00	4·21	3·96	3·87
49·50	4·25	4·00	3·91
50·00	4·30	4·05	3·94
50·50	4·34	4·09	3·98
51·00	4·38	4·13	4·02
51·50	4·42	4·17	4·06
52·00	4·47	4·21	4·10
52·50	4·51	4·25	4·14
53·00	4·55	4·29	4·18
53·50	4·60	4·33	4·22
54·00	4·64	4·37	4·26
54·50	4·68	4·41	4·30
55·00	4·72	4·45	4·34

PART I (*contd.*)

Column 1	Column 2	Column 3	Column 4
Payments of Earnings	Secondary Contributions at rate reduced in accordance with regulation 80(1)(*a*)	Secondary Contributions at rate reduced in accordance with regulation 80(1)(*b*)	Secondary Contributions at rate reduced in accordance with regulation 80(1)(*a*) and (*b*)
£	£	£	£
55·50	4·77	4·49	4·38
56·00	4·81	4·53	4·42
56·50	4·85	4·57	4·45
57·00	4·89	4·61	4·49
57·50	4·94	4·65	4·53
58·00	4·98	4·69	4·57
58·50	5·02	4·73	4·61
59·00	5·07	4·77	4·65
59·50	5·11	4·81	4·69
60·00	5·15	4·85	4·73
60·50	5·19	4·89	4·77
61·00	5·24	4·93	4·81
61·50	5·28	4·97	4·85
62·00	5·32	5·01	4·89
62·50	5·37	5·05	4·93
63·00	5·41	5·09	4·97
63·50	5·45	5·13	5·00
64·00	5·49	5·17	5·04
64·50	5·54	5·21	5·08
65·00	5·58	5·25	5·12
65·50	5·62	5·29	5·16
66·00	5·66	5·33	5·20
66·50	5·71	5·37	5·24
67·00	5·75	5·41	5·28
67·50	5·79	5·45	5·32
68·00	5·84	5·49	5·36
68·50	5·88	5·53	5·40
69·00	5·92	5·57	5·44
69·50	5·96	5·61	5·48
70·00	6·01	5·66	5·51
70·50	6·05	5·70	5·55
71·00	6·09	5·74	5·59
71·50	6·13	5·78	5·63
72·00	6·18	5·82	5·67
72·50	6·22	5·86	5·71
73·00	6·26	5·90	5·75
73·50	6·31	5·94	5·79
74·00	6·35	5·98	5·83
74·50	6·39	6·02	5·87
75·00	6·43	6·06	5·91
75·50	6·48	6·10	5·95
76·00	6·52	6·14	5·99
76·50	6·56	6·18	6·02
77·00	6·60	6·22	6·06
77·50	6·65	6·26	6·10
78·00	6·69	6·30	6·14
78·50	6·73	6·34	6·18
79·00	6·78	6·38	6·22

PART I *(contd.)*

Column 1	Column 2	Column 3	Column 4
Payments of Earnings	Secondary Contributions at rate reduced in accordance with regulation 80(1)(*a*)	Secondary Contributions at rate reduced in accordance with regulation 80(1)(*b*)	Secondary Contributions at rate reduced in accordance with regulation 80(1)(*a*) and (*b*)
£	£	£	£
79·50	6·82	6·42	6·26
80·00	6·86	6·46	6·30
80·50	6·90	6·50	6·34
81·00	6·95	6·54	6·38
81·50	6·99	6·58	6·42
82·00	7·03	6·62	6·46
82·50	7·08	6·66	6·50
83·00	7·12	6·70	6·54
83·50	7·16	6·74	6·57
84·00	7·20	6·78	6·61
84·50	7·25	6·82	6·65
85·00	7·29	6·86	6·69
85·50	7·33	6·90	6·73
86·00	7·37	6·94	6·77
86·50	7·42	6·98	6·81
87·00	7·46	7·02	6·85
87·50	7·50	7·06	6·89
88·00	7·55	7·10	6·93
88·50	7·59	7·14	6·97
89·00	7·63	7·18	7·01
89·50	7·67	7·22	7·05
90·00	7·72	7·27	7·08
90·50	7·76	7·31	7·12
91·00	7·80	7·35	7·16
91·50	7·84	7·39	7·20
92·00	7·89	7·43	7·24
92·50	7·93	7·47	7·28
93·00	7·97	7·51	7·32
93·50	8·02	7·55	7·36
94·00	8·06	7·59	7·40
94·50	8·10	7·63	7·44
95·00 or more	8·12	7·65	7·46

Part II

Monthly Scale

Column 1	Column 2	Column 3	Column 4
Payments of Earnings	Secondary Contributions at rate reduced in accordance with regulation 80(1)(a)	Secondary Contributions at rate reduced in accordance with regulation 80(1)(b)	Secondary Contributions at rate reduced in accordance with regulation 80(1)(a) and (b)
£	£	£	£
56·33	4·89	4·60	4·49
58·00	5·04	4·75	4·63
60·00	5·22	4·91	4·79
62·00	5·39	5·07	4·95
64·00	5·56	5·23	5·10
66·00	5·73	5·39	5·26
68·00	5·90	5·55	5·42
70·00	6·07	5·72	5·57
72·00	6·24	5·88	5·73
74·00	6·41	6·04	5·89
76·00	6·58	6·20	6·04
78·00	6·75	6·36	6·20
80·00	6·93	6·52	6·36
82·00	7·10	6·68	6·52
84·00	7·27	6·84	6·67
86·00	7·44	7·00	6·83
88·00	7·61	7·16	6·99
90·00	7·78	7·33	7·14
92·00	7·95	7·49	7·30
94·00	8·12	7·65	7·46
96·00	8·29	7·81	7·61
98·00	8·46	7·97	7·77
100·00	8·64	8·13	7·93
102·00	8·81	8·29	8·09
104·00	8·98	8·45	8·24
106·00	9·15	8·61	8·40
108·00	9·32	8·77	8·56
110·00	9·49	8·94	8·71
112.00	9·66	9·10	8·87
114·00	9·83	9·26	9·03
116·00	10·00	9·42	9·18
118·00	10·17	9·58	9·34
120·00	10·35	9·74	9·50
122·00	10·52	9·90	9·66
124·00	10·69	10·06	9·81
126·00	10·86	10·22	9·97
128·00	11·03	10·38	10·13
130·00	11·20	10·55	10·28
132·00	11·37	10·71	10·44
134·00	11·54	10·87	10·60
136·00	11.71	11·03	10·75
138·00	11·88	11·19	10·91
140·00	12·06	11·35	11·07
142·00	12·23	11·51	11·23
144·00	12·40	11·67	11·38

PART II (*contd.*)

Column 1	Column 2	Column 3	Column 4
Payments of Earnings	Secondary Contributions at rate reduced in accordance with regulation 80(1)(a)	Secondary Contributions at rate reduced in accordance with regulation 80(1)(b)	Secondary Contributions at rate reduced in accordance with regulation 80(1)(a) and (b)
£	£	£	£
146·00	12·57	11·83	11·54
148·00	12·74	11·99	11·70
150·00	12·91	12·16	11·85
152·00	13·08	12·32	12·01
154·00	13·25	12·48	12·17
156·00	13·42	12·64	12·32
158·00	13·59	12·80	12·48
160·00	13·77	12·96	12·64
162·00	13·94	13·12	12·80
164·00	14·11	13·28	12·95
166·00	14·28	13·44	13·11
168·00	14·45	13·60	13·27
170·00	14·62	13·77	13·42
172·00	14·79	13·93	13·58
174·00	14·96	14·09	13·74
176·00	15·13	14·25	13·89
178·00	15·30	14·41	14·05
180·00	15·48	14·57	14·21
182·00	15·65	14·73	14·37
184·00	15·82	14·89	14·52
186·00	15·99	15·05	14·68
188·00	16·16	15·21	14·84
190·00	16·33	15·38	14·99
192·00	16·50	15·54	15·15
194·00	16·67	15·70	15·31
196·00	16·84	15·86	15·46
198·00	17·01	16·02	15·62
200·00	17·19	16·18	15·78
202·00	17·36	16·34	15·94
204·00	17·53	16·50	16·09
206·00	17·70	16·66	16·25
208·00	17·87	16·82	16·41
210·00	18·04	16·99	16·56
212·00	18·21	17·15	16·72
214·00	18·38	17·31	16·88
216·00	18·55	17·47	17·03
218·00	18·72	17·63	17·19
220·00	18·90	17·79	17·35
222·00	19·07	17·95	17·51
224·00	19·24	18·11	17·66
226·00	19·41	18·27	17·82
228·00	19·58	18·43	17·98
230·00	19·75	18·60	18·13
232.00	19·92	18·76	18·29
234·00	20·09	18·92	18·45
236·00	20·26	19·08	18·60
238·00	20·43	19·24	18·76
240·00	20·61	19·40	18·92

PART II (contd.)

Column 1	Column 2	Column 3	Column 4
Payments of Earnings	Secondary Contributions at rate reduced in accordance with regulation 80(1)(a)	Secondary Contributions at rate reduced in accordance with regulation 80(1)(b)	Secondary Contributions at rate reduced in accordance with regulation 80(1)(a) and (b)
£	£	£	£
242·00	20·78	19·56	19·08
244·00	20·95	19·72	19·23
246·00	21·12	19·88	19·39
248·00	21·29	20·04	19·55
250·00	21·46	20·21	19·70
252·00	21·63	20·37	19·86
254·00	21·80	20·53	20·02
256·00	21·97	20·69	20·17
258·00	22·14	20·85	20·33
260·00	22·32	21·01	20·49
262·00	22·49	21·17	20·65
264·00	22·66	21·33	20·80
266·00	22·83	21·49	20·96
268·00	23·00	21·65	21·12
270·00	23·17	21·82	21·27
272·00	23·34	21·98	21·43
274·00	23·51	22·14	21·59
276·00	23·68	22·30	21·74
278·00	23·85	22·46	21·90
280·00	24·03	22·62	22·06
282·00	24·20	22·78	22·22
284·00	24·37	22·94	22·37
286·00	24·54	23·10	22·53
288·00	24·71	23·26	22·69
290·00	24·88	23·43	22·84
292·00	25·05	23·59	23·00
294·00	25·22	23·75	23·16
296·00	25·39	23·91	23·31
298·00	25·56	24·07	23·47
300·00	25·74	24·23	23·63
302·00	25·91	24·39	23·79
304·00	26·08	24·55	23·94
306·00	26·25	24·71	24·10
308·00	26·42	24·87	24·26
310·00	26·59	25·04	24·41
312·00	26·76	25·20	24·57
314·00	26·93	25·36	24·73
316·00	27·10	25·52	24·88
318·00	27·27	25·68	25·04
320·00	27·45	25·84	25·20
322·00	27·62	26·00	25·36
324·00	27·79	26·16	25·51
326·00	27·96	26·32	25·67
328·00	28·13	26·48	25·83
330·00	28·30	26·65	25·98
332·00	28·47	26·81	26·14
334·00	28·64	26·97	26·30
336·00	28·81	27·13	26·45

PART II (*contd.*)

Column 1	Column 2	Column 3	Column 4
Payments of Earnings	Secondary Contributions at rate reduced in accordance with regulation 80(1)(*a*)	Secondary Contributions at rate reduced in accordance with regulation 80(1)(*b*)	Secondary Contributions at rate reduced in accordance with regulation 80(1)(*a*) and (*b*)
£	£	£	£
338·00	28·98	27·29	26·61
340·00	29·16	27·45	26·77
342·00	29·33	27·61	26·93
344·00	29·50	27·77	27·08
346·00	29·67	27·93	27·24
348·00	29·84	28·09	27·40
350·00	30·01	28·26	27·55
352·00	30·18	28·42	27·71
354·00	30·35	28·58	27·87
356·00	30·52	28·74	28·02
358·00	30·69	28·90	28·18
360·00	30·87	29·06	28·34
362·00	31·04	29·22	28·50
364·00	31·21	29·38	28·65
366·00	31·38	29·54	28·81
368·00	31·55	29·70	28·97
370·00	31·72	29·87	29·12
372·00	31·89	30·03	29·28
374·00	32·06	30·19	29·44
376·00	32·23	30·35	29·59
378·00	32·40	30·51	29·75
380·00	32·58	30·67	29·91
382·00	32·75	30·83	30·07
384·00	32·92	30·99	30·22
386·00	33·09	31·15	30·38
388·00	33·26	31·31	30·54
390·00	33·43	31·48	30·69
392·00	33·60	31·64	30·85
394·00	33·77	31·80	31·01
396·00	33·94	31·96	31·16
398·00	34·11	32·12	31·32
400·00	34·29	32·28	31·48
402·00	34·46	32·44	31·64
404·00	34·63	32·60	31·79
406·00	34·80	32·76	31·95
408·00	34·97	32·92	32·11
410·00	35·13	33·07	32·25
411·67 or more	35·20	33·14	32·32

SCHEDULE C   Regulation 6
Substitution for Schedule 6 to the principal regulations

Schedule 6   Regulation 109(3)

PRESCRIBED SCALES OF CONTRIBUTIONS UNDER THE ACT
FOR MEMBERS OF THE FORCES CALCULATED IN ACCORDANCE
WITH REGULATION 109(3) OF THESE REGULATIONS

PART I

WEEKLY SCALE

Column 1	Column 2	Column 3	Column 4
Payments of Earnings	Primary Contributions at rate reduced in accordance with regulation 109(1)(a)(i)	Primary Contributions at rate reduced in accordance with regulation 109(1)(a)(ii)	Secondary Contributions
£	£	£	£
13·00	0·66	0·24	0·98
13·50	0·68	0·25	1·02
14·00	0·71	0·26	1·05
14·50	0·73	0·27	1·09
15·00	0·75	0·27	1·13
15·50	0·78	0·28	1·17
16·00	0·80	0·29	1·20
16·50	0·83	0·30	1·24
17·00	0·85	0·31	1·28
17·50	0·88	0·32	1·31
18·00	0·90	0·33	1·35
18·50	0·93	0·34	1·39
19·00	0·95	0·35	1·42
19·50	0·98	0·36	1·46
20·00	1·00	0·36	1·50
20·50	1·03	0·37	1·54
21·00	1·05	0·38	1·57
21·50	1·08	0·39	1·61
22·00	1·10	0·40	1·65
22·50	1·13	0·41	1·68
23·00	1·15	0·42	1·72
23·50	1·18	0·43	1·76
24·00	1·20	0·44	1·79
24·50	1·23	0·45	1·83
25·00	1·25	0·45	1·87
25·50	1·27	0·46	1·91
26·00	1·30	0·47	1·94
26·50	1·32	0·48	1·98
27·00	1·35	0·49	2·02
27·50	1·37	0·50	2·05
28·00	1·40	0·51	2·09
28·50	1·42	0·52	2·13
29·00	1·45	0·53	2·16
29·50	1·47	0·54	2·20
30·00	1·50	0·54	2·24

PART I (contd.)

Column 1	Column 2	Column 3	Column 4
Payments of Earnings	Primary Contributions at rate reduced in accordance with regulation 109(1)(a)(i)	Primary Contributions at rate reduced in accordance with regulation 109(1)(a)(ii)	Secondary Contributions
£	£	£	£
30·50	1·52	0·55	2·28
31·00	1·55	0·56	2·31
31·50	1·57	0·57	2.35
32·00	1·60	0·58	2·39
32·50	1·62	0·59	2·42
33·00	1·65	0·60	2·46
33·50	1·67	0·61	2·50
34·00	1·70	0·62	2·53
34·50	1·72	0·63	2·57
35·00	1·74	0·63	2·61
35·50	1·77	0·64	2·65
36·00	1·79	0·65	2·68
36·50	1·82	0·66	2·72
37·00	1·84	0·67	2·76
37·50	1·87	0·68	2·79
38·00	1·89	0·69	2·83
38·50	1·92	0·70	2·87
39·00	1·94	0·71	2·90
39·50	1·97	0·72	2·94
40·00	1·99	0·72	2·98
40·50	2·02	0·73	3·02
41·00	2·04	0·74	3·05
41·50	2·07	0·75	3·09
42·00	2·09	0·76	3·13
42·50	2·12	0·77	3·16
43·00	2·14	0·78	3·20
43·50	2·17	0·79	3·24
44·00	2·19	0·80	3·27
44·50	2·22	0·81	3·31
45·00	2·24	0·81	3·35
45·50	2·26	0·82	3·39
46·00	2·29	0·83	3·42
46·50	2·31	0·84	3·46
47·00	2·34	0·85	3·50
47·50	2·36	0·86	3·53
48·00	2·39	0·87	3·57
48·50	2·41	0·88	3·61
49·00	2·44	0·89	3·64
49·50	2·46	0·90	3·68
50·00	2·49	0·90	3·72
50·50	2·51	0·91	3·76
51·00	2·54	0·92	3·79
51·50	2·56	0·93	3·83
52·00	2·59	0·94	3·87
52.50	2.61	0·95	3·90
53·00	2·64	0·96	3·94
53·50	2·66	0·97	3·98

PART I (*contd.*)

Column 1	Column 2	Column 3	Column 4
Payments of Earnings	Primary Contributions at rate reduced in accordance with regulation 109(1)(a)(i)	Primary Contributions at rate reduced in accordance with regulation 109(1)(a)(ii)	Secondary Contributions
£	£	£	£
54·00	2·69	0·98	4·01
54·50	2·71	0·99	4·05
55·00	2·73	0·99	4·09
55·50	2·76	1·00	4·13
56·00	2·78	1·01	4·16
56·50	2·81	1·02	4·20
57·00	2·83	1·03	4·24
57·50	2·86	1·04	4·27
58·00	2·88	1·05	4·31
58·50	2·91	1·06	4·35
59·00	2·93	1·07	4·38
59·50	2·96	1·08	4·42
60·00	2·98	1·08	4·46
60·50	3·01	1·09	4·50
61·00	3·03	1·10	4·53
61·50	3·06	1·11	4·57
62·00	3·08	1·12	4·61
62·50	3·11	1·13	4·64
63·00	3·13	1·14	4·68
63·50	3·16	1·15	4·72
64·00	3·18	1·16	4·75
64·50	3·21	1·17	4·79
65·00	3·23	1·17	4·83
65·50	3·25	1·18	4·87
66·00	3·28	1·19	4·90
66·50	3·30	1·20	4·94
67·00	3·33	1·21	4·98
67·50	3·35	1·22	5·01
68·00	3·38	1·23	5·05
68·50	3·40	1·24	5·09
69.00	3·43	1·25	5·12
69·50	3·45	1·26	5·16
70·00	3·48	1·26	5·20
70·50	3·50	1·27	5·24
71·00	3·53	1·28	5·27
71·50	3·55	1·29	5·31
72·00	3·58	1·30	5·35
72·50	3·60	1·31	5·38
73·00	3·63	1·32	5·42
73·50	3·65	1·33	5·46
74·00	3·68	1·34	5·49
74·50	3·70	1·35	5·53
75·00	3·72	1·35	5·57
75·50	3·75	1·36	5·61
76·00	3·77	1·37	5·64
76·50	3·80	1·38	5·68
77·00	3·82	1·39	5·72

PART I (contd.)

Column 1	Column 2	Column 3	Column 4
Payments of Earnings	Primary Contributions at rate reduced in accordance with regulation 109(1)(a)(i)	Primary Contributions at rate reduced in accordance with regulation 109(1)(a)(ii)	Secondary Contributions
£	£	£	£
77·50	3·85	1·40	5·75
78·00	3·87	1·41	5·79
78·50	3·90	1·42	5·83
79·00	3·92	1·43	5·86
79·50	3·95	1·44	5·90
80·00	3·97	1·44	5·94
80·50	4·00	1·45	5·98
81·00	4·02	1·46	6·01
81·50	4·05	1·47	6·05
82·00	4·07	1·48	6·09
82·50	4·10	1·49	6·12
83·00	4·12	1·50	6·16
83·50	4·15	1·51	6·20
84·00	4·17	1·52	6·23
84·50	4·20	1·53	6·27
85·00	4·22	1·53	6·31
85·50	4·24	1·54	6·35
86·00	4·27	1·55	6·38
86·50	4·29	1·56	6·42
87·00	4·32	1·57	6·46
87·50	4·34	1·58	6·49
88·00	4·37	1·59	6·53
88·50	4·39	1·60	6·57
89·00	4·42	1·61	6·60
89·50	4·44	1·62	6·64
90·00	4·47	1·62	6·68
90·50	4·49	1·63	6·72
91·00	4·52	1·64	6·75
91·50	4·54	1·65	6·79
92·00	4·57	1·66	6·83
92·50	4·59	1·67	6·86
93·00	4·62	1·68	6·90
93·50	4·64	1·69	6·94
94·00	4·67	1·70	6·97
94·50	4·69	1·71	7·01
95·00 or more	4·70	1·71	7·03

PART II

MONTHLY SCALE

Column 1	Column 2	Column 3	Column 4
Payments of Earnings	Primary Contributions at rate reduced in accordance with regulation 109(1)(a)(i)	Primary Contributions at rate reduced in accordance with regulation 109(1)(a)(ii)	Secondary Contributions
£	£	£	£
56·33	2·83	1·03	4·23
58·00	2·92	1·06	4·37
60·00	3·02	1·10	4·51
62·00	3·12	1·13	4·66
64·00	3·22	1·17	4·81
66·00	3·32	1·21	4·96
68·00	3·42	1·24	5·11
70·00	3·51	1·28	5·25
72·00	3·61	1·31	5·40
74·00	3·71	1·35	5·55
76·00	3·81	1·39	5·70
78·00	3·91	1·42	5·85
80·00	4·01	1·46	5·99
82·00	4·11	1·49	6·14
84·00	4·21	1·53	6·29
86·00	4·31	1·57	6·44
88·00	4·41	1·60	6·59
90·00	4·50	1·64	6·73
92·00	4·60	1·67	6·88
94·00	4·70	1·71	7·03
96·00	4·80	1·75	7·18
98·00	4·90	1·78	7·33
100·00	5·00	1·82	7·47
102·00	5·10	1·85	7·62
104·00	5·20	1·89	7·77
106·00	5·30	1·93	7·92
108·00	5·40	1·96	8·07
110·00	5·49	2·00	8·21
112·00	5·59	2·03	8·36
114·00	5·69	2·07	8·51
116·00	5·79	2·11	8·66
118·00	5·89	2·14	8·81
120·00	5·99	2·18	8·95
122·00	6·09	2·21	9·10
124·00	6·19	2·25	9·25
126·00	6·29	2·29	9·40
128·00	6·39	2·32	9·55
130·00	6·48	2·36	9·69
132·00	6·58	2·39	9·84
134·00	6·68	2·43	9·99
136·00	6·78	2·47	10·14
138·00	6·88	2·50	10·29
140·00	6·98	2·54	10·43
142·00	7·08	2·57	10·58

PART II (*contd.*)

Column 1	Column 2	Column 3	Column 4
Payments of Earnings	Primary Contributions at rate reduced in accordance with regulation 109(1)(*a*)(i)	Primary Contributions at rate reduced in accordance with regulation 109(1)(*a*)(ii)	Secondary Contributions
£	£	£	£
144·00	7·18	2·61	10·73
146·00	7·28	2·65	10·88
148·00	7·38	2·68	11·03
150·00	7·47	2·72	11·17
152·00	7·57	2·75	11·32
154·00	7·67	2·79	11·47
156·00	7·77	2·83	11·62
158·00	7·87	2·86	11·77
160·00	7·97	2·90	11·91
162·00	8·07	2·93	12·06
164·00	8·17	2·97	12·21
166·00	8·27	3·01	12·36
168·00	8·37	3·04	12·51
170·00	8·46	3·08	12·65
172·00	8·56	3·11	12·80
174·00	8·66	3·15	12·95
176·00	8·76	3·19	13·10
178·00	8·86	3·22	13·25
180·00	8·96	3·26	13·39
182·00	9·06	3·29	13·54
184·00	9·16	3·33	13·69
186·00	9·26	3·37	13·84
188·00	9·36	3·40	13·99
190·00	9·45	3·44	14·13
192·00	9·55	3·47	14·28
194·00	9·65	3·51	14·43
196·00	9·75	3·55	14·58
198·00	9·85	3·58	14·73
200·00	9·95	3·62	14·87
202·00	10·05	3·65	15·02
204·00	10·15	3·69	15·17
206·00	10·25	3·73	15·32
208·00	10·35	3·76	15·47
210·00	10·44	3·80	15·61
212·00	10·54	3·83	15·76
214·00	10·64	3·87	15·91
216·00	10·74	3·91	16·06
218·00	10·84	3·94	16·21
220·00	10·94	3·98	16·35
222·00	11·04	4·01	16·50
224·00	11·14	4·05	16·65
226·00	11·24	4·09	16·80
228·00	11·34	4·12	16·95
230·00	11·43	4·16	17·09
232·00	11·53	4·19	17·24
234·00	11·63	4·23	17·39
236·00	11·73	4·27	17·54

PART II (*contd.*)

Column 1	Column 2	Column 3	Column 4
Payments of Earnings	Primary Contributions at rate reduced in accordance with regulation 109(1)(*a*)(i)	Primary Contributions at rate reduced in accordance with regulation 109(1)(*a*)(ii)	Secondary Contributions
£	£	£	£
238·00	11·83	4·30	17·69
240·00	11·93	4·34	17·83
242·00	12·03	4·37	17·98
244·00	12·13	4·41	18·13
246·00	12·23	4·45	18·28
248·00	12·33	4·48	18·43
250·00	12·42	4·52	18·57
252·00	12·52	4·55	18·72
254·00	12·62	4·59	18·87
256·00	12·72	4·63	19·02
258·00	12·82	4·66	19·17
260·00	12·92	4·70	19·31
262·00	13·02	4·73	19·46
264·00	13·12	4·77	19·61
266·00	13·22	4·81	19·76
268·00	13·32	4·84	19·91
270·00	13·41	4·88	20·05
272·00	13·51	4·91	20·20
274·00	13·61	4·95	20·35
276·00	13·71	4·99	20·50
278·00	13·81	5·02	20·65
280·00	13·91	5·06	20·79
282·00	14·01	5·09	20·94
284·00	14·11	5·13	21·09
286·00	14·21	5·17	21·24
288·00	14·31	5·20	21·39
290·00	14·40	5·24	21·53
292·00	14·50	5·27	21·68
294·00	14·60	5·31	21·83
296·00	14·70	5·35	21·98
298·00	14·80	5·38	22·13
300·00	14·90	5·42	22·27
302·00	15·00	5·45	22·42
304·00	15·10	5·49	22·57
306·00	15·20	5·53	22·72
308·00	15·30	5·56	22·87
310·00	15·39	5·60	23·01
312·00	15·49	5·63	23·16
314·00	15·59	5·67	23·31
316·00	15·69	5·71	23·46
318·00	15·79	5·74	23·61
320·00	15·89	5·78	23·75

PART II (contd.)

Column 1	Column 2	Column 3	Column 4
Payments of Earnings	Primary Contributions at rate reduced in accordance with regulation 109(1)(a)(i)	Primary Contributions at rate reduced in accordance with regulation 109(1)(a)(ii)	Secondary Contributions
£	£	£	£
322·00	15·99	5·81	23·90
324·00	16·09	5·85	24·05
326·00	16·19	5·89	24·20
328·00	16·29	5·92	24·35
330·00	16·38	5·96	24·49
332·00	16·48	5·99	24·64
334·00	16·58	6·03	24·79
336·00	16·68	6·07	24·94
338·00	16·78	6·10	25·09
340·00	16·88	6·14	25·23
342·00	16·98	6·17	25·38
334·00	17·08	6·21	25·53
346·00	17·18	6·25	25·68
348·00	17·28	6·28	25·83
350·00	17·37	6·32	25·97
352·00	17·47	6·35	26·12
354·00	17·57	6·39	26·27
356·00	17·67	6·43	26·42
358·00	17·77	6·46	26·57
360·00	17·87	6·50	26·71
362·00	17·97	6·53	26·86
364·00	18·07	6·57	27·01
366·00	18·17	6·61	27·16
368·00	18·27	6·64	27·31
370·00	18·36	6·68	27·45
372·00	18·46	6·71	27·60
374·00	18·56	6·75	27·75
376·00	18·66	6·79	27·90
378·00	18·76	6·82	28·05
380·00	18·86	6·86	28·19
382·00	18·96	6·89	28·34
384·00	19·06	6·93	28·49
386·00	19·16	6·97	28·64
388·00	19·26	7·00	28·79
390·00	19·35	7·04	28·93
392·00	19·45	7·07	29·08
394·00	19·55	7·11	29·23
396·00	19·65	7·15	29·38
398·00	19·75	7·18	29·53
400·00	19·85	7·22	29·67
402·00	19·95	7·25	29·82
404·00	20·05	7·29	29·97
406·00	20·15	7·33	30·12
408·00	20·25	7·36	30·27
410·00	20·34	7·39	30·40
411·67 or more	20·38	7·41	30·46

EXPLANATORY NOTE

(This Note is not part of the Regulations.)

These Regulations amend the Social Security (Contributions) Regulations 1975 ("the principal Regulations") and contain only provisions in consequence of the Social Security (Contributions, Re-rating) Order 1975. Accordingly, by virtue of section 167(2) of, and paragraph 17 of Schedule 15 to, the Social Security Act 1975, no draft of the Regulations has been laid before Parliament for approval by resolution of each House; nor has a reference been made to the National Insurance Advisory Committee.

These Regulations, by amendment of Case C of Part VIII of the principal Regulations (mariners), make provision for contributions payable in respect of mariners' earnings paid on or after 6th April 1976 (the date on which the Social Security (Contributions, Re-rating) Order 1975 comes into operation) in respect of a voyage period which spans that date to be charged in the circumstances and to the extent described in regulation 4 of these Regulations, at the rate which would have been appropriate if that Order had not been made.

The Regulations also increase the rate of contribution payable by share fishermen and substitute scales of contributions which take account of the new earnings limits and rates of contributions imposed by the Order.

STATUTORY INSTRUMENTS

1976 No. 2

CONSUMER PROTECTION

The Children's Clothing (Hood Cords) Regulations 1976

Made - - - - -		*2nd January* 1976
Laid before Parliament	- -	*9th January* 1976
Coming into operation in accordance with Regulation 1(2)	-	

The Secretary of State, after consulting in accordance with the provisions of section 1(5) of the Consumer Protection Act 1961(a) with such persons and bodies of persons as appear to her to be requisite, in exercise of her powers under sections 1 and 2 of that Act and of all other powers enabling her in that behalf, hereby makes the following Regulations:—

1.—(1) These Regulations may be cited as the Children's Clothing (Hood Cords) Regulations 1976.

(2) These Regulations shall come into operation on 1st February 1976 in relation to goods sold, or in the possession of any person for the purpose of being sold, by the manufacturer or importer into Great Britain of those goods and, in any other case, shall come into operation on 1st July 1976.

2.—(1) In these Regulations—

"the Act" means the Consumer Protection Act 1961;

"outer garment" means a raincoat, overcoat, anorak or other garment suitable for use as outer wear;

"child's outer garment" means an outer garment having a measurement not exceeding 44 cm across the chest when the finished garment is laid out as flat as possible without distorting its natural two-dimensional shape and buttoned or otherwise fastened as it is designed to be in normal wear.

(2) Any reference in these Regulations to an enactment shall be construed as a reference to that enactment as amended or extended by or under any other enactment.

(3) The Interpretation Act 1889(b) applies for the interpretation of these Regulations as it applies for the interpretation of an Act of Parliament.

3. The hood of a child's outer garment shall not be designed to be secured by means of a cord drawn through the material.

4. As respects the requirements of these Regulations, subsections (1) and (2) of section 2 of the Act (which prohibits sales and possession for sale of goods and component parts not complying with regulations) shall apply in relation to goods and component parts manufactured before the imposition of those requirements notwithstanding anything in subsection (4) of that section (which exempts such goods and parts unless regulations otherwise provide).

(a) 1961 c. 40. (b) 1889 c. 63.

5. Section 2(1) to (3) of the Act (other than subsection (3)(*d*) and (*e*)) (sale and possession for sale of goods and component parts not complying with regulations) shall, except as provided by the proviso to section 2(6), apply in relation to goods to which these Regulations apply as if references to selling or to a sale included references to letting under a hire-purchase agreement or on hire, and the reference to a sale under a credit-sale agreement were a reference to a letting under a hire-purchase agreement.

6. The Schedule to the Act (which relates to enforcement by local authorities) shall have effect in relation to goods to which these Regulations apply.

Alan Williams,
Minister of State,
Department of Prices and Consumer Protection.

2nd January 1976.

EXPLANATORY NOTE

(This Note is not part of the Regulations.)

These Regulations provide that the hood of a child's outer garment shall not be designed to be secured by means of a cord drawn through the material.

STATUTORY INSTRUMENTS

1976 No. 14 (S. 1)

COURT OF SESSION, SCOTLAND
Act of Sederunt (Sessions of Court) 1976

Made - - - -	*6th January* 1976
Coming into Operation	*1st January* 1977

The Lords of Council and Session by virtue of the powers conferred upon them by section 2 of the Administration of Justice (Scotland) Act 1948(a) DO HEREBY ENACT and DECLARE that the ordinary sessions of the Court of Session during 1977 shall be as follows:—

From Thursday 6th January to Saturday 26th March.

From Tuesday 26th April to Saturday 16th July.

From Tuesday 27th September to Wednesday 21st December.

This Act of Sederunt may be cited as the Act of Sederunt (Sessions of Court) 1976 and shall come into operation on 1st January 1977.

And the Lords appoint this Act of Sederunt to be inserted in the Books of Sederunt.

G. C. Emslie,
I.P.D.

Edinburgh,
6th January 1976.

(a) 12, 13 & 14 Geo. 6 c. 10.

STATUTORY INSTRUMENTS

1976 No. 15

MEDICAL PROFESSION

The Abortion (Amendment) Regulations 1976

Made - - - -	7th January 1976
Laid before Parliament	15th January 1976
Coming into Operation	1st March 1976

The Secretary of State for Social Services, as respects England, and the Secretary of State for Wales, as respects Wales, in exercise of the powers conferred by section 2 of the Abortion Act 1967(a), as amended by the Transfer of Functions (Wales) Order 1969(b), and now vested in them(c), and of all other powers enabling them in that behalf, hereby make the following regulations:—

Citation and commencement

1. These regulations may be cited as the Abortion (Amendment) Regulations 1976, and shall come into operation on 1st March 1976.

Interpretation

2.—(1) In these regulations "the Act" means the Abortion Act 1967, as amended, and "the principal regulations" means the Abortion Regulations 1968(d), as amended(e).

(2) The rules for the construction of Acts of Parliament contained in the Interpretation Act 1889(f) shall apply for the purposes of the interpretation of these regulations as they apply for the purposes of the interpretation of an Act of Parliament.

Amendment of regulation 5 of the principal regulations

3. In regulation 5 of the principal regulations (restriction on disclosure of information) there shall be added after paragraph (*g*) the following paragraph:—

"or (*h*) when requested by the President of the General Medical Council for the purpose of investigating whether there has been serious professional misconduct by a registered medical practitioner, to the President of the General Medical Council or a member of his staff authorised by him.".

Amendment of Schedule 1 to the principal regulations

4. In Schedule 1 to the principal regulations (certificates to be completed before an abortion is performed under section 1 of the Act) for Certificate A there shall be substituted the certificate set out in the Schedule to these regulations.

(a) 1967 c. 87. (b) S.I. 1969/388 (1969 I, p. 1070).
(c) *See* Secretary of State for Social Services Order 1968 (S.I. 1968/1699; 1968 III, p. 4585).
(d) S.I. 1968/390 (1968 I, p. 1060). (e) S.I. 1969/636 (1969 II, p. 1756).
(f) 1889 c. 63.

Amendment of Schedule 2 to the principal regulations

5. In Schedule 2 to the principal regulations (form of notification to be given to the Chief Medical Officer of an abortion performed under section 1 of the Act) immediately before the part of the Schedule headed "*Other information relating to the termination*" there shall be inserted the following:—

"If the operating practitioner joined in giving the certificate did he see/and examine† the pregnant woman before doing so?............................

Has the practitioner named at A certified that he saw/and examined† the pregnant woman before giving the certificate?........................

Has the practitioner named at B (if any) certified that he saw/and examined† the pregnant woman before giving the certificate?........................

†Delete as appropriate".

Barbara Castle,

Secretary of State for Social Services.

2nd January 1976.

John Morris,

Secretary of State for Wales.

7th January 1976.

SCHEDULE   Regulation 4
Certificate A

IN CONFIDENCE

Not to be destroyed within three years of the date of operation

ABORTION ACT 1967

CERTIFICATE TO BE COMPLETED BEFORE AN ABORTION IS PERFORMED UNDER
SECTION 1(1) OF THE ACT

I, ...

(Name and qualifications of practitioner in block capitals)

of ....

....

(Full address of practitioner)

Have/have not* seen/and examined* the pregnant woman to whom this certificate
relates at ....

....

(Full address of place at which patient was seen or examined)

on ....

and I, ...

....

(Name and qualifications of practitioner in block capitals)

of ....

....

(Full address of practitioner)

Have/have not* seen/and examined* the pregnant woman to whom this certificate
relates at ....

....

(Full address of place at which patient was seen or examined)

on ....

We hereby certify that we are of the opinion, formed in good faith, that in the case
of ....

(Full name of pregnant woman in block capitals)

of ....

....

(Usual place of residence of pregnant woman in block capitals)

1. the continuance of the pregnancy would involve risk to the life of the
pregnant woman greater than if the pregnancy were terminated;

2. the continuance of the pregnancy would involve risk of injury to the
physical or mental health of the pregnant woman greater than if the pregnancy
were terminated;

Ring appropriate number(s))

3. the continuance of the pregnancy would involve risk of injury to the
physical or mental health of the existing child(ren) of the family of the pregnant
woman greater than if the pregnancy were terminated;

4. there is substantial risk that if the child were born it would suffer from such
physical or mental abnormalities as to be seriously handicapped.

This certificate of opinion is given before the commencement of the treatment for
the termination of pregnancy to which it refers and relates to the circumstances of the
pregnant woman's individual case.

Signed ....

Date...

Signed ....

Date...

*Delete as appropriate.

1c

EXPLANATORY NOTE

(This Note is not part of the Regulations.)

These Regulations, made under the Abortion Act 1967, further amend the Abortion Regulations 1968 to allow information furnished to the Chief Medical Officers under those regulations to be disclosed to the President of the General Medical Council, or any authorised member of his staff, for the purpose of investigating whether there has been serious professional misconduct by a doctor. Provision is also made for a doctor when giving a certificate under section 1(1) of the Abortion Act 1967 to state therein whether he has or has not seen and examined the pregnant woman before doing so.

STATUTORY INSTRUMENTS

1976 No. 16

EXCHANGE CONTROL

The Exchange Control (Authorised Dealers and Depositaries) (Amendment) Order 1976

Made - - - -		*5th January* 1976
Coming into Operation		*6th February* 1976

The Treasury, in exercise of the powers conferred upon them by sections 42(1) and 36(5) of the Exchange Control Act 1947**(a)**, hereby make the following Order:—

1.—(1) This Order may be cited as the Exchange Control (Authorised Dealers and Depositaries) (Amendment) Order 1976, and shall come into operation on 6th February 1976.

(2) The Interpretation Act 1889**(b)** shall apply for the interpretation of this Order as it applies for the interpretation of an Act of Parliament.

2. Paragraph 2 of Schedule 2 to the Exchange Control (Authorised Dealers and Depositaries) Order 1975**(c)**, as amended **(d)**, (hereinafter called "the said Order") shall be further amended as follows:—

(*a*) by inserting the words "Amex Bank Ltd." after the words "American National Bank and Trust Company of Chicago.";

(*b*) by inserting the words "Banco Central, S.A." after the words "Banca Nazionale del Lavoro.";

(*c*) by inserting the words "Bank Brussels Lambert (U.K.) Ltd." after the words "Bangkok Bank Ltd.";

(*d*) by inserting the words "Bank of Yokohama Ltd., The." after the words "Bank of Tokyo Trust Company, The.";

(*e*) by deleting the words "Banque de Bruxelles Drayton Ltd.";

(*f*) by deleting the words "Banque de l'Indochine." and substituting the words "Banque de l'Indochine et de Suez.";

(*g*) by deleting the words "Rothschild Intercontinental Bank Ltd.";

(*h*) by deleting the words "Standard and Chartered Banking Group Ltd.";

(*i*) by inserting the words "Standard Chartered Bank Ltd." after the words "Standard Bank Ltd., The."; and

(*j*) by inserting the words "Yasuda Trust & Banking Co., Ltd., The." after the words "Western American Bank (Europe) Ltd.".

(a) 1947 c. 14.
(b) 1889 c. 63.
(c) S.I. 1975/571 (1975 I, p. 2091).
(d) S.I. 1975/1495 (1975 I, p. 4998).

3. Paragraph 7 of Schedule 3 to the said Order shall be further amended as follows:—

(*a*) by inserting the words "Hambros Channel Islands Trust Corporation Ltd." after the words "Grindlays Bank (Jersey) Ltd."; and

(*b*) by inserting the words "La Plaiderie Trust Company Ltd." after the words "Joseph & Sons (Guernsey) Ltd., Leopold.".

4. This Order shall extend to the Channel Islands, and any reference in this Order to the Exchange Control Act 1947 includes a reference to that Act as extended by the Exchange Control (Channel Islands) Order 1947**(a)**.

James A. Dunn,
M. Cocks,
Two of the Lords Commissioners
of Her Majesty's Treasury.

5th January 1976.

EXPLANATORY NOTE

(*This Note is not part of the Order.*)

This Order amends the lists of:—

(*a*) the banks and other persons authorised under the Exchange Control Act 1947 to deal in gold and foreign currencies; and

(*b*) those who are entitled to act as authorised depositaries for the purpose of the deposit of securities as required by that Act.

(a) S.R. & O. 1947/2034 (Rev. VI, p. 1001: 1947 I, p. 660).

STATUTORY INSTRUMENTS

1976 No. 17 (L.1)

MATRIMONIAL CAUSES

COUNTY COURTS

The Divorce County Courts (Amendment) Order 1976

Made - - - - *6th January* 1976

Coming into Operation *1st March* 1976

The Lord Chancellor, in exercise of the powers conferred on him by section 1(1) of the Matrimonial Causes Act 1967(a), hereby makes the following Order:—

1.—(1) This Order may be cited as the Divorce County Courts (Amendment) Order 1976 and shall come into operation on 1st March 1976.

(2) The Interpretation Act 1889(b) shall apply to the interpretation of this Order as it applies to the interpretation of an Act of Parliament.

2. The Wandsworth County Court shall be a divorce county court and court of trial for the purposes of section 1(1) of the Matrimonial Causes Act 1967 and accordingly the following entry shall be inserted in Schedule 1 to the Divorce County Courts Order 1971(c), as amended (d), immediately below the reference to Walsall:—

"Wandsworth (T)".

Dated 6th January 1976.

Elwyn-Jones, C.

EXPLANATORY NOTE

(This Note is not part of the Order.)

This Order further amends the Divorce County Courts Order 1971 by designating the Wandsworth County Court as a divorce county court and by adding that court to the list of those at which undefended matrimonial causes may be tried.

(**a**) 1967 c. 56. (**b**) 1889 c. 63. (**c**) S.I. 1971/1954 (1971 III, p. 5271).
(**d**) S.I. 1972/1746, 1973/1278, 1974/1004, 1975/1002, 1869 (1972 III, p. 5070; 1973 II, p. 3878; 1974 II, p. 3783; 1975 II, p. 3459; III, p. 7067).

STATUTORY INSTRUMENTS

1976 No. 18

COMMUNITY LAND

The Community Land (Statutory Undertakers) Order 1976

Made - - -	*8th January* 1976
Laid before Parliament	*19th January* 1976
Coming into Operation	*6th April* 1976

The Secretary of State for the Environment, in relation to England, the Secretary of State for Scotland, in relation to Scotland, and the Secretary of State for Wales, in relation to Wales, in exercise of the powers conferred on them by sections 5(1)(*c*) and 53(2) of the Community Land Act 1975(**a**), and of all other powers enabling them in that behalf, hereby order as follows:—

1. This order shall come into operation on 6th April 1976 and may be cited as the Community Land (Statutory Undertakers) Order 1976.

2. The Interpretation Act 1889(**b**) shall apply for the interpretation of this order as it applies for the interpretation of an Act of Parliament.

3. The authorities, bodies or undertakers specified in the Schedule to this order shall be statutory undertakers for the purposes of the Community Land Act 1975.

SCHEDULE

The British Broadcasting Corporation.

The British Steel Corporation.

The Independent Broadcasting Authority.

The United Kingdom Atomic Energy Authority.

John Silkin,
Minister for Planning and Local Government,
Department of the Environment.

Signed by authority of the
Secretary of State.

8th January 1976.

(**a**) 1975 c. 77.   (**b**) 1889 c. 63.

William Ross,
Secretary of State for Scotland.

7th January 1976.

John Morris,
Secretary of State for Wales.

7th January 1976.

EXPLANATORY NOTE

(This Note is not part of the Order.)

This Order specifies certain material interests in land which are not to be outstanding material interests for the purposes of the Community Land Act 1975.   An authority under that Act may, by order under section 18, be placed under a duty to acquire all outstanding material interests in land which is needed for the purposes of relevant development designated by that order. Under the Act certain planning permissions can be "suspended" under sections 19–22.   These sections do not apply to planning permissions granted in respect of land in which there are no material interests outstanding.

STATUTORY INSTRUMENTS

1976 No. 19

COMMUNITY LAND

The Community Land (Outstanding Material Interests) Order 1976

Made - - -	*8th January* 1976
Laid before Parliament	*19th January* 1976
Coming into Operation	*6th April* 1976

The Secretary of State for the Environment, in relation to England, the Secretary of State for Scotland, in relation to Scotland, and the Secretary of State for Wales, in relation to Wales, in exercise of the powers conferred on them by sections 4(1)(*c*) and 53(2) of the Community Land Act 1975(**a**), and of all other powers enabling them in that behalf, hereby order as follows:—

1. This order shall come into operation on 6th April 1976 and may be cited as the Community Land (Outstanding Material Interests) Order 1976.

2. The Interpretation Act 1889(**b**) shall apply for the interpretation of this order as it applies for the interpretation of an Act of Parliament.

3. A material interest in land (within the meaning of the Community Land Act 1975) shall not be treated as outstanding for the purposes of that Act if it is of a description specified in the Schedule to this order.

SCHEDULE

Any material interest owned by—

The Commission for New Towns.

A co-operative housing association approved for the purposes of section 341 of the Income and Corporation Taxes Act 1970(**c**).

The Highlands and Islands Development Board.

A housing association registered in accordance with section 13(1) of the Housing Act 1974(**d**).

The Housing Corporation.

The Lee Valley Regional Park Authority.

Letchworth Garden City Corporation.

The North Eastern Housing Association.

The Scottish Development Agency.

The Scottish Special Housing Association.

An unregistered self-build society as defined in section 12 of the Housing Act 1974.

The Welsh Development Agency.

John Silkin,
Minister for Planning and Local Government,
Department of the Environment.

Signed by authority of the
Secretary of State.

8th January 1976.

(**a**) 1975 c. 77.	(**b**) 1889 c. 63.
(**c**) 1970 c. 10.	(**d**) 1974 c. 44.

William Ross,
Secretary of State for Scotland.

7th January 1976.

John Morris,
Secretary of State for Wales.

7th January 1976.

EXPLANATORY NOTE

(This Note is not part of the Order.)

This Order specifies the bodies in the Schedule to the Order as statutory undertakers for the purposes of the Community Land Act 1975. The main provisions in that Act relating to statutory undertakers are in section 18, section 22, section 41 and Part III of Schedule 4.

STATUTORY INSTRUMENTS

1976 No. 26

CIVIL AVIATION

The Civil Aviation (Notices) (Second Amendment) Regulations 1976

Made - - - -	12*th January* 1976
Laid before Parliament	13*th January* 1976
Coming into Operation	15*th January* 1976

The Secretary of State in exercise of his powers under section 29(1) and (3) of the Civil Aviation Act 1971(a) and of all other powers enabling him in that behalf hereby makes the following Regulations.

1.—(1) These Regulations may be cited as the Civil Aviation (Notices) (Second Amendment) Regulations 1976 and shall come into operation on 15th January 1976.

(2) The Interpretation Act 1889(b) shall apply for the purpose of the interpretation of these Regulations as it applies for the purpose of the interpretation of an Act of Parliament.

2. The Civil Aviation (Notices) Regulations 1971(c), as amended(d), shall be further amended as follows:—

In Regulation 2 for "Her Majesty's Stationery Office" there shall be substituted "the Civil Aviation Authority".

Stanley Clinton Davis,
Parliamentary Under-Secretary of State,
12th January 1976.   Department of Trade.

EXPLANATORY NOTE

(This Note is not part of the Regulations)

These Regulations, which come into operation on 15th January 1976, further amend the Civil Aviation (Notices) Regulations 1971 by providing that the manner of publishing notices under section 29(1) and (3) of the Civil Aviation Act 1971 shall be by setting forth the notices in a document published by the Civil Aviation Authority instead of by Her Majesty's Stationery Office.

(a) 1971 c. 75   (b) 1889 c. 63.   (c) S.I. 1971/1686 (1971 III, p. 4611).
(d) There is no relevant amending instrument.

STATUTORY INSTRUMENTS

1976 No. 29 (L.2)

COUNTY COURTS

The County Court Districts (North Shields) Order 1976

Made - - - -		*7th January* 1976
Coming into Operation		*2nd February* 1976

The Lord Chancellor, in exercise of the powers conferred on him by section 2 of the County Courts Act 1959(**a**), hereby makes the following Order:—

1.—(1) This Order may be cited as the County Court Districts (North Shields) Order 1976 and shall come into operation on 2nd February 1976.

(2) The Interpretation Act 1889(**b**) shall apply to the interpretation of this Order as it applies to the interpretation of an Act of Parliament.

2. The North Shields County Court shall cease to be held at North Shields and shall be held at Whitley Bay; and accordingly Schedule 2 to the County Court District Order 1970 (**c**), as amended (**d**), shall be further amended by adding in column 1 thereof, in the appropriate alphabetical position, "North Shields" and, opposite thereto in column 2, "Whitley Bay".

Dated 7th January 1976.

Elwyn-Jones, C.

EXPLANATORY NOTE

(This Note is not part of the Order.)

This Order provides for the sittings of the North Shields County Court to be held at Whitley Bay instead of at North Shields.

(**a**) 1959 c. 22.   (**b**) 1889 c. 63.   (**c**) S.I. 1970/16 (1970 I, p. 17).
(**d**) The relevant amending instruments are S.I. 1970/904, 2031, 1973/2045 (1970 II, p. 2833; III, p. 6621; 1973 III, p. 7065).

STATUTORY INSTRUMENTS

1976 No. 30

MEDICINES

The Medicines (Animal Feeding Stuffs) (Enforcement) Regulations 1976

Made - - - -	*8th January* 1976
Laid before Parliament	*26th January* 1976
Coming into Operation	*1st April* 1976

The Minister of Agriculture, Fisheries and Food, the Secretary of State concerned with agriculture in Scotland and the Department of Agriculture for Northern Ireland, acting jointly, in exercise of powers conferred by sections 117(1), (2) and (3) of the Medicines Act 1968(**a**) and now vested in them(**b**) and of all other powers enabling them in that behalf, after consulting such organisations as appear to them to be representative of interests likely to be substantially affected, hereby make the following regulations:—

Citation, commencement and interpretation

1.—(1) These regulations may be cited as the Medicines (Animal Feeding Stuffs) (Enforcement) Regulations 1976, shall come into operation on 1st April 1976 and shall extend to the United Kingdom.

(2) In these regulations, unless the context otherwise requires—

"the Act" means the Medicines Act 1968 and references to sections 112, 113 and 115 of that Act shall be deemed to be references to those sections as modified by these regulations;

"agricultural analyst" means an agricultural analyst appointed under section 67 of the Agriculture Act 1970(**c**) and includes a deputy agricultural analyst so appointed for the same area;

"animal feeding stuff" includes a complete feeding stuff, a feed supplement and a protein concentrate;

"complete feeding stuff" means a substance or a mixture of substances designed for feeding to animals without further mixing with other feeding stuffs;

"feed supplement" means a substance or a mixture of substances designed for further mixing before feeding to animals at an inclusion rate of less than 5 per cent with other animal feeding stuffs;

"inspector" means a person authorised by an enforcement authority for the purposes of the enforcement of the Act;

"protein concentrate" means a substance or a mixture of substances designed for further mixing before feeding to animals at an inclusion rate of 5 per cent or more with other animal feeding stuffs;

(**a**) 1968 c. 67.
(**b**) In the case of the Department of Agriculture for Northern Ireland by virtue of section 40 of, and Schedule 5 to, the Northern Ireland Constitution Act 1973 (c. 36) and paragraph 2(1)(*b*) of Schedule 1 to the Northern Ireland Act 1974 (c. 28).
(**c**) 1970 c. 40.

"sampled portion", in relation to any animal feeding stuff means an amount of that feeding stuff (as prescribed under the provisions of Part I of Schedule 2 to these regulations) from which a sample has been taken or set aside by an inspector in the manner prescribed in Parts II and III of the said Schedule, being an amount—

(*a*) consisting either—

   (i) entirely of feeding stuffs packed in one or more containers; or

   (ii) entirely of feeding stuffs not so packed; and

(*b*) not exceeding, in the case of an amount consisting of feeding stuffs so packed, the requisite quantity, that is to say, five tons or 1,000 gallons, except where—

   (i) it consists of feeding stuffs packed in a single container; or

   (ii) it consists of feeding stuffs packed in two or more containers each of which holds less than the requisite quantity, in which case the prescribed amount may be the contents of the lowest number of those containers which together hold the requisite quantity;

and other expressions have the same meaning as in the Act.

(3) The Interpretation Act 1889(**a**) shall apply to the interpretation of these regulations as it applies to the interpretation of an Act of Parliament.

Modification of certain provisions of the Act

2. For the purposes of the application of the provisions of sections 112, 113 and 115 of the Act in relation to animal feeding stuffs, those provisions shall have effect subject to the modifications specified in Part I of Schedule 1 to these regulations, such provisions as so modified being set out in Part II of the said Schedule.

Sampling and analysis

3.—(1) A sample which is taken in accordance with the provisions of sections 112(2) or 115(1) of the Act, shall be taken, submitted for analysis and dealt with in the manner provided in Schedule 2 to these regulations.

(2) Where pursuant to section 113(2) of the Act a sample is set aside from a substance or article seized in pursuance of section 112(4) of the Act or a substance or article so seized is itself treated as a sample, such a sample or such a substance or article shall be set aside, submitted for analysis and dealt with in the manner provided in Schedule 2 to these regulations, but subject to the modifications set out in Part VI to that Schedule.

(3) Without prejudice to his powers and duties under section 112 of the Act an inspector may for the purposes of the Act take a sample otherwise than in accordance with these regulations of any substance or article appearing to him to be an animal feeding stuff but in all other respects these regulations shall not apply and no proceedings under the Act shall be taken in relation to such a sample.

Methods of analysis

4.—(1) Paragraphs (2) and (3) of this regulation shall have effect for the purposes of proceedings for offences under any of the following provisions

(**a**) 1889 c. 63.

of the Act, that is to say subsections (1), (2), (4) and (5) of section 45, sub-section (2) of section 67, subsections (1) and (2) of section 91 and subsections (1) and (2) of section 123 and for the purposes of proceedings for offences under the Medicines (Labelling of Medicated Animal Feeding Stuffs) Regulations 1973**(a)**.

(2) For the purpose of determining what quantity or proportion (if any) of a substance or article of a description or class specified in Schedule 3 to these regulations has been incorporated in a sample of an animal feeding stuff to be analysed in pursuance of section 112, section 113 or section 115 of the Act the methods of analysis set out in the said Schedule 3 shall, whenever they are applicable, be used.

(3) On the production in the proceedings of a certificate of the results of analysis of a sample of the animal feeding stuff performed by a method pres-cribed by paragraph (2) of this regulation evidence of the results of any analysis of a part of the sample performed by any other method shall not be admissible in the proceedings.

Forms of certificate of analysis or examination

5. A certificate of analysis issued by an agricultural analyst in accordance with Schedule 2 to these regulations shall be in the form set out in Schedule 4 Part I to these regulations, and a certificate of analysis or examination made by any laboratory for the purposes of the said Schedule 2 shall be in the form set out in Schedule 4 Part II to these regulations.

Metric substitutions

6. In the application of these regulations on and after 1st July, 1976 the metric units set out in column 2 of Schedule 5 to these regulations shall be used in substitution for the corresponding imperial units set out in column 1 of the said Schedule.

In Witness whereof the Official Seal of the Minister of Agriculture, Fisheries and Food is hereunto affixed on 22nd December 1975.

Frederick Peart,
Minister of Agriculture, Fisheries
and Food.

(L.S.)

William Ross,
Secretary of State for Scotland.

5th January 1976.

Sealed with the Official Seal of the Department of Agriculture for Northern Ireland this 8th day of January 1976.

(L.S.)

J. A. Young,
Permanent Secretary.

(a) S.I. 1973/1530 (1973 III, p. 4782).

SCHEDULE 1

(Regulation 2)

Part I

Modifications of sections 112, 113 and 115 of the Medicines Act 1968

Section 112

1. In subsection (1), immediately after the words "that authority" there shall be inserted the words "(in this section referred to as an "inspector")", in paragraph (*a*), for the words "a medicinal product" there shall be substituted the words "an animal feeding stuff", in paragraph (*b*), for the words "any medicinal product" there shall be substituted the words "any animal feeding stuff" and for the words "a medicinal product" there shall be substituted the words "an animal feeding stuff", and paragraph (*c*) shall be omitted.

2. In subsection (2), for the words "a person authorised as mentioned in that subsection" there shall be substituted the words "an inspector", for paragraphs (*a*) and (*b*) there shall be substituted the words "an animal feeding stuff" and the words "if he does not obtain the sample by purchase" shall be omitted.

3. In subsection (3), for the words "person authorised as mentioned in that subsection" there shall be substituted the word "inspector", for the words "medicinal products" there shall be substituted the words "animal feeding stuffs" and immediately after the words "medicinal products" there shall be inserted the words "or a business which includes the mixing of animal feeding stuffs for use in the course of that business".

4. In subsection (4), for the words "person so authorised" there shall be substituted the word "inspector" and immediately before the word "document" wherever it appears, there shall be inserted the words "book or".

5. In subsection (5), for the words "subsection (4)" there shall be substituted the words "subsections (1), (2) or (4)", for the words "person having that right" there shall be substituted the word "inspector" and the words "or open any vending machine" shall be omitted.

6. In subsection (6), for the words "a person" there shall be substituted the words "an inspector", immediately before the word "document" there shall be inserted the words "book or" and the words from "and, in the case of" to the end of the subsection shall be omitted.

7. In subsection (7), for the words "person duly authorised in writing by the licensing authority" there shall be substituted the word "inspector" and for the words "a person" there shall be substituted the words "an inspector".

8. In subsection (9), for the words "The provisions of Schedule 3 to" there shall be substituted the words "Regulations made under section 117(2) of".

Section 113

9. In subsections (1) to (5), for the words "authorised officer", wherever they appear, there shall be substituted the word "inspector".

10. In subsection (1), immediately before the word "document" there shall be inserted the words "book or".

11. In subsection (2), immediately after the word "nature" there shall be inserted the words "or quantity".

12. In subsection (3), immediately after the word "nature" there shall be inserted the words "or quantity".

13. In subsection (4), for the words from "into three parts" to the end of the subsection there shall be substituted the words "into such number of parts as shall be required by regulations made under section 117 of this Act".

14. In subsection (5), for the words "Paragraphs 10, 11 and 12 and paragraphs 15 to 27 of Schedule 3 to" there shall be substituted the words "Regulations made under section 117(2) of", and for the words from "as they have effect" to the end of the subsection there shall be substituted the words "and as if any reference to a sample included a reference to a substance or article treated as a sample".

Section 115

15. In subsection (1), for the words from "a medicinal product" to the end of the subsection there shall be substituted the words "an animal feeding stuff shall be entitled to have a sample taken of it by a person authorised in that behalf by an enforcement authority (in this section referred to as an "inspector") and analysed by the agricultural analyst for the inspector's area".

16. At the end of subsection (1) there shall be added the following subsections:—

"(1A) Any request for a sample to be taken and analysed under this section shall be accompanied by such fee as may be fixed by the enforcement authority of the inspector's area; and different fees may be fixed for different animal feeding stuffs and for different analyses of the same animal feeding stuff.

(1B) Regulations made under section 117(2) of this Act shall have effect in relation to a sample taken in accordance with subsection (1) of this section.

(1C) Where a sample of any animal feeding stuff has been taken pursuant to the request of a purchaser under subsection (1) of this section any of the following persons, that is to say, the purchaser, the person who sold the animal feeding stuff to him and any other person against whom a cause of action may lie in respect of the sale of the animal feeding stuff, shall be entitled to require the inspector—

(*a*) to send one of the parts retained by the inspector in accordance with regulations made under section 117 of the Act (hereafter in this section referred to as "the first remaining part") for analysis or other appropriate examination to the Government Chemist;

(*b*) to supply the person making the request with a copy of the Government Chemist's certificate of analysis or other appropriate examination of that first remaining part, whether that part was sent to the Government Chemist for analysis or other appropriate examination in pursuance of the request of that person or otherwise.

(1D) Where a sample of any animal feeding stuff has been taken by an inspector in the prescribed manner and it is intended to institute proceedings against any person for an offence under this Act and to adduce on behalf of the prosecution evidence of the result of an analysis or examination of the sample—

(*a*) the prosecutor, if a person other than the inspector, shall be entitled to require the inspector—

(i) to send the first remaining part of the sample for analysis or other appropriate examination to the Government Chemist;

(ii) to supply the prosecutor with a copy of the Government Chemist's certificate of analysis or other appropriate examination of that first remaining part, whether that part was sent to the Government Chemist for analysis or other appropriate examination in pursuance of the request of the prosecutor or otherwise;

(*b*) the inspector, if he is the prosecutor, shall be entitled himself so to send that first remaining part.

(1E) Where a prosecutor avails himself of his rights under subsection (1D) of this section he shall cause to be served with the summons a copy of the agricultural analyst's certificate of analysis, and of any certificate of analysis or examination of any laboratory to which the sample was referred pursuant to paragraph 7(3) of Part V of Schedule 2 to these regulations, and a copy of the Government Chemist's certificate of analysis or other appropriate examination; and where a prosecutor does not avail himself of his rights under that subsection he shall, not less than fourteen days before the service of the summons, cause to be served on the person charged a copy of the agricultural analyst's certificate of analysis (and of any laboratory certificate above referred to) and a notice of intended prosecution, and if, within the period of fourteen days beginning with the service of the notice, that person sends the prosecutor a written request to that effect accompanied by the amount of the fee payable by the prosecutor for the purpose under subsection (1K) of this section (which shall be refunded to that person by the prosecutor if the prosecution is not brought) the prosecutor shall exercise his rights under subsection (1D) of this section and the proceedings shall not be instituted until he has sent that person a copy of the Government Chemist's certificate of analysis or other appropriate examination.

(1F) Where proceedings are brought against any person for an offence under this Act and evidence is given or sought to be given of the result of an analysis or examination of a sample of any animal feeding stuff taken by an inspector in the prescribed manner but it appears that the sample has not been analysed or examined by the Government Chemist, the court may, of its own motion or on the application of either party, order the remaining part of the sample to be sent for analysis or other appropriate examination to the Government Chemist.

(1G) Where under this section a part of a sample is sent for analysis or other appropriate examination to the Government Chemist there shall be sent with it—

(a) a copy of any document which was sent with the part of the sample sent to the agricultural analyst; and

(b) if the part is sent to the Government Chemist under subsection (1D) or (1F) of this section, a statement of the particulars on which the proceedings or intended proceedings are based.

(1H) The Government Chemist shall analyse or examine or cause to be analysed or examined any part of a sample sent to him under this section but, where the part is accompanied by a statement such as is mentioned in subsection (1G) of this section, the analysis or other appropriate examination shall be made only with respect to the particulars in the statement unless the person or court requesting or ordering the analysis or other appropriate examination requires it to extend also to other matters.

(1J) A certificate of any analysis or other appropriate examination under this paragraph shall be sent by the Government Chemist—

(a) if the material analysed or examined was sent to him in pursuance of subsection (1C) or (1D) of this section, to the inspector;

(b) if it was sent to him in pursuance of an order of the court under subsection (1F) of this section, to the court.

(1K) A request for an analysis or other appropriate examination under subsection (1C) or (1D) of this section shall be of no effect unless accompanied by the appropriate fee; and the appropriate fee for any analysis or other appropriate examination ordered by the court under subsection (1F) of this section shall be paid by such party to the proceedings as the court may direct.

(1L) In the application of this section to Scotland—

(a) for any reference to the court there shall be substituted a reference to the sheriff;

(b) in subsection (1D), in paragraph (a) the words "if a person other than the inspector", and paragraph (b) shall be omitted;

(c) in subsection (1E), for any reference to the summons there shall be substituted a reference to the complaint;

(d) in subsection (1F), for the words "of its own motion" there shall be substituted the words "of his own accord";

(e) for subsection (1K), there shall be substituted the following sub-paragraph—

"(1K) A request for an analysis or other appropriate examination—

(a) under subsection (1C) of this section; or

(b) under subsection (1D) thereof where the request is made at the instance of a person charged with an offence who has received a notice of intended prosecution,

shall be of no effect unless accompanied by the appropriate fee; and the appropriate fee for any analysis or other appropriate examination ordered by the sheriff under subsection (1F) of this section shall be paid by such party to the proceedings as the sheriff may direct.".

(1M) In the application of this section to Northern Ireland—

(a) in subsection (1), for the words "the agricultural analyst for the inspector's area", there shall be substituted the words "an agricultural analyst in Northern Ireland";

(b) in subsection (1A), for the words "the enforcement authority of the inspector's area" there shall be substituted the words "the Department of Agriculture for Northern Ireland";

(c) for any reference to the Government Chemist there shall be substituted a reference to the Chief Agricultural Analyst for Northern Ireland, and the expression "agricultural analyst" shall not include the Chief Agricultural Analyst for Northern Ireland.

(1N) In subsection (1K) of this section "the appropriate fee" means such fee as may be fixed by the Secretary of State for Industry with the approval of the Treasury, and different fees may be fixed for different animal feeding stuffs and for different analyses of the same animal feeding stuff.

(1P) For the purposes of this section, the appropriation of any animal feeding stuff by one person for use under arrangements with another person not constituting a sale of the feeding stuff to that other person, being arrangements which are intended to benefit both the person appropriating the feeding stuff and that other person but under which the probability or extent of any benefit to that other person may be affected by the quality of the feeding stuff, shall be treated as a sale of that feeding stuff to that other person by the person so appropriating it, and references to sale or purchase and cognate expressions shall be construed accordingly."

17. Subsections (2) to (10) shall be omitted.

PART II

SECTIONS 112, 113 AND 115 OF THE MEDICINES ACT 1968 AS MODIFIED IN ACCORDANCE WITH PART I OF THIS SCHEDULE

112.—(1) For the purpose of ascertaining whether there is or has been a contravention of this Act or of any regulations or order made thereunder which, by or under any provisions of sections 108 to 110 of this Act an enforcement authority is required or empowered to enforce, any person duly authorised in writing by that authority (in this section referred to as an "inspector") shall have a right to inspect—

(a) any substance or article appearing to him to be an animal feeding stuff;

(*b*) any article appearing to him to be a container or package used or intended to be used to contain any animal feeding stuff or to be a label or leaflet used or intended to be used in connection with an animal feeding stuff.

(2) Where for the purpose specified in the preceding subsection an inspector requires a sample of any substance or article appearing to him to be an animal feeding stuff he shall have a right to take a sample of that substance or article.

(3) For the purpose specified in subsection (1) of this section, any inspector shall have a right—

(*a*) to require any person carrying on a business which consists of or includes the manufacture, assembly, sale or supply of animal feeding stuffs or a business which includes the mixing of animal feeding stuffs for use in the course of that business, and any person employed in connection with such a business, to produce any books or documents relating to the business which are in his possession or under his control;

(*b*) to take copies of, or of any entry in, any book or document produced in pursuance of the preceding paragraph.

(4) Any inspector shall have a right to seize and detain any substance or article which he has reasonable cause to believe to be a substance or article in relation to which, or by means of which, an offence under this Act is being or has been committed, and any book or document which he has reasonable cause to believe to be a book or document which may be required as evidence in proceedings under this Act.

(5) For the purpose of exercising any such right as is specified in subsections (1), (2) or (4) of this section the inspector may, so far as is reasonably necessary in order to secure that the provisions of this Act and any regulations or order made thereunder are duly observed, require any person having authority to do so to break open any container or package, or to permit him to do so.

(6) Where an inspector seizes any substance or article (including any book or document) in the exercise of such a right as is specified in subsection (4) of this section, he shall inform the person from whom it is seized.

(7) Without prejudice to the preceding provisions of this section, any inspector shall have the rights conferred by those provisions in relation to things belonging to, or any business carried on by, an applicant for a licence or certificate under Part II of this Act, and may exercise those rights for the purpose of verifying any statement contained in the application for the licence or certificate; and, where by virtue of this subsection an inspector exercises any such right as is specified in subsection (4) of this section, he shall be subject to the duty imposed by subsection (6) of this section.

(8) Notwithstanding anything in the preceding provisions of this section, where a person claiming to exercise a right by virtue of this section is required to produce his credentials, the right shall not be exercisable by him except on production of those credentials.

(9) Regulations made under section 117(2) of this Act shall have effect with respect to samples obtained on behalf of enforcement authorities for the purposes of this Act.

113.—(1) The provisions of this section shall have effect where a person (in this section referred to as an "inspector") seizes a substance or article (other than a book or document) in the exercise of such a right as is specified in subsection (4) of section 112 of this Act (including that subsection as applied by subsection (7) of that section).

(2) If any person who in accordance with subsection (6) of that section is entitled to be informed of the seizure so requests, either at the time of the seizure or at any subsequent time, not being later than twenty-one days after he is informed of the seizure, then, subject to the next following subsection, the inspector shall either—

(*a*) set aside a sample of the substance or article seized, or

(*b*) treat that substance or article as a sample,

whichever he considers more appropriate having regard to the nature or quantity of that substance or article.

(3) An inspector shall not be required by virtue of subsection (2) of this section to set aside a sample, or to treat a substance or article as a sample, if the nature or quantity of the substance or article is such that it is not reasonably practicable to do either of those things.

(4) Where in accordance with subsection (2) of this section an inspector sets aside a sample, or treats a substance or article as a sample, he shall divide it into such number of parts as shall be required by regulations made under section 117 of this Act.

(5) Regulations made under section 117(2) of this Act shall have effect in relation to a sample set aside, or a substance or article treated as a sample, in accordance with subsection (2) of this section and as if any reference to a sample included a reference to a substance or article treated as a sample.

115.—(1) A person who, not being a person authorised in that behalf by an enforcement authority, has purchased an animal feeding stuff shall be entitled to have a sample taken of it by a person authorised in that behalf by an enforcement authority (in this section referred to as an "inspector") and analysed by the agricultural analyst for the inspector's area.

(1A) Any request for a sample to be taken and analysed under this section shall be accompanied by such fee as may be fixed by the enforcement authority of the inspector's area; and different fees may be fixed for different animal feeding stuffs and for different analyses of the same animal feeding stuff.

(1B) Regulations made under section 117(2) of this Act shall have effect in relation to a sample taken in accordance with subsection (1) of this section.

(1C) Where a sample of any animal feeding stuff has been taken pursuant to the request of a purchaser under subsection (1) of this section any of the following persons, that is to say, the purchaser, the person who sold the animal feeding stuff to him and any other person against whom a cause of action may lie in respect of the sale of the animal feeding stuff, shall be entitled to require the inspector:—

    (a) to send one of the parts retained by the inspector in accordance with regulations made under section 117 of the Act (hereafter in this section referred to as "the first remaining part") for analysis or other appropriate examination to the Government Chemist;

    (b) to supply the person making the request with a copy of the Government Chemist's certificate of analysis or other appropriate examination of that first remaining part, whether that part was sent to the Government Chemist for analysis or other appropriate examination in pursuance of the request of that person or otherwise.

(1D) Where a sample of any animal feeding stuff has been taken by an inspector in the prescribed manner and it is intended to institute proceedings against any person for an offence under this Act and to adduce on behalf of the prosecution evidence of the result of an analysis or examination of the sample:—

    (a) the prosecutor, if a person other than the inspector, shall be entitled to require the inspector—

        (i) to send the first remaining part of the sample for analysis or other appropriate examination to the Government Chemist;

        (ii) to supply the prosecutor with a copy of the Government Chemist's certificate of analysis or other appropriate examination of that first remaining part, whether that part was sent to the Government Chemist for analysis or other appropriate examination in pursuance of the request of the prosecutor or otherwise;

    (b) the inspector, if he is the prosecutor, shall be entitled himself so to send that first remaining part.

(1E) Where a prosecutor avails himself of his rights under subsection (1D) of this section he shall cause to be served with the summons a copy of the agricultural analyst's certificate of analysis, and of any certificate of analysis or examination of any laboratory to which the sample was referred pursuant to paragraph 7(3) of Part V of Schedule 2 to these regulations, and a copy of the Government Chemist's certificate of analysis or other appropriate examination; and where a prosecutor does not avail himself of his rights under that subsection he shall, not less than fourteen days before the service of the summons, cause to be served on the person charged a copy of the agricultural analyst's certificate of analysis (and of any laboratory certificate above referred to) and a notice of intended prosecution, and if, within the period of fourteen days beginning with the service of the notice, that person sends the prosecutor a written request to that effect accompanied by the amount of the fee payable by the prosecutor for the purpose under subsection (1K) of this section (which shall be refunded to that person by the prosecutor if the prosecution is not brought) the prosecutor shall exercise his rights under subsection (1D) of this section and the proceedings shall not be instituted until he has sent that person a copy of the Government Chemist's certificate of analysis or other appropriate examination.

(1F) Where proceedings are brought against any person for an offence under this Act and evidence is given or sought to be given of the result of an analysis or examination of a sample of any animal feeding stuff taken by an inspector in the prescribed manner but it appears that the sample has not been analysed or examined by the Government Chemist, the court may, of its own motion or on the application of either party, order the remaining part of the sample to be sent for analysis or other appropriate examination to the Government Chemist.

(1G) Where under this section a part of a sample is sent for analysis or other appropriate examination to the Government Chemist there shall be sent with it:—

(a) a copy of any document which was sent with the part of the sample sent to the agricultural analyst; and

(b) if the part is sent to the Government Chemist under subsection (1D) or (1F) of this section, a statement of the particulars on which the proceedings or intended proceedings are based.

(1H) The Government Chemist shall analyse or examine or cause to be analysed or examined any part of a sample sent to him under this section but, where the part is accompanied by a statement such as is mentioned in subsection (1G) of this section, the analysis or other appropriate examination shall be made only with respect to the particulars in the statement unless the person or court requesting or ordering the analysis or other appropriate examination requires it to extend also to other matters.

(1J) A certificate of any analysis or other appropriate examination under this paragraph shall be sent by the Government Chemist—

(a) if the material analysed or examined was sent to him in pursuance of subsection (1C) or (1D) of this section, to the inspector;

(b) if it was sent to him in pursuance of an order of the court under subsection (1F) of this section, to the court.

(1K) A request for an analysis or other appropriate examination under subsection (1C) or (1D) of this section shall be of no effect unless accompanied by the appropriate fee; and the appropriate fee for any analysis or other appropriate examination ordered by the court under subsection (1F) of this section shall be paid by such party to the proceedings as the court may direct.

(1L) In the application of this section to Scotland—

(a) for any reference to the court there shall be substituted a reference to the sheriff;

(b) in subsection (1D), in paragraph (a) the words, "if a person other than the inspector"- and paragraph (b) shall be omitted;

(c) in subsection (1E), for any reference to the summons there shall be substituted a reference to the complaint;

(d) in subsection (1F), for the words "of its own motion" there shall be substituted the words "of his own accord";

(e) for subsection (1K), there shall be substituted the following sub-paragraph—

"(1K) A request for an analysis or other appropriate examination—

(a) under subsection (1C) of this section; or

(b) under subsection (1D) thereof where the request is made at the instance of a person charged with an offence who has received a notice of intended prosecution,

shall be of no effect unless accompanied by the appropriate fee; and the appropriate fee for any analysis or other appropriate examination ordered by the sheriff under subsection (1F) of this section shall be paid by such party to the proceedings as the sheriff may direct".

(1M) In the application of this section to Northern Ireland—

(a) in subsection (1), for the words "the agricultural analyst for the inspector's area" there shall be substituted the words "an agricultural analyst in Northern Ireland";

(b) in subsection (1A), for the words "the enforcement authority of the inspector's area" there shall be substituted the words "the Department of Agriculture for Northern Ireland";

(c) for any reference to the Government Chemist there shall be substituted a reference to the Chief Agricultural Analyst for Northern Ireland, and the expression "agricultural analyst" shall not include the Chief Agricultural Analyst for Northern Ireland.

(1N) In subsection (1K) of this section "the appropriate fee" means such fee as may be fixed by the Secretary of State for Industry with the approval of the Treasury, and different fees may be fixed for different animal feeding stuffs and for different analyses of the same animal feeding stuff.

(1P) For the purposes of this section, the appropriation of any animal feeding stuff by one person for use under arrangements with another person not constituting a sale of the feeding stuff to that other person, being arrangements which are intended to benefit both the person appropriating the feeding stuff and that other person but under which the probability or extent of any benefit to that other person may be affected by the quality of the feeding stuff, shall be treated as a sale of that feeding stuff to that other person by the person so appropriating it, and references to sale or purchase and cognate expressions shall be construed accordingly.

SCHEDULE 2

MANNER OF TAKING OR SETTING ASIDE, DEALING WITH AND SUBMITTING FOR ANALYSIS OR EXAMINATION SAMPLES OF ANIMAL FEEDING STUFFS

(Regulation 3)

PART I

GENERAL PROVISIONS

1. The prescribed amount of animal feeding stuff for the purposes of the definition of sampled portion in regulation 1(2) of these regulations shall be determined in accordance with the following provisions:—

(i) In relation to solid feeding stuff in packages, the prescribed amount shall be the quantity of feeding stuff present or 5 tons, whichever is the less.

(ii) In relation to solid feeding stuff which is packed in bulk containers—

(a) if any of those containers holds not less than 5 tons of feeding stuff, the prescribed amount shall be the contents of any such container;

(*b*) if all the containers together hold not less than 5 tons of feeding stuff and every container holds less than 5 tons, the prescribed amount shall be the contents of the lowest number of containers which together holds not less than 5 tons;

(*c*) if all the containers together hold less than 5 tons of feeding stuff or if all the feeding stuff is in one container, the prescribed amount shall be the quantity of feeding stuff present.

(iii) In relation to solid feeding stuff which is loose in heaps or bays—

(*a*) if the feeding stuff is in more than one heap or bay, any of which contains not less than 5 tons of feeding stuff, the prescribed amount shall be the contents of any heap or bay containing not less than 5 tons;

(*b*) if all the heaps or bays together contain not less than 5 tons of feeding stuff and every heap or bay contains less than 5 tons, the prescribed amount shall be the contents of the lowest number of heaps or bays which together contain not less than 5 tons;

(*c*) if all the heaps or bays together contain less than 5 tons or if all the feeding stuff is in one heap or bay, the prescribed amount shall be the quantity of feeding stuff present.

(iv) In relation to liquid feeding stuff in containers—

(*a*) if any of those containers holds not less than 1 000 gallons of feeding stuff the prescribed amount shall be the contents of any such container;

(*b*) if all the containers together hold not less than 1 000 gallons of feeding stuff and every container holds less than 1 000 gallons, the prescribed amount shall be the contents of the lowest number of containers which together hold not less than 1 000 gallons;

(*c*) if all the containers together hold less than 1 000 gallons of feeding stuff the prescribed amount shall be the quantity of feeding stuff present.

2. In the case of feeding stuff to which paragraphs 1(i) and (iv) of this Part of this Schedule apply, only unopened packages or containers which appear to the inspector proposing to take the sample to be the original packages or containers of the feeding stuff shall be selected for the purpose of the sample.

3. Samples shall not be drawn from any part of the sampled portion which bears the appearance of having received damage.

4. An inspector who proposes to take a sample under section 112 of the Act on premises on which he has reasonable cause to believe that there is any feeding stuff which the occupier of the premises has purchased, not for the purpose of re-sale in the course of trade but for the purpose of use as a feeding stuff, shall satisfy himself that the conditions in which the feeding stuff is stored are not such as might cause deterioration of the feeding stuff and that the feeding stuff appears not to have been contaminated by any other material.

5. In every case the sampling shall be carried out in a manner which will protect the sample from contamination and shall be done as quickly as is possible, consistent with due care, and the feeding stuff shall not be exposed any longer than is necessary.

6. Where a sample has been taken from a feeding stuff in a container which has been opened for the purpose of sampling at a place other than the premises on which the feeding stuff was packed the inspector shall affix to the container a label stating, or otherwise mark the container to the effect, that a portion of the feeding stuff has been withdrawn for the purpose of sampling and the inspector shall, if so required by the person in charge of the container, close and refasten it in an appropriate manner.

PART II

PROVISIONS APPLICABLE TO SOLID FEEDING STUFFS

1. It shall be assumed that the sampled portion is composed of separate approximately equal parts and that the number of such parts is equivalent to—

(*a*) the number of packages to be selected in accordance with paragraph 4(*a*) of this part of this Schedule; or (*b*) the number of portions, where the sampled portion is in bulk, to be taken in accordance with paragraph 4(*b*) of this part of this Schedule.

The packages or portions shall be selected on the basis of at least one from each assumed approximately equal part and shall be drawn at random.

2. Where feeding stuff in packages which an inspector has reasonable cause to believe has been purchased, not for the purpose of resale in the course of trade but for the purpose of use as a feeding stuff has been delivered to the purchaser and is to be sampled but some part of the consignment is no longer present, the number of packages to be selected shall be calculated as if not less than the whole consignment were still present. Where this calculation results in a number of packages larger than that present the number to be selected for sampling shall be the number present.

3. Notwithstanding anything in this Schedule a sampling spear shall not be used if objection is raised. thereto, prior to the taking of a sample, on the ground that the feeding stuff is unsuitable.

Where the feeding stuff is in the state of small lumps or meal

4. (*a*) *In packages*

Where the feeding stuff is in packages, a number of packages shall be selected in accordance with the following table:—

	Number of packages to be selected for sampling
Where the sampled portion consists of one package ...	1
Where the sampled portion consists of two packages ...	2
Where the sampled portion consists of three packages...	3
Where the sampled portion consists of more than three packages but not more than 20 packages	4
Where the sampled portion consists of more than 20 packages but not more than 60 packages ...	6
Where the sampled portion consists of more than 60 packages but not more than 100 packages ...	8
Where the sampled portion consists of more than 100 packages but not more than 400 packages ...	10
Where the sampled portion consists of more than 400 packages	20

When the number of packages has been selected in accordance with this sub-paragraph, either—

    (i) the selected packages shall be emptied separately and worked up with a shovel and one shovelful taken from each, and the shovelfuls so taken shall then be thoroughly mixed together and any lumps broken up; or

    (ii) when the feeding stuff is of a suitable nature, a portion shall be taken from each selected package by means of a closed sampling spear and the separate portions thus taken shall be thoroughly mixed together.

From the mixture so obtained, the samples shall be drawn in the following manner:—

    Heap the feeding stuff to form a "cone"; flatten the cone and quarter it. Reject two diagonally opposite quarters, mix the remainder and continue the quartering and rejection, if necessary, until the remainder is from about 2 lb to 4 lb in weight. Alternatively the reduction of the gross sample by the quartering method may be effected by the use of a mechanical quartering device known as a sample divider or riffle.

(b) *In bulk*

Where the feeding stuff is in bulk, a number of portions shall be taken by a shovel or a closed sampling spear as follows:—

	Portions
Where the sampled portion does not exceed 2 cwt ...	not less than 1 per $\frac{1}{2}$ cwt or part thereof
Where the sampled portion exceeds 2 cwt and does not exceed 1 ton	not less than 6
Where the sampled portion exceeds 1 ton and does not exceed 3 tons	not less than 10
Where the sampled portion exceeds 3 tons and does not exceed 5 tons	not less than 12
Where the sampled portion exceeds 5 tons and does not exceed 25 tons	not less than 20
Where the quantity exceeds 25 tons	not less than 40

The portions, according to whether they have been taken by a shovel or spear, shall be treated in the manner described in paragraph 4(a) and the sample drawn in the manner also described in that paragraph.

Where the feeding stuff is in the form of cake

5. A number of cakes shall be selected from the different parts of the sampled portion equivalent to the number of portions taken in accordance with paragraph 4(b) of this part of this Schedule. The selected cakes shall be broken by a cakebreaker or in some other manner so that the whole will pass through a sieve with meshes one and a quarter inch square and then shall be thoroughly mixed. From the mixture so obtained, a sample of not less than 6 lb in weight shall be drawn in the manner described in paragraph 4(a) of this part of this Schedule.

Where the feeding stuff is in the form of feed blocks or mineral blocks

6. One block shall be selected irrespective of the size of the sampled portion. From this block a sample of 2lb to 4lb shall be taken in any manner.

Where the feeding stuff consists of particles of grossly differing sizes

7. (a) *In packages*

The packages shall be selected according to the appropriate scale in paragraph 4(a) of this part of this Schedule. The selected packages shall be emptied separately, worked up with a shovel and one shovelful from each set aside. The shovelfuls so set aside shall then be thoroughly mixed together and reduced if necessary by the cone and quartering method described in paragraph 4(a) of this part of this Schedule to a quantity of not less than 15lb. Any lumps in the said quantity shall be crushed (and for this purpose may be separated from other material) and the whole then thoroughly remixed. From the mixture a sample of 2lb to 4lb weight shall be drawn.

(b) *In bulk*

Shovelfuls shall be taken according to the appropriate scale in paragraph 4(b) of this part of this Schedule. The shovelfuls thus taken shall be treated, and a sample drawn, in the manner described in paragraph 7(a) above.

Where a portion of the feeding stuff is unsuitable for feeding purposes

8. Where any appreciable portion of the feeding stuff appears to be mouldy, or is otherwise apparently unsuitable for feeding purposes, separate samples shall be drawn of the unsuitable portion and of the residue of the feeding stuff respectively, and in the case of unsuitable cakes, the sample may consist of several large pieces representative thereof.

Part III

Provisions applicable where the feeding stuff is in a liquid or semi-liquid condition

In containers each containing not more than one quart

1. The number of containers to be selected shall be taken at random in accordance with the appropriate scale for solid feeding stuffs in paragraph 4(*a*) of Part II of this Schedule. The entire contents of the selected containers shall be emptied into a clean dry vessel of glass or other suitable material and well mixed by stirring or shaking. From this mixture a sample of between about one quart and about half a gallon shall be drawn, the mixture being stirred or shaken immediately before the sample is drawn.

In containers each containing more than one quart and not more than forty gallons

2. The number of containers to be selected shall be taken at random in accordance with the appropriate scale for solid feeding stuffs in paragraph 4(*a*) of Part II of this Schedule. The selected containers shall be well shaken or the contents agitated or otherwise treated to ensure uniformity. An approximately equal proportion of fluid shall then be taken immediately from each of the selected containers, emptied into a clean dry vessel of glass or other suitable material and well mixed by stirring or shaking. From this mixture a sample of between about one quart and about half a gallon shall be drawn, the mixture being stirred or shaken immediately before the sample is drawn.

In a bulk container or containers containing more than forty gallons

3. (*a*) When a consignment is being withdrawn from the bulk container and there is a tap in the outlet pipe from which it is suitable to draw a sample, a quantity in accordance with the table below shall be drawn from the tap (after first withdrawing sufficient to remove any residues in the pipe) into a clean dry vessel of glass or other suitable material, made up of portions of not less than one pint and of approximately equal size taken at regular intervals; otherwise

(*b*) if the liquid is homogeneous, about one quart shall be drawn from a convenient outlet in the container (after first withdrawing sufficient to remove any residues in the outlet) into a clean dry vessel of glass or other suitable material, or

(*c*) if the liquid is not homogeneous, the contents shall be well stirred or otherwise agitated and sampling shall then proceed as in sub-paragraph (*b*), but

(*d*) if it is not possible to make the liquid homogeneous, in the manner described in sub-paragraph (*c*), the contents shall be sampled by lowering an open tube (which must be long enough to reach the bottom of the container) perpendicularly into the container. One or both ends of the tube shall then be closed and the contents transferred to a clean dry vessel of glass or other suitable material. If sampling by tube is impracticable, portions shall be taken from various levels of the container with a sampling bottle so as to obtain a quantity fairly representative of the whole. The appropriate process shall be repeated until a quantity in accordance with the table below has been withdrawn.

(*e*) Where a sampled portion consists of two or more containers, a sample from each, drawn in the manner described in sub-paragraph (*a*), (*b*), (*c*) or (*d*), as appropriate. shall be placed in a clean dry vessel of glass or other suitable material.

(*f*) The quantity taken as described in sub-paragraphs (*a*), (*d*) and (*e*) shall be thoroughly mixed and a sample of about one quart transferred into a clean dry vessel of glass or other suitable material.

TABLE

QUANTITIES OF LIQUID OR SEMI-LIQUID FEEDING STUFFS TO BE WITHDRAWN
IN ACCORDANCE WITH SUB-PARAGRAPH (3)(*a*) OR (*d*) ABOVE

Where the sampled portion—	Quantity to be withdrawn
does not exceed 1,000 gallons	not less than 2 pints
exceeds 1,000 gallons but does not exceed 5,000 gallons	not less than 3 pints
exceeds 5,000 gallons but does not exceed 10,000 gallons	not less than 4 pints
exceeds 10,000 gallons but does not exceed 15,000 gallons	not less than 5 pints
exceeds 15,000 gallons but does not exceed 20,000 gallons	not less than 6 pints
exceeds 20,000 gallons but does not exceed 50,000 gallons	not less than 7 pints
exceeds 50,000 gallons but does not exceed 100,000 gallons	not less than 10 pints
exceeds 100,000 gallons	not less than 20 pints

PART IV

DIVISION, MARKING, SEALING AND FASTENING OF SAMPLE

1. Where the sample has been taken in the manner prescribed by this Schedule the inspector shall divide it into four parts as nearly as possible equal, in the following manner:—

(*a*) *In the case of dry or powdered substances*

The sample, drawn as described in Part II of this Schedule, shall be thoroughly mixed and divided into four similar and approximately equal parts. Each of these parts shall be placed in an appropriate container such that the composition at the time of sampling of the feeding stuff is preserved.

(*b*) *In the case of substances in a liquid or semi-liquid condition*

The sample, drawn as described in Part III of this Schedule, shall be thoroughly mixed and at once divided into four similar and approximately equal parts by pouring successive portions into each of four appropriate containers. The containers used shall be such that the composition at the time of sampling of the feeding stuff is preserved and shall be so fastened that spillage or evaporation of the contents is prevented.

Each of the containers referred to in sub-paragraphs (*a*) and (*b*) above shall be so secured and sealed that it cannot be opened without breaking the seal; or alternatively the container may be placed in a stout envelope or in a linen, cotton or plastic bag and the envelope or bag then secured and sealed in such a manner that the part of the sample cannot be removed without breaking the seal or the envelope or the bag.

2. Where a sample consists of animal feeding stuffs enclosed in unopened containers, and it appears to the inspector that to open the containers and divide their contents into parts is not reasonably practicable, or may affect the composition, or impede the proper analysis or other appropriate examination of the contents the inspector may divide the containers into four lots without opening them. Each of the said lots shall be regarded as a part of the sample and shall be placed in a bag made of plastic or other suitable material. The bag shall then be secured and sealed in such a manner that the part of the sample cannot be removed without breaking the seal or the bag.

3. Each of the said parts shall be sealed and initialled by the inspector. It may also be sealed or initialled by the person on whose premises the sample is taken, or his representative. Each part shall be marked with the name of the feeding stuff, the manufacturer's reference number of the batch to which the part of the feeding stuff belongs, the date and place of the sampling and some distinguishing reference, in such a manner that the particulars so marked can be seen without breaking the seal or seals.

Part V

Disposal of parts of sample

1. The inspector shall dispose of the four parts of any sample by:

   (a) supplying one part to the agricultural analyst for the inspector's area;

   (b) retaining for 15 months one part for use, if required, by the Government Chemist;

   (c) in the case of a sample taken from an animal feeding stuff in transit from outside the United Kingdom, supplying one part of the sample to the consignee, or in the case of a sample taken from an animal feeding stuff in transit within the United Kingdom, supplying one part of the sample to the consignor;

   (d) in the case of a sample taken from an animal feeding stuff which is not in transit, supplying one part of the sample to the person on whose premises the sample was taken;

   (e) in any case in which the enforcement authority contemplates bringing proceedings against any person for an offence against the Act, supplying one part of the sample to the person against whom proceedings are contemplated (unless he has already received a part under the provisions of sub-paragraph (c) or (d) of this paragraph) and pending disposal (if required) in accordance with this paragraph retaining such part for 15 months.

2. In every case the inspector shall inform the person to whom the part of the sample is supplied that the sample has been obtained for the purpose of analysis or other appropriate examination.

3. In any case in which a part of a sample is supplied to any person pursuant to the provisions of paragraph 1(e) above, the inspector shall when sending it—

   (a) state that the sample has been obtained by him; and

   (b) specify the person from whom and the place from which he obtained it.

4. Section 127 of the Act shall have effect in relation to supplying any part of a sample in pursuance of the preceding paragraphs as it has effect in relation to the service of a document.

5. If after reasonable inquiry the inspector is unable to ascertain the name of a person to whom, or the address at which, a part of a sample ought to be supplied in pursuance of the preceding provisions of this part of this Schedule, he may retain that part of the sample instead of supplying it.

Analysis or examination of sample

6. An inspector who submits a sample for analysis to the agricultural analyst for the inspector's area shall supply with the part of the sample—

   (a) a copy of the label or leaflet relating to the feeding stuff from which the sample was taken, or where this is not reasonably practicable, a copy of each of the particulars as may be necessary for the purposes of analysis by the agricultural analyst as may appear on the label or leaflet; and

   (b) a statement signed by the inspector that the sample was taken or otherwise obtained in the manner prescribed by these Regulations, and, where he requires an analysis to be carried out in respect of some only of the medicinal ingredients stated on the label or leaflet to be present or of any other medicinal ingredient which may be present, he shall also supply instructions appropriate to such an analysis.

7.—(1) Subject to the following sub-paragraphs the agricultural analyst shall analyse the sample, or cause the sample to be analysed by some other person under his direction, as soon as practicable.

(2) If the agricultural analyst determines that for any reason an effective analysis of the sample cannot be performed by him or under his direction, he shall send it to the agricultural analyst for some other area together with any documents received by him with the sample, and that other agricultural analyst shall as soon as practicable analyse the sample or cause it to be analysed by some other person under his direction.

(3) If the agricultural analyst determines that for any reason it is necessary to carry out an analysis or other appropriate examination which he is not in a position to undertake he shall submit the sample for analysis or for such examination to the person having the management or control of any laboratory available for the purpose in accordance with any arrangements made in that behalf by the relevant enforcement authority.

(4) If the agricultural analyst determines that for any reason he is not in a position to undertake the whole of an analysis he shall submit a suitable proportion of the sample for the appropriate part of the analysis to the person referred to in sub-paragraph (3) of this paragraph.

(5) Before any sample which has been unsealed by an agricultural analyst is sent to another agricultural analyst or to a laboratory under the provisions of sub-paragraph (2), (3) or (4) of this paragraph it shall be resealed and initialled by the agricultural analyst so sending it.

8.—(1) An agricultural analyst who has analysed a sample submitted to him under the preceding provisions of this part of this Schedule, or who has caused such a sample to be analysed by some other person under his direction, shall issue and send a certificate of analysis in the form prescribed by these regulations to the inspector, who shall send a copy of it to any person to whom a part of the sample has been supplied in accordance with paragraph 1 of this part of this Schedule.

(2) A person having the management or control of a laboratory in which a sample submitted to him under the preceding provisions of this part of this Schedule has been analysed or examined, or a person appointed by him for the purpose, shall issue and send a certificate of such analysis or examination in the form prescribed by these regulations to the inspector, who shall send a copy of it to any person to whom a part of the sample has been supplied under paragraph 1 of this part of this Schedule.

(3) A person having the management or control of a laboratory in which a proportion only of the sample submitted to him by an agricultural analyst has been analysed, or a person appointed by him for the purpose, shall issue and send a certificate of such analysis in the form prescribed by these regulations to the agricultural analyst, who shall send it, together with his own certificate of analysis in the form prescribed by these regulations, to the inspector; and the inspector shall send a copy of each certificate to any person to whom a part of the sample has been supplied under paragraph 1 of this part of this Schedule.

9. Any certificate issued under the last preceding paragraph shall be signed by the person who issues the certificate.

Provisions as to evidence

10. In any proceedings for an offence under the Act a document produced by one of the parties to the proceedings and purporting to be a certificate issued under paragraph 8 of this part of this Schedule or a certificate of the Government Chemist, shall be sufficient evidence of the facts stated in the document, unless the other party requires that the person who issued the certificate shall be called as a witness; and, in any proceedings in Scotland, if that person is called as a witness, his evidence shall be sufficient evidence of those facts.

11. In any proceedings for an offence under the Act a document produced by one of the parties to the proceedings, which has been supplied to him by the other party as being a copy of such a certificate, shall be sufficient evidence of the facts stated in the document.

Proof by written statement

12. In relation to England and Wales section 9 of the Criminal Justice Act 1967, and in relation to Northern Ireland any corresponding enactment of the Parliament of Northern Ireland or measure of the Northern Ireland Assembly shall not have effect with respect to any document produced as mentioned in paragraph 10 or paragraph 11 of this part of this Schedule or with respect to any certificate transmitted to a court under section 115(1J)(*b*) of the Act.

Payment for sample taken under compulsory powers

13. Where for the purpose of taking a sample of any animal feeding stuff in the exercise of any powers conferred by section 112 of the Act an inspector takes some of it from any parcel of the animal feeding stuff exposed for sale by retail which does not weigh more than fourteen pounds the owners of any such parcel may require the inspector to purchase it on behalf of the authority for whom he acts.

Application of section 64 of the Act to samples

14. Where an animal feeding stuff is taken as a sample by an inspector in the exercise of any power conferred by section 112 of the Act, the provisions of sub-sections (1) to (4) of section 64 of the Act shall have effect as if the taking of the animal feeding stuff as a sample were a sale of it to the inspector by the person from whom it is taken; and, if the animal feeding stuff was prepared in pursuance of a prescription given by a veterinary surgeon or veterinary practitioner, those provisions shall so have effect as if, in subsection (1) of that section, for the words "demanded by the purchaser", there were substituted the words "specified in the prescription".

Application to Northern Ireland

15. In the application of this part of this Schedule to Northern Ireland—

    (*a*) for any reference to the agricultural analyst for the inspector's area there shall be substituted a reference to an agricultural analyst in Northern Ireland, and the expression "agricultural analyst" shall not include the Chief Agricultural Analyst for Northern Ireland;

    (*b*) for any reference to the Government Chemist there shall be substituted a reference to the Chief Agricultural Analyst for Northern Ireland.

PART VI

MODIFICATIONS TO THE FOREGOING PROVISIONS OF THIS SCHEDULE PURSUANT TO REGULATION 3(2)

The following modifications to the foregoing provisions of this Schedule shall be applicable in the case of any sample set aside from a substance or article seized in pursuance of section 112(4) of the Act, or in the case of a substance or article so seized which is itself treated as a sample—

    (*a*) references to a feeding stuff shall be construed as references to any substance or article seized by an inspector in pursuance of section 112(4) of the Act, and the reference in paragraph 1 of Part IV to the taking of a sample in the manner prescribed by this Schedule shall be construed as a reference to the setting aside of a sample in that manner or to the treating of a substance or article as a sample pursuant to section 112(4), as the context requires;

    (*b*) paragraphs 2, 3 and 4 of Part I of this Schedule shall not apply to a sample set aside from a substance or article seized as aforesaid;

    (*c*) Parts I, II and III of this Schedule shall not apply in the case of a substance or article treated as a sample as aforesaid;

(d) in Part V of this Schedule, the following sub-paragraph shall be applicable in place of sub-paragraphs (c) and (d) of paragraph 1:—

"supplying one part of the sample to the person who made the request under section 113(2) of the Act for such sample to be set aside or for such substance or article to be treated as a sample;";

and sub-paragraph (e) of paragraph 1 shall be read as if for the reference to sub-paragraphs (c) and (d) of paragraph 1 aforesaid there were substituted a reference to the foregoing sub-paragraph applicable in place of the said sub-paragraphs (c) and (d);

(e) paragraphs 5, 13 and 14 of Part V of this Schedule shall not apply.

SCHEDULE 3

METHODS OF ANALYSIS

(Section 117(3) and Regulation 4)

The main divisions in this Schedule are as follows:—

1. Introduction

2. Preparation of the sample for analysis

3. Detection and identification of antibiotics of the tetracycline group

4. Determination of acinitrazole

5. Determination of amprolium

6. Determination of buquinolate

7. Determination of chlortetracycline, oxytetracycline and tetracycline by diffusion through agar

8. Determination of chlortetracycline, oxytetracycline and tetracycline by turbidimetry

9. Determination of clopidol

10. Determination of copper by the diethyldithiocarbamate spectrophotometric method

11. Determination of copper by the atomic absorption spectrophotometric method

12. Determination of dinitolmide

13. Determination of furazolidone

14. Determination of ethopabate

15. Determination of nicarbazin

16. Determination of nifursol

17. Determination of nitrofurazone

18. Determination of nitrovin

19. Determination of nitrovin in feed supplements

20. Determination of oleandomycin

21. Determination of sulphaquinoxaline

22. Determination of tylosin

23. Determination of virginiamycin

1. INTRODUCTION

(1) *General*

When two or more methods are prescribed in this Schedule to determine a medicinal component of a feeding stuff the choice of method shall, except where otherwise indicated, be left to the agricultural analyst concerned; the method used must however be indicated in the certificate of analysis.

(2) *Reagents, culture media and apparatus*

(*a*) All reagents used should be of analytical quality.

(*b*) Where water is mentioned this always means purified water as defined in the European Pharmacopoeia.

(*c*) Solutions for which solvents are not prescribed must be aqueous.

(*d*) Aluminium oxide for chromatography must be neutral unless otherwise prescribed.

(*e*) Any commercial culture media of similar composition and giving the same results as those prescribed, may be used.

(*f*) Only special instruments or apparatus requiring special standards are mentioned in the descriptions of the methods of analysis.

(3) *Report on the results*

The results given in the certificates of analysis shall be the average value obtained on the basis of at least two complete tests. Except for special circumstances it shall be expressed as a proportion by weight of the original sample as it reached the laboratory. The result must not include more significant figures than the accuracy of the method of analysis allows.

2. PREPARATION OF THE SAMPLE FOR ANALYSIS

(1) With some materials, fine grinding may lead to loss or gain of moisture, and allowance for this must be made. Grinding should be as rapid as possible and unnecessary exposure to the atmosphere avoided. Grinding in a laboratory mill is usually quicker than grinding in a mortar although the latter is permissible.

(2) If the sample is in a fine condition and passes through a sieve having a nominal aperture size of 1 mm square[1][3], mix thoroughly and transfer a portion of not less than 100g to a non-corrodible container provided with an air-tight closure.

(3) If the sample does not wholly pass through a sieve having a nominal aperture size of 1mm square[1][3], and wholly passes through a sieve having apertures from 2mm to 3mm square[2][3], mix thoroughly and further grind a portion of not less than 100g to pass through a sieve having a nominal aperture size of 1mm square[1][3]. Transfer the portion so prepared to a non-corrodible container provided with an air-tight closure.

(4) If the sample is in a coarse condition as, for example, pieces of broken cake, carefully grind until the whole passes through a sieve having apertures of from 2mm to 3mm square[2][3]. Mix thoroughly and further grind a portion of not less than 100g to pass through a sieve having a nominal aperture size of 1mm square[1][3]. Transfer the portion so prepared to a non-corrodible container provided with an air-tight closure.

(5) Treat by any other suitable means materials which cannot conveniently be ground or passed through a sieve.

---

(1) Test sieves conforming to British Standard 410: 1969 are suitable.

(2) Test sieves of nominal aperture sizes of 2·00, 2·36 or 2·80mm conforming to British Standard 410: 1969 are suitable.

(3) Where an analysis for copper has to be carried out, a stainless steel sieve should be used.

3. DETECTION AND IDENTIFICATION OF ANTIBIOTICS OF THE TETRACYCLINE GROUP

1. SCOPE AND FIELD OF APPLICATION

The method is for the detection and identification of antibiotics of the tetracycline group in complete feeding stuffs, protein concentrates and feed supplements containing at least 0·1ppm.

2. PRINCIPLE

The sample is extracted with acidified methanol, and the extract examined by ascending paper chromatography with standard tetracycline antibiotics for comparison. The antibiotics are detected and identified by comparison of their Rf values with those of standard substances, either by fluorescence in UV light (high levels of antibiotics), or by bio-autography on an agar medium inoculated with *Bacillus cereus*.

3. REAGENTS AND CULTURE MEDIUM

3.1 Buffer solution pH 3·5:

Citric acid monohydrate	10·256g
di Sodium hydrogen phosphate Na_2HPO_4. $2H_2O$	7·45 g
Acetone	300ml
Water to	1,000ml

3.2 Phosphate buffer solution pH 5·5:

Potassium dihydrogen phosphate KH_2PO_4	130·86 g
di Sodium hydrogen phosphate Na_2HPO_4. $2H_2O$	6·947g
Water to	1,000ml

3.3 Eluting solvent I: A mixture of nitromethane, chloroform and 1,3-dichloro-propan-2-ol, in the proportions by volume: 20+10+1·5. Prepare immediately before use.

3.4 Eluting solvent II: A mixture of nitromethane, chloroform and 2-picoline, in the proportions by volume: 20+10+3. Prepare immediately before use.

3.5 Acidified methanol: mix methanol and hydrochloric acid (density 1·18g/ml) in the proportions by volume: 98+2.

3.6 Hydrochloric acid solution 0·1N.

3.7 Ammonia, (density 0·88g per ml).

3.8 Standard substances: chlortetracycline and tetracycline, the activities of which are expressed in terms of the hydrochlorides; oxytetracycline, the activity of which is expressed in terms of the free base.

3.8.1 Standard solutions: dissolve suitable quantities of the standard substances (3.8) in hydrochloric acid (3.6) to give solutions containing respectively 500µg per ml of chlortetracycline hydrochloride, tetracycline hydrochloride and oxytetracycline (free base).

3.8.2 Reference solutions for detection by UV: dilute the standard solutions (3.8.1) with phosphate buffer solution (3.2) to obtain solutions containing 100µg per ml of the antibiotics expressed as in 3.8.1.

3.8.3 Reference solutions for detection by bio-autography: dilute the standard solutions (3.8.1) with phosphate buffer solution (3.2) to obtain solutions containing 5µg per ml of the antibiotics expressed as in 3.8.1.

3.9 MICRO-ORGANISM: *B. cereus* ATCC 11778 (NCIB 8849: NCTC 10320).

3.9.1 Maintenance of the parent strain:
Proceed as described in Division 7, Determination of Chlortetracycline, Oxytetracycline and Tetracycline by Diffusion Through Agar, Sub-Division 3.1.

1d

3.9.2 Preparation of the spore suspension:
Proceed as described in Division 7, Determination of Chlortetracycline, Oxytetracycline and Tetracycline by Diffusion Through Agar Sub-Division 3.2.1.

3.10 Culture medium:

Glucose	1g
Tryptic peptone	10g
Meat extract	1·5g
Yeast extract	3g
Agar	20g
Water to	1,000ml

Adjust the pH to 5·8 immediately before use.

3.11 2, 3, 5-triphenyltetrazolium chloride solution: dissolve 0·1g 2, 3, 5-triphenyltetrazolium chloride and 5g glucose in water and dilute to 100ml.

4. APPARATUS

4.1 Apparatus for ascending paper chromatography (height of paper: 25cm). Schleicher and Schull paper 2040b or 2043b, or equivalent.

4.2 UV lamp for the detection of fluorescence, 350nm.

4.3 Bio-assay plates approximately 20 × 30cm.

5. PROCEDURE

5.1 *Extraction*

5.1.1 Extract, by shaking for a few minutes, the finely divided and mixed sample with acidified methanol (3.5), in suitable proportions to produce a solution containing approximately 100μg per ml of the antibiotic. Centrifuge the mixture, and dilute the clear supernatant if necessary, with acidified methanol (3.5), to give the required concentration of antibiotic.

5.1.2 Dilute the extract from 5.1.1 with acidified methanol (3.5) to give an antibiotic concentration of approximately 5μg per ml.

5.2 *Chromatography*

Immerse the paper in the buffer solution pH 3.5 (3.1) and eliminate the excess liquid by compressing the paper between leaves of dry filter paper. Place volumes of 0·01ml reference solutions (3.8.2 and 3.8.3) and extract (5.1.1 and 5.1.2) on the paper. Adequate separation depends upon the paper having an optimum water content.

Develop by ascending chromatography, use eluting solvent I (3.3) for detection by bio-autography, and eluting solvent II (3.4) for detection by UV light. When the solvent front reaches a height of 15 to 20cm (approximately 1½ hours), remove the paper and dry.

5.3 *Detection by UV light*

For antibiotic concentrations greater than 1μg per ml. Expose the paper to ammonia vapour (3.7) and then examine under the UV lamp (4.2). Golden yellow fluorescent spots indicate the presence of antibiotics of the tetracycline group. (See para 6).

5.4 *Detection by bio-autography*

Pour the culture medium (3.10), previously inoculated with *B. cereus* spore suspension (3.9) into a sterile antibiotic assay plate (4.3) and allow to set. Place the paper on the culture medium and allow to remain in contact for 5 minutes, then transfer it to a fresh position on the culture medium, for the duration of incubation period. Incubate at 30°C overnight. The presence of an antibiotic of the tetracycline group is shown by clear zones of inhibition in the cloudy culture medium. To enhance the contrast between the zones, spray the plate with the 2, 3, 5-triphenyltetrazolium solution (3.11).

6.   IDENTIFICATION

The relative Rf values of antibiotics of the tetracycline group are given as follows. These values may vary slightly according to the quality of the paper and its level of humidity:

Chlortetracycline	0·60
Tetracycline	0·40
Oxytetracycline	0·20
4-epi-Chlortetracycline	0·15
4-epi-Tetracycline	0·13
4-epi-Oxytetracycline	0·10

The "epi" compounds have an antibiotic activity lower than that of normal compounds.

4.   DETERMINATION OF ACINITRAZOLE

(2-acetamido-5-nitrothiazole)

1.   SCOPE AND FIELD OF APPLICATION

The method is for the determination of acinitrazole in complete feeding stuffs, protein concentrates and feed supplements. The lower limit of the determination is 35ppm.

2.   PRINCIPLE

The sample is extracted with hot dimethylformamide. The extract is purified on a column of aluminium oxide, the acinitrazole is eluted with acidified methanol and the eluate treated with sodium hydroxide forming a yellow colour, the absorbance of which is measured at 410nm.

3.   REAGENTS

3.1   Dimethylformamide.

3.2   Methanol.

3.3   Hydrochloric acid solution, 5N.

3.4   Acidified methanol: add 2ml of 5N hydrochloric acid (3.3) to 100ml of methanol (3.2).

3.5   Sodium hydroxide, alcoholic solution: dilute 2·5ml of 10N sodium hydroxide to 100ml with ethanol; stand for two days to allow carbonates to settle.

3.6   Aluminium oxide for column chromatography: transfer 100g aluminium oxide to a suitable container, add 250ml of hydrochloric acid solution (1ml of hydrochloric acid (density 1·18g per ml) diluted to 100ml with water) and stir mechanically for fifteen minutes. Collect the slurry on filter paper in a Buchner funnel. Wash the aluminium oxide on the filter-paper with ten 50ml portions of water and dry by suction. Dry it for at least four hours at 100°C.

3.7   Acinitrazole standard solution: weigh to the nearest 0·1mg, 100mg of acinitrazole (B.Vet.C. grade), dissolve in dimethylformamide (3.1) and dilute to 100ml with dimethylformamide. Dilute 5ml of this solution to 200ml with dimethylformamide. 1ml of this solution contains 25μg acinitrazole.

4.   APPARATUS

4.1   Spectrophotometer with 10mm cells.

4.2   Chromatography columns: glass tubes, internal diameter: 9mm; length: 400 to 500mm, with openings 4 to 5mm diameter at the lower ends. Insert small plugs of glass wool in the lower ends of the tubes and compress the plugs firmly with a glass rod so that a thickness of 2 to 3mm is obtained.

5.   PROCEDURE

5.1 *Extraction*

Weigh to the nearest 0·001g, approximately 20g of the finely divided and mixed sample or a suitable amount expected to contain about 6mg of acinitrazole and transfer it into a 250ml beaker. Add 60ml of boiling dimethylformamide (3.1), boil for two minutes stirring continuously and then cool to room temperature. Filter the liquid through a sintered-glass funnel (porosity G3) under gentle suction. Repeat the extraction with 60ml of boiling dimethylformamide and filter through the funnel. Rinse the beaker with two 30ml portions of cold dimethylformamide and filter through the funnel. Cool the filtrate to room temperature, transfer to a 200ml graduated flask and dilute to volume with dimethylformamide.

5.2 *Purification*

Prepare a slurry of aluminium oxide (3.6) by mixing three volumes of dimethyl-formamide (3.1) with one volume of aluminium oxide. Heat the slurry on a hotplate (do not boil) and then cool to room temperature. Pour the slurry into glass columns (4.2) and allow it to settle to a height of approximately 270mm. Prepare a separate column for each sample. Run a 10ml aliquot of the dimethyl-formamide extract of the sample onto the top of the column and allow the liquid to pass through under gravity. Wash with three successive 10ml portions of dimethylformamide ensuring that the surface of the aluminium oxide is covered throughout. Discard all the dimethylformamide eluates.

Run four successive 10ml portions of acidified methanol (3.4) through the column into a 50ml graduated flask ensuring that the whole of the yellow band of acinitrazole is eluted. Leave about 2ml of the last acidified methanol portion on the top of the column. Add 0·5ml of 5N hydrochloric acid (3.3) to the flask and mix. Dilute to the mark with methanol (3.2).

5.3 *Determination*

Pipette two 20ml aliquots of the sample extract solution (5.2) into each of two 25ml graduated flasks. Dilute the first (A) to the mark with methanol (3.2) and the second (B) with alcoholic sodium hydroxide (3.5). Prepare a reagent blank by adding 5ml of alcoholic sodium hydroxide to a third 25ml graduated flask and diluting to the mark with methanol (3.2). Measure the absorbances of the solutions A and B at 410nm in 10mm cells with the reagent blank as reference. Read the absorbances immediately after the solutions have been prepared.

5.4 *Standard test*

Repeat the entire procedure on a 10ml aliquot of the standard solution (3.7) and a new column of aluminium oxide, commencing at (5.2), "Run a 10ml aliquot of the dimethylformamide . . .".

6.   CALCULATION OF RESULTS

The acinitrazole content in ppm of sample is given by the formula:

$$\frac{(E_A - E_B) \times S \times 200}{(E_A{}^1 - E_B{}^1) \times W \times 10}$$

in which:

E_A =   absorbance of methanolic aliquot from sample;

E_B =   ,,   ,, alcoholic NaOH aliquot from sample;

$E_A{}^1$ =   ,,   ,, methanolic aliquot from standard;

$E_B{}^1$ =   ,,   ,, alcoholic NaOH aliquot from standard;

S   =   weight of acinitrazole standard run onto column (μg); and

W   =   weight of test portion in g.

5.   DETERMINATION OF AMPROLIUM

[1-(4-amino-2-propylpyrimidin-5-yl-methyl)-2-methylpyridinium chloride hydro-chloride]

1.   SCOPE AND FIELD OF APPLICATION

The method is for the determination of the quantity of amprolium in complete feeding stuffs, protein concentrates and feed supplements. The lower limit of the determination is 40ppm.

2.   PRINCIPLE

The sample is extracted with diluted methanol. The extract is purified on a column of aluminium oxide and treated with a methanolic solution of 2,7-dihydroxynaphthalene, potassium ferricyanide, potassium cyanide and sodium hydroxide, forming a purple-coloured complex the absorbance of which is measured at 530nm.

3.   REAGENTS

3.1   Methanol.

3.2   Diluted methanol: mix two volumes of methanol (3.1) with one volume of water.

3.3   Potassium ferricyanide solution: dissolve 0·2g potassium ferricyanide ($K_3Fe(CN)_6$) in water and dilute to 100ml. This solution is stable for two weeks.

3.4   Potassium cyanide solution: dissolve 1g potassium cyanide in water and dilute to 100ml. This solution is stable for two weeks.

3.5   Sodium hydroxide solution: dissolve 2·25g sodium hydroxide in water and dilute to 200ml.

3.6   Methanolic sodium hydroxide solution: dilute 15ml of the solution (3.5) to 200ml with methanol (3.1).

3.7   2,7-dihydroxynaphthalene solution: dissolve 25mg of 2,7-dihydroxynaphthalene in methanol (3.1) and make it up to 1 000ml with methanol (3.1).

3.8   Chromogenic reagent: transfer 90ml of 2,7-dihydroxynaphthalene solution (3.7) to a 250ml conical flask, add 5ml of potassium ferricyanide solution (3.3) and mix well. Then add 5ml of potassium cyanide solution (3.4), stopper the flask and mix well. Leave to stand for 30 to 35 minutes, add 100ml of methanolic sodium hydroxide solution (3.6), mix and filter through a sintered-glass crucible (porosity G3). Use this reagent within 75 minutes of filtering.

3.9   Aluminium oxide for column chromatography: before use, stir 100g of aluminium oxide with 500ml of water for 30 minutes, filter the slurry, wash the aluminium oxide on the filter 3 times with 50ml of methanol (3.1) drying each time by suction, leave to stand overnight and then dry for 2 hours at 100°C in a vacuum oven. Put in a desiccator to cool. Check the activity by subjecting a specified quantity of standard solution (3.11) to analysis, starting from point 5.2. The recovery of the amprolium must be 100%±4%.

3.10 Standard substance: pure amprolium complying with the following characteristics: Melting point (decomposition): 248°C.
Molecular extinction coefficient at both 265 and 235nm in water: $11·0 \times 10^3$.

3.11 Standard solution: weigh to the nearest 0·1mg, 50mg of pure amprolium (3.10). Dissolve in diluted methanol (3.2) in a 500ml graduated flask, make up to volume with the same solvent and mix. Dilute 10·0ml to 50ml with diluted methanol (3.2) in a graduated flask and mix well. 1ml of this solution contains 20μg of amprolium.

4.   APPARATUS

4.1   Glass tube for chromatography (internal diameter: 9mm; length: 400 to 500mm).

4.2   Spectrophotometer, with 10mm cells.

5. PROCEDURE

5.1 *Extraction and purification*

Weigh, to the nearest 0·001g, up to 10g of the finely divided and mixed sample. Place the test portion in a 250ml conical flask and add exactly 100ml of diluted methanol (3.2). Shake for 60 minutes and filter. Dilute with diluted methanol (3.2) as necessary to obtain a solution containing 5 to 15μg of amprolium per ml.

Insert a cotton wool plug into the lower end of a chromatographic tube (4.1), and tamp in 5g of aluminium oxide (3.9) and then run in 25·0ml of the extract. Let the liquid percolate through the column, discard the first 5ml and collect the next 12ml in a graduated test-tube.

5.2 *Determination*

Transfer 5·0ml of the solution obtained in (5.1) into centrifuge tube A. Place 5·0ml of diluted methanol (3.2) in centrifuge tube B. Add to each tube 10·0ml of chromogenic reagent (3.8), stopper the tubes, mix and allow to stand for 20 minutes. Then centrifuge for 3 minutes or until a clear solution is obtained and decant solutions A and B into 50ml conical flasks.

Immediately measure the absorbance of solution A at 530nm against solution B as a reference. Determine the quantity of amprolium by referring to the calibration curve (5.3).

5.3 *Calibration curve*

Pipette into centrifuge tubes volumes of 1·0, 2·0, 3·0, 4·0 and 5·0ml respectively of the standard solution (3.11). Make the contents of the first four tubes up to 5·0ml with diluted methanol (3.2). Add to all five tubes 10·0ml of chromogenic reagent (3.8), stopper the tubes, mix and allow to stand for 20 minutes. Then centrifuge for 3 minutes and decant the solutions into 50ml conical flasks.

Immediately measure the absorbance of the solutions at 530nm against a mixture of 5ml diluted methanol (3.2) and 10ml of chromogenic reagent (3.8) as a reference. Plot the calibration curve, using the absorbances as the ordinates and the corresponding quantities of amprolium in μg as the abscissae.

6. CALCULATION OF RESULTS

The amprolium content in ppm of sample is given by the formula

$$\frac{20 \times A \times F}{W}$$

in which:

A = quantity of amprolium in μg as determined by photometric measurement.

W = weight of the test portion in g.

F = dilution factor (from 5.1).

6. DETERMINATION OF BUQUINOLATE

(ethyl 4-hydroxy-6,7-di-isobutoxyquinoline-3-carboxylate)

1. SCOPE AND FIELD OF APPLICATION

The method is for the determination of the quantity of buquinolate in complete feeding stuffs, protein concentrates and feed supplements. The lower limit of the determination is 10ppm. Decoquinate interferes in the determination.

2. PRINCIPLE

The sample is extracted with chloroform. The extract is evaporated to dryness, the residue dissolved in chloroform and the solution is then subjected to thin-layer chromatography. The buquinolate is eluted with ethanol and determined spectrophotofluorimetrically by comparison with standard solutions.

3.   REAGENTS

3.1   Chloroform.

3.2   Ethanol 96% V/V.

3.3   Mixture of chloroform and ethanol: mix 10 volumes of chloroform (3.1) with 1 volume of ethanol (3.2).

3.4   Ethanol 80% V/V.

3.5   Silica gel G for thin-layer chromatography.

3.6   Standard substance: pure buquinolate.

3.7   Standard solutions:

    3.7.1   Standard solution of 0·2mg of buquinolate per ml: Weigh to the nearest 0·1mg, 50mg of standard substance (3.6). Dissolve in chloroform (3.1) in a 250ml graduated flask by warming in a water-bath at 50°C. Leave to cool to room temperature, make up the volume with chloroform (3.1) and mix.

    3.7.2   Working standard solutions: Transfer 5·0, 10·0, 15·0, 20·0 and 25·0ml portions of the solution (3.7.1) into 25ml graduated flasks. Make up to volume with chloroform (3.1) and mix. Prepare immediately before use. These solutions contain respectively 0·04, 0·08, 0·12, 0·16 and 0·20mg of buquinolate per ml.

4.   APPARATUS

4.1   Glass-plates for thin-layer chromatography, 200 × 200mm, prepared as follows. Spread on the plates a uniform layer 0·5mm thick of silica gel G (3.5) and leave to dry in the air for 15 minutes. Keep the plates in a drying oven at 100°C for 2 hours and transfer into a desiccator containing dehydrating silica gel. Ready-made plates are suitable if they give results similar to those for the plates treated as indicated above.

4.2   Zone collector for thin-layer chromatography.

4.3   Short wavelength ultraviolet lamp, 254nm.

4.4   Spectrophotofluorimeter fitted with a xenon lamp, and two monochromators.

4.5   Rotary vacuum evaporator, with 250ml flask.

5.   PROCEDURE

5.1   *Extraction*

Weigh to within 0·001g, a quantity of the finely divided and mixed sample containing about 1·25mg of buquinolate. Place in a 250ml conical flask and add 100ml of chloroform (3.1). Mix, stopper the flask, and shake for one hour. Decant, filter and discard the first few millilitres of the filtrate. Transfer 80ml of the clear filtrate into a 150ml beaker, or into a 250ml flask fitted to the rotary evaporator (4.5). Evaporate nearly to dryness on a water-bath at 50°C, dissolve the oily residue with a few millilitre portions of chloroform (3.1) and transfer quantitatively the liquids into a 10ml graduated flask. Make up to volume with chloroform (3.1) and mix. If the solution is not clear, centrifuge for three minutes at 3 000 rpm in a stoppered tube.

5.2   *Thin-layer chromatography*

By means of a micropipette, deposit in spots on a plate for thin-layer chromatography (4.1) at intervals of 20mm, volumes of 0·25ml of the extract obtained in 5·1 and of the five working standard solutions (3.7.2). Develop the chromatogram with chloroform (3.1) until the solvent front has nearly reached the upper edge of the plate, then dry in a current of air. Develop with the chloroform-ethanol mixture (3.3) until the solvent front has travelled about 120mm. Allow the solvents to evaporate. Examine the plate under the ultraviolet lamp (4.3) and with a needle, mark the boundary of the buquinolate spots (Rf value 0·4 to 0·6).

5.3 *Elution*

Collect the silica gel from each marked zone, by means of a zone collector (4.2), and place in centrifuge tubes. Add to each tube 10·0ml of 80% V/V ethanol (3.4), shake for 20 minutes, then centrifuge for 5 minutes at 3 000 rpm. Decant the clear solutions into 50ml conical flasks.

5.4 *Measurement of fluorescence*

Set the scale of the spectrophotofluorimeter (4.4) at 100 with the aid of the eluate from the most concentrated standard solution, using the excitation wavelength between 200 and 280nm that gives the most intense fluorescence at an emission wavelength of 375nm. Under these conditions, measure the fluorescence of the other eluates (5.3). From the values obtained, determine the quantity (A) of buquinolate in mg in the 10ml of eluate from the sample.

6.   CALCULATION OF RESULTS

The buquinolate content in ppm of sample is given by the formula

$$\frac{50\ 000\ \times\ A}{W}$$

in which:

A = quantity in mg of buquinolate determined by spectrophotofluorimetric measurement.

W = weight of test portion in grams.

7. DETERMINATION OF CHLORTETRACYCLINE, OXYTETRACYCLINE AND TETRACYCLINE BY DIFFUSION THROUGH AGAR

1.   SCOPE AND FIELD OF APPLICATION

The method is for the determination of the quantity of chlortetracycline, oxytetracycline, and tetracycline in complete feeding stuffs, protein concentrates and feed supplements. The lowest limit of determination is 5ppm. Levels lower than 5ppm may be estimated by graphic extrapolation.

2.   PRINCIPLE

For levels equal to or lower than 50ppm the sample is extracted by diluted formamide. For levels higher than 50ppm, it is extracted by a mixture of acetone, water and hydrochloric acid for the determination of chlortetracycline, and a mixture of methanol and hydrochloric acid for the determination of oxytetracycline and tetracycline.

The extracts are then diluted, and their antibiotic activity is determined by measuring the diffusion of chlortetracycline, oxytetracycline or tetracycline in an agar medium inoculated with *Bacillus cereus*. Diffusion is indicated by the formation of zones of inhibition in the presence of the micro-organism. The diameter of these zones is taken to be in direct proportion to the logarithm of the antibiotic concentration.

3.   MICRO-ORGANISM: *B. cereus* ATCC 11778 (NCIB 8849; NCTC 10320)

3.1 *Maintenance of the parent strain*

Inoculate *B. cereus* onto an agar slope prepared from the culture medium (4.1.1). Incubate overnight at approximately 30°C. Keep the culture in a refrigerator and re-inoculate every 14 days onto agar slopes. At the same time prepare sub-cultures for laboratory use.

3.2 *Preparation of the spore suspension*

    3.2.1   Harvest the bacteria from a recently prepared agar slope (3.1) using 2 to 3ml of physiological saline (4.5). Inoculate this suspension onto 300ml of culture medium (4.1.2) in a Roux flask. Incubate for 3 to 5 days at 28 to 30°C and then confirm by examination under the microscope that sporulation has occurred. Harvest the spores in 15ml of ethanol (4.6) and mix. This suspension may be kept in a refrigerator for at least 5 months.

    3.2.2   Make preliminary tests on the assay plates with the culture medium (4.1.3) to determine the quantity of inoculum needed to obtain the largest possible clear zones of inhibition with the different concentrations of antibiotic used. The quantity will usually be 0·2 to 0·3ml per 1 000ml. Inoculate the culture medium at a temperature between 50 and 60°C.

4.   CULTURE MEDIA AND REAGENTS

    4.1.1   Culture medium I:

Glucose	1g
Tryptic peptone	10g
Meat extract	1·5g
Yeast extract	3g
Agar, according to the quality	10 to 20g
Tween 80	1ml
Phosphate buffer solution pH 5·5 (4.2)	10ml
Water to	1 000ml

    Adjust to pH 5·8 before use.

    4.1.2   Culture medium II:
    As for 4.1.1, but having an agar concentration of 3 to 4%.

    4.1.3   Culture medium III:
    As for 4.1.1, with the following additions:

Methylene blue solution, 0·5g per 100ml in ethanol ...	4ml
Boric acid solution, 5g per 100ml	15ml

4.2   Phosphate buffer solution pH 5·5:

Potassium dihydrogen phosphate, KH_2PO_4	130·86g
di Sodium hydrogen phosphate, Na_2HPO_4. $2H_2O$	6·947g
Water to	1 000ml

4.3   Phosphate buffer solution pH 5·5 (4.2) diluted with water to 1 + 9.

4.4   Phosphate buffer solution pH 8·0:

Potassium dihydrogen phosphate KH_2PO_4	1·407g
di Sodium hydrogen phosphate Na_2HPO_4. $2H_2O$	57·539g
Water to	1 000ml

4.5   Sterile physiological saline (dissolve 9g sodium chloride in water and dilute to 1 000ml).

4.6   Ethanol 20% solution (V/V).

4.7   Hydrochloric acid solution 0·1N.

4.8   Formamide 70% solution (V/V): prepare freshly before use and adjust to pH 4·5 using approximately 2N sulphuric acid.

4.9   A mixture of acetone, water and hydrochloric acid (density 1·18g per ml) in the proportions: 65 + 33 + 2.

4.10 A mixture of methanol and hydrochloric acid (density 1·18g per ml) in the proportions: 98 + 2.

4.11 Standard substances: chlortetracycline hydrochloride, oxytetracycline base, tetracycline hydrochloride of known activities.

5.   STANDARD SOLUTIONS

5.1   *Chlortetracycline*

5.1.1   Prepare from the standard substance (4.11), by using hydrochloric acid (4.7), a standard solution with a concentration of $500\mu g$ chlortetracycline HCl per ml. This solution will keep for one week in a refrigerator.

5.1.2   From this solution (5.1.1) prepare a standard working solution (S_8) with a concentration of $0.2\mu g$ chlortetracycline HCl per ml. Dilution is made with the phosphate buffer solution pH 5·5 diluted to 1/10 (4.3).

5.1.3   Prepare the following concentrations by means of successive dilutions (1 + 1) with the buffer solution (4.3):

S_4 $0.1\mu g$ per ml
S_2 $0.05\mu g$ per ml
S_1 $0.025\mu g$ per ml

5.2   *Oxytetracycline*

5.2.1   Proceed as indicated in 5.1, prepare from a solution with a concentration of $400\mu g$ oxytetracycline per ml, a standard working solution S_8 containing $1.6\mu g$ oxytetracycline per ml, and the following concentrations:

S_4 $0.8\mu g$ per ml
S_2 $0.4\mu g$ per ml
S_1 $0.2\mu g$ per ml

5.3   *Tetracycline*

Proceed as indicated in 5.1, prepare from a solution with a concentration of $500\mu g$ tetracycline HCl per ml, a standard working solution S_8 containing $1.0\mu g$ tetracycline HCl per ml, and the following concentrations:

S_4 $0.5\mu g$ per ml
S_2 $0.25\mu g$ per ml
S_1 $0.125\mu g$ per ml

6.   PROCEDURE

6.1   *Extraction*

6.1.1   Levels not more than 50ppm:

Treat the sample for analysis with formamide (4.8) according to the indications given in the following table. Shake for 30 minutes on a mechanical shaker and then immediately dilute according to the indications given in the following table, with the phosphate buffer solution (4.3). The formamide concentration of this solution must not exceed 40 per cent. Centrifuge or decant to obtain a clear solution, U_8.

Antibiotic	Chlortetracycline		Oxytetracycline		Tetracycline	
Presumed level in mg per kg	10	50	10	50	10	50
Weight of sample in g	10	10	24	9.6	20	10
Volume of formamide (4.8) (ml)	100	100	80	100	80	100
Volume of phosphate buffer solution (4.3) (ml)	dilution 1:5 *(a)*	dilution 1:25 *(b)*	70	200	120	dilution 1:5 *(a)*
U_8 concentration in μg per ml	0.2	0.2	1.6	1.6	1.0	1.0

(*a*)   Dilute 20ml of the extract 100ml with the buffer solution in a graduated flask.
(*b*)   Dilute 4ml of the extract 100ml with the buffer solution in a graduated flask.

Prepare the concentrations U_4, U_2 and U_1 by means of successive dilutions (1 + 1) with the phosphate buffer solution (4.3).

6.1.2 Levels higher than 50ppm:

    6.1.2.1 Chlortetracycline.

        According to the presumed antibiotic level of the sample, treat a sample for analysis of 2 to 10g with 20 times its volume of mixture (4.9). Shake for 30 minutes on a laboratory shaker. Check that the pH remains lower than 3 during extraction and, if necessary, adjust to pH 3 (use 10 per cent acetic acid for mineral compounds). Take an aliquot of the extract and adjust the pH to 5.5 with the phosphate buffer solution pH 8 (4.4) in the presence of bromo-cresol green (colour change yellow to blue). Centrifuge to obtain a clear solution. Dilute the supernatant with phosphate buffer solution pH 5.5 (4.3) to obtain the concentration U_8 (see 6.1). Prepare the concentrations U_4, U_2 and U_1 by means of successive dilutions $(1 + 1)$ with phosphate buffer solution (4.3).

    6.1.2.2 Oxytetracycline and tetracycline.

        Proceed as indicated in 6.1.2.1 replacing the mixture (4.9) by the mixture (4.10).

6.2 *Determination*

Diffusion through agar is carried out in plates with the four concentrations of the standard solution (S_8, S_4, S_2, S_1) and the four concentrations of the extract (U_8, U_4, U_2, U_1). These four concentrations of extract and standard solution must be placed in each plate. To this effect, select plates large enough to allow at least eight holes with a diameter of 10 to 13mm, and not less than 30mm between centres, to be punched out of the agar medium.

Inoculate at 50–60°C, with the spore suspension (3.2.1) a quantity of the melted culture medium (4.1.3), sufficient to give a layer approximately 2mm thick in the assay plates to be employed. Swirl to mix thoroughly, and pour into the sterile assay plates which must be held in a rigorously horizontal position until the agar has set. With a sterile cork borer remove agar plugs to form holes as described above. Pipette into each hole an exactly measured and equal volume (0.10 to 0.15ml) of respectively solutions S_8, S_4, S_2, S_1 and U_8, U_4, U_2, U_1.

Apply each concentration four times so that the determination is subject to an evaluation of 32 zones of inhibition.

Incubate the plates for approximately 18 hours at a temperature of 28–30°C.

6.3 *Evaluation*

Measure the diameter of the zones of inhibition, if possible to the nearest 0·1mm. For each zone, two measurements at right angles should be made. Calculate the mean diameters for each of the concentrations of sample and standard. Plot the mean diameters against the logarithms of the concentrations for both standard solutions and the sample solutions. Draw the best possible straight line for standard and sample. In the absence of any interference the two lines should be approximately parallel.

The logarithm of the relative activity is calculated by the following formula:

$$\frac{(u_1 + u_2 + u_4 + u_8 - s_1 - s_2 - s_4 - s_8) \times 0\cdot602}{u_4 + u_8 + s_4 + s_8 - u_1 - u_2 - s_1 - s_2}$$

Where s and u represent the mean inhibition zone diameters of standard and sample solutions respectively.

Real activity of sample solutions = presumed activity × relative activity.

8. DETERMINATION OF CHLORTETRACYCLINE, OXYTETRACYCLINE AND TETRACYCLINE BY TURBIDIMETRY

1. Scope and Field of Application

The method is for the determination of the quantity of chlortetracycline, oxytetra-cycline, and tetracycline in feeding stuffs at concentrations higher than 1 000ppm, provided that no other substance causes interference by giving rise to cloudy extracts. This method is quicker than the method of diffusion through agar.

2.   PRINCIPLE

The sample is extracted by a mixture of acetone, water and hydrochloric acid for the determination of chlortetracycline, and a mixture of methanol and hydrochloric acid for the determination of oxytetracycline and tetracycline.

The extracts are then diluted and their antibiotic effect is determined by measuring the light transmission from a culture medium which has been inoculated with *Staphylococcus aureus* and to which the antibiotic has been added. The light transmission is a function of the antibiotic concentration.

3.   MICRO-ORGANISM: *S. aureus* K 141.   (NCIB 11182; NCTC 10988)

3.1   *Maintenance of the parent strain*

Inoculate *S. aureus* onto an agar slope of the culture medium II (4.1.2). Incubate overnight at 37°C. Keep the culture in a refrigerator and re-inoculate every 4 weeks onto agar slopes. At the same time prepare sub-cultures for laboratory use.

3.2   *Preparation of the inoculum*

Approximately 24 hours before use, re-inoculate a sub-culture onto a fresh agar slope and incubate overnight at 37°C. Harvest the bacterial growth from the agar slope in approximately 2ml culture medium (4.1), and then decant the suspension into approximately 100ml of the same medium (4.1). Incubate in a water-bath at 37°C for $1\frac{1}{2}$ to 2 hours.

4.   CULTURE MEDIA AND REAGENTS

4.1.1   Culture medium I:

Peptone	5 g
Yeast extract	1·5 g
Meat extract	1·5 g
Sodium chloride	3·5 g
Glucose	1·0 g
Potassium dihydrogen phosphate, KH_2PO_4	1·32g
di Potassium hydrogen phosphate, K_2HPO_4	3·68g
Water to	1 000ml

pH after sterilisation: 6·8 to 7·0.

4.1.2   Culture medium II—as for 4.1.1 with 1·5 to 3·0% agar.

4.2   Phosphate buffer solution pH 4·5:

Potassium dihydrogen phosphate KH_2PO_4	13·6 g
Water to	1 000ml

4.3   Hydrochloric acid solution, 0·1N.

4 4   A mixture of acetone, water and hydrochloric acid (density: 1·18g per ml) in the proportions by volume: 65+33+2.

4.5   Acidified methanol: mix methanol and hydrochloric acid (density: 1·18g per ml) in the proportions by volume: 98+2.

4.6   Formaldehyde solution, containing approximately 10% formaldehyde, (HCHO).

4.7   Standard substances: chlortetracycline hydrochloride, oxytetracycline base, and tetracycline hydrochloride of known activities.

5.   STANDARD SOLUTION

By using hydrochloric acid (4.3), prepare from the standard substance (4.7) a solution with accurately known concentration of 400 to 500μg of the antibiotic per ml. This solution will keep for one week in a refrigerator.

6. PROCEDURE

6.1 *Extraction*

    6.1.1 Chlortetracycline:

        Place 1 to 2g (weighed to the nearest 0·001g) of the sample for analysis in a 200 or 250ml graduated flask. Add approximately 100ml of the mixture (4.4) and shake for 30 minutes on a mechanical shaker. Make up to volume with the phosphate buffer solution pH 4·5 (4.2). Mix and allow to settle.

    6.1.2 Oxytetracycline and tetracycline:

        Place 1 to 2g (weighed to the nearest 0·001g) of the sample for analysis in a 200 or 250ml graduated flask. Add approximately 100ml of the mixture (4.5) and shake for 30 minutes on a mechanical shaker. Make up to volume with the phosphate buffer solution pH 4·5 (4.2). Mix and allow to settle.

6.2 *Determination*

    6.2.1 Preparation of standard and sample extract series:

        Use phosphate buffer solution pH 4·5 (4.2) to dilute the standard solution (5) and the extract (6.1) so as to obtain a series of concentrations making it possible to draw a calibration curve for each determination with the interpolation on this curve of at least two values relative to the extract. The strength of the dilutions must be chosen according to the growth conditions of the strain, which may vary from one laboratory to another. It is usual to proceed as follows:

    6.2.2 Chlortetracycline:

        Use phosphate buffer solution (4.2) to dilute the standard solution (5) to obtain a standard working solution with a concentration corresponding to 0·2μg chlortetracycline HCl per ml. Then, with phosphate buffer solution (4.2), prepare 6 dilutions in the tubes in which the determinations are to be made, repeating each dilution, as indicated below.

Volume of standard working solution (ml)	Volume of phosphate buffer solution (4.2) (ml)	Concentration of Chlortetracycline HCl (μg per ml)
0·7	0·3	0·14
0·6	0·4	0·12
0·55	0·45	0·11
0·45	0·55	0·09
0·4	0·6	0·08
0·3	0·7	0·06

        Use the phosphate buffer solution (4.2) to dilute the extract (6.1) to obtain an expected concentration of chlortetracycline HCl of 0·12μg per ml. Place 1ml of this solution in 2 tubes and 0·75ml (=0·09μg) in 2 other tubes. Make up the volume of the last 2 tubes to 1ml with the phosphate buffer solution (4.2).

    6.2.3 Oxytetracycline and tetracycline:

        Use the phosphate buffer solution (4.2) to dilute the solution (5) to obtain a standard working solution with a concentration corresponding to 0·6μg oxytetracycline or tetracycline HCl per ml. Then, with the phosphate buffer solution (4.2), prepare 7 dilutions in the tubes in which the determinations are to be made, repeating each dilution, as indicated below.

Volume of standard working solution (ml)	Volume of phosphate buffer solution (4.2) (ml)	Concentration of Oxytetracycline or Tetracycline HCl (μg per ml)
0·9	0·1	0·54
0·8	0·2	0·48
0·7	0·3	0·42
0·6	0·4	0·36
0·4	0·6	0·24
0·3	0·7	0·18
0·2	0·8	0·12

Use the phosphate buffer solution (4.2) to dilute the extract (6.2) to obtain an expected concentration of oxytetracycline or tetracycline HCl of 0·48μg per ml. Place 1ml of this solution in 2 tubes and 0·5ml ($=0·24\mu$g) in 2 other tubes. Make up the volume of the last 2 tubes to 1ml with the phosphate buffer solution (4.2).

6.3 Inoculation of the culture medium

Inoculate the culture medium (4.1) with the inoculum (3.2) so as to obtain, with the spectrophotometer at 590nm, a light transmission of 85% in a 50mm cell or 92% in a 20mm cell, having first adjusted the apparatus to give 100% transmission on the culture medium (4.1) before inoculation.

6.4 Seeding

Place in each tube (6.2.2 or 6.2.3) 9ml of inoculated culture medium (6.3). The tubes must be filled in hygienic, but not necessarily sterile conditions.

6.5 Incubation

Incubation must be carried out in a stirred water-bath where the temperature is kept at 37°C$\pm$0·1°C. The time of incubation (generally 2½ to 3 hours) should be chosen so as to obtain transmission curves, the slope of which enables precise measurements to be made. Further growth is then prevented by rapidly injecting 1ml formaldehyde solution (4.6) into each tube.

6.6 Measurement of the growth

Measure the transmissions with the spectrophotometer at 590nm, having first adjusted the apparatus to give 100% transmission on the clearest standard solution (corresponding to the highest antibiotic level). Owing to slight differences of turbidity in the different tubes, cells of at least 20mm, and preferably 50mm, are recommended.

7.   CALCULATION OF RESULTS

Plot a graph of the photometric transmissions against the antibiotic concentrations. Interpolate the transmissions relative to the extract on the curve. Calculate the antibiotic content of the sample.

9. DETERMINATION OF CLOPIDOL
(3,5-dichloro-4-hydroxy-2,6-dimethylpyridine)

1. SCOPE AND FIELD OF APPLICATION

The method is for the determination of the quantity of clopidol in complete feeding stuffs, protein concentrates and feed supplements. The lower limit of the determination is 60ppm.

2. PRINCIPLE

Clopidol is extracted from the feed with methanolic ammonia solution, and a portion of the extract is passed through a column of aluminium oxide onto a column of ion-exchange resin. The clopidol is retained on the resin and interfering substances are removed by washing with 80% methanol. The clopidol is eluted from the resin with 40% acetic acid and the absorbance is measured at 267nm.

3. REAGENTS

Note: The suitability of a batch of aluminium oxide and of the other reagents should be tested before use by analysing a blank feed to which a known amount of clopidol has been added.

3.1 Aluminium oxide for column chromatography, 100 to 250 mesh, alkaline, Brockman activity 1.

3.2 Ammonia (density 0·88g per ml).

3.3 Anion exchange resin, AG1–X8 or Dowex 1–X8, 100 to 200 mesh—
    To convert Dowex resin in the chloride form to the acetate form add 1 litre of 6N hydrochloric acid to 350g of resin in a 3 litre beaker, and heat the mixture on a steam bath for 2 to 3 hours. Pour the slurry into a glass Buchner funnel, and wash the resin with water until the washings are free from chloride (about 6 litres of water are required). Transfer the resin to a 50mm diameter glass column having a coarse sintered-glass disc at the bottom end, and wash with sodium acetate solution (5g sodium acetate, anhydrous, dissolved in water and diluted to 100ml) until the column effluent gives only a cloudy solution on addition of silver nitrate solution. Return the resin to the glass Buchner funnel, and wash with water. Transfer the resin to a 3 litre beaker, add 1 litre of 40% V/V acetic acid solution (3.4) and heat on a steam bath for 3 hours or longer. Filter, and wash the resin again with water until the washings are free from chloride. Store the resin in water.

3.4 Acetic acid solution 40% V/V.

3.5 Methanol.

3.6 Methanol solution, 80% V/V.

3.7 Ammoniacal methanol solution: dilute 1 volume of ammonia (3.2) with 19 volumes of methanol (3.5).

3.8 Clopidol standard solution: weigh, to the nearest 0·1mg, 125mg of clopidol into a beaker, add 25ml of sodium hydroxide solution (2g sodium hydroxide dissolved in water and diluted to 100ml) to dissolve the clopidol, transfer the solution to a 500ml graduated flask, and dilute to the mark with water. This solution contains 250μg per ml clopidol.

4. APPARATUS

4.1 Aluminium Oxide column: constructed as indicated in the diagram opposite.

4.2 Ion exchange column: constructed as indicated in the diagram opposite.

4.3 Spectrophotometer, recording, with 10mm silica cells.

5. PROCEDURE

5.1 *Extraction of clopidol*

Weigh, to the nearest 0·001g, approximately 50g of the finely divided and mixed sample, or a suitable amount expected to contain about 12mg of clopidol, transfer to a 500ml graduated flask, and add 400ml of ammoniacal methanol solution (3.7). Place a magnetic stirring bar in the flask and stir the mixture on a magnetic stirrer for 20 minutes. Remove the stirring bar from the flask, dilute to the mark with ammoniacal methanol solution (3.7), mix the contents well, and set aside for 20 to 30 minutes.

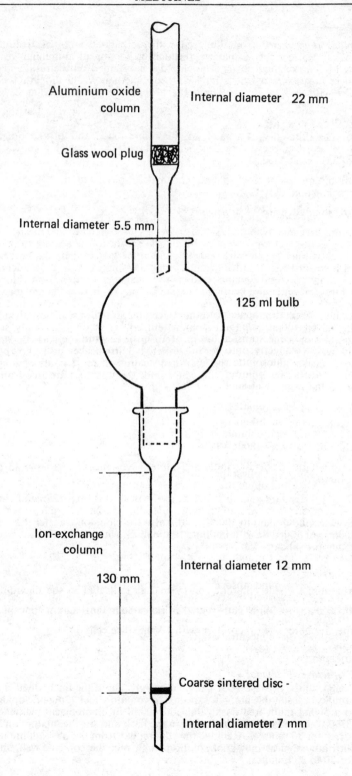

Aluminium oxide column

Internal diameter 22 mm

Glass wool plug

Internal diameter 5.5 mm

125 ml bulb

Ion-exchange column

130 mm

Internal diameter 12 mm

Coarse sintered disc -

Internal diameter 7 mm

5.2 *Purification*

5.2.1   Aluminium oxide column: For each column required weigh approximately 25g of aluminium oxide (3.1) into an aluminium foil dish and place it in an oven at 105 $\pm$ 5°C for 1 hour. Remove the dish from the oven and cool to room temperature in a desiccator. Make a slurry of the aluminium oxide with 25ml of ammoniacal methanol solution (3.7) and filter on a Buchner funnel. Wash the aluminium oxide with methanol (3.5) until the washings are neutral. Form a slurry of the aluminium oxide with 50ml of methanol (3.5) and pour the slurry into the column (4.1). Allow the methanol to drip through the column. Place a plug of glass wool lightly on top of the aluminium oxide and then wash with 25ml of methanol (3.5). Do not allow the liquid in the column to fall below the top of the aluminium oxide. Discard the eluate.

5.2.2   Anion exchange column: Form a slurry in acetic acid (3.4) of sufficient resin (3.3) to fill the columns required. Filter on a Buchner funnel, wash the resin with twice its own volume of acetic acid (3.4), and then with aqueous methanol (3.6) until the washings are neutral. Form a slurry of the resin with aqueous methanol (3.6) and add sufficient to a column (4.2) to give a resin bed 20 to 30mm deep after settling. Place a small plug of glass wool on top of the resin and wash the column with two 13ml portions of aqueous methanol (3.6). Do not allow the liquid level in the column to fall below the top of the resin. Discard the eluate.

5.2.3   Chromatographic procedure: By pipette transfer 10·0ml of the extract of the feed sample (5.1) directly onto an aluminium oxide column and at the same time transfer the same volume of ammoniacal methanol solution (3.7) directly onto a second aluminium oxide column (reagent blank). Allow the solutions to drain to the top of the aluminium oxide and then wash each column with three 12ml portions of aqueous methanol (3.6), allowing the liquid to drain to the top of the aluminium oxide each time. Let all the eluate from each column drain directly into separate ion-exchange columns, and then remove the aluminium oxide columns. Allow the liquid to drain to the top of the ion-exchange resin and then wash each column with four 13ml portions of aqueous methanol (3.6). Discard all eluate.

Elute each column with two 10ml and then one 4ml portions of acetic acid (3.4). Collect the eluates from each column in separate 25ml graduated flasks and dilute the contents of each to the mark with acetic acid (3.4).

5.3 *Determination*

Record the absorption spectrum of the sample extract between 350 and 245nm in 10mm silica cells with the reagent blank solution (5.2.3) as reference. Measure the absorbance of the sample extract at 267nm above a baseline obtained by drawing a line through the absorbance at 327 and 297nm and extending it through 267nm.

(Note: Background absorption due to the feed approaches a linear function that can be described by the points on the curve at 296 and 327nm. Occasionally this is not the case, as can be detected by absorption peaks in the region between 350 and 297nm.)

Determine the concentration of clopidol in the sample by reference to the calibration curve (5.4).

5.4 *Calibration curve*

By pipette transfer 1, 5, 7·5, 10, 12·5 and 15ml portions of clopidol standard solution (3.8) to separate 250ml graduated flasks. Dilute the contents of each flask to the mark with acetic acid (3.4). Record the absorption spectra of these solutions in 10mm silica cells between 350 and 245nm with acetic acid (3.4) as reference. Construct a calibration curve using the absorbances at 267nm as ordinates and the corresponding concentrations of clopidol in μg per ml as abscissae.

6. CALCULATION OF RESULTS

The clopidol content in ppm of sample is given by the formula:

$$\frac{23 \cdot 23 \times C \times 50}{W}$$

in which:

C = concentration of clopidol, in mg per ml, read from the calibration curve equivalent to the absorbance of the test solution;

23·23 = a factor that makes allowance for the volume of the feed sample in the flask; and

W = weight of test portion in g.

Absorbance at 327 and 297nm should not differ by more than 0·05 units and both points should be below 0·2. Results should be satisfactory as long as these criteria are kept in mind along with any obvious distortion in the appearance of the curve. No maximum other than that of clopidol should be present.

10. DETERMINATION OF COPPER BY THE DIETHYLDITHIOCARBAMATE SPECTROPHOTOMETRIC METHOD

1. SCOPE AND FIELD OF APPLICATION

The method is for the determination of the quantity of copper in complete feeding stuffs, protein concentrates and feed supplements.

2. PRINCIPLE

The sample is ashed and the residue treated with hydrochloric acid. Copper is extracted from the resulting solution as its diethyldithiocarbamate complex into carbon tetrachloride. The copper content is measured at 436nm, by reference to a calibration curve.

3. REAGENTS

The water used should be free from copper.

3.1 Carbon tetrachloride, redistilled.

3.2 Sodium diethyldithiocarbamate solution: dissolve 1g sodium diethyldithiocarbamate in water and dilute to 100ml. Filter the solution if it is not clear. The solution may be stored, protected from light, in a refrigerator but should not be used after seven days.

3.3 EDTA-citrate solution: dissolve 20g ammonium citrate and 5g of the disodium salt of ethylenediaminetetra-acetic acid (EDTA) in water and dilute to 100ml. To purify, add 0·1ml sodium diethyldithiocarbamate solution (3.2) and extract with carbon tetrachloride (3.1). Add a further quantity of sodium diethyldithiocarbamate solution (3.2) to ensure that it is in excess.

3.4 Ammonium hydroxide solution approximately 6N: this may be prepared by passing gaseous ammonia into water, or by purifying ammonia solution as described for the EDTA-citrate solution (3.3).

3.5 Sulphuric acid solution, 2N.

3.6 Hydrochloric acid solution, 50% V/V: dilute an appropriate volume of hydrochloric acid (density 1·18g per ml) with an equal volume of water.

3.7 Hydrochloric acid solution, 2N.

3.8 Nitric acid solution, 30% V/V: dilute 30ml of nitric acid (density 1·42g per ml) with water to 100ml.

3.9 Copper standard solution: weigh to the nearest 0·1mg, 393mg of copper sulphate ($CuSO_4.5H_2O$) dissolve in 100ml 2N sulphuric acid (3.5) and dilute to one litre with water.

3.10 Copper standard working solution: dilute 5ml of the copper sulphate standard solution (3.9) to 250ml with 2N sulphuric acid (3.5) immediately before use. 1ml of this solution contains $2\mu g$ copper.

3.11 Thymol blue indicator solution: dissolve 0·1g thymol blue in 2·15ml of 0·1N sodium hydroxide and dilute to 100ml with water.

4. APPARATUS

4.1 Spectrophotometer with 10mm cells.

5. PREPARATION OF THE TEST SAMPLE

Grind the sample to pass through a stainless steel sieve having apertures about 1mm square.

6. PROCEDURE

6.1 *Dissolution of sample*

Weigh, to the nearest 0·001g, approximately 10g of the sample prepared under (5) into a silica dish or basin, and place a silica cover on top. Transfer to a cool muffle furnace. Raise the temperature to $450° \pm 10°C$ and allow to ash until all the carbonaceous matter has disappeared; a slow current of air through the furnace during the initial stages of ashing is desirable. In the case of high-fat content materials, care must be taken to avoid ignition of the sample. When all the organic matter has been destroyed, cool, add 10ml 50% V/V hydrochloric acid solution (3.6) and evaporate to dryness on a water-bath. Extract the soluble salts from the residue with two successive 10ml portions of boiling 2N hydrochloric acid solution (3.7) decanting the solution each time through the same suitable filter-paper (Whatman No 541 or equivalent) into a 50ml graduated flask. Then add 5ml of 50% V/V hydrochloric acid solution (3.6) and about 5ml of 30% V/V nitric acid solution (3.8) to the residue in the basin, and evaporate the mixture to dryness on a hot-plate at low heat. Finally, add a further 10ml of boiling 2N hydrochloric acid solution (3.7) to the residue and filter the solution through the same filter-paper into the flask. Wash the basin and the filter with water, and collect the washings in the flask, make up to the mark with water and mix.

6.2 *Determination*

Transfer to a separating funnel a suitable aliquot of the solution prepared in accordance with (6.1), (or a dilution of this solution in N. hydrochloric acid), containing not more than $50\mu g$ of copper. Add 10ml EDTA-citrate solution (3.3), two drops of thymol blue indicator solution (3.11) and ammonium hydroxide solution (3.4) until the mixture is coloured green or bluish-green. Cool the mixture, add 1ml of sodium diethyldithiocarbamate solution (3.2) and, from a burette, 15ml of carbon tetrachloride (3.1). Stopper the funnel, shake vigorously for two minutes and allow the layers to separate. Place a piece of cotton-wool in the stem of the funnel and run off the carbon tetrachloride layer into a dry 10mm spectrophotometer cell (4.1). Avoid undue exposure of the solution to light.

Measure immediately the absorbance of the sample solution at 436nm, against carbon tetrachloride as reference. Determine the quantity of copper by reference to the calibration curve (6.4).

6.3 *Blank test*

Carry out a blank test omitting only the sample and following the procedure described under (6.2).

6.4 *Calibration curve*

To a series of separating funnels transfer 10ml EDTA-citrate solution (3.3) and the following amounts of copper standard working solution (3.10) and 2N sulphuric acid (3.5).

Copper solution	0	1	2·5	5	10	15	20	25ml
2N H_2SO_4	25	24	22·5	20	15	10	5	0ml

Proceed as for the test solution, as described in (6.2) commencing ". . . two drops thymol blue indicator (3.11) . . .". Measure the absorbances of the solutions and plot the calibration curve using absorbances as the ordinates and the corresponding quantities of copper in μg as the abscissae.

7.　CALCULATION OF RESULTS

The copper content in ppm of sample is given by the formula:

$$A \times \frac{50}{V} \times \frac{F}{W}$$

in which:

A　= weight of copper in aliquot taken for colour development as read from the calibration curve after allowing for blank reading (μg);
V　= volume of aliquot taken for colour development (ml);
W　= weight of test portion in g.
F　= dilution factor (from 6.2).

11.　DETERMINATION OF COPPER BY THE ATOMIC ABSORPTION SPECTROPHOTOMETRIC METHOD

1.　SCOPE AND FIELD OF APPLICATION

The method is for the determination of the quantity of copper in complete feeding stuffs, protein concentrates and feed supplements.

2.　PRINCIPLE

The sample is ashed and the residue treated with hydrochloric acid. The copper content of the sample is determined by atomic absorption spectrophotometry.

3.　REAGENTS

The water used should be free from copper.

3.1　Hydrochloric acid solution 50% V/V: dilute an appropriate volume of hydrochloric acid (density 1·18g per ml) with an equal volume of water.

3.2　Hydrochloric acid solution 2N.

3.3　Hydrochloric acid solution 0·5N.

3.4　Nitric acid solution 30% V/V: dilute 30ml nitric acid (density 1·42g per ml) with water to 100ml.

3.5　Copper standard solution: weigh to the nearest 0·1mg, 393 mg of copper sulphate ($CuSO_4.5H_2O$), dissolve in 0·5N hydrochloric acid solution (3.3) and dilute to 100ml with 0·5N hydrochloric acid solution (3.3). 1ml of this solution contains 1mg of copper.

4.　APPARATUS

4.1　Atomic absorption spectrophotometer with a copper hollow cathode lamp.

5.　PREPARATION OF THE TEST SAMPLE

Grind the sample to pass through a stainless steel sieve having apertures about 1mm square.

6. PROCEDURE

6.1 *Dissolution of sample*

Weigh, to the nearest 0·001g, approximately 10g of the sample as prepared under (5) into a silica dish or basin, and place the silica cover on top. Transfer to a cool muffle furnace. Raise the temperature to 450° ± 10°C and heat until no carbonaceous material remains. A slow current of air through the furnace during the initial stages of the ashing is advantageous. Care must be taken with high-fat content material to avoid ignition of the sample. When all the organic matter has been destroyed, cool, add 10ml 50% V/V hydrochloric acid solution (3.1) and evaporate to dryness on a water-bath. Extract the soluble salts from the residue with two successive 10ml portions of boiling 2N hydrochloric acid solution (3.2), decanting the solution each time through the same suitable filter-paper (Whatman No 541 or equivalent) into a 50ml graduated flask. Then add 5ml 50% V/V hydrochloric acid solution (3.1) and about 5ml 30% V/V nitric acid solution (3.4) to the residue in the basin, and take the mixture to dryness on a hot-plate at low heat. Finally, add a further 10ml of boiling 2N hydrochloric acid solution (3.2) to the residue and filter the solution through the same paper into the flask. Wash the basin and the filter with water, and collect the washings in the graduated flask. Make up to the mark with water and mix.

6.2 *Blank test*

Simultaneously with the test determination prepare a blank of all the reagents which have been used in the preparation of the sample and, starting at 6.1, 'add 10ml 50% V/V hydrochloric acid solution (3.1) to a silica dish'.

6.3 *Determination*

6.3.1 Preparation of sample and blank test solutions:

Take an aliquot of the extract prepared as in 6.1 and dilute with 0·5N hydrochloric acid solution (3.3) to a known volume containing between 0 and 10µg per ml of copper. Treat the blank test solution (6.2) identically.

6.3.2 Preparation of standard solutions for calibration:

Prepare from the copper standard solution (3.5) a series of solutions in 0·5N hydrochloric acid solution (3.3) containing between 0 and 10µg per ml copper.

6.3.3 Measurement:

Set up the instrument at a wavelength of 324·7nm. Spray distilled water into the flame and zero the instrument. Spray successively in triplicate the standard solutions (6.3.2), sample and blank (6.3.1) rinsing the liquid channels with water between each spraying. Plot the calibration curve using the mean absorbances as the ordinates and the corresponding concentrations of copper in µg per ml as the abscissae. Determine the concentration of copper in the blank and test solutions by reference to the calibration curve.

7. CALCULATION OF RESULTS

The copper content in ppm of sample is given by the formula:

$$C \times \frac{V_2}{W} \times \frac{50}{V_1}$$

in which:

C = concentration of copper in final solution after subtracting the blank value (µg per ml);
V_2 = volume of final solution;
V_1 = volume of aliquot taken in para 6.3.2 (ml); and
W = weight of test portion in g.

12. DETERMINATION OF DINITOLMIDE
(3,5-dinitro-*o*-toluamide)

1. SCOPE AND FIELD OF APPLICATION

The method is for the determination of the quantity of dinitolmide in complete feeding stuffs, protein concentrates and feed supplements. Nitrofuran derivatives may interfere. The lower limit of the determination is 40ppm.

2. PRINCIPLE

The sample is extracted with acetonitrile. The extract is purified on aluminium oxide and filtered. An aliquot of the filtrate is evaporated to dryness. The residue is dissolved in dimethylformamide and treated with diaminoethane forming a purple-coloured complex, the absorbance of which is measured at 560nm.

3. REAGENTS

3.1 Acetonitrile 85% (V/V): mix 850ml of acetonitrile, and 150ml of water. Before use distil the mixture and collect the fraction which boils between 75° and 77°C.

3.2 Aluminium oxide for column chromatography: heat at 750°C for at least 2 hours, cool in a desiccator and keep in an amber glass bottle with a ground-glass stopper. Before use de-activate as follows: place in an amber glass bottle 10g of aluminium oxide and 0·7ml of water, stopper, heat for 5 minutes in a bath of boiling water, with occasional shaking and allow to cool, shaking from time to time. Check the activity by subjecting to analysis, starting from point 5.1, a measured quantity of standard solution (3.6). The recovery of the dinitolmide must be 100% ± 2%.

3.3 Dimethylformamide 95% (V/V): mix 95·0ml of dimethylformamide and 5·0ml of water.

3.4 Diaminoethane, colourless, maximum water content: 2·0%.

3.5 Standard substance: pure 3,5-dinitro-2-toluamide complying with the following characteristics:

Melting point: 177°C;

molecular extinction coefficient at 248nm in acetonitrile: $13·1 \times 10^3$;

molecular extinction coefficient at 266nm in dimethylformamide: $10·1 \times 10^3$.

3.6 Standard solution: weigh to the nearest 0·1mg, 40mg of pure dinitolmide (3.5), dissolve in acetonitrile (3.1) in a 200ml graduated flask, make up to volume with the same solvent and mix. Dilute 20·0ml to 100ml with acetonitrile (3.1) in a graduated flask and mix. 1ml of this solution contains 40μg of dinitolmide.

4. APPARATUS

4.1 Sintered-glass crucible, porosity G3, diameter 60mm.

4.2 Spectrophotometer, with 10mm cells.

5. PROCEDURE

5.1 *Extraction and purification*

Weigh, to within 0·001g, approximately 10g of the finely divided and mixed sample. For protein concentrates and feed supplements, weigh, to within 0·001g, approximately 1g. Place the test portion in a 250ml conical flask and add 65ml of acetonitrile (3.1). Mix, fit a reflux condenser to the flask and heat in a water-bath maintained at 50°C for 30 minutes, shaking frequently. Cool under a stream of cold water. Add 20g of aluminium oxide (3.2), shake for 3 minutes, allow to settle.

Filter the solution under suction through the sintered-glass crucible (4.1) transferring as much of the solid material as possible. Transfer the remaining solids to the sintered-glass crucible with a few ml of acetonitrile (3.1) and suck the residue dry. Release the partial vacuum and suspend the filter cake by stirring with a few drops of acetonitrile (3.1). Remove the liquid by applying suction, then repeat the suspension and filtration steps until a total volume of about 90ml has been collected. Transfer this filtrate to a 100ml graduated flask. Rinse the collecting vessel with a few millilitres of acetonitrile (3.1) and add this to the flask. Finally make up to volume and mix. If necessary, dilute an aliquot with acetonitrile (3.1) to obtain a solution containing 5 to 15μg of dinitolmide per ml.

5.2 *Determination*

Pipette into three 50ml beakers A, B and C respectively, 4·0ml of the solution obtained in 5.1. Add to beaker C 1·0ml of standard solution (3.6). Place the three beakers on the water-bath under a well-ventilated hood, and evaporate until dry in a current of dry air. Cool the three beakers to room temperature.

Add 10·0ml of dimethylformamide (3.3) in beaker A and 2·0ml in beakers B and C respectively, leave in contact for a few minutes, stirring a little, until the residue completely dissolves. Then add 8·0ml of diaminoethane (3.4) in beakers B and C and mix. Exactly 5 minutes after adding the diaminoethane measure the absorbance of the three solutions at 560nm against the dimethylformamide (3.3) as a reference.

6. CALCULATION OF RESULTS

The dinitolmide content in ppm of sample is given by the formula:

$$\frac{1\ 000 \times F \times (E_B - E_A)}{W \times (E_C - E_B)}$$

in which:

E_A = absorbance of solution A (blank);
E_B = absorbance of solution B (sample);
E_C = absorbance of solution C (internal standard);
W = weight of test portion in g; and
F = dilution factor (from 5.1).

13. DETERMINATION OF FURAZOLIDONE
[3-(5-nitrofurfurylideneamino)oxazolidin-2-one]

1. SCOPE AND FIELD OF APPLICATION

The method is for the determination of the quantity of furazolidone in complete feeding stuffs, protein concentrates and feed supplements. The lower limit of the determination is 10ppm.

2. PRINCIPLE

After a preliminary extraction with light petroleum to remove fat, the sample is extracted with acetone. The extract is purified on a column of aluminium oxide and the furazolidone is eluted with acetone. The acetone eluate is evaporated to dryness and the residue dissolved in pentanol. Furazolidone is then extracted from the pentanol with aqueous urea solution the absorbance of which is measured at 375nm.

3. REAGENTS

3.1 Acetone.

3.2 Aluminium oxide for chromatography, 100-240 mesh, prepared as follows:

stir 500g of the aluminium oxide with 1 litre of hot water and decant the supernatant liquid. Repeat this procedure twice more, and finally filter through a Buchner funnel. Dry the aluminium oxide at 105°C to constant weight.

3.3 Pentyl acetate.

3.4 Pentan-1-ol. (Material containing mixed isomers is acceptable).

3.5 Light petroleum, boiling range 40–60°C.

3.6 Urea solution. Mix 90g of urea with 100ml of water, dissolve completely by warming gently.

3.7 Standard substance: pure furazolidone.

3.8 Standard solution: Weigh, to the nearest 0.1mg, 25mg of standard substance (3.7), dissolve in acetone (3.1) in a 250ml graduated flask (4.1), make up to volume with acetone (3.1) and mix. 1ml of this solution contains 100μg of furazolidone.

4. APPARATUS

4.1 Amberglass 100 and 250ml volumetric flasks.

4.2 Amberglass 100ml separating funnels.

4.3 Glass tubes for chromatography, internal diameter 10mm, length 300mm.

4.4 Spectrophotometer with 10mm cells.

5. PROCEDURE

Note: All procedures should be carried out in subdued light.

5.1 *Extraction*

Weigh, to within 0·001g, 5 to 20g of the finely divided and mixed sample (containing not more than 1mg of furazolidone) into an extraction thimble and transfer it to an extraction apparatus. Extract with light petroleum (3.5), ensuring, in the case of a Soxhlet apparatus, 13 to 17 cycles of solvent; if other extractors are used, allow not less than 30 minutes for this stage. Remove the thimble from the apparatus, drain off the residual solvent and dry the thimble and the extracted feed in a current of warm air. Place the dried thimble and contents in a clean extraction apparatus and extract with acetone (3.1), allowing at least 25 cycles of solvent when a Soxhlet apparatus is being used. The exact conditions for achieving complete extraction with any particular apparatus should be predetermined. Evaporate the acetone extract to a volume of 5–10ml on a steam bath, and cool to room temperature.

5.2 *Chromatography*

Insert a plug of glass wool into the lower end of a chromatography tube (4.3) and tamp it down with a suitable rod to a thickness of 2 to 3mm. Prepare a slurry of aluminium oxide (3.2) with acetone (3.1), pour into the tube and allow to settle. The prepared column should be about 200mm in height. Allow the acetone layer to drain down to the top of the column.

Transfer the acetone extract obtained in 5.1 from the flask to the column, rinse the flask several times with acetone (3.1) and transfer the liquid onto the column. Place a suitable flask under the column and elute the furazolidone with acetone (3.1); the total volume of acetone used, including that used for rinsing, should be about 150ml.

5.3 *Extraction and measurement of the absorbance*

Evaporate the acetone eluate (5.2) just to dryness on a steam bath. (On occasions a small quantity of diacetone alcohol, produced by condensation of acetone on the aluminium oxide may be left but this will not interfere with the subsequent extractions). Dissolve the residue in 10ml of pentan-1-ol (3.4) and transfer the solution to a separating funnel. Repeat the process using 10ml of pentyl acetate (3.3) as a rinse liquid. Finally rinse the vessel which contained the extract residue with 10ml of urea solution (3.6), add this to the separating funnel and shake fairly vigorously for two minutes.

Allow the phases to separate for a period of three to four minutes before transferring the aqueous extract to a 100ml graduated flask (4.1). Repeat the rinsing and extraction stages with four further 10ml aliquots of urea solution (3.6) and transfer the aqueous extracts to the graduated flask. Dilute the contents of the graduated flask to 100ml with urea solution (3.6) and mix. Measure the absorbance of the solution in the spectrophotometer (4.4) at 375nm against urea solution (3.6) in the reference cell. Determine the quantity of furazolidone by referring to the calibration curve (5.4).

5.4   *Calibration curve*

Prepare four chromatographic columns as described in 5.2. Transfer into separate columns volumes of 2·5, 5·0, 7·5 and 10·0ml respectively of the standard solution (3.8). Wash each of the four columns with 150ml of acetone (3.1) and continue as in paragraph 5.3. Plot the calibration curve, using the absorbance values as ordinates and the corresponding quantities of furazolidone in μg as abscissae.

6.   CALCULATION OF RESULTS

The furazolidone content in ppm is given by the formula:

$$\frac{A}{W}$$

in which:

A = quantity of furazolidone in microgrammes as determined by photometric measurement.
W = weight of test portion in grammes.

14.   DETERMINATION OF ETHOPABATE
(methyl 4-acetamido-2-ethoxybenzoate)

1.   SCOPE AND FIELD OF APPLICATION

The method is for the determination of the quantity of ethopabate in complete feeding stuffs, protein concentrates and feed supplements. The lower limit of the determination is 2ppm.

2.   PRINCIPLE

The sample is extracted with diluted methanol. The solution is acidified and extracted with chloroform. The chloroform extract is washed first with an alkaline solution and then with water. The purified extract is concentrated, the ethopabate is hydrolysed with diluted hydrochloric acid. The amino derivative thus formed is diazotised and coupled with N-2-aminoethyl-1-naphthylamine. The coloured complex is extracted with butanol and the absorbance of the solution is measured at 555nm.

3.   REAGENTS

3.1   Methanol.

3.2   Methanol, 50% (V/V): mix equal volumes of methanol (3.1) and water.

3.3   Hydrochloric acid (density 1·18g per ml).

3.4   Dilute hydrochloric acid: dilute 10·0ml of hydrochloric acid (3.3), to 100ml with water.

3.5   Hydrochloric acid, approximately 0·3N: dilute 25ml of hydrochloric acid (3.3), to 1000ml with water.

3.6   Chloroform.

3.7 Sodium carbonate solution: dissolve 4g sodium carbonate (anhydrous) in water and dilute to 100ml.

3.8 Sodium nitrite solution: dissolve 100mg of sodium nitrite in water and make up to 50ml with water in a graduated flask. Prepare immediately before use.

3.9 Ammonium sulphamate solution: dissolve 500mg of ammonium sulphamate in water and make up to 50ml in a graduated flask. Prepare immediately before use.

3.10 N-2-aminoethyl-1-naphthylamine solution: dissolve 100mg of N-2-aminoethyl-1-naphthylamine dihydrochloride in water and make up to 50ml with water in a graduated flask. Prepare immediately before use.

3.11 Sodium chloride.

3.12 Butan-1-ol.

3.13 Standard substance: pure ethopabate.

3.14 Standard solutions:

3.14.1 Solution of 0·040mg of ethopabate per ml: weigh to the nearest 0·1mg, 40mg of pure ethopabate (3.13). Dissolve in 50% V/V methanol (3.2) in a 100ml graduated flask; make up to volume with the same solvent and mix. Dilute 10·0ml to 100ml with 50% V/V methanol (3.2) in a graduated flask and mix. This solution is stable for a month.

3.14.2 Solution of 0·016mg of ethopabate per 20ml: dilute 5·0ml of the solution (3.14.1) to 250ml with 50% V/V methanol (3.2) in a graduated flask and mix well. Prepare immediately before use.

4. APPARATUS

4.1 Rotary vacuum evaporator, with 250ml flasks.

4.2 Spectrophotometer, with 10mm cells.

5. PROCEDURE

5.1 *Extraction*

Weigh to the nearest 0·001g, a quantity of the finely divided and mixed sample, containing about 80μg of ethopabate. Place the test portion in a 250ml conical flask and add 100·0ml of 50% V/V methanol (3.2). Mix, stopper the flask and shake for 1 hour with the aid of a mechanical shaker. Decant, filter and discard the first 5ml of the filtrate.

5.2 *Purification*

Note: All operations in this sub-section must be carried out rapidly.

Transfer 20·0ml of the clear extract into a 100ml separating funnel, add 5·0ml of dilute hydrochloric acid (3.4) and 20·0ml of chloroform (3.6). Shake, first carefully and then vigorously, for 3 minutes. Allow to stand until the layers separate and collect the chloroform phase in a second 100ml separating funnel.

Extract the acid layer twice more with 20·0ml of chloroform (3.6). Collect the chloroform extracts in the second separating funnel and discard the acid layer. Add to the combined chloroform solution 10ml of sodium carbonate solution (3.7), shake for 3 minutes and allow to stand until the layers separate. Collect the chloroform phase in a third 100ml separating funnel and discard the aqueous layer. Add to the chloroform solution 10ml of sodium carbonate solution (3.7), shake for 3 minutes and allow to stand until the layers separate.

Collect the chloroform phase in a fourth 100ml separating funnel, wash twice with 25·0ml of water each time, separate the aqueous layers and quantitatively collect the chloroform extract in a 250ml round bottom flask. Combine the aqueous layers in one of the separating funnels; rinse each empty funnel with a few millilitres of chloroform; shake the aqueous layer with the chloroform used for rinsing, allow layers to separate, and transfer the chloroform phase to the chloroform extract collected in the flask.

5.3 *Hydrolysis*

Evaporate the chloroform extract down to about 2ml on a water-bath at 50°C with the aid of the rotary vacuum evaporator (4.1). Dissolve the residue in 2 to 3ml of methanol (3.1), and transfer quantitatively the solution to a 50ml centrifuge tube with the aid of two 10ml portions and one 5ml portion of 0·3N hydrochloric acid (3.5). Add a few glass beads, fit an air condenser, shake well, and place the tube in a bath of boiling water for 45 minutes. Then cool under a stream of cold running water.

5.4 *Determination*

Add 1·0ml of sodium nitrite solution (3.8), stir and allow to stand for 2 minutes. Add 1·0ml of ammonium sulphamate solution (3.9), shake and allow to stand for 2 minutes. Add 1·0ml of N-2-aminoethyl-1-naphthylamine solution (3.10), stir and allow to stand for 10 minutes. Add 5·0g of sodium chloride (3.11) and 10·0ml of butan-1-ol (3.12), and shake vigorously until the sodium chloride has completely dissolved.

Draw off the supernatant butanolic solution with the aid of a pipette, and transfer it to a 15ml centrifuge tube and centrifuge. Then measure the absorbance E_A at 555nm against butan-1-ol (3.12) as reference.

5.5 *Reagent blank*

Carry out a blank test, using the same procedure, starting from point 5.2, on 20·0ml of diluted methanol (3.2). Measure the absorbance E_B at 555nm against butan-1-ol (3.12) as reference.

5.6 *Standard test*

Carry out a test, using the same procedure, starting from point 5.2, on 20·0ml of standard solution (3.14.2). Measure the absorbance E_C at 555nm against butan-1-ol (3.12) as reference.

6. CALCULATION OF RESULTS

The ethopabate content in ppm of sample is given by the formula:

$$\frac{80 \times (E_A - E_B)}{W \times (E_C - E_B)}$$

in which:

E_A = absorbance of the solution from the sample;
E_B = absorbance of the solution resulting from the reagent blank;
E_C = absorbance of the solution resulting from the standard test; and
W = weight of test portion in g.

15. DETERMINATION OF NICARBAZIN

(equimolecular mixture of 1,3-bis(4-nitrophenyl)urea and 2-hydroxy-4, 6-dimethylpyrimidine)

1. SCOPE AND FIELD OF APPLICATION

The method is for the determination of the quantity of nicarbazin in complete feeding stuffs, protein concentrates and feed supplements containing not more than 5% grassmeal. Nitrofuran derivatives, acinitrazole and carbadox may interfere. The lower limit of the determination is 20ppm.

2. PRINCIPLE

The sample is extracted with dimethylformamide. The extract is purified by chromatography on a column of aluminium oxide; the nicarbazin is eluted with ethanol. The eluate is treated with ethanolic sodium hydroxide forming a yellow colour, the absorbance of which is measured at 430nm.

3.   REAGENTS

3.1 Dimethylformamide.

3.2 Aluminium oxide for column chromatography: heat at 750°C for at least 2 hours, cool in desiccator and keep in an amber glass bottle with a ground-glass stopper. Before use, check activity by subjecting to analysis, starting from point 5.2, a measured quantity of standard solution (3.8.3). The recovery of the nicarbazin must be 100% ± 2%.

3.3 Ethanol, 95% V/V.

3.4 Ethanol, 80% V/V.

3.5 Sodium hydroxide solution: dissolve 50g sodium hydroxide in water and dilute to 100ml.

3.6 Ethanolic sodium hydroxide: measure 1ml of sodium hydroxide solution (3.5) into a 50ml graduated flask; make up to volume with 80% ethanol (3.4). The solution must be freshly prepared.

3.7 Standard substance: pure nicarbazin, molecular extinction coefficient at 362nm in dimethylformamide: $37·8 \times 10^3$.

3.8 Standard solutions:

Note: Nicarbazin solutions should be protected from light.

3.8.1 Solution of 1·25mg of nicarbazin per ml: weigh to the nearest 0·1mg, 125mg of pure nicarbazin (3.7). Dissolve in 75ml of dimethylformamide (3.1) in a 100ml graduated flask with gentle heat. Allow to cool, make up to volume with the same solvent and mix.

3.8.2 Solution of 0·125mg of nicarbazin per ml: dilute 10·0ml of the solution (3.8.1) to 100ml with dimethylformamide (3.1) in a graduated flask and mix.

3.8.3 Solution of 0·025mg of nicarbazin per ml: dilute 20·0ml of the solution (3.8.2) to 100ml with dimethylformamide (3.1) in a graduated flask and mix.

4.   APPARATUS

4.1 Glass tube for chromatography (internal diameter: 25mm; length: 300mm).

4.2 Spectrophotometer, with 10mm cells.

5.   PROCEDURE

5.1 *Extraction*

Weigh, to within 0·001g, approximately 10g of the finely divided and mixed sample. For protein concentrates and feed supplements, weigh to the nearest 0·001g approximately 1g. Transfer the test portion to a 250ml conical flask and add exactly 100ml of dimethylformamide (3.1). Mix, fit a reflux condenser to the flask and heat on a water-bath for 15 minutes, shaking from time to time. Cool under a stream of cold water. Pour the supernatant layer into a centrifuge tube and centrifuge for about 3 minutes. If necessary, dilute 25·0ml of the supernatant layer with dimethylformamide (3.1), to obtain a solution containing 2·0 to 10µg of nicarbazin per ml.

5.2 *Chromatography*

Pour into the chromatographic tube (4.1) a slurry of 30g of aluminium oxide (3.2) in dimethylformamide (3.1). Allow the liquid level to fall to 10mm above the column of aluminium oxide and then put onto the column 25·0ml of the extract obtained in 5.1. Allow the liquid to flow through, not allowing the column to become dry, and wash the column with three 10ml portions of dimethyl-formamide (3.1). Then elute with 70ml of 95% ethanol (3.3). Discard the first 10ml of the eluate and collect the three fractions in the following order:

(a)   a 5ml fraction;

(b)   a 50ml fraction in a graduated flask;

(c)   a 5ml fraction.

Check that fractions (a) and (c) do not turn yellow when ethanolic sodium hydroxide (3.6) is added. Continue the operations on fraction (b) as shown in 5.3.

5.3   *Determination*

Pipette two 20·0ml portions of fraction (b) into separate 25ml graduated flasks A and B. Add to flask A 5·0ml of ethanolic sodium hydroxide (3.6) and to flask B 5·0ml of 95% ethanol (3.3). Mix well.

Within five minutes measure the absorbance of both solutions at 430nm, against a mixture of 20·0ml of 95% ethanol (3.3) and 5·0ml of ethanolic sodium hydroxide (3.6) as a reference.

Subtract the value of the absorbance of solution B from that of solution A. From this value determine the quantity of nicarbazin by reference to the calibration curve (5.4).

5.4   *Calibration curve*

Chromatograph 25·0ml of the standard solution (3.8.3) as described in 5.2. Transfer 2·0, 4·0, 6·0, 8·0, and 10·0ml portions (corresponding to 25, 50, 75, 100 and 125µg of nicarbazin respectively) of fraction (b) into 25ml graduated flasks from a burette. To each flask add 5·0ml of ethanolic sodium hydroxide (3.6), make up to volume with 95% ethanol (3.3) and mix well.

Within five minutes measure the absorbance of the solutions at 430nm, against a mixture of 20·0ml of 95% ethanol (3.3) and 5·0ml of ethanolic sodium hydroxide (3.6) as a reference.

Plot the calibration curve, using the absorbance values as the ordinates and the corresponding quantities of nicarbazin in µg as the abscissae.

6.   CALCULATION OF RESULTS

The nicarbazin content in ppm of sample is given by the formula:

$$\frac{10 \times A \times F}{W}$$

in which:

A   =   quantity of nicarbazin in µg as determined by photometric measurement;
W   =   weight of test portion in grams; and
F   =   dilution factor (from 5.1).

16.   DETERMINATION OF NIFURSOL
[3,5-dinitro-2'-(nitrofurfurylidene)salicylohydrazide]

1.   SCOPE AND FIELD OF APPLICATION

The method is for the determination of the quantity of nifursol in complete feeding stuffs, protein concentrates and feed supplements. Other substances that will provide a nitro group under the conditions of the method, eg. nitrofurazone and furazolidone, will interfere. The lower limit of the determination is 20ppm.

2.   PRINCIPLE

The sample is extracted with dimethylformamide and the extract is purified on a column of aluminium oxide. A portion of the purified extract containing the nifursol is treated with phenylhydrazine hydrochloride and the resulting phenylhydrazone extracted into toluene. The addition of hyamine hydroxide to the toluene solution produces a blue colour, the absorbance of which is measured at 515nm.

3. REAGENTS

3.1 Toluene.

3.2 Aluminium oxide for column chromatography, 80 to 200 mesh, alkaline, Brockman activity 1. To 100 parts of the aluminium oxide add 6 parts of powdered magnesium hydroxide. Shake in a screw-cap bottle to mix, add 8 parts of water, and mix until free from lumps.

3.3 Sand: acid washed.

3.4 Dimethylformamide solution, 95% V/V.

3.5 Dimethylformamide solution, 50% V/V.

3.6 Phenylhydrazine hydrochloride solution: shake 0.25 ± 0.005g of phenylhydrazine hydrochloride in 25ml of water, add 25ml of concentrated hydrochloric acid, and shake to dissolve the solid, filtering if necessary. Prepare this reagent immediately before use.

3.7 Hyamine 10-X hydroxide solution: about 10% in methanol. (Note: Hyamine is a trade mark of the Rohm & Haas Company. The reagent solution can be obtained from BDH Chemicals Ltd.)

3.8 Nifursol standard solution: weigh, to the nearest 0.1mg, 25mg of pure nifursol into a 100ml graduated flask, add 5ml of 95% V/V dimethylformamide solution (3.4), and mix until all the solid has dissolved. Dilute to the mark with methanol. Prepare this solution freshly each day.

4. APPARATUS

4.1 Chromatographic column—A glass column, internal diameter: 20 to 25mm; length: 100 to 150mm plugged at the lower end with glass wool.

4.2 Spectrophotometer, with 10mm cells.

5. PROCEDURE

5.1 *Extraction*
Weigh to the nearest 0.001g, approximately 5g of the finely divided and mixed sample, or a suitable amount expected to contain about 350µg of nifursol and transfer to a 125ml conical flask. Add 50.0ml of 95% V/V dimethylformamide solution (3.4), insert a stopper loosely, and place the flask in a water-bath at $60° \pm 5°$C for 30 minutes. Swirl the contents of the flask occasionally during this period. Shake the flask on a mechanical shaker for 30 minutes and then filter the contents through a rapid filter-paper, preferably under reduced pressure on a Buchner funnel. Transfer 40.0ml of the filtrate to a beaker, add 40.0ml of water, and stir. Set the beaker aside, protected from light, for 30 minutes.

5.2 *Purification*
Pack the chromatographic column (4.1) to a depth of 70mm with the prepared aluminium oxide (3.2) and on top of the aluminium oxide add a layer of sand (3.3) 15mm deep. Wash the column with 50ml of 50% V/V dimethylformamide solution (3.5) and then pass the dimethylformamide extract of the test sample through the column; reject the first 45ml of eluate and collect the next 17ml.

5.3 *Determination*
Pipette 5.0ml of the eluate to a 20ml centrifuge tube, add 5ml of phenylhydrazine hydrochloride solution (3.6), mix, and place the tube in a water-bath at $40° \pm 2°$C for 20 minutes. Remove the tube from the water-bath and cool it in running water for 5 minutes. Add 5.0ml of toluene (3.1) to the contents of the tube, insert a glass or plastic stopper (a rubber stopper must not be used), and shake vigorously 40 times. Centrifuge for 5 minutes to clear the toluene layer, and transfer 3.0ml of the toluene layer to a 10mm spectrophotometer cell. Add 0.2ml of hyamine hydroxide solution (3.7), mix immediately, and measure the absorbance of the solution within one minute at 515nm with toluene as reference. Determine the quantity of nifursol by reference to the calibration curve (5.4).

5.4 *Calibration curve*

Pipette 5·0ml of nifursol standard solution (3.8) to a 200ml graduated flask, add 100ml of 95% V/V dimethylformamide solution (3.4), dilute to the mark with water and mix. Into separate 20ml centrifuge tubes transfer by pipette 1, 2, 3, 4 and 5ml portions of this solution and dilute the contents of each tube to 5ml with 50% V/V dimethylformamide solution (3.5).

Treat the contents of each tube as described under "Determination" (5.3) beginning at ". . . add 5ml of phenylhydrazine hydrochloride solution (3.6) . . .". Plot the calibration curve using the absorbances as the ordinates and the corresponding quantities of nifursol in μg as abscissae.

6. CALCULATION OF RESULTS

The nifursol content in ppm of sample is given by the formula:

$$\frac{20 \times A}{W}$$

in which:

A = micrograms of nifursol read from the calibration curve; and
W = weight of the test portion in g.

17. DETERMINATION OF NITROFURAZONE
(5-nitrofurfuraldehyde semicarbazone)

1. SCOPE AND FIELD OF APPLICATION

The method is for the determination of the quantity of nitrofurazone in complete feeding stuffs, protein concentrates and feed supplements. The lower limit of the determination is 30ppm.

2. PRINCIPLE

The sample is treated with light petroleum in order to remove interfering substances. The sample is then extracted with acetone and the extract then evaporated to dryness. The residue containing the nitrofurazone is treated with alkaline dimethylformamide to form a coloured solution the absorbance of which is measured at 530nm.

3. REAGENTS

3.1 Acetone.

3.2 Dimethylformamide: test the suitability of the reagent by developing the colour from nitrofurazone with solutions of phenol and sodium hydroxide (see 5.2 and 5.3 below); the colour should remain stable for at least two hours.

3.3 Light petroleum, boiling range 40° to 60°C.

3.4 Phenol solution: Dissolve 5g of phenol in dimethylformamide (3.2) and dilute to 100ml with dimethylformamide.

3.5 Potassium permanganate, 0·1N solution.

3.6 Sodium dithionite solution: dissolve 1g of sodium dithionite, $Na_2S_2O_4$ in N sodium hydroxide solution and dilute to 100ml with N sodium hydroxide solution. Prepare this solution immediately before use.

3.7 Sodium hydroxide, N solution.

3.8 Nitrofurazone standard solution: weigh to the nearest 0·1mg, 100mg of nitrofurazone (B.Vet.C grade) dissolve in dimethylformamide and dilute to 100ml with dimethylformamide. Dilute 10ml of this solution to 100ml with dimethylformamide. 1ml of this solution contains 100μg nitrofurazone. Prepare the dilute solution immediately before use.

4.   APPARATUS

4.1   Spectrophotometer with 10mm glass cells.

4.2   Rotary evaporator.

5.   PROCEDURE

5.1   *Extraction of interfering substances*

Weigh to the nearest 0·001g an amount of the finely divided and mixed sample expected to contain 1mg of nitrofurazone into an extraction thimble; cover the sample with a small pad of cottonwool. Insert the packed thimble into an extraction apparatus and extract the sample with light petroleum (3.3); use an electric heating mantle as the source of heat, so adjusted that the solvent cycles twenty times in about 45 minutes, and sufficient solvent so that the volume in the flask throughout the operation is not less than 25ml.

Remove the packed thimble, allow the solvent to drain, and carefully remove any residual solvent in a current of warm air at a temperature not exceeding 60°C.

5.2   *Extraction of the nitrofurazone*

Transfer the packed thimble to a clean extraction apparatus, and extract the sample with acetone (3.1); use an electric heating mantle as a source of heat so that the solvent cycles twenty times in about one hour; and sufficient solvent so that the volume in the flask throughout the operation is not less than 25ml. During the extraction shield the apparatus from light with a cardboard cylinder containing a small inspection window, or by any other suitable means. When the extraction is complete, rapidly cool the flask containing the extract to 20°C, and add 0·1N potassium permanganate solution (3.5), drop by drop, until a faint pink colour is obtained that persists for about two seconds (about four drops are required). Evaporate the extract on a water-bath to a volume of about 5ml, shielding the extract from light. It is important at this stage to avoid evaporating to dryness.

Remove the flask from the water-bath, place an externally ribbed conical filter funnel into the neck of the flask, and evaporate off the residual acetone under vacuum or by blowing a current of warm air (temperature not exceeding 60°C) across the top of the funnel in such a way that a slight turbulence is produced on the surface of the liquid in the flask. A rotary evaporator (4.2) may be used for the evaporation stages.

Dissolve the residue in dimethylformamide (3.2), transfer the solution quantitatively to a 50ml graduated flask, suitably shielded from light, and dilute to the mark at 20°C with dimethylformamide. Transfer a suitable portion containing about 200μg of nitrofurazone to each of two 50ml graduated flasks containing 5ml of phenol solution (3.4).

5.3   *Determination*

To the contents of one flask add 2·5ml of N sodium hydroxide solution (3.7) and dilute to the mark at 20°C with dimethylformamide (3.2); this is the sample solution. To the contents of the other flask add 2·5ml of sodium dithionite solution (3.6), and dilute to the mark at 20°C with dimethylformamide; this is the blank solution and it should be a pale lemon-yellow colour free from any red or purplish tinge. Centrifuge until clear solutions are obtained. Measure the absorbance of the sample solution in a 10mm cell at 530nm against the blank solution as reference. Determine the quantity of nitrofurazone by reference to the calibration curve (5.4).

5.4   *Calibration curve*

Transfer amounts of nitrofurazone standard solution (3.8) corresponding to 100, 150, 200, 250 and 300μg of nitrofurazone into two series of 50ml graduated flasks each containing 5ml of phenol solution (3.4), and proceed as described under 5.3. Plot the calibration curve using the absorbances as the ordinates and the corresponding quantities of nitrofurazone in μg as abscissae.

6.   CALCULATION OF RESULTS

The nitrofurazone content in ppm of sample is given by the formula:

$$\frac{A}{W} \times \frac{50}{V}$$

in which:

A = weight of nitrofurazone in aliquot taken for colour development as read from the calibration curve (μg);

V = volume of aliquot taken for colour development (ml); and

W = weight of test portion in g.

18. DETERMINATION OF NITROVIN

[1,5-di-(5-nitro-2-furyl)pentadien-3-one amidinohydrazone hydrochloride]

1.   SCOPE AND FIELD OF APPLICATION

The method is for the determination of nitrovin in complete feeding stuffs and protein concentrates. The lower limit of the determination is 5ppm.

2.   PRINCIPLE

After a preliminary extraction with hexane the sample is extracted with dimethyl-formamide. This extract is cleaned up on a column of aluminium oxide and the nitrovin is eluted with dimethylformamide containing ammonium hydroxide. The absorbance of the eluate is measured at 495nm, a portion of the eluate is acidified and the absorbance of this solution is subtracted from the absorbance of the alkaline solution to give the corrected absorbance, from which the nitrovin content is calculated by reference to a standard curve.

3.   REAGENTS

3.1 Aluminium oxide, for column chromatography: heat overnight in a muffle furnace at 600°C. Test the suitability of each batch of aluminium oxide by adding 15ml of dilute nitrovin standard solution (3.7) to the column and eluting as described in paragraph 5.4. At least 95% recovery should be indicated.

3.2 Dimethylformamide.

3.3 Eluting solution: dilute 20ml of ammonium hydroxide solution (density 0·88g per ml) to 1 litre with dimethylformamide.

3.4 Hexane: fraction from petroleum.

3.5 Hydrochloric acid solution: dilute a suitable volume of hydrochloric acid (density 1·18g per ml) with an equal volume of water.

3.6 Dichloromethane.

3.7 Nitrovin standard solution: weigh to the nearest 0·1mg, 100mg of pure nitrovin and transfer it to a 100ml graduated flask. Dissolve in, and dilute to volume with the eluting solution (3.3), and mix well. Transfer by pipette 10·0ml of this solution to a 100ml graduated flask, dilute to volume with the eluting solution (3.3) and mix well. This gives a solution containing 100μg per ml. Transfer by pipette 10·0ml of the 100μg per ml solution to a 100ml calibrated flask, dilute to volume with the eluting solution (3.3) and mix well. This gives a solution containing 10μg per ml (solution 3.7).

4.   APPARATUS

4.1 Chromatographic column—diameter: 15mm; length: 250mm, with polytetra-fluoroethylene stopcock and 250ml reservoir.

1e

4.2   Filter-paper, glass fibre (Whatman GF/A or equivalent).

4.3   Spectrophotometer with 10mm cells.

5.   PROCEDURE

Warning: It is necessary that the glassware used should be completely dry, as a small amount of water in the feed extract will adversely affect the aluminium oxide chromatography by causing the band to become diffuse, which could lead to low recovery.

5.1   *Extraction of interfering substances*

Weigh, to the nearest 0·001g, approximately 50g of the finely divided and mixed sample, transfer to a bottle of not less than 350ml capacity fitted with a polyethylene lined screw cap. Add 5ml of hexane (3.4) for each gram of feed taken, close the bottle and shake for 1 hour. Filter the contents of the bottle through two layers of glass fibre filter-paper (4.2) on a Buchner funnel, and wash with an equal amount of fresh hexane (3.4). Continue to suck air through the filter for 15 minutes. Transfer the filter-paper and sample to an aluminium tray and dry in a vacuum oven at 65°C for 1 hour.

5.2   *Extraction of nitrovin*

Transfer the dried sample and glass fibre filter-paper (5.1) to a bottle, add 2·5ml of dimethylformamide (3.2) for each gram of feed present, cap with a polyethylene lined screw cap and shake for 1 hour. Filter the extract through two layers of glass fibre paper (4.2) on a Buchner funnel.

5.3   *Purification*

Place a plug of glass wool in the bottom of the 15mm diameter glass tube (4.1), close the stopcock and fill the barrel of the column with dichloromethane (3.6). Tamp with a glass rod to remove air bubbles, and add 15g of aluminium oxide (3.1). Allow the aluminium oxide to settle by gravity, and drain the solvent until the surface reaches the level of the aluminium oxide bed. Close the stopcock. Transfer by pipette 20·0ml of the feed extract to the column. Allow the extract and subsequent washes to percolate through the column at a rate of 30 drops per minute. When the surface of the extract has reached the level of the aluminium oxide bed, wash the column with two 5ml portions of dimethylformamide (3.2). When the surface of the second wash has reached the level of the aluminium oxide bed, wash the column with sufficient dimethylformamide to wash out the rapidly descending yellow band without eluting any of the slower moving red nitrovin band. When the surface of the final wash reaches the surface of the aluminium oxide bed, discard the effluent that has been collected and place a 100ml graduated flask under the column. Add about 125ml of the eluting solution (3.3) to the reservoir and allow it to percolate through the column at a rate of 30 drops per minute. Collect 100ml of the eluate.

5.4   *Determination*

Mix the eluate well and measure its absorbance at 495nm with the eluting solution as reference. Withdraw a further 25ml of the eluate from the flask and add to this 2ml of hydrochloric acid solution (3.5) (no correction is made for the additional volume as the reading is small). Mix well, measure the absorbance of the acidified eluate at 495nm against the eluting solution, and subtract this value from the absorbance of the alkaline eluate to determine the corrected absorbance. Determine the concentration of nitrovin in the sample solution by reference to the calibration curve (5.5).

5.5   *Calibration curve*

Transfer by pipette 2·0, 4·0, 6·0 and 8·0ml portions of nitrovin standard solution (3.7) to separate 50ml graduated flasks. Dilute the contents of each to volume with the eluting solution (3.3), and mix well. These solutions have concentrations of 0·4, 0·8, 1·2 and 1·6µg of nitrovin per ml, respectively. Measure the absorbances of these solutions at 495nm against the eluting solution as reference.

Add 2ml of hydrochloric acid solution (3.5) to each of the solutions remaining in the flasks, and mix well. If any of these solutions become turbid clarify them by spinning in a centrifuge. Measure the absorbances of the acidified solutions in the same manner as for the alkaline solutions and subtract the reading from the absorbance of the appropriate alkaline solution to give the corrected absorbance. Plot the calibration curve using the absorbances as the ordinates and the corresponding concentrations of nitrovin in μg per ml as abscissae.

6. CALCULATION OF RESULTS

The nitrovin content in ppm of sample is given by the formula:

$$\frac{5 \times C \times V}{W}$$

in which:

C = concentration of nitrovin in eluate, μg per ml;
V = volume of extract, ml;
W = weight of the test portion in g.

19. DETERMINATION OF NITROVIN IN FEED SUPPLEMENTS

[1,5-di-(5-nitro-2-furyl)pentadien-3-one amidinohydrazone hydrochloride]

1. SCOPE AND FIELD OF APPLICATION

The method is for the determination of the quantity of nitrovin in feed supplements, made with inert or cereal carriers.

2. PRINCIPLE

Nitrovin is extracted from the sample with dimethylformamide containing ammonium hydroxide and the absorbance of this solution before and after acidification is measured at 495nm.

3. REAGENTS

3.1 Dimethylformamide solvent: dilute 20ml of ammonia solution (density 0·88g per ml) to 1 litre with dimethylformamide.

3.2 Hydrochloric acid solution: dilute a suitable volume of hydrochloric acid (density 1·18g per ml) with an equal volume of water.

3.3 Nitrovin standard solution: weigh to the nearest 0·1mg, 100mg of pure nitrovin and transfer it to a 200ml graduated flask. Dissolve in and dilute to volume with the dimethylformamide solvent (3.1), and mix well. Transfer by pipette 10·0ml of this solution to a 100ml graduated flask, dilute to volume with the dimethylformamide solvent, and mix well. This solution contains 50μg of nitrovin per ml.

4. APPARATUS

4.1 Spectrophotometer with 10mm cells.

5. PROCEDURE

5.1 *Extraction of nitrovin*

Weigh, to the nearest 0·001g about 1g of the finely divided and mixed sample and transfer it to a 200ml graduated flask. Add 100ml of the dimethylformamide solvent (3.1), and place on a mechanical shaker and shake for 20 minutes. Dilute to the mark with the dimethylformamide solvent (3.1) and mix well. Filter the solution through a suitable filter-paper (Whatman No 41 or equivalent), discarding the first 20ml of filtrate. By pipette transfer 2·0ml of filtrate to a 100ml graduated flask, dilute to the mark with the dimethylformamide solvent, and mix well. Measure the absorbance of this solution at 495nm with dimethylformamide as reference. Add 2ml of hydrochloric acid solution (3.2) to the remainder of the solution in the flask, and measure the absorbance of the acidified solution in the same manner. Subtract the absorbance of the acidified solution from that of the untreated solution to give the corrected absorbance. Determine the concentration of nitrovin in the sample by reference to the calibration curve (5.2).

5.2   Calibration curve

Transfer by pipette, 1·0, 2·0, 4·0, 6·0, 8·0 and 10·0ml of nitrovin standard solution (3.3) to separate 50ml graduated flasks. Dilute the contents of each to volume with the dimethylformamide solvent, (3.1) and mix well. These solutions will have concentrations of 1·0, 2·0, 4·0, 6·0, 8·0 and 10·0μg of nitrovin per ml, respectively. Measure the absorbance of these solutions at 495nm with dimethylformamide as reference. Add 2ml of hydrochloric acid solution (3.2) to each of the solutions remaining in the flasks and mix well. If any of these solutions has become turbid clarify it by spinning in a centrifuge. Measure the absorbances of the acidified solutions in the same manner as for the alkaline solutions and subtract the reading from the absorbance of the appropriate alkaline solution to give the corrected absorbance. Plot the calibration curve using the absorbances as the ordinates and the corresponding concentrations of nitrovin in μg per ml as the abscissae.

6.   CALCULATION OF RESULTS

The nitrovin content per cent of sample is given by the formula:

$$\frac{C}{W}$$

in which:

C = concentration of nitrovin in the final solution, μg per ml; and
W = weight of the test portion in g.

20.   DETERMINATION OF OLEANDOMYCIN

1.   SCOPE AND FIELD OF APPLICATION

The method is for the determination of the quantity of oleandomycin in complete feeding stuffs, protein concentrates and feed supplements. The lower limit of determination is 0·5ppm.

2.   PRINCIPLE

The sample is extracted with a solution of aqueous methanol containing 'Tris-buffer'. After centrifuging, the extract is diluted and its antibiotic activity is determined by measuring the diffusion of the oleandomycin in an agar medium inoculated with *Bacillus cereus*. Diffusion is shown by the formation of zones of inhibition in the presence of the micro-organism. The diameter of these zones is taken to be in direct proportion to the logarithm of the antibiotic concentration.

3.   MICRO-ORGANISM: *B. cereus* K 250 TR (RESISTANT TO TETRACYCLINES) (NCIB 11183; NCTC 10989)

3.1   Maintenance of the parent strain

Inoculate *B. cereus* onto an agar slope prepared from the culture medium (4.1) to which has been added 100μg oxytetracycline per 5ml. Incubate overnight at approximately 30°C. Keep the culture in a refrigerator and re-inoculate onto agar slopes every 4 weeks.

3.2 *Preparation of the spore suspension*

Harvest the bacteria from the agar slope (3.1) in 2 to 3ml of physiological saline (4.2). Inoculate this suspension onto 300ml of culture medium (4.1.2) in a Roux flask. Incubate for 3 to 5 days at 28 to 30°C and then confirm by examination under the microscope that sporulation has occurred. Harvest the spores in 15ml of ethanol (4.3) and mix. This suspension may be kept in a refrigerator for at least 5 months.

Make preliminary tests on the assay plates with the culture medium (4.1.3) to determine the quantity of inoculum needed to obtain the largest possible clear zones of inhibition with the different concentrations of antibiotic used. The quantity will usually be 0·2 to 0·3ml per 1 000ml. Inoculate the culture medium at a temperature between 50 and 60°C.

4. CULTURE MEDIA AND REAGENTS

4.1.1 Culture Medium I:

Glucose	1g
Tryptic peptone	10g
Meat extract	1·5g
Yeast extract	3g
Agar, according to quality	10 to 20g
Water to	1 000ml

Adjust the pH to 6·5 before use.

4.1.2 Culture Medium II:
As for 4.1.1 with agar concentration of 3 to 4%.

4.1.3 Culture Medium III:
As for 4.1.1 with pH 8·8.

4.2 Sterile physiological saline: dissolve 9g sodium chloride in water and dilute to 1 000ml.

4.3 Ethanol, 20% solution (V/V).

4.4 Methanol.

4.5 'Tris-buffer' solution: dissolve 0·5g 2-amino-2-hydroxymethylpropanediol in water and dilute to 100ml.

4.6 *Extraction solution*

Methanol	50ml
Water	50ml
2-amino-2-hydroxymethylpropanediol	0·5g

4.7 Standard substance: oleandomycin chloroform adduct of known activity.

5. STANDARD SOLUTION

Dissolve an accurately weighed quantity of between 10 and 50mg of the standard substance (4.7) in about 5ml methanol (4.4) in a graduated flask, and dilute with solution (4.5) to obtain an oleandomycin concentration of 100μg per ml.

Prepare from this solution, diluting with solution (4.5), a standard working solution S_8 containing 0·1μg oleandomycin per ml. Then prepare the following concentrations by means of successive dilutions (1 + 1) with solution (4.5):

S_4 0·05μg per ml
S_2 0·025μg per ml
S_1 0·0125μg per ml

6. PROCEDURE

6.1 *Extraction*

According to the presumed level of oleandomycin of the sample, take a sample for analysis of 2 to 10g, weighed to the nearest 0·001g, add 100ml of solution (4.6) and shake for 30 minutes on a mechanical shaker.

Centrifuge, and dilute a suitable volume of the clear supernatant with the solution (4.5) to obtain an expected concentration of oleandomycin of $0 \cdot 1 \mu g$ per ml (U_8). Then prepare the concentrations U_4, U_2 and U_1 by means of successive dilutions (1 + 1) with solution (4.5).

6.2 *Determination*

Diffusion through agar is carried out in plates with the four concentrations of the standard solution (S_8, S_4, S_2, S_1) and the four concentrations of the extract (U_8, U_4, U_2, U_1). These four concentrations of extract and standard solution must be placed in each plate. To this effect, select plates large enough to allow at least 8 holes with a diameter of 10 to 13mm, and not less than 30mm between centres, to be punched out of the agar medium.

Inoculate at 50–60°C with the spore suspension (3.2) a quantity of the melted culture medium (4.1.3), sufficient to give a layer approximately 2mm thick in the assay plates to be employed. Swirl to mix thoroughly, and pour into the sterile assay plates which must be held in a rigorously horizontal position until the agar has set. With a sterile cork borer remove agar plugs to form holes as described above.

Pipette into each hole an exactly measured and equal volume ($0 \cdot 10$ to $0 \cdot 15$ml) of respectively solutions S_8, S_4, S_2, S_1 and U_8, U_4, U_2, U_1.

Apply each concentration 4 times so that the determination is subject to an evaluation of 32 zones of inhibition.

Incubate the plates for approximately 18 hours at 28–30°C.

6.3 *Evaluation*

Measure the diameter of the zones of inhibition, if possible to the nearest $0 \cdot 1$mm. For each zone, two measurements at right angles should be made. Calculate the mean diameters for each of the concentrations of sample and standard. Plot the mean diameters against the logarithms of the concentrations for both standard solutions and the sample solutions. Draw the best possible straight line for standard and sample. In the absence of any interference the two lines should be approximately parallel.

The logarithm of the relative activity is calculated by the following formula:

$$\frac{(u_1 + u_2 + u_4 + u_8 - s_1 - s_2 - s_4 - s_8) \times 0 \cdot 602}{u_4 + u_8 + s_4 + s_8 - u_1 - u_2 - s_1 - s_2}$$

where s and u represent the mean inhibition zone diameters of standard and sample solutions respectively.

Real activity of sample solutions = presumed activity $\times$ relative activity.

21. DETERMINATION OF SULPHAQUINOXALINE

[2-(4-aminobenzenesulphonamido)quinoxaline]

1. SCOPE AND FIELD OF APPLICATION

The method is for the determination of the quantity of sulphaquinoxaline in complete feeding stuffs, protein concentrates and feed supplements. The lower limit of the determination is 20ppm.

2. PRINCIPLE

The sample is extracted with a mixture of dimethylformamide and chloroform, and the extract treated with an alkaline brine solution. After acidifying the aqueous phase, the sulphaquinoxaline is diazotised and coupled with N-2-aminoethyl-1-naphthylamine, forming a red colour, the absorbance of which is measured at 545nm.

3. REAGENTS.

3.1 Dimethylformamide.

3.2   Chloroform.

3.3   Ethanol absolute.

3.4   Alkaline brine: dissolve 10g sodium hydroxide and 25g sodium chloride in water. Make up to 500ml with water.

3.5   Hydrochloric acid (density 1·18g per ml).

3.6   Sodium nitrite solution: dissolve 0·1g sodium nitrite in water and dilute to 100ml. Prepare immediately before use.

3.7   Ammonium sulphamate solution: dissolve 0·5g ammonium sulphamate in water and dilute to 100ml. Prepare immediately before use.

3.8   N-2-aminoethyl-1-naphthylamine dihydrochloride solution: dissolve 0·1g of N-2-aminoethyl-1-naphthylamine dihydrochloride in dilute hydrochloric acid (0·2ml hydrochloric acid (3.5) diluted to 200ml with water) and make up to 100ml with the same acid. Prepare immediately before use.

3.9   Sulphaquinoxaline standard solution: weigh to the nearest 0·1mg, 250mg of pure sulphaquinoxaline, dissolve in 50ml sodium hydroxide solution (25ml 0.1N sodium hydroxide solution + 25ml water) and make up to 500ml with water. Dilute 5·0ml to 100ml with water. 1ml of this solution contains $25\mu g$ of sulphaquinoxaline.

4.   APPARATUS

4.1   Sintered-glass funnel, porosity: G3, diameter 80mm, with filter flask.

4.2   Spectrophotometer, with 20mm cells.

5.   PROCEDURE

5.1   *Extraction*

Weigh, to the nearest 0·001g, a quantity of the finely divided and mixed sample expected to contain between 0·25 and 1·25mg of sulphaquinoxaline. Place the test portion in a 250ml conical flask and add 20ml dimethylformamide (3.1). Mix and heat the flask on a steam-bath for 20 minutes, then allow to cool under a stream of cold water. Add 60ml of chloroform (3.2), stopper the flask and shake mechanically for 30 minutes.

Filter the liquid through the sintered-glass funnel (4.1) under mild suction. Rinse the filter flask with four 5ml portions of chloroform (3.2) and pass the rinsings through the funnel. Transfer the filtrate to a separating funnel, rinse the filter flask with about 15ml chloroform (3.2) and transfer the rinsings to the funnel.

Add to the funnel 50ml of alkaline brine (3.4) and 5ml ethanol (3.3). Mix the layers thoroughly, avoiding emulsion formation, either by slow inversion of the funnel about twenty times or by rotating it about the horizontal axis of the stem and the stopper. Allow the layers to separate (separation is usually complete in about 15 minutes).

Transfer the upper (aqueous) layer to a 250ml graduated flask. Repeat the extraction of the chloroform layer with three further 50ml portions of alkaline brine (3.4), adding each aqueous extract to the contents of the graduated flask.

Make up the volume with water and mix.

Transfer 25·0ml of the solution to a 50ml graduated flask, add 5ml hydrochloric acid (3.5), make up the volume with water and mix. Filter if necessary, discarding the first 15ml of filtrate. Transfer 10·0ml aliquots of the solution to two boiling tubes A and B.

5.2 Determination

To each tube add 2·0ml of sodium nitrite solution (3.6), mix and allow to stand for three minutes. Add 2·0ml of ammonium sulphamate solution (3.7), mix and allow to stand for two minutes. Add 1·0ml of N-2-aminoethyl-1-naphthylamine dihydrochloride solution (3.8) to tube A and 1·0ml water to tube B. Mix thoroughly the contents of each tube. By means of a water pump apply a partial vacuum to the tubes through rubber connections in order to remove dissolved nitrogen. After 10 minutes measure the absorbances E_A and E_B of the solutions in 20mm cells at 545nm against water as reference. From the value $E_A - E_B$ determine the amount (A) of sulphaquinoxaline present in the sample solution by reference to the calibration curve (5.3).

5.3 Calibration curve

Transfer into a series of 100ml graduated flasks volumes of 2·0, 4·0, 6·0, 8·0 and 10·0ml of the standard solution (3.9) corresponding to 50, 100, 150, 200 and 250 micrograms of sulphaquinoxaline. Add 8ml hydrochloric acid (3.5) to each flask, make up the volume with water and mix. Transfer by pipette 10·0ml of each solution (equivalent to 5, 10, 15, 20 and 25 micrograms sulphaquinoxaline) into boiling tubes. Develop the colour reaction as indicated under (5.2). Measure the absorbances in 20mm cells at 545nm against water as reference. Plot the calibration curve, using the absorbances as the ordinates and the corresponding quantities of sulphaquinoxaline in micrograms as the abscissae.

6. CALCULATION OF RESULTS

The sulphaquinoxaline content in ppm of sample is given by the formula:

$$\frac{A \times 50}{W}$$

in which:

A = quantity of sulphaquinoxaline in micrograms as determined by photo-metric measurement;

W = weight of test portion in g.

22. DETERMINATION OF TYLOSIN

1. SCOPE AND FIELD OF APPLICATION

The method is for the determination of the quantity of tylosin in complete feeding stuffs, protein concentrates and feed supplements. The lower limit of determination is 2 ppm.

2. PRINCIPLE

The sample is treated with pH 8·0 phosphate buffer solution which has been heated to a temperature of 80°C, and then extracted by methanol. After centrifuging, the extract is diluted and its antibiotic activity is determined by measuring the diffusion of the tylosin in an agar medium inoculated with *Micrococcus luteus*. Diffusion is indicated by the formation of zones of inhibition in the presence of the micro-organism. The diameter of the zones is taken to be in direct proportion to the logarithm of the antibiotic concentration.

3. MICRO-ORGANISM: *M. luteus* ATCC 9341 (NCIB 8553; NCTC 8340)

3.1 Maintenance of the parent strain

Inoculate *M. luteus* on to an agar slope prepared from the culture medium (4.1.1). Incubate overnight at approximately 35°C. Keep the culture in a refrigerator and re-inoculate on to agar slopes every two weeks.

3.2 *Preparation of the bacterial suspension*

Harvest the bacteria from a recently-prepared agar slope (3.1) with 2 to 3ml physiological saline (4.4). Inoculate this suspension into 250ml culture medium (4.1.1) contained in a Roux flask. Incubate for 24 hours at 35°C, and harvest the bacteria in 25ml physiological saline (4.4). Mix and dilute this suspension to obtain a light transmission of approximately 75% at 650nm, in a 10mm cell using physiological saline as reference. This suspension is usable for one week if kept in a refrigerator.

Make preliminary tests on the assay plates with the culture medium (4.1.3) to determine the quantity of inoculum needed to obtain the largest possible clear zones of inhibition with the different concentrations of antibiotic used. The quantity will usually be 0·2 to 0·3ml per 1 000ml. Inoculate the culture medium at a temperature between 48 and 50°C.

4. CULTURE MEDIA AND REAGENTS

    4.1.1 Culture Medium I:

Glucose	1g
Tryptic peptone	10g
Meat extract	1.5g
Yeast extract	3g
Agar, according to quality	10 to 20g
Water to	1 000ml

    pH after sterilisation 7·0.

    4.1.2 Culture Medium II:

    As for 4.1.1 but pH after sterilisation of 8·0.

4.2 Phosphate buffer solution pH 8·0:

Potassium dihydrogen phosphate KH_2PO_4	0·523g
di Potassium hydrogen phosphate K_2HPO_4	16·730g
Water to	1 000ml

4.3 Phosphate buffer solution pH 7·0:

Potassium dihydrogen phosphate KH_2PO_4	5·5g
di Potassium hydrogen phosphate K_2HPO_4	13·6g
Water to	1 000ml

4.4 Sterile physiological saline: dissolve 9g sodium chloride in water and dilute to 1 000ml.

4.5 Methanol.

4.6 Methanol, 10% solution (V/V).

4.7 A mixture of phosphate buffer solution (4.2) and methanol, in the proportions: 60 + 40.

4.8 Standard substance: tylosin base of known activity.

5. STANDARD SOLUTIONS

Dry the standard substance (4.8) for 3 hours at 60°C in a vacuum oven (5mm mercury). Accurately weigh 10 to 50mg in a graduated flask, dissolve in 5ml methanol (4.5) and dilute the solution with the phosphate buffer solution pH 7·0 (4.3) to obtain a concentration of tylosin base of 1 000μg per ml.

Diluting with the mixture (4.7), prepare from this solution a standard working solution S_8 containing 2μg tylosin base per ml.

Then by means of successive dilutions (1 + 1) with the mixture (4.7), prepare the following concentrations:

        S_4 1μg per ml
        S_2 0·5μg per ml
        S_1 0·25μg per ml.

6.   PROCEDURE

6.1   *Extraction*

For feed supplements take a sample for analysis of 10g, weighed to the nearest 0·001g; for protein concentrates and complete feeding stuffs, take a sample for analysis of 20g, weighed to the nearest 0·001g. Add 60ml phosphate buffer solution pH8 (4.2), heat to a temperature of 80°C, and homogenise for 2 minutes in a blender.

Allow to stand for 10 minutes, add 40ml methanol (4.5) and homogenise again for 5 minutes. Centrifuge, take an aliquot of the clear supernatant and dilute with the mixture (4.7) to obtain an expected concentration of tylosin of 2μg per ml (U_8). Then by means of successive dilutions (1+1) prepare the concentrations U_4, U_2 and U_1 with the mixture (4.7). For levels lower than 10mg per kg, concentrate the extract in a rotary evaporator at 35°C, dissolve the residue in 10% methanol (4.6) and dilute to a known volume to give a concentration of 2μg per ml.

6.2   *Determination*

Diffusion through agar is carried out in plates with the four concentrations of the standard solution (S_8, S_4, S_2, S_1) and the four concentrations of the extract (U_8, U_4, U_2, U_1). These four concentrations of extract and standard solution must be placed in each plate. To this effect, select plates large enough to allow at least 8 holes with a diameter of 10 to 13mm, and not less than 30mm between centres, to be punched out of the agar medium.
Inoculate at 48–50°C with the bacterial suspension (3.2) a quantity of the melted culture medium (4.1.2), sufficient to give a layer approximately 2mm thick in the assay plates to be employed. Swirl to mix thoroughly, and pour into the sterile assay plates which must be held in a rigorously horizontal position until the agar has set. With a sterile cork borer remove agar plugs to form holes as described above.
Pipette into each hole an exactly measured and equal volume (0·10 to 0·15ml) of respectively solutions S_8, S_4, S_2, S_1 and U_8, U_4, U_2, U_1.

Apply each concentration 4 times so that the determination is subject to an evaluation of 32 zones of inhibition.

Incubate the plates overnight at 35–37°C.

6.3   *Evaluation*

Measure the diameter of the zones of inhibition, if possible to the nearest 0·1mm. For each zone, two measurements at right angles should be made. Calculate the mean diameters for each of the concentrations of sample and standard. Plot the mean diameters against the logarithms of the concentrations for both standard solutions and the sample solutions. Draw the best possible straight line for standard and sample. In the absence of any interference the two lines should be approximately parallel.

The logarithm of the relative activity is calculated by the following formula:

$$\frac{(u_1+u_2+u_4+u_8-s_1-s_2-s_4-s_8) \times 0\cdot602}{u_4+u_8+s_4+s_8-u_1-u_2-s_1-s_2}$$

where s and u represent the mean inhibition zone diameters of standard and sample solutions respectively.

Real activity of sample solutions = presumed activity × relative activity.

23.   DETERMINATION OF VIRGINIAMYCIN

1.   SCOPE AND FIELD OF APPLICATION

The method is for the determination of the quantity of virginiamycin in complete feeding stuffs, protein concentrates and feed supplements. The lower limit of determination is 2ppm.

2. PRINCIPLE

The sample is extracted with a methanol solution of a non-ionic surfactant. After centrifuging or filtering, the extract is diluted and its antibiotic activity is determined by measuring the diffusion of the virginiamycin in an agar medium inoculated with *Micrococcus luteus*. Diffusion is shown by the formation of zones of inhibition in the presence of the micro-organism. The diameter of these zones is taken to be in direct proportion to the logarithm of the antibiotic concentration.

3. MICRO-ORGANISM: *M. luteus* ATCC 9341 (NCIB 8553; NCTC 8340)

3.1 *Maintenance of the parent strain*

Inoculate *M. luteus* onto an agar slope prepared from the culture medium (4.1). Incubate overnight at approximately 35°C. Keep the culture in a refrigerator and re-inoculate onto agar slopes every two weeks.

3.2 *Preparation of the bacteria suspension*

Harvest the bacteria from a recently-prepared agar slope (3.1) with 2 to 3ml physiological saline (4.3). Inoculate this suspension into 250ml culture medium (4.1) contained in a Roux flask. Incubate for 24 hours at 35°C, and harvest the bacteria using 25ml physiological saline (4.3).

Mix well, and dilute this suspension to obtain a light transmission of approximately 75% at 650nm, in a 10mm cell using physiological saline as reference. This suspension is usable for one week if kept in a refrigerator.

Make preliminary tests on the assay plates using the culture medium (4.1) to determine the quantity of inoculum needed to obtain the largest possible clear zones of inhibition with the different concentrations of antibiotic used. Inoculate the culture medium at a temperature between 48 and 50°C.

4. CULTURE MEDIUM AND REAGENTS

4.1 Culture medium:

Glucose	1 g
Tryptic peptone	10 g
Meat extract	1·5g
Yeast extract	3 g
Agar, according to quality	10 to 20 g
Water to	1 000ml

Adjust the pH to 6·5 before use.

4.2 Phosphate buffer solution pH 6·0:

Potassium dihydrogen phosphate, KH_2PO_4	8·0g
di Potassium hydrogen phosphate, K_2HPO_4	2·0g
Water to	1 000ml

4.3 Sterile physiological saline: dissolve 9g sodium chloride in water and dilute to 1 000ml.

4.4 Methanol.

4.5 A mixture of phosphate buffer solution (4.2) and methanol (4.4) in the proportions by volume: 80+20.

4.6 Tween 80: dissolve 1g in methanol and dilute to 200ml.

4.7 Standard substance: virginiamycin of known activity.

5. STANDARD SOLUTION

Dissolve an accurately weighed quantity of the standard substance (4.7) in methanol (4.4) in a graduated flask, to give a solution containing 800µg virginiamycin per ml.

Prepare from this solution, diluting with solution (4.5), a standard working solution S_8 containing $1\mu g$ virginiamycin per ml. Then prepare the following concentrations by means of successive dilutions $(1+1)$ using the solution (4.5):

S_4 $0\cdot5\mu g$ per ml
S_2 $0\cdot25\mu g$ per ml
S_1 $0\cdot125\mu g$ per ml

6.   PROCEDURE

6.1   *Extraction*

6.1.1   Levels of virginiamycin not more than 50ppm:
Take 10 to 20g of the sample, weighed to the nearest 0·001g, add 100ml of solution (4.6) and shake for 30 minutes. Centrifuge or filter, take 20ml of the clear solution and evaporate to dryness in a rotary evaporator. Take up the residue with 20ml or more of the mixture (4.5) to obtain an expected concentration of virginiamycin of $1\mu g$ per ml (U_8).
Then prepare the concentrations U_4, U_2 and U_1 by means of successive dilutions $(1 + 1)$ using the mixture (4.5).

6.1.2   Levels of virginiamycin in excess of 50ppm:
Take 1 to 10g of the sample, weighed to the nearest 0·001g, add 100ml of solution (4.6) and shake for 30 minutes. Centrifuge or filter, and then dilute with the mixture (4.5) to obtain an expected concentration of virginiamycin of $1\mu g$ per ml (U_8). Then prepare the concentrations U_4, U_2 and U_1 as described in (6.1.1).

6.2   *Determination*

Diffusion through agar is carried out in plates with the four concentrations of the standard solution (S_8, S_4, S_2, S_1) and the four concentrations of the extract (U_8, U_4, U_2, U_1). These four concentrations of extract and standard solution must be placed in each plate. To this effect, select plates large enough to allow at least 8 holes with a diameter of 10 to 13mm, and not less than 30mm between centres, to be punched out of the agar medium.

Inoculate at 48–50°C with the bacterial suspension (3.2) a quantity of the melted culture medium (4.1), sufficient to give a layer approximately 2mm thick in the assay plates to be employed. Swirl to mix thoroughly, and pour into the sterile assay plates which must be held in a rigorously horizontal position until the agar has set. With a sterile cork borer remove agar plugs to form holes as described above.

Pipette into each hole an exactly measured and equal volume (0·10 to 0·15ml) of respectively solutions S_8, S_4, S_2, S_1 and U_8, U_4, U_2, U_1.

Apply each concentration 4 times so that the determination is subject to an evaluation of 32 zones of inhibition.

Incubate the plates for approximately 18 hours at 28–30°C.

6.3   *Evaluation*

Measure the diameter of the zones of inhibition, if possible to the nearest 0·1mm. For each zone, two measurements at right angles should be made. Calculate the mean diameters for each of the concentrations of sample and standard. Plot the mean diameters against the logarithms of the concentrations for both standard solutions and the sample solutions. Draw the best possible straight lines for standard and sample. In the absence of any interference the two lines should be approximately parallel.

The logarithm of the relative activity is calculated by the following formula:

$$\frac{(u_1 + u_2 + u_4 + u_8 - s_1 - s_2 - s_4 - s_8) \times 0\cdot602}{u_4 + u_8 + s_4 + s_8 - u_1 - u_2 - s_1 - s_2}$$

where s and u represent the mean inhibition zone diameters of standard and sample solutions respectively.

Real activity of sample solutions = presumed activity $\times$ relative activity.

SCHEDULE 4

FORMS OF CERTIFICATE OF ANALYSIS OR EXAMINATION

(Regulation 5)

PART I

CERTIFICATE OF ANALYSIS OF ANIMAL FEEDING STUFF (1)

I, the undersigned, agricultural analyst for the (2)

in pursuance of the provisions of the Medicines Act 1968, hereby certify that I received
on the   day of   , 19   , from (3)

one part of a sample of (4)   for analysis;
which was duly sealed and fastened up and marked (5)
and was accompanied by a (6)   ,
as follows:— (7)

and also by a signed statement that the sample was taken or otherwise obtained in
the manner prescribed by the Medicines (Animal Feeding Staffs) (Enforcement)
Regulations 1976; and that the said part has been analysed by me or under my
direction. I further certify the results of analysis to be as follows:—(8)

(9)
and I am of the opinion that (10)

The analysis was made in accordance with the Medicines (Animal Feeding Stuffs)
(Enforcement) Regulations 1976.

As witness my hand this   day of   19   .

                                    (Signature and address of analyst)

NOTES

These notes and the numbers referring to them are for guidance only and do not
form part of and need not appear on the certificate.

(1) Statements made in certificates are to be confined to matters which are
relevant to the presence in the feeding stuff of a medicinal product, as defined
in section 130(1) of the Act, or of a substance used for a medicinal purpose,
being a purpose defined in section 130(2) of the Act.

(2) Here insert the name of the local authority.

(3) Here insert the name of the inspector who submitted the sample for analysis.

(4) Here insert the name or description applied to the feeding stuff.

(5) Here insert the distinguishing mark on the sample and the date of sampling
shown thereon.

(6) Here insert either "copy of the label or leaflet" or "copy of such particulars
as may be necessary for the purpose of analysis", or otherwise as the case
may be.

(7) Here insert the relevant particulars for which analyses have been made and
which are contained in the items indicated at (6) above.

(8) Here insert relevant results including, if appropriate, the identification and quantity of any medicinal ingredient not specified in the items indicated at (6) above and an indication of any medicinal ingredient in respect of which it has not been possible to carry out a satisfactory determination.

(9) Here indicate the method of analysis used, where alternative methods are prescribed.

(10) (a) If a full analysis has been performed, ie one where the work is not shared with a person having the management or control of a laboratory, here enter information as follows:
    (i) If the composition of the feeding stuff agrees with or does not differ by more than the limits of variation from the statement of particulars contained in the copy of the label or leaflet or other relevant particulars indicated at item (6) above, state that the particulars are correct within the limits of variation.
    (ii) If the composition of the feeding stuff differs by more than the limits of variation from the statement of particulars contained in the copy of the label or leaflet or other relevant particulars indicated at item (6) above, state the difference between the amount found and the amount stated.

(b) If a part analysis only has been performed, ie one where the work is shared with a person having the management or control of a laboratory, here enter the information as under (i) or (ii) above which is appropriate to the part analysis.

PART II

CERTIFICATE OF ANALYSIS OR EXAMINATION OF ANIMAL FEEDING STUFF (1)

I, the undersigned, having management or control of the (2)

with which arrangements have been made in pursuance of the provisions of the Medicines Act 1968 hereby certify that I received on the   day of
19   , from (3)

one part of a sample of (4)   for *analysis/examination;
which was duly sealed and fastened up and marked (5)
and was accompanied by a (6)
as follows (7):—

and also by a signed statement that the sample was taken or otherwise obtained in the manner prescribed by the Medicines (Animal Feeding Stuffs) (Enforcement) Regulations 1976 (8)†, and that the said part has been *analysed/examined by me or under my direction. I further certify the results of *analysis/examination to be as follows (9):—

(10)†
and I am of the opinion that (11)

The *analysis/examination was made in accordance with the Medicines (Animal Feeding Stuffs) (Enforcement) Regulations 1976.

As witness my hand this   day of   19   .

(Signature and address of analyst
or examiner).

*Delete as necessary.
†Delete if not required.

NOTES

These notes and the numbers referring to them are for guidance only and do not form part of and need not appear on the certificate.

(1) Statements made in certificates are to be confined to matters which are relevant to the presence in the feeding stuff of a medicinal product, as defined in section 130(1) of the Act, or of a substance used for a medicinal purpose, being a purpose defined in section 130(2) of the Act.

(2) Here insert the name of the laboratory.

(3) Here insert the name of the agricultural analyst who submitted the sample for analysis or examination.

(4) Here insert the name or description applied to the feeding stuff.

(5) Here insert the distinguishing mark on the sample and the date of sampling shown thereon.

(6) Here insert either "copy of the label or leaflet", "copy of such particulars as may be necessary for the purpose of analysis or examination" or otherwise as the case may be.

(7) Here insert the relevant particulars for which analyses or examinations have been made and which are contained in the items indicated at (6) above.

(8) A statement, signed by the inspector, that the sample was taken or otherwise obtained in the manner prescribed by the Medicines (Animal Feeding Stuffs) (Enforcement) Regulations, 1976, will accompany the sample only if a full analysis, ie one where the work is *not* shared with the agricultural analyst or an examination is to be carried out at the laboratory with which special arrangements have been made.

(9) Here insert relevant results including, if appropriate, the identification and quantity of any medicinal ingredient not specified in the items indicated at (6) above and an indication of any medicinal ingredient in respect of which it has not been possible to carry out a satisfactory determination or examination.

(10) Here indicate the method of analysis used, where alternative methods are prescribed.

(11) (*a*) If a full analysis has been performed, ie one where the work is not shared with the agricultural analyst (or an examination has been performed) here enter information as follows:—
    (i) If the composition of the feeding stuff agrees with or does not differ by more than the limits of variation from the statement of particulars contained in the copy of the label or leaflet or other relevant particulars indicated at item (6) above, state that the particulars are correct within the limits of variation.
    (ii) If the composition of the feeding stuff differs by more than the limits of variation from the statement of particulars contained in the copy of the label or leaflet or other relevant particulars indicated at item (6) above, state the difference between the amount found and the amount stated.

(b) If a part analysis only has been performed, ie one where the work is shared with the agricultural analyst, here enter the information as under (i) or (ii) above which is appropriate to the part analysis.

SCHEDULE 5

METRIC SUBSTITUTIONS TO REPLACE IMPERIAL UNITS

(Regulation 6)

	Column 1 Imperial Unit	Column 2 Metric Substitution
1. Capacity		
	1 Pint	0·5 Litre
	2 Pints (1 Quart)	1·0 Litre
	3 Pints	1·5 Litre
	4 Pints (½ Gallon)	2·0 Litre
	5 Pints	2·5 Litre
	6 Pints	3·0 Litre
	7 Pints	3·5 Litre
	10 Pints	5·0 Litre
	20 Pints	10·0 Litre
	40 Gallons	200 Litre
	1 000 Gallons	5 000 Litre
	5 000 Gallons	25 000 Litre
	10 000 Gallons	50 000 Litre
	15 000 Gallons	75 000 Litre
	20 000 Gallons	100 000 Litre
	50 000 Gallons	250 000 Litre
	100 000 Gallons	500 000 Litre
2. Weight		
	2–4 lb	1–2 Kg
	6 lb	2·5 Kg
	14 lb	6·0 Kg
	15 lb	7·0 Kg
	½ cwt	25 Kg
	2 cwt	100 Kg
	1 ton	1 tonne
	3 ton	3 tonne
	5 ton	5 tonne
	25 ton	25 tonne
3. Sieve aperture size		
	1¼ inch square	31·8 mm square
4. Ratios		
	parts per million (ppm)	mg per kg

EXPLANATORY NOTE

(This Note is not part of the Regulations.)

These Regulations, made under section 117 of the Medicines Act 1968, apply throughout the United Kingdom. The principal provisions of the regulations are as follows:—

1. Modifications of sections 112, 113 and 115 of the Medicines Act 1968 (which sections contain powers of inspecting, sampling, etc., medicinal products and lay down procedures for analysis of samples) are made for the purposes of the application under the Medicines Act of those sections to animal feeding stuffs. (Regulation 2 and Schedule 1 Part I). (The full provisions of those sections as so modified are set out in Schedule 1 Part II).

2. The methods by which samples of animal feeding stuffs shall be taken, set aside and submitted for analysis by an agricultural analyst, and the steps to be taken by such analyst when samples are received for analysis are set out (Regulation 3 and Schedule 2).

3. The methods by which analysis of animal feeding stuffs is to be carried out are prescribed (Regulation 4 and Schedule 3), and also the forms of certificate of analysis or examination (Regulation 5 and Schedule 4) and the metric substitutions to replace imperial units (Regulation 6 and Schedule 5).

The Regulations implement certain of the provisions of Directive 70/373/EEC of the Council of the European Economic Community of 20th July, 1970 (O.J. No. L.170, 3.8.70, p. 2) (SE 1970 (II), p. 535) on the introduction of Community methods of sampling and analysis for the official control of feeding stuffs; and Commission Directives 72/199/EEC (O.J. No. L.123, 29.5.72, p. 6) (SE 1966–72, p. 74), 74/203/EEC (O.J. No. L.108, 22.4.74, p. 7) and 75/84/EEC (O.J. No. L.32, 5.2.75, p. 26) establishing Community methods of analysis for the official control of feeding stuffs.

STATUTORY INSTRUMENTS

1976 No. 31

MEDICINES

The Medicines (Feeding Stuffs Limits of Variation) Order 1976

Made - - - -	*8th January* 1976
Laid before Parliament	*26th January* 1976
Coming into Operation	*1st April* 1976

The Minister of Agriculture, Fisheries and Food, the Secretary of State concerned with agriculture in Scotland and the Department of Agriculture for Northern Ireland, acting jointly, in exercise of powers conferred by section 117(4) and (5) of the Medicines Act 1968(a), as read with and modified by the Medicines (Feeding Stuffs Additives) Order 1975(b), and now vested in them (c), and of all other powers enabling them in that behalf, and after consulting such organisations as appear to them to be representative of interests likely to be substantially affected, hereby make the following order:—

Citation and commencement

1. This order may be cited as the Medicines (Feeding Stuffs Limits of Variation) Order 1976, and shall come into operation on 1st April 1976.

Interpretation

2.—(1) In this order—

"the Act" means the Medicines Act 1968;

"the Agriculture Ministers" means the Minister of Agriculture, Fisheries and Food, the Secretary of State concerned with agriculture in Scotland and the Department of Agriculture for Northern Ireland, acting jointly;
and other expressions have the same meaning as in the Act.

(2) The Interpretation Act 1889(d) shall apply to the interpretation of this order as it applies to the interpretation of an Act of Parliament.

Limits of variation

3.—(1) In relation to the incorporation in animal feeding stuffs of any substance of any description or class specified in column 1 of the Schedule to this order, the limits of variation for the purposes of section 117(4) of the Act (which provides that so much of any licence granted or animal test certificate issued under Part II of the Act as imposes any restriction or requirement by

---

(a) 1968 c. 67.   (b) S.I. 1975/1349, 1975 II, p. 4586.

(c) In the case of the Department of Agriculture for Northern Ireland by virtue of section 40 of, and Schedule 5 to, the Northern Ireland Constitution Act 1973(c. 36), and paragraph 2(1)(b) of Schedule 1 to the Northern Ireland Act 1974 (c. 28).

(d) 1889 c. 63.

reference to the quantity to be incorporated, or the proportion in which any such substance may be incorporated, in any animal feeding stuff shall not be taken to be contravened in any particular case if the discrepancy does not exceed such limit as the Agriculture Ministers may specify) shall be those specified in column 3 of the said Schedule in relation to the substances of the descriptions or classes specified in column 1 thereof when such substances are to be incorporated in animal feeding stuffs at the levels specified in column 2 of the said Schedule.

(2) Where a label or mark on a container or package containing any animal feeding stuff, or a leaflet supplied or to be supplied with any animal feeding stuff specifies a quantity or proportion of a medicinal product of a particular description, or of a substance other than a medicinal product (but incorporated for a medicinal purpose), as being incorporated in the animal feeding stuff, the limits of variation for the purposes of section 117(5) of the Act (which provides that section 90(2) (creating offences relating to false or misleading descriptions of medicated animal feeding stuffs) of the Act shall not be taken to be contravened by reason only that the quantity or proportion actually incorporated in the animal feeding stuff is greater or less than that so specified, if the discrepancy does not exceed such limit as the Agriculture Ministers may specify) shall be those specified in column 3 of the Schedule to this order in relation to the medicinal products or substances of the descriptions or classes specified in column 1 thereof when such medicinal products or substances are specified as incorporated in animal feeding stuffs at the levels specified in column 2 of the said Schedule.

In Witness whereof the Official Seal of the Minister of Agriculture, Fisheries and Food is hereunto affixed on 22nd December 1975.

(L.S.)

Frederick Peart,
Minister of Agriculture, Fisheries and Food.

William Ross,
Secretary of State for Scotland.

5th January 1976.

Sealed with the Official Seal of the Department of Agriculture for Northern Ireland this 8th day of January 1976.

(L.S.)

J. A. Young,
Permanent Secretary.

Article 3

SCHEDULE

Column 1 Description or class of medicinal product or substance	Column 2 Quantity or proportion of medicinal product or substance to be incorporated in any animal feeding stuff for a medicinal purpose under any restriction or requirement of a licence or animal test certificate, or specified as incorporated in any animal feeding stuff by a label, mark or leaflet.	Column 3 Limits of variation
Anthelmintics anti-blackhead drugs anti-coccidial agents anti-microbial substances anti-scour agents arsenicals growth promoters (except copper) hormones (including synthetic hormones) tranquillisers	1. Not exceeding 50 parts per million or 50 milligrams per kilogram	50%
	2. Exceeding 50 parts per million or 50 milligrams per kilogram but not exceeding 500 parts per million or 500 milligrams per kilogram	40%
	3. Exceeding 500 parts per million or 500 milligrams per kilogram but not exceeding 0·5%	30%
	4. Exceeding 0·5% but not exceeding 5%	20%
	5. Exceeding 5%	10%
copper	1. Not exceeding 200 parts per million or 200 milligrams per kilogram	50%
	2. Exceeding 200 parts per million or 200 milligrams per kilogram	30%

EXPLANATORY NOTE

(This Note is not part of the Order.)

This Order specifies limits of variation under the Medicines Act 1968 within which—

(1) levels at which incorporation in animal feeding stuffs of specified substances actually takes place may depart from levels required under any licence or animal test certificate issued under Part II of the Act without contravention of so much of the licence or animal test certificate as imposes the required levels; and

(2) levels at which specified medicinal products or other substances added for a medicinal purpose are actually incorporated in an animal feeding stuff may depart from the levels at which such medicinal products or substances are stated to have been incorporated on any label, mark or leaflet relating to such animal feeding stuffs, without contravening section 90(2) of the Act (which creates offences relating to false or misleading descriptions of medicated animal feeding stuffs).

S T A T U T O R Y   I N S T R U M E N T S

1976 No. 32

ANIMALS

DISEASES OF ANIMALS

The Diseases of Animals (Approved Disinfectants) (Amendment) Order 1976

Made - - - -	*9th January* 1976
Coming into Operation	*30th January* 1976

The Minister of Agriculture, Fisheries and Food and the Secretary of State, acting jointly, in exercise of the powers conferred by sections 1(1), 11(vi) and (vii), 20(viii) and (ix), 50(1) and 85(1) of the Diseases of Animals Act 1950(a) and now vested in them(b), and all other powers enabling them in that behalf, hereby order as follows:—

Citation, extent and commencement

1. This order, which may be cited as the Diseases of Animals (Approved Disinfectants) (Amendment) Order 1976, shall apply to Great Britain and shall come into operation on 30th January 1976.

Interpretation

2. This order shall be construed as one with the Diseases of Animals (Approved Disinfectants) Order 1972(c) as amended(d) (hereinafter referred to as "the principal order").

Amendment of Article 3 of the principal order

3. For paragraph (4) of Article 3 of the principal order (which specifies the periods for which approved disinfectants remain approved) there shall be substituted the following paragraph:—

"(4) An approved disinfectant listed in Part I–B of the Schedule to this order shall remain an approved disinfectant until 31st July 1976, and an approved disinfectant listed in any other part of the said Schedule shall remain an approved disinfectant until deleted therefrom by subsequent order of the Minister."

Amendment of the Schedule to the principal order

4. For the Schedule to the principal order (which contains lists of disinfectants approved by the Minister of Agriculture, Fisheries and Food and the Secretary of State) there shall be substituted the Schedule to this order.

(a) 1950 c. 36.

(b) By the Transfer of Functions (Animal Health) Order 1955 (S.I. 1955/958 (1955 I, p. 1184)).

(c) S.I. 1972/1413 (1972 III, p. 4281).

(d) S.I. 1974/799; S.I. 1975/95; 1975/1051 (1974 II, p. 3059; 1975 I, p. 280; II, p. 3665).

Transitional Provisions

5. Notwithstanding the amendment of the principal order effected by Article 4 above, it shall continue to be lawful until 30th June 1976 to use for the purposes of any special disease order or general order in which a reference to a disinfectant or an approved disinfectant occurs any disinfectant previously, but no longer, listed in the Schedule to the principal order which it was lawful to use for such purposes immediately before the coming into operation of this order.

In Witness whereof the Official Seal of the Minister of Agriculture, Fisheries and Food is hereunto affixed on 6th January 1976.

(L.S.)

Frederick Peart,
Minister of Agriculture, Fisheries and Food.

9th January 1976.

William Ross,
Secretary of State for Scotland.

SCHEDULE

Part I—A

Disinfectants approved by the Minister in respect of the Foot-and-Mouth Disease Order of 1938, as amended(a) and the Foot-and-Mouth Disease (Infected Areas Restrictions) Order of 1938(b) as amended(c).

Column 1 Disinfectant	Column 2 Dilution Rate
Action Approved Disinfectant	240
Agridyne	240
Agridyne 2	250
Agrisan Master Approved Disinfectant	120
Alodine	240
Battles Improved Iofarm Disinfectant	250
Boots Lysol BP 1968	9
Castrol Solvex ICD 109	50
Centaur Approved Agricultural Disinfectant	240
Centaur New Approved Agricultural Disinfectant	250
Citric Acid BP	500
Combat	240
Combat 74	250
Compass Agricultural Disinfectant	50
Compass Lysol BP 1968	9
Crown Special Detergent Disinfectant	240
Delta Farm Disinfectant	240
Dexadyne	240
Disteola	240
Fakta Four Plus	300
FAM	240
FAM 30	250
Famclor	200
Famosan Mark II	139
Famosan Mark III	120
Farm Aid	240
Farmicide	40
Farmiod	50
Formalin BP (containing not less than 34% formaldehyde) ...	9
Halamid	20
Hygasan	20
Hykil	40
Iodel FD	130
Iodel X	130
Iodet	240
Iodicide Plus	240
Iofarm	240
Iosan 4	240
Jeyes Farm Fluid	219
Jeyes New Formula Farm Fluid	300
Killgerm Iodair	250
Kryptol	60
Lysol BP Evansol	10
Lysovet J Forte	50

(a) S.R. & O. 1928/133, 1938/192 (Rev. II, p. 499: 1928, p. 94; 1938 I, p. 151); S.I. 1969/1444 (1969 III, p. 4661).

(b) S.R. & O. 1938/1434 (Rev. II, p. 528: 1938 I, p. 155).

(c) The relevant amending instrument is S.I. 1969/1445 (1969 III, p. 4667).

Items in italics indicate additions to the Schedule as printed in S.I. 1975/1051.

PART I—A continued

Column 1 Disinfectant	Column 2 Dilution Rate
Marstan Dairy Hygiene Iodair	250
Microdine D	160
Novagen FP	240
Nutosan 1	250
1 Stroke Environ...	10
Ortho-phosphoric acid (Technical Grade)	330
pbi Iodophor Disinfectant	240
Pharmicide	40
Phiodin	220
Phorpass	240
Phorpass 75	300
Polykil	240
Polykil Plus	250
Professional No. 1	300
Resiguard F	80
Ropolik	240
Safeguard Abattoir Sanitiser	20
Safeguard Iodophor Concentrate	100
Sanol FM	140
Sodium Carbonate (Decahydrate) (Complying with BS 3674 of 1963)	24
Special Ropolik	250
Steriguard...	90
Sulphamic Acid	500
Young's All-Purpose Farm Disinfectant	240

Items in italics indicate additions to the Schedule as printed in S.I. 1975/1051.

SCHEDULE

Part I—B

Disinfectants approved by the Minister in respect of the Foot-and-Mouth Disease Order of 1938, as amended, the Foot-and-Mouth Disease (Infected Areas Restrictions) Order of 1938, as amended, as applied to Swine Vesicular Disease by the Swine Vesicular Disease Order 1972(a).

Column 1 Disinfectant	Column 2 Dilution Rate
Action Approved Disinfectant	160
Agridyne	160
Alodine	160
Centaur Approved Agricultural Disinfectant	160
Combat	160
Compass Agricultural Disinfectant	30
Crown Special Detergent Disinfectant	160
Delta Farm Disinfectant	160
Disteola	160
Fakta Four Plus	200
FAM	160
Famosan Mark II	90
Famosan Mark III	80
Farm Aid	160
Formalin BP (containing not less than 34% formaldehyde) + detergent	9
Iodel X	85
Iodet	160
Iodicide Plus	160
Iofarm	160
Iosan 4	160
Jeyes Farm Fluid	140
Killgerm Iodair	160
Marstan Dairy Hygiene Iodair	160
Novagen FP	160
pbi Iodophor Disinfectant	160
Phorpass	160
Polykil	160
Professional No. 1	200
Ropolik	160
Sanol FM	90
Sodium Hydroxide	100
Steriguard	60
Young's All-Purpose Farm Disinfectant	160

(a) S.I. 1972/1980 (1972 III, p. 5902).

SCHEDULE

Part II

Disinfectants approved by the Minister in respect of the Fowl Pest Order of 1936(a), as amended(b) and the Fowl Pest (Infected Areas Restrictions) Order 1956(c), as amended(d).

Column 1 Disinfectant	Column 2 Dilution Rate
Absol Emulsion	30
Action Approved Disinfectant	80
Agridyne	80
Agridyne 2	110
Agrisan Master Approved Disinfectant	59
Alodine	80
Basol 99	20
Battles Improved Iofarm Disinfectant	110
Boots Farm Disinfectant	30
Boots Lysol BP 1968	39
Byro Disinfectant Fluid	30
Centaur Approved Agricultural Disinfectant	80
Centaur New Approved Agricultural Disinfectant	110
Combat	80
Combat 74	110
Compass Agricultural Disinfectant	100
Compass Lysol BP 1968	39
Coopers Farm Disinfectant	29
Cophen	60
Cresl Improved	100
Crown Special Detergent Disinfectant	80
Dellaphen General Purpose Soluble Disinfectant	60
Delsol	100
Delta Farm Disinfectant	80
Dexadyne	91
Disteola	80
Fakta Four Plus	80
FAM	80
FAM 30	110
Famosan Mark II	79
Famosan Mark III	59
Farm Aid	80
Farmicide	50
Farmiod	35
Fensol	60
Gloquat SD Extra	50
Halamid	200
Hygasan	60
Hykil	50
Iodel FD	60
Iodel X	49
Iodet	80

(a) S.R. & O. 1936/1297 (Rev. XVIII, p. 422: 1936 II, p. 2086).

(b) The relevant amending instruments are S.I. 1963/629, 1971/2053 (1963 I, p. 760; 1971 III, p. 6130).

(c) S.I. 1956/1611 (1956 II, p. 1883).

(d) The amending order is not relevant to the subject matter of this order.

Items in italics indicate additions to the Schedule as printed in S.I. 1975/1051.

PART II continued

Column 1 Disinfectant	Column 2 Dilution Rate
Iodicide Plus	90
Iofarm	80
Iosan 4	80
Izal Germicide	30
Izal Green Label Germicide	30
Jeyes Farm Fluid	39
Jeyes Longlife	60
Jeyes New Formula Farm Fluid	70
Jeyes White Farm Disinfectant	30
Killgerm Iodair	61
Killgerm Black Disinfectant RW Coefficient 18/22	41
Killgerm Lysol BP	50
Killgerm White Farm Disinfectant	21
Lethane 100	55
Lysol BP Evansol	50
Lysovet	49
Lysovet J Forte	60
Margisons Farm Disinfectant	30
Marstan Dairy Hygiene Iodair	61
Microdine P	90
Microl–Plus	60
Microsan	70
Microzol	100
New Tekresol	90
Novagen FP	80
Nutosan I	110
Nutosan II	100
1 Stroke Environ	50
Parasept	100
pbi Iodophor Disinfectant	90
Pharmicide	50
Phiodin	80
Phorpass	90
Phorpass 75	150
Polykil	80
Polykil Plus	110
Professional No. 1	80
Ropolik	80
Rygenitas Farm Disinfectant	30
Safeguard Abattoir Sanitiser	10
Safeguard Iodophor Concentrate	100
SEP 55	100
Special Ropolik	110
Steriguard	79
Sterilite Farm Disinfectant	30
Sudol	60
Summit	30
Vapulin Black Disinfectant	41
White Cresanol	30
Young's All-Purpose Farm Disinfectant	80

Items in italics indicate additions to the Schedule as printed in S.I. 1975/1051.

SCHEDULE

Part III

Disinfectants approved by the Minister in respect of The Tuberculosis Order 1964(a), as amended(b) and The Tuberculosis (Scotland) Order 1964(c), as amended(d).

Column 1 Disinfectant	Column 2 Dilution Rate
Absol Emulsion	90
Action Approved Disinfectant	25
Agridyne	25
Agridyne 2	30
Alodine	25
Applied 8-57 White Disinfectant	49
Basol 99	20
Battles Improved Iofarm Disinfectant	30
Boots Farm Disinfectant	90
Boots Lysol BP 1968	39
Byro Disinfectant Fluid	90
Carbo White Disinfectant	49
Centaur Approved Agricultural Disinfectant	25
Centaur New Approved Agricultural Disinfectant	30
Clearsol	45
Combat	25
Combat 74	30
Compass Agricultural Disinfectant	50
Compass Lysol BP 1968	39
Coopers Farm Disinfectant	99
Cophen	65
Cresl Improved	100
Crown Special Detergent Disinfectant	25
Dellaphen General Purpose Soluble Disinfectant	65
Delsol	100
Delta Farm Disinfectant	25
Disteola	25
Fakta Four Plus	62
FAM	25
FAM 30	30
Farm Aid	25
Fensol	65
Focal Biokil Disinfectant	49
Halamid	20
Hullite Disinfectant Fluid	49
Iodel FD	15
Iodet	25
Iodicide Plus	30
Iofarm	25
Iosan 4	15
Izal Germicide	90
Izal Green Label Germicide	80
Jeyes Farm Fluid	24
Jeyes New Formula Farm Fluid	30
Jeyes White Farm Disinfectant...	90
Killgerm Lysol BP	39

(a) S.I. 1964/1151 (1964 II, p. 2634).   (b) S.I. 1973/2030 (1973 III, p. 7051).
(c) S.I. 1964/1109 (1964 II, p. 2463).   (d) S.I. 1973/2101 (S.154) (1973 III, p. 7269).

Items in italics indicate additions to the Schedule as printed in S.I. 1975/1051.

PART III continued

Column 1 Disinfectant	Column 2 Dilution Rate
Killgerm White Farm Disinfectant	66
Lenfectant White Fluid	49
Lysovet	45
Margisons Farm Disinfectant	90
Microdine D	18
Microl-Plus	65
Microzol	100
New Tekresol	80
Novagen FP	25
Nutosan I	30
Nutosan II	100
1 Stroke Environ...	70
Parasept	100
pbi Iodophor Disinfectant	25
Phiodin	11
Phorpass	30
Phorpass 75	100
Polykil	25
Polykil Plus	30
Premier White Disinfectant	49
Professional No. 1	62
Ropolik	25
Hygenitas Farm Disinfectant	90
SEP 55	100
Special Ropolik	30
Sterilite Farm Disinfectant	90
Sterilite WD White Disinfectant	49
Sudol	65
Summit	90
Superlin Black Disinfectant	70
Warden Black Disinfectant	160
White Cresanol	90
White Zenos Disinfectant	49
Young's All-Purpose Farm Disinfectant	25
Young's White Septol 'B'	100

Items in italics indicate additions to the Schedule as printed in S.I. 1975/1051.

SCHEDULE
PART IV
Disinfectants approved by the Minister in respect of general orders.

Column 1 Disinfectant	Column 2 Dilution Rate
Absol Emulsion ...	100
Action Approved Disinfectant ...	145
Agridyne ...	145
Agridyne 2	180
Agrisan Master Approved Disinfectant	59
Alodine ...	145
Applied 8-57 White Disinfectant	89
Basol 99 ...	20
Battles Improved Iofarm Disinfectant	180
Boots Farm Disinfectant	100
Boots Lysol BP 1968 ...	49
Byro Disinfectant Fluid	100
Carbo White Disinfectant	89
Centaur Approved Agricultural Disinfectant	145
Centaur New Approved Agricultural Disinfectant ...	180
Combat ...	145
Combat 74	180
Compass Agricultural Disinfectant	100
Compass Lysol BP 1968	49
Coopers Farm Disinfectant	99
Cophen ...	70
Cresl Improved ...	120
Crown Special Detergent Disinfectant	145
Dellaphen General Purpose Soluble Disinfectant	70
Delsol ...	120
Delta Farm Disinfectant	145
Disteola ...	100
Fakta Four Plus ...	150
FAM ...	145
FAM 30 ...	180
Famosan Mark III	59
Farm Aid	145
Farmicide ...	40
Fensol ...	70
Focal Biokil Disinfectant	89
Halamid ...	199
Hullite Disinfectant Fluid	89
Hykil ...	40
Iodel FD	65
Iodet ...	145
Iodicide Plus	85
Iofarm ...	145
Iosan 4 ...	80
Izal Germicide ...	90
Izal Green Label Germicide ...	120
Jeyes Fluid ...	50
Jeyes Farm Fluid	29
Jeyes Longlife ...	60
Jeyes New Formula Farm Fluid	65
Jeyes White Farm Disinfectant	100
Kilcrobe WO Disinfectant Fluid Special Grade	99

Items in italics indicate additions to the Schedule as printed in S.I. 1975/1051.

PART IV—continued

Column 1 Disinfectant	Column 2 Dilution Rate
Killgerm Black Disinfectant RW Coefficient 18/22	80
Killgerm Lysol BP	49
Killgerm White Farm Disinfectant	100
Kryptol	20
Lenfectant White Fluid	89
Lethane 100	49
Lysol BP Evansol	50
Lysovet	49
Lysovet J Forte	100
Margisons Farm Disinfectant	100
Microdine D	100
Microl-Plus	70
Microzol	120
New Tekresol	135
Novagen FP	145
Nutosan I	180
Nutosan II	120
1 Stroke Environ	55
Parasept	120
Pharmicide	40
Phiodin	90
Phorpass	85
Phorpass 75	180
Polykil	145
Polykil Plus	180
Premier White Disinfectant	89
Professional No. 1	150
Ropolik	145
Rygenitas Farm Disinfectant	100
Safeguard Abattoir Sanitiser	3
Safeguard Iodophor Concentrate	74
San Izal	16
SEP 55	120
Special Ropolik	180
Steriguard	49
Sterilite Farm Disinfectant	100
Sterilite WD White Disinfectant	89
Sudol	70
Summit	100
Superlin Black Disinfectant	70
Texol	95
Triphenol	50
Vapulin Black Disinfectant	80
Warden Black Disinfectant	60
White Cresanol	100
White Zenos Disinfectant	89
Young's All-Purpose Farm Disinfectant	145
Young's White Septol 'B'	100

Items in italics indicate additions to the Schedule as printed in S.I. 1975/1051.

EXPLANATORY NOTE

(This Note is not part of the Order.)

This Order revokes and re-enacts with amendments the lists of disinfectants approved by the Minister and the Secretary of State in the Schedule to the Diseases of Animals (Approved Disinfectants) Order 1972, as amended.

The Schedule, as re-enacted, contains lists of approved disinfectants in relation to orders under the Diseases of Animals Act 1950 dealing with Foot-and-Mouth Disease (Part I–A), Swine Vesicular Disease (Part I–B), Fowl Pest (Part II), Tuberculosis (Part III) and disinfectants approved until further notice in relation to other general orders made under the Diseases of Animals Act (Part IV).

The Order also extends until 31st July 1976 the period for which disinfectants approved in respect of swine vesicular disease shall remain approved.

Provision is also made for the continued use of approved disinfectants now deleted from the Schedule for a transitional period from the coming into operation of this order until 30th June 1976.

STATUTORY INSTRUMENTS

1976 No. 37

PUBLIC HEALTH, ENGLAND AND WALES
The Control of Noise (Measurement and Registers) Regulations 1976

Made - - - -	13*th January* 1976
Laid before Parliament	23*rd January* 1976
Coming into Operation	13*th February* 1976

The Secretary of State for the Environment, as respects England and the Secretary of State for Wales, as respects Wales, in exercise of the powers conferred on them by section 64(2) and (8) and section 104(1) of the Control of Pollution Act 1974(a) and of all other powers enabling them in that behalf, hereby make the following regulations:—

Citation and commencement

1. These regulations may be cited as the Control of Noise (Measurement and Registers) Regulations 1976 and shall come into operation on 13th February 1976.

Interpretation

2.—(1) In these regulations, unless the context otherwise requires—

"the Act" means the Control of Pollution Act 1974, and any reference in these regulations to a numbered section shall be construed as a reference to the section bearing that number in the Act;

"local authority" has the meaning given to it in section 73(1)(*a*) of the Act;

"classified premises" means premises of any specified class to which a noise abatement order under section 63 of the Act for the time being applies;

"the scheduled memorandum" means the memorandum on measurement and calculation of noise levels incorporated in the Schedule to these regulations, and expressions used in that memorandum have the meanings given to them therein.

(2) The Interpretation Act 1889(**b**) shall apply for the interpretation of these regulations as it applies for the interpretation of an Act of Parliament.

Application and extent

3. These regulations apply to the measurement and calculation by local authorities in England and Wales of levels of noise emanating from classified premises and to the keeping by local authorities of registers in which those levels, levels of noise determined for such premises under section 67 and other relevant matters are recorded.

Measurement and calculation of noise levels

4.—(1) Subject to the following paragraph, the methods described in the scheduled memorandum are, according to circumstances as indicated therein, the methods by which levels of noise emanating from classified premises are to

---

(a) 1974 c. 40.　　　　　　(b) 1889 c. 63.

be measured, or, in so far as they cannot be measured by such methods, calculated, for the purposes of sections 64 to 66 (including section 66 as it has effect by virtue of section 67(5)).

(2) If it appears to the Secretary of State, whether in consequence of representations made to him or otherwise, that, in order to facilitate the effective, or more effective, performance by a local authority of its functions in pursuance of any of the provisions of sections 64 to 66, it is necessary or expedient in any circumstances to provide for the measurement or calculation of noise levels by methods other than those described in the scheduled memorandum, or by those methods with modifications, he may in those circumstances determine the methods by which levels of noise emanating from premises are to be measured or calculated by the local authority and may give directions to the authority accordingly.

Effect of calculation of noise levels

5. Noise levels calculated in accordance with these regulations or in accordance with directions given by the Secretary of State under the preceding regulation may be treated, for the purposes of the provisions of section 64 relating to the measurement of noise levels, to the recording of measurements in the noise level register and to measurements when so recorded, as measured by a method determined in pursuance of section 64(8)(*a*).

The Noise Level Register

6.—(1) The noise level register which, by virtue of section 64(2), a local authority is required to keep for the purpose of recording levels of noise from classified premises shall be so kept as to show, in relation to each of the premises in respect of which an entry falls to be made—

   (*a*) the address, or other sufficient identification, of the premises and the specified class to which they belong, or, where section 67(1) applies, will belong;

   (*b*) such of the particulars required by paragraph (2) below as are appropriate;

   (*c*) any cancellation or alteration of an entry in the register and the reason for the cancellation or alteration;

   (*d*) the date on which each entry, cancellation or alteration is made.

(2) The record in the register of a noise level which has been ascertained by methods of measurement or calculation, or by a combination of such methods, shall contain particulars of the methods employed, particulars, where appropriate, of any methods determined by the Secretary of State under regulation 4(2) above, and the details of all relevant measurements and calculations including—

   (*a*) the location (including height) of each point at which the measurements were taken, or for which the calculations were made;

   (*b*) relevant details of any equipment used for the purpose;

   (*c*) the dates and times when any such measurements were taken and relevant details of the prevailing weather conditions.

(3) The register shall include an index, which may be in the form of, or may incorporate, a map.

(4) Subject to the foregoing provisions, the noise level register shall be kept in such a form (whether in one or more parts), and may include such additional material (including plans, drawings and photographs) in relation to any of the matters recorded therein, as the local authority considers appropriate.

SCHEDULE

Memorandum on Measurement and Calculation of Noise Levels

Interpretation

1. In this memorandum—

"dB(A)" is a measure of sound pressure level in decibels indicated by measuring equipment using A-scale frequency weighting (A-weighting) as described in the British Standard Specification for a precision sound level meter which was published on 14th September 1967 under the number B.S. 4197: 1967;

"L_{eq}" has the meaning given to it in paragraph 6(1) below;

"period of interest", in relation to any measurement or calculation of a sound level, means the period for which the measurement or calculation in question is taken or made.

Where to measure

2.—(1) Noise emanating from classified premises in a noise abatement zone should be measured at points on a line ("the noise control boundary") drawn so as to enclose all significant noise sources on the premises. The precise alignment of the noise control boundary will depend on particular circumstances. In general the perimeter of the premises would be the appropriate line, but special factors (e.g. the presence of obstructions) may make it impracticable or inappropriate to measure noise from the premises at the perimeter.

(2) The simplest situation is one where all the noise sources are close to the ground, where there is open land between the sources and the site perimeter and where the perimeter is marked by fencing of open construction. In such circumstances it will be convenient to locate the measurement points around the perimeter (as indicated below) at a height of 1·2 metres.

Determination of measurement points

3.—(1) The number and position of measurement points will be dictated by the degree of control proposed to be exercised over the level of noise from any premises. The most complete control will be obtained by adopting the approach illustrated in Fig. 1 supplemented as necessary by the additional measurement points referred to in paragraph 3(3). The first measurement point is designated A in Fig. 1. A measurement made at point A will adequately take account of the noise leaving the area XY of the building. A measurement at point B will cover the noise from the area YZ. The distance between points A and B will be determined by the angle θ. This angle should be between 45° and 65° if rigorous control is to be maintained. Where θ is less than 45° the number of measuring points is unnecessarily increased. Where θ is greater than 65° there will be fewer measurement points, and this will have implications for the subsequent control of noise emanating from the premises.

(2) It is essential that measurement points can be re-located for the purpose of future monitoring of noise levels. Hence it is important that a reliable way of noting the positions of points is used. A plan on which the positions are marked may be advantageous, supplemented, if necessary, by further description, photographs, etc.

(3) For rigorous control the basic coverage provided by the method described in paragraph 3(1) may need to be supplemented for a variety of reasons, for example where there is a permanent noise source, such as a ventilator, close to the perimeter, or where it is anticipated that new noise generating sources might be introduced in the future. Where the noise has noticeable pure tone (i.e. single frequency) components, standing wave patterns of noise (which are characteristically indicated by significant variations in noise level over short distances) may occasionally result. The effect is generally only noticeable at some distance from the source. Since the standing wave pattern may vary from time to time it is possible for the levels at a fixed position to change where the power output of the source has not changed. Where standing wave patterns are encountered, measurements made at fixed points on the boundary should be supplemented by a record of the maximum noise levels between the fixed positions.

(4) Where the perimeter of the premises comprises the external walls of a building which flank directly onto the highway, the noise control boundary must be outside the perimeter of the site as indicated in Fig. 2. In this case the pavement width will probably limit the distance between the noise control boundary and the perimeter of the site, unless it is convenient to take measurements on the opposite sides of the surrounding roads. As a general rule more measuring positions will be required in such a case than where the external walls of a building do not flank directly onto the highway. The number of measuring positions using an angle equal to 60°–65° would be about half the number of positions with the angle equal to 45°, and should give adequate coverage. Here it is particularly important to take account of any prominent noise sources (such as ventilation or cooling equipment, windows and doors along the perimeter), either by introducing extra positions or by varying the angle around the noise control boundary so that there are measuring positions close to such sources.

Height of measuring positions

4.—(1) As previously indicated the convenient height in a simple case would be 1·2 metres but the appropriate height at any particular point will depend on the circumstances.

(2) For the maximum noise level emanating from the premises to be measured, the points from which noise is emanating should be visible from the measurement point. Where the site is enclosed by a wall or other sound-opaque structure at the perimeter, the measuring positions should normally be established at points high enough to measure the noise coming over the top of the wall.

(3) Fig. 3 illustrates a situation where measurement along the site perimeter on top of the wall would not adequately measure noise from the ventilation equipment on the roof of the premises, because of shading from the edge of the building. In some situations it might be practicable to increase the height of the microphone without moving away from the perimeter, but it would usually be more convenient to take measurements at a normal measuring height at a point away from the perimeter which, though still as close as possible to the premises, will give a view of the ventilation equipment from the measuring height.

When to measure

5.—(1) The aim should be to determine typical levels of noise from the premises. Measurements should therefore be made when activity is as near normal as possible. When making measurements the following situations should be borne in mind:—

    (i) In some cases plant may be running below its maximum capacity for a long period, e.g. 6 months or a year. If the registered noise levels are determined during this period a note should be made for inclusion in the noise level register that plant was operating below full capacity.

    (ii) Noise levels at the perimeter of the premises may vary between summer and winter because doors and windows are left open in the summer in order to increase ventilation. Where doors and windows must be opened for ventilation the registered noise levels should be determined with them open.

(2) The intervals or continuous periods in which measurements are taken should be selected to meet the particular needs at each measurement point. Within the constraints set by the availability of resources, the period will be determined by the pattern of variation of noise and the type of control of the noise that is needed.

(3) For rigorous control of noise which varies throughout the day and between weekdays and the weekend the noise levels should be measured over appropriate day-time and night-time periods and registered accordingly, allowing separate control of noise levels over these periods. For less rigorous control the separate noise levels may be combined to form an equivalent noise level over a longer period. Where the noise level is measured for several periods for registration separately, the object of the measurements should be to determine the typical noise level for each of the periods chosen.

Methods of measurement: general

6.—(1) The noise level to be measured at each measuring position is the equivalent continuous noise level (L_{eq}), measured in dB(A), over a stated period of time. The definition of L_{eq} is that level of continuous noise which has, over any defined period the same energy content as the actual noise during that period. Where appropriate (eg. for impulsive noise), measurements of L_{eq} should be supplemented by measurements of the maximum noise level during the period. The method of measurement of L_{eq} to be used will depend on the way in which the noise level varies, and different methods are described in the paragraphs which follow. This is not intended to preclude the noting of characteristics of the noise, such as pure tones or impulsive character, and the activities giving rise to the noise at a particular measurement point which might be relevant to future control.

(2) No matter which measuring technique is used, the measurements should be carried out by competent staff and detailed records kept of the measurements, so that the techniques can be repeated during the different stages of noise monitoring and control.

(3) The acoustic performance of the measuring equipment must conform to the relevant standards (see paragraphs 7 to 10 below). Its calibration must be maintained and the overall acoustic performance checked before and after each measurement, using high-quality calibration equipment with a calibration level known within ± 0.5 dB(A). A microphone windshield of a type which does not appreciably affect the calibration should be used in all measurements.

(4) The effects of extraneous noise on the measurements should always be considered carefully. In some situations it may be possible temporarily to silence the sources of extraneous noise while noise from the premises is measured, or to silence sources of noise within the premises while extraneous noise is measured. Measurements will not be affected where the extraneous noise is 10 dB(A) or more below the noise from the premises. Where extraneous noise is 7 to 10 dB(A) below the noise from the premises the measurements will only be affected slightly. Where extraneous noise is 6 dB(A) or less below the noise from the premises a subtractive correction to the noise level of between 1 and 3 dB(A), using Fig. 6, should be made in registering the noise level at the point. Where extraneous noise dominates noise from the premises, and it is not possible to measure the noise in the way described above, a calculation method should be used (see paragraph 11).

Steady noise

7.—(1) A sound level meter which meets the requirements of B.S. 4197: 1967 is adequate for the purpose of measuring steady noise. The meter should incorporate A-weighting and be set at the "SLOW" dynamic characteristic (as defined in B.S. 4197: 1967). The noise is deemed steady for this purpose if fluctuations of the meter reading do not exceed ± 4 dB(A).

(2) If the sound level averaged visually from the meter over a short time (i.e. 30–60 seconds) remains substantially unchanged throughout the period of interest, the indicated reading is numerically equal to L_{eq} for that period.

Noise having distinguishable levels

8.—(1) Noise which changes in level from time to time, remaining steady at each separate step, can be measured adequately with a sound level meter as described in paragraph 7. The separate levels should be determined and their durations ("on-times") noted. For each level the extraneous noise level should be taken into account when the noise level from the premises is measured.

(2) The pattern of the distinguishable levels is unlikely to recur exactly each day, and it would usually be unnecessarily restrictive to enter the levels separately in the noise level register. Instead the period of measurement should be chosen as described in paragraph 5, and the distinguishable levels observed during the period should be combined to form the L_{eq} for the period. To do this the duration of each distinguish-

able level should be expressed as a percentage of the period of measurement. A correction should be made, using Fig. 4, to convert each level to the equivalent continuous level over the period of measurement, and the corrected levels should be combined to give a value of L_{eq} for entry in the noise level register. (The procedure for combining the corrected levels is the conventional one for adding sound levels, as indicated in the example in paragraph 8(3)). This single figure specification of the noise level would allow very high noise levels over short periods unless accompanied by some further specification of the noise level. Where appropriate (i.e. where control of the maximum noise level is required) the maximum noise level measured should be noted for entry in the noise level register in addition to the L_{eq} level.

(3) The following example illustrates this method of measurement of noise. Fig. 5 shows the pattern of noise levels from a factory during the period 0700 to 1700 hours over which registered noise levels are to be determined. At a particular measuring position three noise levels occur at different times during the period of measurement. Noise A is a continuous level of 60 dB(A) present throughout the period. Noise B comprises this continuous noise plus noise from riveting, typically present for two separate half-hour periods, and gives a measurable level of 65 dB(A). Noise C comprises the continuous noise, plus the noise of hammering, and occurs typically for one half-hour period at a level of 75 dB(A). The duration corrections should be applied as follows (using Fig. 4):—

Noise	Noise level	Percentage "on-time"	Correction	Corrected level
A	60 dB(A)	85	— 1 dB(A)	59 dB(A)
B	65 dB(A)	10	— 10 dB(A)	55 dB(A)
C	75 dB(A)	5	— 13 dB(A)	62 dB(A)

The corrected noise levels should then be combined, using Fig. 7. Combining 59 and 55 dB(A) gives 60·5 dB(A) which is then combined with 62 dB(A) to give a single value of 64·3 dB(A) as the L_{eq} noise level for the period to be entered in the noise level register. In addition it will be appropriate to note the maximum noise level of 75 dB(A) for entry in the noise level register where control over the maximum noise level is required.

Varying noise levels

9.—(1) Where the noise level varies so that there are no distinguishable steady noise levels, the methods described above cannot be applied. The method described here, or the method in paragraph 10, should be used instead. The method of measurement described here is not appropriate for noise with impulsive character.

(2) The noise level should be measured with equipment providing a statistical analysis of the sound levels, and L_{eq} calculated as described in paragraph 9(3). A typical set of equipment comprises a microphone and microphone amplifier, a graphic level recorder (producing a visual record of the noise level over the period of measurement) and a statistical analyser performing the analysis required by paragraph 9(3). An alternative would be to use data-logging equipment which samples (i.e. periodically measures) the noise level and produces an output in digital form on magnetic tape. L_{eq} is then derived by replaying the tape through a suitably programmed calculator. The equipment used should have the same overall acoustic performance as a sound level meter used under similar conditions (see paragraph 7(1)).

(3) For the purpose of analysis the sound levels should be grouped in classes with widths of 5, 2·5 or 1 dB(A) as appropriate. The total duration within the overall period of measurement chosen for which the noise level lies in each class should be recorded.

L_{eq} can then be calculated from the formula:

$$L_{eq} \text{ (period specified)} = 10 \log_{10} \left[\frac{1}{100} \left(f_1.10^{L_1/10} + f_2.10^{L_2/10} + f_3.10^{L_3/10} \right.\right.$$

$$\left.\left. \cdots\cdots + f_n.10^{L_n/10} \right) \right]$$

where L_{eq} (period specified) is the equivalent continuous sound level in dB(A) over the period for registering noise levels;

    f_1 is the percentage of the period for which the noise level lies within the first class-interval with centre-point L_1;

    f_2 is the percentage of the period for which the noise level lies within the second class-interval with centre-point L_2;

    f_3 is the percentage of the period for which the noise level lies within the third class-interval with centre-point L_3;

and so on up to f_n where n is the total number of sound level class-intervals.

Rapidly varying noise levels

10.—(1) Varying noise levels including those which fluctuate over a wide range of levels, or have an impulsive characteristic, can be measured by a meter giving a direct reading of L_{eq} (i.e. an integrating meter). The meter should incorporate A-weighting in the measuring circuit and should give a value of L_{eq} according to the equation:

$$L_{eq} = 10 \log_{10} \frac{1}{T} \int_0^T \left[\frac{p_A(t)}{p_O} \right]^2 dt$$

where L_{eq} is the equivalent continuous sound level in dB(A) over the period of the measurement, T;

    $p_A(t)$ is the instantaneous A-weighted sound pressure in newtons per square metre (pascals), varying with time t;

    p_O is the reference sound pressure whose value is 20×10^{-6} newtons per square metre (pascals).

(2) The integrating meter should meet all the relevant requirements of B.S. 4197: 1967. A dynamic range of at least 60 dB(A), and preferably 80 dB(A), is necessary when the instrument is required to measure impulse noise. The instrument should incorporate an instantaneous overload indicator to show if the noise level to be measured has exceeded the maximum level which the meter is capable of measuring.

(3) To measure maximum levels of impulsive noise the measurement equipment should have a response equivalent to that of the "FAST" response defined in B.S. 4197: 1967.

Dominant extraneous noise

11.—(1) The extraneous noise at any point on the noise control boundary is all noise which does not emanate from the premises in question. The following simple calculation method may be used where for the period of interest extraneous noise dominates the noise emanating from the premises, and makes direct measurement of the noise emanating impracticable. This calculation method may be used for any period for which a noise level is to be registered. Measurements should be taken of the ambient noise at the noise control boundary (X dB(A) expressed as the L_{eq} over the period of interest), comprising the sum of the noise emanating from the premises and the extraneous noise. To calculate the level of noise emanating from the premises (i.e. the level to be treated as the measured level for entry in the noise level register) subtract from the measured ambient level:

(a) 6 dB(A) L_{eq} where the extraneous noise level is recognisably more than twice as loud as the level of noise emanating from the premises;

(b) 3 dB(A) L_{eq} where the extraneous noise is less dominant than described in (a) above.

(2) The method of measurement used may be any of those set out in paragraphs 7 to 10 which are appropriate to the situation.

(3) Where extraneous noise dominates the noise emanating from the premises at the perimeter of the premises, but does not dominate it at all points within the grounds belonging to the premises, the need to use the method described above may be avoided by locating the noise control boundary along a line (within or partly within the perimeter) on which extraneous noise is not dominant. There are limitations to this approach where sources of noise are likely to be introduced between the noise control boundary and the perimeter of the site.

(4) Calculation of the noise level at points on the line of the noise control boundary, as described above, may be supplemented where more rigorous control over noise is needed, by measurements to establish the noise level at isolated points close to the sources of the noise emanating from the premises. The measured levels should be recorded for entry in the noise level register. This may facilitate control over noise from these sources, but it would not by itself provide complete control over noise from the premises because of the possible addition of new noise sources.

Meteorological conditions

12.—(1) The effects of meteorological conditions on sound propagation are complex, and are most marked when either the source or the receiver, or both, are close to the ground and when sound is propagated over large distances. The meteorological conditions which are suitable for making measurements of noise levels are indicated in paragraph 12(2) to (5).

(2) Wind has a major influence over sound propagation:

(i) Particular care is required when the noise source is more than 50 metres from the measuring position. A positive wind component of up to 2 m/sec towards the measuring position, to ensure that the measured noise level is at a maximum, is desirable.

(ii) When the noise source is 25 metres to 50 metres from the measuring position, calm or a positive wind component of up to 2 m/sec towards the measuring position is desirable.

(iii) When the noise source is less than 25 metres from the measuring position, calm or any wind direction is acceptable.

(3) A temperature gradient (i.e. variation of temperature with height) can also have a significant effect on sound propagation. In particular, measurements of noise levels should not normally be made in conditions of temperature inversion (often associated with calm, clear nights and a tendency for the formation of mist or fog).

(4) Strong winds can themselves create noise at the microphone and affect the readings. The use of a microphone windshield is effective in some situations, but not always. As a general guide, measurements should not be made if the wind-generated noise is within 10 dB(A) of the total noise reading. Wind-generated noise should be checked in some relatively quiet situation exposed to wind conditions similar to those experienced at the noise measuring positions on the noise control boundary.

(5) The reception of noise can also be affected by a layer of snow on the ground, and measurements should not normally be made in these conditions. As a general rule, noise measurements should not be taken in adverse meteorological conditions such as snow, rain, or fog, but frost alone would not affect measurements.

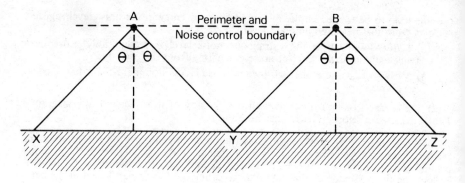

Figure 1

Determination of measuring positions.

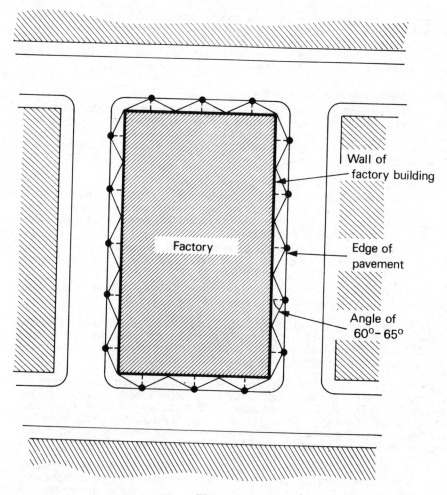

Figure 2

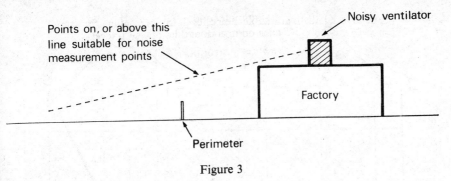

Figure 3

Correction to observed distinguishable noise level for percentage "on-time". (The correction should be subtracted from the observed level.)

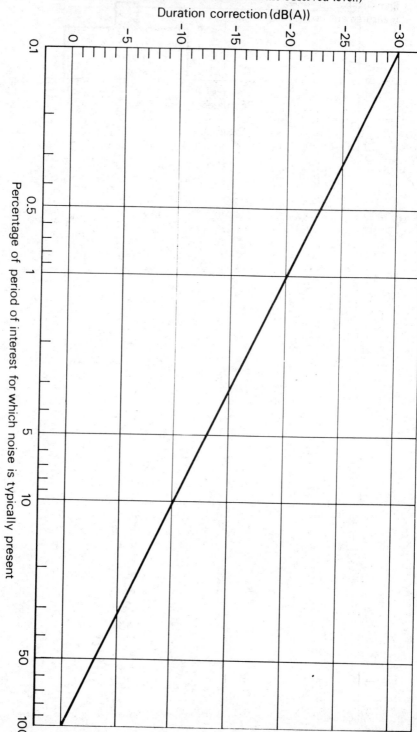

Figure 4

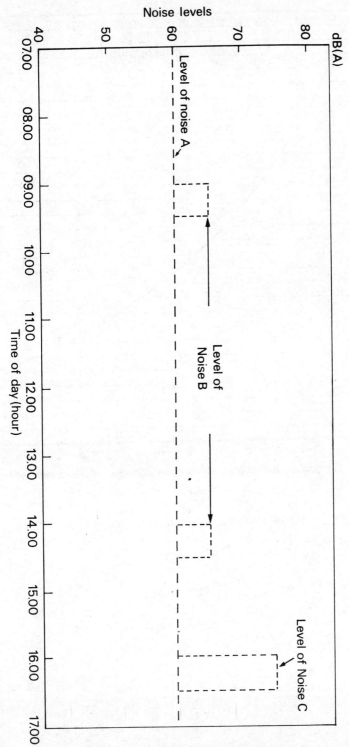

Figure 5. An example of the variation with time of the noise levels from a factory.

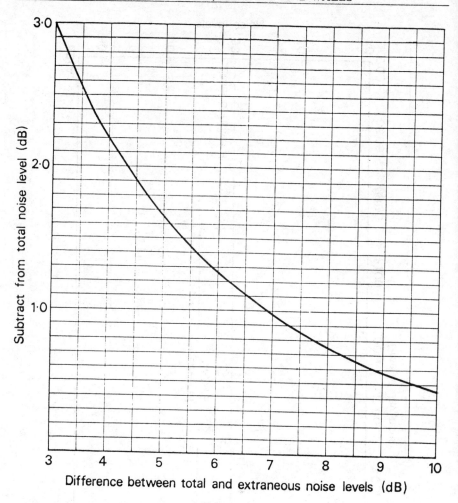

Figure 6
The subtraction of one noise level from another.

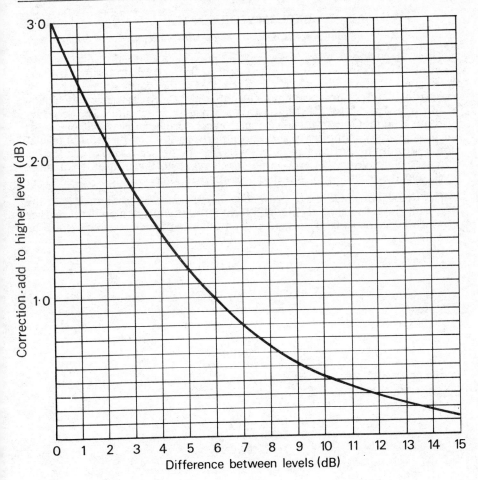

Figure 7

The addition of two noise levels.

Anthony Crosland,
Secretary of State for the Environment.

8th January 1976.

John Morris,
Secretary of State for Wales.

13th January 1976.

EXPLANATORY NOTE

(This Note is not part of the Regulations.)

These Regulations make provision, in pursuance of section 64(8) of the Control of Pollution Act 1974, with respect to the methods to be used by local authorities in England and Wales when measuring, and, where necessary, calculating, levels of noise from premises of any specified class in a noise abatement zone. Methods for general use are described in the schedule. The Secretary of State is authorised in certain circumstances to determine special methods for use by a local authority (reg. 4(2)). In pursuance of section 64(8)(*b*) regulation 5 provides that calculated noise levels may be treated as measured for the purposes of provisions of section 64 which relate to the measuring of noise levels and the recording of measurements in a register.

The Regulations also make provision, in pursuance of section 64(2) of the Act, with respect to the keeping by a local authority of the noise level register in which measurements of noise levels and other particulars are required to be recorded.

STATUTORY INSTRUMENTS

1976 No. 38

SEA FISHERIES

LANDING AND SALE OF SEA FISH

The Herring By-Catch (Restrictions on Landing) Order 1976

Made - - -	*9th January* 1976
Laid before Parliament	*23rd January* 1976
Coming into Operation	*1st February* 1976

The Minister of Agriculture, Fisheries and Food and the Secretaries of State respectively concerned with the sea fishing industry in Scotland and Northern Ireland, in exercise of the powers conferred on them by sections 6 and 15 of the Sea Fish (Conservation) Act 1967(a) as the latter section is amended by section 22(1) of, and paragraph 38 of Part II of Schedule 1 to, the Sea Fisheries Act 1968(b) and of all other powers enabling them in that behalf, after consultation with the Secretary of State for Trade(c), hereby make the following order:—

Citation and commencement

1. This order may be cited as the Herring By-Catch (Restrictions on Landing) Order 1976 and shall come into operation on 1st February 1976.

Interpretation

2.—(1) In this order unless the context otherwise requires—

"herring by-catch" means any herring (*Clupea harengus*) comprised in a catch of mixed fisheries;

"mixed fisheries" means any catch of which more than 50 per cent. consists of one or more of the species described in Schedule 1 to this order;

"specified waters" means the waters described in Schedule 2 to this order.

(2) The Interpretation Act 1889(d) shall apply for the interpretation of this order as it applies for the interpretation of an Act of Parliament.

Prohibition on landing

3. During the period 1st February 1976 to 31st December 1976, both dates inclusive, the landing in the United Kingdom of any herring by-catch caught in specified waters is hereby prohibited.

(a) 1967 c. 84.   (b) 1968 c. 77.

(c) For transfer of functions from the Board of Trade to the Secretary of State for Trade and Industry, and subsequently to the Secretary of State for Trade, see the Secretary of State for Trade and Industry Order 1970 (S.I. 1970/1537) (1970 III, p. 5293) and the Secretary of State (New Departments) Order 1974 (S.I. 1974/692) (1974 I, p. 2711).

(d) 1889 c. 63.

Exceptions from prohibition on landing

4. Notwithstanding the prohibition contained in Article 3 of this order and the prohibitions contained in Article 2 of the North Sea Herring (Restrictions on Landing) Order 1974(**a**) (which prohibits the landing in the United Kingdom of any herring caught in the waters comprised in the North Sea) and in Article 3 of the West Coast Herring (Restrictions on Landing) Order 1974(**b**) (which prohibits the landing in the United Kingdom of under-sized herring and herring taken within waters off the West Coast) a herring by-catch caught in the specified waters may be landed in the United Kingdom if—

(*a*) the herring are comprised in a catch of sprats (*Sprattus sprattus*) caught in the specified waters and do not exceed in weight 10 per cent. of the total weight of the catch determined on the basis of a sample selected by a British sea-fishery officer and being a quantity not less than two kilograms in weight taken from any part of the catch; or

(*b*) the herring are comprised in mixed fisheries (excluding sprats) caught in the specified waters and do not exceed in weight 5 per cent. of the total weight of the catch determined on the basis of a sample selected in accordance with paragraph (*a*) of this Article.

Powers of British sea-fishery officers

5. For the purposes of the enforcement of this order there are hereby conferred on every British sea-fishery officer all the powers of a British sea-fishery officer under section 8(2) to (4) of the Sea Fisheries Act 1968.

In Witness whereof the official seal of the Minister of Agriculture, Fisheries and Food is hereunto affixed on 7th January 1976.

Frederick Peart,
Minister of Agriculture, Fisheries and Food.

William Ross,
Secretary of State for Scotland.

19th December 1975.

Merlyn Rees,
Secretary of State for Northern Ireland.

9th January, 1975.

(**a**) S.I. 1974/881 (1974 II, p. 3357).   (**b**) 1974/2207 (1974 III, p. 8631).

SCHEDULE 1   *Article* 2

Mackerel (*Scomber scombrus*)   Shrimps
Clupeoid fish other than herring   Prawns
Sand-eels (*Ammodytes*)   Nephrops
Norway pout (*Trisopterus esmarkii*)   Molluscs
Smelts (*Osmerus*)   Saury (*Scombresox saurus*)
Great Weevers (*Trachinus draco*)
Capelin (*Mallotus villosus*)
Horse Mackerel (*Trachurus trachurus*)
Blue Whiting (*Micromesistius poutassou*)
Polar Cod (*Boreogadus saida*)

SCHEDULE 2   *Article* 2

The waters, excluding the Kattegat, bounded on the south by a line running due west from a point on the coast of France at 48° 00′ north latitude to the meridian of 18° 00′ west longitude; thence due north to the parallel of 60° 00′ north latitude; thence due east to the meridian of 5° 00′ west longitude; thence due north to the parallel of 60° 30′ north latitude; thence due east to the meridian of 4° 00′ west longitude; thence due north to the parallel of 62° 00′ north latitude; thence due east to the coast of Norway.

EXPLANATORY NOTE

(*This Note is not part of the Order.*)

This Order prohibits from 1st February 1976 until 31st December 1976, both dates inclusive, the landing in the United Kingdom of any by-catches of herring taken in mixed fisheries caught in the North Sea and other waters surrounding the United Kingdom. Exemptions are provided when the weight of the herring by-catch amounts to 10 per cent. or less of the total weight of any sprat catch landed or 5 per cent. or less of the total weight of mixed fisheries. The order takes account of existing orders governing the landing in the United Kingdom of herring taken from the North Sea and from West Coast waters.

STATUTORY INSTRUMENTS

1976 No. 41

INDUSTRIAL DEVELOPMENT

The Investment Grants Termination (No. 6) Order 1976

Made - - -	14th January 1976
Laid before Parliament	19th January 1976
Coming into Operation	9th February 1976

The Secretary of State in exercise of his powers under section 1(6) of the Investment and Building Grants Act 1971(a) and all other powers in that behalf enabling him, hereby orders as follows:—

Citation, commencement and interpretation

1.—(1) This Order may be cited as the Investment Grants Termination (No. 6) Order 1976 and shall come into force on 9th February 1976.

(2) The Interpretation Act 1889(b) shall apply to the interpretation of this Order as it applies to the interpretation of an Act of Parliament.

Dates before which certain applications for grant are to be made

2.—(1) Applications for grant under Part I of the Industrial Development Act 1966(c) in respect of expenditure incurred during the period 1st April 1975 to 30th June 1975 (both dates inclusive) are to be made before 1st January 1977.

(2) Such applications in respect of expenditure incurred during the period 1st July 1975 to 30th September 1975 (both dates inclusive) are to be made before 1st April 1977.

(3) Such applications in respect of expenditure incurred during the period 1st October 1975 to 31st December 1975 (both dates inclusive) are to be made before 1st July 1977.

(4) Such applications in respect of expenditure incurred during the period 1st January 1976 to 31st March 1976 (both dates inclusive) are to be made before 1st October 1977.

(a) 1971 c. 51   (b) 1889 c. 63   (c) 1966 c. 34

Form and manner of applications

3. The applications for grant to which this Order applies are to be made in such form and manner, and to contain such particulars and be accompanied by such documents, as the Secretary of State may direct.

Gregor Mackenzie,
Minister of State,
14th January 1976.   Department of Industry.

EXPLANATORY NOTE

(This Note is not part of the Order.)

The Investment Grants Termination (No .1) Order 1971 (S.I. 1971/1275), the Investment Grants Termination (No. 2) Order 1972 (S.I. 1972/34), the Investment Grants Termination (No. 3) Order 1973 (S.I. 1973/384), the Investment Grants Termination (No. 4) Order 1974 (S.I. 1974/646) and the Investment Grants Termination (No. 5) Order 1975 (S.I. 1975/32) each specified certain dates by which applications for investment grant in respect of expenditure incurred before a related date or in related periods must be made. This Order specifies further dates by which such applications in respect of expenditure in further related periods must be made.

The Order also provides for the making of directions as to the form of such applications, the particulars they must contain and the documents to accompany them.

STATUTORY INSTRUMENTS

1976 No. 42

PESTS

The Prevention of Damage by Pests (Threshing and Dismantling of Ricks) (Amendment) Regulations 1976

Made - - -	12*th January* 1976
Laid before Parliament	26*th January* 1976
Coming into Operation	16*th February* 1976

The Minister of Agriculture, Fisheries and Food in exercise of the powers vested in him by section 8(1) and (2) of the Prevention of Damage by Pests Act 1949(a), and all other powers enabling him in that behalf, hereby makes the following regulations:—

Citation and Commencement

1. These regulations may be cited as the Prevention of Damage by Pests (Threshing and Dismantling of Ricks) (Amendment) Regulations 1976, and shall come into operation on 16th February 1976.

Amendment of principal regulations

2. Regulation 3(*a*) of the Prevention of Damage by Pests (Threshing and Dismantling of Ricks) Regulations 1950(b) is hereby amended by substituting for the words " thirty inches ", the expression "750 mm " and for the words " one half of an inch ", the expression " 13 mm ".

(L.S.)

In Witness whereof the Official Seal of the Minister of Agriculture, Fisheries and Food is hereto affixed on 12th January 1976.

Frederick Peart,
Minister of Agriculture, Fisheries and Food.

EXPLANATORY NOTE

(This Note is not part of the regulations.)

These regulations amend the Prevention of Damage by Pests (Threshing and Dismantling of Ricks) Regulations 1950 by substituting the approximate metric measurements for the imperial measurements referred to in the principal regulations.

(a) 1949 c. 55.   (b) S.I. 1950/1172 (1950 II, p. 317).

STATUTORY INSTRUMENTS

1976 No. 46 (S.3)

LANDLORD AND TENANT

The Notices to Quit (Prescribed Information) (Protected Tenancies and Part VII Contracts) (Scotland) Regulations 1976

Made - - - -	*9th January* 1976
Laid before Parliament	*26th January* 1976
Coming into Operation	*31st March* 1976

In exercise of the powers conferred upon me by section 131 of the Rent (Scotland) Act 1971**(a)** as amended by section 123(1) of the Housing Act 1974**(b)**, and of all other powers enabling me in that behalf, I hereby make the following regulations:—

1. These regulations may be cited as the Notices to Quit (Prescribed Information) (Protected Tenancies and Part VII Contracts) (Scotland) Regulations 1976 and shall come into operation on 31st March 1976.

2.—(1) In these regulations—

"Part VII contract" means a contract to which section 85(1) of the Rent (Scotland) Act 1971 applies; and

"protected tenancy" means a protected tenancy within the meaning of section 1 of the Rent (Scotland) Act 1971.

(2) The Interpretation Act 1889**(c)** shall apply for the interpretation of these regulations as it applies for the interpretation of an Act of Parliament.

(3) Any reference in these regulations to any enactment shall be construed, except where the context otherwise requires, as a reference to that enactment as amended, and as including a reference thereto as applied, or treated as applying, by any other enactment.

3. Where a notice to quit is given by a landlord on or after the coming into operation of these regulations to determine a tenancy which is—

(*a*) a protected tenancy, or

(*b*) a Part VII contract,

that notice shall contain, in such form as may be, the information in the Schedule to these regulations.

William Ross,
One of Her Majesty's Principal
Secretaries of State.

New St. Andrew's House,
Edinburgh.
9th January 1976.

(**a**) 1971 c. 28. (**b**) 1974 c. 44. (**c**) 1889 c. 63.

SCHEDULE

Information to be Contained in the Notice to Quit

1. Even after the notice to quit has run out, before the tenant can lawfully be evicted, the landlord must get an order for possession, that is to say a decree of removing or warrant of ejection, from the court.

2. If the tenancy is a protected tenancy under the Rent Acts, the court can normally give the landlord such an order only on the grounds set out in those Acts.

3. Where the tenancy is not a protected tenancy, the tenant may be able to ask the rent tribunal to postpone the date when the notice to quit expires for up to six months, as long as he does so before the notice runs out.

4. If the tenant does not know whether his tenancy is a protected tenancy or is otherwise unsure of his rights, he can obtain advice from a solicitor. Help with all or part of the cost of legal advice and assistance may be available under the Legal Aid Scheme. He can also seek information from a rent officer, rent tribunal office, citizens' advice bureau or a housing aid centre.

EXPLANATORY NOTE

(This Note is not part of the Regulations.)

These Regulations prescribe the information to be contained in a notice to quit, given by a landlord on or after 31st March 1976 to determine a tenancy which is either a protected tenancy under the Rent (Scotland) Act 1971, or a contract to which Part VII of that Act applies. Failure to include such information will in terms of section 131 of the Act render the notice to quit invalid.

STATUTORY INSTRUMENTS

1976 No. 47

CUSTOMS AND EXCISE

RELIEFS AND REDUCED DUTIES (CUSTOMS)

The Agricultural Levy Reliefs (Frozen Beef and Veal) Order 1976

Made - - - -	13*th January* 1976
Laid before the House of Commons	27*th January* 1976
Coming into Operation	28*th January* 1976

The Minister of Agriculture, Fisheries and Food, the Secretary of State for Scotland, the Secretary of State for Northern Ireland (being the Secretaries of State respectively concerned with agriculture in Scotland and Northern Ireland) and the Secretary of State for Wales, acting jointly, in exercise of the powers conferred upon them by section 5(4) of the Import Duties Act 1958(a), as amended by section 4(1) of, and paragraph 1 of Schedule 4 to, the European Communities Act 1972(b) and as applied by section 6(5) of that Act, as read with the Transfer of Functions (Wales) Order 1969(c) and of all other powers enabling them in that behalf, hereby make the following order:—

1. This order may be cited as the Agricultural Levy Reliefs (Frozen Beef and Veal) Order 1976, and shall come into operation on 28th January 1976.

2.—(1) In this order, unless the context otherwise requires—

"the Board" means the Intervention Board for Agricultural Produce established under section 6 of the European Communities Act 1972;

"licence" means an import licence issued by the Board under the provisions of Council Regulation (EEC) No. 805/68 of 27th June 1968(d), on the common organisation of the market in beef and veal, as amended(e), Commission Regulation (EEC) No. 193/75 of 17th January 1975(f), laying down common detailed rules for the application of the system of import and export licences and advance fixing certificates for agricultural products and Commission Regulation (EEC) No. 2045/75 of 25th July 1975(g) on special detailed rules for the application of the system of import licences and advance fixing certificates for beef and veal;

"the Minister" means the Minister of Agriculture, Fisheries and Food;

"the quota" means the Community tariff quota for the importation of frozen beef and veal provided for by Council Regulation (EEC) No. 3288/75 of 16th December 1975(h), on the opening, apportionment and method of

---

(a) 1958 c. 6. (b) 1972 c. 68.
(c) S.I. 1969/388 (1969 I, p. 1070). (d) OJ No. L148, 28.6.68, p. 24.
(e) There is no amendment which relates expressly to the subject matter of this order.
(f) OJ No. L25, 31.1.75, p. 10.
(g) OJ No. L213, 11.8.75, p. 21. (h) OJ No. L327, 19.12.75, p. 1.

administration of a Community tariff quota for frozen beef and veal falling within subheading 02.01 A II a) 2 of the Common Customs Tariff (1976).

(2) The Interpretation Act 1889(a) shall apply to the interpretation of this order as it applies to the interpretation of an Act of Parliament.

3.—(1) The Minister shall determine the allocation of the United Kingdom's share of the quota.

(2) The determination mentioned in paragraph (1) of this article shall be made by the Minister by allocating an amount not exceeding one third of the United Kingdom's share to Government Departments, and allocating the remainder to importers of frozen beef and veal by reference to the amounts of frozen beef and veal which such importers have previously imported from outside the European Economic Community into the United Kingdom during the period from 1st July 1972 to 30th June 1974. Any such allocation shall be made subject to such conditions as appear to the Minister to be expedient to secure the object or prevent the abuse of the relief.

4. Any entitlement to relief under the United Kingdom's share of the quota shall be subject to:

(a) the production of the licence in respect of the goods on which relief is sought appropriately endorsed by the Board with a statement that the amount of frozen beef or veal appearing in the licence may be imported free of levy under the quota;

(b) the observance by the importer of any conditions subject to which the allocation was made.

5. No licence, endorsed with the statement referred to in article 4(a) of this order, may be issued to an importer unless the Board is satisfied, after taking into account any levy-free imports of beef or veal authorised under previous licences issued to that importer, that the amount of levy-free beef or veal allocated to him in pursuance of this order will not be exceeded by the import of beef or veal under that licence.

6. Goods shall be treated as forming part of the quota when they are entered for home use in the United Kingdom, within the meaning of the Customs and Excise Act 1952(b) and regulation 8 of the Warehousing Regulations 1975(c), under the authority of a licence endorsed with the statement referred to in article 4(a) of this order.

In Witness whereof the Official Seal of the Minister of Agriculture, Fisheries and Food is hereunto affixed on 5th January 1976.

(L.S.)   *Frederick Peart,*
Minister of Agriculture, Fisheries and Food.

(a) 1889 c. 63.   (b) 1952 c. 44.
(c) S.I. 1975/1789 (1975 III, p. 6764).

6th January 1976.

William Ross,
Secretary of State for Scotland.

8th January 1976.

Merlyn Rees,
Secretary of State for Northern Ireland.

13th January 1976.

John Morris,
Secretary of State for Wales.

EXPLANATORY NOTE

(This Note is not part of the Order.)

This Order, which comes into operation on 28th January 1976 and applies throughout the United Kingdom, requires the Minister of Agriculture, Fisheries and Food to allocate the United Kingdom's share of a quota for the levy-free import of frozen beef and veal under the provisions of Council Regulation (EEC) No. 3288/75.

The Order provides that not more than one third of the United Kingdom's share of the quota shall be allocated to Government Departments and that the remainder shall be allocated to importers of frozen beef and veal by reference to the amounts of frozen beef and veal which they have previously imported from outside the European Economic Community into the United Kingdom during the period 1st July 1972 to 30th June 1974.

STATUTORY INSTRUMENTS

1976 No. 48

LAND CHARGES

The Local Land Charges (Amendment) Rules 1976

Made - - - -	15*th January* 1976
Coming into Operation	19*th February* 1976

The Lord Chancellor, in exercise of the powers conferred on him by section 19 of the Land Charges Act 1925**(a)**, as set out in Schedule 4 to the Land Charges Act 1972**(b)**, and with the concurrence of the Treasury as to fees, hereby makes the following Rules:—

1.—(1) These Rules may be cited as the Local Land Charges (Amendment) Rules 1976 and shall come into operation on 19th February 1976.

(2) The Interpretation Act 1889**(c)** shall apply to the interpretation of these Rules as it applies to the interpretation of an Act of Parliament.

2. The Schedule set out in the Schedule to these Rules shall be substituted for Schedule 4 to the Local Land Charges Rules 1966**(d)**, as amended by the Local Land Charges (Amendment) Rules 1970**(e)**.

3. The Local Land Charges (Amendment) Rules 1970 are hereby revoked.

Dated 8th January 1976.

Elwyn-Jones, C.

We, the undersigned, two of the Lords Commissioners of Her Majesty's Treasury, do hereby concur in the above Rules and in the Schedule thereto.

Dated 15th January 1976.

Donald R. Coleman,
M. Cocks,

(a) 1925 c. 22.   **(b)** 1972 c. 61.   **(c)** 1889 c. 63.
(d) S.I. 1966/579 (1966 II, p. 1318).   **(e)** S.I. 1970/1775 (1970 III, p. 5775).

SCHEDULE
Fees

Item	*Fee* *£*
1. Registration of a charge in Part 11 of the register	15·00
2. Filing a further certificate of the Lands Tribunal under rule 16(3)...	0·60
3. Filing a judgement or order, or written request for the variation or cancellation of any entry, in Part 11 of the register	1·25
4. Inspection of documents filed in the registry relating to an entry in Part 11 of the register, in respect of each parcel of land	0·60
5. Variation or cancellation of any entry in Part 11 of the register	0·35
6. Personal search in the whole or any part of the register	0·50
And in addition, but subject to a maximum additional fee of £3·50 in respect of each parcel of land above one, where the search extends to more than one parcel	0·25
7. Official search (including issue of official certificate of search) in:	
(*a*) any one part of the register	0·50
(*b*) the whole of the register	1·25
And in addition, but subject to a maximum additional fee of £5 in respect of each parcel of land above one, where several parcels are included in the same requisition under rule 24(3), whether the requisition is for search in the whole or any part of the register	0·25
8. Office copy of any entry in the register (not including a copy or extract of any plan or document filed in the register)	0·35
9. Office copy of any plan or other document filed in the registry	such reasonable fee as may be fixed by the local registrar according to the time and labour involved.

EXPLANATORY NOTE
(This Note is not part of the Rules.)

These Rules, which supersede the Local Land Charges (Amendment) Rules 1970, increase the fees payable in connection with the registration of local land charges.

STATUTORY INSTRUMENTS

1976 No. 50

ASSOCIATED STATES
The Anguilla (Constitution) Order 1976

Made - - - - *19th January 1976*
Coming into Operation *10th February 1976*

At the Court at Buckingham Palace, the 19th day of January 1976

Present,

The Queen's Most Excellent Majesty in Council

Her Majesty, by virtue of the powers conferred upon Her by section 1(1) of the Anguilla Act 1971(**a**) is pleased, by and with the advice of Her Privy Council, to order, and it is hereby ordered as follows :—

1.—(1) This Order may be cited as the Anguilla (Constitution) Order 1976 and shall come into operation on 10th February 1976. Citation, commencement and interpretation.

(2) The Interpretation Act 1889(**b**) shall apply with the necessary adaptations for the purpose of interpreting and otherwise in relation to this Order as it applies for the purpose of interpreting and in relation to an Act of Parliament.

2.—(1) The Schedule to this Order shall have effect as the Constitution of Anguilla as from the date on which the Anguilla Council is next dissolved after the coming into operation of this Order: and the Anguilla (Administration) Order 1971(**c**) is revoked with effect from that date. Constitution of Anguilla and revocation.

(2) The Schedule to this Order may be cited as the Constitution of Anguilla, and references in any law made before this Order to the Anguilla (Administration) Order 1971 or to any particular provision thereof shall be construed, as from the commencement of this Order, as references to the Constitution of Anguilla and to the corresponding provision thereof.

(3) So long as the Constitution of Anguilla is in force the Constitution of the associated state of St. Christopher, Nevis and Anguilla(**d**) shall not apply in and in relation to Anguilla.

3. At any time between the commencement of this Order and the date on which the Constitution of Anguilla comes into effect, the Commissioner may by regulation make provision for any matter with respect to which a law could be made under section 45 of the Constitution in order that elections to the Legislative Assembly established by the Constitution may be held immediately or shortly after the Constitution comes into effect. Provisions relating to elections.

(**a**) 1971 c. 63.   (**b**) 1889 c. 63.   (**c**) S.I. 1971/1235 (1971 II, p. 3587).
(**d**) Schedule 2 to S.I. 1967/228 (1967 I, p. 594).

Discharge of functions of Supreme Court.
4.—(1) The Commissioner, acting in pursuance of instructions given by Her Majesty through a Secretary of State, may appoint fit and proper persons to exercise in or in relation to Anguilla any powers, duties or jurisdiction conferred upon the Court of Appeal or, as the case may be, the High Court established by the Courts Order or upon the Chief Justice or any other judge of either of those courts, or upon any officer of either of those courts, by the Constitution of Anguilla or any other law for the time being in force in, or having effect in relation to, Anguilla and, subject to the provisions of any such instructions concerning the tenure of office of any such person, may terminate any such appointment.

(2) Any powers, duties or jurisdiction exercisable in or in relation to Anguilla by any person or persons appointed under the preceding subsection shall, to the extent that it is so provided in any instructions given to the Commissioner by Her Majesty through a Secretary of State, be so exercisable by that person or those persons, as the case may be, to the exclusion of any other person or persons.

(3) Any reference in the Constitution of Anguilla or any other law for the time being in force in, or having effect in relation to, Anguilla to the Court of Appeal or, as the case may be, the High Court established by the Courts Order or to the Chief Justice or any other judge of either of those courts or to any officer of either of those courts shall, to the extent that any person or persons appointed under subsection (1) of this section are authorised to exercise in or in relation to Anguilla any powers, duties or jurisdiction, have effect in relation to such powers, duties or jurisdiction as if that reference included a reference to that person or, as the case may be, those persons.

(4) Persons appointed under subsection (1) of this section shall, for the purposes of any law for the time being in force in Anguilla, be regarded as holding offices constituted for Anguilla.

(5) In this section the Courts Order means the West Indies Associated States Supreme Court Order 1967(e).

Stamp of Anguilla.
5. Until such time as a public seal is provided for Anguilla, a stamp bearing the words " Government of Anguilla " and countersigned by the Commissioner may be used instead of such seal.

N. E. Leigh

(e) S.I. 1967/223 (1967 I, p. 364).

THE SCHEDULE TO THE ORDER
THE CONSTITUTION OF ANGUILLA

CHAPTER I

Protection of Fundamental Rights and Freedoms

1. Whereas every person in Anguilla is entitled to the fundamental rights and freedoms of the individual, that is to say, the right, whatever his race, place of origin, political opinions, colour, creed or sex, but subject to respect for the rights and freedoms of others and for the public interest, to each and all of the following, namely— *Fundamental rights and freedoms of the individual.*

(a) life, liberty, security of the person, the enjoyment of property and the protection of the law;

(b) freedom of conscience, of expression and of peaceful assembly and association; and

(c) respect for his private and family life,

the subsequent provisions of this Chapter shall have effect for the purpose of affording protection to the aforesaid rights and freedoms, subject to such limitations of that protection as are contained in those provisions, being limitations designed to ensure that the enjoyment of the said rights and freedoms by any individual does not prejudice the rights and freedoms of others or the public interest.

2.—(1) No person shall be deprived of his life intentionally save in execution of the sentence of a court in respect of a criminal offence under the law of Anguilla of which he has been convicted. *Protection of right to life.*

(2) A person shall not be regarded as having been deprived of his life in contravention of this section if he dies as the result of the use, to such extent and in such circumstances as are permitted by law, of such force as is reasonably justifiable—

(a) for the defence of any person from violence or for the defence of property;

(b) in order to effect a lawful arrest or to prevent the escape of a person lawfully detained;

(c) for the purpose of suppressing a riot, insurrection or mutiny; or

(d) in order lawfully to prevent the commission by that person of a criminal offence,

or if he dies as the result of a lawful act of war.

3.—(1) No person shall be deprived of his personal liberty save as may be authorised by law in any of the following cases, that is to say— *Protection of right to personal liberty.*

(a) in consequence of his unfitness to plead to a criminal charge;

(b) in execution of the sentence or order of a court, whether established for Anguilla or some other country, in respect of a criminal offence of which he has been convicted;

(c) in execution of an order of the High Court or the Court of Appeal or such other court as may be prescribed by the Legislature on the grounds of his contempt of any such court or of another court or tribunal;

(d) in execution of the order of a court made in order to secure the fulfilment of any obligation imposed on him by law;

(e) for the purpose of bringing him before a court in execution of the order of a court;

(f) upon reasonable suspicion of his having committed or of being about to commit a criminal offence under the law of Anguilla;

(g) under the order of a court or with the consent of his parent or guardian, for his education or welfare during any period ending not later than the date when he attains the age of eighteen years;

(h) for the purpose of preventing the spread of an infectious or contagious disease;

(i) in the case of a person who is, or is reasonably suspected to be, of unsound mind, addicted to drugs or alcohol, or a vagrant, for the purpose of his care or treatment or the protection of the community;

(j) for the purpose of preventing the unlawful entry of that person into Anguilla, or for the purpose of effecting the expulsion, extradition or other lawful removal of that person from Anguilla or for the purpose of restricting that person while he is being conveyed through Anguilla in the course of his extradition or removal as a convicted prisoner from one country to another; or

(k) to such extent as may be necessary in the execution of a lawful order requiring that person to remain within a specified area within Anguilla or prohibiting him from being within such an area or to such extent as may be reasonably justifiable for the taking of proceedings against that person relating to the making of any such order, or to such extent as may be reasonably justifiable for restraining that person during any visit that he is permitted to make to any part of Anguilla in which, in consequence of any other such order, his presence would otherwise be unlawful.

(2) Any person who is arrested or detained shall be informed orally and in writing as soon as reasonably practicable, in a language which he understands, of the reasons for his arrest or detention.

(3) Any person who is arrested or detained—

(a) for the purpose of bringing him before a court in execution of the order of a court; or

(b) upon reasonable suspicion of his having committed or being about to commit a criminal offence under the law of Anguilla,

and who is not released, shall be brought without delay before a court; and if any person arrested or detained upon reasonable suspicion of his having committed or being about to commit a criminal offence under the law of Anguilla is not tried within a reasonable time, then, without prejudice to any further proceedings which may be brought against him, he shall be released either unconditionally or upon reasonable conditions, including in particular such conditions as are reasonably necessary to ensure that he appears at a later date for trial or for proceedings preliminary to trial.

(4) Any person who is unlawfully arrested or detained by any other person shall be entitled to compensation therefor from that person or from any other person or authority on whose behalf that person was acting.

(5) Where any person is brought before a court in execution of the order of a court in any proceedings or upon suspicion of his having committed or being about to commit an offence, he shall not be thereafter further held in custody in connection with those proceedings or that offence save upon the order of a court.

(6) For the purposes of subsection (1)(*b*) of this section a person charged before a court with a criminal offence in respect of whom a special verdict has been returned that he was guilty of the act or omission charged but was insane when he did the act or made the omission shall be regarded as a person who has been convicted of an offence and the detention of a person in consequence of such a verdict shall be regarded as detention in execution of the order of a court.

4.—(1) No person shall be held in slavery or servitude.

(2) No person shall be required to perform forced labour.

(3) For the purposes of this section, the expression " forced labour " does not include—

(*a*) any labour required in consequence of the sentence or order of a court;

(*b*) labour required of any person while he is lawfully detained that, though not required in consequence of the sentence or order of a court, is reasonably necessary in the interests of hygiene or for the maintenance of the place at which he is detained;

(*c*) any labour required of a member of a disciplined force in pursuance of his duties as such or, in the case of a person who has conscientious objections to service as a member of a naval, military or air force, any labour that that person is required by law to perform in place of such service;

(*d*) any labour required during any period of public emergency or in the event of any other emergency or calamity that threatens the life and well-being of the community, to the extent that the requiring of such labour is reasonably justifiable in the circumstances of any situation arising or existing during that period or as a result of that other emergency or calamity, for the purpose of dealing with that situation.

Protection from slavery and forced labour.

5.—(1) No person shall be deprived of his freedom of movement, and, for the purposes of this section the said freedom means the right to move freely throughout Anguilla, the right to reside in any part of Anguilla, the right to enter Anguilla, the right to leave Anguilla and immunity from expulsion from Anguilla.

Protection of freedom of movement.

(2) Any restriction on a person's freedom of movement which is involved in his lawful detention shall not be held to be inconsistent with or in contravention of this section.

(3) Nothing contained in or done under the authority of any law shall be held to be inconsistent with or in contravention of this section to the extent that the law in question makes provision—

(*a*) for the imposition of restrictions on the movement or residence within Anguilla of any person or on any person's right to leave Anguilla that are reasonably required in the interests of defence, public safety or public order;

(*b*) for the imposition of restrictions on the movement or residence within Anguilla or on the right to leave Anguilla of persons generally or any class of persons in the interests of defence, public safety, public order, public morality or public health and except so far as that provision or, as the case may be, the thing done under the authority thereof is shown not to be reasonably justifiable in a democratic society;

(*c*) for the imposition of restrictions on the movement or residence within Anguilla of any person who does not belong to Anguilla or the exclusion or expulsion from Anguilla of any such person;

(*d*) for the imposition of restrictions on the acquisition or use by any person of land or other property in Anguilla;

(*e*) for the imposition of restrictions on the movement or residence within Anguilla of public officers, or on the right of public officers to leave Anguilla;

(*f*) for the removal of a person from Anguilla to be tried or punished in some other country for a criminal offence under the law of that other country or to undergo imprisonment in that other country in execution of the sentence of a court in respect of a criminal offence under the law of Anguilla of which he has been convicted; or

(*g*) for the imposition of restrictions on the right of any person to leave Anguilla that are reasonably required in order to secure the fulfilment of any obligations imposed on that person by law and except so far as that provision or, as the case may be, the thing done under the authority thereof is shown not to be reasonably justifiable in a democratic society.

(4) If any person whose freedom of movement has been restricted by virtue only of such a provision as is referred to in subsection (3)(*a*) of this section so requests at any time during the period of that restriction not earlier than six months after the restriction was imposed or six months after he last made such a request during that period, his case shall be reviewed by an independent and impartial tribunal established by law and presided over by a person appointed by the Chief Justice from among persons who hold the office of magistrate in Anguilla or who are entitled to practise or to be admitted to practise in Anguilla as barristers.

(5) On any review by a tribunal in pursuance of subsection (4) of this section of the case of any person whose freedom of movement has been restricted, the tribunal may make recommendations concerning the necessity or expediency of continuing that restriction to the authority by whom it was ordered and, unless it is otherwise provided by law, that authority shall be obliged to act in accordance with any such recommendations.

Protection from inhuman treatment.   6.—(1) No person shall be subjected to torture or to inhuman or degrading punishment or other treatment.

(2) Nothing contained in or done under the authority of any law shall be held to be inconsistent with or in contravention of this section to the extent that the law in question authorises the infliction of any description of punishment that was lawful in Anguilla immediately before the coming into operation of this Constitution.

S.I. 1976/50 165

7.—(1) No interest in or right over any property of any description shall be compulsorily acquired, and no such property shall be compulsorily taken possession of, except by or under the provisions of a written law which—

(a) prescribes the principles on which and the manner in which adequate compensation thereto is to be determined;

(b) requires the prompt payment of such adequate compensation;

(c) prescribes the manner in which the compensation is to be given; and

(d) the manner of enforcing the right to any such compensation.

Protection from deprivation of property.

(2) Nothing in this section shall be construed as affecting the making or operation of any law so far as that law provides for the taking of possession or acquisition of any property, interest or right—

(a) in satisfaction of any tax, rate or due; or

(b) by way of penalty for breach of the law, whether under civil process or after conviction of a criminal offence under the law of Anguilla; or

(c) upon the attempted removal of the property in question out of or into Anguilla in contravention of any law; or

(d) by way of the taking of a sample for the purpose of any law; or

(e) where the property consists of an animal upon its being found trespassing or straying; or

(f) as an incident of a lease, tenancy, licence, mortgage, charge, bill of sale, pledge or contract; or

(g) by way of the vesting or administration of trust property, enemy property, or the property of persons adjudged or otherwise declared bankrupt or insolvent, persons of unsound mind, deceased persons, or bodies corporate or unincorporate in the course of being wound up; or

(h) in the execution of judgments or orders of courts; or

(i) by reason of its being in a dangerous state or injurious to the health of human beings, animals or plants; or

(j) in consequence of any law with respect to the limitation of actions; or

(k) for so long only as may be necessary for the purposes of any examination, investigation, trial or inquiry or, in the case of land, the carrying out thereon—

  (i) of work of soil conservation or of conservation of other natural resources; or

  (ii) of work relating to agricultural development or improvement which the owner or occupier of the land has been required, and has without reasonable excuse refused or failed, to carry out.

(3) Nothing in this section shall be construed as affecting the making or operation of any law so far as it provides for the orderly marketing or production or growth or extraction of any agricultural product or mineral or any article or thing prepared for market or manufactured therefore or for the reasonable restriction of the use of any property for the purpose of safeguarding the interests of others or the protection of tenants, licensees or others having rights in or over such property.

(4) Nothing in this section shall be construed as affecting the making or operation of any law for the compulsory taking of possession in the public interest of any property, or the compulsory acquisition in the public interest of any interest in or right over property, where that property, interest or right is held by a body corporate which is established for public purposes by any law and in which no monies have been invested other than monies provided by the Legislature.

(5) In this section " compensation " means the consideration to be given to a person for any interest or right which he may have in or over property which has been compulsorily taken possession of or compulsorily acquired as prescribed and determined in accordance with the provisions of the law by or under which the property or such right or interest has been compulsorily taken possession of or compulsorily acquired.

Protection from arbitrary search or entry.

8.—(1) Except with his own consent, no person shall be subjected to the search of his person or his property or the entry by others on his premises.

(2) Nothing contained in or done under the authority of any law shall be held to be inconsistent with or in contravention of this section to the extent that the law in question makes provision—

(a) that is reasonably required in the interests of defence, public safety, public order, public morality, public health, public revenue, town and country planning or the development and utilisation of any property in such a manner as to promote the public benefit;

(b) that authorises an officer or agent of the Government of Anguilla, a local government authority or a body corporate established by law for public purposes to enter on the premises of any person in order to inspect those premises or anything thereon for the purpose of any tax, rate or due or in order to carry out work connected with any property that is lawfully on those premises and that belongs to that Government, authority or body corporate, as the case may be;

(c) that is reasonably required for the purpose of preventing or detecting crime;

(d) that is reasonably required for the purpose of protecting the rights or freedoms of other persons; or

(e) that authorises, for the purpose of enforcing the judgment or order of a court in any civil proceedings, the search of any person or property by order of a court or entry upon any premises by such order,

and except so far as that provision or, as the case may be, anything done under the authority thereof is shown not to be reasonably justifiable in a democratic society.

Provisions to secure protection of law.

9.—(1) Whenever any person is charged with a criminal offence he shall, unless the charge is withdrawn, be afforded a fair hearing within a reasonable time by an independent and impartial court established by law.

(2) Any court or other authority prescribed by law for the determination of the existence or the extent of civil rights or obligations shall be established by law and shall be independent and impartial; and where

roceedings for such a determination are instituted by any person before uch a court or other authority, the case shall be given a fair hearing ·ithin a reasonable time.

(3) Except with the agreement of all the parties thereto all proceed 1gs of every court and proceedings relating to the determination of the xistence or the extent of a person's civil rights or obligations before any ·ther authority, including the announcement of the decision of the ·ourt or other authority, shall be held in public.

(4) Nothing in subsection (3) of this section shall prevent any court ·r any other authority such as is mentioned in that subsection from xcluding from the proceedings persons other than the parties thereto nd their legal representatives—

(a) in interlocutory civil proceedings; or

(b) in appeal proceedings under any law relating to income tax; or

(c) to such extent as the court or other authority—

    (i) may consider necessary or expedient in circumstances where publicity would prejudice the interests of justice; or

    (ii) may be empowered or required by law to do so in the interests of defence, public safety, public order, public morality, the welfare of persons under the age of eighteen years or the protection of the private lives of persons concerned in the proceedings.

(5) Every person who is charged with a criminal offence shall be ·resumed to be innocent until he is proved or has pleaded guilty:

Provided that nothing contained in or done under the authority of any law shall be held to be inconsistent with or in contravention of this subsection to the extent that the law in question imposes upon any person charged as aforesaid the burden of proving particular facts.

(6) Every person who is charged with a criminal offence—

(a) shall be informed orally and in writing as soon as reasonably practicable, in a language which he understands, of the nature of the offence charged;

(b) shall be given adequate time and facilities for the preparation of his defence;

(c) shall be permitted to defend himself in person or, at his own expense, by a legal representative of his own choice;

(d) shall be afforded facilities to examine in person or by his legal representative the witnesses called by the prosecution before any court and to obtain the attendance of witnesses, subject to the payment of their reasonable expenses, and carry out the examination of such witnesses to testify on his behalf before the court on the same condition as those applying to witnesses called by the prosecution; and

(e) shall be permitted to have without payment the assistance of an interpreter if he cannot understand the English language.

(7) No person shall be held to be guilty of a criminal offence on ·ccount of any act or omission which did not, at the time it took place, ·onstitute such an offence, and no penalty shall be imposed for any

criminal offence which is severer in degree or description than the maximum penalty which might have been imposed for that offence at the time when it was committed.

(8) No person who shows that he has been tried by any competent court for a criminal offence and either convicted or acquitted shall again be tried for that offence or for other criminal offence of which he could have been convicted at the trial for that offence save upon the order of a superior court made in the course of appeal proceedings relating to the conviction or acquittal; and no person shall be tried for a criminal offence if he shows that he has been pardoned for that offence:

Provided that nothing contained in or done under the authority of any law shall be held to be inconsistent with or in contravention of this subsection to the extent that the law in question authorises any court to try a member of a disciplined force for a criminal offence notwithstanding any trial and conviction or acquittal of that member under the disciplinary law of that force; but any court so trying such a member and convicting him shall in sentencing him to any punishment take into account any punishment awarded him under that disciplinary law.

(9) When a person is tried for any criminal offence, the accused person or any person authorised by him in that behalf shall, if he so requires and subject to payment of such reasonable fee as may be prescribed by law, be given within a reasonable time after judgment a copy for the use of the accused person of any record of the proceedings made by or on behalf of the court.

(10) No person who is tried for a criminal offence shall be compelled to give evidence at the trial.

(11) In the case of any person who is held in lawful detention the provisions of subsection (1), subsection (3) and paragraphs (c) and (d) of subsection (5) of this section shall not apply in relation to his trial for a criminal offence under the law regulating the discipline of persons held in such detention.

(12) In this section "criminal offence" means a criminal offence under the law of Anguilla.

Protection of freedom of conscience.

10.—(1) Except with his own consent, no person shall be hindered in the enjoyment of his freedom of conscience, including freedom of thought and of religion, freedom to change his religion or belief and freedom, either alone or in community with others, and both in public and in private, to manifest and propagate his religion or belief in worship, teaching, practice and observance.

(2) Except with his own consent (or, if he is a person under the age of eighteen years, the consent of his parent or guardian) no person attending any place of education shall be compelled to receive religious instruction or to take part in or attend any religious ceremony or observance if that instruction, ceremony or observance relates to a religion other than his own.

(3) Every religious community shall be entitled, at its own expense, to establish and maintain places of education and to manage any place of education which it wholly maintains; and no such community shall be prevented from providing religious instruction for persons of that

community in the course of any education provided at any places of education which it wholly maintains or in the course of any education which it otherwise provides.

(4) No person shall be compelled to take any oath which is contrary to his religion or belief or to take any oath in a manner which is contrary to his religion or belief.

(5) Nothing contained in or done under the authority of any law shall be held to be inconsistent with or in contravention of this section to the extent that the law in question makes provision which is reasonably required—

(a) in the interests of defence, public safety, public order, public morality or public health;

(b) for the purpose of protecting the rights and freedoms of other persons, including the right to observe and practise any religion without the unsolicited intervention of members of any other religion; or

(c) for the purpose of regulating educational institutions in the interests of persons who receive or may receive instruction in them,

and except so far as that provision or, as the case may be, the thing done under the authority thereof is shown not to be reasonably justifiable in a democratic society.

(6) References in this section to a religion shall be construed as including references to a religious denomination, and cognate expressions shall be construed accordingly.

11.—(1) Except with his own consent, no person shall be hindered in the enjoyment of his freedom of expression, and for the purposes of this section the said freedom includes the freedom to hold opinions and to receive and impart ideas and information without interference, and freedom from interference with his correspondence and other means of communication. *Protection of freedom of expression.*

(2) Nothing contained in or done under the authority of any law shall be held to be inconsistent with or in contravention of this section to the extent that the law in question makes provision—

(a) that is reasonably required in the interests of defence, public safety, public order, public morality or public health;

(b) that is reasonably required for the purpose of protecting the reputations, rights and freedoms of other persons or the private lives of persons concerned in legal proceedings, preventing the disclosure of information received in confidence, maintaining the authority and independence of the courts or regulating telephony, telegraphy, posts, wireless, broadcasting or television; or

(c) that imposes restrictions upon public officers:

Provided that the provision or, as the case may be, the thing done under the authority thereof is shown to be reasonably justifiable in a democratic society.

12.—(1) Except with his own consent, no person shall be hindered in the enjoyment of his freedom of peaceful assembly and association, that is to say, his right peacefully to assemble freely and associate with other persons and in particular to form or belong to trade unions or other associations for the protection of his interests. *Protection of freedom of assembly and association.*

(2) Nothing contained in or done under the authority of any law shall be held to be inconsistent with or in contravention of this section to the extent that the law in question makes provision—

(*a*) that is reasonably required—

    (i) in the interests of defence, public safety, public order, public morality or public health; or

    (ii) for the purpose of protecting the rights or freedoms of other persons; or

(*b*) that imposes restrictions upon public officers:

Provided that:—

    (i) paragraph (*a*)(ii) of this subsection shall not apply in relation to a provision that operates so as to prohibit a trade union or other association from carrying out activities preventing or restricting persons who are not members of that trade union or other association from pursuing a particular trade, profession or employment unless that provision is contained in a written law;

    (ii) the provision or, as the case may be, the thing done under the authority of any such law is shown to be reasonably justifiable in a democratic society.

Protection from discrimination on the grounds of race, etc.

13.—(1) Subject to the provisions of subsections (4), (5) and (7) of this section, no law shall make any provision which is discriminatory either of itself or in its effect.

(2) Subject to the provisions of subsections (6), (7) and (8) of this section, no person shall be treated in a discriminatory manner by any person acting by virtue of any written law or in the performance of the functions of any public office or any public authority.

(3) In this section, the expression " discriminatory " means affording different treatment to different persons attributable wholly or mainly to their respective descriptions by race, place of origin, political opinions, colour or creed whereby persons of one such description are subjected to disabilities or restrictions to which persons of another such description are not made subject or are accorded privileges or advantages which are not accorded to persons of another such description.

(4) Subsection (1) of this section shall not apply to any law so far as that law makes provision—

(*a*) with respect to persons who do not belong to Anguilla;

(*b*) for the application, in the case of persons of any such description as is mentioned in subsection (3) of this section (or of persons connected with such persons), of the law with respect to adoption, marriage, divorce, burial, devolution of property on death or other like matters which is the personal law of persons of that description; or

(*c*) for the imposition of taxation or appropriation of revenue by the Government of Anguilla or any local authority or body for local purposes.

(5) Nothing contained in any law shall be held to be inconsistent with or in contravention of subsection (1) of this section to the extent that it makes provision with respect to qualifications for service as a

public officer, or as a member of a disciplined force or for the service of a local government authority or a body corporate established by any law for public purposes.

(6) Subsection (2) of this section shall not apply to anything which is expressly or by necessary implication authorised to be done by any such provision of law as is referred to in subsection (4) or (5) of this section.

(7) Nothing contained in or done under the authority of any law shall be held to be inconsistent with or in contravention of this section to the extent that the law in question makes provision whereby persons of any such description as is mentioned in subsection (3) of this section may be subjected to any restriction on the rights and freedoms guaranteed by sections 5, 8, 10, 11 and 12 of this Constitution, being such a restriction as is authorised by paragraph (*a*), (*b*) or (*g*) of subsection (3) of section 5, subsection (2) of section 8, subsection (6) of section 10, subsection (2) of section 11, or subsection (2) of section 12, as the case may be.

(8) Nothing in subsection (2) of this section shall affect any discretion relating to the institution, conduct or discontinuance of civil or criminal proceedings in any court that is vested in any person by or under this Constitution or any other law.

14. Nothing contained in or done under the authority of any law shall be held to be inconsistent with or in contravention of section 3 or section 13 of this Constitution to the extent that the law authorises the taking during any period of public emergency of measures that are reasonably justifiable for dealing with the situation that exists in Anguilla during that period. *Derogations from fundamental rights and freedoms under emergency powers.*

15.—(1) When a person is detained by virtue of any such law as is referred to in section 14 of this Constitution the following provisions shall apply, that is to say— *Protection of persons detained under emergency laws.*

(*a*) he shall, as soon as reasonably practicable and in any case not more than four days after the commencement of his detention, be furnished with a statement in writing in a language that he understands specifying in detail the grounds upon which he is detained:

(*b*) not more than fourteen days after the commencement of his detention, a notification shall be published in the Official Gazette stating that he has been detained and giving particulars of the provision of law under which his detention is authorised;

(*c*) not more than one month after the commencement of his detention and thereafter during his detention at intervals of not more than six months, his case shall be reviewed by an independent and impartial tribunal established by law and presided over by a person appointed by the Chief Justice from among persons who are or have been judges of the High Court or the Court of Appeal or are qualified for appointment as such judges:

(*d*) he shall be afforded reasonable facilities to consult a legal representative of his own choice who shall be permitted to make representations to the tribunal appointed for the review of the case of the detained person: and

(e) at the hearing of his case by the tribunal appointed for the review of his case he shall be permitted to appear in person or by a legal representative of his own choice.

(2) On any review by a tribunal in pursuance of this section of the case of a detained person, the tribunal may make recommendations concerning the necessity or expediency of continuing his detention to the authority by which it was ordered but, unless it is otherwise provided by law, that authority shall not be obliged to act in accordance with any such recommendations.

(3) Nothing contained in subsection (1)(d) or subsection (1)(e) of this section shall be construed as entitling a person to legal representation at public expense.

(4) The reference in subsection (1)(c) of this section to the High Court and Court of Appeal shall be construed as including a reference to the Supreme Court established by the Windward Islands and Leeward Islands (Courts) Order in Council 1959(a) and the British Caribbean Court of Appeal established by the British Caribbean Court of Appeal Order in Council 1962(b).

Enforcement of protective provisions.

16.—(1) If any person alleges that any of the provisions of sections 2 to 15 (inclusive) of this Constitution has been, or is being, contravened in relation to him (or, in the case of a person who is detained, if any other person alleges such a contravention in relation to the detained person), then, without prejudice to any other action with respect to the same matter which is lawfully available, that person may apply to the High Court for redress.

(2) The High Court shall have original jurisdiction to hear and determine any application made by any person in pursuance of subsection (1) of this section and may make such orders, issue such writs and give such directions as it may consider appropriate for the purpose of enforcing, or securing the enforcement of, any of the provisions of the said sections 2 to 15 (inclusive) to the protection of which the person concerned is entitled:

Provided that the High Court may decline to exercise its powers under this subsection if it is satisfied that adequate means of redress for the contravention alleged are or have been available to the person concerned under any other law.

(3) If in any proceedings in any court (other than the Court of Appeal, the High Court or a court martial) any question arises as to the contravention in any of the provisions of sections 2 to 15 (inclusive) of this Constitution, the person presiding in that court may, and shall if any party to the proceedings so requests, refer the question to the High Court unless, in his opinion, the raising of the question is merely frivolous or vexatious.

(4) Where any question is referred to the High Court in pursuance of subsection (3) of this section, the High Court shall give its decision upon the question and the court in which the question arose shall

---

(a) S.I. 1959/2197 (1959 I, p. 563).
(b) S.I. 1962/1086, 1962/1245 (1962 II, p. 1247; II, p. 1367).

dispose of the case in accordance with that decision or, if that decision is the subject of an appeal to the Court of Appeal or to Her Majesty in Council, in accordance with the decision of the Court of Appeal or, as the case may be, of Her Majesty in Council.

(5) The Legislature may confer or authorise the conferment on the High Court of such powers in addition to those conferred by this section as may appear to be necessary or desirable for the purpose of enabling the Court more effectively to exercise the jurisdiction conferred on it by this section.

(6) The Chief Justice may make rules with respect to the practice and procedure of the High Court in relation to the jurisdiction and powers conferred on it by or under this section (including rules with respect to the time within which applications may be brought and references shall be made to the High Court).

Declaration of emergency.

17.—(1) The Commissioner may, by Proclamation which shall be published in the Official Gazette, declare that a state of emergency exists for the purposes of this Chapter.

(2) A declaration of emergency may at any time be revoked by the Commissioner, by Proclamation which shall be published in the Official Gazette, and, unless sooner revoked, shall, without prejudice to the making of a further declaration in like manner, expire at the expiration of ninety days from the date on which it was made.

Interpretation and savings.

18.—(1) In this Chapter, unless the context otherwise requires—

" contravention ", in relation to any requirement, includes a failure to comply with that requirement, and cognate expressions shall be construed accordingly;

" court " means any court of law having jurisdiction in Anguilla other than a court established by a disciplinary law, and includes Her Majesty in Council and in section 2 of this Constitution a court established by a disciplinary law;

" disciplinary law " means a law regulating the discipline of any disciplined force;

" disciplined force " means—

(a) a naval, military or air force;

(b) the Police Force; or

(c) a prison service;

" legal representative " means a person entitled to be in or to enter Anguilla and entitled to practise as a barrister in Anguilla or, except in relation to proceedings before a court in which a solicitor has no right of audience, so entitled to practise as a solicitor; and

" member ", in relation to a disciplined force, includes any person who, under the law regulating the discipline of that force, is subject to that discipline.

(2) In this Chapter " a period of public emergency " means any period during which—

(a) Her Majesty is at war; or

(b) a declaration of emergency is in force under section 17 of this Constitution.

(3) In relation to any person who is a member of a disciplined force raised under the law of Anguilla, nothing contained in or done under the authority of the disciplinary law of that force shall be held to be inconsistent with or in contravention of any of the provisions of this Chapter other than sections 2, 4 and 5 of this Constitution.

(4) In relation to any person who is a member of a disciplined force raised otherwise than as aforesaid and lawfully present in Anguilla, nothing contained in or done under the authority of the disciplinary law of that force shall be held to be inconsistent with or in contravention of any of the provisions of this Chapter.

(5) For the purposes of this Chapter a person shall be regarded as belonging to Anguilla if that person is—

(a) a citizen of the United Kingdom and Colonies born in Anguilla; or

(b) a citizen of the United Kingdom and Colonies born outside Anguilla—

(i) whose father or mother was born in Anguilla; or

(ii) who is domiciled in Anguilla and whose father or mother became a citizen of the United Kingdom and Colonies by virtue of naturalisation or registration in Anguilla; or

(c) a citizen of the United Kingdom and Colonies by virtue of having been naturalised or registered as such in Anguilla; or

(d) a Commonwealth citizen who is domiciled in Anguilla and has been ordinarily resident in Anguilla for not less than seven years; or

(e) the spouse, widow or widower of such a person referred to in any of the preceding paragraphs of this subsection, and, in the case of a spouse, is not living apart from the other spouse under a decree of a competent court or a deed of separation; or

(f) under the age of eighteen years and is the child, stepchild, or child adopted in a manner recognised by law, of such a person as is referred to in any of the preceding paragraphs of this subsection.

Chapter II

The Commissioner

19.—(1) For the purpose of administering the Government of Anguilla, the Commissioner shall have such powers and duties as are conferred or imposed on him by this Constitution or any other law and such other powers as Her Majesty may from time to time be pleased to assign to him. The Commissioner.

(2) Subject to the provisions of this Constitution and of any other law by which any such powers or duties are conferred or imposed upon him, the Commissioner shall do and execute all things that belong to his office according to such Instructions, if any, as Her Majesty may from time to time see fit to give him; but no court shall enquire whether or not he has complied with any such Instructions.

(3) A person appointed to the office of Commissioner shall, before entering upon the functions of that office, make oaths of allegiance and for the due execution of that office in the forms set out in the Schedule to this Constitution.

20.—(1) Whenever the Commissioner— Commissioner's Deputy.

(*a*) has occasion to be absent from Anguilla for a period which he has reason to believe will be of short duration; or

(*b*) is suffering from illness which he has reason to believe will be of short duration,

he may, by writing under his hand, appoint the Chief Secretary, or, in the absence of the Chief Secretary, the Attorney-General or, in the absence of the Attorney-General, such other suitable person in Anguilla to be his deputy during such absence or illness and in that capacity to perform on his behalf such of the functions of the office of Commissioner as may be specified in the instrument by which he is appointed.

(2) The powers and authority of the Commissioner shall not be abridged, altered or in any way affected by the appointment of a deputy under this section, and a deputy shall conform to and observe all instructions that the Commissioner, acting in his discretion, may from time to time address to him; but no court shall enquire whether or not he has complied with any such instructions.

(3) A person appointed as a deputy under this section shall hold that appointment for such period as may be specified in the writing by which he is appointed, and his appointment may be revoked at any time by Her Majesty by instructions given through a Secretary of State, or by the Commissioner, acting in his discretion.

Chapter III

The Executive

Executive
Authority
for
Anguilla.

21.—(1) The executive authority of Anguilla shall be vested in Her Majesty.

(2) Subject to the provisions of this Constitution, the executive authority of Anguilla may be exercised on behalf of Her Majesty by the Commissioner either directly or through officers subordinate to him, but nothing in this subsection shall operate so as to prejudice the provisions of any laws for the time being in force in Anguilla whereby functions are, or may be, conferred on persons or authorities other than the Commissioner.

Executive
Council.

22. There shall be an Executive Council in and for Anguilla which shall consist of the Chief Minister, two other Ministers and two ex-officio members, namely, the Attorney-General and the Financial Secretary.

Appoint-
ment of
Ministers.

23.—(1) The Commissioner, acting in his discretion, shall appoint as the Chief Minister the elected member of the Assembly who, in his judgment, is best able to command the support of a majority of the elected members of the Assembly.

(2) The other Ministers shall be appointed by the Commissioner in accordance with the advice of the Chief Minister from among the elected members of the Assembly.

(3) If occasion arises for making an appointment of any Minister between a dissolution of the Assembly and the polling in the next following general election a person who was an elected member of the Assembly immediately before the dissolution may be appointed as if he were still a member of the Assembly.

(4) Appointments made under this section shall be made by instrument under the public seal.

Tenure of
Office of
members.

24.—(1) If a motion that the Assembly should declare a lack of confidence in the Government of Anguilla receives in the Assembly the affirmative votes of two-thirds of all the elected members thereof the Commissioner shall, by instrument under the public seal, revoke the appointment of the Chief Minister:

Provided that before so revoking the Chief Minister's appointment the Commissioner shall consult with the Chief Minister and, if the Chief Minister so requests, the Commissioner, acting in his discretion, may dissolve the Assembly instead of revoking the appointment.

(2) The Chief Minister shall vacate his office if, after the polling in a general election and before the Assembly first meets thereafter, the Commissioner, acting in his discretion, informs him that he is about to appoint another person as the Chief Minister.

(3) Any Minister shall vacate his office if—

(*a*) he ceases to be a member of the Assembly for any reason other than a dissolution;

(*b*) he is not an elected member of the Assembly when it first meets after a general election;

(c) he is required under the provisions of section 38 of this Constitution to cease to perform his functions as a member of the Assembly;

(d) he resigns it by writing under his hand addressed to the Commissioner; or

(e) if he is absent from Anguilla without having given the Commissioner prior notice of such absence.

(4) A Minister other than the Chief Minister shall also vacate his office if—

(a) the Chief Minister vacates his office; or

(b) his appointment is revoked by the Commissioner acting in accordance with the advice of the Chief Minister, by instrument under the public seal.

25.—(1) If the Chief Minister is unable, by reason of his illness or absence from Anguilla, to perform the functions of his office, the Commissioner may, by instrument under the public seal, authorise any other Minister to perform the functions conferred on the Chief Minister by this Constitution (other than the functions conferred upon him by subsection (3) of this section). *Performance of functions of Chief Minister in certain events.*

(2) The Commissioner may, by instrument under the public seal, revoke any authority given under this section.

(3) The powers conferred upon the Commissioner by this section shall be exercised by him acting in his discretion if, in his judgment, it is impracticable to obtain the Chief Minister's advice owing to his illness or absence, and in any other case shall be exercised in accordance with the advice of the Chief Minister.

26.—(1) The Commissioner, acting in accordance with the advice of the Chief Minister, may, by directions in writing, assign to any Minister responsibility for the conduct (subject to the provisions of this Constitution and of any other law) of any business of the Government of Anguilla including responsibility for the administration of any department of government: *Assignment of responsibilities to Ministers.*

Provided that a Minister shall not be charged with responsibility under this section for any of the matters mentioned in subsection (2) (a) and (b) of the next following section, nor for the matter of finance, responsibility for which shall always be assigned to the Financial Secretary.

(2) The Commissioner, acting in his discretion, may at any time call for any official papers or seek any official information or advice available to a Minister with respect to a matter for which that Minister is responsible under this section.

27.—(1) Subject to the provisions of this section and the next following section, the Commissioner shall consult with the Executive Council in the formulation of policy and in the exercise of all powers conferred upon him by this Constitution or by any other law for the time being in force in Anguilla and act in accordance with the advice of the Council. *Commissioner to consult Council.*

(2) The Commissioner shall not be obliged to consult with nor act upon the advice of the Executive Council with respect to the following—

(a) any matter that in his opinion relates to defence, external affairs or internal security, including the police;

(*b*) the appointment (including the appointment on promotion or transfer, appointment on contract and appointment to act in an office) of any person to any public office, the suspension, termination of employment, dismissal, or retirement of any public officer or taking of disciplinary action in respect of such an officer, the application to any public officer of the terms or conditions of employment of the public service (including salary scales, allowances, leave, passages or pensions) for which financial provision has been made, or the organisation of the public service to the extent that it does not involve new financial provision;

(*c*) any power conferred upon him by this Constitution which he is empowered to exercise in his discretion or in pursuance of instructions given to him by Her Majesty;

(*d*) any power conferred by any law other than this Constitution which he is empowered or directed, either expressly or by necessary implication, by that or any other law to exercise without consulting the Council;

(*e*) any matter in which, in his judgment, the service of Her Majesty would sustain material prejudice thereby;

(*f*) where the matter to be decided is in his judgment too unimportant to require the advice of the Council; or

(*g*) where the urgency of the matter requires him to act before the Council can be consulted:

Provided that in exercising his powers in relation to—

(i) the matters referred to in (*a*) hereof the Commissioner shall keep the Council informed of any matters that in his judgment may involve the economic or financial interests of Anguilla;

(ii) the matters referred to in (*g*) hereof the Commissioner shall as soon as practicable communicate to the Council the measures which he has adopted and the reasons for those measures.

(3) The question whether the Commissioner has exercised any power after consultation with or in accordance with the advice of the Executive Council shall not be inquired into by any court.

Commissioner's reserved executive power.

28.—(1) In any case where the Commissioner is required by the last foregoing section to consult with the Executive Council, he may act otherwise than in accordance with the advice given him by the Council if in his opinion it would be inexpedient in the interests of public order, public faith or good government to act in accordance with that advice:

Provided that he shall not so act against the advice of the Council without first obtaining the approval of a Secretary of State, unless in his judgment the matter is so urgent that it is necessary for him to act before obtaining such approval, in which case he shall forthwith report his action to a Secretary of State with the reasons therefor.

(2) Whenever the Commissioner acts otherwise than in accordance with the advice given to him by the Executive Council, any member of the Council may require that there be recorded in the minutes the grounds of any advice or opinion which he may have given on the question, and the Commissioner shall as soon as is practicable forward a copy of the resulting entry in the minutes to a Secretary of State.

29. Every member of the Executive Council shall, before entering upon the duties of his office as a member, make before the Commissioner an oath or affirmation of allegiance in the form set out in the Schedule to this Constitution and an oath or affirmation for the due execution of that office in such form as may be prescribed by any law in force in Anguilla or, if no law in that behalf is for the time being in force, in the form set out in the Schedule to this Constitution. *Oaths to be taken by members.*

30. The Commissioner may summon any public officer to a meeting of the Executive Council whenever, in his opinion, the business before the Council renders the presence of that officer desirable. *Summoning of persons to the Council.*

31.—(1) The Executive Council shall not be summoned except by the authority of the Commissioner, acting in his discretion: *Summoning of Council and transaction of business.*

Provided that the Commissioner shall summon the Council if not less than two elected members of the Council so request in writing.

(2) No business shall be transacted at any meeting of the Executive Council unless there are four members present besides the Commissioner or other person presiding.

(3) Subject to the provisions of the last foregoing subsection, the Executive Council shall not be disqualified for the transaction of business by reason of any vacancy in the membership of the Council (including any vacancy not filled when the Council is first constituted or is reconstituted at any time) and the validity of the transaction of business in the Council shall not be affected by reason only of the fact that some person who was not entitled to do so took part therein.

32.—(1) The Commissioner shall, so far as is practicable, attend and preside at meetings of the Executive Council. *Proceedings in the Executive Council.*

(2) In the absence of the Commissioner there shall preside at any meeting of the Executive Council such member of the Council as the Commissioner, acting in his discretion, may appoint.

(3) No business shall be transacted at any meeting of the Executive Council if there are less than two elected members present besides the Commissioner or other person presiding.

(4) Subject to the last foregoing subsection, the Executive Council shall not be disqualified for the transaction of business by reason of any vacancy in the membership of the Council (including any vacancy not filled when the Council is first constituted or is reconstituted at any time) and the validity of the transaction of business in the Council shall not be affected by reason only of the fact that some person who was not entitled so to do took part in the proceedings.

(5) The Chief Secretary shall be the Secretary of the Executive Council, but if at any time he cannot conveniently discharge the functions of Secretary of the Council, those functions shall be discharged by such public officer as may be designated in that behalf by the Commissioner, acting in his discretion.

33.—(1) The Attorney-General shall have power, in any case in which he considers it desirable so to do— *Attorney-General.*

    (*a*) to institute and undertake criminal proceedings against any person before any civil court in respect of any offence against any law in force in Anguilla;

(*b*) to take over and continue any such criminal proceedings that have been instituted by any other person or authority; and

(*c*) to discontinue at any stage before judgment is delivered any criminal proceedings instituted or undertaken by himself or any other person or authority.

(2) The powers of the Attorney-General under the last foregoing subsection may be exercised by him in person or by officers subordinate to him acting under and in accordance with his general or special instructions.

(3) The powers conferred upon the Attorney-General by paragraphs (*b*) and (*c*) of subsection (1) of this section shall be vested in him to the exclusion of any other person or authority:

Provided that where any other person or authority has instituted criminal proceedings, nothing in this subsection shall prevent the withdrawal of those proceedings by or at the instance of that person or authority at any stage before the person against whom the proceedings have been instituted has been charged before the court.

(4) For the purposes of this section, any appeal from any determination in any criminal proceedings before any court, or any case stated or question of law reserved for the purpose of any such proceedings, to any other court or to Her Majesty in Council shall be deemed to be part of those proceedings.

Chapter IV

The Legislative Assembly

34.—(1) There shall be a Legislative Assembly for Anguilla.

(2) Subject to the provisions of this Constitution, the Assembly shall consist of—

    (*a*) the Commissioner, or at any time when there is a person holding the office of Speaker, the Speaker;

    (*b*) three ex-officio members, namely the Chief Secretary, the Financial Secretary and the Attorney-General;

    (*c*) not less than seven elected members, who shall be persons qualified for election in accordance with the provisions of this Constitution and elected in the manner provided by any law in force in Anguilla; and

    (*d*) two nominated members, who shall be persons who belong to Anguilla for the purposes of Chapter I of this Constitution of the age of twenty-one years or upwards and shall be appointed by the Commissioner, one on the advice of the Chief Minister and the other after consultation with the Chief Minister, by instrument under the public seal.

(margin: Legislative Assembly.)

35. Subject to the provisions of the next following section, a person shall be qualified to be elected as a member of the Assembly if, and shall not be qualified to be so elected unless, he is a British subject of twenty-one years or upwards and either—

    (*a*) was born in Anguilla and is domiciled there at the date of his nomination for election; or

    (*b*) has resided in Anguilla for a period of not less than three years immediately before the date of his nomination for election and is domiciled there at that date and is the son or daughter of parents at least one of whom was born in Anguilla.

(margin: Qualifications for elected membership.)

36.—(1) No person shall be qualified to be nominated or elected as a member of the Assembly who—

    (*a*) is, by virtue of his own act, under any acknowledgement of allegiance, obedience or adherence to a foreign power or state;

    (*b*) is a minister of religion;

    (*c*) holds or is acting in any office of emolument in the service of the Crown;

    (*d*) is an undischarged bankrupt, having been adjudged or otherwise declared bankrupt under any law in force in any part of the Commonwealth;

    (*e*) is a person certified to be insane or otherwise adjudged to be of unsound mind under any law in force in Anguilla;

    (*f*) is under sentence of death imposed on him by a court in any part of the Commonwealth or is under a sentence of imprisonment (by whatever name called) exceeding twelve months imposed on him by such a court or substituted by competent authority for some other sentence imposed on him by such a court; or

    (*g*) is disqualified for membership of the Assembly by any law in force in Anguilla relating to offences connected with elections.

(margin: Disqualifications for nominated or elected membership.)

(2) In this section " minister of religion " means any person in holy orders and any other person the functions of whose principal occupation include teaching or preaching in any congregation for religious worship.

(3) For the purposes of paragraph (*f*) of subsection (1) of this section—

(*a*) two or more terms of imprisonment that are required to be served consecutively shall be regarded as a single term of imprisonment for the aggregate period of those terms; and

(*b*) no account shall be taken of a sentence of imprisonment imposed as an alternative to, or in default of the payment of, a fine.

(4) Paragraph (*c*) of subsection (1) of this section shall not be construed as precluding a member of the Assembly from receiving emoluments in respect of his services as such a member.

Tenure of office of members of Assembly.

37. The seat of a nominated or elected member of the Assembly shall become vacant—

(*a*) upon a dissolution of the Assembly;

(*b*) if, without prior notice to the Commissioner, he is absent from three consecutive meetings of the Assembly;

(*c*) if he ceases to be a British subject;

(*d*) if he ceases to be resident in Anguilla;

(*e*) if he resigns his seat by writing under his hand addressed to the Commissioner;

(*f*) if any of the circumstances arise that, if he were not a member of the Assembly, would cause him to be disqualified for election thereto by virtue of paragraph (*a*), (*b*), (*c*), (*d*), (*e*), or (*g*) of subsection (1) of the last foregoing section; or

(*g*) in the circumstances specified in the next following section.

Vacation of seat on sentence.

38.—(1) Subject to the provisions of this section, if a nominated or elected member of the Assembly is sentenced by a court in any part of the Commonwealth to death or to imprisonment (by whatever name called) for a term exceeding twelve months, he shall forthwith cease to perform his functions as a member of the Assembly, and his seat in the Assembly shall become vacant at the expiration of a period of thirty days thereafter:

Provided that the Commissioner may, at the request of the member, from time to time extend that period for thirty days to enable the member to pursue any appeal in respect of his conviction or sentence, so however that extensions of time exceeding in the aggregate three hundred and thirty days shall not be given without the approval of the Assembly signified by resolution.

(2) If at any time before the member vacates his seat he is granted a free pardon or his conviction is set aside or his sentence is reduced to a term of imprisonment of less than twelve months or a punishment other than imprisonment is substituted, his seat in the Assembly shall not become vacant under the provisions of the last foregoing subsection and he may again perform his functions as a member of the Assembly.

(3) For the purposes of this section—

(*a*) where a person is sentenced to two or more terms of imprisonment that are required to be served consecutively account shall be taken only of any of those terms that exceeds twelve months; and

(b) no account shall be taken of a sentence of imprisonment imposed as an alternative to or in default of the payment of a fine.

39.—(1) Whenever an ex-officio member of the Assembly is by reason of his illness or absence from Anguilla or for any other reason incapable of performing the functions of his office, the Commissioner acting in his discretion may, by instrument under the public seal, appoint any public officer to be temporarily a member of the Assembly in his place.

(2) A person appointed under this section to be temporarily a member of the Assembly—

(a) shall hold his seat in the Assembly during Her Majesty's pleasure; and

(b) shall vacate his seat when he is informed by the Commissioner that the member on account of whose incapacity he was appointed is again able to perform his functions as a member of the Assembly.

(3) The Commissioner shall forthwith report to Her Majesty through a Secretary of State any appointment made under this section.

(4) Subject to the provisions of this section the provisions of this Constitution shall apply to a person appointed to be temporarily a member of the Assembly as they apply to the member on account of whose incapacity he was appointed.

Temporary members of Assembly.

40.—(1) Any question whether a person has been validly appointed as a nominated or a temporary member of the Assembly, or whether a nominated or a temporary member of the Assembly has vacated his seat therein, shall be determined by the Commissioner acting in his discretion.

(2) Any question whether a person has been validly elected as a member of the Assembly, or whether an elected member of the Assembly has vacated his seat therein, shall be determined by the High Court, whose decision shall be final and not subject to any appeal.

(3) (a) An application to the High Court for the determination of any question whether a person has been validly elected as a member of the Assembly may be made by—

(i) a person who voted or had the right to vote at the election to which the application relates;

(ii) a person claiming to have had the right to be returned at such election;

(iii) a person alleging himself to have been a candidate at such election; or

(iv) the Attorney-General.

(b) An application to the High Court for the determination of any question whether an elected member of the Assembly has vacated his seat therein may be made by—

(i) any elected member of the Assembly; or

(ii) the Attorney-General.

Determination of questions as to membership of Assembly.

(c) If any application referred to in paragraph (a) or (b) of this subsection is made by a person other than the Attorney-General, the Attorney-General may intervene and may then appear or be represented in the proceedings.

Penalty for sitting or voting in Assembly when un-qualified.

41.—(1) Any person who sits or votes in the Assembly knowing or having reasonable grounds for knowing that he is not entitled to do so shall be liable to a penalty not exceeding EC$100·00 for each day upon which he sits or votes.

(2) Any such penalty shall be recoverable by civil action in the High Court at the suit of the Commissioner.

Qualification of voters.

42.—(1) Subject to the next following subsection a person shall be qualified to be registered as a voter in an electoral district if he is of the age of eighteen years and upwards and—

(a) is a citizen of the United Kingdom and Colonies born in Anguilla, and is domiciled there at the qualifying date; or

(b) (i) is a citizen of the United Kingdom and Colonies or a Commonwealth citizen who has resided in Anguilla for a period of not less than twelve months immediately before the qualifying date, and is domiciled there at that date, and is the lawful spouse, widow or widower, or the son or daughter or the spouse of such son or daughter of a person who was born in Anguilla; or

(ii) is a Commonwealth citizen domiciled in Anguilla and has resided there for a period of at least five years immediately before the qualifying date; and

(c) is at the qualifying date resident in the electoral district in which he claims to be registered.

(2) Every person who is qualified to be registered as a voter in any electoral district shall be entitled to be so registered provided that a person shall not be registered as a voter in more than one electoral district.

Disqualification of voters.

43.—(1) No person shall be qualified to be registered as a voter who—

(a) is under sentence of death imposed on him by a court in any part of the Commonwealth, or is under a sentence of imprisonment (by whatever name called) exceeding twelve months imposed on him by such a court or substituted by competent authority for some other sentence imposed on him by such a court;

(b) is a person certified to be insane or otherwise adjudged to be of unsound mind under any law in force in Anguilla; or

(c) is disqualified for registration as a voter by any law in force in Anguilla relating to offences connected with elections.

(2) For the purposes of paragraph (a) of the preceding subsection—

(a) two or more terms of imprisonment that are required to be served consecutively shall be regarded as a single term of imprisonment for the aggregate period of those terms; and

(b) no account shall be taken of a sentence of imprisonment imposed as an alternative to, or in default of the payment of, a fine.

44.—(1) Any person who is registered as a voter in an electoral Right to district shall, while so registered, be entitled to vote at any election vote at election for that district unless he is prohibited from so voting by any law in elections. force in Anguilla—

(*a*) because he is a returning officer; or

(*b*) because he has been concerned in any offence connected with elections.

(2) No person shall vote at any election for any electoral district who—

(*a*) is not registered as a voter in that district;

(*b*) has voted in another electoral district at the same election;

(*c*) is in lawful custody; or

(*d*) is for any other reason unable to attend to vote in person (except in so far as it may be provided by law that persons unable so to attend may vote).

45.—Subject to the provisions of this Constitution, the Legislature Law as to may provide for the election of members of the Assembly, including election. (without prejudice to the generality of the foregoing power) the following matters, that is to say—

(*a*) the qualifications and disqualifications of voters;

(*b*) the registration of voters;

(*c*) the ascertainment of the qualification of voters and of candidates for election;

(*d*) the division of Anguilla into electoral districts for the purpose of elections;

(*e*) the holding of elections;

(*f*) the determination of any question whether any person has been validly elected a member of the Assembly or whether the seat of any elected member in the Assembly has become vacant;

(*g*) the definition and trial of offences connected with elections and the imposition of penalties therefor, including the disqualification for membership of the Assembly, or for registration as a voter or for voting at elections, of any person concerned in any such offence; and

(*h*) the disqualification for election as members of the Assembly of persons holding or acting in any office the functions of which involve any responsibility for, or in connection with, the conduct of any election or the compilation or revision of any electoral register.

CHAPTER V

Powers and Procedure in Legislative Assembly

Power to make laws.

46. Subject to the provisions of this Constitution, the Commissioner, with the advice and consent of the Assembly may make laws for the peace, order and good government of Anguilla.

Royal Instructions.

47. Subject to the provisions of this Constitution, the Commissioner and the Assembly shall, in the transaction of business and the making of laws, conform as nearly as may be to the directions contained in any Instructions under Her Majesty's Sign Manual and Signet which may from time to time be addressed to the Commissioner in that behalf.

Rules of procedure.

48. Subject to the provisions of this Constitution and of any Instructions under Her Majesty's Sign Manual and Signet, the Assembly may from time to time make, amend and revoke rules of procedure for the regulation and orderly conduct of its own proceedings and the despatch of business, and for the passing, intituling and numbering of Bills for the presentation thereof to the Commissioner for assent; but no such rules of procedure or amendment or revocation thereof shall have effect until the Commissioner shall by writing under his hand approve the same.

Presiding in Assembly.

49.—(1) At sittings of the Assembly there shall preside—

(*a*) the Commissioner; or

(*b*) at any time when there is a person holding the office of Speaker, the Speaker; or

(*c*) in the absence of the Commissioner or, as the case may be, of the Speaker, the senior ex-officio member of the Assembly.

(2) The Commissioner, acting in his discretion, may appoint a Speaker of the Assembly, who shall be a person, whether or not a member of the Assembly, who is qualified and not disqualified to be a member of the Assembly:

Provided that this subsection shall not come into force until the Assembly has passed a resolution that there shall be an office of Speaker.

Assembly may transact business notwithstanding vacancies.

50. The Assembly shall not be disqualified for the transaction of business by reason of any vacancy in the membership thereof (including any vacancy not filled when the Assembly is first constituted or is reconstituted at any time) and any proceedings therein shall be valid notwithstanding that some person who was not entitled to do so sat or voted in the Assembly or otherwise took part in those proceedings.

Quorum.

51.—(1) If at any sitting of the Assembly a quorum is not present and any member of the Assembly who is present objects on that account to the transaction of business and, after such interval as may be prescribed in the rules of procedure of the Assembly, the person presiding at the sitting ascertains that a quorum is still not present, he shall adjourn the Assembly.

(2) For the purposes of this section a quorum shall consist of two-thirds of the members of the Assembly in addition to the person presiding.

52.—(1) Save as otherwise provided in this Constitution, all questions proposed for decision in the Assembly shall be determined by a majority of votes of the members present and voting.

(2) The Commissioner or other member presiding shall not vote unless on any question the votes are equally divided, in which case he shall have and exercise a casting vote.

53.—(1) The Commissioner or other person presiding may, when in his opinion the business before the Assembly makes it desirable, summon any person to a meeting of the Assembly notwithstanding that that person is not a member of the Assembly.

(2) Any person so summoned shall be entitled to take part as if he was a member in the proceedings of the Assembly relating to the matter in respect of which he was summoned, except that he may not vote.

54.—(1) Subject to the provisions of this Constitution and of the rules of procedure of the Assembly, any member may introduce any Bill or propose any motion for debate in, or may present any petition to, the Assembly, and the same shall be debated and disposed of according to the rules of procedure of the Assembly.

(2) Except on the recommendation of the Commissioner, the Assembly shall not—

(*a*) proceed upon any Bill (including any amendment to a Bill) which in the opinion of the person presiding in the Assembly, makes provision for imposing or increasing any tax, for imposing or increasing any charge on the revenues or other funds of Anguilla or for altering any such charge otherwise than by reducing it or for compounding or remitting any debt due to Anguilla;

(*b*) proceed upon any motion (including any amendment to a motion) the effect of which, in the opinion of the person presiding in the Assembly, is that provision would be made for any of the purposes aforesaid; or

(*c*) receive any petition which, in the opinion of the person presiding in the Assembly, requests that provision be made for any of the purposes aforesaid.

55.—(1) If the Commissioner considers that it is expedient—

(*a*) in the interests of public order, public faith or good government (which expressions shall, without prejudice to their generality, include the responsibility of Anguilla as a territory within the Commonwealth and all matters pertaining to the creation or abolition of any public office or to the salary or other conditions of service of any public officer); or

(*b*) in order to secure detailed control of the finances of Anguilla during such time as, by virtue of the receipt of financial assistance by Anguilla from Her Majesty's Exchequer in the United Kingdom for the purpose of balancing the annual budget or otherwise, such control rests with Her Majesty's Government,

that any Bill introduced or motion proposed, in the Assembly relating to the matters referred to in subsection (1) hereof should have effect, then, if the Assembly fail to pass the Bill or to carry the motion within such time and in such form as the Commissioner thinks reasonable and expedient, the Commissioner, acting in his discretion, may, at any time that he thinks fit, and notwithstanding any provision of this Constitution or of any other law in force in Anguilla or of any rules of procedure of the Assembly declare that the Bill or motion shall have effect as if it had been passed or carried by the Assembly either in the form in which it was introduced or proposed or with such amendments as the Commissioner thinks fit which have been moved or proposed in the Assembly or any Committee thereof; and the Bill or the motion shall be deemed thereupon to have been so passed or carried, and the provisions of this Constitution, and in particular the provisions relating to assent to Bills and disallowance of laws, shall have effect accordingly:

Provided that the Commissioner shall not exercise his powers under this subsection without prior written instructions from a Secretary of State, unless in his judgment the matter is so urgent that it is necessary for him to do so before having consulted a Secretary of State.

(2) The Commissioner shall forthwith report to a Secretary of State every case in which he makes any such declaration and the reasons therefor.

(3) If any member of the Assembly objects to any declaration made under this section, he may, within fourteen days of the making thereof, submit to the Commissioner a statement in writing of his reasons for so objecting, and a copy of the statement shall (if furnished by the member) be forwarded by the Commissioner as soon as is practicable to a Secretary of State.

(4) Any declaration made under this section other than a declaration relating to a Bill may be revoked by a Secretary of State and the Commissioner shall forthwith cause notice of the revocation to be published by notice in the Official Gazette; and from the date of such publication any motion that is deemed to have been carried by virtue of the declaration shall cease to have effect and the provisions of sub-section (2) of section 38 of the Interpretation Act 1889(a) shall apply to the revocation as they apply to the repeal of an Act of Parliament.

Assent to Bills.

56.—(1) A Bill shall not become a law until—

(a) the Commissioner has assented to it in Her Majesty's name and on Her Majesty's behalf and has signed it in token of his assent; or

(b) Her Majesty has given Her assent to it through a Secretary of State and the Commissioner has signified Her assent by Proclamation.

(2) When a Bill is presented to the Commissioner for his assent, he shall, subject to the provisions of this Constitution and of any Instructions addressed to him under Her Majesty's Sign Manual and Signet or through a Secretary of State, declare that he assents to it, or that he reserves the Bill for the signification of Her Majesty's pleasure:

Provided that the Commissioner shall reserve for the signification of Her Majesty's pleasure—

(a) any Bill which appears to him to be in any way repugnant to, or inconsistent with, the provisions of this Constitution; and

(b) any Bill which determines or regulates the privileges, immunities or powers of the Assembly or of its members,

unless he has been authorised by a Secretary of State to assent to it.

(a) 1889 c. 63.

(3) This section shall have effect in relation to any Bill passed by the Anguilla Council subsisting immediately before the appointed day but not assented to before that day as it has effect in relation to Bills passed after the appointed day.

57. The Commissioner may return to the Assembly any Bill presented to him for assent, transmitting therewith any amendment which he may recommend, and the Assembly shall deal with such recommendation. Return of Bills by Commissioner.

58.—(1) Any law to which the Commissioner has given his assent may be disallowed by Her Majesty through a Secretary of State. Disallowance of laws.

(2) Whenever a law has been disallowed by Her Majesty the Commissioner shall, as soon as practicable, cause notice of the disallowance to be published in the Official Gazette and the law shall be annulled with effect from the date of the publication of that notice.

(3) The provisions of subsection (2) of section 38 of the Interpretation Act 1889, shall apply to the annulment of any law under this section as they apply to the repeal of an Act of Parliament, save that any enactment repealed or amended by or in pursuance of that law shall have effect as from the date of the annulment as if that law had not been made.

59. Except for the purpose of enabling this section to be complied with, no ex-officio, nominated or elected member of the Assembly shall be permitted to take part in its proceedings until he has made before the Commissioner, or some other person authorised in that behalf by the Commissioner, acting in his discretion, an oath of allegiance in the form set out in the Schedule to this Constitution. Oath of allegiance.

60. A law enacted under this Constitution may determine and regulate the privileges, immunities and powers of the Assembly and its members, but no such privileges, immunities or powers shall exceed those of the Commons' House of Parliament of the United Kingdom or of the members thereof. Privileges of Assembly and members.

61.—(1) Subject to the provisions of this Constitution, the sessions of the Assembly shall be held at such places and begin at such times as the Commissioner may from time to time by Proclamation appoint. Sessions.

(2) The first session of the Assembly shall begin within twelve months after the appointed day; and thereafter there shall be at least one session of the Assembly in every year, so however that there shall be an interval of less than twelve months between the last sitting in one session and the first sitting in the next session.

62.—(1) The Commissioner, acting in accordance with the advice of the Chief Minister, may at any time, by Proclamation published in the Official Gazette, prorogue the Assembly. Prorogation and dissolution.

(2) The Commissioner, acting after consultation with the Chief Minister, may at any time, by Proclamation published in the Official Gazette, dissolve the Assembly.

(3) The Commissioner shall dissolve the Assembly at the expiration of four years from the date when the Assembly first meets after any general election unless it has been sooner dissolved.

63. There shall be a general election at such time within two months after every dissolution of the Assembly as the Commissioner shall by Proclamation appoint. General elections.

Chapter VI

THE PUBLIC SERVICE

Public Service—General

Public
Service
Commission.

64.—(1) There shall be in and for Anguilla a Public Service Commission which shall consist of five members of whom three shall be appointed by the Commissioner, acting in his discretion, and two shall be appointed by the Commissioner, acting after consultation with the public service staff associations.

(2) The Commissioner, acting after consultation with the Chief Minister, shall appoint one of the members of the Public Service Commission to be Chairman of the Commission.

(3) No person shall be qualified to be appointed as a member of the Public Service Commission if he is a member of, or a candidate for election to the Assembly, or holds or is acting in any public office.

(4) The office of a member of the Public Service Commission shall become vacant—

(a) at the expiration of three years from the date of his appointment or such earlier time as may be specified in the instrument by which he was appointed;

(b) if he resigns his office by writing under his hand addressed to the Commissioner;

(c) if he becomes a member of, or a candidate for election to, the Assembly or is appointed to or to act in any public office; or

(d) if the Commissioner, acting in his discretion, directs that he shall be removed from office for inability to discharge the functions thereof (whether arising from infirmity of body or mind or any other cause) or for misbehaviour.

(5) If the office of a member of the Public Service Commission is vacant or a member is for any reason unable to perform the functions of his office, the Commissioner acting in the manner prescribed by subsection (1) of this section for the appointment of that member may appoint a person who is qualified for appointment as a member of the Commission to act as a member of the Commission, and any person so appointed shall, subject to the provisions of the preceding subsection, continue so to act until he is notified by the Commissioner acting in his discretion, that the circumstances giving rise to the appointment have ceased to exist:

Provided that, in the case of a vacancy in the office of the Chairman or the inability of the holder thereof to perform his functions, the functions of the office of Chairman shall be performed by such member of the Commission or person acting as a member as the Commissioner, acting after consultation with the Chief Minister, may designate.

(6) There shall be charged on the revenues of Anguilla and paid thereout to the members of the Public Service Commission such emoluments as may be prescribed by any law for the time being in force in Anguilla:

Provided that the emoluments of a member of the Commission shall not be reduced during his continuance in office.

65.—(1) Power to make appointments to public offices and to remove and to exercise disciplinary control over persons holding or acting in such offices shall vest in the Commissioner, acting in his discretion in relation to the offices of Chief Secretary, Attorney-General and Financial Secretary and in relation to all other offices acting after consultation with the Public Service Commission.

Power to appoint, etc., to public offices.

(2) The Commissioner, acting after consultation with the Public Service Commission, may, by regulations published in the Official Gazette, delegate to any member of the Commission or any public officer or class of public officer, to such extent and subject to such conditions as may be prescribed in the regulations, any of the powers vested in him by the last foregoing subsection.

(3) The provisions of subsection (1) of this section shall not apply to—

(a) any office to which section 67 of this Constitution applies; or

(b) any office in the Police Force below the rank of Assistant Superintendent to the extent that the Chief of Police or some other officer of the Police Force is empowered by any law for the time being in force in Anguilla to exercise the powers mentioned in that subsection.

66. There shall be for Anguilla a Judicial Service Commission which shall consist of—

Judicial Service Commission.

(a) the Chief Justice, who shall be Chairman;

(b) another judge of the Court of Appeal or the High Court nominated by the Chief Justice after consultation with the Commissioner; and

(c) the Chairman of the Public Service Commission.

67.—(1) Power to make appointments to the offices to which this section applies and to remove and exercise disciplinary control over persons holding or acting in such offices shall vest in the Commissioner, acting after consultation with the Judicial Service Commission.

Power to appoint, etc., to judicial offices.

(2) This section applies to the office of Magistrate, to any office in the public service of any registrar or other officer of the High Court who is required to possess legal qualifications and to such other offices in the public service, for appointment to which persons are required to possess legal qualifications, as may be prescribed by any law for the time being in force in Anguilla.

Pensions

68.—(1) Subject to the provisions of section 70 of this Constitution, the law applicable to the grant and payment to any officer, or to his widow, children, dependants or personal representatives, of any pension gratuity or other like allowance (in this section and the two next following sections referred to as an " award ") in respect of the service of that officer in a public office shall be that in force on the relevant day or any later law not less favourable to the person concerned.

Applicability of pensions law.

(2) For the purposes of this section the relevant day is—

(a) in relation to an award granted before the appointed day, the day on which the award was granted;

(b) in relation to an award granted or to be granted on or after the appointed day to or in respect of a person who was a public officer before that day, the day immediately before that day;

(c) in relation to an award granted or to be granted to or in respect of a person who first becomes a public officer on or after the appointed day, the day on which he becomes a public officer.

(3) For the purposes of this section, in so far as the law applicable to an award depends on the option of the person to or in respect of whom it is granted or to be granted, the law for which he opts shall be taken to be more favourable to him than any other law for which he might have opted.

Pensions, etc., charged on revenues of Anguilla.

69. Awards granted under any law for the time being in force in Anguilla shall be charged on and paid out of the revenues of Anguilla.

Grant and withholding of pensions, etc.

70.—(1) The power to grant any award under any pensions law in force in Anguilla (other than an award to which, under that law, the person to whom it is payable is entitled as of right) and, in accordance with any provisions in that behalf contained in any such law, to withhold, reduce in amount or suspend any award payable under any such law is hereby vested in the Commissioner acting in his discretion.

(2) In this section "pensions law" means any law relating to the grant to any person, or to the widow, children, dependants or personal representatives of that person, of an award in respect of the services of that person in a public office, and includes any instrument made under any such law.

Chapter VII

Miscellaneous

71.—(1) In the following cases, an appeal shall lie from decisions of the High Court to the Court of Appeal and thence to Her Majesty in Council as of right, that is to say— Appeals to Her Majesty in Council.

(*a*) final decisions, in any civil or criminal proceedings, on questions as to the interpretation of this Constitution;

(*b*) final decisions in any civil proceedings where the matter in dispute on the appeal is of the value of EC$2,500 or upwards or where the appeal involves, directly or indirectly, a claim to or a question respecting property or a right of the value of EC$2,500 or upwards;

(*c*) final decisions in proceedings under section 16 of this Constitution;

(*d*) final decisions in proceedings for dissolution or nullity of marriage; and

(*e*) in such other cases as may be prescribed by the Legislature.

(2) In the following cases, an appeal shall lie from decisions of the High Court to the Court of Appeal with the leave of the High Court or of the Court of Appeal and thence to Her Majesty in Council with the leave of the Court of Appeal, that is to say—

(*a*) where the decision appealed against is a final decision in civil proceedings and, in the opinion of the court giving leave, the question involved in the appeal is one that, by reason of its great general or public importance or otherwise, ought to be submitted to the Court of Appeal or to Her Majesty in Council, as the case may be; and

(*b*) in such other cases as may be prescribed by the Legislature.

(3) The foregoing provisions of this section shall be subject to the provisions of section 40(2) of this Constitution.

(4) In this section the references to final decisions of a court do not include any determination thereof that any application made thereto is merely frivolous or vexatious.

(5) Nothing in this section shall affect any right of Her Majesty to grant special leave to appeal to Her Majesty in Council from the decision of any court in any civil or criminal matter.

72.—(1) In this Constitution unless it is otherwise provided or required by the context— Interpretation.

" appointed day " means the date as from which this Constitution has effect under section 2(1) of the Anguilla (Constitution) **Order** 1976;

" Assembly " means the Legislative Assembly of Anguilla established by this Constitution;

" Chief Justice " means the Chief Justice of the West Indies Associated States;

" Commissioner " means such person as Her Majesty may appoint by instrument under Her Sign Manual and Signet to be Her Majesty's Commissioner in Anguilla, and includes any person

1h

appointed by Her Majesty by instructions given through a Secretary of State to act in that office and, to the extent to which a deputy appointed under section 20 of this Constitution is authorised to act, that deputy;

"Courts Order" means the West Indies Associated States Supreme Court Order 1967(a).

"Court of Appeal" means the Court of Appeal established by the Courts Order.

"functions" includes jurisdictions, powers and duties;

"High Court" means the High Court established by the Courts Order;

"law" includes any instrument having the force of law made in exercise of a power conferred by a law;

"Legislature" means the legislature established by Chapter V of this Constitution and includes Her Majesty in Council;

"the Order of 1971" means the Anguilla (Administration) Order 1971(b);

"public office" means, subject to the provisions of the next following subsection, an office of emolument in the public service;

"public officer" means the holder of any public office, and includes a person appointed to act in any public office;

"the public service" means the service of the Crown in a civil capacity in respect of the government of Anguilla;

"session" means the meetings of the Assembly commencing when the Assembly first meets after being constituted under this Constitution, or after its prorogation or dissolution at any time, and and terminating when the Assembly is prorogued or is dissolved without having been prorogued.

"sitting" means a period during which the Assembly is sitting continuously without adjournment and includes any period during which the Assembly is in committee.

(2) For the purposes of this Constitution, a person shall not be considered to hold a public office by reason only that he—

(a) is in receipt of any remuneration or allowance as a member of the Executive Council or the Assembly;

(b) is in receipt of a pension or other like allowance in respect of service under the Crown; or

(c) holds an office the holder of which is declared by any law in force in Anguilla not to be disqualified for election as a member of the Assembly.

(3) Any person who has vacated his seat in any body, or has vacated any office established by this Constitution may, if qualified, again be appointed or elected as a member of that body or to that office, as the case may be, from time to time.

(4) A reference in this Constitution to the holder of an office by the term designating his office shall be construed as a reference to any person for the time being lawfully performing the functions of that office.

(a) S.I. 1967/223 (1967 I, p. 364).   (b) S.I. 1971/1235 (1971 II, p. 3587).

(5) Without prejudice to the last foregoing subsection—

(a) where the holder of any office constituted by or under this Constitution is on leave of absence pending the relinquishment of that office, the person or authority having power to make appointments to that office may appoint another person thereto; and

(b) where two or more persons concurrently hold the same office by virtue of the foregoing paragraph, the person last appointed shall in respect of any function conferred on the holder of that office be deemed to be the sole holder thereof.

(6) Any power conferred by this Constitution to make any Proclamation or order or to give any directions shall be construed as including a power exercisable in like manner to amend or revoke any such Proclamation, order or directions.

(7) Where a person is required by this Constitution to make an oath he shall if he so desires be permitted to comply with that requirement by making an affirmation in accordance with the provisions of the Schedule to this Constitution.

(8) For the purpose of this Constitution the resignation of a member of any body or holder of any office thereby established that is required to be addressed to any person shall, unless otherwise expressly provided, be deemed to have effect from the time at which it is received by that person.

73. The Commissioner shall keep and use the public seal for sealing all things that should pass that seal. *Public Seal.*

74. Subject to the provisions of any law for the time being in force in Anguilla, the Commissioner or any person duly authorised by him in writing under his hand may, in Her Majesty's name and on Her behalf, make and execute under the public seal grants and dispositions of any land or other immovable property within Anguilla that may be lawfully granted or disposed of by Her Majesty. *Grants of land.*

75. Subject to any Instructions given to him by Her Majesty under Her Sign Manual and Signet, the Commissioner may, in Her Majesty's name and on Her behalf— *Commissioner's power of pardon.*

(a) grant to any person concerned in the commission of any offence for which he may be tried in Anguilla, or to any person convicted of any offence under any law in force in Anguilla, a pardon, either free or subject to lawful conditions;

(b) grant to any person so convicted a respite, either indefinite or for a specified period, of the execution of any sentence passed on him in respect of the conviction;

(c) substitute a less severe form of punishment for that imposed on any such person by any such sentence; or

(d) remit the whole or any part of any such sentence or of any penalty or forfeiture due to Her Majesty by reason of the conviction.

76. The Commissioner, in Her Majesty's name and on Her behalf, may constitute such offices for Anguilla as may lawfully be constituted by Her Majesty and, subject to the provisions of any law in force in *Offices and appointments.*

Anguilla, may make appointments (including appointments on promotion and transfer) to any such office; and any person so appointed shall, unless it is otherwise provided by any such law, hold office during Her Majesty's pleasure.

Discipline.

77.—(1) Subject to the provisions of any law in force in Anguilla, the Commissioner may for cause shown to his satisfaction dismiss or suspend from the exercise of his office any person holding a public office, or take such disciplinary action as may seem to him to be desirable.

(2) The reference in this section to the power to dismiss any person holding a public office shall be construed as including a reference to any power to require or permit a person to retire.

Existing offices and authorities.

78.—(1) Subject to the provisions of this section offices and authorities established by or under the Order of 1971 and existing immediately before the appointed day shall on and after that day, so far as consistent with the provisions of the Constitution, continue as if they had been established by or under this Constitution; and any person who immediately before that day is holding or acting in any such office or as a member of any such authority shall on and after that day continue to hold or act in that office or to be such a member as if he had been appointed thereto or as the case may be elected as such in accordance with this Constitution and had made any oath thereby required.

(2) The provisions of this section shall be without prejudice to any powers conferred by or under this Constitution upon any person or authority to make provision for any matter, including (but without prejudice to the generality of the foregoing words) the establishment and abolition of offices, courts of law and authorities and the appointment, election or selection of persons to hold or act in any office or to be members of any court or authority and their removal from office.

Existing laws.

79.—(1) All Acts, Ordinances, rules, regulations, orders and other instruments made under or having effect by virtue of the Order of 1971 and having effect as part of the law of Anguilla immediately before the appointed day shall on and after the appointed day have effect as if they had been made under or by virtue of this Constitution.

(2) Subject to the provisions of the next following subsection, the existing laws shall on and after the appointed day be construed with such modifications, adaptations, qualifications and exceptions as are necessary to bring them into conformity with this Constitution.

(3) Subject to the provisions of this Constitution, the Commissioner may by regulations at any time within eighteen months from the appointed day make such amendments to any existing law as appear to him to be necessary or expedient for bringing that law into conformity with the provisions of this Constitution or otherwise for giving effect or enabling effect to be given to those provisions.

(4) In this section the expression "existing laws" means laws and instruments (other than Acts of Parliament and instruments made thereunder) having effect as part of the law of Anguilla immediately before the appointed day.

Power reserved to Her Majesty.

80. Her Majesty hereby reserves to Herself power, with the advice of Her Privy Council, to make laws for the peace, order and good government of Anguilla.

THE SCHEDULE TO THE CONSTITUTION

Forms of Oaths and Affirmations

1. *Oath of Allegiance*

Sections
19(3), 29
and 59.

I .... do swear that I will be faithful and bear true allegiance to Her Majesty Queen Elizabeth the Second, Her Heirs and Successors, according to law. So help me God.

2. *Oath for due execution of office*

I .... do swear that I will well and truly serve Her Majesty Queen Elizabeth the Second, Her Heirs and Successors, in the office (*here insert the description of the office*). So help me God.

3. *Affirmations*

In the forms above respectively set forth, for the word "swear" there shall be substituted the words "solemnly and sincerely affirm and declare", and the words "So help me God" shall be omitted.

EXPLANATORY NOTE

(*This Note is not part of the Order.*)

This Order, which is made under section 1 of the Anguilla Act 1971, confers a new constitution on Anguilla, and supersedes the Anguilla (Administration) Order 1971, which is revoked.

The Constitution contains provision with regard to the office of Commissioner, the Executive Council, the Legislature and the Judicature.

The Anguilla Council is replaced by an Executive Council and a Legislative Assembly, each consisting of ex-officio and elected members, with nominated members in addition in the case of the Assembly.

While the Constitution requires the Commissioner in general to exercise his functions in accordance with the advice of the Executive Council, it provides for him to be responsible in his discretion for defence, external affairs, internal security, including the police, and certain matters relating to the public service.

Provision is made for the assignment of responsibility for business or departments of the Government to members of the Executive Council.

STATUTORY INSTRUMENTS

1976 No. 51

DIPLOMATIC AND INTERNATIONAL IMMUNITIES AND PRIVILEGES

The Commonwealth Countries and Republic of Ireland (Immunities and Privileges) (Amendment) Order 1976

Made - - - -	*19th January* 1976
Laid before Parliament	*26th January* 1976
Coming into Operation	*17th February* 1976

At the Court at Buckingham Palace, the 19th day of January 1976

Present,

The Queen's Most Excellent Majesty in Council

Her Majesty, by virtue and in exercise of the powers conferred on Her by sections 12 and 14 of the Consular Relations Act 1968(a), as amended by section 4 of the Diplomatic and other Privileges Act 1971(b), or otherwise in Her Majesty vested, is pleased, by and with the advice of Her Privy Council, to order, and it is hereby ordered, as follows:—

1. This Order may be cited as the Commonwealth Countries and Republic of Ireland (Immunities and Privileges) (Amendment) Order 1976 and shall come into operation on 17th February 1976.

2. The Interpretation Act 1889(c) shall apply for the interpretation of this Order as it applies for the interpretation of an Act of Parliament.

3. After Article 8 of the Commonwealth Countries and Republic of Ireland (Immunities and Privileges) Order 1971(d) as amended(e) there shall be inserted a new Article as follows:

" 8A. The like relief from general rates as is accorded under Article 32 in Schedule 1 to the Act to consular premises and the residence of the career head of a consular post shall be extended to the office (known as the Hong Kong Government Office) and the residence respectively of the Hong Kong Commissioner.".

N. E. Leigh

(a) 1968 c. 18.   (b) 1971 c. 64.   (c) 1889 c. 63.
(d) S.I. 1971/1237 (1971 II, p. 3597).
(e) S.I. 1974/109, 1709 (1974 I, p. 405; III, p. 6146).

EXPLANATORY NOTE

(This Note is not part of the Order.)

This Order further amends the Commonwealth Countries and Republic of Ireland (Immunities and Privileges) Order 1971 by extending partial relief from general rates to the office and residence of the Hong Kong Commissioner.

STATUTORY INSTRUMENTS

1976 No. 52

SOUTH ATLANTIC TERRITORIES

The Falkland Islands (Legislative Council) (Amendment) Order 1976

Made - - - -	*19th January* 1976
Laid before Parliament	*26th January* 1976
Coming into Operation	*31st January* 1976

At the Court at Buckingham Palace, the 19th day of January 1976

Present,

The Queen's Most Excellent Majesty in Council

Her Majesty, by virtue and in exercise of the powers vested in Her by the British Settlements Acts 1887 and 1945(a), and of all other powers enabling Her in that behalf, is pleased, by and with the advice of Her Privy Council, to order, and it is hereby ordered, as follows: —

Citation, construction and commencement

1.—(1) This Order may be cited as the Falkland Islands (Legislative Council) (Amendment) Order 1976 and shall be construed as one with the Falkland Islands (Legislative Council) Orders 1948 to 1975(b), which Orders are hereinafter referred to as " the principal Order ".

(2) This Order and the principal Order may be cited together as the Falkland Islands (Legislative Council) Orders 1948 to 1976.

(3) This Order shall come into operation on 31st January 1976.

Extension of life of existing Legislative Council

2. Notwithstanding the provisions of section 26(3) of the principal Order, the existing Legislative Council shall not stand dissolved on 31st January 1976, but, unless it is sooner dissolved, it shall stand dissolved on 28th February 1976.

N. E. Leigh

EXPLANATORY NOTE

(This Note is not part of the Order.)

This Order further amends the Falkland Islands (Legislative Council) Orders 1948 to 1975 so as to prolong the life of the existing Legislative Council (which has already been prolonged for about ten weeks) for a further four weeks, unless it is sooner dissolved.

(a) 1887 c. 54; 1945 c. 7.
(b) S.I. 1948/2573 (Rev. VII, p. 591: 1948 I, p. 1018), 1950/1184, 1951/1946, 1955/1650, 1964/1397, 1972/668, 1973/598, 1975/1706 (1950 I, p. 683; 1951 I, p. 682; 1955 I, p. 833; 1964 III, p. 3204; 1972 I, p. 2150; 1973 I, p. 1908; 1975 III, p. 5813).

STATUTORY INSTRUMENTS

1976 No. 53

MERCHANT SHIPPING

The Merchant Shipping (Oil Pollution) (Gibraltar) Order 1976

Made - - - -	*19th January,* 1976
Laid before Parliament	*26th January* 1976
Coming into Operation	*17th February* 1976

At the Court at Buckingham Palace, the 19th day of January 1976

Present,

The Queen's Most Excellent Majesty in Council

Her Majesty, in exercise of the powers conferred upon Her by section 18 (1) of the Merchant Shipping (Oil Pollution) Act 1971(a), by section 20 (1) of the Merchant Shipping Act 1974(b) and all other powers enabling Her in that behalf, is pleased, by and with the advice of Her Privy Council, to order, and it is hereby ordered, as follows:

1. This Order may be cited as the Merchant Shipping (Oil Pollution) (Gibraltar) Order 1976 and shall come into operation on 17th February 1976.

2. The Interpretation Act 1889(c) shall apply, with the necessary adaptations, for the purpose of interpreting this Order and otherwise in relation thereto as it applies for the purpose of interpreting, and in relation to, Acts of Parliament.

3. The provisions of the Merchant Shipping (Oil Pollution) Act 1971 (except sections 17 and 18 thereof), subject to the exemptions, modifications and adaptations as set out in Schedule 1 hereto, shall extend to Gibraltar.

4. The provisions of Part I and sections 22, 23 and 24 of, and Schedule 1 to the Merchant Shipping Act 1974, subject to the exceptions, modifications and adaptations as set out in Schedule 2 hereto, shall extend to Gibraltar.

5. Save as is expressly provided otherwise therein, any reference in the Schedules to this Order to any enactment of the United Kingdom shall be construed as a reference to that enactment as applying or extended to Gibraltar.

N. E. Leigh

(a) 1971 c. 59.   (b) 1974 c. 43.   (c) 1889 c. 63.

ARTICLE 3   SCHEDULE I TO THE ORDER

THE MERCHANT SHIPPING (OIL POLLUTION) ACT 1971

Liability for oil pollution. 1.—(1) Where, as a result of any occurrence taking place while a ship is carrying a cargo of persistent oil in bulk, any persistent oil carried by the ship (whether as part of the cargo or otherwise) is discharged or escapes from the ship, the owner of the ship shall be liable, except as otherwise provided by this Act,—

(a) for any damage caused in the area of Gibraltar by contamination resulting from the discharge or escape ; and

(b) for the cost of any measures reasonably taken after the discharge or escape for the purpose of preventing or reducing any such damage in the area of Gibraltar ; and

(c) for any damage caused in the area of Gibraltar by any measures so taken.

(2) Where a person incurs a liability under subsection (1) of this section he shall also be liable for any damage or cost for which he would be liable under that subsection if the references therein to the area of Gibraltar included the area of any other Convention country.

(3) Where persistent oil is discharged or escapes from two or more ships and—

(a) a liability is incurred under this section by the owner of each of them ; but

(b) the damage or cost for which each of the owners would be liable cannot reasonably be separated from that for which the other or others would be liable ;

each of the owners shall be liable, jointly with the other or others, for the whole of the damage or cost for which the owners together would be liable under this section.

(4) For the purposes of this Act, where more than one discharge or escape results from the same occurrence or from a series of occurrences having the same origin, they shall be treated as one ; but any measures taken after the first of them shall be deemed to have been taken after the discharge or escape.

(5) The Contract and Tort Ordinance(a) shall apply in relation to any damage or cost for which a person is liable under this section, but which is not due to his fault, as if it were due to his fault.

Exceptions from liability under s. 1. 2. The owner of a ship from which persistent oil has been discharged or has escaped shall not incur any liability under section 1 of this Act if he proves that the discharge or escape—

(a) resulted from an act of war, hostilities, civil war, insurrection or an exceptional, inevitable and irresistible natural phenomenon ; or

(b) was due wholly to anything done or left undone by another person, not being a servant or agent of the owner, with intent to do damage ; or

(c) was due wholly to the negligence or wrongful act of a government or other authority in exercising its function of maintaining lights or other navigational aids for the maintenance of which it was responsible.

(a) Laws of Gibraltar Revised Ed. 1964, Cap. 32.

3. Where, as a result of any occurrence taking place while a ship is carrying a cargo of persistent oil in bulk, any persistent oil carried by the ship is discharged or escapes then, whether or not the owner incurs a liability under section 1 of this Act,— Restriction of liability for oil pollution.

(a) he shall not be liable otherwise than under that section for any such damage or cost as is mentioned therein ; and

(b) no servant or agent of the owner nor any person performing salvage operations with the agreement of the owner shall be liable for any such damage or cost.

4.—(1) Where the owner of a ship incurs a liability under section 1 of this Act by reason of a discharge or escape which occurred without his actual fault or privity— Limitation of liability under s. 1.

(a) section 503 of the Merchant Shipping Act 1894(a) (limitation of liability) shall not apply in relation to that liability ; but

(b) he may limit that liability in accordance with the provisions of this Act, and if he does so his liability (that is to say, the aggregate of his liabilities under section 1 resulting from the discharge or escape) shall not exceed 2,000 gold francs for each ton of the ship's tonnage nor (where that tonnage would result in a greater amount) 210 million gold francs.

(2) For the purposes of this section the tonnage of a ship shall be ascertained as follows : —

(a) if the ship is a British ship (whether registered in Gibraltar or elsewhere) or a ship to which an Order under section 84 of the Merchant Shipping Act 1894 applies, its tonnage shall be taken to be its registered tonnage increased, where a deduction has been made for engine room space in arriving at that tonnage, by the amount of that deduction ;

(b) if the ship is not such a ship as is mentioned in the preceding paragraph and it is possible to ascertain what would be its registered tonnage if it were registered in Gibraltar, that paragraph shall apply (with the necessary modifications) as if the ship were so registered ;

(c) if the ship is not such a ship as is mentioned in paragraph (a) of this subsection and is of a description with respect to which no provision is for the time being made by regulations under section 1 of the Merchant Shipping Act 1965(b) (tonnage regulations) its tonnage shall be taken to be 40 per cent. of the weight (expressed in tons of 2,240 lbs.) of oil which the ship is capable of carrying ;

(d) if the tonnage of the ship cannot be ascertained in accordance with the preceding paragraphs a surveyor appointed under section 214 of the Merchant Shipping Ordinance(c) shall, if so directed by the court, certify what, on the evidence specified in the direction, would in his opinion be the tonnage of the ship if ascertained in accordance with those paragraphs, and the tonnage stated in his certificate shall be taken to be the tonnage of the ship.

(3) For the purposes of this section a gold franc shall be taken to be a unit of sixty-five and a half milligrams of gold of millesimal fineness nine hundred.

(4) The Governor may from time to time by order made by statutory instrument specify the amounts which for the purposes of this section are to be taken as equivalent as 2,000 gold francs and 210 million gold francs respectively.

(a) 1894 c. 60.   (b) 1965 c. 47; S.I. 1971/383 (1971 I, p. 1175).
(c) Laws of Gibraltar Revised Ed. 1964, Cap. 106.

(5) Where the amounts specified by an order under the preceding sub-section are varied by a subsequent order the variation shall not affect the limit of any liability under section 1 of this Act if, before the variation comes into force, an amount not less than that limit (ascertained in accordance with the order then in force) has been paid into court in proceedings for the limitation of that liability in accordance with this Act.

Limitation actions.

5.—(1) Where the owner of a ship has or is alleged to have incurred a liability under section 1 of this Act he may apply to the court for the limitation of that liability to an amount determined in accordance with section 4 of this Act.

(2) If on such an application the court finds that the applicant has incurred such a liability and is entitled to limit it, the court shall, after determining the limit of the liability and directing payment into court of the amount of that limit,—

(a) determine the amounts that would, apart from the limit, be due in respect of the liability to the several persons making claims in the proceedings ; and

(b) direct the distribution of the amount paid into court (or, as the case may be, so much of it as does not exceed the liability) among those persons in proportion to their claims, subject to the following provisions of this section.

(3) No claim shall be admitted in proceedings under this section unless it is made within such time as the court may direct or such further time as the court may allow.

(4) Where any sum has been paid in or towards satisfaction of any claim in respect of the damage or cost to which the liability extends,—

(a) by the owner or the person referred to in section 12 of this Act as " the insurer " ; or

(b) by a person who has or is alleged to have incurred a liability, otherwise than under section 1 of this Act, for the damage or cost and who is entitled to limit his liability in connection with the ship by virtue of the Merchant Shipping (Liability of Shipowners and Others) Act 1958(a) ;

the person who paid the sum shall, to the extent of that sum, be in the same position with respect to any distribution made in proceedings under this section as the person to whom it was paid would have been.

(5) Where the person who incurred the liability has voluntarily made any reasonable sacrifice or taken any other reasonable measures to prevent or reduce damage to which the liability extends or might have extended he shall be in the same position with respect to any distribution made in proceedings under this section as if he had a claim in respect of the liability equal to the cost of the sacrifice or other measures.

(6) The court may, if it thinks fit, postpone the distribution of such part of the amount to be distributed as it deems appropriate having regard to any claims that may later be established before a court of any country outside Gibraltar.

Restriction on enforcement of claims after establishment of limitation fund.

6.—(1) Where the court has found that a person who has incurred a liability under section 1 of this Act is entitled to limit that liability to any amount and he has paid into court a sum not less than that amount—

(a) the court shall order the release of any ship or other property arrested in connection with a claim in respect of that liability or any security given to prevent or obtain release from such an arrest ; and

(b) no judgment or decree for any such claim shall be enforced, except so far as it is for costs ;

(a) 1958 c. 62.

if the sum paid into court, or such part thereof as corresponds to the claim, will be actually available to the claimant or would have been available to him if the proper steps in the proceedings under section 5 of this Act had been taken.

7. Where, as a result of any discharge or escape of persistent oil from a ship, the owner of the ship incurs a liability under section 1 of this Act and any other person incurs a liability, otherwise than under that section, for any such damage or cost as is mentioned in subsection (1) of that section, then, if— **Concurrent liabilities of owners and others.**

  (a) the owner has been found, in proceedings under section 5 of this Act, to be entitled to limit his liability to any amount and has paid into court a sum not less than that amount ; and

  (b) the other person is entitled to limit his liability in connection with the ship by virtue of the Merchant Shipping (Liability of Shipowners and Others) Act 1958 ;

no proceedings shall be taken against the other person in respect of his liability, and if any such proceedings were commenced before the owner paid the sum into court, no further steps shall be taken in the proceedings except in relation to costs.

8. Where the events resulting in the liability of any person under section 1 of this Act also resulted in a corresponding liability under the law of another Convention country sections 6 and 7 of this Act shall apply as if the references to sections 1 and 5 of this Act included references to the corresponding provisions of that law and the references to sums paid into court included references to any sums secured under those provisions in respect of the liability. **Establishment of limitation fund outside Gibraltar.**

9. No action to enforce a claim in respect of a liability incurred under section 1 of this Act shall be entertained by any court in Gibraltar unless the action is commenced not later than three years after the claim arose nor later than six years after the occurrence or first of the occurrences resulting in the discharge or escape by reason of which the liability was incurred. **Extinguishment of claims.**

10.—(1) Subject to the provisions of this Act relating to Government ships, subsection (2) of this section shall apply to any ship carrying in bulk a cargo of more than 2,000 tons of persistent oil of a description specified in regulations made by the Governor. **Compulsory insurance against liability for pollution.**

  (2) The ship shall not enter or leave a port in Gibraltar or arrive at or leave a terminal in the territorial sea of Gibraltar nor, if the ship is registered in Gibraltar, a port in any other country or a terminal in the territorial sea of any other country, unless there is in force a certificate complying with the provisions of subsection (3) of this section and showing that there is in force in respect of the ship a contract of insurance or other security satisfying the requirements of Article VII of the Convention (cover for owner's liability).

  (3) The certificate must be—

  (a) if the ship is registered in Gibraltar, a certificate issued by the Governor ;

  (b) if the ship is registered in a Convention country other than Gibraltar, a certificate issued by or under the authority of the government of the other Convention country ; and

  (c) if the ship is registered in a country which is not a Convention country, a certificate recognised for the purposes of this paragraph by regulations made under this section.

(4) The Governor may by regulations provide that certificates in respect of ships registered in any, or any specified, country which is not a Convention country shall, in such circumstances as may be specified in the regulations, be recognised for the purposes of subsection (3)(c) of this section if issued by or under the authority of the government of the country designated in the regulations in that behalf ; and the country that may be so designated may be either or both of the following, that is to say—

(a) the country in which the ship is registered ; and

(b) any country specified in the regulations for the purposes of this paragraph.

(5) Any certificate required by this section to be in force in respect of a ship shall be carried in the ship and shall, on demand, be produced by the master to the Captain of the Port.

(6) If a ship enters or leaves, or attempts to enter or leave, a port or arrives at or leaves, or attempts to arrive at or leave, a terminal in contravention of subsection (2) of this section, the master or owner shall be liable on conviction on indictment to a fine, or on summary conviction to a fine not exceeding £35,000.

(7) If a ship fails to carry, or the master of a ship fails to produce, a certificate as required by subsection (5) of this section the master shall be liable on summary conviction to a fine not exceeding £400.

(8) If a ship attempts to leave a port in Gibraltar in contravention of this section the ship may be detained.

Issue of certificate by Governor.

11.—(1) Subject to subsection (2) of this section, if the Governor is satisfied, on an application for such a certificate as is mentioned in section 10 of this Act in respect of a ship registered in Gibraltar that there will be in force in respect of the ship, throughout the period for which the certificate is to be issued, a contract of insurance or other security satisfying the requirement of Article VII of the Convention, the Governor shall issue such a certificate to the owner.

(2) If the Governor is of opinion that there is a doubt whether the person providing the insurance or other security will be able to meet his obligations thereunder, or whether the insurance or other security will cover the owner's liability under section 1 of this Act in all circumstances, he may refuse the certificate.

(3) The Governor may make regulations—

(a) prescribing the fee to be paid on an application for a certificate to be issued by him under this section ; and

(b) providing for the cancellation and delivery up of such a certificate in such circumstances as may be prescribed by the regulations.

(4) If a person required by regulations under subsection (3)(b) of this section to deliver up a certificate fails to do so he shall be liable on summary conviction to a fine not exceeding £200.

(5) The Governor shall send a copy of any certificate issued by him under this section in respect of a ship registered in Gibraltar to the Captain of the Port, and the Captain of the Port shall make the copy available for public inspection.

Rights of third parties against insurers.

12.—(1) Where it is alleged that the owner of a ship has incurred a liability under section 1 of this Act as a result of any discharge or escape of oil occurring while there was in force a contract of insurance or other security to which such a certificate as is mentioned in section 10 of this

Act related, proceedings to enforce a claim in respect of the liability may be brought against the person who provided the insurance or other security (in the following provisions of this section referred to as " the insurer ").

(2) In any proceedings brought against the insurer by virtue of this section it shall be a defence (in addition to any defence affecting the owner's liability) to prove that the discharge or escape was due to the wilful misconduct of the owner himself.

(3) The insurer may limit his liability in respect of claims made against him by virtue of this section in like manner and to the same extent as the owner may limit his liability but the insurer may do so whether or not the discharge or escape occurred without the owner's actual fault or privity.

(4) Where the owner and the insurer each apply to the court for the limitation of his liability any sum paid into court in pursuance of either application shall be treated as paid also in pursuance of the other.

13.—(1) Paragraph (*d*) of section 1(1) of the Administration of Justice Act 1956 as applied in Gibraltar by the Admiralty Jurisdiction (Gibraltar) Order in Council, 1961(a) (Admiralty jurisdiction in claims for damage done by ships) shall be construed as extending to any claim in respect of a liability incurred under this Act. Jurisdiction of Gibraltar courts and registration of foreign judgments.

(2) Where any persistent oil is discharged or escapes from a ship but does not result in any damage caused by contamination in the area of Gibraltar and no measures are reasonably taken to prevent or reduce such damage in that area, no court in Gibraltar shall entertain an action (whether *in rem* or *in personam*) to enforce a claim arising from—

(*a*) any damage caused in the area of another Convention country by contamination resulting from the discharge or escape ;

(*b*) any cost incurred in taking measures to prevent or reduce such damage in the area of another Convention country ; or

(*c*) any damage caused by any measures so taken.

(3) The Judgments (Reciprocal Enforcement) Ordinance(b) shall apply, whether or not it would so apply apart from this section, to any judgment given by a court in a Convention country to enforce a claim in respect of a liability incurred under any provision corresponding to section 1 of this Act ; and in its application to such a judgment the said Ordinance shall have effect with the omission of subsections (2) and (3) of section 7 of that Ordinance.

14.—(1) Nothing in the preceding provisions of this Act applies in relation to any warship or any ship for the time being used by the government of any State for other than commercial purposes. Government ships.

(2) In relation to a ship owned by a State and for the time being used for commercial purposes it shall be a sufficient compliance with subsection (2) of section 10 of this Act if there is in force a certificate issued by the government of that State and showing that the ship is owned by that State and that any liability for pollution damage as defined in Article I of the Convention will be met up to the limit prescribed by Article V thereof.

(3) Every Convention State shall, for the purposes of any proceedings brought in a court in Gibraltar to enforce a claim in respect of a liability incurred under section 1 of this Act, be deemed to have submitted to the jurisdiction of that court, and accordingly rules of court may provide for

---

(a) S.I. 1961/2031 (1961 III, p. 3694).
(b) Laws of Gibraltar Revised Ed. 1964, Cap. 80.

the manner in which such proceedings are to be commenced and carried on ; but nothing in this subsection shall authorise the issue of execution against the property of any State.

Liability for cost of preventive measures where s. 1 does not apply.

15.—(1) **Where,**—

(*a*) after an escape or discharge of persistent oil from a ship, measures are reasonably taken for the purpose of preventing or reducing damage in the area of Gibraltar which may be caused by contamination resulting from the discharge or escape ; and

(*b*) any person incurs, or might but for the measures have incurred, a liability, otherwise than under section 1 of this Act, for any such damage ;

then, notwithstanding that subsection (1)(*b*) of that section does not apply, he shall be liable for the cost of the measures, whether or not the person taking them does so for the protection of his interests or in the performance of a duty.

(2) For the purposes of section 503 of the Merchant Shipping Act 1894(a) (limitation of liability) any liability incurred under this section shall be deemed to be a liability to damages in respect of such loss, damage or infringement as is mentioned in subsection (1)(*d*) of that section.

Saving for recourse actions.

16. Nothing in this Act shall prejudice any claim, or the enforcement of any claim, a person incurring any liability under this Act may have against another person in respect of that liability.

Meaning of " the Convention ", " Convention country " and " Convention State ".

19.—(1) **In this Act**—

" the Convention " means the International Convention on Civil Liability for Oil Pollution Damage signed in Brussels in 1969 ;

" Convention country " means a country in respect of which the Convention is in force ; and

" Convention State " means a State which is a party to the Convention.

(2) If Her Majesty by Order in Council made under this subsection as it applies in the United Kingdom declares that any State specified in the Order is a party to the Convention in respect of any country so specified the Order shall, while in force, be conclusive evidence that that State is a party to the Convention in respect of that country.

Interpretation of other expressions.

20.—(1) **In this Act**—

" damage " includes loss ;

" owner ", in relation to a registered ship, means the person registered as its owner, except that in relation to a ship owned by a State which is operated by a person registered as the ship's operator, it means the person registered as its operator ;

" the court " means the Supreme Court of Gibraltar.

(2) In relation to any damage or cost resulting from the discharge or escape of any oil carried in a ship references in this Act to the owner of the ship are references to the owner at the time of the occurrence or first of the occurrences resulting in the discharge or escape.

(3) References in this Act to the area of any country include the territorial sea of that country.

(a) 1894 c. 60.

21.—(2) This Act shall be construed as one with the Merchant Shipping Construction Acts 1894 to 1967.

and commence-

(3) This Act shall come into force on such day as the Governor may by ment. order appoint, and different days may be so appointed for different provisions of this Act.

SCHEDULE II TO THE ORDER   Article 4

THE MERCHANT SHIPPING ACT 1974

PART I

THE INTERNATIONAL OIL POLLUTION COMPENSATION FUND

1.—(1) In this Part of this Act—

(a) the " Liability Convention " means the International Convention on Civil Liability for Oil Pollution Damage opened for signature in Brussels on 29th November 1969 ;

Interpretation of Part I.

(b) the " Fund Convention " means the International Convention on the Establishment of an International Fund for Compensation for Oil Pollution Damage opened for signature in Brussels on 18th December 1971 ;

(c) " the Fund " means the International Fund established by the Fund Convention ; and

(d) " Fund Convention country " means a country in respect of which the Fund Convention is in force.

(2) If Her Majesty by Order in Council made under this subsection as it applies in the United Kingdom declares that any State specified in the Order is a party to the Fund Convention in respect of any country so specified the Order shall, while in force, be conclusive evidence that that State is a party to the Convention in respect of that country.

(3) In this Part of this Act, unless the context otherwise requires—

the " Act of 1971 " means the Merchant Shipping (Oil Pollution) Act 1971(a),

" damage " includes loss,

" discharge or escape ", in relation to pollution damage, means the discharge or escape of oil carried by the ship,

" guarantor " means any person providing insurance or other financial security to cover the owner's liability of the kind described in section 10 of the Act of 1971,

" oil ", except in sections 2 and 3, means persistent hydrocarbon mineral oil,

" owner " means the person or persons registered as the owner of the ship or, in the absence of registration, the person or persons owning the ship, except that in relation to a ship owned by a State which is operated by a person registered as the ship's operator, it means the person registered as its operator,

" pollution damage " means damage caused outside the ship carrying oil by contamination resulting from the escape or discharge of oil from the ship, wherever the escape or discharge may occur, and includes the cost of preventive measures and further damage caused by preventive measures,

---

(a) 1971 c. 59.

PART I

"preventive measures" means any reasonable measures taken by any person after the occurrence to prevent or minimise pollution damage,

"ship" means any sea-going vessel and any seaborne craft of any type whatsoever carrying oil in bulk as cargo.

(4) For the purposes of this Part of this Act a ship's tonnage shall be the net tonnage of the ship with the addition of the amount deducted from the gross tonnage on account of engine room space for the purpose of ascertaining the net tonnage.

If the ship cannot be measured in accordance with the normal rules, its tonnage shall be deemed to be 40 per cent. of the weight in tons (of 2240 lbs.) of oil which the ship is capable of carrying.

(5) For the purposes of this Part of this Act, where more than one discharge or escape results from the same occurrence or from a series of occurrences having the same origin, they shall be treated as one.

(6) In this Part of this Act a franc shall be taken to be a unit of $65\frac{1}{2}$ milligrammes of gold of millesimal fineness 900.

(7) The Governor may from time to time by order made by statutory instrument specify the amounts which for the purposes of this Part of this Act are to be taken as equivalent to any specified number of francs.

Contributions to Fund

Contributions by importers of oil and others.

2.—(1) Contributions shall be payable to the Fund in respect of oil carried by sea to ports or terminal installations in Gibraltar.

(2) Subsection (1) above applies whether or not the oil is being imported, and applies even if contributions are payable in respect of carriage of the same oil on a previous voyage.

(3) Contributions shall also be payable to the Fund in respect of oil when first received in any installation in Gibraltar after having been carried by sea and discharged in a port or terminal installation in a country which is not a Fund Convention country.

(4) The person liable to pay contributions is—

(a) in the case of oil which is being imported into Gibraltar, the importer, and

(b) otherwise, the person by whom the oil is received.

(5) A person shall not be liable to make contributions in respect of the oil imported or received by him in any year if the oil so imported or received in the year does not exceed 150,000 tonnes.

(6) For the purpose of subsection (5) above—

(a) all the members of a group of companies shall be treated as a single person, and

(b) any two or more companies which have been amalgamated into a single company shall be treated as the same person as that single company.

(7) The contributions payable by a person for any year shall—

(a) be of such amount as may be determined by the Assembly of the Fund under Articles 11 and 12 of the Fund Convention and notified to him by the Fund;

(b) be payable in such instalments, becoming due at such times, as may be so notified to him;

and if any amount due from him remains unpaid after the date on which it became due, it shall from then on bear interest, at a rate determined from time to time by the said Assembly, until it is paid.

(8) The Governor may by regulations contained in a statutory instrument impose on persons who are or may be liable to pay contributions under this section obligations to give security for payment to the Governor, or to the Fund.

Regulations under this subsection—

(*a*) may contain such supplemental or incidental provisions as appear to the Secretary of State expedient, and

(*b*) may impose penalties for contravention of the regulations punishable on summary conviction by a fine not exceeding £400, or such lower limit as may be specified in the regulations.

(9) In this and the next following section, unless the context otherwise requires—

" company " means a body incorporated under the law of Gibraltar, or of any other country ;

" group " in relation to companies, means a holding company and its subsidiaries as defined by section 119 of the Companies Ordinance(a) subject, in the case of a company incorporated outside Gibraltar, to any necessary modifications of those definitions ;

" importer " means the person by whom or on whose behalf the oil in question is entered for customs purposes on importation, and

" import " shall be construed accordingly ;

" oil " means crude oil and fuel oil, and

(*a*) " crude oil " means any liquid hydrocarbon mixture occurring naturally in the earth whether or not treated to render it suitable for transportation, and includes—

(i) crude oils from which distillate fractions have been removed, and

(ii) crude oils to which distillate fractions have been added,

(*b*) " fuel oil " means heavy distillates or residues from crude oil or blends of such materials intended for use as a fuel for the production of heat or power of a quality equivalent to the " American Society for Testing and Materials' Specification for Number Four Fuel Oil (Designation D 396-69) ", or heavier.

" terminal installation " means any site for the storage of oil in bulk which is capable of receiving oil from waterborne transportation, including any facility situated offshore and linked to any such site.

3.—(1) For the purpose of transmitting to the Fund the names and Power to addresses of the persons who under the last preceding section are liable obtain to make contributions to the Fund for any year, and the quantity of oil information. in respect of which they are so liable, the Governor may by notice require any person engaged in producing, treating, distributing or transporting oil to furnish such information as may be specified in the notice.

(2) A notice under this section may require a company to give such information as may be required to ascertain whether its liability is affected by subsection (6) of the last preceding section.

(3) A notice under this section may specify the way in which, and the time within which, it is to be complied with.

(a) Laws of Gibraltar Revised Ed. 1964, Cap. 30.

(4) In proceedings by the Fund against any person to recover any amount due under the last preceding section, particulars contained in any list transmitted by the Governor to the Fund shall, so far as those particulars are based on information obtained under this section, be admissible as evidence of the facts stated in the list ; and so far as particulars which are so admissible are based on information given by the person against whom the proceedings are brought, those particulars shall be presumed to be accurate until the contrary is proved.

(5) If a person discloses any information which has been furnished to or obtained by him under this section, or in connection with the execution of this section, he shall, unless the disclosure is made—

(a) with the consent of the person from whom the information was obtained, or

(b) in connection with the execution of this section, or

(c) for the purposes of any legal proceedings arising out of this section or of any report of such proceedings,

be liable on summary conviction to a fine not exceeding £400.

(6) A person who—

(a) refuses or wilfully neglects to comply with a notice under this section, or

(b) in furnishing any information in compliance with a notice under this section makes any statement which he knows to be false in a material particular, or recklessly makes any statement which is false in a material particular,

shall be liable—

(i) on summary conviction to a fine not exceeding £400, and

(ii) on conviction on indictment to a fine, or to imprisonment for a term not exceeding twelve months, or to both.

Compensation for persons suffering pollution damage

Liability of
the Fund.

4.—(1) The Fund shall be liable for pollution damage in Gibraltar if the person suffering the damage has been unable to obtain full compensation under section 1 of the Act of 1971 (which gives effect to the Liability Convention)—

(a) because the discharge or escape causing the damage—

(i) resulted from an exceptional, inevitable and irresistible phenomenon, or

(ii) was due wholly to anything done or left undone by another person (not being a servant or agent of the owner) with intent to do damage, or

(iii) was due wholly to the negligence or wrongful act of a government or other authority in exercising its function of maintaining lights or other navigational aids for the maintenance of which it was responsible,

(and because liability is accordingly wholly displaced by section 2 of the Act of 1971), or

(b) because the owner or guarantor liable for the damage cannot meet his obligations in full, or

(c) because the damage exceeds the liability under section 1 of the Act of 1971 as limited—

(i) by section 4 of the Act of 1971, or

(ii) (where the said section 4 is displaced by section 9 of this Act) by section 503 of the Merchant Shipping Act 1894(a).

(2) Subsection (1) above shall apply with the substitution for the word " Gibraltar " of the words " a Fund Convention country " where the incident has caused pollution damage both in Gibraltar and in another Fund Convention country, and proceedings under the Liability Convention for compensation for the pollution damage have been brought in a country which is not a Fund Convention country or in Gibraltar.

(3) Where the incident has caused pollution damage both in Gibraltar and in another country in respect of which the Liability Convention is in force, references in this section to the provisions of the Act of 1971 shall include references to the corresponding provisions of the law of any country giving effect to the Liability Convention.

(5) For the purposes of this section an owner or guarantor is to be treated as incapable of meeting his obligations if the obligations have not been met after all reasonable steps to pursue the legal remedies available have been taken.

(6) Expenses reasonably incurred, and sacrifices reasonably made, by the owner voluntarily to prevent or minimise pollution damage shall be treated as pollution damage for the purposes of this section, and accordingly he shall be in the same position with respect to claims against the Fund under this section as if he had a claim in respect of liability under section 1 of the Act of 1971.

(7) The Fund shall incur no obligation under this section if—

(a) it proves that the pollution damage—

(i) resulted from an act of war, hostilities, civil war or insurrection, or

(ii) was caused by oil which has escaped or been discharged from a warship or other ship owned or operated by a State and used, at the time of the occurrence, only on Government non-commercial service, or

(b) the claimant cannot prove that the damage resulted from an occurrence involving a ship identified by him, or involving two or more ships one of which is identified by him.

(8) If the Fund proves that the pollution damage resulted wholly or partly—

(a) from an act or omission done with intent to cause damage by the person who suffered the damage, or

(b) from the negligence of that person,

the Fund may be exonerated wholly or partly from its obligation to pay compensation to that person:

Provided that this subsection shall not apply to a claim in respect of expenses or sacrifices made voluntarily to prevent or minimise pollution damage.

(9) Where the liability under section 1 of the Act of 1971 is limited to any extent by subsection (5) of that section (contributory negligence), the Fund shall be exonerated to the same extent.

(10) The Fund's liability under this section shall be subject to the limits imposed by paragraphs 4, 5 and 6 of Article 4 of the Fund Convention which impose an overall liability on the liabilities of the owner and of the Fund, and the text of which is set out in Schedule 1 to this Act.

(a) 1894 c. 60.

PART I

(11) Evidence of any instrument issued by any organ of the Fund or of any document in the custody of the Fund, or any entry in or extract from such a document, may be given in any legal proceedings by production of a copy certified as a true copy by an official of the Fund ; and any document purporting to be such a copy shall be received in evidence without proof of the official position or handwriting of the person signing the certificate.

(12) For the purpose of giving effect to the said provisions of Article 4 of the Fund Convention a court giving judgment against the Fund in proceedings under this section shall notify the Fund, and—

(a) no steps shall be taken to enforce the judgment unless and until the court gives leave to enforce it,

(b) that leave shall not be given unless and until the Fund notifies the court either that the amount of the claim is not to be reduced under the said provisions of Article 4 of the Fund Convention, or that it is to be reduced to a specified amount, and

(c) in the latter case the judgment shall be enforceable only for the reduced amount.

Indemnification of shipowners

Indemnification where damage is caused by ship registered in Fund Convention country.

5.—(1) Where a liability is incurred under section 1 of the Act of 1971 in respect of a ship registered in a Fund Convention country the Fund shall indemnify the owner and his guarantor for that portion of the aggregate amount of the liability which—

(a) is in excess of an amount equivalent to 1,500 francs for each ton of the ship's tonnage or of an amount of 125 million francs, whichever is the less, and

(b) is not in excess of an amount equivalent to 2,000 francs for each ton of the said tonnage or an amount of 210 million francs, whichever is the less.

(2) Where proceedings under the Liability Convention for compensation for pollution damage have been brought in a country which is not a Fund Convention country (but is a country in respect of which the Liability Convention is in force), and the incident has caused pollution damage in Gibraltar (as well as in that other country) subsection (1) above shall apply with the omission of the words " under section 1 of the Act of 1971 ".

(3) The Fund shall not incur an obligation under this section where the pollution damage resulted from the wilful misconduct of the owner.

(4) In proceedings to enforce the Fund's obligation under this section the court may exonerate the Fund wholly or partly if it is proved that, as a result of the actual fault or privity of the owner—

(a) the ship did not comply with such requirements as the Governor may by order prescribe for the purposes of this section, and

(b) the occurrence or damage was caused wholly or partly by that non-compliance.

(5) The requirements referred to in subsection (4) above are such requirements as appear to the Governor appropriate to implement the provisions of—

(a) article 5(3) of the Fund Convention (marine safety conventions), and

(b) article 5(4) of the Fund Convention (which enables the Assembly of the Fund to substitute new conventions).

(6) An order made under subsection (4) above—

(a) may be varied or revoked by a subsequent order so made, or

(b) may contain such transitional or other supplemental provisions as Part I
appear to the Governor to be expedient.

(7) Expenses reasonably incurred, and sacrifices reasonably made, by the owner voluntarily to prevent or minimise the pollution damage shall be treated as included in the owner's liability for the purposes of this section.

Supplemental

6.—(1) Paragraph (d) of section 1(1) of the Administration of Justice Jurisdiction Act 1956 as applied in Gibraltar by the Admiralty Jurisdiction (Gibraltar) and effect of Order in Council 1961(a) (Admiralty jurisdiction in claims for damage judgments. done by ships) shall be construed as extending to any claim in respect of a liability falling on the Fund under this Part of this Act.

(2) Where in accordance with rules of court made for the purposes of this subsection the Fund has been given notice of proceedings brought against an owner or guarantor in respect of liability under section 1 of the Act of 1971, any judgment given in the proceedings shall, after it has become final and enforceable, become binding upon the Fund in the sense that the facts and evidence in the judgment may not be disputed by the Fund even if the Fund has not intervened in the proceedings.

(3) Where a person incurs a liability under the law of a Fund Convention country corresponding to the Act of 1971 for damage which is partly in the area of Gibraltar, subsection (2) above shall, for the purpose of proceedings under this Part of this Act, apply with any necessary modifications to a judgment in proceedings under that law of the said country.

(4) Subject to subsection (5) below, the Judgments (Reciprocal Enforcement) Ordinance(b) shall apply, whether or not it would so apply apart from this subsection, to any judgment given by a court in a Fund Convention country to enforce a claim in respect of liability incurred under any provision corresponding to section 4 or 5 of this Act ; and in its application to such a judgment the said Ordinance shall have effect with the omission of subsections (2) and (3) of section 7 of that Ordinance.

(5) No steps shall be taken to enforce such a judgment unless and until the court in which it is registered under the said Ordinance gives leave to enforce it: and—

(a) that leave shall not be given unless and until the Fund notifies the court either that the amount of the claim is not to be reduced under paragraph 4 of Article 4 of the Fund Convention (as set out in Schedule 1 to this Act) or that it is to be reduced to a specified amount ; and

(b) in the latter case, the judgment shall be enforceable only for the reduced amount.

7.—(1) No action to enforce a claim against the Fund under this Part Extinguishof this Act shall be entertained by a court in Gibraltar unless— ment of
claims.
(a) the action is commenced, or

(b) a third-party notice of an action to enforce a claim against the owner or his guarantor in respect of the same damage is given to the Fund,

not later than three years after the claim against the Fund arose.

(a) S.I. 1961/2031 (1961 III, p. 3694).
(b) Laws of Gibraltar Revised Ed. 1964, Cap. 80.

PART I   In this subsection " third-party notice " means a notice of the kind
described in subsections (2) and (3) of the last preceding section.

(2) No action to enforce a claim against the Fund under this Part of
this Act shall be entertained by a court in Gibraltar unless the action is
commenced not later than six years after the occurrence, or first of the
occurrences, resulting in the discharge or escape by reason of which the
claim against the Fund arose.

(3) Notwithstanding the preceding provisions of this section, a person's
right to bring an action under section 5 of this Act shall not be extinguished
before six months from the date when that person first acquired knowledge of the bringing of an action against him under the Act of 1971
(that is to say an action to enforce a liability against which he seeks
indemnity), or under the corresponding provisions of the law of any
country outside Gibraltar giving effect to the Liability Convention.

Subrogation   8.—(1) In respect of any sum paid under section 4(1)(b) of this Act
and rights of (default by owner or guarantor on liability for pollution damage) the
recourse.   Fund shall acquire by subrogation the rights of the recipient against the
owner or guarantor.

(2) The right of the Fund under subsection (1) above is subject to any
obligation of the Fund under section 5 of this Act to indemnify the
owner or guarantor for any part of the liability on which he has defaulted.

(3) In respect of any sum paid—
(a) under paragraph (a) or paragraph (c) of section 4(1) ; or
(b) under section 5,

the Fund shall acquire by subrogation any rights of recourse or subrogation which the owner or guarantor or any other person has in respect of
his liability for the damage in question.

(4) In respect of any sum paid by a public authority in Gibraltar as
compensation for pollution damage, that authority shall acquire by subrogation any rights which the recipient has against the Fund under this
Part of this Act.

Modification   9. In the Act of 1971 after section 8 there shall be inserted the following
of limitation section—
of liability
under Act   Cases   " 8A.—(1) Sections 4 to 8 of this Act shall not apply to a
of 1971.   excluded   ship which at the time of the discharge or escape was regis-
              from   tered in a country—
              sections
              4 to 8.   (a) which was not a Convention country, and
                                 (b) which was a country in respect of which the 1957 Con-
                                     vention was in force.

(2) In this section ' the 1957 Convention ' means the International Convention relating to the Limitation of the Liability
of Owners of Seagoing Ships signed in Brussels on 10th October
1957.

(3) If Her Majesty by Order in Council made under this
subsection as it applies in the United Kingdom declares that
any country—
     (a) is not a Convention country within the meaning of this
         Act, and
     (b) is a country in respect of which the 1957 Convention
         is in force,
or that it was such a country at a time specified in the Order
the Order shall, while in force, be conclusive evidence of the
facts stated in the Order."

PART V

Supplemental

22. Where an offence under this Act, or under regulations made under Offences by any of its provisions, which has been committed by a body corporate bodies is proved to have been committed with the consent or connivance of, or corporate. to be attributable to any neglect on the part of, a director, manager, secretary or other similar officer of the body corporate, or any person who was purporting to act in any such capacity, he, as well as the body corporate, shall be guilty of that offence and shall be liable to be proceeded against and punished accordingly.

In this section "director", in relation to a body corporate established by or under any enactment for the purpose of carrying on under public ownership any industry or part of an industry or undertaking, being a body corporate whose affairs are managed by its members, means a member of that body corporate.

23.—(1) This Act shall be construed as one with the Merchant Shipping Construc Acts 1894 to 1971, and without prejudice to the generality of this provi tion and sion, references in those Acts to the Merchant Shipping Acts shall be interpreta construed as including references to this Act. tion.

(2) References in this Act to the area of any country include the territorial sea of that country, and references to pollution damage in Gibraltar shall be construed accordingly.

(4) Except so far as the context otherwise requires, any reference in this Act to an enactment shall be construed as a reference to that enactment as amended or extended by or under any other enactment.

24. (2) This Act shall come into force on such day as the Governor may Commence by Order appoint and different days may be appointed for different pro ment. visions, or for different purposes.

(3) An order under subsection (2) above may make such transitional provision as appears to the Governor to be necessary or expedient in connection with the provisions thereby brought into force, including such adaptations of those provisions, or any provisions of this Act then in force, as appear to him to be necessary or expedient in consequence of the partial operation of this Act (whether before or after the day appointed).

SCHEDULE 1 TO THE ACT

Sections 4(10), 6(5).

OVERALL LIMIT ON LIABILITY OF FUND

Article 4—paragraphs 4, 5 and 6

4. (*a*) Except as otherwise provided in sub-paragraph (*b*) of this paragraph, the aggregate amount of compensation payable by the Fund under this Article shall in respect of any one incident be limited, so that the total sum of that amount and the amount of compensation actually paid under the Liability Convention for pollution damage caused in the territory of the Contracting States, including any sums in respect of which the Fund is under an obligation to indemnify the owner pursuant to Article 5, paragraph 1, of this Convention, shall not exceed 450 million francs.

(*b*) The aggregate amount of compensation payable by the Fund under this Article for pollution damage resulting from a natural phenomenon of an exceptional, inevitable and irresistible character shall not exceed 450 million francs.

5. Where the amount of established claims against the Fund exceeds the aggregate amount of compensation payable under paragraph 4, the amount available shall be distributed in such a manner that the proportion between any established claim and the amount of compensation actually recovered by the claimant under the Liability Convention and this Convention shall be the same for all claimants.

6. The Assembly of the Fund may, having regard to the experience of incidents which have occurred and in particular the amount of damage resulting therefrom and to changes in the monetary values, decide that the amount of 450 million francs referred to in paragraph 4, sub-paragraph (a) and (b), shall be changed ; provided, however, that this amount shall in no case exceed 900 million francs or be lower than 450 million francs. The changed amount shall apply to incidents which occur after the date of the decision effecting the change.

EXPLANATORY NOTE

(This Note is not part of the Order.)

This Order extends to Gibraltar the provisions of the Merchant Shipping (Oil Pollution) Act 1971, with the necessary adaptations, enabling effect to be given to the International Convention on Civil Liability for Oil Pollution Damage opened for signature in Brussels on 29th November 1969 (Cmnd. 4403). The Order also extends the provisions of Parts I and V of, and of Schedule 1 to the Merchant Shipping Act 1974, with the necessary adaptations, enabling effect to be given to the International Convention on the Establishment of an International Fund for Compensation for Oil Pollution Damage opened for signature in Brussels on 18th December 1971 (Cmnd. 5061). The 1969 Convention provides uniform rules and procedures for determining questions of liability and for awarding compensation when damage is caused by pollution resulting from the escape or discharge of oil from ships. The 1971 Convention sets up an international fund to provide a supplementary system for compensation and indemnification for such damage.

STATUTORY INSTRUMENTS

1976 No. 54

OVERSEAS TERRITORIES

The Statute Law (Repeals) Act 1973 (Colonies) Order 1976

Made - - - -	19*th January* 1976
Coming into Operation	10*th February* 1976

At the Court at Buckingham Palace, the 19th day of January 1976

Present,

The Queen's Most Excellent Majesty in Council

Her Majesty, in exercise of the powers conferred on Her by section 2(2) of the Statute Law (Repeals) Act 1973(a), is pleased, by and with the advice of Her Privy Council, to order, and it is hereby ordered, as follows:

Citation and commencement

1. This Order may be cited as the Statute Law (Repeals) Act 1973 (Colonies) Order 1976 and shall come into operation on 10th February 1976.

Extension of certain repeals to colonies

2. The repeal by the Statute Law (Repeals) Act 1973 of the enactments specified in Schedule 1 to this Order (the said repeal thereof being to the extent specified in column 3 of that Schedule) shall on the coming into operation of this Order extend to the colonies mentioned in Schedule 2 to this Order or, where the enactment concerned forms part of the law of some but not all of those colonies, to the colonies so mentioned of whose law it forms part.

N. E. Leigh

(a) 1973 c. 39.

SCHEDULE 1

ENACTMENTS REPEALED

Chapter	Short Title	Extent of Repeal
6 Anne c. 41.	The Succession to the Crown Act 1707	Section 8.
18 Geo. 3. c. 12.	The Taxation of Colonies Act 1778	The whole Act.
52 Geo. 3. c. 156.	The Prisoners of War (Escape) Act 1812	The whole Act.
1 & 2 Geo. 4. c. 121.	The Commissariat Accounts Act 1821	The whole Act.
1 Will. 4. c. 4.	The Colonial Offices Act 1830	The whole Act.
1 & 2 Vict. c. 67.	The West Indian Prisons Act 1838	The whole Act.
24 & 25 Vict. c. 11.	The Foreign Law Ascertainment Act 1861	The whole Act.
26 & 27 Vict. c. 76.	The Colonial Letters Patent Act 1863	The whole Act.
36 & 37 Vict. c. 60.	The Extradition Act 1873	In the Schedule, in the entry relating to the Theft Act 1968, the words " which is not included in the First Schedule to the principal Act ".
57 & 58 Vict. c. 17.	The Colonial Officers (Leave of Absence) Act 1894	The whole Act.

SCHEDULE 2

COLONIES TO WHICH REPEALS EXTEND

Belize
Bermuda
British Antarctic Territory
British Indian Ocean Territory
British Virgin Islands
Cayman Islands
Falkland Islands
Gibraltar
Gilbert Islands
Hong Kong
Montserrat
Pitcairn
Saint Helena and its dependencies
Seychelles
Sovereign Base Areas of Akrotiri and Dhekelia in Cyprus
Turks and Caicos Islands
Tuvalu

EXPLANATORY NOTE

(This Note is not part of the Order.)

The Statute Law (Repeals) Act 1973 repealed certain enactments which are no longer of practical utility. Section 2(2) of the Act declared that the Act does not repeal any enactment so far as the enactment forms part of the law of a country outside the United Kingdom, and enables Her Majesty by Order in Council to provide that the repeal by the Act of any enactment specified in the Order shall extend to any colony for whose external relations the United Kingdom is responsible. This Order provides for the extension of the repeals of the enactments specified in Schedule 1 to the Order to the colonies mentioned in Schedule 2 to the Order.

STATUTORY INSTRUMENTS

1976 No. 55

CARIBBEAN AND NORTH ATLANTIC TERRITORIES

The Turks and Caicos Islands (Electoral Provisions) Order 1976

Made - · - -	*19th January* 1976
Laid before Parliament	*26th January* 1976
Coming into Operation	*17th February* 1976

At the Court at Buckingham Palace, the 19th day of January 1976

Present,

The Queen's Most Excellent Majesty in Council

Whereas it is proposed that there shall be established for the Turks and Caicos Islands a Legislative Council (in this Order referred to as " the proposed Council "), eleven members of which shall be elected from eleven constituencies, and that there shall be established new qualifications for registration as voters:

Now, therefore, Her Majesty, by virtue and in exercise of the powers conferred upon Her by section 5 of the West Indies Act 1962(a), or otherwise in Her Majesty vested, is pleased, by and with the advice of Her Privy Council, to order, and it is hereby ordered, as follows: —

Citation and commencement

1. This Order may be cited as the Turks and Caicos Islands (Electoral Provisions) Order 1976 and shall come into operation on 17th February 1976.

Electoral Regulations

2.—(1) The Governor, acting in his discretion, may by regulation published in the Gazette make provision, for the purposes of the election of members of the proposed Council, for—

(*a*) the division of the Turks and Caicos Islands into constituencies ;

(*b*) the qualifications and registration of voters ; and

(*c*) any matter that appears to him to be incidental thereto or consequential thereon.

(2) Any such regulations may come into force at any time after the coming into operation of this Order.

N. E. Leigh

(a) 1962 c. 19.

EXPLANATORY NOTE

(This Note is not part of the Order.)

This Order enables the Governor of the Turks and Caicos Islands to make provision under which preparations may be made for the election of members of a new Legislative Council which it is proposed to establish for the Turks and Caicos Islands to replace the present State Council acting in its legislative capacity.

STATUTORY INSTRUMENTS

1976 No. 56

CIVIL AVIATION

The Carriage by Air (Parties to Convention) (Supplementary) Order 1976

Made -   -   -   -   19*th January* 1976

At the Court at Buckingham Palace, the 19th day of January 1976

Present,

The Queen's Most Excellent Majesty in Council

Her Majesty, in exercise of the powers conferred on Her by section 2(1) of the Carriage by Air Act 1961(a) (which provides that Her Majesty may by Order in Council from time to time certify who are the High Contracting Parties to the Warsaw Convention as amended at the Hague, 1955, relating to international carriage by air, in respect of what territories they are respectively parties and to what extent they have availed themselves of the provisions of the Additional Protocol to the said Convention) and by that section as applied to international carriage under the unamended Warsaw Convention by Article 5 of the Carriage by Air Acts (Application of Provisions) Order 1967(b), and of all other powers enabling Her in that behalf is pleased, by and with the advice of Her Privy Council, to order, and it is hereby ordered, as follows:—

1.—(1) It is hereby certified that the High Contracting Parties to the Warsaw Convention and to the Warsaw Convention as amended at The Hague, 1955, and the territories in respect of which they are respectively parties are, in addition to those certified in Schedule 1 to the Carriage by Air (Parties to Convention) Order 1975(c), as specified in the Schedule to this Order.

(2) In the said Schedule an asterisk in a column opposite the name of a territory means that this Order does not certify that a state is a party, in respect of that territory, to the Convention named at the head of the column.

2. This Order may be cited as the Carriage by Air (Parties to Convention) (Supplementary) Order 1976.

N. E. Leigh

(a) 1961 c. 27.   (b) S.I. 1967/480 (1967 I, p. 1475).
(c) S.I. 1975/430 (1975 I, p. 1359).

SCHEDULE

High Contracting Parties	Territories in respect of which they are respectively parties	Dates on which the Warsaw Convention came into force	Dates on which the Warsaw Convention as amended at the Hague came in force
Iran	Iran	*	6th October 1975
The Democratic Republic of The Sudan ...	The Sudan ...	*	12th May 1975

EXPLANATORY NOTE

(This Note is not part of the Order.)

The Carriage by Air Act 1961 gives effect in the United Kingdom to the Warsaw Convention as amended at the Hague, 1955, relating to international carriage by air, and the Carriage by Air Acts (Application of Provisions) Order 1967 makes transitional provision for the application of that Act to carriage still governed by the unamended Warsaw Convention, to which the United Kingdom remains a party.

Under section 2(1) of the Act and Article 5 of that Order, Her Majesty may, by Order in Council, from time to time certify, inter alia, who are the High Contracting Parties to the Warsaw Convention as amended at the Hague and to the unamended Warsaw Convention, and such an Order is conclusive evidence of the matters so certified.

This Order, which is supplementary to the Carriage by Air (Parties to Convention) Order 1975, certifies additional High Contracting Parties to the Conventions and the territories in respect of which they are Parties.

STATUTORY INSTRUMENTS

1976 No. 60 (S.2)

LEGAL AID AND ADVICE, SCOTLAND

Act of Sederunt (Legal Aid Rules Amendment) 1976

Made - - - -	*14th January* 1976
Coming into Operation	*11th February* 1976

The Lords of Council and Session, under and by virtue of the powers conferred upon them by section 16 of the Legal Aid (Scotland) Act 1967(a), and of all other powers competent to them in that behalf, do hereby enact and declare:

1. For Rules 3 and 4 of the Act of Sederunt (Legal Aid Rules) 1964(b) there are substituted the following Rules:

"3. On an application being made, the Court shall either order the applicant to lodge a statement on oath of his grounds for claiming payment out of the legal aid fund of the whole or any part of the expenses incurred by him, together with an estimate of the probable amount of those expenses, or dismiss the application forthwith.

4. In the event of an applicant being ordered to lodge his grounds for claiming payment out of the legal aid fund of the whole or any part of the expenses incurred by him, together with an estimate of the probable amount of those expenses, the Court shall order intimation of the statement of grounds and of the estimate to be made by the applicant to the Law Society who shall be entitled to be represented at the hearing when the Court disposes of the application and to cite any party to the cause to attend that hearing".

2. This Act of Sederunt may be cited as the Act of Sederunt (Legal Aid Rules Amendment) 1976, and shall come into operation on 11th February 1976.

And the Lords appoint this Act of Sederunt to be inserted in the Books of Sederunt.

G.C. Emslie,
I.P.D.

Edinburgh.
14th January 1976.

(a) 1967 c. 43. (b) S.I. 1964/1622 (1964 III, p. 3594).

EXPLANATORY NOTE

(This Note is not part of the Act of Sederunt.)

This Act of Sederunt requires the Court considering an application for payment out of the legal aid fund of the whole or any part of the expenses incurred by a successful unassisted party either to order the applicant to lodge a statement on oath of his grounds for so claiming payment, together with an estimate of the probable amount of those expenses, or to dismiss the application, and gives the Law Society powers to cite a party to the cause to attend the hearing of the Court disposing of the application.

STATUTORY INSTRUMENTS

1976 No. 63 (S.4)

ROADS AND BRIDGES, SCOTLAND

The Stopping Up of Roads and Private Accesses (Procedure) (Scotland) Regulations 1976

Made - - - -	14th January 1976
Laid before Parliament	28th January 1976
Coming into Operation	18th February 1976

In exercise of the powers conferred on me by sections 12 and 13 of the Roads (Scotland) Act 1970(a), and of all other powers enabling me in that behalf, I hereby make the following regulations:—

PART I

GENERAL

Citation and commencement

1. These regulations may be cited as the Stopping Up of Roads and Private Accesses (Procedure) (Scotland) Regulations 1976 and shall come into operation on 18th February 1976.

Interpretation

2. In these regulations unless the context otherwise requires, the following expressions have the meaning hereby respectively assigned to them:—

"the Act" means the Roads (Scotland) Act 1970;

"highway authority" means, in relation to a highway other than a trunk road, a regional or islands council and, in relation to a trunk road, the Secretary of State;

"local highway authority" means a highway authority other than the Secretary of State;

"local authority" means a regional or islands council;

"owner" in relation to premises means the person for the time being entitled to receive, or who would, if the same were let, be entitled to receive, the rents of the premises, and includes a trustee, factor, tutor or curator; and in the case of public or municipal property applies to the persons to whom the management thereof is entrusted;

"occupier" means the person in occupation or having the charge, management or control of premises, either on his own account or as the agent of another person.

3. The Interpretation Act 1889(b), shall apply for the interpretation of these regulations as it applies for the interpretation of an Act of Parliament.

(a) 1970 c. 20.   (b) 1889 c. 63.

PART II

FORM AND CONTENT OF ORDERS

Orders under section 12

4. An order made by a highway authority under section 12 of the Act (which provides for the stopping up of roads) shall be in the Form A set out in the Schedule hereto, or a form substantially to the like effect.

5. The plan accompanying an order made under section 12 shall be to a scale of not less than 1/2500, showing in zebra hatching the road to be closed. Any means of passage to be reserved to pedestrians shall be outlined and marked "footpath".

Orders under section 13

6. An order made by a highway authority under section 13 of the Act (which provides for the stopping up of accesses from a highway to premises) shall be in Form B set out in the Schedule hereto, or a form substantially to the like effect.

7. The plan accompanying an order under section 13 shall be to a scale of not less than 1/2500 showing:—

   (a) in solid black the access to be closed up;

   (b) by a thin diagonal hatching any new means of access to be provided; and

   (c) outlined and marked "footpath" any means of access for pedestrians which is to be reserved.

The plan shall indicate the proposed method of closing the access.

PART III

PROCEDURE FOR THE MAKING AND APPROVAL OF ORDERS

Publication of notice

8. Where a highway authority proposes to make an order under section 12 or section 13 of the Act, the authority shall publish in each of two successive weeks in at least one newspaper circulating in the area in which the road or private access to which the order relates is situated and in the Edinburgh Gazette a notice in the Form C set out in the Schedule hereto or a form substantially to the like effect.

9. Not later than the date on which the notice under regulation 8 is first published the highway authority shall serve a copy thereof together with a copy of the draft order and of any relevant map or plan and of a statement of the reasons for making the order:—

   (a) on every local authority in whose areas any road or private access to which the order relates is situated, on the district planning authority, and on any other highway authority affected;

   (b) where the order relates to a private access, on the owner and occupier of any premises to which the order relates and on the owner and occupier of any land which it is proposed to acquire for the provision of a new means of access;

(c) where the order relates to a road to be stopped up under the order, on any statutory undertakers having apparatus under, in, on, over, along or across the said road; and

(d) where the order is made by a local highway authority, on the Secretary of State.

10. Not later than the date on which the said notice is published as aforesaid the highway authority shall cause a copy thereof to be displayed in a prominent position at or near the ends of so much of any road as it is proposed to stop up, and shall keep it exhibited in such a position and in a legible condition for a period of not less than 28 days.

Objections

11. Any person desiring to object to a proposal to make an order shall send to the Secretary of State within the period and to the address specified in the notice of proposal published as required by regulation 8 above, a written statement of his objections and of the grounds thereof.

12. In the case of a proposal made by a local highway authority, the Secretary of State shall, on receipt of any objection, send a copy to the local highway authority who shall send to the objector any comments they may wish to make relevant to the objection and shall inform the Secretary of State accordingly.

13. The Secretary of State may at any time require a local highway authority to furnish him with any further information which appears to him to be relevant.

Public inquiries

14. If in any case objections are made and are not withdrawn the Secretary of State may before taking a decision cause a public local inquiry to be held:

Provided that except where an objection is made by any local authority, owner or occupier or statutory undertaker on whom a notice is required to be served under regulation 9 the Secretary of State may dispense with such an inquiry if he is satisfied that in the circumstances of the case the holding of such an inquiry is unnecessary.

15. In relation to any inquiry under regulation 14 the provisions of subsections (2), (3), and (8) of section 210 of the Local Government (Scotland) Act 1973(a) shall apply as they apply in relation to local inquiries under that section.

Confirmation of order

16. After considering any objections to the order which are not withdrawn and, where a local inquiry is held, the report of the person who held the inquiry, the Secretary of State may confirm the order either without modification or subject to such modification as he thinks fit or may decide not to confirm it.

(a) 1973 c. 65.

17. In any case where no objections are made to a proposal by a highway authority the highway authority which has published the proposal shall confirm the order:

Provided that a local highway authority before so doing shall satisfy themselves that no objection to the making of the order has been received by the Secretary of State or that any such objection has been withdrawn.

PART IV

DECISION

Notice of making, confirmation of or refusal to confirm orders

18. Immediately after an order has been made or confirmed, the highway authority shall publish in the manner prescribed by regulation 8, a notice in the Form D or E set out in the Schedule hereto, or a form substantially to the like effect and regulations 9 and 10 above shall apply to any such notice as they apply to the notice required to be published by the said regulation 8.

19. In any case where the Secretary of State decides not to confirm an order he shall notify the local highway authority accordingly. On receipt of such notification the local highway authority shall publish in the manner prescribed by regulation 8, a notice in the Form F set out in the Schedule hereto, or a form substantially to the like effect and regulations 9 and 10 above shall apply to any such notices as they apply to the notice required to be published by the said regulation 8.

Date of operation

20. An order to which these regulations apply shall become operative on the date on which the notice required by regulation 18 is first published or on such later date, if any, as may be specified in the order:

Provided that a private means of access shall not be stopped-up before the expiry of 6 weeks from the date of the first public notification of the order under regulation 8 and in a case where a new means of access is to be provided by the highway authority, before it has been so provided.

William Ross

New St. Andrew's House,   One of Her Majesty's Principal
Edinburgh.   Secretaries of State.
14th January 1976.

SCHEDULE

Form A

Form of order stopping up a road

ROADS (SCOTLAND) ACT 1970

The [*Name of Council*] [*name of road*] (Stopping Up) Order 19

Whereas the [*name of highway authority*] consider that the road specified in the Schedule to this order has become *[unnecessary] [dangerous to the public] and are satisfied that *[a suitable alternative road exists] [no alternative road is necessary] in exercise of the powers conferred on them by section 12 of the Roads (Scotland) Act 1970 and of all other powers enabling them in that behalf, hereby make the following order: —

(1)   This order may be cited as [*as in the heading*].

(2)   The Interpretation Act 1889 shall apply for the interpretation of this order as it applies for the interpretation of an Act of Parliament.

(3)   The stopping up of the road in the [of Area] specified in the Schedule to this order is hereby ordered, (subject to the reservation of the means of passage for pedestrians specified in that Schedule).

(4)   Where there is immediately before the date on which the said road is stopped up under this order any apparatus under, in, on, over, along or across the road belonging to any statutory undertakers for the purpose of carrying on their undertaking, the undertakers shall thereafter have all such rights of continuing and maintaining or renewing the apparatus as they then had.

Given under the seal of the [*name of highway authority*]

on   19

Signatures

SCHEDULE

ROAD TO BE STOPPED UP

(*Description of road, or length of road, sufficient for identification with reference to a plan accompanying the order, specifying accurately the terminal points and measurement of the length to be stopped up by reference to some permanent feature (e.g. a road junction) together with a description of any means of passage reserved for pedestrians, also related to the plan. The plan should be signed and sealed and identified by a heading embodying the title to the order*).

Delete where inapplicable.

SCHEDULE

Form B

Form of order stopping up a private access

ROADS (SCOTLAND) ACT 1970

The [*name of council*] [*name of highway*] (Stopping Up of Access) Order 19

Whereas the [*name of highway authority*] consider the private means of access from the [*name of highway*] specified in the Schedule to this order is likely to *[cause danger to] [interfere unreasonably with] traffic on the highway and are satisfied that *[a reasonably convenient alternative means of access is available] [no alternative means of access is necessary] [in a case where they are satisfied that an alternative means of access is necessary but that a reasonably convenient alternative means of access is not available they are capable of providing a new means of access] in exercise of the powers conferred on them by section 13 of the Roads (Scotland) Act 1970 and of all other powers enabling them in that behalf, hereby make the following order: —

(1)   This order may be cited as the [*as in the heading*].

(2)   The Interpretation Act 1889 shall apply for the interpretation of this order as it applies for the interpretation of an Act of Parliament.

(3)   The stopping up of the private access to [*name of highway*] specified in the Schedule to this order is hereby ordered [subject to the reservation of the means of passage for pedestrians specified in that Schedule]. [The [*name of highway authority*] shall provide the new means of access specified in the Schedule].

Given under the seal of the [*name of highway authority*] on   19

Signature

SCHEDULE

PRIVATE ACCESS TO BE STOPPED UP

(Description of access together with a description of any means of passage reserved for pedestrians and any new access proposed by the highway authority all sufficient for identification with reference to a plan accompanying the order. The plan should be signed and sealed and identified by a heading embodying the title to the order).

Delete where inapplicable.

SCHEDULE

Form C

Form of notice by a local highway
authority of intention to make an
order stopping up a road or
private means of access

ROADS (SCOTLAND) ACT 1970

NOTICE IS HEREBY GIVEN that the [*name of highway authority*] propose to make an order under section *[12] [13] of the Roads (Scotland) Act 1970 *[stopping up the road] [stopping up the private means of access] described in the Schedule hereto. The title of the order is the [*insert title*].

A copy of the draft order and of the plan referred to therein showing the *[road] [private access] to be stopped up, together with a statement of the reason for making the order may be inspected at the office of [*name and address of highway authority*] without payment of fee at all reasonable hours between [*dates when documents will be on display*].

ANY PERSON may, within 28 days from [*date of first publication of the notice*], object to the making of the order by notice in writing to the Secretary, Scottish Development Department, New St. Andrew's House, Edinburgh EH1 3SZ stating the grounds of objection.

Dated this   day of   19 .

                    Signature of Chief Executive of the
                    local highway authority

SCHEDULE

(Here insert such a description of the road or private means of access to which the order relates as may be sufficient for identification, specifying the terminal points of any length of road to be stopped up).

Delete where inapplicable.

SCHEDULE

Form D

Form of notice of confirmation of an order
stopping up a road or private means of access

ROADS (SCOTLAND) ACT 1970

The [*title of order*]

NOTICE IS HEREBY GIVEN that, on [*date*] the Secretary of State, in exercise of the powers conferred on him by section *[12(4)] [13(4)] of the Roads (Scotland) Act 1970, *[confirmed] [confirmed with modifications] the above-mentioned order stopping up *[the road] [the private means of access] described in the Schedule hereto.

Copies of the order as confirmed and of the plan referred to therein have been deposited for inspection at [*name and address of highway authority*] and may be seen there without payment of fee at all reasonable hours.

The order as confirmed becomes operative from [*date*]†.

Dated this   day of   19 .

Signature of Chief Executive of the local
highway authority

SCHEDULE

(*Here insert such a description of the road or private access to which the order relates as may be sufficient for identification*).

*Delete where inapplicable.

†Insert date of coming into operation of order. In the case of a private access where a new access has to be provided, this will be a date subsequent to the provision of the new means of access (section 13(4)(ii) of the Act).

SCHEDULE

Form E

*Form of notice of making of an order by a
local highway authority stopping up a road
or private means of access*

ROADS (SCOTLAND) ACT 1970

The [*title of order*]

NOTICE IS HEREBY GIVEN that, on [*date*] the [*name of highway
authority*] in exercise of the powers conferred on them by section *[12(4)]
[13(4)] of the Roads (Scotland) Act 1970 made and confirmed the above-
mentioned order stopping up the *[road] [private means of access] described
in the Schedule hereto.

Copies of the order as confirmed and of the plan referred to therein have been
deposited for inspection at [*name and address of highway authority*] and may
be seen there without payment of fee at all reasonable hours.

The order becomes operative from [*date*]†.

Dated this   day of   19   .

Signature of Chief Executive of the local
highway authority

SCHEDULE

*(Here insert such a description of the road or private means of access to which
the order relates as may be sufficient for identification).*

Delete where inapplicable.

†*Insert date of coming into operation of order. In the case of a private access
this will be a date at least six weeks after first publication of intention to
make the order or, where a new access has to be provided, a date subsequent
to the provision of the new means of access. (Section 13(4) (ii) of the Act).*

SCHEDULE

Form F

Form of Notice of Secretary of State's Refusal to Confirm an Order Stopping Up a Road or Private Means of Access

ROADS (SCOTLAND) ACT 1970

The [*title of draft order*].

NOTICE IS HEREBY GIVEN that, on [*date*] the Secretary of State, in exercise of the powers conferred on him by section *[12(4)] [13(4)] of the Roads (Scotland) Act 1970 refused to confirm the above-mentioned draft order to stop up *[the road] [the private means of access] described in the Schedule hereto.

Dated this   day of   19 .

Signature of Chief Executive of the
local highway authority

SCHEDULE

(*Here insert such a description of the road or private access to which the order relates as may be sufficient for identification*).

*Delete where inapplicable.

EXPLANATORY NOTE

(This Note is not part of the Regulations.)

Sections 12 and 13 of the Roads (Scotland) Act 1970 authorise highway authorities by order to stop-up roads which are considered unnecessary or dangerous to the public, and private means of accesses from highways which are likely to cause danger to, or interfere unreasonably with, traffic on the highways. These regulations prescribe the procedure to be followed in connection with the making of orders under sections 12 and 13.

Part II specifies the form and content of the orders and Part III lays down the procedure for making and confirming orders and provides for public and private notification, objections, inquiries and confirmation.

Part IV makes provision as to the date of operation of orders under the said sections 12 and 13.

STATUTORY INSTRUMENTS

1976 No. 66 (S. 5)

EDUCATION, SCOTLAND

The Central Institutions (Scotland) Amendment Regulations 1976

Made - - -	16*th January* 1976
Laid before Parliament	29*th January* 1976
Coming into Operation	19*th February* 1976

In exercise of the powers conferred upon me by sections 76(1) and 81(1) and (4) of the Education (Scotland) Act 1962(a) as said section 81 is set out in section 15 of the Education (Scotland) Act 1969(b) and of section 144(1) and (5) of the Education (Scotland) Act 1962 and of all other powers enabling me in that behalf, and being of the opinion mentioned in regulation 5 of these regulations, I hereby make the following regulations:—

Citation, construction and commencement

1. These regulations, which may be cited as the Central Institutions (Scotland) Amendment Regulations 1976, shall be construed as one with the Central Institutions (Scotland) Regulations 1972(c), with the Central Institutions (Scotland) Regulations 1974(d), with the Central Institutions (Scotland) Amendment Regulations 1974(e) and with the Central Institutions (Scotland) Amendment Regulations 1975(f) and shall come into operation on 19th February 1976.

Interpretation

2.—(1) In these regulations the expression "the principal regulations" means the Central Institutions (Scotland) Regulations 1974 as amended by the Central Institutions (Scotland) Amendment Regulations 1974 and the Central Institutions (Scotland) Amendment Regulations 1975.

(2) In these regulations any reference to any enactment or scheme shall be construed as a reference to that enactment or scheme as amended or extended and as including a reference thereto as applied by or under any other enactment or scheme.

(3) The Interpretation Act 1889(g) shall apply for the interpretation of these regulations as it applies for the interpretation of an Act of Parliament.

Duncan of Jordanstone College of Art

3. The Duncan of Jordanstone College of Art Scheme 1975(h) shall be amended as follows:

    (i) for sub-paragraph 3(*b*) of paragraph 4 there shall be substituted the following sub-paragraph:—

        "(*b*) 2 persons appointed by the Regional Council of Tayside;";

(a) 1962 c. 47.
(c) S.I. 1972/1753 (1972 III, p. 5082).
(e) S.I. 1974/1410 (1974 II, p. 5453).
(g) 1889 c. 63.

(b) 1969 c. 49.
(d) S.I. 1974/102 (1974 I, p. 351).
(f) S.I. 1975/520 (1975 I, p. 1707).
(h) S.I. 1975/697.

(ii) for sub-paragraphs (1) and (2) of paragraph 35 there shall be substituted the following sub-paragraphs:—

"(1) The governing body shall appoint a principal and, where appropriate, a vice-principal of the College and such other members of staff as they may require.

(2) The governing body may delegate to a committee appointed by the Academic Council and consisting wholly of academic staff such powers with regard to the appointment of academic staff below the level of head of department as the governing body think fit.";

(iii) in sub-paragraph 2(*b*)(i) of paragraph 43 the words "ex officio" shall be inserted after the word "College";

(iv) for sub-paragraph (3) of paragraph 43 there shall be substituted the following sub-paragraph:—

"(3) The governing body acting jointly with the governing body of the College of Technology shall determine the periods of office, not exceeding 4 years, of the appointed members of the Joint Standing Committee. The appointed members of the said Committee shall be eligible for reappointment after the lapse of such period of time, not being less than 1 year, following the expiry of a period of office as may be determined by the governing body.".

Dundee College of Technology

4. The Dundee College of Technology Scheme 1975(**a**) shall be amended as follows:

(i) for sub-paragraph 3(*b*) of paragraph 4 there shall be substituted the following sub-paragraph:—

"(*b*) 2 persons appointed by the Regional Council of Tayside;";

(ii) for sub-paragraphs (1) and (2) of paragraph 35 there shall be substituted the following sub-paragraph:—

"(1) The governing body shall appoint a principal and, where appropriate, a vice-principal of the College and such other members of staff as they may require.

(2) The governing body may delegate to a committee appointed by the Academic Council and consisting wholly of academic staff such powers with regard to the appointment of academic staff below the level of head of department as the governing body think fit.";

(iii) in sub-paragraph 2(*b*)(i) of paragraph 45 the words "ex officio" shall be inserted after the word "College";

(iv) for sub-paragraph (3) of paragraph 45 there shall be substituted the following sub-paragraph:—

"(3) The governing body acting jointly with the governing body of the College of Art shall determine the periods of office, not exceeding 4 years, of the appointed members of the Joint Standing Committee. The appointed members of the said Committee shall be eligible for reappointment after the lapse of such period of time, not being less than 1 year, following the expiry of a period of office as may be determined by the governing body.".

(**a**) S.I. 1975/698.

Revocations of instruments

5. The Articles of Association specified in column (1) of the Schedule to these regulations are hereby revoked to the extent (being the extent to which the provisions of such Articles of Association are in the opinion of the Secretary of State inconsistent with the principal regulations) specified opposite such Articles of Association in column (2) of that Schedule.

Savings

6.—(1) The provision of any instrument relating to any of the Central Institutions specified in these regulations and in force immediately before the date of coming into operation of these regulations shall, except as otherwise expressly varied or revoked by these regulations, continue in force after the said date as if these regulations had not been made.

(2) Section 38(2) of the Interpretation Act 1889 shall apply as if these regulations were an Act of Parliament and as if any provision of any instrument hereby revoked by these regulations were an Act of Parliament repealed by an Act of Parliament.

William Ross,

One of Her Majesty's
Principal Secretaries of State

New St Andrew's House,
Edinburgh

16th January 1976.

Regulation 5

SCHEDULE

REVOCATIONS OF THE PROVISIONS OF INSTRUMENTS

Instrument Column (1)	Extent of Revocation Column (2)
Articles of Association of the Scottish College of Textiles dated 26th October 1922 as amended by Special Resolutions passed on 27th December 1949 and 27th December 1967 and by the principal regulations.	In Article 65 the words ", one of whom shall be the person appointed by the County of Selkirk. The remaining Members of the Executive shall be appointed by the Governors" shall be deleted.

EXPLANATORY NOTE

(This Note is not part of the Regulations.)

These Regulations amend the Duncan of Jordanstone College of Art Scheme 1975 and the Dundee College of Technology Scheme 1975 by increasing from one to two the number of persons who may be appointed to the governing body of each of those colleges by the Tayside Regional Council. They also make certain other minor amendments relating to the administration of the colleges.

The Regulations also revoke a provision in the Articles of Association of the Scottish College of Textiles which is, in the opinion of the Secretary of State, inconsistent with the Central Institutions (Scotland) Regulations 1974 as amended.

STATUTORY INSTRUMENTS

1976 No. 70 (C. 1)

INCOME TAX

The Income Tax (Certification of Life Policies) (Appointed Day) Order 1976

Made - - - - *20th January* 1976

The Treasury, in exercise of the powers conferred on them by paragraph 1(1) of Part I of Schedule 2 to the Finance Act 1975(a), hereby make the following Order:—

Citation

1. This Order may be cited as the Income Tax (Certification of Life Policies) (Appointed Day) Order 1976.

Appointed Day

2. The day appointed for the purposes of paragraph 1(1) of Part I of Schedule 2 to the Finance Act 1975 is 1st April 1976.

3. The Interpretation Act 1889(b) shall apply for the interpretation of this Order as it applies for the interpretation of an Act of Parliament.

> *M. Cocks,*
> *James A. Dunn,*
> Two of the Lords Commissioners
> of Her Majesty's Treasury.

20th January 1976.

EXPLANATORY NOTE

(This Note is not part of the Order.)

Part I of Schedule 2 to the Finance Act 1975 provides for the function of certifying life policies as "qualifying" policies for income tax purposes, at present exercised by the life offices issuing the policies, to be taken over as from an Appointed Day by the Board of Inland Revenue. This Order fixes 1st April 1976 as the Appointed Day.

(a) 1975 c. 7.   (b) 1889 c. 63.

STATUTORY INSTRUMENTS

1976 No. 71

COUNTER-INFLATION

The Counter-Inflation (Price Code) (Amendment) Order 1976

Made - - - -	*22nd January* 1976
Laid before Parliament	*22nd January* 1976
Coming into Operation	*1st February* 1976

The Secretary of State in exercise of the powers conferred by section 2 of the Counter-Inflation Act 1973(a) as amended (b), and of all other powers enabling her in that behalf, and having consulted the Price Commission and representatives of consumers, persons experienced in the supply of goods or services, employers and employees and other persons in accordance with subsection (4) of the said section 2, hereby makes the following Order:—

1.—(1) This Order may be cited as the Counter-Inflation (Price Code) (Amendment) Order 1976 and shall come into operation on 1st February 1976.

(2) The Interpretation Act 1889(c) shall apply for the interpretation of this Order as it applies for the interpretation of an Act of Parliament.

2. The Schedule to the Counter-Inflation (Price Code) Order 1974(d) as amended (e) shall have effect subject to the amendments specified in the Schedule to this Order.

3. The Counter-Inflation (Price Code) (Amendment) Order 1975(f) is hereby amended in the Schedule thereto by the deletion of paragraphs 2 and 3.

Shirley Williams,
Secretary of State for
Prices and Consumer Protection.

22nd January 1976.

(a) 1973 c. 9.
(b) *See* S.I. 1974/1218 (1974 II, p. 4631).
(c) 1889 c. 63.
(d) S.I. 1974/2113 (1974 III, p. 8253).
(e) S.I. 1974/2158. 1975/864, 1293 (1974 III, p. 8441; 1975 II, pp. 3072, 4400).
(f) S.I. 1975/864 (1975 II, p. 3072).

(*Article 2*)

SCHEDULE
●
AMENDMENTS TO THE SCHEDULE TO THE COUNTER-INFLATION
(PRICE CODE) ORDER 1974

1. For paragraph 79 there shall be substituted—

"*Relief for investment*

79.—(1) Enterprises may increase net profit margin reference levels, the levels of gross percentage margins and prices, by reference to their estimated capital expenditure on investment physically located (or, in the case of road vehicles, based) in the United Kingdom, in accordance with the provisions of this paragraph.

(2) In this paragraph and in paragraph 80—

"expenditure on investment" means expenditure, approved in the case of a company by the board of directors, which it is estimated will actually become due and payable in the investment year (any estimate being revised from time to time on the basis of fact or of revised estimates, as circumstances may require) being—

(*a*) capital expenditure on new and second-hand plant and machinery other than under agreements within (*b*) below;

(*b*) payments—

(i) under leasing and hiring agreements for terms of not less than 2 years; and

(ii) under hire-purchase, credit sale and conditional sale agreements; relating to new and second-hand plant and machinery; and

(*c*) capital expenditure on the construction of industrial buildings and of warehouses;

less the disposal value of any plant and machinery, industrial buildings and warehouses disposed of in the investment year:

Provided that—

(i) expenditure relating to trading operations outside the control (except by virtue only of paragraph 5) shall be left out of account; and

(ii) expenditure which cannot be appropriated to each activity within the meaning of paragraph 17 shall be apportioned in proportion to the turnover of all the activities concerned in the year of account ended not more than 12 months before the beginning of the investment year;

and in this definition, "plant and machinery" does not include mechanically propelled vehicles other than—

(*a*) vehicles of a construction primarily suited for the conveyance of goods or burden of any description;

(*b*) vehicles of a type not commonly used as private vehicles and unsuitable to be so used; and

(*c*) vehicles provided wholly or mainly for hire to, or for the carriage of, members of the public in the ordinary course of a trade;

"the investment year" means a period of 12 months chosen by the enterprise beginning on or after 1st December 1974 and not later than the beginning of the relief year;

"the relief year" means a period of 12 months chosen by the enterprise—

(*a*) in the case of an enterprise required to furnish periodical returns pursuant to an order (a) under section 15 of the Counter-Inflation Act 1973, beginning not earlier than 56 days after the enterprise concerned has informed the Commission that it intends to apply this paragraph; and

(b) in the case of any other enterprise, beginning not earlier than 1st December 1974;

"relevant expenditure" means an amount (revised from time to time to take account of revision of expenditure on investment) being 20 per cent of expenditure on investment;

"turnover", in relation to the relief year, means the turnover on trading operations within the control which may reasonably be expected to be achieved in the year in question, revised from time to time on the basis of fact or as circumstances may require.

(3) The permitted increases in net profit margin reference levels, the levels of gross percentage margins and prices shall be calculated in accordance with the following provisions of this paragraph. An enterprise—

(a) may, for the relief year, treat the net profit margin reference level as increased by the addition of a figure found by expressing the relevant expenditure as a percentage of turnover;

(b) in respect of its distribution activities, may, for the relief year, treat the level of the gross percentage margin from time to time ascertained under paragraph 86 as increased by the addition of a figure found by expressing the relevant expenditure as a percentage of turnover; and

(c) in respect of its manufacturing and service activities, may increase any price within control for a period of 12 months beginning in the relief year by an amount the additional yield from which, taken with the additional yield from all other such increases, will not exceed the relevant expenditure; and the total increase under this head in the price for any individual product shall not exceed a percentage equal to four times the percentage points by which the net profit margin reference level may be increased under head (a) above but, where an increase to be made in any price under this head is less than a whole number of pence, the increased price may be rounded up to the next halfpenny.

(4) If the application of sub-paragraph (3) has not caused the relevant expenditure to be recovered in sales, an enterprise for so long as may be necessary—

(a) may, in respect of its manufacturing and service activities, treat the reference level as increased by an amount sufficient to permit a price calculated under sub-paragraph (3)(c) to remain in force until the relevant expenditure has been recovered;

(b) may, in respect of its distribution activities, treat the reference level and the level of the gross percentage margin ascertained under paragraph 86 as increased by an amount sufficient to permit the recovery of any part of the relevant expenditure which has not been recovered:

Provided that where the amount of the relevant expenditure has been recovered (and any adjustments required under paragraph 80 to the amount actually recovered have had effect) net profit margin reference levels, gross percentage margins and prices may until 31st July 1976 continue at levels determined under sub-paragraph (3).

(5) Investment expenditure in respect of which the enterprise has benefited from a modification under paragraph 81 or any provision which it replaces may not be included in the calculation of relevant expenditure—

(a) *See* S.I. 1974/2115 (1974 III, p. 8306).

(a) where the modification is to the provisions relating to profit margins, for the purposes of sub-paragraph (3)(a):

Provided that, for the purposes of sub-paragraph (3)(c), sub-paragraph (3)(a) shall have effect without adaptation; and

(b) where the modification is to the provisions relating to allowable cost increases or to increases in total costs, for the purposes of sub-paragraph (3)(b) and (c).

(6) Increases in prices under this paragraph and under this paragraph as applied by paragraph 79A must be disregarded in determining increases in any price under any other provisions of this Code."

2. After paragraph 79 as substituted by paragraph 1 above there shall be inserted the following paragraph—

"*Further relief for investment*

79A.—(1) An enterprise which has obtained relief under paragraph 79 may obtain further relief under that paragraph as applied by this paragraph; and for that purpose the provisions of paragraph 79 shall have effect accordingly and subject to the following provisions of this paragraph.

(2) For the purposes of this paragraph, the definitions of "the investment year" and "the relief year" in sub-paragraph (2) of paragraph 79 shall not have effect and "the investment year" and "the relief year" shall mean respectively a period of 12 months beginning immediately after the end of the investment year or of the relief year, as the case may be, by reference to which relief under paragraph 79 was calculated.

(3) In the case of an enterprise required to furnish periodical returns pursuant to an order(a) under section 15 of the Counter-Inflation Act 1973(b), no relief shall be taken under this paragraph earlier than 28 days after the enterprise concerned has informed the Commission that it intends to apply this paragraph.

(4) Where relief is obtained under this paragraph, the proviso to paragraph 79(4) shall cease to have effect.

(5) References to paragraph 79 in any provisions of the Code, other than paragraph 79 and the foregoing provisions of this paragraph, include references to paragraph 79 as applied by this paragraph."

3. After paragraph 136 there shall be inserted the following paragraphs—

"*Special provisions facilitating selective price restraint*
Restricted price products

137.—(1) If the Secretary of State is satisfied that a substantial number of enterprises, which sell products or provide services of a description appearing to the Secretary of State to be of special importance in family expenditure, are able to restrain prices for those products and services in accordance with the policy set out in the document "The Attack on Inflation" laid before Parliament by command of Her Majesty in July 1975 (Cmnd. 6151), the Secretary of State may so certify in relation to any description of such products and services ("restricted price product").

(2) Paragraphs 138 to 141 shall have effect for facilitating price restraint in relation to restricted price products and apply to all manufacturing and service enterprises and to all distributors but not to the nationalised industries listed in paragraph 97 of the Code.

(a) *See* S.I. 1974/2115 (1974 III, p. 8306).   **(b)** 1973 c. 9.

Transfer of revenue from restricted price products

138.—(1) Where an enterprise—

(a) may, under the Code, implement an increase in the price of a restricted price product, and

(b) does not at any time implement any increase, including an increase under paragraph 79 (relief for investment), which would bring the price of that product to a level which is more than 5 per cent above the base price together with such amount (if any) as will bring the price up to the next whole multiple of the unit of currency in which it is the established practice of the enterprise to express prices for products of the same description,

the enterprise may, in accordance with this paragraph, implement an increase in the price of one or more transferred revenue products chosen by the enterprise, whether sold in the course of an activity within the same unit for profit margin control or another.

(2) Under this paragraph, an enterprise—

(a) may increase the price of any transferred revenue product by an amount the yield of which over a period of 6 months will, taken with the corresponding yield of all other such increases in respect of the same transferable revenue, result in the receipt of an increase in revenue of not more than the amount of the transferable revenue; and

(b) may, in respect of its distribution activities, treat the level of the gross percentage margin as increased by an amount sufficient to permit the receipt in revenue over 6 months of the amount of any transferable revenue relating to restricted price products sold in the course of its manufacturing and service activities and not transferred under this paragraph to transferred revenue products sold in the course of those activities.

(3) The Commission shall under this paragraph permit an enterprise to implement different price increases in different parts of the United Kingdom where they are satisfied that differentials in price between different parts of the United Kingdom are in accord with the established practice of the enterprise.

(4) An increase in price under this paragraph may be made notwithstanding anything in the foregoing provisions of the Code including, in particular, paragraph 18 (which provides for the limitation of price increases by reference to increases in total costs per unit of output) and paragraph 29 (which limits the frequency of price increases).

Savings for provisions relating to net profit margins and gross percentage margins

139. For the purposes of paragraphs 37 to 40, 60, 77, 78, 88 and 93 (safeguards), and 66 and 94 (which specify action to be taken where margins likely to be exceeded)—

(a) in the case of any enterprise, the level of the net profit margin, and

(b) in the case of a distributor, the level of the gross percentage margin,

shall be taken to be what it would have been if no adjustment in prices, whether of restricted price products or of transferred revenue products, had been made under paragraph 138.

Prices of products adjusted under paragraph 138

140. Adjustments in prices, whether of restricted price products or of transferred revenue products, under paragraph 138 must be disregarded in determining permitted prices under other provisions of the Code.

Interpretation of paragraphs 137 *to* 141

141. For the purposes of paragraphs 137 to 140 and of this paragraph—

(*a*) "base price", in relation to a restricted price product, means the price charged by an enterprise for comparable transactions immediately before 1st February 1976 (or, in the case of a service, 14th February 1976) or—

    (i) in the case of a restricted price product in relation to which there is no such comparable transaction or of a restricted price product which is not on sale immediately before 1st February 1976 because of seasonal factors (not being, in either case, a product within (ii) below), the first price charged after 31st January 1976 (or, in the case of a service, 13th February 1976); or

    (ii) in the case of a restricted price product which was sold by the enterprise only at a special offer price immediately before 1st February 1976 (or, in the case of a service, 14th February 1976), the price at which the enterprise last sold the product before the beginning of the period of the special offer;

and includes any excise duty charged, or which may be charged, on the product;

(*b*) "special offer price", in relation to a restricted price product, means the price—

    (i) at which an enterprise sells the product during a continuous period, including 31st January 1976 (or, in the case of a service, 14th February 1976) and of not more than 6 months, and

    (ii) which is lower than the price at which it last sold such products before it began selling them at the price first mentioned in this sub-paragraph;

(*c*) "restricted price product" means a product or service specified in a certificate under paragraph 137(1);

(*d*) "transferable revenue" in relation to a restricted price product, means the yield over a period (being a period of 6 months, beginning not earlier than 1st February 1976, chosen by the enterprise or, in a case where the price of the product is to be increased, beginning when the increase is implemented) from sales of the product at a price permitted under the Code (apart from paragraph 138) after deduction of the yield over that period from sales of the product at its price at the beginning of that period, including any increase then implemented; and

(*e*) "transferred revenue product" means any product or service (including a restricted price product)."

EXPLANATORY NOTE

(This Note is not part of the Order.)

This Order further amends the Price Code contained in the Schedule to the Counter-Inflation (Price Code) Order 1974.

First, in a new paragraph 79A, it extends the provision for relief for expenditure on investment provided by paragraph 79. The new paragraph permits companies to apply a second year's entitlement to investment relief on the same basis as provided in paragraph 79. Paragraph 79 itself is also included in a form which consolidates earlier amendments with, in sub-paragraph (4), an amendment permitting companies which do not invoke the new paragraph 79A to maintain prices and profit margins established under the existing relief until 31st July 1976, and, in sub-paragraph (6), a technical amendment consequential upon the introduction of paragraph 79A.

Second, in furtherance of the policy contained in the White Paper *The Attack on Inflation* (Cmnd. 6151), the Order introduces, as paragraphs 137 to 141, provisions to facilitate selective price restraint by permitting the recovery of revenue, which may be forgone by restraint in the prices of certain products, by increasing the prices of other products.

STATUTORY INSTRUMENTS

1976 No. 72

COUNTER-INFLATION

The Counter-Inflation (Prices and Charges) (Information) (Amendment) Order 1976

Made - - - -	*22nd January* 1976
Coming into Operation	*1st February* 1976

The Secretary of State, in exercise of powers conferred on her by section 15 of the Counter-Inflation Act 1973(a), as amended(b), and of all other powers enabling her in that behalf, hereby makes the following Order:—

1.—(1) This Order may be cited as the Counter-Inflation (Prices and Charges) (Information) (Amendment) Order 1976 and shall come into operation on 1st February 1976.

(2) The Interpretation Act 1889(c) shall apply for the interpretation of this Order as it applies for the interpretation of an Act of Parliament.

2. The Counter-Inflation (Prices and Charges) (Information) Order 1974(d) as varied(e) is hereby further varied—

(a) by the insertion after article 6A of the following article—

"6B. The provisions of articles 6, 7 and 8 (except in so far as they refer to paragraph 10 of the Schedule) and of paragraphs 9, 11 and 12 of the Schedule apply in relation to paragraph 79A (further provision for relief for investment) of the code as they apply in relation to paragraph 79 of the code save that, for the purposes of those provisions as applied by this article, "the investment year" and "the relief year" have the meanings assigned to them respectively in paragraph 79A(2) of the code."

(b) in the Schedule, by the insertion after paragraph 12 of the following paragraph—

"*Price Restraint*

12A. In a case where an increase in a price or charge is implemented or the level of gross percentage margin is increased under paragraph 138 of the code (which permits increases in certain prices and gross percentage margins to facilitate restraint in other prices)—

(a) any transferred revenue product and any increase in its price;

(a) 1973 c. 9.
(b) *See* S.I. 1974/1218 (1974 II, p. 4631).
(c) 1889 c. 63.
(d) S.I. 1974/2115 (1974 III, p. 8306).
(e) S.I. 1975/865, 1295, 1948, 2209 (1975 II, pp. 3075, 4406; III, p. 7242).

(b) any restricted price product to which the transferable revenue justifying any increase referred to in (a) above relates;

(c) the name and address of the person selling each restricted price product, if different from the person specified pursuant to paragraph 1(1);

(d) the unit for profit margin control within which each restricted price product is sold, if different from that within which the goods or services to which the return or record relates are sold or provided;

(e) the amount of all transferable revenue and the manner of its calculation, including the relevant base prices and the dates by reference to which they are respectively ascertained;

(f) any increase in revenue arising from increases in prices and margins under paragraph 138 of the code; and

(g) in the case of a distributor, any modification in the level of the gross percentage margin under paragraph 138 of the code;

and in this paragraph, "base price", "restricted price product", "transferable revenue" and "transferred revenue product" have the meanings assigned to them respectively in paragraph 141 of the code."

Shirley Williams,
Secretary of State
22nd January 1976.   for Prices and Consumer Protection.

EXPLANATORY NOTE

(This Note is not part of the Order.)

This Order further amends the Counter-Inflation (Prices and Charges) (Information) Order 1974.

It requires enterprises, which are obliged under the 1974 Order to make returns to the Price Commission or to keep records, to include in such returns or records information relating to changes in prices, charges and margins under paragraph 79A of the Price Code (which extends relief for investment under paragraph 79 for a further period) or under paragraphs 137 to 141 of the Code (which permit increases in the prices of certain products and changes in the levels of certain gross percentage margins to facilitate restraint in other prices and gross percentage margins in furtherance of the policy contained in the White Paper *The Attack on Inflation* (Cmnd. 6151)).

Paragraphs 79A and 137 to 141 are inserted in the Price Code by the Counter-Inflation (Price Code) (Amendment) Order 1976 (S.I. 1976/71).

1976 No. 73

COUNTER-INFLATION

The Counter-Inflation (Notification of Increases in Prices and Charges) (Amendment) Order 1976

Made - - - -	*22nd January* 1976
Laid before Parliament	*22nd January* 1976
Coming into Operation	*1st February* 1976

The Secretary of State, in exercise of powers conferred on her by sections 5 and 15 of, and paragraph 1(1), (2), (4) and (6) of Schedule 3 to, the Counter-Inflation Act 1973(a) as amended(b), and of all other powers enabling her in that behalf, hereby makes the following Order:—

1.—(1) This Order may be cited as the Counter-Inflation (Notification of Increases in Prices and Charges) (Amendment) Order 1976 and shall come into operation on 1st February 1976.

(2) The Interpretation Act 1889(c) shall apply for the interpretation of this Order as it applies for the interpretation of an Act of Parliament.

2. The Counter-Inflation (Notification of Increases in Prices and Charges) (No. 2) Order 1974(d) as varied(e) is hereby further varied in Schedule 4—

(*a*) by the insertion after paragraph 7A of the following paragraph—

"*Price Restraint*

7B. In a case where the grounds specified pursuant to paragraph 7(1) above as those upon which the person required to make the notification considers the increase specified pursuant to paragraph 4 above to be justified consist of or include an increase in price under paragraph 138 of the code (which permits increases in certain prices to facilitate restraint of others), particulars of—

(*a*) the restricted price product or products to which the transferable revenue relates;

(*b*) the amount of the transferable revenue and the manner of its calculation, including the base price and the date by reference to which it is ascertained;

(*c*) the name and address of the person selling each restricted price product, if different from the person specified pursuant to paragraph 1;

(a) 1973 c. 9.
(c) 1889 c. 63.
(b) *See* S.I. 1974/1218 (1974 II, p. 4631).
(d) S.I. 1974/2114 (1974 III, p. 8291).
(e) The variation Orders are not relevant to the subject matter of this Order.

(*d*) the unit for profit margin control within which each re-stricted price product is sold, if different from that within which the goods or services to which the notification relates are sold or provided;

(*e*) the amount which the increase specified pursuant to paragraph 4(1) may reasonably be estimated to yield over a period of 6 months; and

(*f*) the amount which all other increases, whether in the same unit for profit margin control or another, specified in any notifi-cation to the Commission relating to an increase under para-graph 138 of the code and all increases which would have been required to be so specified apart from any provision of articles 7 to 10 may reasonably be estimated to yield in total;

and in this paragraph "base price", "restricted price product" and "transferable revenue" have the meanings assigned to them respectively in paragraph 141 of the code."

(*b*) in paragraph 10, by the insertion after the words "paragraph 79" of the words "or paragraph 79A" and in sub-paragraph (*a*), by the substitution for the words "paragraph 3" of the words "paragraph 4(1)".

22nd January 1976.	*Shirley Williams,* Secretary of State for Prices and Consumer Protection.

EXPLANATORY NOTE

(This Note is not part of the Order.)

This Order further amends the Counter-Inflation (Notification of Increases in Prices and Charges) (No. 2) Order 1974.

It requires an enterprise, which is obliged under the 1974 Order to notify proposed increases in prices and charges to the Price Commission to include additional information in notifications which rely on paragraph 79A of the Price Code (which extends relief for investment under paragraph 79 for a further period) or under paragraphs 137 to 141 of the Code (which permit increases in the prices of certain products to facilitate restraint in other prices in furtherance of the policy contained in the White Paper *The Attack on Inflation* (Cmnd. 6151)).

Paragraphs 79A and 137 to 141 are inserted in the Price Code by the Counter-Inflation (Price Code) (Amendment) Order 1976 (S.I.1976/71).

STATUTORY INSTRUMENTS

1976 No. 74 (C. 2)

MEDICINES

The Medicines Act 1968 (Commencement No. 5) Order 1976

Made	-	-	-	-	*22nd January* 1976

The Secretaries of State respectively concerned with health in England and in Wales, the Secretary of State concerned with health and with agriculture in Scotland, the Minister of Agriculture, Fisheries and Food, the Department of Health and Social Services for Northern Ireland and the Department of Agriculture for Northern Ireland, acting jointly, in exercise of powers conferred by section 136(3) of the Medicines Act 1968(a) and now vested in them(b) and of all other powers enabling them in that behalf, after consulting such organisations as appear to them to be representative of interests likely to be substantially affected by the following order, hereby make the following order:—

1.—(1) The 20th February 1976 shall be the day appointed for the coming into operation of section 135(2) (repeal of enactments) of the Medicines Act 1968 (hereinafter referred to as "the Act") for the purpose of—

(a) section 1 of the Therapeutic Substances Act 1956(c) (hereinafter referred to as "the Act of 1956") to the extent specified in paragraph (2) of this Article, and

(b) section 2 of the Act of 1956.

(2) The repeal of section 1 of the Act of 1956 shall have effect in respect of—

(a) the substances specified in paragraphs 2 and 4 of Schedule 1 to the Act of 1956,

(b) the substances specified in paragraphs 1 and 3 of that Schedule in so far as those substances are substances to which the restrictions imposed by sections 7(3) and 31(4) of the Act apply or, in the case of the said section 7(3), would apply but for any exemption from that subsection conferred under or by any provision of the Act, and

---

(a) 1968 c. 67.

(b) In the case of the Secretaries of State concerned with health in England and in Wales by virtue of Article 2(2) of, and Schedule 1 to, the Transfer of Functions (Wales) Order 1969 (S.I. 1969/388; 1969 I, p. 1070), and in the case of the Northern Ireland Departments by virtue of section 40 of, and Schedule 5 to, the Northern Ireland Constitution Act 1973 (c. 36), and paragraph 2(1)(b) of Schedule 1 to the Northern Ireland Act 1974 (c. 28).

(c) 1956 c. 25.

(*c*) all the substances added to that Schedule by regulations made under section 5(1)(*d*) of the Act of 1956 except the following in so far as they are not substances to which the restrictions imposed by sections 7(3) and 31(4) of the Act apply or, in the case of the said section 7(3), would apply but for any exemption from that subsection conferred under or by any provision of the Act:—

  (i) preparations of the pituitary (posterior lobe) or the active principles thereof (whether obtained by fractionation of the gland or by synthesis) or of derivatives of those principles with the same specific biological action, which are intended for use by parenteral injection(**a**),

  (ii) corticotrophin and preparations thereof(**a**),

  (iii) heparin and preparations thereof intended for use by parenteral injection(**b**),

  (iv) hyaluronidase and preparations thereof intended for use by parenteral injection(**b**).

2. This order may be cited as the Medicines Act 1968 (Commencement No. 5) Order 1976.

Signed by authority of the Secretary of State for Social Services.

D. A. L. Owen,
Minister of State,
Department of Health and Social Security.

12th January 1976.

John Morris,
Secretary of State for Wales.

12th January 1976.

William Ross,
Secretary of State for Scotland.

15th January 1976.

In witness whereof the official seal of the Minister of Agriculture, Fisheries and Food is hereunto affixed on 16th January 1976.

(L.S.)

Frederick Peart,
Minister of Agriculture, Fisheries and Food.

(**a**) *See* S.I. 1966/502 (1966 I, p. 1025).   (**b**) *See* S.I. 1966/501 (1966 I, p. 1015).

Sealed with the official seal of the Department of Health and Social Services or Northern Ireland this 21st day of January 1976.

(L.S.)

N. *Dugdale*,
Permanent Secretary.

Sealed with the official seal of the Department of Agriculture for Northern Ireland this 22nd day of January 1976.

(L.S.)

J. A. *Young*,
Permanent Secretary.

EXPLANATORY NOTE

(*This Note is not part of the Order.*)

This Order brings into operation on 20th February 1976 certain parts of section 135(2) of the Medicines Act 1968 so as to repeal section 1 of the Therapeutic Substances Act 1956 to the extent specified and the whole of section 2.

STATUTORY INSTRUMENTS

1976 No. 77

INDUSTRIAL TRAINING

The Industrial Training Levy (Petroleum) Order 1976

Made - - -	*21st January* 1976
Laid before Parliament	*2nd February* 1976
Coming into Operation	*25th February* 1976

Whereas proposals made by the Petroleum Industry Training Board for the raising and collection of a levy have been submitted to, and approved by, the Manpower Services Commission under section 7 of the Industrial Training Act 1964(a) ("the 1964 Act"), as amended by section 6 of and Schedule 2 to the Employment and Training Act 1973(b) ("the 1973 Act") and have thereafter been submitted by the said Commission to the Secretary of State under section 7(1C) of the 1964 Act as inserted by the 1973 Act;

And whereas in pursuance of section 7(1A)(*a*) of the 1964 Act as inserted by the 1973 Act the said proposals include provision for the exemption from the levy of employers who, in view of the small number of their employees, ought in the opinion of the Secretary of State to be exempted from it;

And whereas the Secretary of State estimates that the amount which, disregarding any exemptions, will be payable by virtue of this Order by any employer in the petroleum industry, does not exceed an amount which the Secretary of State estimates is equal to one per cent. of the aggregate of the emoluments and payments intended to be disbursed as emoluments which have been paid or are payable by any such employer to or in respect of persons employed in the industry, in respect of the period specified in the said proposals as relevant, that is to say the period of twelve months that commenced on 1st June 1974;

And whereas the Secretary of State is satisfied that proposals published by the said Board in pursuance of section 4A of the 1964 Act, as inserted by the 1973 Act, provide for exemption certificates relating to the levy in such cases as he considers appropriate;

Now, therefore, the Secretary of State in exercise of the powers conferred by section 4 of the 1964 Act, as amended by section 6 of and Schedule 2 to the 1973 Act, and of all other powers enabling him in that behalf hereby makes the following Order:—

Citation and commencement

1. This Order may be cited as the Industrial Training Levy (Petroleum) Order 1976 and shall come into operation on 25th February 1976.

(a) 1964 c. 16.   (b) 1973 c. 50.

Interpretation

2.—(1) In this Order unless the context otherwise requires:—

(a) "agriculture" has the same meaning as in section 109(3) of the Agriculture Act 1947(**a**) or, in relation to Scotland, as in section 86(3) of the Agriculture (Scotland) Act 1948(**b**);

(b) "an appeal tribunal" means an industrial tribunal established under section 12 of the Industrial Training Act 1964;

(c) "assessment" means an assessment of an employer to the levy;

(d) "average number" in relation to the persons employed at or from a petroleum establishment of an employer means the number that is equal to the average (calculated to the lowest whole number) of the numbers of the persons employed at or from the establishment by the employer on the relevant dates;

(e) "the Board" means the Petroleum Industry Training Board;

(f) "business" means any activities of industry or commerce;

(g) "charity" has the same meaning as in section 360 of the Income and Corporation Taxes Act 1970(**c**);

(h) "employer" means a person who is an employer in the petroleum industry at any time in the seventh levy period;

(i) "exemption certificate" means a certificate issued by the Board under section 4B of the 1964 Act, as inserted by the 1973 Act;

(j) "the industrial training order" means the Industrial Training (Petroleum Board) Order 1967(**d**) as amended by the Industrial Training (Petroleum Board) Order 1970(**e**);

(k) "the levy" means the levy imposed by the Board in respect of the seventh levy period;

(l) "notice" means a notice in writing;

(m) "petroleum establishment" means an establishment in Great Britain engaged wholly or mainly in the petroleum industry for a total of twenty-seven or more weeks in the period of twelve months that commenced on 1st June 1974 or, being an establishment that commenced to carry on business in the said period, for a total number of weeks exceeding one half of the number of weeks in the part of the said period commencing with the day on which business was commenced and ending on the last day thereof;

(n) "the petroleum industry" means any one or more of the activities which, subject to the provisions of paragraph 2 of the Schedule to the industrial training order, are specified in paragraph 1 of that Schedule as the activities of the petroleum industry;

(o) "the relevant dates" means 2nd September 1974 and 3rd March 1975;

(p) "the seventh levy period" means the period commencing with the day upon which this Order comes into operation and ending on 31st March 1976.

(a) 1947 c. 48. (b) 1948 c. 45.
(c) 1970 c. 10. (d) S.I. 1967/648 (1967 I, p. 2032).
(e) S.I. 1970/205 (1970 I, p. 926).

(2) Any reference in this Order to persons employed at or from a petroleum establishment shall in any case where the employer is a company be construed as including a reference to any director of the company (or any person occupying the position of director by whatever name he was called) who devoted substantially the whole of his time to the service of the company.

(3) For the purposes of this Order no regard shall be had—

(a) to any person employed at or from a petroleum establishment, being on either or both of the relevant dates—

(i) a person normally employed by the employer for less than twenty-two hours a week; or

(ii) a male person aged sixty-five years or more or a female person aged sixty years or more; or

(iii) a person employed under a contract for services;

(b) to any person employed wholly in agriculture or in the supply of food or drink for immediate consumption; or

(c) to any person who is employed as the master or a member of the crew of a ship or who, being ordinarily employed as a seaman, is employed in or about a ship in port by the owner or charterer thereof on work of a kind ordinarily done by a seaman on a ship while it is in port.

(4) In the case where a petroleum establishment is taken over (whether directly or indirectly) by an employer in succession to, or jointly with, another person, a person employed at or from the establishment on either or both of the relevant dates by a person other than the employer carrying on the establishment on the day upon which this Order comes into operation shall be deemed for the purposes of this Order to have been employed by the last mentioned employer, and any reference in this Order to persons employed by an employer at or from a petroleum establishment on either or both of the relevant dates shall be construed accordingly.

(5) Any reference in this Order to an establishment that commences to carry on business or that ceases to carry on business shall not be taken to apply where the location of the establishment is changed but its business is continued wholly or mainly at or from the new location, or where the suspension of activities is of a temporary or seasonal nature.

(6) The Interpretation Act 1889(a) shall apply to the interpretation of this Order as it applies to the interpretation of an Act of Parliament.

Imposition of the levy

3.—(1) The levy to be imposed by the Board on employers in respect of the seventh levy period shall be assessed in accordance with the provisions of this Article.

(2) The levy shall be assessed by the Board separately in respect of each relevant establishment (that is to say, each petroleum establishment other than one which is exempted by an exemption certificate or one which is an establishment of an employer who is exempted by virtue of paragraph (5) of this Article), but in agreement with the employer one assessment may be made in respect of any number of relevant establishments, in which case those establishments shall be deemed for the purpose of that assessment to constitute one establishment.

(a) 1889 c. 63.

(3) Subject to the provisions of this Article, the levy in respect of a petroleum establishment of an employer shall be assessed by reference to the average number of the persons employed at or from the establishment by the employer as follows—

(a) where the said average number of persons exceeded ten but did not exceed twenty, by multiplying the sum of £10 by that average number and by subtracting from the amount so obtained the sum of £60; or

(b) where the said average number of persons exceeded twenty, by multiplying the sum of £7 by the said average number of persons.

(4) The amount of the levy imposed in respect of a petroleum establishment that ceases to carry on business in the seventh levy period shall be in the same proportion to the amount that would otherwise be due under paragraph (3) of this Article as the number of days between the commencement of the said levy period and the date of cessation of business (both dates inclusive) bears to the number of days in the said levy period.

(5) There shall be exempt from the levy—

(a) an employer in whose case the average number of all the persons employed by him at or from the petroleum establishment or establishments of the employer (including any persons employed at or from a petroleum establishment by an associated company of the employer) was less than eleven;

(b) a charity.

Assessment notices

4.—(1) The Board shall serve an assessment notice on every employer assessed to the levy, but one notice may comprise two or more assessments.

(2) An assessment notice shall state the Board's address for the service of a notice of appeal or of an application for an extension of time for appealing.

(3) An assessment notice may be served on the person assessed to the levy either by delivering it to him personally or by leaving it, or sending it to him by post, at his last known address or place of business in the United Kingdom or, if that person is a corporation, by leaving it, or sending it by post to the corporation, at such address or place of business or at its registered or principal office.

Payment of the levy

5.—(1) Subject to the provisions of this Article and of Articles 6 and 7, the amount of the levy payable under an assessment notice served by the Board shall be due and payable to the Board one month after the date of the notice.

(2) The amount of an assessment shall not be recoverable by the Board until there has expired the time allowed for appealing against the assessment by Article 7(1) of this Order and any further period or periods of time that the Board or an appeal tribunal may have allowed for appealing under paragraph (2) or (3) of that Article, or, where an appeal is brought, until the appeal is decided or withdrawn.

Withdrawal of assessment

6.—(1) The Board may, by a notice served on the person assessed to the levy in the same manner as an assessment notice, withdraw an assessment if that person has appealed against that assessment under the provisions of Article 7 of this Order and the appeal has not been entered in the Register of Appeals kept under the appropriate Regulations specified in paragraph (5) of that Article.

(2) The withdrawal of an assessment shall be without prejudice to the power of the Board to serve a further assessment notice in respect of any establishment to which that assessment related and, where the withdrawal is made by reason of the fact that an establishment has ceased to carry on business in the seventh levy period, the said notice may provide that the whole amount payable thereunder in respect of the establishment shall be due one month after the date of the notice.

Appeals

7.—(1) A person assessed to the levy may appeal to an appeal tribunal against the assessment within one month from the date of the service of the assessment notice or within any further period or periods of time that may be allowed by the Board or an appeal tribunal under the following provisions of this Article.

(2) The Board by notice may for good cause allow a person assessed to the levy to appeal to an appeal tribunal against the assessment at any time within the period of four months from the date of the service of the assessment notice or within such further period or periods as the Board may allow before such time as may then be limited for appealing has expired.

(3) If the Board shall not allow an application for extension of time for appealing an appeal tribunal shall upon application made to the tribunal by the person assessed to the levy have the like powers as the Board under the last foregoing paragraph.

(4) In the case of an establishment that ceases to carry on business in the seventh levy period on any day after the date of the service of the relevant assessment notice the foregoing provisions of this Article shall have effect as if for the period of four months from the date of the service of the assessment notice mentioned in paragraph (2) of this Article there were substituted the period of six months from the date of the cessation of business.

(5) An appeal or an application to an appeal tribunal under this Article shall be made in accordance with the Industrial Tribunals (England and Wales) Regulations 1965(a) as amended by the Industrial Tribunals (England and Wales) (Amendment) Regulations 1967(b), except where the establishment to which the relevant assessment relates is wholly in Scotland, in which case the appeal or application shall be made in accordance with the Industrial Tribunals (Scotland) Regulations 1965(c) as amended by the Industrial Tribunals (Scotland) (Amendment) Regulations 1967(d).

(6) The powers of an appeal tribunal under paragraph (3) of this Article may be exercised by the President of the Industrial Tribunals (England and Wales) or by the President of the Industrial Tribunals (Scotland) as the case may be.

(a) S.I. 1965/1101 (1965 II, p. 2805).   (b) S.I. 1967/301 (1967 I, p. 1040).
(c) S.I. 1965/1157 (1965 II, p. 3266).   (d) S.I. 1967/302 (1967 I, p. 1050).

vidence

8.—(1) Upon the discharge by a person assessed to the levy of his liability ⌐nder an assessment the Board shall if so requested issue to him a certificate ⌐ that effect.

(2) The production in any proceedings of a document purporting to be ⌐rtified by the Secretary of the Board to be a true copy of an assessment or ⌐ther notice issued by the Board or purporting to be a certificate such as is ⌐entioned in the foregoing paragraph of this Article shall, unless the contrary proved, be sufficient evidence of the document and of the facts stated therein.

⌐igned by order of the Secretary of State.

⌐st January 1976.

Harold Walker,
Joint Parliamentary Under Secretary of State,
Department of Employment.

EXPLANATORY NOTE

(*This Note is not part of the Order.*)

This Order gives effect to proposals of the Petroleum Industry Training Board which were submitted to and approved by the Manpower Services Commission, and thereafter submitted by the Manpower Services Commission to the Secretary of State. The proposals are for the imposition of a levy on employers in the petroleum industry for the purpose of encouraging adequate training in the industry.

The levy is to be imposed in respect of the seventh levy period commencing with the date upon which this Order comes into operation and ending on 31st March 1976. The levy will be assessed by the Board and there will be a right of appeal against an assessment to an industrial tribunal.

STATUTORY INSTRUMENTS

1976 No. 86

FRIENDLY SOCIETIES

The Friendly Societies (Limits of Benefits) Order 1976

Made - - - -	*22nd January* 1976
Laid before Parliament	*30th January* 1976
Coming into Operation	*23rd February* 1976

The Chief Registrar of Friendly Societies, with the consent of the Treasury, pursuant to the powers conferred upon him by section 64(3) of the Friendly Societies Act 1974(a) and to all other powers enabling him in that behalf, hereby makes the following Order:—

1.—(1) This Order may be cited as the Friendly Societies (Limits of Benefits) Order 1976 and shall come into operation on 23rd February, 1976.

(2) The Interpretation Act 1889(b) shall apply to the interpretation of this Order as it applies to the interpretation of an Act of Parliament.

2. The limits in paragraphs (c) and (d) of section 64 (1) of the Friendly Societies Act 1974, (which govern the amount which members of registered friendly societies and branches may be entitled to receive under life or endowment business which is not tax exempt), shall be increased as follows—

(a) the limit in paragraph (c) (relating to gross sums) shall be increased to £10,000, whether or not the entitlement or any part thereof is under any mortgage protection policy or policies.

(b) the limit in paragraph (d) (relating to annuities) shall be increased to £1,000.

K. Brading,
Chief Registrar of Friendly Societies.

Dated 19th January 1976.

We consent to this Order.

M. Cocks,
James A. Dunn,
Two of the Lords Commissioners
of Her Majesty's Treasury.

Dated 22nd January 1976.

(a) 1974 c. 46   (b) 1889 c. 63

EXPLANATORY NOTE
(This Note is not part of the Order.)

This Order raises the limits of the amounts which a member of a registered friendly society or branch may be entitled to receive from any one or more of such societies or branches under non tax exempt business. The new limits are (i) £10,000 by way of life or endowment business whether or not any part of the entitlement is under any mortgage protection policy or policies and (ii) £1,000 by way of annuity.

STATUTORY INSTRUMENTS

1976 No. 87

INSURANCE

The Insurance Companies (Valuation of Assets) Regulations 1976

Made - - -	23rd January 1976
Laid before Parliament	2nd February 1976
Coming into Operation	1st May 1976

The Secretary of State, in exercise of his powers under sections 78 and 86 of the Insurance Companies Act 1974(a), hereby makes the following Regulations:

Citation, commencement and revocation

1.—(1) These Regulations may be cited as the Insurance Companies (Valuation of Assets) Regulations 1976 and shall come into operation on 1st May 1976.

(2) The Insurance Companies (Valuation of Assets) Regulations 1974(b) are hereby revoked.

Interpretation

2.—(1) In these Regulations, unless the context otherwise requires—

"the Act" means the Insurance Companies Act 1974;

"approved financial institution" means any of the following:—

    (a) the Bank of England,

    (b) the National Savings Bank,

    (c) a trustee savings bank within the meaning of the Trustee Savings Bank Act 1969(c),

    (d) a banking or discount company within the meaning of paragraph 23 of the Eighth Schedule to the Companies Act 1948(d),

    (e) a banking or discount company within the meaning of the Protection of Depositors Act 1963(e),

    (f) a person duly authorised by the Treasury to act for the purposes of the Exchange Control Act 1947(f) as an authorised dealer in relation to any foreign currency,

    (g) Finance for Industry Limited,
the International Bank for Reconstruction and Development,
the Inter-American Development Bank,
the African Development Bank,
the Asian Development Bank, and
the Caribbean Development Bank, and

    (h) the National Giro;

(a) 1974 c. 49.   (b) S.I. 1974/2203 (1974 III, p. 8615).
(c) 1969 c. 50.   (d) 1948 c. 38.
(e) 1963 c. 16.   (f) 1947 c. 14.

"asset" includes part of an asset;

"associate" has the same meaning as in section 7(6) of the Act;

"building society" means a building society within the meaning of the Building Societies Act 1962(**a**) or the Building Societies Act (Northern Ireland) 1967(**b**);

"company" includes any body corporate;

"computer equipment" means the electro-mechanical and electronic units which make up a computer configuration;

"debenture" includes debenture stock and bonds, whether constituting a charge on assets or not, and loan stock or notes;

"debenture option" means a right exercisable within a specified period, at the option of the holder of the right, to acquire or dispose of any debenture at a specified price;

"debt" includes an obligation to pay a sum of money under a negotiable instrument;

"equity share" means a share of equity share capital;

"equity share capital" has the same meaning as in section 154(5) of the Companies Act 1948;

"general business amount" has the meaning assigned to it in Regulation 15(2) below;

"general business assets" and "general business liabilities" mean respectively assets and liabilities of an insurance company which are not long term business assets or long term business liabilities;

"holding company" shall be construed in accordance with section 154 of the Companies Act 1948;

"industrial and provident society" means any society registered (or deemed to be registered) under the Industrial and Provident Societies Act 1965(**c**) or the Industrial and Provident Societies Act (Northern Ireland) 1969(**d**);

"insurance company" includes, in relation to the application of these Regulations for the purposes of section 4 of the Act, a body proposing to carry on insurance business;

"insurance liabilities" means, in relation to an insurance company, any debt due from or other liabilities of the company under any contract of insurance to which it is a party;

"intermediary" means a person who in the course of any business or profession invites other persons to make offers or proposals or to take other steps with a view to entering into contracts of insurance with an insurance company, other than a person who only publishes such invitations on behalf of, or to the order of, some other person;

"land" includes any interest in land;

"liability" includes a contingent or prospective liability and a part of a liability, but does not include a liability in respect of share capital;

"linked assets" means, in relation to an insurance company, long term business assets of the company which are, for the time being, identified in the records of the company as being assets by reference to the value of which property linked benefits are to be determined;

(**a**) 1962 c. 37.   (**b**) 1967 c. 31 (N.I.).

(**c**) 1965 c. 12.   (**d**) 1969 c. 24 (N.I.).

"long term business amount" has the meaning assigned to it in Regulation 15(2) below;

"long term business assets" and "long term business liabilities" mean respectively assets of an insurance company which are, for the time being, identified as representing the long term fund or funds maintained by the company in respect of its long term business and liabilities of the company which are attributable to its long term business;

"middle market price" means—

    (a)   in relation to an investment for which two prices are quoted in the official list published for the relevant market, the average of the two prices so quoted for the relevant date or, if no official list has been published for that day, for the most recent day prior to that day for which the official list has been published; and

    (b)   in relation to an investment for which one price is quoted in the official list published for the relevant market, the price so quoted for the relevant date or, if no official list has been published for that day, for the most recent day prior to that day for which the official list has been published; and

    (c)   in any other case, the nearest equivalent to the average referred to in paragraph *(a)* above which is published or can be reasonably ascertained from information which is published;

"price earnings ratio" means the Financial Times-Actuaries estimated price earnings ratio (net) relating to the Industrial Group;

"proper valuation" means, in relation to land, a valuation made by a qualified valuer not more than three years before the relevant date which determined the amount which would be realised at the time of the valuation on an open market sale of the land free from any mortgage or charge;

"property linked benefits" means benefits provided for under any contracts of the kind mentioned in section 83(2) of the Act, the amount of which is to be determined by reference to the value of property of any description (whether specified in the contract or not);

"qualified valuer" means a person who—

    (a)   is a fellow or professional associate of the Royal Institution of Chartered Surveyors or a fellow or associate of the Incorporated Society of Valuers and Auctioneers or the Rating and Valuation Association, and has knowledge and experience in the valuation of land, or

    (b)   is approved for the time being by the Secretary of State for the purposes of these Regulations;

"quoted" means, in relation to an investment—

    (a)   that there has been granted a quotation or permission to deal in respect of that investment on a stock exchange which is a recognised stock exchange within the meaning of the Companies Act 1948;

    (b)   that there has been granted such a quotation or permission on any stock exchange of repute outside Great Britain; or

    (c)   that dealings in that investment are effected in a securities market of repute outside Great Britain being a market in which prices of all securities of which there are dealings are publicly quoted and which is supervised by a public authority;

and "unquoted" shall be construed accordingly;

"related company" means, in relation to an insurance company—
  (*a*) a dependent of the insurance company,
  (*b*) a company of which the insurance company is a dependent, or
  (*c*) a dependent of a company of which the insurance company is a dependent;

"relevant date" means, in relation to the valuation of any asset for any purpose for which these Regulations apply, the date when the asset falls to be valued for that purpose;

"salvage right" means any right of an insurance company under a contract of insurance to take possession of and to dispose of property by virtue of the fact that the company has made a payment or has become liable to make a payment in respect of a loss thereof;

"share" includes stock;

"share option" means a right exercisable within a specified period, at the option of the holder of the right, to acquire or dispose of any share at a specified price;

"subsidiary" shall be construed in accordance with section 154 of the Companies Act 1948.

(2) For the purposes of these Regulations, a company is a dependent of another company if—
  (*a*) that other company, either alone or with any associate or associates, is entitled to exercise, or control the exercise of, one-third or more of the voting power at any general meeting of the first-mentioned company, or
  (*b*) the first-mentioned company is a dependent of any company which is that other company's dependent.

(3) The Interpretation Act 1889(a) shall apply for the interpretation of these Regulations as it applies for the interpretation of an Act of Parliament and as if these Regulations and the Regulations hereby revoked were Acts of Parliament.

Application
3.—(1) Subject to the provisions of paragraph (2) below, these Regulations apply with respect to the determination of the value of assets of insurance companies for the purposes of sections 4, 24(6), 26, 28(2)(*b*), 31 and 44 of the Act, any investigation to which section 14 of the Act applies and any investigation made in pursuance of a requirement under section 34 of the Act.

(2) Where an insurance company has entered into any contracts providing for the payment of property linked benefits, these Regulations shall not apply with respect to the determination of the value of the linked assets by reference to the value of which those benefits are to be determined.

(3) Any asset to which these Regulations apply (other than cash) for the valuation of which no provision is made in these Regulations shall be left out of account for the purposes specified in paragraph (1) above.

(4) Where in accordance with these Regulations the value of any asset is to be not greater than any specified amount and, in all the circumstances of the case, it appears that the asset is of a lesser value than that amount, such lesser value shall be the value of the asset.

(a) 1889 c. 63.

Shares in and debts due or to become due from dependents

4.—(1) The value of any share in a dependent of an insurance company shall be not greater than that part of the net asset value of the dependent which would be payable in respect of the share if the dependent were in liquidation and the net asset value were the amount distributable to the shareholders in the winding up.

(2) In this Regulation, "net asset value" means, in relation to a dependent, the amount by which the value of its assets, as determined in accordance with Regulation 5 below, exceeds the amount of its liabilities as determined in the case of a dependent which is an insurance company, in accordance with the said Regulation 5.

(3) The value of any debt due, or to become due, to an insurance company from a dependent (other than a debt to which Regulation 6(2) or (3) below applies) shall be the amount which would reasonably be expected to be recovered in respect of that debt (due account being taken of any security held in respect thereof) if the dependent were in liquidation and—

> (*a*) in the case of a dependent which is an insurance company, the amount realised from its assets and the amount of its liabilities in the liquidation were equal to the value of those assets and the amount of those liabilities, as determined in accordance with Regulation 5 below, and

> (*b*) in the case of a dependent which is not an insurance company, the amount realised from its assets in the liquidation were equal to the value of those assets, as determined in accordance with the said Regulation 5.

(4) Any share in a dependent—

> (*a*) in which there is no such excess of assets over liabilities as is mentioned in paragraph (2) above, or

> (*b*) in relation to which an insurance company cannot reasonably ascertain the amount of the liabilities of the dependent for the purposes of the said paragraph (2),

shall be left out of account for the purposes for which these Regulations apply.

(5) Where an insurance company is unable to determine the value of any debt due or to become due to the company from a dependent because it cannot reasonably ascertain the amount of the liabilities of the dependent for the purpose of ascertaining what would reasonably be expected to be recovered in respect of that debt in accordance with paragraph (3) above, the debt shall be left out of account for the purposes for which these Regulations apply.

Valuation of assets and liabilities of dependents for the purposes of Regulation 4

5.—(1) The provisions of this Regulation shall apply with respect to the determination of the value of the assets and the amount of the liabilities of a dependent for the purposes of Regulation 4 above.

(2) In the case of a dependent which is an insurance company—

> (*a*) subject to the provisions of paragraph (4) below and paragraph 3 of Schedule 1 hereto, the value of its assets shall be determined in accordance with these Regulations;

(b) the amount of its liabilities shall be determined in accordance with any valuation regulations applicable for the purpose of section 44 of the Act, in the case of general business liabilities, and for the purpose of any investigation to which section 14 of the Act applies, in the case of long term business liabilities; and

(c) where the dependent carries on general business, an amount equal to—

    (i) in the case of a dependent which has completed its first financial year, the relevant amount, for the time being, for the purposes of section 4(1)(a) of the Act, and

    (ii) in any other case, the amount specified, for the time being, in section 4(1)(b) of the Act,

shall be deemed to be a liability of the dependent.

(3) In the case of a dependent which is not an insurance company—

(a) the value of its assets shall be determined in accordance with these Regulations, subject to the provisions of and the modifications provided for in paragraphs 3 and 4 of Schedule 1 hereto; and

(b) subject to the provisions of paragraph (4) below, assets of the dependent which are of a relevant description shall be taken into account only to the extent that their value does not exceed the permitted limit applicable to the dependent in relation to those assets.

(4) Where—

(a) the dependent is an insurance company and has general business assets of a relevant description or is not an insurance company and has assets of a relevant description,

(b) the value of such assets exceeds the permitted limit applicable to the dependent in relation to those assets, and

(c) the insurance company has no assets of the same description of the relevant class, or has assets of the same description of the relevant class and their value is less than the permitted limit applicable to the insurance company in relation to those assets,

then, for the purpose of determining the value of the assets of the dependent, there shall be added to the permitted limit applicable to the dependent in relation to the assets referred to in sub-paragraph (a) above an amount equal to the supplementary amount determined in accordance with the provisions of Part I of Schedule 1 hereto.

(5) In this Regulation and Schedule 1 hereto—

"assets of a relevant description" means assets of a description specified in Part I of Schedule 2 hereto or, in the case of a dependent which is not an insurance company, assets which would be of such a description if it were an insurance company;

"the insurance company" means the company the value of whose shares in or debt due or to become due from the dependent is being determined in accordance with Regulation 4 above;

"permitted limit" means, in relation to assets of a relevant description—

(a) in the case of the insurance company, or a dependent which is an insurance company, an amount equal to the percentage of the general business amount or, as the case may be, the long term business amount applicable in relation to assets of that description in accordance with Regulation 15 below (as applied in the case of a dependent pursuant to paragraph (2) above); and

(b) in the case of a dependent which is not an insurance company, an amount equal to the percentage specified in Schedule 2 hereto, with respect to assets of that description, of the liabilities of the dependent, other than liabilities to the insurance company or any other related company of the insurance company;

and references to assets held by any company being of the same description as assets held by a dependent mean—

(i) in relation to land of the dependent of a description specified in paragraph 1 of Schedule 2 hereto, any interest of that other company in that land,

(ii) in relation to assets of the dependent of a description specified in paragraph 2 of the said Schedule, any debt due or to become due to that other company which is secured on the land on which the debt due or to become due to the dependent is secured, and

(iii) in relation to assets of the dependent of a description specified in paragraphs 3 to 11 of the said Schedule, assets of that other company which, if held by the dependent, would be assets of that description.

(6) Save as otherwise provided in paragraph 3(5) of Schedule 1 hereto, references in this Regulation and in the said Schedule to assets of the insurance company being of a relevant class mean—

(a) where this Regulation and the said Schedule are being applied for the purpose of determining the value of a long term business asset of the insurance company, assets of the insurance company which are long term business assets, and

(b) in any other case, assets of the insurance company which are general business assets.

(7) Where the insurance company cannot reasonably ascertain in accordance with the provisions of this Regulation—

(a) the value of any asset of the dependent, or

(b) the amount of the permitted limit applicable in relation to any asset of the dependent,

such asset shall be left out of account in determining the value of the assets of the dependent under this Regulation.

Debts and other rights

6.—(1) The value of any debt due, or to become due, to an insurance company, other than a debt to which Regulation 4(3) above, paragraphs (2), (3) or (4) of this Regulation or Regulations 9, 12 or 14 below apply, shall be—

(a) in the case of any such debt which is due, or will become due within twelve months of the relevant date (including any debt which would become due within that period if the company were to exercise any right to which it is entitled to require payment of the same), the amount which can reasonably be expected to be recovered in respect of that debt (due account being taken of any security being held in respect thereof); and

(b) in the case of any other such debt, the amount which would reasonably be paid by way of consideration for an immediate assignment of the debt together with the benefit of any security held in respect thereof.

(2) The value of any debt due or to become due to the company which is secured on a policy of insurance issued by the company and which (together with any other debt secured on that policy) does not exceed the amount payable on a surrender of that policy at the relevant date shall be the amount of that debt.

(3) Any debt due, or to become due, to the company from an intermediary in respect of money advanced on account of commission to which that intermediary is not absolutely entitled at the relevant date shall be left out of account for the purposes for which these Regulations apply.

(4) The value of any debt due to, or other rights of, the company under any contract of reinsurance to which the company is a party (other than a debt to which Regulation 4(3) above applies) shall be the amount which can reasonably be expected to be recovered in respect of that debt or right.

(5) The value of any salvage right of the company shall be the amount which can reasonably be expected to be recovered by virtue of the exercise of that right.

Land

7. The value of any land of an insurance company (other than land held by the company as security for a debt or to which Regulation 13 below applies) shall be not greater than the amount which (after deduction of the reasonable expenses of sale) would be realised if the land were sold at a price equal to the most recent proper valuation of that land which has been provided to the company and any such land of which there is no proper valuation shall be left out of account for the purposes for which these Regulations apply.

Equipment

8.—(1) The value of any computer equipment of an insurance company—
  (a) in the financial year of the company in which it is purchased, shall be not greater than three-quarters of the cost thereof to the company;
  (b) in the first financial year thereafter, shall be not greater than one-half of that cost;
  (c) in the second financial year thereafter, shall be not greater than one-quarter of that cost; and
  (d) in any subsequent financial year, shall be left out of account for the purposes for which these Regulations apply.

(2) The value of any office machinery (other than computer equipment), furniture, motor vehicles and other equipment of an insurance company, shall be, in the financial year of the company in which it is purchased, not greater than one-half of the cost thereof and shall be, in any subsequent financial year, left out of account for the purposes for which these Regulations apply.

Amounts unpaid on partly paid shares

9.—(1) Where an insurance company has issued any share which is partly paid and that share is paid up to an amount equal to or greater than one-quarter of its nominal value or, in the case of a share issued at a premium, of the aggregate of its nominal value and the premium, the value of any moneys unpaid on that share and not already due shall be not greater than one-half of the amount of such moneys.

(2) There shall be left out of account for the purposes for which these Regulations apply—
  (a) any moneys unpaid but already due on a share which is partly paid; and

(b) any moneys unpaid on a share which is not paid up to an amount equal to, or greater than, one-quarter of its nominal value or, in the case of a share issued at a premium, of the aggregate of its nominal value and the premium.

Unquoted shares

10.—(1) The value of any unquoted equity share, other than a share in a dependent of the insurance company, shall be not greater than—

(a) where the company in which the share is held has been carrying on business for more than three financial years, the multiple of the price earnings ratio for the relevant date (or, if no price earnings ratio has been published for that date, for the most recent date prior to that date for which a price earnings ratio has been published) and the proportionate amount attributable to that share of the average amount of the profits of the company for the last three financial years; and

(b) where the company has been carrying on business for less than three but more than one financial year, the multiple of such price earnings ratio and the proportionate amount attributable to that share of the average amount of the profits of the company for its two financial years or the profits of the company available for distribution to shareholders in its only financial year (as the case may be).

(2) For the purposes of this Regulation, the average amount of the profits of a company for any specified years shall be determined as follows:—

(a) there shall be ascertained the aggregate amount of the profits of the company available for distribution to shareholders in each of the specified years;

(b) there shall be deducted therefrom—

(i) any loss made by the company in any of the specified years in which there were no profits available for distribution to shareholders, and

(ii) any undistributed profits brought forward into any of the specified years from any previous year (whether being a specified year or not); and

(c) the amount ascertained in accordance with sub-paragraphs (a) and (b) above shall be divided by the number of years specified.

(3) In this Regulation, the proportionate amount attributable to any share of the average amount or the amount of any profits of the company in which the share is held for any specified years, shall be the amount which could reasonably be expected to be received in respect of that share if the average amount or the amount (as the case may be) of the profits in question were to be distributed by the company among its shareholders.

(4) Where the value of any share cannot be determined in accordance with the provisions of paragraph (1) above because the amount of the profits available for distribution, or the amount of losses incurred, by the company in the last financial year cannot be reasonably ascertained, then the value of that share shall be determined—

(a) in the case of a company which has been carrying on business for not less than four financial years, by reference to the average amount of the profits of the company for the three financial years preceding the last financial year; and

(b) in the case of a company which has been carrying on business for less than four but more than two financial years, by reference to the average amount or the amount (as the case may be) of the profits of the company in any specified years other than the last financial year.

(5) Any share to be valued in accordance with the foregoing provisions of this Regulation shall be left out of account for the purposes for which these Regulations apply if—

(a) no amount is attributable thereto in accordance with the provisions of paragraph (1) above;

(b) the company in which the share is held has been carrying on business for less than one financial year; or

(c) the value of the share cannot be ascertained in accordance with paragraph (1) above because the amount of the profits available for distribution, or the amount of the losses incurred, by the company in any of the specified years cannot reasonably be ascertained and no provision is made for its valuation in paragraph (4) above.

(6) The value of any unquoted share, which is neither an equity share nor a share in a dependent of the insurance company, shall be the amount which would reasonably be paid by way of consideration for an immediate transfer of that share.

Unit trusts

11. The value of any holding of units, or other beneficial interest, under a unit trust scheme authorised for the purposes of the Prevention of Fraud Investments) Act 1958(a) or the Prevention of Fraud (Investments) Act Northern Ireland) 1940(b) shall be the price at which the managers under the unit trust scheme would purchase the holding of units or other beneficial interest if required to do so.

Quoted investments

12.—(1) The value of any quoted debenture which is not a debenture issued by a dependent of the insurance company, and of any quoted share which is not a share in such a dependent nor a share in any body specified in Regulation 14(2)(a) below, shall be the middle market price.

(2) Where the quotation of any quoted debenture or quoted share, the value of which falls to be determined in accordance with this Regulation, has been suspended for the time being, then that debenture or share shall be left out of account for the purposes for which these Regulations apply.

Life interests, reversionary interests, etc.

13. The value of any asset consisting of an interest in property which—

(a) is determinable upon the death of any person or upon the happening of some other future event or at some future time or is a remainder, reversionary interest, right of fee subject to a liferent or other future interest, whether vested or contingent, and

(b) is not a lease or reversionary interest expectant upon the determination of a lease,

shall be the amount which would reasonably be paid by way of consideration for an immediate transfer or assignment thereof.

(a) 1958 c. 45.   (b) 1940 c. 9 (N.I.).

Other assets

14.—(1) The value of any securities issued or guaranteed by any government or public authority shall be—

(*a*) in the case of quoted securities, the middle market price;

(*b*) in the case of securities which are not transferable, the amount payable on a surrender or redemption of such securities at the relevant date; and

(*c*) in any other case, the amount which would reasonably be paid by way of consideration for an immediate transfer or assignment thereof.

(2) The value of—

(*a*) shares in any building society or industrial and provident society, and

(*b*) share options and debenture options,

shall be the amount which would reasonably be paid by way of consideration for an immediate transfer or assignment thereof.

Assets to be taken into account only to a specified extent

15.—(1) Assets of an insurance company of any of the descriptions specified in Schedule 2 hereto shall be taken into account only to the extent that the value of those assets does not exceed—

(*a*) in the case of general business assets of a description specified in Part I of the said Schedule, an amount equal to the percentage of the general business amount specified in the said Schedule with respect to assets of that description;

(*b*) in the case of long term business assets of a description specified in Part I of the said Schedule, an amount equal to the percentage of the long term business amount so specified;

(*c*) in the case of general business assets of the description specified in Part II of the said Schedule, an amount equal to the percentage specified in the said Schedule of the net premium income of the company in respect of general business (other than premium income in respect of treaty reinsurance accepted) for the twelve months preceding the relevant date; and

(*d*) in the case of long term business assets of the description specified in Part II of the said Schedule, an amount equal to the percentage so specified of the net premium income of the company in respect of long term business (other than premium income in respect of treaty reinsurance accepted) for the twelve months preceding the relevant date.

(2) In this Regulation—

"general business amount" means the aggregate of—

(*a*) the company's general business liabilities; and

(*b*) in the case of a company which carries on general business, an amount equal to—

(i) in the case of a company which has completed its first financial year, the relevant amount for the time being for the purposes of section 4(1)(*a*) of the Act, and

(ii) in any other case, the amount for the time being specified in section 4(1)(*b*) of the Act;

less the amount of the deduction specified in paragraph (3) below;

"long term business amount" means the aggregate of the company's long term business liabilities less the amount of the deduction specified in paragraph (3) below; and "the net premium income" of a company for any specified period means the gross amounts first recorded in the company's books during that period as paid or due to the company by way of premiums, less any rebates, refunds and commission so recorded during that period as allowed or paid on those gross amounts or on any such gross amounts so recorded in any previous period.

(3) The deduction to be made in determining the general business amount or the long term business amount in accordance with paragraph (2) above shall be the aggregate of the following:—

(*a*) the amount of any general business or, as the case may be, long term business liabilities of the company to related companies, other than insurance liabilities, and

(*b*) the value of the debts due or to become due to and other rights of the company under contracts of reinsurance ceded by it (but excluding any rights of recovery in respect of insurance liabilities already discharged by the company) which are general business or, as the case may be, long term business assets of the company, and

(*c*) in the case of the long term business amount, the amount of any liabilities of the company in respect of property linked benefits.

(4) For the purposes of this Regulation, the amount of the liabilities of an insurance company shall be determined in accordance with any valuation regulations applicable for the purposes of section 44 of the Act, in the case of general business liabilities and for the purpose of any investigation to which section 14 of the Act applies, in the case of long term business liabilities.

Stanley Clinton Davis,
Parliamentary Under-Secretary of State,
Department of Trade.

23rd January 1976.

Regulation 5

SCHEDULE 1

PART I

THE SUPPLEMENTARY AMOUNT

1. Subject to the provisions of paragraph 2(1) below, the supplementary amount in relation to assets of a relevant description held by a dependent of the insurance company shall be determined in accordance with the following formula:—

$$A = \frac{B}{C} \times D$$

in which

A is the supplementary amount;

B is the amount by which the value of assets of that description held by the dependent, excluding any long term business assets of the dependent if it is an insurance company, exceeds the permitted limit applicable to the dependent in relation to those assets;

C is the aggregate of the amount specified in B above and of the amounts by which the value of assets of the same description held by other relevant dependents, excluding any long term business assets of a dependent which is an insurance company, exceeds respectively the permitted limits applicable to such other relevant dependents in relation to those assets;

D is—

    (*a*) where the insurance company holds no assets of the same description of the relevant class, the amount of the permitted limit that would be applicable to the insurance company in relation to such assets were it to hold them; and

    (*b*) where the insurance company holds assets of the same description of the relevant class, the amount by which the permitted limit applicable to the insurance company in relation to those assets exceeds the value of those assets.

2.—(1) Where for the purpose of determining any supplementary amount in accordance with paragraph 1 above, the insurance company cannot reasonably ascertain—

    (*a*) the value of any asset of a relevant dependent, or

    (*b*) the amount of the permitted limit applicable in relation to any asset of a relevant dependent,

such asset shall be left out of account for that purpose.

(2) In this Part of this Schedule—

"relevant dependent" means—

    (*a*) where this Schedule is being applied in relation to the determination of the value of a share in, or debt due or to become due from, a dependent of the insurance company which is a long term business asset of the insurance company, any dependent of the insurance company—

        (i) a share in which, or in any company of which it is a dependent, is a long term business asset of the insurance company, or

        (ii) from which a debt is due, or will become due, to the insurance company which is a long term business asset of that company; and

    (*b*) in any other case, any dependent of the insurance company—

        (i) a share in which, or in any company of which it is a dependent, is a general business asset of the insurance company, or

        (ii) from which a debt is due, or will become due, to the insurance company which is a general business asset of that company.

PART II

FURTHER PROVISIONS AND MODIFICATIONS OF THE REGULATIONS APPLICABLE WITH RESPECT TO THE DETERMINATION OF THE VALUE OF DEPENDENTS

3.—(1) This paragraph applies where, for the purpose of ascertaining the value of the assets of the subject company under the Regulation 5 above, any determination falls to be made in accordance with the said Regulation 5 of the value of the assets of a dependent of the insurance company, a share in which, or a debt due or to become due from which, is an asset of the subject company; and references herein to a determination of the value of assets of a dependent to which this paragraph applies are references to any such determination.

(2) Regulation 5(4) shall not apply with respect to a determination of the value of assets of a dependent to which this paragraph applies.

(3) Where, in the case of a determination of the value of assets of a dependent to which this paragraph applies—

    (*a*) the dependent is an insurance company and has general business assets of a relevant description or is not an insurance company and has assets of a relevant description,

    (*b*) the value of such assets exceeds the permitted limit applicable to the dependent in relation to those assets, and

    (*c*) any controller of the dependent has no assets of the same description of the relevant class, or has assets of the same description of the relevant class and their value is less than the permitted limit applicable to that controller in relation to those assets;

then, for the purposes of such determination, there shall be added to the permitted limit applicable to the dependent in relation to the assets referred to in subparagraph (*a*) above an amount equal to the supplementary amount or, if there is more than one such controller, to the aggregate of the supplementary amounts, determined with respect to any such controller in accordance with the provisions of Part I of this Schedule, subject, where the controller is not the insurance company, to the modifications specified in subparagraph (5) below.

(4) In this paragraph, "a controller" means, in relation to a dependent—

    (*a*) the insurance company,

    (*b*) the subject company, if it is an insurance company, and

    (*c*) a dependent of the insurance company which is an insurance company and of which the subject company is a dependent.

(5) Where subparagraph (3) above is being applied in relation to a controller, other than the insurance company—

    (*a*) Part I of this Schedule, as applied in accordance with the said subparagraph, shall have effect as if, for the references to the insurance company, there were substituted references to the controller, and

    (*b*) the references to assets being of a relevant class in the said subparagraph and in Part I of this Schedule, as so applied, shall be construed as referring to long term business assets of the controller, if the said subparagraph is being applied in connection with the determination of the value of a long term business asset of the controller, and to general business assets of the controller, in any other case.

4. The modifications of these Regulations applicable (in addition to that specified in paragraph 3(2) above) with respect to the determination of the value of the assets of the subject company where it is not an insurance company, are as follows:—

    (*a*) these Regulations shall apply to the subject company as if it were an insurance company and its assets were being valued for a purpose specified in Regulation 3(1);

    (*b*) Regulation 3(2) shall not apply; and

    (*c*) Regulation 15 shall not apply.

5. In this Schedule, "subject company" means the dependent of the insurance company the value of whose assets is being determined in accordance with Regulation 5(2) or (3) (as the case may be).

Regulation 15   **SCHEDULE 2**

ASSETS TO BE TAKEN INTO ACCOUNT ONLY TO A SPECIFIED EXTENT

PART I

Descriptions of Asset	Percentage of general business or long term business amount
1. A piece of land (not being land held as a security for a debt) or a number of pieces of such land to which in the most recent proper valuation of such pieces of land an aggregate value is ascribed which is greater than the aggregate of the value of each of such pieces of land valued separately	5%
2. A debt (other than a quoted debenture) due or to become due to the insurance company from any person (not being an individual nor a dependent of the insurance company) which is fully secured on land or a number of such debts all of which are secured on the same land	5%

	Percentage of general business or long term business amount
Descriptions of Asset	

3. Debts (other than quoted debentures, debts to which Regulation 6(2), (3) or (4) above apply, and debts of the descriptions specified in paragraph 2 above or paragraph 12 below) which are due or will become due to the insurance company within twelve months of the relevant date (including debts which would become due within that period if the company were to exercise any right to which it is entitled to require repayment of the same) from—

(a)	any one company and any of its connected companies (not being a dependent of the insurance company nor an approved financial institution);	$2\frac{1}{2}\%$
(b)	any one unincorporated body of persons (not being an approved financial institution)	$2\frac{1}{2}\%$

4. Debts (other than quoted debentures, debts to which Regulation 6(2), (3) or (4) above apply and debts of the descriptions specified in paragraphs 2 or 3 above or paragraph 12 below) which will become due to the insurance company from—

(a)	any one company and any of its connected companies (not being a dependent of the insurance company nor an approved financial institution)	1%
(b)	any one unincorporated body of persons (not being an approved financial institution)	1%

5. Quoted equity shares in any one company and any of its connected companies (not being a dependent of the insurance company) — $2\frac{1}{2}\%$

6. Quoted shares (including quoted equity shares but only to the extent that such shares may be taken into account in accordance with paragraph 5 above) and quoted debentures in any one company and any of its connected companies (not being a dependent of the insurance company) — 5%

7. Unquoted shares in any one company and any of its connected companies (not being a dependent of the insurance company) — 1%

8. Debts and shares of the descriptions specified in paragraphs 3, 4, 5, 6 and 7 above due or to become due from or held in any one company and any of its connected companies to the extent that such debts and shares may be taken into account in accordance with the provisions of those paragraphs — $7\frac{1}{2}\%$

9. Debts due or to become due to the insurance company from any individual (other than debts of the descriptions specified in Regulation 6(2) above or in paragraphs 3(b) or 4(b) above or paragraph 12 below) — $\frac{1}{4}\%$

10. Computer equipment — 5%

11. Office machinery (other than computer equipment), furniture, motor vehicles and other equipment — $2\frac{1}{2}\%$

PART II

Description of Asset	Percentage of general business or long term business net premium income
12. Amounts recorded in the insurance company's books as due in respect of premiums (other than premiums in respect of treaty reinsurance accepted) which either—	30%

(a) have not been paid, or

(b) have been received by an intermediary on behalf of the company, but have not been paid to the company by the intermediary,

less any rebates, refunds and commission recorded in the company's books as allowable or payable in respect of any such amounts

PART III

13. In this Schedule, a company is a connected company of another company if it is—

(a) a subsidiary of that other company,

(b) the holding company of that other company, or

(c) a subsidiary of the holding company of that other company.

14. In this Schedule, a debt is fully secured on land if the amount that would be realised on a sale of that land at a price equal to the most recent proper valuation of that land would (after deducting the reasonable expenses of sale) be sufficient to enable that debt (and any other obligation secured on that land which has priority to or ranks equally with that debt) to be discharged in full.

EXPLANATORY NOTE

(This Note is not part of the Regulations.)

The Regulations revoke and replace with modifications and additions the Insurance Companies (Valuation of Assets) Regulations 1974 (S.I. No. 2203) which provided for the valuation of the assets of insurance companies for the purposes of provisions in the Insurance Companies Act 1974 requiring the value of such assets to be determined in accordance with valuation regulations. The main additions to the previous Regulations are comprised in Regulation 15 and Schedule 2 which impose limitations on the extent to which the value of certain descriptions of assets of insurance companies may be taken into account for the purposes for which the Regulations apply. The provisions relating to the valuation of shares held in and debts owing from dependent companies have also been revised and additional provisions have been included covering the adaptation and application of the provisions of Regulation 15 and Schedule 2 in relation to valuation of such shares and debts.

STATUTORY INSTRUMENTS

1976 No. 88

SOCIAL SECURITY

The Social Security (Contributions) Amendment Regulations 1976

Made - - -	*23rd January* 1976
Laid before Parliament	*4th February* 1976
Coming into Operation	*25th February* 1976

The Secretary of State for Social Services, in exercise of the powers conferred upon her by sections 1(6), 3, 8(1) and 11(3) of, and paragraphs 3(1), 6(1)(c) and (m), 6(3) and 8 of Schedule 1 to, the Social Security Act 1975(a), and of all other powers enabling her in that behalf, after considering the report of the National Insurance Advisory Committee on the draft submitted to them in accordance with section 139 of that Act, hereby makes the following regulations:—

Citation, interpretation and commencement

1. These regulations, which may be cited as the Social Security (Contributions) Amendment Regulations 1976, shall be read as one with the Social Security (Contributions) Regulations 1975(b) (hereinafter referred to as the "principal regulations") and shall come into operation on 25th February 1976.

Amendment of regulation 17 of the principal regulations

2. In regulation 17(1) of the principal regulations (payments to be disregarded) after sub-paragraph (*f*) there shall be added the following sub-paragraph—

"(*g*) any payment by way of a pension."

Amendment of regulation 20 of the principal regulations

3. In regulation 20(1) of the principal regulations (exception from liability for Class 2 contributions)—

(*a*) in sub-paragraph (*a*) for the words "injury benefit, or unemployability supplement" there shall be substituted the words "or injury benefit";

(*b*) after sub-paragraph (*d*) there shall be added the following—

"or

(*e*) in respect of any part of which the earner is in receipt of unemployability supplement or invalid care allowance."

(a) 1975 c. 14.   (b) S.I. 1975/492 (1975 I, p. 1516).

Amendment of regulation 25 of the principal regulations

4. In regulation 25 of the principal regulations (Class 3 contributions not paid within prescribed periods)—

(*a*) for the words "a contribution under the provisions or regulation 24 of these regulations (Class 3 contributions)" there shall be substituted the words "a Class 3 contribution under the provisions of regulation 24, 114(2)(*b*) or 115 of these regulations";

(*b*) for the words "in the period provided for payment in the said provision applicable" there shall be substituted the words "in the appropriate period prescribed therefor".

Insertion of regulation 36A in the principal regulations

5. After regulation 36 of the principal regulations there shall be inserted the following regulation—

"*Treatment for the purpose of any contributory benefit of contributions paid under an arrangement.*

36A. For the purposes of the foregoing provisions of this Part of these regulations—

(*a*) where a contribution is paid under an arrangement to which regulations 41 and 41A or, as the case may be, regulation 46(3) apply the date by which but for those provisions the contribution would have fallen due to be paid shall in relation to that contribution be the due date;

(*b*) any payment made of, or as on account of, a contribution in accordance with any such arrangement shall, on and after the due date, be treated as a contribution paid on the due date."

Insertion of regulations 41A and 41B in the principal regulations

6. After regulation 41 of the principal regulations there shall be inserted the following regulations—

"*Special provisions relating to primary Class 1 contributions*

41A.—(1) Where by virtue of an arrangement authorised under the last preceding regulation an earner has agreed that, notwithstanding the provisions of paragraph 3(1) of Schedule 1 to the Act (method of paying Class 1 contributions), he himself will pay any primary Class 1 contribution payable in respect of earnings paid to or for his benefit in respect of an employed earner's employment, the Secretary of State shall notify the secondary contributor in writing of the arrangement and of the period to which the arrangement relates.

(2) During the said period the said paragraph 3(1) shall not apply to the secondary contributor unless and until the arrangement has been cancelled before the end of the period and the secondary contributor has been notified in writing of the cancellation.

Exception in relation to earnings to which regulation 41A applies

41B.—(1) Where in any year an earner has earnings from more than one employed earner's employments and to the earnings paid in respect of at least one of those employments the provisions of the last preceding regulation apply and to the earnings paid in respect of at least one of those employments those provisions do not apply, the following provisions of this regulation shall have effect.

(2) If in respect of any payment made in that year of earnings to which the provisions of the last preceding regulation do not apply the earner has paid by way of contributions a sum equal to at least the smaller of the two amounts specified in the next succeeding paragraph, he shall be excepted from liability to pay contributions in respect of any payment made in that year of earnings to which the said provisions apply.

(3) The amounts referred to in the last preceding paragraph are—

    (a) 52 primary Class 1 contributions at the rate applicable to the earner on earnings at the upper earnings limit, or

    (b) 12 primary Class 1 contributions at the rate applicable to the earner on earnings at the upper earnings limit for persons paid monthly."

Amendment of regulation 42 of the principal regulations

7. In regulation 42(1)(b) of the principal regulations (special provisions relating to secondary contributors exempted by treaty etc. from enforcement of the Act or from liability under it) for the words "who is willing" there shall be substituted the words "who is not willing".

Amendment of regulation 115 of the principal regulations

8. In regulation 115(3)(a) of the principal regulations (Class 2 and 3 contributions for periods abroad) for the words following the words "contributions under the Act" there shall be substituted the words "the earnings factor derived from which is not less than 50 times the lower earnings limit for the time being for Class 1 contributions".

Minor amendments of the principal regulations

9. The provisions of the principal regulations specified in column 2 of Schedule A to these regulations shall be amended in accordance with the provisions set out opposite thereto in column 4 of that Schedule.

Barbara Castle,
Secretary of State for Social Services.

23rd January 1976.

SCHEDULE A   Regulation 9

MINOR AMENDMENTS OF PRINCIPAL REGULATIONS

Column 1	Column 2	Column 3	Column 4
Item	Provision of Principal Regulations	Description	Amendment
1	Regulation 12	Change of earnings period.	In paragraph (4) after the words "the old period" there shall be inserted the word "and".
2	Regulation 17	Payments to be disregarded.	In paragraph (1) for the words "is it" there shall be substitued the words "it is". In paragraph (4) after the words "an earner in" there shall be inserted the words "respect of any".
3	Regulation 20	Exception from liability for Class 2 contributions	In paragraph (1)(c)— (a) for the words "in is" there shall be substituted the words "is in"; (b) there shall be deleted the word "or".
4	Regulation 47	Deduction of contributions from pensions etc.	In paragraph (a)(ii) for the reference "24(b)" there shall be substituted the reference "24(4)(b)".
5	Schedule 3, (so far as it relates to section 13 of the Stamp Duties Management Act 1891).	Certain offences in relation to stamps.	In paragraph (6) for the words "any stamp which" there shall be substituted the words "any stamp, any stamp or part of a stamp which".

EXPLANATORY NOTE

(This Note is not part of the Regulations.)

These Regulations amend the Social Security (Contributions) Regulations 1975 ("the principal Regulations").

They make provision for paragraph 3(1) of Schedule 1 to the Social Security Act 1975 (liability in the first instance of secondary contributor to pay primary Class 1 contributions) not to apply in respect of earnings from any employed earner's employment where by virtue of an arrangement under regulation 41 of the principal Regulations the earner has agreed himself to pay any primary Class 1 contribution payable in respect of those earnings. They also make piovision in such a case for the earner to be excepted from liability to pay those contributions if he has paid in respect of his earnings from an employment which is not subject to the arrangement an amount equal to 52 primary Class 1 contributions at the rate applicable to him on earnings at the upper earnings limit. They further make provision for contributions paid in accordance with the arrangement to be treated as paid on the due date.

The Regulations also provide for payments by way of pensions to be disregarded in the calculation of earnings; and for a self-employed earner to be excepted from liability for Class 2 contributions for any week in which he is in receipt of an invalid care allowance.

The Regulations also extend the provisions of regulation 25 of the principal Regulations (Class 3 contributions not paid within prescribed periods) to Class 3 contributions payable for periods abroad.

The other amendments are of a minor nature.

The report of the National Insurance Advisory Committee on the draft of these regulations dated 13th January 1976 is contained in House of Commons Paper No. 138 (Session 1975–76) published by Her Majesty's Stationery Office.

STATUTORY INSTRUMENTS

1976 No. 90

CUSTOMS AND EXCISE
The Import Duties (Temporary Reductions and Exemptions) Order 1976

Made - - - -	*24th January* 1976
Coming into Operation	*26th January* 1976
Laid before the House of Commons	*26th January* 1976

The Lords Commissioners of Her Majesty's Treasury, by virtue of the powers conferred on them by sections 1, 3(6) and 13 of the Import Duties Act 1958(a), as amended by section 5(5) of, and paragraph 1 of Schedule 4 to, the European Communities Act 1972(b), and of all other powers enabling them in that behalf, on the recommendation of the Secretary of State(c), hereby make the following Order:—

1.—(1) This Order may be cited as the Import Duties (Temporary Reductions and Exemptions) Order 1976 and shall come into operation on 26th January 1976.

(2) The Interpretation Act 1889(d) shall apply for the interpretation of this Order as it applies for the interpretation of an Act of Parliament.

2. Up to and including 28th March 1976, no import duty shall be charged on the following goods, namely potatoes which fall within subheading 07.01 A.III b)2 of the Customs Tariff 1959.

3. Where any import duty for the time being chargeable on the goods has been removed by a directly applicable Community provision the import duty shall, to the extent of that removal, not be regarded as removed by virtue of this Order and the reference to it in this Order shall be treated as merely indicative of the rate of import duty payable in respect of the goods.

M. Cocks,

Donald R. Coleman,

24th January 1976.

Two of the Lords Commissioners
of Her Majesty's Treasury

(a) 1958 c. 6.
(c) *See* S.I. 1970/1537 (1970 III, p. 5293).

(b) 1972 c. 68.
(d) 1889 c. 63.

EXPLANATORY NOTE

(This Note is not part of the Order.)

This Order provides exemption from import duty as from 26th January 1976 up to and including 28th March 1976 in the case of certain potatoes which are subject to total suspension of duty in the Common Customs Tariff of the European Economic Community; the exemption is made in accordance with the United Kingdom's Community obligations.

STATUTORY INSTRUMENTS

1976 No. 91

CAR TAX

The Car Tax (Sale or Return) Regulations 1976

Made - - - -	*23rd January* 1976
Laid before the House of Commons -	*4th February* 1976
Coming into Operation	*1st March* 1976

The Commissioners of Customs and Excise, in exercise of the powers conferred upon them by paragraphs 4(1)(*b*) and 26(1) of Schedule 7 to the Finance Act 1972(**a**) and of all other powers enabling them in that behalf, hereby make the following Regulations:—

1.—(1) These Regulations may be cited as the Car Tax (Sale or Return) Regulations 1976 and shall come into operation on 1st March 1976.

(2) The Interpretation Act 1889(**b**) shall apply for the interpretation of these Regulations as it applies for the interpretation of an Act of Parliament.

2. Where a registered person delivers a chargeable vehicle under an agreement providing for its sale or return then, whether or not the person to whom it is so delivered delivers the vehicle to some other party under a further agreement for sale or return and notwithstanding any other event upon which it ceases to be the property of that registered person in accordance with the terms of that agreement with him, any one of the following events shall be treated for the purposes of car tax as an event upon which the vehicle ceases to be his property:

    (*a*) the acceptance by a customer of an offer for sale of the vehicle when the offer is made by a person to whom it is so delivered;

    (*b*) the acceptance by a person to whom it is so delivered of an offer to purchase the vehicle when the offer is made by a customer;

    (*c*) the despatch by hand or by post of an application for the registration of the vehicle under any enactment relating to vehicle excise duty;

    (*d*) the commencement of, the despatch of the vehicle to another party for, or the giving of written instructions for, any alteration, adaptation or addition to the vehicle or the equipment fitted to it, other than—

      (i) maintenance or repair,

      (ii) the addition of any "slip-on" type of accessory for sales promotion, or

      (iii) any alteration, adaptation or addition carried out on the instructions of the registered person;

(**a**) 1972 c. 41.   (**b**) 1889 c. 63.

(e) the hiring out of the vehicle or the making of it the subject of a legally enforceable hiring agreement;

(f) the making of the vehicle the subject of a legally enforceable hire purchase agreement, credit sale agreement, charge, lien or bill of sale other than a charge or lien created by the registered person;

(g) the use of the vehicle on the public road for demonstration purposes or its use for any purpose otherwise than for display by a person to whom it is so delivered;

(h) the purchase of the vehicle by a person to whom it is so delivered or the appropriation of it by him as stock or to his own use or that of any other person;

(i) the transfer of the vehicle by the person to whom it is so delivered to another person otherwise than under an agreement for sale or return made with the consent of the registered person;

(j) the expiry of 365 days, or such longer period as the Commissioners may allow generally or in any particular case, after the date of the first delivery of the vehicle from the premises of the registered person under the agreement;

(k) the doing of any act by a person to whom it is so delivered which is inconsistent with his right or ability to return the vehicle.

Dorothy Johnstone,
Commissioner of Customs and Excise.

23rd January 1976.

King's Beam House,
Mark Lane,
London EC3R 7HE.

EXPLANATORY NOTE

(This Note is not part of the Regulations.)

These Regulations made under Schedule 7 to the Finance Act 1972 provide for a chargeable vehicle which has been delivered by a registered person under a sale or return agreement to be treated as ceasing to be his property when any one of specified events occurs.

STATUTORY INSTRUMENTS

1976 No. 95

AGRICULTURE

GUARANTEED PRICES AND ASSURED MARKETS

The Milk (Guaranteed Prices) (Amendment) Order 1976

Made - - - -	21*st January* 1976
Laid before Parliament	3*rd February* 1976
Coming into Operation	1*st April* 1976

The Minister of Agriculture, Fisheries and Food, the Secretary of State for Scotland, the Secretary of State for Northern Ireland (being the Secretaries of State respectively concerned with agriculture in Scotland and Northern Ireland) and the Secretary of State for Wales, acting jointly, in exercise of the powers conferred on them by sections 1 and 35(3) of the Agriculture Act 1957(a), as read with the Transfer of Functions (Wales) Order 1969(b), and of all other powers enabling them in that behalf, with the consent of the Treasury and after consultation with such bodies of persons as appear to the said Ministers to represent the interests of producers of milk, hereby make the following order:—

Citation, commencement and interpretation

1.—(1) This order may be cited as the Milk (Guaranteed Prices) (Amendment) Order 1976 and shall come into operation on 1st April 1976.

(2) The Interpretation Act 1889(c) shall apply to the interpretation of this order as it applies to the interpretation of an Act of Parliament.

Amendment of principal order

2. The Milk (Guaranteed Prices) Order 1956(d) shall be amended by substituting therein for the word "gallon" wherever it appears the word "litre", so however that in relation to any period before the commencement of this order the said order of 1956 shall continue to operate as if this order had not been made.

(a) 1957 c. 57.
(c) 1889 c. 63.

(b) S.I. 1969/388 (1969 I, p. 1070).
(d) S.I. 1956/363 (1956 I, p. 130).

In Witness whereof the Official Seal of the Minister of Agriculture, Fisheries and Food is hereunto affixed on 13th January, 1976.

(L.S.)

Frederick Peart,
Minister of Agriculture, Fisheries and Food.

14th January 1976.

William Ross,
Secretary of State for Scotland.

15th January 1976.

Merlyn Rees,
Secretary of State for Northern Ireland.

16th January 1976.

John Morris,
Secretary of State for Wales.

We consent

21st January 1976.

M. Cocks,
James A. Dunn,
Two of the Lords Commissioners
of Her Majesty's Treasury.

EXPLANATORY NOTE

(This Note is not part of the Order.)

This Order, which comes into operation with effect from the beginning of the year 1st April 1976 to 31st March 1977, amends the Milk (Guaranteed Prices) Order 1956 by substituting for the word "gallon" wherever it appears the word "litre". This Order will not affect the operation of the principal order in relation to any period before 1st April 1976.

STATUTORY INSTRUMENTS

1976 No. 96 (S.7)

SCOTTISH LAND COURT

The Scottish Land Court (Fees) Amendment Rules 1976

Made - - - -	*20th January* 1976
Coming into operation	*18th February* 1976

The Scottish Land Court in exercise of the powers conferred upon them by section (12) of the Small Landholders (Scotland) Act 1911 (a) and all other powers enabling them in that behalf with the approval of the Treasury hereby make the following rules:—

1. For the Table of Fees contained in Schedule 3 to the Rules of the Scottish Land Court (b) as amended (c) there shall be substituted the Table set out in the Schedule hereto.

2. These rules may be cited as the Scottish Land Court (Fees) Amendment Rules 1976 and shall come into operation on 18th February 1976.

Harald R. Leslie,
John McVicar,
D. W. Cunningham,
A. Gillespie.

Scottish Land Court,
1 Grosvenor Crescent,
Edinburgh.

19th January 1976.

We approve,

M. Cocks,
J. Dormand.
Two of the Lords Commissioners of
Her Majesty's Treasury.

20th January 1976.

(a) 1911 c. 49.   (b) S.R. & O. 1912/1750 (Rev. XII, p. 235: 1912, p. 269).
(c) S.R. & O. 1932/439 (Rev. XII, p. 235: 1932, p. 714); S.I. 1949/144; 1957/1955; 1963/1518; 1970/1764 (1949 I, p. 2418; 1957 II, p. 2260; 1963 III, p. 2799; 1970 III, p. 5753).

SCHEDULE

TABLE OF FEES

(1) SMALL LANDHOLDERS (SCOTLAND) ACTS 1886-1931 AND
    CROFTERS (SCOTLAND) ACTS 1955 AND 1961

		£	p
(a) Application for a Record of a holding or a croft Principal Application (each Applicant)		1	00
For each Respondent		–	25
(b) Recording Agreements for loan by (1) the Department of Agriculture and Fisheries for Scotland and...			
(2) the Highlands and Islands Development Board			
Each Agreement		–	75
(c) Other Applications			
Principal Application (each crave)		–	50
When more than one Applicant (each Applicant)		–	50
For each Respondent		–	25

(2) SHEEP STOCKS VALUATION (SCOTLAND) ACT 1937 AND HILL FARMING
    ACT 1946

	£	p
(a) Valuations of sheep stocks		
Awards not exceeding £100	2	00
Awards exceeding £100, £2 for the first £100 and for every additional £100 or fractional part thereof awarded	–	50
Where Application dismissed or withdrawn before valuation ...	4	50
(b) Determination of questions under section 5 and section 39 (b) Hill Farming Act 1946		
Principal Application	3	75
For each Respondent	–	75

(3) AGRICULTURE (SCOTLAND) ACT 1948, AGRICULTURAL HOLDINGS
    (SCOTLAND) ACT 1949 AND AGRICULTURE ACT 1958

	£	p
(a) Arbitrations as to rents		
Rental, as fixed by Court, not exceeding £50	2	50
Rental, as fixed by Court, exceeding £50 but not exceeding £100 ...	5	00
Rental, as fixed by Court, exceeding £100, £5 for first £100 and for every additional £100 or fractional part thereof	2	00
Where Application dismissed or withdrawn before rent fixed ...	4	50
(b) Claims for compensation		
Awards not exceeding £50	2	50
Awards exceeding £50 but not exceeding £100	5	00
Awards exceeding £100, £5 for first £100 and for every additional £100 or fractional part thereof awarded	2	00
Where Application dismissed or withdrawn before compensation fixed	4	50

(c) Other Applications

Principal Application (each crave)	3	75
When more than one Applicant (each Applicant)	3	75
For each Respondent	–	75

(4) MISCELLANEOUS

(a) Appeals and Motions for Rehearing ... ...

Each Appellant, or Motioner for Rehearing	–	75

(b) For making at the request of any party to an Application a certified copy or copies of the Principal Application, or any part of it, or any Order in it, or any original deed, writ, or document in process

Per sheet of 250 typed or written words	–	30

(c) Applications not otherwise specified

Principal Application (each crave)	3	75
When more than one Applicant (each Applicant)	3	75
For each Respondent	–	75

EXPLANATORY NOTE

(This Note is not part of the Rules.)

These Rules introduce a new table of fees payable in respect of applications to the Scottish Land Court.

STATUTORY INSTRUMENTS

1976 No. 97

PRICES

The Cheese Prices (Amendment) Order 1976

Made - - - -	*27th January* 1976
Laid before Parliament	*27th January* 1976
Coming into Operation	*30th January* 1976

The Secretary of State, after consulting in accordance with subsection (6) of section 2 of the Prices Act 1974(a) as amended(b) with the organisations therein referred to, in exercise of her powers under subsections (1) and (8) of that section and of all other powers enabling her in that behalf, hereby makes the following Order:—

1.—(1) This Order may be cited as the Cheese Prices (Amendment) Order 1976 and shall come into operation on 30th January 1976.

(2) The Interpretation Act 1889(c) shall apply for the interpretation of this Order as it applies for the interpretation of an Act of Parliament, and as if this Order and the Order hereby revoked were Acts of Parliament.

2. Article 5 of the Cheese Prices (No. 2) Order 1975(d), as varied (e), is hereby further varied by the substitution for the Table set out in that article of the following Table—

(a) 1974 c. 24.
(c) 1889 c. 63.
(e) S.I. 1975/1953 (1975 III, p. 7257).

(b) 1975 c. 32.
(d) S.I. 1975/1244 (1975 II, p. 4247).

TABLE

Column 1 Category of Cheese	Column 2 Price in pence per 1lb weight
Cheddar produced in New Zealand (other than farmhouse or matured)	61
Cheddar (including Dunlop) produced in the United Kingdom (other than farmhouse or matured)	61
Farmhouse or matured Cheddar (including Dunlop) produced in the United Kingdom	71
Cheddar produced in a member State (other than the United Kingdom) of the European Economic Community (other than farmhouse or matured)	61
Farmhouse or matured Cheddar produced in a member State (other than the United Kingdom) of the European Economic Community	71
Cheshire produced in the United Kingdom (other than farmhouse or matured)	59
Farmhouse or matured Cheshire produced in the United Kingdom	69
Caerphilly, Derby, Double Gloucester, Lancashire, Leicester, Wensleydale, and White Stilton produced in the United Kingdom (other than farmhouse or matured)	61
Edam and Gouda (other than farmhouse or matured)... ...	61

Revocation

3. The Cheese Prices (No. 2) (Second Amendment) Order 1975(**a**) is hereby revoked.

Robert Maclennan,
Parliamentary Under-Secretary of State,
Department of Prices and Consumer Protection.

27th January 1976.

EXPLANATORY NOTE

(This Note is not part of the Order.)

This Order varies the Cheese Prices (No. 2) Order 1975 by increasing the maximum retail prices of cheese subsidised under section 1 of the Prices Act 1974.

(**a**) S.I. 1975/1953 (1975 III, p. 7257).

STATUTORY INSTRUMENTS

1976 No. 98

FAIR TRADING

The Restrictive Trade Practices (Services) Order 1976

Laid before Parliament in draft

Made - - - -   *26th January* 1976

Coming into Operation   *22nd March* 1976

Whereas a notice has been published by the Secretary of State complying with the terms of section 111(2) of the Fair Trading Act 1973(a) (hereinafter referred to as "the Act of 1973") and all the representations made with respect thereto have been taken into consideration:

And whereas a draft of this Order has been laid before Parliament and approved by resolution of each House of Parliament:

Now, therefore, the Secretary of State in exercise of powers conferred on her by sections 107 and 110 of the Act of 1973 hereby makes the following Order:—

1.—(1) This Order may be cited as the Restrictive Trade Practices (Services) Order 1976 and shall come into operation on 22nd March 1976.

(2) The Interpretation Act 1889(b) shall apply for the interpretation of this Order as it applies for the interpretation of an Act of Parliament.

2.—(1) The services brought under control by this Order are all services without exception.

(2) The services described in this Order as designated services are all services except those described in Schedule 4 to the Act of 1973.

3.—(1) It is directed that, subject to the provisions of Part X of the Act of 1973, the agreements to which Part I of the Restrictive Trade Practices Act 1956(c) applies shall include agreements (whether made before or after the passing of the Act of 1973 and whether before or after the making of this Order) which—

(*a*) are agreements between two or more persons carrying on business

---

(a) 1973 c. 41.
(c) 1956 c. 68.
                                     (b) 1889 c. 63.

within the United Kingdom in the supply of services brought under control by this Order, or between two or more such persons together with one or more other parties, and

(b) are agreements under which restrictions, in respect of the matters specified in paragraph (2) below for the purposes of section 107(1)(b) of the Act of 1973, are accepted by two or more parties, and

(c) are not agreements described in the Schedule hereto.

(2) The matters specified for the purposes of the said section 107(1)(b) are the following, that is to say—

(a) the charges to be made, quoted or paid for designated services supplied, offered or obtained;

(b) the terms or conditions on or subject to which designated services are to be supplied or obtained;

(c) the extent (if any) to which, or the scale (if any) on which, designated services are to be made available, supplied or obtained;

(d) the form or manner in which designated services are to be made available, supplied or obtained;

(e) the persons or classes of persons for whom or from whom, or the areas or places in or from which, designated services are to be made available or supplied or are to be obtained.

Alan Williams,
Minister of State,
Department of Prices and Consumer
Protection.

26th January 1976.

SCHEDULE

1. For the purposes of determining whether any agreement to which such an association as is mentioned in section 112 of the Act of 1973 is a party falls within a paragraph of this Schedule—

(a) if the association does not carry on business in the supply of the relevant service or belong to the relevant class of persons, but represents persons who do, it shall be deemed to carry on such a business or belong to that class; and

(b) there shall be disregarded any person who does not carry on the relevant business or belong to the relevant class and who is a party to the agreement by virtue only of the operation of that section.

2.—(1) An agreement to which the only parties are operators of international sea transport services and the only restrictions accepted thereunder are in respect of such services.

(2) An agreement to which the only parties are such operators and persons for whom such services are being supplied and the only restrictions accepted thereunder are in respect of such services so far as those services relate to goods.

(3) An agreement to which the only parties are operators of international sea transport services and one other person carrying on business in the supply of another service and the only restrictions accepted under the agreement relate to the supply or acquisition of that other service in connection with the operation of international sea transport services.

(4) In this paragraph "international sea transport services" means the international carriage of passengers or goods wholly or partly by sea; and where the carriage is not wholly by sea, the carriage by sea and the carriage otherwise than by sea form part of the same service.

3.—(1) An agreement to which the only parties are air transport undertakings and the only restrictions accepted thereunder are in respect of carriage by air.

(2) An agreement entered into between an air transport undertaking and its agent and the only restrictions accepted thereunder are accepted in pursuance of such an agreement as is described in (1) above.

(3) In this paragraph "air transport undertaking" shall have the same meaning as in the Air Navigation Order 1974**(a)**.

4.—(1) An agreement to which the only parties are road passenger transport operators, and the only restrictions accepted thereunder relate to the provision of stage carriages or express carriages or both.

(2) For the purposes of this paragraph "stage carriage" and "express carriage" shall have the meaning given those expressions by sections 117 and 118 of the Road Traffic Act 1960**(b)**.

5.—(1) An agreement entered into between the Treasury or both the Treasury and the Secretary of State and building societies and the only restrictions accepted thereunder relate to the raising of funds or the making of loans.

(2) An agreement to which the only parties are building societies and the only restrictions accepted thereunder are accepted in pursuance of such an agreement as is described in (1) above.

(3) An agreement to which the only parties are building societies, and the only restrictions accepted thereunder relate to the rates of interest charged or to be charged for loans, or to the rates of interest paid or to be paid to shareholders or depositors.

(4) In this paragraph a "building society" means a society incorporated under the Building Societies Act 1962**(c)** or any enactment repealed by that Act (and includes a Northern Ireland society defined in section 134 of that Act).

6. An agreement to which the Bank of England or the Treasury or both are parties and which relates exclusively to the exercise of control by the Bank of England and the Treasury or one of them, as the case may be, over financial institutions or over the monetary system generally, or to the conduct of markets in money, in public sector debt instruments or in foreign currencies.

(a) S.I. 1974/1114 (1974 II, p. 4057).   (b) 1960 c. 16.
(c) 1962 c. 37.

7. An agreement to which the only parties carry on business in the supply of banking services and the only restrictions accepted thereunder relate to the supply of such services in Northern Ireland, or in Northern Ireland and the Republic of Ireland.

8. An agreement to which the only parties are persons permitted by or under Part I of the Insurance Companies Act 1974(a) or Part II of the Insurance Companies Act (Northern Ireland) 1968(b) to carry on insurance business and the only restrictions accepted thereunder relate to the provision of insurance services.

9. An agreement to which the only parties are trustees or managers of unit trust schemes authorised under the provisions of the Prevention of Fraud (Investments) Act 1958(c), or of the Prevention of Fraud (Investments) Act (Northern Ireland) 1940(d), and the only restrictions accepted thereunder relate to the management of, or the sale and purchase of units of, unit trust schemes authorised as aforesaid.

10. An agreement arising by virtue of a recommendation made by an association such as is described in section 112(1) of the Act of 1973 and which is either represented on the body known as the Panel on Take-overs and Mergers or is a member of such an association represented thereon, being a recommendation to comply with the provisions of the City Code on Take-overs and Mergers or a recommendation made for the purpose of implementing a decision of the Panel.

(a) 1974 c. 49. (b) 1968 c. 6. (N.I.).
(c) 1958 c. 45. (d) 1940 c. 9. (N.I.).

EXPLANATORY NOTE
(This Note is not part of the Order.)

This Order applies Part I of the Restrictive Trade Practices Act 1956 (which relates to the registration and judicial investigation of agreements about goods) to restrictive agreements in the supply and acquisition of services.

All services are brought under control by the Order, and all services are designated services with the exception of those listed in Schedule 4 to the Fair Trading Act 1973. As a consequence agreements between two or more persons carrying on business in the supply of any services under which restrictions in respect of the matters specified in Article 3(2) of the Order are accepted in relation to those or other services (other than those listed in Schedule 4) will in general be brought within Part I of the 1956 Act.

Part I will not however apply to agreements of the particular descriptions specified in the Schedule to this Order. These, subject to the conditions laid down in the Schedule, relate to—

    (*a*) international sea transport services;

    (*b*) carriage by air;

    (*c*) road passenger transport;

    (*d*) the raising of funds and making of loans by building societies;

    (*e*) the exercise of financial control by the Treasury or the Bank of England;

    (*f*) banking services in Northern Ireland;

    (*g*) the provision of insurance services;

    (*h*) Unit Trust schemes;

    (*i*) the implementation of decisions of the Panel on Take-overs and Mergers.

Particulars of agreements existing at the date of operation of this Order must be furnished for registration within three months from that date, unless the agreement is terminated within that time, and particulars of other agreements must be furnished before the relevant restrictions become effective and in any event within three months of their making.

STATUTORY INSTRUMENTS

1976 No. 103

FOOD AND DRUGS

LABELLING

The Skimmed Milk with Non-Milk Fat (Amendment) Regulations 1976

Made - - - -	*26th January* 1976
Laid before Parliament	*4th February* 1976
Coming into Operation	*25th February* 1976

The Minister of Agriculture, Fisheries and Food and the Secretary of State for Social Services, acting jointly, in exercise of the powers conferred on them by sections 7 and 123 of the Food and Drugs Act 1955(a), as read with the Secretary of State for Social Services Order 1968(b), and of all other powers enabling them in that behalf, hereby make the following regulations after consultation with such organisations as appear to them to be representative of interests substantially affected by the regulations and after reference to the Food Hygiene Advisory Council under section 82 of the said Act:—

Citation, commencement and interpretation

1.—(1) These regulations may be cited as the Skimmed Milk with Non-Milk Fat (Amendment) Regulations 1976, and shall come into operation on 25th February 1976.

(2) The Interpretation Act 1889(c) shall apply to the interpretation of these regulations as it applies to the interpretation of an Act of Parliament.

Amendment of principal regulations

2. The Skimmed Milk with Non-Milk Fat Regulations 1960(d), as amended(e), shall be further amended by substituting for Schedule 2 thereto the Schedule to these regulations.

Revocation

3. The Skimmed Milk with Non-Milk Fat (Amendment) Regulations 1968(f) and the Skimmed Milk with Non-Milk Fat (Amendment) Regulations 1973(g) are hereby revoked.

In Witness whereof the Official Seal of the Minister of Agriculture, Fisheries and Food is hereunto affixed on 22nd January 1976.

(L.S.)

Frederick Peart,
Minister of Agriculture, Fisheries and Food.

Barbara Castle,
Secretary of State for Social Services.

26th January 1976.

(a) 4 & 5 Eliz. 2. c. 16.   (b) S.I. 1968/1699 (1968 III, p. 4585).
(c) 1889 c. 63.   (d) S.I. 1960/2331 (1960 II, p. 1483).
(e) the relevant amending instruments are S.I. 1968/1474 (1968 III, p. 4214) and S.I. 1973/161 (1973 I, p. 664).
(f) S.I. 1968/1474 (1968 III, p. 4214).   (g) S.I. 1973/161 (1973 I, p. 664).

THE SCHEDULE

PART I

FOODS IN RESPECT OF WHICH THE WORDS "UNFIT FOR BABIES" [OR "NOT TO BE USED FOR BABIES"] MAY BE OMITTED FROM THE LABEL

C & G V.Formula, manufactured by or for Cow and Gate.

Efalac, manufactured by or for L E Pritchitt and Company Limited.

Osterfood, manufactured by or for Glaxo-Farley Foods Limited.

S–M–A and S–M–A/S–26, manufactured by or for John Wyeth and Brother Limited.

PART II

REQUIREMENTS RELATING TO THE FOODS SPECIFIED IN PART I OF THIS SCHEDULE

1. Every food specified in Part I of this Schedule—
   (*a*) shall contain poly-unsaturated fatty acids of the cis-cis form to the extent of not less than 12 per cent. of the total fatty acids present in such food;
   (*b*) shall not contain any protein other than protein derived from milk; and
   (*c*) shall not contain any ingredient of no nutritional value.

2.—(1) C & G V.Formula in powder form shall contain—
   (*a*) not less than 14·5 per cent. of protein derived from milk;
   (*b*) not less than 24·0 per cent. of fat;
   (*c*) ergocalciferol (vitamin D or D_2) or cholecalciferol (vitamin D or D_3) or any mixture thereof equivalent to not less than 1·25 microgrammes and not more than 3·13 microgrammes of cholecalciferol per ounce or to not less than 4·41 microgrammes and not more than 11·0 microgrammes of cholecalciferol per 100 grammes;
   (*d*) retinol (vitamin A) or biologically active carotenoids or any mixture thereof equivalent to not less than 180 microgrammes of retinol per ounce or to not less than 635 microgrammes of retinol per 100 grammes;
   (*e*) ascorbic acid (vitamin C) or dehydroascorbic acid (vitamin C) or any mixture thereof equivalent to not less than 12·0 milligrammes of ascorbic acid per ounce or to not less than 42·3 milligrammes of ascorbic acid per 100 grammes.

(2) C & G V.Formula in condensed liquid form shall contain—
   (*a*) not less than 3·6 per cent. of protein derived from milk;
   (*b*) not less than 6·0 per cent. of fat;
   (*c*) ergocalciferol (vitamin D or D_2) or cholecalciferol (vitamin D or D_3) or any mixture thereof equivalent to 0·63 ±0·31 microgrammes of cholecalciferol per fluid ounce or to 2·20±1·10 microgrammes of cholecalciferol per 100 millilitres;
   (*d*) retinol (vitamin A) or biologically active carotenoids or any mixture thereof equivalent to not less than 45·0 microgrammes of retinol per fluid ounce or to not less than 158 microgrammes of retinol per 100 millilitres;
   (*e*) ascorbic acid (vitamin C) or dehydroascorbic acid (vitamin C) or any mixture thereof equivalent to not less than 3·00 milligrammes of ascorbic acid per fluid ounce or to not less than 10·6 milligrammes of ascorbic acid per 100 millilitres.

(3) C & G V.Formula in liquid, diluted ready for use form shall contain—
   (*a*) not less than 1·8 per cent. of protein derived from milk;
   (*b*) not less than 3·0 per cent. of fat;

(c) ergocalciferol (vitamin D or D₂) or cholecalciferol (vitamin D or D₃) or any mixture thereof equivalent to 0·31 ±0·16 microgrammes of cholecalciferol per fluid ounce or to 1·10 ±0·55 microgrammes of cholecalciferol per 100 millilitres;

(d) retinol (vitamin A) or biologically active carotenoids or any mixture thereof equivalent to not less than 22·5 microgrammes of retinol per fluid ounce or to not less than 79·2 microgrammes of retinol per 100 millilitres;

(e) ascorbic acid (vitamin C) or dehydroascorbic acid (vitamin C) or any mixture thereof equivalent to not less than 1·50 milligrammes of ascorbic acid per fluid ounce or to not less than 5·28 milligrammes of ascorbic acid per 100 millilitres.

3. Efalac shall contain—

(a) not less than 23·1 per cent. of protein derived from milk;

(b) not less than 28·6 per cent. of fat;

(c) ergocalciferol (vitamin D or D₂) or cholecalciferol (vitamin D or D₃) or any mixture thereof equivalent to 2·50 ±0·78 microgrammes of cholecalciferol per ounce or to 8·82 ±2·73 microgrammes of cholecalciferol per 100 grammes;

(d) retinol (vitamin A) or biologically active carotenoids or any mixture thereof equivalent to not less than 107 microgrammes of retinol per ounce or to not less than 378 microgrammes of retinol per 100 grammes.

4.—(1) *Osterfood in liquid, diluted ready for use form shall contain—*

(a) *not less than 1·7 per cent. of protein derived from milk;*

(b) *not less than 2·65 per cent. of fat;*

(c) *ergocalciferol (vitamin D or D₂) or cholecalciferol (vitamin D or D₃) or any mixture thereof equivalent to 0·37 ±0·11 microgrammes of cholecalciferol per fluid ounce or to 1·30 ±0·39 microgrammes of cholecalciferol per 100 millilitres;*

(d) *retinol (vitamin A) or biologically active carotenoids or any mixture thereof equivalent to not less than 28·4 microgrammes of retinol per fluid ounce or to not less than 100 microgrammes of retinol per 100 millilitres;*

(e) *ascorbic acid (vitamin C) or dehydroascorbic acid (vitamin C) or any mixture thereof equivalent to not less than 1·99 milligrammes of ascorbic acid per fluid ounce or to not less than 7·00 milligrammes of ascorbic acid per 100 millilitres.*

(2) *Osterfood in powder form shall contain—*

(a) *not less than 11·4 per cent. of protein derived from milk;*

(b) *not less than 18·0 per cent. of fat;*

(c) *ergocalciferol (vitamin D or D₂) or cholecalciferol (vitamin D or D₃) or any mixture thereof equivalent to 2·55 ±0·77 microgrammes of cholecalciferol per ounce or to 9·00 ±2·70 microgrammes of cholecalciferol per 100 grammes;*

(d) *retinol (vitamin A) or biologically active carotenoids or any mixture thereof equivalent to not less than 198 microgrammes of retinol per ounce or to not less than 700 microgrammes of retinol per 100 grammes;*

(e) *ascorbic acid (vitamin C) or dehydroascorbic acid (vitamin C) or any mixture thereof equivalent to not less than 13·0 milligrammes of ascorbic acid per ounce or to not less than 46·0 milligrammes of ascorbic acid per 100 grammes.*

5.—(1) S-M-A and S-M-A/S-26 in powder form shall each contain—

(a) not less than 11·6 per cent. of protein derived from milk;

(b) not less than 27·0 per cent. of fat;

(c) ergocalciferol (vitamin D or D₂) or cholecalciferol (vitamin D or D₃) or any mixture thereof equivalent to 2·30 ±0·70 microgrammes of cholecalciferol per ounce or to 8·11 ±2·47 microgrammes of cholecalciferol per 100 grammes;

(*d*) retinol (vitamin A) or biologically active carotenoids or any mixture thereof equivalent to not less than 96·3 microgrammes of retinol per ounce or to not less than 340 microgrammes of retinol per 100 grammes;

(*e*) ascorbic acid (vitamin C) or dehydroascorbic acid (vitamin C) or any mixture thereof equivalent to not less than 11·5 milligrammes of ascorbic acid per ounce or to not less than 40·6 milligrammes of ascorbic acid per 100 grammes.

(2) S–M–A and S–M–A/S–26 in concentrated liquid form shall each contain—

(*a*) not less than 2·6 per cent. of protein derived from milk;

(*b*) not less than 6·2 per cent. of fat;

(*c*) ergocalciferol (vitamin D or D_2) or cholecalciferol (vitamin D or D_3) or any mixture thereof equivalent to 0·56 ±0·18 microgrammes of cholecalciferol per fluid ounce or to 1·98 ±0·62 microgrammes of cholecalciferol per 100 millilitres;

(*d*) retinol (vitamin A) or biologically active carotenoids or any mixture thereof equivalent to not less than 42·0 microgrammes of retinol per fluid ounce or to not less than 148 microgrammes of retinol per 100 millilitres;

(*e*) ascorbic acid (vitamin C) or dehydroascorbic acid (vitamin C) or any mixture thereof equivalent to not less than 2·80 milligrammes of ascorbic acid per fluid ounce or to not less than 9·86 milligrammes of ascorbic acid per 100 millilitres.

(3) S–M–A and S–M–A/S–26 in liquid, diluted ready for use form shall each contain—

(*a*) not less than 1·3 per cent. of protein derived from milk;

(*b*) not less than 3·1 per cent. of fat;

(*c*) ergocalciferol (vitamin D or D_2) or cholecalciferol (vitamin D or D_3) or any mixture thereof equivalent to 0·28 ±0·09 microgrammes of cholecalciferol per fluid ounce or to 0·97 ±0·31 microgrammes of cholecalciferol per 100 millilitres;

(*d*) retinol (vitamin A) or biologically active carotenoids or any mixture thereof equivalent to not less than 21·0 microgrammes of retinol per fluid ounce or to not less than 73·9 microgrammes of retinol per 100 millilitres;

(*e*) ascorbic acid (vitamin C) or dehydroascorbic acid (vitamin C) or any mixture thereof equivalent to not less than 1·40 milligrammes of ascorbic acid per fluid ounce or to not less than 4·93 milligrammes per 100 millilitres.

6. In this Schedule, each reference to any percentage means that percentage by weight and in any provision requiring that any food specified in this Schedule shall contain retinol, ascorbic acid, dehydroascorbic acid, ergocalciferol or cholecalciferol, any reference to dehydroascorbic acid or ergocalciferol and the first of any two references in such provision to retinol, ascorbic acid or cholecalciferol shall include the biologically active equivalents or derivatives of those substances. For the purposes of calculating the retinol equivalent of biologically active carotenoids, the factors set out in Part I of Schedule 4 to the Labelling of Food Regulations 1970(**a**), as amended(**b**), shall apply.

(**a**) S.I. 1970/400 (1970 I, p. 1383).   (**b**) S.I. 1972/1510 (1972 III, p. 4441).

EXPLANATORY NOTE

(This Note is not part of the Regulations.)

These Regulations further amend the Second Schedule to the Skimmed Milk with Non-Milk Fat Regulations 1960—

(*a*) by exempting Osterfood from the requirement under regulation 3(1) and the First Schedule to bear on the label the declaration "Unfit for babies" (or the permitted alternatives);

(*b*) by replacing expressions of the existing requirements in Part II of the Second Schedule in terms of international units of vitamins A and D and milligrammes of ascorbic acid per ounce or per fluid ounce with expressions of those requirements in the following terms:—

retinol (vitamin A) or biologically active carotenoids or any mixture thereof—their equivalent in microgrammes of retinol per ounce or 100 grammes or per fluid ounce or 100 millilitres;

ergocalciferol (vitamin D or D_2) or cholecalciferol (vitamin D or D_3) or any mixture thereof—their equivalent in microgrammes of cholecalciferol per ounce or 100 grammes or per fluid ounce or 100 millilitres;

ascorbic acid (vitamin C) or dehydroascorbic acid (vitamin C) or any mixture thereof—their equivalent in milligrammes of ascorbic acid per ounce or 100 grammes or per fluid ounce or 100 millilitres.

The amendments at (*a*) and (*b*) are consolidated with previous amendments to the Second Schedule and exemptions relating to foods no longer marketed, Alfonal, Alfonal Evaporated, White Dove Brand and Enfamil, are withdrawn.

The new material, insofar as it relates to Osterfood, appears in italics.

STATUTORY INSTRUMENTS

1976 No. 104

TOWN AND COUNTRY PLANNING, ENGLAND AND WALES

The Town and Country Planning (Repeal of Provisions No. 5) (Herefordshire) Order 1976

Made - - - -		*26th January* 1976
Coming into Operation		*1st March* 1976

The Secretary of State for the Environment in exercise of the powers conferred on him by sections 21(2) and 287 of the Town and Country Planning Act 1971(**a**) hereby makes the following order:—

1.—(1) This order may be cited as the Town and Country Planning (Repeal of Provisions No. 5) (Herefordshire) Order 1976 and shall come into operation on 1st March 1976.

(2) In this order "the Act" means the Town and Country Planning Act 1971; and "the Order area" means the area described in the Schedule to this order.

2. The provisions of the Act contained in Part I of Schedule 5 and in Schedule 6 to the Act are hereby repealed as respects the Order area.

SCHEDULE

THE ORDER AREA

1. In the County of Hereford and Worcester:

(*a*) The City of Hereford;

(*b*) the District of South Herefordshire;

(**a**) 1971 c. 78.

(c) the following parishes in the District of Malvern Hills:—

Acton Beauchamp
Ashperton
Avenbury
Aylton
Bishop's Frome
Bosbury
Bredenbury
Brockhampton
Bromyard
Canon Frome
Castle Frome
Coddington
Collington
Colwall
Cradley
Donnington
Eastnor
Edvin Loach
Edwyn Ralph
Eggleton
Evesbatch
Felton
Grendon Bishop
Hampton Charles
Ledbury Rural
Ledbury Town
Linton
Little Cowarne
Little Marcle

Mathon Rural
Moreton Jeffries
Much Cowarne
Much Marcle
Munsley
Norton
Ocle Pychard
Pencombe with Grendon Warren
Pixley
Putley
Saltmarshe
Stanford Bishop
Stoke Lacy
Stretton Grandison
Tarrington
Tedstone Delamere
Tedstone Wafer
Thornbury
Ullingswick
Upper Sapey
Wacton
Wellington Heath
Whitbourne
Winslow
Wolferlow
Woolhope
Yarkhill

(d) the following parishes in the District of Leominster:—

Adforton
Almeley
Aymestrey
Birley
Bishopstone
Blakemere
Bodenham
Brampton Bryan
Bridge Sollers
Brilley
Brimfield
Brinsop
Brobury
Buckton and Coxall
Burrington
Byford
Byton
Canon Pyon
Combe
Croft
Dilwyn
Docklow
Downton
Eardisland
Eardisley
Elton

Eye, Moreton and Ashton
Eyton
Ford
Hampton Wafer
Hatfield
Hope under Dinmore
Humber
Huntington
Kimbolton
Kingsland
King's Pyon
Kington Rural
Kington
Kinnersley
Kinsham
Knill
Laysters
Leinthall Starkes
Leintwardine
Leominster
Letton
Lingen
Little Hereford
Lower Harpton
Lucton
Luston

Lyonshall
Mansell Gamage
Mansell Lacy
Middleton on the Hill
Moccas
Monkland
Monnington on Wye
New Hampton
Newton
Norton Canon
Orleton
Pembridge
Pipe Aston
Preston on Wye
Pudlestone
Richards Castle (Hereford)
Rodd, Nash and Little Brampton
Sarnesfield

Shobdon
Stapleton
Staunton on Arrow
Staunton on Wye
Stoke Prior
Stretford
Titley
Walford, Letton and Newton
Weobley
Whitney
Wigmore
Willey
Willersley
Winforton
Wormsley
Yarpole
Yazor

Anthony Crosland,

26th January 1976.

Secretary of State for the Environment.

EXPLANATORY NOTE

(This Note is not part of the Order.)

This Order, which is made in consequence of the approval of the structure plan for that part of the County of Hereford and Worcester defined in the Schedule to the order (formerly the administrative county of Hereford), repeals for the area covered by that structure plan the provisions of the Town and Country Planning Act 1971 relating to development plans which are contained in Part I of Schedule 5 and in Schedule 6 to that Act. Those provisions which substantially re-enacted the provisions of the former Town and Country Planning Act 1962 (c. 38) relating to development plans are now superseded, in the area to which this order relates, by the provisions relating to structure and local plans contained in Part II of the Act of 1971.

Following this repeal, the development plan for the area to which this order relates is, by virtue of the provisions of paragraph 2 of Schedule 7 to the Act, the above mentioned structure plan read together with the development plan (within the meaning of Schedule 5) which is in force in that area at the date when this order comes into operation. The structure plan prevails in any case of conflict between the provisions of the two plans.

STATUTORY INSTRUMENTS

1976 No. 105 (C. 3)

TOWN AND COUNTRY PLANNING, ENGLAND AND WALES

The Town and Country Planning Act 1971 (Commencement No. 33) (Herefordshire) Order 1976

Made - - - - *26th January* 1976

The Secretary of State for the Environment, in exercise of the powers conferred on him by sections 21 and 287 of the Town and Country Planning Act 1971**(a)** hereby makes the following order:—

1.—(1) This order may be cited as the Town and Country Planning Act 1971 (Commencement No. 33) (Herefordshire) Order 1976.

(2) In this order—

"the Act" means the Town and Country Planning Act 1971;

"the Order area" means the area described in Schedule I to the order.

2. The provisions of the Act which are specified in the first column of Schedule 2 hereto (which relate to the matters specified in the second column of the said Schedule) shall come into operation in the Order area on 1st March 1976.

3. Notwithstanding the bringing into operation of those provisions of Part I of Schedule 23 to the Act specified in Schedule 2 to the order, any reference in the Land Compensation Act 1961**(b)** to an area defined in the current development plan as an area of comprehensive development shall continue to be construed as including a reference to an area so defined in any development plan currently in force.

(a) 1971 c. 78. (b) 1961 c. 33.

SCHEDULE I

THE ORDER AREA

1. In the County of Hereford and Worcester:

(*a*) The City of Hereford;

(*b*) the District of South Herefordshire;

(*c*) the following parishes in the District of Malvern Hills:—

Acton Beauchamp	Mathon Rural
Ashperton	Moreton Jeffries
Avenbury	Much Cowarne
Aylton	Much Marcle
Bishop's Frome	Munsley
Bosbury	Norton
Bredenbury	Ocle Pychard
Brockhampton	Pencombe with Grendon Warren
Bromyard	Pixley
Canon Frome	Putley
Castle Frome	Saltmarshe
Coddington	Stanford Bishop
Collington	Stoke Lacy
Colwall	Stretton Grandison
Cradley	Tarrington
Donnington	Tedstone Delamere
Eastnor	Tedstone Wafer
Edvin Loach	Thornbury
Edwyn Ralph	Ullingswick
Eggleton	Upper Sapey
Evesbatch	Wacton
Felton	Wellington Heath
Grendon Bishop	Whitbourne
Hampton Charles	Winslow
Ledbury Rural	Wolferlow
Ledbury Town	Woolhope
Linton	Yarkhill
Little Cowarne	
Little Marcle	

(*d*) the following parishes in the District of Leominster:—

Adforton	Dilwyn
Almeley	Docklow
Aymestrey	Downton
Birley	Eardisland
Bishopstone	Eardisley
Blakemere	Elton
Bodenham	Eye, Moreton and Ashton
Brampton Bryan	Eyton
Bridge Sollers	Ford
Brilley	Hampton Wafer
Brimfield	Hatfield
Brinsop	Hope under Dinmore
Brobury	Humber
Buckton and Coxall	Huntington
Burrington	Kimbolton
Byford	Kingsland
Byton	King's Pyon
Canon Pyon	Kington Rural
Combe	Kington
Croft	Kinnersley

SCHEDULE 1 (cont.)

Kinsham	Pipe Aston
Knill	Preston on Wye
Laysters	Pudlestone
Leinthall Starkes	Richards Castle (Hereford)
Leintwardine	Rodd, Nash and Little Brampton
Leominster	Sarnesfield
Letton	Shobdon
Lingen	Stapleton
Little Hereford	Staunton on Arrow
Lower Harpton	Staunton on Wye
Lucton	Stoke Prior
Luston	Stretford
Lyonshall	Titley
Mansell Gamage	Walford, Letton and Newton
Mansell Lacy	Weobley
Middleton on the Hill	Whitney
Moccas	Wigmore
Monkland	Willey
Monnington on Wye	Willersley
New Hampton	Winforton
Newton	Wormsley
Norton Canon	Yarpole
Orleton	Yazor
Pembridge	

SCHEDULE 2

PROVISIONS COMING INTO OPERATION IN THE ORDER AREA ON 1ST MARCH 1976

Provisions of the Act	Subject matter of provisions
Section 20	Meaning of "development plan" for the purposes of the Act and of certain other enactments.
In Schedule 23 that paragraph in Part I which relates to the Land Compensation Act 1961	Meaning of "area of comprehensive development" in the Land Compensation Act 1961.

26th January 1976.

Anthony Crosland,
Secretary of State for the Environment.

EXPLANATORY NOTE

(This Note is not part of the Order.)

This Order brings into force for that part of the County of Hereford and Worcester defined in the Schedule to the order (formerly the administrative county of Hereford), section 20 of, and certain of the provisions of Part I of Schedule 23 to, the Town and Country Planing Act 1971 specified in Schedule 2 to the order. Section 20 provides, for the purposes of the Act of 1971, any other enactment relating to town and country planning, the Land Compensation Act 1961 and the Highways Act 1959 (c. 25), that the development plan for any district shall consist of the structure and local plans for that area. The provision in Part I of Schedule 23 which is specified in Schedule 2 to this order provides for references in the Land Compensation Act 1961 to areas defined in the current development plan as areas of comprehensive development to be construed as references to action areas for which a local plan is in force.

The Order contains a transitional provision relating to old-style development plans (which remain in existence alongside structure plans until revoked by order of the Secretary of State). The provision secures that references to areas of comprehensive development in the Land Compensation Act 1961 are continued to be construed as including references to areas so defined in any old-style development plan.

STATUTORY INSTRUMENTS

1976 No. 106

MINES AND QUARRIES

The Ironstone Restoration Fund (Standard Rate) Order 1976

Made - - - -	*27th January* 1976
Laid before Parliament	*5th February* 1976
Coming into Operation	*1st April* 1976

The Secretary of State for the Environment, in exercise of the powers conferred on him by section 3 of the Mineral Workings Act 1971(a) and after consultation with those persons and bodies of persons appearing to him to be representative of ironstone operators and of owners of interests in land from which ironstone is extracted, hereby makes the following order:—

1.—(1) This order may be cited as the Ironstone Restoration Fund (Standard Rate) Order 1976 and shall come into operation on 1st April 1976.

(2) The Interpretation Act 1889(b) shall apply for the interpretation of this order as it applies for the interpretation of an Act of Parliament.

2. In respect of all work of the kinds specified in section 9(1) of the Mineral Workings Act 1951(c) which is completed after 31st March 1976 the standard rate for the purposes of section 9 of that Act (payment to operators from the Ironstone Restoration Fund by reference to excess of cost of works of restoration over the standard rate) shall be £510 per acre.

3. The Ironstone Restoration Fund (Standard Rate) Order 1975(d) is hereby revoked, but without prejudice to any payments due to operators under section 9 of the Mineral Workings Act 1951 in respect of work completed on or before 31st March 1976.

27th January 1976.

Anthony Crosland,
Secretary of State for the Environment.

(a) 1971 c. 71.　　　　(b) 1889 c. 63.
(c) 1951 c. 60.　　　　(d) S.I. 1975/181 (1975 I, p. 457).

EXPLANATORY NOTE

(This Note is not part of the Order.)

Section 9 of the Mineral Workings Act 1951, as amended by the Mineral Workings Act 1971, provides that the rate of payments out of the Ironstone Restoration Fund to be made to ironstone operators in respect of the restoration of worked ironstone land in compliance with conditions of a planning permission shall represent the amount by which the estimated cost per acre of the work of restoration exceeds such standard rate as the Secretary of State may from time to time determine. The existing standard rate, prescribed by the Ironstone Restoration Fund (Standard Rate) Order 1975, is £410 per acre: this order raises it to £510 per acre in respect of all work completed after 31st March 1976.

STATUTORY INSTRUMENTS

1976 No. 107

MINES AND QUARRIES

The Ironstone Restoration Fund (Rates of Contribution) (Amendment) Order 1976

Made - - - -	27th January 1976
Laid before Parliament	5th February 1976
Coming into Operation	1st April 1976

The Secretary of State for the Environment after consultation with such persons and bodies of persons appearing to him to be representative of ironstone operators and of owners of interests in land from which ironstone is extracted, in exercise of his powers under sections 1(2) and (3) and 2 of the Mineral Workings Act 1971(a) and of all other powers enabling him in that behalf hereby makes the following order:—

1.—(1) This order may be cited as the Ironstone Restoration Fund (Rates of Contribution) (Amendment) Order 1976 and the Ironstone Restoration Fund (Rates of Contribution) Order 1972(b) and this order may be cited together as the Ironstone Restoration Fund (Rates of Contribution) Orders 1972 and 1976.

(2) This order shall come into operation on 1st April 1976.

(3) The Interpretation Act 1889(c) shall apply for the interpretation of this order as it applies for the interpretation of an Act of Parliament.

2. For articles 2 and 3 of the Ironstone Restoration Fund (Rates of Contribution) Order 1972 there shall be substituted the following articles:—

"2. The full rate of contribution payable to the Secretary of State under the provisions of section 1(2) of the 1971 Act shall be—

(a) in respect of ironstone extracted on or after 1st April 1971 but before 1st April 1975, 3p per ton; and

(b) in respect of ironstone extracted on or after 1st April 1975, 4p per ton.

3. The reduced rate of contribution payable to the Secretary of State in respect of ironstone extracted in the circumstances specified in section 1(3) of the 1971 Act shall be—

(a) in respect of ironstone so extracted on or after 1st April 1971 but before 1st April 1975, 1·5p per ton; and

(b) in respect of ironstone so extracted on or after 1st April 1975, 2p per ton.".

	Anthony Crosland,
27th January 1976.	Secretary of State for the Environment.

(a) 1971 c. 71.   (b) S.I. 1972/210 (1972 I, p. 698).   (c) 1889 c. 63.

EXPLANATORY NOTE

(This Note is not part of the Order.)

This Order varies the rates of contribution, as set out in the Ironstone Restoration Fund (Rates of Contribution) Order 1972, to be paid by ironstone operators towards the Ironstone Restoration Fund under section 1 of the Mineral Workings Act 1971. Under the provisions of the Order of 1972, the full rate of contribution (in respect of ironstone extracted on or after 1st April 1971) is 3p per ton and the reduced rate (payable in respect of ironstone extracted in the circumstances set out in section 1(3) of the Act of 1971) is 1·5p per ton. This order provides that, in respect of ironstone extracted on and after 1st April 1975, the full rate is to be 4p per ton and the reduced rate 2p per ton.

STATUTORY INSTRUMENTS

1976 No. 110

COMMUNITY LAND

The Community Land (Operational Land of Water Authorities) Order 1976

Made - - -	*27th January* 1976
Laid before Parliament	*6th February* 1976
Coming into Operation	*6th April* 1976

The Secretary of State for the Environment, in relation to England, the Secretary of State for Scotland, in relation to Scotland, and the Secretary of State for Wales, in relation to Wales (being also, in each case, the appropriate Minister in relation to the statutory undertakers herein mentioned), in exercise of the powers conferred on them by sections 5(3) and 53(2) of the Community Land Act 1975(a) and of all other powers enabling them in that behalf, hereby order as follows:—

1. This order shall come into operation on 6th April 1976, and may be cited as the Community Land (Operational Land of Water Authorities) Order 1976.

2. The Interpretation Act 1889(b) shall apply for the interpretation of this order as it applies for the interpretation of an Act of Parliament.

3. In England and Wales, "operational land" as respects any water authority shall mean—

(a) land which is used for the purpose of carrying on any of the functions of the Authority, and

(b) land in which an interest is held for that purpose,

not being land which in respect of its nature and situation is comparable rather with land in general than with land which is used, or in which interests are held, for the purpose of the carrying on of statutory undertakings.

4. In Scotland, "operational land" as respects any statutory undertakers carrying on any undertaking for the supply of water (other than an authority within the meaning of section 1(1)(b) of the Community Land Act 1975) shall mean—

(a) land which is used for the purpose of carrying on any of the functions of those undertakers, and

(b) land in which an interest is held for that purpose,

not being land which in respect of its nature and situation is comparable rather with land in general than with land which is used, or in which interests are held, for the purpose of the carrying on of statutory undertakings.

(a) 1975 c. 77.   (b) 1889 c. 63.

Signed by authority of
the Secretary of State
21st January 1976.

John Silkin,
Minister for Planning and Local Government,
Department of the Environment.

22nd January 1976.

William Ross,
Secretary of State for Scotland.

27th January 1976.

John Morris,
Secretary of State for Wales.

EXPLANATORY NOTE

(This Note is not part of the Order.)

The operational land of statutory undertakers is treated differently from other land for some of the purposes of the Community Land Act 1975. The duty which the Secretary of State may, under section 18 of the Act, impose on an authority—this is a duty to acquire all land needed for the relevant development designated by that order—cannot be imposed on the operational land of statutory undertakers (see section 18(4)(*d*)). Similarly, the provisions of sections 19 to 22 of the Act ("suspension" of certain planning permissions) do not apply to planning permissions granted in respect of operational land of statutory undertakers, or land which would be operational land if it were used or held by statutory undertakers for the purposes covered by the planning permission.

Water authorities in England and Wales and the Central Scotland Water Development Board in Scotland are statutory undertakers as defined in section 5(1)(*a*) of the Act, as they carry on undertakings for the supply of water. The definition of "operational land" in section 5(2) of the Act is linked to the statutory undertaking of statutory undertakers. However, those statutory undertakers have other statutory functions, e.g., sewerage and water conservation, and developing held sources of supply, and land held for the purpose of these functions does not come within the definition of "operational land" in section 5(2).

This Order accordingly defines "operational land" in relation to those statutory undertakers as land which is used for the purpose of *any* of their statutory functions, if it is land in which they hold an interest for the purpose of those functions, and is land comparable with land used or held for the purpose of statutory undertakings, rather than with land in general.

In Scotland, the functions of water authorities and sewerage functions are carried out by regional and islands councils who are authorities for the purposes of the Act, and accordingly any land held by them for the purposes of those functions does not require to be dealt with for the purposes of sections 18 and 19 to 22 of the Act.

STATUTORY INSTRUMENTS

1976 No. 111

WEIGHTS AND MEASURES

The Weights and Measures Act 1963 (Biscuits and Shortbread) Order 1976

Laid before Parliament in draft

Made	-	-	-	*27th January* 1976

Coming into Operation   1st *January* 1978

Whereas the Secretary of State pursuant to section 54(2) of the Weights and Measures Act 1963(a) (hereinafter referred to as "the Act") has consulted with organisations appearing to her to be representative of interests substantially affected by this Order and considered the representations made to her by such organisations with respect to the subject matter of this Order:

And whereas a draft of this Order has been laid before Parliament and approved by resolution of each House of Parliament pursuant to section 54(3) of the Act:

Now, therefore, the Secretary of State, in exercise of powers conferred by section 21(2), (3) and (5) of the Act and now vested in her(b) and of all other powers enabling her in that behalf, hereby makes the following Order:

1.—(1) This Order may be cited as the Weights and Measures Act 1963 (Biscuits and Shortbread) Order 1976 and shall come into operation on 1st January 1978.

(2) The Interpretation Act 1889(c) shall apply for the interpretation of this Order as it applies for the interpretation of an Act of Parliament.

2. Part XI of Schedule 4 to the Act shall cease to apply to biscuits and shortbread.

3.—(1) Except where the quantity does not exceed 8 biscuits or 8 shortbread pieces, as the case may be, biscuits (other than wafer biscuits which are not cream-filled), and shortbread, being biscuits and shortbread which are not pre-packed, shall be sold by retail only by net weight.

(2) Wafer biscuits which are not cream-filled and which are not pre-packed shall be sold by retail only by number.

(a) 1963 c. 31.   (b) S.I. 1970/1537 (1970 III, p. 5293).   (c) 1889 c. 63.

4.—(1) Subject to Articles 5 and 6, biscuits (other than wafer biscuits which are not cream-filled) shall be pre-packed:—

> (*a*) except where made up in a quantity not exceeding 85g or exceeding 5kg, only if made up in one of the following quantities by net weight, that is to say:—
>
>> (i) 3½oz, 7oz. 10½oz. 14oz, and subsequent multiples of 3½oz; or
>>
>> (ii) 100g, 125g. 150g. 200g, 250g. 300g, and subsequent multiples of 100g; or
>>
>> (iii) if made up before 1st January 1981, 175g; and
>
> (*b*) except where made up in a quantity not exceeding 50g, only if the container is marked with an indication of quantity by net weight.

(2) Subject to Article 6, shortbread, except where made up in a quantity not exceeding 50g or except where the shortbread consists of a piece or pieces each weighing 200g or more, shall be pre-packed only if the container is marked with an indication of quantity by net weight.

(3) Subject to Article 6, wafer biscuits which are not cream-filled shall be pre-packed only if the container is marked with an indication of quantity by number.

5.—(1) Article 4(1) shall not apply in relation to biscuits which have been pre-packed on the same premises as those on which they were produced, and either:—

> (*a*) the biscuits are in possession of the producer for sale by him by retail on those premises; or
>
> (*b*) if the producer has agreed to sell or has sold the biscuits, he agreed to sell or sold them by retail on those premises.

(2) Subject to Article 6 and except where the biscuits are made up in a quantity not exceeding 100g, biscuits specified in paragraph (1) above shall be pre-packed only if the container is marked with an indication of quantity by net weight.

6.—(1) Where two or more identical marked inner packs are enclosed within an outer container, nothing in Articles 4 or 5 shall require the outer container to be marked with any information or to enclose goods of a particular weight if either:—

> (i) the marking of the net weight or the number on at least one of the packs, and the total number of packs, is clearly visible through the outer container; or
>
> (ii) the information as to the matters mentioned in (i) above is marked on the outer container.

(2) Where two or more marked inner packs which are not identical are enclosed within an outer container, nothing in Article 4 or Article 5 shall require the outer container to be marked with any informaton or to enclose goods of a particular weight if the outer container is marked with the net weight or the number of the biscuits or pieces of shortbread in each pack and with the number of packs of each such net weight or number.

(3) Where two or more biscuits (other than wafer biscuits which are not cream-filled) each of which is separately wrapped and is of a net weight of not more than 50g are enclosed in an outer container, nothing in Article 4(1) or Article 5 shall require the outer container to be marked with any information or to enclose goods of a particular weight if the outer container is marked with an indication of quantity by number.

(4) In this Article a "marked inner pack", in relation to any goods, means the goods and the immediate container in which they are made up, being:

    (i) in the case of goods to which Article 4(1) relates, goods made up in a quantity for the time being permitted by that paragraph for pre-packed goods of a quantity exceeding 85g and not exceeding 5kg or in a quantity exceeding 50g but not exceeding 85g, and being a container marked with an indication of quantity by net weight:

    (ii) in the case of goods to which Article 4(2) or Article 5(2) relates, goods made up in a container marked with an indication of quantity by net weight;

    (iii) in the case of goods to which Article 4(3) relates, goods made up in a container marked with an indication of quantity by number;

and packs shall be taken as being identical if the goods in each pack are of the same weight or of the same number, as the case may be.

Alan Williams.

Minister of State.
Department of Prices and Consumer
Protection.

27th January 1976.

EXPLANATORY NOTE

(This Note is not part of the Order.)

This Order provides that Part XI of Schedule 4 to the Weights and Measures Act 1963 shall cease to apply to biscuits and shortbread on 1st January 1978 when the provisions of that Part are replaced by those of this Order. It introduces prescribed imperial and metric quantities for pre-packed biscuits intended for general retail sale, and provisions for the sale of biscuits and shortbread when not pre-packed.

Where the quantity exceeds 85g (approximately 3oz) and does not exceed 5kg (approximately 11lb), biscuits (other than those pre-packed for sale by retail on the premises where they were produced and pre-packed, and wafer biscuits which are not cream-filled), may be pre-packed only in prescribed imperial and metric weights. The container of such biscuits, when made up in a quantity exceeding 50g (approximately 1¾oz) must be marked with an indication of quantity by net weight.

Shortbread in a quantity exceeding 50g (approximately 1¾oz) which does not consist of a piece or pieces each weighing 200g (approximately 7ozs) or more and biscuits which are made up in a quantity exceeding 100g (approximately 3½oz) on the premises on which they were produced for sale by retail on those premises may only be pre-packed if the container is marked with an indication of quantity by net weight.

The container of pre-packed wafer biscuits which are not cream-filled must be marked with an indication of quantity by number. When not pre-packed such wafer biscuits shall be sold by retail only by number. Other biscuits and shortbread covered by the Order, when not pre-packed, shall be sold by retail only by net weight except where the quantity does not exceed 8.

Special provisions are included to cover multi-packs containing more than one pre-package or individually wrapped product.

STATUTORY INSTRUMENTS

1976 No. 112

CUSTOMS AND EXCISE

The Anti-Dumping Duty (Temporary Suspension) Order 1976

Made - - - -	27th January 1976
Laid before the House of Commons -	28th January 1976
Coming into Operation	21st February 1976

The Secretary of State, in exercise of powers conferred by sections 1, 10(3) and 15(4) of the Customs Duties (Dumping and Subsidies) Act 1969(a) and now vested in him (b), and of all other powers enabling him in that behalf, hereby makes the following Order:

1. This Order may be cited as the Anti-Dumping Duty (Temporary Suspension) Order 1976 and shall come into operation on 21st February 1976.

2. The Interpretation Act 1889(c) shall apply for the interpretation of this Order as it applies for the interpretation of an Act of Parliament.

3. The anti-dumping duties imposed by the Anti-Dumping Duty (No. 2) Order 1972(d) on machinery for wrapping pre-formed individual pieces of confectionery originating in the German Democratic Republic and Berlin (East), which were temporarily suspended by the Anti-Dumping Duty (Temporary Suspension) Order 1975(e) for a period of twelve months beginning with 21st February 1975, shall not be chargeable on such machinery imported into the United Kingdom during a period beginning on 21st February 1976 and ending on 30th June 1977.

Eric Deakins,
Parliamentary Under-Secretary of State,
Department of Trade.

27th January 1976.

(a) 1969 c. 16.
(c) 1889 c. 63.
(e) S.I. 1975/54 (1975 I, p. 163).

(b) S.I. 1970/1537 (1970 III, p. 5293).
(d) S.I. 1972/1371 (1972 III, p. 4223).

EXPLANATORY NOTE

(This Note is not part of the Order.)

This Order suspends for a further period up to and including 30th June 1977 the anti-dumping duties imposed by the Anti-Dumping Duty (No. 2) Order 1972 on machinery for wrapping pre-formed individual pieces of confectionery originating in the German Democratic Republic and Berlin (East).

STATUTORY INSTRUMENTS

1976 No. 116

PROBATION AND AFTER-CARE

The Probation (Allowances) (Amendment) Rules 1976

Made - - - -	*27th January* 1976
Laid before Parliament	*5th February* 1976
Coming into Operation	*1st March* 1976

In exercise of the powers conferred upon me by Schedule 3 of the Powers of Criminal Courts Act 1973(a). I hereby make the following Rules:—

1. These Rules may be cited as the Probation (Allowances) (Amendment) Rules 1976 and shall come into operation on 1st March 1976.

2. The Probation (Allowances) Rules 1971(b) as amended(c) shall be amended—

(a) by substituting, for Rule 5 (which relates to financial loss allowances), the following Rule: —

"5.—(1) Subject to paragraph (2) below, the rate of financial loss allowance payable under paragraph 13 of Schedule 3 to the Powers of Criminal Courts Act 1973 to a member where for the purposes of enabling him to perform any of his duties as a member there is incurred by him any expenditure (other than expenses on account of travelling or subsistence) to which he would not otherwise be subject or there is suffered by him any loss of earnings or of benefit under enactments relating to social security, which he would otherwise have made or received shall be the amount of that expenditure or loss:

Provided that the allowance payable in respect of any one period of 24 hours shall not exceed—

(a) where the period of time over which earnings or benefit are lost additional expense incurred is not more than 4 hours, the sum of £4.00; or

(b) where the said period of time is more than 4 hours, the sum of £8.00.

(2) For the purposes of paragraph (1) above, a member sha'l not be treated as having incurred any expenditure or suffered any loss for the purpose of enabling him to perform any of his duties as a member insofar as the expenditure was also incurred or the loss also suffered for

---

(a) 1973 c. 62. (b) S.I. 1971/414 (1971 I, p. 1225).
(c) The relevant amending Rules are S.I. 1974/1954 (1974 III. p. 6758).

the purpose of enabling the member to perform an approved duty within the meaning of the Local Government Act 1972(**a**).".

b) by inserting in Schedule 3, in the form of application for financial loss allowance, after "the [Petty Sessional Division] of........................",
the following sentence: —

"I declare that no claim is made in respect of any expenditure or loss also incurred for the purpose of enabling me to perform an approved duty within the meaning of the Local Government Act 1972.".

Roy Jenkins,

One of Her Majesty's Principal
Secretaries of State.

Home Office,
  Whitehall.
27th January 1976.

EXPLANATORY NOTE

(This Note is not part of the Rules.)

These Rules amend the Probation (Allowances) Rules 1971 by replacing Rule 5 (which relates to financial loss allowance). The amendment prevents claims being made for financial loss allowance in respect of loss or expenditure for which a member may also receive an attendance allowance or a financial loss allowance under the Local Government Act 1972. A consequential amendment is made to the form of application for financial loss allowance. The other main consequence of the amendment is an increase in the maximum rates of financial loss allowance from £3.35 to £4.00, for a period of less than 4 hours, and from £6.70 to £8.00, for a period of more than 4 hours in any 24 hours.

(**a**) 1972 c. 70.

STATUTORY INSTRUMENTS

1976 No. 117

JUSTICES OF THE PEACE

The Justices' Allowances Regulations 1976

Made	-	-	-	*27th January* 1976
Laid before Parliament				*5th February* 1976
Coming into Operation				*1st March* 1976

In exercise of the powers conferred upon me by Part III of Schedule 1 to the Administration of Justice Act 1973(**a**), I hereby make the following Regulations:—

1. These Regulations may be cited as the Justices' Allowances Regulations 1976 and shall come into operation on 1st March 1976.

2.—(1) In these Regulations unless the context otherwise requires—

"authority" means any authority responsible by virtue of paragraph 8(4) of Schedule 1 to the Act, for the payment of allowances under that paragraph;

"the Act" means the Administration of Justice Act 1973.

(2) The Interpretation Act 1889(**b**) shall apply to the interpretation of these Regulations as it applies to the interpretation of an Act of Parliament, and as if these Regulations and the Regulations revoked by these Regulations were Acts of Parliament.

3. The Regulations contained in Schedule 4 to these Regulations are hereby revoked.

4. The rates of travelling and subsistence allowance payable under paragraph 8 of Schedule 1 to the Act to a justice of the peace for any area in England or Wales in respect of expenditure on travelling, or, as the case may be, on subsistence, necessarily incurred by him for the purpose of enabling him to perform any of his duties as a justice shall be the rates set out in Schedules 1 and 2 to these Regulations respectively.

5.—(1) The rate of financial loss allowance payable under paragraph 8 of Schedule 1 to the Act to a justice of the peace for any area in England or Wales where for the purpose of enabling him to perform any of his duties as a justice there is incurred by him any expenditure (other than expense on account of travelling or subsistence) to which he would not otherwise be subject or there is suffered by him any loss of earnings or of benefit under the enactments relating to social security which he would otherwise have made or received shall be the amount of that expenditure or loss:

(**a**) 1973 c. 15.   (**b**) 1889 c. 63.

Provided that the allowance payable in respect of any one period of 24 hours shall not exceed—

(a) where the period of time over which earnings or benefit are lost or additional expense incurred is not more than 4 hours, the sum of £4.00; or

(b) where the said period of time is more than 4 hours, the sum of £8.00.

(2) For the purposes of paragraph (1) above, a justice shall not be treated as having incurred any expenditure or suffered any loss for the purpose of enabling him to perform any of his duties as a justice in so far as the expenditure was also incurred or the loss also suffered for the purpose of enabling the justice to perform an approved duty within the meaning of the Local Government Act 1972(**a**).

6. A justice who desires to claim financial loss, travelling or subsistence allowance shall complete and submit to the authority an application in the appropriate form set out in Schedule 3 to these Regulations or in a form substantially to the like effect.

7. An authority shall, so far as practicable, arrange for the issue to a justice of a ticket, or a document which can be exchanged for a ticket, to cover a journey in respect of which a travelling allowance would otherwise fall to be paid.

8.—(1) An authority shall keep a record of every payment made under paragraph 8 of Schedule 1 to the Act showing the amount and nature of the payment and the name of the justice to whom it is paid; and payments made in respect of duties as chairman, deputy chairman or member of the Crown Court shall be kept separate from other payments in the said record.

(2) For the purposes of this Regulation, expenditure incurred in the issue to a justice of a ticket or other document under Regulation 7 of these Regulations shall be deemed to be an amount paid to that justice.

9. Where any expenditure or loss entitles a person to receive an allowance under paragraph 8 of Schedule 1 to the Act in respect of duties as a justice and an allowance of the same nature, by whatever name called, under any other enactment in respect of duties in respect of some other capacity, the aggregate amount which that person shall be entitled to receive under the said paragraph 8 on account of the said expenditure or loss shall be reduced by the aggregate amount received by him on that account under the other enactment, and any claim made under the said paragraph 8 shall contain particulars of any amount so received or claimed, or which it is intended to claim, under the other enactment.

Roy Jenkins,
One of Her Majesty's Principal
Secretaries of State.

Home Office,
Whitehall.
27th January 1976.

(**a**) 1972 c. 70.

Regulation 4   SCHEDULE 1

RATES OF TRAVELLING ALLOWANCE

1.—(1) The rate for travel by public service shall be the amount of the fare of the class in which the justice chooses to travel but, subject to any supplementary allowances payable under sub-paragraph (2) of this paragraph, shall not exceed the lowest available first class fare.

(2) The rate payable under the foregoing sub-paragraph shall, if the justice so claims, be increased by supplementary allowances not exceeding the expenditure incurred on deposit or porterage of luggage, on reservation of seats, or on Pullman Car or similar supplements (other than expenditure on refreshment or sleeping accommodation).

2. The rate for travel by hired motor vehicle shall be—

(a) in cases of urgency or where no public service is reasonably available, the amount of the fare and any reasonable gratuity paid; and

(b) in any other case, the amount of the fare for travel by the appropriate public service.

3.—(1) The rate for travel by a justice's own motor-cycle of cylinder capacity not exceeding 500 cubic centimetres shall be—

(a) for the use of a motor cycle of cylinder capacity not exceeding 120 cubic centimetres, of an autocycle or of a motor-assisted pedal cycle, 1·7p a mile;

(b) for the use of a motor cycle of cylinder capacity exceeding 120 cubic centimetres but not exceeding 150 cubic centimetres, 2·1p a mile;

(c) for the use of a motor cycle of cylinder capacity exceeding 150 cubic centimetres but not exceeding 500 cubic centimetres, 2·6p a mile.

(2) The rate for travel by a justice's own private motor vehicle, or one belonging to a member of his family or otherwise provided for his use, other than a motor cycle of cylinder capacity not exceeding 500 cubic centimetres shall be 3·0p a mile unless such travel—

(a) results in a substantial saving of the justice's time; or

(b) is otherwise reasonable, in which case the rate shall be—

(i) for the use of a motor cycle of cylinder capacity exceeding 500 cubic centimetres, a motor cycle combination, or a motor car of cylinder capacity not exceeding 500 cubic centimetres, 3·5p a mile;

(ii) for the use of a motor car of cylinder capacity—

(a) exceeding 500 c.c. but not exceeding 999 c.c., 7·1p a mile;

(b) exceeding 999 c.c. but not exceeding 1199 c.c., 7·9p a mile;

(c) exceeding 1199 c.c., 9·0p a mile.

(3) The appropriate rate specified in the foregoing provisions of this paragraph shall, if the justice so claims, be increased—

(a) where the rate exceeds 3·0p a mile, by 0·21p a mile for the carriage, otherwise than by motor cycle, of each additional person to whom an allowance for travelling would otherwise be payable under any enactment;

(b) where the rate is 3·0p a mile, by 0·5p a mile for the carriage, otherwise than by motor cycle, of each additional person as aforesaid, so, however, that the rate when so increased shall not exceed 4·0p a mile;

(c) in the case of an absence overnight from the usual place of residence, by the amount of any expenditure incurred on garaging a motor vehicle, not exceeding 12·5p a night in the case of a motor car or 7·5p a night in the case of a vehicle of any other type;

(d) in any case, by the amount of any expenditure incurred on tolls, ferries or parking fees.

(4) For the purposes of this paragraph—

"motor car" includes a tri-car;

"motor cycle combination" means a motor cycle with a side car;

"motor cycle" means a motor cycle without a side car.

4. The rate for travel by air shall not exceed the fare paid but, subject thereto, shall be the rate applicable to travel by the appropriate public service together with an allowance equivalent to the amount of any saving in subsistence allowance consequent upon travel by air.

5. In this Schedule "public service" means any service provided for travel by the public by railway, ship, vessel, omnibus, trolley vehicle or tramway.

SCHEDULE 2   Regulation 4

RATES OF SUBSISTENCE ALLOWANCE

1.—(1) The rate of subsistence allowance shall be—

(a) in the case of an absence, not involving an absence overnight, from the usual place of residence—

(i) of more than four but not more than eight hours, £1.65;

(ii) of more than eight but not more than twelve hours, £2.90;

(iii) of more than twelve but not more than sixteen hours, £4.10;

(iv) of more than sixteen hours, £4.90;

(b) in the case of an absence overnight from the usual place of residence, £10.40:

Provided that for such an absence overnight in Greater London the rate may be increased by a supplementary allowance not exceeding £1.00.

(2) Any rate determined under the preceding sub-paragraph shall be deemed to cover a continuous period of absence of twenty-four hours.

2.—(1) The rates specified in the preceding paragraph shall be reduced by an appropriate amount in respect of any meal provided free of charge by any local authority during the period to which the allowance relates.

(2) In the preceding sub-paragraph "local authority" means the corporation of the City of London, the Greater London Council, a county council, a district council, a London borough council or a parish or community council.

Regulation 6

SCHEDULE 3

FORM OF APPLICATION FOR TRAVELLING AND SUBSISTENCE ALLOWANCES

1	2	3	4	5	6	7	8	9	10
Date	Place and time of departure	Place and time of return	Description of duties	Mode and class of travel	Number of miles travelled by private motor vehicle and rate applicable	Fares and other authorised payments	Toll, ferry and parking fees and garaging allowance	Travelling allowance claimed	Subsistence allowance claimed

TOTALS   ⋮

If the rate claimed is related to the type of vehicle and cylinder capacity, state what these are:—

If the rate claimed is more than 3·0p a mile, state grounds on which higher rate is claimed:—

Particulars of amounts received or claimed, or which it is intended to claim, under any other enactment by way of travelling allowance or subsistence allowance, or any equivalent allowance by whatever name called, in connection with any journey or absence claimed for above.

AMOUNTS NOW CLAIMED   ⋮

SCHEDULE 3—*(continued)*

I declare that I have actually and necessarily incurred expenditure on travelling and subsistence for the purpose of enabling me to perform duties as a justice of the peace and that I have actually paid the fares and made the other payments shown in column 7 and paid the fees shown in column 8 above. The amounts claimed do not exceed the amounts which I am entitled to receive in accordance with the rates prescribed by the Justices' Allowances Regulations 1976.

I declare that the statements above are correct. Except as shown above I have not made, and will not make, any claim under any enactment for travelling or subsistence expenses or allowances in connection with the duties indicated above.

Date ....

Signature of Justice ....

Address (usual place of residence) ....

FORM OF APPLICATION FOR FINANCIAL LOSS ALLOWANCE

1	2	3	4	5	6
Date	Place and time of departure	Place and time of return	Description of duties	Period of time over which earnings were lost or expense was incurred	Amount claimed

TOTALS ...

Particulars of amounts received or claimed, or which it is intended to claim, under any other enactment by way of financial loss allowance, or any equivalent allowance by whatever name called, in connection with the duties indicated above.

AMOUNTS NOW CLAIMED ...

I declare that I have actually and necessarily—

*(a) suffered loss of earnings which I would otherwise have made,

*(b) incurred additional expense, other than expense on account of travelling or subsistence, to which I would not otherwise have been subject,

for the purpose of enabling me to perform duties as a justice of the peace. I declare that no claim is made in respect of any expenditure or loss also incurred for the purpose of enabling me to perform an approved duty within the meaning of the Local Government Act 1972. The amounts claimed do not exceed the amounts which I am entitled to receive in accordance with the rates prescribed by the Justices' Allowances Regulations 1976.

I declare that the statements above are correct. Except as shown above I have not made, and will not make, any claim under any enactment for financial loss allowance in connection with the duties indicated above.

Date..   Signature of justice ....

Address ....
(usual place of residence)

* Delete as appropriate

SCHEDULE 4 Regulation 3

REGULATIONS REVOKED

Regulations	References
The Justices' Allowances Regulations 1971	1971/413 (1971 I, p. 1217)
The Justices' Allowances (Amendment) Regulations 1972	1972/1401 (1972 III, p. 4262)
The Justices' Allowances (Amendment) Regulations 1973	1973/1174 (1973 II, p. 3552)
The Justices' Allowances (Amendment) (No. 2) Regulations 1973	1973/1560 (1973 III, p. 4865)
The Justices' Allowances (Amendment) Regulations 1974	1974/530 (1974 II, p. 2172)
The Justices' Allowances (Amendment) (No. 2) Regulations 1974	1974/1507 (1974 III, p. 5772)
The Justices' Allowances (Amendment) Regulations 1975	1975/593 (1975 I, p. 2166)

EXPLANATORY NOTE

(This Note is not part of the Regulations.)

These Regulations consolidate with amendments the Regulations revoked by Regulation 3 which relate to the payment of certain allowances to justices of the peace, and increase the maximum rates of financial loss allowance payable. The new maximum rates are £8.00, if the time involved exceeds 4 hours in a 24 hour period, and £4.00 in other cases.

STATUTORY INSTRUMENTS

1976 No. 118

CUSTOMS AND EXCISE

The Import Duties (Quota Relief) Order 1976

Made - - - -	28th January 1976
Laid before the	
House of Commons -	29th January 1976
Coming into Operation	30th January 1976

The Secretary of State, in exercise of the powers conferred on him by section 5(1) and (4) of, and paragraph 8 of Schedule 3 to, the Import Duties Act 1958(a), as amended by paragraph 1 of Schedule 4 to the European Communities Act 1972(b), and of all other powers enabling him in that behalf, hereby makes the following Order:—

1. This Order may be cited as the Import Duties (Quota Relief) Order 1976 and shall come into operation on 30th January 1976.

2.—(1) In this Order:—

references to a "subheading" are references to a subheading of the Customs Tariff 1959;

the "relevant quota" means, in relation to goods which fall within a subheading specified in column 1 of the Schedule hereto and are of a description specified in column 2 thereof, the quantity of such goods which are to be exempt from duty on import into the United Kingdom by virtue of Regulation (EEC) 126/76(c) in relation to the goods.

(2) The Interpretation Act 1889(d) shall apply for the interpretation of this Order as it applies for the interpretation of an Act of Parliament.

3. Up to and including 31st December 1976, no import duty shall be charged on goods which fall within a subheading specified in column 1 of the Schedule hereto and are of a description specified in column 2 thereof if they form part of the relevant quota.

4.—(1) For the purposes of this Order goods shall be treated as forming part of the relevant quota in the order in which the importer delivers an entry thereof for home use (within the meaning of section 28 of the Customs and Excise Act 1952(e) and Regulation 8 of the Warehousing Regulations 1975(f)), containing a claim for relief from import duty under the quota in the United Kingdom on or after 30th January 1976.

(2) For the purposes of this Order the following classes of goods shall not be treated as forming part of the relevant quota, namely—

(a) goods on which, apart from this Order, import duty would not be chargeable (whether because the goods originate in a particular country or area or in a developing country or otherwise);

(b) goods on which by virtue of Article 5 below import duty would not be chargeable.

(a) 1958 c. 6.
(c) O.J. No. L14, 23.1.1976.
(e) 1952 c. 44.

(b) 1972 c. 68.
(d) 1889 c. 63.
(f) S.I. 1975/1789 (1975 III, p. 6764).

5.—(1) So long as relief is available in respect of the relevant quota of goods which fall within subheading 77.01 A.I. and are of a description specified in column 2 of the Schedule hereto in relation to that subheading no import duty shall be charged in the case of goods of that description which satisfy the requisite conditions to benefit from Regulation (EEC) 385/73(a) (relating to goods entitled to benefit from the eventual abolition of customs duties in trade between the United Kingdom and the other member States of the European Communities).

(2) For the purpose of paragraph (1) above relief shall be treated as being available in respect of the relevant quota until two days after the end of the last day on which goods of that description are entitled to exemption from import duty by virtue of the preceding Articles of this Order.

6. Any description of goods in column 2 of the Schedule hereto shall be taken to comprise all goods which would be classified under an entry in the same terms constituting a subheading in the relevant heading of the Customs Tariff 1959.

7. Where any import duty for the time being chargeable on any goods has been removed by a directly applicable Community provision the import duty shall, to the extent of that removal, not be regarded as removed by virtue of this Order and the reference to it in the Order shall be treated as merely indicative of the rate of import duty payable in respect of the goods.

Eric Deakins,
Parliamentary Under-Secretary of State,
Department of Trade.

28th January 1976.

(a) O.J. No. L42, 14.2.1973, p. 1.

SCHEDULE

(1) Tariff Subheadings	(2) Description of Goods
ex 77.01 A.II.	Unwrought magnesium containing not less than 99·95% by weight of pure magnesium, intended for the nuclear industry and under Customs control or the administrative equivalent.
ex 77.01 A.II.	Unwrought magnesium containing not less than 99·8% but less than 99·95% by weight of pure magnesium.
77.01 A.I. ex 77.01 A.II. }	Unwrought magnesium containing less than 99·8% by weight of pure magnesium.

EXPLANATORY NOTE

(This Note is not part of the Order.)

This Order, which comes into operation on 30th January 1976, provides for the implementation and administration of the United Kingdom's shares of the tariff quota opened by the European Economic Community for certain grades of unwrought magnesium under the provisions of the Community Instrument specified in the Order.

The Order provides, up to and including 31st December 1976, for exemption from duty in respect of imports of the goods within the United Kingdom's shares of the tariff quota. Any goods which constitute part of the relevant quota do so in the order in which an entry for home use is made containing a claim for relief from import duty on or after 30th January 1976.

The Order also provides that goods shall not constitute part of the quota if duty apart from this Order would not be chargeable, and that no duty shall be chargeable on certain goods of tariff subheading 77.01 A.I. satisfying the requisite conditions to benefit from the eventual abolition of customs duties between the United Kingdom and other member States of the European Communities until after the relevant quota has been exhausted.

STATUTORY INSTRUMENTS

1976 No. 123

PLANT BREEDERS' RIGHTS

The Plant Breeders' Rights (Fees) Regulations 1976

Made - - - -	*28th January* 1976
Laid before Parliament	*6th February* 1976
Coming into Operation	*27th February* 1976

The Minister of Agriculture, Fisheries and Food, the Secretary of State for Scotland and the Secretary of State for Northern Ireland (being the Secretary of State concerned with agriculture in Northern Ireland), acting jointly, in exercise of the powers vested in them by sections 9(1) and 36 of the Plant Varieties and Seeds Act 1964(a), (extended to Northern Ireland by the Plant Varieties and Seeds (Northern Ireland) Order 1964(b) and to the Isle of Man by the Plant Varieties and Seeds (Isle of Man) Order 1969(c)) and of all other powers enabling them in that behalf, with the approval of the Treasury, hereby make the following regulations:—

Citation and commencement

1. These regulations may be cited as the Plant Breeders' Rights (Fees) Regulations 1976 and shall come into operation on 27th February 1976.

Revocation of previous regulations

2. The Plant Breeders' Rights (Fees) Regulations 1972(d) are hereby revoked.

Interpretation

3.—(1) In these regulations unless the context otherwise requires—

"the Act" means the Plant Varieties and Seeds Act 1964;

"the Controller" means the Controller of Plant Variety Rights;

"plant breeders' rights" means rights which may be granted in accordance with Part 1 of the Act;

(a) 1964 c. 14.
(b) S.I. 1964/1574 (1964 III, p. 3543).
(c) S.I.. 1969/1829 (1969 III, p. 5701).
(d) S.I. 1972/506 (1972 I, p. 1749).

"the principal Regulations" means the Plant Breeders' Rights Regulations 1969(a) as amended (b) or any subsequent amendment or re-enactment thereof;

and other expressions have the same meaning as they have in the Act.

(2) The Interpretation Act 1889(c) shall apply to the interpretation of these regulations as it applies to the interpretation of an Act of Parliament and as if these regulations and the regulations hereby revoked were Acts of Parliament.

Payment of fees

4. There shall be paid to the Controller in respect of the matters relating to plant breeders' rights arising under the Act or the principal regulations—

(i) a fee on making an application for a grant of plant breeders' rights, being a fee of the amount set out in the third column of Part I of the Schedule to these regulations opposite the reference in the second column of the said Part I to the plant variety of the kind to which the application relates, such fee being payable on making the said application;

(ii) a fee payable in respect of tests or examination of a plant variety which is the subject of an application for a grant of plant breeders' rights, being a fee of the amount set out in the fourth column of Part II of the Schedule to these regulations opposite the reference in the second column of the said Part II to the plant variety of the kind to which the tests or examination relate, such fee being payable for the tests or examination referred to in the third column of the said Part II and so payable within fourteen days of demand made by the Controller;

(iii) a fee payable in respect of the continued exercise of plant breeders' rights in a plant variety, being a fee of the amount set out in relation to the particular year of the exercise of such rights in the third to the tenth columns of Part III of the Schedule to these regulations opposite the reference in the second column of the said Part III to the plant variety of the kind for which the rights were granted, such fee being payable on, but not more than three months before, the anniversary of the date of the grant of the rights with which the particular year begins or within such later period as may have been allowed;

(iv) the fees payable in respect of the matters referred to in the second column of Part IV of the Schedule to these regulations being the fees of the amounts set out in the fourth column of the said Part IV opposite the respective references to those matters, such fees being payable at the times specified in respect of each such matter in the third column of the said Part IV.

(a) S.I. 1969/1021 (1969 II, p. 2976).
(b) S.I. 1971/1094, 1972/84 (1971 II, p. 3253; 1972 I, p. 244).
(c) 1889 c. 63.

Renewal fees

5.—(1) The fee payable in respect of the continued exercise of plant breeders' rights in a plant variety (hereinafter referred to as the "renewal fee") shall be paid only by the holder of those rights or by a person acting on his behalf, being either an agent duly authorised in accordance with Regulation 16 of the principal regulations or a person who shall deliver to the Controller with the fee an authority in writing to pay the same, signed by the holder of the rights and if any such fee is tendered or paid otherwise than in accordance with this paragraph, the liability to pay the same shall not be regarded as having been thereby discharged.

(2) In a case where the period for which any plant breeders' rights are exercisable has been terminated in accordance with the principal regulations on the ground that a renewal fee has not been paid there shall only be recoverable by the Controller such a proportion of the said fee as the period during which the said rights have continued to be enjoyed since the date when the said fee became payable bears to the period of 12 months.

(3) Notwithstanding Regulation 4 of these regulations and the last preceding paragraph of this regulation, in a case where the period for which any plant breeders' rights are exercisable has been terminated in accordance with the principal regulations on the ground that a renewal fee has not been paid and—

(a) the person entitled to exercise those rights shall, not later than 14 days before the date when the said fee became payable, have informed the Controller that he did not propose to exercise any of such rights at any time after such date, and

(b) such person shall not have exercised any of the said rights during the period beginning with the date when the said fee became payable and ending with the date when the said period was terminated,

the Controller shall not be entitled to recover from such person, by any legal proceedings or otherwise, the said fee or any part thereof.

In Witness whereof the official seal of the Minister of Agriculture, Fisheries and Food is hereunto affixed on 21st January 1976.

L.S.

Frederick Peart,

Minister of Agriculture, Fisheries and Food.

26th January 1976.

William Ross,

Secretary of State for Scotland.

27th January 1976.

Merlyn Rees,

Secretary of State for Northern Ireland.

Approved on 28th January 1976.

M. Cocks,

J. Dormand,

Two of the Lords Commissioners of
Her Majesty's Treasury.

Regulation 4

SCHEDULE

PART I

FEES PAYABLE ON AN APPLICATION FOR A GRANT OF PLANT BREEDERS' RIGHTS

No.	Plant Variety	Amount
		£
1.	A wheat, oats or barley variety	60.00
2.	A potato variety	30.00
3.	A ryegrass or lucerne variety	50.00
4.	A pea, French bean, runner bean or lettuce variety	30.00
5.	A rose, perennial chrysanthemum, perpetual flowering carnation, raspberry, black currant, strawberry, rhubarb, apple, apple rootstock, pear, pear rootstock, plum, plum rootstock, damson or damson rootstock variety	25.00
6.	A border carnation, pink, narcissus, freesia, gladiolus, dahlia, rhododendron, perennial delphinium, pelargonium, streptocarpus, cymbidium, herbaceous perennial, tree, shrub, woody climber, conifer or taxad variety	20.00

PART II

FEES PAYABLE IN RESPECT OF TESTS OR EXAMINATION OF A PLANT VARIETY WHICH IS THE SUBJECT OF AN APPLICATION FOR A GRANT OF PLANT BREEDERS' RIGHTS

No.	Plant Variety	Tests or examination for which payable	Amount
			£
1.	A wheat, oats or barley variety	(a) Tests in the first year of a testing cycle ...	150.00
		(b) Tests in any one subsequent year of a testing cycle	100.00
2.	A potato variety	Tests in any one year ...	55.00
3.	A ryegrass or lucerne variety	Tests in any one year ...	70.00
4.	A pea, French bean, runner bean or lettuce variety	Tests in any one year ...	60.00
5.	A rose variety	Tests in any one year ...	60.00
6.	A year-round perennial chrysanthemum variety	Tests in each flowering season	60.00
7.	A perpetual flowering carnation variety	Tests in any one year ...	60.00
8.	A cymbidium variety	Each examination ...	25.00
9.	A rhododendron, perennial delphinium, conifer, taxad, tree, shrub or woody climber variety	(a) Tests in any one year in which plants of the variety are being established	15.00
		(b) Tests in any one year other than one in which plants of the variety are being established	25.00
10.	A narcissus, freesia, gladiolus, border carnation, pink, dahlia, pelargonium, streptocarpus, herbaceous perennial, or perennial chrysanthemum (other than a year-round perennial chrysanthemum) variety	Tests in any one year ...	25.00
11.	A strawberry, raspberry, black currant or rhubarb variety	Tests in any one year ...	40.00
12.	An apple, pear, plum or damson variety	(a) Tests in any one year before one or more of the trees undergoing tests comes into fruit	20.00
		(b) Tests in any one subsequent year	40.00
13.	An apple rootstock, pear rootstock, plum rootstock or damson rootstock variety	Tests in any one year ...	40.00

PART III

FEES PAYABLE FOR THE CONTINUED EXERCISE OF PLANT BREEDERS' RIGHTS IN A PLANT VARIETY

No.	Plant Variety	Fees payable for the continued exercise of plant breeders' rights during the years indicated below							
		Second year of the exercise of plant breeders' rights	Third year of the exercise of plant breeders' rights	Fourth year of the exercise of plant breeders' rights	Fifth year of the exercise of plant breeders' rights	Sixth year of the exercise of plant breeders' rights	Seventh year of the exercise of plant breeders' rights	Eighth year of the exercise of plant breeders' rights	Ninth and each subsequent year of the exercise of plant breeders' rights
		£	£	£	£	£	£	£	£
1.	A wheat, oats or barley variety	45.00	65.00	85.00	105.00	135.00	135.00	135.00	135.00
2.	A potato, pea, French bean, runner bean or lettuce variety	30.00	40.00	50.00	60.00	70.00	70.00	70.00	70.00
3.	A ryegrass or lucerne variety	30.00	40.00	45.00	55.00	65.00	65.00	65.00	65.00
4.	A strawberry, raspberry, black currant or rhubarb variety	35.00	45.00	50.00	55.00	65.00	65.00	65.00	65.00
5.	A year-round perennial chrysanthemum or perpetual flowering carnation variety	40.00	50.00	60.00	70.00	75.00	75.00	75.00	75.00

PART III (*Cont'd.*)

Fees Payable for the continued Exercise of Plant Breeders' Rights in a Plant Variety

No.	Plant Variety	Fees payable for the continued exercise of plant breeders' rights during the years indicated below							
		Second year of the exercise of plant breeders' rights	Third year of the exercise of plant breeders' rights	Fourth year of the exercise of plant breeders' rights	Fifth year of the exercise of plant breeders' rights	Sixth year of the exercise of plant breeders' rights	Seventh year of the exercise of plant breeders' rights	Eighth year of the exercise of plant breeders' rights	Ninth and each subsequent year of the exercise of plant breeders' rights
		£	£	£	£	£	£	£	£
6.	A narcissus, freesia, gladiolus, border carnation, pink, cymbidium, dahlia, rhododendron, pelargonium, perennial delphinium, streptocarpus, herbaceous perennial, perennial chrysanthemum (other than a year-round perennial chrysanthemum,) conifer, taxad, tree, shrub, woody climber, apple rootstock, pear rootstock, plum	25.00	30.00	35.00	35.00	45.00	45.00	45.00	45.00

· PART III (*Cont'd.*)

FEES PAYABLE FOR THE CONTINUED EXERCISE OF PLANT BREEDERS' RIGHTS IN A PLANT VARIETY

No.	Plant Variety	Fees payable for the continued exercise of plant breeders' rights during the years indicated below							
		Second year of the exercise of plant breeders' rights	Third year of the exercise of plant breeders' rights	Fourth year of the exercise of plant breeders' rights	Fifth year of the exercise of plant breeders' rights	Sixth year of the exercise of plant breeders' rights	Seventh year of the exercise of plant breeders' rights	Eighth year of the exercise of plant breeders' rights	Ninth and each subsequent year of the exercise of plant breeders' rights
		£	£	£	£	£	£	£	£
6.	*Cont'd.* rootstock or damson rootstock variety								
7.	An apple, pear, plum or damson variety	25.00	25.00	35.00	35.00	45.00	55.00	60.00	65.00
8.	A rose variety, other than a glass-house variety	30.00	40.00	50.00	60.00	70.00	70.00	70.00	70.00
9.	A rose variety, being a glass-house variety	40.00	50.00	60.00	65.00	75.00	75.00	75.00	75.00

PART IV

FEES PAYABLE IN RESPECT OF OTHER MATTERS

No.	Matter	When payable	Amount
			£
1.	Application for an extension of the period for which plant breeders' rights are exercisable.	On making the application	15.00
2.	Application for a compulsory licence.	On making the application	7.50
3.	Application to extend, limit, vary or revoke a compulsory licence	On making the application	7.50
4.	Application to amend a document in any application or proceeding.	On making the application	1.50
5.	Application to rectify an error or omission in the register of plant varieties.	On making the application	1.50
6.	Application for extension of time for the service or delivery of a document or thing or for the doing of an act.	On making the application	1.50
7.	Making representations in writing to the Controller, by any person other than the applicant, in connection with any application.	On delivering the representations	1.00
8.	Making representations in writing to the Controller, by any person other than the holder of plant breeders' rights, in connection with a proposal to terminate those rights or to revoke or terminate any extensions of such rights.	On delivering the representations	1.00
9.	On attending to be heard by the Controller or by a person appointed by him for the purpose.	Before the hearing	7.50
10.	The grant of plant breeders' rights in respect of	Before the issue of the document constituting evidence of the grant	
	(a) a wheat, oats or barley variety.		40.00
	(b) a ryegrass, lucerne, potato, pea, French bean, runner bean or lettuce variety.		30.00
	(c) any other plant variety.		35.00

PART IV (Cont'd)
FEES PAYABLE IN RESPECT OF OTHER MATTERS

No.	Matter	When payable	Amount
			£
11.	The grant of an extension of the period for which plant breeders' rights are exercisable.	Before the issue of the document constituting evidence of the extension.	15.00
12.	The giving of a protective direction.	Before the issue of the document constituting evidence of the giving of the protective direction.	7.50
13.	Application for an extension of the period for payment of a renewal fee.	On making the application	7.50
14.	Payment of a renewal fee after the expiration of 7 days from the date when it fell due, except in a case where an application has been made for the period for payment to be extended.	On payment of the renewal fee.	4.00
15.	Application for the approval of a substituted name for a plant variety.	On making the application.	7.50
16.	Application for the amendment of the register of plant varieties, except in a case where the plant breeders' rights are transferred to another person.	On making the application.	1.50
17.	Registration of title and amendment of the register of plant varieties on a transfer of plant breeders' rights or a share in such rights.	On making the application for registration.	7.50
18.	Inspection of the register of plant varieties or of a document in the possession of the Controller.	Before the inspection.	.50
19.	Supplying copies of documents,	Before the delivery of the copies.	
	(a) foolscap or smaller, per page.		.15
	(b) larger than foolscap, per page.		.20
20.	Supplying a duplicate of a document constituting evidence of a grant of plant breeders' rights or protective direction or of an extension of the period for which plant breeders' rights are exercisable.	On ordering the duplicate.	3.00

EXPLANATORY NOTE

(This Note is not part of the Regulations.)

These Regulations, made under the Plant Varieties and Seeds Act 1964, supersede the Plant Breeders' Rights (Fees) Regulations 1972, which are revoked. They prescribe the fees payable to the Controller of Plant Variety Rights in regard to matters arising out of the application for granting and continuance of plant breeders' rights.

STATUTORY INSTRUMENTS

1976 No. 124

SEEDS

The Seeds (National Lists of Varieties) (Fees) Regulations 1976

Made - - - -	*27th January* 1976
Laid before Parliament	*6th February* 1976
Coming into Operation	*27th February* 1976

The Minister of Agriculture, Fisheries and Food, the Secretary of State for Scotland and the Secretary of State for Northern Ireland (being the Secretary of State concerned with agriculture in Northern Ireland), acting jointly, in exercise of the powers vested in them by section 16(1), (1A)(e) and (8) of the Plant Varieties and Seeds Act 1964(a), as amended by section 4(1) of and paragraph 5(1), (2) and (3) of Schedule 4 to the European Communities Act 1972(b) (extended to Northern Ireland by the Plant Varieties and Seeds (Northern Ireland) Order 1964(c) and the Plant Varieties and Seeds (Northern Ireland) Order 1973(d)) and of all other powers enabling them in that behalf, after consultation with representatives of such interests as appear to them to be concerned, hereby make the following regulations:—

Citation and commencement

1. These regulations may be cited as the Seeds (National Lists of Varieties) (Fees) Regulations 1976 and shall come into operation on 27th February 1976.

2.—(1) The Interpretation Act 1889(e) shall apply to the interpretation of these regulations as it applies to the interpretation of an Act of Parliament.

(2) In these regulations—

"maintainer" means a person indicated in a National List as responsible for the maintenance of a plant variety;

"the Ministers" means the Minister of Agriculture, Fisheries and Food, the Secretary of State for Scotland and the Secretary of State concerned with agriculture in Northern Ireland;

"plant breeders' rights" means rights which may be granted in accordance with Part I of the Plant Varieties and Seeds Act 1964.

Fees

3.—(1) There shall be paid to the Minister of Agriculture, Fisheries and Food in respect of the matters arising under the Seeds (National Lists of Varieties) Regulations 1973(f) specified in the first column of the Schedule to

---

(a) 1964 c. 14.
(c) S.I. 1964/1574 (1964 III, p. 3543).
(e) 1889 c. 63.
(b) 1972 c. 68.
(d) S.I. 1973/609 (1973 I, p. 1934).
(f) S.I. 1973/994 (1973 II, p. 3024).

these regulations the fees specified in the third column of the said Schedule opposite the respective references to such matters, such fees being payable at the times respectively indicated in the second column of the said Schedule.

(2) If the prescribed fee payable by a person in connection with an application or with tests or trials of a plant variety shall not have been paid at the appropriate time indicated in the second column of the said Schedule the Ministers shall not be obliged to take any further steps in relation to the application or to the tests or trials until the fee shall have been paid.

(3) The prescribed fees for the tests for distinctness, uniformity and stability of a plant variety shall, if at the time of the application an application for a grant of plant breeders' rights is made or has previously been made, be payable only to the extent by which they exceed the amount of any fees which have been paid or which are or will become payable for the tests and trials of the plant variety in connection with the application for a grant of plant breeders' rights.

(4) A fee in respect of the continuance of the period during which a plant variety will remain in a National List shall be paid by the maintainer who is indicated in the National List in compliance with Regulation 13(1) of the Seeds (National Lists of Varieties) Regulations 1973.

(5) Where two or more maintainers are indicated in a National List as responsible for the maintenance of a plant variety there shall when the occasion arises be paid by each of them, in place of the prescribed fee for the continuance of the period during which the plant variety will remain in the National List, a fee equal to one-half of such fee and if a fee so payable by a maintainer is not paid the Ministers shall remove from the National List the reference to such person as a maintainer of the plant variety.

(6) The Ministers may extend the time for the payment of a fee payable in respect of the continuance of the period of entry in a National List if they consider that it is reasonable in all the circumstances to do so.

In Witness whereof the Official Seal of the Minister of Agriculture, Fisheries and Food is hereunto affixed on 22nd January 1976.

(L.S.)

Frederick Peart,
Minister of Agriculture, Fisheries and Food.

26th January 1976.

William Ross,
Secretary of State for Scotland.

27th January 1976.

Merlyn Rees,
Secretary of State for Northern Ireland.

SCHEDULE

Matter	When payable	Amount
		£
Application for the addition to a National List of—	On making the application	
a cereal variety		60·00
a beet variety		60·00
a fodder plant or an oil or fibre plant variety		50·00
a potato variety		30·00
a vegetable variety		30·00
Tests for distinctness, uniformity and stability of—	Within 14 days of demand by the Minister of Agriculture, Fisheries and Food	
a cereal variety		
(i) first year of a testing cycle		150·00
(ii) a subsequent year of a testing cycle		100·00
Tests for one year for distinctness, uniformity and stability of—	Within 14 days of demand by the Minister of Agriculture, Fisheries and Food	
a beet variety		75·00
a fodder plant or an oil or fibre plant variety		70·00
a potato variety		55·00
Tests for one season for distinctness, uniformity and stability of—	Within 14 days of demand by the Minister of Agriculture, Fisheries and Food	
a vegetable variety		60·00
Trials for one year for value for cultivation and use of—	Within 14 days of demand by the Minister of Agriculture, Fisheries and Food	
a cereal variety—		
(i) first year of a trials cycle		200·00
(ii) a subsequent year of a trials cycle		150·00
a beet variety—		
(i) first year		100·00
(ii) second and subsequent years		150·00
a fodder plant variety (other than a Westerwold ryegrass or a fodder radish variety) or an oil or fibre plant variety		120·00
a Westerwold ryegrass or a fodder radish variety		70·00
a potato variety		100·00
The continuance of the period during which a plant variety will remain in a National List being—	Before the beginning of the particular year of entry in a National List	
a cereal variety, a beet variety or a potato variety—		
(i) for the second year of entry in a National List		20·00
(ii) for the third year of entry in a National List		30·00
(iii) for the fourth year of entry in a National List		40·00
(iv) for the fifth year of entry in a National List		50·00
(v) for the sixth year and each subsequent year of entry in a National List		60·00
a fodder plant or an oil or fibre plant variety—		
(i) for the second year of entry in a National List		20·00

Matter	When payable	Amount
		£
(ii) for the third year of entry in a National List		30·00
(iii) for the fourth year of entry in a National List		35·00
(iv) for the fifth year of entry in a National List		40·00
(v) for the sixth and each subsequent year of entry in a National List		45·00
a vegetable variety—		
(i) for the second year of entry in a National List		10·00
(ii) for the third year of entry in a National List		10·00
(iii) for the fourth year of entry in a National List		10·00
(iv) for the fifth year of entry in a National List		20·00
(v) for the sixth year of entry in a National List		20·00
(vi) for the seventh year and each subsequent year of entry in a National List		30·00
Application for the substitution of a name in a National List	On making the application	7·50
Making written representations to the Ministers	On delivering the representations	1·00
Attending to be heard by a person appointed by the Ministers	Before the hearing	7·50
Inspection of the National List record	Before the inspection	0·50
Inspection of the file maintained for a plant variety in a National List	Before the inspection	0·50

EXPLANATORY NOTE

(This Note is not part of the regulations.)

These regulations prescribe fees in respect of matters arising under the Seeds (National Lists of Varieties) Regulations 1973.

STATUTORY INSTRUMENTS

1976 No. 125

CUSTOMS AND EXCISE

The Import Duties (General) (No. 1) Order 1976

Made - - - - - -	*28th January* 1976
Laid before the House of Commons	*29th January* 1976
Coming into Operation - - -	*1st February* 1976

The Lords Commissioners of Her Majesty's Treasury, by virtue of the powers conferred on them by sections 1, 3(6) and 13 of the Import Duties Act 1958(**a**), as amended by section 5(5) of, and paragraph 1 of Schedule 4 to, the European Communities Act 1972(**b**), and of all other powers enabling them in that behalf, on the recommendation of the Secretary of State(**c**), hereby make the following Order:—

1.—(1) This Order may be cited as the Import Duties (General) (No. 1) Order 1976 and shall come into operation on 1st February 1976.

(2) The Interpretation Act 1889(**d**) shall apply for the interpretation of this Order as it applies for the interpretation of an Act of Parliament.

(3) This Order does not increase duties of customs otherwise than in pursuance of a Community obligation.

2. Schedules 1 and 3 to the Import Duties (General) (No. 5) Order 1975(**e**), as amended(**f**), shall be further amended as specified in Schedule 1 hereto.

3. The Import Duties (Spain) (Reductions) Order 1975(**g**) shall be amended as specified in Schedule 2 hereto.

4. Part I of Schedule 2 to the Import Duties (Israel) (Reductions) Order 1975(**h**) shall be amended as specified in Schedule 3 hereto.

J. Dormand,

M. Cocks,

Two of the Lords Commissioners
of Her Majesty's Treasury.

28th January 1976.

(**a**) 1958 c. 6.	(**b**) 1972 c. 68.
(**c**) *See* S.I. 1970/1537 (1970 III, p. 5293).	(**d**) 1889 c. 63.
(**e**) S.I. 1975/1744 (1975 III, p. 5912).	(**f**) There is no relevant amending instrument.
(**g**) S.I. 1975/2093 (1975 III, p. 7786).	(**h**) S.I. 1975/1998 (1975 III, p. 7392).

SCHEDULE 1

Article 2

AMENDMENTS TO SCHEDULE 1 TO THE IMPORT DUTIES (GENERAL) (No. 5) ORDER 1975

1. In paragraph (B) of Additional Note 2. to Chapter 15 (on page 114) after "olive oil" there shall be inserted "obtained by refining virgin olive oil, whether or not blended with virgin olive oil, and".

2. For paragraph (D) of the said Additional Note (on page 115) there shall be inserted the following paragraph:

"(D) For the purposes of subheadings 15.07 A.I.a) and 15.07 A.II.a), "virgin olive oil" means natural olive oil obtained exclusively by mechanical processes, including pressure, apart from mixtures with olive oil obtained otherwise, and having the following characteristics:

(a) a K_{270} extinction coefficient after treatment of the sample of oil on activated alumina, not higher than 0·11; in exceptional cases certain oils of high acidity, after being passed over activated alumina, may have a K_{270} extinction coefficient higher than 0·11. In such cases, after neutralization and decolourization in the laboratory, they must have the characteristics of the oils falling within subheading 15.07 A.I.a);

(b) an extinction coefficient variation, in the 270 nm range, not higher than 0·01;

(c) no positive reaction of oils from olive residues."

3. For the entries in columns 2, 3, 4 and 5 of subheading 15.07 A.II. (on page 117) there shall be substituted the following entries:

(2)				(3)	(4)	(5)
II. Other:						
a) Virgin olive oil ...	...	...	...	—	—	—
b) Other ...	...	...	...	...	—	—	—

AMENDMENTS TO PART II OF SCHEDULE 3 TO THE IMPORT DUTIES (GENERAL) (No. 5) ORDER 1975 (on page 746):

1. In column 1 subheadings 48.21 C.II., III. and IV. shall be deleted.

2. In column 1 for "48.21 C.V." there shall be substituted "48.21 C.II."

3. In column 1 for "48.21 C.VI." there shall be substituted "48.21 C.III."

SCHEDULE 2

Article 3

AMENDMENTS TO THE IMPORT DUTIES (SPAIN) (REDUCTIONS) ORDER 1975

1. Article 4 shall be renumbered as 3 and in Article 2(1) for "Article 4(1)" there shall be substituted "Article 3(1)".

2. On page 7, in column 2 of subheadings 18.06 D.I.a) and 18.06 D.II.a)1. in Part II of the Schedule for "6%" there shall be substituted "9·6%".

3. On page 20, in column 1 of heading 38.19 in Part II of the Schedule for "T" there shall be substituted "U" wherever it occurs.

4. On page 20, in columns 1 and 2 of Part II of the Schedule there shall be inserted after subheading 38.19 S.II.:

(1)	(2)
"38.19 T.	8%"

5. On page 26, in column 2 of subheading 58.02 B.I. in Part II of the Schedule for "18·4%" there shall be substituted "8·4%".

Article 4   SCHEDULE 3

AMENDMENTS TO PART I OF SCHEDULE 2 TO THE IMPORT DUTIES (ISRAEL) (REDUCTIONS)
ORDER 1975

1. The following entries shall be deleted:—

(1)	(2)	(3)
"20.02 C.II.a)1.	Tomato concentrate	7·5%"

2. In the entries in column 2 of tariff headings 20.02 C.II.a)2. and 20.02 C.II.b) "Tomato concentrate and" shall be deleted.

EXPLANATORY NOTE

(This Note is not part of the Order.)

This Order, which comes into operation on 1st February 1976, provides for further amendments to the Import Duties (General) (No. 5) Order 1975 which sets out the United Kingdom Customs Tariff and the protective import duties chargeable in accordance with it.

The amendments are made to alter Additional Note 2. to Chapter 15 of the Tariff and to re-structure subheading 15.07 A.II. relating to olive oil in Schedule 1 to the Order in accordance with Regulation (EEC) No. 3366/75, and to correct certain errors in Part II of Schedule 3 relating to sub-heading 48.21 C. (certain articles of paper pulp, paper, paperboard or cellulose wadding of EFTA countries).

This Order also amends the Import Duties (Spain) (Reductions) Order 1975 by correcting the numbering of one of the Articles to that Order and certain typographical errors in Part II of the Schedule. It also provides consequential changes in the Schedule arising out of the re-structuring of tariff heading 38.19 as a result of the Import Duties (General) (No. 8) Order.

The Order also amends the Import Duties (Israel) (Reductions) Order 1975 by removing the preferential import duty on tomato concentrate originating in Israel, in accordance with Regulation (EEC) No. 119/76.

STATUTORY INSTRUMENTS

1976 No. 126

CUSTOMS AND EXCISE

The Import Duties (Temporary Reductions and Exemptions)
(No. 2) Order 1976

Made - - - - - -	*28th January* 1976
Laid before the House of Commons	*29th January* 1976
Coming into Operation - - -	*2nd February* 1976

The Lords Commissioners of Her Majesty's Treasury, by virtue of the powers
conferred on them by sections 1, 3(6) and 13 of the Import Duties Act 1958(**a**),
as amended by section 5(5) of, and paragraph 1 of Schedule 4 to, the European
Communities Act 1972(**b**), and of all other powers enabling them in that behalf,
on the recommendation of the Secretary of State(**c**), hereby make the following
Order:—

Citation, operation, interpretation

1.—(1) This Order may be cited as the Import Duties (Temporary Reductions
and Exemptions) (No. 2) Order 1976 and shall come into operation on
2nd February 1976.

(2) In this Order a reference to a heading is a reference to a heading of the
Customs Tariff 1959.

(3) The Interpretation Act 1889(**d**) shall apply for the interpretation of this
Order as it applies for the interpretation of an Act of Parliament.

Intra-Community trade

2. Up to and including 31st March 1976. no import duty shall be charged on
goods which fall within the heading specified in column 1 of the Schedule hereto
and are of the description specified in column 2 thereof if they satisfy the
requisite conditions to benefit from Regulation (EEC) 385/73(**e**) (relating to
goods entitled to benefit from the eventual abolition of customs duties in trade
between member States of the European Communities).

The full rate

3.—(1) Up to and including 31st March 1976, in the case of goods which fall
within the heading specified in column 1 of the Schedule hereto and are of the
description specified in column 2 thereof import duty shall be charged at the
rate shown in column 3 thereof in relation to the goods instead of any higher
rate which would otherwise apply.

(**a**) 1958 c. 6.   (**b**) 1972 c. 68.   (**c**) *See* S.I. 1970/1537 (1970 III, p. 5293).
(**d**) 1889 c. 63.   (**e**) O.J. No. L42, 14.2.1973, p.1.

(2) Paragraph (1) above shall operate without prejudice to the exemptions provided for by Article 2 above and any exemptions or greater reductions provided for by Articles 4 and 5 below.

Cyprus, Egypt

4. Up to and including 31st March 1976, any import duty for the time being chargeable on goods which fall within the heading specified in column 1 of the Schedule hereto and are of the description specified in column 2 thereof shall be charged:

    (a) at the rate shown in column 4 thereof in relation to the description if the goods originate in Cyprus; and

    (b) at the rate shown in column 5 thereof in relation to the description if the goods originate in Egypt.

Greece, Morocco and Tunisia

5. Up to and including 31st March 1976, no import duty shall be charged on goods which fall within the heading specified in column 1 of the Schedule hereto and are of the description specified in column 2 thereof if the goods originate in Greece, Morocco or Tunisia.

6. For the purposes of Articles 4 and 5 above goods shall be regarded as originating:

    (a) in Cyprus if they are to be so regarded under the Agreement, signed on 19th December 1972, between the European Economic Community and Cyprus(**a**);

    (b) in Egypt if they are to be so regarded under the Agreement, signed on 18th December 1972, between the European Economic Community and Egypt(**b**);

    (c) in Greece if they are to be regarded as being in free circulation in Greece under Article 7 of the Agreement, signed on 9th July 1961, establishing an association between the European Economic Community and Greece(**c**) as modified by the Additional Protocol, signed on 28th April 1975, between the European Economic Community and Greece(**d**);

    (d) in Morocco if they are to be so regarded under the Agreement, signed on 31st March 1969, between the European Economic Community and Morocco(**e**);

    (e) in Tunisia if they are to be so regarded under the Agreement, signed on 28th March 1969, between the European Economic Community and Tunisia(**f**).

Miscellaneous

7.—(1) Articles 4 and 5 above shall operate without prejudice to any reliefs from import duty to which the goods therein referred to may be entitled as goods of developing countries or of a particular country or area or otherwise.

(**a**) The Agreement is annexed to Regulation (EEC) 1246/73 (O.J. No. L133, 21.5.1973, p.1).
(**b**) The Agreement is annexed to Regulation (EEC) 2409/73 (O.J. No. L251, 7.9.1973, p.1).
(**c**) The Agreement is annexed to Decision (EEC) 63/106 (O.J. No. 26, 18.2.1963, p.293/63).
(**d**) See O.J. No. 123, 15.5.1975, p.1.
(**e**) The Agreement is annexed to Regulation (EEC) 2285/73 (O.J. No. L239, 27.8.1973, p.1).
(**f**) The Agreement is annexed to Regulation (EEC) 2286/73 (O.J. No. L239, 27.8.1973, p.105).

(2) Any description of goods in column 2 of the Schedule hereto shall be taken to comprise all goods which would be classified under an entry in the same terms constituting a subheading of the relevant heading in the Customs Tariff 1959, provided that the Additional Note to Chapter 29 shall not apply for the purposes of classification.

(3) For the purposes of classification under the Customs Tariff 1959, in so far as that depends on the rate of duty, any goods to which this Order applies shall be treated as chargeable with the same duty as if this Order had not been made.

(4) Where any import duty for the time being chargeable on any goods has been removed or reduced by a directly applicable Community provision the import duty shall, to the extent of that removal or reduction, not be regarded as removed or reduced by virtue of this Order and the reference to it in the Schedule hereto shall be treated as merely indicative of the rate of import duty payable in respect of the goods.

J. Dormand,

M. Cocks,

28th January 1976.   Two of the Lords Commissioners
                                     of Her Majesty's Treasury

SCHEDULE

Goods subject to Temporary Reduction in or Exemption from
Import Duty

Tariff Heading	Description	Rates of Duty %		
		Full	Cyprus	Egypt
(1)	(2)	(3)	(4)	(5)
29.14	Ethyl acrylate	12	3.6	5.4

EXPLANATORY NOTE

(This Note is not part of the Order.)

This Order provides for exemption from or reduction in import duty in the case of the goods specified in the Schedule to this Order as from 2nd February 1976 to 31st March 1976.

Exemption from import duties is provided in the case of the goods in the Schedule if they satisfy the requisite conditions to benefit from the eventual abolition of customs duties in trade between member States of the European Communities.

In the case of goods in the Schedule not satisfying those conditions import duty is reduced to the rate specified in column 3 instead of any higher rate which would otherwise apply.

In the case of goods in the Schedule originating in Cyprus or Egypt, reductions to lower rates of import duty are made in accordance with the Agreements between the European Economic Community (EEC) and those countries, such reduced rates being shown in column 4 (Cyprus) and column 5 (Egypt) of the Schedule.

In the case of goods in the Schedule originating in Greece, Morocco or Tunisia, exemption from import duty is provided in accordance with the Agreements between the EEC and those countries.

STATUTORY INSTRUMENTS

1976 No. 127 (S. 8)

MEDICAL PROFESSION

The Abortion (Scotland) Amendment Regulations 1976

Made - - - -	*23rd January* 1976
Laid before Parliament	*5th February* 1976
Coming into Operation	*1st March* 1976

In exercise of the powers conferred on me by section 2 of the Abortion Act 1967(a) and of all other powers enabling me in that behalf, I hereby make the following regulations:—

Citation, commencement and interpretation

1.—(1) These regulations may be cited as the Abortion (Scotland) Amendment Regulations 1976 and shall come into operation on 1st March 1976.

(2) In these regulations "the Act" means the Abortion Act 1967, and "the principal regulations" means the Abortion (Scotland) Regulations 1968(b), as amended(c).

(3) The Interpretation Act 1889(d) shall apply for the interpretation of these regulations as it applies for the interpretation of an Act of Parliament.

Amendment of the principal regulations

2. The principal regulations shall be amended as follows:—

(*a*) in regulation 5 (restriction on disclosure of information) there shall be added after paragraph (*g*) the following paragraph:—

"or

(*h*) when requested by the President of the General Medical Council for the purpose of investigating whether there has been serious professional misconduct by a registered practitioner, to the President of the General Medical Council or a member of his staff authorised by him.";

(*b*) in Schedule 1 (certificates to be completed before an abortion is performed under section 1 of the Act) for Certificate A there shall be substituted the certificate set out in the Schedule to these regulations;

(*c*) in Schedule 2 (form of notification to be given to the Chief Medical Officer of an abortion performed under section 1 of the Act)

(a) 1967 c. 87.
(b) S.I. 1968 /505 (1968 I, p. 1231).
(c) S.I. 1974/1309 (1974 II, p. 4988).
(d) 1889 c. 63.

immediately before the words "NOTE: This form is to be completed by the operating practitioner" there shall be inserted the following:—

"If the operating practitioner joined in giving the certificate did he see/and examine* the pregnant woman before doing so?............

Has the practitioner named at A certified that he saw/and examined* the pregnant woman before giving the certificate?.............

Has the practitioner named at B (if any) certified that he saw/and examined* the pregnant woman before giving the certificate?.............

*Delete as appropriate".

William Ross,
One of Her Majesty's Principal
Secretaries of State.

New St. Andrew's House,
Edinburgh.
23rd January 1976.

SCHEDULE   *Regulation* 3(*b*)

Certificate A

Not to be destroyed within three years of the date of operation

ABORTION ACT 1967

CERTIFICATE TO BE COMPLETED BEFORE AN ABORTION IS PERFORMED UNDER SECTION 1(1)
OF THE ACT

I, ...
(Name and qualifications of practitioner in block capitals)

of ....
(Full address of practitioner)

....

have/have not* seen/and examined* the pregnant woman to whom this certificate

relates at ....
(Full address of place at which patient was seen or examined)

....

on ....

and I, ...
(Name and qualifications of practitioner in block capitals)

of ....
(Full address of practitioner)

....

have/have not* seen/and examined* the pregnant woman to whom this certificate

relates at ....
(Full address of place at which patient was seen or examined)

....

on ....

We hereby certify that we are of the opinion, formed in good faith, that in the case of

....
(Full name of pregnant woman in block capitals)

of ....

....
(Usual place of residence of pregnant woman in block capitals)

1. the continuance of the pregnancy would involve risk to the life of   (Ring
the pregnant woman greater than if the pregnancy were terminated;   appropriate
                                                                     number(s)

2. the continuance of the pregnancy would involve risk of injury
to the physical or mental health of the pregnant woman greater than if
the pregnancy were terminated;

*Delete as appropriate

3. the continuance of the pregnancy would involve risk of injury to the physical or mental health of the existing child(ren) of the family of the pregnant woman greater than if the pregnancy were terminated;

4. there is substantial risk that if the child were born it would suffer from such physical or mental abnormalities as to be seriously handicapped.

This certificate of opinion is given before the commencement of the treatment for the termination of pregnancy to which it refers and relates to the circumstances of the pregnant woman's individual case.

Signed ....

Date...

Signed ....

Date...

EXPLANATORY NOTE

(This Note is not part of the Regulations.)

These Regulations, made under the Abortion Act 1967, further amend the Abortion (Scotland) Regulations 1968 to allow information furnished to the Chief Medical Officer of the Scottish Home and Health Department under these Regulations to be disclosed to the President of the General Medical Council, or any authorised member of his staff, for the purpose of investigating whether there has been serious professional misconduct by a doctor. Provision is also made for a doctor when giving a certificate under section 1(1) of the Abortion Act 1967 to state therein whether he has seen and examined the pregnant woman before doing so.

STATUTORY INSTRUMENTS

1976 No. 128

VALUE ADDED TAX

The Value Added Tax (Consolidation) Order 1976

Made - - - - -	29th January 1976
Laid before the House of Commons	10th February 1976
Coming into Operation - -	2nd March 1976

The Treasury, in exercise of the powers conferred on them by sections 12(4), 13(2) and 43(1) of the Finance Act 1972(a) and section 17(2) of the Finance (No. 2) Act 1975(b) and of all other powers enabling them in that behalf, hereby make the following Order:—

1. This Order may be cited as the Value Added Tax (Consolidation) Order 1976 and shall come into operation on 2nd March 1976.

2. The Interpretation Act 1889(c) shall apply for the interpretation of this Order as it applies for the interpretation of an Act of Parliament.

3. Save and except for item 5 of Group 9, Schedule 4 to the Finance Act 1972 shall be varied by substituting the descriptions specified in Schedule 1 to this Order for the descriptions in the Schedule as originally enacted.

4. Schedule 5 to the Finance Act 1972 shall be varied by substituting the descriptions specified in Schedule 2 to this Order for the descriptions in the Schedule as originally enacted.

5. Schedule 7 to the Finance (No. 2) Act 1975 shall be varied by substituting the descriptions specified in Schedule 3 to this Order for the descriptions in the Schedule as originally enacted.

6. The Orders listed in Schedule 4 to this Order (the effect of which is reproduced in this Order, and which are all superseded by this Order) shall be revoked.

M. Cocks,

James A. Dunn,

Two of the Lords Commissioners
of Her Majesty's Treasury.

29th January 1976.

(a) 1972 c. 41.   (b) 1975 c. 45.   (c) 1889 c. 63.

SCHEDULE 1

<small>SUBSTITUTED DESCRIPTIONS</small>

"SCHEDULE 4

<small>ZERO-RATING</small>

<small>GROUP 1—FOOD</small>

The supply of anything comprised in the general items set out below, except—

(*a*) a supply in the course of catering; and

(*b*) a supply of anything comprised in any of the excepted items set out below, unless it is also comprised in any of the items overriding the exceptions set out below which relates to that excepted item.

General items

Item No.

1. Food of a kind used for human consumption.

2. Animal feeding stuffs.

3. Seeds or other means of propagation of plants comprised in item 1 or 2.

4. Live animals of a kind generally used as, or yielding or producing, food for human consumption.

Excepted items

Item No.

1. Ice cream, ice lollies, frozen yogurt, water ices and similar frozen products, and prepared mixes and powders for making such products.

2. Chocolates, sweets and similar confectionery (including drained, glacé or crystallized fruits); and biscuits and other confectionery (not including cakes) wholly or partly covered with chocolate or some product similar in taste and appearance.

3. Beverages chargeable with any duty of excise specifically charged on spirits, beer, wine or made-wine and preparations thereof.

4. Other manufactured beverages, including fruit juices and bottled waters, and syrups, concentrates, essences, powders, crystals or other products for the preparation of beverages.

5. Any of the following when packaged for human consumption without further preparation, namely, potato crisps, potato sticks, potato puffs, and similar products made from the potato, or from potato flour, or from potato starch, and savoury food products obtained by the swelling of cereals or cereal products; and salted or roasted nuts other than nuts in shell.

6. Pet foods, canned, packaged or prepared; packaged foods (not being pet foods) for birds other than poultry or game; and biscuits and meal for cats and dogs.

Items overriding the exceptions

Item No.

1. Yogurt unsuitable for immediate consumption when frozen.

2. Drained cherries.

3.   Candied peels.

4.   Tea, maté, herbal teas and similar products, and preparations and extracts thereof.

5.   Cocoa, coffee and chicory and other roasted coffee substitutes, and preparations and extracts thereof.

6.   Preparations and extracts of meat, yeast, egg or milk.

Notes:

(1) 'Food' includes drink.

(2) 'Animal' includes bird, fish, crustacean and mollusc.

(3) A supply of anything in the course of catering includes any supply of it for consumption on the premises on which it is supplied.

(4) Item 1 of the items overriding the exceptions relates to item 1 of the excepted items; items 2 and 3 of the items overriding the exceptions relate to item 2 of the excepted items and items 4 to 6 of the items overriding the exceptions relate to item 4 of the excepted items.

GROUP 2—WATER

Item No.

1.   Water other than—

(a) distilled water, deionised water and water of similar purity; and

(b) water comprised in the excepted items set out in Group 1.

GROUP 3—BOOKS, ETC.

Item No.

1.   Books, booklets, brochures, pamphlets and leaflets.

2.   Newspapers, journals and periodicals.

3.   Children's picture books and painting books.

4.   Music (printed, duplicated or manuscript).

5.   Maps, charts and topographical plans.

6.   Covers, cases and other articles supplied with items 1 to 5 and not separately accounted for.

Note: This group does not include plans or drawings for industrial, architectural, engineering, commercial or similar purposes.

GROUP 4—TALKING BOOKS FOR THE BLIND AND HANDICAPPED AND
WIRELESS SETS FOR THE BLIND

Item No.

1.   The supply to the Royal National Institute for the Blind, the National Listening Library or other similar charities of—

(a) magnetic tape specially adapted for the recording and reproduction of speech for the blind or severely handicapped;

(b) tape recorders designed for the reproduction of sound from such tape;

(c) parts and accessories for goods comprised in paragraphs (a) and (b) above.

2.   The supply to a charity of wireless receiving sets solely for gratuitous loan to the blind.

GROUP 5—NEWSPAPER ADVERTISEMENTS

Item No.

1. The publication in any newspaper, journal or periodical of any advertisement.

2. The preparation of any advertisement intended for publication solely or mainly in one or more newspapers, journals or periodicals.

3. The supply of services for the purpose of securing such a publication or a preparation as is mentioned in item 1 or 2.

GROUP 6—NEWS SERVICES

Item No.

1. The supply to newspapers or to the public of information of a kind published in newspapers.

Note: This item does not include the supply of photographs.

GROUP 7—FUEL AND POWER

Item No.

1. Coal, coke and other solid substances held out for sale solely as fuel.

2. Coal gas, water gas, producer gases and similar gases.

3. Petroleum gases and other gaseous hydrocarbons, whether in a gaseous or liquid state.

4. Hydrocarbon oil within the meaning of the Hydrocarbon Oil (Customs & Excise) Act 1971(a).

5. Electricity, heat and air-conditioning.

6. Lubricating oils other than those included in item 4.

Notes:

(1) Item 1 shall be deemed to include combustible materials put up for sale for kindling fires but shall not include matches upon which a duty of customs or excise has been or is to be charged.

(2) 'Lubricating oils' means agents for lubrication which are neither:—

    (*a*) solid or semi-solid at a temperature of 60°F, nor

    (*b*) gaseous at a temperature of 60°F and under a pressure of one atmosphere.

(3) Items 2 and 3 do not include any gas (within the meaning of section 3 of the Finance Act 1971(b)) for use as fuel in road vehicles and on which a duty of excise has been charged or is chargeable.

(4) Item 4 does not include hydrocarbon oil on which a duty of customs or excise has been or is to be charged without relief from, or rebate of, such duty by virtue of the provisions of the Hydrocarbon Oil (Customs & Excise) Act 1971.

GROUP 8—CONSTRUCTION OF BUILDINGS, ETC.

Item No.

1. The granting, by a person constructing a building, of a major interest in, or in any part of, the building or its site.

2. The supply, in the course of the construction, alteration or demolition of any building or of any civil engineering work, of any services other than the services of an architect, surveyor or any person acting as consultant or in a supervisory capacity.

(a) 1971 c. 12.   **(b)** 1971 c. 68.

3.　　The supply, by a person supplying services within item 2 and in connection with those services, of materials or of builder's hardware, sanitary ware or other articles of a kind ordinarily installed by builders as fixtures.

Notes:

(1) Where the benefit of the consideration for the grant of a major interest as described in item 1 accrues to the person constructing the building but that person is not the grantor, he shall for the purposes of that item be treated as the person making the grant.

(2) Item 2 does not include—

　(*a*)　any work of repair or maintenance; or

　(*b*)　the supply of any services in the course of the construction or alteration of any civil engineering work within the grounds or garden of a building used or to be used wholly or mainly as a private residence; or

　(*c*)　the supply by a person of any services which consist of or include any services supplied to him by some other person otherwise than in the course of a business carried on by that other person.

(3) 'Major interest' has the same meaning as in section 5(6) of this Act.

(4) Section 12(3) of this Act does not apply to goods forming part of a description of supply in this group.

GROUP 9—SERVICES TO OVERSEAS TRADERS OR FOR OVERSEAS PURPOSES

Item No.

1.　　Any services supplied by an agent to his principal if the principal is an overseas trader or overseas resident.

2.　　The application of any treatment or process to goods imported on behalf of an overseas trader or overseas resident for subsequent re-export and in fact re-exported.

3.　　The preparation, publication or dissemination of any advertisement in the United Kingdom on behalf of an overseas trader or an overseas authority.

4.　　The supply of any services for the purpose of securing the preparation, publication or dissemination of any advertisement in the United Kingdom on behalf of an overseas trader or an overseas authority.

*

6.　　The supply to an overseas trader or overseas resident of any services not used by a person present in the United Kingdom and not included in items 1 to 5 of this group nor in any group in Schedule 5 to this Act.

7.　　The supply to an overseas authority of any services not comprised in item 5 of this group nor in any group in Schedule 5 to this Act.

8.　　The supply to an overseas trader—

　(*a*)　of services consisting of the storage at or transport to or from a port or customs airport (within the meanings of the Customs and Excise Act 1952(**a**)) of goods which respectively are to be exported or have been imported or of the handling or storage of such goods in connection with such transport; or

　(*b*)　of services comprised in paragraph (*a*) of item 6, item 9 and paragraph (*a*) of item 10 of Group 10 of this Schedule.

---

*For item 5 see Schedule 4 to the Finance Act 1972 as originally enacted. The current Order made under item 5 is the Value Added Tax (Finance and Insurance) (No. 2) Order 1973 (S.I. 1973/2150 (1973 III, p. 7427)).

(**a**) 1952 c. 44.

9.   The preparation of plans and specifications for construction operations outside the United Kingdom.

10.   The granting, assignment or surrender or any right solely exercisable or exercised outside the United Kingdom.

Notes:

(1) For the purposes of this group a person is an overseas trader if he carries on a business and has his place of business or principal place of business outside the United Kingdom.

(2) 'Overseas authority' means any country other than the United Kingdom or any part of or place in such a country or the Government of any such country, part or place.

(3) 'Overseas resident' means a person who is not resident in the United Kingdom.

(4) Items 3 and 4 do not apply where the overseas trader is a person, or the agent or subsidiary of a person, who carries on a business in the United Kingdom or is resident or (if a company) incorporated in the United Kingdom.

(5) Items 3, 4 and 7 do not include the supply of any services to any agency or establishment in the United Kingdom.

(6) Item 6 does not include the supply of any services in connection with the care, management, repair or maintenance of a building or parts of a building in the United Kingdom.

GROUP 10—TRANSPORT

Item No.

1.   The supply, repair or maintenance of any ship which is neither—

        (*a*) a ship of a gross tonnage of less than 15 tons; nor

        (*b*) a ship designed or adapted for use for recreation or pleasure.

2.   The supply, repair or maintenance of any aircraft which is neither—

        (*a*) an aircraft of a weight of less than 8,000 kilogrammes; nor

        (*b*) an aircraft designed or adapted for use for recreation or pleasure.

3.   The supply to and repair or maintenance for the Royal National Lifeboat Institution of any lifeboat.

4.   Transport of passengers—

        (*a*) in any vehicle, ship or aircraft designed or adapted to carry not less than twelve passengers; or

        (*b*) by the Post Office; or

        (*c*) on any scheduled flight.

5.   Transport of passengers or freight outside the United Kingdom or to or from a place outside the United Kingdom.

6.   Any services provided for—

        (*a*) the handling of ships or aircraft in a port or customs airport; or

        (*b*) the handling, in a port or customs airport or on land adjacent to a port, of goods carried in a ship or aircraft.

7.   Pilotage services.

8.   Salvage or towage services.

9.   Any services supplied within or outside the United Kingdom for or in connection with the surveying of any ship or aircraft or the classification of any ship or aircraft for the purposes of any register.

10.   The making of arrangements for—

       (*a*) the supply of, or of space in, any ship or aircraft; or

       (*b*) the supply of any service included in items 1 to 9.

Notes:

(1) 'Port' and 'customs airport' have the same meanings as in the Customs and Excise Act 1952.

(2) The supply of any ship or aircraft includes the supply of any services under a charter of the ship or aircraft.

(3) 'Lifeboat' includes any ship used as a lifeboat.

(4) For the purposes of this group paragraph (*a*) of item 6, item 9 and paragraph (*a*) of item 10 do not include the supply of any services where the ships or aircraft referred to therein are of the descriptions specified in paragraphs (*a*) and (*b*) of item 1 or in paragraphs (*a*) and (*b*) of item 2 respectively.

GROUP 11—CARAVANS AND HOUSEBOATS

Item No.

1.   Caravans exceeding the limits of size for the time being permitted for the use on roads of a trailer drawn by a motor vehicle having an unladen weight of less than 2,030 kilogrammes.

2.   Houseboats being boats or other floating decked structures designed or adapted for use solely as places of permanent habitation and not having means of, or capable of being readily adapted for, self-propulsion.

Note:

Items 1 and 2 do not include—

(*a*) removable contents other than goods of a kind mentioned in item 3 of Group 8; or

(*b*) the supply of holiday accommodation including any accommodation advertised or held out as such.

GROUP 12—GOLD

Item No.

1.   The supply of any gold bullion.

2.   The supply of gold coins by an authorised dealer in gold to another such dealer.

Notes:

(1) 'Authorised dealer in gold' means a person for the time being authorised by an order of the Treasury under the Exchange Control Act 1947(a) to act for the purposes of that Act as an authorised dealer in relation to gold; and 'gold bullion' means any newly mined gold and refined bar gold or gold grain of not less than 995 millesimal fineness.

(2) Section 12(3) of this Act does not apply to gold coins.

GROUP 13—BANK NOTES

Item No.

1.   The issue by a bank of a note payable to bearer on demand.

(a) 1947 c. 14.

GROUP 14—DRUGS, MEDICINES, MEDICAL AND SURGICAL APPLIANCES, ETC.

Item No.

1.   The supply of any goods dispensed, by a person registered in the register of pharmaceutical chemists kept under the Pharmacy Act 1954(a) or the Pharmacy and Poisons Act (Northern Ireland) 1925(b), on the prescription of a person registered in the register of medical practitioners, the register of temporarily registered medical practitioners or the dentists' register.

2.   The supply to the order of a person registered in the register of medical practitioners or the register of temporarily registered medical practitioners, to a chronically sick or disabled person, for domestic use, of medical or surgical appliances designed solely for the relief of a severe abnormality or severe injury.

3.   The supply to a chronically sick or disabled person, for domestic use, of the following:—

         (a)   electrically or mechanically adjustable beds designed for invalids;

         (b)   commode chairs, commode stools, devices incorporating a bidet jet and warm air drier and frames or other devices for sitting over or rising from a sanitary appliance;

         (c)   chair lifts or stair lifts designed for use in connection with invalid wheel chairs;

         (d)   hoists and lifters designed for use by invalids.

Notes:

(1) Section 12(3) of this Act does not apply to goods forming part of a description of supply in this group.

(2) In item 2 'appliances' shall not include hearing aids, dentures, spectacles and contact lenses but shall be deemed to include—

     (a) clothing, footwear and wigs;

     (b) invalid wheel chairs, and invalid carriages other than mechanically propelled vehicles intended or adapted for use on roads; and

     (c) renal haemodialysis units, oxygen concentrators, artificial respirators and other similar apparatus.

(3) In item 3 'chronically sick or disabled person' shall include only a person who is under the care of a person registered in the register of medical practitioners or the register of temporarily registered medical practitioners as a chronically sick or disabled person.

GROUP 15—IMPORTS, EXPORTS, ETC.

Item No.

1.   The supply of imported goods before the delivery of an entry (within the meaning of section 28 of the Customs and Excise Act 1952) under an agreement requiring the purchaser to make such entry.

2.   The transfer of goods or services from the United Kingdom by a person carrying on a business both inside and outside the United Kingdom to his place of business outside the United Kingdom.

3.   The supply to or by an overseas authority, overseas body or overseas trader, charged with the management of any Defence project which is the subject of an international collaboration arrangement or under direct contract with any government or government sponsored international body participating in a Defence project under such an arrangement, of goods or services in the course of giving effect to that arrangement.

(a) 1954 c. 61.   **(b)** 1925 c. 8 (N.I.).

Notes:

(1) Item 2 does not apply where the person makes other taxable supplies.

(2) An 'international collaboration arrangement' means any arrangement made—

    (*a*) between the United Kingdom Government and the government of one or more other countries, or any government sponsored international body for collaboration in a joint project of research, development or production; and

    (*b*) which includes provision for participating governments to relieve the cost of the project from taxation.

(3) 'Overseas authority' means any country other than the United Kingdom or any part of or place in such a country or the government of any such country, part or place.

(4) 'Overseas body' means a body established outside the United Kingdom.

(5) 'Overseas trader' means a person who carries on a business and has his principal place of business outside the United Kingdom.

GROUP 16—CHARITIES, ETC.

Item No.

1. The supply by a charity established primarily for the relief of distress of any goods which have been donated for sale.

2. The export of any goods by a charity.

3. The supply, for donation to a designated hospital or research institution, of medical or scientific equipment solely for use in medical research, diagnosis or treatment, where such equipment is purchased with funds provided:—

    (*a*) by a charity; or

    (*b*) from voluntary contributions.

Notes:

(1) Where the goods have been donated from his stock in trade by a taxable person item 1 shall only apply to the extent of the exception contained in paragraph 6 of Schedule 3 to this Act.

(2) Item 1 shall apply only if the supply is a sale by the first donee of the goods.

(3) 'The relief of distress' means—

    (*a*) the relief of poverty; or

    (*b*) the making of provision for the cure or mitigation or prevention of, or for the care of persons suffering from or subject to, any disease or infirmity or disability affecting human beings (including the care of women before, during and after child birth).

(4) Item 3 does not apply where—

    (*a*) the supply is to a person other than the donor of the equipment; or

    (*b*) the activities of the hospital or research institution are carried on for profit; or

    (*c*) the donee of the equipment has contributed wholly or in part to the funds provided for the purchase thereof.

GROUP 17—CLOTHING AND FOOTWEAR

Item No.

1. Articles designed as clothing or footwear for young children and not suitable for older persons except articles within item 1 of Group 6 of Schedule 7 to the Finance (No. 2) Act 1975(a).

(a) 1975 c. 45.

2.   Protective boots and helmets for industrial use.

3.   Protective helmets for wear by a person driving or riding a motor bicycle.

Notes:

(1) 'Clothing' includes hats and other headgear.

(2) Items 2 and 3 apply only where the articles referred to therein are manufactured to standards for boots or helmets approved by the British Standards Institution and bear a marking indicating compliance with the specification relating thereto.".

SCHEDULE 2

SUBSTITUTED DESCRIPTIONS

"SCHEDULE 5

EXEMPTIONS

GROUP 1—LAND

Item No.

1.   The grant, assignment or surrender of any interest in or right over land or of any licence to occupy land, other than—

 (*a*) the provision of accommodation in a hotel, inn, boarding house or similar establishment or of holiday accommodation in a house, flat, caravan or houseboat;

 (*b*) the granting of facilities for camping in tents or caravans;

 (*c*) the granting of facilities for parking a vehicle;

 (*d*) the granting of any right to take game or fish;

 (*e*) the granting of any right to fell and remove standing timber;

 (*f*) the granting of facilities for housing, or storage of, an aircraft or for mooring, or storage of, a ship, boat or vessel; and

 (*g*) the provision to an exhibitor of a site or space at any exhibition, or similar event, organised wholly or mainly for the display or advertisement of goods or services.

Notes:

(1) 'Holiday accommodation' includes any accommodation advertised or held out as such.

(2) 'Houseboat' includes a houseboat within the meaning of Group 11 of Schedule 4.

(3) 'Mooring' includes anchoring or berthing.

GROUP 2—INSURANCE

Item No.

1.   The provision of insurance of any description.

2.   The making of arrangements for the provision of any insurance.

GROUP 3—POSTAL SERVICES

Item No.

1.   The conveyance of postal packets by the Post Office.

2.   The supply by the Post Office of any services in connection with the conveyance of postal packets.

Note: 'Postal packet' has the same meaning as in the Post Office Act 1953(a), except that it does not include a telegram.

(a) 1953 c. 36.

GROUP 4—BETTING, GAMING AND LOTTERIES

Item No.

1.   The provision of any facilities for the placing of bets or the playing of any games of chance.

2.   The granting of a right to take part in a lottery.

Notes:

(1) Item 1 does not include—

(*a*) admission to any premises; or

(*b*) the granting of a right to take part in a game in respect of which a charge may be made by virtue of regulations under section 14 of the Gaming Act 1968(**a**); or

(*c*) the provision by a club of such facilities to its members as are available to them on payment of their subscription but without further charge; or

(*d*) the provision of a gaming machine.

(2) 'Game of chance' has the same meaning as in the Gaming Act 1968.

(3) 'Lottery' includes any competition for prizes which is authorised by a licence under the Pool Competitions Act 1971(**b**).

(4) 'Gaming machine' means a machine in respect of which the following conditions are satisfied, namely—

(*a*) it is constructed or adapted for playing a game of chance by means of it; and

(*b*) a player pays to play the machine (except where he has an opportunity to play payment-free as the result of having previously played successfully), either by inserting a coin or token into the machine or in some other way; and

(*c*) the element of chance in the game is provided by means of the machine.

GROUP 5—FINANCE

Item No.

1.   The issue, transfer or receipt of, or any dealing with, money, any security for money or any note or order for the payment of money.

2.   The making of any advance or the granting of any credit.

3.   The making of arrangements for any transaction comprised in item 1 or 2.

4.   The issue, transfer or receipt of, or any dealing with, any security or secondary security within the definition in section 42 of the Exchange Control Act 1947(**c**).

5.   The operation of any current, deposit or savings account.

Note: Item 1 does not include anything included in item 4.

GROUP 6—EDUCATION

Item No.

1.   The provision of education if—

(*a*) it is provided by a school or university; or

(*b*) it is of a kind provided by a school or university and is provided otherwise than for profit.

(**a**) 1968 c. 65.   (**b**) 1971 c. 57.   (**c**) 1947 c. 14.

2.   The supply of any goods or services incidental to the provision of any education included in item 1.

3.   The provision of any instruction supplemental to the provision of any education included in item 1.

4.   The provision by a youth club of the facilities available to its members.

Notes:

(1) 'School' means any institution providing primary or secondary education or both within the meaning of the Education Acts 1944 to 1971, the Education (Scotland) Acts 1939 to 1971 or the Education Acts (Northern Ireland) 1947 to 1971.

(2) 'Education' includes training in any form of art.

(3) 'University' includes a university college and the college, school or hall of a university.

(4) Items 2 and 3 apply only where the supplies are made by the supplier of the education described in item 1 to persons receiving the education from that supplier.

GROUP 7—HEALTH

Item No.

1.   The supply of services and, in connection with it, the supply of goods, by a person registered or enrolled in any of the following:—

    (*a*) the register of medical practitioners or the register of temporarily registered medical practitioners;

    (*b*) the dentists' register;

    (*c*) either of the registers of ophthalmic opticians or the register of dispensing opticians kept under the Opticians Act 1958(**a**) or either of the lists kept under section 4 of that Act of bodies corporate carrying on business as ophthalmic opticians or as dispensing opticians;

    (*d*) any register kept under the Professions Supplementary to Medicine Act 1960(**b**);

    (*e*) the register of nurses or the roll of nurses maintained in pursuance of section 2(1) of the Nurses Act 1957(**c**) or kept under section 2 or section 3 of the Nurses (Scotland) Act 1951(**d**) or section 17(1) of the Nurses and Midwives Act (Northern Ireland) 1970(**e**);

    (*f*) the roll of certified midwives kept under section 2 of the Midwives Act 1951(**f**), section 3 of the Midwives (Scotland) Act 1951(**g**) or section 17(1) of the Nurses and Midwives Act (Northern Ireland) 1970;

    (*g*) any roll of ancillary dental workers established under section 41 of the Dentists Act 1957(**h**);

    (*h*) the register of dispensers of hearing aids and the register of persons employing such dispensers maintained under section 2 of the Hearing Aid Council Act 1968(**i**).

2.   The supply of any goods or services by a dental technician.

3.   The supply of any services by a person registered in the register of pharmaceutical chemists kept under the Pharmacy Act 1954(**j**) or the Pharmacy and Poisons Act (Northern Ireland) 1925(**k**).

(**a**) 1958 c. 32.	(**b**) 1960 c. 66.	(**c**) 1957 c. 15.
(**d**) 1951 c. 55.	(**e**) 1970 c. 11 (N.I.).	(**f**) 1951 c. 53.
(**g**) 1951 c. 54.	(**h**) 1957 c. 28.	(**i**) 1968 c. 50.
(**j**) 1954 c. 61.	(**k**) 1925 c. 8 (N.I.).	

4. The provision of care or medical or surgical treatment and, in connection with it, the supply of any goods, in any hospital or other institution approved, licensed, registered or exempted from registration by any Minister or other authority.

GROUP 8—BURIAL AND CREMATION

Item No.

1. The disposal of the remains of the dead.

2. The making of arrangements for or in connection with the disposal of the remains of the dead.".

SCHEDULE 3

SUBSTITUTED DESCRIPTIONS

"SCHEDULE 7

HIGHER RATE

GROUP 1—DOMESTIC APPLIANCES

Item No.

1. Goods of a kind suitable for domestic use which are operated by electricity or, in the case of horticultural appliances, by electricity or by an internal combustion engine, except—

   (a) boiling rings, ovens, ranges and stoves;

   (b) space heaters;

   (c) appliances for water heating ordinarily installed as fixtures;

   (d) light fittings and torches;

   (e) telephones of a kind supplied by the Post Office and ancillary equipment of a kind so supplied;

   (f) tools of a kind used wholly or mainly for carpentry, metalwork or masonry work;

   (g) clocks, watches and timing devices;

   (h) mechanical lighters;

   (i) hearing aids;

   (j) goods suitable for domestic use as, and only as, parts of goods (whether operated by electricity or not) of a kind mentioned in paragraphs (a) to (i);

   (k) goods within Group 2 or Group 5.

2. Refrigerators and freezers of a kind suitable for domestic use, not being goods within item 1.

3. Accessories to goods within item 1 or item 2.

4. Accessories to goods excepted from item 1 by paragraph (f) of that item, if the accessories are for horticultural use.

5. Goods of a kind suitable for use as parts of goods comprised in items 1 to 4, except—

   (a) nuts, bolts, screws, screw caps, nails, washers, eyelets, rivets, pins, studs, buckles, engineers' keys, hose fittings, tube fittings, springs, bushes, bearings and magnets;

   (b) hinges, brackets, latches, catches, locks and keys;

   (c) electric batteries, fuses, mains plugs, electric filament light bulbs, fluorescent tubes, tags and terminals;

(*d*) wheels (other than steering wheels), castors and tyres and parts of such goods;

(*e*) goods of a kind used mainly as parts of engines for road vehicles;

(*f*) sewing machine needles.

6. The installation, alteration, testing, repair or maintenance of, or the provision of similar services in respect of, goods comprised in items 1 to 5.

7. The supply of goods in connection with a supply of services within item 6.

Notes:

(1) The goods excepted from item 1 by paragraph (*a*) of that item do not include hotplates or other appliances for keeping food hot.

(2) 'Mechanical lighters' has the meaning assigned to it by section 221(4) of the Customs and Excise Act 1952(**a**).

GROUP 2—RADIO AND TELEVISION SETS, ETC.

Item No.

1. Goods of a kind suitable for domestic or recreational use which are, or are capable of use as, goods within the following paragraphs—

(*a*) television sets;

(*b*) radio receivers or transmitters;

(*c*) gramophones or tape recorders;

(*d*) electronic musical instruments.

2. Microphones, radio-tuners, turntables, amplifiers, loudspeakers and other goods capable of use as components of goods within item 1, being of a kind suitable for domestic or recreational use.

3. Combinations of goods within item 2.

4. Accessories to goods comprised in items 1 to 3.

5. Goods of a kind suitable for use as parts of goods comprised in items 1 to 4, except goods within the exceptions from item 5 of Group 1.

6. The installation, alteration, testing, repair or maintenance of, or the provision of similar services in respect of, goods comprised in items 1 to 5.

7. The supply of goods in connection with a supply of services within item 6.

Notes:

(1) Items 1 and 2 include goods which can be adapted to produce goods within those items.

(2) 'Television sets' and 'radio receivers' include apparatus designed to receive programmes transmitted by wire.

(3) 'Gramophones or tape recorders' includes video cassette machines and other equipment for recording or reproducing sound or visual images by means of gramophone records, magnetic tape or similar recording media.

(4) 'Electronic musical instruments' means musical instruments which incorporate or are designed for use with, an amplifier.

(5) On and after 1st August 1975 item 1 shall not include any television set which was, and so long as it remains, supplied under a contract of hire entered into prior to 16th April 1975.

(**a**) 1952 c. 44.

(6) Item 3 does not include hearing aids.

(7) 'Accessories' includes aerials.

(8) Item 4 does not include—

    (a) gramophone records, magnetic tape or other recording media;

    (b) goods for cleaning or storing goods within paragraph (a);

    (c) tape splicers.

(9) Items 1 and 3 do not include radio receivers or transmitters of a kind used solely on boats and designed to be operated solely on radio frequencies designated for distress calls at sea.

(10) Items 1 and 3 do not include the following equipment—

    (a) very high frequency receivers or transmitters;

    (b) very high frequency omni-directional radio range equipment;

    (c) automatic direction finding equipment;

    (d) distance measuring equipment;

    (e) instrument landing system receivers;

    (f) other radio navigation equipment;

if in each case it is of a kind used solely on aircraft and complies with the requirements of the rules for the time being in force under the Civil Aviation Acts 1949 to 1971(a).

Group 3—Boats and Aircraft

Item No.

1.   Boats—

    (a) of a gross tonnage of less than 15 tons; or

    (b) designed for use for recreation or pleasure;

    except boats which are of a kind used solely as liferafts and comply with the requirements of the rules for the time being in force under section 427 of the Merchant Shipping Act 1894(b) in relation to liferafts.

2.   Boats adapted for use for recreation or pleasure.

3.   Aircraft—

    (a) of a weight of less than 8,000 kilogrammes; or

    (b) designed or adapted for use for recreation or pleasure.

4.   Hovercraft designed or adapted for use for recreation or pleasure.

5.   The following accessories to goods within item 1 or item 2, namely—

    (a) outboard motors and other engines;

    (b) electricity generators;

    (c) sails;

    (d) logs, wind speed, wind direction and boat speed indicators, and other navigational and meteorological instruments and recorders except compasses, echo sounders and radar sets;

    (e) automatic pilots and automatic steering gear;

    (f) trailers and trolleys.

6.   Goods of a kind suitable for use as parts of goods within item 1 or item 5, except goods within the exceptions from item 5 of Group 1.

(a) 1949 c. 67; 1968 c. 61; 1971 c. 75.   (b) 1894 c. 60.

7. Parts of aircraft which are of a weight of less than 8,000 kilogrammes and of a kind used for recreation or pleasure, except parts within the exceptions from item 5 of Group 1.

8. The alteration, testing, repair or maintenance of, or the provision of similar services in respect of, goods within item 1, item 5 or item 6.

9. The supply of materials or parts in connection with a supply of services within item 8.

10. The classification or surveying of goods within item 1, 2, 4 or 5.

11. The making of arrangements for the supply of goods comprised in items 1 to 5.

Notes:

(1) 'Boats' includes ships, inflatable craft and submersibles.

(2) 'Aircraft' includes gliders and balloons.

(3) 'Hovercraft' has the same meaning as in the Hovercraft Act 1968(a).

(4) This group does not include the letting on hire of a boat—

(a) as holiday accommodation for a period not exceeding 28 consecutive days by a person who customarily hires out boats to the public for such purposes; or

(b) for a period of less than a day if the boat is customarily held out for letting for such periods;

or the making of arrangements for any such letting.

GROUP 4—CARAVANS

Item No.

1. Caravans suitable for use as trailers drawn by motor vehicles having an unladen weight of less than 2,030 kilogrammes.

2. Caravan units designed to be mounted and carried on, and de-mounted from, motor vehicles.

3. Goods of a kind suitable for use as parts of goods within item 1 or item 2, except goods within the exceptions from item 5 of Group 1.

4. The alteration, repair or maintenance of, or the provision of similar services in respect of, goods comprised in items 1 to 3.

5. The supply of materials or parts in connection with a supply of services within item 4.

6. The making of arrangements for the supply of goods within item 1 or item 2.

Notes:

(1) Items 1 and 2 do not include removable contents of a kind not ordinarily installed as fixtures.

(2) This group does not include the letting on hire of a caravan—

(a) for use solely on a specified site; or

(b) as holiday accommodation for a period not exceeding 28 consecutive days by a person who customarily hires out caravans to the public for such purposes;

or the making of arrangements for any such letting.

(a) 1968 c. 59.

GROUP 5—PHOTOGRAPHIC EQUIPMENT, BINOCULARS, ETC.

Item No.

1. Goods within the following paragraphs if they are of a kind suitable for domestic or recreational use—

   (*a*) photographic and cinematographic cameras;

   (*b*) apparatus for developing, printing, reproducing, enlarging, reducing, editing or otherwise processing photographic or cinematographic images on film, plates or paper;

   (*c*) cinematographic, film strip or slide projectors, slide viewers, epidiascopes, projector screens and other apparatus for viewing photographic or cinematographic images.

2. Binoculars, monoculars, field glasses, opera glasses and terrestrial telescopes.

3. Accessories to goods comprised in items 1 and 2.

4. Goods of a kind suitable for use as parts of goods comprised in items 1 to 3, except goods within the exceptions from item 5 of Group 1.

5. The installation, alteration, testing, repair or maintenance of, or the provision of similar services in respect of, goods comprised in items 1 to 4.

6. The supply of goods in connection with a supply of services within item 5.

Notes:

(1) Item 1 includes goods which can be adapted to produce goods within that item.

(2) Items 1 and 3 do not include—

   (*a*) film, plates and paper;

   (*b*) chemicals;

   (*c*) disposable flash bulbs;

   (*d*) albums, mounts, wallets and other photographic stationery;

   (*e*) slide boxes and other storage equipment for developed film, plates or prints.

GROUP 6—FURS

Item No.

1. Clothing made wholly or partly of fur skin, except—

   (*a*) headgear;

   (*b*) gloves;

   (*c*) footwear;

   (*d*) buttons, belts and buckles;

   (*e*) any garment merely trimmed with fur skin unless the trimming has an area greater than one-fifth of the area of the outside material or, in the case of a new garment, represents a cost to the manufacturer greater than the cost to him of the other components.

2. Rugs, other than goat skin rugs, made wholly or partly of fur skin.

3. Fur skin, whether or not tanned or dressed.

4. The application to goods comprised in items 1 to 3 of any process or treatment, except the cleaning of goods comprised in items 1 and 2.

5. The supply of goods in connection with a supply of services within item 4.

6. The storage of goods comprised in items 1 to 3.

Notes:

(1) 'Fur skin' means any skin with fur, hair or wool attached except—

    (*a*) rabbit skin;

    (*b*) woolled sheep or lamb skin; and

    (*c*) the skin, if neither tanned nor dressed, of bovine cattle (including buffalo), equine animals, goats or kids (other than Yemen, Mongolian and Tibetan goats or kids), swine (including peccary), chamois, gazelles, deer or dogs.

(2) Item 3 does not include goods comprised in items 1 and 2 or excepted from item 1 but does include other goods made of fur skin and capable of being made into or incorporated in such goods.

(3) Item 4 includes the repair or alteration of goods comprised in items 1 to 3.

Group 7—Jewellery, Goldsmiths' and Silversmiths' Wares, etc.

Item No.

1. Jewellery, goldsmiths' and silversmiths' wares and similar goods made (in each case) wholly or partly from—

    (*a*) precious metal;

    (*b*) precious stones;

    (*c*) semi-precious stones mounted, set or strung;

    (*d*) real or cultured pearls.

2. Precious stones, except—

    (*a*) uncut diamonds;

    (*b*) diamond powder or dust.

3. Semi-precious stones in the form of gems, jewels or beads.

4. Real or cultured pearls.

5. Jade and articles of jade.

6. The design or valuation of, the application of any process or treatment to, or the provision of similar services in respect of, goods comprised in items 1 to 5.

7. The supply of goods in connection with a supply of services within item 6.

Notes:

(1) 'Precious metal' means gold, silver, platinum and any alloy containing any of those metals.

(2) 'Platinum' includes iridium, osmium, palladium, rhodium and ruthenium.

(3) 'Precious stones' means diamonds, rubies, sapphires and emeralds; and 'precious stones' and 'semi-precious stones' include synthetic stones which are similar to natural stones in respect of their physical properties and chemical composition.

(4) In item 1 'similar goods' includes—

    (*a*) articles of personal use of a kind normally carried in the pocket or handbag;

    (*b*) trophy cups, shields and similar articles of a kind awarded as prizes;

    (*c*) medals, medallions and the insignia of orders and decorations, and miniatures or reproductions of medals, medallions or such insignia.

(5) Goods do not fall within item 1 by reason only of one or more of the following—

    (*a*) that they are coated or plated with precious metal;

    (*b*) in the case of clocks and watches, that they contain precious or semi-precious stones as part of the movement;

    (*c*) in the case of fountain pens, that the nib contains precious metal.

(6) Item 1 does not include goods of a kind suitable only for use—

    (*a*) in churches, chapels or other buildings used mainly as places of meeting for religious worship; or

    (*b*) by ministers of religion.

(7) Item 6 does not include the cleaning, repair or maintenance of the movements of clocks or watches.

GROUP 8—PETROL, ETC.

Item No.

1.   Light oil, except where it is in containers not exceeding 20 fluid ounces and is intended for sale in those containers solely as fuel for mechanical lighters.

2.   Petrol substitute.

3.   Power methylated spirits.

Notes:

(1) 'Light oil', 'petrol substitute' and 'power methylated spirits' have the same meanings as in the Hydrocarbon Oil (Customs & Excise) Act 1971(a).

(2) 'Mechanical lighters' has the meaning assigned to it by section 221(4) of the Customs and Excise Act 1952(b).".

SCHEDULE 4

SUPERSEDED ORDERS

Column 1 Orders revoked	Column 2 References
The Value Added Tax (Consolidation) Order 1974	S.I. 1974/1146 (1974 II, p. 4374).
The Value Added Tax (Donated Medical Equipment) Order 1974	S.I. 1974/1331 (1974 II, p. 5039).
The Value Added Tax (Fuel and Power) Order 1974 ...	S.I. 1974/2080 (1974 III, p. 8128).
The Value Added Tax (Construction of Buildings, etc.) Order 1975	S.I. 1975/517 (1975 I, p. 1700).
The Value Added Tax (Construction of Buildings, etc.) (No. 2) Order 1975	S.I. 1975/746 (1975 II, p. 2760).
The Value Added Tax (Betting, Gaming and Lotteries) Order 1975	S.I. 1975/1185 (1975 II, p. 4089).
The Value Added Tax (Higher Rate) Order 1975	S.I. 1975/1297 (1975 II, p. 4411).
The Value Added Tax (Education) Order 1975	S.I. 1975/2008 (1975 III, p. 7417).
The Value Added Tax (Exhibition Sites) Order 1975 ...	S.I. 1975/2009 (1975 III, p. 7418).
The Value Added Tax (Higher Rate) (No. 2) Order 1975 ...	S.I. 1975/2010 (1975 III, p. 7419).
The Value Added Tax (Construction of Buildings, etc.) (No. 3) Order 1975	S.I. 1975/2011 (1975 III, p. 7420).
The Value Added Tax (Containers) (Variation) Order 1975...	S.I. 1975/2012 (1975 III, p. 7421).
The Value Added Tax (Food) Order 1975	S.I. 1975/2013 (1975 III, p. 7422).

(a) 1971 c. 12.   (b) 1952 c. 44.

EXPLANATORY NOTE

(This Note is not part of the Order.)

This Order consolidates, with one exception, the descriptions of supplies of goods or services which are either zero-rated for, or exempt from, value added tax. These reliefs were originally included in Schedules 4 and 5 to the Finance Act 1972, varied by subsequent Treasury Orders, and consolidated in the Value Added Tax (Consolidation) Order 1974 (S.I. 1974/1146). These schedules have been further varied by ten Treasury Orders made between 31st July 1974 and 5th December 1975 and by section 17 of the Finance (No. 2) Act 1975, and also take account of the provisions of sections 8 and 15 and Schedule 3 to the Act which came into force on 1st January 1976. The one exception, namely item 5, Group 9 of Schedule 4 to the Finance Act 1972, has not been included in the consolidation, this item itself conferring power on the Treasury to make orders.

This Order also consolidates the descriptions of supplies of goods or services which are higher rated for value added tax by virtue of Schedule 7 to the Finance (No. 2) Act 1975 as varied by two subsequent Treasury Orders.

STATUTORY INSTRUMENTS

1976 No. 133

AGRICULTURE

The Potato Marketing Scheme (Amendment) Order 1976

Made - - - - 28*th January* 1976

Whereas the Potato Marketing Board duly submitted to the Minister of Agriculture, Fisheries and Food, the Secretary of State concerned with agriculture in Scotland and the Secretary of State for Wales (hereinafter called "the Ministers") certain amendments of the Potato Marketing Scheme 1955(a), as amended(b), and the Ministers, as required by section 2 of, and Schedule 1 to, the Agricultural Marketing Act 1958(c) duly published notice of the submission of the said amendments and of the time within which objections and representations with respect thereto might be made;

And whereas no such objections were made and the Ministers made certain modifications, to which the said Board assented, in the said amendments which, as so modified, are set forth in the Schedule hereto;

Now, therefore, the Ministers in pursuance of section 2 of the Agricultural Marketing Act 1958 and Schedule 1 to that Act, as read with the Transfer of Functions (Wales) Order 1969(d), acting jointly, hereby make the following order:—

1. This order may be cited as the Potato Marketing Scheme (Amendment) Order 1976.

2. The amendments of the Potato Marketing Scheme 1955, as amended, which are set forth in the Schedule hereto, are hereby approved and shall come into operation on 1st March 1976.

In Witness whereof the Official Seal of the Minister of Agriculture, Fisheries and Food is hereunto affixed on 23rd January 1976.

(L.S.)

Frederick Peart,
Minister of Agriculture, Fisheries and Food.

28th January 1976.

William Ross,
Secretary of State for Scotland.

27th January 1976.

John Morris,
Secretary of State for Wales.

(a) S.I. 1955/690 (1955 I, p. 148).
(b) S.I. 1962/883, 1971/711 (1962 I, p. 1009; 1971 I, p. 1926).
(c) 1958 c. 47.   (d) S.I. 1969/388 (1969 I, p. 1070).

SCHEDULE

The Potato Marketing Scheme 1955, as amended, shall be further amended as follows:—

1. By substituting in paragraph 3 thereof for the word "acreage" the word "area" and for the word "acres" wherever it occurs the word "hectares".

2. By substituting in paragraph 5(1) thereof for the word "acres" wherever it occurs the word "hectares" and for the words "an acre" wherever they occur the words "a hectare".

3. By substituting in paragraph 5(1) thereof for the words "quarters of an acre, as the case may require, any fraction of a quarter of an acre being reckoned as a quarter of an acre" the words "tenths of a hectare, as the case may require, any fraction of a tenth of a hectare being reckoned as a tenth of a hectare".

4. By substituting in the proviso to paragraph 10 thereof for the word "acreage" the word "area".

5. By deleting from paragraph 14(1) thereof the words "designed so as to be capable of being returned through the post without a covering envelope and so that the voter may seal it if he wishes".

6. By inserting at the end of paragraph 14(1) thereof the following:—

"At the option of the Board, the voting paper shall either—

(a) be designed so as to be capable of being returned through the post without a covering envelope and so that the voter may seal it if he wishes, or

(b) be accompanied by an envelope addressed for return of the voting paper to the Board."

7. By deleting from paragraph 14(2) thereof the words "by means of adhesive stamps of the proper value affixed to the voting paper itself".

8. By substituting in paragraph 14(4) for the word "acreage" wherever it occurs the word "area".

9. By substituting for paragraph 14(5) thereof the following paragraph:—

"(5) The standard number of votes of a registered producer shall be calculated in relation to the appropriate area as follows and the expression "standard number of votes" shall be construed accordingly:—

(a) where the area does not exceed four hectares—one vote;

(b) where the area exceeds four hectares and does not exceed eight hectares—two votes;

(c) where the area exceeds eight hectares—two votes plus one additional vote for every twenty hectares of such excess: provided that if such excess does not amount to an even twenty hectares or a multiple of twenty hectares the odd fraction of such excess shall be taken to be an additional twenty hectares."

10. By substituting for paragraph 16 thereof the following paragraph:—

"16.—(1) If a district or special member of the Board dies, or pursuant to paragraph 17 of this Scheme ceases to hold office, then the Board may co-opt in his place any person who, in their opinion, is qualified to represent the registered producers producing potatoes in the district or territory for which the member was elected or co-opted:

Provided that this paragraph shall not apply if the vacancy occurs less than six months before the beginning of September in the year in which the next election for that district or territory would be held under the foregoing provisions of this Part of this Scheme.

(2) The term of office of any person co-opted to the Board under this paragraph shall cease not later than the date on which the term of office of his immediate predecessor would have ceased if such predecessor had not died or, pursuant to paragraph 17 of this Scheme, ceased to hold office."

11. By substituting for the stop at the end of paragraph 20 thereof a colon and adding thereafter the following proviso:—

"Provided that, where it is for the Board, or where the Board decide under paragraph 16 of this Scheme, to take action in relation to the filling of any vacancy, the Board shall do so as soon as they consider this reasonably practicable."

12. By substituting in paragraph 23 thereof for the word "and" a comma.

13. By deleting the stop at the end of paragraph 23 thereof and inserting the following:—

"and (subject to any directions from the Board) the provisions of paragraph 20 of this Scheme relating to the Board's power to act shall apply mutatis mutandis to the Executive Committee:

Provided that, where it is for the Board, or where the Board decide under paragraph 16 of this Scheme, to take action in relation to the filling of any vacancy, the Board shall do so as soon as they consider this reasonably practicable."

14. By inserting after sub-paragraph (c) of paragraph 28 thereof the following sub-paragraph:—

"(d) subject to any directions from the Board, the provisions of paragraph 20 of this Scheme relating to the Board's power to act shall apply mutatis mutandis to the Committee:

Provided that, where it is for the Board, or where the Board decide under paragraph 16 of this Scheme, to take action in relation to the filling of any vacancy, the Board shall do so as soon as they consider this reasonably practicable."

15. By substituting for paragraph 39 thereof the following paragraph:—

"39. A producer whose potato area is less than four tenths of a hectare shall be exempt from registration."

16. By substituting in paragraph 40(1) thereof for the words "the office of the Board in England" the words "such office of the Board in England as the Board may from time to time decide".

17. By deleting from paragraph 47(1) thereof the words "and designed so as to be capable of being returned through the post without a covering envelope and so that the voter may seal it if he wishes".

18. By inserting at the end of paragraph 47(1) thereof the following:—

"At the option of the Board, the voting paper shall either—

(a) be designed so as to be capable of being returned through the post without a covering envelope and so that the voter may seal it if he wishes, or

(b) be accompanied by an envelope addressed for return of the voting paper to the returning officer."

19. By deleting from paragraph 48 thereof the words "by means of adhesive stamps of the proper value affixed to the voting paper itself".

20. By substituting in paragraphs 50, 62 and 63(2) thereof for the word "acreage" wherever it occurs the word "area".

21. By substituting in sub-paragraph (c) of paragraph 75(4) thereof for the words "112 lbs." wherever they occur the words "50 kilograms" and for the words "19 cwt." the words "950 kilograms".

22. By substituting in sub-paragraph (b) of paragraph 83(1) thereof for the words "£5 per acre of his potato acreage" the words "£12 per hectare of his potato area".

23. By substituting for sub-paragraph (b) of paragraph 84(2) thereof the following sub-paragraph:—

"(b) an excess area contribution at a rate per hectare not exceeding five times the formula rate as defined in paragraph 84(3)(a), and proportionately for each tenth of a hectare, of the excess area in the case of a producer who, if that year is a quota year, has exceeded his quota area in that year."

24. By substituting in sub-paragraph (*a*) of paragraph 84(3) thereof for the words "sub-paragraph (3)" the word "paragraph".

25. By substituting in sub-paragraph (*a*) of paragraph 84(3) thereof for the words "tons per acre" the words "tonnes per hectare" and for the words "0·1 of a ton" the words "one tenth of a tonne".

26. By substituting for sub-paragraph (ii) of the proviso to sub-paragraph (*a*) of paragraph 84(3) thereof the following sub-paragraph:—

"(ii) for the purpose of calculating the formula rate for the calendar year 1976 the formula rate for the calendar year 1975 shall be deemed to have been £15·94 per hectare;"

27. By substituting in sub-paragraph (*a*) of paragraph 84(3) thereof for the words "Agriculture Act 1957**(b)**" the words "Agriculture Act 1957**(a)**".

28. By substituting in sub-paragraph (*b*) of paragraph 84(3) thereof for the word "acre" the word "hectare", for the words "quarter of an acre" the words "tenth of a hectare" and for the word "acreage" the word "area".

29. By substituting in sub-paragraph (*c*) of paragraph 84(3) thereof for the date "1971" the date "1975".

30. By deleting sub-paragraphs (*d*) and (*e*) of paragraph 84(3) thereof and re-lettering sub-paragraph (*f*) as sub-paragraph (*d*).

31. By substituting in paragraph 84(4) thereof for the word "acreage" wherever it occurs the word "area" and for the word "acre" the word "hectare".

32. By substituting in sub-paragraph (*b*) of paragraph 84(5) thereof, in sub-paragraphs (*a*) and (*b*) of paragraph 84(6) thereof and in paragraph 84(7) thereof, for the word "acreage" wherever it occurs the word "area".

33. By inserting after paragraph 84(9) thereof the following paragraph:—

"(10) A certificate purporting to be signed by the Secretary, Registration Officer or Assistant Registration Officer for the time being of the Board specifying the basic area of any registered producer as determined under the provisions of Schedule D of this Scheme for a stated date shall be evidence of the facts stated therein."

34. By substituting in paragraphs 88(2) and 88(3) thereof for the words "acreage of at least 20,000 acres" the words "area of at least 8,000 hectares".

35. By substituting in paragraph 89(2) thereof for the word "acres" the word "hectares" and for the words "1s. per acre" the words "12½p per hectare".

36. By substituting in Schedule B thereof for the words "highest acreage" wherever they occur the words "largest area", for the word "Acres" wherever it occurs the word "Hectares", for the word "acreage" wherever it occurs the word "area" and for the word "acreages" the word "areas".

37. By deleting from Schedule B thereof the words "by means of adhesive stamps of the proper value affixed to the voting paper itself".

38. By deleting from Note (*a*) at the foot of Schedule B thereof the letter "(*a*)" and the whole of Note (*b*).

39. By substituting in Schedule D thereof for the words "ACREAGES", "acreage", "an acre", "acres", "quarters", "a quarter" and "acreages" wherever they occur the words "AREAS", "area", "a hectare", "hectares", "tenths", "one tenth" and "areas" respectively.

(a) 1957 c. 57.

EXPLANATORY NOTE

(This Note is not part of the order.)

This order approves further amendments to the Potato Marketing Scheme 1955, as amended, which are set out in the Schedule. The amendments provide for—

(1) the removal of the requirement for the consent of producers to any increase exceeding 6 per cent. from one year to the next in the rate of the ordinary annual contribution which registered producers are required to pay to the Board;

(2) the maximum rate of excess acreage contribution for any year to be five times the maximum rate of the ordinary contribution for the same year instead of £25 per acre as at present;

(3) the substitution of metric units for imperial units;

(4) certain changes in the Board's administrative arrangements, such as the filling of vacancies on the Board and its Committees pending the election or appointment of new members and the return of voting papers.

STATUTORY INSTRUMENTS

1976 No. 137 (S. 9)

COURT OF SESSION, SCOTLAND
Act of Sederunt (Rules of Court Amendment) 1976

Made - - -		*30th January* 1976
Coming into Operation		*27th February* 1976

The Lords of Council and Session, under and by virtue of the powers conferred upon them by section 16 of the Administration of Justice (Scotland) Act 1933(a), and of all other powers competent to them in that behalf, do hereby enact and declare:

1. The Rules of Court(b) as amended, are hereby further amended as follows:—

(1) In Rule 112, by adding at the end the following sentence:—

"An application by any party by motion under this rule shall be heard in the Single Bills and it shall not be necessary for any documents to be lodged in support of the application unless the Court otherwise directs."

(2) In Rule 114, by substituting for paragraphs (*a*) to (*d*) the following paragraphs:—

"(*a*) In a cause, being a cause appropriate for jury trial, where—

(i) the parties agree at the closing of the record, or at any time thereafter up to and including the appearance of the cause in the By Order Adjustment Roll that the cause be so tried and the Court so allows; or

(ii) the Court, after hearing the parties, or any of them, in Procedure Roll, allows the cause to be so tried, the pursuer shall, within 14 days from the date of an interlocutor allowing issues, lodge in process a proposed issue or proposed issues for the trial, with a copy for the Court, and shall at the same time deliver a copy to the solicitor acting for the other party or parties.

(*b*) Notwithstanding that an interlocutor has been pronounced allowing issues, where a pursuer fails to lodge a proposed issue for the trial and to deliver a copy thereof in accordance with paragraph (*a*) of this Rule, he shall, unless on special cause shown, the Court otherwise determines, be held to have passed from his application for trial of the cause by jury, and any inquiry into the facts of the cause shall be taken by a proof, provided that the other party or parties to the cause on such failure, may if he or they maintain that the cause should be tried by jury, within 7 days after the expiry of the said period of 14 days, enrol a motion to have the cause sent to the Procedure Roll.

(a) 1933 c. 41.

(b) S.I. 1965/321 (1965 I, p. 803).

(c) Where a proposed issue has been lodged in pursuance of paragraph (a) of this Rule, the other party or parties to the cause may, within 7 days after the day on which such issue is lodged, lodge a proposed counter-issue or proposed counter-issues, and the provisions of paragraph (a) of this Rule relating to the lodging and delivery of copies of a proposed issue shall apply to a proposed counter-issue under this paragraph as they apply to a proposed issue under that paragraph.

(d) A proposed counter-issue lodged by a party or parties to the cause in pursuance of paragraph (c) of this Rule may include any question of fact which is made the subject of specific averment on the record or is relevant to his or their pleas, notwithstanding that it does not in terms meet the proposed issue or issues.

(e) The pursuer shall, not later than 7 days after any such proposed counter-issue has been lodged and intimated or, if no proposed counter-issue has been lodged, on the expiry of the period allowed for lodging a proposed counter-issue in paragraph (c) of this Rule, enrol a motion for the approval of the proposed issue and on intimation being made to him of that motion, any party who has lodged a proposed counter-issue under paragraph (c) of this Rule, shall, within 7 days of such intimation, enrol a motion for the approval of the proposed counter-issue and any such motion may be marked as opposed in accordance with Rule 93.";

and by substituting for the letters (e), (f) and (g) in the remaining paragraphs the letters (f), (g) and (h) respectively.

(3) By substituting for Rule 116 the following Rule:—

"116 (a) The Court after hearing parties in Procedure Roll in pursuance of an order made under Rule 91 or Rule 114 shall dispose of the contentions and pleas of parties as shall seem just; and in the event of the cause being found, in whole or in part, relevant for enquiry, the Court may either allow or dispense with issues, or if the Court thinks that such enquiry or any part thereof should not be taken before a jury, the Court may pronounce an interlocutor allowing a proof.

(b) In a cause tried by jury with an issue and counter-issue, the presiding judge may, after the evidence has been led, submit to the jury in writing along with the issue and counter-issue such further question or questions as may appear to him to be required by the circumstances of the case, but where he does so the powers exercisable under Rule 128 in relation to a special verdict shall not be exercisable by him."

(4) In Rule 158 by adding at the end the following paragraphs:—

"(d) The applicant in an application for an order under section 27(1)(a) of the said Act of 1964 reducing or varying any settlement or disposition of property belonging to a defender made by him in favour of any third party within the period mentioned in the said section, shall intimate the minute mentioned in paragraph (b) of this Rule to any such third party and to any other person having an interest in the settlement or disposition, and any such third party or other person may lodge answers thereto within such period as the Court may allow.

(*e*) On cause shown, the Court may dispense with intimation under paragraph (*d*) of this Rule."

2. This Act may be cited as the Act of Sederunt (Rules of Court Amendment) 1976 and shall come into operation on 27th February 1976.

And the Lords appoint this Act of Sederunt to be inserted in the Books of Sederunt.

G. C. Emslie,

I.P.D.

Edinburgh,
30th January 1976.

EXPLANATORY NOTE

(This Note is not part of the Act of Sederunt.)

This Act of Sederunt amends the Rules of Court (*a*) by expressly providing that an application to the Inner House arising from the retiral of a judge in the course of a case is to be heard as a Single Bill without any documents being required to be lodged; (*b*) by altering the circumstances in and the time limits within which proposed issues and counter-issues are to be lodged; and (*c*) by providing for minutes in divorce actions to have settlements or dispositions reduced to be served on persons having an interest, and for answers by them.

STATUTORY INSTRUMENTS

1976 No. 138

BURIAL, ENGLAND AND WALES

The Human Remains Removal Licence (Variation of Maximum Fee) Order 1976

Made - - - -	*2nd February* 1976
Laid before Parliament	*10th February* 1976
Coming into Operation	*20th February* 1976

In exercise of the powers conferred upon me by section 5 of and Schedule 3 to the Public Expenditure and Receipts Act 1968(a), I hereby make the following Order:—

1. This Order may be cited as the Human Remains Removal Licence (Variation of Maximum Fee) Order 1976 and shall come into operation on 20th February 1976.

2. The Interpretation Act 1889(b) applies for the interpretation of this Order as it applies for the interpretation of an Act of Parliament.

3. Section 7(1) of the Fees (Increase) Act 1923(c) (which relates to fees for licences to remove bodies after burial) shall be amended by substituting the words "four pounds" for the words "two pounds".

Roy Jenkins,

One of Her Majesty's Principal Secretaries of State.

Home Office.
 Whitehall.
2nd February 1976.

EXPLANATORY NOTE

(This Note is not part of the Order.)

This Order amends section 7(1) of the Fees (Increase) Act 1923 to increase from £2 to £4 the maximum amount which may be prescribed by the Secretary of State, with the consent of the Treasury, for a fee in respect of a licence issued under section 25 of the Burial Act 1857 (c.81) for the removal of human remains interred in a place of burial.

(a) 1968 c. 14.   (b) 1889 c. 63.   (c) 1923 c. 4.

STATUTORY INSTRUMENTS

1976 No. 140

PENSIONS

The Occupational Pension Schemes (Preservation of Benefit) Amendment Regulations 1976

Made - - - -	*3rd February* 1976
Laid before Parliament	*10th February* 1976
Coming into Operation	*2nd March* 1976

The Secretary of State for Social Services, in exercise of the powers conferred upon her by paragraphs 9(2), 13(5), 23 and 26 of Schedule 16 to the Social Security Act 1973(a) and of all other powers enabling her in that behalf, after considering the report of the Occupational Pensions Board on the preliminary draft submitted to them, hereby makes the following regulations:—

Citation, interpretation and commencement

1.—(1) These regulations, which may be cited as the Occupational Pension Schemes (Preservation of Benefit) Amendment Regulations 1976, shall be read as one with the Occupational Pension Schemes (Preservation of Benefit) Regulations 1973(b) (hereinafter called "the principal regulations"), as amended by the Occupational Pension Schemes (Preservation of Benefit) Amendment Regulations 1974(c) (hereinafter called "the 1974 regulations"), and shall come into operation on 2nd March 1976.

(2) In these regulations, the expression "the payment of a lump sum by way of a refund of contributions" means the payment of a lump sum to or in respect of a member of a scheme which is made under a provision made by that scheme, the amount of the lump sum being equal to the amount of the member's contributions to one or more schemes in respect of a particular period or periods; and for the purpose of deciding whether these amounts are equal there shall be disregarded any addition made to the latter amount in respect of interest, and any deduction made from it in order to do any or all of the following, namely—

(*a*) to pay taxes arising out of the member's participation in the scheme or schemes to which he contributed;

(*b*) to reflect the cost of life insurance premiums paid or other provision made for benefits payable in the event of the member's death;

(*c*) to provide equivalent pension benefits for the purposes of the former legislation (within the meaning of section 33(5) to (7) of the Social Security Pensions Act 1975(d)); and

---

(a) 1973 c. 38.
(c) S.I. 1974/1324 (1974 II, p. 5023).
(b) S.I. 1973/1469 (1973 II, p. 4471).
(d) 1975 c. 60.

(*d*) to pay sums which are payable under section 60(1) of the National Insurance Act 1965(**a**), as continued in force and modified by the National Insurance (Non-participation—Transitional Provisions) Regulations 1974(**b**), to persons liable for payments in lieu of contributions.

(3) In these regulations, the expression "the period in respect of which the contributions were made" means the period or periods in respect of which the contributions referred to in paragraph (2) above were made by the member to the scheme or schemes in question, and any period or periods in respect of which he would have been required to make contributions to that scheme or any of those schemes but for the fact that—

(*a*) his contributions were waived by the trustees or managers of the scheme; or

(*b*) he was excused from making contributions under a specific provision in the rules of the scheme (other than a provision relating to a period at the beginning of a member's pensionable service during which long service benefit does not accrue to him).

Transfer credits to be treated in part as bonus credits in certain cases

2. In cases where a person is a member of 2 or more schemes relating to employment with the same employer or with an employer and his successor or successors, and under the rules of one of those schemes the person is entitled to transfer credits by reference to a transfer to that scheme of his accrued rights from another of those schemes, and the transfer credits are greater in value than those accrued rights, short service benefit shall be computed under paragraph 13(3) of Schedule 16 as if the difference in value between those credits and those rights were a bonus credit awarded on the date when the transfer was made.

Refunds of contributions and extinguishment of benefits

3.—(1) Regulation 6(1) of the principal regulations shall be amended by the substitution, for sub-paragraphs (*c*) and (*d*), of the following, namely—

"(*c*) subject to the provisions of regulation 3(2) of the Occupational Pension Schemes (Preservation of Benefit) Amendment Regulations 1976, the payment, at any time after the termination of the service in relevant employment, of a lump sum (whether or not being or including a payment by way of refund of contributions) in respect of any period of qualifying service before 6th April 1975;

"(*d*) subject to the provisions of regulation 3(2) of the Occupational Pension Schemes (Preservation of Benefit) Amendment Regulations 1976, the payment, at any time after the termination of the service in relevant employment, of a lump sum in respect of any period of qualifying service after 5th April 1975, in the following circumstances, namely—

(i) that a payment under paragraph (1)(*c*) of this regulation is being or has been made to the member in question under the scheme in question,

(**a**) 1965 c. 51.   (**b**) S.I. 1974/2057 (1974 III, p. 8011).

(ii) that if the lump sum in respect of the period after 5th April 1975 is or includes a payment by way of refund of contributions, so also is or does the lump sum in respect of the period before 6th April 1975, and

(iii) that the duration of the period described in paragraph (2), or, as the case may be, the aggregate duration of the periods described in paragraph (3), of this regulation is less than 5 years, so however that for the purposes of this calculation no period shall be counted more than once;".

(2) The payment of a lump sum by way of a refund of contributions shall be a prescribed alternative to the following descriptions of short service benefit (and no others), namely—

(a) short service benefit (excluding any transfer credits or bonus credits) in respect of the period in respect of which the contributions were made;

(b) short service benefit consisting of bonus credits which were awarded by reference to the period in respect of which the contributions were made;

(c) short service benefit consisting of bonus credits which were awarded by reference to any period of service which was not pensionable service in relation to any scheme applying to employment with either—

(i) the same employer as the one to whose employment of the person in question the scheme under whose provisions the lump sum is paid applies, or

(ii) his predecessor,

but only to the extent that, applying the assumptions mentioned in paragraph 13(3) of Schedule 16, the credits accrued during the period in respect of which the contributions were made;

(d) in a case where the period of service the termination of which gave rise to the payment of the lump sum included a waiting period within the meaning of regulation 4 of the 1974 regulations, short service benefit which is deemed in accordance with the said regulation 4 to accrue over, or short service benefit which consists of bonus credits awarded by reference to, the whole, or part or parts, of the waiting period, but only if—

(i) the total duration of the waiting period is less than 5 years,

(ii) during the period or periods over which that short service benefit was so deemed to accrue or (as the case may be) by reference to which it was awarded, any member of the scheme in question to whom long service benefit was (apart from the said regulation 4) accruing was required to contribute to it, except in the circumstances referred to in regulation 1(3)(a) and (b) above, and

(iii) the lump sum is by way of a refund of all the member's contributions (and for the purpose of deciding whether it is or not there shall be disregarded any such addition or deduction as is mentioned in regulation 1(2) above) in respect of the period of service the termination of which gave rise to the payment of the lump sum; and

(e) short service benefit consisting of transfer credits, where and to the extent that, in the opinion of the trustees or managers of the scheme under whose provisions the lump sum is paid—

    (i) the member is entitled to that benefit by virtue of having been entitled to benefit under another scheme (whether or not the scheme from which the member's accrued rights were transferred into the scheme under whose provisions the lump sum is paid), and

    (ii) a lump sum by way of a refund of contributions, if it had been paid under the provisions of that other scheme, would have been a prescribed alternative under the foregoing provisions of this paragraph to the benefit to which he was entitled under that other scheme (assuming, if it is not so, that that benefit was short service benefit).

Special provision for schemes to which no contributions are made by a particular member

4.—(1) This regulation applies to cases where—

(a) a person is a member of 2 or more schemes relating to the same employment;

(b) payment of a lump sum by way of a refund of contributions made to one of the schemes (referred to in paragraph (2) below as "the contributory scheme") is made as an alternative to the provision of short service benefit; and

(c) that person has made no contributions to the other schemes, or to at least one of the others if there are more than one (the scheme or schemes to which he has made no contributions being referred to in paragraph (2) below as "the non-contributory scheme").

(2) In a case to which this regulation applies, the preservation requirements shall apply subject to the exception that there need not be provided for that person—

(a) short service benefit of any of the descriptions specified in sub-paragraphs (a) to (c) of regulation 3(2) above; or

(b) short service benefit in respect of any period or periods which was, or were, in relation to that person and his membership of the contributory scheme, a waiting period or part or parts thereof within the meaning of regulation 4 of the 1974 regulations, but only if the conditions specified in regulation 3(2)(d) above are fulfilled,

under the non-contributory scheme, or short service benefit under any scheme to the extent that it would consist of transfer credits allowed, in the opinion of the trustees or managers of the latter scheme, by reference to that person's rights under the non-contributory scheme to short service benefit of the descriptions specified in sub-paragraphs (a) and (b) above.

(3) For paragraph (3)(a) of regulation 6 of the principal regulations there shall be substituted the following, namely—

"(a) any period before 6th April 1975 during which the member in question was in qualifying service relevant to another non-centralised scheme (not being a scheme which, by virtue of regulation 4(2) of the Occupational Pension Schemes (Preservation of Benefit) Amendment Regulations 1976, was not required to provide short service benefit for or in respect of that member in respect of that period) which applied to the same employment as the scheme in question, no payment being or having been made under paragraph (1)(*c*) of this regulation under that scheme in respect of that service; and".

Bonus credits to be extinguished in certain cases of refunds

5.—(1) This regulation applies to cases where—

(*a*) a person is a member of 2 or more schemes relating to the same employment; and

(*b*) payment of a lump sum by way of a refund of contributions is made under a provision of one of the schemes as an alternative to the provision of short service benefit.

(2) In a case to which this regulation applies, the preservation requirements shall apply subject to the exception that the other scheme or schemes need not provide for the inclusion in short service benefit of any bonus credits to which that person has become entitled to the extent that those credits were awarded by reference to any period of service which coincided with the whole or any part of—

(*a*) the period in respect of which the contributions were made; and

(*b*) if the conditions specified in regulation 3(2)(*d*) above are fulfilled, a period which was, in relation to that person and his membership of the scheme under the provisions of which the lump sum is paid, a waiting period within the meaning of regulation 4 of the 1974 regulations.

Barbara Castle,
Secretary of State for Social Services.

3rd February 1976.

EXPLANATORY NOTE
(This Note is not part of the Regulations.)

These Regulations make special provision regarding entitlement to, and computation of, short service benefit (within the meaning of Schedule 16 to the Social Security Act 1973).

Regulation 2 deals with certain cases where a person's accrued rights to retirement benefits have been transferred from one scheme to another, both schemes relating to employment with the same employer or with an employer and his successor; and Regulations 3, 4 and 5 deal with cases where a lump sum is paid to or in respect of a scheme member by way of a refund of his contributions.

The report of the Occupational Pensions Board on the preliminary draft of these regulations, dated 6th November 1975, is contained in House of Commons Paper No. 156 (Session 1975–76) published by Her Majesty's Stationery Office.

1976 No. 141 (C. 4)

SOCIAL SECURITY

The Social Security Pensions Act 1975 (Commencement No. 5) Order 1976

Made - - - -	*3rd February* 1976
Laid before Parliament	*10th February* 1976
Coming into Operation	*6th April* 1978

The Secretary of State for Social Services, in exercise of the powers conferred on her by section 67(1) of the Social Security Pensions Act 1975(a) and of all other powers enabling her in that behalf, hereby makes the following order:—

Citation and commencement

1. This order may be cited as the Social Security Pensions Act 1975 (Commencement No. 5) Order 1976 and shall come into operation on 6th April 1978.

Appointed day

2. The day appointed for the coming into operation of each of the provisions of the Social Security Pensions Act 1975 specified in column (1) of the Schedule to this Order shall be 6th April 1978.

Barbara Castle,
Secretary of State for Social Services.

3rd February 1976.

(a) 1975 c. 60.

Article 2

SCHEDULE

Provisions of the Social Security Pensions Act 1975 for which 6th April 1978 is appointed as the day of coming into operation.

Provision of the Act (1)	Subject matter (2)
Section 30(5)	Amendment of the Contracts of Employment Act 1972(a).
Section 42	Premium on termination of contracted-out employment.
Section 43	Premium under section 42: additional provisions.
Section 44	Premium on termination of contracted-out scheme.
Section 45	Premium where guaranteed minimum pension excluded from full revaluation.
Section 46	Provisions as to actuarial tables.
Section 47	Deduction of premium from refund of contributions.
Section 58 (so far as it relates to paragraph 3 of Schedule 3) and paragraph 3 of Schedule 3	Priority in bankruptcy etc.
Section 65(1) (so far as it relates to paragraphs 54 to 57 of Schedule 4) and paragraphs 54 to 57 of Schedule 4	Amendments of enactments.

EXPLANATORY NOTE

(This Note is not part of the Order.)

This Order appoints 6th April 1978 as the date for the coming into force of all those provisions of the Social Security Pensions Act 1975 for which dates have not already been appointed. It does not affect section 22 and certain related paragraphs in Schedule 4, which relate to mobility allowance and are already in operation for certain purposes only.

(a) 1972 c. 53.

STATUTORY INSTRUMENTS

1976 No. 142

PENSIONS

The Occupational Pension Schemes (Equal Access to Membership) Regulations 1976

Made - - - -	*3rd February* 1976
Laid before Parliament	*10th February* 1976
Coming into Operation	*6th April* 1978

The Secretary of State for Social Services, in exercise of powers conferred upon her by sections 53(3) and (6), 55(2) and 66(3) and (4) of the Social Security Pensions Act 1975(a) and of all other powers enabling her in that behalf, hereby makes the following regulations:—

Citation, commencement and interpretation

1.—(1) These regulations may be cited as the Occupational Pension Schemes (Equal Access to Membership) Regulations 1976, and shall come into operation on 6th April 1978.

(2) In these regulations, unless the context otherwise requires—

"the Act" means the Social Security Pensions Act 1975;

"the Board" means the Occupational Pensions Board;

"the Equal Pay Act" means the Equal Pay Act 1970(b) as amended by the Sex Discrimination Act 1975(c) and the Employment Protection Act 1975(d);

"maximum age for admission", in relation to a person and a scheme, means the highest age at which, under the rules of that scheme, that person can become a member of that scheme;

"relevant employment", in relation to a scheme, means any employment with an employer who contributes or is liable to contribute to the resources of the scheme, or with any successor to such an employer;

"replacing scheme", in relation to another scheme, means a scheme to which persons who would otherwise be admitted to that other scheme would be admitted if that other scheme were wound up or ceased to admit new members;

"scheme" means an occupational pension scheme;

and other expressions have the same meanings as in the Act.

(3) Any reference in these regulations to any provision made by or contained in any enactment or instrument shall, except in so far as the context otherwise requires, be construed as a reference to that provision as amended or extended by any enactment or instrument and as including a reference to any provision which it re-enacts or which may re-enact or replace it, with or without modification.

(a) 1975 c. 60.	(b) 1970 c. 41.
(c) 1975 c. 65.	(d) 1975 c. 71.

(4) The rules for the construction of Acts of Parliament contained in the Interpretation Act 1889(a) shall apply for the purposes of the interpretation of these regulations as they apply for the purposes of the interpretation of an Act of Parliament.

Meaning of expressions "member", "prospective member" and "employer" in relation to a scheme

2.—(1) The following provisions of this regulation shall apply for the purposes of sections 53 to 56 of the Act (equal access requirements).

(2) Any person is to be regarded as a member of a scheme during, or at any time after, a period when his service in relevant employment is or was such that at the time it is or was given it either—

(*a*) qualifies or qualified him for benefits under the scheme; or

(*b*) is or was certain so to qualify him subsequently if it continues or continued for a sufficiently long time and the rules of the scheme and the terms of his contract of service remain or remained unaltered during that time.

(3) There are to be regarded as prospective members of a scheme any persons in relevant employment who are not members but—

(*a*) who, by virtue of the terms of their contracts of service, are able to become members at their own option or the option of any other person; or

(*b*) who, by virtue of the terms of their contracts of service, will become so able, if their service in relevant employment continues for a sufficiently long time and the terms of their contracts of service remain unaltered during that time; or

(*c*) who, by virtue of the rules of the scheme or the terms of their contracts of service, will become members in any event, if their service in relevant employment continues for a sufficiently long time and the rules of the scheme or, as the case may be, the terms of their contracts of service remain unaltered during that time.

(4) Any person, government department, public authority or body of persons who under the Social Security Act 1975(b) is, or is to be treated as, the secondary Class 1 contributor shall be treated as the employer of the earner in respect of whom the Class 1 contributions are payable.

(5) Without prejudice to paragraph (4) above, there shall be treated as the employer of a self-employed earner to whom a scheme applies any person (other than that self-employed earner), government department, public authority or body of persons who makes or is to make payments towards the resources of that scheme in respect of that self-employed earner (either under actual or contingent legal obligation or in the exercise of a power conferred, or duty imposed, on a Minister of the Crown, government department or any other person, being a power or duty which extends to the disbursement or allocation of public money).

Persons competent to apply for determination

3. In relation to a scheme which makes different provision for men and women with regard to access to membership, any persons who, if they were of the

---

(**a**) 1889 c. 63.   (**b**) 1975 c. 14.

opposite sex, would be members or prospective members of the scheme shall be proper persons to make an application for the purposes of section 55 of the Act (determination of questions whether a scheme, other than a public service scheme, conforms with the equal access requirements).

Upper age limit for membership

4. The equal access requirements shall apply with the modification that, in a case where the rules of a scheme are such that the normal pension age applicable to a member of a scheme may be different from what it would be if he were of the opposite sex, membership of that scheme may be open to men and women on terms which differ as to the maximum age for admission, so however that where the normal pension age applicable to a person (if he becomes a member) is higher than it would be if he were of the opposite sex—

(*a*) the maximum age for admission for that person must not be lower than it would be if he were of the opposite sex; and

(*b*) the difference between the maximum age for admission applicable to that person and the maximum age for admission which would be applicable if he were of the opposite sex shall not exceed the difference between the normal pension age applicable to him and the normal pension age which would be applicable to him if he were of the opposite sex.

Interpretation of "age" and "length of service"

5. In the case of a scheme which provides for admission to membership to be by reference not to the attainment of a precise age or length of service but to the falling of a particular day of the week, month or year bearing some relationship to the date of attainment of an age or length of service, the equal access requirements shall apply with the modification that membership of the scheme must be open to men and women, not on terms which are the same as to the age and length of service needed for becoming a member, but on terms which are the same with regard to any qualification for becoming a member which is related to attainment of an age or a length of service.

Schemes to be considered together in certain cases

6. In a case where 2 or more schemes apply to employment with an employer, the equal access requirements shall apply with the modification that any one of those schemes which apart from this regulation does not comply with those requirements shall nevertheless be treated as doing so if that scheme and another or others of those schemes—

(*a*) were both or all set up on or before 5th April 1978;

(*b*) are both or all continuing to admit new members; and

(*c*) would comply with those requirements if treated as a single scheme.

Schemes with an overseas element

7.—(1) This regulation applies to any scheme which has any overseas element, that is to say, a scheme established, or relating to employment, or with parties domiciled, resident or carrying on business, in any part of the world outside Great Britain, or otherwise not confined in its operation to Great Britain (being a scheme to which the equal access requirements apply or but for the provisions of this regulation would apply).

(2) In the case of a scheme to which this regulation applies, the equal access requirements shall be so modified as not to apply to that scheme unless—

(*a*) at least one of its members is employed in the United Kingdom in employment to which the scheme relates; and

(*b*) either the scheme is established in Great Britain or it has a representative appointed to carry out the functions of a trustee or manager in Great Britain.

(3) In the case of a scheme to which this regulation applies and in respect of which conditions (*a*) and (*b*) in paragraph (2) of this regulation are fulfilled, the equal access requirements shall be so modified as to apply only in relation to men and women whose employment is in the United Kingdom, or whose earnings give rise to liability for primary Class 1 contributions or would do so if the level of their earnings were not below the lower earnings limit.

Schemes closed to new members

8.—(1) This regulation applies to any scheme which has ceased to admit any new members.

(2) In the case of a scheme to which this regulation applies, the equal access requirements shall be so modified as to apply only in relation to persons who, if they had been of the opposite sex, would have had access to membership of the scheme after 5th April 1978 but before the date on which the scheme ceased to admit new members.

Special provision for membership of a scheme to be or remain voluntary

9.—(1) This regulation applies to cases where it is or has been necessary to modify the rules of a scheme in order to make them comply with the equal access requirements because in the scheme's application to any class of persons membership of the scheme is or has been obligatory for members of that class who are of one sex but either voluntary for, or not available to, members of that class who are of the other sex.

(2) In a case to which this regulation applies, the equal access requirements shall apply subject to the exceptions that—

(*a*) while to become a member of the scheme is obligatory for the generality of members of that class, it may be voluntary for any member of that class who on 5th April 1978 is employed in relevant employment but is not a member of the scheme; and

(*b*) until his service in the employment of the person who was his employer on 5th April 1978 is terminated—

(i) it may continue to be voluntary for him to become a member of that scheme, and

(ii) it may be voluntary for him to become a member of any replacing scheme.

(3) For the purposes of paragraph (2) above, and except as mentioned in paragraph (4) below, a person's service in an employment is to be treated as terminated when his contract of service expires or is terminated, or, in a case where there is no contract, when the service itself ends.

(4) A person's service in an employment is not to be treated as terminated if that employment is followed by another employment with the same employer or his successor and either—

(*a*) there is no interval, or an interval not exceeding one month, between the 2 employments; or (*b*) the second employment results from the exercise of a right to return to work under section 48(1) of the Employment Protection Act 1975(**a**) (right to return to work following pregnancy or confinement).

Modification, in relation to the equal access requirements, of the provisions of the Equal Pay Act as to equality clauses

10.—(1) Subject to paragraphs (2) to (4) below, the Equal Pay Act shall be so modified, in its application to the equal access requirements, as to have effect as if there were substituted, for references to less favourable terms of a contract and less favourable terms and conditions of employment, references to—

(*a*) terms (or, as the case may be, terms and conditions) which do not enable persons to have access to membership of a scheme (as compared with terms, or terms and conditions, which do enable persons to have such access), and

(*b*) terms (or, as the case may be, terms and conditions) which enable persons to have access to membership of a scheme at a higher minimum or (subject to regulation 4 above) lower maximum age, after a greater length of service or on a voluntary (as compared with an obligatory) basis.

(2) In relation to a person who on 5th April 1978 is not a member of a scheme but is employed in relevant employment, paragraphs (3) and (4) below shall apply until his service in the employment of the person who was his employer on 5th April 1978 is terminated (which expression is to be construed in accordance with paragraphs (3) and (4) of regulation 9 above).

(3) In its application to any such person as is specified in paragraph (2) above, the Equal Pay Act shall be further modified so as to provide that where, by virtue of paragraph (1) above and apart from the provisions of this paragraph, an equality clause would be a provision making it obligatory for that person to become a member of the scheme in question or any replacing scheme, an equality clause shall be a provision making that obligatory unless, but voluntary if, the scheme makes such provision as is referred to in paragraph (4) below, so however that any question whether the scheme has made such provision shall not fall to be determined in any proceedings brought in respect of a failure to comply with the equality clause, or in respect of a dispute in relation to the effect of that clause.

(4) The scheme's provision referred to in paragraph (3) above is that in the application of the scheme to any class of persons which includes the person referred to in paragraph (3) above, membership is obligatory for the generality of members of that class but voluntary for any member of that class who on 5th April 1978 is employed in relevant employment but is not a member of the scheme.

(5) The Equal Pay Act shall be further modified, in its application to the equal access requirements, so as to have effect as if for the references in section 1(2) to treating a contract as including a term there were substituted references to treating a contract as so modified as to include a term.

Damages not to be awarded for failure to comply with the equal access requirements

11. The Equal Pay Act shall be so modified that there shall be no power for

---

(**a**) 1975 c. 71.

a court or an industrial tribunal to award damages in respect of any failure to comply with the equal access requirements.

Power for court or industrial tribunal to declare right to admission to scheme, and employer's duty to provide additional resources

12.—(1) The Equal Pay Act shall be so modified as to provide that where a court or an industrial tribunal finds that there has been a breach of a term in a contract of employment which has been included in the contract, or modified, by virtue of an equality clause and which relates to membership of a scheme, or where it makes an order declaring the right of an employee to admission to membership of a scheme in pursuance of the equal access requirements, it may declare that the employee has a right to be admitted to the scheme in question with effect from such date ("the deemed entry date") as it may specify, not being earlier than whichever is the later of the following dates, namely—

(*a*) 6th April 1978; and

(*b*) the date 2 years before the institution of the proceedings in which the order was made.

(2) The Equal Pay Act shall be so modified as to require that if the deemed entry date is earlier than the date of the declaration, the employer shall provide any such resources as are specified in paragraph (3) below.

(3) The resources referred to in paragraph (2) above are any additional resources which may be necessary for the scheme to secure to the employee, without contribution or further contribution by the employee or by other members of the scheme, the same prospective entitlement to benefit arising from past service (other than benefit by way of refund of contributions) as if he had been a member of the scheme since the deemed entry date.

Employer's duty to provide additional resources when scheme is modified

13.—(1) This regulation applies to cases where—

(*a*) an employer has failed to comply with a term of employment relating to membership of a scheme; and

(*b*) the Board by order modify the scheme retrospectively (within the meaning of section 56(4) of the Act), or authorise or direct other persons to modify the scheme retrospectively, in order to make it comply with the equal access requirements.

(2) In a case to which this regulation applies, the employer of every person (not being a person who by virtue of regulation 9 above has, and is exercising, a right not to become a member of the scheme) who could have been, but because of the employer's failure to comply with a term of employment relating to membership of the scheme was not, a member of the scheme during a period ending on the date on which the order is made and beginning not earlier than the latest of the following dates, namely—

(*a*) the date 2 years earlier than that on which the order is made;

(*b*) the date with effect from which the scheme is to be modified; and

(*c*) 6th April 1978,

shall provide any such resources as are specified in paragraph (3) below.

(3) The resources referred to in paragraph (2) above are any additional resources which may be necessary for the scheme to secure to that person, without contribution or further contribution by him or by other members of

the scheme, the same prospective entitlement to benefit arising from past service (other than benefit by way of refund of contributions) as if he had been a member of the scheme since whichever is the later of—

(a) the date on which, but for the employer's failure mentioned in paragraph (2) above, he would have become a member of the scheme; and

(b) the date on which the period mentioned in paragraph (2) above began.

Additional power of Board to modify or authorise modification of schemes

14.—(1) Where—

(a) there has been an alteration under the Equal Pay Act of any terms of employment relating to access to membership of a scheme; and

(b) a competent person (within the meaning of paragraph (2) below) has applied to the Board to make or authorise such a modification of the rules of the scheme as is specified in paragraph (3) below,

the Board shall have power by order themselves to make, or to authorise the trustees or managers of the scheme or other persons named in the order to make, such a modification of the rules of the scheme.

(2) For the purposes of paragraph (1)(b) above, a competent person is any of the following, namely—

(a) the trustees or managers of the scheme;

(b) any person other than the trustees or managers who has power to alter any of the rules of the scheme; and

(c) any person who is an employer of persons in service in an employment to which the scheme applies.

(3) Paragraph (1) above refers to a modification of the scheme's rules which is consequential upon the alteration of terms of employment referred to in that paragraph.

(4) Subsections (2) to (4) of section 56 of the Act shall apply to orders and modifications under this regulation as they apply to orders and modifications under that section.

Barbara Castle,
Secretary of State for Social Services.

3rd February 1976.

EXPLANATORY NOTE

(This Note is not part of the Regulations.)

These Regulations make miscellaneous provisions with regard to the equal access requirements of sections 53 to 56 of the Social Security Pensions Act 1975, which relate to the access of men and women to membership of occupational pension schemes. Regulation 3 provides for a category of persons (additional to those specified in section 55(2)) to be competent to apply for a determination whether the rules of a scheme conform with those requirements.

Regulation 4 modifies those requirements in their application to upper age limits for membership; regulation 6 modifies them in their application to cases where there is (on or before 5th April 1978) a group of schemes some of which do not comply with those requirements unless the group is treated as a single scheme; and regulations 7 and 8 modify them in their application to schemes with an overseas element and schemes closed to new members respectively. Regulations 9 and 10 make a transitional provision for membership of a scheme to be or to remain voluntary for certain persons for whom it would otherwise be obligatory; and regulation 10 also modifies the references in the Equal Pay Act 1970 to "less favourable" terms and conditions of employment. Regulations 11, 12 and 13 modify the provisions of that Act in its application to the equal access requirements so that a court or industrial tribunal may not award damages but may declare the right of employees to be admitted to schemes, and so that in certain circumstances employers are required to make additional contributions to the resources of schemes so as to provide appropriate benefits for employees who, through a breach of the equal access requirements, have been admitted to schemes later than they should have been. Regulation 14 confers upon the Occupational Pensions Board power to order or effect the consequential modification of a scheme where there has been an alteration under the Equal Pay Act 1970 of terms of employment relating to membership of that scheme. The remaining regulations are concerned with interpretation.

STATUTORY INSTRUMENTS

1976 No. 143

PENSIONS

The Contracted-out Employment (Notifications, Premium Payment and Miscellaneous Provisions) Regulations 1976

Made - - - -	*3rd February* 1976
Laid before Parliament	*10th February* 1976
Coming into Operation-	
Regulation 9	*2nd March* 1976
Remainder -	*6th April* 1978

The Secretary of State for Social Services, in exercise of the powers conferred upon her by sections 39(1), 43(4) and (6), 44(2), (3) and (6), 45(1) to (3) and 47(7) and (11) of, and paragraphs 1, 3, 6 and 9 of Schedule 2 to, the Social Security Pensions Act 1975(a), and section 166(2)(b)(ii) of the Social Security Act 1975(b), and of all other powers enabling her in that behalf, hereby makes the following regulations:—

Citation, commencement and interpretation

1.—(1) These regulations may be cited as the Contracted-out Employment (Notifications, Premium Payment and Miscellaneous Provisions) Regulations 1976, and shall come into operation in the case of regulation 9 on 2nd March 1976 and in the case of the remainder of the regulations on 6th April 1978.

(2) In these regulations, unless the context otherwise requires—

"the Act" means the Social Security Pensions Act 1975;

"administrator", in relation to an occupational pension scheme, means the person or persons resident in the United Kingdom having the management of the scheme;

"the Board" means the Occupational Pensions Board;

"the Contracting-out regulations" means the Occupational Pension Schemes (Contracting-out) Regulations 1975(c);

"employer" includes a person who, by virtue of regulation 3(2) below, is treated as an employer for the purposes of these regulations;

"responsible paying authority" means—

(*a*) in relation to a public service scheme, the authority responsible for paying the benefits of that scheme;

(*b*) in relation to a scheme, not being a scheme set up or established under an irrevocable trust, where the benefits, or so much of the benefits as represent guaranteed minimum pensions, are secured by means of a

---

(a) 1975 c. 60.   (b) 1975 c. 14.   (c) S.I. 1975/2101 (1975 III, p. 7879).

policy of insurance or annuity contract in accordance with regulation 4 of the Contracting-out regulations, the insurance company or friendly society with which the policy of insurance is taken out or the contract entered into;

(c) in relation to a deferred annuity under regulation 4(3) of the Contracting-out regulations, the insurance company or friendly society with which the insurance policy is taken out or the contract entered into; and

(d) in any other case, the trustees of the scheme;

"scheme" means an occupational pension scheme;

"trustees", in relation to a scheme which is not set up or established under a trust, means the administrator of the scheme;

and other expressions have the same meanings as in the Act.

(3) Any reference in these regulations to any provision made by or contained in any enactment or instrument shall, except in so far as the context otherwise requires, be construed as a reference to that provision as amended or extended by any enactment or instrument and as including a reference to any provision which it re-enacts or replaces, or which may re-enact or replace it, with or without modification.

(4) The rules for the construction of Acts of Parliament contained in the Interpretation Act 1889(a) shall apply for the purposes of the interpretation of these regulations as they apply for the purposes of the interpretation of an Act of Parliament.

Notifications to the Secretary of State

2.—(1) Whenever an earner's service in contracted-out employment is treated as terminated under the provisions of regulation 10 of the Contracting-out regulations the employer of that earner in that service shall, except where the termination is due to the death of the earner or occurs on a date later than the end of the tax year preceding that in which he attains pensionable age, or where the amount of a contributions equivalent premium in respect of that service would not exceed £5, notify the Secretary of State of that termination.

(2) A notification required to be given under paragraph (1) above may be given at any time within the period of one month before the expected date of termination but if not so given shall be given within 6 months from the date on which the service terminated or, if the Secretary of State is satisfied that the notification could not reasonably have been given within that period, such longer period as he may approve in a particular case or class of case.

(3) A notification required to be given under paragraph (1) above shall be given in writing in such form as the Secretary of State may direct and shall contain such information as the Secretary of State may reasonably require for calculating guaranteed minimum pensions and state scheme premiums and for related purposes.

(a) 1889 c. 63.

(4) In any case where, subsequent to the giving of a notification under paragraph (1) above, a responsible paying authority transfers its responsibility for a guaranteed minimum pension to another responsible paying authority, the responsible paying authority making the transfer shall, within one month from the date of such transfer, notify the Secretary of State in writing of the transfer giving such particulars as the Secretary of State may reasonably require to enable him to identify the new responsible paying authority.

(5) An employer to whom a contracting-out certificate has been issued or the trustees of the scheme to which the certificate relates shall, if required to do so by the Secretary of State, in such manner and at such times as the Secretary of State may reasonably require, furnish to the Secretary of State such information relating to members of the scheme to which the contracting-out certificate relates as he may reasonably require for the purpose of calculating guaranteed minimum pensions and for related purposes.

Liability for payment of state scheme premiums

3.—(1) For the purposes of section 44(2) of the Act (payment of accrued rights premiums and pensioner's rights premiums) the prescribed person is the trustees of the scheme.

(2) For the purposes of sections 42 to 45 of the Act the person to be treated as the employer of an employed earner is—

(*a*) subject to sub-paragraphs (*b*) to (*e*) below, in the case of an employed earner, including an employed earner such as is mentioned in paragraph 6 (2) of Schedule 2 to the Act, any person, government department, public authority or body of persons who, under Part I of the Social Security Act 1975, is, or is to be treated as, the secondary Class 1 contributor in respect of that earner;

(*b*) in a case where the employer (within the meaning of sub-paragraph (*a*) above) of an employed earner in contracted-out employment is insolvent, the trustees of the scheme by reference to which the earner's employment is contracted-out employment, so however that except in the case of a premium under section 42(3) of the Act the trustees of the scheme shall be liable by virtue of this sub-paragraph only for so much of any state scheme premium as is not recovered from the insolvent employer as a priority debt by virtue of the provisions of paragraph 3 of Schedule 3 to the Act;

(*c*) in a case where a scheme ceases to be contracted-out, and by virtue of arrangements approved by the Board under section 44(1) of the Act a limited revaluation premium is payable under section 45(1) of the Act, the trustees of that scheme;

(*d*) in a case where an employed earner's employer (within the meaning of sub-paragraph (*a*) above) dies or otherwise ceases to be his employer and the business is. taken over by a new employer and the earner's employment in contracted-out employment is to be treated as con-tinuing under the new employer by virtue of regulation 10(5) of the Contracting-out regulations, that new employer; and

(*e*) in a case where a holding company within the meaning of section 154 of the Companies Act 1948(**a**) or a company which is treated by

---

a) 1948 c. 38.

the Board under regulation 13(1)(*b*)(ii) of the Occupational Pension Schemes (Certification of Employments) Regulations 1975(**a**) as a holding company, has made an election to contract-out in respect of earners employed by one or more subsidiary companies of that company, that holding company or, as the case may be, that company which is treated as a holding company.

(3) Where the amount of a state scheme premium payable under the Act does not exceed £5 the person who would otherwise be liable to pay that premium shall not be so liable, but may nevertheless choose to pay it; and if any such premium is not paid, then for the purpose of extinguishing the earner's entitlement to the guaranteed minimum pension to which the premium relates the premium shall be treated as if it had been paid.

(4) In the event of a contracted-out scheme ceasing to be contracted-out then for the purposes of section 44 (accrued rights premiums and pensioner's rights premiums) and section 45 (limited revaluation premiums) of the Act the Board shall certify to the Secretary of State whether or not an earner's accrued rights to guaranteed minimum pension or a pensioner's rights to guaranteed minimum pension are subject to approved arrangements as mentioned in that section, and in the event of rights which are so subject ceasing to be so subject the Board shall certify to the Secretary of State the date on which those rights ceased to be so subject.

(5) Any liability for the payment of a state scheme premium which is, by any provisions of these regulations, imposed on the trustees of a scheme shall be a liability to make that payment out of the resources of the scheme.

Elections to pay state scheme premiums

4.—(1) An employer's obligation under section 43(4) of the Act (not to discriminate between different earners when making or abstaining from making elections to pay contributions equivalent premiums) shall not apply to—

(*a*) cases where an earner's accrued rights are transferred under section 38 of the Act;

(*b*) married women and widows who, by virtue of regulations made under section 3(2) of the Act, have elected to pay primary Class 1 contributions under the Social Security Act 1975 at a reduced rate;

(*c*) cases where a refund of the earner's contributions to the scheme is precluded to enable the scheme to qualify for the approval of the Commissioners of Inland Revenue for the purposes of Section 208 of the Income and Corporation Taxes Act 1970(**b**) or of Chapter II of Part II of the Finance Act 1970(**c**);

(*d*) cases where, on the death of an earner, his widow becomes entitled to a widow's pension which comprises an amount of pension which has accrued by reference to the earner's service in employment which was not contracted-out employment and a widow's guaranteed minimum pension by reference to the earner's service in contracted-out employment; and

---

(**a**) S.I. 1975/1927 (1975 III, p. 7163). (**b**) 1970 c. 10. (**c**) 1970 c. 24.

(e) cases where the earner has completed less than 5 years' qualifying service for the purposes of Schedule 16 to the Social Security Act 1973(a) (preservation) but where, nevertheless, he is entitled under the rules of the scheme to elect, and he has elected, that his accrued rights shall be preserved:

Provided that in respect of any of the classes of case mentioned in this paragraph an employer shall not discriminate between different earners falling within the same class of case.

(2) An election under section 42(2) or (3), or section 44(6) or 45(3) of he Act shall be notified to the Secretary of State in writing in such form as he Secretary of State may reasonably require for the purpose of identifying he earner to whom the election relates, and such notification shall be given—

(a) in the case of an election under section 42(2) of the Act, within the period beginning one month before the date of termination of the contracted-out employment to which the election relates and ending 6 months after that date;

(b) in the case of an election under section 42(3) of the Act, within a period of 6 months from the date of death in respect of which the election is made; and

(c) in the case of an election under section 44(6) or 45(3) of the Act, within a period ending 6 months after the date on which the Board certify to the Secretary of State, under regulation 3(4) above, that the earner's accrued rights to guaranteed minimum pension or as the case may be the pensioner's rights to guaranteed minimum pension are not, or, as the case may be, have ceased to be, subject to approved arrangements.

(3) On application being made to him for that purpose the Secretary of State may, in any particular case or class of case, extend the periods mentioned in paragraph (2) above for the making of an election to pay a state scheme premium if it appears to him that the circumstances are such that an election could not reasonably be made within the specified period.

Time for payment of state scheme premiums

5.—(1) Subject to paragraph (3) below any state scheme premium payable under the Act shall be paid on or before whichever is the later of the following days—

(a) the day 6 months after the date of termination of contracted-out employment in respect of which the premium is payable; and

(b) the day one month after the day on which the Secretary of State sends to the person liable to pay the premium a notice certifying the amount of the premium payable.

(2) On application made to him for that purpose the Secretary of State may, in any particular case or class of case, extend the period within which, under paragraph (1) above, a state scheme premium is required to be paid—

---

a) 1973 c. 38.

(*a*) by up to 6 months if he is satisfied that the circumstances are such that payment of the premium could not reasonably be required to be made within that period; and

(*b*) by such further period as he considers reasonable if he is satisfied that to require earlier payment of the premium would be prejudicial to the interests of the earner in respect of whom the premium is payable or of the generality of members of the scheme.

(3) In cases where a state scheme premium has become payable by reason of the fact that a contracted-out scheme has ceased to be contracted-out and an earner's accrued rights to guaranteed minimum pension or a pensioner's rights to guaranteed minimum pension under that scheme which are not the subject of approved arrangements under section 44 of the Act or, having been so subject, have ceased to be so subject, references in paragraph (1)(*a*) above to the date of termination of contracted-out employment shall be read as references to the date on which the Board certify under regulation 3(4) above that the earner's rights are not subject to approved arrangements or have ceased to be so subject.

Payment in lieu of benefit and delay in refund for purposes of employer's right of recovery

6.—(1) For the purposes of section 47(10) of the Act (payments in lieu of benefit) a payment in lieu of benefit shall include a payment made or to be made out of the resources of the scheme in or towards the provision of deferred benefits for the earner.

(2) Where on the coming to an end of an employed earner's service in contracted-out employment he (or, by virtue of a connection with him, any other person) is or may be entitled to a refund of any payments made under a contracted-out scheme by or in respect of him towards the provision of benefits under the scheme, the following provisions of this regulation shall apply for the purpose of enabling any right of recovery conferred by section 47 of the Act to be exercised.

(3) Where in such a case a state scheme premium falls to be paid in respect of the earner under the Act, the person liable for the refund shall not, after he has been given such notice for the purpose of this regulation as is hereinafter described (hereafter in this regulation called a "notice of delay"), make the refund in whole or in part until the expiration of the period of delay specified in paragraph (4) of this regulation:

Provided that this paragraph shall not apply to so much, if any, of the refund as exceeds the amount certified by the Secretary of State under section 47(2) of the Act.

(4) The period of delay referred to in paragraph (3) of this regulation shall be the period beginning with the giving of the notice of delay and ending with the expiration of 4 weeks after the payment of the state scheme premium or any part of it, or 4 weeks after the end of the prescribed period for the payment of the state scheme premium, whichever first occurs.

(5) A notice of delay shall be a notice in writing given by the person who is liable for the payment of the state scheme premium (hereafter in this

egulation called "the liable person"), relating either to a particular case or
o a class or classes of case and containing the following particulars: —

> (a) the name of the earner or such particulars as will sufficiently identify
> the class or classes of cases concerned;

> (b) such particulars as will sufficiently identify the refund or refunds
> concerned; and

> (c) a memorandum in a form approved by the Secretary of State giving
> brief particulars of the effect of paragraphs (3) and (4) of this regulation.

(6) Every liable person who has given a notice of delay shall from time to
time inform any person to whom he has given that notice of the ending of
the period of delay in relation to any refund affected by the notice.

Alternative to limited revaluation premium

7.—(1) For the purposes of section 45(1)(b) of the Act (exclusion from
liability to pay a limited revaluation premium), where a scheme provides,
under section 35(7) of the Act, for the earnings factors of an earner whose
service in contracted-out employment by reference to the scheme is terminated
before he attains the scheme's normal pension age to be determined without
reference to any order that comes into force under section 21 of the Act after
the relevant year in which his service is terminated, then, subject to the
following provisions of this regulation, there shall be no liability to pay a
limited revaluation premium in respect of such an earner if the provisions
made by the scheme under section 35(7) of the Act conform with the following
additional requirement, namely that the rate of increase specified by the
scheme for the purposes of the said section 35(7) is at least $8\frac{1}{2}$ per cent com-
pound for each relevant year after the year in which the earner's service is
terminated, notwithstanding that the amount by which an earnings factor for
that year equal to that weekly equivalent would be increased by any order
or orders that come into force under section 21 of the Act before the end
of the final relevant year is less than the amount produced by that rate.

(2) Paragraph (1) above applies only so as to permit the same such provision to be made for all members of the scheme.

(3) Regulation 8(7) of these regulations applies for the purposes of this
regulation as it applies for the purposes of section 35(7) of the Act.

Miscellaneous provisions

8.—(1) Where a contracted-out scheme is being wound up and the person
who is liable to pay an accrued rights premium or a pensioner's rights
premium fails to pay that premium within the period prescribed by regulation
5(1) above, or such longer period as the Secretary of State may allow under
regulation 5(2) above, then, if the Secretary of State is satisfied that the failure
to pay was not with the consent or connivance of, or attributable to any
negligence on the part of, the person in respect of whom the premium is
payable, that premium shall, for the purpose of extinguishing the earner's
or pensioner's accrued rights to guaranteed minimum pension under the
scheme, be treated as having been paid within the prescribed period.

(2) Where a state scheme premium is wrongly paid, or paid as to the wrong amount, the Secretary of State may treat all or part of that premium as paid (wholly or in part) in discharge of a liability for another premium (where the premium was paid by the employer within the meaning of regulation 3(2) (*a*) above) for contributions under Part I of the Social Security Act 1975.

(3) Subject to paragraph (2) above the Secretary of State shall refund a state scheme premium if—

　(*a*) that premium was paid in error; or

　(*b*) he is satisfied that the employment to which the premium relates will be linked with another employment in the circumstances set out in regulation 10(2) and (3) of the Contracting-out regulations; or

　(*c*) he is satisfied that the earner in respect of whom the premium was paid has entered into employment which is contracted-out employment by reference to the same contracted-out scheme as that by which the employment to which the premium relates was contracted-out employment, and that for the purpose of calculating the earner's accrued rights under the scheme the 2 employments will be linked; or

　(*d*) he is satisfied that a transfer of the earner's accrued rights will be made in accordance with section 38 of the Act,

and where a premium is refunded under the provisions of this paragraph the earner's accrued rights under the scheme, which were extinguished by payment of the premium, shall be restored.

(4) A refund shall be made under paragraph (3) above only if an application is made in writing, in such form as the Secretary of State may reasonably require for the purpose.

(5) In paragraph (3) above "error" means, and means only, an error which—

　(*a*) is made at the time of the payment, and

　(*b*) relates to some present or past matter.

(6) Where an earner has been employed concurrently in 2 or more contracted-out employments, on the termination of one or more of which one or more contributions equivalent premiums are paid the amount, or the aggregate amount, of which has the effect that the National Insurance Fund has gained in all, by reference to the employment or employments in respect of which the premium or premiums have been paid, a greater amount than it would have gained from Class 1 contributions under the Social Security Act 1975 if the employment or employments had not been contracted-out, there shall be paid out of the National Insurance Fund to the earner (or his estate) an amount equal to that amount which bears the same proportion to the amount of the excess as the reduction, under section 27(2) of the Act, in the normal percentage of primary Class 1 contributions bears to the total reduction under that sub-section in the total normal percentage of Class 1 contributions.

(7) Where, under section 38 of the Act, a transfer of an earner's accrued rights under a contracted-out scheme is made, or is to be made, to another

ontracted-out scheme the earner's service in contracted-out employment by
eference to the first mentioned scheme shall, for the purposes of section 35(7)
f the Act (exclusion of guaranteed minimum pension from full revaluation)
e treated as not having terminated, notwithstanding that, by virtue of the
rovisions of regulation 10 of the Contracting-out regulations, it is otherwise
reated as having terminated.

Amendment of the Contracting-out regulations

9.—(1) The Contracting-out regulations shall be amended in accordance
with the following provisions of this regulation.

(2) Regulation 8 of the Contracting-out regulations shall be amended by
adding at the end the following new paragraph—

"(4) The condition in paragraph (1)(b) above shall not apply in cases
where the scheme is being wound up or an earner retires before the age of
65 if a man or 60 if a woman and if a premium under section 42 (contributions equivalent), section 44 (accrued rights) or section 45 (limited
revaluation) of the Act has been paid, or is treated under regulation 3(3)
of the Contracted-out Employment (Notifications, Premium Payment and
Miscellaneous Provisions) Regulations 1976 as having been paid, or where
provision has been made under regulation 7 of those regulations, provided
that—

(a) for the purpose of paragraph (1)(c) above the aggregate amount of
benefit which has accrued to the earner at the date of winding up or, as
the case may be, of his retirement, increased, where appropriate, in
accordance with section 35(7) of the Act or in accordance with provision made under regulation 7 of the Contracted-out Employment
(Notifications, Premium Payment and Miscellaneous Provisions)
Regulations 1976, in either case to the amount that would have been
payable at pensionable age, shall be treated as the amount of benefit
currently payable to him under the scheme;

(b) in the case of early retirement commutation is not permitted before
the date on which the pension would otherwise become payable; and

(c) in cases where the earner is a member of more than one scheme
relating to the same employment all those schemes are being wound up
or, as the case may be, he is treated by all those schemes as having
retired and, in each case, all those schemes have paid a contributions
equivalent premium, accrued rights premium or a limited revaluation
premium, or have made provision under regulation 7 of the Contracted-
out Employment (Notifications, Premium Payment and Miscellaneous
Provisions) Regulations 1976."

(3) Regulation 10 of the Contracting-out regulations shall be amended as
follows: —

(a) in the first line of paragraph (1) for "paragraph" substitute "paragraphs", and after "(2)" insert "and (7)";

(b) at the end add the following new paragraph—

"(7) In cases where an earner is employed concurrently in 2 or more
contracted-out employments by reference to the same scheme and with
the same employer his employment in any one of those employments

shall not be treated as having terminated by reason only of th
circumstances mentioned in paragraph (1)(*a*) and (*b*) above until bot
or all such employments are treated as having so terminated."

Barbara Castle,
Secretary of State for Social Services
3rd February 1976.

EXPLANATORY NOTE

(This Note is not part of the Regulations.)

These Regulations contain provisions relating to the giving to the Secretary
of State of notification of various matters connected with contracted-out
employment under the Social Security Pensions Act 1975; liability for, and
payment of, state scheme premiums, and miscellaneous matters arising, under
that Act. These regulations also amend the Occupational Pension Schemes
(Contracting-out) Regulations 1975.

Regulation 2 contains provisions as to the circumstances, time and manner
in or within which a notification of termination of contracted-out employment
is to be given. Regulation 3 relates to liability for payment of state scheme
premiums. Regulation 4 relates to the making of elections to pay state scheme
premiums. Regulation 5 prescribes the period within which a state scheme
premium must be paid. Regulation 6 contains provisions as to payments in
lieu of benefit and to delay in making refunds for the purposes of an
employer's right of recovery under the Act. Regulation 7 provides an alternative to limited revaluation premiums under section 45 of the Act. Regulation 8
contains miscellaneous provisions and regulation 9 amends the Occupational
Pension Schemes (Contracting-out) Regulations 1975.

STATUTORY INSTRUMENTS

1976 No. 144 (C.5)

TERMS AND CONDITIONS OF EMPLOYMENT

The Employment Protection Act 1975 (Commencement No. 2) Order 1976

Made - - - - 3rd February 1976

The Secretary of State, in exercise of the powers conferred on him by section 129 of the Employment Protection Act 1975(**a**) and of all other powers enabling him in that behalf, hereby makes the following Order:—

Citation

1. This Order may be cited as the Employment Protection Act 1975 (Commencement No. 2) Order 1976.

Commencement

2. The provisions of the Employment Protection Act 1975 specified in the Schedules hereto shall come into operation—

    (*a*) in the case of the provisions mentioned in Schedule 1, on 8th March 1976; and

    (*b*) in the case of the provisions mentioned in Schedule 2, on 20th April 1976.

Transitional provisions and savings

3.—(1) Sections 99 and 100 shall not apply to any dismissal which, pursuant to a qualifying notice given before the date on which those sections come into operation, is to take effect before the expiry of the period of 90 days beginning with that date.

(2) In determining for the purposes of section 99(3) or section 100(1) whether an employer is proposing to dismiss as redundant 100 or more, or, as the case may be, 10 or more employees, no account shall be taken of employees whose proposed dismissals, pursuant to a qualifying notice given before the date on which those sections come into operation, are to take effect before the expiry of the period of 90 days beginning with that date.

(3) For the purposes of paragraphs (1) and (2) above a qualifying notice is a notice complying with the requirements of section 1(1) of the Contracts of Employment Act 1972(**b**) (rights of employee to minimum period of notice) and the relevant terms of the contract of employment.

(4) Section 99(3) shall not apply to any dismissal which is to take effect on or after the date on which section 99 comes into operation where consultation with trade union representatives began before that date.

(**a**) 1975 c. 71.   (**b**) 1972 c. 53.

(5) For the purposes of paragraph (4) above consultation shall not be taken to have begun unless the employer has disclosed in writing to the relevant trade union representatives the matters specified in paragraphs (*a*), (*b*) and (*c*) of section 99(5).

(6) In a case falling within paragraph (4) above section 100(1) shall have effect as if the words "at least 90 days" and "at least 60 days" in paragraphs (i) and (ii) respectively were omitted.

3rd February 1976.

Michael Foot,

Secretary of State for Employment.

Article 2

SCHEDULE 1
PROVISIONS COMING INTO OPERATION ON 8TH MARCH 1976

Provisions of the Act	Subject matter of provisions
Section 85(1), so far as it relates to the purposes of section 102	Calculation of normal working hours and a week's pay
Section 99	Duty of employer to consult trade union representatives on redundancy
Section 100	Duty of employer to notify Secretary of State of certain redundancies
Section 101	Complaint by trade union and protective award
Section 102	Entitlement under protective award
Section 103	Complaint by employee to industrial tribunal
Section 104	Reduction of rebate on failure to notify redundancies
Section 105	Offence and proceedings
Section 106	Supplementary
Section 107	Power to adapt foregoing provisions in case of collective agreements on redundancies
Section 108	General provisions as to industrial tribunals and conciliation officers
Section 110, so far as it relates to sections 99 to 107	Death of employee or employer
Section 113, so far as it relates to remuneration paid under a protective award under section 101	Payments which are to be treated as earnings for social security purposes
Section 117, so far as it relates to any offence under section 105	Offences by bodies corporate
Section 119, so far as it relates to sections 99 and 100	Excluded classes of employment
Section 126(1), so far as it relates to the definition of "business", "dismiss", "dismissal" and "effective date of termination", (5), (6) and (7)	Interpretation
Schedule 4, to the extent mentioned above in relation to section 85	Calculation of normal working hours and a week's pay
Schedule 12, to the extent mentioned above in relation to section 110	Death of employee or employer

SCHEDULE 2 Article 2

PROVISIONS COMING INTO OPERATION ON 20TH APRIL 1976

Provisions of the Act	Subject matter of provisions
Section 63(1) and (2)(d)	Priority of certain debts on insolvency
Section 64, apart from paragraph (d) of subsection (3) and subsection (6)	Employee's rights on insolvency of employer
Section 65	Payment of unpaid contributions to occupational pension scheme
Section 66	Complaint to industrial tribunal
Section 67	Transfer to the Secretary of State of rights and remedies
Section 68	Power of Secretary of State to obtain information in connection with applications
Section 69	Interpretation of sections 64 to 68
Section 110, so far as it relates to sections 63 to 69	Death of employee or employer
Section 119, so far as it relates to sections 64 and 65	Excluded classes of employment
Section 117, so far as it relates to any offence under section 68	Offences by bodies corporate
Section 125(2), so far as it relates to paragraph 8 of Schedule 17	Transitional provisions in relation to sections 64 and 65
Schedule 12, to the extent mentioned above in relation to section 110	Death of employee or employer
Schedule 17, paragraph 8	Transitional provisions in relation to sections 64 and 65

EXPLANATORY NOTE

(*This Note is not part of the Order.*)

This Order brings into operation on 8th March, 1976 the provisions of the Employment Protection Act 1975 specified in Schedule 1. These provisions relate to the procedure for handling redundancies.

The Order also brings into operation on 20th April, 1976 the provisions of the Employment Protection Act 1975 specified in Schedule 2. These provisions relate to the rights of employees on the insolvency of their employer.

STATUTORY INSTRUMENTS

1976 No. 146

PENSIONS

The Pensions Increase (Northern Ireland Reserved Services) Regulations 1976

Made - - - -	*2nd February* 1976
Laid before Parliament	11*th February* 1976
Coming into Operation	4*th March* 1976

The Minister for the Civil Service, in exercise of the powers conferred on him by section 5(2) and (4) of the Pensions (Increase) Act 1971(a) and of all other powers enabling him in that behalf, hereby makes the following Regulations:—

1. These Regulations may be cited as the Pensions Increase (Northern Ireland Reserved Services) Regulations 1976, and shall come into operation on 4th March 1976.

2.—(1) Any reference in these Regulations to any enactment is a reference to that enactment as amended by or under, and includes a reference to that enactment as extended or applied by, any other enactment; and in this paragraph "enactment" includes an enactment of the Parliament of Northern Ireland.

(2) The Interpretation Act 1889(b) shall apply for the interpretation of these Regulations as it applies for the interpretation of an Act of Parliament.

3. The Pensions (Increase) Act 1971 shall have effect in relation to the pensions specified in the Schedule to these Regulations as if they were specified in Part I of Schedule 2 to that Act.

4. Any increase of pension payable by virtue of these Regulations shall take effect from 1st October 1975.

Given under the official seal of the Minister for the Civil Service on 2nd February 1976.

(L.S.)

C. R. Morris,
Minister of State,
Civil Service Department.

(a) 1971 c. 56.   (b) 1889 c. 63.

SCHEDULE

PENSIONS TO WHICH THE PENSIONS (INCREASE) ACT 1971 IS TO APPLY

1. A pension payable out of moneys provided by Parliament by virtue of section 12 of the Administration of Justice Act (Northern Ireland) 1954(a) (caretakers of court-houses).

2. A pension payable by way of compensation to Civil Defence employees under Regulations made under section 4 of the Public Expenditure and Receipts Act (Northern Ireland) 1968(b).

3. A pension payable by virtue of section 6 of the Summary Jurisdiction and Criminal Justice Act (Northern Ireland) 1935(c) (resident magistrates).

EXPLANATORY NOTE

(This Note is not part of the Regulations.)

These Regulations apply the Pensions (Increase) Act 1971 to the pensions payable in respect of service in certain offices and occupations in Northern Ireland which are now reserved services by virtue of the Northern Ireland Constitution Act 1973, and the pensions are payable out of the Consolidated Fund of the United Kingdom or out of moneys provided by the Parliament of the United Kingdom.

(a) 1954 c. 9 (N.I.).
(b) 1968 c. 8 (N.I.).
(c) 1935 c. 13 (N.I.).

STATUTORY INSTRUMENTS

1976 No. 147

CHARITIES

The Charities (The Marine Society) Order 1976

Laid before Parliament in draft

Made -	-	-	-	*2nd February* 1976
Coming into Operation			16*th February* 1976	

Whereas the Charity Commissioners for England and Wales have, in pursuance of section 19(1) of the Charities Act 1960(**a**), settled the Scheme set out in the Appendix to this Order with a view to its being given effect under that section:

And Whereas the said Scheme does not alter any statutory provision contained in or having effect under any public general Act of Parliament:

Now, therefore, I, the Right Honourable Roy Harris Jenkins, one of Her Majesty's Principal Secretaries of State, in pursuance of section 19(2) of the Charities Act 1960, hereby make the following Order:—

1. This Order may be cited as the Charities (The Marine Society) Order 1976 and shall come into operation on the fourteenth day after the day on which it is made.

2. The Scheme set out in the Appendix to this Order shall have effect.

Roy Jenkins,
One of Her Majesty's Principal
Secretaries of State.

Home Office,
    Whitehall.

2nd February 1976.

(**a**) 1960 c. 58.

APPENDIX

Scheme for the Administration of the Charity Called The Marine Society

Whereas the Charity called The Marine Society is now regulated by:

(1) the Act of Parliament of the year 1772 intituled An Act for incorporating the Members of a Society, commonly called The Marine Society, and their Successors, to be elected as therein is mentioned; and for the better empowering and enabling them to carry on their charitable and useful Designs(a);

(2) the Marine Society Act 1957(b);

(3) the Marine Society Act, 1963(c):

And Whereas the Charity has made application to the Charity Commissioners for a Scheme for the administration thereof:

And Whereas it appears to the Charity Commissioners that a Scheme should be established for the administration of the Charity but that it is necessary for the Scheme to alter the provisions made by the said Acts of 1772, 1957 and 1963:

And Whereas in pursuance of section 21 of the Charities Act 1960 public notice of the Charity Commissioners' proposals for this Scheme has been given and no representations have been received by the Charity Commissioners in respect thereof:

Now, therefore, the Charity Commissioners for England and Wales, in pursuance of section 19(1) of the Charities Act 1960, hereby settle the following Scheme:—

SCHEME

1. *Variation of trusts.*—The provisions of the above-mentioned Acts of 1772, 1957 and 1963, other than the provisions of the said Act of 1772 relating to the incorporation of the Charity called The Marine Society shall henceforth cease to have effect in relation to the Charity.

2. *Administration of Charity.*—(1) Subject to the Bye-laws made and to any directions, restrictions or conditions given or imposed by the Governors of the Charity, the persons comprising from time to time the Council of the Charity hereinafter constituted shall have the general control and management of the day to day administration of the Charity.

(2) The Council shall in particular:

(*a*) manage the financial and other business of the Charity;

(*b*) keep proper books of account with respect to the affairs of the Charity and prepare consecutive statements of account consisting on each occasion of an Income and Expenditure Account relating to a period of not more than fifteen months and a balance sheet relating to the end of that period;

(*c*) appoint a secretary and other paid officers and servants and determine the terms and conditions of their employment within the limits permitted by law; and

(*d*) perform such other functions as the Governors from time to time direct.

(3) Subject to and in accordance with the Bye-laws the Council may from time to time appoint such committees as it thinks fit consisting either wholly or as to not less than two-thirds of persons who are members of the Council, and may delegate to such committees the exercise of any of its powers and functions.

(a) 12 Geo. 3 c. 67.   (b) 5 & 6 Eliz. 2 c. ix.   (c) 1963 c. xiii.

OBJECT

3. *Object*.—(1) The object of the Charity shall be the advancement of the educatio and the relief in need of seafarers in one or more of the following ways:

(*a*) The provision in ships and on shore of a comprehensive library service for the use of seafarers;

(*b*) The assistance of persons preparing for, or entering upon, a seafaring career by the provision of training, the payment of fees, maintenance and other expenses and the making of loans;

(*c*) The award to seafarers of scholarships, bursaries and maintenance allowances tenable at any nautical or other school or training establishment;

(*d*) The making of grants or loans to nautical or other schools or training establishments which are Charities or to other organisations established for charitable purposes only which provide facilities for and encourage young persons to become seafarers;

(*e*) The promotion in other ways of the education of seafarers;

(*f*) The promotion of scientific or other research of particular benefit to seafarers;

(*g*) The provision and carrying on of hostels providing accommodation for seafarers in need of the same;

(*h*) The provision in the interests of the social welfare of seafarers of facilities for recreation and other leisure-time occupation, being facilities which will improve their conditions of life and of which they have need by reason of their social and economic circumstances; and

(*i*) The relief of poverty and distress among seafarers, their widows, children and other dependants, by the making of grants or loans or otherwise.

(2) In this clause the expression "seafarers" means persons of all ranks and grades who have served, are serving or intend to serve in the Royal Navy and the British Merchant Navy and Fishing Fleets and persons who are serving in the navies, merchant navies and fishing fleets of such other countries as the Governors of the Charity from time to time determine.

(3) In furthering the said object the Governors, Council and officers of the Charity shall have regard to maintaining the efficiency of the Royal Navy and the British Merchant Navy and Fishing Fleets.

GOVERNORS

4. *Governors*.—(1) Notwithstanding the provisions of the said Act of 1772 relating to the constitution of the Corporation, the Governors of the Charity shall consist henceforth of the following persons—

the President for the time being of the Charity,

the Vice-Presidents for the time being of the Charity,

Life Governors, being all persons who have subscribed to the funds of the Charity such sum or aggregate sums or such sums for such periods as shall from time to time be prescribed in the Bye-laws of the Charity as qualifying the subscriber for Life Governorship,

Nominated Governors, being all persons who have been appointed by corporations, societies or charities which have subscribed to the funds of the Charity such sum or aggregate sums or such sums for such periods as shall from time to time be prescribed in the Bye-laws as qualifying the subscriber to nominate a Nominated Governor, and

Annual Governors, being all persons who have subscribed to the funds of the Charity such sum as shall from time to time be prescribed in the Bye-laws as qualifying the subscriber for Annual Governorship.

(2) The appointment of a Nominated Governor shall be made at a meeting convened and held according to the ordinary practice of the nominating body. The person appointed may be but need not be a member of the nominating body.

(3) Every Life Governor shall hold office for life. Every Nominated Governor shall hold office until the date of the appointment of his successor by the body nominating him. Every Annual Governor shall hold office for one year from the date of the receipt of the last subscription made by him to the funds of the Charity.

(4) The persons holding office as Governors of the Charity at the date of the coming into effect of this Scheme shall continue to hold office as Life Governors under the provisions of this Scheme.

5. *Annual courts.*—The Governors of the Charity shall hold an annual court in the month of May in every year or as soon as practicable thereafter at such time and place as the Governors shall determine. At the annual court the Governors shall receive and consider the report and accounts of the Charity for the preceding year, shall elect officers of the Charity, members of the Council of the Charity and auditors for the ensuing year and shall transact any other business of which one month's notice shall have been given.

6. *Special courts.*—A special court of the Governors may be summoned at any time by the President of the Charity, the Council or any 20 Governors upon one month's notice being given to all the other Governors of the matters to be discussed.

7. *President.*—(1) Except at first as hereinafter provided the Governors shall at an annual court of the Governors elect one of their number to be President of the Charity. The President shall hold office for a period which shall be determined at his election by the Governors or until resignation.

(2) In the event of a vacancy in the office of President the Chairman of the Council of the Charity hereinafter referred to or, if he refuses to act or there is no Chairman, a person nominated by the Council shall be the President of the Charity and shall hold office until the election of his successor at the next ensuing annual court of the Governors.

8. *First President.*—The first President of the Charity shall be the Right Honourable Walter Leslie, Viscount Runciman of Doxford, O.B.E., A.F.C., and shall hold office for life or until resignation.

9. *Vice-Presidents.*—Except at first as hereinafter provided the Governors shall at an annual court of the Governors elect such number of Vice-Presidents as the Governors from time to time determine. Every Vice-President shall hold office for life or until resignation. A Vice-President may be elected to the Council of the Charity.

10. *First Vice-Presidents.*—The following persons shall be the first Vice-Presidents of the Charity:

The Right Honourable Charles Marsham Earl of Romney, D.L., J.P.,
Sir Gilmour Jenkins, K.C.B., K.B.E., M.C.,
Admiral Sir Geoffrey John Audley Miles, K.C.B., K.C.S.I.,
Admiral Sir Alan Kenneth Scott-Moncrieff, K.C.B., C.B.E., D.S.O.,
Charles Frederick Bernard Arthur,
Frank George Griffith Carr, C.B., C.B.E.,
Ernest Charles de Rougemont, C.B.E.,
Frederick John Alfred Beatty Everard,
William Marcus Graham,
George Palmer Holt,
Michael Henry Marsham,
Sidney Arthur Newton,
Commander Alan Westbury Preston, R.N.,
Captain George Whalley Wakeford, O.B.E.

11. *Quorum.*—There shall be a quorum when seven Governors are present at a court of the Governors.

12. *Voting.*—Every matter shall be determined by the majority of votes of the Governors present and voting on the question. In case of equality of votes the President shall have a casting vote whether he has or has not voted previously on the same question but no Governor in any other circumstances shall give more than one vote.

13. *General power to make bye-laws.*—Within the limits prescribed by this Scheme the Governors shall have power to make and alter bye-laws for the management of the Charity and for the conduct of their business and in particular but without prejudice to the generality of this provision with respect to all, or any, of the following matters:

(a) the proceedings at courts of the Governors,

(b) the election of officers of the Charity and members of the Council,

(c) the sums to be subscribed to the funds of the Charity for the purpose of qualifying persons to be Life Governors or Annual Governors, and corporations, societies or charities to nominate a Nominated Governor,

(d) the appointment, dismissal, remuneration and duties of persons employed by the Charity,

(e) the keeping of minute books and books of account,

(f) the deposit of money at a bank and the signing of cheques,

(g) the appointment, proceedings and business of committees of the Council and of sub-committees of such committees.

14. *Treasurer.*—(1) There shall be a Treasurer of the Charity who, except at first as hereinafter provided, shall be elected at an annual court of the Governors, and shall hold office for the period for which he is elected or until resignation.

(2) The first Treasurer of the Charity shall be Christopher Edward Thornton, F.C.A., of Great House Close, Souldern, in the County of Oxfordshire, Esquire.

(3) In the event of a vacancy in the office of Treasurer the Council shall appoint one of its number to be the Treasurer until the election of a successor.

THE COUNCIL

15. *Constitution of Council.*—The Council of the Charity shall consist of the following persons (hereinafter referred to as Members):

The President of the Charity, and

The Treasurer of the Charity, both for the time being,

Not more than 30 and not less than 15 Elected Members, who shall be elected, except at first as hereinafter provided, at an annual court of the Governors, and

Not more than five Co-optative Members, who shall be appointed by a resolution of the Council.

16. *Elected Members.*—(1) The term of office of an Elected Member of the Council shall, except at first as hereinafter provided, commence at the termination of the annual court at which he is elected.

(2) At every annual court one-third of the Elected Members of the Council for the time being, or, if the number of Elected Members of the Council is not a multiple of three then the number nearest to but not exceeding one-third, shall retire. A retiring Elected Member of the Council shall retain his office until the termination of the annual court at which his successor is elected or until it is determined not to fill his place. The Elected Members of the Council to retire shall for the first three annual courts from the date of the coming into effect of this Scheme in the absence of agreement be selected from among them by ballot and thereafter the Elected Members of the Council to retire shall be those who have been longest in office since their last election. As between Elected Members of equal seniority, the Elected Members to retire shall

in the absence of agreement be selected from among them by ballot. A retiring Elected Member shall be eligible for re-election. The Charity at the annual court at which an Elected Member of the Council retires in manner aforesaid may fill up the vacated office by electing a member thereto, and in default the retiring Member shall be deemed to have been re-elected unless at such meeting it is resolved not to fill up such vacated office.

17. *Co-optative Members.*—The term of office of a Co-optative Member of the Council shall commence on the passing of the resolution of the Council by which he is appointed and be as specified therein; and on the expiration thereof he shall be eligible for re-appointment.

18. *Termination of membership.*—Any Member of the Council who is adjudicated a bankrupt or who makes a composition or arrangement with his creditors or who is incapacitated from acting or who communicates in writing to the Council a wish to resign shall thereupon cease to be a Member.

19. *First Elected Members.*—The following persons shall be the first Elected Members of the Council and shall hold office from the date of the coming into effect of this Scheme:

Lieutenant-Commander Kenneth Roy Alger, R.D., R.N.R.,
Roy Austin Arnold,
Commander William Ashton, D.S.C., R.N.,
Captain John Arthur Neale Bezant, D.S.C., R.D., R.N.R.,
Glynden Ewart Carter,
Bernard Gilbert Stancombe Cayzer,
Geoffrey Ernest Cook,
Rear-Admiral Edward Findlay Gueritz, C.B., O.B.E., D.S.C.,
Captain Raymond Hart, C.B.E., D.S.O., D.S.C., R.N.,
Richard Henry Hobhouse,
Captain Gilbert Roy Hughes, M.B.E.,
William Furlonger Hunt,
Richard Ewart Hutson,
Philip Charles Izard,
Sir Gilmour Jenkins, K.C.B., K.B.E., M.C.,
The Reverend Prebendary Thomas Phoebus Kerfoot, M.B.E., A.L.C.D.,
Walter Kerr,
George Alfred Brown King,
Captain Alan Coulson Manson, C.B.E.,
Captain Ronald Charles Marsh,
Walter Marshall,
Michael Henry Marsham,
Captain Robert Novis Mayo, C.B.E.,
Captain George William Merrick,
Kevin Anthony Murphy,
Eric Nevin,
David Royden Rooper,
Rear-Admiral Maurice James Ross, C.B., D.S.C.,
Captain George Whalley Wakeford, O.B.E.,
William Laurence Woof.

20. *Chairman and Vice-Chairman.*—(1) There shall be a Chairman and Vice-Chairman of the Council who shall be Members thereof and shall be appointed at its first meeting in each year after the termination of the annual court of the Governors or on the occurrence of a vacancy.

(2) The Chairman and Vice-Chairman shall each hold office until resignation, ceasing to be a Member of the Council or the termination of the annual court of the Governors held next after his appointment whichever shall first occur.

(3) Any Member of the Council who has previously held office as Chairman or Vice-Chairman shall be eligible for re-appointment.

MEETINGS AND PROCEEDINGS OF COUNCIL

21. *Ordinary Meetings.*—The Council shall hold not less than three ordinary meetings in each year. A special meeting may be summoned at any time by the Chairman or any two Members upon seven days' notice being given to all the other Members of the matters to be discussed.

22. *First Meeting.*—The first meeting of the Council under this Scheme shall be summoned by Captain Charles Wickham Malins, D.S.O., D.S.C., R.N., of Old Farm Place, Catsfield, in the County of East Sussex, as soon as conveniently may be after the date on which this Scheme comes into effect or, if he fails to summon a meeting for two months after that date, by any two Members.

23. *Quorum.*—There shall be a quorum when not less than seven Members are present at a meeting.

24. *Chairman.*—The Chairman of the Council or, in his absence, the Vice-Chairman shall preside at meetings of the Council. If both the Chairman and Vice-Chairman are absent from any meeting or part of a meeting, the Members present shall appoint a Chairman before any other business is transacted.

25. *Voting.*—Every matter shall be determined by a majority of the Members present at a meeting and voting on the question. In the case of equality of votes on any question the Chairman of the meeting shall have a casting vote.

26. *Attendance of non-members.*—The Council may invite persons who are not Members to attend any of its meetings and any such person may be heard but shall not be entitled to vote thereat.

27. *Validation of proceedings.*—The proceedings of the Council shall not be invalidated by any vacancy in their number or by any defect in the appointment or qualification of any Member.

28. *General power to make regulations.*—Within the limits prescribed by the foregoing provisions of this Scheme and subject to the provisions of the Bye-laws the Council shall make regulations for the conduct of its proceedings and management of its business in such manner as it from time to time determines.

POWERS OF COUNCIL

29. *Powers of Council.*—In furthering the object of the Charity and for the purpose of the exercise of its functions under this Scheme the Council may—

(1) accept any donations, grants and legacies for the general purposes of the Charity or for any special purpose connected therewith and take steps to procure such donations, grants and legacies;

(2) co-operate with and assist other charitable organisations financially, by co-ordination of activities or otherwise;

(3) collect, circulate, publish and distribute (gratuitously or otherwise) information relating to the activities of the Charity;

(4) purchase, print, manufacture, publish and distribute newspapers, journals, books, leaflets, video-tapes, films, records and other means of communication whether or not of a wholly novel kind;

(5) pay or subscribe to funds or schemes for the provision of pensions and retirement benefits for employees of the Charity, their widows, children and other dependants;

(6) grant pensions and retirement benefits to or for employees and former employees of the Charity and to the widows, children and other dependants of deceased employees who are in necessitous circumstances; and

(7) do all such other lawful acts and things as are incidental or conducive thereto.

POWERS OF INVESTMENT

30. *Powers of investment.*—(1) The Charity may divide property now or hereafter belonging to the Charity or held by the Charity upon special trusts administered in connection with the Charity (but subject in the case of the last-mentioned property to any special powers or provisions affecting that property) into two parts in the proportions following, namely—

One fourth to a part consisting of narrower-range investments within the meaning of the Trustee Investments Act 1961(a), and

Three-fourths to a part consisting of wider-range investments within the meaning of that Act.

(2) In all other respects the powers of investment of the Charity shall be exercised in accordance with the provisions of the last-mentioned Act.

GENERAL PROVISIONS

31. *Saving of interests.*—Any exhibition, bursary, maintenance allowance, grant, loan or other like emolument or payment awarded or made on or before the date on which this Scheme comes into effect shall be maintained, held and continued, as nearly as may be, as if this Scheme had not been made.

32. *Governors, etc. not to be personally interested.*—No Governor, Member or any member of any committee or sub-committee exercising powers or functions under the provisions of this Scheme shall take or hold any interest in any property belonging to or held in trust for the Charity otherwise than as a Trustee for the purpose thereof, or receive any remuneration or be interested in the supply of work or goods, at the cost of the Charity.

33. *Questions of construction.*—Any question as to the construction of this Scheme may be referred to the Charity Commissioners for their opinion or advice in accordance with the provisions of section 24 of the Charities Act 1960.

Sealed by Order of the Charity Commissioners on the 29th day of October 1975.

(L.S.)

EXPLANATORY NOTE

(This Note is not part of the Order.)

This Order gives effect to a Scheme of the Charity Commissioners relating to the Marine Society which was founded in 1756 principally for placing men and boys in service at sea. The Scheme makes new provision for the government and administration of the charity and for its purposes. The new purposes are set out in clause 3 of the Scheme.

(a) 1961 c. 62.

STATUTORY INSTRUMENTS

1976 No. 154

MERCHANT SHIPPING

OIL POLLUTION

The Oil Pollution (Compulsory Insurance) (Amendment) Regulations 1976

Made - - - -	*4th February* 1976
Laid before Parliament	*11th February* 1976
Coming into Operation	*7th March* 1976

The Secretary of State, in exercise of his powers under section 10(4) of the Merchant Shipping (Oil Pollution) Act 1971(**a**) and of all other powers enabling him in that behalf, hereby makes the following Regulations:—

1. These Regulations may be cited as the Oil Pollution (Compulsory Insurance) (Amendment) Regulations 1976 and shall come into operation on 7th March 1976.

2. The Oil Pollution (Compulsory Insurance) Regulations 1975(**b**), as amended(**c**), shall have effect as though in Article 3 (recognition of certificates of insurance)—

(*a*) in paragraph (1), after the reference to Norway there were inserted a reference to Spain; and

(*b*) in paragraph (2), the reference to Spain were omitted.

Stanley Clinton Davis,
Parliamentary Under-Secretary of State,
Department of Trade.

4th February 1976.

(**a**) 1971 c. 59.   (**b**) S.I. 1975/869 (1975 II, p. 3081).
(**c**) S.I. 1975/1234, 1759, 2002 (1975 II, p. 4229, II, p. 6695 ,III, p. 7405).

EXPLANATORY NOTE

(This Note is not part of the Regulations.)

The Oil Pollution (Compulsory Insurance) Regulations 1975 provide, inter alia, for the recognition of certificates of insurance against liability for oil pollution damage caused by ships in the case of certificates issued by or under the authority of the governments of certain countries specified in the Regulations. This provision is made for the purposes of the Merchant Shipping (Oil Pollution) Act 1971, which gives effect to the International Convention on Civil Liability for Oil Pollution Damage signed in Brussels in 1969 (Cmnd. 4403).

Regulations 2(*a*) and (*b*) amend the 1975 Regulations in this regard. The effect is that a certificate for a ship registered in a country which is not a party to the Convention is recognised for the purposes mentioned above if it is issued by or under the authority of the government of Spain.

STATUTORY INSTRUMENTS

1976 No. 155

INDUSTRIAL DEVELOPMENT

The Financial Assistance For Industry (Increase of Limit) (No. 2) Order 1976

Laid before the House of Commons in draft

Made - - - -	*4th February* 1976
Coming into Operation	*5th February* 1976

The Secretary of State in exercise of his powers under section 8(7) of the Industry Act 1972(a) and with the consent of the Treasury hereby makes the following order:—

1.—(1) The Interpretation Act 1889(b) shall apply to the interpretation of this Order as it applies to the interpretation of an Act of Parliament.

(2) This Order may be cited as the Financial Assistance For Industry (Increase of Limit) (No. 2) Order 1976, and shall come into operation on the day after it is made.

2. The limit of £150 million specified in section 8(7) of the Industry Act 1972 in respect of the aggregate at any time of the sums paid by the Secretary of State under that section plus the liabilities of the Secretary of State under guarantees under that section, as increased by the Financial Assistance For Industry (Increase of Limit) Order 1975(c) shall be further increased by £100 million.

Eric Varley,
Secretary of State for Industry.

3rd February 1976.

We consent to the making of this Order.

J. Dormand,
Donald R. Coleman,
Lords Commissioners of
Her Majesty's Treasury.

4th February 1976.

(a) 1972 c. 63.   (b) 1889 c. 63.   (c) S.I. 1975/383 (1975 I, p. 1195).

STATUTORY INSTRUMENTS

1976 No. 157

OPTICIANS

The General Optical Council (Registration and Enrolment Rules) (Amendment) Order of Council 1976

Made - - - - *5th February* 1976

At the Council Chamber, Whitehall, the 5th day of February 1976

By the Lords of Her Majesty's Most Honourable Privy Council

Whereas in pursuance of section 7 of the Opticians Act 1958(a) the General Optical Council have made rules entitled "The Registration and Enrolment (Amendment) Rules 1975":

And whereas by subsection (5) of the said section such rules shall not come into force until approved by Order of the Privy Council:

Now, therefore, Their Lordships, having taken the said rules into consideration, are hereby pleased to approve the same as set out in the Schedule to this Order.

This Order may be cited as the General Optical Council (Registration and Enrolment Rules) (Amendment) Order of Council 1976.

N. E. Leigh

SCHEDULE

THE REGISTRATION AND ENROLMENT (AMENDMENT) RULES 1975

In pursuance of their powers under section 7 of the Opticians Act 1958, the General Optical Council hereby make the following rules:—

1. These rules may be cited as the Registration and Enrolment (Amendment) Rules 1975.

2. The Registration and Enrolment Rules 1973 (scheduled to the General Optical Council (Registration and Enrolment Rules) Order of Council 1973)(b) as subsequently amended (c) shall be further amended as follows:

(1) in the definition of "practice address" in Rule 2 all the words after "services" (on the second occasion where it appears) shall be replaced by the words, "in an emergency or in the place of a registered optician who is ill or on holiday";

(2) Rule 5 shall be re-numbered 5(1);

(a) 1958 c. 32.   (b) S.I. 1973/1450 (1973 II, p. 4418).
(c) S.I. 1973/2215, 1975/51 (1973 III, p. 7817; 1975 I, p. 161).

(3) at the end of Rule 5(1)(*b*) there shall be added the words "and the name under which any practice is carried on at such address";

(4) item (*c*) of Rule 5(1) shall be replaced by the following item:—

(*c*) subject to paragraph (2) of this rule, practice addresses, if any, other than the permanent address including, in each case, the name under which the practice is carried on at the practice address;

(5) after Rule 5(1) there shall be added the following paragraph:—

"(2) Notwithstanding item (*c*) of paragraph (1) of this rule it will be sufficient compliance with this rule if an entry in the register contains one practice address only (whether or not such practice address is also the permanent address) in the following cases that is to say—

(*a*) in relation to an optician who practises as an employee of a registered optician, the permanent address of his employer may be included as the employee's practice address;

(*b*) in relation to an optician who practises as an employee of a registered medical practitioner or of an authority or person carrying on a hospital, clinic, nursing home or other institution providing medical or surgical treatment, or of a Minister of the Crown or Government department (including a department of the Government of Northern Ireland), any single address of his employer from which ophthalmic services are provided may be included as his practice address;

(*c*) in relation to an optician who practises as a director, secretary or employee of an enrolled body corporate, the principal place of business of that enrolled body corporate may be included as his practice address.";

(6) in Rule 23(1) the words, "other than a permanent address" shall be replaced by the words, "whether or not that practice address is also a permanent address";

(7) in Rule 24(2) the words, "other than a permanent address" shall be deleted;

(8) in Rule 29(1) the words, "other than the address of the principal place of business of a body corporate" shall be replaced by the words, "from which ophthalmic services are provided by a body corporate, whether or not that address is also the principal place of business of the body corporate.";

(9) in Rule 30(2) the words, "other than the address of a principal place of business" shall be deleted;

(10) In the Appendix—

(i) the figure "£7", on each occasion where it appears, shall be replaced by the figure "£9";

(ii) the figure "£3", on each occasion where it appears, shall be replaced by the figure "£4";

(iii) the figure "£1·50", on each occasion where it appears, shall be replaced by the figure "£2";

(iv) the figure "£2", on each occasion where it appears, shall be replaced by the figure "£3";

(v) in Table A the words, "other than a permanent address" shall be replaced by the words, "included in the register";

(vi) in Table B the words, "other than the address of the principal place of business" shall be replaced by the words, "from which ophthalmic services are provided".

3. These rules shall come into operation on the 1st day of April 1976, and shall apply to applications for registration, enrolment and retention to take effect on or after 1st day of April 1976, whether made before, on or after that date.
Sealed on the 20th day of November 1975.

Attested by:—

Eric Richardson,
Member of Council.

(L.S.)

J. P. Quilliam,
Member of Council.

J. Daniel Devlin,
Registrar.

EXPLANATORY NOTE
(This Note is not part of the Order.)

The rules approved by this Order increase with effect from 1st April 1976 the fees payable to the General Optical Council by ophthalmic and dispensing opticians and bodies corporate carrying on business as opticians for registration, retention and other purposes.

Provision is also made for additional fees to be charged in respect of certain addresses entered in the register or list.

STATUTORY INSTRUMENTS

1976 No. 159 (C. 6)

ANIMALS

The Diseases of Animals Act 1975 (Commencement No. 1) Order 1976

Made - - - - *5th February* 1976

The Minister of Agriculture, Fisheries and Food and the Secretary of State, acting jointly in exercise of the power conferred upon them by section 5(2) of the Diseases of Animals Act 1975(a), hereby make the following Order:—

1.—(1) This Order may be cited as the Diseases of Animals Act 1975 (Commencement No. 1) Order 1976.

(2) In this Order "the Act" means the Diseases of Animals Act 1975.

(3) The Interpretation Act 1889(b) shall apply to this Order as it applies to an Act of Parliament.

2. The following provisions of the Act shall come into operation on 5th February 1976:—

Section 1 (extended power to prevent introduction and spread of diseases of animals and poultry);

Section 2 (powers of entry);

Section 3 (prosecution on indictment of certain offences connected with importation);

Section 4 (1) and (2) (transitional provisions);

Schedule 1 (provisions to be substituted for Schedule 1 to the Diseases of Animals Act 1950)(c).

In witness whereof the Official Seal of the Minister of Agriculture, Fisheries and Food is hereunto affixed on 3rd February 1976.

(L.S.)

Frederick Peart,
Minister of Agriculture, Fisheries and Food.

William Ross,
Secretary of State for Scotland.

5th February 1976.

(a) 1975 c. 40. (b) 1889 c. 63. (c) 1950 c. 36.

EXPLANATORY NOTE

(This Note is not part of the Order.)

This Order brings into force on 5th February 1976 all the provisions of the Diseases of Animals Act 1975 except section 4(3) and Schedule 2 thereof which relate to enactments to be repealed.

STATUTORY INSTRUMENTS

1976 No. 160

TRADE DESCRIPTIONS

The Trade Descriptions (Indication of Origin) (Exemptions No. 9) Directions 1976

Made - - - *5th February* 1976

Coming into Operation *1st March* 1976

The Secretary of State, in exercise of the powers conferred on her by section 1(5) of the Trade Descriptions Act 1972(**a**), hereby gives the following Directions:—

1. These Directions may be cited as the Trade Descriptions (Indication of Origin) (Exemptions No. 9) Directions 1976, and shall come into operation on 1st March 1976.

2. In these Directions the expression "dried molassed beet pulp" has the meaning assigned thereto by the Fertilisers and Feeding Stuffs Regulations 1973(**b**) at the date of the making of these Directions.

3. Subsection (2) of section 1 of the Trade Descriptions Act 1972 shall be excluded in relation to dried molassed beet pulp until the beginning of 1st January 1977.

C. E. Coffin,
An Under-Secretary of the
Department of Prices and Consumer
Protection.

5th February 1976.

EXPLANATORY NOTE

(*This Note is not part of the Directions.*)

These Directions exclude, until 1st January 1977, section 1(2) of the Trade Descriptions Act 1972 (which requires that a United Kingdom name or mark applied to imported goods be accompanied by an indication of the country of origin of those goods) in relation to dried molassed beet pulp.

(**a**) 1972 c. 34.   (**b**) S.I. 1973/1521 (1973 II, p. 4604).

1976 No. 163

INDUSTRIAL TRAINING

The Industrial Training Levy (Paper and Paper Products) Order 1976

Made - - - -	*5th February* 1976
Laid before Parliament	*16th February* 1976
Coming into Operation	*7th April* 1976

Whereas proposals made by the Paper and Paper Products Industry Training Board for the raising and collection of a levy have been submitted to, and approved by, the Manpower Services Commission under section 7 of the Industrial Training Act 1964(a) ("the 1964 Act"), as amended by section 6 of and Schedule 2 to the Employment and Training Act 1973(b) ("the 1973 Act") and have thereafter been submitted by the said Commission to the Secretary of State under section 7(1C) of the 1964 Act as inserted by the 1973 Act;

And whereas in pursuance of section 7(1A)(*a*) of the 1964 Act, as inserted by the 1973 Act, the said proposals include provision for the exemption from the levy of employers who, in view of the small number of their employees, ought in the opinion of the Secretary of State to be exempted from it;

And whereas the Secretary of State estimates that the amount which, disregarding any exemptions, will be payable by virtue of this Order by any employer in the paper and paper products industry, does not exceed an amount which the Secretary of State estimates is equal to one per cent. of the aggregate of the emoluments and payments intended to be disbursed as emoluments which have been paid or are payable by any such employer to or in respect of persons employed in the industry, in respect of the period specified in the said proposals as relevant, that is to say the period hereafter referred to in this Order as "the eighth base period";

And whereas the Secretary of State is satisfied that proposals published by the said Board in pursuance of section 4A of the 1964 Act, as inserted by the 1973 Act, provide for exemption certificates relating to the levy in such cases as he considers appropriate;

Now, therefore, the Secretary of State in exercise of the powers conferred by section 4 of the 1964 Act, as amended by section 6 of and Schedule 2 to the 1973 Act, and of all other powers enabling him in that behalf hereby makes the following Order:—

Citation and commencement

1. This Order may be cited as the Industrial Training Levy (Paper and Paper Products) Order 1976 and shall come into operation on 7th April 1976.

(a) 1964 c. 16.   (b) 1973 c. 50.

Interpretation

2.—(1) In this Order unless the context otherwise requires:—

(*a*) "agriculture" has the same meaning as in section 109(3) of the Agriculture Act 1947(**a**) or, in relation to Scotland, as in section 86(3) of the Agriculture (Scotland) Act 1948(**b**);

(*b*) "an appeal tribunal" means an industrial tribunal established under section 12 of the Industrial Training Act 1964;

(*c*) "assessment" means an assessment of an employer to the levy;

(*d*) "the Board" means the Paper and Paper Products Industry Training Board;

(*e*) "business" means any activities of industry or commerce;

(*f*) "charity" has the same meaning as in section 360 of the Income and Corporation Taxes Act 1970(**c**);

(*g*) "dock work" and "registered dock worker" have the same meanings as in the Docks and Harbours Act 1966(**d**);

(*h*) "emoluments" means all emoluments assessable to income tax under Schedule E (other than pensions), being emoluments from which tax under that Schedule is deductible, whether or not tax in fact falls to be deducted from any particular payment thereof;

(*i*) "the eighth base period" means the period of twelve months that commenced on 6th April 1975;

(*j*) "the eighth levy period" means the period commencing with the day upon which this Order comes into operation and ending on 5th April 1977;

(*k*) "employer" means a person who is an employer in the paper and paper products industry at any time in the eighth levy period;

(*l*) "exemption certificate" means a certificate issued by the Board under section 4B of the 1964 Act, as inserted by the 1973 Act;

(*m*) "the industrial training order" means the Industrial Training (Paper and Paper Products Board) Order 1968(**e**);

(*n*) "the levy" means the levy imposed by the Board in respect of the eighth levy period;

(*o*) "notice" means a notice in writing;

(*p*) "paper and paper products establishment" means an establishment in Great Britain engaged in the eighth base period wholly or mainly in the paper and paper products industry for a total of twenty-seven or more weeks or, being an establishment that commenced to carry on business in the eighth base period, for a total number of weeks exceeding one-half of the number of weeks in the part of the said period commencing with the day on which business was commenced and ending on the last day thereof;

(*q*) "the paper and paper products industry" does not include any activities of an establishment which have been transferred from the industry of the Board to the industry of another industrial training board by one of the transfer orders but save as aforesaid means any one or more of the activities which, subject to the provisions of paragraph 2 of the Schedule to the industrial training order, are specified in paragraph 1 of the Schedule as activities of the paper and paper products industry or, in relation to an establishment whose activities have been transferred to the industry of the Board by one of the transfer orders, any activities so transferred;

(a) 1947 c. 48.   (b) 1948 c. 45.
(c) 1970 c. 10.   (d) 1966 c. 28.
(e) S.I. 1968/787 (1968 II, p. 2194).

(r) "the transfer orders" means—

   (i) the Industrial Training (Transfer of Activities of Establishments) Order 1974(a);

   (ii) the Industrial Training (Transfer of Activities of Establishments) (No. 2) Order 1974(b);

   (iii) the Industrial Training (Transfer of Activities of Establishments) Order 1975(c); and

   (iv) the Industrial Training (Transfer of Activities of Establishments) (No. 2) Order 1975(d);

(s) other expressions have the same meanings as in the industrial training order.

(2) In the case where a paper and paper products establishment is taken over (whether directly or indirectly) by an employer in succession to, or jointly with, another person, a person employed at any time in the eighth base period at or from the establishment shall be deemed, for the purposes of this Order, to have been so employed by the employer carrying on the said establishment on the day upon which this Order comes into operation, and any reference in this Order to persons employed by an employer at or from a paper and paper products establishment in the eighth base period shall be construed accordingly.

(3) Any reference in this Order to an establishment that commences to carry on business or that ceases to carry on business shall not be taken to apply where the location of the establishment is changed but its business is continued wholly or mainly at or from the new location, or where the suspension of activities is of a temporary or seasonal nature.

(4) The Interpretation Act 1889(e) shall apply to the interpretation of this Order as it applies to the interpretation of an Act of Parliament.

Imposition of the levy

3.—(1) The levy to be imposed by the Board on employers in respect of the eighth levy period shall be assessed in accordance with the provisions of this Article.

(2) The levy shall be assessed by the Board separately in respect of each relevant establishment (that is to say, each paper and paper products establishment other than one which is exempted by an exemption certificate or one which is an establishment of an employer who is exempted by virtue of paragraph (4) of this Article), but in agreement with the employer one assessment may be made in respect of any number of relevant establishments, in which case those establishments shall be deemed for the purpose of that assessment to constitute one establishment.

(3) Subject to the provisions of this Article, the levy assessed in respect of a paper and paper products establishment of an employer shall be an amount equal to 1·0 per cent. of the sum of the emoluments of all the persons employed by the employer at or from that establishment in the eighth base period.

   (a) S.I. 1974/1154 (1974 II, p. 4402).
   (b) S.I. 1974/1495 (1974 III, p. 5739).
   (c) S.I. 1975/434 (1975 I, p.1371).
   (d) S.I. 1975/1157 (1975 II, p. 4019).
   (e) 1889 c. 63.

(4) There shall be exempt from the levy—

(*a*) an employer in whose case the sum of the emoluments of all the persons employed by him in the eighth base period at or from the paper and paper products establishment or establishments of the employer (including any persons employed in that period at or from a paper and paper products establishment by an associated company of the employer) is less than £65,000;

(*b*) a charity.

(5) Where any persons whose emoluments are taken into account for the purposes of this Article were employed at or from an establishment that ceases to carry on business in the eighth levy period the sum of the emoluments of those persons shall, for the purposes of this Article, be reduced in the same proportion as the number of days between the commencement of the said levy period and the date of cessation of business (both dates inclusive) bears to the number of days in the said levy period.

(6) For the purposes of this Order no regard shall be had to the emoluments of any person wholly engaged—

(*a*) in agriculture;

(*b*) as a registered dock worker in dock work; or

(*c*) in the supply of food or drink for immediate consumption.

Assessment notices

4.—(1) The Board shall serve an assessment notice on every employer assessed to the levy, but one notice may comprise two or more assessments.

(2) The amount of any assessment payable under an assessment notice shall be rounded down to the nearest £1.

(3) An assessment notice shall state the Board's address for the service of a notice of appeal or of an application for an extension of time for appealing.

(4) An assessment notice may be served on the person assessed to the levy either by delivering it to him personally or by leaving it, or sending it to him by post, at his last known address or place of business in the United Kingdom or, if that person is a corporation, by leaving it, or sending it by post to the corporation, at such address or place of business or at its registered or principal office.

Payment of the levy

5.—(1) Subject to the provisions of this Article and of Articles 6 and 7, the amount of each assessment appearing in an assessment notice served by the Board shall be due and payable to the Board one month after the date of a further notice requiring payment of that amount, which notice shall be served by the Board on the person assessed to the levy in the same manner as an assessment notice.

(2) The amount of an assessment shall not be recoverable by the Board until there has expired the time allowed for appealing against the assessment by Article 7(1) of this Order and any further period or periods of time that the Board or an appeal tribunal may have allowed for appealing under paragraph (2) or (3) of that Article or, where an appeal is brought, until the appeal is decided or withdrawn.

Withdrawal of assessment

6.—(1) The Board may, by a notice served on the person assessed to the levy in the same manner as an assessment notice, withdraw an assessment if that person has appealed against that assessment under the provisions of Article 7 of this Order and the appeal has not been entered in the Register of Appeals kept under the appropriate Regulations specified in paragraph (5) of that Article.

(2) The withdrawal of an assessment shall be without prejudice to the power of the Board to serve a further assessment notice in respect of any establishment or, as the case may be, persons to which that assessment related.

Appeals

7.—(1) A person assessed to the levy may appeal to an appeal tribunal against the assessment within one month from the date of the service of the assessment notice or within any further period or periods of time that may be allowed by the Board or an appeal tribunal under the following provisions of this Article.

(2) The Board by notice may for good cause allow a person assessed to the levy to appeal to an appeal tribunal against the assessment at any time within the period of four months from the date of the service of the assessment notice or within such further period or periods as the Board may allow before such time as may then be limited for appealing has expired.

(3) If the Board shall not allow an application for extension of time for appealing, an appeal tribunal shall upon application made to the tribunal by the person assessed to the levy have the like powers as the Board under the last foregoing paragraph.

(4) In the case of an assessment that has reference to an establishment that ceases to carry on business in the eighth levy period on any day after the date of the service of the relevant assessment notice, the foregoing provisions of this Article shall have effect as if for the period of four months from the date of the service of the assessment notice mentioned in paragraph (2) of this Article there were substituted the period of six months from the date of the cessation of business.

(5) An appeal or an application to an appeal tribunal under this Article shall be made in accordance with the Industrial Tribunals (England and Wales) Regulations 1965(**a**) as amended by the Industrial Tribunals (England and Wales) (Amendment) Regulations 1967(**b**) except where the relevant assessment relates to an establishment that is wholly in Scotland or, as the case may be, to persons employed at or from any such establishment or establishments and to no other persons, in which case the appeal or application shall be made in accordance with the Industrial Tribunals (Scotland) Regulations 1965(**c**) as amended by the Industrial Tribunals (Scotland) (Amendment) Regulations 1967(**d**).

(6) The powers of an appeal tribunal under paragraph (3) of this Article may be exercised by the President of the Industrial Tribunals (England and Wales) or by the President of the Industrial Tribunals (Scotland) as the case may be.

(**a**) S.I. 1965/1101 (1965 II, p. 2805). (**b**) S.I. 1967/301 (1967 I, p. 1040).
(**c**) S.I. 1965/1157 (1965 II, p. 3266). (**d**) S.I. 1967/302 (1967 I, p. 1050).

Evidence

8.—(1) Upon the discharge by a person assessed to the levy of his liability under an assessment the Board shall if so requested issue to him a certificate to that effect.

(2) The production in any proceedings of a document purporting to be certified by the Secretary of the Board to be a true copy of an assessment or other notice issued by the Board or purporting to be a certificate such as is mentioned in the foregoing paragraph of this Article shall, unless the contrary is proved, be sufficient evidence of the document and of the facts stated therein.

Signed by order of the Secretary of State.

5th February 1976.

Harold Walker,
Joint Parliamentary Under Secretary of State,
Department of Employment.

EXPLANATORY NOTE

(This Note is not part of the Order.)

This Order gives effect to proposals of the Paper and Paper Products Industry Training Board which were submitted to and approved by the Manpower Services Commission, and thereafter submitted by the Manpower Services Commission to the Secretary of State. The proposals are for the imposition of a levy on employers in the paper and paper products industry for the purpose of encouraging adequate training in the industry.

The levy is to be imposed in respect of the eighth levy period commencing with the date upon which this Order comes into operation and ending on 5th April 1977. The levy will be assessed by the Board and there will be a right of appeal against an assessment to an industrial tribunal.

STATUTORY INSTRUMENTS

1976 No. 169

EDUCATION, ENGLAND AND WALES

The Remuneration of Teachers (Burnham Further Education Committee) Order 1976

Made - - - -	*6th February* 1976
Laid before Parliament	*13th February* 1976
Coming into Operation	*24th February* 1976

The Secretary of State for Education and Science, in exercise of the powers conferred on him by section 1(3) and (4) of the Remuneration of Teachers Act 1965(a), hereby orders as follows:—

Citation and commencement

1. This order may be cited as the Remuneration of Teachers (Burnham Further Education Committee) Order 1976 and shall come into operation on 24th February 1976.

Cessation of representation

2. It is hereby determined that the National Federation of Continuative Teachers' Associations shall cease to be represented on the committee constituted under section 1 of the Remuneration of Teachers Act 1965 for the purpose of considering the remuneration payable to teachers in establishments of further education maintained by local education authorities.

Given under the Official Seal of the Secretary of State for Education and Science on 6th February 1976.

(L.S.)

William Pile,
Secretary,
Department of Education and Science.

EXPLANATORY NOTE

(This Note is not part of the Order.)

This Order ends the representation of the National Federation of Continuative Teachers' Associations on the Burnham Further Education Committee.

(a) 1965 c. 3.

1p.

STATUTORY INSTRUMENTS

1976 No. 172 (S 11)

HIGH COURT OF JUSTICIARY, SCOTLAND
SHERIFF COURT, SCOTLAND

Act of Adjournal (Form of Oaths) 1976

Made - - - -	*6th February* 1976
Coming into Operation	*3rd May* 1976

The Lord Justice General, the Lord Justice Clerk and the Lords Commissioners of Justiciary, under and by virtue of the powers conferred upon them by sections 282 and 457 of the Criminal Procedure (Scotland) Act 1975(a) and of all other powers competent to them in that behalf, do hereby enact and declare:—

1. (*a*) Where the clerk of court administers the oath to the jury in pursuance of the provisions of section 135 of the said Act of 1975, he shall do so in accordance with the forms set out in Part 1 of the Schedule to this Act of Adjournal.

(*b*) In the case of any juror who elects to affirm the clerk shall administer the affirmation in accordance with the form set out in Part 2 of the said Schedule.

(*c*) The oath or the affirmation so administered shall be deemed to have been administered in common form for the purposes of the said section 135.

2. (*a*) Where in any criminal proceedings in Scotland the Judge administers the oath to a witness, he shall do so in accordance with the form set out in Part 3 of the said Schedule.

(*b*) In the case of any witness who elects to affirm the Judge shall administer the affirmation in accordance with the form set out in Part 4 of the said Schedule.

(*c*) The oath or the affirmation so administered shall be deemed to have been administered in common form.

3. This Act of Adjournal may be cited as the Act of Adjournal (Form of Oaths) 1976, and shall come into operation on 3rd May 1976.

And the Lords appoint this Act of Adjournal to be recorded in the Books of Adjournal and to be published in the Edinburgh Gazette.

G. C. Emslie,

I.P.D.

Edinburgh.
6th February 1976.

(a) 1975 c. 21.

SCHEDULE

PART 1

FORM OF OATH FOR JURORS

The jurors to raise their right hands and the clerk of court to ask them: "Do you swear by Almighty God that you will well and truly try the accused and give a true verdict according to the evidence?" The jurors to reply: "I do".

PART 2

FORM OF AFFIRMATION FOR JURORS

The juror to repeat after the clerk of court: "I, [name], do solemnly, sincerely and truly declare and affirm that I will well and truly try the accused and give a true verdict according to the evidence".

PART 3

FORM OF OATH FOR WITNESSES

The witness to raise his right hand and repeat after the judge: "I swear by Almighty God that I will tell the truth, the whole truth and nothing but the truth".

PART 4

FORM OF AFFIRMATION FOR WITNESSES

The witness to repeat after the judge: "I solemnly, sincerely and truly declare and affirm that I will tell the truth, the whole truth and nothing but the truth".

EXPLANATORY NOTE

(This Note is not part of the Act of Adjournal.)

This Act of Adjournal gives effect to Recommendation 116 of the second report of the Thomson Committee on Criminal Procedure in Scotland (Cmnd. 6218) by providing simpler forms of oaths and affirmations for jurors and witnesses in criminal trials.

STATUTORY INSTRUMENTS

1976 No. 173

CUSTOMS AND EXCISE

The Import Duties (Temporary Reductions and Exemptions) (No. 3) Order 1976

Made - - - - - -		*9th February* 1976
Laid before the House of Commons		*10th February* 1976
Coming into Operation - - -		*2nd March* 1976

The Lords Commissioners of Her Majesty's Treasury, by virtue of the powers conferred on them by sections 1, 3(6) and 13 of the Import Duties Act 1958**(a)**, as amended by section 5(5) of, and paragraph 1 of Schedule 4 to, the European Communities Act 1972**(b)**, and of all other powers enabling them in that behalf, on the recommendation of the Secretary of State**(c)**, hereby make the following Order:—

Citation, operation, interpretation

1.—(1) This Order may be cited as the Import Duties (Temporary Reductions and Exemptions) (No. 3) Order 1976 and shall come into operation on 2nd March 1976.

(2) In this Order—

a reference to a heading is a reference to a heading of the Customs Tariff 1959;

"the relevant date" in relation to any goods specified in column 2 of Schedule 1 or 2 hereto means 30th June 1977, or, if an earlier date is specified in relation to the goods, the date so specified.

(3) The Interpretation Act 1889**(d)** shall apply for the interpretation of this Order as it applies for the interpretation of an Act of Parliament.

Intra-Community Trade

2. Up to and including the relevant date, no import duty shall be charged on goods which fall within a heading specified in column 1 of Schedule 1 or 2 hereto and are of a description specified in column 2 thereof if they satisfy the requisite conditions to benefit from Regulation (EEC) 385/73**(e)** (relating to goods entitled to benefit from the eventual abolition of customs duties in trade between member States of the European Communities).

The full rate

3.—(1) Up to and including the relevant date, in the case of goods which fall within a heading specified in column 1 of Schedule 1 hereto and are of a description specified in column 2 thereof:

(*a*) if a rate of duty is shown in column 3 thereof in relation to the goods,

---

(a) 1958 c. 6.
(c) *See* S.I. 1970/1537 (1970 III, p. 5293).
(e) O.J. No. L42, 14.2.1973, p. 1.

(b) 1972 c. 68.
(d) 1889 c. 63.

import duty shall be charged at the rate so shown instead of any higher rate which would otherwise apply;

(b) if the entry "free" appears in the said column 3 in relation to them, no import duty shall be charged; and

(c) if no entry appears in the said column 3 in relation to them, no exemption from, or reduction in, import duty applies by virtue of this Article.

(2) Paragraph (1) above shall operate without prejudice to the exemptions provided for by Article 2 above and any exemptions or greater reductions provided for by Articles 4 and 5 below.

Cyprus, Egypt

4. Up to and including the relevant date, any import duty for the time being chargeable on goods which fall within a heading specified in column 1 of Schedule 1 hereto and are of a description specified in column 2 thereof shall be charged:

(a) at the rate, if any, shown in column 4 thereof in relation to the description if the goods originate in Cyprus; and

(b) at the rate, if any, shown in column 5 thereof in relation to the description if the goods originate in Egypt.

Greece, Morocco and Tunisia

5. Up to and including the relevant date, no import duty shall be charged on goods which fall within a heading specified in column 1 of Schedule 1 hereto and are of a description specified in column 2 thereof if the goods originate in Greece, Morocco or Tunisia.

6. For the purposes of Articles 4 and 5 above goods shall be regarded as originating:

(a) in Cyprus if they are to be so regarded under the Agreement, signed on 19th December 1972, between the European Economic Community and Cyprus**(a)**;

(b) in Egypt if they are to be so regarded under the Agreement, signed on 18th December 1972, between the European Economic Community and Egypt**(b)**;

(c) in Greece if they are to be regarded as being in free circulation in Greece under Article 7 of the Agreement, signed on 9th July 1961, establishing an association between the European Economic Community and Greece**(c)** as modified by the Additional Protocol, signed on 28th April 1975, between the European Economic Community and Greece**(d)**;

(d) in Morocco if they are to be so regarded under the Agreement, signed on 31st March 1969, between the European Economic Community and Morocco**(e)**;

(e) in Tunisia if they are to be so regarded under the Agreement, signed on 28th March 1969, between the European Economic Community and Tunisia**(f)**.

(a) The Agreement is annexed to Regulation (EEC) 1246/73 (O.J. No. L133, 21.5.1973, p. 1).   (b) The Agreement is annexed to Regulation (EEC) 2409/73 (O.J. No. L251, 7.9.1973, p. 1).   (c) The Agreement is annexed to Decision (EEC) 63/106 (O.J. No. 26, 18.2.1963, p. 293/63).   (d) *See* O.J. No. 123, 15.5.1975, p. 1.   (e) The Agreement is annexed to Regulation (EEC) 2285/73 (O.J. No. L239, 27.8.1973, p. 1.).   (f) The Agreement is annexed to Regulation (EEC) 2286/73 (O.J. No. L239, 27.8.1973, p. 105).

Miscellaneous

7.—(1) Articles 4 and 5 above shall operate without prejudice to any relief from import duty to which any goods therein referred to may be entitled as goods of developing countries or of a particular country or area or otherwise

(2) Any description of goods in column 2 of Schedule 1 or 2 hereto shall be taken to comprise all goods which would be classified under an entry in the same terms constituting a subheading of the relevant heading in the Customs Tariff 1959, provided that the Additional Note to Chapter 29 shall not apply for the purposes of classification.

(3) For the purposes of classification under the Customs Tariff 1959, in so far as that depends on the rate of duty, any goods to which this Order applies shall be treated as chargeable with the same duty as if this Order had not been made.

(4) Where any import duty for the time being chargeable on any goods has been removed or reduced by a directly applicable Community provision the import duty shall, to the extent of that removal or reduction, not be regarded as removed or reduced by virtue of this Order and the reference to it in the Schedules hereto shall be treated as merely indicative of the rate of import duty payable in respect of the goods.

8. In column 2 of heading 29.23 in the Schedule to the Import Duties (Temporary Reductions and Exemptions) (No. 21) Order 1975**(a)** for "15-Methylprostaglandin $F_{z\alpha}$, trometamol salt" there shall be substituted "15-Methylprostaglandin $F_{2\alpha}$, trometamol salt".

9th February 1976.

James A. Dunn,
M. Cocks,
Two of the Lords Commissioners
of Her Majesty's Treasury.

(a) S.I. 1975/2027 (1975 III, p. 7437).

NOTE: Where no rate of duty is shown in column 3 there is no reduction in he full rate.

SCHEDULE 1

GOODS SUBJECT TO TEMPORARY REDUCTION IN OR EXEMPTION
FROM IMPORT DUTY

Tariff Heading (1)	Description (2)	Rates of Duty %		
		Full (3)	Cyprus (4)	Egypt (5)
25.07	Kyanite, sillimanite and mullite of which less than 10 per cent. by weight is retained on a sieve having a nominal width of aperture of 4·75 millimetres	Free	—	—
29.22	3,4-Dichloroaniline (up to and including 3 May 1976)	12·8	3·8	5·7
59.03	Bonded-fibre fabrics of spunbonded polyethylene man-made fibres not exceeding 110 grammes per square metre in weight, in reels (up to and including 30 June 1976)	12	3·6	5·4
73.14	Copper coated iron or steel wire with a diameter of not less than 0·790 millimetre and not more than 0·840 millimetre for telephone and telegraphic purposes (up to and including 3 May 1976) ..	8	2·4	3·6
85.15	The following apparatus for use in aircraft: (a) automatic radio direction finding apparatus covering a frequency range of at least 200 KHz to 850 KHz;	10	3	4·5
	(b) distance measuring apparatus for determining the slant range from aircraft to ground transponder and operating within the frequency range of 960 MHz to 1,215 MHz;	10	3	4·5
	(c) panel-mounted secondary surveillance radar transponder apparatus, operating within a 12 or 24 volt electrical power system, having an integral control panel and capable of interrogation at a frequency of 1,030 MHz on each of the modes A and C and replying on these modes at a frequency of 1,090 MHz;	10	3	4·5
	(d) very high frequency omni-directional radio range apparatus (VOR), instrument landing system localiser apparatus (ILS/LOC), instrument landing system glide path apparatus (ILS/G.PATH);	10	3	4·5

SCHEDULE 1—*continued*

Tariff Heading	Description	Rates of Duty %		
		Full	Cyprus	Egypt
(1)	(2)	(3)	(4)	(5)
	(e) very high frequency communications apparatus (VHF/COM) (receivers or combined transmitter receivers) covering a frequency band of at least 118 to 135·95 MHz with not less than 180 channels and capable of operating in areas where 50 KHz or 25 KHz channel spacing is in force, provided that the apparatus includes the very high frequency function of the apparatus specified in (d) and is capable of operating apparatus having the functions and capabilities specified in (d) but no other function or capability;			
	—falling within subheading AII b) ..	11	3·3	4·9
	—falling within subheading AIII b)2 ..	—	4·2	6·3
	—falling within subheading BII;	10	3	4·5
	being apparatus of a type approved by the Civil Aviation Authority, at the date of this Order, under Article 14(5) of the Air Navigation Order 1974, for use in aircraft of not more than 5,700 kilogrammes maximum total weight authorised, flying in controlled airspace in accordance with the Instrument Flight Rules as defined in the said Air Navigation Order, but not for use in other aircraft (up to and including 3 May 1976)			

SCHEDULE 2

Temporary Exemption from Import Duty Only in the case of Goods in Intra-Community Trade

Tariff Heading	Description
(1)	(2)
73·07	Slabs of iron or steel, rolled (ECSC) (up to and including 3 May 1976).
73.08	Hot rolled steel coils for re-rolling not less than 630 millimetres nor more than 1,090 millimetres in width and not less than 1·9 millimetres nor more than 2·8 millimetres in thickness (ECSC) (up to and including 3 May 1976).

EXPLANATORY NOTE
(This Note is not part of the Order.)

This Order provides for exemption from or reduction in import duty in the case of goods specified in Schedule 1 or 2 to this Order as from 2nd March 1976 to 30th June 1977 or such earlier dates as may be there specified in relation to the goods.

Exemption from import duties is provided in the case of all goods in Schedule 1 or 2 if the goods satisfy the requisite conditions to benefit from the eventual abolition of customs duties in trade between member States of the European Communities.

In the case of goods in Schedule 1 not satisfying those conditions, where a rate of import duty is specified in column 3, the duty is reduced to that rate instead of any higher rate which would otherwise apply and where "free" appears in column 3 in relation to the goods, they are exempt from import duty.

In the case of goods in Schedule 1 originating in Cyprus or Egypt, reductions to lower rates of import duty are made in certain cases in accordance with the Agreements between the European Economic Community (EEC) and those countries, such reduced rates being shown in column 4 (Cyprus) and column 5 (Egypt) of Schedule 1.

In the case of goods in Schedule 1 originating in Greece, Morocco or Tunisia exemption from import duty is provided in accordance with the Agreements between the EEC and those countries.

As regards the exemption for equipment for use in aircraft under heading 85.15, apparatus of a type approved by the Civil Aviation Authority is listed in Civil Aviation Publication CAP 208, Airborne Radio Apparatus Volume 2, published by Her Majesty's Stationery Office. This Publication is subject to amendment, and confirmation that apparatus is of a type approved at the date of this Order should be obtained from the Civil Aviation Authority, Controllerate of National Air Traffic Services, Tels N2s(c), 19/29 Woburn Place, London WC1H 0LX.

This Order also amends the Import Duties (Temporary Reductions and Exemptions) (No. 21) Order 1975 by altering part of the description in column 2 of the Schedule to that Order relating to tariff heading 29.23.

STATUTORY INSTRUMENTS

1976 No. 177 (S. 12)

RATING AND VALUATION

The Valuation (Post Office Telecommunication Services) (Scotland) Amendment Order 1976

Made - - - -	*5th February* 1976
Laid before Parliament	*18th February* 1976
Coming into Operation	*15th March* 1976

In exercise of the powers conferred on me by section 53 of the Post Office Act 1969(**a**), as amended by paragraph 74 of Schedule 9 to the Local Government (Scotland) Act 1973(**b**) and of all other powers enabling me in that behalf, and after consultation with the Post Office and such associations of local authorities and such local authorities as I consider appropriate, I hereby make the following order:—

Citation and commencement

1. This order may be cited as the Valuation (Post Office Telecommunication Services) (Scotland) Amendment Order 1976 and shall come into operation on 15th March 1976.

Interpretation

2.—(1) The Interpretation Act 1889(**c**) shall apply for the interpretation of this order as it applies for the interpretation of an Act of Parliament.

(2) In this order—

"the principal order" means the Valuation (Post Office Telecommunication Services) (Scotland) Order 1971(**d**) and other words and expressions have the same meanings as in the principal order.

Amendment of principal order

3. For the purposes of the re-determination of the aggregate amount of rateable values for each of the years 1976-77 and 1977-78 and the apportionment of the aggregate amount of those values for each of those years among rating areas the principal order shall be varied as follows:—

(*a*) In article 2(1) after the definition of "Article" there shall be inserted " "rating area" means the area of an islands council or of a district council; "year" has the meaning given to the financial year of a local authority in section 96(5) of the Local Government (Scotland) Act 1973, as substituted by section 18 of the Local Government (Scotland) Act 1975"(**e**).

(**a**) 1969 c. 48.
(**c**) 1889 c. 63.
(**e**) 1975 c. 30.

(**b**) 1973 c. 65.
(**d**) S.I. 1971/1210 (1971 II, p. 3534).

(*b*) In article 5—

    (i) in paragraph 1 the words "in the valuation roll made up by him" shall be omitted;

    (ii) in sub-paragraph 1(*b*) for the words "the rating area" there shall be substituted the words "each rating area"; and for the words "16th May in" in both places where they occur, there shall be substituted the words "the commencement of";

    (iii) in paragraph (2) after the words "of this Article," there shall be added "(*a*) any changes in the boundaries of rating areas which take place at the commencement of the year 1976-77 or the year 1977-78 shall be deemed to have taken place at the commencement of the preceding year; and (*b*)"; and for the word "area" there shall be substituted the word "areas".

(*c*) In the Schedule—

    in column 1 below "1975-76" there shall be added "1976-77
                                                   1977-78";

    in column 2 below "30 per cent" there shall be added "$37\frac{1}{2}$ per cent
                                                  45 per cent".

William Ross,
One of Her Majesty's Principal
Secretaries of State.

New St. Andrew's House,
Edinburgh.

5th February 1976.

EXPLANATORY NOTE

(*This Note is not part of the Order.*)

This Order extends the Valuation (Post Office Telecommunication Services) (Scotland) Order 1971 to the years 1976-77 and 1977-78 following the postponement of the next revaluation until the year 1978-79. It determines for the years 1976-77 and 1977-78 the manner in which the aggregate amount of the rateable values of the posts, wires, underground cables and ducts, telephone kiosks and other equipment not within a building used by the Post Office for telecommunication services is to be determined. It also determines how the aggregate rateable values for each of these years are to be apportioned among rating areas.

STATUTORY INSTRUMENTS

1976 No. 183

RESTRICTIVE TRADE PRACTICES

The Registration of Restrictive Trading Agreements Regulations 1976

Made - - - -	10*th February* 1976
Laid before Parliament	19*th February* 1976
Coming into Operation	22*nd March* 1976

The Director General of Fair Trading (in these regulations referred to as "the Director") in exercise of the powers conferred on him by sections 11 and 19 of the Restrictive Trade Practices Act 1956(a), as amended by section 8 of the Restrictive Trade Practices Act 1968(b) and section 94 of, and Schedule 10 to, the Fair Trading Act 1973(c) (in these regulations referred to respectively as "the Act of 1956", "the Act of 1968" and "the Act of 1973"), hereby makes the following regulations:—

Citation, commencement, revocation and interpretation

1.—(1) These regulations may be cited as the Registration of Restrictive Trading Agreements Regulations 1976 and shall come into operation on 22nd March 1976.

(2) The Registration of Restrictive Trading Agreements Regulations 1968(d) are hereby revoked.

(3) In these regulations—

"agreement", except in regulation 3, means an agreement subject to registration under Part I of the Act of 1956 and includes an agreement so subject by virtue of the application of that Part by or under any other enactment; and

"association" means an association as defined in section 112 of the Act of 1973 or a trade association within the meaning of section 6(8) of the Act of 1956.

(4) The Interpretation Act 1889(e) shall apply to the interpretation of these regulations as it applies to the interpretation of an Act of Parliament.

Furnishing of particulars of agreements

2.—(1) Subject to the following provisions of these regulations, a person furnishing particulars of an agreement to the Director pursuant to section 10 of the Act of 1956 shall send or deliver to him within the time specified in section 6 of the Act of 1968 for furnishing those particulars the documents mentioned in paragraph (2) below.

(2) The documents to be sent or delivered pursuant to paragraph (1) are—

(*a*) three copies of any document setting out the terms of the agreement so far as they are in writing;

(**a**) 1956 c. 68. (**b**) 1968 c. 66.
(**c**) 1973 c. 41. (**d**) S.I. 1968/1755 (1968 III, p. 4764).
(**e**) 1889 c. 63.

(b) where the agreement or part of it is not in writing, three copies of a memorandum in writing signed by the person furnishing particulars and setting out the terms thereof or such of the terms thereof as are not in writing, as the case may be.

(3) Where the documents sent or delivered pursuant to paragraph (1) above do not disclose the name and the address of any person party to the agreement, there shall also be sent or delivered therewith three copies of a document indicating that person's name and address:

Provided that where the members of an association, or persons represented thereon by members, are parties to an agreement as such or are to be treated as parties for the purposes of Part I of the Act of 1956, this paragraph shall not require the name or address of any of them to be provided if their number exceeds 100 and the certificate sent or delivered in accordance with regulation 7 indicates their number or their approximate number.

(4) At least one of the copies of any document mentioned in paragraph (2)(a) or (3) above shall be signed by, or identified by the signature of, the person furnishing particulars.

(5) In relation to an agreement in which a term is to be implied by virtue of section 6(7) of the Act of 1956 or section 112(3) of the Act of 1973 (specific recommendations to members of associations) references in this regulation to the terms of an agreement include references to the terms of any relevant recommendations.

Newly registrable agreements varied before registration

3. In the case of an agreement becoming subject to registration by virtue of an order made under section 5 of the Act of 1968 (information agreements relating to goods) or Part X of the Act of 1973 (agreements relating to services) which was made before the commencement of the relevant order and is varied not later than three months after such commencement but before particulars of the agreement are furnished to the Director, regulation 2(2) above shall have effect—

(a) in a case where the original agreement was in writing, as if it referred to three copies of the original agreement incorporating the variations; or

(b) in a case where the original agreement was not in writing, as if it referred to three copies of a memorandum signed by the person furnishing particulars and setting out the agreement as varied.

Common form agreements

4.—(1) Where particulars of an agreement are being or have been furnished to the Director pursuant to section 10 of the Act of 1956 and a person party thereto is also party to other agreements differing therefrom only as respects the other party thereto or the date of making, it shall be a sufficient compliance with regulation 2 in relation to those other agreements to send or deliver to the Director three copies of a memorandum which—

(a) refers to the agreement of which the particulars are being or have been furnished;

(b) indicates the dates of the other agreements and the names and addresses of the parties thereto; and

(c) states that those agreements are otherwise identical to the agreement of which particulars are being or have been furnished.

(2) At least one of the copies of a memorandum sent or delivered pursuant to paragraph (1) above shall be signed by the person furnishing particulars.

(3) The proviso to regulation 2(3) above shall apply in relation to paragraph (1)(*b*) above as it applies in relation to the said regulation 2(3).

Extent of the obligation to furnish particulars of variations of agreements

5. The obligation to furnish particulars of any variation of an agreement to the Director pursuant to section 10 of the Act of 1956 shall apply only to variations whereby—

(*a*) a further restriction is accepted by one or more of the parties; or

(*b*) a restriction ceases to have effect; or

(*c*) the application of an existing restriction is extended or reduced as regards the areas or places or the classes of persons, goods, processes of manufacture or services to which it relates; or

(*d*) so far as restrictions are accepted as to the terms or conditions on which goods are to be supplied or acquired or any process of manufacture is to be applied to goods or any designated service is to be supplied or obtained, the terms or conditions are varied.

Furnishing of particulars of the variation or determination of an agreement

6.—(1) A person furnishing particulars of the variation or determination of an agreement to the Director pursuant to section 10 of the Act of 1956 shall send or deliver to him within the time specified in section 6 of the Act of 1968 for furnishing those particulars the documents hereinafter specified.

(2) The documents to be sent or delivered pursuant to paragraph (1) above are—

(*a*) in a case where the variation or determination is effected by an instrument in writing, three copies of the instrument;

(*b*) in a case where the variation or determination is not effected by an instrument in writing, three copies of a memorandum in writing signed by the person furnishing particulars and setting out complete particulars of the variation or determination.

(3) At least one of the copies of any document mentioned in paragraph (2)(*a*) above shall be signed by, or identified by the signature of, the person furnishing particulars.

Certificate of particulars

7. A person sending or delivering documents to the Director in accordance with these regulations shall send or deliver therewith a certificate signed by him or on his behalf in whichever of the forms set out in the Schedule hereto (or forms commonly used before the commencement of these regulations) is appropriate.

Contents of the register

8.—(1) The particulars of agreements which shall be entered or filed in the register shall be—

(*a*) copies of the documents duly sent or delivered to the Director pursuant to these regulations;

(*b*) any documents or information obtained by him under sections 14 or 15 of the Act of 1956; and

(*c*) any other particulars which any party to an agreement may furnish to him and which the Director thinks it appropriate to include in the register.

(2) Nothing in paragraph (1) above shall apply to any details as to parties or other persons, prices, terms or other matters as are material for the purpose only of defining the particular application from time to time of a continuing restriction accepted under an agreement of which particulars are entered or filed in the register, being details which the Director considers it unnecessary to enter or file therein.

The special section of the register

9.—(1) There shall be maintained a special section of the register which shall not be open to public inspection.

(2) There shall be entered or filed in the special section such particulars described in section 11(3) of the Act of 1956 (information the publication of which may be contrary to the public interest or may substantially damage legitimate business interests) as the Secretary of State may by virtue of that subsection direct.

(3) Where particulars are being furnished to the Director by a person who considers that any of them should be included in the special section of the register he shall send or deliver therewith a signed memorandum indicating the particulars in question and the grounds on which he considers that they should be included in that section.

Public inspection of the register

10. The public section of the register shall be open to public inspection between 10.00 a.m. and 4.30 p.m. except on Saturdays, Sundays and official holidays on which the Office of Fair Trading is closed.

Addressing of documents

11. Any documents to be sent or delivered to the Director pursuant to these regulations shall be addressed to—

> The Office of Fair Trading (Registration),
> Chancery House,
> Chancery Lane,
> London WC2A 1SP.

Application for extension of time for furnishing particulars

12.—(1) Any application to the Director for further time for furnishing any particulars in relation to any agreement beyond the time specified by section 6 of the Act of 1968 (as modified by the Act of 1973) shall be made in writing within the time so specified.

(2) Any such application shall—

(a) identify the agreement to which it relates;

(b) indicate the further time requested; and

(c) state why it is impracticable to furnish particulars within the time so specified.

10th February 1976.

M. J. Methven,
Director General of Fair Trading.

SCHEDULE

Regulation 7   FORMS OF CERTIFICATE

(obtainable free of charge from the Office of Fair Trading)

Association Agreements   Form C.1/76

Restrictive Trade Practices Acts 1956 to 1973

CERTIFICATE in respect of an agreement constituted by

(a)...

of the (b)..

being an agreement relating to (c)......................................

....

....

and to which the only parties are members of the association or persons represented by those members.

I, ...

herewith send/deliver to the Director General of Fair Trading in accordance with the Registration of Restrictive Trading Agreements Regulations 1976 copies of particulars of an agreement which is subject to registration under Part I of the Restrictive Trade Practices Act 1956.

I CERTIFY

that the whole of the terms of that agreement (d) are contained in the following documents (three copies of each of which are attached):—

Delete whichever alternative is inappropriate

and that [the names and addresses of the persons who are parties to it (e) are so contained] [the number of parties to it (e) exceeds 100, namely, approximately ....]

(i) Copies of Instruments in writing (f)

....

....

....

(ii) Copies of a Memorandum of particulars not contained in Instruments mentioned in (i) above

....

....

and that I have identified one copy of each of the documents at (i) above by my signature and have signed one copy of the memorandum at (ii) above.

Dated.........................   Signed.........................

Status (g) and address of signatory   On behalf of.....................

....

....

....

       (a party to the above agreement)

NOTES

1. This Form should be used for the initial submission of particulars of an agreement which is constituted by the articles of association, rules, resolutions or bye-laws etc. of a trade association (as defined in section 6(8) of the Restrictive Trade Practices Act 1956) or an association of persons supplying services (as defined in section 112(1) of the Fair Trading Act 1973).

2. Notes referred to on the Form

    (*a*) Insert the title or some description identifying the document(s) constituting the agreement.

    (*b*) Insert the name of the association.

    (*c*) Insert a brief description of the goods, processes or services to which the agreement relates.

    (*d*) The whole of the terms of the agreement and not merely those involving restrictions must be provided. The documents must also include any recommendations by the association of the kind referred to in Section 6(7) of the Restrictive Trade Practices Act 1956 or Section 112(3) of the Fair Trading Act 1973.

    (*e*) The Acts regard all members of an association and persons (including companies, partnerships, etc.) represented on it by members as parties to the agreement. The documents supplied must include a list of all such members and represented persons and their addresses, *unless* they exceed 100 in number when only their approximate number must be stated.

    (*f*) Insert the title or some description identifying each document.

    (*g*) e.g. "Secretary of the.........................Association", "a partner of Messrs. ....Solicitors", etc.

Form C.2/76

Common form agreements

RESTRICTIVE TRADE PRACTICES ACTS 1956 TO 1973

CERTIFICATE in respect of agreements in common form between
(a)..
....
relating to (b)...
....

     I, ...
herewith send/deliver to the Director General of Fair Trading in accordance
with the Registration of Restrictive Trading Agreements Regulations 1976
copies of particulars of (c)..
....
agreements subject to registration under Part I of the Restrictive Trade Practices
Act 1956.

CERTIFI-
CATE A   I CERTIFY that all the agreements referred to above have a party or parties
in common and are in the same form except for the identity of another party
or parties or the date thereof or both, and that the whole of the terms (d) of
those agreements together with the name(s) and address(es) of the common
party or parties (e) to all of them

delete if
inappropriate   [other than the names of the members or persons represented by the members
of the..
....
who number approximately...]
and the separate party or parties to each of them are contained in the following
documents (three copies of each of which are attached):—

      (i) Copies of Instruments in writing (f)
....
....

     (ii) Copies of a Memorandum of particulars not contained in instruments
          mentioned in (i) above
....

     (iii) Copies of a Memorandum of the name(s) and address(es) of the separate
           party or parties and dates of agreements similar to the agreement
           whose terms are set out in the documents mentioned in (i) or (ii)
           above

and that I have identified one copy of each of the documents at (i) above by
my signature and have signed one copy of the memoranda at (ii) and (iii)
above.

CERTIFI-
CATE B   I CERTIFY that the Memorandum (three copies of which are attached and
one copy of which I have signed) sets out in accordance with regulation 4 of
the Registration of Restrictive Trading Agreements Regulations 1976 particulars
of agreements subject to registration under Part I of the Restrictive Trade
Practices Act 1956.

Dated..........................   Signed..........................

Status (g) and address of signatory   On behalf of.....................
....
....
....

           (a party to all the above agreements)

NOTES

1. This Form (Certificate A) should be used for the initial submission of particulars of a series of agreements in common form. Where particulars are being furnished of subsequent agreements made in common form to agreements of which particulars have already been furnished, complete Certificate B.

2. Notes referred to on the Form

(a) Insert the name of the party (or parties) common to all agreements together with a description of the business of the other parties e.g. wholesalers, etc.

(b) Insert a brief description of the goods, processes or services to which the agreements relate.

(c) Insert the number (in figures) of agreements to which the certificate applies.

(d) The whole of the terms of the agreements and not merely those involving restrictions must be provided.

(e) Where an association is party to an agreement the Acts regard its members and persons (including companies, partnerships, etc.) represented on it by members as parties. The documents supplied must include a list of all such members and represented persons and their addresses, *unless* they exceed 100 in number when only their approximate number must be stated.

(f) Insert the title or some description identifying each document.

(g) e.g. "Secretary of the .... Association", "a partner of Messrs. ...., Solicitors", etc.

Form C.3/76

Agreements other than association and common form agreements

RESTRICTIVE TRADE PRACTICES ACTS 1956 TO 1973

CERTIFICATE in respect of an agreement between

(a)..

....

relating to (b)..

....

I, ...
herewith send/deliver to the Director General of Fair Trading in accordance
with the Registration of Restrictive Trading Agreements Regulations 1976
copies of particulars of an agreement subject to registration under Part I of
the Restrictive Trade Practices Act 1956.

complete
or delete as
appropriate

I CERTIFY that the whole of the terms of that agreement (c) and the names
and addresses of the persons who are parties (d) to it [(d) other than the names
and addresses of the members or persons represented by the members of the

....

....

who number approximately...]
are contained in the following documents (three copies of each of which are
attached):—

    (i) Copies of Instruments in writing (e)

....

....

....

    (ii) Copies of a Memorandum of particulars not contained in Instruments
    mentioned in (i) above

and that I have identified one copy of each of the documents at (i) above by
my signature and have signed one copy of the memorandum at (ii) above.

Dated...........................   Signed...........................

Status (f) and address of signatory   On behalf of.....................

....

....

....

                           (a party to the above agreement)

NOTES

1. This Form should be used for the initial submission of particulars of any agreement other than

(i) an agreement which is constituted by the articles of association, rules, resolutions, bye-laws etc. of a trade association (as defined in section 6(8) of the Restrictive Trade Practices Act 1956) or an association of persons supplying services (as defined in section 112(1) of the Fair Trading Act 1973); and

(ii) a series of agreements in common form where one party (or group of parties) is common to all of them while the other is different in each case.

2. Notes referred to on the Form

(a) Insert the names of at least two parties and indicate whether there are also other parties. If an association is a party, insert its name—but see also (d) below.

(b) Insert a brief description of the goods, processes or services to which the agreement relates.

(c) The whole of the terms of the agreement and not merely those involving restrictions must be provided.

(d) Where an association is party to an agreement the Acts regard its members and persons (including companies, partnerships, etc.) represented on it by members as parties. The documents supplied must include a list of all such members and represented persons and their addresses, *unless* they exceed 100 in number when only their approximate number must be stated.

(e) Insert the title or some description identifying each document.

(f) e.g. "Secretary of the.........................Association", "a partner of Messrs. ...., Solicitors", etc.

Form C.4/76

Variation or Determination

RESTRICTIVE TRADE PRACTICES ACTS 1956 TO 1973

CERTIFICATE in respect of the variation or determination of an agreement particulars of which have already been furnished to the Director General.

I, ...
herewith send/deliver to the Director General of Fair Trading in accordance with the Registration of Restrictive Trading Agreements Regulations 1976 copies of particulars of the variation/determination (a) of the agreement [entered on the Register of Restrictive Trading Agreements under the number (b)............] [of which the Director General's reference number is ....] made between..

....

I CERTIFY that the whole of the particulars of that variation/determination (a) are contained in the following documents (three copies of each of which are attached):—

(i) Copies of Instruments in writing (c)

....

....

....

....

(ii) Copies of a Memorandum of particulars not contained in Instruments mentioned in (i) above

....

....

and that I have identified one copy of each of the documents at (i) above by my signature and have signed one copy of the memorandum at (ii) above.

Dated..........................   Signed..........................

Status (d) and address of signatory   On behalf of.....................

....

....

....

(a party to the above agreement)

NOTES

Notes referred to on the Form

(a) Delete whichever word is inappropriate.

(b) Insert the number of the agreement on the Register or the reference number used by the Office in any correspondence relating to the original agreement and delete whichever wording in square brackets is inappropriate.

(c) Insert the title of or some description identifying each document sent.

(d) e.g. "Secretary of the .... Association", or "A partner of Messrs. ...., Solicitors".

EXPLANATORY NOTE

(This Note is not part of the Regulations.)

These regulations relate to the furnishing of particulars of restrictive trading agreements to the Director General of Fair Trading in accordance with the Restrictive Trade Practices Acts 1956 to 1973, and to the keeping by him under those Acts of a register of such agreements.

The regulations replace the Registration of Restrictive Trading Agreements Regulations 1968 (S.I. 1968/1755) which are revoked.

The main changes are—

    (*a*) provision is made in relation to restrictive agreements affecting the supply of services, particulars of which must be furnished to the Director once the Registration of Restrictive Trading Agreements (Services) Order comes into operation on 22nd March 1976;

    (*b*) the number of copies of any agreement or memorandum of an agreement to be furnished is reduced from four to three;

    (*c*) the procedure for furnishing particulars of a series of standard form agreements is simplified; and

    (*d*) the exemption from the obligation to furnish the names and addresses of persons party to agreements as members of trade associations applies where more than 100 names and addresses are involved (instead of more than 200).

STATUTORY INSTRUMENTS

1976 No. 184

PUBLIC OFFICE

Court of Session (Scotland) (Fees) Order 1976

Made - - - - 10th February 1976

Coming into Operation 1st April 1976

The Treasury, in exercise of the powers conferred on them by section 2 of the Public Offices Fees Act 1879(a) and of all other powers enabling them in that behalf, hereby make the following Order:—

1. This Order may be cited as the Court of Session (Scotland) (Fees) Order 1976 and shall come into operation on 1st April 1976.

2. The Interpretation Act 1889(b) shall apply for the interpretation of this Order as it applies for the interpretation of an Act of Parliament.

3. All fees payable to the Court of Session Scotland shall be collected in money.

4. The Treasury Minute dated 25th March 1873 is hereby revoked.

M. Cocks,
James A. Dunn,
Two of the Lords Commissioners of
10th February 1976. Her Majesty's Treasury.

EXPLANATORY NOTE
(This Note is not part of the Order.)

This Order directs that fees payable to the Court of Session Scotland shall be collected in money and not by means of stamps.

(a) 1879 c. 58. (b) 1889 c. 63.

STATUTORY INSTRUMENTS

1976 No. 185

PENSIONS

The Occupational Pensions Board (Determinations and Review Procedure) Regulations 1976

Made - - - -	11*th February* 1976
Laid before Parliament	19*th February* 1976
Coming into Operation	11*th March* 1976

The Secretary of State for Social Services, in exercise of the powers conferred upon her by sections 66(7) and 67(4) of the Social Security Act 1973(a) (as amended by section 65(1) of and Schedule 4 to the Social Security Pensions Act 1975(b)) and section 31(5) and (7) of the Social Security Pensions Act 1975 and of all other powers enabling her in that behalf, after considering the report of the Occupational Pensions Board on the preliminary draft submitted to them and after consultation with the Council on Tribunals as required by sections 66(9) and 67(5) of the said Act of 1973, hereby makes the following regulations:—

Citation, interpretation and commencement

1.—(1) These regulations may be cited as the Occupational Pensions Board (Determinations and Review Procedure) Regulations 1976 and shall come into operation on 11th March 1976.

(2) In these regulations, unless the context otherwise requires—

"the Act" means the Social Security Act 1973;

"administrator", in relation to an occupational pension scheme, means the person or persons resident in the United Kingdom having the management of the scheme;

"the Board" means the Occupational Pensions Board;

"the 1973 regulations" means the Occupational Pensions Board (Determinations and Review Procedure) Regulations 1973(c);

"the Certification Regulations" means, in the application of these regulations to Great Britain, the Occupational Pension Schemes (Certification of Employments) Regulations 1975(d), and in the application of these regulations to Northern Ireland, the Occupational Pension Schemes (Certification of Employments) Regulations (Northern Ireland) 1976(e);

"employer" has the same meaning as in the Certification Regulations;

"the Northern Ireland Order" means the Social Security Pensions (Northern Ireland) Order 1975(f);

(a) 1973 c. 38.
(c) S.I. 1973/1776 (1973 III, p. 5427).
(e) S.R. 1976/5 (N.I.).

(b) 1975 c. 60.
(d) S.I. 1975/1927 (1975 III, p. 7163).
(f) S.I. 1975/1503 (N.I. 15).

"scheme" means occupational pension scheme;

"trade union recognised to any extent" includes a trade union which is treated as recognised to any extent under section 31(9) of the Social Security Pensions Act 1975 as amended by section 125 of and Schedule 16 to the Employment Protection Act 1975(a);

and other expressions have the same meaning as in the Act.

(3) Any reference in these regulations to any provision made by or contained in any enactment or instrument shall, except in so far as the context otherwise requires, be construed as a reference to that provision as amended or extended by any enactment or instrument and as including a reference to any provision which it re-enacts or replaces, or which may re-enact or replace it, with or without modification.

(4) The rules for the construction of Acts of Parliament contained in the Interpretation Act 1889(b) shall apply in relation to this instrument and in relation to the revocation effected by it as if this instrument and the regulations revoked by it were Acts of Parliament and as if the revocation were a repeal.

Determination of question arising on an election with a view to the issue of a contracting-out certificate

2.—(1) Subject to the provisions of this regulation, the Board shall treat an election made with a view to the issue of a contracting-out certificate as an application for the determination of the question whether the employments included in it should be treated as contracted-out employments, and shall allow 14 days to elapse after the date of expiry of the notice (or, if there was more than one such notice, the later or latest notice) of intention to make the election; subject to the provisions of paragraphs (3) and (4) below they shall then determine the question as soon as practicable.

(2) The Board may refuse to give effect to an election made by an employer if they are not satisfied that he has complied with the provisions of regulations 2 to 6 of the Certification Regulations.

(3) The Board, if they think fit, may defer making a determination to enable the election to be further considered in the light of any representations made by or on behalf of persons to whom notice of the election is required to be given by regulation 3 of the Certification Regulations.

(4) The Board may defer making a determination until such documents and information as are mentioned in regulation 6(3) of the Certification Regulations have been supplied.

(5) Where under this regulation the Board determine that an employment should be treated as contracted-out employment they shall issue a contracting-out certificate in accordance with regulation 8 of the Certification Regulations, and inform the Secretary of State or, as the case may be, the Department of Health and Social Services for Northern Ireland, that they have done so.

(6) Where the Board's determination under this regulation does not give effect, or gives only partial effect, to the election, the Board shall notify the employer in writing of the determination and of the reasons for it and shall refer him to the Board's powers of review under section 67 of the Act or, as the

---

(a) 1975 c. 71.   (b) 1889 c. 63.

case may be, Article 62 of the Northern Ireland Order; and the employer shall give notice of the determination and the Board's reasons for it, in the manner mentioned in regulation 3(3) of the Certification Regulations, to—

(a) those earners whose employment will be contracted-out as a result of the determination but would not have been if the determination had given full effect to the election;

(b) those earners whose employment will not be contracted-out as a result of the determination but would have been if the determination had given full effect to the election;

(c) the trustees (if any) and administrator of the scheme to which the election related;

(d) where there is a policy of insurance or annuity contract as a means of securing the guaranteed minimum pensions to be payable under the scheme, the insurance company or friendly society concerned; and

(e) all independent trade unions recognised to any extent for the purpose of collective bargaining in relation to the earners mentioned in this paragraph.

Determination of question arising on an election with a view to the variation or surrender of a contracting-out certificate

3.—(1) Subject to the provisions of this regulation, the Board shall treat an election made with a view to the variation or surrender of a contracting-out certificate as an application for the determination of the question whether the employments concerned should be treated or, as the case may be, cease to be treated as contracted-out employments; subject to the provisions of paragraphs (3) and (4) below they shall determine the question as soon as practicable, but not (except in a case where the Board have under paragraph (1) of regulation 10 of the Certification Regulations approved the making of the election without compliance with paragraphs (1)(a) and (b) and (2) to (5) of that regulation) before 14 days have elapsed after the date of expiry of the notice (or, if there was more than one such notice, the later or latest notice) of intention to make the election.

(2) The Board may refuse to give effect to an election made by an employer if they are not satisfied that he has complied with the provisions of paragraphs (1) to (5) of regulation 10 of the Certification Regulations, except in a case where the Board have under paragraph (1) of that regulation approved the making of the election without such compliance.

(3) The Board, if they think fit, may defer making a determination to enable the election to be further considered in the light of any representations made by or on behalf of persons to whom notice of the election is required to be given by regulation 10(2) of the Certification Regulations.

(4) The Board may defer making a determination until such documents and information as are mentioned in regulation 10(6) of the Certification Regulations have been supplied.

(5) When the Board have made a determination under paragraph (1) above, they shall vary or accept the surrender of the certificate if such action would give effect to their determination, and inform the Secretary of State or, as the case may be, the Department of Health and Social Services for Northern Ireland, that they have done so.

(6) The variation or surrender of a certificate under paragraph (5) above shall have effect from such date as the Board may specify, which may, where the Board consider it appropriate, be earlier than the date of the determination, but not earlier than the date from which the certificate had effect.

(7) Where the Board have made a determination under paragraph (1) above and it does not give effect, or gives only partial effect, to the application, the Board shall notify the employer in writing of the determination and of the reasons for it and shall refer him to the Board's powers of review under section 67 of the Act or, as the case may be, Article 62 of the Northern Ireland Order; and the employer shall give notice of the determination and the Board's reasons for it, in the manner mentioned in regulation 3(3) of the Certification Regulations, to—

(a) those earners whose employment will be contracted-out as a result of the determination but would not have been if the determination had given full effect to the election;

(b) those earners whose employment will not be contracted-out as a result of the determination but would have been if the determination had given full effect to the election;

(c) the trustees (if any) and administrator of the scheme to which the election related;

(d) where there is a policy of insurance or annuity contract as a means of securing the guaranteed minimum pensions to be payable under the scheme, the insurance company or friendly society concerned; and

(e) all independent trade unions recognised to any extent for the purpose of collective bargaining in relation to the earners mentioned in this paragraph.

Other circumstances in which the Board may vary or cancel a contracting-out certificate

4.—(1) Where the Board have reason to suppose that any employment to which a contracting-out certificate applies should not continue to be contracted-out employment and the employer has not shown to the satisfaction of the Board that it should so continue, the Board may determine that the employment should not continue to be treated as contracted-out employment; where they so determine, they shall cancel or, as the case may be, vary the certificate with effect from such date as they may specify (subject to paragraph (2) below); the Board shall notify the employer in writing of their determination and of the reasons for it and shall refer him to the Board's powers of review under section 67 of the Act or, as the case may be, Article 62 of the Northern Ireland Order, and shall also notify the Secretary of State or, as the case may be, the Department of Health and Social Services for Northern Ireland, of their determination.

(2) The date from which the cancellation or variation is to have effect may not be earlier than the date of the cancellation or variation, as the case may be, except in a case where the Board consider that the resources of the scheme have not been maintained at a sufficient level for meeting all claims in respect of guaranteed minimum pensions so far as falling to be met out of those resources, in which case the date may be the latest date on which in the opinion of the Board those resources were maintained at such a sufficient level.

(3) In any case where the Board have cancelled or varied a certificate under the provisions of paragraph (1) above they may require the employer to give notice of the cancellation or variation, in the manner mentioned in regulation 3(3) of the Certification Regulations, to—

(a) the earners in relation to whom the employment was contracted-out by virtue of the certificate immediately before its cancellation or variation;

(*b*) the trustees (if any) and administrator of the scheme by reference to which the employment was contracted-out immediately before the cancellation or variation of the certificate; and

(*c*) the persons or bodies mentioned in regulation 3(1)(*c*) and (*d*) of the Certification Regulations,

and they may require any such notice to include such particulars (including particulars of the consequences of the cancellation or variation) as they may consider appropriate.

Amendments of the 1973 *regulations*

5.—(1) The 1973 regulations shall be amended as mentioned in the following paragraphs of this regulation.

(2) In regulation 1(2), for the definition of "referred question" there shall be substituted the following definition, namely—

" 'referred question' means a question referred to the Board under section 55(4) or 60(2) of the Social Security Pensions Act 1975 or under Article 57(4) or 70(2) of the Social Security Pensions (Northern Ireland) Order 1975(**a**)";

and there shall be inserted after it the following definition, namely—

" 'referring authority', in relation to a question referred to the Board under section 55(4) of that Act or Article 57(4) of that Order, means the court, the tribunal or the Industrial Arbitration Board (as the case may be) before which the proceedings were held in which the question arose; in relation to a question referred to the Board under section 60(2) of that Act, means the Secretary of State; and in relation to a question referred to the Board under Article 70(2) of that Order, means the Department of Health and Social Services for Northern Ireland".

(3) Regulation 2 shall be amended by—

(*a*) the insertion, after the word "Act" in paragraph (1), of the words "or Article 62(2) of the Social Security Pensions (Northern Ireland) Order 1975"; and

(*b*) the substitution, for the words "Secretary of State" in paragraph (6), of the words "referring authority".

(4) Regulation 5 shall be amended by—

(*a*) the omission of the words "by the Secretary of State" from the heading;

(*b*) the substitution, for the words "the Secretary of State" in paragraph (1), of the words "a referring authority";

(*c*) the addition, at the end of paragraph (2), of the words "and before determining any question referred under section 55(4) of the Social Security Pensions Act 1975 or Article 57(4) of the Social Security Pensions (Northern Ireland) Order 1975 they shall also notify in writing the trustees or managers of the scheme concerned"; and

(*d*) the substitution, for the words "the Secretary of State" in paragraph (3), of the words "the referring authority", and the addition, at the end of that paragraph, of the words "or, as the case may be, Article 62 of the Social Security Pensions (Northern Ireland) Order 1975".

(a) S.I. 1975/1503 (N.I. 15).

(5) Regulation 7 shall be amended by—

(*a*) the omission, from paragraph (1), of the words "51 to", and the substitution for the words "Schedules 15 and 16 to, the Act," in that paragraph, of the following words, namely—

"Schedule 16 to, the Act, Part III and sections 53 to 56 of, and Schedule 2 to, the Social Security Pensions Act 1975, and Part IV and Articles 55 to 59 and 62 of, and Schedules 2 and 3 to, the Social Security Pensions (Northern Ireland) Order 1975,"; and

(*b*) the addition, after the word "Act" in paragraph (2), of the words "or Article 62 of the Social Security Pensions (Northern Ireland) Order 1975".

Revocation

6. The Occupational Pension Schemes (Certification of Employments) Regulations 1973(**a**), so far as they are still in force, are hereby revoked.

Northern Ireland

7. Regulations 2(2), 3(2) and (6) and 4(2) above shall not apply to Northern Ireland.

Barbara Castle,

Secretary of State for Social Services.

11th February 1976.

(a) S.I. 1973/1498 (1973 II, p. 4575).

EXPLANATORY NOTE

(This Note is not part of the Regulations.)

These Regulations make provision for the determination by the Occupational Pensions Board of questions whether employments should be treated as contracted-out employments or whether contracting-out certificates should be varied, surrendered or cancelled; and for the procedure on such determinations.

These Regulations also modify the Occupational Pensions Board (Determinations and Review Procedure) Regulations 1973 in such a way as to extend their application to the determination of questions referred to the Board by a court or tribunal or by the Industrial Arbitration Board under section 55(4) of the Social Security Pensions Act 1975 or Article 57(4) of the Social Security Pensions (Northern Ireland) Order 1975, by the Secretary of State under section 60(2) of that Act, or by the Department of Health and Social Services for Northern Ireland under Article 70(2) of that Order; and as to extend the Board's power to require the production of documents and the furnishing of information to cases where the Board are exercising their functions under that Act or that Order.

The report of the Occupational Pensions Board on the preliminary draft of these regulations, dated 17th December 1975, is contained in House of Commons Paper No. 180 (Session 1975–76) published by Her Majesty's Stationery Office.

STATUTORY INSTRUMENTS

1976 No. 189

POULTRY

THE IMPORTATION OF CAPTIVE BIRDS ORDER 1976

Made - - - -	*9th February* 1976
Laid before Parliament	*18th February* 1976
Coming into Operation	*1st March* 1976

The Minister of Agriculture, Fisheries and Food and the Secretary of State, acting jointly, in exercise of the powers conferred by sections 1 and 84(2) of the Diseases of Animals Act 1950(a), and now vested in them (b), and of the powers conferred on them by section 24 of the said Act, as amended by the Diseases of Animals Act 1975(c), and of all their other enabling powers, hereby order as follows:—

Citation, extent and commencement

1. This order, which may be cited as the Importation of Captive Birds Order 1976, shall apply throughout Great Britain, and shall come into operation on 1st March 1976.

Interpretation

2.—(1) For the purposes of the Act in its application to this order, the definition of the expression "poultry" in section 84(2) thereof is hereby extended so as to comprise birds of every species.

(2) In this order, unless the context otherwise requires—

"the Act" means the Diseases of Animals Act 1950, as amended or extended by any subsequent enactment;

"the appropriate Minister" means, in the application of this order to England and Wales, the Minister of Agriculture, Fisheries and Food, and, in its application to Scotland, the Secretary of State;

"bird" means a captive bird of any species, other than a bird of a species within the meaning of "poultry";

"disease" means any disease of birds or poultry;

"egg" means the egg of a bird;

"inspector" means a person appointed to be an inspector for the purposes of the Act by the Minister of Agriculture, Fisheries and Food or by a local authority, and, when used in relation to a person so appointed by the said Minister, includes a veterinary inspector;

"licence" means a licence issued under Article 3(2) of this order authorising a bird or egg to be landed in Great Britain;

(a) 1950 c. 36.
(b) By the Transfer of Functions (Animal Health) Order 1955 (S.I. 1955/958 (1955 I, p. 1184)).
(c) 1975 c. 40.

"poultry" means all species of fowls, turkeys, geese, ducks, guinea-fowls, pheasants, partridges and quails;

"veterinary inspector" means a veterinary inspector appointed by the Minister of Agriculture, Fisheries and Food.

(3) The Interpretation Act 1889(a) applies for the interpretation of this order as it applies for the interpretation of an Act of Parliament.

Prohibition on landing in Great Britain of birds and eggs

3.—(1) Subject to the provisions of this order, the landing in Great Britain of a bird or egg brought from a place outside Great Britain is hereby prohibited.

(2) The prohibition contained in paragraph (1) above shall not apply to the landing in Great Britain of a bird or egg when that landing takes place under the authority of a licence in writing previously issued by the appropriate Minister, and in accordance with the terms and conditions of that licence.

(3) A licence may be either general or specific, and may in either case be issued subject to such conditions specified therein as the appropriate Minister may see fit to impose for the purpose of preventing the introduction or spreading of disease into or within Great Britain.

(4) A general licence shall be issued by publication of the provisions thereof in such manner and to such extent as appears to the appropriate Minister to be sufficient to bring the terms of that licence to the attention of those persons likely to be affected by it.

Detention of birds and eggs in quarantine

4.—(1) Subject to Article 5(3) below, every bird and egg landed in Great Britain shall, except where the licence otherwise provides, be detained in quarantine at its owner's expense for such period, and at such premises and subject to such conditions, as may be specified in the licence.

(2) Notwithstanding the provisions of paragraph (1) above, a veterinary inspector may, for the purpose of preventing the introduction or spreading of disease into or within Great Britain, by notice in writing served on the owner or other person in charge of a bird or egg landed in Great Britain, require that bird or egg to be detained in quarantine at its owner's expense for such period, or (where the bird or egg is detained in quarantine at the time when the notice is served) for such further period, as may be specified in the notice, and subject to such conditions as may be so specified; and where a notice is served under the foregoing provisions of this paragraph in respect of a bird or egg which was not required to be detained in quarantine by the licence under the authority of which it was landed in Great Britain, that notice shall specify the premises at which that bird or egg is to be so detained.

(3) It shall be the duty of the person for the time being in charge of a bird or egg required by the foregoing provisions of this Article to be detained in quarantine to ensure that, until such time as the bird or egg arrives at the premises at which it is to be so detained, it is kept separate from—

(a) any other bird or egg, other than a bird or egg which forms part of the same shipment, and

(b) any poultry or poultry eggs.

(a) 1889 c. 63.

(4) Where a bird or egg is or has been detained in quarantine under the foregoing provisions of this Article, no person shall remove or attempt to remove that bird or egg, or cause or permit its removal or attempted removal from the premises at which it is or has been so detained, except with the written authority of a veterinary inspector, and in accordance with any conditions subject to which that authority is given.

Control of birds and eggs passing through Great Britain

5.—(1) The provisions of Articles 3 and 4 above shall not apply to a bird or egg landed in Great Britain in respect of which satisfactory arrangements have previously been made for it to be either—

    (a) moved by air from the airport at which it is landed direct to another airport in Great Britain for exportation therefrom, or

    (b) exported from the port or airport at which it is landed within a period of 48 hours after that landing takes place;

and it shall be for the person who purports to land a bird or egg under the foregoing provisions of this paragraph to prove to the satisfaction of an inspector or officer of Customs and Excise if required so to do that the arrangements referred to in those provisions have been made in respect of that bird or, as the case may be, that egg.

(2) Where a bird or egg to which paragraph (1)(b) above applies has not been exported from the port or airport at which it was landed at the end of the period of 48 hours after that landing took place, the person for the time being in charge of the bird or egg shall forthwith report the fact to an inspector, and inform him of the reason for the delay.

(3) The provisions of Article 4 above shall not apply to a bird or egg landed in Great Britain under the authority of a licence, and moved otherwise than by air direct to a port or airport in Great Britain for exportation therefrom in accordance with the terms and conditions of that licence.

(4) It shall be the duty of the person for the time being in charge of a bird or egg to which the foregoing provisions of this Article apply to ensure that, while in Great Britain, the bird or egg is kept separate from—

    (a) any other bird or egg, other than a bird or egg to which those provisions apply, or which forms part of the same shipment, and

    (b) any poultry or poultry eggs.

Powers of veterinary inspectors in relation to disease

6.—(1) Where a veterinary inspector suspects that—

    (a) a bird or egg which has been landed in Great Britain (whether or not that bird or egg is, or is required to be, detained in quarantine under any provision of this order), or

    (b) a bird or egg or any poultry or poultry eggs, which may have been in contact with a bird or egg which has been landed in Great Britain,

is or are or may be affected with disease, he may require the owner or other person in charge thereof to submit—

    (i) that bird or egg, or, as the case may be, that poultry or those poultry eggs, or a sample of that poultry or those eggs, and

    (ii) any litter, droppings or other excreta, and any other material or thing which may have been in contact with that bird, egg or poultry, or with those poultry eggs,

to such diagnostic or other tests as he may specify.

(2) A veterinary inspector may, without prejudice to paragraph (4) below, serve on the owner or other person in charge of any bird, egg, poultry or poultry eggs to which paragraph (1) above applies (whether or not any test in respect thereof has been carried out in accordance with that paragraph) a notice in writing requiring him, at the owner's expense, immediately—

(a) in the case of a bird or egg which has been landed in Great Britain—

(i) to export it therefrom, or

(ii) to slaughter or, as the case may be, destroy it; or

(b) in any other case—

(i) to place that bird, egg or poultry, or those poultry eggs, in quarantine for such period, and at such premises and subject to such conditions, as may be specified in the notice, or

(ii) to slaughter that bird or poultry or, as the case may be, destroy that egg or those poultry eggs.

(3) Where any person fails to comply—

(a) with a requirement of a veterinary inspector under paragraph (1) above, or

(b) with the terms of a notice served under paragraph (2) above,

a veterinary inspector may seize or cause to be seized the bird, egg, poultry or poultry eggs to which the requirement or notice relates, and arrange for any such test to be carried out or, as the case may be, the terms of the notice to be complied with.

(4) A veterinary inspector may at any time seize or cause to be seized, and may thereafter slaughter or cause to be slaughtered or, as the case may be, destroy or cause to be destroyed, any bird, egg, poultry or poultry eggs to which paragraph (1) above applies.

Action in case of contravention of the order, etc.

7.—(1) Without prejudice to paragraph (2) below, where—

(a) a bird or egg is landed in Great Britain in contravention of this order or of a licence, or

(b) there is, in respect of a bird or egg which has been landed in Great Britain, any contravention of or failure to comply with any provision of this order or of a licence, or any contravention of or failure to comply with any provision of any notice served or authority given under this order,

an inspector may, by notice in writing served on the owner or other person in charge of a bird or egg, require him, at the owner's expense, immediately—

(i) to slaughter or, as the case may be, destroy it,

(ii) to export it from Great Britain, or

(iii) to place it in quarantine for such period, and at such premises and subject to such conditions, as may be specified in the notice;

and where any person on whom a notice is served under the foregoing provisions of this paragraph fails to comply with the terms thereof, a veterinary inspector may seize or cause to be seized the bird or egg to which the notice relates, and arrange for the requirements of the notice to be complied with.

(2) A veterinary inspector may at any time seize or cause to be seized, and may thereafter slaughter or cause to be slaughtered or, as the case may be destroy or cause to be destroyed—

(a) any bird or egg to which paragraph (1) above applies, and

(b) any bird or egg, or any poultry or poultry eggs, which may have been in contact with a bird or egg to which that paragraph applies.

(3) Nothing in this Article shall affect the powers of the Commissioners of Customs and Excise to seize or detain as liable to forfeiture under the Customs and Excise Acts any bird or egg which is landed in Great Britain in contravention of this order or of a licence, or to institute legal proceedings under those Acts in respect of such contravention.

Supplementary provisions

8.—(1) Any reasonable expenses arising out of or in connection with the exercise of any power conferred on an inspector by the foregoing provisions of this order shall, without prejudice to any proceedings for an offence against the Act or this order, be recoverable on demand by the appropriate Minister or, as the case may be, the local authority, as a civil debt from the owner of the bird, egg, poultry or poultry eggs in respect of which the power was exercised, or from any other person for the time being in charge thereof.

(2) Nothing in Articles 6 and 7 above shall be construed as precluding the owner of any bird, egg, poultry or poultry eggs to which any provision of those Articles applies from slaughtering that bird or poultry or, as the case may be, destroying that egg or those poultry eggs.

Production of licences, etc.

9. Any licence issued, authority given or notice served under the foregoing provisions of this order shall, upon demand, be produced to a police officer, a veterinary inspector, an officer of the appropriate Minister or of a local authority, or an officer of Customs and Excise.

Indictable offence

10. Without prejudice to Article 11 below—

(a) the landing in Great Britain by any person, with intent to evade the provisions of this order, of a bird or egg in contravention of Article 3(1) above, and

(b) the failure by any person, with a like intent, to observe any condition subject to which a licence is issued,

are hereby declared to be offences against the Act to which section 3 of the Diseases of Animals Act 1975 applies, and accordingly prosecutable on indictment.

Summary offences

11. Any person who lands or attempts to land a bird or egg in Great Britain in contravention of Article 3(1) above, or who contravenes any other provision of this order or of a licence, or any provision of an authority given or notice

erved under this order, or who fails to comply with any such provision, or who causes or permits any such landing or attempted landing, or any such other contravention or non-compliance, commits an offence against the Act.

Local authority to enforce order

12. The provisions of this order shall, except where otherwise expressly provided, be executed and enforced by the local authority.

In Witness whereof the Official Seal of the Minister of Agriculture, Fisheries and Food is hereunto affixed on 6th February 1976.

(L.S.)
Frederick Peart,
Minister of Agriculture, Fisheries and Food.

9th February 1976.
William Ross,
The Secretary of State for Scotland.

EXPLANATORY NOTE

(This Note is not part of the Order.)

The principal provision of the Order is the prohibition on the landing in Great Britain, without a licence issued by the appropriate Agriculture Minister, of any captive bird or egg brought from any country.

The Order contains detailed provisions relating to quarantine and to the movement and control of birds and eggs in transit through Great Britain. It also confers on veterinary inspectors of the Agriculture Departments powers to deal with birds and eggs suspected of being diseased, and on inspectors of the Agriculture Departments and of local authorities power to deal with any illegal landing or any other contravention of the Order.

The Order introduces the possibility of prosecution on indictment in respect of certain offences, with a liability on conviction to imprisonment for a maximum term of 12 months or to an unlimited fine or to both.

STATUTORY INSTRUMENTS

1976 No. 191

CONSUMER CREDIT

The Consumer Credit Licensing (Representations) Order 197

Made - - -	11*th February* 1976
Laid before Parliament	19*th February* 1976
Coming into Operation	12*th March* 1976

The Secretary of State, after consulting with the Council on Tribunals i accordance with section 10 of the Tribunals and Inquiries Act 1971(a) a amended by section 3 of the Consumer Credit Act 1974(b), in exercise of he powers under sections 2(1)(*b*) and 182(2) of the Consumer Credit Act 197 and of all other powers enabling her in that behalf, hereby makes the followin Order:—

Citation, commencement and interpretation

1.—(1) This Order may be cited as the Consumer Credit Licensin (Representations) Order 1976 and shall come into operation on 12th Marc 1976.

(2) In this Order—

"the Act" means the Consumer Credit Act 1974;

"the person affected" means a person who is required under section 34(1 of the Act to be invited to submit representations to the Director and

"oral representations" means oral representations made under section 3 of the Act.

(3) The Interpretation Act 1889(c) shall apply for the interpretation of thi Order as it applies for the interpretation of an Act of Parliament.

Powers of the Director

2. Except as expressly provided herein, nothing in this Order restricts o abridges any right or power of the Director to do anything in the performance of any of his functions under the Act.

Notice of hearing

3. Where the person affected gives notice to the Director under section 34(1 of the Act that he wishes to make oral representations the Director shall, not less than 21 days before the day on which he arranges for those representations to be heard, or such shorter period before that day as the Director shall with the consent of the person affected determine, give notice to the person affected of the date, time and place at which they are to be heard.

(a) 1971 c. 62.   (b) 1974 c. 39.   (c) 1889 c. 63.

Conduct of hearing

4.—(1) In the course of the hearing of oral representations the Director shall—

    (*a*) at the request of the person affected permit any other person (in addition to the person affected) to make representations on his behalf or to give evidence or introduce documents for him; and

    (*b*) if he adjourns the hearing, inform the person affected a reasonable time before its resumption of the date, time and place of that resumption.

(2) The Director shall permit any member of the Council on Tribunals or of the Scottish Committee of the Council to attend any hearing of oral representations in his capacity as such a member.

(3) The Director shall not refuse to admit evidence solely on the ground that it would not be admissible in a court of law.

Making of determination under section 29(5) or 32(5) of the Act

5. Where the Director makes a determination to refuse to renew a licence in the terms applied for or to revoke or suspend a licence he shall not later than the time when he gives notice of his determination also determine whether to give or to refuse directions under section 29(5) or 32(5) of the Act as the case may require authorising a licensee to carry into effect agreements made by him.

Notice of the Director's determination

6.—(1) Where any notice which is required to be given under section 34(3) of the Act is notice of a determination that an application is refused, or granted in terms different from those applied for, or that the person affected is excluded from a group licence or that a licence is varied compulsorily, suspended or revoked, that notice shall in addition contain a statement—

    (*a*) setting out the Director's reasons for the determination;

    (*b*) setting out the findings of fact upon which the Director relies; and

    (*c*) declaring that if any person who is aggrieved by any such determination wishes to appeal to the Secretary of State under section 41 of the Act he must do so within the period and in the manner prescribed under subsection (1) of that section.

(2) Where the Director determines to refuse directions under section 29(5) or 32(5) of the Act authorising a licensee to carry into effect agreements made by him, the Director shall at the time when he gives notice under section 34(3) of the Act of his determination in relation to the licence—

    (*a*) in the case of a standard licence, give notice of the refusal to give directions to the licensee;

    (*b*) in the case of a group licence which the Director has determined to refuse to renew, give notice of the refusal to give directions to the applicant for its renewal;

    (*c*) in the case of a group licence which the Director has determined to suspend or revoke, give notice of the refusal to give directions to the original applicant for the licence, if any; and (*d*) in the case of any group licence—

(i) give notice of the refusal to give directions to the licensee in respect of whom such directions are refused; or

(ii) give general notice of the refusal to give directions;

and any notice given under this paragraph shall contain a statement setting out and declaring the matters mentioned in paragraph (1)(*a*) to (*c*) above.

Alan Williams,
Minister of State,
Department of Prices and
Consumer Protection.

11th February 1976.

EXPLANATORY NOTE

(This Note is not part of the Order.)

This Order regulates the carrying out of certain functions of the Director General of Fair Trading under the Consumer Credit Act 1974 relating to the provision of consumer credit, consumer hire and ancillary credit business. The functions concerned are—

(*a*) the hearing by the Director under section 34(1) of that Act of representations in relation to determinations which he is minded to make about the issue, renewal, variation, suspension and revocation of licences and about rendering enforceable certain agreements which would otherwise not be enforceable (articles 3 and 4);

(*b*) the making of determinations under sections 29(5) and 32(5) of that Act (which confer on the Director a power to authorise a licensee to carry into effect agreements made by him before the expiry, revocation or suspension of the licence) (article 5); and

(*c*) the giving of notice of the Director's determinations (article 6).

STATUTORY INSTRUMENTS

1976 No. 194

CUSTOMS AND EXCISE

The Import Duties (Temporary Reductions and Exemptions) (No. 4) Order 1976

Made - - - - - -	12th February 1976
Laid before the House of Commons	13th February 1976
Coming into Operation - - -	14th February 1976

The Lords Commissioners of Her Majesty's Treasury, by virtue of the powers conferred on them by sections 1, 3(6) and 13 of the Import Duties Act 1958(a), as amended by section 5(5) of, and paragraph 1 of Schedule 4 to, the European Communities Act 1972(b), and of all other powers enabling them in that behalf, on the recommendation of the Secretary of State(c), hereby make the following Order:—

Citation, operation, interpretation

1.—(1) This Order may be cited as the Import Duties (Temporary Reductions and Exemptions) (No. 4) Order 1976 and shall come into operation on 14th February 1976.

(2) In this Order—

a reference to a heading or subheading is a reference to a heading or subheading of the Customs Tariff 1959;

"the relevant date" in relation to any goods specified in column 2 of Schedule 1 or 2 hereto means 30th June 1977, or, if an earlier date is specified in that column in relation to the goods, the date so specified.

(3) If a period of time is specified in column 2 of Schedule 2 hereto in relation to any goods, the reductions in duty provided for by Article 2 below shall apply to such goods only during that period.

(4) The Interpretation Act 1889(d) shall apply for the interpretation of this Order as it applies for the interpretation of an Act of Parliament.

Intra-Community trade

2. Subject to the provisions of Article 1(3) hereof, up to and including the relevant date no import duty shall be charged on goods which fall within a heading or subheading specified in column 1 of Schedule 1 or 2 hereto and are of a description specified in column 2 thereof if they satisfy the requisite conditions to benefit from Regulation (EEC) 385/73(e) (relating to goods entitled to benefit from the eventual abolition of customs duties in trade between member States of the European Communities).

The full rate

3.—(1) Up to and including the relevant date, in the case of goods which fall within a heading specified in column 1 of Schedule 1 hereto and are of a description specified in column 2 thereof:

(a) 1958 c. 6.   (b) 1972 c. 68.   (c) *See* S.I. 1970/1537 (1970 III, p. 5293).
(d) 1889 c. 63.   (e) O.J. No. L42, 14.2.1973, p. 1.

(a) if a rate of duty is shown in column 3 thereof in relation to the goods, import duty shall be charged at the rate so shown instead of any higher rate which would otherwise apply; and

(b) if no entry appears in the said column 3 in relation to them, no reduction in import duty applies by virtue of this Article.

(2) Paragraph (1) above shall operate without prejudice to the exemptions provided for by Article 2 above and any exemptions or greater reductions provided for by Articles 4 and 5 below.

Cyprus, Egypt

4.—(1) Up to and including the relevant date, any import duty for the time being chargeable on goods which fall within a heading specified in column 1 of Schedule 1 hereto and are of a description specified in column 2 thereof shall be charged:

(a) at the rate, if any, shown in column 4 thereof in relation to the description if the goods originate in Cyprus; and

(b) at the rate, if any, shown in column 5 thereof in relation to the description if the goods originate in Egypt.

(2) If no entry appears in columns 4 or 5 of Schedule 1 in relation to goods of a description specified in column 2 thereof, no reduction in import duty applies by virtue of this Article to goods of that description originating in Cyprus or Egypt.

Greece, Morocco and Tunisia

5.—(1) Subject to the provisions of paragraph (2) of this Article, up to and including the relevant date, no import duty shall be charged on goods which fall within a heading specified in column 1 of Schedule 1 hereto and are of a description specified in column 2 thereof if the goods originate in Greece, Morocco or Tunisia.

(2) The exemptions provided for by paragraph (1) above shall not apply to goods which are of a description specified in column 2 of Schedule 1 hereto followed by the letters "ECSC".

6. For the purposes of Articles 4 and 5 above goods shall be regarded as originating:

(a) in Cyprus if they are to be so regarded under the Agreement, signed on 19th December 1972, between the European Economic Community and Cyprus(**a**);

(b) in Egypt if they are to be so regarded under the Agreement, signed on 18th December 1972, between the European Economic Community and Egypt(**b**);

(c) in Greece if they are to be regarded as being in free circulation in Greece under Article 7 of the Agreement, signed on 9th July 1961, establishing an association between the European Economic Community and Greece(**c**) as modified by the Additional Protocol, signed on 28th April 1975, between the European Economic Community and Greece(**d**);

(**a**) The Agreement is annexed to Regulation (EEC) 1246/73 (O.J. No. L133, 21.5.1973, p. 1).
(**b**) The Agreement is annexed to Regulation (EEC) 2409/73 (O.J. No. L251, 7.9.1973, p. 1).
(**c**) The Agreement is annexed to Decision (EEC) 63/106 (O.J. No. 26, 18.2.1963, p. 293/63).
(**d**) *See* O.J. No. L123, 15.5.1975, p. 1.

(d) in Morocco if they are to be so regarded under the Agreement, signed on 31st March 1969, between the European Economic Community and Morocco(a);

(e) in Tunisia if they are to be so regarded under the Agreement, signed on 28th March 1969, between the European Economic Community and Tunisia(b).

7. Up to and including 28th March 1976, no import duty shall be charged on the following goods, namely new potatoes which fall within subheading 07.01 A.II.a) and seed potatoes which fall within subheading 07.01 A.I.c).

Miscellaneous

8.—(1) Articles 4 and 5 above shall operate without prejudice to any reliefs from import duty to which any goods therein referred to may be entitled as goods of developing countries or of a particular country or area or otherwise.

(2) Any description of goods in column 2 of Schedule 1 or 2 hereto (other than one covering a whole heading or subheading) shall be taken to comprise all goods which would be classified under an entry in the same terms constituting a subheading of the relevant heading.

(3) For the purposes of classification under the Customs Tariff 1959, in so far as that depends on the rate of duty, any goods to which this Order applies shall be treated as chargeable with the same duty as if this Order had not been made.

(4) Where any import duty for the time being chargeable on any goods has been removed or reduced by a directly applicable Community provision the import duty shall, to the extent of that removal or reduction, not be regarded as removed or reduced by virtue of this Order and the reference to it in this Order shall be treated as merely indicative of the rate of import duty payable in respect of the goods.

(5) The abbreviations used in Schedule 1 hereto (being those used in the Customs Tariff 1959) have the meanings given in Article 11(5) of the Import Duties (General) (No. 5) Order 1975(c).

M. Cocks,

T. Pendry,

12th February 1976.

Two of the Lords Commissioners of Her Majesty's Treasury.

(a) The Agreement is annexed to Regulation (EEC) 2285/73 (O.J. No. L239, 27.8.1973, p. 1).
(b) The Agreement is annexed to Regulation (EEC) 2286/73 (O.J. No. L239, 27.8.1973, p. 105).
(c) S.I. 1975/1744 (1975 III, p. 5912).

SCHEDULE 1

GOODS SUBJECT TO TEMPORARY REDUCTION IN OR EXEMPTION FROM IMPORT DUTY

Tariff Heading (1)	Description (2)	RATES OF DUTY %		
		Full (3)	Cyprus (4)	Egypt (5)
73.11	Rolled steel section in lengths of not less than 488 centimetres and not more than 503 centimetres, being not less than 63 millimetres and not more than 76 millimetres wide, with a ridge, projecting at right angles from one face, not less than 19 millimetres and not more than 32 millimetres high, parallel to, and at not less than 10 millimetres and not more than 16 millimetres from one edge, the thickness of the ridge being not less than 4 millimetres and not more than 10 millimetres (ECSC)	6	—	—
73.12	Strip of iron or steel, coated with tin, of a width not less than 304 millimetres and not more than 500 millimetres, of a thickness of not less than 0·12 millimetre and not more than 0·5 millimetre, and of a length of not more than 1016 millimetres			
	—tinplate (ECSC)...	7	—	—
	—other ... ... (up to and including 3 May 1976)	—	1·9%+wig of 0·4% or £0·3306 per tonne	2·8%+wig of 0·7% or £0·4960 per tonne
	Strip of iron or steel, in coil form, coated with tin of a width of not less than 140 millimetres, and not more than 500 millimetres, and of a thickness of not less than 0·12 millimetre and not more than 0·5 millimetre			
	—tinplate (ECSC)...	7	—	—
	—other ... ... (up to and including 3 May 1976)	—	1·9%+wig of 0·4% or £0·3306 per tonne	2·8%+wig of 0·7% or £0·4960 per tonne
73.13	Sheets of iron or steel, cold-rolled but not coated or otherwise worked, not exceeding 3 millimetres in thickness —more than 1 millimetre but less 3 millimetres (ECSC) ... —1 millimetre or less (ECSC) ... (up to and including 31 March 1976)	6 —	—	—
	Sheets of iron or steel, hot-rolled but not coated or otherwise worked, not exceeding 3 millimetres in thickness: —more than 2 millimetres but less than 3 millimetres (ECSC) ... —less than 2 millimetres (ECSC) ... (up to and including 31 March 1976)	7 6	—	—

SCHEDULE 1—*continued*

Tariff Heading (1)	Description (2)	RATES OF DUTY %		
		Full (3)	Cyprus (4)	Egypt (5)
73.13 (contd)	Sheets of iron or steel, coated with tin, of a width exceeding 500 millimetres but not more than 966 millimetres, of a thickness of not less than 0·12 millimetre and not more than 0·5 millimetre, and of a length of not more than 1016 millimetres:			
	—tinplate (ECSC)	7	—	—
	—other	7	1·6%+wig of 0·4% or £0·3424 per tonne	2·2%+wig of 0·7% or £0·5137 per tonne
	(up to and including 3 May 1976)			
	Sheets of iron or steel, in coil form, coated with tin, of a width exceeding 500 millimetres but not more than 966 millimetres, and of a thickness of not less than 0·12 millimetre and not more than 0·5 millimetre:			
	—tinplate (ECSC)	7	—	—
	—other	7	1·6%+wig of 0·4% or £0·3424 per tonne	2·2%+wig of 0·7% or £0·5137 per tonne
	(up to and including 3 May 1976)			

SCHEDULE 2

TEMPORARY EXEMPTION FROM IMPORT DUTY ONLY IN THE CASE OF GOODS IN INTRA-COMMUNITY TRADE

Tariff Heading (1)	Description (2)
07.01. A.II. (a)	New Potatoes—29th March 1976 to 15th May 1976
07.01. A.II. (b)	New Potatoes—16th May 1976 to 30th June 1976

EXPLANATORY NOTE
(This Note is not part of the Order.)

This Order provides for exemption from or reduction in import duty in the case of goods specified in Schedule 1 or 2 to this Order as from 14th February 1976 to 30th June 1977 or such earlier dates as may be there specified in relation to the goods.

There is exemption from import duties in the case of all goods in Schedule 1 or 2 if the goods satisfy the requisite conditions to benefit from the eventual abolition of customs duties in trade between member States of the European Communities.

In the case of goods in Schedule 1 not satisfying those conditions, where a rate of import duty is specified in column 3, the duty is reduced to that rate instead of any higher rate which would otherwise apply.

In the case of goods in Schedule 1 originating in Cyprus or Egypt reductions to lower rates of import duty are made in accordance with the Agreements between the European Economic Community (EEC) and those countries, such reduced rates being shown in column 4 (Cyprus) and 5 (Egypt) of Schedule 1.

In the case of goods in Schedule 1 originating in Greece, Morocco or Tunisia, exemption from import duty is provided in accordance with the Agreements between the EEC and those countries except for goods whose description in the said Schedule 1 is followed by the letters "ECSC".

The Order also provides exemption from import duty up to and including 28th March 1976 in the case of certain new potatoes and seed potatoes which are subject to total suspension of duty in the Common Customs Tariff of the EEC; the exemption is made in accordance with the United Kingdom's Community obligations.

1976 No. 195

PREVENTION OF FRAUD

The Authorised Unit Trust Schemes Regulations 1976

Made - - -	12*th February* 1976
Laid before Parliament	20*th February* 1976
Coming into Operation	12*th March* 1976

The Secretary of State, being a Minister designated(a) for the purposes of section 2(2) of the European Communities Act 1972(b) in relation to authorisation of unit trust schemes where persons who are managers or trustees under the scheme are or include corporations incorporated under the law of a Member State, in exercise of powers conferred by that section, hereby makes the following Regulations:—

1.—(1) These Regulations may be cited as the Authorised Unit Trust. Schemes Regulations 1976 and shall come into operation on 12th March 1976.

(2) The Interpretation Act 1889(c) shall apply for the interpretation of these Regulations as it applies for the interpretation of an Act of Parliament.

2. In paragraph (a) of section 17(1) of the Prevention of Fraud (Investments) Act 1958(d) for the words "under the law of some part of the United Kingdom" there shall be substituted the words "under the law of, or of some part of, the United Kingdom or any other State which is a member of the European Economic Community".

Stanley Clinton Davis,

Parliamentary Under-Secretary of State,
Department of Trade.

12th February 1976.

(a) The European Communities (Designation) Order 1973, S.I. 1973/1889 (1973 III, p. 6561).   (b) 1972 c. 68.   (c) 1889 c. 63.   (d) 1958 c. 45.

EXPLANATORY NOTE

(This Note is not part of the Regulations.)

These Regulations implement the obligation imposed on Great Britain by Council Directive No. 73/183/EEC (O.J. No. L 194, 16.7.73, p. 1) to abolish the restriction contained in section 17(1)*(a)* of the Prevention of Fraud (Investments) Act 1958 under which only United Kingdom corporations may be trustees and managers of authorised unit trust schemes. A unit trust scheme may now be authorised if the manager and the trustee are corporations incorporated under the law of any Member State of the European Economic Community, provided that the other conditions contained in section 17(1) are satisfied.

STATUTORY INSTRUMENTS

1976 No. 198

COMMUNITY LAND

The Community Land (Appropriate Minister for the National Coal Board) Order 1976

Made - - - -	*11th February* 1976
Laid before Parliament	*23rd February* 1976
Coming into Operation	*15th March* 1976

The Secretary of State for the Environment, in relation to England, the Secretary of State for Scotland, in relation to Scotland, and the Secretary of State for Wales, in relation to Wales, in exercise of the powers conferred on them by sections 5(4)(b) and 53(2) of the Community Land Act 1975(a), and of all other powers enabling them in that behalf, hereby order as follows:—

1. This order shall come into operation on 15th March 1976 and may be cited as the Community Land (Appropriate Minister for the National Coal Board) Order 1976.

2. The Interpretation Act 1889(b) shall apply for the interpretation of this order as it applies for the interpretation of an Act of Parliament.

3. In the Community Land Act 1975, the expression "the appropriate Minister" in relation to the National Coal Board shall mean the Secretary of State for Energy.

4. In relation to the National Coal Board, any reference in the Community Land Act 1975 to the Secretary of State and the appropriate Minister shall have effect as if it were a reference—

(a) in England, to the Secretary of State for the Environment and the Secretary of State for Energy;

(b) in Scotland, to the Secretary of State for Scotland and the Secretary of State for Energy;

(c) in Wales, to the Secretary of State for Wales and the Secretary of State for Energy.

(a) 1975 c. 77.   (b) 1889 c. 63.

John Silkin,
Minister for Planning and Local Government,
Department of the Environment.

Signed by authority of the
Secretary of State

5th February 1976.

William Ross,
Secretary of State for Scotland.

10th February 1976.

John Morris,
Secretary of State for Wales.

11th February 1976.

EXPLANATORY NOTE

(This Note is not part of the Order.)

Some provisions of the Community Land Act 1975 refer to "the appropriate Minister" in relation to statutory undertakers (examples are section 5(3) and paragraphs 5, 17, 18, 19 and 21 of Schedule 4). Section 5(4)(*b*) of the Act empowers the Secretary of State by order to designate the appropriate Minister for those statutory undertakers who are not statutory undertakers for the purposes of Part XI of the Town and Country Planning Act 1971 (c. 78) and Part XI of the Town and Country Planning (Scotland) Act 1972 (c. 52).

This Order, therefore, names the Secretary of State for Energy as the appropriate Minister for the National Coal Board.

Section 5(4)(*b*) also empowers the Secretary of State to give a meaning to references to the Secretary of State and the appropriate Minister. This order provides that, as respects the National Coal Board, the Secretary of State and the appropriate Minister shall mean the Secretary of State for the Environment, for Scotland or for Wales (as appropriate) and the Secretary of State for Energy.

STATUTORY INSTRUMENTS

1976 No. 199

COMMUNITY LAND

The Community Land (Appropriate Minister) Order 1976

Made - - -	11*th February* 1976
Laid before Parliament	23*rd February* 1976
Coming into Operation	6*th April* 1976

The Secretary of State for the Environment, in relation to England, the Secretary of State for Scotland, in relation to Scotland, and the Secretary of State for Wales, in relation to Wales, in exercise of the powers conferred on them by sections 5(4)(*b*) and 53(2) of the Community Land Act 1975(a), and of all other powers enabling them in that behalf, hereby order as follows:—

1. This order shall come into operation on 6th April 1976 and may be cited as the Community Land (Appropriate Minister) Order 1976.

2. The Interpretation Act 1889(b) shall apply for the interpretation of this order as it applies for the interpretation of an Act of Parliament.

3. In the Community Land Act 1975, the expression "the appropriate Minister" in relation to the statutory undertakers set out in column 1 in the following Table shall have the meaning given in column 2 of that Table as respects those undertakers—

Statutory Undertakers	*Appropriate Minister*
The British Broadcasting Corporation.	The Secretary of State for the Home Department.
The British Steel Corporation.	The Secretary of State for Industry.
The Independent Broadcasting Authority.	The Secretary of State for the Home Department.
The United Kingdom Atomic Energy Authority.	The Secretary of State for Energy.

4. In relation to the statutory undertakers set out in column 1 of the above Table, any reference in the Community Land Act 1975 to the Secretary of State and the appropriate Minister shall have effect as if it were a reference—

(*a*) in England, to the Secretary of State for the Environment and the appropriate Minister specified as respects those undertakers in column 2 of that Table,

(*b*) in Scotland, to the Secretary of State for Scotland and the appropriate Minister specified as respects those undertakers in column 2 of that Table,

---

(a) 1975 c. 77.　　　　　　　　　　　　(b) 1889 c. 63.

(c) in Wales, to the Secretary of State for Wales and the appropriate Minister specified as respects those undertakers in column 2 of that Table.

John Silkin,
Signed by authority of   Minister for Planning and Local Government
the Secretary of State   Department of the Environment.

5th February 1976.

William Ross,
Secretary of State for Scotland.

10th February 1976.

John Morris,
Secretary of State for Wales.

11th February 1976

EXPLANATORY NOTE

(This Note is not part of the Order.)

Some provisions in the Community Land Act 1975 refer to "the appropriate Minister" in relation to statutory undertakers (examples are section 5(3) and paragraphs 5, 17, 18, 19 and 21 of Schedule 4). Section 5(4)(a) of the Act provides that, in relation to those statutory undertakers who are also statutory undertakers for the purposes of Part XI of the Town and Country Planning Act 1971 (c. 78) and Part XI of the Town and Country Planning (Scotland) Act 1972 (c. 52), the expression "the appropriate Minister" has the meaning it has for Part XI of those Acts.

For those statutory undertakers who are not statutory undertakers for the purposes of Part XI of the Planning Acts, section 5(4)(b) empowers the Secretary of State by order to designate the appropriate Minister. This order sets out who are to be the appropriate Ministers for the statutory undertakers named in the order.

Section 5(4)(b) also empowers the Secretary of State to give a meaning to references to the Secretary of State and the appropriate Minister. This order provides that, as respects the statutory undertakers named in it, the Secretary of State and the appropriate Minister shall mean the Secretary of State for the Environment, for Scotland or for Wales (as appropriate) and the appropriate Minister designated by the order for those undertakers.

STATUTORY INSTRUMENTS

1976 No. 201 (L.3)

COUNTY COURTS

The County Court Districts (Miscellaneous) (Amendment) Order 1976

Made - - - - 11th February 1976

Coming into Operation 16th March 1976

The Lord Chancellor, in exercise of the powers conferred on him by section 2 of the County Courts Act 1959(a), hereby makes the following Order:—

1.—(1) This Order may be cited as the County Court Districts (Miscellaneous) (Amendment) Order 1976 and shall come into operation on 16th March 1976.

(2) The Interpretation Act 1889(b) shall apply to the interpretation of this Order as it applies to the interpretation of an Act of Parliament.

2. The County Court Districts (Miscellaneous) Order 1970(c), which amends the County Court Districts Order 1970(d), shall be amended as follows:—

(a) in section 2 of Schedule 2 thereto, for the words "After the entry relating to the Bridport Rural District insert the following two entries:—", where they appear with reference to Dorchester, there shall be substituted the words "After the entry relating to the Blandford Rural District insert the following two entries:—"; and

(b) in section 3 of Schedule 2 thereto, for the words—

"In the entry relating to the Stratton Rural District:—

For "Holsworthy" substitute "Bideford"	Insert "Jacobstow, St. Genny's".",

where they appear with reference to Launceston, there shall be substituted the words—

"Immediately after the entry relating to the Launceston Rural District insert the following entry:—

Stratton Rural District (part). *Other part* in Bideford County Court District.	Jacobstow, St. Genny's.".

Dated 11th February 1976.

Elwyn-Jones, C.

(a) 1959 c. 22.
(c) S.I. 1970/904 (1970 II, p. 2833).
(b) 1889 c. 63.
(d) S.I. 1970/16 (1970 I, p. 17).

EXPLANATORY NOTE

(This Note is not part of the Order.)

This Order corrects two formal errors in the County Court Districts (Miscellaneous) Order 1970.

STATUTORY INSTRUMENTS

1976 No. 202

TRADE DESCRIPTIONS

The Textile Products (Determination of Composition) Regulations 1976

Made - - - -	13*th February* 1976
Laid before Parliament	23*rd February* 1976
Coming into Operation	19*th March* 1976

The Secretary of State, being a Minister designated (a) for the purposes of section 2(2) of the European Communities Act 1972(b) concerning the composition, marketing, labelling, classification or description of textiles and products incorporating textiles, in exercise of the powers conferred by that section, hereby makes the following Regulations:—

1. These Regulations may be cited as the Textile Products (Determination of Composition) Regulations 1976 and shall come into operation on 19th March 1976.

2.—(1) In these Regulations:—

"B.S. 4407" means the British Standard of that number published by the British Standards Institution in November 1975;

"textile product" has the same meaning as in the Textile Products (Indications of Fibre Content) Regulations 1973(c), as amended (d).

(2) The Interpretation Act 1889(e) shall apply for the interpretation of these Regulations as it applies for the interpretation of an Act of Parliament.

(3) For the purposes of these Regulations a reference in B.S. 4407 to another British Standard shall be construed as a reference to that other British Standard as it has effect on the date on which these Regulations are made.

3.—(1) These Regulations shall apply for determining for the purposes of the Textile Products (Indications of Fibre Content) Regulations 1973 in the course of any official test the composition of any textile product comprising a binary textile fibre mixture or a ternary textile fibre mixture.

(2) In this Regulation "official test" means a test carried out by or on behalf of a person whose duty it is to enforce the said Regulations of 1973.

4. Test samples and test specimens of a textile product shall be prepared for analysis in accordance with the provisions of Schedule 1 hereto.

(a) The European Communities (Designation) Order 1972, S.I. 1972/1811 (1972 III, p. 5216).
(b) 1972 c. 68.
(c) S.I. 1973/2124 (1973 III, p. 7301).
(d) S.I. 1975/928 (1975 II, p. 3239).
(e) 1889 c. 63.

5.—(1) Wherever possible the fibre components of the textile product being analysed shall be separated manually. Where this is not possible the method used shall be based on the selective solution of the individual components.

(2) Where manual separation is possible the analysis shall be carried out in accordance with sections two and three of B.S. 4407, and the results shall be calculated and expressed in accordance with the said section two.

(3) Where manual separation is not possible the analysis shall be carried out in accordance with section two of B.S. 4407 and (subject to Regulation 7 below) with the appropriate method set out in section four thereof; and in the case of a ternary mixture in accordance with one or more of the four variants set out in section five thereof. The results shall be calculated and expressed in accordance with the said section four.

Nothing in the foregoing provisions of this paragraph shall be taken as restricting the choice of which of the four variants is or are to be used in the analysis of any particular ternary mixture.

(4) The test report shall comply with the provisions of clause 10 of B.S. 4407, and in the case of a ternary mixture, shall also indicate the variant or variants used to carry out the analysis.

6. The composition of a textile product comprising a binary textile fibre mixture other than one for which a special method of test is set out in section four of B.S. 4407 shall be ascertained by the use of any valid method of analysis; and the test report shall set out the result obtained and, so far as is known, the degree of accuracy of the method used.

7. Regulations 5(3) and 6 shall have effect as if methods 3 and 14 were omitted from section four of B.S. 4407:

Provided that nothing in this Regulation shall be taken as prohibiting the use of those methods in appropriate cases.

8. The provisions of Schedule 2 hereto shall apply in relation to tests carried out for the purposes of these Regulations.

Neil G. Carmichael,
Parliamentary Under-Secretary of State,
Department of Industry.

13th February 1976.

Regulation 4

SCHEDULE 1

PREPARATION OF TEST SAMPLES AND TEST SPECIMENS TO DETERMINE THE
FIBRE COMPOSITION OF TEXTILE PRODUCTS

Field of application

1. This Schedule gives procedures for obtaining laboratory test samples of a suitable size for pre-treatment for quantitative analysis (i.e. of a mass not exceeding 100 g) from laboratory bulk samples, and for selecting test specimens from the laboratory test samples that have been pre-treated to remove non-fibrous matter[1].

Definitions

2. In this Schedule—

"bulk source" means that quantity of material which is judged on the basis of one series of test results. This may comprise, for example, all the material in one delivery of cloth; all the cloth woven from a particular beam; a consignment of yarn, a bale or a group of bales of raw fibre;

"laboratory bulk sample" means that portion of the bulk source taken to be representative of the whole, and which is available to the laboratory. The size and nature of the laboratory bulk sample should be sufficient to overcome adequately the variability of the bulk source and to facilitate ease of handling in the laboratory[2];

"laboratory test sample" means that portion of the laboratory bulk sample that is subjected to pre-treatment to remove non-fibrous matter, and from which test specimens are taken. The size and nature of the laboratory test sample should be sufficient to overcome adequately the variability of the laboratory bulk sample;[3]

"test specimen" means the portion of material required to give an individual test result, and selected from the laboratory test sample.

Principle

3. The laboratory test sample is selected so that it is representative of the laboratory bulk sample.

The test specimens are taken from the laboratory test sample in such a way that each of them is representative of the laboratory test sample.

Sampling from loose fibres

4.—(1) Unorientated fibres—Obtain the laboratory test sample by selecting at random tufts from the laboratory bulk sample. Mix thoroughly the whole of the laboratory test sample by means of a laboratory carder.[4] Subject the web or mixture, including loose fibres and fibres adhering to the equipment used for mixing, to the pre-treatment Then select test specimens, in proportion to the respective masses, from the web or mixture, from the loose fibres and from the fibres adhering to the equipment.

If the card web remains intact after pre-treatment, select the test specimens in the manner described in sub-paragraph (2) below. If the card web is disturbed by the pre-treatment, select each test specimen by removing at random at least 16 small tufts of suitable and approximately equal size and then combine them.

(2) Orientated fibres (cards, webs, slivers, rovings)—From randomly selected parts of the laboratory bulk sample cut not less than ten cross-sections each of mass approximately 1 g. Subject the laboratory test sample so formed to the pre-treatment. Recombine the cross-sections by laying them side by side and obtain the test specimen by cutting through them so as to take a portion of each of the ten lengths.

---

[1] In some cases it is necessary to pre-treat the individual test specimen.
[2] For made-up and finished articles see paragraph 7.
[3] See paragraph 1.
[4] The laboratory carder may be replaced by a fibre blender, or the fibres may be mixed by the method of "tufts and rejects".

Sampling yarn

5.—(1) Yarn in packages or in hanks—Sample all the packages in the bulk laboratory sample.

Withdrawn the appropriate continuous equal lengths from each package either by winding skeins of the same number of turns on a wrap-reel,[1] or by some other means, Unite the lengths side by side either as a single skein or as a tow to form the laboratory test sample, ensuring that there are equal lengths from each package in the skein or tow.

Subject the laboratory test sample to the pre-treatment.

Take test specimens from the laboratory test sample by cutting a bunch of threads of equal length from the skein or tow, taking care to see that the bunch contains all the threads in the sample.

If the tex of the yarn is t and the number of packages selected from the laboratory bulk sample is n, then to obtain a test sample of 10 g, the length of yarn to be withdrawn from each package is $\dfrac{10^6}{nt}$ cm.

If nt is high, i.e. more than 2000, wind a heavier skein and cut it across in two places to make a tow of suitable mass. The ends of any sample in the form of a tow should be securely tied before pre-treatment and test specimens taken from a place remote from the tie bands.

(2) Yarn on warp—Take the laboratory test sample by cutting a length from the end of the warp, not less than 20 cm long and comprising all the yarns in the warp except the selvedge yarns, which are rejected. Tie the bunch of threads together near one end. If the sample is too large for pre-treatment as a whole divide it into two or more portions, each tied together for pre-treatment, and reunite the portions after each has been pre-treated separately. Take a test specimen by cutting a suitable length from the laboratory test sample from the end remote from the tie band, and comprising all the threads in the warp. For warp of N threads of tex t, the length of a specimen of mass 1 g is $\dfrac{10^5}{Nt}$ cm.

Sampling fabric

6.—(1) From a laboratory bulk sample consisting of a single cutting representative of the cloth—Cut a diagonal strip from one corner to the other and remove the selvedges. This strip is the laboratory test sample. To obtain a laboratory test sample of x g, the strip area shall be $\dfrac{x \times 10^4}{G}$ cm^2, where G is the mass of the cloth in g/m^2.

Subject the laboratory test sample to the pre-treatment and then cut the strip transversely into four equal lengths and superimpose them.

Take test specimens from any part of the layered material by cutting through all the layers so that each specimen contains an equal length of each layer.

If the fabric has a woven design, make the width of the laboratory test sample, measured parallel to the warp direction, not less than one warp repeat of the design. If, with this condition satisfied, the laboratory test sample is too large to be treated as a whole, cut it into equal parts, pre-treat them separately, and superimpose these parts before selection of the test specimen, taking care that corresponding parts of the design do not coincide.

(2) From a laboratory bulk sample consisting of several cuttings—Treat each cutting as described in sub-paragraph (1) above, and give each result separately.

Sampling made-up and finished articles

7. The bulk laboratory sample is normally a complete made-up or finished article or a representative fraction of one.

---

[1] If the packages can be mounted in a convenient creel a number can be wound simultaneously.

Where appropriate determine the percentage of the various parts of the article not having the same fibre content, in order to check compliance with Regulation 3(4) of the Textile Products (Indications of Fibre Content) Regulations 1973.

Select a laboratory test sample representative of the part of the made-up or finished article, whose composition must be shown by the label. If the article has several labels, select laboratory test samples representative of each part corresponding to a given label.

If the article whose composition is to be determined is not uniform, it may be necessary to select laboratory test samples from each of the parts of the article and to determine the relative proportions of the various parts in relation to the whole article in question.

Then calculate the percentages taking into account the relative proportions of the sampled parts.

Subject the laboratory test samples to the pre-treatment.
Then select test specimens representative of the pre-treated laboratory test samples.

Regulation 8

SCHEDULE 2

1. Substances that are to be left out of account in calculating the percentage fibre content of the textile product by virtue of paragraph 7(1)(*d*) of Schedule 1 to the Textile Products (Indications of Fibre Content) Regulations 1973 (that is to say, fatty substances, bindings, sizings, dressings, additional dyeing and printing products and other textile processing products) shall before analysis be removed by the appropriate method of pre-treatment provided for in B.S. 4407.

2. At least two determinations shall be made, either by manual separation or by chemical separation. If the results of duplicate tests differ by more than 2%, two repeat determinations shall be made.

EXPLANATORY NOTE

(*This Note is not part of the Regulations.*)

These Regulations implement Council Directive No. 72/276/EEC (O.J. No. L173, 31.7.1972, p. 1) (O.J./S.E. 1972 (III), p. 787) as amended (Supplement to the first series of Special Editions (1952-1972) of the Official Journal of the European Communities—Consolidated edition of Corrigenda, p. 100, published in July 1975) and Council Directive No. 73/44/EEC (O.J. No. L83, 30.3.1973, p. 1).

The Regulations specify the test methods to be used to determine the composition of textile products comprising a binary textile fibre mixture or a ternary fibre mixture for the purposes of enforcement of the Textile Products (Indications of Fibre Content) Regulations 1973.

STATUTORY INSTRUMENTS

1976 No. 206

RATING AND VALUATION

The Post Office (Rateable Values) Order 1976

Made - - - -	*7th January* 1976
Laid before Parliament	*15th January* 1976
Coming into Operation	*13th February* 1976

The Secretary of State for the Environment, in exercise of the powers conferred upon him by section 19 of the Local Government Act 1974(**a**) and section 114 of the General Rate Act 1967(**b**) as applied by section 22(3) of the Local Government Act 1974 and of all other powers enabling him in that behalf, after consultation with such associations of local authorities appearing to him to be concerned and with the local authority and the person carrying on an undertaking with whom consultations appeared to him to be desirable, hereby makes the following order:—

Title and Commencement

1. This Order may be cited as the Post Office (Rateable Values) Order 1976 and shall come into operation on the day following the day on which it has been approved by a resolution of each House of Parliament.

Interpretation

2.—(1) In this order,

"the Commissioners" means the Commissioners of Inland Revenue;

"the Kingston upon Hull Telephone Area" means the area described in the Schedule to this order;

"rate year" means the year for which apportionment of the rateable value of the relevant Post Office hereditaments is being determined;

"relevant Post Office hereditaments" means all those hereditaments occupied by the Post Office referred to in paragraph 5(a) of Schedule 3 to the Local Government Act 1974; and

"year" means a period of 12 months beginning with 1st April.

(2) The Interpretation Act 1889(**c**) shall apply for the interpretation of this order as it applies for the interpretation of an Act of Parliament.

(**a**) 1974 c. 7.   (**b**) 1967 c. 9.   (**c**) 1889 c. 63.

Determination of rateable value

3. For the year 1976-7 and subsequent years the rateable value of the relevant Post Office hereditaments in rating areas and rating districts shall be determined by the method specified in the following articles of this order.

4.—(1) The Commissioners shall calculate the rateable value of the relevant Post Office hereditaments in all rating areas and districts in accordance with the following formula:—

$$£13,500,000 \times \frac{E + T}{8,975,000}$$

E being the number of exchange connections on 31st March in the year penultimate to the rate year, and

T being one-third of the number of television relay connections on 31st March in the year penultimate to the rate year.

(2) Where the sum calculated under paragraph (1) above includes a sum of pounds less than £100,000 then where that sum is £50,000 or more it shall be rounded up to the nearest £100,000 and where that sum is less than £50,000 it shall be disregarded.

(3) In this article—

(a) the expression "number of exchange connections" means the aggregate of the number of exclusive exchange lines and the number of subscribers sharing party lines of the Post Office in England and Wales, and

(b) the expression "number of television relay connections" means the number of subscribers to wires of the Post Office used for the diffusion of television programmes in England and Wales.

(4) The Post Office shall calculate the sum of the number of exchange connections and one-third of the number of television relay connections and certify that sum to the Commissioners as the correct figure for the expression E + T.

(5) Where the sum of the number of exchange connections and the number of television relay connections includes a figure less than 1000 it shall be sufficient where that figure is 500 or more for the certificate required by paragraph (4) above to state that number rounded up to the nearest 1000 and where that figure is less than 500 to disregard it.

(6) It shall be the duty of the Post Office, before 30th September in the year preceding the rate year, to transmit to the Commissioners the certificate required by paragraph (4) above; but for the rate year 1976-7 it shall be sufficient for the certificate to be transmitted to the Commissioners before 31st March 1976.

Apportionment of rateable value

5.—(1) The Commissioners shall, in accordance with the following provisions of this article, apportion the sum calculated in accordance with article 4 of this order among rating areas and rating districts and shall, before 31st January preceding the rate year, notify each rating authority of the amount of the rateable value of the relevant Post Office hereditaments occupied by the Post Office during the rate year in the area of that rating authority and shall include any apportionment made under paragraph (3) of this article;

but for the rate year 1976-7 it shall be sufficient for the Commissioners to notify each rating authority as aforesaid by 1st June 1976.

(2) Subject to article 6 below and paragraphs (5) and (6) of this article the sum calculated in accordance with article 4 of this order shall be apportioned among individual rating areas in accordance with the following formula:—

$$\left(\frac{R}{4} \times \frac{A1}{A2} \right) \; + \; \left(\frac{R}{4} \times \frac{ND1}{ND2} \right) \; + \; \left(\frac{R}{2} \times \frac{H1}{H2} \right)$$

R being the sum calculated in accordance with article 4 of this order;

A1 being the acreage of the individual rating area as at 1st April in the rate year;

A2 being the total acreage of all rating areas in England and Wales as at 1st April in the rate year but including one-tenth only of the acreage of the Kingston upon Hull Telephone Area;

ND1 being the non-domestic rateable value of the individual rating area;

ND2 being the aggregate of the non-domestic rateable values of all rating areas in England and Wales but including one-tenth only of the non-domestic rateable value of the Kingston upon Hull Telephone Area;

H1 being the number of domestic hereditaments in the individual rating area as at 1st April in the year preceding the rate year; and

H2 being the aggregate of the number of domestic hereditaments in all rating areas in England and Wales as at 1st April in the year preceding the rate year but including one-tenth only of the number of domestic hereditaments in the Kingston upon Hull Telephone Area.

(3) Where a rating area consists of more than one rating district the rateable value apportioned to that area in accordance with the formula in paragraph (2) above shall be further apportioned to each rating district within that area in accordance with the following formula:—

$$AR \times \frac{V1}{V2}$$

AR being the apportioned rateable value determined for the individual rating area in accordance with the formula in paragraph (2) above;

V1 being the total rateable value of the individual rating district; and

V2 being the total rateable value of the individual rating area.

(4) Where the Commissioners make the notification required by paragraph (1) above the valuation officer, at or as soon as may be after the beginning of the rate year shall cause such alteration, if any, to be made in the valuation list as may be requisite for showing the Post Office in the list as the occupier of a hereditament of that rateable value; and if any such alteration is made after the beginning of the rate year, it shall be treated as having been made at the beginning of the rate year:

Provided that if the rate year referred to is one beginning with the date on which a new valuation list comes into force this paragraph shall not apply but the valuation officer shall include the Post Office in the list as the occupier of a hereditament of the said rateable value.

(5) In this article—

(*a*) the total rateable value of a rating district or a rating area shall be taken to be the aggregate of the rateable values of every hereditament as assessed in the valuation list for the district or area on 1st April in the year preceding the rate year excluding any hereditament there appearing in pursuance of sections 33(3) and (5) and 34(3) of the General Rate Act 1967, section 52(1) (a) of the Post Office Act 1969(a) or this order and which the Commissioners, for the purpose of computing the apportionment required by paragraph (1) above certify to be the correct figures for the expressions V1 and V2;

(*b*) the non-domestic rateable value of a rating area shall be taken to be the total rateable value represented by the expression V2 excluding the rateable value of domestic hereditaments as assessed in the valuation list for the area on 1st April in the year preceding the rate year and which the Commissioners, for the purpose of computing the apportionment required by paragraph (1) above, certify to be the correct figure for the expression ND1;

(*c*) domestic hereditaments shall be taken to be the dwelling houses and single assessed caravan sites upon which there is no rateable structure; and

(*d*) the number of domestic hereditaments in a rating area shall be taken to be the number of all those domestic hereditaments the rateable value of which is excluded from non-domestic rateable value and which the Commissioners, for the purpose of computing the apportionment required by paragraph (1) above, certify to be the correct figure for the expression H1.

(6) For the purposes of calculating the apportionment required by this article—

(*a*) the areas in the District of Beverley described in the Schedule to this order shall be deemed to constitute a rating area and the remaining parishes of that district shall be deemed to constitute another rating area; and

(*b*) the parishes in the District of Holderness named in the Schedule to this order shall be deemed to constitute a rating area and the remaining areas of that district shall be deemed to constitute another rating area.

Special provision for the Kingston upon Hull Telephone Area

6.—(1) The provisions of article 5 above shall apply to the rating areas and rating districts in the Kingston upon Hull Telephone Area subject to the following modifications.

(2) For the expressions A1, ND1 and H1 the acreage, non-domestic rateable value, and the number of domestic hereditaments of a rating area in the Kingston upon Hull Telephone Area shall be reduced by 90%.

(3) The certificates of the Commissioners shall, where they relate to the rating areas to which this article applies, be modified accordingly.

(a) 1969 c. 48.

Amendment and Repeals

7. In section 52 of the Post Office Act 1969—

(*a*) in subsection (4), after the words "by virtue of this section", there shall be inserted the words "or of an order under section 19 of the Local Government Act 1974", and

(*b*) the following provisions are hereby repealed—

(i) in subsection (1)—paragraph (a), paragraph (i) and the words "so much of the amount determined under paragraph (*a*) above as is apportioned to a rating district shall be the rateable value of such of the hereditaments mentioned in that paragraph as are in that district, and", and

(ii) subsections (2) and (3).

SCHEDULE

KINGSTON UPON HULL TELEPHONE AREA

The District of Kingston upon Hull.

In the District of Beverley, the areas of the former borough of Beverley and urban district of Haltemprice and the Parishes of Brantingham, Elloughton, Molescroft, North Ferriby, Rowley, Skidby, Swanland, Tickton, Walkington, Wawne, Welton and Woodmansey.

In the District of Holderness, the Parishes of Bilton, Coniston, Hedon, Paull, Preston, Sproatley and Swine.

Anthony Crosland,
Secretary of State for the Environment.

7th January 1976.

EXPLANATORY NOTE

(This Note is not part of the Order.)

This Order specifies a method for determining the rateable value of certain Post Office hereditaments, namely, property (not in a building) used for tele-communication purposes, for the year 1976-7 and subsequent years in place of that specified in the Post Office (Rateable Values) Order 1972 (S.I. 1972/1794). The order continues the method previously provided in that Order save that there is introduced into the formula for determining the rateable value of those hereditaments in all rating areas and districts an element for the number of subscribers to wires of the Post Office used for the diffusion of television programmes. It also amends section 52(4) of the Post Office Act 1969 so as to apply that provision to valuations shown in a valuation list by virtue of this Order.

The Order repeals provisions in section 52 of the Post Office Act 1969 under which the 1972 Order (so far as it relates to the hereditaments dealt with in this Order), was made.

STATUTORY INSTRUMENTS

1976 No. 207

RATING AND VALUATION
The Post Office (Rateable Values) (Amendment) Order 1976

Made - - - -	*2nd February* 1976
Laid before Parliament	*2nd February* 1976
Coming into Operation	*13th February* 1976

The Secretary of State for the Environment, in exercise of the powers conferred upon him by section 19 of the Local Government Act 1974(a) and section 114 of the General Rate Act 1967(b) as applied by section 22(3) of the Local Government Act 1974 and all other powers enabling him in that behalf, after consultation with such associations of local authorities appearing to him to be concerned and with the local authority and the person carrying on an undertaking with whom consultations appeared to him to be desirable, hereby makes the following order:—

Title, commencement and interpretation

1.—(1) This order may be cited as the Post Office (Rateable Values) (Amendment) Order 1976 and shall come into operation on the day following the day on which it has been approved by a resolution of each House of Parliament.

(2) The Interpretation Act 1889(c) shall apply for the interpretation of this order as it applies for the interpretation of an Act of Parliament.

2. The Post Office (Rateable Values) Order 1976(d) shall have effect as if in article 4(5) thereof, after the words "exchange connections and", there were inserted the words "one-third of".

2nd February 1976.	*Anthony Crosland,* Secretary of State for the Environment.

(a) 1974 c. 7.   (b) 1967 c. 9.   (c) 1889 c. 63.   (d) S.I. 1976/206 (1976 I, p. 508).

EXPLANATORY NOTE
(This Note is not part of the Order.)

This Order makes a minor drafting amendment to the provision of the Post Office (Rateable Values) Order 1976 relating to the calculation of the rateable value of certain Post Office hereditaments.

STATUTORY INSTRUMENTS

1976 No. 208

AGRICULTURE

The Agricultural Land Tribunals (Areas) (Amendment) Order 1976

Made - - - -	*13th February* 1976
Laid before Parliament	*24th February* 1976
Coming into Operation	*17th March* 1976

The Lord Chancellor, in exercise of the powers conferred on him by section 73(1) of the Agriculture Act 1947(a), as amended by paragraph 3 of Schedule 1 to the Agriculture Act 1958(b), hereby makes the following Order:—

1.—(1) This Order may be cited as the Agricultural Land Tribunals (Areas) (Amendment) Order 1976 and shall come into operation on 17th March 1976.

(2) The Interpretation Act 1889(c) shall apply to the interpretation of this Order as it applies to the interpretation of an Act of Parliament.

(3) In this Order "the principal Order" means the Agricultural Land Tribunals (Areas) Order 1974(d).

2. The principal Order is hereby amended by attaching the Boston and South Holland districts of Lincolnshire (formerly comprised in the Eastern Area) to the East Midland Area:

Provided that nothing in this Article shall affect the jurisdiction of the Agricultural Land Tribunal for the Eastern Area to deal with proceedings pending in that tribunal on the coming into operation of this Order.

3. The Schedule to the principal Order shall accordingly be amended:

(*a*) in respect of the entry relating to the East Midland Area:—
   (i) in column 2, by adding "Lincolnshire";
   (ii) in column 3, by deleting the words "all districts of Lincolnshire except Boston and South Holland";

(*b*) in respect of the entry relating to the Eastern Area, in column 3, by deleting the item relating to the districts of Lincolnshire.

Dated 13th February 1976.

Elwyn-Jones, C.

(**a**) 1947 c. 48.
(**c**) 1889 c. 63.

(**b**) 1958 c. 71.
(**d**) S.I. 1974/66 (1974 1, p. 212).

EXPLANATORY NOTE

(This Note is not part of the Order.)

This Order amends the Agricultural Land Tribunals (Areas) Order 1974 by transferring the districts of Boston and South Holland from the Eastern Area to the East Midland Area.

STATUTORY INSTRUMENTS

1976 No. 210 (S. 14)

TOWN AND COUNTRY PLANNING, SCOTLAND

The Town and Country Planning (Determination of Appeals by Appointed Persons) (Prescribed Classes) (Scotland) Regulations 1976

Made - - - -	13th February 1976
Laid before Parliament	26th February 1976
Coming into Operation	1st April 1976

In exercise of the powers conferred on me by section 273 of and paragraph 1 of Schedule 7 to the Town and Country Planning (Scotland) Act 1972(a) and of all other powers enabling me in that behalf, I hereby make the following regulations:—

Citation and commencement

1. These regulations may be cited as the Town and Country Planning (Determination of Appeals by Appointed Persons) (Prescribed Classes) (Scotland) Regulations 1976 and shall come into operation on 1st April 1976.

Interpretation

2.—(1) In these regulations, unless the context otherwise requires—

"the Act" means the Town and Country Planning (Scotland) Act 1972;

"planning authority" shall be construed in accordance with section 172 of the Local Government (Scotland) Act 1973(b);

"local authority" has the meaning assigned to it by section 275(1) of the Act;

"dwellinghouse" means a building used for residential purposes and includes a flat or other separate dwelling which is comprised in a larger building of which it forms part;

"operational land", except in relation to land of the Post Office, has the meaning assigned to it by section 211 of the Act as read with section 212 of the Act, and in relation to land of the Post Office means, subject to section 212 of the Act so far as applicable, land of the Post Office of any such class as may be specified in regulations made pursuant to paragraph 93(4) of Schedule 4 to the Post Office Act 1969(c);

"statutory undertakers" means persons authorised by any enactment to carry on any railway, light railway, tramway, road transport, water transport, canal, inland navigation, dock, harbour, pier or lighthouse undertaking or any undertaking for the supply of electricity, gas, hydraulic power or water

---

(a) 1972 c. 52.   (b) 1973 c. 65.   (c) 1969 c. 48.

and includes the British Airports Authority, the Post Office and companies which are deemed to be statutory undertakers by virtue of section 141(2) of the Transport Act 1968(a).

(2) References in these regulations to the use of land or buildings for residential purposes shall be construed as excluding a use falling within any of Classes X, XI, or XIII of the Schedule to the Town and Country Planning (Use Classes) (Scotland) Order 1973(b) and references to development for residential purposes shall be construed accordingly.

(3) For the purposes of Schedule 2 to these regulations development or land is concurrently the subject of another appeal to the Secretary of State or of an application referred to him or of an order where that appeal, application or order comes into the jurisdiction of the Secretary of State within the period of one month before or after the giving of notice of the appeal to which Schedule 1 of these regulations relates.

(4) The Interpretation Act 1889(c) applies to the interpretation of these regulations as it applies to the interpretation of an Act of Parliament.

Classes of appeal for determination by Appointed Persons

3. Subject to Regulation 4 hereof, the Secretary of State hereby prescribes the following classes of appeal to be determined by a person appointed for the purpose by the Secretary of State instead of by the Secretary of State, namely:—

    (*a*) appeals under section 33 of the Act (appeals against planning decisions), as originally enacted or as applied by section 34 of the Act (appeals in default of planning decisions), where the appeal relates to an application for planning permission to carry out development of land or for approval of matters reserved by a planning permission for development of land, being in either case development wholly within any one or more of the descriptions in the classes of appeal specified in Schedule 1 to these regulations;

    (*b*) appeals under section 85 of the Act (appeals against enforcement notices) where the breach of planning control alleged in the enforcement notice consists in the carrying out of development wholly within any one or more of the descriptions in the classes of appeal specified in Schedule 1 to these regulations or failure to comply with a condition or limitation on a grant of planning permission for any such development.

Classes of appeal reserved for determination by the Secretary of State

4. Regulation 3 hereof shall not apply to:—

    (*a*) any such appeal as mentioned therein if it relates to an application in respect of development falling within any one or more of the classes of case specified in Schedule 2 to these regulations, or to an enforcement notice alleging a breach of planning control in respect of development falling within any one or more of the classes of case specified in the said Schedule; or

    (*b*) any such appeal as is mentioned in paragraph (*b*) of that regulation where the grounds upon which the appeal is made (as originally indicated in the notice of appeal or as amended at any time before the expiry of the period specified in the notice as the period at the end of which the notice is to take effect) include any of the grounds set out in paragraphs (*b*) to (*e*) of section 85(1) of the Act.

Publicity for Directions under paragraph 1 *of schedule* 7 *to the Act*

5. On the making by the Secretary of State of a direction under paragraph 1 of Schedule 7 to the Act he may by notice in writing enclosing a copy of the direction require the planning authority of any area for which the direction has effect to publish as soon as may be a notice in at least one newspaper circulating in the area; and this notice shall contain a concise statement of the effect of the direction and shall specify the place or places where a copy of the direction may be seen at all reasonable hours.

Saving

6. These regulations shall not apply to any appeal of which notice was given before the coming into operation of these regulations.

William Ross,
One of Her Majesty's Principal
Secretaries of State.

New St. Andrew's House,
Edinburgh.
13th February 1976.

SCHEDULE 1
Classes of Appeals to be determined by Appointed Persons

Appeals in respect of Development by Operations

1. The development for residential purposes of land not exceeding 0·8 hectare (2 acres) in extent where the application for planning permission is an outline application within the terms of Article 5(2) of the Town and Country Planning (General Development) (Scotland) Order 1975(a) and the appeal arises therefrom or on an application for approval required under Article 6 of that Order.

2. The erection, enlargement or other alteration of a building or buildings for use as not more than 10 dwellinghouses, where the application for planning permission is not an outline application.

3. The carrying out of building, engineering or other operations on land for a purpose ancillary to the existing use of land for residential purposes, or ancillary or incidental to development of land for residential purposes.

4. The formation, laying out or widening of a means of access or the laying down of hard standing for the parking of vehicles.

Appeals in respect of change of use

5. The change in the use of a building or buildings to use as not more than 10 dwellinghouses.

6. The change in the use of a building or buildings in use as not more than 10 dwellinghouses to another use for residential purposes.

SCHEDULE 2
Classes of Cases excepted from Schedule 1

1. Development in respect of which the Secretary of State has given a direction under Article 8 of the General Development Order restricting the grant of planning permission, e.g. where a trunk road or special road was affected.

2. Development by a local authority.

3. Development by statutory undertakers on operational land or on land in the case of which the circumstances mentioned in section 214(2) of the Act apply.

4. Development by the National Coal Board on land of a class specified in regulations made under section 259 of the Act.

5. Development for which planning permission has been refused by a planning authority, or granted subject to conditions, following an expression of views by a Government Department or new town development corporation that the application should either not be granted or be granted only subject to conditions.

6. Development where the same development is concurrently the subject or part of the subject of another appeal to the Secretary of State or of an application referred to him under any provisions of the Act.

7. Development where the same land is concurrently the subject or part of the subject of another appeal to the Secretary of State or of an application referred to him in respect of development wholly or partly outside the classes specified in Schedule 1 to these regulations.

8. Land or buildings used as boarding or guest houses, hotels with sleeping accommodation, residential schools and homes etc. (i.e. any use falling within classes X XI and XIII of the Town and Country Planning (Use Classes) (Scotland) Order 1973).

(a)   S.I. 1975/679 (1975 I, p. 2410).

EXPLANATORY NOTE

(This Note is not part of the Regulations.)

These Regulations prescribe classes of appeals (set out in Schedule 1) which are to be determined by persons appointed for the purpose by the Secretary of State instead of being determined by the Secretary of State.

Regulation 4 provides that certain excepted classes of appeals (set out in Schedule 2) which would otherwise fall within the prescribed classes are to continue to be determined by the Secretary of State. Insofar as appeals against enforcement notices which are included in the appeals covered by these regulations are concerned, regulation 4 also excepts from the prescribed classes appeals made on grounds which include any of the grounds set out in paragraphs (b) to (e) of section 85(1) of the Town and Country Planning (Scotland) Act 1972.

Regulation 5 provides for the advertisement by planning authorities of any direction made by the Secretary of State under paragraph 1 of Schedule 7 to the Town and Country Planning (Scotland) Act 1972 whereby specified classes of appeals are to be determined by him instead of by an appointed person.

STATUTORY INSTRUMENTS

1976 No. 211 (S.15)

LOCAL GOVERNMENT, SCOTLAND

The Local Authorities (Staff Transfer and Protection) (Scotland) Amendment Order 1976

Made - - -	*13th February* 1976
Laid before Parliament	*26th February* 1976
Coming into Operation	*18th March* 1976

In exercise of the powers conferred on me by section 215 of the Local Government (Scotland) Act 1973 **(a)**, and of all other powers enabling me in that behalf, I hereby make the following order:—

Title and commencement

1. This order may be cited as the Local Authorities (Staff Transfer and Protection) (Scotland) Amendment Order 1976 and shall come into operation on 18th March 1976.

Interpretation

2.—(1) In this order, unless the context otherwise requires—
"the principal order" means the Local Authorities (Staff Transfer and Protection) (Scotland) Order 1975 **(b)**.

(2) The Interpretation Act 1889 **(c)** shall apply for the interpretation of this order as it applies for the interpretation of an Act of Parliament.

Amendments to the principal order

3. In Article 4(2) of the principal order there shall be substituted the following preamble to sub-paragraphs (*a*) (*b*) and (*c*)—
"No provision of articles 5 to 11 inclusive of this order for the transfer of officers, in their application to any local authority applies to — "

4. In line 2 of article 12(7) of the principal order the word 'or' where it first occurs shall be deleted.

(a) 1973 c. 65.   (b) S.I. 1975/703 (1975 I, p. 2538).   (c) 1889 c. 63.

5. The following article shall be inserted in the principal Order.

"Protection of Officers appointed before 16th May 1975".

   12A. Any question by an officer appointed before 16th May 1975 to hold any office or employment before or as from that date (and who but for the appointment would be transferred on 16th May 1975 by virtue of this Order or the Local Authorities (Staff Transfer Schemes) (Scotland) Order 1975 **(a)**) as to (a) whether the duties of such office or employment are reasonably comparable to those in which he was engaged immediately before the appointment or (b) whether the terms and conditions of his employment are not less favourable than those which he enjoyed immediately before the appointment shall be determined in accordance with the arrangements set out in the Appeals Memorandum.

William Ross,

One of Her Majesty's Principal
Secretaries of State.

New St. Andrew's House,
Edinburgh.
13th February 1976.

EXPLANATORY NOTE

(This Note is not part of the Order.)

   This Order affords a right of appeal to officers appointed before 16 May 1975 who were not covered by any transfer and whose appointment is subject to the requirements of article 6 of the Local Government (New Councils, etc.) (Scotland) Order 1974 (S.I. 1974/653).

(a) S.I. 1975/574 (1975 I, p. 2106).

STATUTORY INSTRUMENTS

1976 No. 212

EXCHANGE CONTROL

The Exchange Control (Purchase of Foreign Currency) (Amendment) Order 1976

Made - - - -	16*th February* 1976
Laid before Parliament	26*th February* 1976
Coming into Operation	18*th March* 1976

The Treasury, in exercise of the powers conferred upon them by sections 31 and 36(5) of the Exchange Control Act 1947(a), hereby make the following Order:—

1.—(1) This Order may be cited as the Exchange Control (Purchase of Foreign Currency) (Amendment) Order 1976, and shall come into operation on 18th March 1976.

(2) The Interpretation Act 1889(b) shall apply for the interpretation of this Order as it applies for the interpretation of an Act of Parliament.

2. The Schedule to the Exchange Control (Purchase of Foreign Currency) Order 1970(c), as amended (d), shall be further amended as follows:—

    (*a*) by inserting the words "American Express International Banking Corporation." after the words "Allied Irish Banks Ltd.";

    (*b*) by deleting the words "Morris Wigram Ltd."; and

    (*c*) by inserting the words "Schlesinger Ltd." and "Standard Chartered Bank Ltd." after the words "Royal Bank of Scotland Ltd., The.".

3. This Order shall extend to the Channel Islands, and any reference in this Order to the Exchange Control Act 1947 includes a reference to that Act as extended by the Exchange Control (Channel Islands) Order 1947(e).

James A. Dunn,

T. Pendry,

Two of the Lords Commissioners
of Her Majesty's Treasury.

16th February 1976.

(**a**) 1947 c. 14.
(**b**) 1889 c. 63.
(**c**) S.I. 1970/789 (1970 II, p. 2499).
(**d**) S.I. 1973/1997, 1975/313 (1973 III, p. 6879; 1975 I, p. 839).
(**e**) S.R. & O. 1947/2034 (Rev. VI, p. 1001; 1947 I, p. 660).

EXPLANATORY NOTE

(This Note is not part of the Order.)

The Exchange Control (Purchase of Foreign Currency) Order 1970 *inter alia* exempts from section 1(1) of the Exchange Control Act 1947 the purchase abroad by travellers resident here of foreign currency for travel expenditure if the traveller holds a cheque card issued by a bank named in the Schedule to that Order and encashes his cheque within the limits imposed on the use of his cheque card by the bank which issued it.

This Order adds certain banks to the Schedule to the 1970 Order, so that the exemption is now extended to holders of cheque cards issued by those banks, and the other amendments take account of a change of name.

STATUTORY INSTRUMENTS

1976 No. 213

LONDON GOVERNMENT

The London Councillors Order 1976

Laid before Parliament in draft

Made	-	-	-	*17th February* 1976
Coming into Operation				*2nd March* 1976

The Secretary of State for the Environment, in exercise of the powers conferred upon him by section 8(2) of, and paragraph 9(2) of Schedule 2 to, the Local Government Act 1972(**a**) and of all other powers enabling him in that behalf, hereby makes the following order in the terms of a draft approved by resolution of each House of Parliament:—

1. This order may be cited as the London Councillors Order 1976 and shall come into operation on the fourteenth day after the day on which it is made.

2. The Interpretation Act 1889(**b**) shall apply for the interpretation of this order as it applies for the interpretation of an Act of Parliament.

3. In Schedule 2 to the Local Government Act 1972, in sub-paragraphs (2) and (3) of paragraph 6 (term of office and retirement of councillors of the Greater London Council and London boroughs)—

for "every third year" there shall be substituted "every fourth year";

for "three years" there shall be substituted "four years"; and

for "such third year" there shall be substituted "such fourth year".

4.—(1) The year 1977 is hereby specified for the purposes of paragraph 9 (2)(*a*) of the said Schedule (date on which the offices of alderman of the Greater London Council are to cease to exist).

(2) The year 1978 is hereby specified for the purposes of paragraph 9(2)(*b*) of the said Schedule (date on which the offices of alderman of the London boroughs are to cease to exist).

Anthony Crosland,
Secretary of State for the Environment.

17th February 1976.

(**a**) 1972 c. 70.   (**b**) 1889 c. 63.

EXPLANATORY NOTE
(This Note is not part of the Order.)

On the existing arrangements—

councillors of the Greater London Council were elected in 1973, and will be elected in 1976 and every third year thereafter;

London borough councillors were elected in 1974, and will be elected in 1977 and every third year thereafter.

This Order substitutes quadrennial elections, for the Greater London Council in 1977 and every fourth year thereafter, and for the London boroughs in 1978 and every fourth year thereafter.

The Order also specifies the years in which aldermen of the Greater London Council and the London boroughs are to cease to exist. The basic provision is contained in Schedule 2 to the Act of 1972, but that Schedule empowered the specification of years of elections of councillors for the years 1976 and 1977, which were apt on the system of triennial elections.

STATUTORY INSTRUMENTS

1976 No. 214

LOCAL GOVERNMENT, ENGLAND AND WALES

The Rate Support Grant (Specified Bodies) Regulations 1976

Made - - - -	16*th February* 1976
Laid before Parliament	26*th February* 1976
Coming into Operation	1*st April* 1976

The Secretary of State for the Environment, after consultation with such associations of local authorities as appear to him to be concerned, in exercise of his powers under section 2(7)(*a*) of the Local Government Act 1974(**a**) and of all other powers enabling him in that behalf, hereby makes the following regulations:—

Title, commencement and interpretation

1.—(1) These regulations may be cited as the Rate Support Grant (Specified Bodies) Regulations 1976, and shall come into operation on 1st April 1976.

(2) The Interpretation Act 1889(**b**) shall apply for the interpretation of these regulations as it applies for the interpretation of an Act of Parliament.

Specified bodies

2. The following bodies are hereby specified for the purposes of section 2(7)(*a*) of the Local Government Act 1974, namely:—

a. The National Committee for Audio Visual Aids in Education;

b. The Field Studies Council;

c. The Further Education Staff College;

d. The Local Authorities Conditions of Service Advisory Board.

Signed by authority of
the Secretary of State
16th February 1976.

John Silkin,
Minister for Planning and Local Government,
Department of the Environment.

(**a**) 1974 c. 7. (**b**) 1889 c. 63.

EXPLANATORY NOTE

(This Note is not part of the Regulations.)

Section 2(7) of the Local Government Act 1974 empowers the Secretary of State to defray any expenditure incurred in any year in the provision of services for local authorities by any body specified by him in regulations, and enables him to make an appropriate deduction from the needs element of rate support grant. These regulations specify bodies (in addition to those bodies specified in the Rate Support Grant (Specified Bodies) Regulations 1974 (S.I. 1974/788) and the Rate Support Grant (Specified Bodies) Regulations 1975 (S.I. 1975/5)) in relation to whose services the power to defray expenditure applies.

STATUTORY INSTRUMENTS

1976 No. 215

DIPLOMATIC SERVICE

The Consular Fees Order 1976

Made - - - - 18*th February* 1976
Coming into Operation 15*th March* 1976

At the Court at Buckingham Palace, the 18th day of February 1976

Present,

The Queen's Most Excellent Majesty in Council

Her Majesty, by virtue and in exercise of the powers in that behalf by section 2(1) of the Consular Salaries and Fees Act 1891(a) and section 8(1) of the Fees (Increase) Act 1923(b) or otherwise in Her Majesty vested, is pleased, by and with the advice of Her Privy Council, to order, and it is hereby ordered, as follows:—

1. This Order shall come into operation on 15th March 1976 and may be cited as the Consular Fees Order 1976.

2.—(1) The Interpretation Act 1889(c) shall apply for the interpretation of this Order as it applies for the interpretation of an Act of Parliament and as if this Order and the Orders hereby revoked were Acts of Parliament.

(2) In this Order " consular officer " has the same meaning as in section 3 of the Consular Salaries and Fees Act 1891, read with section 13(4) of the Consular Relations Act 1968(d).

(3) In this Order " consular employee " and " consular premises " have the same meanings as in Article 1 of Schedule 1 to the Consular Relations Act 1968.

3. The several fees set forth in the table in the Schedule annexed to this Order are hereby established to be levied by consular officers, by public officers in Great Britain acting under the authority of a Secretary of State, and by marriage officers under the Foreign Marriage Act 1892(e) and the Marriage with Foreigners Act 1906(f) in the execution of their duties, and the said table shall be construed as part of the Order.

4. The following Orders in Council are hereby revoked:—

The Consular Fees Order 1971(g)
The Consular Fees (Amendment) Order 1973(h)
The Consular Fees (Amendment) (No. 2) Order 1973(i)
The Consular Fees (Amendment) Order 1975(j)
The Consular Fees (Amendment) (No. 2) Order 1975(k).

N. E. Leigh.

(a) 1891 c. 36.   (b) 1923 c. 4.   (c) 1889 c. 63.   (d) 1968 c. 18.   (e) 1892 c. 23.
(f) 1906 c. 40.   (g) S.I. 1971/211 (1971 I, p. 601).
(h) S.I. 1973/597 (1973 I, p. 1907).   (i) S.I. 1973/1082 (1973 II, p. 3320).
(j) S.I. 1975/806 (1975 II, p. 2887).   (k) S.I. 1975/2161 (1975 III, p. 7997).

SCHEDULE

TABLE OF CONSULAR FEES

PART I

NOTARIAL AND KINDRED MATTERS

Fee   £

1 Preparing any certificate, declaration or document not otherwise
   provided for—
   (*a*) in standard form, per copy ...   .   4·00
   (*b*) not in standard form, per 100 words:
       (i) in English   ...   .   4·00
       (ii) in any other language   ...   .   6·00

2 Preparing or signing, or both, a declaration of existence   ...   3·00
   except in connexion with pay or pensions payable by a department of the Government of the United Kingdom or of any
   other Government within the Commonwealth

3 Administering an oath or receiving a declaration or affirmation
   or attesting or legalising a signature or seal   ...   .   3·00
   except where—
   (*a*) the oath, declaration or affirmation is made under the
       Merchant Shipping Acts or in connexion with the loss of a
       passport, or
   (*b*) fee 20, 25, 26, 28, 37 or 38 is to be taken, or
   (*c*) the signature or seal is on a certificate or survey of foreign
       passenger ships running to or from the United Kingdom, or
   (*d*) the signature or seal is on a document required for the
       deposit or withdrawal of money in or from any British Post
       Office or other Government Savings Bank, or
   (*e*) the signature or seal is in connexion with stocks or bonds
       on the registers of the Post Office, with Savings Bank
       Annuities or with annuities granted direct by the National
       Debt Commissioners

   When an oath of allegiance is taken on the form set out in the
   Thirteenth Schedule to the British Nationality Regulations
   1975(a) at the same time as a declaration is made under those
   Regulations, the fee shall be charged once only

4 Supplying witnesses, for each witness   ...   .   2·00

5 Initialling alterations in any document not prepared by the
   consular officer or marking exhibits, for each initialling or
   marking   ...   .   0·50

6 Making or verifying (including certifying where necessary) a copy
   of a document—
   (*a*) in typescript or made by photographic process outside the
       consular premises, for every 100 words   ...   .   3·00
   (*b*) by photographic process, if the copy is made in the consular
       premises, for each page (with a minimum charge of £2·00)   0·50
   (*c*) by photographic process, copies of treaty texts, for each
       paper (with minimum charge of £1·00)   ...   .   0·10

7 Uniting documents and sealing the fastening   ...   .   1·50
   except where fee 38 is to be taken

8 Obtaining a legalisation or other certification from another
   authority upon any document   ...   .   2·00
   in addition to costs, if any

(a) S.I. 1975/225 (1975 I, p. 573).

Fee £

9 Supplying certified copies of documents forming part of the records of a court which is, or was formerly, established under the Foreign Jurisdiction Acts 1890(a) and 1913(b)—
for every page ... ... 1·00

10 Making or verifying (including certifying where necessary) a translation in writing of a document or part of document, for each 100 words or characters (or part thereof) in the foreign language—
(*a*) from or into Amharic, Chinese, Japanese or Korean (three Japanese *Kana* being counted as one character when used independently) ... ... 8·00
(*b*) from or into any other language ... ... 4·00
except where fee 28 or 40 is to be taken

11 Translating and interpreting *viva voce* (except when necessary for the performance of official duties)—
for every 15 minutes ... ... 2·50

PART II

PASSPORTS, VISAS AND KINDRED MATTERS

12 Issuing a passport of not more than 32 pages except where fee 13 is to be taken 8·00

12A Issuing a passport of 94 pages ... ... 16·00

13 Issuing an additional passport of not more than 32 pages of restricted validity ... ... 4·00
except in replacement of a passport lost or temporarily unavailable

14 Issuing a British Visitor's passport ... ... 4·00

15 Issuing a collective passport ... ... 8·00

16 Renewing a passport issued before the introduction of passports of 10 years validity at the office of issue, a certificate of identity or other travel document ... ... 4·00
except where fee 17, 23 or 24 is to be taken

17 Extending for the first time the validity of an additional passport 4·00
except of one in replacement of a passport lost or temporarily unavailable

18 Amending an existing passport in one of the following ways—
(*a*) adding the particulars of a child or children
(*b*) amending the holder's name at the request of the holder
(*c*) adding a fresh photograph or amending the holder's description, except where the holder is under 21 years of age 2·00

19 Making or forwarding, or both, a request or recommendation to an authority of Her Majesty's Government in the United Kingdom, or of a foreign State or Commonwealth country, Colony, Protectorate, Protected State or Trust Territory for the issue or renewal of—
(*a*) a visa or entry permit (except a visa or entry certificate for the United Kingdom) ... ... 1·00
(*b*) any certificate or document (except a Home Office travel document) or any application for registration or naturalization ... ... 2·00
in addition to costs, if any

(a) 1890 c. 37.   (b) 1913 c. 16.

Fee £

20 Issuing and, where required, preparing an Emergency Passport or other document not otherwise provided for in lieu of a passport, or accepting a Declaration of Identity on which a visa is to be granted and issuing a certificate on such declaration describing the applicant ... ... 2·00

21 Granting a visa or entry permit—
for an ordinary visa or entry permit ... ... 3·00
for a transit visa or permit ... ... 1·00
or for any visa or entry permit such sums, being the equivalents of fees charged by the authorities of any State for granting a visa or entry permit to a citizen of the United Kingdom and Colonies, as the Secretary of State, with the consent of the Treasury, directs to be taken for granting a visa or entry permit to a national or citizen of that State
except where a United Kingdom visa is issued on a foreign passport held by a British subject

22 Issuing a Travel Certificate on behalf of Nigeria, Ghana, or The Gambia ... ... 3·00

23 Renewing a Travel Certificate, a certificate of identity or other travel document on behalf of—
(*a*) Nigeria, Ghana or The Gambia ... ... 2·00
(*b*) Hong Kong ... ... 4·00
except where fee 24 is to be taken

24 Revalidating or renewing a Seaman's Certificate of Nationality and Identity or a Seaman's Identity Book ... ... 1·00
in addition to fee 19 where applicable

PART III
MARRIAGES, BIRTHS AND DEATHS

25 Receiving notice of an intended marriage ... ... 4·00

26 Solemnising or attending a marriage under the Foreign Marriage Acts 1892 to 1947(a), administering oaths to the parties and registering the marriage ... ... 12·00

27 Issuing in English or in the local language a certificate that no impediment to an intended marriage has been shown to exist 4·00

28 Transmitting a record of a marriage under the local law to the appropriate Registrar General in accordance with Article 7(1) of the Foreign Marriage Order 1970(b), including the provision of any necessary certification ... ... 6·00

29 Issuing a " certificat de coutume " for an intended marriage in accordance with the local law ... ... 4·00

30 Registering a birth or death or making an addition to or correction in the register at the request of the parties concerned ... ... 3·00

31 Referring an application for registration of a birth (or births) where the permission of the Secretary of State is required ... 4·00
in addition to fees 30 and 32 where applicable

32 Furnishing a certified copy of an entry in the consular register of births, deaths or marriages—
(*a*) at the time of registration ... ... 1·00
(*b*) subsequently ... ... 2·00
in addition to fee 33 where applicable

(a) 1892 c. 23; 1934 c. 13; 1947 c. 33.   (b) S.I. 1970/1539 (1970 III, p. 5299).

Fee   £

PART IV

SEARCHES

33 Making a search in

(*a*) the consular registers of births, deaths or marriages where the number or date of entry is not provided   ...   ...   1·00

(*b*) any other records or archives of Her Majesty's Government in addition to fee 32 where applicable   3·00

34 Having a search made for, or obtaining copies of, or both, entries in the local registers or records not kept by a consular officer—

for an entry in a local register of births, deaths or marriages   5·00

for any other document   ...   .   5·00

in addition to costs exceeding £1·00

PART V

ESTATES

35 Administering in full or in part, safeguarding, or arranging the transmission of all or part of the personal effects and other estate of a deceased person or proceeds thereof, other than the wages and personal effects of a seaman—

on the amount up to £2,000, if over £30, of the gross current market value   2% rounded upwards to the nearest £1·00

on the amount over £2,000   ...   .   1% rounded upwards to the nearest £1·00

with a minimum, to be taken also where a local lawyer is employed and the matters or things to be done by the consular officer are nominal, of   ...   .   10·00

PART VI

ATTENDANCES

36 Attending (except in connexion with commercial enquiries) for each hour or lesser period, including the time taken in proceeding from a reasonable point of departure and in returning to a reasonable point—

during customary business hours but elsewhere than at the consular premises   ...   .   10·00

outside customary business hours—

at the consular residence   ...   .   12·00

elsewhere   ...   .   20·00

with—

(*a*) a maximum in any period of 24 hours of   ...   ...   60·00

(*b*) an increase of one-half where the consular officer is accompanied away from the consular premises or residence by another consular officer or a consular employee with a maximum in this event of   ...   ...   90·00

Fee   £

PART VII

MATTERS RELATING TO LEGAL PROCEEDINGS

37 Presiding at the taking of evidence under a commission or order
    from a Court, including any matter or thing done by the
    consular officer as examiner—
    (*a*) for the first two hours or less on the first day   ...   ...   30·00
    (*b*) for the first two hours or less on each subsequent day   ...   20·00
    (*c*) for each additional hour on any day   ...   .   10·00

38 Providing evidence of service or attempted service   ...   ...   6·00
    in addition to fee 36 or 39.

39 Providing the services of a consular officer or consular employee—
    (*a*) to assist the consular officer in the taking of evidence under
        a commission or order from a Court, for each such person—
            for each sitting of two hours or less   ...   .   6·00
            for each additional hour at each sitting ...   .   2·00
    (*b*) to effect or endeavour to effect service of a document, for
        each hour or shorter period elsewhere than at the consular
        premises—
            during customary business hours ...   .   6·00
            outside customary business hours   ...   .   10·00

40 Forwarding a request to a local authority for the taking of
    evidence or the service of a document and, where necessary,
    certifying the accuracy of a translation accompanying the
    document   ...   .   6·00

PART VIII

REPATRIATION

41 Arranging the repatriation of a person or a group of persons of
    the same family and travelling together ...   .   12·00

PART IX

SHIPPING, SEAMEN AND KINDRED MATTERS

42 Receiving or recording a declaration under Part I of the Merchant
    Shipping Act 1894(**a**) with a view to the registry, transfer and
    transmission of ships, interests in ships, or mortgages of ships   8·00

43 Endorsing a memorandum of change of master upon the certifi-
    cate of registry and initialling, where required, the new master's
    signature on the agreement with the crew   ...   .   4·00

44 Granting a provisional certificate of registry   ...   .   21·00
    in addition to fee 42 where applicable

45 Recording a mortgage of a ship or of shares in a ship ...   ...   21·00

46 Recording the transfer of a mortgage of a ship or of shares in a
    ship ...   .   21·00

47 Recording the discharge of a mortgage of a ship or of shares in a
    ship ...   .   21·00

48 Making an interposition in the sale of a ship or of shares in a
    ship ...   .   21·00

(**a**) 1894 c. 60.

Fee		£
49	Receiving a return of the birth or death of any person on board a ship and endorsing the agreement with the crew accordingly...	2·00
50	Certifying a form of claim for wages and other matters, if any, of a deceased seaman or apprentice	3·00
51	Examining or arranging for the examination of provisions or water, payable by the party who proves to be in default . ... in addition to the cost, if any, of survey	10·00
52	Preparing and attesting a salvage bond executed in pursuance of section 560(1) of the Merchant Shipping Act 1894, payable by the master or owner of the property salved	40·00
53	Noting a marine protest and furnishing one certified copy if required	8·00
	for every further copy	4·00
54	Extending a marine protest, filing the original and furnishing one certified copy if required—	
	for any number of words up to 200, excluding the declaratory clause	21·00
	for every subsequent 100 words or less	4·00
	in addition to fees 1 and 3 where applicable	
55	Filing a request for survey and issuing an order of survey ...	10·00
56	Receiving a report of a survey, filing the original and furnishing one certified copy, if required, of the request, order and report of survey—	
	for any number of words up to 200, excluding the words in the consular certificate	21·00
	for every subsequent 100 words or less	4·00
57	Issuing a bill of health	8·00
58	Addressing at the request of the master an application to local authorities for the arrest, imprisonment or release of seamen or apprentices—	
	for each seaman or apprentice	5·00
59	Granting such certificates as to the number of the crew and other matters as may be required by local authorities for the clearance inwards and outwards of a ship ... ... in addition to fee 70 or 63 where applicable	6·00
60	Drawing up, in the form and language required by local authorities, a muster-roll or detailed list giving the names and other details of each member of the crew ... ... in addition to fee 59 unless a certificate in the form of a muster-roll or list is required for the clearance of the vessel	4·00
61	Signing and, if required, sealing the original of a ship's manifest and signing any copies on the same occasion	5·00
62	Signing and, if required, sealing any entry in the official log-book of a ship where such entry is not required under the Merchant Shipping Acts	3·00
63	Inspecting a ship's papers when required to enable a consular officer to do any matter or thing in respect of a ship ... ... except where—	4·00
	(a) the papers are already in the custody of the consular officer and fee 70 has been taken, or	
	(b) the master opens a new agreement at the consular premises	

Fee £

64 Inspecting the marking of a ship, irrespective of the number of
    visits   ...   .   4·00
    in addition to fee 36

65 Making a request for survey and arranging for the issue of a
    certificate in accordance with the International Convention for
    the Safety of Life at Sea 1960(a) ...   .   4·00

*The following fees are to be levied only in respect of British ships not registered in
the United Kingdom:—*

66 Sanctioning the engagement of seamen—
    for each seaman   ...   .   2·00
    with—
      (*a*) a maximum where a crew or part of a crew transfer from
           one British ship to another, or
      (*b*) a maximum in respect of each ship where crews or parts
           of crews transfer between British ships,
    of   ...   .   40·00
    in addition to fee 71 or 63 where applicable

67 Attesting alterations in the agreement with the crew—
    for each alteration in respect of each seaman concerned   ...   2·00
    with a maximum on each separate occasion of...   ...   ...   40·00

68 Sanctioning the discharge of seamen or leaving behind of seamen
    and apprentices—
    for each seaman or apprentice   ...   .   2·00
    with—
      (*a*) a maximum where a crew or part of a crew transfer from
           one British ship to another, or
      (*b*) a maximum in respect of each ship where crews or parts
           of crews transfer between British ships,
    of   ...   .   40·00
    except where an apprentice—
      (*a*) is transferred whilst overseas from one ship to another, or
      (*b*) having come to the end of his indentures, signs on as a
           seaman
    in addition to fee 63 where applicable

69 Certifying desertions of seamen and apprentices—
    for each seaman or apprentice   ...   .   2·00

70 Taking custody of a ship's papers, making any necessary endorse-
    ments thereon, and giving the certificate required by section
    257(2) of the Merchant Shipping Act 1894   ...   .   4·00

71 Preparing a fresh agreement with the crew when a new agreement
    is opened at a foreign port and furnishing the copy which must
    be made accessible to the crew—
    for each seaman ...   .   2·00
    with a minimum of   ...   .   20·00
    and a maximum of   ...   .   40·00
    in addition to fee 66

EXPLANATORY NOTE
(This Note is part of the Order.)

This Order revokes and replaces the Consular Fees Order 1971 and
subsequent amending Orders.   It increases all consular fees and makes a few
minor amendments to the services for which fees are charged.

(a) Cmnd. 2812

1976 No. 216

DIPLOMATIC AND INTERNATIONAL IMMUNITIES AND PRIVILEGES

The European Centre for Medium-Range Weather Forecasts (Immunities and Privileges) (Amendment) Order 1976

Laid before Parliament in draft
Made -   -   -   -   18th February 1976
Coming into operation   On a date to be notified in the London, Edinburgh and Belfast Gazettes.

At the Court at Buckingham Palace, the 18th day of February 1976

Present,

The Queen's Most Excellent Majesty in Council

Whereas a draft of this Order has been laid before Parliament in accordance with section 10(1) of the International Organisations Act 1968(**a**) (hereinafter referred to as the Act) and has been approved by a resolution of each House of Parliament:

Now, therefore, Her Majesty, by virtue and in exercise of the powers conferred on Her by sections 1 and 10(3) of the Act, or otherwise in Her Majesty vested, is pleased, by and with the advice of Her Privy Council to order, and it is hereby ordered as follows:—

1. This Order may be cited as the European Centre for Medium-Range Weather Forecasts (Immunities and Privileges) (Amendment) Order 1976. It shall come into operation on the date on which the Headquarters Agreement between the Government of the United Kingdom of Great Britain and Northern Ireland and the European Centre for Medium-Range Weather Forecasts(**b**) enters into force. This date shall be notified in the London, Edinburgh and Belfast Gazettes.

2. The Interpretation Act 1889(**c**) shall apply for the interpretation of this Order as it applies for the interpretation of an Act of Parliament.

3. The European Centre for Medium-Range Weather Forecasts (Immunities and Privileges) Order 1975(**d**) shall be amended as follows:

(*a*) In Article 6(2), after the word " mission " there shall be inserted the words " provided that nothing in this paragraph shall preclude service of legal process by post ";

(*b*) Article 13 shall be replaced by the following:

" **13.**—(1) Except in so far as in any particular case any privilege or immunity is waived by the Government of the Member State whom they

---

(**a**) 1968 c. 48.   (**b**) Cmnd. 6368.   (**c**) 1889 c. 63.   (**d**) S.I. 1975/158 (1975 I, p. 428).

represent, representatives of Member States of the Centre attending meetings of the Council of the Centre or of the Finance Committee, and members of the Scientific Advisory Committee attending meetings of that Committee, shall enjoy:—

(a) immunity from suit and legal process in respect of things done or omitted to be done by them in the exercise of their functions, except in the case of a traffic offence committed by them or in the case of damage caused by a vehicle belonging to or driven by them ;

(b) while exercising their functions and during their journeys to and from the place of meetings:

(i) the like immunity from personal arrest or detention as is accorded to a diplomatic agent, provided that they shall not enjoy such immunity if there are reasonable grounds for suspecting that they are in the course of committing, attempting to commit, or have just committed an offence ;

(ii) the like immunity for all their official papers and documents as is accorded to a diplomatic agent ; and

(iii) the like exemptions and privileges in respect of their personal baggage as, in accordance with Article 36 of the 1961 Convention Articles, are accorded to a diplomatic agent.

(2) Part IV of Schedule 1 to the Act shall not operate so as to confer any privilege or immunity on the official staff of representatives, other than their alternates and advisers, or of members of the Scientific Advisory Committee.

(3) Neither the provisions of the preceding paragraphs of this Article, nor those of Part IV of Schedule 1 to the Act, shall operate so as to confer any privilege or immunity on any person as the representative or alternate representative of, or adviser to, Her Majesty's Government in the United Kingdom or on any person who is a citizen of the United Kingdom and Colonies.

(4) Part IV of Schedule 1 to the Act shall not operate so as to confer any privilege or immunity on families of representatives, alternate representatives or advisers, or of members of the Scientific Advisory Committee.".

N. E. Leigh.

EXPLANATORY NOTE

(This Note is not part of the Order.)

This Order amends the European Centre for Medium-Range Weather Forecasts (Immunities and Privileges) Order 1975 in order to enable legal process to be served on the Centre, to apply the provisions regarding representatives to advisers and to members of the Scientific Advisory Committee and to accord to them (as well as to representatives and alternate representatives) the same customs facilities as are accorded to diplomatic agents. These amendments are required by the provisions of a Headquarters Agreement the text of which has been agreed between the Government of the United Kingdom and the Centre (Cmnd. 6368). This Order will enable Her Majesty's Government to give effect to the Headquarters Agreement which will enter into force on signature.

STATUTORY INSTRUMENTS

1976 No. 217

EUROPEAN COMMUNITIES

The European Communities (Definition of Treaties) Order 1976

Laid before Parliament in draft

Made -   -   -   -   18*th February* 1976

Coming into Operation in accordance with Article 1

At the Court at Buckingham Palace, the 18th day of February 1976

Present,

The Queen's Most Excellent Majesty in Council

Whereas a draft of this Order has been laid before Parliament in accordance with section 1 of the European Communities Act 1972(**a**) and has been approved by a resolution of each House of Parliament:

Now, therefore, Her Majesty, by virtue and in exercise of the powers conferred on Her by section 1(3) of the European Communities Act 1972 or otherwise in Her Majesty vested, is pleased, by and with the advice of Her Privy Council, to order, and it is hereby ordered, as follows:—

1. This Order may be cited as the European Communities (Definition of Treaties) Order 1976. It shall come into operation in respect of each treaty specified in the Schedule to this Order on the date on which the treaty enters into force for the United Kingdom. These dates will be notified in the London, Edinburgh and Belfast Gazettes.

2. The Interpretation Act 1889(**b**) shall apply for the interpretation of this Order as it applies for the interpretation of an Act of Parliament.

3. The treaties specified in the Schedule to this Order are to be regarded as Community Treaties as defined in section 1(2) of the European Communities Act 1972.

N. E. Leigh.

(**a**) 1972 c. 68.   (**b**) 1889 c. 63.

SCHEDULE

1. Treaty amending certain Provisions of the Protocol on the Statute of the European Investment Bank signed at Brussels on 10th July 1975 (Cmnd. 6253).

2. Treaty amending certain Financial Provisions of the Treaties establishing the European Communities and of the Treaty establishing a Single Council and a Single Commission of the European Communities signed at Brussels on 22nd July 1975 (Cmnd. 6252).

EXPLANATORY NOTE

(This Note is not part of the Order.)

This Order declares the treaties mentioned in the Schedule to be Community Treaties as defined in section 1(2) of the European Communities Act 1972.

STATUTORY INSTRUMENTS

1976 No. 218

EUROPEAN COMMUNITIES

The European Communities (Definition of Treaties) (No. 2) Order 1976

Laid before Parliament in draft
Made - 18th February 1976
Coming into Operation in accordance with Article 1

At the Court at Buckingham Palace, the 18th day of February 1976

Present,

The Queen's Most Excellent Majesty in Council

Whereas a draft of this Order has been laid before Parliament in accordance with section 1 of the European Communities Act 1972(**a**) and has been approved by a resolution of each House of Parliament:

Now, therefore, Her Majesty, by virtue and in exercise of the powers conferred on Her by section 1(3) of the European Communities Act 1972 or otherwise in Her Majesty vested, is pleased, by and with the advice of Her Privy Council, to order, and it is hereby ordered, as follows:—

1. This Order may be cited as the European Communities (Definition of Treaties) (No. 2) Order 1976. It shall come into operation in respect of the treaty specified in Part I of the Schedule to this Order on the date on which the Order is made. In respect of each treaty specified in Part II of the Schedule to this Order, the Order shall come into operation on the date on which the treaty enters into force for the United Kingdom, which date will be notified in the London, Edinburgh and Belfast Gazettes.

2. The Interpretation Act 1889(**b**) shall apply for the interpretation of this Order as it applies for the interpretation of an Act of Parliament.

3. The treaties specified in the Schedule to this Order are to be regarded as Community Treaties as defined in section 1(2) of the European Communities Act 1972.

N. E. Leigh.

(**a**) 1972 c. 68. (**b**) 1889 c. 63.

SCHEDULE

Part I

1. Decision of 26 June 1975 of the Representatives of the Governments of the Member States of the European Coal and Steel Community, meeting within the Council, opening tariff preferences for products covered by that Community and originating in Israel (Cmnd. 6265).

Part II

2. Protocol on the Accession of Greece to the Convention on the Provision of Mutual Assistance by their Customs Authorities, concluded between the Member States of the European Economic Community, signed at Rome on 7 September 1967 (Cmnd. 6331).

3. Additional Protocol to the Agreement establishing an Association between the European Economic Community and Greece consequent on the Accession of new Member States to the Community, signed at Brussels on 28 April 1975 (Cmnd. 6289).

4. Agreement between the Member States of the European Coal and Steel Community, of the one part, and the State of Israel, of the other part, signed at Brussels on 11 May 1975 (Cmnd. 6265).

5. Agreement in the form of an Exchange of Letters renewing the Agreement on Trade and Technical Co-operation between the European Economic Community and the Member States, of the one part, and the Lebanese Republic, of the other part, signed at Brussels on 13 October 1975 (Cmnd. 6304).

EXPLANATORY NOTE

(This Note is not part of the Order.)

This Order declares the treaties mentioned in the Schedule to be Community Treaties as defined in section 1(2) of the European Communities Act 1972.

STATUTORY INSTRUMENTS

1976 No. 219

DIPLOMATIC AND INTERNATIONAL IMMUNITIES AND PRIVILEGES

The European Free Trade Association (Immunities and Privileges) (Revocation) Order 1976

Laid before Parliament in draft

Made - - - - 18th February 1976
Coming into Operation 19th February 1976

At the Court at Buckingham Palace, the 18th day of February 1976

Present,

The Queen's Most Excellent Majesty in Council

Whereas a draft of this Order has been laid before Parliament in accordance with section 10(1) of the International Organisations Act 1968(**a**) and has been approved by a resolution of each House of Parliament:

Now, therefore, Her Majesty, by virtue and in exercise of the powers conferred on Her by sections 10(3) and 12(6) of the said Act, or otherwise in Her Majesty vested, is pleased, by and with the advice of Her Privy Council, to order, and it is hereby ordered, as follows:—

1. This Order may be cited as the European Free Trade Association (Immunities and Privileges) (Revocation) Order 1976 and shall come into operation on 19th February 1976.

2. The Interpretation Act 1889(**b**) shall apply for the interpretation of this Order as it applies for the interpretation of an Act of Parliament, and as if this Order and the Order hereby revoked were Acts of Parliament.

3. The European Free Trade Association (Immunities and Privileges) Order 1961(**c**) is hereby revoked.

N. E. Leigh.

EXPLANATORY NOTE

(This Note is not part of the Order.)

This Order revokes the Order conferring immunities and privileges on the European Free Trade Association and persons connected with it.

(**a**) 1968 c. 48.   (**b**) 1889 c. 63.   (**c**) S.I. 1961/1000 (1961 II, p. 1929).

1976 No. 220

FOREIGN COMPENSATION

The Foreign Compensation (Financial Provisions) Order 1976

Made - - - -	18*th February* 1976
Laid before Parliament	25*th February* 1976
Coming into Operation	22*nd March* 1976

At the Court at Buckingham Palace, the 18th day of February 1976

Present,

The Queen's Most Excellent Majesty in Council

Her Majesty, by virtue and in exercise of the powers conferred on Her by section 7(2) of the Foreign Compensation Act 1950(a) and section 3(3) of the Foreign Compensation Act 1962(b) or otherwise in Her Majesty vested, is pleased, by and with the advice of Her Privy Council, to order, and it is hereby ordered, as follows:—

1. This Order may be cited as the Foreign Compensation (Financial Provisions) Order 1976 and shall come into operation on 22nd March 1976.

2. The Foreign Compensation Commission shall pay into the Exchequer not later than 30th March 1976 out of each of the Funds named in Column 1 of the Schedule to this Order the amount specified in respect of that Fund in Column 2 of the Schedule which is hereby determined to be the amount of the expenses of the Commission during the period 1st October 1974 to 30th September 1975 attributable to the discharge by the Commission of their functions in relation to the distribution of sums from that Fund.

N. E. Leigh.

SCHEDULE

Column 1 Name of Fund	Column 2 Amount
	£
The Egyptian Compensation Fund	3,089
The Egyptian Nationalised Property Compensation Fund ...	156,368

(a) 1950 c. 12. (b) 1962 c. 4.

EXPLANATORY NOTE

(This Note is not part of the Order.)

This Order, which is made under section 7(2) of the Foreign Compensation Act 1950 and section 3(3) of the Foreign Compensation Act 1962, directs the Foreign Compensation Commission to pay into the Exchequer, out of the funds paid to the Commission for the purpose of being distributed under the said Acts, amounts in respect of the Commission's expenses during the period 1st October 1974 to 30th September 1975 in relation to the distribution of those funds.

STATUTORY INSTRUMENTS

1976 No. 221

DIPLOMATIC AND INTERNATIONAL IMMUNITIES AND PRIVILEGES

The International Organisations (Immunities and Privileges) Miscellaneous Provisions Order 1976

Laid before Parliament in draft

Made	-	-	-	18*th February* 1976
Coming into Operation				19*th February* 1976

At the Court at Buckingham Palace, the 18th day of February 1976

Present,

The Queen's Most Excellent Majesty in Council

Whereas a draft of this Order has been laid before Parliament in accordance with section 3(4) of the International Finance Corporation Act 1955(a), section 3(4) of the International Development Association Act 1960(b) and section 10(1) of the International Organisations Act 1968(c) and has been approved by resolution of each House of Parliament :

Now, therefore, Her Majesty, by virtue and in exercise of the powers conferred on Her by section 3(1) and (3) of the Bretton Woods Agreements Act 1945(d), section 3(1) and (3) of the International Finance Corporation Act 1955, section 3(1) and (3) of the International Development Association Act 1960 and sections 1 and 10(3) of the International Organisations Act 1968 or otherwise in Her Majesty vested, is pleased, by and with the advice of Her Privy Council, to order, and it is hereby ordered, as follows :—

1. This Order may be cited as the International Organisations (Immunities and Privileges) Miscellaneous Provisions Order 1976 and shall come into operation on 19th February 1976.

2. The Interpretation Act 1889(e) shall apply for the interpretation of this Order as it applies for the interpretation of an Act of Parliament.

3. In paragraph (*b*) of the proviso to Article 3 of the Bretton Woods Agreements Order in Council 1946(f), after " sold " shall be inserted " , except that the Fund and the Bank shall have relief, under arrangements made by the Secretary of State, by way of refund of car tax paid on any vehicles and value added tax paid on the supply of any goods and services which are necessary for the exercise of the official activities of the Fund or the

---

(a) 1955 c. 5.   (b) 1960 c. 35.   (c) 1968 c. 48.   (d) 1945 c. 19.
(e) 1889 c. 63.   (f) S.R. & O. 1946/36 (Rev. III, p. 165: 1946 I, p. 43).

Bank, such relief to be subject to compliance with such conditions as may be imposed in accordance with the arrangements ".

4. In paragraph (*b*) of the proviso to Article 3 of the International Finance Corporation Order 1955(**a**) and in paragraph (*b*) of the proviso to Article 3 of the International Development Association Order 1960(**b**), after the word " sold " shall be inserted " , except that it shall have relief, under arrangements made by the Secretary of State, by way of refund of car tax paid on any vehicles and value added tax paid on the supply of any goods and services which are necessary for the exercise of its official activities, such relief to be subject to compliance with such conditions as may be imposed in accordance with the arrangements ".

5. The International Organisations (Immunities and Privileges of Western European Union) Order 1955(**c**) shall be amended by inserting after Article 6 the following new Article:

" 6A. The Organisation shall have relief, under arrangements made by the Secretary of State, by way of refund of car tax paid on any vehicles and value added tax paid on the supply of any goods and services which are necessary for the exercise of the official activities of the Organisation, such relief to be subject to compliance with such conditions as may be imposed in accordance with the arrangements.".

N. E. Leigh.

EXPLANATORY NOTE
(This Note is not part of the Order.)

This Order makes amendments to certain Orders which confer privileges and immunities on the International Monetary Fund, the International Bank for Reconstruction and Development, the International Finance Corporation, the International Development Association and the Western European Union consequential upon the introduction of car tax and value added tax. Such amendments are necessary in order to implement our international obligations to the organisations concerned. Similar provisions in respect of other international organisations were made by the International Organisations (Immunities and Privileges) Miscellaneous Provisions Order 1975 (S.I., 1975/1209).

(**a**) S.I. 1955/1954 (1955 I, p. 663).   (**b**) S.I. 1960/1383 (1960 I, p. 1201).
(**c**) S.I. 1955/1209 (1955 I, p. 671).

1976 No. 222

DIPLOMATIC AND INTERNATIONAL IMMUNITIES AND PRIVILEGES

The Inter-American Development Bank (Immunities and Privileges) Order 1976

Laid before Parliament in draft
Made - - - - *18th February* 1976
Coming into operation On a date to be notified
in the London, Edin-
burgh and Belfast
Gazettes.

At the Court at Buckingham Palace, the 18th day of February 1976

Present,

The Queen's Most Excellent Majesty in Council

Whereas a draft of this Order has been laid before Parliament in accordance with section 10(1) of the International Organisations Act 1968(a) (hereinafter referred to as the Act) and has been approved by a resolution of each House of Parliament:

Now, therefore, Her Majesty, by virtue and in exercise of the powers conferred on Her by section 1 of the Act or otherwise in Her Majesty vested, is pleased, by and with the advice of Her Privy Council, to order, and it is hereby ordered, as follows:—

PART I

GENERAL

1. This Order may be cited as the Inter-American Development Bank (Immunities and Privileges) Order 1976. It shall come into operation on a date on which the Agreement establishing the Inter-American Development Bank (with proposed amendments, including those to admit non-regional countries as members of the Bank) and the Declaration of Madrid of 17th December 1974(b), enters into force in respect of the United Kingdom. This date shall be notified in the London, Edinburgh and Belfast Gazettes.

2.—(1) In this Order " the 1961 Convention Articles " means the Articles (being certain Articles of the Vienna Convention on Diplomatic Relations signed in 1961) which are set out in Schedule 1 to the Diplomatic Privileges Act 1964(c).

(2) The Interpretation Act 1889(d) shall apply for the interpretation of this Order as it applies for the interpretation of an Act of Parliament.

(a) 1968 c. 48.   (b) Cmnd. 6271.   (c) 1964 c. 81.   (d) 1889 c. 63.

PART II
THE BANK

3. The Inter-American Development Bank (hereinafter referred to as the Bank) is an organisation of which the United Kingdom and foreign sovereign Powers are members.

4. The Bank shall have the legal capacities of a body corporate.

5.—(1) The Bank shall have immunity from suit and legal process, except :

(*a*) to the extent that it shall have expressly waived such immunity in a particular case ; or

(*b*) if it has an office, has appointed an agent for the purpose of accepting service or notice of process, or has issued or guaranteed securities, in the United Kingdom,

provided that no proceedings may be brought against the Bank by a member or any person acting for or deriving a claim from a member.

(2) The provisions of paragraph (1) of this Article shall not prevent the taking of such measures as may be permitted by law in relation to the execution of judgment against the Bank.

6. The Bank shall have the like inviolability of official archives as, in accordance with the 1961 Convention Articles, is accorded in respect of the official archives of a diplomatic mission. Premises of the Bank shall be immune from search, requisition, confiscation, expropriation or any other form of taking or foreclosure.

7. The Bank shall have the like exemption or relief from taxes, other than customs duties and taxes on the importation of goods, as is accorded to a foreign sovereign Power.

8. The Bank shall have the like relief from rates as, in accordance with Article 23 of the 1961 Convention Articles, is accorded in respect of the premises of a diplomatic mission.

9. The Bank shall have exemption from customs duties and taxes on the importation of goods imported by or on behalf of the Bank for its official use in the United Kingdom, such exemption to be subject to compliance with such conditions as the Commissioners of Customs and Excise may prescribe for the protection of the Revenue.

10. The Bank shall have exemption from prohibitions and restrictions on importation or exportation in the case of goods imported or exported by the Bank for its official use and in the case of any publications of the Bank imported or exported by it.

11. The Bank shall have relief, under arrangements made by the Commissioners of Customs and Excise, by way of refund of excise duty paid on or value added tax paid on the importation of any hydrocarbon oil (within the meaning of the Hydrocarbon Oil (Customs & Excise) Act 1971(a)) which is bought in the United Kingdom and used for the official purposes of the Bank, such relief to be subject to compliance with such conditions as may be imposed in accordance with the arrangements.

(a) 1971 c. 12.

12. The Bank shall have relief, under arrangements made by the Secretary of State, by way of refund of car tax paid on any vehicles and value added tax paid on the supply of any goods or services which are used for the official purposes of the Bank, such relief to be subject to compliance with such conditions as may be imposed in accordance with the arrangements.

PART III
OFFICERS AND EMPLOYEES

13. Except in so far as in any particular case any privilege or immunity is expressly waived by the Bank, any governor, executive director, alternate, officer and employee of the Bank shall enjoy:—

(*a*) immunity from suit and legal process in respect of things done or omitted to be done by him in his official capacity ; and

(*b*) unless he is a citizen of the United Kingdom and Colonies, exemption from income tax in respect of emoluments received by him as an officer or employee of the Bank.

N. E. Leigh.

EXPLANATORY NOTE

(This Note is not part of the Order.)

This Order confers privileges and immunities upon the Inter-American Development Bank, its officers and employees. It will enable the United Kingdom to give effect to Article XI of the Agreement establishing the Bank (Cmnd. 6271) signed at Washington on 8 April 1956. It will come into operation on the date on which the Agreement enters into force with respect to the United Kingdom.

STATUTORY INSTRUMENTS

1976 No. 223

MERCHANT SHIPPING

The Merchant Shipping (Oil Pollution) (Turks and Caicos Islands) Order 1976

Made - - - -	*18th February* 1976
Laid before Parliament	*25th February* 1976
Coming into Operation	*17th March* 1976

At the Court at Buckingham Palace, the 18th day of February 1976

Present,

The Queen's Most Excellent Majesty in Council

Her Majesty, in exercise of the powers conferred upon Her by section 18(1) of the Merchant Shipping (Oil Pollution) Act 1971(a), by section 20 (1) of the Merchant Shipping Act 1974(b) and all other powers enabling Her in that behalf, is pleased, by and with the advice of Her Privy Council, to order, and it is hereby ordered, as follows:

1. This Order may be cited as the Merchant Shipping (Oil Pollution) (Turks and Caicos Islands) Order 1976 and shall come into operation on 17th March 1976.

2. The Interpretation Act 1889(c) shall apply, with the necessary adaptations, for the purpose of interpreting this Order and otherwise in relation thereto as it applies for the purpose of interpreting, and in relation to, Acts of Parliament.

3. The provisions of the Merchant Shipping (Oil Pollution) Act 1971 (except sections 17 and 18 thereof), subject to the exemptions, modifications and adaptations as set out in Schedule 1 hereto, shall extend to the Turks and Caicos Islands.

4. The provisions of Part I and sections 22, 23 and 24 of, and Schedule 1 to the Merchant Shipping Act 1974, subject to the exceptions, modifications and adaptations as set out in Schedule 2 hereto, shall extend to the Turks and Caicos Islands.

5. Save as is expressly provided otherwise therein, any reference in the Schedules to this Order to any enactment of the United Kingdom shall be construed as a reference to that enactment as applying or extended to the Turks and Caicos Islands.

N. E. Leigh.

(a) 1971 c. 59.   (b) 1974 c. 43.   (c) 1889 c. 63.

Article 3   SCHEDULE 1 TO THE ORDER

THE MERCHANT SHIPPING (OIL POLLUTION) ACT 1971

Liability for oil pollution.

1.—(1) Where, as a result of any occurrence taking place while a ship is carrying a cargo of persistent oil in bulk, any persistent oil carried by the ship (whether as part of the cargo or otherwise) is discharged or escapes from the ship, the owner of the ship shall be liable, except as otherwise provided by this Act,—

(a) for any damage caused in the area of the Turks and Caicos Islands by contamination resulting from the discharge or escape ; and

(b) for the cost of any measures reasonably taken after the discharge or escape for the purpose of preventing or reducing any such damage in the area of the Turks and Caicos Islands ; and

(c) for any damage caused in the area of the Turks and Caicos Islands by any measures so taken.

(2) Where a person incurs a liability under subsection (1) of this section he shall also be liable for any damage or cost for which he would be liable under that subsection if the references therein to the area of the Turks and Caicos Islands included the area of any other Convention country.

(3) Where persistent oil is discharged or escapes from two or more ships and—

(a) a liability is incurred under this section by the owner of each of them ; but

(b) the damage or cost for which each of the owners would be liable cannot reasonably be separated from that for which the other or others would be liable ;

each of the owners shall be liable, jointly with the other or others, for the whole of the damage or cost for which the owners together would be liable under this section.

(4) For the purposes of this Act, where more than one discharge or escape results from the same occurrence or from a series of occurrences having the same origin, they shall be treated as one ; but any measures taken after the first of them shall be deemed to have been taken after the discharge or escape.

(5) The Contributory Negligence Ordinance 1970(a) shall apply in relation to any damage or cost for which a person is liable under this section, but which is not due to his fault, as if it were due to his fault.

Exceptions from liability under s. 1.

2. The owner of a ship from which persistent oil has been discharged or has escaped shall not incur any liability under section 1 of this Act if he proves that the discharge or escape—

(a) resulted from an act of war, hostilities, civil war, insurrection or an exceptional, inevitable and irresistible natural phenomenon ; or

(b) was due wholly to anything done or left undone by another person, not being a servant or agent of the owner, with intent to do damage ; or

(c) was due wholly to the negligence or wrongful act of a government or other authority in exercising its function of maintaining lights or other navigational aids for the maintenance of which it was responsible.

Restriction of liability for oil pollution.

3. Where, as a result of any occurrence taking place while a ship is carrying a cargo of persistent oil in bulk, any persistent oil carried by the

(a) Laws of the Turks and Caicos Islands, No. 11 of 1970.

ship is discharged or escapes then, whether or not the owner incurs a liability under section 1 of this Act,—

(a) he shall not be liable otherwise than under that section for any such damage or cost as is mentioned therein ; and

(b) no servant or agent of the owner nor any person performing salvage operations with the agreement of the owner shall be liable for any such damage or cost.

4.—(1) Where the owner of a ship incurs a liability under section 1 of this Act by reason of a discharge or escape which occurred without his actual fault or privity— *Limitation of liability under s. 1.*

(a) section 503 of the Merchant Shipping Act 1894(a) (limitation of liability) shall not apply in relation to that liability ; but

(b) he may limit that liability in accordance with the provisions of this Act, and if he does so his liability (that is to say, the aggregate of his liabilities under section 1 resulting from the discharge or escape) shall not exceed 2,000 gold francs for each ton of the ship's tonnage nor (where that tonnage would result in a greater amount) 210 million gold francs.

(2) For the purposes of this section the tonnage of a ship shall be ascertained as follows : —

(a) if the ship is a British ship (whether registered in the Turks and Caicos Islands or elsewhere) or a ship to which an Order under section 84 of the Merchant Shipping Act 1894 applies, its tonnage shall be taken to be its registered tonnage increased, where a deduction has been made for engine room space in arriving at that tonnage, by the amount of that deduction ;

(b) if the ship is not such a ship as is mentioned in the preceding paragraph and it is possible to ascertain what would be its registered tonnage if it were registered in the Turks and Caicos Islands, that paragraph shall apply (with the necessary modifications) as if the ship were so registered ;

(c) if the ship is not such a ship as is mentioned in paragraph (a) of this subsection and is of a description with respect to which no provision is for the time being made by regulations under section 1 of the Merchant Shipping Act 1965(b) (tonnage regulations) its tonnage shall be taken to be 40 per cent. of the weight (expressed in tons of 2,240 lbs.) of oil which the ship is capable of carrying ;

(d) if the tonnage of the ship cannot be ascertained in accordance with the preceding paragraphs a surveyor of ships appointed by the Governor shall, if so directed by the court, certify what, on the evidence specified in the direction, would in his opinion be the tonnage of the ship if ascertained in accordance with those paragraphs, and the tonnage stated in his certificate shall be taken to be the tonnage of the ship.

(3) For the purposes of this section a gold franc shall be taken to be a unit of sixty-five and a half milligrams of gold of millesimal fineness nine hundred.

(4) The Governor may from time to time by order specify the amounts which for the purposes of this section are to be taken as equivalent to 2,000 gold francs and 210 million gold francs respectively.

(5) Where the amounts specified by an order under the preceding subsection are varied by a subsequent order the variation shall not affect the limit of any liability under section 1 of this Act if, before the variation comes into force, an amount not less than that limit (ascertained in accordance with the order then in force) has been paid into court in proceedings for the limitation of that liability in accordance with this Act.

(a) 1894 c. 60.   (b) 1965 c. 47; S.I. 1971/383 (1971 I, p. 1175).

Limitation
actions.

5.—(1) Where the owner of a ship has or is alleged to have incurred a liability under section 1 of this Act he may apply to the court for the limitation of that liability to an amount determined in accordance with section 4 of this Act.

(2) If on such an application the court finds that the applicant has incurred such a liability and is entitled to limit it, the court shall, after determining the limit of the liability and directing payment into court of the amount of that limit,—

(a) determine the amounts that would, apart from the limit, be due in respect of the liability to the several persons making claims in the proceedings ; and

(b) direct the distribution of the amount paid into court (or, as the case may be, so much of it as does not exceed the liability) among those persons in proportion to their claims, subject to the following provisions of this section.

(3) No claim shall be admitted in proceedings under this section unless it is made within such time as the court may direct or such further time as the court may allow.

(4) Where any sum has been paid in or towards satisfaction of any claim in respect of the damage or cost to which the liability extends,—

(a) by the owner or the person referred to in section 12 of this Act as " the insurer " ; or

(b) by a person who has or is alleged to have incurred a liability, otherwise than under section 1 of this Act, for the damage or cost and who is entitled to limit his liability in connection with the ship by virtue of the Merchant Shipping (Liability of Shipowners and Others) Act 1958(a) ;

the person who paid the sum shall, to the extent of that sum, be in the same position with respect to any distribution made in proceedings under this section as the person to whom it was paid would have been.

(5) Where the person who incurred the liability has voluntarily made any reasonable sacrifice or taken any other reasonable measures to prevent or reduce damage to which the liability extends or might have extended he shall be in the same position with respect to any distribution made in proceedings under this section as if he had a claim in respect of the liability equal to the cost of the sacrifice or other measures.

(6) The court may, if it thinks fit, postpone the distribution of such part of the amount to be distributed as it deems appropriate having regard to any claims that may later be established before a court of any country outside the Turks and Caicos Islands.

Restriction
on
enforcement
of claims
after
establish-
ment of
limitation
fund.

6.—(1) Where the court has found that a person who has incurred a liability under section 1 of this Act is entitled to limit that liability to any amount and he has paid into court a sum not less than that amount—

(a) the court shall order the release of any ship or other property arrested in connection with a claim in respect of that liability or any security given to prevent or obtain release from such an arrest ; and

(b) no judgment or decree for any such claim shall be enforced, except so far as it is for costs ;

if the sum paid into court, or such part thereof as corresponds to the claim, will be actually available to the claimant or would have been available to him if the proper steps in the proceedings under section 5 of this Act had been taken.

Concurrent
liabilities
of owners
and others.

7. Where, as a result of any discharge or escape of persistent oil from a ship, the owner of the ship incurs a liability under section 1 of this Act and any other person incurs a liability, otherwise than under that

(a) 1958 c. 62; S.I. 1964/1658 (1964 III, p. 3758).

section, for any such damage or cost as is mentioned in subsection (1) of that section, then, if—

(a) the owner has been found, in proceedings under section 5 of this Act, to be entitled to limit his liability to any amount and has paid into court a sum not less than that amount; and

(b) the other person is entitled to limit his liability in connection with the ship by virtue of the Merchant Shipping (Liability of Shipowners and Others) Act 1958;

no proceedings shall be taken against the other person in respect of his liability, and if any such proceedings were commenced before the owner paid the sum into court, no further steps shall be taken in the proceedings except in relation to costs.

8. Where the events resulting in the liability of any person under section 1 of this Act also resulted in a corresponding liability under the law of another Convention country sections 6 and 7 of this Act shall apply as if the references to sections 1 and 5 of this Act included references to the corresponding provisions of that law and the references to sums paid into court included references to any sums secured under those provisions in respect of the liability. *Establishment of limitation fund outside Turks and Caicos Islands.*

9. No action to enforce a claim in respect of a liability incurred under section 1 of this Act shall be entertained by any court in the Turks and Caicos Islands unless the action is commenced not later than three years after the claim arose nor later than six years after the occurrence or first of the occurrences resulting in the discharge or escape by reason of which the liability was incurred. *Extinguishment of claims.*

10.—(1) Subject to the provisions of this Act relating to Government ships, subsection (2) of this section shall apply to any ship carrying in bulk a cargo of more than 2,000 tons of persistent oil of a description specified in regulations made by the Governor. *Compulsory insurance against liability for pollution.*

(2) The ship shall not enter or leave a port in the Turks and Caicos Islands or arrive at or leave a terminal in the territorial sea of the Turks and Caicos Islands nor, if the ship is registered in the Turks and Caicos Islands, a port in any other country or a terminal in the territorial sea of any other country, unless there is in force a certificate complying with the provisions of subsection (3) of this section and showing that there is in force in respect of the ship a contract of insurance or other security satisfying the requirements of Article VII of the Convention (cover for owner's liability).

(3) The certificate must be—

(a) if the ship is registered in the Turks and Caicos Islands, a certificate issued by the Governor;

(b) if the ship is registered in a Convention country other than the Turks and Caicos Islands, a certificate issued by or under the authority of the government of the other Convention country; and

(c) if the ship is registered in a country which is not a Convention country, a certificate recognised for the purposes of this paragraph by regulations made under this section.

(4) The Governor may by regulations provide that certificates in respect of ships registered in any, or any specified, country which is not a Convention country shall, in such circumstances as may be specified in the regulations, be recognised for the purposes of subsection (3)(c) of this section if issued by or under the authority of the government of the country designated in the regulations in that behalf; and the country that may be so designated may be either or both of the following, that is to say—

(a) the country in which the ship is registered; and

(b) any country specified in the regulations for the purposes of this paragraph.

(5) Any certificate required by this section to be in force in respect of a ship shall be carried in the ship and shall, on demand, be produced by the master to any officer of customs.

(6) If a ship enters or leaves, or attempts to enter or leave, a port or arrives at or leaves, or attempts to arrive at or leave, a terminal in contravention of subsection (2) of this section, the master or owner shall be liable on conviction on indictment to a fine, or on summary conviction to a fine not exceeding 90,000 dollars.

(7) If a ship fails to carry, or the master of a ship fails to produce, a certificate as required by subsection (5) of this section the master shall be liable on summary conviction to a fine not exceeding 1,000 dollars.

(8) If a ship attempts to leave a port in the Turks and Caicos Islands in contravention of this section the ship may be detained.

Issue of certificate by Governor.

11.—(1) Subject to subsection (2) of this section, if the Governor is satisfied, on an application for such a certificate as is mentioned in section 10 of this Act in respect of a ship registered in the Turks and Caicos Islands, that there will be in force in respect of the ship, throughout the period for which the certificate is to be issued, a contract of insurance or other security satisfying the requirements of Article VII of the Convention, the Governor shall issue such a certificate to the owner.

(2) If the Governor is of opinion that there is a doubt whether the person providing the insurance or other security will be able to meet his obligations thereunder, or whether the insurance or other security will cover the owner's liability under section 1 of this Act in all circumstances, he may refuse the certificate.

(3) The Governor may make regulations—

(a) prescribing the fee to be paid on an application for a certificate to be issued by him under this section; and

(b) providing for the cancellation and delivery up of such a certificate in such circumstances as may be prescribed by the regulations.

(4) If a person required by regulations under subsection (3)(b) of this section to deliver up a certificate fails to do so he shall be liable on summary conviction to a fine not exceeding 500 dollars.

(5) The Governor shall send a copy of any certificate issued by him under this section in respect of a ship registered in the Turks and Caicos Islands to the Registrar General of Shipping and Seamen, and the Registrar shall make the copy available for public inspection.

Rights of third parties against insurers.

12.—(1) Where it is alleged that the owner of a ship has incurred a liability under section 1 of this Act as a result of any discharge or escape of oil occurring while there was in force a contract of insurance or other security to which such a certificate as is mentioned in section 10 of this Act related, proceedings to enforce a claim in respect of the liability may be brought against the person who provided the insurance or other security (in the following provisions of this section referred to as " the insurer ").

(2) In any proceedings brought against the insurer by virtue of this section it shall be a defence (in addition to any defence affecting the owner's liability) to prove that the discharge or escape was due to the wilful misconduct of the owner himself.

(3) The insurer may limit his liability in respect of claims made against him by virtue of this section in like manner and to the same extent as the owner may limit his liability but the insurer may do so whether or not the discharge or escape occurred without the owner's actual fault or privity.

(4) Where the owner and the insurer each apply to the court for the limitation of his liability any sum paid into court in pursuance of either application shall be treated as paid also in pursuance of the other.

13.—(1) Paragraph (*d*) of section 1(1) of the Administration of Justice Act 1956 as applied in Turks and Caicos Islands by the Admiralty Jurisdiction (Turks and Caicos Islands) Order 1965(a) (Admiralty jurisdiction in claims for damage done by ships) shall be construed as extending to any claim in respect of a liability incurred under this Act.

Jurisdiction of Turks and Caicos Islands courts and registration of foreign judgments.

(2) Where any persistent oil is discharged or escapes from a ship but does not result in any damage caused by contamination in the area of the Turks and Caicos Islands and no measures are reasonably taken to prevent or reduce such damage in that area, no court in the Turks and Caicos Islands shall entertain an action (whether *in rem* or *in personam*) to enforce a claim arising from—

(*a*) any damage caused in the area of another Convention country by contamination resulting from the discharge or escape ;

(*b*) any cost incurred in taking measures to prevent or reduce such damage in the area of another Convention country ; or

(*c*) any damage caused by any measures so taken.

(3) Where a judgment has been obtained in a court in a Convention country to enforce a claim in respect of a liability incurred under any provision corresponding to section 1 of this Act the judgment creditor may apply to the court in the Turks and Caicos Islands to have the judgment registered in the said court and on any such application the said court shall, subject to the provisions of this subsection and of subsection (5) of this section, order the judgment to be registered accordingly :

Provided that no judgment shall be ordered to be registered under this subsection if :

(*a*) the judgment has been wholly satisfied ; or

(*b*) the judgment was obtained by fraud ; or

(*c*) the judgment debtor was not given reasonable notice and a fair opportunity to present his case ; or

(*d*) the judgment debtor satisfies the court in the Turks and Caicos Islands either that an appeal is pending or that he is entitled and intends to appeal against the judgment.

(4) Where a judgment is registered under this section :

(*a*) the judgment shall, as from the date of registration, be of the same force and effect and proceedings may be taken thereon as if it had been a judgment originally obtained or entered up on the date of registration in the registering court ; and

(*b*) the registering court shall have the same control and jurisdiction over the judgment as it has over similar judgments given by itself but insofar only as relates to execution under this section.

(5) The Judge of the court in the Turks and Caicos Islands may make rules of court for regulating the practice and procedure in respect of proceedings for the registration and enforcement of judgments under subsections (3) and (4) of this section and such rules of court shall (*inter alia*) provide :

(*a*) for service on the judgment debtor of notice of the registration of a judgment under subsection (3) of this section ; and

(*b*) for enabling the registering court on an application by the judgment debtor to set aside the registration of a judgment under subsection (3) of this section on such terms as the court thinks fit ; and

---

(a) S.I. 1965/1529 (1965 II, p. 4437).

(c) for suspending the execution of a judgment registered under this section until the expiration of the period during which the judgment debtor may apply to have the registration set aside.

Government ships.

14.—(1) Nothing in the preceding provisions of this Act applies in relation to any warship or any ship for the time being used by the government of any State for other than commercial purposes.

(2) In relation to a ship owned by a State and for the time being used for commercial purposes it shall be a sufficient compliance with sub-section (2) of section 10 of this Act if there is in force a certificate issued by the government of that State and showing that the ship is owned by that State and that any liability for pollution damage as defined in Article I of the Convention will be met up to the limit prescribed by Article V thereof.

(3) Every Convention State shall, for the purposes of any proceedings brought in a court in the Turks and Caicos Islands to enforce a claim in respect of a liability incurred under section 1 of this Act, be deemed to have submitted to the jurisdiction of that court, and accordingly rules of court may provide for the manner in which such proceedings are to be commenced and carried on ; but nothing in this subsection shall authorise the issue of execution, against the property of any State.

Liability for cost of preventive measures where s. 1 does not apply.

15.—(1) Where,—

(a) after an escape or discharge of persistent oil from a ship, measures are reasonably taken for the purpose of preventing or reducing damage in the area of the Turks and Caicos Islands which may be caused by contamination resulting from the discharge or escape ; and

(b) any person incurs, or might but for the measures have incurred, a liability, otherwise than under section 1 of this Act, for any such damage ;

then, notwithstanding that subsection (1)(b) of that section does not apply, he shall be liable for the cost of the measures, whether or not the person taking them does so for the protection of his interests or in the performance of a duty.

(2) For the purposes of section 503 of the Merchant Shipping Act 1894(a) (limitation of liability) any liability incurred under this section shall be deemed to be a liability to damages in respect of such loss, damage or infringement as is mentioned in subsection (1)(d) of that section.

Saving for recourse actions.

16. Nothing in this Act shall prejudice any claim, or the enforcement of any claim, a person incurring any liability under this Act may have against another person in respect of that liability.

Meaning of " the Convention ", " Convention country " and " Convention State ".

19.—(1) In this Act—

" the Convention " means the International Convention on Civil Liability for Oil Pollution Damage signed in Brussels in 1969 ;

" Convention country " means a country in respect of which the Convention is in force ; and

" Convention State " means a State which is a party to the Convention.

(2) If Her Majesty by Order in Council made under this subsection as it applies in the United Kingdom declares that any State specified in the Order is a party to the Convention in respect of any country so specified the Order shall, while in force, be conclusive evidence that that State is a party to the Convention in respect of that country.

(a) 1894 c. 60.

20.—(1) In this Act—

Interpretation of other expressions.

" damage " includes loss ;

" owner ", in relation to a registered ship, means the person registered as its owner, except that in relation to a ship owned by a State which is operated by a person registered as the ship's operator, it means the person registered as its operator ;

" the court " means the Supreme Court of the Turks and Caicos Islands ;

" dollars " means United States dollars.

(2) In relation to any damage or cost resulting from the discharge or escape of any oil carried in a ship references in this Act to the owner of the ship are references to the owner at the time of the occurrence or first of the occurrences resulting in the discharge or escape.

(3) References in this Act to the area of any country include the territorial sea of that country.

21.—(2) This Act shall be construed as one with the Merchant Shipping Acts 1894 to 1967.

Construction and commencement

(3) This Act shall come into force on such day as the Governor may by order appoint, and different days may be so appointed for different provisions of this Act.

SCHEDULE 2 TO THE ORDER ARTICLE 4

THE MERCHANT SHIPPING ACT 1974

PART I

THE INTERNATIONAL OIL POLLUTION COMPENSATION FUND

1.—(1) In this Part of this Act—

Interpretation of Part I.

(a) the " Liability Convention " means the International Convention on Civil Liability for Oil Pollution Damage opened for signature in Brussels on 29th November 1969 ;

(b) the " Fund Convention " means the International Convention on the Establishment of an International Fund for Compensation for Oil Pollution Damage opened for signature in Brussels on 18th December 1971 ;

(c) " the Fund " means the International Fund established by the Fund Convention ; and

(d) " Fund Convention country " means a country in respect of which the Fund Convention is in force.

(2) If Her Majesty by Order in Council made under this subsection as it applies in the United Kingdom declares that any State specified in the Order is a party to the Fund Convention in respect of any country so specified the Order shall, while in force, be conclusive evidence that that State is a party to the Convention in respect of that country.

(3) In this Part of this Act, unless the context otherwise requires—

the " Act of 1971 " means the Merchant Shipping (Oil Pollution) Act 1971(a),

" damage " includes loss,

" discharge or escape ", in relation to pollution damage, means the discharge or escape of oil carried by the ship,

" dollars " means United States dollars.

(a) 1971 c. 59.

"guarantor" means any person providing insurance or other financial security to cover the owner's liability of the kind described in section 10 of the Act of 1971,

"oil", except in sections 2 and 3, means persistent hydrocarbon mineral oil,

"owner" means the person or persons registered as the owner of the ship or, in the absence of registration, the person or persons owning the ship, except that in relation to a ship owned by a State which is operated by a person registered as the ship's operator, it means the person registered as its operator,

"pollution damage" means damage caused outside the ship carrying oil by contamination resulting from the escape or discharge of oil from the ship, wherever the escape or discharge may occur, and includes the cost of preventive measures and further damage caused by preventive measures,

"preventive measures" means any reasonable measures taken by any person after the occurrence to prevent or minimise pollution damage,

"ship" means any sea-going vessel and any seaborne craft of any type whatsoever carrying oil in bulk as cargo.

(4) For the purposes of this Part of this Act a ship's tonnage shall be the net tonnage of the ship with the addition of the amount deducted from the gross tonnage on account of engine room space for the purpose of ascertaining the net tonnage.

If the ship cannot be measured in accordance with the normal rules, its tonnage shall be deemed to be 40 per cent. of the weight in tons (of 2240 lbs.) of oil which the ship is capable of carrying.

(5) For the purposes of this Part of this Act, where more than one discharge or escape results from the same occurrence or from a series of occurrences having the same origin, they shall be treated as one.

(6) In this Part of this Act a franc shall be taken to be a unit of 65½ milligrammes of gold of millesimal fineness 900.

(7) The Governor may from time to time by order specify the amounts which for the purposes of this Part of this Act are to be taken as equivalent to any specified number of francs.

Contributions to Fund

Contributions by importers of oil and others.

2.—(1) Contributions shall be payable to the Fund in respect of oil carried by sea to ports or terminal installations in the Turks and Caicos Islands.

(2) Subsection (1) above applies whether or not the oil is being imported, and applies even if contributions are payable in respect of carriage of the same oil on a previous voyage.

(3) Contributions shall also be payable to the Fund in respect of oil when first received in any installation in the Turks and Caicos Islands after having been carried by sea and discharged in a port or terminal installation in a country which is not a Fund Convention country.

(4) The person liable to pay contributions is—

(a) in the case of oil which is being imported into the Turks and Caicos Islands, the importer, and

(b) otherwise, the person by whom the oil is received.

(5) A person shall not be liable to make contributions in respect of the oil imported or received by him in any year if the oil so imported or received in the year does not exceed 150,000 tonnes.

(6) For the purpose of subsection (5) above—

(a) all the members of a group of companies shall be treated as a single person, and

(b) any two or more companies which have been amalgamated into a single company shall be treated as the same person as that single company.

(7) The contributions payable by a person for any year shall—

(a) be of such amount as may be determined by the Assembly of the Fund under Articles 11 and 12 of the Fund Convention and notified to him by the Fund ;

(b) be payable in such instalments, becoming due at such times, as may be so notified to him ;

and if any amount due from him remains unpaid after the date on which it became due, it shall from then on bear interest, at a rate determined from time to time by the said Assembly, until it is paid.

(8) The Governor may by regulations impose on persons who are or may be liable to pay contributions under this section obligations to give security for payment to the Governor, or to the Fund.

Regulations under this subsection—

(a) may contain such supplemental or incidental provisions as appear to the Governor expedient, and

(b) may impose penalties for contravention of the regulations punishable on summary conviction by a fine not exceeding 1,000 dollars, or such lower limit as may be specified in the regulations.

(9) In this and the next following section, unless the context otherwise requires—

" company " means a body incorporated under the law of the Turks and Caicos Islands, or of any other country ;

" group " in relation to companies, means a holding company and any subsidiary or community controlled entity, subject, in the case of a company incorporated outside the Turks and Caicos Islands, to any necessary modification of this definition ;

" importer " means the person by whom or on whose behalf the oil in question is entered for customs purposes on importation, and " import " shall be construed accordingly ;

" oil " means crude oil and fuel oil, and

(a) " crude oil " means any liquid hydrocarbon mixture occurring naturally in the earth whether or not treated to render it suitable for transportation, and includes—

(i) crude oils from which distillate fractions have been removed, and

(ii) crude oils to which distillate fractions have been added,

(b) " fuel oil " means heavy distillates or residues from crude oil or blends of such materials intended for use as a fuel for the production of heat or power of a quality equivalent to the " American Society for Testing and Materials' Specification for Number Four Fuel Oil (Designation D 396-69) ", or heavier,

" terminal installation " means any site for the storage of oil in bulk which is capable of receiving oil from waterborne transportation, including any facility situated offshore and linked to any such site.

3.—(1) For the purpose of transmitting to the Fund the names and addresses of the persons who under the last preceding section are liable to make contributions to the Fund for any year, and the quantity of oil in respect of which they are so liable, the Governor may by notice

Power to obtain information.

PART I   require any person engaged in producing, treating, distributing or transport-
              ing oil to furnish such information as may be specified in the notice.

              (2) A notice under this section may require a company to give such
              information as may be required to ascertain whether its liability is affected
              by subsection (6) of the last preceding section.

              (3) A notice under this section may specify the way in which, and the
              time within which, it is to be complied with.

              (4) In proceedings by the Fund against any person to recover any
              amount due under the last preceding section, particulars contained in any
              list transmitted by the Governor to the Fund shall, so far as those
              particulars are based on information obtained under this section, be
              admissible as evidence of the facts stated in the list ; and so far as
              particulars which are so admissible are based on information given by
              the person against whom the proceedings are brought, those particulars
              shall be presumed to be accurate until the contrary is proved.

              (5) If a person discloses any information which has been furnished to
              or obtained by him under this section, or in connection with the execution
              of this section, he shall, unless the disclosure is made—

                  (a) with the consent of the person from whom the information was
                  obtained, or

                  (b) in connection with the execution of this section, or

                  (c) for the purposes of any legal proceedings arising out of this section
                  or of any report of such proceedings,

              be liable on summary conviction to a fine not exceeding 1,000 dollars.

              (6) A person who—

                  (a) refuses or wilfully neglects to comply with a notice under this
                  section, or

                  (b) in furnishing any information in compliance with a notice under
                  this section makes any statement which he knows to be false in a
                  material particular, or recklessly makes any statement which is false
                  in a material particular,

              shall be liable—

                      (i) on summary conviction to a fine not exceeding 1,000 dollars, and

                      (ii) on conviction on indictment to a fine, or to imprisonment for
                      a term not exceeding twelve months, or to both.

              Compensation for persons suffering pollution damage

Liability of   4.—(1) The Fund shall be liable for pollution damage in the Turks and
the Fund.   Caicos Islands if the person suffering the damage has been unable to
              obtain full compensation under section 1 of the Act of 1971 (which gives
              effect to the Liability Convention)—

                  (a) because the discharge or escape causing the damage—

                      (i) resulted from an exceptional, inevitable and irresistible pheno-
                      menon, or

                      (ii) was due wholly to anything done or left undone by another
                      person (not being a servant or agent of the owner) with intent
                      to do damage, or

                      (iii) was due wholly to the negligence or wrongful act of a govern-
                      ment or other authority in exercising its function of maintaining
                      lights or other navigational aids for the maintenance of which
                      it was responsible,

                  (and because liability is accordingly wholly displaced by section 2 of
                  the Act of 1971), or

(b) because the owner or guarantor liable for the damage cannot meet PART I
his obligations in full, or

(c) because the damage exceeds the liability under section 1 of the
Act of 1971 as limited—

    (i) by section 4 of the Act of 1971, or

    (ii) (where the said section 4 is displaced by section 9 of this Act)
by section 503 of the Merchant Shipping Act 1894(a).

(2) Subsection (1) above shall apply with the substitution for the words
" the Turks and Caicos Islands " of the words " a Fund Convention
country " where the incident has caused pollution damage both in the
Turks and Caicos Islands and in another Fund Convention country, and
proceedings under the Liability Convention for compensation for the
pollution damage have been brought in a country which is not a Fund
Convention country or in the Turks and Caicos Islands.

(3) Where the incident has caused pollution damage both in the Turks
and Caicos Islands and in another country in respect of which the Liability
Convention is in force, references in this section to the provisions of the
Act of 1971 shall include references to the corresponding provisions of the
law of any country giving effect to the Liability Convention.

(5) For the purposes of this section an owner or guarantor is to be
treated as incapable of meeting his obligations if the obligations have not
been met after all reasonable steps to pursue the legal remedies available
have been taken.

(6) Expenses reasonably incurred, and sacrifices reasonably made, by
the owner voluntarily to prevent or minimise pollution damage shall be
treated as pollution damage for the purposes of this section, and accordingly he shall be in the same position with respect to claims against the
Fund under this section as if he had a claim in respect of liability under
section 1 of the Act of 1971.

(7) The Fund shall incur no obligation under this section if—

(a) it proves that the pollution damage—

    (i) resulted from an act of war, hostilities, civil war or insurrection,
or

    (ii) was caused by oil which has escaped or been discharged from
a warship or other ship owned or operated by a State and used,
at the time of the occurrence, only on Government non-commercial service, or

(b) the claimant cannot prove that the damage resulted from an occurrence involving a ship identified by him, or involving two or more
ships one of which is identified by him.

(8) If the Fund proves that the pollution damage resulted wholly or
partly—

(a) from an act or omission done with intent to cause damage by the
person who suffered the damage, or

(b) from the negligence of that person,

the Fund may be exonerated wholly or partly from its obligation to pay
compensation to that person:

Provided that this subsection shall not apply to a claim in respect of
expenses or sacrifices made voluntarily to prevent or minimise pollution
damage.

(9) Where the liability under section 1 of the Act of 1971 is limited to
any extent by subsection (5) of that section (contributory negligence), the
Fund shall be exonerated to the same extent.

(a) 1894 c. 60.

(10) The Fund's liability under this section shall be subject to the limits imposed by paragraphs 4, 5 and 6 of Article 4 of the Fund Convention which impose an overall liability on the liabilities of the owner and of the Fund, and the text of which is set out in Schedule 1 to this Act.

(11) Evidence of any instrument issued by any organ of the Fund or of any document in the custody of the Fund, or any entry in or extract from such a document, may be given in any legal proceedings by production of a copy certified as a true copy by an official of the Fund ; and any document purporting to be such a copy shall be received in evidence without proof of the official position or handwriting of the person signing the certificate.

(12) For the purpose of giving effect to the said provisions of Article 4 of the Fund Convention a court giving judgment against the Fund in proceedings under this section shall notify the Fund, and—

(a) no steps shall be taken to enforce the judgment unless and until the court gives leave to enforce it,

(b) that leave shall not be given unless and until the Fund notifies the court either that the amount of the claim is not to be reduced under the said provisions of Article 4 of the Fund Convention, or that it is to be reduced to a specified amount, and

(c) in the latter case the judgment shall be enforceable only for the reduced amount.

Indemnification of shipowners

Indemnifica-
tion where
damage is
caused by
ship
registered
in Fund
Convention
country.

5.—(1) Where a liability is incurred under section 1 of the Act of 1971 in respect of a ship registered in a Fund Convention country the Fund shall indemnify the owner and his guarantor for that portion of the aggregate amount of the liability which—

(a) is in excess of an amount equivalent to 1,500 francs for each ton of the ship's tonnage or of an amount of 125 million francs, whichever is the less, and

(b) is not in excess of an amount equivalent to 2,000 francs for each ton of the said tonnage or an amount of 210 million francs, whichever is the less.

(2) Where proceedings under the Liability Convention for compensation for pollution damage have been brought in a country which is not a Fund Convention country (but is a country in respect of which the Liability Convention is in force), and the incident has caused pollution damage in the Turks and Caicos Islands (as well as in that other country) subsection (1) above shall apply with the omission of the words " under section 1 of the Act of 1971 ".

(3) The Fund shall not incur an obligation under this section where the pollution damage resulted from the wilful misconduct of the owner.

(4) In proceedings to enforce the Fund's obligation under this section the court may exonerate the Fund wholly or partly if it is proved that, as a result of the actual fault or privity of the owner—

(a) the ship did not comply with such requirements as the Governor may by order prescribe for the purposes of this section, and

(b) the occurrence or damage was caused wholly or partly by that non-compliance.

(5) The requirements referred to in subsection (4) above are such requirements as appear to the Governor appropriate to implement the provisions of—

(a) article 5(3) of the Fund Convention (marine safety conventions), and

(*b*) article 5(4) of the Fund Convention (which enables the Assembly of   Part I
the Fund to substitute new conventions).

(6) An order made under subsection (4) above—

(*a*) may be varied or revoked by a subsequent order so made, or

(*b*) may contain such transitional or other supplemental provisions as
appear to the Governor to be expedient.

(7) Expenses reasonably incurred, and sacrifices reasonably made, by
the owner voluntarily to prevent or minimise the pollution damage shall
be treated as included in the owner's liability for the purposes of this
section.

Supplemental

6.—(1) Paragraph (*d*) of section 1(1) of the Administration of Justice   Jurisdiction
Act 1956 as applied in Turks and Caicos Islands by the Admiralty Juris- and effect of
diction (Turks and Caicos Islands) (Order) 1965(a) (Admiralty jurisdiction judgments.
in claims for damage done by ships) shall be construed as extending to
any claim in respect of a liability falling on the Fund under this Part
of this Act.

(2) Where in accordance with rules of court made for the purposes of
this subsection the Fund has been given notice of proceedings brought
against an owner or guarantor in respect of liability under section 1 of
the Act of 1971, any judgment given in the proceedings shall, after it has
become final and enforceable, become binding upon the Fund in the sense
that the facts and evidence in the judgment may not be disputed by the
Fund even if the Fund has not intervened in the proceedings.

(3) Where a person incurs a liability under the law of a Fund Convention
country corresponding to the Act of 1971 for damage which is partly in
the area of the Turks and Caicos Islands, subsection (2) above shall, for
the purpose of proceedings under this Part of this Act, apply with any
necessary modifications to a judgment in proceedings under that law of
the said country.

(4) Subject to subsection (5) below, the provisions of subsections (3),
(4) and (5) of section 13 of the Merchant Shipping (Oil Pollution) Act 1971
shall apply, whether or not they would so apply apart from this subsection,
to any judgment given by a court in a Fund Convention country to
enforce a claim in respect of liability incurred under any provision corresponding to section 4 or 5 of this Act.

(5) No steps shall be taken to enforce such a judgment unless and
until the court in which it is registered under the said subsections (3), (4)
and (5) of section 13 of the Merchant Shipping (Oil Pollution) Act 1971
gives leave to enforce it: and—

(*a*) that leave shall not be given unless and until the Fund notifies the
court either that the amount of the claim is not to be reduced under
paragraph 4 of Article 4 of the Fund Convention (as set out in
Schedule 1 to this Act) or that it is to be reduced to a specified
amount; and

(*b*) in the latter case, the judgment shall be enforceable only for the
reduced amount.

7.—(1) No action to enforce a claim against the Fund under this Part Extinguishof this Act shall be entertained by a court in the Turks and Caicos Islands ment of
unless—   claims.

(*a*) the action is commenced, or

(a) S.I. 1965/1529 (1965 II, p. 4437).

PART I (*b*) a third-party notice of an action to enforce a claim against the owner or his guarantor in respect of the same damage is given to the Fund,

not later than three years after the claim against the Fund arose.

In this subsection "third-party notice" means a notice of the kind described in subsections (2) and (3) of the last preceding section.

(2) No action to enforce a claim against the Fund under this Part of this Act shall be entertained by a court in the Turks and Caicos Islands unless the action is commenced not later than six years after the occurrence, or first of the occurrences, resulting in the discharge or escape by reason of which the claim against the Fund arose.

(3) Notwithstanding the preceding provisions of this section, a person's right to bring an action under section 5 of this Act shall not be extinguished before six months from the date when that person first acquired knowledge of the bringing of an action against him under the Act of 1971 (that is to say an action to enforce a liability against which he seeks indemnity), or under the corresponding provisions of the law of any country outside the Turks and Caicos Islands giving effect to the Liability Convention.

Subrogation and rights of recourse.

8.—(1) In respect of any sum paid under section 4(1)(*b*) of this Act (default by owner or guarantor on liability for pollution damage) the Fund shall acquire by subrogation the rights of the recipient against the owner or guarantor.

(2) The right of the Fund under subsection (1) above is subject to any obligation of the Fund under section 5 of this Act to indemnify the owner or guarantor for any part of the liability on which he has defaulted.

(3) In respect of any sum paid—

(*a*) under paragraph (*a*) or paragraph (*c*) of section 4(1) ; or

(*b*) under section 5,

the Fund shall acquire by subrogation any rights of recourse or subrogation which the owner or guarantor or any other person has in respect of his liability for the damage in question.

(4) In respect of any sum paid by a public authority in the Turks and Caicos Islands as compensation for pollution damage, that authority shall acquire by subrogation any rights which the recipient has against the Fund under this Part of this Act.

Modification of limitation of liability under Act of 1971.

9. In the Act of 1971 after section 8 there shall be inserted the following section—

"Cases excluded from sections 4 to 8.

8A.—(1) Sections 4 to 8 of this Act shall not apply to a ship which at the time of the discharge or escape was registered in a country—

(*a*) which was not a Convention country, and

(*b*) which was a country in respect of which the 1957 Convention was in force.

(2) In this section 'the 1957 Convention' means the International Convention relating to the Limitation of the Liability of Owners of Seagoing Ships signed in Brussels on 10th October 1957.

(3) If Her Majesty by Order in Council made under this subsection as it applies in the United Kingdom declares that any country—

(*a*) is not a Convention country within the meaning of this Act, and (*b*) is a country in respect of which the 1957 Convention is in force,

or that it was such a country at a time specified in the Order, the Order shall, while in force, be conclusive evidence of the the facts stated in the Order."

PART V

Supplemental

22. Where an offence under this Act, or under regulations made under Offences by any of its provisions, which has been committed by a body corporate is bodies proved to have been committed with the consent or connivance of, or to be corporate. attributable to any neglect on the part of a director, manager, secretary or other similar officer of the body corporate, or any person who was purporting to act in any such capacity, he, as well as the body corporate, shall be guilty of that offence and shall be liable to be proceeded against and punished accordingly.

In this section " director ", in relation to a body corporate established by or under any enactment for the purpose of carrying on under public ownership any industry or part of an industry or undertaking, being a body corporate whose affairs are managed by its members, means a member of that body corporate.

23.—(1) This Act shall be construed as one with the Merchant Shipping Construc-Acts 1894 to 1971, and without prejudice to the generality of this provision, tion and references in those Acts to the Merchant Shipping Acts shall be construed interpreta-as including references to this Act. tion.

(2) References in this Act to the area of any country include the territorial sea of that country, and references to pollution damage in the Turks and Caicos Islands shall be construed accordingly.

(4) Except so far as the context otherwise requires, any reference in this Act to an enactment shall be construed as a reference to that enactment as amended or extended by or under any other enactment.

24.—(2) This Act shall come into force on such day as the Governor may Commence-appoint and different days may be appointed for different provisions, or for ment. different purposes.

(3) An order under subsection (2) above may make such transitional provision as appears to the Governor to be necessary of expedient in connection with the provisions thereby brought into force, including such adaptations of those provisions, or any provisions of this Act then in force, as appear to him to be necessary or expedient in consequence of the partial operation of this Act (whether before or after the day appointed).

SCHEDULE 1 TO THE ACT

Sections 4(10), 6(6).

OVERALL LIMIT ON LIABILITY OF FUND

Article 4—paragraphs 4, 5 and 6

4. (*a*) Except as otherwise provided in sub-paragraph (*b*) of this paragraph, the aggregate amount of compensation payable by the Fund under this Article shall in respect of any one incident be limited, so that the total sum of that amount and the amount of compensation actually paid under the Liability Convention for pollution damage caused in the territory of the Contracting States, including any sums in respect of which the Fund is under an obligation to indemnify the owner pursuant to Article 5, paragraph 1, of this Convention, shall not exceed 450 million francs.

PART V   (*b*) The aggregate amount of compensation payable by the Fund under this Article for pollution damage resulting from a natural phenomenon of an exceptional, inevitable and irresistible character shall not exceed 450 million francs.

5. Where the amount of established claims against the Fund exceeds the aggregate amount of compensation payable under paragraph 4, the amount available shall be distributed in such a manner that the proportion between any established claim and the amount of compensation actually recovered by the claimant under the Liability Convention and this Convention shall be the same for all claimants.

6. The Assembly of the Fund may, having regard to the experience of incidents which have occurred and in particular the amount of damage resulting therefrom and to changes in the monetary values, decide that the amount of 450 million francs referred to in paragraph 4, sub-paragraph (*a*) and (*b*), shall be changed ; provided, however, that this amount shall in no case exceed 900 million francs or be lower than 450 million francs. The changed amount shall apply to incidents which occur after the date of the decision effecting the change.

EXPLANATORY NOTE

(*This Note is not part of the Order.*)

This Order extends to the Turks and Caicos Islands the provisions of the Merchant Shipping (Oil Pollution) Act 1971, with the necessary adaptations, enabling effect to be given to the International Convention on Civil Liability for Oil Pollution Damage opened for signature in Brussels on 29th November 1969 (Cmnd. 4403). The Order also extends the provisions of Parts I and V of, and of Schedule 1 to the Merchant Shipping Act 1974, with the necessary adaptations, enabling effect to be given to the International Convention on the Establishment of an International Fund for Compensation for Oil Pollution Damage opened for signature in Brussels on 18th December 1971 (Cmnd. 5061). The 1969 Convention provides uniform rules and procedures for determining questions of liability and for awarding compensation when damage is caused by pollution resulting from the escape or discharge of oil from ships. The 1971 Convention sets up an international fund to provide a supplementary system for compensation and indemnification for such damage.

STATUTORY INSTRUMENTS

1976 No. 224

DIPLOMATIC AND INTERNATIONAL IMMUNITIES AND PRIVILEGES

The OECD Financial Support Fund (Immunities and Privileges) Order 1976

Laid before Parliament in draft

Made -   -   -   -   18th February 1976
Coming into operation On a date to be notified
in the London, Edin-
burgh and Belfast
Gazettes.

At the Court at Buckingham Palace, the 18th day of February 1976

Present,

The Queen's Most Excellent Majesty in Council

Whereas a draft of this Order has been laid before Parliament in accordance with section 10(1) of the International Organisations Act 1968(a) and has been approved by a resolution of each House of Parliament:

Now, therefore, Her Majesty, by virtue and in exercise of the powers conferred on Her by section 1 of the said Act or otherwise in Her Majesty vested, is pleased, by and with the advice of Her Privy Council, to order, and it is hereby ordered, as follows: —

1. This Order may be cited as the OECD Financial Support Fund (Immunities and Privileges) Order 1976. It shall come into operation on the date on which the Agreement establishing a Financial Support Fund of the Organisation for Economic Co-operation and Development(b), opened for signature at Paris on 9th April 1975, enters into force in respect of the United Kingdom. This date shall be notified in the London, Edinburgh and Belfast Gazettes.

2.—(1) In this Order " the 1961 Convention Articles " means the Articles (being certain Articles of the Vienna Convention on Diplomatic Relations signed in 1961) which are set out in Schedule 1 to the Diplomatic Privileges Act 1964(c).

(2) The Interpretation Act 1889(d) shall apply for the interpretation of this Order as it applies for the interpretation of an Act of Parliament.

3. The Financial Support Fund of the Organisation for Economic Co-operation and Development (hereinafter referred to as the Fund) is an

---

(a) 1968 c. 48.   (b) Cmnd. 6242.   (c) 1964 c. 81.   (d) 1889 c. 63.

organisation of which the United Kingdom and foreign sovereign Powers are members.

4. The Fund shall have the legal capacities of a body corporate.

5.—(1) The Fund shall have immunity from suit and legal process except:

(*a*) to the extent that the Governing Committee of the Fund shall have expressly waived such immunity in a particular case ; or

(*b*) if the Fund has borrowed money or issued securities in the United Kingdom, in respect of any proceedings (other than proceedings brought against the Fund by any member, or any agency of a member, or any person acting for or deriving claims from a member or an agency of a member) arising out of or in connection with the exercise of any of the powers of the Fund to borrow money or to buy and sell securities.

(2) The provisions of paragraph (1) of this Article shall not prevent the taking of such measures as may be permitted by law in relation to the execution of judgment against the Fund.

6. The Fund shall have the like inviolability of official archives as, in accordance with the 1961 Convention Articles, is accorded in respect of the official archives of a diplomatic mission.

7. Within the scope of its official activities, the Fund shall have the like exemption or relief from taxes, other than customs duties and taxes on the importation of goods, as is accorded to a foreign sovereign Power.

8. The Fund shall have the like relief from rates on its official premises as, in accordance with Article 23 of the 1961 Convention Articles, is accorded in respect of the premises of a diplomatic mission.

N. E. Leigh.

EXPLANATORY NOTE

(This Note is not part of the Order.)

This Order confers certain privileges and immunities upon the OECD Financial Support Fund. It will enable the United Kingdom to give effect to Article XVII of the Agreement establishing the Fund (Cmnd. 6242) opened for signature at Paris on 9th April 1975. It will come into operation on the date on which the Agreement enters into force with respect to the United Kingdom.

STATUTORY INSTRUMENTS

1976 No. 225

SOCIAL SECURITY

The Social Security (Reciprocal Agreements) Order 1976

Made - - - -	18*th February* 1976
Coming into Operation	18*th February* 1976

At the Court at Buckingham Palace, the 18th day of February 1976

Present

The Queen's Most Excellent Majesty in Council

Whereas the Orders in Council specified in Schedule 1 to this Order modified certain enactments so as to give effect to the agreements set out in the Schedules to those Orders:

And Whereas Her Majesty's Government have proposed to each of the parties with whom the United Kingdom has made a relevant agreement set out in a Schedule to the Orders in Council mentioned in Schedule 1 to this Order to enter into agreements with them for modifying the existing agreements so as to take account of changes in the legislation of the United Kingdom but without otherwise altering the effect of the existing agreements:

And Whereas by virtue of section 2 of, and paragraph 10 of Schedule 3 to, the Social Security (Consequential Provisions) Act 1975(a) it is provided that Her Majesty may by Order in Council provide that an Order in Council made under section 105 of the National Insurance Act 1965(b) or section 84 of the National Insurance (Industrial Injuries) Act 1965(c) shall have effect with such modifications as may be specified in the Order and, in the case of an Order under the said section 105, shall have effect for the purposes of section 143 of the Social Security Act 1975(d) and as if the reference in the said sections 105 and 143 to an agreement included a reference to a proposed agreement:

Now, therefore, Her Majesty, in pursuance of the said section 2, and the said paragraph 10 and of all other powers enabling Her in that behalf, is pleased, by and with the advice of Her Privy Council, to order, and it is hereby ordered, as follows:—

Citation, commencement and interpretation

1.—(1) This Order may be cited as the Social Security (Reciprocal Agreements) Order 1976 and shall come into operation forthwith.

(2) In this Order, unless the context otherwise requires—

"the Act" means the Social Security Act 1975;

"the other country" means the party with whom the United Kingdom has made the relevant agreement set out in a Schedule to the Orders in Council mentioned in Schedule 1 to this Order;

(a) 1975 c. 18. (b) 1965 c. 51.
(c) 1965 c. 52. (d) 1975 c. 14.

"year" means the period of twelve months beginning with 6th April in any year;

and other expressions have the same meanings as in the Act.

(3) Any reference in this Order to any provision made by, or contained in, any enactment or instrument shall, except insofar as the context otherwise requires, be construed as a reference to that provision as amended or extended by any enactment or instrument, and as including a reference to any provision which it re-enacts or replaces, or which may re-enact or replace it, with or without modification.

(4) The rules for the construction of Acts of Parliament contained in the Interpretation Act 1889(a) shall apply for the purposes of this Order and the revocation effected by it as they would apply if this Order and the Order which it revokes were Acts of Parliament and the revocation were a repeal.

Modification of Orders made under the National Insurance Act 1965

2.—(1) Any Order in Council specified in Schedule 1 to this Order which was made under section 105 of the National Insurance Act 1965 shall, for the purposes of section 143 of the Social Security Act 1975, have effect subject to the modifications contained in the following provisions of this Order.

(2) Any such Order in Council shall have effect as if the agreement proposed by Her Majesty's Government for modifying the agreement set out in the Schedule to such Order, so as to take account of changes in the legislation of the United Kingdom without otherwise altering the effect of such agreement, had been entered into.

(3) Any reference in any such Order in Council specified in Schedule 1 to this Order to any matter dealt with by, or provision contained in, the National Insurance Acts 1965 to 1974 shall have effect as if it were a reference to the corresponding or most nearly corresponding matter dealt with by, or provision contained in, the Act.

(4) Where in any agreement set out in the Schedule to any such Order in Council there is any reference or provision to the effect set out in any paragraph of column 1 of Schedule 2 to this Order, the modifications of any such Order made by the preceding provisions of this Order shall have effect as if the reference or provision set out in the corresponding paragraph of column 2 of the said Schedule 2 were substituted for the former reference or provision so however that this paragraph shall not apply to any act, omission or event occurring before 6th April 1975 or to the National Insurance (Isle of Man Reciprocal Agreement) Order 1948(b).

Modifications of Orders made under the National Insurance (Industrial Injuries) Act 1965

3. Any reference in any Order in Council specified in Schedule 1 to this Order which was made under section 84 of the National Insurance (Industrial Injuries) Act 1965 to any matter dealt with by, or provision contained in, the National Insurance (Industrial Injuries) Acts 1965 to 1974 shall have effect as if it were a reference to the corresponding or most nearly corresponding matter dealt with by, or provision contained in, the Act.

(a) 1889 c. 63.
(b) S.I. 1948/1844 (Rev. XVI, p. 363: 1948 I, p. 2902).

Revocation of Order

4. The Social Security (Reciprocal Agreements) Order 1975(a) is hereby revoked.

N. E. Leigh.

Articles 2(1) and 3   SCHEDULE 1

ORDERS IN COUNCIL MODIFIED BY THIS ORDER

Title of Order in Council	Reference
The National Insurance (Isle of Man Reciprocal Agreement) Order 1948	S.I. 1948/1844 (Rev. XVI, p. 363: 1948 I, p. 2902)
The National Insurance (Industrial Injuries) (Isle of Man Reciprocal Agreement) Order 1948	S.I. 1948/2350 (Rev. XVI, p. 538: 1948 I, p. 3027)
The National Insurance and Industrial Injuries (Reciprocal Agreement with Italy) Order 1953	S.I. 1953/884 (1953 I, p. 1395)
The National Insurance and Industrial Injuries (Luxembourg) Order 1955	S.I. 1955/420 (1955 I, p. 1636)
The National Insurance and Industrial Injuries (Netherlands) Order 1955	S.I. 1955/874 (1955 I, p. 1653)
The National Insurance and Industrial Injuries (Malta) Order 1956	S.I. 1956/1897 (1956 I, p. 1663)
The National Insurance and Industrial Injuries (Sweden) Order 1957	S.I. 1957/856 (1957 I, p. 1667)
The National Insurance and Industrial Injuries (Israel) Order 1957	S.I. 1957/1879 (1957 I, p. 1658)
The Family Allowances, National Insurance and Industrial Injuries (Norway) Order 1958	S.I. 1958/423 (1958 II, p. 1614)
The National Insurance and Industrial Injuries (France) Order 1958	S.I. 1958/597 (1958 II, p. 1641)
The Family Allowances, National Insurance and Industrial Injuries (Belgium) Order 1958	S.I. 1958/771 (1958 II, p. 1599)
The National Insurance and Industrial Injuries (Malta) Order 1958	S.I. 1958/772 (1958 II, p. 1657)
The Family Allowances, National Insurance and Industrial Injuries (Yugoslavia) Order 1958	S.I. 1958/1263 (1958 II, p. 1628)
The Family Allowances and National Insurance (Canada) Order 1959	S.I. 1959/2216 (1959 II, p. 1898)
The Family Allowances, National Insurance and Industrial Injuries (Denmark) Order 1960	S.I. 1960/211 (1960 II, p. 2301)
The Family Allowances, National Insurance and Industrial Injuries (Finland) Order 1960	S.I. 1960/212 (1960 II, p. 2316)
The National Insurance and Industrial Injuries (Republic of Ireland) Order 1960	S.I. 1960/707 (1960 II, p. 2328)
The National Insurance and Industrial Injuries (Turkey) Order 1961	S.I. 1961/584 (1961 I, p. 1290)
The Family Allowances, National Insurance and Industrial Injuries (Germany) Order 1961	S.I. 1961/1202 (1961 II, p. 2371)
The National Insurance (Germany) Order 1961	S.I. 1961/1513 (1961 II, p. 3090)
The National Insurance (Canada) Order 1962	S.I. 1962/173 (1962 I, p. 181)
The National Insurance (Republic of Ireland) Order 1966	S.I. 1966/270 (1966 I, p. 722)

Title of Order in Council	Reference
The National Insurance and Industrial Injuries (Republic of Ireland) Order 1968	S.I. 1968/1655 (1968 III, p. 4478)
The Family Allowances, National Insurance and Industrial Injuries (Switzerland) Order 1969	S.I. 1969/384 (1969 I, p. 1050)
The National Insurance (United States of America) Order 1969	S.I. 1969/1493 (1969 III, p. 4775)
The National Insurance and Industrial Injuries (Cyprus) Order 1969	S.I. 1969/1494 (1969 III, p. 4779)
The National Insurance and Industrial Injuries (Bermuda) Order 1969	S.I. 1969/1686 (1969 III, p. 5309)
The Family Allowances and National Insurance (New Zealand) Order 1970	S.I. 1970/150 (1970 I, p. 650)
The National Insurance (Republic of Ireland) Order 1971	S.I. 1971/1742 (1971 III, p. 4745)
The Family Allowances, National Insurance and Industrial Injuries (Austria) Order 1972	S.I. 1972/1586 (1972 III, p. 4592)
The National Insurance and Industrial Injuries (Jamaica) Order 1972	S.I. 1972/1587 (1972 III, p. 4616)
The National Insurance and Industrial Injuries (Jersey and Guernsey) Order 1972	S.I. 1972/1588 (1972 III, p. 4627)
The National Insurance (Canada) Order 1973	S.I. 1973/763 (1973 I, p. 2425)
The Family Allowances, National Insurance and Industrial Injuries (Gibraltar) Order 1974	S.I. 1974/555 (1974 I, p. 2279)
The Family Allowances, National Insurance and Industrial Injuries (Spain) Order 1975	S.I. 1975/415 (1975 I, p. 1293)

Article 2(4)   SCHEDULE 2

SPECIFIC MODIFICATIONS OF CERTAIN ORDERS IN COUNCIL

Reference or Provision in Agreement 1	Modification of Order in Council 2
1. insurance periods, contribution periods or periods of employment completed in the other country by a person to whom the agreement applies to be treated as if those periods were periods for which contributions had been paid under the legislation of the United Kingdom.	1. each complete week in any such period during which the person was an employed person in the other country to be treated as a week in which he had paid a contribution on earnings equal to two-thirds of the upper earnings limit within the meaning of section 4(1) of the Act for the year which includes the first day of that week.
2. a period of residence in the other country by a person to whom the agreement applies to be treated as a period for which contributions have been paid under the legislation of the United Kingdom.	2. that person to be treated as having paid as many Class 3 contributions under section 8 of the Act as there are complete weeks in any such period.
3. that, for the purposes of any claim by a married woman to receive a retirement pension under the legislation of the United Kingdom by virtue of her own insurance and her residence in the other country, she shall have paid 156 contributions under the legislation of the United Kingdom for any period after the date of her marriage.	3. the number of contributions paid to be ascertained by dividing that person's earnings factor derived from contributions paid in any relevant year under the legislation of the United Kingdom by the lower earnings limit for that year within the meaning of section 4(1) of the Act; provided that the number of contributions so ascertained shall not exceed the number of weeks the person was subject to the legislation of the United Kingdom.
4. that, for the purposes of entitlement to receive in the other country any benefit under the legislation of the United Kingdom, a specified period of insurance shall have been completed by the relevant person. 5. where the amount of any benefit is to be determined by reference to the relationship which the insurance periods completed under the legislation of the United Kingdom bear to the total of the insurance periods completed under the legislation of both countries.	4. & 5. the period of insurance to be ascertained as complete weeks equal in number to the number resulting from dividing the person's earnings factor derived from contributions paid or credited for any year under the legislation of the United Kingdom by the lower earnings limit for that year within the meaning of section 4(1) of the Act; provided that the number shall not exceed the number of weeks the person was subject to the legislation of the United Kingdom.

Reference or Provision in Agreement 1	Modification of Order in Council 2
6. for the purposes of a claim for guardian's allowance under the legislation of the United Kingdom the parent of the child in question who had been insured or resident in the other country to be treated as having been insured under the legislation of the United Kingdom.	6. that parent to be deemed to satisfy the conditions set out in regulation 6 of the Social Security (Guardian's Allowances) Regulations 1975(a).
7. the exclusion of contributions related to wages or earnings.	7. only such contributions paid in respect of periods before 6th April 1975 to be excluded.
8. persons to be treated as having paid contributions as non-employed persons.	8. those persons to be treated as having paid Class 3 contributions.

EXPLANATORY NOTE

(This Note is not part of the Order.)

This Order provides for the Orders in Council listed in Schedule 1 (which give effect to the agreements made between the Governments of the United Kingdom and other countries providing for reciprocity in certain social security matters) to have effect subject to modifications to take account of changes contained in the Social Security Act 1975 and for such Orders made under the National Insurance Act 1965 to have effect for the purposes of section 143 of the 1975 Act. The Social Security (Reciprocal Agreements) Order 1975, which is replaced by this Order, is revoked.

(a) S.I. 1975/515 (1975 I, p. 1693).

STATUTORY INSTRUMENTS

1976 No. 227

COPYRIGHT

The Copyright (International Conventions) (Amendment) Order 1976

Made - - -	18*th February* 1976
Laid before Parliament	25*th February* 1976
Coming into Operation	18*th March* 1976

At the Court at Buckingham Palace, the 18th day of February 1976

Present,

The Queen's Most Excellent Majesty in Council

Her Majesty, by and with the advice of Her Privy Council, and by virtue of the authority conferred upon Her by sections 31, 32 and 47 of the Copyright Act 1956(**a**) and of all other powers enabling Her in that behalf, is pleased to order, and it is hereby ordered, as follows:—

1.—(1) This Order may be cited as the Copyright (International Conventions) (Amendment) Order 1976 and shall come into operation on 18th March 1976.

(2) The Interpretation Act 1889(**b**) shall apply to the interpretation of this Order as it applies to the interpretation of an Act of Parliament.

2. The Copyright (International Conventions) Order 1972(**c**), as amended(**d**), shall be further amended by including in Schedules 4 and 5 (countries whose broadcasting organisations have copyright protection in relation to their sound and television broadcasts) references to Luxembourg and related references to 18th March 1976 in the list of dates in those two Schedules.

3. This Order shall extend to Gibraltar and Bermuda.

N. E. Leigh.

EXPLANATORY NOTE

(This Note is not part of the Order.)

This Order further amends the Copyright (International Conventions) Order 1972. It takes account of the accession by Luxembourg to the International Convention for the Protection of Performers, Producers of Phonograms and Broadcasting Organisations. The Order extends to Gibraltar and Bermuda.

(**a**) 1956 c. 74. (**b**) 1889 c. 63. (**c**) S.I. 1972/673 (1972 I, p. 2172).
(**d**) The amendments are not relevant to the subject matter of this Order.

STATUTORY INSTRUMENTS

1976 No. 228

COUNTER-INFLATION

The Counter-Inflation Act 1973 (Continuation) Order 1976

Made - - - -	*18th February* 1976
Laid before Parliament	*18th February* 1976
Coming into Operation	*31st March* 1976

At the Court at Buckingham Palace, the 18th day of February 1976

Present,

The Queen's Most Excellent Majesty in Council

Her Majesty, in exercise of the power conferred upon Her by section 2(4) of the Remuneration, Charges and Grants Act 1975(**a**), is pleased, by and with the advice of Her Privy Council, to order, and it is hereby ordered, as follows—

1.—(1) This Order may be cited as the Counter-Inflation Act 1973 (Continuation) Order 1976.

(2) The Interpretation Act 1889(**b**) shall apply for the interpretation of this Order as it applies for the interpretation of an Act of Parliament.

(3) This Order shall come into operation on 31st March 1976.

2. The following provisions (as amended)(**c**) of Part II of the Counter-Inflation Act 1973(**d**), namely, sections 5, 6, 8, 9 and 10, shall continue in force until the expiration of the period ending with 31st July 1976.

N. E. Leigh.

EXPLANATORY NOTE

(This note is not part of the Order.)

Section 4 of the Counter-Inflation Act 1973 provides that Part II of that Act shall cease to have effect on the 31st March 1976. This Order, made in exercise of the power contained in section 2(4) of the Remuneration, Charges and Grants Act 1975, continues in force certain provisions of that Part until the end of July 1976, namely sections 5 (notification of price increases, and approvals and consents, 6 (powers of the Price Commission), 8 (power to modify Acts about prices), 9 (restrictions on insurance premiums) and 10 (restrictions on dividends).

(**a**) 1975 c. 57.   (**b**) 1889 c. 63.
(**c**) S.I. 1974/1218 (1974 II, p. 4631) and see section 3 of the Prices Act 1974, c. 24.
(**d**) 1973 c. 9.

STATUTORY INSTRUMENTS

1976 No. 229

MINISTERS OF THE CROWN

The Transfer of Functions (Treasury and Lord Chancellor) Order 1976

Made - - - -	*18th February* 1976
Laid before Parliament	*25th February* 1976
Coming into Operation	*1st April* 1976

At the Court at Buckingham Palace, the 18th day of February 1976

Present,

The Queen's Most Excellent Majesty in Council

Her Majesty, in pursuance of section 1 of the Ministers of the Crown Act 1975 **(a)**, is pleased, by and with the advice of Her Privy Council, to order, and it is hereby ordered, as follows:—

Citation, interpretation and commencement

1.—(1) This Order may be cited as the Transfer of Functions (Treasury and Lord Chancellor) Order 1976.

(2) The Interpretation Act 1889**(b)** applies for the interpretation of this Order as it applies for the interpretation of an Act of Parliament.

(3) This Order shall come into operation on 1st April 1976.

Transfer of functions from Treasury to Lord Chancellor

2. There are hereby transferred to the Lord Chancellor the functions conferred on the Treasury by the following enactments, namely:—

(*a*) sections 29 and 30 of the Criminal Law Act 1826**(c)** (repayment of sums paid out by sheriff by way of reward or compensation);

(*b*) sections 23 to 26, 28, 31 and 33 of the Fines Act 1833**(d)** (receipt of fines etc. and accounts, and power to stay process); and

(*c*) sections 21 and 22 of the Sheriffs Act 1887**(e)** (allowance or repayment of sums claimed by sheriff, and audit of his accounts).

Supplemental and consequential

3.—(1) This Order shall not affect the validity of anything done by or in relation to the Treasury before the coming into operation of this Order, and

---

(a) 1975 c. 26.   (b) 1889 c. 63.
(c) 1826 c. 64.   (d) 1833 c. 99.   (e) 1887 c. 55

anything which at the coming into operation of this Order is in process of being done by or in relation to the Treasury may be continued by or in relation to the Lord Chancellor.

(2) Any authorisation given (by way of approval or otherwise), requirement imposed or appointment made by the Treasury for the purposes of any functions transferred by this Order shall, if in force at the coming into operation of this Order, have effect as if given, imposed or made by the Lord Chancellor, in so far as that is required for continuing its effect after the coming into operation of this Order.

4. In consequence of the transfer of functions effected by Article 2 above—

(*a*) in the enactments specified in that Article for " the Treasury ", wherever those words occur, there shall be substituted " the Lord Chancellor " ;

(*b*) in section 33 of the Fines Act 1833(**a**) for " they are " there shall be substituted " he is " ;

(*c*) in section 23 of the Queen's Remembrancer Act 1859(**b**) for " the Treasury " there shall be substituted " the Lord Chancellor " ;

(*d*) in the Sheriffs Act 1887(**c**)—

(i) in section 21(1), for " they may " there shall be substituted " he may ", and

(ii) in section 22(3), for " require " and " them " there shall be respectively substituted " requires " and " him ".

N. E. Leigh

EXPLANATORY NOTE

(This Note is not part of the Order.)

This Order transfers to the Lord Chancellor those remaining functions of the Treasury which are concerned with receipts and payments by sheriffs in England and Wales and the related administration of the collection of certain fines and forfeited recognizances.

(**a**) 1833 c. 99.   (**b**) 1859 c. 21 (22 & 23 Vict.).   (**c**) 1887 c. 55.

STATUTORY INSTRUMENTS

1976 No. 230

COMMUNITY LAND

The Community Land (Prescribed Forms) (England) Regulations 1976

Made - - - - 16th February 1976

Coming into Operation 6th April 1976

The Secretary of State for the Environment, in exercise of his powers under sections 19(2), 21(4)(c), 23(7)(b) and 53 of, and paragraph 2(3) of Schedule 6, paragraphs 4(2), 5(2) and 6(2) of Schedule 7, and paragraph 3(2) of Schedule 8 to, the Community Land Act 1975(a), and of all other powers enabling him in that behalf, hereby makes the following regulations:

Application, commencement and citation

1. These regulations apply to England, come into effect on 6th April 1976 and may be cited as the Community Land (Prescribed Forms) (England) Regulations 1976.

Interpretation

2.—(1) In these regulations, "the Act" means the Community Land Act 1975.

(2) In these regulations, any reference to a numbered form is a reference to the form bearing that number in the Schedule hereto, or a form substantially to the like effect.

(3) In these regulations, unless the context otherwise requires, references to any enactment shall be construed as references to that enactment as amended, extended or applied by or under any other enactment.

(4) The Interpretation Act 1889(b) shall apply for the interpretation of these regulations as it applies for the interpretation of an Act of Parliament.

Prescribed forms

3. The prescribed forms for the provisions of the Act set out below shall be as follows:—

(*a*) for the purpose of paragraph 2(3) of Schedule 6, the form of an application by an owner to negotiate shall be form 1, and the form of application by an applicant for planning permission to negotiate shall be form 2;

(*b*) for the purpose of section 19(2), the form of a notice of election to be served on an authority shall be form 3;

(a) 1975 c. 77. (b) 1889 c. 63.

(c) for the purpose of paragraph 4(2) of Schedule 7 (planning permission to which section 19 applies) the form of a notice stating that an authority intend or do not intend to acquire the land to which the planning permission relates shall be form 4;

(d) for the purpose of paragraph 5(2) of Schedule 7 (planning permission to which section 20 applies), the form of a notice stating that an authority intend or do not intend to acquire land to which the planning application relates shall be form 5, or where planning permission is granted following an enforcement notice, form 6;

(e) for the purpose of paragraph 6(2) of Schedule 7, the form of a notice by an authority that, having served a notice that they intend to acquire, they have decided not to acquire the land shall be form 7;

(f) for the purpose of section 21(4)(c), the form of a certificate stating that an authority are satisfied that subsections (a) and (b) of section 21(4) have been complied with shall be form 8;

(g) for the purpose of paragraph 3(2) of Schedule 8, the form of a notice of intention to dispose of land in a disposal notification area shall be form 9;

(h) for the purpose of section 23(7)(b), the form of a counter-notice by an authority shall be form 10.

SCHEDULE

FORM 1   *Regulation* 3(a)

COMMUNITY LAND ACT 1975

APPLICATION BY OWNER UNDER PARAGRAPH 2 OF SCHEDULE 6

To (a)

1. This notice relates to land at   (b) details of which are set out at the end of this notice.

2. I/We own a material interest in the land. The material interest which I/we own is   (c).

3. If you acquire the land and make it available for development, I/we apply for an opportunity to negotiate [the purchase of a material interest in the land in order to carry out the development for which it is being made available on terms acceptable to you] [or] [to carry out the development for which the land is being made available on terms acceptable to you].

Particulars of the land
(d)

Signed:

Date:

Full name and address of owner of the material interest.

Full name and address of Agent (if any) to whom correspondence should be sent.

Notes to Form 1

(a) State name and address of authority on which the notice is served.

(b) State briefly the location of the land.

(c) State the material interest, e.g. freehold or lease. If lease state number of years unexpired.

(d) Give full description of the land and enclose a plan on which it is identified.

Regulation 3(a) FORM 2

COMMUNITY LAND ACT 1975

APPLICATION BY APPLICANT FOR PLANNING PERMISSION UNDER
PARAGRAPH 2 OF SCHEDULE 6

To (*a*)

1. This notice relates to land at   (*b*) details of which are set out at the end of this notice.

2. [I am] [We are] an applicant for planning permission for development of the land. The application was dated   (*c*) and was submitted to (*c*).

3. If you acquire the land and make it available for development and if the development for which you make the land available is development of the same class as the development for which I am/we are an applicant for planning permission, I/we apply for an opportunity to negotiate [the purchase of a material interest in the land in order to carry out the development for which it is being made available on terms acceptable to you] [or] [to carry out the development for which the land is being made available on terms acceptable to you].

4. This application is accompanied by the written consent of the owner of every outstanding material interest in the land which has not already been acquired by you.

Particulars of the land

(*d*)

      Signed:

      Date:

      Full name and address of the applicant for planning permission.

      Full name and address of Agent (if any) to whom correspondence should be sent.

Notes to Form 2

(*a*) State name and address of authority on which the notice is served.

(*b*) State briefly the location of the land.

(*c*) State date of planning application and name and address of planning authority to which it was submitted.

(*d*) Give full description of the land and enclose a plan on which it is identified.

Regulation 3(b) FORM 3

COMMUNITY LAND ACT 1975

NOTICE OF ELECTION UNDER SECTION 19(2)

To (*a*)

1. This notice relates to land which is covered by planning permission the details of which are set out at the end of this notice.

2. [I/We own] [I/We have entered into a binding contract to acquire] a material interest in the whole of the land covered by the planning permission. The material interest which I/we [own] [have contracted to acquire] is   (*b*).

3. [I am] [We are] entitled to possession of the land as against

    (i) every other owner (if any) of a material interest in any of the land, and

    (ii) every other person (if any) who has entered into a binding contract to acquire a material interest in any of the land.

4. By this notice I/we require all the authorities under the Community Land Act 1975 whose areas include the land to state within 3 months of the date when this notice was served whether or not any of them intend to acquire the land or any part of it.

Particulars of the planning permission (c)

      (i) date of the application for permission;

      (ii) name of authority which granted the permission;

      (iii) date of the permission;

      (iv) reference number of the application or permission.

    Signed:

    Date:

    Full name and address of owner or person with binding contract.

    Full name and address of Agent (if any) to whom correspondence should be sent.

Notes to Form 3

(*a*) State name and address of authority on which the notice is served.

(*b*) State the material interest, e.g. freehold or lease. If lease, state number of years unexpired.

(*c*) Give details of all the planning permissions if more than one.

FORM 4   *Regulation* 3(*c*)

COMMUNITY LAND ACT 1975

NOTICE OF INTENTION BY AUTHORITY UNDER PARAGRAPH 4 OF SCHEDULE 7

To (*a*)

1. You served a notice of election under section 19(2) of the Community Land Act 1975 on   (*b*). This notice of election was served on   (*c*) and related to land which is covered by planning permission the details of which are set out at the end of this notice and were set out at the end of the notice of election.

2. By the notice of election you required all the authorities under the Community Land Act 1975 whose areas include the land to state within 3 months of the date when the notice was served whether or not any of them intended to acquire the land or any part of it. The authorities concerned are—

(*d*)

3. This notice is given by   (*e*) who [INTEND TO ACQUIRE all the land covered by the planning permission and shown (*h*) on the plan accompanying this notice] [INTEND TO ACQUIRE that part of the land covered by the planning permission which is shown   (*h*) on the plan accompanying this notice] [do NOT intend to acquire any part of the land covered by the planning permission] [and shown   (*h*) on the plan accompanying this notice subject to the following conditions] [and] [do NOT intend to acquire that part of the land covered by the planning permission shown   (*h*) on the plan accompanying this notice] [subject to the following conditions]:—

(*f*)

[4. This notice is also given on behalf of   (*g*)
who [INTEND TO ACQUIRE all the land covered by the planning permission and
shown   (*h*) on the plan accompanying this notice] [INTEND TO
ACQUIRE that part of the land covered by the planning permission which is shown
                              (*h*) on the plan accompanying this notice] [do NOT intend to
acquire any part of the land covered by the planning permission] [and shown
                              (*h*) on the plan accompanying this notice subject to the following
conditions] [and] [do NOT intend to acquire that part of the land covered by the
planning permission shown   (*h*) on the plan accompanying this
notice] [subject to the following conditions]:—

(*f*)

]．

Particulars of the Planning Permission (*i*)

  (i) date of the application for permission;

  (ii) name of authority which granted the permission;

  (iii) date of the permission;

  (iv) reference number of the application or permission.

  Signed:

  On behalf of (*j*):

  Date:

Notes to Form 4

(*a*) State name and address of the person who served the notice of election.

(*b*) State name of authority on whom notice of election was served.

(*c*) State date of service of notice of election.

(*d*) Give the names of all the authorities whose areas include any of the land.

(*e*) Give name of authority actually giving the notice.

(*f*) Set out the conditions (if any).

(*g*) State the names of any of the other authorities whose areas include any of the land on whose behalf the notice is being served.

(*h*) Describe the colouring or other method used to identify the land on the plan.

(*i*) Give details of all the planning permissions (if more than one) as set out on the notice of election.

(*j*) State the name of the authority actually giving the notice and any others on whose behalf it is given.

Regulation 3(*d*)   Form 5

COMMUNITY LAND ACT 1975

NOTICE OF INTENTION BY AUTHORITY UNDER PARAGRAPH 5 OF SCHEDULE 7

To (*a*)

1. An application for planning permission dated   (*b*) made

by   (*c*) was on   (*d*) received by

                              (*e*). This application was for   (*f*).

2. Under the Community Land Act 1975 it is the duty of all authorities whose areas include the land to which an application for relevant development relates to state whether or not any of them intend to acquire the land or any part of it. The authorities concerned are—

(*g*)

3. This notice is given by *(h)* who consider the application to be an application for relevant development and (if planning permission is granted in accordance with the application) [INTEND TO ACQUIRE all the land to which the application relates (shown *(k)* on the plan accompanying this notice)] [INTEND TO ACQUIRE that part of the land to which the planning application relates which is shown *(k)* on the plan accompanying this notice] [do NOT intend to acquire any part of the land to which the planning application relates] [and shown *(k)* on the plan accompanying this notice subject to the following conditions] [and] [do NOT intend to acquire that part of the land to which the planning application relates shown *(k)* on the plan accompanying this notice] [subject to the following conditions]:—

(i)

[4. This notice is also given on behalf of *(j)* who consider the application to be an application for relevant development and (if planning permission is granted in accordance with the application) [INTEND TO ACQUIRE all the land to which the application relates (shown *(k)* on the plan accompanying this notice)] [INTEND TO ACQUIRE that part of the land to which the planning application relates which is shown *(k)* on the plan accompanying this notice] [do NOT intend to acquire any part of the land to which the planning application relates] [and shown *(k)* on the plan accompanying this notice subject to the following conditions] [and] [do NOT intend to acquire that part of the land to which the planning application relates shown *(k)* on the plan accompanying this notice] [subject to the following conditions]:—

(i)   ].

Signed:

On behalf of *(l)*:

Date:

Notes to Form 5

(a) State name and address of the person on whom the notice is served. Notice must be served on the applicant for planning permission and on any other person named in a certificate under section 27 of the Town and Country Planning Act 1971 which is submitted with the application.

(b) Give date of application for planning permission.

(c) State name of applicant for permission.

(d) Give date when a valid planning application was received.

(e) State name of local planning authority who received the application.

(f) Give brief details of development applied for sufficient to identify the application.

(g) Give the names of all the authorities whose areas include any of the land.

(h) Give name of authority actually giving the notice.

(i) Set out the conditions (if any).

(j) State the names of any of the other authorities whose areas include any of the land on whose behalf the notice is being served.

(k) Describe the colouring or other method used to identify the land on the plan.

(l) State the name of the authority actually giving the notice and any others on whose behalf it is given.

Regulation 3(*d*)   FORM 6

COMMUNITY LAND ACT 1975

NOTICE OF INTENTION BY AUTHORITY UNDER PARAGRAPH 5 OF SCHEDULE 7
WHERE ENFORCEMENT NOTICE HAS BEEN SERVED

To (*a*)

1. Following the service of an enforcement notice, the Secretary of State granted planning permission for   (*b*) being the development to which the enforcement notice related, and details of the permission are set out at the end of this notice.

2. Under the Community Land Act 1975 it is the duty of all authorities whose areas include the land to which planning permission for relevant development relates to state whether or not any of them intend to acquire the land or any part of it. The authorities concerned are—

(*c*)

3. This notice is given by   (*d*) who consider the permission to be a permission for relevant development and [INTEND TO ACQUIRE all the land to which the permission relates and shown   (*g*) on the plan accompanying this notice] [INTEND TO ACQUIRE that part of the land to which the permission relates which is shown   (*g*) on the plan accompanying this notice] [do NOT intend to acquire any part of the land to which the permission relates] [and shown   (*g*) on the plan accompanying this notice subject to the following conditions] [and] [do NOT intend to acquire that part of the land to which the permission relates shown   (*g*) on the plan accompanying this notice] [subject to the following conditions]:—

(*e*)

[4. This notice is also given on behalf of   (*f*) who consider the permission to be a permission for relevant development and [INTEND TO ACQUIRE all the land to which the permission relates and shown (*g*) on the plan accompanying this notice] [INTEND TO ACQUIRE that part of the land to which the permission relates which is shown   (*g*) on the plan accompanying this notice] [do NOT intend to acquire any part of the land to which the permission relates] [and shown   (*g*) on the plan accompanying this notice subject to the following conditions] [and] [do NOT intend to acquire that part of the land to which the permission relates shown   (*g*) on the plan accompanying this notice] [subject to the following conditions]:—

(*e*)].

Particulars of the planning permission

    (i) name and address of person to whom letter of Secretary of State was addressed;

    (ii) date of letter;

    (iii) brief details of development;

    (iv) reference number of the Secretary of State.

Signed:

On behalf of (*h*):

Date:

Notes to Form 6

(*a*) State name and address of person on whom notice is served. Notice must be served on the applicant for planning permission and on any other person on whom the enforcement notice was served.

(*b*) Give brief details of the development.

(*c*) Give names of all the authorities whose areas include any of the land.

(*d*) Give name of authority actually giving the notice.

(*e*) Set out the conditions (if any).

(*f*) State the names of any of the other authorities whose areas include any of the land on whose behalf the notice is being served.

(*g*) Describe the colouring or other method used to identify the land on the plan.

(*h*) State the name of the authority actually giving the notice and any others on whose behalf it is given.

FORM 7   *Regulation* 3(*e*)

COMMUNITY LAND ACT 1975

NOTICE BY AUTHORITY UNDER PARAGRAPH 6 OF SCHEDULE 7
OF CHANGE OF INTENTION

To (*a*)

1. This notice is given by   (*b*) who on (*c*) served a notice under paragraph [4] [5] of Schedule 7 to the Community Land Act 1975 that they intended to acquire the land shown   (*d*) on the plan accompanying this notice. The authority have changed their intention.

2. Accordingly notice is given that   (*b*) [do NOT intend to acquire any part of the land shown   (*d*) on the plan accompanying this notice] [do NOT intend to acquire that part of the land shown   (*d*) on the plan accompanying this notice] [subject to the following conditions]:—

(*e*)

Signed:

On behalf of (*b*):

Date:

Notes to Form 7

(*a*) State name and address of person on whom notice is served. Notice must be served on all the persons on whom the notice of intention to acquire was required to be served and where the authority have made a compulsory purchase order before serving this notice, this notice must also be served on the persons on whom notice of the making of the compulsory purchase order was required to be served.

(*b*) State name of authority who have changed their intention.

(*c*) State date of notice of intention to acquire.

(*d*) Describe the colouring or other method used to identify the land on the plan.

(*e*) Set out the conditions (if any).

Regulation 3(*f*)   FORM 8

COMMUNITY LAND ACT 1975

CERTIFICATE BY AUTHORITY UNDER SECTION 21(4)

This certificate is given by   (*a*) who certify that they are
satisfied that:

    (i) a material interest in the land shown   (*b*) on the plan accompanying this certificate has been disposed of by them.

    (ii) immediately before the disposal there were no material interests in the land outstanding.

    (iii) they have approved for the purposes of section 21 of the Community Land Act 1975 the carrying out of the development for which planning permission has been granted by the permission the details of which are set out at the end of this notice.

    [(iv) a material interest in the land was disposed of by them before 6th April 1976 and they approve the interest disposed of by them as being an interest appropriate for the purposes of section 21 of the Community Land Act 1975].

Particulars of the planning permission

    (i) date of the application for permission;

    (ii) name of authority which granted the permission;

    (iii) date of the permission;

    (iv) reference number of the application or permission.

Signed:

On behalf of (*a*):

Date:

Notes to Form 8

(*a*) State name of authority giving the certificate.

(*b*) Describe the colouring or other method used to identify the land on the plan.

FORM 9   *Regulation* 3(*g*)

COMMUNITY LAND ACT 1975

NOTICE UNDER SECTION 23(5) OF INTENTION TO DISPOSE

To (*a*)

1. This notice is given by   (*b*) and relates to
   (*c*).

2. At the time of serving this notice the interest which I/we own in the land is
   (*d*).

3. I/we propose in not less than 4 weeks and not more than 6 months [to enter into a binding contract to dispose of a material interest (*e*) in the land] [to dispose of a material interest in the land].

4. [When I/we have carried out the disposal I/we will not retain any material interest in the land or any part of it.] [When the disposal has been carried out I/we will retain a material interest consisting of   (*f*) in [the whole of the land] part of the land i.e.   (*g*)].

Signed:

Date:

Full name and address of person owning the interest in the land.

Full name and address of Agent (if any) to whom correspondence should be sent.

Notes to Form 9

(*a*) State the name and address of the authority who have declared the area to be a disposal notification area.

(*b*) Give the name and address of the person furnishing the notice. The address should be the place of abode or place of business of the person owning the material interest or, in the case of a company, its registered office.

(*c*) Give the address of and any further information necessary to identify the land to which the notice relates. To the extent that it is capable to being so given, this information may be given by reference to a plan accompanying the notice.

(*d*) State whether freehold or leasehold. If lease state number of years unexpired.

(*e*) A material interest is a freehold or a lease with not less than 7 years still to run.

(*f*) Give details of the material interest being retained.

(*g*) Give sufficient information to identify the part of the land in which the person giving the notice will retain an interest. This can be indicated on a plan.

Regulation 3(*h*)   FORM 10

COMMUNITY LAND ACT 1975

COUNTER-NOTICE BY AUTHORITY UNDER SECTION 23(7)

To (*a*)

1. This notice is given by   (*b*) on whom you served a
notice dated   (*c*) that you [proposed to enter into a binding
contract to dispose of a material interest] [proposed to dispose of a material interest]
in the land described in your notice.

2. Under the Community Land Act 1975 we are required to tell you whether or
not we propose to purchase the land or any part of it. Accordingly we give you notice
that [we do not propose to purchase the land or any part of it] [we propose to purchase
the land to which your notice related and which is shown   (*d*) on the
plan accompanying this notice] [we propose to purchase that part of the land which
is shown   (*d*) on the plan accompanying this notice].

Signed:

On behalf of (*b*):

Date:

Notes to Form 10

(*a*) State name and address of person who served the notice of intention to dispose.

(*b*) State name and address of authority giving the notice.

(*c*) Give the date of the notice of intention to dispose.

(*d*) Describe the colouring or other method used to identify the land on the plan.

John Silkin,

Signed by authority of   Minister for Planning and Local Government,
the Secretary of State   Department of the Environment.

16th February 1976.

EXPLANATORY NOTE

(This Note is not part of the Regulations.)

These Regulations prescribe the following forms for use under the Community Land Act 1975:—

Form 1 —Application by Owner under Paragraph 2 of Schedule 6.

Form 2 —Application by Applicant for Planning Permission under Paragraph 2 of Schedule 6.

Form 3 —Notice of Election under section 19(2).

Form 4 —Notice of Intention by Authority under Paragraph 4 of Schedule 7.

Form 5 —Notice of Intention by Authority under Paragraph 5 of Schedule 7.

Form 6 —Notice of Intention by Authority under Paragraph 5 of Schedule 7 where Enforcement Notice has been served.

Form 7 —Notice by Authority under Paragraph 6 of Schedule 7 of Change of Intention.

Form 8 —Certificate by Authority under section 21(4).

Form 9 —Notice under section 23(5) of Intention to Dispose.

Form 10—Counter-Notice by Authority under section 23(7).

STATUTORY INSTRUMENTS

1976 No. 231

OVERSEAS AID

The Asian Development Bank (Extension of Limit on Guarantees) Order 1976

Laid before the House of Commons in draft

Made - - - -	16*th February* 1976
Coming into operation	17*th February* 1976

Whereas it is provided in section 3(2) of the Overseas Aid Act 1968(a) that the aggregate of the sums which may be paid out of moneys to be provided by Parliament for making, on behalf of Her Majesty's Government in the United Kingdom, payments in fulfilment of any undertaking given by that Government in pursuance of paragraph 3 of Article 3 of the Asian Development Bank Agreement (undertaking by a member of the Asian Development Bank to be responsible for obligations under the Agreement of another member for whose external relations the first mentioned member is responsible) shall not exceed £5,000,000, or such greater sums as may from time to time be specified in an order made by Statutory Instrument by the Minister of Overseas Development with the approval of the Treasury:

And whereas under the Asian Development Bank (Extension of Limit on Guarantees) Order 1972(b), the said sum was increased to £25,000,000:

Now, therefore, the Minister of Overseas Development in the exercise of the powers conferred upon him by section 3 of the Overseas Aid Act 1968 and with the approval of the Treasury, hereby makes the following Order:—

1.—(1) This Order may be cited as the Asian Development Bank (Extension of Limit on Guarantees) Order 1976 and shall come into operation on 17th February 1976.

(2) The Interpretation Act 1889(c) shall apply to the interpretation of, and otherwise in relation to, this Order as it applies to the interpretation of, and otherwise in relation to, an Act of Parliament.

2. The aggregate amount of the sums which may be paid out of moneys provided by Parliament under section 3(1) of the Overseas Aid Act 1968 shall not exceed £45,000,000.

James Callaghan,
Minister of Overseas Development.

Date: 13th February 1976.

We approve,

James A. Dunn,
T. Pendry,
Two of the Lords Commissioners
of Her Majesty's Treasury.

Date: 16th February 1976.

(a) 1968 c. 57.　　(b) S.I. 1972/1046 (1972 II, p. 3151).　　(c) 1889 c. 63.

EXPLANATORY NOTE

(This Note is not part of the Order.)

The Overseas Aid Act 1968, section 3(1) provides that there may be paid out of moneys provided by Parliament sums required by the Minister of Overseas Development for making payments in fulfilment of any undertaking given by Her Majesty's Government in the United Kingdom in pursuance of paragraph 3 of Article 3 of the Asian Development Bank Agreement, being an undertaking to be responsible for obligations under the Agreement of another member for whose external relations Her Majesty's Government in the United Kingdom is responsible. Section 3(2) of the said Act provides that the aggregate amount of the sums which may be paid under section 3(1) of the Act shall not exceed £5,000,000 or such greater sum as the Minister of Overseas Development, with the approval of the Treasury, may from time to time specify in an Order made by Statutory Instrument.

The Asian Development Bank (Extension of Limit on Guarantees) Order 1972 provided that the aggregate amount of the sums which may be paid under section 3(1) of the said Act be increased from £5,000,000 to £25,000,000.

This Order provides that the aggregate amount of the sums which may be paid under section 3(1) of the said Act shall be increased from £25,000,000 to £45,000,000.

STATUTORY INSTRUMENTS

1976 No. 232

CURRENCY AND BANK NOTES

The Fiduciary Note Issue (Extension of Period) Order 1976

Made - - - -	17*th February* 1976
Laid before Parliament	20*th February* 1976
Coming into Operation	14*th March* 1976

The Treasury, in exercise of the powers conferred upon them by section 2(7) of the Currency and Bank Notes Act 1954(a) and of all other powers enabling them in that behalf, hereby make the following Order:—

1. This Order may be cited as the Fiduciary Note Issue (Extension of Period) Order 1976, and shall come into operation on 14th March 1976.

2. The Interpretation Act 1889(b) shall apply for the interpretation of this Order as it applies for the interpretation of an Act of Parliament.

3. The period of two years during which, by virtue of section 2(7) of the Currency and Bank Notes Act 1954, the fiduciary note issue may stand at amounts continuously exceeding fifteen hundred and seventy-five million pounds as extended by the Fiduciary Note Issue (Extension of Period) Order 1974(c), shall be further extended by a period of two years beginning with 14th March 1976.

4. The Fiduciary Note Issue (Extension of Period) Order 1974 is hereby revoked.

James A. Dunn,
T. Pendry,
Two of the Lords Commissioners
of Her Majesty's Treasury.

17th February 1976.

EXPLANATORY NOTE

(This Note is not part of the Order.)

This Order extends for a further two years the period during which the Fiduciary Note Issue may stand at amounts continuously exceeding £1,575 million.

(a) 1954 c. 12.   (b) 1889 c. 63.   (c) S.I. 1974/405 (1974 I, p. 1275).

STATUTORY INSTRUMENTS

1976 No. 233

ACQUISITION OF LAND

COMPENSATION

The Acquisition of Land (Rate of Interest after Entry) Regulations 1976

Made - - - -	16*th February* 1976
Laid before Parliament	25*th February* 1976
Coming into Operation	17*th March* 1976

The Treasury, in exercise of the powers conferred upon them by section 32(1) of the Land Compensation Act 1961(a), and of all other powers enabling them in that behalf, hereby make the following Regulations:—

1. These Regulations may be cited as the Acquisition of Land (Rate of Interest after Entry) Regulations 1976, and shall come into operation on 17th March 1976.

2. The Interpretation Act 1889(b) shall apply for the interpretation of these Regulations as it applies for the interpretation of an Act of Parliament.

3. The rate of interest on any compensation in respect of the compulsory acquisition of an interest in any land on which entry has been made before the payment of the compensation shall be $12\frac{1}{2}$ per cent. per annum.

4. The Acquisition of Land (Rate of Interest after Entry) (No. 3) Regulations 1975(c) are hereby revoked.

James A. Dunn,
T. Pendry,
Two of the Lords Commissioners
of Her Majesty's Treasury.

16th February 1976.

(a) 1961 c. 33.   (b) 1889 c. 63.   (c) S.I. 1975/1856 (1975 I, p. 6983).

EXPLANATORY NOTE

(This Note is not part of the Regulations.)

These Regulations reduce from $13\frac{1}{2}$ per cent. to $12\frac{1}{2}$ per cent. per annum, in respect of any period after the coming into operation of these Regulations, the rate of interest payable where entry is made, before payment of compensation, on land in England and Wales which is being purchased compulsorily, and revoke the Acquisition of Land (Rate of Interest after Entry) (No. 3) Regulations 1975.

1976 No. 234

ACQUISITION OF LAND

COMPENSATION

The Acquisition of Land (Rate of Interest after Entry) (Scotland) Regulations 1976

Made - - - -	*16th February* 1976
Laid before Parliament	*25th February* 1976
Coming into Operation	*17th March* 1976

The Treasury, in exercise of the powers conferred upon them by section 40(1) of the Land Compensation (Scotland) Act 1963(a), and of all other powers enabling them in that behalf, hereby make the following Regulations:—

1.—(1) These Regulations may be cited as the Acquisition of Land (Rate of Interest after Entry) (Scotland) Regulations 1976, and shall come into operation on 17th March 1976.

(2) These Regulations shall extend to Scotland only.

2. The Interpretation Act 1889(b) shall apply for the interpretation of these Regulations as it applies for the interpretation of an Act of Parliament.

3. The rate of interest on any compensation in respect of the compulsory acquisition of an interest in any land on which entry has been made before the payment of the compensation shall be 12½ per cent. per annum.

4. The Acquisition of Land (Rate of Interest after Entry) (Scotland) (No. 3) Regulations 1975(c) are hereby revoked.

James A. Dunn,
T. Pendry,
Two of the Lords Commissioners
of Her Majesty's Treasury.

16th February 1976.

(a) 1963 c. 51.   (b) 1889 c. 63.   (c) S.I. 1975/1857 (1975 I, p. 7045).

EXPLANATORY NOTE

(This Note is not part of the Regulations.)

These Regulations reduce from 13½ per cent. to 12½ per cent. per annum, in respect of any period after the coming into operation of these Regulations, the rate of interest payable where entry is made, before payment of compensation, on land in Scotland which is being purchased compulsorily, and revoke the Acquisition of Land (Rate of Interest after Entry) (Scotland) (No. 3) Regulations 1975.

STATUTORY INSTRUMENTS

1976 No. 235

COAL INDUSTRY

The Opencast Coal (Rate of Interest on Compensation) Order 1976

Made - - - -	16*th February* 1976
Laid before Parliament	25*th February* 1976
Coming into Operation	17*th March* 1976

The Treasury, in exercise of the powers conferred upon them by sections 35(8) and 49(4) of the Opencast Coal Act 1958(a) and of all other powers enabling them in that behalf, hereby make the following Order:—

1. This Order may be cited as the Opencast Coal (Rate of Interest on Compensation) Order 1976, and shall come into operation on 17th March 1976.

2. The Interpretation Act 1889(b) shall apply for the interpretation of this Order as it applies for the interpretation of an Act of Parliament.

3. The rate of interest for the purposes of section 35 of the Opencast Coal Act 1958 shall be 11 per cent. per annum.

4. The Opencast Coal (Rate of Interest on Compensation) (No. 3) Order 1975(c) is hereby revoked.

James A. Dunn,
T. Pendry,
Two of the Lords Commissioners
of Her Majesty's Treasury.

16th February 1976.

EXPLANATORY NOTE

(This Note is not part of the Order.)

Section 35 of the Opencast Coal Act 1958 provides that interest shall be payable in addition to compensation in certain circumstances. This Order reduces the rate of interest from 12 per cent to 11 per cent. per annum and revokes the Opencast Coal (Rate of Interest on Compensation) (No. 3) Order 1975.

(a) 1958 c. 69.   **(b)** 1889 c. 63.   **(c)** S.I. 1975/1858 (1975 III, p. 7046).

STATUTORY INSTRUMENTS

1976 No. 236 (C.7) (S.16)

SHERIFF COURT, SCOTLAND

The Sheriff Courts (Scotland) Act 1971 (Commencement No. 3) Order 1976

Made - - - - *13th February* 1976

In exercise of the powers conferred on me by section 47 of the Sheriff Courts (Scotland) Act 1971(**a**), I hereby make the following order:

1. This order may be cited as the Sheriff Courts (Scotland) Act 1971 (Commencement No. 3) Order 1976.

2. The provisions of the Sheriff Courts (Scotland) Act 1971 (hereinafter referred to as the "Act") specified in the Schedule to this order shall come into operation on 1st September 1976.

William Ross,
One of Her Majesty's Principal
Secretaries of State.

New St. Andrew's House,
Edinburgh.
13th February 1976.

SCHEDULE

PROVISIONS COMING INTO FORCE ON 1ST SEPTEMBER 1976

Provisions of the Act	Subject matter of provisions
Section 31	Civil jurisdiction
Sections 35 to 38	Summary causes
Sections 39 to 42	Miscellaneous and supplemental
Schedule 1, paragraph 2 to 4	Minor and consequential amendment of enactments
Schedule 2, Part II	Repeal of enactments

EXPLANATORY NOTE

(*This Note is not part of the Order.*)

This Order brings into force on 1st September 1976 those provisions of the Sheriff Courts (Scotland) Act 1971 which are not already in operation.

(**a**) 1971 c. 58.

STATUTORY INSTRUMENTS

1976 No. 237 (S. 17)

PRISONS

The Local Review Committee (Scotland) Amendment Rules 1976

Made - - - -	10*th February* 1976
Laid before Parliament	25*th February* 1976
Coming into Operation	22*nd March* 1976

In exercise of the powers conferred on me by section 59(6) of the Criminal Justice Act 1967**(a)** and of all other powers enabling me in that behalf, I hereby make the following rules:—

1.—(1) These rules may be cited as the Local Review Committee (Scotland) Amendment Rules 1976 and shall come into operation on 22nd March 1976.

(2) In these rules the expression "the principal rules" means the Local Review Committee (Scotland) Rules 1967**(b)** as amended **(c)**.

2. The principal rules shall be amended as follows:—

by the addition of "Glenochil young offenders institution" to the Schedule of the principal rules.

William Ross,
One of Her Majesty's Principal
Secretaries of State.

New St. Andrew's House,
Edinburgh.

10th February 1976.

(a) 1967 c. 80.   (b) S.I. 1967/1699 (1967 III, p. 4623).
(c) S.I. 1969/1256, 1975/1528 (1969 III, p. 3761; 1975 III, p. 5108).

EXPLANATORY NOTE

(This Note is not part of the Rules.)

These Rules amend the Local Review Committee (Scotland) Rules 1967 by providing for the establishment of a local review committee at Glenochil young offenders institution.

STATUTORY INSTRUMENTS

1976 No. 242

ROAD TRAFFIC

The Goods Vehicles (Plating and Testing) (Amendment) Regulations 1976

Made - - - -	*16th February* 1976
Laid before Parliament	*3rd March* 1976
Coming into Operation	*1st April* 1976

The Secretary of State for the Environment, in exercise of the powers conferred by section 45(1) of the Road Traffic Act 1972(a) and of all other enabling powers, and after consultation with representative organisations in accordance with the provisions of section 199(2) of that Act, hereby makes the following Regulations:—

1. These Regulations may be cited as the Goods Vehicles (Plating and Testing) (Amendment) Regulations 1976 and shall come into operation on 1st April 1976.

2. The Goods Vehicles (Plating and Testing) Regulations 1971(b), as amended (c), shall be further amended so as to have effect in accordance with the following provisions of these Regulations.

3. In Regulations 12(2) (applications for first examination and fees therefor) and 31(2) (applications for periodical tests and fees therefor) the proviso shall be omitted.

4. In Schedule 4 (fees payable on examinations)—

 (*a*) in Part I (fees payable on first examinations), in column 2, for "£5·50" and "£3·50" there shall be substituted "£11·00" and "£6·50" respectively;

 (*b*) in Part II (fees payable on Part II re-tests), in paragraph 1, for "£3·50" and "£2" shall be substituted "£6·50" and "£4·00" respectively;

 (*c*) in Part III (fees payable on periodical tests), in column 2, for "£5·50" and "£3·50" there shall be substituted "£11·00" and "£6·50" respectively; and

 (*d*) in Part IV (fees payable on Part III re-tests), in paragraph 1, for "£3·50" and "£2" there shall be substituted "£6·50" and "£4·00" respectively.

Signed by authority of the Secretary of State 16th February 1976.	*John Gilbert,* Minister for Transport, Department of the Environment.

(**a**) 1972 c. 20.   (**b**) S.I. 1971/352 (1971 I, p. 1098).
(**c**) The relevant amending instrument is S.I. 1974/99 (1974 I, p. 347).

EXPLANATORY NOTE

(This Note is not part of the Regulations.)

These Regulations further amend the Goods Vehicles (Plating and Testing) Regulations 1971, by increasing the fees payable for examinations, tests and re-tests of motor vehicles. The increased fees will be payable on applications made after 1st April 1976 for the examination, test or re-test of a vehicle. Certain spent provisions are deleted from the 1971 Regulations.

STATUTORY INSTRUMENTS

1976 No. 243

INDUSTRIAL TRAINING

The Industrial Training Levy (Iron and Steel) Order 1976

Made - - - -	18*th February* 1976
Laid before Parliament	27*th February* 1976
Coming into Operation	7*th April* 1976

Whereas proposals made by the Iron and Steel Industry Training Board for the raising and collection of a levy have been submitted to, and approved by, the Manpower Services Commission under section 7 of the Industrial Training Act 1964(a) ("the 1964 Act"), as amended by section 6 of and Schedule 2 to the Employment and Training Act 1973(b) ("the 1973 Act") and have thereafter been submitted by the said Commission to the Secretary of State under section 7(1C) of the 1964 Act as inserted by the 1973 Act;

And whereas in pursuance of section 7(1A)(a) of the 1964 Act as inserted by the 1973 Act the said proposals include provision for the exemption from the levy of employers who, in view of the small number of their employees, ought in the opinion of the Secretary of State to be exempted from it;

And whereas the Secretary of State estimates that the amount which, disregarding any exemptions, will be payable by virtue of this Order by any employer in the iron and steel industry, does not exceed an amount which the Secretary of State estimates is equal to one per cent. of the aggregate of the emoluments and payments intended to be disbursed as emoluments which have been paid or are payable by any such employer to or in respect of persons employed in the industry, in respect of the period specified in the said proposals as relevant, that is to say the period of twelve months that commenced on 1st April 1975;

And whereas the Secretary of State is satisfied that proposals published by the said Board in pursuance of section 4A of the 1964 Act, as inserted by the 1973 Act, provide for exemption certificates relating to the levy in such cases as he considers appropriate;

Now, therefore, the Secretary of State in exercise of the powers conferred on him by section 4 of the 1964 Act, as amended by section 6 of and Schedule 2 to the 1973 Act, and of all other powers enabling him in that behalf hereby makes the following Order: —

Citation and commencement

1. This Order may be cited as the Industrial Training Levy (Iron and Steel) Order 1976 and shall come into operation on 7th April 1976.

(a) 1964 c. 16.   (b) 1973 c. 50.

Interpretation

2.—(1) In this Order unless the context otherwise requires:—

(*a*) "agriculture" has the same meaning as in section 109(3) of the Agriculture Act 1947(**a**), or, in relation to Scotland, as in section 86(3) of the Agriculture (Scotland) Act 1948(**b**);

(*b*) "an appeal tribunal" means an industrial tribunal established under section 12 of the Industrial Training Act 1964;

(*c*) "assessment" means an assessment of an employer to the levy;

(*d*) "average number" in relation to the persons employed at or from an iron and steel establishment of an employer means the number that is equal to the average (calculated to the lowest whole number) of the numbers of the persons employed, or deemed under the provisions of paragraph (3) of this Article to have been employed, at or from the establishment by the employer on 4th April 1975 and on 3rd October 1975;

(*e*) "the Board" means the Iron and Steel Industry Training Board;

(*f*) "business" means any activities of industry or commerce;

(*g*) "charity" has the same meaning as in section 360 of the Income and Corporation Taxes Act 1970(**c**);

(*h*) "employer" means a person who is an employer in the iron and steel industry at any time in the twelfth levy period;

(*i*) "exemption certificate" means a certificate issued by the Board under section 4B of the 1964 Act, as inserted by the 1973 Act;

(*j*) "the industrial training order" means the Industrial Training (Iron and Steel Board) Order 1969(**d**);

(*k*) "iron and steel establishment" means an establishment in Great Britain engaged wholly or mainly in the iron and steel industry for a total of twenty-seven or more weeks in the period of twelve months that commenced on 4th October 1974 or, being an establishment that commenced to carry on business in the said period, for a total number of weeks exceeding one half of the number of weeks in the part of the said period commencing with the day on which business was commenced and ending on the last day thereof;

(*l*) "the iron and steel industry" means any one or more of the activities which subject to the provisions of paragraph 2 of the Schedule to the industrial training order, are specified in paragraph 1 of that Schedule as the activities of the iron and steel industry or are activities which have been transferred to the industry of the Board from the industry of another industrial training board by one of the transfer orders;

(*m*) "the levy" means the levy imposed by the Board in respect of the twelfth levy period;

(*n*) "notice" means a notice in writing;

(**a**) 1947 c. 48.   (**b**) 1948 c. 45.
(**c**) 1970 c. 10.   (**d**) S.I. 1969/884 (1969 II, p. 2517).

(o) "the transfer orders" mean—

    (i) the Industrial Training (Transfer of Activities of Establishments) Order 1974(a);

    (ii) the Industrial Training (Transfer of Activities of Establishments) (No. 2) Order 1974(b);

    (iii) the Industrial Training (Transfer of the Activities of Establishments) Order 1975(c).

(p) "the twelfth levy period" means the period commencing with the day upon which this Order comes into operation and ending on 31st March 1977;

(q) other expressions have the same meanings as in the industrial training order.

(2) For the purposes of this Order no regard shall be had to any person employed wholly in agriculture or in the supply of food or drink for immediate consumption.

(3) In the case where an iron and steel establishment is taken over (whether directly or indirectly) by an employer in succession to, or jointly with, another person, a person employed at or from the establishment on either or both of the days specified in paragraph (1)(d) of this Article by a person other than the employer carrying on the establishment on the day upon which this Order comes into operation shall be deemed for the purposes of this Order to have been employed by the last mentioned employer.

(4) Any reference in this Order to an establishment that commences to carry on business or that ceases to carry on business shall not be taken to apply where the location of the establishment is changed but its business is continued wholly or mainly at or from the new location, or where the suspension of activities is of a temporary or seasonal nature.

(5) The Interpretation Act 1889(d) shall apply to the interpretation of this Order as it applies to the interpretation of an Act of Parliament.

Imposition of the levy

3.—(1) The levy to be imposed by the Board on employers in respect of the twelfth levy period shall be assessed in accordance with the provisions of this Article.

(2) The levy shall be assessed by the Board separately in respect of each relevant establishment of an employer (that is to say each iron and steel establishment other than any establishment in respect of which an exemption certificate has been issued to the employer, or one which is an establishment of an employer who is exempted by virtue of paragraph (6) of this Article), but in agreement with the employer one assessment may be made in respect of any number of such establishments, in which case those establishments shall be deemed for the purposes of that assessment to constitute one establishment.

(a) S.I. 1974/1154 (1974 II, p. 4402).   (b) S.I. 1974/1495 (1974 III, p. 5739).
(c) S.I. 1975/434 (1975 I, p. 1371).   (d) 1889 c. 63.

(3) Subject to the provision of this Article, the levy assessed in respect of an iron and steel establishment of an employer shall be the amount obtained by multiplying the sum of £13.50 by the average number of the persons employed at or from the establishment by the employer.

(4) The amount of the levy imposed in respect of an iron and steel establishment that ceases to carry on business in the twelfth levy period shall be in the same proportion to the amount that would otherwise be due under paragraph (3) of this Article as the number of days between the commencement of the said levy period and the date of cessation of business (both dates inclusive) bears to the number of days in the said levy period.

(5) Where in any case the amount of levy payable by an employer in respect of his iron and steel establishment or establishments under the foregoing provisions of this Article exceeds an amount equal to 1 per cent. of the aggregate of the emoluments and payments intended to be disbursed as emoluments which have been paid or are payable by the employer to or in respect of persons employed in the industry in respect of the period of twelve months that commenced on 1st April 1975, the amount of the levy shall be reduced to that amount.

(6) There shall be exempt from the levy: —

(a) an employer in whose case the average number of all the persons employed by him under contracts of service at or from the iron and steel establishment or establishments of the employer (including any such persons employed at or from an iron and steel establishment by an associated company of the employer) was less than twenty-six;

(b) a charity.

Assessment notices

4.—(1) The Board shall serve an assessment notice on every employer assessed to the levy, but one notice may comprise two or more assessments.

(2) An assessment notice shall state the Board's address for the service of a notice of appeal or of an application for an extension of time for appealing.

(3) An assessment notice may be served on the person assessed to the levy either by delivering it to him personally or by leaving it, or sending it to him by post, at his last known address or place of business in the United Kingdom or, if that person is a corporation, by leaving it, or sending it by post, to the corporation, at such address or place of business or at its registered or principal office.

Payment of the levy

5.—(1) Subject to the provisions of this Article and of Articles 6 and 7 the amount of each assessment appearing in an assessment notice served by the Board shall be due and payable to the Board one month after the date of the notice.

(2) The amount of an assessment shall not be recoverable by the Board until there has expired the time allowed for appealing against the assessment by Article 7(1) of this Order and any further period or periods of time that the Board or an appeal tribunal may have allowed for appealing under paragraph (2) or (3) of that Article or, where an appeal is brought, until the appeal is decided or withdrawn.

Withdrawal of assessment

6.—(1) The Board may, by a notice served on the person assessed to the levy in the same manner as an assessment notice, withdraw an assessment if that person has appealed against that assessment under the provisions of Article 7 of this Order and the appeal has not been entered in the Register of Appeals kept under the appropriate Regulations specified in paragraph (5) of that Article.

(2) The withdrawal of an assessment shall be without prejudice to the power of the Board to serve a further assessment notice in respect of any establishment to which that assessment related and, where the withdrawal is made by reason of the fact that an establishment has ceased to carry on business in the twelfth levy period, the said notice may provide that the whole amount payable thereunder in respect of the establishment shall be due one month after the date of the notice.

Appeals

7.—(1) A person assessed to the levy may appeal to an appeal tribunal against the assessment within one month from the date of the service of the assessment notice or within any further period or periods of time that may be allowed by the Board or an appeal tribunal under the following provisions of this Article.

(2) The Board by notice may for good cause allow a person assessed to the levy to appeal to an appeal tribunal against the assessment at any time within the period of four months from the date of the service of the assessment notice or within such further period or periods as the Board may allow before such time as may then be limited for appealing has expired.

(3) If the Board shall not allow an application for extension of time for appealing, an appeal tribunal shall upon application made to the tribunal by the person assessed to the levy have the like powers as the Board under the last foregoing paragraph.

(4) In the case of an establishment that ceases to carry on business in the twelfth levy period on any day after the date of the service of the relevant assessment notice, the foregoing provisions of this Article shall have effect as if for the period of four months from the date of the service of the assessment notice mentioned in paragraph (2) of this Article there were substituted the period of six months from the date of the cessation of business.

(5) An appeal or an application to an appeal tribunal under this Article shall be made in accordance with the Industrial Tribunals (England and Wales) Regulations 1965(a) as amended by the Industrial Tribunals (England and Wales) (Amendment) Regulations 1967(b) except where the establishment to which the relevant assessment relates is wholly in Scotland in which case the appeal or application shall be made in accordance with the Industrial Tribunals (Scotland) Regulations 1965(c) as amended by the Industrial Tribunals (Scotland) (Amendment) Regulations 1967(d).

(6) The powers of an appeal tribunal under paragraph (3) of this Article may be exercised by the President of the Industrial Tribunals (England and Wales) or by the President of the Industrial Tribunals (Scotland) as the case may be.

(a) S.I. 1965/1101 (1965 11, p. 2805).   (b) S.I. 1967/301 (1967 I, p. 1040).
(c) S.I. 1965/1157 (1965 II, p. 3266).   (d) S.I. 1967/302 (1967 I, p. 1050).

Evidence

8.—(1) Upon the discharge by a person assessed to the levy of his liability under an assessment the Board shall if so requested issue to him a certificate to that effect.

(2) The production in any proceedings of a document purporting to be certified by the Director of the Board to be a true copy of an assessment or other notice issued by the Board or purporting to be a certificate such as is mentioned in the foregoing paragraph of this Article shall, unless the contrary is proved, be sufficient evidence of the document and of the facts stated therein.

Signed by order of the Secretary of State.

18th February 1976.

Harold Walker,

Joint Parliamentary Under Secretary of State,

Department of Employment.

EXPLANATORY NOTE

(This Note is not part of the Order.)

This Order gives effect to proposals of the Iron and Steel Industry Training Board which were submitted to and approved by the Manpower Services Commission, and thereafter submitted by the Manpower Services Commission to the Secretary of State for Employment. The proposals are for the imposition of a further levy on employers in the iron and steel industry for the purpose of encouraging adequate training in the industry.

The levy is to be imposed in respect of the twelfth levy period commencing with the day upon which this Order comes into operation and ending on 31st March 1977. The levy will be assessed by the Board and there will be a right of appeal against an assessment to an industrial tribunal.

STATUTORY   INSTRUMENTS

1976 No. 244

ANIMALS

DISEASES OF ANIMALS

The Brucellosis (Area Eradication) (England and Wales) (Amendment) Order 1976

Made - - - -	16*th February* 1976
Coming into Operation	28*th February* 1976

The Minister of Agriculture, Fisheries and Food, in exercise of the powers conferred on him by sections 1, 5 and 85(1) of the Diseases of Animals Act 1950(a), as read with the Diseases of Animals (Extension of Definitions) Order 1971(b), and as extended in the case of the said section 5 by section 106(3) of the Agriculture Act 1970(c), and of all his other enabling powers, hereby orders as follows:—

Citation and commencement

1. This order, which may be cited as the Brucellosis (Area Eradication) (England and Wales) (Amendment) Order 1976, shall come into operation on 28th February 1976.

Interpretation

2.—(1) In this order, "the principal order" means the Brucellosis (Area Eradication) (England and Wales) Order 1971(d), as amended(e).

(2) The Interpretation Act 1889(f) applies for the interpretation of this order as it applies for the interpretation of an Act of Parliament.

Amendment of principal order

3.—(1) In Article 2(1) of the principal order (interpretation) there shall be inserted—

(*a*) in the definition of "licence", after the word "Ministry", the words "or by an officer of the Secretary of State"; and

(*b*) after the definition of "premises", the following definition:—
  " 'reactor' means a bovine animal which gives rise to a reaction consistent with its being affected with brucellosis when tested for that disease either by or on behalf of the Minister or the Secretary of State or otherwise, as

---

(a) 1950 c. 36.
(c) 1970 c. 40.
(e) S.I. 1972/1173 (1972 II, p. 3486).

(b) S.I. 1971/531 (1971 I, p. 1530).
(d) S.I. 1971/1717 (1971 III, p. 4673).
(f) 1889 c. 63.

the case may be, provided that in the case of a test otherwise so carried out the result thereof has been reported to the Minister or the Secretary of State;".

(2) Article 3 of the principal order (application of order) shall be amended—

(*a*) by the insertion, at the beginning of paragraph (1) thereof, of the words "subject to paragraph (1A) below", and by the inclusion at the end of that paragraph of the following paragraph:—

"(1A) Notwithstanding the provisions of paragraph (1) above, the provisions of this order shall not apply to an export quarantine station or an approved landing place which is situated in an Eradication Area or Attested Area unless those provisions are applied thereto by the order declaring the Area to be an Eradication Area or Attested Area, as the case may be, for purposes connected with the control of brucellosis."; and

(*b*) by the addition at the end of that Article of the following paragraph:—

"(3) In this Article—

(*a*) 'export quarantine station' means an export quarantine station within the meaning of section 36(1) of the Diseases of Animals Act 1950, and

(*b*) 'approved landing place' means a landing place for the time being approved by the Minister for the purposes of the Animals (Landing from Channel Islands, Isle of Man, Northern Ireland and Republic of Ireland) Order 1955(a), as amended(b), or the Importation of Canadian Cattle Order of 1933(c), as amended (d).".

(3) In Article 4 of the principal order (movement of cattle into or through Eradication Areas or Attested Areas)—

(*a*) paragraph (1) shall be amended by the deletion of the comma after the word "Ministry", and the insertion after that word of the words "or, in the case of cattle being moved from a place in Scotland, an officer of the Secretary of State"; and

(*b*) paragraph (2) shall cease to have effect, and the following paragraphs shall be substituted therefor:—

"(2) The provisions of paragraph (1) above shall not apply to the movement, otherwise than on foot,—

(*a*) of cattle through an Eradication Area or Attested Area from a place outside that Area direct to another place outside that Area;

(*b*) of cattle into an Eradication Area or Attested Area direct to a slaughterhouse in that Area (from which they shall not be removed alive) for the purpose of unloading and slaughter there;

(*c*) of cattle (other than a reactor) into an Eradication Area or Attested Area direct to premises in that Area for the purpose of unloading and sale there, being premises used for the time being in connection with the holding of a market under the

(a) S.I. 1955/1310 (1955 I, p. 190).
(b) S.I. 1962/757, 1963/736, 1967/171 (1962 I, p. 752; 1963 I, p. 892; 1967 I, p. 281).
(c) S.R. & O. 1933/15 (Rev. II, p. 377: 1933, p. 361).
(d) S.I. 1972/1644. 1973/1698 (1972 III, p. 4841; 1973 III, p. 5184).

authority of a licence issued under Article 15 of this order imposing a condition that cattle in the premises may only be sold there for immediate slaughter;

(*d*) of cattle under the age of 6 months into an Eradication Area direct to premises in that Area for the purpose of unloading and sale there, being premises used for the time being in connection with the holding of a market under the authority of a licence issued under Article 15 of this order; or

(*e*) of cattle from one Attested Area to another Attested Area by a route which, disregarding any part thereof which involves the carriage of the cattle by sea or air, is entirely over land comprised in an Attested Area.

(3) The exemption from the provisions of paragraph (1) of this Article conferred by paragraph (2)(*c*) above shall not apply in respect of the movement into an Attested Area of cattle which—

(*a*) are lactating,

(*b*) have calved within the preceding 14 days, or

(*c*) are showing signs of vaginal discharge.

(4) When cattle are moved into or through an Eradication Area or Attested Area in circumstances referred to in any of sub-paragraphs (*a*) to (*d*) of paragraph (2) above, the person in charge of the cattle shall ensure that they do not come into contact with any cattle, other than cattle with which they were in contact immediately before they entered the Area, and that they are not (except in case of emergency) unloaded within the Area from the vehicle by means of which they are transported otherwise than as provided for in the relevant sub-paragraph.''.

(4) Article 5(1) of the principal order (movement of cattle within an Eradication Area or Attested Area) shall be amended by the deletion of the comma after the word "Ministry", and the insertion after that word of the words "or, in the case of cattle being moved on to those premises from a place in Scotland, an officer of the Secretary of State,".

(5) After Article 5 of the principal order there shall be inserted the following Articles:—

"*Movement of cattle to temporary accommodation for cattle intended for export*

5A.—(1) Nothing in Articles 4(1) and 5(1) above shall apply to cattle being moved otherwise than on foot into an Eradication Area or Attested Area direct to approved premises within that Area.

(2) In this Article, 'approved premises' means premises which have been approved under Article 3(1) of the Exported Animals Protection Order 1964(a) for the resting of animals immediately before their exportation from Great Britain, and also approved in writing for the purposes of this order by an officer of the Ministry.

(a) S.I. 1964/704 (1964 II, p. 1352).

Control of slaughterhouses in Attested Areas

5B. No slaughterhouse in an Attested Area, other than a slaughterhouse which has been approved for the purposes of this order by a veterinary inspector, shall admit, or be used for the purpose of slaughtering, a reactor.

Supplementary provision as to approvals

5C.—(1) An approval to which Article 5A or Article 5B above refers may be given subject to compliance by the owner or occupier of the premises or, as the case may be, the slaughterhouse to which it relates with such conditions as may be specified in the approval.

(2) Such an approval may, by notice in writing served on such owner or occupier, be withdrawn or varied at any time by a veterinary inspector, but without prejudice to anything lawfully done pursuant to such approval before such withdrawal or variation has taken effect.

Restriction of vaccination in Attested Areas

5D. No person other than—

(*a*) a veterinary inspector,

(*b*) a veterinary surgeon authorised for the purpose by the Minister, or

(*c*) a person acting under the authority of a licence issued for the purpose by a veterinary inspector employed by the Minister, and who complies with the conditions (if any) subject to which the licence is issued,

shall vaccinate cattle in an Attested Area against brucellosis.".

In Witness whereof the Official Seal of the Minister of Agriculture, Fisheries and Food is hereunto affixed on 16th February 1976.

(L.S.)

Frederick Peart,
Minister of Agriculture, Fisheries and Food.

EXPLANATORY NOTE

(This Note is not part of the order.)

The Brucellosis (Area Eradication) (England and Wales) Order 1971 (as amended in 1972) sets out the controls to be applied to cattle in areas designated by the Minister of Agriculture, Fisheries and Food as Eradication Areas or Attested Areas for purposes connected with the eradication of brucellosis. Under Article 4 of that order a general prohibition is imposed on the movement of cattle into or through Eradication or Attested Areas otherwise than in accordance with a licence issued by an officer of the Ministry, but the Article contains a number of exceptions from this prohibition. The present order introduces certain additional exceptions in readiness for the declaration of the first Attested Areas. It also provides that licences under both Article 4 and Article 5 of the 1971 Order may in future be issued by an officer of the Secretary of State for Scotland where they relate to cattle being moved into or through an Eradication or Attested Area in England or Wales from a place in Scotland.

By an amendment to Article 3 of the 1971 Order, export quarantine stations and approved landing places (both of which expressions are defined in the present order) which are situated within Eradication or Attested Areas are generally exempted from its provisions. In addition, by a new Article 5A introduced into the 1971 Order, the prohibitions imposd by Articles 4 and 5 thereof are disapplied in respect of cattle moved directly to premises within Eradication or Attested Areas which have been aproved for the purpose of resting animals immediately before export under the Exported Animals Protection Order 1964, and which have also been approved for the purposes of the 1971 Order.

By two further new Articles inserted in the 1971 Order, slaughterhouses within Attested Areas (other than slaughterhouses which have been approved by a veterinary inspector of the Ministry) are prohibited from accepting for slaughter cattle which are brucellosis reactors, and a prohibition is imposed on the vaccination of cattle against brucellosis within Attested Areas, except where such vaccination is carried out on behalf of the Minister or in accordance with a licence issued by a veterinary inspector. A definition of the term "reactor" is introduced for the purposes of the 1971 Order.

STATUTORY INSTRUMENTS

1976 No. 246

LOCAL GOVERNMENT, ENGLAND AND WALES
The Local Government Area Changes Regulations 1976

Made - - - -	16*th February* 1976
Laid before Parliament	8*th March* 1976
Coming into Operation	29*th March* 1976

ARRANGEMENT OF REGULATIONS

SCHEDULES

The Secretary of State for the Environment and the Secretary of State for Wales, in exercise of the powers conferred upon them by sections 67(1) and (2) and 255(1) and (3) of, and paragraph 9 of Schedule 10 to, the Local Government Act 1972(a) and of all other powers enabling them in that behalf, hereby make the following regulations:—

Title and commencement

1. These regulations may be cited as the Local Government Area Changes Regulations 1976 and shall come into operation on 29th March 1976.

Application: extent of exercise of powers

2. These regulations make incidental, consequential, transitional or supplementary provision for the purposes or in consequence of orders made under Part IV of the Local Government Act 1972 by the Secretary of State for the Environment or the Secretary of State for Wales, or both, or under paragraph 7 of Schedule 10 to the said Act by the Secretary of State for Wales, and are made—

by the Secretary of State for the Environment in so far as they are made in relation to orders made by him;

by the Secretary of State for Wales in so far as they are made in relation to orders made by him; and

by both such Secretaries in so far as they are made in relation to orders made by both.

Interpretation

3.—(1) The Interpretation Act 1889(b) shall apply for the interpretation of these regulations as it applies for the interpretation of an Act of Parliament.

(2) In these regulations—

"the appointed day" means the day on which the order comes into operation otherwise than for any purposes set out in regulation 4(1);

"as altered" means as altered by any orders under Part IV of the Local Government Act 1972, or paragraph 7 of Schedule 10 thereto, coming into operation on the appointed day;

"byelaws" includes any regulation, scale of charges, list of tolls or table of fees and payments;

"charity", "charity trustees", "court" and "trust" have the same meanings as in the Charities Act 1960(c);

"the City" means the City of London;

"the City Corporation" means the mayor and commonalty and citizens of the City of London;

"the Common Council" means the Common Council of the City of London;

"dissolved authority" means an authority dissolved by the order;

"exercisable", in relation to functions, means exercisable otherwise than by virtue of section 101, 110 or 187(2) or (3) of the Local Government Act 1972, section 15 of the Water Act 1973(d) or article 19 of the Local Authorities etc. (Miscellaneous Provision) Order 1974(e);

"local Act" includes an Act confirming a provisional order;

"officer", in relation to any authority, includes the holder of any office or employment under that authority;

(a) 1972 c. 70. (b) 1889 c. 63. (c) 1960 ‑
(d) 1973 c. 37. (e) S.I. 1974/462 (1974 I, p. 1690).

"the order" means the order under Part IV of the Local Government Act 1972, or paragraph 7 of Schedule 10 thereto, for the purposes or in consequence of which the provisions in these regulations become applicable;

"parish authority" means in the case of a parish having a separate parish council that council, and in any other case the parish meeting or the parish trustees of the parish, as may be appropriate;

except in regulation 49 "the proper officer", in relation to any purpose and any body, means the officer appointed for that purpose by that body;

"residuary successor", in relation to any dissolved authority, means the authority specified as such in the order;

except in paragraph 6 of Schedule 3 "the Secretary of State", without more, means the Secretary of State or the Secretaries of State by whom the order is made;

"the Sub-Treasurer" means the Sub-Treasurer of the Inner Temple;

"the Temples" means the Inner Temple and the Middle Temple; and

"the Under Treasurer" means the Under Treasurer of the Middle Temple.

(3) These regulations have effect subject to the provisions of the order.

(4) For the purposes of these regulations and of the order—

(a) an area shall be treated as transferred from any relevant area wherever it ceases on the appointed day to be comprised in that relevant area, whether that area continues to exist or not, and if it does not whether the first-mentioned area constitutes only part of it or the whole;

(b) an area shall be treated as transferred to any relevant area wherever it first comes on the appointed day to be comprised in that relevant area, whether that area previously existed or not, and if it did not whether the first-mentioned area constitutes only part of it or the whole.

In this paragraph, "relevant area" means a county, district, London borough, parish, community, petty sessions area, police area or the area of an area health authority.

(5) In these regulations and in the order, unless the context otherwise requires—

(a) references to any enactment shall be construed as references to that enactment as amended, extended or applied by or under any other enactment;

(b) references to any instrument shall be construed as references to that instrument as amended, extended or applied by any other instrument.

(6) Any reference in these regulations to a numbered regulation or schedule shall, unless the reference is to a regulation or schedule of a specified instrument, be construed as a reference to the regulation or schedule bearing that number in these regulations.

(7) Any reference in any regulation or schedule of these regulations to a numbered paragraph shall, unless the reference is to a paragraph of a specified instrument, be construed as a reference to the paragraph bearing that number in the first-mentioned regulation or schedule.

(8) Any reference in any paragraph of a regulation or schedule to a numbered sub-paragraph shall, unless the reference is to a sub-paragraph of a specified paragraph, be construed as a reference to the sub-paragraph bearing that number in the first-mentioned paragraph.

Coming into operation of order

4.—(1) The following are purposes for which the order shall come into operation on such day earlier than the appointed day as may be specified therein—

(*a*) the application of sections 39 and 40 of the Local Government Act 1972;

(*b*) the preparation or the alteration of any register of electors under the Representation of the People Acts;

(*c*) any local government election under the said Acts or the Local Government Act 1972 for any area consisting of or comprising any area established or altered by the order and proceedings preliminary or relating thereto;

(*d*) any action under Part IV of, or Schedule 9 or 10 to, the Local Government Act 1972 in relation to electoral areas;

(*e*) the constitution of any body established by the order and proceedings preliminary or relating to the first meeting thereof;

(*f*) the annual assembly of any parish meeting;

(*g*) the making of any scheme under regulation 67 or 68;

(*h*) the appointment of any officer or the taking of any other action, and the incurring of any expenditure in relation thereto, by any authority to ensure their effective operation as from the appointed day;

(*i*) the alteration of any valuation list to take effect on the appointed day, the preparation or revision of any estimate of the product of a rate of a new penny in the pound, the preparation or service of any precept to be made in respect of a period commencing on the appointed day and the preparation or approval of any rate to be made in respect of a period commencing on the appointed day; and

(*j*) any provision of these regulations or of the order which expressly refers to the coming into operation of the order or requires or enables action to be taken before the appointed day.

(2) If new valuation lists are to come into force on the appointed day, and the order comes into operation more than 5 months before that day, in item (*i*) of paragraph (1) for the first 13 words there shall be substituted "the preparation of any valuation list to come into force on the appointed day,".

(3) Nothing in this regulation authorises the appointment of the chief officer of a new fire brigade to take effect before the appointed day.

Maps

5.—(1) A print of any map referred to in the order shall be deposited in the offices of the Secretary of State.

(2) A print of any such map shall be deposited—

with the council of any district or London borough affected by the changes of areas made by the order;

where the City is so affected, with the Common Council;

where the Inner Temple is so affected, with the Sub-Treasurer; and

where the Middle Temple is so affected, with the Under Treasurer.

A print deposited under this paragraph shall at all reasonable times be open to inspection by any person affected by the changes of areas made by the order, and on payment of a reasonable fee (to be determined by the body with whom the print is deposited) any such person shall be entitled to a copy of or an extract from it, certified by the proper officer of such body to be a true copy or extract, which shall be received in all courts of justice and elsewhere as prima facie evidence of the contents of the map as regards the changes of areas made by the order.

(3) In addition—

(a) prints shall be supplied to—

(i) the councils of the counties affected by the order or if Greater London is affected the Greater London Council;
the Commissioners of Inland Revenue;
the Secretary of State for Employment;
the Secretary of State for Industry;
the Secretary of State for Prices and Consumer Protection;
the Treasury Valuer;
the Boundary Commission for England or the Boundary Commission for Wales;
the Registrar General;
Ordnance Survey; and
the Land Registry.

(ii) if the map is relevant to any changes in the boundaries of districts or London boroughs, or the City, the Inner Temple or the Middle Temple, the Secretary of State for Social Services;

(b) if the map is relevant to any change in the boundaries of a parish, a print thereof, or an extract therefrom, shall be supplied to the parish authority;

(c) if the map is relevant to any change in the boundaries of a community having a community council, a print thereof, or an extract therefrom, shall be supplied to that council.

(4) Any print or extract supplied under (b) or (c) of paragraph (3) shall be deposited with the records of the parish or community.

Mereing of boundaries

6. The boundaries established by the order shall be mered by Ordnance Survey. Any boundary defined on any map referred to in the order by reference to proposed works shall, if such works have not been executed at the time of the completion of the first survey including such boundary made after the coming into operation of the order for a new edition of Ordnance Survey large scale plans, be mered as if the boundary had not been so defined.

General continuance of matters

7. Subject to the other provisions of these regulations, any of the following things done or treated by virtue of any enactment as having been done by, or to, or in relation to, any authority from whom any area is transferred by the order in connection with the discharge of any of their functions in relation to such area, that is to say—

any written agreement or other instrument in writing or any determination or declaration made or treated as made by such an authority;

any notice or direction given or treated as given by, or to, such an authority;

any licence, permission, consent, approval, exemption, dispensation or relaxation granted or treated as granted by, or to, such an authority;

any application, proposal or objection made or treated as made by, or to, such an authority;

any condition or requirement imposed or treated as imposed by, or on, such an authority; or

any appeal allowed by, or in favour of, or against, such an authority,

shall, as from the appointed day, be treated as having been done by, to, or in relation to, the authority by whom the functions become exercisable in the area on and after that day by virtue of the order, and any such thing shall as from that day have effect as if any reference therein to the first-mentioned authority were a reference to the authority secondly mentioned.

Councillors

8.—(1) Any person in office at the appointed day as councillor for any electoral area which is altered by the order shall represent the area as altered until the date on which he would have retired if the order had not been made. Any casual vacancy which exists at the coming into operation of the order or occurs before the appointed day in the office of councillor for any such area shall (except where notice of the election has at the coming into operation of the order already been given) be deemed to have arisen in the representation of the area as altered. Where notice of the election has at the coming into operation of the order already been given the person elected shall represent the area as altered until the date on which he would have retired if the order had not been made.

(2) In relation to the qualification of any person to be elected and to be a member of any county council, district council, London borough council, parish council or community council, of the Greater London Council or the Common Council, or of any committee, joint board or joint committee, the order shall be deemed, for the purposes of section 79 of the Local Government Act 1972, to have been in operation during the whole of the twelve months preceding the relevant day within the meaning of that section.

(3) No person who remains in office after the appointed day as a member of any county council, district council, London borough council, parish council or community council, of the Greater London Council or the Common Council, or of any committee, joint board or joint committee, shall, during the term for which he remains in office, lose his qualification for being a member by reason of the changes of areas made by the order.

Local government electors

9. If in relation to any election, parish meeting or community meeting for any area consisting of or comprising any area established or altered by the order the register of local government electors has not been prepared and published on the basis that the changes of areas made by the order had become operative, the registration officer shall make such alteration of the register as may be proper for the purpose of such election or meeting.

Grouped parishes

10.—(1) The provisions of this regulation shall have effect where parishes are grouped.

(2) There shall be a separate parish meeting for each parish.

(3) Where under the provisions of any enactment or instrument the consent of the parish meeting for a parish is required in respect of any act done, or proposed to be done, by a parish council, the consent of the parish meeting of each parish affected by the act shall be necessary in respect of such act done, or proposed to be done, by the common parish council.

(4) For the purposes of the application to the parishes of all or any of the provisions of section 37 of the Charities Act 1960 and of any of the provisions of the Local Government Act 1972 with respect to the custody of parish documents, so as to preserve the separate rights of each parish, the common parish council shall be deemed to be the separate parish council for each parish:

Provided that the consent of the parish meeting for any parish shall be required to any act of the common parish council under the said provisions which relates only to the affairs of that parish.

Grouped communities

11.—(1) The provisions of this regulation shall have effect where communities are grouped.

(2) For the purposes of the application to the communities of all or any of the provisions of section 37 of the Charities Act 1960 and of any of the provisions of the Local Government Act 1972 with respect to the custody of community documents, so as to preserve the separate rights of each community, the common community council shall be deemed to be the separate community council for each community.

Dissolution of charter trustees

12.—(1) The provisions of this regulation shall have effect where the city or town for which charter trustees have been constituted under subsection (4) of section 246 of the Local Government Act 1972—

(*a*) becomes a parish;

(*b*) becomes wholly comprised in a parish; or

(*c*) becomes wholly comprised in two or more parishes,

and the said subsection (4) therefore, in accordance with subsection (8) of the said section 246, ceases to apply to the city or town.

(2) Any reference in this regulation to "the parish council" shall be construed—

(*a*) in the cases described in (*a*) and (*b*) in paragraph (1), as a reference to the parish council for the parish so described;

(*b*) in the case described in (*c*) in paragraph (1), as a reference to the parish council specified in relation to this paragraph in respect of the city or town in the order.

(3) The charter trustees shall be dissolved.

(4) Any mayor or deputy mayor of the city or town shall cease to hold office as such.

(5) Any local officer of dignity appointed under paragraph (*c*) of the said subsection (4) shall hold office as if he had been appointed by the parish council.

(6) All property and liabilities vested in or attaching to the charter trustees shall by virtue of the order be transferred to and vest in or attach to the parish council.

All contracts, deeds, bonds, agreements and other instruments subsisting in favour of, or against, and all notices in force which were given (or have effect as if they had been given) by, or to, the charter trustees shall be of full force and effect in favour of, or against, the parish council.

Any action or proceeding or any cause of action or proceeding, pending or existing at the dissolution of the charter trustees, by, or against, the charter trustees shall not be prejudicially affected by reason of the dissolution, and may be continued, prosecuted and enforced by, or against, the parish council.

(7) The accounts of the charter trustees and of the committees and officers thereof shall be made up to the dissolution of the charter trustees and shall be audited in like manner and subject to the same incidents and consequences as if the charter trustees had not been dissolved:

Provided that where the audit is carried out by a district auditor the expression "the body in question" in section 161(2)(a) (orders for repayment of expenditure declared unlawful) and (4) (certification of sums not brought into account or losses) of the Local Government Act 1972 shall include the parish council.

(8) Any officer of the charter trustees shall be transferred to the employment of the parish council, and regulation 71 shall apply to such officer as it applies to officers transferred by regulation 70.

(9) In this regulation, "city or town" means an area for which charter trustees act under section 246(4) to (8) of the Local Government Act 1972.

(10) This regulation applies only to England.

Honorary freedoms

13. Nothing in the order shall affect the status of any person who is immediately before the appointed day an honorary freeman of any place being a London borough or a district having the status of a city, borough or royal borough or of any body which at such time enjoys privileges of a similar nature to honorary freedom of any such place.

Honorary aldermen

14. Services rendered to any dissolved authority may be treated for the purposes of section 249(1) of the Local Government Act 1972 as services rendered to any principal council to whose area any area of the dissolved authority is transferred.

Privileges or rights of inhabitants of cities and boroughs

15. Any privileges or rights belonging immediately before the appointed day, by virtue of the provision of any charter granted under section 245 of the Local Government Act 1972, to the inhabitants of the whole of any city or borough altered by the order shall belong to the inhabitants of the whole of the city or borough as altered.

Appointments to bodies

16.—(1) Any power to appoint any person to any body belonging to an authority in respect of any property or liability transferred by regulation 12 or 62 shall be transferred to the authority to whom such property or liability is transferred.

(2) Any other power to appoint any person to any body belonging to a dissolved authority shall be transferred to the residuary successor of that authority.

(3) In this regulation any reference to a power to appoint includes references to powers to elect or to nominate any persons for appointment.

High sheriffs

17.—(1) This regulation shall apply where an area is transferred from one relevant area to another such area, and in this regulation—

"the transferred area" means the area so transferred; and

"relevant area" means a county or Greater London other than the City and the Temples.

(2) If any person is immediately before the appointed day qualified to be appointed high sheriff of a relevant area by reason of holding land in the transferred area, he shall continue to be so qualified for a period of two years from the appointed day.

(3) On or about the appointed day the high sheriff of the relevant area from which the transferred area is transferred shall perform all the duties required by section 28(1) of the Sheriffs Act 1887**(a)** to be performed by a high sheriff at the expiration of his term of office so far as they relate to persons or things in the transferred area and accordingly—

    (*a*) that high sheriff shall transfer to the custody of the high sheriff of the relevant area to which the transferred area is transferred all documents relating to the transferred area; and

    (*b*) any reference in that subsection, so far as it applies by virtue of this paragraph, to an incoming sheriff shall be construed as a reference to the high sheriff secondly mentioned in (*a*).

Agency arrangements

18.—(1) Any arrangements made under section 101 or 110 of the Local Government Act 1972 for the discharge of functions of one authority by another authority which would apart from the changes of areas effected by the order be in force on and after the appointed day throughout any relevant area altered by the order shall be in force throughout the area as altered.

In this paragraph, "relevant area" means a district, London borough, parish or community or the City, the Inner Temple or the Middle Temple.

(2) Any arrangements made under section 15 of the Water Act 1973 for the discharge by a relevant authority within the meaning of that section of functions of a water authority which would apart from the changes of areas effected by the order be in force on and after the appointed day throughout the area of the relevant authority or throughout so much of that area as is situated in the water authority's area shall be in force throughout the area of the relevant authority as altered or throughout so much of that area as is situated in the water authority's area, as the case may be.

Justices

19.—(1) The justices for any county or London commission area shall have jurisdiction in respect of anything done or omitted before the appointed day in an area transferred to the county or London commission area.

(2) The provisions of Part I of Schedule 1 shall have effect wherever an area is transferred from one petty sessions area to another such area. The provisions of Part II of that schedule shall have effect where a petty sessions area is abolished by the order. The provisions of Part III of that schedule shall have effect where a new petty sessions area is constituted by the order.

(a) 1887 c. 55.

Licensing

20. The permitted hours in licensed premises in an area transferred from any petty sessions area shall not be affected by, or by reason of, the changes of areas made by the order except by alteration by the licensing justices at a general annual licensing meeting or under the provisions of section 66 of the Licensing Act 1964**(a).**

Police

21.—(1) Where any area is transferred from a police area, the appropriate part of any register kept in pursuance of any enactment by the chief constable, the Commissioner of City of London Police or the Commissioner of Police of the Metropolis shall be transferred by him, as soon as may be after the appointed day, to such officer for the police area to which the area is transferred, and as from that day shall be deemed to form part of the corresponding register kept by such officer.

(2) (*a*) This paragraph shall have effect in relation to any member of a police force transferred by the order, and in this paragraph "the officer" means such a person.

(*b*) Where a report or allegation is received before the appointed day from which it appears that the officer may have committed an offence against discipline, within the meaning of any regulations in force under section 33 of the Police Act 1964**(b)**—

    (i) if the police force from which the officer is transferred is to continue to exist on and after the appointed day, the chief constable of that police force may postpone the transfer of the officer for the purpose of facilitating the investigation of the matter and any disciplinary proceedings arising therefrom, including any appeal to the Secretary of State for the Home Department under section 37 of the Police Act 1964, and the provision of the order transferring him shall apply in the case of the officer as if for any reference therein to the appointed day there were substituted a reference to such day as may be determined by such chief constable after consultation with the chief constable of the police force to which the officer is transferred;

    (ii) otherwise, any investigation and any disciplinary proceedings, including any such appeal, may be continued as if the alleged offence had been committed while he is a member of the police force to which he is transferred.

(3) (*a*) This paragraph shall have effect in relation to any officer of a county council or a police authority employed for police purposes, including the purposes of section 81 of the Road Traffic Regulation Act 1967**(c)**, and transferred by the order, and in this paragraph "the officer" means such a person.

(*b*) The officer shall, so long as he continues to be an officer or servant of the body to whom he is transferred and until he is served with a statement in writing referring to the order and specifying new terms and conditions of employment, enjoy terms and conditions of employment not less favourable than those which he enjoyed immediately before the appointed day.

(*c*) Paragraphs (2) to (11) of regulation 71 shall apply to the statement referred to in sub-paragraph (*b*) above with the substitution for the reference in paragraph (5) to paragraph (1) of a reference to sub-paragraph (*b*) above.

    (a) 1964 c. 26.   **(b)** 1964 c. 48.   **(c)** 1967 c. 76.

Fire services

22.—(1) This regulation shall have effect in relation to any member of a fire brigade transferred by the order, and in this regulation "the officer" means such a person.

(2) Where a report, complaint or other allegation is received before the appointed day from which it appears that the officer may have committed an offence against discipline, within the meaning of any regulations in force under the Fire Services Act 1947**(a)**, then—

(*a*) if the fire brigade from which the officer is transferred is to continue to exist on and after the appointed day, the chief officer of that fire brigade may postpone the transfer of the officer for the purpose of facilitating the investigation of the matter and any disciplinary proceedings, including any appeal, arising therefrom, and the provision of the order transferring him shall apply in the case of the officer as if for any reference therein to the appointed day there were substituted a reference to such day as may be determined by such chief officer after consultation with the chief officer of the fire brigade to which he is transferred;

(*b*) otherwise, any investigation and any disciplinary proceedings, including any appeal, arising therefrom under any such regulations may be continued as if the alleged offence had been committed while he is a member of the fire brigade to which he is transferred and, accordingly, the said regulations shall have effect subject to any necessary modifications.

(3) The officer shall be transferred in the rank which he held immediately before the appointed day.

(4) Without prejudice to section 27(4) of the Fire Services Act 1947, in relation to an officer in whose case the Firemen's Pension Scheme for the time being in force under section 26 of the said Act had effect immediately before the appointed day subject to the modifications set out in section 27(3) thereof, the fire brigade from which he is transferred and the fire brigade to which he is transferred shall be treated as one for the purposes of section 27(2).

(5) (*a*) The officer shall, so long as he continues to be a member of the fire brigade to which he is transferred and until he is served with a statement in writing referring to the order and specifying new terms and conditions of employment, enjoy terms and conditions of employment not less favourable than those which he enjoyed immediately before the appointed day.

(*b*) Paragraphs (2) to (11) of regulation 71 shall apply to the statement referred to in sub-paragraph (*a*) above with the substitution for the reference in paragraph (5) to paragraph (1) of a reference to sub-paragraph (*a*) above.

Education

23.—(1) The managers or governors of any school in any area transferred by the order shall (unless a new instrument of management or instrument of government is made for the school) remain in office until the date on which they would have retired if the order had not been made.

(2) (*a*) This paragraph shall apply where an area is transferred from the area of one local education authority to the area of another such authority and in this paragraph—

"the specified enactments" means sections 50, 61(2) and 81 of the

---

(a) 1947 c. 41.

Education Act 1944(a), section 6 of the Education (Miscellaneous Provisions) Act 1953(b) and sections 1 and 2 of the Education Act 1962(c);

"the transferor authority" means the local education authority from whose area the area is transferred; and

"the transferee authority" means the local education authority to whose area the area is transferred.

In the application of this paragraph to a county, district or London borough regulation 3(4) shall apply.

(b) Any instrument made by the transferor authority in connection with the discharge of any of their functions, and any other thing done by, to or in relation to such authority in connection therewith, shall in relation to the area transferred be treated as having been made by, or done by, to or in relation to, the transferee authority, and any instrument relating to the exercise of those functions, or to things done in their exercise, or to property held or maintained for the purposes of those functions, shall so far as it relates to such area have effect as if any reference to the transferor authority or their area were a reference to the transferee authority or their area.

This sub-paragraph does not extend to any byelaws or order to which paragraph (6) or (7) of regulation 62 applies.

(c) Where, in the case of any grant made before the appointed day under any of the specified enactments by the transferor authority in respect of a pupil who has not completed his course by the appointed day, the transferee authority would, if the changes of areas made by the order had been made at the date of the making of the grant, have been the appropriate authority to make it, it shall be the duty of such authority to make the remaining payments in pursuance of that grant, subject to the same conditions, if any, as to satisfactory work, financial need or other matters as were attached to the grant or as would be attached to the grant by such authority, whichever are the most favourable.

Charities

24.—(1) (a) The provisions of this paragraph shall have effect in relation to property held, immediately before the appointed day, as sole trustee, exclusively for charitable purposes, by any authority described in column (1) of the following table affected by the order.

(b) Where such property is held for the benefit of, or of the inhabitants of, or of any particular class or body of persons in, a specified area the whole or the greater part of which is transferred from the authority so described to an authority specified in respect thereof in column (2), that property shall by virtue of this paragraph be transferred to and vest (on the same trusts) in the authority so specified.

(c) Where the authority so described is dissolved any other property to which this paragraph applies shall by virtue of this paragraph be transferred to and vest (on the same trusts) in the authority specified in respect of such authority in column (2) to whom the whole or the greater part of the area of the first-mentioned authority is transferred.

(a) 1944 c. 31.   (b) 1953 c. 33.   (c) 1962 c. 12.

TABLE

(1)	(2)
The council of a county	The council of another county or the Greater London Council
The council of a district	The council of another district or the corporation or council of a London borough
The parish council of a parish, or the community council of a community	The corporation or council of a London borough, the parish council (or where there is no parish council the parish meeting or parish trustees) of a parish, the community council of a community or where there is in a district in England no parish or in Wales no community council the council of the district
The parish meeting or parish trustees of a parish	The corporation or council of a London borough, the parish meeting or parish trustees of a parish not having a separate parish council, the parish meeting or in the case of real property the parish council of a parish having a separate parish council, the community council of a community or where there is in a district in England no parish or in Wales no community council the council of the district
The Greater London Council	The council of a county
The Inner London Education Authority	The corporation or council of an outer London borough
The corporation or council of a London borough, the City Corporation or the Common Council, the Honourable Society of the Inner Temple or the Honourable Society of the Middle Temple	Any authority described in column (1) or the council of a district

1. In relation to property held by the council of a non-metropolitan county or a metropolitan district for the purposes of a charity which, before 1st February 1974, was registered in the register established under section 4 of the Charities Act 1960 in any part of that register maintained by the Secretary of State for Education and Science or the Secretary of State for Wales by virtue of section 2 of that Act, the first and second entries in column (2) shall have effect with the substitution for references to the council of another county or the council of another district of references to the council of a non-metropolitan county or of a metropolitan district.

2. The entries in respect of the Inner London Education Authority shall have effect only in relation to property held by that Authority for the purposes of a charity registered as specified in paragraph 1.

3. In relation to property held by the corporation or council of an outer London borough for the purposes of a charity registered as so specified, the last entry in column (2) shall have effect with the substitution for the corporation or council of any inner London borough of the Inner London Education Authority.

(*d*) All liabilities attaching to any authority in respect of any property transferred by sub-paragraph (*b*) or (*c*) shall by virtue of this paragraph be transferred to and attach to the authority to whom such property is transferred.

(*e*) All contracts, deeds, bonds, agreements and other instruments subsisting in favour of, or against, and all notices in force which were given (or have effect as if they had been given) by, or to, the authority first mentioned in sub-paragraph (*d*) in respect of any property transferred by sub-paragraph (*b*) or (*c*), or in respect of liabilities transferred by sub-paragraph (*d*), shall be of full force and effect in favour of, or against, the authority to whom such property and liabilities are transferred.

(*f*) Any action or proceeding or any cause of action or proceeding, pending or existing at the appointed day, by, or against, the authority first mentioned in sub-paragraph (*d*) in respect of any property transferred by sub-paragraph (*b*) or (*c*), or in respect of liabilities transferred by sub-paragraph (*d*), shall not be prejudicially affected by reason of this paragraph, and may be continued, prosecuted and enforced by, or against, the authority to whom such property and liabilities are transferred.

(2) (*a*) Where, immediately before the appointed day, any power with respect to a charity, not being a charity incorporated under the Companies Acts or by charter, is under the trusts of the charity or by virtue of any enactment vested in, or in the holder of an office connected with, an authority to whom paragraph (1)(*b*) or (*c*) applies, that power shall vest in, or in the holder of the corresponding office connected with, the authority in whom, had property of the charity been vested in the first-mentioned authority, that property would have been transferred by paragraph (1).

(*b*) If there is no corresponding office the power shall vest in the authority described in sub-paragraph (*a*).

(3) (*a*) References in paragraph (2) to a power with respect to a charity do not include references to a power of any person by virtue of being a charity trustee thereof, but where under the trusts of any charity, not being a charity incorporated under the Companies Acts or by charter, the charity trustees immediately before the appointed day include either an authority to whom paragraph (1) (*b*) or (*c*) applies or the holder of an office connected with such an authority, those trustees shall instead include the authority specified in paragraph 2(*a*) or, as the case may require, the holder of the corresponding office connected with that authority.

(*b*) If there is no corresponding office, the charity trustees shall include the person appointed for that purpose by the authority.

(4) (*a*) Where, immediately before the appointed day, any power with respect to a charity to which paragraphs (1) to (3) do not apply, not being a charity incorporated under the Companies Acts or by charter, is under the trusts of the charity or by virtue of any enactment vested in, or in the holder of an office connected with, the local authority of any area affected by the order, that power shall be exercisable, if the Charity Commissioners so direct, by such other authority or persons as may be specified in the direction.

(*b*) In this paragraph, "local authority" includes a parish meeting, the Common Council, the Honourable Society of the Inner Temple or the Honourable Society of the Middle Temple.

(5) Nothing in this regulation shall affect any power of Her Majesty, the court or any other person to alter the trusts of any charity.

Commons

25.—(1) Any agreement under section 2(2) of the Commons Registration Act 1965(a) (one council to be registration authority for land which spans the boundaries of counties or Greater London) which is in force immediately before the appointed day in relation to any common affected by the changes of areas effected by the order shall cease to have effect, without prejudice to the making of a new agreement under the said subsection.

(2) Where any common regulated by a scheme under the Commons Act 1899(b) is transferred from one district or London borough to another such area, any functions under the scheme of the council of the district or London borough from which the common is transferred shall be exercised by the council of the district or London borough to which the common is transferred.

(3) Where any common so regulated—

(a) is immediately before the appointed day comprised in a single district or London borough; and

(b) comes on the appointed day to be comprised in two or more districts or London boroughs,

any functions under the scheme of the council of the area described in (a) shall be exercised by the council of the area described in (b) in which the greater part of the common is situated unless all such councils agree that they shall be exercised by the council of any other such area.

Food and drugs

26.—(1) This regulation shall apply wherever an area is transferred from the area of one food and drugs authority or local authority under the Food and Drugs Act 1955(c) to the area of another such authority, and in this regulation—

"the transferor authority" means the food and drugs authority or the local authority, as the case may be, from whose area the area is transferred; and

"the transferee authority" means the food and drugs authority or the local authority, as the case may be, to whose area the area is transferred.

In the application of this paragraph to a county, district or London borough regulation 3(4) shall apply.

(2) Anything duly done before the appointed day in the area transferred by, to or in relation to the transferor authority or an authorised officer of such authority in the exercise of any function under the said Act or regulations having effect thereunder shall be deemed to have been duly done by, to or in relation to the transferee authority or, as the case may be, an authorised officer of such authority, and any instrument made in the exercise of such functions in force immediately before the appointed day shall continue in force on and after that day until varied or revoked in relation to the area transferred in the exercise of such functions by the transferee authority.

Social services

27.—(1) This regulation shall apply where an area is transferred from the area of one local authority for the purposes of the Local Authority Social Services Act 1970(d) to the area of another such authority and in this regulation "the transferred area" means the area so transferred and—

(a) 1965 c. 64.　　　　　　　　　(b) 1899 c. 30.
(c) 4 & 5 Eliz. 2. c. 16.　　　　　(d) 1970 c. 42.

"the transferor authority" means the authority for the purposes aforesaid from whose area the area is transferred; and

"the transferee authority" means the authority for the purposes aforesaid to whose area the area is transferred.

In the application of this paragraph to a county, district or London borough regulation 3(4) shall apply.

(2) The transferee authority shall be authorised to continue to provide in the transferred area any services, accommodation and facilities which the transferor authority were required or authorised to provide in such area immediately before the appointed day under the enactments specified in the first column of Schedule 1 to the said Act and the other enactments conferring functions designated under section 2(2) of that Act as being appropriate for discharge by a local authority's social services committee.

(3) Where any person is immediately before the appointed day deemed under section 24(5), 24(6) or 29(7) of the National Assistance Act 1948(a) to continue to be ordinarily resident in the area of the transferor authority by reason of having been ordinarily resident in the transferred area immediately before entering residential accommodation, becoming a patient in hospital, or being accepted for work, as the case may be, that person shall be deemed on and after the appointed day to be ordinarily resident in the area of the transferee authority.

Family practitioner services

28. The provisions of Schedule 2 shall apply wherever an area is transferred from the area of one area health authority to the area of another such authority.

Mental health

29.—(1) This regulation shall apply where an area is transferred from one relevant area to another such area, and in this regulation "the transferred area" means the area so transferred and—

"the Act of 1959" means the Mental Health Act 1959(b);

"dissolved authority" means a local authority dissolved by the order;

"local authority" means the local authority for the purposes of the Local Authority Social Services Act 1970 for a relevant area; and

"relevant area" means a non-metropolitan county, a metropolitan district, a London borough or the City.

(2) Anything duly done before the appointed day for the purposes of any provision of the Act of 1959 by or in relation to the local authority from whose area any area is transferred, or a mental welfare officer appointed by them, in relation to any person in the transferred area shall not be affected by the changes of areas made by the order but may be continued by or in relation to the local authority to whose area the transferred area is transferred, or a mental welfare officer appointed by them, as the case may be.

(3) Where immediately before the appointed day a patient is in the guardianship under the Act of 1959 of a dissolved authority his guardianship shall vest in the local authority for the area comprising the place where he resided immediately before he was received into guardianship or if that place cannot with reasonable diligence be ascertained, or is disputed, in such local authority as shall have been designated by the dissolved authority (or is designated by the residuary successor of that authority), and—

(*a*) in the case of a patient subject to guardianship by virtue of a guardian-

_____

(a) 1948 c. 29.   (b) 1959 c. 72.

ship application, the provisions of Part IV of the Act of 1959 shall apply to him as if the application for his reception into guardianship had been for his reception into the guardianship of that local authority and had been accepted at the time when it was originally accepted;

(b) in the case of a patient subject to guardianship by virtue of a guardian-ship order, the provisions of Part IV of the Act of 1959 shall apply to him as if the order by virtue of which he is subject to guardianship were an order placing him under the guardianship of that local authority.

(4) Any order made by a county court under section 52 of the Act of 1959 directing that the functions under Part IV of that Act of the nearest relative of a patient shall be exercisable by a dissolved authority shall have effect as if it had directed those functions to be exercised by the local authority in whose area the patient resided on the appointed day, or if he is then in hospital by the local authority in whose area on that day the place at which he was resident immediately before he was admitted to hospital is situated.

(5) For the purposes of regulation 26 of the Mental Health (Hospital and Guardianship) Regulations 1960(a) a patient in hospital at the time when his age is to be determined who resided before the date of his admission to hospital in the transferred area shall be deemed to have resided at that time in the area of a local authority to which the transferred area is transferred.

Infectious disease notification

30. Any order made or having effect as if made under section 147 of the Public Health Act 1936(b) or section 52 of the Health Services and Public Health Act 1968(c) in force immediately before the appointed day throughout a relevant area which is altered by the order shall apply to such area as altered.

In this regulation, "relevant area" means a district or London borough or the City, the Inner Temple or the Middle Temple.

Registration service

31. Any reference in any scheme made under section 14 of the Registration Service Act 1953(d) or article 4 of the Local Government (Registration Service) Order 1973(e) to a relevant area which is altered by the order shall be read as a reference to such area as altered.

Any such reference to a relevant area which is abolished by the order shall cease to have effect.

In this regulation, "relevant area" means a county, district, London borough, parish or community, the City, the Inner Temple or the Middle Temple, or any ward of a district, London borough, parish or community or the City.

Marriages: registration of births and deaths

32.—(1) Nothing in the order or in any scheme made in accordance with any provision thereof shall affect the validity of any certificate or licence issued or notice given under the Marriage Act 1949(f) (hereinafter referred to as "the Act of 1949") before the appointed day. A marriage solemnised on or after that day in any registration district altered or established in consequence of the order on the authority of such a certificate or licence shall not be void, and a person solemnising a marriage in accordance with paragraph (2)(b)(iii) shall not be guilty of an offence under section 75 of the Act of 1949, by reason of the fact that the marriage is solemnised in an office other than that specified in the notice of marriage or certificate.

(a) S.I. 1960/1241 (1960 II, p. 1903).　　(b) 1936 c. 49.　　(c) 1968 c. 46.
(d) 1953 c. 37.　　(e) S.I. 1973/1654 (1973 III, p. 5117).　　(f) 1949 c. 76.

(2) Where notice of marriage is given before the appointed day to any superintendent registrar whose district will be altered or abolished on that day, and the marriage has not been solemnised before that day, the following provisions shall apply—

(a) Where the district is altered, the provisions of the Act of 1949 with regard to the issue of a certificate or a certificate and licence shall apply as if the alteration had not taken place;

(b) Where the district is abolished, the notice shall have effect as if it had been given to the superintendent registrar designated by the Registrar General for the purposes of section 15(1) of the Registration Service Act 1953 as the successor to the superintendent registrar whose district is abolished (which successor is hereinafter referred to as "the succeeding superintendent registrar"); and—

(i) the succeeding superintendent registrar shall cause any notice or exact copy of the particulars entered in the marriage notice book, required to be displayed under section 31(1) of the Act of 1949, to be affixed in some conspicuous place in his office from the appointed day for any unexpired portion of the period mentioned in the said section 31(1);

(ii) the succeeding superintendent registrar, and any other superintendent registrar so empowered by the Act of 1949, may, in accordance with the provisions of that Act, issue his certificate or, as the case may be, his certificate and licence for the solemnisation of the marriage notwithstanding that the building in which the marriage is to be solemnised is not within his district or within the district within which one of the persons to be married has resided; and

(iii) the succeeding superintendent registrar may arrange for the solemnisation of the marriage in his office where the persons to be married had stated in the notice that they wished to be married in the office of the superintendent registrar to whom the notice was given.

(3) For the purposes of any notice of marriage to be given on or after the appointed day the alteration or the establishment of any registration district by the order or any scheme made in accordance with any provision thereof shall be deemed to have taken effect 32 days before the appointed day.

(4) The superintendent registrar of any district which will be abolished on the appointed day shall for one month before that day display in a conspicuous position in his office and inform every person giving notice of marriage the name and address of the succeeding superintendent registrar.

(5) Nothing in the order or in any scheme made in accordance with any provision thereof shall prejudice or affect the registration of any building for the solemnisation of marriages under section 41 of the Act of 1949 or the appointment of any person as an authorised person under section 43 of that Act.

(6) Where any birth (including a still-birth) or death occurring in any registration sub-district which is altered or abolished on the appointed day in consequence of the order has not been registered before that day, it shall be registered by the registrar of births and deaths for the sub-district in which is situated on that day the place of birth or death, as the case may be.

Town and country planning

33.—(1) (*a*) This paragraph shall apply where any area is transferred from a county, district or London borough or from Greater London, the City, the Inner Temple or the Middle Temple.

(*b*) Any development plan scheme under section 10C of the Town and Country Planning Act 1971(**a**) shall cease to have effect in relation to the area transferred.

(*c*) Regulation 7 shall apply to anything required by the said Act to be done in the preparation or the submission for approval of any structure plan or local plan.

(*d*) That part of any definitive map and statement under Part IV of the National Parks and Access to the Countryside Act 1949(**b**) which relates to the area transferred shall be deemed to be the definitive map and statement for such area and to have been prepared by the surveying authority for the area to which such area is transferred.

(2) Any industrial development certificate under section 67 of the Town and Country Planning Act 1971 or office development permit under section 74 of that Act issued in respect of any land in a relevant area which is altered or abolished by the order shall continue on and after the appointed day to have effect as if the order had not been made.

In this paragraph, "relevant area" means a district or London borough or the City and the Temples.

Clean air

34. Any order under section 11 of the Clean Air Act 1956(**c**) shall, in so far as it extends to an area transferred to a district or London borough, or to the City, the Inner Temple or the Middle Temple—

(*a*) if at the appointed day it has not been confirmed, be considered, and if confirmed come into operation and have effect;

(*b*) if at such day it has been confirmed but has not come into operation, come into operation and have effect;

(*c*) if at such day it has already come into operation, continue to have effect,

as if it had been made by the council of such district or London borough, or by the Common Council, the Sub-Treasurer or the Under Treasurer.

Cemeteries

35.—(1) Nothing in the order shall affect any right of burial, to construct a walled grave or vault or to place and maintain, or to put any additional inscription on, a tombstone or other memorial which any person may have acquired before the appointed day or affect the amount of any fee payable by him in respect of any such right.

(2) This paragraph shall have effect where an area (hereinafter referred to as "the transferred area") is transferred by the order from an area for which a cemetery to which the Local Authorities' Cemeteries Order 1974(**d**) applies has been provided (hereinafter referred to as "the cemetery area").

In the period of 25 years beginning on the appointed day—

(*a*) any inhabitant or parishioner of the transferred area shall be entitled

---

(**a**) 1971 c. 78.   (**b**) 1949 c. 97.   (**c**) 1956 c. 52.
(**d**) S.I. 1974/628 (1974 I, p. 2489).

to the same rights of burial as the inhabitants or parishioners of the cemetery area as altered;

(*b*) any provisions in relation to inhabitants or parishioners in any table of fees in force in respect of the cemetery shall apply to the inhabitants or parishioners of the transferred area as they apply to the inhabitants or parishioners of the cemetery area as altered;

(*c*) no differential charges shall be imposed on the inhabitants or parishioners of the transferred area.

(3) Subject to paragraph (2), any provisions in relation to inhabitants or parishioners of any area which is altered by the order in any table of fees in force in respect of any cemetery to which the Local Authorities' Cemeteries Order 1974 applies shall apply to the inhabitants or parishioners of the area as altered.

(4) In the area in which the Church of England was disestablished by the Welsh Church Act 1914(**a**) the references in this regulation to inhabitants and parishioners shall be read as references to inhabitants.

Maintenance of highways

36. Where the council of a district altered by the order have, under section 187(2)(*a*) of the Local Government Act 1972, undertaken the maintenance of all the footpaths, bridleways and urban roads which are neither trunk roads nor classified roads in the district, the undertaking shall extend to all such highways in the district as altered.

Road traffic and highways

37.—(1) Subject to paragraph (2), the provisions of Schedule 3 shall have effect, and—

(*a*) the provision of regulation 7 shall not apply in relation to any matter as to which provision is made in any such provisions; and

(*b*) the provisions of regulation 62 shall not apply in relation to any matter as to which provision is made in paragraph 6 of the said Schedule.

(2) The provisions of paragraph 5 of the said Schedule shall not apply in relation to any matter for which provision is made in regulation 38.

Private street works

38.—(1) The provisions of this regulation shall apply wherever an authority (in this regulation referred to as "the new street works authority") becomes the street works authority under Part IX of the Highways Act 1959(**b**) in place of another authority (in this regulation referred to as "the former street works authority").

(2) In respect of any sum paid or secured under section 192 of the said Act before the appointed day the new street works authority shall be the street works authority for the purposes of sections 192 to 198 of the said Act.

(3) The changes of areas made by the order shall not affect any notices given or proceedings taken by, or on behalf of, the former street works authority under the code of 1892 (within the meaning of the said Act) in relation to the street, and such proceedings, and any works commenced under the said code, may be continued and completed, in accordance with the provisions of the

---

said code, by the new street works authority as if they had given the notices, taken the proceedings or commenced the works.

(4) Where, at the appointed day, any works under the said code have been commenced but not·completed in the street the new street works authority shall be entitled to recover—

(a) such of the expenses incurred by the former street works authority as that authority could have recovered under the said code; and

(b) such of the expenses incurred by themselves as the said authority could have recovered under the said code had they completed the works,

and the new street works authority shall have all such powers for the recovery of such expenses as they would have had if they had executed the whole of the works, and all the provisions of the said code shall apply accordingly.

(5) Where, at the appointed day, any works under the said code have been completed in the street the new street works authority shall have all such powers for the recovery of the expenses incurred in the execution of the works as they would have had if they had undertaken the works, and all the provisions of the said code shall apply accordingly.

(6) Paragraphs (3) to (5) shall extend to notices, proceedings and works under sections 189 to 191 of the Highways Act 1959 or under any local Act to which article 7 of the Local Government (Road Traffic and Highways) (Transitional Provisions) Order 1974(a) applied, with the substitution, for any reference to the code of 1892, of a reference to the said sections or the local Act, as the case may be.

Land registration

39. Where an area is transferred from a district in which registration of title to land under the Land Registration Acts 1925 to 1971(b) is compulsory on sale to another such district such registration shall continue to be compulsory.

Statutory definitions of areas

40.—(1) (a) This paragraph applies to any provision of any Act or of any order, rules or regulations made by a Minister under any Act defining an area for any purpose wholly by reference to entire relevant areas.

In this sub-paragraph, "relevant areas" means—

(i) counties, districts, London boroughs, parishes and communities;

(ii) areas common to parishes or communities;

(iii) Greater London, the City, the Inner Temple and the Middle Temple;

(iv) electoral divisions of counties or of Greater London and wards of districts, London boroughs, parishes, communities and the City;

(v) the areas of former counties, boroughs, urban districts and rural districts;

(vi) any area described in (i) to (v) other than another such area;

(vii) any area described in (i) or (iii) other than an area expressly defined;

(viii) any part of an area described in (i) or (iv) defined wholly by reference to circumstances existing immediately before 1st April 1974;

(ix) any petty sessions area.

(b) In any provision to which this paragraph applies, subject to sub-paragraph (c)—

(a) S.I. 1974/142 (1974 I, p. 461).
(b) 1925 c. 21; 1936 c. 26; 1966 c. 39; 1971 c. 54.

(i) any reference to any relevant area altered by the order shall be construed as a reference to such area as altered,

(ii) any reference to any relevant area abolished by the order shall cease to have effect, and

(iii) there shall be deemed to be included a reference to any county, district, London borough, parish or community formed by the order and wholly comprised in the area.

(c) Notwithstanding the provision of sub-paragraph (b), the extent of—

any district of a county court;

any bailiwick for which an under-sheriff acts;

any licensing planning area;

any area specified for the purposes of subsection (3) of section 76 of the Licensing Act 1964 in an order made under that subsection;

any area specified in regulations made under section 22(3) of the Gaming Act 1968(a);

any area specified in an order made under section 9(1) of the Protection of Birds Act 1954(b);

the order area of any order made under section 21 of the Town and Country Planning Act 1971;

the Metropolitan Police District; and

the Cheshire brine subsidence compensation district,

shall not be altered except by express provision in the order.

(2) Any provision of any Act or of any order, rules or regulations made under any Act defining an area for any purpose to which paragraph (1) does not apply shall not be affected by the order except by express provision therein.

(3) If the order alters any of the counties of Buckinghamshire, Essex, Hertfordshire and Kent the references to those counties in Schedule 1 to the Home Counties (Music and Dancing) Licensing Act 1926(c) as amended by section 204(7) of the Local Government Act 1972 shall be construed as a reference to those counties as altered.

Local Acts, orders and byelaws—General

41.—(1) This regulation shall apply to—

(a) any provision of any local Act,

any order made under any Act, or

any byelaws,

which would apart from the changes of areas effected by the order be in force on the appointed day throughout a relevant area;

(b) any provision of any Act other than a local Act which would be in force as aforesaid by reason of any application thereof by any Act, instrument or resolution,

other than—

(i) a provision relating to any railway, light railway, tramway, road transport, water transport, canal, inland navigation, ferry, dock, harbour, pier or lighthouse undertaking, any telephone undertaking, any market undertaking or any undertaking for the supply of electricity, gas, hydraulic power or district heating;

(a) 1968 c. 65.   (b) 1954 c. 30.   (c) 1926 c. 31.

  (ii) a provision relating to any person's status, or the right of any person to be admitted, as a freeman of any place or the rights of any person by virtue of any relationship or association with such a freeman;

  (iii) a protective provision for the benefit of any person; or

  (iv) a provision contained in the Green Belt (London and Home Counties) Act 1938(a).

(2) In this regulation, "relevant area" means a county, district, London borough, parish or community, Greater London, the City, the Inner Temple or the Middle Temple, the Metropolitan Police District or so much of a district as is not within the said District.

(3) Any provision to which this regulation applies in force immediately before the appointed day throughout a relevant area which is altered by the order shall be in force throughout the area as altered.

(4) Any provision to which this regulation applies in force throughout such relevant areas as may be specified in relation to this paragraph in the order shall be in force throughout the area so specified in relation to the areas specified.

(5) Subject to paragraphs (3) and (4), any provision to which this regulation applies shall cease to have effect in relation to any area transferred by the order.

(6) In any provision in relation to which paragraph (3) or (4) has effect any reference to a relevant area shall have effect as a reference to the area as altered or the area specified in accordance with paragraph (4), as the case may be.

(7) Nothing in this regulation shall apply to any provision applying to property held on a charitable trust.

Local Acts and orders—Protective provisions

42.—(1) Paragraphs (2) to (4) shall have effect in relation to protective provisions for the benefit of authorities described in column (1) of Part I or II of Schedule 4, or their predecessors, contained in any local Act or in any order made under any Act.

(2) Any such provision for the benefit of an authority described in column (1) of the said Part I, or their predecessors, so far as it relates to or affects an area specified in respect of such authority in column (2), shall enure to the benefit of the authority so specified in column (3).

(3) Any such provision for the benefit of an authority described in column (1) of the said Part II, or their predecessors, so far as it relates to or affects an area specified in respect of such authority in column (2), shall, if it is appropriate that it should enure for the benefit of the authority so specified in column (3), so enure.

(4) Any provision which under paragraph (2) or (3) enures in respect of any area shall in relation thereto be construed as if a reference to the authority specified in column (3) were substituted for any reference to the authority described in column (1) or their predecessors.

Proceedings for the enforcement of byelaws

43.—(1) Paragraphs (2) and (3) shall have effect in relation to proceedings which if the order had not been made might have been taken by an authority described in column (1) of Part I or II of Schedule 4 for any offence against any byelaw alleged to have been committed before the appointed day in an area specified in respect of such authority in column (2).

(a) 1938 c. xciii.

(2) Any such proceedings which might have been taken by an authority described in column (1) of the said Part I for any offence alleged to have been committed in an area specified in column (2) may be taken by the authority specified in respect of the first-mentioned authority in column (3).

(3) Any such proceedings which might have been taken by an authority described in column (1) of the said Part II for any offence alleged to have been committed in an area specified in column (2) shall, if it is appropriate that they should be taken by the authority specified in respect of the first-mentioned authority in column (3), be so taken.

Compulsory purchase orders and other instruments

44.—(1) Any order authorising the compulsory acquisition of land (hereinafter referred to as a "compulsory purchase order"), whether confirmed before the coming into operation of the order for the purposes mentioned in regulation 4(1) or submitted for confirmation before or after such coming into operation, may be amended by the Minister by whom it was confirmed, or by whom it falls to be confirmed, by the substitution, as the authority to be authorised to acquire the land comprised therein, or any part thereof, of such authority as seems to him to be appropriate, and thereafter the order shall have effect, or be considered and if confirmed have effect, accordingly.

(2) Any compulsory purchase order which has not been submitted to a Minister for confirmation before the appointed day may be so submitted by any authority, and any action which requires to be taken prior to the submission of the order which has not already been taken shall be taken by such authority.

(3) Any instrument other than a compulsory purchase order which has been submitted to a Minister for confirmation before the appointed day may be amended by such Minister by the substitution of references to the whole or parts of one or more specified areas or of references to one or more specified authorities, and thereafter the instrument may be considered and if confirmed have effect accordingly.

(4) Any instrument which has not been submitted to a Minister for confirmation before the appointed day may be so submitted by a specified authority, and—

(a) any action which requires to be taken prior to the submission of the instrument which has not already been taken shall be taken by such authority; and

(b) paragraph (3) shall apply to such instrument as it applies to the instruments therein described.

(5) In paragraphs (3) and (4)—

"instrument" includes a draft scheme under section 30 of the Land Drainage Act 1961**(a)**;

"specified area" means a county, district, London borough, water authority area or passenger transport area or Greater London, the City, the Inner Temple or the Middle Temple; and

"specified authority" means a county council, district council, London borough council, water authority or passenger transport executive, or the Greater London Council, the Common Council, the Sub-Treasurer or the Under Treasurer.

(a) 1961 c. 48.

Instruments made by Ministers

45. Any instrument which has been made by a Minister before the appointed day may be amended by the appropriate Minister by the substitution of references to—

the whole or parts of one or more specified areas (as defined in regulation 44); or

one or more specified authorities (as so defined);

and thereafter the instrument shall have effect, or be proceeded with, accordingly.

In this regulation, "the appropriate Minister", in relation to any instrument, means the Minister in charge of any government department concerned with the subject matter of the instrument, but the validity of any action shall not be affected by any question as to whether or not any Minister was the appropriate Minister for the purpose.

Instruments subject to special parliamentary procedure

46.—(1) Regulations 44 and 45 shall not apply to any instrument which at the appointed day is subject to the procedure regulated in the Statutory Orders (Special Procedure) Acts 1945 and 1965(a) until the completion of such procedure.

(2) In any such procedure—

(a) any notice given by a Minister that he desires that rights and functions conferred on him shall be exercisable by any authority shall have effect; but

(b) otherwise, the instrument subject to the procedure shall be dealt with as if the order had not been made.

Inspection of parish and community books, etc.

47. Any person shall at all times be entitled to the rights to which he would have been entitled if the order had not been made of inspecting and making extracts from the public books, writings and papers of a parish or community (including any photographic copies thereof) and all documents directed by law to be kept therewith.

Registration—General

48.—(1) Subject to paragraph (2), in this regulation—

"register" means any register under any enactment, rule, order or regulation and includes any index of local charities maintained under section 10 of the Charities Act 1960;

"registration" means inclusion in any register; and

"exemption" means exemption from any obligation in respect of registration.

(2) This regulation does not extend to—

(a) any register of parliamentary and local government electors;

(b) any register of births, marriages or deaths;

(c) any register maintained under the Local Authorities' Cemeteries Order 1974;

(d) any register to which regulation 49 applies.

(a) 9 & 10 Geo. 6. c. 18; 1965 c. 43.

(3) Immediately before the appointed day the proper officer of any dissolved authority shall deliver any register of the authority to the proper officer of the following authority, namely—

    (a) if the register is not appropriate for the residuary successor of the dissolved authority and is appropriate for one other authority only, to that authority;

    (b) in any other case, to the residuary successor of the dissolved authority.

(4) As soon as may be after the appointed day the proper officer of any authority shall—

    (a) send to the proper officer of any other authority a copy of every entry in any register of the authority by whom he is employed or received by him under paragraph (3)(b) which is appropriate for the register of that other authority; and

    (b) incorporate or include in the appropriate register of the authority by whom he is employed, with any necessary modifications—

        (i) the entries in the registers delivered to him under paragraph (3)(b) of which copies have not been sent, under (a), to the proper officer of any other authority; and

        (ii) the particulars of every entry furnished to him under (a) in its application to the proper officer of any other authority,

and every entry so incorporated or included shall continue in force as fully and effectively as if it had originally been made in the register in which it is incorporated or included.

Where any register is kept in such manner that the entries therein are separable, (a) may be complied with, as regards any entry, by sending the entry to the proper officer specified therein, and if the entry is so sent (b)(ii) may be complied with, as regards that entry, by the inclusion of the entry in the appropriate register.

(5) Any application made before the appointed day for registration in any register, or for exemption from any obligation in respect of inclusion in such register, which concerns or has effect in relation to any area transferred from the authority to whom the application is made or to any person, property, matter or thing therein, shall be treated as having been made to the authority for whose register the application is appropriate.

(6) Any order, decision, notice or certificate made, taken, given or issued before the appointed day by any authority in relation to—

any entry in any register of the authority; or

any application for registration or exemption,

which concerns or has effect in relation to any area transferred from such authority shall have effect as if it had been made, taken, given or issued by the authority in whose register the entry falls to be incorporated or included or in relation to whose register the application is appropriate.

(7) Paragraphs (5) and (6) shall have effect in relation to any area transferred within a county, or within Greater London, in relation to matters which on and after the appointed day are appropriate for the register of an authority other than the county council or the Greater London Council, as if the area had been transferred from the county, or from Greater London.

Local land charges

49.—(1) This regulation shall apply where an area is transferred from one relevant area to another such area, and in this regulation "the transferred area" means the area so transferred and—

"proper officer" means the officer appointed to act as local registrar under rules made under the Land Charges Act 1925(a) as set out in Schedule 4 to the Land Charges Act 1972(b);

"register" means a register of local land charges kept in pursuance of section 15 of the said Act of 1925 as set out in the said Schedule 4;

"relevant area" means a district or London borough or the City and the Temples;

"the transferor authority", in relation to any transferred area, means the local authority for the relevant area from which the transferred area is transferred; and

"the transferee authority", in relation to any transferred area, means the local authority for the relevant area to which the transferred area is transferred.

(2) The proper officer of the transferor authority shall immediately before the appointed day supply to the proper officer of the transferee authority an office copy of every entry in the register for the transferor authority relating to any land in the transferred area.

(3) The proper officer of the transferee authority shall, within 14 days after the receipt of an office copy under paragraph (2), enter the particulars contained therein, with any necessary modifications, in the appropriate part of the register for the transferee authority.

(4) Until all the entries required by paragraph (3) have been made, the following provisions shall have effect in relation to land in the transferred area—

    (a) where application is made for a personal search in the register for the transferee authority, the proper officer of that authority shall notify the applicant that additional search should be made in the register for the transferor authority;

    (b) where application is made for an official search in the register for the transferee authority, the proper officer of that authority shall issue to the applicant free of charge a certificate of official search in that register and shall forward the application to the proper officer of the transferor authority, together with the fees paid in respect thereof, or where there is more than one transferor authority equal portions of such fees;

    (c) the proper officer of the transferor authority shall permit and make such searches and furnish such office copies and certificates as he would have been required to permit, make and furnish, and shall in relation thereto have the same powers and be subject to the same obligations, as if this regulation and the order had not been made;

    (d) where a local land charge, registration of which was effected prior to the appointed day in the register for the transferor authority, is required under the foregoing provisions of this regulation to be entered in the register for the transferee authority it shall not be unenforceable by reason only that it has not been entered in that register.

(a) 1925 c. 22.   (b) 1972 c. 61.

Licences, etc.

50. Where any enactment will become applicable to any area transferred to a district or London borough, or to the City or the Temples, only as from the appointed day, any licence, certificate, permit, consent or exemption under such enactment, to become effective on or after the appointed day, may be granted before that day.

Rate support grants

51. In any calculations of the rate support grants for the year beginning on the appointed day the changes of areas made by the order shall be deemed to have been made at the date by reference to which, for the purposes of paragraph 9(1) of Part III of Schedule 2 to the Local Government Act 1974(a) the effective rateable values therein referred to are to be generally determined for that year.

Civil defence grants

52. For the purpose of determining whether any, and if so what, deductions should be made from grants payable in accordance with regulations under section 3 of the Civil Defence Act 1948(b) to any authority, any land or article acquired by, or article provided for, any authority for the purposes of functions conferred on them by section 2 of the said Act and transferred to the first-mentioned authority by regulation 62 shall be treated as having been acquired by or, as the case may be, provided by such authority for those purposes.

Precepts

53.—(1) This regulation shall apply where any estimate of the product of a rate of a new penny in the pound in the year commencing on the appointed day has not been made on the basis that the changes of areas made by the order had become operative.

(2) The proper officer of a county council or the Greater London Council, or the Receiver for the Metropolitan Police District, shall make such adaptation of and alteration in the estimate as may be necessary as the result of the changes of areas made by the order.

(3) The rating authority shall supply any such proper officer or Receiver with such information as he may require for the purposes of giving effect to paragraph (2).

Valuation of water hereditaments of statutory water undertakings

54. Where new valuation lists are to come into force on the appointed day, then, in the application of Schedule 4 to the General Rate Act 1967(c) as amended by the Rating (Water hereditaments) Order 1975(d) the changes of areas made by the order shall be deemed to have been operative at all material times.

Rating of British Gas Corporation and electricity boards

55.—(1) In the application of section 33 of and Schedule 6 to the General Rate Act 1967 (as set out in Schedule 5 to the Gas Act 1972(e)) to the British Gas Corporation and of section 34 of and Schedule 7 to the said Act to the Central Electricity Generating Board and any Area Board in relation to any

---

(a) 1974 c. 7.   (b) 12, 13 & 14 Geo. 6. c. 5.   (c) 1967 c. 9.
(d) S.I. 1975/540 (1975 1, p. 1785).   (e) 1972 c. 60.

rate period beginning on or after the appointed day, the changes of rating areas made by the order shall be deemed to have been operative at all material times.

(2) The provisions of Schedule 5 shall have effect in relation to matters provided for by the said Schedules 6 and 7.

Valuation of hereditaments of National Coal Board

56.—(1) This regulation shall have effect in relation to any rating districts in which coal is brought to bank or under which coal is worked.

(2) For the purposes of article 7 of the National Coal Board (Valuation) Order 1963**(a)** in relation to any year beginning on or after the appointed day the changes of areas made by the order shall be deemed to have been effective at all material times.

(3) Where amounts have been certified by the National Coal Board under article 21(3)(*b*) and (*c*) of the said order of 1963, the Board shall as soon as may be after the coming into operation of the order certify to the Commissioners of Inland Revenue any variation of such amounts which is necessary.

(4) Where the Commissioners of Inland Revenue have notified to the National Coal Board and to the rating authority or authorities the particulars required by article 21(4) of the said order of 1963, they shall as soon as may be notify the particulars which would have been required to have been notified before the end of October if the order had come into operation on 1st April, and the notifications under article 21(4) shall cease to have effect.

(5) Where the Commissioners of Inland Revenue have notified to the National Coal Board and to the rating authority or authorities the rateable values required by article 21(5) or (6) of the said order of 1963 to be notified, they shall as soon as may be notify the rateable values which would have been required to have been notified before the end of December if the order had come into operation on 1st April, and the notifications under article 21(5) or (6) shall cease to have effect.

(6) In this regulation—

any reference to the end of October or the end of December is a reference to the end of such month last preceding the appointed day; and

any reference to 1st April is a reference to such date last preceding the appointed day.

Valuation of hereditaments of Post Office

57.—(1) For the purposes of articles 6 and 7 of the Post Office (Rateable Values) Order 1972**(b)** in relation to any year beginning on and after the appointed day the changes of areas made by the order shall be deemed to have been operative at all material times.

(2) Where the Commissioners of Inland Revenue have notified the amounts of rateable values under paragraph (1) of the said article 6, they shall as soon as may be after the coming into operation of the order notify to the rating authorities any variation of such amounts which is necessary, and the valuation officer in his action under paragraph (4) of such article shall proceed accordingly.

(a) S.I. 1963/636 (1963 I, p. 785).   (b) S.I. 1972/1794 (1972 III, p. 5184).

Valuation lists

58. The appropriate valuation officer of the Commissioners of Inland Revenue shall cause such alterations to be made in the valuation lists as may be necessary as a result of the changes of areas made by the order, and—

(*a*) any area transferred from any county, district, London borough, parish or community or from the City, the Inner Temple or the Middle Temple, or any other area which becomes part of a parish, may be treated in a valuation list as a rating district;

(*b*) nothing in the rules prescribing the form of valuation lists for the time being in force shall preclude any such alteration being made by—

(i) the deletion of hereditaments from a valuation list;

(ii) the repositioning in a valuation list of any sheets therein;

(iii) the insertion of sheets in a valuation list, or copies thereof, in another valuation list;

(iv) the amalgamation of existing valuation lists to form a new valuation list;

(v) such revisions in the sheets, copies or lists mentioned in (ii), (iii) or (iv) (in particular the deletion of hereditaments) as may be necessary.

Proposals for alteration of valuation lists

59.—(1) This regulation shall apply (except where new valuation lists are to come into force on the appointed day) wherever an area is transferred from one rating area to another, and—

(*a*) regulation 3(4) shall apply where such rating area is a district or London borough;

(*b*) any area so transferred is in this regulation referred to as a transferred area;

(*c*) "transferor authority", in relation to any transferred area, means the rating authority from whose area the transferred area is transferred; and

(*d*) "transferee authority", in relation to any transferred area, means the rating authority to whose area the transferred area is transferred.

(2) Subject to the provision of paragraph (3), any proposal for the alteration of a valuation list in respect of a hereditament in a transferred area shall have effect as from the appointed day as if it had been made for the alteration of the valuation list for the rating area to which the area is transferred in respect of such hereditament, and any action in relation to such proposal taken by, or in relation to, the transferor authority shall have effect as if it had been taken by, or in relation to, the transferee authority.

(3) Paragraph (2) shall not apply where notice of the date, time and place for the hearing of an appeal arising out of the proposal has been given before the appointed day, and such appeal shall continue with the substitution of the transferee authority for the transferor authority, but otherwise in all respects as if the order had not been made.

(4) Any reference in any scheme for the purposes of section 88 of the General Rate Act 1967 to any relevant area which is altered by the order shall be construed as a reference to the area as altered.

In this paragraph, "relevant area" means a county, district, London borough, parish or community, or Greater London, the City, the Inner Temple or the Middle Temple.

Rating of owners and discount for rates: rating of unoccupied property

60. Any direction for the rating of owners or the allowance of a discount in respect of rates or resolution with respect to the rating of unoccupied property in force immediately before the appointed day in a rating area which is altered by the order shall apply to the rating area as altered.

Arrears of rates

61. All rates made but not collected at the appointed day in respect of hereditaments in an area transferred to a rating area shall be collected and recovered by the rating authority for that area.

In the application of this regulation to a district or London borough regulation 3(4) shall apply.

Property, liabilities, contracts, etc., notices and proceedings

62.—(1) Nothing in this regulation shall apply to—

(a) property held for the purposes of, and liabilities incurred, contracts, deeds, bonds, agreements and other instruments subsisting, notices given, actions and proceedings pending, and causes of action or proceeding existing in relation to, any charitable trust;

(b) any property specified in relation to this sub-paragraph in the order, and liabilities incurred, contracts, deeds, bonds, agreements and other instruments subsisting, notices given, actions and proceedings pending, and causes of action or proceeding existing in relation thereto,

and nothing in paragraph (2) shall apply to property held for the purposes of, and liabilities incurred, contracts, deeds, bonds, agreements and other instruments subsisting, notices given, actions and proceedings pending, and causes of action or proceeding existing in relation to the functions of any authority in relation to smallholdings and cottage holdings.

(2) Subject to the provision of paragraph (1)—

(a) all property vested in an authority described in column (1) of the table in Part I of Schedule 6 or in any extension thereof made in the order for the purposes of this paragraph and specified in respect of such authority in column (2) (whether by reason of its inclusion in any description of matters or particularly), and all liabilities attaching to the said authority in respect of any such property, shall by virtue of this paragraph be transferred to and vest in or attach to the authority specified in respect of such property in column (3);

(b) all other liabilities attaching to an authority described in the said column (1) and within any description of matters specified in respect of such authority in column (2) shall by virtue of this paragraph be transferred to and attach to the authority specified in respect of such description of matters in column (3);

(c) all contracts, deeds, bonds, agreements and other instruments subsisting in favour of, or against, and all notices in force which were given (or have effect as if they had been given) by, or to, an authority described in the said column (1) in respect of any property or liability transferred by sub-paragraph (a) or (b) shall be of full force and effect in favour of, or against, the authority to whom such property or liability is transferred;

(*d*) all other contracts, deeds, bonds, agreements and other instruments subsisting in favour of, or against, and all notices in force which were given (or have effect as if they had been given) by, or to, an authority described in the said column (1) and within any description of matters specified in respect of such authority in column (2) shall be of full force and effect in favour of, or against, the authority specified in respect of such description of matters in column (3);

(*e*) any action or proceeding or any cause of action or proceeding, pending or existing at the appointed day, by, or against, an authority described in the said column (1) in respect of any property or liability transferred by sub-paragraph (*a*) or (*b*) shall not be prejudicially affected by reason of the order, and may be continued, prosecuted and enforced by, or against, the authority to whom such property or liability is transferred;

(*f*) any other action or proceeding or any other cause of action or proceeding, pending or existing at the appointed day, by, or against, an authority described in the said column (1) and within any description of matters specified in respect of such authority in column (2) shall not be prejudicially affected by reason of the order, and may be continued, prosecuted and enforced by, or against, the authority specified in respect of such description of matters in column (3).

Paragraphs 1 to 7 in Part I of Schedule 6 shall have effect in relation to the table in that Part.

Part II of Schedule 6 shall have effect in the application of this paragraph.

(3) Subject to the provisions of paragraphs (1) and (2)—

(*a*) all property and liabilities vested in or attaching to a dissolved authority shall by virtue of this paragraph be transferred to and vest in or attach to the residuary successor of that authority;

(*b*) all contracts, deeds, bonds, agreements and other instruments subsisting in favour of, or against, and all notices in force which were given, or have effect as if they had been given, by, or to, a dissolved authority shall be of full force and effect in favour of, or against, the residuary successor of that authority;

(*c*) any action or proceeding or any cause of action or proceeding, pending or existing at the appointed day, by, or against, a dissolved authority shall not be prejudicially affected by reason of the order, and may be continued, prosecuted and enforced by, or against, the residuary successor of that authority.

(4) The authority to whom any property other than land is transferred by paragraph (2) or (3) (otherwise than by its particular inclusion in an extension of the table in Part I of Schedule 6 made in the order for the purposes of paragraph (2)) may by resolution agree—

(*a*) that the property shall not be transferred; or

(*b*) that it shall be transferred to any other authority named in the resolution, and in the case of (*b*) sub-paragraph (*a*) of paragraph (2) in so far as it relates to liabilities, and sub-paragraphs (*c*) and (*e*) thereof, shall apply accordingly.

(5) (*a*) Subject to sub-paragraph (*b*), any interest in any property or any liability transferred by paragraph (2) or (3) to the authority for any county, district, London borough, parish or community, or for Greater London, the City, the Inner Temple or the Middle Temple, shall be held or discharged by them in respect of such area as existing on and after the appointed day.

(b) Sub-paragraph (a)—

(i) shall not apply in respect of any interest in any property or any liability which by reason of agreements made (or having effect as if made) by the transferor authority falls to be held or discharged in respect of any specified area; and

(ii) shall have effect subject to the provision of subsections (4) and (5) of section 248 of the Local Government Act 1972 (freemen and inhabitants of boroughs existing prior to 1st April 1974).

(6) Any byelaws in force for the regulation of any property transferred by paragraph (2) or (3) shall have effect as if they had been made by the authority to whom such property is transferred (but in the case of property transferred to a parish meeting or parish trustees only if such byelaws could have been made by the parish meeting).

(7) Any provision of any local Act or of any order made under any Act which applies to any property transferred by paragraph (2) or (3) to any authority shall have effect with the substitution of references to that authority for any references to (or having effect as references to) the authority from whom the property is transferred.

(8) Any authorisation of the borrowing of money in force in respect of any property or liability transferred by paragraph (2) or (3) to any authority may, subject to the terms applicable thereto, be acted on by such authority.

(9) Any excise licence, operators' licence, public service vehicle licence, road service licence, plating certificate or other document issued in respect of any vehicle transferred by paragraph (2) or (3) to any authority shall have effect as if it had been issued to such authority, and any reference to the authority from whom the vehicle is transferred in any such licence or certificate or in any registration book or other document issued in respect of such vehicle shall have effect as a reference to the authority to whom the vehicle is transferred.

(10) The expression "market authority" in Part III of the Food and Drugs Act 1955 shall include any district council to whom such a market as is described in section 49(2) of that Act is transferred by paragraph (2) or (3).

(11) Where parts of any land are in consequence of paragraph (2) or (3), or of both such paragraphs, vested in two different authorities, and any easement or other right over one part is required to enable the other part to be used, the authority in whom the said other part is vested may within the 6 months following the appointed day serve notice on the authority in whom the said one part is vested specifying such easement or other right and requiring the authority in whom the said one part is vested to grant the same to them on terms specified in the notice.

Any question—

(a) whether any easement or other right is required to enable the said other part to be used; or

(b) as to the terms on which any easement or other right shall be conferred, shall be determined by the decision of a person agreed on by the authorities or in default of agreement appointed by the Secretary of State.

(12) The provision made by this regulation is without prejudice to—

(a) any agreement which may be made for payment in respect of any property transferred by paragraph (2) or (3);

(*b*) any agreement which may be made under section 68 of the Local Government Act 1972, or arbitration in default of such agreement—

- (i) as to the use of any property transferred as aforesaid;
- (ii) in relation to any matter not so transferred.

Audit of accounts

63.—(1) Sections 154 to 167 (accounts and audit) of the Local Government Act 1972 shall apply in relation to the accounts of any county or district council established by the order, and of the committees and officers thereof, with the substitution in section 154(2)(*a*) (resolutions as to audit), for "before 1st January 1974" of "within the 6 weeks following the date of their first meeting".

(2) The said sections shall apply in relation to the accounts of the parish councils, parish meetings or community councils of each of the parishes or communities in a district established by the order and of every joint committee of the councils of two or more parishes or communities, both or all of which are situated in that district, and of the committees and officers of any such body, with the substitution in section 154(2)(*d*) (resolutions as to audit), for "before 1st January 1974" of "within the 6 weeks following the date of their first meeting".

(3) The accounts of any dissolved authority (other than charter trustees) and of the committees and officers thereof shall be made up to the appointed day and shall be audited in like manner and subject to the same incidents and consequences as if the order had not been made:

Provided that where the audit of the accounts of a dissolved authority is carried out by a district auditor the expression "the body in question" in section 161(2)(*a*) (orders for repayment of expenditure declared unlawful) and (4) (certification of sums not brought into account or losses) shall include the residuary successor of the dissolved authority.

Security for loans

64. Where under these regulations, the order or any agreement made under section 68 of the Local Government Act 1972 any liability or part of a liability charged indifferently on all the revenues of a public body or on any particular revenues of such body is transferred to another public body, the liability or part of the liability shall be charged indifferently to all the revenues of the public body to whom it is transferred and shall cease to be a charge on any revenues or fund of the public body from whom it is transferred.

Legal proceedings

65. All legal proceedings pending at the appointed day shall be amended in such manner as may be necessary or proper in consequence of these regulations and the order.

Liabilities to certain funds

66.—(1) Where by virtue of these regulations or of the order any matter for the purposes of which in pursuance of paragraph 19 of Schedule 13 to the Local Government Act 1972 moneys forming part of a fund to which that paragraph applies have been used is transferred to an authority other than the authority by whom such fund is maintained on and after the appointed day, the provisions of sub-paragraph (2) of that paragraph, and sub-paragraph (3) thereof in so far as it relates to the debiting of accounts, shall be applicable to the first-mentioned authority.

(2) Where by virtue of these regulations or of the order any matter for the purposes of which in pursuance of regulation B.6 of the Local Government Superannuation Regulations 1974(a) moneys forming part of a superannuation fund have been used is transferred to an authority other than the authority by whom the fund is maintained on and after the appointed day, the said regulation shall apply as if the moneys had been lent to the first-mentioned authority.

(3) Where by virtue of these regulations or of the order any matter in respect of which any advance from a capital fund established under paragraph 16 of Schedule 13 to the Local Government Act 1972 or under any local Act is not fully repaid is transferred to an authority other than the authority by whom such fund is maintained on and after the appointed day, the first-mentioned authority may treat the outstanding amount of the advance as an advance to the capital fund established by them and make such payments to that fund as they consider appropriate, but otherwise any liability to make repayments in respect of the advance shall cease.

(4) Where by virtue of these regulations or of the order any matter in respect of which advances from a consolidated loans fund or loans pool would have fallen to be repaid is transferred to any authority other than the authority by whom such fund or pool is maintained on and after the appointed day—

(a) sums which would have become due and owing to the fund or pool shall be paid by the authority first mentioned to the authority last mentioned:

Provided that the authorities concerned and the lender may agree for the transfer to the authority first mentioned of the liability with respect to any outstanding loan;

(b) the outstanding amount in respect of any such advances shall be shown in the accounts of the authority first mentioned as loans from other local authorities and as advances to the appropriate borrowing account, and in the accounts of the authority last mentioned as loans to other authorities.

(5) In relation to a London borough, any provision of this regulation which applies to the corporation of the borough shall be given effect to by the borough council.

Schemes for the allocation of officers for transfer—Local authorities

67.—(1) Schemes for the allocation of officers for transfer shall be made by the councils of counties, districts, London boroughs, parishes and communities, the Greater London Council and the Common Council in accordance with the provisions of this regulation and regulation 69.

(2)(a) Where the area of any authority to be dissolved by the order is not transferred as a whole to the area of one relevant authority a scheme for the allocation of all their officers for transfer shall be made by the first-mentioned authority unless the relevant authorities other than one notify the first-mentioned authority that no officers need be allocated for transfer to them.

(b) In sub-paragraph (a), "relevant authorities" means, in relation to any authority described in column (1) of the following table, the authorities specified in respect thereof in column (2).

(a) S.I. 1974/520 (1974 I, p. 1986).

TABLE

(1)	(2)
The council of any county	The councils of the counties in which the area of the county is to be comprised, and if any area of the county is to be comprised in Greater London the Greater London Council
The council of any district or London borough	The councils of the districts and London boroughs in which the area of the district or London borough is to be comprised, and if any area of a London borough is to be comprised in the City the Common Council
The parish authority of any parish or the community council of any community	The parish authorities of the parishes, and the community councils of communities with such councils, in which the area of the parish or community is to be comprised

(c) In sub-paragraph (a), the reference to all the officers of the authority does not include—

(i) any person who will by virtue of any agreement entered into between him and any authority enter into the employment of that authority before or on the appointed day; and

(ii) any person as regards any employment which, otherwise than by virtue of the dissolution of the authority, is to be terminated before or on the appointed day.

(3) Where any non-metropolitan county is to become a metropolitan county, with or without any alteration in its area, a scheme for the allocation of officers for transfer to the councils of the districts in the county shall be made by the council of the county.

(4) Where the area of any non-metropolitan district is to be wholly or substantially comprised in a metropolitan county, a scheme for the allocation of officers of the council of the non-metropolitan county for transfer to the councils of the metropolitan county and district shall be made by the council of the non-metropolitan county.

(5) Where any metropolitan district is to be wholly or substantially comprised in a non-metropolitan county a scheme for the allocation of officers for transfer to the council of the non-metropolitan county shall be made by the council of the district unless the council of the county notify the council of the district that no officers need be allocated for transfer to them.

(6) A scheme for the allocation of officers for transfer may be made by any council described in paragraph (1) in any other circumstances in which they consider it appropriate to make a scheme and shall be made by such a council if they are notified by any other such council that they require a scheme to be made.

(7) Nothing in this regulation applies to—

any member of a police force;

any officer of a county council employed for police purposes, including the purposes of section 81 of the Road Traffic Regulation Act 1967; or

any member of a fire brigade.

(8) Subject to paragraphs (2)(*c*) and (7), paragraph (2)(*a*), in its application to any authority, applies to any officer who, immediately before the appointed day, will be in the employment of the authority.

Schemes for the allocation of officers for transfer—Other authorities

68. A scheme for the allocation of officers (other than the officers specified in regulation 67(7)) for transfer may be made by any authority to whom regulation 67 does not apply but who are affected by the order.

Provision as to schemes

69.—(1) Any scheme made under regulation 67 or 68 or under any provision of the order shall allocate the officers covered by it on the basis of the likely needs of the services to be provided on and after the appointed day.

(2) In any scheme made under regulation 67 any arrangements made under section 101 or 110 of the Local Government Act 1972, or any direction given under the said section 110, shall be taken into account.

(3) In preparing any scheme under regulation 67 or 68 or under any provision of the order an authority shall—

(*a*) consult the authorities and bodies representative of officers appearing to them to be concerned; and—

(*b*) (i) notify any officer likely to be allocated for transfer otherwise than to the residuary successor of the authority of such likelihood and supply to him a copy of regulations 67 to 79; and

(ii) take into consideration any representations made by such officer.

(4) Upon making any such scheme an authority shall—

(*a*) transmit copies thereof to the authorities and bodies representative of officers appearing to them to be concerned; and

(*b*) notify every officer allocated of such allocation and (unless such copy has already been supplied) supply to him a copy of regulations 67 to 79.

(5) Any such scheme may be amended by the authority by whom it was made, but—

no substantive amendment shall be made in a matter in respect of which there has been no consultation under paragraph (3) with any authority or body representative of staff appearing to the first-mentioned authority to be concerned without such consultation; and

no officer shall be allocated for transfer unless the action described in paragraph (3)(*b*) has been taken in relation to him.

Upon making any amendment an authority shall—

(*a*) transmit copies of the scheme as amended or of the amendments to the authorities and bodies representative of officers appearing to them to be concerned; and

(*b*) notify every officer affected by the amendments of his allocation and (unless such copy has already been supplied) supply him with a copy of regulations 67 to 79.

(6) If notice is given by any authority that they are dissatisfied with the provisions of any such scheme as made or amended the question shall be determined by agreement between the authorities concerned or failing such agreement by the decision of a person agreed on by such authorities or in default of agreement appointed by the Secretary of State.

Upon any determination which involves a variation of the scheme the authority by whom the scheme was made shall vary it in accordance with the determination and—

(a) transmit copies of the scheme as amended or of the amendments to the authorities and bodies representative of staff appearing to them to be concerned; and

(b) notify every officer affected by the variation of his allocation and (unless such copy has already been supplied) supply him with a copy of regulations 67 to 79.

(7) In the application of paragraph (2)(a), (3), (4), (5) or (6) of regulation 67, regulation 68 or any provision of the order to any authority, any allocation of a person not in the whole-time employment of the authority shall be limited to the extent of his employment with the authority.

(8) Any question by an officer of any authority in relation to the application of a scheme to him may be determined in accordance with the arrangements applicable to the determination of disputes as to employment and terms and conditions thereof between the officer and the authority, and on the determination of such question by any body, any necessary amendment of the scheme shall be made by that body.

(9) No scheme made under any provision of the order shall extend to the officers specified in regulation 67(7).

Transfer of officers

70.—(1) Every officer allocated by any scheme made under regulation 67 or 68 or under any provision of the order for transfer to any authority shall, to the extent of the allocation, be transferred to the employment of that authority.

(2) (a) Any other officer of the council of a county, district or London borough or of the Greater London Council or the Common Council employed in the discharge of functions which will after the appointed day be exercisable in an area transferred by the order by another such council, and

(i) being so employed wholly or mainly in premises which will be transferred by regulation 62 to such other council; or

(ii) operating wholly or mainly from such premises; or

(iii) being otherwise so employed wholly or substantially so in relation to the area transferred,

shall on the appointed day be transferred to the employment of such other council.

Sub-paragraphs (b) to (d) shall have effect in the application of this sub-paragraph.

(b) Where on the appointed day any officer has not taken up the duties of his employment he shall be deemed to be employed in, or to be operating from, the premises in which he would be employed or from which he would be operating if he had taken up such duties.

(c) Where any officer is on the appointed day absent from his normal duties for the purposes of undergoing training sub-paragraph (a) shall apply—

(i) if it was part of the arrangements under which he is so absent that at the completion of such training he should be employed in a place, situation or employment different from the place, situation or employment which he occupied prior to the commencement of the training, as if he was, on the appointed day, occupying such different place, situation or employment;

(ii) otherwise as if he was, on the appointed day, occupying the place, situation or employment which he occupied immediately prior to the commencement of such training.

(*d*) Where any officer is on the appointed day absent from his normal duties otherwise than for the purpose of undergoing training he shall be deemed to be discharging such duties, and to be discharging them in, or from, the premises in, or from, which he normally discharges them.

(3) Any other officer of a dissolved authority (other than charter trustees) shall be transferred to the employment of the residuary successor of that authority.

(4) Nothing in paragraph (2) or (3) applies to any person described in (i) or (ii) of sub-paragraph (2)(*c*) of regulation 67 or in paragraph (7) of that regulation.

(5) Subject to paragraph (4), paragraph (2) or (3), in its application to any authority, applies to any officer who immediately before the appointed day is in the employment of the authority, but in the case of a person not in the whole-time employment of the authority the transfer effected by such paragraph in such application is limited to the extent of his employment with the authority.

(6) Any officer who will be transferred by paragraph (2) or (3) shall be notified by the authority employing him of such transfer not later than one month before the appointed day, and (unless such copy has already been supplied) shall be supplied with a copy of regulations 67 to 79.

(7) (*a*) The following questions by an officer of any authority, namely—
    (i) any question of hardship; and
    (ii) any question whether he is or is not employed in any manner specified in paragraph (2)(*a*);
may be determined in accordance with the arrangements applicable to the determination of disputes as to employment and terms and conditions thereof between the officer and the authority.

(*b*) Any question described in item (ii) of sub-paragraph (*a*) shall be raised as soon as may be and in any case not later than the expiration of 2 months (or such longer period as may be agreed by the authority) from the notification under paragraph (6).

(*c*) Where any question described in sub-paragraph (*a*) has been determined before the appointed day in such manner that no transfer of the officer is appropriate the officer shall not be transferred by this regulation.

(*d*) Where any such question is so determined in such manner that a transfer of the officer otherwise than in accordance with the provisions of paragraphs (1) to (3) is appropriate the officer shall be transferred on the appointed day in accordance with the determination.

(*e*) Where any such question is determined on or after the appointed day in such manner that a transfer or further transfer of the officer is appropriate the officer shall be transferred in accordance with the determination at the expiration of 28 days from the date thereof or such other date as may be agreed by the authorities concerned and the officer.

(*f*) Where it is determined that an officer will sustain or has sustained hardship in consequence of his transfer (and sub-paragraph (*c*), (*d*) or (*e*) is not applicable) the authority to whom he will be or has been transferred shall in consultation with the officer and representatives of their employees seek a remedy and, not later than the expiration of one month (or such longer period as may be agreed by the officer) following the notification of the determination, notify the officer of any remedy which they are able to offer him or that they are unable to offer him any remedy but that an allowance would be paid to him in respect of the hardship.

(g) In either event, the officer shall be informed that he may, subject to sub-paragraph (j), request that his employment be terminated and of his entitlements if it is so terminated.

(h) Any remedy offered under sub-paragraph (f) may be accepted by the officer within the 2 months following the notification thereof, or within such longer period as may be agreed by the authority.

(i) An allowance in respect of hardship shall be by periodic payments of such amount as may be determined by agreement between the officer and the authority or failing such agreement in accordance with the arrangements applicable to the determination of disputes as to employment and terms and conditions thereof between them.

(j) No such request as is described in sub-paragraph (g) shall be made after the expiration of 2 months from the determination of the amount of the periodic payments of the allowance.

(k) Regulation 77 shall not apply to any officer to whom an allowance is payable under this paragraph.

(l) If the remedy offered is, with the agreement of the authority from whose employment the officer was transferred, transfer back to the employment of that authority, and that remedy is accepted by the officer and he is so transferred, paragraph (12) of regulation 71, and regulations 72 to 78, shall cease to apply to him. Otherwise, such provisions shall apply to any officer transferred under sub-paragraph (f) as they apply to officers transferred by this regulation.

Protection of officers transferred

71.—(1) Every officer transferred by or under regulation 70 to the employment of any body (other than an officer transferred under paragraph (7)(f) of that regulation back to the employment of the authority from whose employment he was transferred) shall, so long as he continues in that employment by virtue of the transfer and until he is served with a statement in writing referring to these regulations and specifying new terms and conditions of employment, enjoy terms and conditions of employment not less favourable than those which he enjoyed immediately before the appointed day.

(2) A statement of new terms and conditions of employment shall not be served on any officer in relation to whom a question has been referred under regulation 70 (7) until the determination of the question has been notified.

A statement of new terms and conditions of employment shall not be served on any officer to whom sub-paragraphs (f) to (l) of regulation 70(7) apply until the remedy offered under the said sub-paragraph (f) or the allowance there referred to has been accepted by the officer.

(3) Subject to paragraph (2), a statement of new terms and conditions of employment may be served before the appointed day.

(4) Subject to paragraph (2), a statement of new terms and conditions of employment shall be served before the expiry of 12 months after the appointed day.

(5) If after service of a statement of new terms and conditions of employment upon any officer (whether before the appointed day or otherwise) a question is

referred under regulation 70(7), the statement shall cease to have effect and paragraphs (1) and (2) shall have effect as if the statement had not been served.

(6) The new terms and conditions of employment shall be such that—

(a) so long as the officer is engaged in duties reasonably comparable to those in which he was engaged immediately before the appointed day, the scale of his salary or remuneration is not less favourable than that which he enjoyed immediately before the appointed day; and

(b) the other terms and conditions of his employment are not less favourable than those which he enjoyed immediately before the appointed day.

(7) Where between the appointed day and the service of the statement of new terms and conditions of employment upon any officer the scale of the salary or remuneration which such officer enjoyed immediately before the appointed day is improved, paragraph (6)(a) shall have effect as if the scale as improved has been so enjoyed.

(8) Where the new terms and conditions of employment involve any diminution of the scale of the salary or remuneration of an officer they shall not come into effect until the date, not earlier than the expiration of 3 months from the service of the statement thereof, specified in that statement.

(9) Any question by an officer of any authority—

whether duties are reasonably comparable within the meaning of paragraph (6);

whether the scale of his salary or remuneration is such as is required by paragraphs (6) and (7); or

whether the other terms and conditions of his employment are not less favourable than those which he enjoyed immediately before the appointed day,

shall be determined in accordance with the arrangements applicable to the determination of disputes as to employment and terms and conditions thereof between the officer and the authority.

(10) In this regulation, "terms and conditions of employment" includes any restriction arising under any Act or any instrument made under any Act on the termination of the employment of any officer.

(11) A written statement given in accordance with section 4(1) of the Contracts of Employment Act 1972(a) shall not be regarded as a statement of new terms and conditions of employment for the purposes of this regulation unless the statement so indicates.

(12) A notice to terminate the contract of employment of any officer transferred by regulation 70, given by reason of the fact that the officer to whom it is given has become redundant in consequence of the order, shall, unless such officer otherwise agrees, not come into operation earlier than the expiration of 3 months from the service thereof.

Secondary transfers

72. Any officer transferred by regulation 70 to the employment of any authority may, within the 2 years following the appointed day, be transferred

---

(a) 1972 c. 53.

by the said authority, with the agreement of any other authority, and of the officer, to the employment of that other authority, and regulation 71 shall thereupon apply to such officer as it applies to officers transferred by regulation 70.

Apprenticeships

73. Any contract of apprenticeship entered into between any person and a dissolved authority shall have effect as a contract entered into between such person and the authority to whose employment he is transferred by regulation 70 or under regulation 72 or would have been so transferred if he had been in the employment of such dissolved authority.

Saving for training arrangements

74. Where any officer transferred by regulation 70 or under regulation 72 is undergoing training under arrangements which have not been discharged before the appointed day, those arrangements shall continue to apply with the substitution, for the authority in whose employment the officer was prior to the commencement of the training, of the authority to whose employment he has been transferred as aforesaid.

Saving for dispensations

75. Any dispensation from the requirements of any Act or of any instrument made under any Act granted to the authority from whom any officer is transferred by regulation 70 or under regulation 72 shall have effect, in relation to such officer, as if it had been granted to the authority to whose employment he has been transferred as aforesaid.

Saving for extensions of service

76. Any extension of service under regulation L.15 of the Local Government Superannuation Regulations 1974 effective on the appointed day in relation to an officer transferred by regulation 70 or under regulation 72 shall continue to have effect as if it had been made by the authority to whose employment he has been transferred as aforesaid.

Travelling and removal expenses

77. Any additional travelling expenses, and any removal or incidental expenses, reasonably incurred by any officer in consequence of the order shall be reimbursed by the authority to whose employment he is transferred by regulation 70 or under regulation 72.

Commencing points on scales

78. Where in relation to any officer—

(*a*) on the scale of salary or remuneration applicable to him immediately before the appointed day he would have become entitled to an increment on that day; and

(*b*) by reason of any appointment effective as from the appointed day made by the authority to whose employment he is transferred by regulation 70 or under regulation 72, any other scale of salary or remuneration becomes applicable to him as from that day,

any term of his employment as to his commencing point on such other scale shall be applicable as if his employment before, and on and after, the said day were one continuous employment under one authority.

Continuity of employment

79. Where, apart from this regulation, a person's continuity of employment would be broken by any transfer referred to in (*a*) or (*b*) then nevertheless, for the purposes of the Redundancy Payments Act 1965**(a)**, section 28 of the Industrial Relations Act 1971**(b)** as re-enacted in paragraph 10 of Schedule 1 to the Trade Union and Labour Relations Act 1974**(c)** (qualifying period for protection from unfair dismissal), sections 1 and 2 of the Contracts of Employment Act 1972 (minimum periods of notice) and section 61 of the Employment Protection Act 1975**(d)**—

> (*a*) the period of his employment in the employment from which he is transferred by paragraph (1), (2), (3) or (7)(*d*) or (*e*) of regulation 70 and the period of his employment in the employment to which he is transferred by such provision shall in the case of an officer further transferred by or under paragraph (7)(*e*) or (*f*) of the said regulation or under regulation 72 count as a period of employment in the employment to which he is so further transferred;

> (*b*) the period of his employment in the employment from which he is transferred by paragraph (1), (2), (3) or (7)(*d*) or (*e*) of regulation 70 shall in the case of any other officer so transferred count as a period of employment in the employment to which he is so transferred; and

> (*c*) no change of employment covered by (*a*) or (*b*) shall break the continuity of the period of employment.

Appointment of officers before appointed day

80.—(1) Where before the appointed day the local authority for any area established or altered by the order appoint to hold any office or employment before or as from that day any person (hereinafter referred to as "the officer") who is in the employment of the local authority for any area so altered or abolished, the appointment shall be on such terms and conditions that—

> (*a*) so long as the officer is engaged in duties reasonably comparable to those in which he was engaged immediately before the appointment, the scale of his salary or remuneration; and

> (*b*) the other terms and conditions of his employment,

are not less favourable than those he enjoyed immediately before the appointment.

Any question by the officer—

> whether duties are reasonably comparable as aforesaid; or

> whether the scale of his salary or remuneration or the other terms and conditions of his employment are not less favourable than those which he enjoyed immediately before the appointment,

shall be determined in accordance with the arrangements applicable to the determination of disputes as to employment and terms and conditions thereof between the officer and the first-mentioned authority.

In this paragraph, "terms and conditions of employment" includes any restriction arising under any Act or any instrument made under any Act on the termination of the employment of any officer.

(a) 1965 c. 62.   **(b)** 1971 c. 72.
(c) 1974 c. 52.   **(d)** 1975 c. 71.

(2) This paragraph may be applied by the order in respect of any authority (hereinafter referred to as "the new employing authority") and of any authority specified in relation thereto (hereinafter referred to as "the existing employing authority") and in this paragraph "the officer" means a person appointed as mentioned in paragraph (1).

The appointment of an officer to hold any office or employment before the appointed day shall not result in his employment by the new employing authority until that day, and his employment by the existing employing authority shall continue to that day, unless determined otherwise than by reason of the said appointment; and—

(a) the existing employing authority shall place the services of the officer at the disposal of the new employing authority to such extent as may be agreed between the said authorities;

(b) the salary or remuneration payable by the existing employing authority to the officer at any time shall be the aggregate of the following amounts, namely—

    (i) the amount of the salary or remuneration which would have been payable by the existing employing authority apart from their action under (a) hereof which is for the time being agreed between the existing employing authority and the officer to be appropriate having regard to such action; and

    (ii) the amount for the time being agreed between the new employing authority and the officer in respect of the office or employment; and

(c) the new employing authority shall reimburse to the existing employing authority—

    (i) the amounts described in (b)(ii) hereof paid by the existing employing authority; and

    (ii) such proportion of all other payments to or in respect of the officer as may be agreed between the said authorities or, failing such agreement, as may be determined by a person agreed on by them or in default of agreement appointed by the Secretary of State:

Provided that the said authorities may, in any particular case, agree that no reimbursement shall be made.

(3) Paragraphs (1) and (2) shall apply, where an officer appointed by the new employing authority is in the employment of two or more existing employing authorities, and paragraph (1) shall apply, where the officer is in two or more employments of one such authority, as if he were only in the employment in respect of which there is paid to him the highest salary or remuneration, or if two or more salaries or remunerations are equal such employment as the new employing authority shall determine.

(4) Where an adjustment of superannuation funds is required to be made in respect of any person to whom paragraphs (1) to (3) apply and in consequence of action taken under those paragraphs his remuneration is higher or lower than it would have been if those paragraphs had not applied to him, no account shall be taken of that increase or decrease in determining his remuneration for the purposes of calculating the amount payable by way of adjustment but the said amount shall be increased or decreased as the case may be by a sum equivalent to the aggregate of the contributions payable or which would have been payable

by the employing authority and the employee in respect of the amount by which his remuneration was increased or decreased during the period for which the said paragraphs apply to him.

Gratuities and pensions

81.—(1) Where at any time before the appointed day a gratuity or allowance, by way of periodical payment or an annuity—

(*a*) has been granted to any person by any authority on his ceasing to be employed by them; or

(*b*) has been granted to the widow or other dependant of a person who died while in or after leaving the employment of any authority,

and, if payment in respect of the gratuity or allowance had continued in accordance with the terms of the grant or any subsequent increase, one or more payments would have been made on or after the appointed day (whether under legal obligation or otherwise) by a dissolved authority, those payments shall be made by the specified authority.

(2) Without prejudice to paragraph (1), where, if the order had not been made, any dissolved authority would for the purposes of any statutory provision relating to pensions have been the employing authority or former employing authority in relation to a person who died before the appointed day while in the employment of, or otherwise ceased to be employed by, any authority, or the widow or other dependant of such a person, the specified authority shall be treated as being at that time the employing authority or former employing authority for those purposes in relation to that person, his widow or other dependant.

(3) In paragraphs (1) and (2), "the specified authority" means—

(*a*) if the person described in (*a*) or (*b*) of paragraph (1) or in paragraph (2) was—

    (i) in the case of a person who died while in the employment of the authority, last employed before he died; or

    (ii) otherwise, last employed before he ceased to hold the employment referred to,

exclusively in the discharge of functions in relation to any area transferred by the order and those functions are, on and after the appointed day, exercisable in relation to that area by an authority other than the residuary successor of the dissolved authority, that other authority; and

(*b*) otherwise, the residuary successor of the dissolved authority.

Inspection of documents

82.—(1) This regulation shall apply in the circumstances set out in the entries in column (1) of the following table and in this regulation "transferred area" means an area described in any such entry, and—

"transferor authority", in relation to any transferred area, means an authority specified in respect of the area in column (2) in whose area the transferred area is comprised before the appointed day; and

"transferee authority", in relation to any transferred area, means an authority specified in respect of the transferor authority in column (3) in whose area the transferred area is comprised on and after the appointed day.

TABLE

(1)	(2)	(3)
Where an area is transferred from a metropolitan county and district to a non-metropolitan county and district	The county council The district council	The county council { The county council The district council
Where an area is transferred from a non-metropolitan county and district to a metropolitan county and district	The county council The district council	{ The county council The district council The district council
Where an area is otherwise transferred from a county and district to another county and district	The county council The district council	The county council The district council
Where an area is transferred from a district to another district in the same county	The district council	The district council
Where an area is transferred from a county and district to Greater London and a London borough	The county council The district council }	{ The Greater London Council The London borough council
Where an area is transferred from Greater London and a London borough to a county and district	The Greater London Council The London borough council }	{ The county council The district council
Where an area is transferred from a London borough to another such borough	The London borough council	The London borough council
Where an area is transferred from a London borough to the City, the Inner Temple or the Middle Temple	The London borough council	The Common Council The Sub-Treasurer The Under Treasurer
Where an area is transferred from the City, the Inner Temple or the Middle Temple to a London borough	The Common Council The Sub-Treasurer The Under Treasurer }	{ The Greater London Council The London borough council
Where an area is transferred from the City to the Inner Temple or the Middle Temple	The Common Council	The Sub-Treasurer The Under Treasurer
Where an area is transferred from the Inner Temple or the Middle Temple to the City	The Sub-Treasurer The Under Treasurer }	The Common Council
Where an area is transferred from a parish or community to another such area	The parish authority or community council or where in Wales there is no community council the district council	The parish authority or community council or where in Wales there is no community council the district council
Where an area in England becomes or becomes part of a parish	The district council	The parish authority
Where an area in England ceases to be part of any parish	The parish authority	The district council

(2) As from the coming into operation of the order any officer of a transferee authority, duly authorised in that behalf, shall for the purposes of the functions of the authority by whom he is employed, be entitled during ordinary office hours to inspect and take copies of or extracts from any books or documents of a transferor authority relating to the transferred area not in the custody of the transferee authority, and a transferor authority shall supply such information and afford such assistance in relation to such books and documents as a transferee authority may reasonably require.

(3) In relation to any highways in an area transferred from a district to another district in the same county—

(a) if such highways are immediately before the appointed day being maintained by the district council by virtue of section 187(2)(a) of the Local Government Act 1972 but will on and after that day be maintained by the county council, paragraph (2) shall apply as if the county council were a transferee authority; and

(b) if such highways are immediately before the appointed day being maintained by the county council but will on and after that day be maintained by the district council by virtue of the said section 187(2)(a), paragraph (2) shall apply as if the county council were a transferor authority.

Minutes of last meetings

83.—(1) This regulation shall apply to any dissolved authority other than parish trustees and to the committees and sub-committees thereof.

(2) The minutes of the last meeting of any body to whom this regulation applies shall if practicable be signed at such meeting.

(3) If it is not practicable for the minutes to be so signed they may be signed by the person who presided at the meeting in accordance with paragraph (4), (5) or (6), and—

(a) any minute purporting to be so signed shall be received in evidence without further proof; and

(b) until the contrary is proved, the meeting in respect of the proceedings whereof a minute has been made and so signed shall be deemed to have been duly convened and held, and all the members present at the meeting shall be deemed to have been duly qualified, and where the proceedings are the proceedings of a committee or sub-committee the committee or sub-committee shall be deemed to have been duly consti-tuted and to have had power to deal with the matters referred to in the minutes.

(4) Minutes of the proceedings of the last meeting of any body to whom this regulation applies other than a committee or sub-committee or a parish meeting may be signed as aforesaid on or after the 7th day following the transmission to every member of the body of a copy of the minutes and of a notification of the purport of paragraph (3) and this paragraph. The person who presided at the meeting shall take into consideration any representations made by any such member.

(5) Minutes of the proceedings of the last meeting of a committee or sub-committee may be signed as aforesaid on or after the 7th day following the transmission to every member of the committee or sub-committee of a notifica-tion of the purport of paragraph (3) and this paragraph, with a copy of the minutes or information as to the availability of a copy for inspection. The person

who presided at the meeting shall take into consideration any representations made by any such member.

(6) Minutes of the proceedings of the last meeting of a parish meeting may be signed as aforesaid after such consultation as the person presiding at the meeting shall think appropriate.

(7) If the person who presided at the meeting is not able to sign the minutes in accordance with paragraph (4), (5) or (6), paragraph (3) and such paragraph shall have effect with the substitution for any reference to the person who presided at the meeting of a reference to such person as the Secretary of State may direct.

General provision as to disputes

84.—(1) Any question as to the interpretation of these regulations (other than regulation 24) or of the order may be determined by the decision of a person agreed on by the authorities concerned or in default of agreement appointed by the Secretary of State.

(2) Where a determination required by any provision in Part II of Schedule 6 has not been made by the transferor authority before the appointed day notice that a question exists may be given within the 12 months following the appointed day by any authority concerned.

(3) Where—

    (*a*) at the appointed day—

        (i) notice has been given by any authority under any provision in Part II of Schedule 6; or

        (ii) notice has been given by any authority that the interpretation of any provision made by paragraphs (2) or (3) of regulation 62 is in dispute;

    and the question has not been determined; or

    (*b*) thereafter, but within the 12 months following the appointed day—

        (i) notice is given by any authority under any provision in Part II of Schedule 6;

        (ii) notice is so given under paragraph (2); or

        (iii) notice is so given that the interpretation of any provision made by paragraphs (2) or (3) of regulation 62 is in dispute,

then from the appointed day or from the later day on which the notice is given, as the case may be—

    (*k*) paragraph (2) of regulation 62 shall cease to have effect in relation to the property;

    (*l*) where the transferor authority is dissolved by the order, paragraph (3) of that regulation shall apply to the property and to any liabilities incurred, contracts, deeds, bonds, agreements and other instruments subsisting, notices given, actions and proceedings pending and causes of action or proceeding existing in relation thereto, as temporary provision pending the determination of the question:

    Provided that the authorities concerned may by instrument in writing agree that any authority may in such application be substituted for the residuary successor of the dissolved authority;

    (*m*) where notice has been given under paragraph (2), the question shall be determined by agreement between the authorities concerned or failing such agreement by the decision of a person agreed on by such authorities or in default of agreement appointed by the Secretary of State; and

(*n*) on the determination of the question whether under (*m*) or otherwise—

(*x*) the determination shall specify the authority to whom the property is to be transferred; and

(*y*) if paragraph (3) of regulation 62 has been applied by (*l*) it shall cease to have effect; and

(*z*) the property shall by virtue of the determination be transferred to and vest in the authority specified in the determination, and the provisions of these regulations which would have applied to the property if the transfer had been effected by paragraph (2) of regulation 62 shall apply to it.

(4) Any reference in any provision of these regulations for the decision of any question by a person shall be construed as including a reference to three persons.

(5) Section 31 of the Arbitration Act 1950(a) shall have effect for the purposes of the determination of any question by any person or persons under any provision of these regulations as if such determination were an arbitration under any other Act within the meaning of that section.

General savings

85.—(1) Nothing in these regulations or the order shall affect—

(*a*) the definition of any parliamentary constituency, the division of any parliamentary constituency into polling districts or the designation of polling places;

(*b*) any ecclesiastical parish or district;

(*c*) the area for the supply of electricity of any Area Electricity Board;

(*d*) the area for any purposes of any water authority;

(*e*) the area for the supply of water of any company;

(*f*) the functions of the conservators of any common;

(*g*) any order in force under the Shops Act 1950(b);

(*h*) any inquest begun before the appointed day;

(*i*) any right or interest under any inclosure award.

(2) Save as provided in the order, nothing in these regulations or the order shall affect—

(*a*) any electoral area;

(*b*) any petty sessions area or coroner's district;

(*c*) the trusts of any charity.

(a) 1950 c. 27.   (b) 1950 c. 28.

Regulation 19   SCHEDULE 1

PETTY SESSIONS AREAS

PART I

PROVISIONS APPLYING WHERE AN AREA IS TRANSFERRED FROM
ONE PETTY SESSIONS AREA TO ANOTHER SUCH AREA

1. In this Part, "transferred area" means an area transferred from one petty sessions area to another such area, and—

"community service order" means an order made under section 14 of the Powers of Criminal Courts Act 1973(a);

"probation order" means a probation order made or having effect as if made under section 2 of that Act;

"supervision order" means any of the following orders, namely—

a supervision order within the meaning of section 11 of the Children and Young Persons Act 1969(b) or to which paragraph 12 of Schedule 4 to that Act applies;

an order under section 2(1)(f) of the Matrimonial Proceedings (Magistrates' Courts) Act 1960(c);

an order under section 2(2)(a) of the Guardianship Act 1973(d);

a supervision order within the meaning of section 26 of the Powers of Criminal Courts Act 1973;

"the transferor area" means the petty sessions area from which the transferred area is transferred, and "the transferor justices" means the justices who ordinarily act for such petty sessions area; and

"the transferee area" means the petty sessions area to which the transferred area is transferred, and "the transferee justices" means the justices who will, on and after the appointed day, ordinarily act for such petty sessions area.

2. Subject to the following paragraphs, any process issued, order made, sentence passed, appeal brought, case stated, licence granted, recognizance entered into, proceeding begun, appointment made or other thing done before the appointed day by, from, to or before any of the transferor justices in relation to any matter arising in or concerning the transferred area, shall, on and after that day, be deemed to have been issued, made, passed, brought, stated, granted, entered into, begun or done by, from, to or before the transferee justices or their clerk, as the case may be.

3. Any order made, licence granted or other thing done under the Licensing Act 1964 by the transferor justices in relation to any premises in the transferred area, being an order or licence in force or other thing having effect immediately before the appointed day, shall continue to have like effect on and after that day as if the order had not been made but shall be treated as if it had been made, granted or done by the transferee justices.

4. Anything done under the Betting, Gaming and Lotteries Act 1963(e) or the Gaming Act 1968(f) by or in relation to the betting licensing committee for the transferor area in relation to any matter arising in or concerning the transferred area, being a thing having effect immediately before the appointed day, shall continue to have effect on or after that day as if the order had not been made but shall be treated as if it had been done by or in relation to the betting licensing committee for the transferee area; and anything done under either of those Acts by or in relation to any other person or body shall have effect accordingly.

5.—(1) Any order made by a magistrates' court directing the payment of money to the clerk or any other officer of a magistrates' court acting for the transferor area,

---

(a) 1973 c. 62.   (b) 1969 c. 54.   (c) 1960 c. 48.   (d) 1973 c. 29.
(e) 1963 c. 2.   (f) 1968 c. 65.

SCHEDULE 1—*continued*

in relation to any matter arising in or concerning the transferred area, shall have effect as if it had directed payment to be made to the clerk to the justices for the transferee area.

(2) Where on the appointed day periodical payments are by virtue of sub-paragraph (1) payable under section 52 of the Magistrates' Courts Act 1952(a) through the clerk to the justices for the transferor area to a person who resides outside that area, in relation to any matter arising in or concerning the transferred area, the said clerk may amend the order so as to require payments to be made through the clerk to the justices for the transferee area and, if he does so, shall give notice of the amendment to the person entitled to the payments, to the person required to make the payments and to the justices' clerk for the transferee area.

6. Where the transferor area is named in a community service order, probation order or supervision order, and the person named in the order is immediately before the appointed day residing in the transferred area, the powers and functions of the transferor justices in relation to the order shall vest in and be discharged by the transferee justices, and the order, unless amended in regard to the petty sessions area named therein, shall have effect in all respects as if the transferee area were named therein.

7. Any process, records or other document in relation to any matter arising in or concerning the transferred area in the custody, by virtue of his office as such, of the clerk to the justices for the transferor a. a shall—

    (*a*) if such clerk is the clerk to the justices for the transferee area, be retained by him in that capacity;

    (*b*) otherwise, be transferred by him to the clerk to the justices for the transferee area.

Copies of or extracts from any such record or document made or certified by the clerk to the justices for the transferee area shall be of the same effect as if they had been made or certified by the clerk to the justices for the transferor area.

Part II

Provision Applying where a Petty Sessions Area Ceases to Exist

Where a community service order, probation order or supervision order (within the meanings set out in paragraph 1 of Part I) is in force, and the offender, probationer or person under supervision is residing outside any area transferred by the order, the justices for any petty sessions area may amend the order in regard to the petty sessions area named therein as if the offender, probationer or person under supervision, as the case may be, had changed his residence.

Part III

Provisions Applying where a Petty Sessions Area is Constituted

1. The justices for the area shall appoint, in the prescribed manner, so far as may be applicable, and for the prescribed term, to take office on the appointed day—

    (*a*) a chairman and one or more deputy chairmen;

    (*b*) a juvenile court panel;

    (*c*) one or more case committees;

    (*d*) a justice or justices to serve as member of the magistrates' courts committee for the county or London commission area;

    (*e*) a divisional licensing committee; and

(a) 1952 c. 55.

SCHEDULE 1—*continued*

(*f*) a betting licensing committee.

In this paragraph, "the prescribed manner" and "the prescribed term" mean respectively—

(i) in relation to the election of a chairman or deputy chairman, the manner prescribed by rules made under section 13 of the Justices of the Peace Act 1949(a) and a term ending at the expiration of the month of December next following the appointed day;

(ii) in relation to the election of the juvenile court panel, the manner prescribed by rules made under section 15 of that Act and a term ending at the expiration of the month of October in 1976, 1979 or a third year thereafter;

(iii) in relation to the appointment of a case committee, the manner prescribed by rules made or having effect as if made under Schedule 3 to the Powers of Criminal Courts Act 1973 and a term ending at the expiration of the month of December next following the appointed day;

(iv) in relation to the appointment of a member of the magistrates' courts committee, the manner prescribed by regulations made under Schedule 4 to the Justices of the Peace Act 1949 and a term ending at the expiration of the month of November next following the appointed day;

(v) in relation to the appointment of the divisional licensing committee, the manner prescribed by Part I of Schedule 1 to the Licensing Act 1964 and a term ending at the expiration of the month of December next following the appointed day; and

(vi) in relation to the appointment of the betting licensing committee, the manner prescribed by the Betting (Licensing) Regulations 1960(b) and a term ending at the expiration of the month of December next following the appointed day.

2. In relation to the appointment of a justices' clerk for the area, any consultation with the justices for the area required by section 19(9) of the Justices of the Peace Act 1949 may take place before the appointed day.

(a) 1949 c. 101.   (b) S.I. 1960/1701 (1960 I, p. 363).

SCHEDULE 2

Regulation 28

FAMILY PRACTITIONER SERVICES

1. In this Schedule "the transferred area" means the area transferred from the rea of one area health authority (hereinafter referred to as "the transferor authority") o the area of another such authority (hereinafter referred to as "the transferee uthority"), and—

"the Secretary of State" means the Secretary of State for Social Services or the Secretary of State for Wales;

"the transferor area" means the area of the transferor authority and "the transferor committee" means the family practitioner committee established for that area; and

"the transferee area" means the area of the transferee authority and "the transferee committee" means the family practitioner committee established for that area.

2. Subject to the following paragraphs—

(a) all arrangements for the provision of general medical services, general dental services, general ophthalmic services and pharmaceutical services made by the transferor committee shall, so far as they relate to the transferred area, remain of full force and effect as if made on behalf of the transferee authority by the transferee committee;

(b) any decision given before the appointed day by the local medical committee, local dental committee, local optical committee or local pharmaceutical committee for the transferor area shall, in so far as it relates to the transferred area, have effect as if it had been given by the corresponding committee for the transferee area; and

(c) any reference in any instrument to the local medical committee, local dental committee, local optical committee or local pharmaceutical committee for the transferor area shall, in so far as it relates to the transferred area, have effect as if it had been a reference to the corresponding committee for the transferee area.

3. Any services provided as part of general medical services, general dental services, general ophthalmic services or pharmaceutical services which have been commenced in the transferred area but not completed before the appointed day, and any matters arising in consequence of such services completed before that day, may be continued with the substitution for the transferor committee, as regards any responsibility for the administration (including payment) of those services, of the transferee committee.

4. Any proceedings under Part II of the National Health Service (Service Committees and Tribunal) Regulations 1974(a) in relation to services provided before the appointed day in the transferred area may be instituted and carried on, or as the case may be, continued in all respects as if the order had not been made. Any direction for the withholding of remuneration following such proceedings may be given to such family practitioner committee as the Secretary of State may think fit.

5. Any proceedings before the transferor committee instituted before the appointed day for determining whether the replacement or repair of an appliance is necessitated—

(a) in the case of an optical appliance, by lack of care on the part of the person supplied; or

(b) in the case of a dental appliance, by an act or omission of the person supplied or (if it occurred when such person was under 16 years of age) of him or of the person having charge of him when it occurred;

shall where the practice premises given on the application for the replacement or repair of the appliance are situated in the transferred area be continued with the substitution for the transferor committee of the transferee committee.

(a) S.I. 1974/455 (1974 I, p. 1511).

SCHEDULE 2—*continued*

6. Any medical practitioner who immediately before the appointed day is included in the medical list of the transferor committee and who at that date—

(*a*) has a surgery in the transferred area, or

(*b*) has on his list any patient permanently residing in such area,

shall be entitled to be included in the medical list of the transferee committee for the provision of services in those parts of the transferred area in which he was entitled to provide services immediately before the appointed day.

7. Any practitioner who immediately before the appointed day is providing services under section 38(1) of the National Health Service Act 1946(a) as set out in section 42 of the National Health Service Reorganisation Act 1973(b) or under section 40 or 41 of the said Act of 1946 from premises within the transferred area shall be included in the dental, ophthalmic or pharmaceutical list, as appropriate, of the transferee committee.

8. Anything duly done by, and any application duly made, or direction, authorisation or notice duly given to—

(*a*) the Secretary of State;

(*b*) the transferor committee;

(*c*) the Prescription Pricing Authority;

(*d*) the Welsh Health Technical Services Organisation;

(*e*) the Dental Estimates Board; or

(*f*) any other body dealing with family practitioner services,

in connection with the exercise, by such body, of any function which, by virtue of directions given under section 7 of the National Health Service Reorganisation Act 1973 or of any other provision of that Act, is a function exercisable by an area health authority or family practitioner committee, shall, in so far as it relates to the transferred area, be deemed to have been duly done by, or made or given to, the body exercising such function on the appointed day in place of the body by which such thing was done or to which such application was made, or such direction, authorisation or notice was given.

9. Any instrument made by any of the bodies specified in paragraph 8, in so far as it was made in the exercise of any function referred to in that paragraph, shall continue in force until it is varied or revoked by the body exercising such function in place of the body by which such instrument was made.

10. Any form supplied by any of the bodies specified in paragraph 8 in the exercise, by such body, of a function which by virtue of any directions given under section 7 of the National Health Service Reorganisation Act 1973 or of any other provision of that Act is a function exercisable by an area health authority or a family practitioner committee shall continue to be a valid form in connection with the exercise of any function until it is cancelled or withdrawn by the Secretary of State or by the body exercising the function in place of the body by which the form was supplied, and as if any reference contained in such a form to a body by which the function was exercisable before the appointed day was a reference to the body exercising that function on and after that day.

(a) 1946 c. 81.   (b) 1973 c. 32.

SCHEDULE 3   Regulation 37

ROAD TRAFFIC AND HIGHWAYS

oad traffic orders and schemes

1. Any order or scheme made or having effect as if made under any provision f the Road Traffic Regulation Act 1967 or section 31 of the Road Traffic Act 972(a) by any authority shall, so far as it relates to any road in any area transferred y the order from the area of that authority, have effect as if it had been made by ne authority empowered to make such an order or scheme for the road on and fter the appointed day and if the power under which the order or scheme would ave been made by that authority is one different from the power under which it ʼas made as if it had been made under the power first mentioned.

2.—(1) Sub-paragraphs (2) to (4) shall apply in relation to—

parts of roads authorised for use as parking places under section 28 of the Road Traffic Regulation Act 1967; and

parking places on highways designated under section 35 (parking places where charges made) of that Act.

(2) In relation to such parking places in any area transferred to a county and district in Wales the reference in paragraph 1 to the authority empowered to make uch an order or scheme shall be construed—

in the case of an order made by a county council, as a reference to the council of the county to which the area is transferred;

in the case of an order made by a district council, as a reference to the council of the district to which the area is transferred.

(3) In relation to such parking places in any other area transferred to a district n Wales the said reference shall be construed, in the case of an order made by a district council, as a reference to the council of the district to which the area is transferred.

(4) In relation to such parking places in any area transferred to Greater London the said reference shall be construed as a reference to the Greater London Council.

3. Paragraphs 1 and 2 shall have effect subject to the provision of paragraph 4.

Division of instruments affecting highways

4. Where provision as respects any length of highway is contained in an instrument made, submitted or published in draft before the appointed day under any enactment and on and after that day parts of that length are situated in the areas of two or more authorities so that, if provision had been made on or after that day as respects that length, separate instruments made, submitted or published in draft by each of those authorities would have been required, then—

(*a*) the instrument shall have effect on and after the appointed day as such number of separate instruments as would then be required for that provision, each instrument relating to the part of that length of highway situated in the area of one authority and containing references to that authority instead of references to the authority by whom it was made, submitted or published in draft, and

(*b*) if the instrument is an order or scheme in relation to which some, but not all, of the necessary procedural steps have been taken before the appointed day—

(i) any notice given or published and any other document made or issued in connection with the order or scheme before that day shall similarly have effect on and after that day as such number of separate notices and documents (each containing references to the authority first mentioned in (*a*)) as may be requisite;

(a) 1972 c. 20.

SCHEDULE 3—*continued*

(ii) any remaining procedural steps required to be taken by the authority by whom the scheme was made, submitted or published in draft may be carried out separately by the several authorities concerned; and

(iii) the orders and schemes as made, confirmed or approved shall (so far as practicable) reflect the division into separate instruments.

General provisions relating to highways

5.—(1) This paragraph shall apply where—

(a) an area is transferred from the area of one highway authority to the area of another such authority; or

(b) an area is transferred from one district to another district in the same county, and in this paragraph "transferred area" means an area so transferred, and "the transferee district", in relation to any transferred area, means the district council to whose area the transferred area is transferred.

In the application of (a) to a county, district or London borough regulation 3(4) shall apply.

(2) Where, at the appointed day, in relation to any highway in a transferred area, under the provisions of any enactment or otherwise, any act has been done by, any notice or payment has been given or made to, or any right or duty has been conferred or imposed on—

(a) the highway authority in their capacity as highway authority for the highway; or

(b) the district council in their maintenance of the highway undertaken under section 187(2)(a) of the Local Government Act 1972,

then, on and after the appointed day, that act shall be deemed to have been done, that notice or payment shall be deemed to have been given or made, and that right or duty shall be deemed to have been conferred or imposed—

(i) if the act, notice, payment, right or duty relates to the maintenance of a highway which under regulation 36 or otherwise under section 187(2) of the Act the transferee district council are entitled to maintain, by, to or on that council;

(ii) otherwise, by, to or on the highway authority,

and accordingly any document comprising or relating to the act, notice, payment, right or duty shall have effect on and after the appointed day as if for any reference therein to the highway authority or district council mentioned in (a) or (b) there were substituted a reference to the district council or highway authority specified in (i) or (ii).

(3) Where, at the appointed day, in relation to any highway in a transferred area, under the provisions of any enactment, any act has been done by, any notice or payment has been given or made to, or any right or duty has been conferred or imposed on, a local authority (other than a parish council or community council) otherwise than as highway authority, then, subject to sub-paragraph (4), on and after the appointed day that act shall be deemed to have been done by, that notice or payment shall be deemed to have been given or made to, or that right or duty shall be deemed to have been conferred or imposed on, the specified authority, and accordingly any document comprising or relating to the act, notice, payment, right or duty shall have effect on and after the appointed day as if for any reference therein to the said local authority there were substituted a reference to the specified authority.

In this paragraph, "the specified authority" means the council of the county, district or London borough in which the highway is situated, or in the case of a highway situated in Greater London or the City the Greater London Council or the Common Council, by whom the function in connection with which the act was done, the notice was given, the payment was made or the right or duty was conferred or imposed becomes exercisable on and after the appointed day.

SCHEDULE 3—*continued*

(4) In a case where the function referred to in sub-paragraph (3) is exercisable on and after the appointed day either by the council of the county or the council of the district in which the highway is situated, that function shall be regarded for he purposes of that sub-paragraph as becoming exercisable—

> (a) by the district council alone, where the act was done by, the notice or payment was given or made to, or the right or duty was conferred or imposed on, a district council or a London borough council;

> (b) by the county council alone, where the act was done by, the notice or payment was given or made to, or the right or duty was conferred or imposed on, a county council or the Greater London Council.

This sub-paragraph shall apply to any act, notice, payment, right or duty which by virtue of article 6(2) and (3) of the Local Government (Road Traffic and Highways) Transitional Provisions) Order 1974 is deemed to have been done by, given or made to, or conferred or imposed on a county council or district council as if it had been done by, made or given to or conferred or imposed on such council.

(5) Sub-paragraphs (2) to (4) shall have effect subject to the provision of paragraph 4.

(6) In this paragraph—

> any reference to any act done by an authority shall include a reference to any scheme, order (other than any order to which regulation 44 applies), regulation, byelaw, agreement, requirement, application, apportionment or demand for payment made, resolution passed, charge conferred, authorisation granted, notice, direction, consent, approval, licence, permit or certificate given, building line or improvement line prescribed, or other thing done by that authority;

> any reference to any notice given to an authority shall include a reference to any direction, consent or approval given to that authority; and

> any reference to any right or duty conferred or imposed on an authority shall include a reference to an obligation assumed by or a requirement made upon or a deposit or lodgement made with that authority, a transfer of a highway to that authority or a provision for that authority to become the highway authority for a highway.

(7) In so far as provision is made by paragraphs 1, 2, 4 or 6 for any matter, the provisions of this paragraph shall not apply in relation to that matter.

Adaptation of certain agreements between Secretaries of State and local authorities

6.—(1) This paragraph applies to agreements made under section 10(1) and (4) of the Highways Act 1959, section 30(1) and (4) of the Local Government Act 1966**(a)** and section 27(1) and (3) of the Highways Act 1971**(b)** made before the appointed day between the Secretary of State for the Environment or the Secretary of State for Wales and a council described in column (1) of the following table and in force at the appointed day.

TABLE

(1)	(2)
The council of a county or the Greater London Council	The councils of counties and the Greater London Council
The council of a district or a London borough or the Common Council	The councils of districts and London boroughs and the Common Council

(a) 1966 c. 42.   **(b)** 1971 c. 41.

SCHEDULE 3—*continued*

(2) Where the matter to which the agreement applies is situated in a single transferred area, an agreement made between a Secretary of State and a council described in column (1) of the said table shall on and after the appointed day have effect as an agreement made between the Secretary of State and the authority specified in respect of the said council in column (2) to whose area the transferred area is transferred and as if for references therein to the said council there were substituted references to such authority, and any rights or liabilities of the said council under any such agreement which immediately before the appointed day are subsisting against or, as the case may be, are enforceable by, the Secretary of State shall on and after the appointed day be rights and liabilities of such authority.

(3) Where the matter to which the agreement applies is not so situated, an agreement made between a Secretary of State and a council described in column (1) of the said table shall have effect as separate agreements between the Secretary of State and—

   (*a*) if the matter remains in part situated in the area of the said council, that council, and

   (*b*) the councils specified in respect of the said council in column (2) in whose areas parts of the matter are situated,

each such agreement referring to the authority described in (*a*) or (*b*) and relating to so much of the matter as is situated in the area of such authority, and any rights or liabilities of the council described in column (1) under the agreement as in force at the appointed day shall be divided between the said authorities in a manner which has regard to the nature of such rights and liabilities and also to the extent of the matter in the area of each such authority.

(4) Where any action, measure or procedure has been begun before the appointed day by the council described in column (1) of the said table in pursuance of an agreement to which sub-paragraph (2) or (3) applies but has not been completed at the appointed day, that action, measure or procedure may be continued and completed by the authority or authorities specified in sub-paragraph (2) or (3), and any notice given or published and any other document made or issued by or to the said council before the appointed day for the purpose of, or in connection with, that action, measure or procedure shall have effect on and after that day as if for references therein to the said council there were substituted references to such authority or authorities.

SCHEDULE 4   Regulations 42 and 43

LOCAL ACTS AND ORDERS—PROTECTIVE PROVISIONS
PROCEEDINGS FOR THE ENFORCEMENT OF BYELAWS

PART I

(1)	(2)	(3)
The council of a county or district	Any area transferred to a county and a district	The council of the county or district, as may be appropriate
	Any area transferred to Greater London and a London borough	The Greater London Council or the council of the borough, as may be appropriate
The council of a district	Any area transferred to another district in the same county	The council of the district, or, if appropriate, the county council
The Greater London Council or the council of a London borough	Any area transferred to a county and a district	The council of the county or district, as may be appropriate
The council of a London borough or the Common Council	Any area transferred to a London borough or the City	The council of the London borough or the Common Council
The Council of the City of Westminster or the Common Council	Any area transferred to the Inner Temple or the Middle Temple	The Sub-Treasurer or the Under Treasurer
The Sub-Treasurer or the Under Treasurer	Any area transferred to the City of Westminster or the City	The Council of the City of Westminster or the Common Council

PART II

(1)	(2)	(3)
The council of a county	Any area transferred from a district to another district in the same county	The council of the district
The Greater London Council	Any area transferred to a London borough, the City, the Inner Temple or the Middle Temple	The council of the London borough, the Common Council, the Sub-Treasurer or the Under Treasurer

Regulation 55 SCHEDULE 5

RATING OF BRITISH GAS CORPORATION AND ELECTRICITY BOARDS

1. In this Schedule—

any reference to Schedule 6 of the General Rate Act 1967 is a reference to that Schedule as set out in Schedule 5 to the Gas Act 1972;

any reference to 1st April, 31st May, 1st November, 15th November, 16th November, 31st December or 1st January is a reference to such date last preceding the appointed day; and

the reference to the end of the month of October is a reference to the end of such month last preceding the appointed day.

RATING OF BRITISH GAS CORPORATION

2. Where the order comes into operation for the purposes mentioned in regulation 4(1) between 31st May and 1st November, then as soon as may be after the coming into operation of the order the British Gas Corporation shall, whether or not they have already transmitted the statements which would have been required by paragraph 7 of Schedule 6 to the General Rate Act 1967 to have been transmitted before the end of the month of October if the order had not been made, transmit to the rating authorities of the rating areas and to the valuation officer for such areas the statements which would have been required by such paragraph to have been so transmitted if the order had come into operation on 1st April, and—

(i) paragraph 8 of the said Schedule 6 shall have effect as if the statements had been transmitted under the said paragraph 7 but with the substitution for the words following "rating authority" of "as soon as may be"; and

(ii) any statements already transmitted as aforesaid shall cease to have effect.

3. Where the order comes into operation for the said purposes between 31st October and 1st January, then as soon as may be after the coming into operation of the order, and in any case before the expiration of 28 days, the British Gas Corporation shall transmit to the rating authorities of the rating areas and to the valuation officer for such areas the statements which would have been required by paragraph 7 of the said Schedule 6 to have been transmitted before 31st October if the order had come into operation on 1st April, and as soon as may be after receiving such statements the valuation officer shall calculate the rateable values of any hereditaments which the Corporation are to be treated as occupying in the rating areas during any rate period consisting or forming part of the year commencing on the appointed day, and shall notify the amounts so calculated to the rating authorities aforesaid, and—

(i) paragraph 10 of the said Schedule 6 shall apply as if the said notifications had been made under paragraph 8 thereof; and

(ii) the statements transmitted in accordance with the said paragraph 7 and any notifications under the said paragraph 8 shall cease to have effect.

4. Where the order comes into operation for the said purposes after 31st December, then as soon as may be after the coming into operation of the order, and in any case before the expiration of 28 days, the British Gas Corporation shall transmit to the rating authorities of the rating areas and to the valuation officer for such areas the statements which would have been required by paragraph 7 of the said Schedule 6 to have been transmitted before 31st October if the order had come into operation on 1st April, and as soon as may be after receiving such statements the valuation officer shall calculate the rateable values of any hereditaments which the Corporation are to be treated as occupying in the rating areas during any rate period consisting or forming part of the year commencing on the appointed day, and shall notify the amounts so calculated to the rating authorities aforesaid, and—

(i) paragraph 10 of the said Schedule 6 shall apply as if the said notifications had been made under paragraph 8 thereof; and

(ii) the notifications under the said paragraph 8 shall cease to have effect.

SCHEDULE 5—*continued*

RATING OF ELECTRICITY BOARDS

5. Where the order comes into operation for the purposes mentioned in regulation 4(1) between 31st May and 16th November, then as soon as may be after the coming into operation of the order, the Commissioners of Inland Revenue shall, whether or not they have already transmitted and notified the particulars which would have been required by paragraphs 11 and 12 of Schedule 7 to the General Rate Act 1967 to have been transmitted and notified before 15th November if the order had not been made, transmit and notify the particulars which would have been required by such paragraphs to have been so transmitted and notified if the order had come into operation on 1st April; and—

   (i) any particulars already transmitted and notified shall cease to have effect; and

   (ii) paragraph 13 of the said Schedule shall have effect with the substitution for the words following "rating authority" of "as soon as may be".

6. Where the order comes into operation for the said purposes between 15th November and 1st January, then as soon as may be after the coming into operation of the order the Commissioners of Inland Revenue shall transmit and notify the particulars which would have been required by paragraphs 11 and 12 of the said Schedule 7 to have been transmitted and notified before 15th November if the order had come into operation on 1st April, and as soon as may be thereafter the Commissioners shall calculate the rateable values of any hereditaments which the Central Electricity Generating Board or any Area Board are to be treated as occupying in the rating areas during any rate period consisting or forming part of the year commencing on the appointed day, and shall notify the amounts so calculated to the rating authorities of the rating areas, and—

   (i) paragraph 14 of the said Schedule 7 shall apply as if the said notifications had been made under paragraph 13 thereof; and

   (ii) the particulars transmitted and notified under the said paragraphs 11 and 12 and any notifications under the said paragraph 13 shall cease to have effect.

7. Where the order comes into operation for the said purposes after 31st December, then as soon as may be after the coming into operation of the order the Commissioners of Inland Revenue shall transmit and notify the particulars which would have been required by paragraphs 11 and 12 of the said Schedule 7 to have been transmitted and notified before 15th November if the order had come into operation on 1st April, and as soon as may be thereafter the Commissioners shall calculate the rateable values of any hereditaments which the Central Electricity Generating Board or any Area Board are to be treated as occupying in the rating areas during any rate period consisting or forming part of the year commencing on the appointed day, and shall notify the amounts so calculated to the rating authorities of the rating areas, and—

   (i) paragraph 14 of the said Schedule 7 shall apply as if the said notifications had been made under paragraph 13 thereof; and

   (ii) the notifications under the said paragraph 13 shall cease to have effect.

Regulation 62   SCHEDULE 6

TRANSFER OF SPECIFIED CLASSES OF PROPERTY, ETC.

PART I

1. "Local matters", in relation to any area, means—

    (a) in the case of property—

        (i) sited property situated in the area;

        (ii) specified property in relation to buildings or other land constituting local matters in relation to the area, except in so far as such property is excluded by the agreement of the transferee authority; and

        (iii) other property held exclusively in respect of the area;

    (b) in the case of liabilities, liabilities incurred exclusively in respect of the area;

    (c) in the case of contracts, deeds, bonds, agreements and other instruments, and notices, such instruments subsisting and notices given exclusively in respect of the area;

    (d) in the case of actions and proceedings and causes of action or proceeding, such actions and proceedings pending or causes existing exclusively in respect of the area.

In this paragraph—

    "sited property" means—

        land, including any interest in land and any easement in, to or over land;

        buildings not within the meaning of the term "land";

        fittings, furniture, equipment and stores supplied in respect of a voluntary school or a controlled community home;

        lamps, lamp posts and other apparatus forming part of a system not constituting highway matters under paragraph 3;

    "specified property", in relation to any building, means—

        the fittings, furniture, equipment and records of the building;

        any stores in the building which have been provided for the discharge of functions therein;

        any vehicle or other mobile equipment used wholly or mainly in the performance of the functions carried out in the building;

    and in the case of any other land means any vehicle or other mobile equipment used wholly or mainly in the performance of the functions carried out on the land.

2. "County matters", "district matters", "parish matters", "community matters", "Greater London matters" and "borough matters", in relation to any area, mean the following classes of local matters—

    (a) in the case of property, property held for the purposes of functions not exercisable in the area on and after the appointed day by the transferor authority or the authority of the relevant class in relation to the transferor authority but so exercisable by the authority specified in respect of the matters transferred in column (3) of the table;

    (b) in the case of liabilities, liabilities incurred in relation to such functions;

    (c) in the case of contracts, deeds, bonds, agreements and other instruments, and notices, such instruments subsisting and notices given in relation to such functions;

    (d) in the case of actions and proceedings and causes of action or proceeding, such actions and proceedings pending or causes existing in relation to such functions.

SCHEDULE 6—*continued*

In this paragraph, the relevant class of authorities, in relation to any transferor authority described in column (1) below, means the class specified in respect thereof in column (2).

(1)	(2)
A county council or the Greater London Council	County councils and the Greater London Council
A district council or a London borough council	District councils and London borough councils
A parish authority or a community council	Parish authorities and community councils

3. "Highway matters", in relation to any highway, means—

    (*a*) the interest of the former highway authority, as such, in the highway, in so far as such interest is not vested in a county council, the Greater London Council or a London borough council by virtue of section 226 of the Highways Act 1959;

    (*b*) any land held by the former highway authority, as such, for the purposes of their functions in relation to the highway or which has been acquired by them as highway authority for the highway and not appropriated for any other purpose;

    (*c*) any equipment on or near the highway belonging to the former highway authority as such, including any road lighting system within the meaning of Part III of the Local Government Act 1966 and any other lighting system belonging to the former highway authority as highway authority for the highway; and

    (*d*) any traffic sign (in the meaning attached to that expression in section 54(1) of the Road Traffic Regulation Act 1967) on or near the highway, belonging to the former highway authority and not comprised in (*c*).

4. "Magistrates' court matters", "police matters" and "probation and after-care matters" mean the following classes of local matters—

    (i) in the case of property, property held for the purposes of the relevant functions;

    (ii) in the case of liabilities, liabilities incurred in relation to such functions;

    (iii) in the case of contracts, deeds, bonds, agreements and other instruments, and notices, such instruments subsisting and notices given in relation to such functions; and

    (iv) in the case of actions and proceedings and causes of action or proceeding, such actions and proceedings pending or causes existing in relation to such functions,

and for the purposes of the foregoing definitions "the relevant functions" means—

    (*a*) in the case of magistrates' court matters, functions exercisable for the purposes of the Magistrates' Courts Acts 1952 and 1957(a);

    (*b*) in the case of police matters, functions exercisable for police purposes, including the purposes of section 81 of the Road Traffic Regulation Act 1967; and

    (*c*) in the case of probation and after-care matters, functions exercisable in relation to the probation and after-care service.

(**a**) 1952 c. 55; 1957 c. 29.

SCHEDULE 6—*continued*

5. "The appropriate authority" means—

in the case of an area transferred to a county for which there is a combined police authority, that authority;

in the case of an area transferred to the Metropolitan Police District, the Receiver for that District;

in the case of any other area, the county council of, or the police committee for, the county to which the area is transferred.

6. No entry in column (2) of the table in this Part of this Schedule shall extend to any property included in any extension of the table effected by the order.

7. No entry other than the first in the said table shall extend to any property described in such first entry.

TABLE

(1) Transferor authority	(2) Matters transferred	(3) Transferee authority
The council of a county or a London borough or the Greater London Council	Highway matters in relation to any highway in an area transferred from a county or Greater London to another such area	The highway authority in relation to the highway
The council of a county from which any area is transferred to a county and district	District matters in relation to the area	The council of the district to which the area is transferred
	Police matters in relation to the area	The appropriate authority in relation to the area
	Other local matters in relation to the area	The council of the county to which the area is transferred
The council of a county from which any area is transferred to Greater London and a London borough	Borough matters in relation to the area	The corporation or council of the London borough to which the area is transferred
	Police matters in relation to the area	The Receiver for the Metropolitan Police District
	Other local matters in relation to the area	The Greater London Council
The council of a county within which any area is transferred from one district to another	District matters in relation to the area	The council of the district to which the area is transferred
The council of a district from which any area is transferred to a county and district or to another district in the same county	County matters in relation to the area	The council of the county in which the area is comprised on and after the appointed day
	If the area is transferred to a parish, parish matters in relation to the area	The parish authority for the parish

SCHEDULE 6—*continued*

(1) Transferor authority	(2) Matters transferred'	(3) Transferee authority
	If the area is transferred to a community with a community council, community matters in relation to the area	The community council
	Other local matters in relation to the area	The council of the district to which the area is transferred
The council of a district within which any area is transferred from one parish or community to a parish or a community with a community council	Parish or community matters in relation to the area	The parish authority for the parish or the community council for the community
The council of a district in England	Parish matters in relation to any area which becomes or becomes part of a parish	The parish authority for the parish
The council of a district or the parish authority of a parish from which any area is transferred to Greater London and a London borough	Greater London matters in relation to the area	The Greater London Council
	Other local matters in relation to the area	The corporation or council of the London borough to which the area is transferred
The parish authority for a parish, or the community council for a community, from which any area is transferred otherwise than to Greater London and a London borough	District matters in relation to the area	The council of the district in which the area is comprised on and after the appointed day
	Other local matters in relation to the area	In England, the parish authority for the parish, or if the area is not transferred to a parish, the council of the district, to which the area is transferred In Wales, the community council for the community, or if there is no community council the council of the district, to which the area is transferred
The Greater London Council	District matters in relation to any area transferred to a county and district	The council of the district to which the area is transferred
	Other local matters in relation to such area	The council of the county to which the area is transferred

SCHEDULE 6—*continued*

(1) Transferor authority	(2) Matters transferred	(3) Transferee authority
	Borough matters in relation to an area transferred from a London borough, the City, the Inner Temple or the Middle Temple to another such area	The corporation or council of the London borough to which the area is transferred, the City Corporation or the Common Council, the Honourable Society of the Inner Temple or the Honourable Society of the Middle Temple
	Magistrates' court matters in relation to an area transferred from an outer London borough to an inner London borough	The Receiver for the Metropolitan Police District
The corporation or council of any London borough from which any area is transferred to a county and district	County matters in relation to such area	The council of the county to which the area is transferred
	If the area is transferred to a parish, parish matters in relation to the area	The parish authority for the parish
	Other local matters in relation to such area	The council of the district to which the area is transferred
The corporation or council of any London borough, the City Corporation or the Common Council, the Honourable Society of the Inner Temple or the Honourable Society of the Middle Temple	Greater London matters in relation to any area transferred within Greater London	The Greater London Council
	Other local matters in relation to such area	The corporation or council of the London borough to which the area is transferred, the City Corporation or the Common Council, the Honourable Society of the Inner Temple or the Honourable Society of the Middle Temple
The police committee for any county, or the combined police authority for any combined police area, from which any area is transferred	Local matters in relation to the area	The appropriate authority
The Receiver for the Metropolitan Police District	Local matters in relation to any area of the Metropolitan Police District transferred to another police area other than the City and the Temples	The appropriate authority

SCHEDULE 6—*continued*

(1) Transferor authority	(2) Matters transferred	(3) Transferee authority
	Local matters in relation to any such area transferred to the City and the Temples	The City Corporation or the Common Council
	Magistrates' court matters in relation to an area transferred from an inner London borough to an outer London borough	The Greater London Council
	Probation and after-care matters in relation to such an area	The probation and after-care committee for the area to which the area is transferred
The City Corporation or the Common Council	Police matters in relation to any area transferred to the Metropolitan Police District	The Receiver for the Metropolitan Police District
The probation and after-care committee for the area from which any area is transferred	Local matters in relation to any area transferred to an inner London borough	The Receiver for the Metropolitan Police District
	Local matters in relation to any other area	The probation and after-care committee for the area to which the area is transferred

PART II

1.—(*a*) Any question as to the functions for the purposes of which any property is held, any liabilities have been incurred, any contract, deed, bond, agreement or other instrument subsists, any notice has been given or any action or proceeding or cause of action or proceeding relates shall, subject to the provision of sub-paragraph (*b*), be determined by the transferor authority.

(*b*) If notice is given by any authority that they are dissatisfied with any determination under sub-paragraph (*a*), the question shall be determined by agreement between the authorities concerned or failing such agreement by the decision of a person agreed on by such authorities or in default of agreement appointed by the Secretary of State.

2. The provisions of section 187(2) and (3) of the Local Government Act 1972 shall be disregarded.

3.—(*a*) This paragraph applies to—

  (i) any property held for the purposes of section 132 or 133 of the Local Government Act 1972;

  (ii) any land acquired under section 112, 114 or 119(1)(*a*) of the Town and Country Planning Act 1971 or any earlier provision corresponding to any such enactment;

  (iii) any land acquired under section 120(1)(*b*) of the said Act of 1972, section 124(1)(*b*) thereof or any other provision empowering the acquisition of land for the benefit, improvement or development of any area and not allocated or appropriated for any statutory purpose; and

  (iv) any property acquired by a local authority as a gift otherwise than for charitable purposes;

SCHEDULE 6—*continued*

(*b*) Where any property to which this paragraph applies is, immediately before the appointed day—

> (i) in the case of property referred to in sub-paragraph (*a*)(i), used wholly or substantially so for the purposes of a particular function being purposes authorised by enactments other than the said sections 132 and 133;

> (ii) in the case of property referred to in sub-paragraph (*a*)(ii), used wholly or mainly for the purposes of a statutory function other than those exercised under the Town and Country Planning Acts 1971 and 1972(**a**); or

> (iii) in the case of property referred to in sub-paragraph (*a*)(iii) or (iv), used wholly or mainly for the purpose of any statutory function,

it shall for the purposes of paragraph (2) of regulation 62 be deemed to be held for the purposes of the function for which it is so used.

(*c*) In the application of sub-paragraph (*b*) any temporary use of the property shall be disregarded.

(*d*) Two (but not more) functions shall be treated as a single function in the application of sub-paragraph (*b*).

(*e*) Any property to which sub-paragraph (*b*) applies shall be held by the authority to whom it is transferred for the purposes of the function described in (i), (ii) or (iii) of that sub-paragraph or where two functions have been treated as a single function for the purposes of such one of those functions as is determined by the authority to whom the property is transferred.

(*f*) Any question whether any property to which this paragraph applies is, immediately before the appointed day, used as described in (i), (ii) or (iii) of sub-paragraph (*b*) shall, subject to the provision of sub-paragraph (*g*), be determined by the authority in whom the property is, before the appointed day, vested.

(*g*) If notice is given by any authority that they are dissatisfied with any such determination the question shall be determined by agreement between the authorities concerned or failing such agreement by the decision of a person agreed on by such authorities or in default of agreement appointed by the Secretary of State, and sub-paragraph (*e*) shall apply accordingly. Sub-paragraphs (*c*) and (*d*) shall apply in the application of this sub-paragraph.

4.—(*a*) The provisions of this paragraph shall apply where—

> (i) at the appointed day any building or part of a building is to be wholly or substantially so replaced by another building which is completed or in the course of erection or for the erection of which a contract has been entered into, or by part of such building;

> (ii) it has been resolved by the transferor authority before the coming into operation of the order that the first-mentioned building or part of a building or the site thereof is to be used for some function other than the one for which it is held; and

> (iii) the nature of the building or the location of its site is such as to make it peculiarly suited for use for the purposes of such function rather than for other local government purposes,

and apart from the provisions of this paragraph the two buildings or parts of buildings would be transferred to the same authority.

(*b*) The transferor authority may determine that for the purposes of paragraph (2) of regulation 62 the land on which the building or part of a building first mentioned in sub-paragraph (*a*) is erected shall be deemed to be held for the purposes for which by the resolution described in (ii) thereof it is to be used.

(*c*) If notice is given by any authority concerned that they question whether (i), (ii) or (iii) in sub-paragraph (*a*) is satisfied, the determination shall be of no effect and

---

(**a**) 1971 c. 78; 1972 c. 42.

SCHEDULE 6—*continued*

the question of the purpose for which the land is to be deemed to be held shall be determined by agreement between the authorities concerned or failing such agreement by the decision of a person agreed on by such authorities or in default of agreement appointed by the Secretary of State.

5.—(*a*) The provisions of this paragraph shall have effect in relation to any land appropriated within the 12 months preceding the appointed day and to any financial adjustment made on the appropriation.

(*b*) Any such land shall for the purposes of paragraph (2) of regulation 62 be treated as held for the purposes for which it has been appropriated, and any financial adjustment made on the appropriation shall be of full effect, unless an authority give notice that the land falls to be treated for the purposes of the said paragraph as being held for the purpose for which it was held before the appropriation, or that the financial adjustment falls to be varied. If such notice is given the question of the purpose for which the land is held, or as the case may be the adjustment to be made, shall be determined by agreement between the authorities concerned or failing such agreement by the decision of a person agreed on by such authorities or in default of agreement appointed by the Secretary of State.

Anthony Crosland,
Secretary of State for the Environment.

12th February 1976.

John Morris,
Secretary of State for Wales.

16th February 1976.

EXPLANATORY NOTE
(This Note is not part of the Regulations.)

Part IV of the Local Government Act 1972 makes provision for changes of local government areas, to be effected by orders. Section 67(1) and (2) of the Act of 1972 empowers the making of provision incidental, consequential, transitional or supplementary to the orders by regulations of general application. These Regulations contain such provision. This also extends to the orders made under the provisions of Schedule 10 to the Act of 1972 for the initial review of the communities in Wales.

STATUTORY   INSTRUMENTS

1976 No. 247

ROAD TRAFFIC

The Cycle Racing on Highways (Special Authorisation) (England and Wales) Regulations 1976

Made - - - -		*18th February* 1976
Laid before Parliament		*27th February* 1976
Coming into Operation		*19th March* 1976

The Secretary of State for the Environment (in relation to England) and the Secretary of State for Wales (in relation to Wales) hereby make these Regulations in exercise of the powers conferred on them by section 20(2) and (3) of the Road Traffic Act 1972**(a)** and of all other enabling powers, after consultation with representative organisations in accordance with section 199(2) of the said Act:—

1.—(1) These Regulations shall come into operation on 19th March 1976 and may be cited as the Cycle Racing on Highways (Special Authorisation) (England and Wales) Regulations 1976.

(2) In these Regulations—

(*a*) "specified events" means the cycle racing events proposed to be held on or between 21st March and 12th September 1976, particulars of which as notified to the Secretary of State for the Environment or, as the case may be, the Secretary of State for Wales by the British Cycling Federation are specified in the Schedule to these Regulations;

(*b*) "the principal Regulations" means the Cycle Racing on Highways Regulations 1960**(b)**, as amended by the Cycle Racing on Highways (Amendment) Regulations 1963**(c)**;

(*c*) expressions to which a meaning is assigned by the principal Regulations shall have that meaning.

(3) The Interpretation Act 1889**(d)** shall apply for the interpretation of these Regulations as it applies for the interpretation of an Act of Parliament.

2.—(1) The principal Regulations shall have effect in their application to any bicycle race comprised in any of the specified events as if in Regulation 5(1)(*a*)(i) for the condition that the number of competitors must not exceed 40 there were substituted the condition that the number of competitors must not exceed,—

(a) 1972 c. 20.
(c) S.I. 1963/929 (1963 II, p. 1556).
(b) S.I. 1960/250 (1960 III, p. 3047).
(d) 1889 c. 63.

(*a*) in the case of a bicycle race comprised in the event specified in the Schedule to these Regulations under the title "Tour of Britain (Milk Race)", 84, and

(*b*) in the case of a bicycle race comprised in any of the other specified events, 60.

(2) The foregoing provisions of this Regulation shall have effect in relation to any bicycle race comprised in any of the specified events notwithstanding that after the coming into operation of these Regulations the title of that event is changed from that specified in column 1 of the Schedule to these Regulations or that some person other than the person specified in column 3 of the said Schedule becomes the promoter of that event.

(3) Save as otherwise provided by the foregoing provisions of these Regulations, the principal Regulations shall apply to a bicycle race comprised in any of the specified events as they apply to any other bicycle race.

Anthony Crosland,
Secretary of State for the Environment.

17th February 1976.

John Morris,
Secretary of State for Wales.

18th February 1976.

SCHEDULE

CYCLE RACING EVENTS—1976

1. Title of event	2. Proposed time for the holding of the event	3. Name and address of the promoter of the event
1. Grand Prix of Essex ...	21st March	D. Worsley Esq., Bramble Rise, Colne Engaine, Essex, CO6 2JB.
2. Heineken Grand Prix ...	4th April	R. Whinnerah Esq., 1, Harrogate Street, Barrow-in-Furness, Cumbria.
3. Grand Prix Pernod International.	11th April	L. Docker Esq., 233, Droop Street, London, W10.

SCHEDULE—(*continued*)

1. Title of event	2. Proposed time for the holding of the event	3. Name and address of the promoter of the event
4. Ras Tri Niwrnod de Cymru	17th to 19th April (inclusive)	R. Phillips Esq., 12, Harriet Town, Troedyrhiw, Merthyr Tydfil, Glamorgan.
5. Manchester-Rhyl 200 ...	24th to 25th April (inclusive)	N. A. Shelmerdine Esq., 1, Fircroft Close, Tilehurst, Reading, Berkshire.
6. Leyland Grand Prix ...	2nd May	A. Williams Esq., c/o Sam Williams Cycles, Deepdale Road, Preston, Lancashire.
7. VAT Watkins Grand Prix	9th May	P. Whelan Esq., 164, Scotland Green Road, Enfield, Middlesex, EN3 7AT.
8. Zerny 2-Day Road Race ...	15th to 16th May (inclusive)	D. J. Bishop Esq., 67, Grandale, Sutton Park, Hull.
9. Lincoln Grand Prix ...	23rd May	M. Griffin Esq., 17, Larkin Avenue, Cherry Willingham, Lincoln.
10. Tour of Britain (Milk Race).	30th May to 12th June (inclusive)	P. Liggett Esq., 65, Cotswold Way, Enfield, Middlesex.
11. National Professional Road Race Championship.	20th June	M. A. Cumberworth Esq., Hebden Hall Park, Hebden, Near Skipton, North Yorks. BD23 5DX.
12. Five Valley Road Race ...	3rd July	R. S. Budd Esq., 11, Oakland Drive, Neath, Glamorgan, SA10 7ED.
13. Golden Wonder Classic ...	11th July	J. R. Partridge Esq., 45, Gotch Road, Barton Seagrave, Kettering, Northants
14. Zorbit Grand Prix ...	18th July	J. D. Greenhalgh Esq., 12, Lovell Drive, Newton, Hyde, Cheshire.

SCHEDULE—(*continued*)

1. Title of event	2. Proposed time for the holding of the event	3. Name and address of the promoter of the event
15. Tour of the Cotswolds Road Race.	1st August	R. T. Griffin Esq., 37, Courtenay Street, Cheltenham, Gloucester.
16. Bromsgrove Grand Prix ...	15th August	G. W. Calcutt Esq., 'Stet', Withybed Lane, Inkberrow, Worcester, WR7 4JJ.
17. National Amateur Road Race Championship.	22nd August	K. L. White Esq., 60, Goldthorne Road, Goldthorne Hill, Wolverhampton.
18. Celtic 3-Day	28th to 30th August (inclusive)	J. A. Richards Esq., 97, Oak Street, Abertillery, Gwent.
19. Gibbsport Tour of the Peak.	5th September	A. Pickburn Esq., 48, Mostyn Road, Hazel Grove, Cheshire.
20. Ansells Skol Classic ...	12th September	B. Moss Esq., 18, Arden Close, Balsall Common, Coventry, CV7 7NY.

EXPLANATORY NOTE

(*This Note is not part of the Regulations.*)

The Cycle Racing on Highways Regulations 1960, which apply to England and Wales, authorise certain races or trials of speed between bicycles or tricycles, not being motor vehicles, (described in those Regulations as bicycle races) to be held on public highways subject to certain conditions including the condition that the number of competitors taking part must not exceed 40. These Regulations provide for varying this condition in the case of any bicycle race (as defined in the 1960 Regulations) which is comprised in the 20 cycle racing events proposed to be held in 1976 which are specified in the Schedule, by increasing to 84 the maximum number of competitors who may take part in the case of the event specified under the title "Tour of Britain (Milk Race)" and to 60 in the case of the other events so specified.

STATUTORY INSTRUMENTS

1976 No. 249

AGRICULTURE

GUARANTEED PRICES AND ASSURED MARKETS

The Fat Sheep (Guarantee Payments) Order 1976

Made - - -	*18th February* 1976
Laid before Parliament -	*26th February* 1976
Coming into Operation—	
Article 4(2) - -	*3rd January* 1977
Remainder - -	*27th February* 1976

The Minister of Agriculture, Fisheries and Food, the Secretary of State for Scotland, the Secretary of State for Northern Ireland (being the Secretaries of State respectively concerned with agriculture in Scotland and Northern Ireland) and the Secretary of State for Wales, acting jointly, in exercise of the powers conferred upon them by sections 1, 9(4) and 35(3) of the Agriculture Act 1957(a), as read with the Transfer of Functions (Wales) Order 1969(b), and of all other powers enabling them in that behalf, with the consent of the Treasury and after consultation with such bodies of persons as appear to the said Ministers to represent the interests of producers of fat sheep, hereby make the following order:—

PART I

Citation, commencement, interpretation and revocation

1. This order may be cited as the Fat Sheep (Guarantee Payments) Order 1976, and shall come into operation on 27th February 1976, except that article 4(2) hereof shall come into operation on 3rd January 1977.

2.—(1) In this order, except where the context otherwise requires—

"certification centre" means a place for the time being approved by the Minister for the certification for the purposes of this order of all or any particular class of fat sheep;

"certified", in relation to any fat sheep, means certified as being eligible for any relevant payment under this order by the proper officer in pursuance of this order in such manner and after compliance by the producer of such fat sheep with such conditions as may from time to time be specified by or on behalf of the Minister;

(a) 1957 c. 57.   (b) S.I. 1969/388 (1969 I, p. 1070).

"deadweight", in relation to any fat sheep, means the weight of an animal's carcase ascertained after such preparation of the carcase, and by weighing in such conditions, as may from time to time be specified by or on behalf of the Minister;

"deadweight certification centre" means a certification centre at which carcases are certified;

"description", in relation to any fat sheep, includes quality and, without prejudice to the general meaning of the expression, any kind of fat sheep distinguished by reference—

(a) to the area in which, or the season of the year in which it is produced, sold or dispatched or delivered on sale;

(b) to the purpose for which it is sold or used;

(c) to the methods by which it is marketed, including the places to which it is delivered on sale;

"determined" means determined by the Minister with the approval of the Treasury and, as respects any guaranteed price to be determined in pursuance of this order, means so determined by the Minister from time to time in the light of the conclusions of the Ministers from a review held under section 2 of the Agriculture Act 1947(a);

"fat sheep" includes the carcases of such animals;

"grade", in relation to fat sheep of any guarantee class, means the classification of fat sheep within that class by reference to such standards of quality, weight or other factors as may be determined for that grade;

"guarantee class" has the meaning assigned to it by article 3 of this order;

"guarantee period" means the period commencing on the last Monday before 2nd April in any year and ending at midnight on the Sunday immediately preceding the last Monday before 2nd April in the succeeding year;

"guaranteed price" means a price or prices determined by the Minister in pursuance of this order;

"liveweight certification centre" means a certification centre at which live animals are certified;

"the Minister", in relation to any part of the United Kingdom, means either that one of the Ministers who is concerned with agriculture in that part, or that Minister and any one or all of the others acting jointly;

"the Ministers" means the Minister of Agriculture, Fisheries and Food and the Secretaries of State respectively concerned with agriculture in Scotland and Northern Ireland, and the Secretary of State for Wales acting jointly;

"producer", in relation to any fat sheep, means the person in whose name such fat sheep are presented for certification;

"proper officer" for any of the purposes of this order means the person for the time being authorised by the Minister to act for that purpose;

"standard price" means a price determined, by reference to the guaranteed price, in accordance with article 8;

(a) 1947 c. 48.

"week" means a period of seven days commencing with a Monday, except that when the period includes Christmas Day the expression shall, if the Minister so decides, mean that period and the immediately preceding or succeeding period as the Minister shall specify.

(2) The Interpretation Act 1889(a) shall apply to the interpretation of this order as it applies to the interpretation of an Act of Parliament, and as if this order and the order hereby revoked were Acts of Parliament.

(3) The Fatstock (Guarantee Payments) Order 1973(b) is hereby revoked.

PART II

Provisions as to guarantee class, rate of payment, etc.

3. This order shall apply to such description of fat sheep as may be determined from time to time as guarantee classes for the purposes of this order, and any class so determined is in this order referred to as a "guarantee class".

4.—(1) Any guaranteed price, standard price, average market price, or average return to producers determined or ascertained in accordance with this order shall be at a rate per pound actual or estimated deadweight.

(2) On the day on which this paragraph comes into operation paragraph (1) of this article shall be amended by substituting for the word "pound" the word "kilogramme".

5. A guaranteed price shall be determined in respect of each guarantee period and each guarantee class.

6. The Minister may, if he thinks fit, and subject to the provisions of this order, make payments to producers of fat sheep of sums ascertained in accordance with articles 8 and 9 of this order.

7.—(1) Any rate of payment—

(*a*) ascertained in accordance with this order for any guarantee class of fat sheep may be subject to such modifications as may be determined by the Minister in respect of grades or descriptions of fat sheep within such guarantee class;

(*b*) may be ascertained in accordance with this order to such nearest unit or fraction of a unit of currency as may from time to time be specified by or on behalf of the Minister and the amount of any individual payment to a producer made under this order may be calculated to such nearest unit or fraction of a unit of currency as may from time to time be specified by or on behalf of the Minister.

(2) In relation to animals imported or brought into the United Kingdom from any place outside the United Kingdom, or to carcases produced by the slaughter within the United Kingdom of animals which have been so imported or brought in, any rate of payment for any description of such animals or carcases may be reduced by such amount as may be determined for that description of animal or carcase and any payment in respect of any such description of animal or carcase shall be subject to such terms and conditions as may from time to time be specified by or on behalf of the Minister.

(a) 1889 c. 63.　　　　(b) S.I. 1973/352 (1973 I, p. 1235).

Part III

Guarantee Payments

8. For the purpose of ascertaining the rate of payment which may be made under this order to producers of fat sheep of a guarantee class the Minister may determine for each week of a guarantee period a standard price and for those weeks of a guarantee period that he considers payment may be made under article 6 of this order he shall ascertain an average market price in accordance with the Schedule to this order.

9. Subject to the provisions of this order where the average market price of fat sheep ascertained as aforesaid is lower than the standard price, determined as aforesaid, the rate of any payment which may be made in respect of each guarantee class of fat sheep certified during any week shall be a rate equal to the difference between the standard price and the average market price.

Part IV

Provisions as to certification and payments, etc.

10.—(1) The proper officer may, subject to the provisions of this article, certify any fat sheep by the issue of a certificate in respect of such fat sheep in such manner and subject to such conditions as may from time to time be specified by or on behalf of the Minister.

(2) No animal or carcase shall be certified unless—

 (*a*) it is presented for certification at a certification centre for the time being approved by the Minister; and

 (*b*) the proper officer is satisfied that it is of a guarantee class.

(3) No live animal shall be certified unless—

 (*a*) it has been sold by auction at the liveweight certification centre at which it is presented for certification; provided that the purchase of any animal by or on behalf of the vendor shall not constitute a sale for the purpose of this sub-paragraph; or

 (*b*) the producer has made a declaration that it has been sold by private treaty; or

 (*c*) the producer has made a declaration that it is to be slaughtered for sale in the producer's own butchery business.

(4) No carcase shall be certified unless the producer has made a declaration that—

 (*a*) it has been sold; or

 (*b*) it will be sold by or on behalf of the producer in a butchery business and is not intended for consumption in the producer's household; or

 (*c*) it has been or will be transferred by the producer from the carcase owner's agricultural undertaking to another undertaking (not being an agricultural undertaking) in the same ownership for consumption therein.

In any case where a declaration has been made pursuant to sub-paragraph (*c*) above the carcase shall not be certified unless the Minister is satisfied that the carcase owner's agricultural undertaking is managed as a separate concern.

(5) No carcase shall be certified if the whole of that carcase has been condemned by virtue of any enactment as unfit for human consumption, and, if a carcase has been presented for certification and a part thereof has been so condemned, no payment shall be made under this order in respect of that part.

(6) No animal or carcase shall be certified unless the proper officer is satisfied that it has not been previously certified under this order or under the Fatstock (Guarantee Payments) Order 1973.

(7) No payment shall be made under this order in respect of—

(a) any excess weight of an animal or carcase of any description above such weight as may be determined for that description of animal or carcase;

(b) any live animal certified in accordance with paragraph (3)(c) of this article unless the proper officer receives from the producer within such time as may be specified by or on behalf of the Minister a declaration in a form so specified, that the animal has been slaughtered for sale in the producer's own butchery business.

(8) For the purposes of certification and payment under this order, where two or more animals or carcases are presented for certification in a single lot, the price and weight of each individual animal or carcase shall be taken to be the average price or, as the case may be, the average weight of the animals or carcases comprised in that lot.

(9) Except under arrangements approved by or on behalf of the Minister no carcase shall be certified unless it is derived from an animal slaughtered at the deadweight certification centre at which such carcase was presented for certification.

11. The Minister may in respect of any fat sheep presented for certification require an application for a guarantee payment, in such form as he may specify, to be completed by the producer of such fat sheep and submitted to the proper officer at the certification centre where such fat sheep is presented for certification and he may from time to time specify such conditions in relation to the presentation of any fat sheep for certification or in relation to the certification of any fat sheep as seem to him to be necessary or expedient and where the Minister is not satisfied that any such requirement or condition has been complied with in relation to any fat sheep he may, if he thinks fit, withhold certification of, or payment in respect of, such fat sheep, notwithstanding that such fat sheep has or have been marked under the provisions of the Fat Sheep (Protection of Guarantees) Order 1976(a), or any order amending or replacing it.

12. The Minister may, to such extent and in such manner as he may from time to time direct, delegate to the Meat and Livestock Commission (established under section 1 of the Agriculture Act 1967(b)) any of the functions in relation to Great Britain (other than the function of determining guaranteed prices or factors relevant to the operation of such prices) conferred or imposed on him by this order.

13. The functions of the Minister under this order (other than the function of determining guaranteed prices or factors relevant to the operation of such

---

(a) S.I. 1976/250. (1976 I, p. 702).   (b) 1967 c. 22.

prices) may be exercised in relation to Northern Ireland by the Department of Agriculture for Northern Ireland.

In Witness whereof the Official Seal of the Minister of Agriculture, Fisheries and Food is hereunto affixed on 4th February 1976.

(L.S.)

Frederick Peart,
Minister of Agriculture, Fisheries and Food.

6th February 1976.

William Ross,
Secretary of State for Scotland.

10th February 1976.

Mervyn Rees,
Secretary of State for Northern Ireland.

16th February 1976.

John Morris,
Secretary of State for Wales.

We consent

18th February 1976.

Donald R. Coleman,
J. Dormand,
Two of the Lords Commissioners of Her Majesty's Treasury.

Article 8

THE SCHEDULE

Weekly Average Market Prices

For the purpose of article 8 of this order, the average market price for any guarantee class of fat sheep in respect of any week shall be ascertained after the end of that week in such manner as appears to the Minister proper by reference to—

    (*a*) market prices received in respect of fat sheep of that guarantee class certified during the week in respect of which the average market price is ascertained; and

    (*b*) any other matter which the Minister may consider relevant.

EXPLANATORY NOTE

(This Note is not part of the Order.)

This Order replaces the Fatstock (Guarantee Payments) Order 1973 to provide for changes in the arrangements for guarantee payments to producers of fatstock.   The principal changes are—

(a) the arrangements for guarantee payments to producers of fat sheep will operate on a metric basis on and after 3rd January 1977;

(b) the provisions relating to the adjustment of guarantee payments by reference to the difference between a weekly average market price and an estimated price are discontinued;

(c) the provisions relating to the payment of further amounts ascertained by reference to an annual average market price and an annual average estimated price after each guarantee period are discontinued;

(d) the references to guarantee payments to producers of fat pigs are removed.

The system of guaranteed prices applicable in the United Kingdom in the market in pigmeat terminated in July 1975 in accordance with Council Regulation (EEC) No. 749/73 of 19th March 1973 (OJ No. L 72, 20.3.73, p. 1) and Commission Regulation (EEC) No. 1822/75 of 15th July 1975 (OJ No. L185, 16.7.75, p. 10).

STATUTORY INSTRUMENTS

1976 No. 250

AGRICULTURE

GUARANTEED PRICES AND ASSURED MARKETS

The Fat Sheep (Protection of Guarantees) Order 1976

Made - - - -	16*th February* 1976
Laid before Parliament	26*th February* 1976
Coming into Operation—	
Paragraph 3 *of Schedule* 2	3*rd January* 1977
Remainder	27*th February* 1976

The Minister of Agriculture, Fisheries and Food, the Secretary of State for Scotland, the Secretary of State for Northern Ireland (being the Secretaries of State respectively concerned with agriculture in Scotland and Northern Ireland) and the Secretary of State for Wales, acting jointly, in exercise of the powers conferred upon them by sections 5 (as amended by sections 3(2) and 70(1) of the Agriculture Act 1967(**a**)), 9(4) and 35(3) of the Agriculture Act 1957(**b**), as read with the Transfer of Functions (Wales) Order 1969(**c**), and of all other powers enabling them in that behalf, hereby make the following order:—

Citation and commencement

1. This order may be cited as the Fat Sheep (Protection of Guarantees) Order 1976, and shall come into operation on 27th February 1976, except that paragraph 3 of Schedule 2 to this order shall come into operation on 3rd January 1977.

Interpretation and revocation

2.—(1) In this order, unless the context otherwise requires—

"the appropriate Minister" means—

(*a*) in relation to England, the Minister of Agriculture, Fisheries and Food;

(*b*) in relation to Scotland and Northern Ireland, respectively, the Secretary of State concerned with agriculture therein; and

(*c*) in relation to Wales—

(i) for the purpose of the making, receipt or recovery of any payment, the Minister of Agriculture, Fisheries and Food;

(ii) for all other purposes, that Minister and the Secretary of State for Wales, acting jointly;

(**a**) 1967 c. 22.   (**b**) 1957 c. 57.
(**c**) S.I. 1969/388 (1969 I, p. 1070).

"approved animal" means any animal approved by the proper officer for certification for a guarantee payment;

"approved carcase" means any carcase approved by the proper officer for certification for a guarantee payment;

"certified", in relation to an animal or carcase, means certified by the proper officer as being eligible for a guarantee payment and "certification" shall be construed accordingly;

"deadweight certification centre" means any place for the time being approved by the appropriate Minister for the certification of the carcases of livestock for a guarantee payment;

"fat sheep" includes the carcases of such animals;

"guarantee payment" means any sum payable by the appropriate Minister under the provisions of the Fat Sheep (Guarantee Payments) Order 1976 **(a)** or any order amending or replacing it;

"liveweight certification centre" means any place for the time being approved by the appropriate Minister for the certification of livestock for a guarantee payment;

"the Ministers" means the Minister of Agriculture, Fisheries and Food, the Secretaries of State respectively concerned with agriculture in Scotland and Northern Ireland and the Secretary of State for Wales, acting jointly;

"Proper officer" means, in relation to any purpose referred to in this order, a person for the time being authorised by the appropriate Minister to act for that purpose.

(2) The Interpretation Act 1889**(b)** shall apply to the interpretation of this order as it applies to the interpretation of an Act of Parliament and as if this order and the orders hereby revoked were Acts of Parliament.

(3) The orders specified in Schedule 1 hereto are hereby revoked.

Marking of fat sheep

3. Every approved animal and every approved carcase before being removed from a liveweight or a deadweight certification centre, as the case may be, at which such animal or carcase has been approved, shall, unless the appropriate Minister otherwise directs, be marked by or under the supervision of the proper officer with one of the appropriate marks prescribed in Schedule 2 to this order and in addition, if the appropriate Minister so requires, the ear or ears of any approved carcase shall be removed or mutilated.

Prohibition relating to removal of approved fat sheep

4. No person shall—

(*a*) remove any approved animal from a liveweight certification centre or, within a liveweight certification centre, from a pen or other place which is allocated for the marking of livestock;

(*b*) remove any approved carcase from a deadweight certification centre

unless any such approved animal or approved carcase, as the case may be, has been dealt with in accordance with article 3 of this order.

(a) S.I. 1976/249 (1976 I,p. 695).   **(b)** 1889 c. 63.

Prohibition relating to approved fat sheep

5.—(1) No person shall—

    (*a*) present for certification any approved animal or approved carcase or the carcase of any approved animal;

    (*b*) use or permit or cause to be used any approved animal for breeding or permit or cause any such approved animal to have access to any animal with which it may mate.

(2) In any proceedings in respect of a contravention of any of the provisions of paragraph (1) of this article, if any animal or any carcase bears one of the marks prescribed for live animals in Schedule 2 hereto, it shall be deemed to be an approved animal or the carcase of an approved animal, as the case may be, and if any carcase bears one of the marks prescribed for carcases in Schedule 2 hereto it shall be deemed to be an approved carcase, unless the contrary be proved.

Records

6.—(1) Every person who buys, sells or transports any fat sheep and who is required by virtue of the Movement of Animals (Records) Order 1960(**a**), as amended(**b**), or the Transit of Animals (Amendment) (Northern Ireland) Order 1941(**c**), to keep or retain a record of the movement of animals shall produce on request such record or register for inspection by a person authorised by or on behalf of the appropriate Minister for the purposes of this order.

(2) Any reference in paragraph (1) of this article to any order includes any modification or re-enactment thereof for the time being in force.

Keeping and retention of records

7.—(1) Every person who presents any fat sheep for certification shall keep an accurate record, showing, in respect of every purchase and sale by him of such fat sheep,

    (*a*) the date of the transaction and the description of fat sheep;

    (*b*) in the case of a purchase or sale of a live animal by auction at an auction market, the name and address of the auctioneer, and in any other case the name and address of the other party to the transaction; and

    (*c*) the price paid or received in respect of the fat sheep.

(2) The retention by any person of an invoice or similar account or of a copy of such invoice or similar account shall, in relation to the particulars mentioned in such document, be a sufficient compliance by that person with the provisions of this article.

(3) Every person who is required by this article to keep any record shall retain it for at least two years from the date of the transaction to which it relates and shall produce it for inspection if so required by any person authorised by or on behalf of the appropriate Minister to require its production.

(a) S.I. 1960/105 (1960 I, p. 302).   (b) S.I. 1961/1493 (1961 II, p. 3016).
(c) S.R. & O. (N.I.) 1941/145.

Keeping and production of books, accounts and records

8. Any person who carries on any undertaking by way of trade or business in the course of which he buys or sells any approved animal or approved carcase shall if a notice in writing is served upon him by or on behalf of the appropriate Minister keep such books accounts or records relating to the purchase sale or use of livestock or the carcases of livestock or the slaughter of livestock as may be specified in the notice and shall produce such books accounts or records for inspection if required to do so by any person authorised by or on behalf of the appropriate Minister to require their production.

Powers of entry and to obtain evidence

9.—(1) Any authorised officer of the appropriate Minister or any authorised officer of the Meat and Livestock Commission where accompanying an authorised officer of the appropriate Minister may at all reasonable times enter upon land used for the production, slaughter or sale of fat sheep or for the storage, grading, packing or sale of the carcases of fat sheep and may inspect any fat sheep or carcases of fat sheep found thereon.

(2) In any case where an authorised person has reason to suspect that there has been a contravention of this order, or of section 7 of the Agriculture Act 1957 or that a guarantee payment has been illegally obtained or that there has been an attempt to obtain a guarantee payment illegally he may—

> (*a*) take possession of any ear of any carcase presented for certification for a guarantee payment; and

> (*b*) take possession of any book, account or record required to be kept by or under this order or take any copy or extract from any such book, account or record.

(3) In paragraph (2) of this article—

"authorised person" means in relation to sub-paragraph (*a*) of that paragraph any person authorised by or on behalf of the appropriate Minister or a proper officer for the purpose of the approval or certification for a guarantee payment of any carcase of any livestock; and in relation to sub-paragraph (*b*) of that paragraph any person authorised by or on behalf of the appropriate Minister.

Service of notices

10.—(1) Any notice required or authorised by this order to be given to or served on any person shall be sufficiently given or served if it is delivered to him personally or left at his last known place of abode or business or sent by post addressed to him at the aforesaid place of abode or business.

(2) Any notice required or authorised by this order to be given to or served on an incorporated company or body shall be sufficiently given or served if given to or served on the secretary or clerk of the company or body. For the purposes of this order and of section 26 of the Interpretation Act 1889, the proper address of such secretary or clerk shall be that of the registered or principal office of the company or body.

Delegation of functions

11.—(1) The appropriate Minister may, to such extent and in such manner as he may from time to time direct, delegate to the Meat and Livestock Commission (established under section 1 of the Agriculture Act 1967(**a**)) any of the functions in relation to Great Britain conferred or imposed on him by this order.

(**a**) 1967 c. 22.

(2) The functions of the appropriate Minister under this order may be exercised in relation to Northern Ireland by the Department of Agriculture for Northern Ireland.

In Witness whereof the Official Seal of the Minister of Agriculture, Fisheries and Food is hereunto affixed on 4th February 1976.

(L.S.)

Frederick Peart,
Minister of Agriculture, Fisheries and Food.

6th February 1976.

William Ross,
Secretary of State for Scotland.

10th February 1976.

Merlyn Rees,
Secretary of State for Northern Ireland.

16th February 1976.

John Morris,
Secretary of State for Wales.

SCHEDULE 1

Orders revoked	References
The Fatstock (Protection of Guarantees) Order 1958	S.I. 1958/958 (1958 I, p. 84)
The Fatstock (Protection of Guarantees) (Amendment) Order 1960	S.I. 1960/293 (1960 I, p. 103)
The Fatstock (Protection of Guarantees) (Amendment) Order 1968	S.I. 1968/399 (1968 I, p. 1080)

Articles 3 and 5

SCHEDULE 2

APPROPRIATE MARKS FOR THE PURPOSES OF ARTICLES 3 AND 5 OF THIS ORDER

1. For live sheep: any of the following marks—
   (a) a tattoo mark consisting of dots in a rectangular pattern measuring approximately three quarters of an inch across the diagonal, or
   (b) a circular punch hole of approximately a quarter of an inch diameter surrounded by a tattoo mark consisting of dots in a rectangular pattern measuring approximately three quarters of an inch across the diagonal, or
   (c) a circular punch hole of approximately half an inch in diameter surrounded by a tattoo mark consisting of dots in a circular or rectangular pattern measuring approximately one inch across the diameter or diagonal as the case may be

such mark to be placed—
   (a) in the case of home-bred sheep, in the right ear,
   (b) in the case of imported sheep, in the left ear.

2. For the carcases of sheep:
   (a) approved in England and Wales—a mark comprising a circle of approximately one and one half inch diameter with the letters and word "M.A.F.F. Certified" on the inner circumference around the number allocated to the proper officer for the time being using the instrument which applies the mark. Such mark to be applied at least once to the outer surface of the carcase;
   (b) approved in Scotland and Northern Ireland—a mark comprising a diagonal (or St Andrew's) cross within a circle of approximately one and a half inch diameter. Such mark to be applied at least once to the outer surface of the carcase.

3. On the day on which this paragraph comes into operation for the measures mentioned in paragraphs 1 and 2 of this Schedule there shall be substituted new measures as follows:—

Old Measure	New Measure
quarter of an inch	six millimetres
half an inch	thirteen millimetres
three quarters of an inch	nineteen millimetres
one inch	twenty-five millimetres
one and one half inch	thirty-eight millimetres

EXPLANATORY NOTE
(This Note is not part of the Order.)

This Order replaces the Fatstock (Protection of Guarantees) Order 1958, as amended, to provide for changes in the arrangements for the protection of guarantee payments to producers of fatstock following the discontinuance of guaranteed prices for fat pigs in July 1975. The order re-enacts the provisions of the Fatstock (Protection of Guarantees) Order 1958, as amended, in so far as they relate to fat sheep except that

(*a*) the appropriate Minister is enabled to direct that approved animals shall not be marked with one of the marks prescribed in the Schedule to this order; and

(*b*) such marks as are applied shall be on a metric basis on and after 3rd January 1977.

STATUTORY INSTRUMENTS

1976 No. 251

CUSTOMS AND EXCISE

The Import Duties (Temporary Reductions and Exemptions) (No. 5) Order 1976

Made -	-	-	-	-	-	*19th February* 1976

Laid before the House of Commons   20th February 1976

Coming into Operation—

for all purposes of Articles 5 and 6 23rd February 1976

for all other purposes   1st March 1976

The Lords Commissioners of Her Majesty's Treasury, by virtue of the powers conferred on them by sections 1, 2, 3(6) and 13 of the Import Duties Act 1958(a), as amended by section 5(5) of, and paragraph 1 of Schedule 4 to, the European Communities Act 1972(b), and of all other powers enabling them in that behalf, on the recommendation of the Secretary of State(c), hereby make the following Order:

Citation, operation, interpretation

1.—(1) This Order may be cited as the Import Duties (Temporary Reductions and Exemptions) (No. 5) Order 1976 and shall come into operation for all purposes of Articles 5 and 6 on 23rd February 1976 and for all other purposes on 1st March 1976.

(2) In this Order a reference to a heading or subheading is a reference to a heading or subheading of the Customs Tariff 1959.

(3) The Interpretation Act 1889(d) shall apply for the interpretation of this Order as it applies for the interpretation of an Act of Parliament.

The full rate

2.—(1) Up to and including 31st December 1976, in the case of goods which fall within the subheading specified in column 1 of Schedule 1 hereto and are of the description specified in column 2 thereof, import duty shall be charged at the rate shown in column 3 thereof in relation to the goods instead of any higher rate which would otherwise apply.

(2) Paragraph (1) above shall operate without prejudice to any greater reduction provided for by Article 3 below.

The Commonwealth preference area

3. Up to and including 31st December 1976, in the case of goods which fall within the subheading specified in column 1 of Schedule 1 hereto and are of the description specified in column 2 thereof and qualify for Commonwealth preference, import duty shall be charged at the rate shown in column 4 thereof in relation to the goods instead of any higher rate which would otherwise apply.

(a) 1958 c. 6.   (b) 1972 c. 68.   (c) *See* S.I. 1970/1537 (1970 III, p. 5293).
(d) 1889 c. 63.

Miscellaneous

4.—(1) Article 3 above shall operate without prejudice to any reliefs from import duty to which any goods therein referred to may be entitled as goods of developing countries or of a particular country or area or otherwise.

(2) Any description of goods in column 2 of Schedule 1 hereto shall be taken to comprise all goods which would be classified under an entry in the same terms constituting a subheading of the relevant heading of the Customs Tariff 1959.

(3) For the purposes of classification under the Customs Tariff 1959 in so far as that depends on the rate of duty, any goods to which this Order applies shall be treated as chargeable with the same duty as if this Order had not been made.

(4) Where any import duty for the time being chargeable on any goods has been reduced by a directly applicable Community provision the import duty shall, to the extent of that reduction, not be regarded as reduced by virtue of this Order and the reference to it in Schedule 1 hereto shall be treated as merely indicative of the rate of import duty payable in respect of the goods.

5. In Schedule 1 to the Import Duties (Temporary Reductions and Exemptions) (No. 22) Order 1975**(a)** in column 2 of subheading ex 16.05 A for the word "canning" there shall be substituted "processing".

6. Schedule 1 to the Import Duties (Temporary Reductions and Exemptions) (No. 4) Order 1976**(b)** shall be amended as specified in Schedule 2 hereto.

J. Dormand,
Donald R. Coleman,
Two of the Lords Commissioners
of Her Majesty's Treasury.

19th February 1976.

SCHEDULE 1

Tariff Heading (1)	Description (2)	Rate of Duty	
		Full (3)	Commonwealth (4)
ex 06.04 BIa) 2.	Foliage of asparagus plumosus	4.8% + £0.0734 per kg.	4.8%

SCHEDULE 2

AMENDMENTS TO SCHEDULE 1 TO THE IMPORT DUTIES (TEMPORARY REDUCTIONS AND EXEMPTIONS) (NO. 4) ORDER 1976

(1) In columns 2, 3, 4 and 5 of heading 73.13 before the words "—more than 1 millimetre but less than 3 millimetres (ECSC)" there shall be inserted the following entries:

" (2)	(3)	(4)	(5)
—3 millimetres	7	2.1	3.1 "

(2) In column 2 of heading 73.13 for the words "—more than 2 millimetres but less than 3 millimetres (ECSC)" there shall be substituted "—2 millimetres or more but not more than 3 millimetres (ECSC)".

EXPLANATORY NOTE

(This Note is not part of the Order.)

This Order provides for reduction in import duty in the case of goods specified in Schedule 1 to this Order as from 1st March 1976 to 31st December 1976.

In the case of goods in Schedule 1 import duty is reduced to the rate specified in column 3 instead of any higher rate which would otherwise apply, and in the case of goods in Schedule 1 of the Commonwealth preference area a reduction to a lower rate of import duty is available, such reduced rate being shown in column 4. The goods specified in Schedule 1 are subject to reduction of duty in the Common Customs Tariff of the European Economic Community and the reductions provided by this Order are made in accordance with the United Kingdom's Community obligations.

The Order also amends, as from 23rd February 1976, the Import Duties (Temporary Reductions and Exemptions) (No. 22) Order 1975 by altering part of the description in tariff subheading 16.05 A in Schedule 1 to that Order. It also amends as from 23rd February 1976 the Import Duties (Temporary Reductions and Exemptions) (No. 4) Order 1976 by altering part of the description of tariff heading 73.13 in Schedule 1 to that Order and provides for reduction in duty in the case of certain other goods of the same tariff heading specified in Schedule 2 to this Order.

STATUTORY INSTRUMENTS

1976 No. 256

ANIMALS

DISEASES OF ANIMALS

The Tuberculosis (Compensation) (Amendment) Order 1976

Made - - - -	*23rd February* 1976
Laid before Parliament	*24th February* 1976
Coming into Operation	*25th February* 1976

The Minister of Agriculture, Fisheries and Food, in exercise of the powers conferred on him by sections 17(3), 19(7) and 85(1) of the Diseases of Animals Act 1950(a), and of all his other enabling powers, with the approval of the Treasury, hereby orders as follows:—

Citation and commencement

1. This order, which may be cited as the Tuberculosis (Compensation) (Amendment) Order 1976, shall come into operation on 25th February 1976.

Interpretation

2.—(1) This order shall be construed as one with the Tuberculosis (Compensation) Order 1964(b), as amended (c), hereinafter referred to as "the principal order".

(2) The Interpretation Act 1889(d) applies for the interpretation of this order as it applies for the interpretation of an Act of Parliament.

Amendment of principal order

3. Article 4(2) of the principal order (which prescribes scales of compensation for bovine animals slaughtered on account of tuberculosis) shall be amended by the substitution in sub-paragraph (*a*) thereof for the reference to "£180" of a reference to "£300".

In Witness whereof the Official Seal of the Minister of Agriculture, Fisheries and Food is hereunto affixed on 20th February 1976.

(L.S.)   *Frederick Peart,*
Minister of Agriculture, Fisheries and Food.

We approve,
23rd February 1976.

Donald R. Coleman,
M. Cocks,
Two of the Lords Commissioners
of Her Majesty's Treasury.

(a) 1950 c. 36.
(c) S.I. 1972/814 (1972 II, p. 2621).
(b) S.I. 1964/1150 (1964 II, p. 2630).
(d) 1889 c. 63.

EXPLANATORY NOTE

(*This Note is not part of the Order.*)

This Order amends the Tuberculosis (Compensation) Order 1964 (as amended) by increasing from £180 to £300 the maximum limit of compensation payable for cattle slaughtered by the Minister because they are affected by tuberculosis or have reacted to a tuberculin test. In respect of cattle slaughtered by the Minister because they have been exposed to the infection of tuberculosis by contact with an affected animal or a reactor, compensation remains payable at he full market value.

STATUTORY INSTRUMENTS

1976 No. 257

ANIMALS

DISEASES OF ANIMALS

The Brucellosis (England and Wales) Compensation (Amendment) Order 1976

Made - - - -	*23rd February* 1976
Laid before Parliament	*24th February* 1976
Coming into Operation	*25th February* 1976

The Minister of Agriculture, Fisheries and Food, in exercise of the powers conferred on him by sections 17(3), 19(7) and 85(1) of the Diseases of Animals Act 1950(a), as extended by Article 3(1) of the Diseases of Animals (Extension of Definitions) Order 1971(b), and of all his other enabling powers, with the approval of the Treasury, hereby orders as follows:—

Citation and commencement

1. This order, which may be cited as the Brucellosis (England and Wales) Compensation (Amendment) Order 1976, shall come into operation on 25th February 1976.

Interpretation

2.—(1) This order shall be construed as one with the Brucellosis (England and Wales) Compensation Order 1972(c), hereinafter referred to as "the principal order".

(2) The Interpretation Act 1889(d) applies for the interpretation of this order as it applies for the interpretation of an Act of Parliament.

Amendment of principal order

3. Article 3(2) of the principal order (which prescribes scales of compensation payable for bovine animals slaughtered on account of brucellosis) shall be amended by—

(a) the substitution in sub-paragraph (a) thereof for the reference to "£180" of a reference to "£300", and

(b) the substitution in sub-paragraph (b) thereof for the reference to "£240" of a reference to "£400".

(a) 1950 c. 36.
(c) S.I. 1972/1500 (1972 III, p. 4416).

(b) S.I. 1971/531 (1971 I, p. 1530).
(d) 1889 c. 63.

In Witness whereof the Official Seal of the Minister of Agriculture, Fisheries and Food is hereunto affixed on 20th February 1976.

(L.S.)

Frederick Peart,
Minister of Agriculture, Fisheries and Food.

We approve,
23rd February 1976.

Donald R. Coleman,
M. Cocks,
Two of the Lords Commissioners
of Her Majesty's Treasury.

EXPLANATORY NOTE

(This Note is not part of the Order.)

This Order amends the Brucellosis (England and Wales) Compensation Order 1972 so as to raise the limit of the amount of compensation payable for cattle slaughtered by the Minister because they are affected with brucellosis or are reactors. The limit is increased from £180 to £300 where the animal slaughtered was comprised in an accredited herd, and from £240 to £400 in any other case. In respect of cattle slaughtered by the Minister because they have been exposed to the infection of brucellosis, compensation remains payable at the full market value.

STATUTORY INSTRUMENTS

1976 No. 258 (S. 18)

ANIMALS

DISEASES OF ANIMALS

The Brucellosis Compensation (Scotland) Amendment Order 1976

Made - - - -	*23rd February* 1976
Laid before Parliament	*24th February* 1976
Coming into Operation	*25th February* 1976

In exercise of the powers conferred by sections 17(3), 19(7) and 85(1) of the Diseases of Animals Act 1950(a) and now vested in me (b), and as extended by Article 3(1) of the Diseases of Animals (Extension of Definitions) Order 1971(c), and of all other powers enabling me in that behalf and with the approval of the Treasury, I hereby make the following order:—

Citation and commencement

1. This order, which may be cited as the Brucellosis Compensation (Scotland) Amendment Order 1976, shall come into operation on 25th February 1976.

Interpretation

2.—(1) This order shall be construed as one with the Brucellosis Compensation (Scotland) Order 1972(d), hereinafter referred to as "the principal order".

(2) The Interpretation Act 1889(e) applies for the interpretation of this order as it applies for the interpretation of an Act of Parliament.

Amendment of principal order

3. Article 3(2) of the principal order (which prescribes scales of compensation payable for bovine animals slaughtered on account of brucellosis) shall be amended by the substitution—

    (*a*) in sub-paragraph (*a*) thereof for the reference to "£180" of a reference to "£300"; and

---

  (a) 1950 c. 36.
  (b) By the Transfer of Functions (Animal Health) Order 1955 (S.I. 1955/958 (1955 I, p. 1184)).
                                 (c) S.I. 1971/531 (1971 I, p. 1530).
  (d) S.I. 1972/1538 (1972 III, p. 4524).   **(e)** 1889 c. 63.

    (*b*) in sub-paragraph (*b*) thereof for the reference to "£240" of a reference to "£400".

William Ross,
One of Her Majesty's Principal
Secretaries of State.

New St. Andrew's House,
Edinburgh.

20th February 1976.

We approve,

Donald R. Coleman,
M. Cocks,
Two of the Lords Commissioners
of Her Majesty's Treasury.

23rd February 1976.

EXPLANATORY NOTE

(This Note is not part of the Order.)

    This Order amends the Brucellosis Compensation (Scotland) Order 1972 by increasing the maximum limits of compensation which may be paid for cattle slaughtered by the Secretary of State either because they are affected with brucellosis or because they have reacted to a diagnostic test for the disease. The limit for such cattle comprised in an accredited herd is increased from £180 to £300 and the limit for such cattle comprised in other herds from £240 to £400. In respect of cattle slaughtered by the Secretary of State because they have been exposed to the infection of brucellosis, compensation remains payable at full market value.

STATUTORY INSTRUMENTS

1976   No. 259 (S. 19)

ANIMALS

DISEASES OF ANIMALS

The Tuberculosis (Compensation) (Scotland) Amendment Order 1976

Made	- - -	*23rd February* 1976
Laid before Parliament		*24th February* 1976
Coming into Operation		*25th February* 1976

In exercise of the powers conferred by sections 17(3), 19(7) and 85(1) of the Diseases of Animals Act 1950(**a**), and now vested in me(**b**), and of all other powers enabling me in that behalf, and with the approval of the Treasury, I hereby make the following order:—

Citation and commencement

1. This order, which may be cited as the Tuberculosis (Compensation) (Scotland) Amendment Order 1976, shall come into operation on 25th February 1976.

Interpretation

2.—(1) This order shall be construed as one with the Tuberculosis (Compensation) (Scotland) Order 1964(**c**), as amended(**d**), hereinafter referred to as "the principal order".

(2) The Interpretation Act 1889(**e**) applies for the interpretation of this order as it applies for the interpretation of an Act of Parliament.

Amendment of the principal order

3. Article 4(2) of the principal order (which prescribes scales of compensation for bovine animals slaughtered on account of tuberculosis) shall be amended by the substitution in sub-paragraph (*a*) thereof for the reference to "£180" of a reference to "£300".

William Ross,
One of Her Majesty's Principal
Secretaries of State.

New St. Andrew's House,
Edinburgh.
20th February 1976.

(**a**) 1950 c. 36.
(**b**) By the Transfer of Functions (Animal Health) Order 1955 (S.I. 1955/958 (1955I, p.1184)).
(**c**) S.I. 1964/1152 (1964 II, p. 2643).   (**d**) S.I. 1972/825 (1972 II, p. 2656).
(**e**) 1889 c. 63.

We approve,

> Donald R. Coleman,
> M. Cocks,
> Two of the Lords Commissioners
> of Her Majesty's Treasury.

23rd February 1976.

EXPLANATORY NOTE

(This Note is not part of the Order.)

This Order amends the Tuberculosis (Compensation) (Scotland) Order 1964 by increasing from £180 to £300 the maximum limit of compensation which may be paid for cattle slaughtered by the Secretary of State because they are affected with tuberculosis or have reacted to a tuberculin test. In respect of cattle slaughtered by the Secretary of State because they have been exposed to the infection of tuberculosis by contact with an affected animal or a reactor, compensation remains payable at full market value.

STATUTORY INSTRUMENTS

1976 No. 260

TRADE DESCRIPTIONS

The Trade Descriptions (Indication of Origin) (Exemptions No. 10) Directions 1976

Made - - - -	*23rd February* 1976
Coming into Operation	*1st April* 1976

The Secretary of State, in exercise of the powers conferred on her by section 1(5) of the Trade Descriptions Act 1972(a), hereby gives the following Directions:—

1.—(1) These Directions may be cited as the Trade Descriptions (Indication of Origin) (Exemptions No. 10) Directions 1976, and shall come into operation on 1st April 1976.

(2) The Directions listed in the Schedule hereto are hereby revoked.

(3) The Interpretation Act 1889(b) shall apply for the interpretation of these Directions as it applies for the interpretation of an Act of Parliament and as if these Directions and the Directions hereby revoked were Acts of Parliament.

2. In these Directions "prepacked" means made up in advance ready for supply by retail in or on a container.

3. Subsection (2) of section 1 of the Trade Descriptions Act 1972 shall be excluded in relation to prepacked uncooked bacon, other than canned or bottled uncooked bacon, if any United Kingdom name or mark applied thereto, which that subsection would, but for the provisions of this paragraph, have required to be accompanied by an indication of the country in which the bacon was manufactured or produced, is accompanied by the word "imported" appearing conspicuously.

C. E. Coffin,
An Under-Secretary of the
Department of Prices and Consumer Protection.

23rd February 1976.

(a) 1972 c. 34.   (b) 1889 c. 63.

SCHEDULE

The Trade Descriptions (Indication of Origin) (Exemptions No. 2) Directions 1972.	S.I. 1972/1887 (1972 III, p. 5511).
The Trade Descriptions (Indication of Origin) (Exemptions) (Amendment) Directions 1973.	S.I. 1973/1027 (1973 II, p. 3102).
The Trade Descriptions (Indication of Origin) (Exemptions No. 7) Directions 1974.	S.I. 1974/1046 (1974 II, p. 3900).
The Trade Descriptions (Indication of Origin) (Exemptions) (Amendment) Directions 1974.	S.I. 1974/2032 (1974 III, p. 7862).
The Trade Descriptions (Indication of Origin) (Exemptions) (Amendment) Directions 1975.	S.I. 1975/949 (1975 II, p. 3301).
The Trade Descriptions (Indication of Origin) (Exemptions No. 7) (Amendment No. 2) Directions 1975.	S.I. 1975/2047 (1975 III, p. 7488).
The Trade Descriptions (Indication of Origin) (Exemptions No. 8) Directions 1975.	S.I. 1975/1758 (1975 III, p. 6693).

EXPLANATORY NOTE

(This Note is not part of the Directions.)

These Directions exclude indefinitely section 1(2) of the Trade Descriptions Act 1972 (which requires that a United Kingdom name or mark applied to imported goods be accompanied by an indication of origin of those goods) in relation to prepacked uncooked bacon, other than canned or bottled bacon, if a United Kingdom name or mark applied to such bacon is accompanied by the word "imported".

STATUTORY INSTRUMENTS

1976 No. 261

CRIMINAL PROCEDURE, ENGLAND AND WALES

The Fixed Penalty (Procedure) (Amendment) Regulations 1976

Made - - - -	*20th February* 1976
Laid before Parliament	*1st March* 1976
Coming into Operation	*1st April* 1976

In exercise of the powers conferred upon me by section 80(11) of the Road Traffic Regulation Act 1967**(a)**, I hereby make the following Regulations:—

1. These Regulations may be cited as the Fixed Penalty (Procedure) (Amendment) Regulations 1976 and shall come into operation on 1st April 1976.

2. In Schedule 2 to the Fixed Penalty (Procedure) (No. 2) Regulations 1974**(b)** as amended**(c)**—

(*a*) there shall be inserted in the appropriate places the entries contained in Part I of the Schedule to these Regulations;

(*b*) there shall be substituted for the entries relating to the non-metropolitan county of Norfolk the entry set out in Part II of the Schedule to these Regulations.

Roy Jenkins,
One of Her Majesty's Principal
Secretaries of State.

Home Office,
Whitehall.
20th February 1976.

(a) 1967 c. 76.   (b) S.I. 1974/1475 (1974 III, p. 5633).
(c) The relevant amending instrument is S.I. 1975/312 (1975 I, p. 834).

Regulation 2   SCHEDULE

PART I

The non-metropolitan county of Durham.	The clerk to the justices for the Darlington petty sessional division.
The non-metropolitan county of Gwent.	The clerk to the justices for the Usk petty sessional division.

PART II

The non-metropolitan county of Norfolk.	The clerk to the justices for the Norwich petty sessional division.

EXPLANATORY NOTE

(This Note is not part of the Regulations.)

These Regulations amend the Fixed Penalty (Procedure) (No. 2) Regulations 1974 as amended so as to provide that the payment of a fixed penalty for an offence committed in the non-metropolitan counties of Durham, Gwent and Norfolk shall be paid to the clerks to the justices for the petty sessional divisions of Darlington, Usk and Norwich respectively.

STATUTORY INSTRUMENTS

1976 No. 270 (S. 20)

SOCIAL WORK, SCOTLAND

Residential Establishments (Payments by Local Authorities) (Scotland) Amendment Order 1976

Made - - - -	18*th February* 1976
Coming into Operation	1*st April* 1976

In exercise of the powers conferred on me by section 90(3) of and paragraph 2(2) of Schedule 7 to the Social Work (Scotland) Act 1968(a), and of all other powers enabling me in that behalf, I hereby make the following order:—

Citation, commencement and interpretation

1.—(1) This order may be cited as the Residential Establishments (Payments by Local Authorities) (Scotland) Amendment Order 1976 and shall come into operation on 1st April 1976.

(2) The Interpretation Act 1889(b) shall apply for the interpretation of this order as it applies for the interpretation of an Act of Parliament.

Increase in rate of payment

2. Article 3 of the Residential Establishments (Payments by Local Authorities) (Scotland) Order 1971(c) as amended **(d)** (which prescribes weekly payments to be made by local authorities in respect of the expenses of carrying on the establishments which were approved schools immediately before the commencement of Part III of the Social Work (Scotland) Act 1968) shall be further amended by the substitution of £51·31 for £36·75.

William Ross,
One of Her Majesty's Principal
Secretaries of State.

New St. Andrew's House,
Edinburgh.
18th February 1976.

(a) 1968 c. 49.   (b) 1889 c. 63.
(c) S.I. 1971/249 (1971 I, p. 857).
(d) The relevant amending instrument is S.I. 1975/359 (1975 I, p. 1119).

EXPLANATORY NOTE

(This Note is not part of the Order.)

This Order amends the Residential Establishments (Payments by Local Authorities) (Scotland) Order 1971 as amended by increasing from £36·75 to £51·31 the weekly payments to be made by local authorities in respect of the expenses of carrying on the establishments which were approved schools immediately before the commencement of Part III of the Social Work (Scotland) Act 1968 and in relation to which functions were transferred to local authorities under section 1(5) of that Act.

STATUTORY INSTRUMENTS

1976 No. 271

HOUSING, ENGLAND AND WALES

The Rent Refunds (Housing Authorities) (Amendment) Regulations 1976

Made - - - -	*24th February* 1976
Laid before Parliament	*2nd March* 1976
Coming into Operation	*23rd March* 1976

The Secretary of State for the Environment as respects England and the Secretary of State for Wales as respects Wales, in exercise of the powers conferred on them by sections 15(1) and 17(3) of and paragraph 15 of Schedule 1 to the Housing Rents and Subsidies Act 1975(a) and of all other powers enabling them in that behalf, hereby make the following regulations:—

1.—(1) These regulations may be cited as the Rent Refunds (Housing Authorities) (Amendment) Regulations 1976 and shall come into operation on 23rd March 1976.

(2) The Interpretation Act 1889(b) shall apply for the interpretation of these regulations as it applies for the interpretation of an Act of Parliament.

(3) In these regulations "the principal regulations" means the Rent Refunds (Housing Authorities) Regulations 1975(c).

2. In regulation 4(1) of the principal regulations there shall be substituted for the date "31st March 1976" the date "30th June 1976".

Anthony Crosland,

23rd February 1976. Secretary of State for the Environment.

John Morris,

24th February, 1976. Secretary of State for Wales.

(a) 1975 c. 6.   (b) 1889 c. 63.   (c) S.I. 1975/909 (1975 II, p. 3145).

EXPLANATORY NOTE

(This Note is not part of the Regulations.)

These Regulations, which apply to England and Wales, amend the Rent Refunds (Housing Authorities) Regulations 1975 ("the principal regulations") so as to extend the time limit for making applications for rent refunds payable pursuant to the principal regulations. Such applications (which under the principal regulations must be in writing) are required to be made to the authority concerned not later than 30th June 1976, instead of not later than 31st March 1976.

STATUTORY INSTRUMENTS

1976 No. 273

NATIONAL HEALTH SERVICE, ENGLAND AND WALES

The National Health Service
(Transferred Local Authority Property) Amendment Order 1976

Made - - - -	*24th February* 1976
Laid before Parliament	*2nd March* 1976
Coming into Operation	*31st March* 1976

The Secretary of State for Social Services, as respects England, and the Secretary of State for Wales, as respects Wales, in exercise of powers conferred on them by sections 16(2) and 56(3) of the National Health Service Reorganisation Act 1973(a) and of all other powers enabling them in that behalf, hereby make the following Order:—

Citation, commencement and interpretation

1.—(1) This Order may be cited as the National Health Service (Transferred Local Authority Property) Amendment Order 1976 and shall come into operation on 31st March 1976.

(2) The rules for the construction of Acts of Parliament contained in the Interpretation Act 1889(b) shall apply for the purpose of the interpretation of this Order as they apply for the purposes of the interpretation of an Act of Parliament.

Abolition of time limit for giving notices

2. In the National Health Service (Transferred Local Authority Property) Order 1974(c), as amended by the National Health Service (Transferred Local Authority Property) Amendment Order 1975(d), in—

(*a*) article 3(2) (Power of Secretary of State to give notice that he is dissatisfied with the determination of a local authority); and

(*b*) article 3(3) (Power of Secretary of State to give notice that a question exists),

"before 1st April 1976" shall be omitted.

(a) 1973 c. 32.
(c) S.I. 1974/330 (1974 I, p. 1088).

(b) 1889 c. 63.
(d) S.I. 1975/325 (1975 I, p. 880).

Barbara Castle,
Secretary of State for Social Services.

24th February 1976.

John Morris,
Secretary of State for Wales.

24th February 1976.

EXPLANATORY NOTE

(This Note is not part of the Order.)

This Order abolishes the time limit (1st April 1976) within which the Secretary of State may give notice that he is dissatisfied with the determination of a local authority under Article 3(1) of the Order of 1974 or that a question exists in a case where a local authority has failed to make such a determination.

STATUTORY INSTRUMENTS

1976 No. 275

INDUSTRIAL TRAINING

The Industrial Training Levy (Knitting, Lace and Net) Order 1976

Made	-	-	- *23rd February* 1976
Laid before Parliament			*5th March* 1976
Coming into Operation			*1st April* 1976

Whereas proposals made by the Knitting, Lace and Net Industry Training Board for the raising and collection of a levy have been submitted to, and approved by, the Manpower Services Commission under section 7 of the Industrial Training Act 1964(a) ("the 1964 Act"), as amended by section 6 of and Schedule 2 to the Employment and Training Act 1973(b) ("the 1973 Act") and have thereafter been submitted by the said Commission to the Secretary of State under section 7(IC) of the 1964 Act as inserted by the 1973 Act;

And whereas in pursuance of section 7(1A)(*a*) of the 1964 Act as inserted by the 1973 Act the said proposals include provision for the exemption from the levy of employers who, in view of the small number of their employees, ought in the opinion of the Secretary of State to be exempted from it;

And whereas the Secretary of State estimates that the amount which, disregarding any exemptions, will be payable by virtue of this Order by any employer in the knitting, lace and net industry, does not exceed an amount which the Secretary of State estimates is equal to one per cent. of the aggregate of the emoluments and payments intended to be disbursed as emoluments which have been paid or are payable by any such employer to or in respect of persons employed in the industry, in respect of the period specified in the said proposals as relevant, that is to say the period hereafter referred to in this Order as "the tenth base period";

And whereas the Secretary of State is satisfied that proposals published by the said Board in pursuance of section 4A of the 1964 Act, as inserted by the 1973 Act, provide for exemption certificates relating to the levy in such cases as he considers appropriate;

Now, therefore, the Secretary of State in exercise of the powers conferred on him by section 4 of the 1964 Act, as amended by section 6 of and Schedule 2 to the 1973 Act, and of all other powers enabling him in that behalf hereby makes the following Order:—

Citation and commencement

1. This Order may be cited as the Industrial Training Levy (Knitting, Lace and Net) Order 1976 and shall come into operation on 1st April 1976.

(a) 1964 c. 16.   (b) 1973 c. 50.

Interpretation

2.—(1) In this Order unless the context otherwise requires:—

(*a*) "agriculture" has the same meaning as in section 109(3) of the Agriculture Act 1947(**a**) or, in relation to Scotland, as in section 86(3) of the Agriculture (Scotland) Act 1948(**b**);

(*b*) "an appeal tribunal" means an industrial tribunal established under section 12 of the Industrial Training Act 1964;

(*c*) "assessment" means an assessment of an employer to the levy;

(*d*) "the Board" means the Knitting, Lace and Net Industry Training Board;

(*e*) "business" means any activity of industry or commerce;

(*f*) "charity" has the same meaning as in section 360 of the Income and Corporation Taxes Act 1970(**c**);

(*g*) "emoluments" means all emoluments assessable to income tax under Schedule E (other than pensions), being emoluments from which tax under that Schedule is deductible, whether or not tax in fact falls to be deducted from any particular payment thereof;

(*h*) "employer" means a person who is an employer in the knitting, lace and net industry at any time in the tenth levy period;

(*i*) "an exemption certificate" means a certificate issued by the Board under section 4B of the 1964 Act, as inserted by the 1973 Act;

(*j*) "the industrial training order" means the Industrial Training (Knitting, Lace and Net Industry Board) Order 1966(**d**);

(*k*) "knitting, lace and net establishment" means an establishment in Great Britain engaged in the tenth base period wholly or mainly in the knitting, lace and net industry for a total of twenty-seven or more weeks or, being an establishment that commenced to carry on business in the tenth base period, for a total number of weeks exceeding one-half of the number of weeks in the part of the said period commencing with the day on which business was commenced and ending on the last day thereof;

(*l*) "the knitting, lace and net industry" means any one or more of the activities which, subject to the provisions of paragraph 2 of Schedule 1 to the industrial training order, are specified in paragraph 1 of that Schedule as the activities of the knitting, lace and net industry or, in relation to an establishment whose activities have been transferred to the industry of the Board by the transfer order, any activities so transferred;

(*m*) "the levy" means the levy imposed by the Board in respect of the tenth levy period;

(*n*) "notice" means a notice in writing;

(*o*) "the tenth base period" means the period of twelve months that commenced on 6th April 1974;

(*p*) "the tenth levy period" means the period commencing with the day upon which this Order comes into operation and ending on 31st March 1977;

(*q*) "the transfer order" means the Industrial Training (Transfer of Activities of Establishments) Order 1975(**e**).

(2) In the case where a knitting, lace and net establishment is taken over (whether directly or indirectly) by an employer in succession to, or jointly with, another person, a person employed at any time in the tenth base period at or

---

(a) 1947 c. 48.   (b) 1948 c. 45.   (c) 1970 c. 10.
(d) S.I. 1966/246 (1966 I, p. 506).   (e) S.I. 1975/434 (1975 I, p. 1371).

from the establishment shall be deemed, for the purposes of this Order, to have been so employed by the employer carrying on the said establishment on the day upon which this Order comes into operation, and any reference in this Order to persons employed by an employer in the tenth base period at or from a knitting, lace and net establishment shall be construed accordingly.

(3) In reckoning the amount of emoluments for the purposes of this Order no regard shall be had to the emoluments of any person wholly engaged in agriculture or in the supply of food or drink for immediate consumption.

(4) Any reference in this Order to an establishment that commences to carry on business or that ceases to carry on business shall not be taken to apply where the location of the establishment is changed but its business is continued wholly or mainly at or from the new location, or where the suspension of activities is of a temporary or seasonal nature.

(5) The Interpretation Act 1889(a) shall apply to the interpretation of this Order as it applies to the interpretation of an Act of Parliament.

Imposition of the levy

3.—(1) The levy to be imposed by the Board on employers in respect of the tenth levy period shall be assessed in accordance with the provisions of this Article.

(2) The levy shall be assessed by the Board separately in respect of each relevant establishment of an employer (that is to say the knitting, lace and net establishment of an employer other than any establishment in respect of which an exemption certificate has been issued to the employer, or one which is an establishment of an employer who is exempt from the levy by virtue of paragraph (5) of this Article), but in agreement with the employer one assessment may be made in respect of any number of such establishments, in which case those establishments shall be deemed for the purposes of that assessment to constitute one establishment.

(3) Subject to the provisions of this Article, the levy assessed in respect of a knitting, lace and net establishment of an employer shall be an amount equal to 0·425 per cent. of the sum of the emoluments of all the persons employed in the tenth base period by the employer at or from that establishment.

(4) The amount of the levy imposed in respect of a knitting, lace and net establishment that ceases to carry on business in the tenth levy period shall be in the same proportion to the amount that would otherwise be due under paragraph (3) of this Article as the number of days between the commencement of the said levy period and the date of cessation of business (both dates inclusive) bears to the number of days in the said levy period.

(5) There shall be exempt from the levy—

(*a*) an employer in whose case the sum of the emoluments of all the persons employed by him in the tenth base period at or from the knitting, lace and net establishment or establishments of the employer was less than £25,000 or in whose case the number of the persons employed by him under contracts of service in the week which included 5th April 1975 did not exceed twenty-four;

(*b*) a charity.

(a) 1889 c. 63.

Assessment notices

4.—(1) The Board shall serve an assessment notice on every employer assessed to the levy, but one notice may comprise two or more assessments.

(2) An assessment notice shall state the amount of the levy payable by the person assessed to the levy, and that amount shall be equal to the total amount (rounded down where necessary to the nearest £1) of the levy assessed by the Board under Article 3 of this Order in respect of each establishment included in the notice.

(3) An assessment notice shall state the Board's address for the service of a notice of appeal or of an application for an extension of time for appealing.

(4) An assessment notice may be served on the person assessed to the levy either by delivering it to him personally or by leaving it, or sending it to him by post, at his last known address or place of business in the United Kingdom or, if that person is a corporation, by leaving it, or sending it by post to the corporation, at such address or place of business or at its registered or principal office.

Payment of the levy

5.—(1) Subject to the provisions of this Article and of Articles 6 and 7, the amount of the levy payable under an assessment notice served by the Board shall be due and payable to the Board on 1st May 1976.

(2) An assessment shall not be recoverable by the Board until there has expired the time allowed for appealing against the assessment by Article 7(1) of this Order and any further period or periods of time that the Board or an appeal tribunal may have allowed for appealing under paragraph (2) or (3) of that Article or, where an appeal is brought, until the appeal is decided or withdrawn.

Withdrawal of assessment

6.—(1) The Board may, by a notice served on the person assessed to the levy in the same manner as an assessment notice, withdraw an assessment if that person has appealed against that assessment under the provisions of Article 7 of this Order and the appeal has not been entered in the Register of Appeals kept under the appropriate Regulations specified in paragraph (5) of that Article.

(2) The withdrawal of an assessment shall be without prejudice to the power of the Board to serve a further assessment notice in respect of any establishment to which that assessment related and, where the withdrawal is made by reason of the fact that an establishment has ceased to carry on business in the tenth levy period, the said notice may provide that the whole amount payable thereunder in respect of the establishment shall be due one month after the date of the notice.

Appeals

7.—(1) A person assessed to the levy may appeal to an appeal tribunal against the assessment within one month from the date of the service of the assessment notice or within any further period or periods of time that may be allowed by the Board or an appeal tribunal under the following provisions of this Article.

(2) The Board by notice may for good cause allow a person assessed to the levy to appeal to an appeal tribunal against the assessment at any time within the

period of four months from the date of the service of the assessment notice or within such further period or periods as the Board may allow before such time as may then be limited for appealing has expired.

(3) If the Board shall not allow an application for extension of time for appealing, an appeal tribunal shall upon application made to the tribunal by the person assessed to the levy have the like powers as the Board under the last foregoing paragraph.

(4) In the case of an establishment that ceases to carry on business in the tenth levy period on any day after the date of the service of the relevant assessment notice the foregoing provisions of this Article shall have effect as if for the period of four months from the date of the service of the assessment notice mentioned in paragraph (2) of this Article there were substituted the period of six months from the date of the cessation of business.

(5) An appeal or an application to an appeal tribunal under this Article shall be made in accordance with the Industrial Tribunals (England and Wales) Regulations 1965(a) as amended by the Industrial Tribunals (England and Wales) (Amendment) Regulations 1967(b) except where the establishment to which the relevant assessment relates is wholly in Scotland in which case the appeal or application shall be made in accordance with the Industrial Tribunals (Scotland) Regulations 1965(c) as amended by the Industrial Tribunals (Scotland) (Amendment) Regulations 1967(d).

(6) The powers of an appeal tribunal under paragraph (3) of this Article may be exercised by the President of the Industrial Tribunals (England and Wales) or by the President of the Industrial Tribunals (Scotland) as the case may be.

Evidence

8.—(1) Upon the discharge by a person assessed to the levy of his liability under an assessment the Board shall if so requested issue to him a certificate to that effect.

(2) The production in any proceedings of a document purporting to be certified by the Secretary of the Board to be a true copy of an assessment or other notice issued by the Board or purporting to be a certificate such as is mentioned in the foregoing paragraph of this Article shall, unless the contrary is proved, be sufficient evidence of the document and of the facts stated therein.

Signed by order of the Secretary of State.

23rd February 1976.

Harold Walker,
Joint Parliamentary Under Secretary of State,
Department of Employment.

(a) S.I. 1965/1101 (1965 II, p. 2805).   (b) S.I. 1967/301 (1967 I, p. 1040).
(c) S.I. 1965/1157 (1965 II, p. 3266).   (d) S.I. 1967/302 (1967 I, p. 1050).

EXPLANATORY NOTE
(This Note is not part of the Order.)

This Order gives effect to proposals of the Knitting, Lace and Net Industry Training Board, which were submitted to and approved by the Manpower Services Commission, and thereafter submitted by the Manpower Services Commission to the Secretary of State. The proposals are for the imposition of a levy on employers in the knitting, lace and net industry for the purpose of encouraging adequate training in the industry.

The levy is to be imposed in respect of the tenth levy period commencing with the day upon which this Order comes into operation and ending on 31st March 1977. The levy will be assessed by the Board and there will be a right of appeal against an assessment to an industrial tribunal.

STATUTORY INSTRUMENTS

1976 No. 276

CONTINENTAL SHELF

PETROLEUM

The Petroleum (Production) (Amendment) Regulations 1976

Made - - - -	24th *February* 1976
Laid before Parliament	26th *February* 1976
Coming into Operation	20th *March* 1976

The Secretary of State in exercise of the powers conferred by section 6 of the Petroleum (Production) Act 1934(a) and by that section as applied by section 1(3) of the Continental Shelf Act 1964(b), and now vested in him (c), hereby makes the following Regulations:—

1.—(1) These Regulations may be cited as the Petroleum (Production) (Amendment) Regulations 1976 and shall come into operation on 20th March 1976.

(2) The Interpretation Act 1889(d) shall apply to the interpretation of these Regulations as it applies to the interpretation of an Act of Parliament.

2. The Petroleum (Production) Regulations 1966(e), as amended (f), shall have effect with the substitution for Regulation 6 (non-invited applications) of the following regulation:—

"6.—(1) An application for a production licence in accordance with the provisions of this regulation (in these regulations called a "non-invited application") may, subject to paragraphs (2) to (5), be made in respect of any landward area and may, subject to paragraphs (6) and (7), be made in respect of any seaward area.

(2) No non-invited application may be made in respect of a landward area which is, or is comprised in, an area in respect of which the Secretary of State has published a Gazette notice in accordance with regulation 7(2) unless it is made in respect of any landward area which is, or is comprised in, an area in respect of which the Secretary of State has published a Gazette notice to the effect that he is once more prepared to receive non-invited applications in respect of the area therein described or thereby specified by reference to a map deposited at the principal office of the Department of Energy and at such other places (if any) as may be specified in that notice, being a notice published after the last Gazette notice in accordance with regulation 7(2) comprising that area.

(a) 1934 c. 36.   (b) 1964 c. 29.
(c) S.R. & O. 1942/1132 (Rev. XV, p. 99), the Ministry of Fuel and Power Act 1945 (c. 19), S.I. 1969/1498, 1970/1537 (1969 III, p. 4797; 1970 III, p. 5293).
(d) 1889 c. 63.   (e) S.I. 1966/898 (1966 II, p. 2109).
(f) S.I. 1971/814, 1972/1522 (1971 II, p. 2327; 1972 III, p. 4477), the Petroleum and Submarine Pipe-lines Act 1975 (c. 74).

(3) Every landward area in respect of which a non-invited application is made shall be a clearly defined area which shall as far as possible be compact and shall be described in the application which shall be accompanied by two copies of the 1:25,000 Ordnance Survey Map or such other map or chart as may be required by the Secretary of State, upon which shall be delineated the boundaries of the landward area in respect of which a licence is applied for.

(4) No licence shall be granted pursuant to a non-invited application in respect of a landward area of more than 250 square kilometres or less than 10 square kilometres unless the Secretary of State otherwise determines.

(5) Where an applicant desires to make non-invited applications for two or more separate landward areas, a separate application shall be made in respect of each such area, but a licence may be granted in respect of two or more landward areas provided that the sum of such areas shall not exceed 250 square kilometres.

(6) No non-invited application in respect of a seaward area, other than an application which is made by the British National Oil Corporation, the British Gas Corporation or any body corporate which is a wholly owned subsidiary of either of those Corporations, may be made unless—

(a) the whole of the area to which the application relates is, or has been, comprised in a production licence which was granted in pursuance of an invited application;

(b) the whole of that area is proposed to be, or has been, surrendered by the holder for the time being of that licence otherwise than by virtue of a provision of that licence requiring the compulsory surrender of part of the licensed area; and

(c) the Secretary of State has served notice in writing on such persons as appear to him to be concerned that he would be prepared to consider the application in such circumstances as may be specified in the notice.

(7) For the purposes of paragraph (6) the expression "wholly owned subsidiary" shall be construed in accordance with section 150(4) of the Companies Act 1948(a) or section 144(5) of the Companies Act (Northern Ireland) 1960(b)."

24th February 1976.

John Smith,
Minister of State,
Department of Energy.

(a) 1948 c. 38.   (b) 1960 c. 22 (N.I.).

EXPLANATORY NOTE
(This Note is not part of the Regulations.)

These Regulations further amend the provisions of the Petroleum (Production) Regulations 1966 which relate to the making of applications for petroleum production licences.

The Regulations extend the category of licences for which application may be made otherwise than by virtue of the invited application procedure prescribed by Regulation 7 of the 1966 Regulations to include two classes of seaward production licence. These are licences in respect of areas formerly comprised in production licences issued pursuant to invited applications and licences issued to the British National Oil Corporation, the British Gas Corporation or their wholly owned subsidiaries.

STATUTORY INSTRUMENTS

1976 No. 281 (L. 4)

COUNTY COURTS

The County Court Districts (Thanet) Order 1976

Made	-	-	-	*23rd February* 1976
Coming into Operation				*25th March* 1976

The Lord Chancellor, in exercise of the powers conferred on him by section 2 of the County Courts Act 1959(a), hereby makes the following Order:—

1.—(1) This Order may be cited as the County Court Districts (Thanet) Order 1976 and shall come into operation on 25th March 1976.

(2) The Interpretation Act 1889(b) shall apply to the interpretation of this Order as it applies to the interpretation of an Act of Parliament.

2.—(1) The districts of the Margate and Ramsgate County Courts shall be consolidated and courts shall be held for the consolidated district at Margate under the name of the Thanet County Court; and accordingly Schedule 1 to the County Court Districts Order 1970(c), as amended(d), shall be further amended:—

    (*a*) by inserting therein, immediately after the entry relating to the Taunton County Court, the entry set out in Schedule 1 to this Order; and

    (*b*) by deleting the entries therein relating to the Margate and Ramsgate County Courts.

(2) The Thanet County Court shall have jurisdiction to deal with proceedings commenced in the Margate County Court or the Ramsgate County Court before this Order comes into operation.

3. The amendments set out in column 2 of Schedule 2 to this Order shall be made in the corresponding columns of Schedule 1 to the County Court District Order 1970 opposite the name of the court mentioned in column 1.

Dated 23rd February 1976.

Elwyn-Jones, C.

(a) 1959 c. 22.   (b) 1889 c. 63.   (c) S.I. 1970/16 (1970 I, p. 17).
(d) There are no relevant amendments.

SCHEDULE 1

THANET COUNTY COURT

Column 1	Column 2	Column 3
Thanet ...	Broadstairs and St. Peter's Urban District.	Broadstairs and St. Peter's.
	Eastry Rural District (part). *Other parts* in Canterbury, Deal and Dover County Court Districts.	Acol, Minster, Monkton, St. Nicholas at Wade, Sarre.
	Margate Municipal Borough.	Margate.
	Ramsgate Municipal Borough.	Ramsgate.

SCHEDULE 2

THANET COUNTY COURT

AMENDMENTS CONSEQUENT ON CONSOLIDATION

Column 1	Column 2
Canterbury	In the entry relating to the Eastry Rural District:— For "*Other parts* in Deal, Dover, Margate and Ramsgate County Court Districts." substitute "*Other parts* in Deal, Dover and Thanet County Court Districts."
Deal ...	In the entry relating to the Eastry Rural District:— For "*Other parts* in Canterbury, Dover, Margate and Ramsgate County Court Districts." substitute "*Other parts* in Canterbury, Dover and Thanet County Court Districts."
Dover ...	In the entry relating to the Eastry Rural District:— For "*Other parts* in Canterbury, Deal, Margate and Ramsgate County Court Districts." substitute "*Other parts* in Canterbury, Deal and Thanet County Court Districts.".

EXPLANATORY NOTE

(*This Note is not part of the Order.*)

This Order amalgamates the Ramsgate and Margate County Courts under the name of the Thanet County Court; the court for the new district will sit at Margate.

STATUTORY INSTRUMENTS

1976 No. 282 (S.21)

COURT OF SESSION, SCOTLAND

Act of Sederunt (Rules of Court Amendment No. 2) 1976

Made - - - -	*24th February* 1976
Coming into Operation	*1st April* 1976

The Lords of Council and Session, under and by virtue of the powers conferred upon them by section 2 of the Courts of Law Fees (Scotland) Act 1895(a) and section 16 of the Administration of Justice (Scotland) Act 1933(b), and of all other powers competent to them in that behalf, with the approval of the Treasury, do hereby enact and declare:

Citation, interpretation and commencement

1.—(1) This Act of Sederunt may be cited as the Act of Sederunt (Rules of Court Amendment No. 2) 1976, and shall come into operation on 1st April 1976.

(2) The Interpretation Act 1889(c) shall apply to the interpretation of this Act of Sederunt as it applies to an Act of Parliament.

Amendment of rules relating to Fee-Fund Dues

2. The Rules of Court(d) are amended—

(*a*) in rule 341—

(i) by substituting for the first two sentences the following sentence: "All the fees mentioned in Rule 340 shall be collected in cash.";

(ii) by deleting the words "whether in money or by means of stamps,";

(iii) by deleting the words "and, where appropriate, for the due cancellation of the stamps.";

(*b*) in rule 344, by deleting the last sentence;

(*c*) in rule 346, in head A II, in the note to item 8, by deleting the first sentence.

And the Lords appoint this Act of Sederunt to be inserted in the Books of Sederunt.

G. C. Emslie,
I.P.D.

Edinburgh,
24th February 1976.

(a) 1895 c. 14.   (b) 1933 c. 41.
(c) 1889 c. 63.   (d) S.I. 1965/321 (1965 I, p. 803).

EXPLANATORY NOTE

(This Note is not part of the Act of Sederunt.)

This Act of Sederunt amends the Rules of Court to reflect the authorisation by the Treasury of collection of fee-fund dues in cash.

STATUTORY INSTRUMENTS

1976 No. 283 (S. 22)

COURT OF SESSION, SCOTLAND

Act of Sederunt (Letters of Request) 1976

Made -	-	-	-	*24th February* 1976

Coming into Operation   *4th May* 1976

The Lords of Council and Session, by virtue of the powers conferred upon them by section 16 of the Administration of Justice (Scotland) Act 1933(a), by sections 2 and 5 of the Evidence (Proceedings in Other Jurisdictions) Act 1975(b), and of all other powers competent to them in that behalf do hereby enact and declare:

Citation, interpretation and commencement

1.—(1) This Act of Sederunt may be cited as the Act of Sederunt (Letters of Request) 1976 and shall come into operation on 4th May 1976.

(2) The Interpretation Act 1889(c) shall apply for the interpretation of this Act of Sederunt as it applies for the interpretation of an Act of Parliament.

Amendment of Rules of Court

2. In the Rules of Court(d)—

(*a*) there are substituted for rule 102 the following rules:—

"102.—(1) This rule applies to applications to the Court for a letter of request to a court or tribunal outside Scotland to obtain evidence of the kind specified in paragraph (2) of this rule, being evidence obtainable within the jurisdiction of that court or tribunal, for the purposes of civil proceedings commenced before the Court of Session.

(2) An application under paragraph (1) of this rule may be made in relation to a request—

(*a*) for the examination of witnesses;

(*b*) for the production of documents;

(*c*) for the inspection, photographing, preservation, custody or detention of any property;

(*d*) for the taking of samples of any property and the carrying out of any experiments on or with any property.

(3) An application to which this rule applies shall be made by way of a minute lodged in process and framed in accordance with Form 10, to which is appended a proposed letter of request framed in accordance with Form 11.

(4) On consideration of the minute and proposed letter of request, and after allowing the other parties to lodge answers, and after hearing any objections, the application may be granted and a letter of request authorised to be issued.

(a) 1933 c. 41.   (b) 1975 c. 34.   (c) 1889 c. 63.
(d) S.I. 1965/321 (1965 I, p. 803).

(5) Unless the court or tribunal to which a letter of request is addressed under this rule, is a court or tribunal in a country or territory—

(a) where the official language or one of the official languages is English; or

(b) in relation to which the Deputy Principal Clerk certifies that no translation is required,

then the applicant shall, before the issue of the letter, lodge in process a translation of the letter and relative interrogatories, if any, into the language of that court or tribunal.

(6) It shall be a condition of granting any such letter of request that the solicitor for the applicant shall become personally liable for the whole expenses which may become due and payable in respect thereof to the court or tribunal obtaining the evidence and to any witnesses who may be examined for that purpose; and he shall consign such sums in respect of such expenses as the court shall think proper.

(7) The letter of request when duly issued shall together with any interrogatories adjusted according to the present practice and the relative translations, be forwarded forthwith by the Deputy Principal Clerk to such person and in such manner as the Lord President may direct.

102A.—(1) This rule applies to applications made to the Court of Session for an order for evidence to be obtained in Scotland in pursuance of a request issued—

(a) by or on behalf of a court or tribunal exercising jurisdiction outside Scotland, being evidence to be obtained for the purposes of civil proceedings commenced or contemplated before that court or tribunal; or

(b) by or on behalf of a court or tribunal exercising jurisdiction outside the United Kingdom, being evidence to be obtained by the examination of witnesses, either orally or in writing, or the production of documents, for the purpose of criminal proceedings commenced before that court or tribunal.

(2) An application to which this rule applies shall be made by way of Petition to the Inner House, and shall have a certificate appended—

(a) certifying that the application is made in pursuance of a request issued by or on behalf of a court or tribunal exercising jurisdiction outside Scotland, or where the request relates to criminal proceedings, outside the United Kingdom;

(b) certifying that the evidence to be obtained is for the purposes of civil proceedings commenced or contemplated, or criminal proceedings commenced, as the case may be, before that court or tribunal;

(c) in the case of criminal proceedings, certifying that the proceedings are not of a political nature; and

(d) signed by a duly authorised diplomatic or consular representative of the country or territory within which the court or tribunal exercises jurisdiction.

(3) (a) Where in pursuance of an order of the Court granting the prayer of a Petition under this rule, a witness is cited to attend to give evidence, and he claims that he is not a compellable witness by virtue of the provisions

of section 3 of the Evidence (Proceedings in Other Jurisdictions) Act 1975, the Court, or a Commissioner appointed by the Court to take the evidence of that witness, may, if the claim is not supported by a statement in the request issued by or on behalf of the foreign court or tribunal or is not conceded by the applicant, take his evidence and have it recorded in a separate document.

(b) If a Commissioner appointed to take evidence refuses to do so on the ground that the witness is not a compellable witness, the applicant may apply to the Court to order him to do so.

(c) Where a Commissioner takes evidence under sub-paragraph (a) or (b) of this paragraph of this rule, he shall certify the claim and the grounds upon which it was made, and send the certificate to the Court, which shall cause the certificate to be sent to the foreign court or tribunal with a request to them to determine the claim.

(d) On receipt of the determination of the foreign court or tribunal the Court shall give notice of the determination to the person who made the claim and shall, in accordance with the determination, send the document in which that person's evidence is recorded to the foreign court or tribunal, or return it to that person, as the case may be.";

(b) paragraph (vi) of Rule 190 is deleted, and the following paragraphs are renumbered accordingly;

(c) there are substituted for Forms 10 and 11 the following forms:

"FORM 10

FORM OF MINUTE FOR LETTERS OF REQUEST

Minute for A.B. (design)

Counsel for the Minuter states that the evidence specified in the Schedule is required for the purpose of these proceedings and prays the Court to issue a letter of request to (specify the Court or tribunal having powers to obtain the evidence) to obtain the evidence so specified.

(signed by Counsel).

SCHEDULE

(Specify the evidence to be obtained)

FORM 11

FORM OF LETTER OF REQUEST

Whereas an action for [divorce] is now pending in the Court of Session, Supreme Court of Scotland, in which A.B. is pursuer and is represented by C.D., counsel, and E.F., solicitors, and E.F., is defender and is represented by G.H., counsel, and I.J., solicitors, and whereas it has been represented to the said Court that it is necessary, for the purposes of justice and for the due determination of the matters in dispute between the parties that the following persons should be examined as witnesses upon oath [or affirmation], that is to say:

K.L., of   , who will give evidence to the effect that
M.N., of   , who will give evidence to the effect that
and O.P., of   , who will give evidence to the effect that

and who may competently refuse to give evidence on the following grounds [or that the following evidence shall be obtained, that is to say,   ] and it appearing that such witnesses are resident [or such evidence is] within the jurisdiction of your honourable Court [or tribunal]:

Now I, the Right Honourable   as the President of the   Division of said Court [or, I, the Right Honourable [or the Honourable] Lord   , one of the Judges of said Court], have the honour to request, and do hereby request, that for the reasons aforesaid, and for the assistance of the said Court, you as the President and judges of the said Court [or tribunal] or some one or more of you, will be pleased to summon the said witnesses to attend at such time and place as you shall appoint before some one or more of you, or such other person as, according to the procedure of your Court [or tribunal], is competent to take the examination of witnesses, and that you will cause such witnesses to be examined upon the interrogatories which accompany this letter of request in the presence of the solicitors, procurators or attorneys of the pursuer and defender, or such of them as shall, on due notice given, attend such examination [or will be pleased to take such steps as, according to the procedure of your Court (or tribunal), are competent to obtain such evidence].

And I have further the honour to request that you will be pleased to cause the answers by the witnesses to the said interrogatories to be reduced to writing, and all books, letters, papers and documents produced upon such examination, [or evidence so obtained] to be duly marked for identification; and that you will be further pleased to authenticate such examination [or evidence] by the seal of your Court [or tribunal], or in such other way as is in accordance with your procedure, and to return the same through Her Majesty's Secretary of State for Foreign Affairs, for transmission to the said Court of Session.

(signed by the Judge)

(address of Foreign Court or tribunal)

(date)   .''

And the Lords appoint this Act of Sederunt to be inserted in the Books of Sederunt.

G. C. Emslie,

I.P.D.

Edinburgh,
24th February 1976.

EXPLANATORY NOTE

(This Note is not part of the Act of Sederunt.)

This Act of Sederunt amends the Rules of Court relating to Letters of Request by making new provision in respect of Letters received from foreign courts or tribunals to give effect to the provisions of the Evidence (Proceedings in Other Jurisdictions) Act 1975, and corresponding provision in respect of Letters sent out by the Court of Session in relation to civil proceedings that have been commenced before the Court.

STATUTORY INSTRUMENTS

1976 No. 289

SOCIAL SECURITY

The Family Income Supplements (Child Interim Benefit) (Consequential) Regulations 1976

Made - - - -	*26th February* 1976
Laid before Parliament	*4th March* 1976
Coming into Operation	*5th April* 1976

The Secretary of State for Social Services, in exercise of the powers conferred upon her by sections 4(2)(*a*), 6(3) (as substituted by section 3 of the Pensioners and Family Income Supplement Payments Act 1972(**a**)) and 10(2)(*h*) of the Family Income Supplements Act 1970(**b**), and of all other powers enabling her in that behalf, hereby makes the following regulations:—

Citation, commencement and interpretation

1.—(1) These regulations may be cited as the Family Income Supplements (Child Interim Benefit) (Consequential) Regulations 1976 and shall come into operation on 5th April 1976.

(2) In these regulations, unless the context otherwise requires—

"the Act" means the Family Income Supplements Act 1970;

"benefit" means a family income supplement under the Act;

"child interim benefit" means benefit under section 16 of the Child Benefit Act 1975(**c**) (interim benefit for unmarried or separated parents with children);

"determination" means a determination under the Act by the Supplementary Benefits Commission or the Appeal Tribunal;

"relevant date" means the date on which the prescribed amount in section 2(1) and the maximum amount in section 3(1) of the Act are both next increased,

and other expressions have the same meanings as in the Act.

(3) The rules for the construction of Acts of Parliament contained in the Interpretation Act 1889(**d**) shall apply for the purposes of the interpretation of these regulations as they apply for the purposes of the interpretation of an Act of Parliament.

Deduction of child interim benefit in determining a person's normal gross income

2. For any period falling before the relevant date, regulation 2(5) of the Family Income Supplements (General) Regulations 1971(**e**), as amended (**f**), shall have effect as if there were included among the sums referred to in that

---

(a) 1972 c. 75.   (b) 1970 c. 55.   (c) 1975 c. 61.
(d) 1889 c. 63.   (e) S.I. 1971/226 (1971 I, p. 662).
(f) The relevant amending instruments are S.I. 1972/1282, 1975/1360 (1972 II, p. 3857; 1975 II, p. 4634).

regulation, the whole of which are to be deducted in calculating or estimating a person's normal gross income, the whole of any sums by way of child interim benefit.

Circumstances in which entitlement to child interim benefit is to be taken into account in determinations awarding benefit

3.—(1) Where—

(a) pursuant to a claim for benefit made before the relevant date a determination is made whereby benefit is payable for a family for a period which includes that date; and

(b) a person by whom sums by way of benefit are receivable under that determination is entitled to child interim benefit for the week which includes that date,

that determination may, with effect from that date, take account of or, as the case may be, be reviewed by the Supplementary Benefits Commission so as to take account of that person's entitlement to child interim benefit.

(2) A determination made by the Supplementary Benefits Commission on a review under paragraph (1) of this regulation shall be subject to appeal in like manner as an original determination by the Supplementary Benefits Commission.

Barbara Castle,
Secretary of State for Social Services.

26th February 1976.

EXPLANATORY NOTE
(This Note is not part of the Regulations.)

These Regulations modify the legislation relating to family income supplements under the Family Income Supplements Act 1970 to take account of the introduction on 5th April 1976 of the interim benefit under section 16 of the Child Benefit Act 1975 (interim benefit for unmarried or separated parents with children).

The Regulations make provision whereby the interim benefit under the 1975 Act is not to be taken into account in determining a person's normal gross income for the purposes of the 1970 Act before the date on which the prescribed amount in section 2(1) and the maximum amount payable by way of family income supplement in section 3(1) of the 1970 Act are next both increased and whereby the interim benefit may be taken into account for those purposes from and including that date.

STATUTORY INSTRUMENTS

1976 No. 292

ROAD TRAFFIC

The Goods Vehicles (Operators' Licences) (Amendment) Regulations 1976

Made - - - -	*23rd February* 1976
Laid before Parliament	*10th March* 1976
Coming into Operation	*1st April* 1976

The Secretary of State for the Environment in exercise of the powers conferred by sections 63(4) and 91(1) of the Transport Act 1968**(a)** and now vested in him **(b)**, and of all other enabling powers, and after consultation with representative organisations in accordance with the provisions of section 91(8) of that Act, hereby makes the following Regulations:—

1. These Regulations shall come into operation on 1st April 1976 and may be cited as the Goods Vehicles (Operators' Licences) (Amendment) Regulations 1976.

2. The Goods Vehicles (Operators' Licences) Regulations 1969**(c)** shall have effect as if the following were substituted for Schedule 2 (Notice of objections):—

"SCHEDULE 2 (see Regulation 9)

NOTICE OF OBJECTION

TRANSPORT ACT 1968 AND ROAD TRAFFIC ACT 1974

Operators' Licensing

Notice of Objection

To the LICENSING AUTHORITY,   TRAFFIC AREA
We, being an objector under Section 63(3) of the Transport Act 1968 hereby give notice of objection to the application for the grant/variation of an operator's licence made by ....
and numbered .... in Applications and Decisions dated
.... and numbered .... on the
following grounds:—

*(*a*) that the applicant is not a fit person to hold an operator's licence having regard to relevant activities of himself or others before the making of the application and/or relevant convictions of himself or others during the 5 years preceding the making of the application or since the application was made.

Details are as follows:— ....
....

(a) 1968 c. 73.   (b) S.I. 1970/1681 (1970 III, p. 5551).
(c) S.I. 1969/1636 (1969 III, p. 5141).

*(b) that the applicant will not make satisfactory arrangements for securing that Part VI of the Transport Act 1968 including the international rules (i.e. the provisions relating to the statutory limits on drivers' hours) will be complied with.
Details are as follows:— ....
....

*(c) that the applicant will not make satisfactory arrangements for securing that his vehicles will not be overloaded.
Details are as follows: —..
....

*(d) (i) that the applicant will not provide satisfactory facilities and arrangements for maintaining his vehicles in a fit and serviceable condition or

(ii) that a place which is to be an operating centre for his vehicles is not suitable for that purpose.
Details are as follows: —..
....

*(e) that the provision of satisfactory maintenance facilities and arrangements and of a suitable operating centre by the applicant will be prejudiced by reason of his having insufficient financial resources.
Details are as follows: —..
....

A copy of this objection has been sent to the applicant.
Body or person by whom objection is made...
Signature of (person authorised by*) the above-named objector.

....

Position held by signatory   ....

Address of objector   ....

....

Date...................................".

*Delete if not applicable. In each case where a ground of objection is included, give reasons.

Signed by authority of
the Secretary of State
23rd February 1976.

John Gilbert,
Minister for Transport,
Department of the Environment.

EXPLANATORY NOTE
(This Note is not part of the Regulations.)

These Regulations amend Schedule 2 to the Goods Vehicles (Operators' Licences) Regulations 1969 which specifies the form of a notice of objection (pursuant to section 63(3) and (4) and 68(4) of the Transport Act 1968) to the grant or variation of an operator's licence under Part V of that Act. The change in the form is a consequence of the amendment of section 64(2) of the Act by paragraph 2 of Schedule 4 to the Road Traffic Act 1974 (c. 50).

STATUTORY INSTRUMENTS

1976 No. 293

TRIBUNALS AND INQUIRIES

The Tribunals and Inquiries (Discretionary Inquiries) (Amendment) Order 1976

Made	-	-	*24th February* 1976
Laid before Parliament			*5th March* 1976
Coming into Operation			*29th March* 1976

The Lord Chancellor and the Lord Advocate, in exercise of the powers conferred on them by sections 16 and 19(2) of the Tribunals and Inquiries Act 1971(a), as amended by the Transfer of Functions (Secretary of State and Lord Advocate) Order 1972(b), hereby make the following Order:—

1. This Order may be cited as the Tribunals and Inquiries (Discretionary Inquiries) (Amendment) Order 1976 and shall come into operation on 29th March 1976.

2. The Interpretation Act 1889(c) shall apply to the interpretation of this Order as it applies to the interpretation of an Act of Parliament.

3. Part 1 of the Schedule to the Tribunals and Inquiries (Discretionary Inquiries) Order 1975(d) shall be amended as follows:—

(*a*) after paragraph 15 there shall be inserted the following paragraph:—

"15A. Any inquiry or hearing held under paragraph 4 of Schedule 1 to the Acquisition of Land (Authorisation Procedure) Act 1946(e), as modified by paragraph 2 of Schedule 4 to the Community Land Act 1975(f), not being an inquiry the holding of which is, under paragraph 4 as modified, obligatory."; and

(*b*) after paragraph 20 there shall be inserted the following paragraph:—

"20A. Any inquiry or hearing held under paragraph 4 of Schedule 1 to the Acquisition of Land (Authorisation Procedure)

(a) 1971 c. 62.
(c) 1889 c. 63.
(e) 1946 c. 49.

(b) S.I. 1972/2002 (1972 III, p. 5957).
(d) S.I. 1975/1379 (1975 II, p. 4730).
(f) 1975 c. 77.

(Scotland) Act 1947(**a**), as modified by paragraph 2 of Schedule 4 to the Community Land Act 1975, not being an inquiry the holding of which is, under paragraph 4 as modified, obligatory.".

Dated 17th February 1976.

Elwyn-Jones, C.

Dated 24th February 1976.

Ronald King Murray,
Lord Advocate.

EXPLANATORY NOTE

(*This Note is not part of the Order.*)

This Order amends the Tribunals and Inquiries (Discretionary Inquiries) Order 1975 by including in the Schedule to that Order the discretionary inquiries specified, thus applying sections 1 and 11 of the Tribunals and Inquiries Act 1971 to those inquiries. This brings the specified inquiries within the jurisdiction of the Council on Tribunals and gives the Lord Chancellor and, in Scotland, the Lord Advocate power to make rules for regulating their procedure.

(**a**) 1947 c. 42.

STATUTORY INSTRUMENTS

1976 No. 294 (S.23)

FOOD AND DRUGS

LABELLING

The Skimmed Milk with Non-Milk Fat (Scotland) Amendment Regulations 1976

Made - - - -	*20th February* 1976
Laid before Parliament	*5th March* 1976
Coming into Operation	*26th March* 1976

In exercise of the powers conferred upon me by sections 7 and 56 of the Food and Drugs (Scotland) Act 1956(a), and of all other powers enabling me in that behalf, and after consultation with such organisations as appear to me to be representative of interests substantially affected by these regulations and after reference to the Scottish Food Hygiene Council under section 25 of the said Act (in so far as the regulations relate to the labelling, marking or description of food), I hereby make the following regulations:—

Citation, commencement and interpretation

1.—(1) These regulations may be cited as the Skimmed Milk with Non-Milk Fat (Scotland) Amendment Regulations 1976, and shall come into operation on 26th March 1976.

(2) The Interpretation Act 1889(b) shall apply for the interpretation of these regulations as it applies for the interpretation of an Act of Parliament.

Amendment of principal regulations

2. The Skimmed Milk with Non-Milk Fat (Scotland) Regulations 1960(c) as amended(d) shall be further amended as follows:—

(a) by substituting for the Second Schedule thereto the Schedule to these regulations;

(b) by deleting from regulation 2(1) thereof the words " 'local authority' means the Council of a county or a large burgh within the meaning of the Local Government (Scotland) Act, 1947 and any small burgh within the meaning of that Act shall, for the purposes of these regulations, be included in the county in which it is situated;";

(c) by substituting for paragraph (5) of regulation 2 the following paragraph:—

"(5) The Regional or Islands Council of any area shall enforce and execute the provisions of these regulations within their area.".

(a) 1956 c. 30.   (b) 1889 c. 63.   (c) S.I. 1960/2437 (1960 II, p. 1491).
(d) The relevant amending instruments are S.I. 1968/1495, 1973/249 (1968 III, p. 4249; 1973 I, p. 915).

Revocation

3. The Skimmed Milk with Non-Milk Fat (Scotland) Amendment Regulations 1968(a) and the Skimmed Milk with Non-Milk Fat (Scotland) Amendment Regulations 1973(b) are hereby revoked.

William Ross,
One of Her Majesty's Principal
Secretaries of State.

New St. Andrew's House,
Edinburgh.
20th February 1976.

(a) S.I. 1968/1495 (1968 III, p. 4249).   (b) S.I. 1973/249 (1973 I, p. 915).

Regulation 2

SCHEDULE

"THE SECOND SCHEDULE

Part I

Foods in respect of which the words "Unfit for babies" [or "Not to be used for babies"] may be omitted from the label

C & GV. Formula, manufactured by or for Cow and Gate.

Efalac, manufactured by or for L. E. Pritchitt and Company Limited.

Osterfood, manufactured by or for Glaxo-Farley Foods Limited.

S-M-A and S-M-A/S-26, manufactured by or for John Wyeth and Brother Limited.

Part II

Requirements relating to the foods specified in Part I of this Schedule

1. Every food specified in Part I of this Schedule—

   (a) shall contain poly-unsaturated fatty acids of the cis-cis form to the extent of not less than 12 per cent. of the total fatty acids present in such food;

   (b) shall not contain any protein other than protein derived from milk; and

   (c) shall not contain any ingredient of no nutritional value.

2.—(1) C & GV. Formula in powder form shall contain—

   (a) not less than 14·5 per cent. of protein derived from milk;

   (b) not less than 24·0 per cent. of fat;

   (c) ergocalciferol (vitamin D or D_2) or cholecalciferol (vitamin D or D_3) or any mixture thereof equivalent to not less than 1·25 microgrammes and not more than 3·13 microgrammes of cholecalciferol per ounce or to not less than 4·41 microgrammes and not more than 11·0 microgrammes of cholecalciferol per 100 grammes;

   (d) retinol (vitamin A) or biologically active carotenoids or any mixture thereof equivalent to not less than 180 microgrammes of retinol per ounce or to not less than 635 microgrammes of retinol per 100 grammes;

   (e) ascorbic acid (vitamin C) or dehydroascorbic acid (vitamin C) or any mixture thereof equivalent to not less than 12·0 milligrammes of ascorbic acid per ounce or to not less than 42·3 milligrammes of ascorbic acid per 100 grammes.

   (2) C & GV. Formula in condensed liquid form shall contain—

   (a) not less than 3·6 per cent. of protein derived from milk;

   (b) not less than 6·0 per cent. of fat;

   (c) ergocalciferol (vitamin D or D_2) or cholecalciferol (vitamin D or D_3) or any mixture thereof equivalent to 0·63 ±0·31 microgrammes of cholecalciferol per fluid ounce or to 2·20 ±1·10 microgrammes of cholecalciferol per 100 millilitres;

   (d) retinol (vitamin A) or biologically active carotenoids or any mixture thereof equivalent to not less than 45·0 microgrammes of retinol per fluid ounce or to not less than 158 microgrammes of retinol per 100 millilitres;

   (e) ascorbic acid (vitamin C) or dehydroascorbic acid (vitamin C) or any mixture thereof equivalent to not less than 3·00 milligrammes of ascorbic acid per fluid ounce or to not less than 10·6 milligrammes of ascorbic acid per 100 millilitres.

(3) C & GV. Formula in liquid, diluted ready for use form shall contain—

(a) not less than 1·8 per cent. of protein derived from milk;

(b) not less than 3·0 per cent. of fat;

(c) ergocalciferol (vitamin D or D₂) or cholecalciferol (vitamin D or D₃) or any mixture thereof equivalent to 0·31 ±0·16 microgrammes of cholecalciferol per fluid ounce or to 1·10 ±0·55 microgrammes of cholecalciferol per 100 millilitres;

(d) retinol (vitamin A) or biologically active carotenoids or any mixture thereof equivalent to not less than 22·5 microgrammes of retinol per fluid ounce or to not less than 79·2 microgrammes of retinol per 100 millilitres;

(e) ascorbic acid (vitamin C) or dehydroascorbic acid (vitamin C) or any mixture thereof equivalent to not less than 1·50 milligrammes of ascorbic acid per fluid ounce or to not less than 5·28 milligrammes of ascorbic acid per 100 millilitres.

3. Efalac shall contain—

(a) not less than 23·1 per cent. of protein derived from milk;

(b) not less than 28·6 per cent. of fat;

(c) ergocalciferol (vitamin D or D₂) or cholecalciferol (vitamin D or D₃) or any mixture thereof equivalent to 2·50 ±0·78 microgrammes of cholecalciferol per ounce or to 8·82 ±2·73 microgrammes of cholecalciferol per 100 grammes;

(d) retinol (vitamin A) or biologically active carotenoids or any mixture thereof equivalent to not less than 107 microgrammes of retinol per ounce or to not less than 378 microgrammes of retinol per 100 grammes.

4.—(1) *Osterfood in liquid, diluted ready for use form shall contain—*

(a) *not less than 1·7 per cent. of protein derived from milk;*

(b) *not less than 2·65 per cent. of fat;*

(c) *ergocalciferol (vitamin D or D₂) or cholecalciferol (vitamin D or D₃) or any mixture thereof equivalent to 0·37 ±0·11 microgrammes of cholecalciferol per fluid ounce or to 1·30 ±0·39 microgrammes of cholecalciferol per 100 millilitres;*

(d) *retinol (vitamin A) or biologically active carotenoids or any mixture thereof equivalent to not less than 28·4 microgrammes of retinol per fluid ounce or to not less than 100 microgrammes of retinol per 100 millilitres;*

(e) *ascorbic acid (vitamin C) or dehydroascorbic acid (vitamin C) or any mixture thereof equivalent to not less than 1·99 milligrammes of ascorbic acid per fluid ounce or to not less than 7·00 milligrammes of ascorbic acid per 100 millilitres.*

(2) *Osterfood in powder form shall contain—*

(a) *not less than 11·4 per cent. of protein derived from milk;*

(b) *not less than 18·0 per cent. of fat;*

(c) *ergocalciferol (vitamin D or D₂) or cholecalciferol (vitamin D or D₃) or any mixture thereof equivalent to 2·55 ±0·77 microgrammes of cholecalciferol per ounce or to 9·00 ±2·70 microgrammes of cholecalciferol per 100 grammes;*

(d) *retinol (vitamin A) or biologically active carotenoids or any mixture thereof equivalent to not less than 198 microgrammes of retinol per ounce or to not less than 700 microgrammes of retinol per 100 grammes;*

(e) *ascorbic acid (vitamin C) or dehydroascorbic acid (vitamin C) or any mixture thereof equivalent to not less than 13·0 milligrammes of ascorbic acid per ounce or to not less than 46·0 milligrammes of ascorbic acid per 100 grammes.*

5.—(1) S-M-A and S-M-A/S-26 in powder form shall each contain—

(a) not less than 11·6 per cent. of protein derived from milk;

(*b*) not less than 27·0 per cent. of fat;

(*c*) ergocalciferol (vitamin D or D₂) or cholecalciferol (vitamin D or D₃) or any mixture thereof equivalent to 2·30 ±0·70 microgrammes of cholecalciferol per ounce or to 8·11 ±2·47 microgrammes of cholecalciferol per 100 grammes;

(*d*) retinol (vitamin A) or biologically active carotenoids or any mixture thereof equivalent to not less than 96·3 microgrammes of retinol per ounce or to not less than 340 microgrammes of retinol per 100 grammes;

(*e*) ascorbic acid (vitamin C) or dehydroascorbic acid (vitamin C) or any mixture thereof equivalent to not less than 11·5 milligrammes of ascorbic acid per ounce or to not less than 40·6 milligrammes of ascorbic acid per 100 grammes.

(2) S-M-A and S-M-A/S-26 in concentrated liquid form shall each contain—

(*a*) not less than 2·6 per cent. of protein derived from milk;

(*b*) not less than 6·2 per cent. of fat;

(*c*) ergocalciferol (vitamin D or D₂) or cholecalciferol (vitamin D or D₃) or any mixture thereof equivalent to 0·56 ±0·18 microgrammes of cholecalciferol per fluid ounce or to 1·98 ±0·62 microgrammes of cholecalciferol per 100 millilitres;

(*d*) retinol (vitamin A) or biologically active carotenoids or any mixture thereof equivalent to not less than 42·0 microgrammes of retinol per fluid ounce or to not less than 148 microgrammes of retinol per 100 millilitres;

(*e*) ascorbic acid (vitamin C) or dehydroascorbic acid (vitamin C) or any mixture thereof equivalent to not less than 2·80 milligrammes of ascorbic acid per fluid ounce or to not less than 9·86 milligrammes of ascorbic acid per 100 millilitres.

(3) S-M-A and S-M-A/S-26 in liquid, diluted ready for use form shall each contain—

(*a*) not less than 1·3 per cent. of protein derived from milk;

(*b*) not less than 3·1 per cent. of fat;

(*c*) ergocalciferol (vitamin D or D₂) or cholecalciferol (vitamin D or D₃) or any mixture thereof equivalent to 0·28 ±0·09 microgrammes of cholecalciferol per fluid ounce or to 0·97 ±0·31 microgrammes of cholecalciferol per 100 millilitres;

(*d*) retinol (vitamin A) or biologically active carotenoids or any mixture thereof equivalent to not less than 21·0 microgrammes of retinol per fluid ounce or to not less than 73·9 microgrammes of retinol per 100 millilitres;

(*e*) ascorbic acid (vitamin C) or dehydroascorbic acid (vitamin C) or any mixture thereof equivalent to not less than 1·40 milligrammes of ascorbic acid per fluid ounce or to not less than 4·93 milligrammes per 100 millilitres.

6. In this Schedule, each reference to any percentage means that percentage by weight and in each requirement for any food specified therein containing retinol, ascorbic acid, dehydroascorbic acid, ergocalciferol or cholecalciferol any reference to dehydroascorbic acid or ergocalciferol and the first of any two references to retinol, ascorbic acid or cholecalciferol shall include the biologically active equivalents or derivatives of those substances. For the purposes of calculating the retinol equivalent of biologically active carotenoids, the factors set out in Part I of Schedule 4 to the Labelling of Food (Scotland) Regulations 1970(**a**), as amended(**b**), shall apply."

(**a**) S.I. 1970/1127 (1970 II, p. 3559).   (**b**) S.I. 1972/1790 (1972 III, p. 5163).

EXPLANATORY NOTE

(This Note is not part of the Regulations.)

These Regulations which come into operation on 26th March 1976, further amend the Second Schedule to the Skimmed Milk with Non-Milk Fat (Scotland) Regulations 1960—

(*a*) by exempting Osterfood from the requirement under regulation 3(1) and the First Schedule to bear on the label the declaration "Unfit for babies" (or the permitted alternatives);

(*b*) by replacing expressions of the existing requirements in Part II of the Second Schedule in terms of international units of vitamins A and D and milligrammes of ascorbic acid per ounce or per fluid ounce with expressions of those requirements in the following terms—

retinol (vitamin A) or biologically active carotenoids or any mixture thereof—their equivalent in microgrammes of retinol per ounce or 100 grammes or per fluid ounce or 100 millilitres.

ergocalciferol (vitamin D or D_2) or cholecalciferol (vitamin D or D_3) or any mixture thereof—their equivalent in microgrammes of cholecalciferol per ounce or 100 grammes or per fluid ounce or 100 millilitres.

ascorbic acid (vitamin C) or dehydroascorbic acid (vitamin C) or any mixture thereof—their equivalent in milligrammes of ascorbic acid per ounce or 100 grammes or per fluid ounce or 100 millilitres;

(*c*) by amending the wording of Regulation 2(5) to comply with the provisions of the Local Government (Scotland) Act 1973 (c. 65).

The amendments at (*a*) and (*b*) are consolidated with previous amendments to the Second Schedule and exemptions relating to foods no longer marketed, Alfonal, Alfonal Evaporated, White Dove Brand and Enfamil, are withdrawn.

The new material, in so far as it relates to Osterfood, appears in italics.

STATUTORY INSTRUMENTS

1976 No. 295

FOOD AND DRUGS

COMPOSITION AND LABELLING

The Soft Drinks (Amendment) Regulations 1976

Made - - -	*26th February* 1976
Laid before Parliament	*5th March* 1976
Coming into Operation	*26th March* 1976

The Minister of Agriculture, Fisheries and Food and the Secretary of State for Social Services, acting jointly, in exercise of the powers conferred on them by sections 4, 7 and 123 of the Food and Drugs Act 1955(a), as read with the Secretary of State for Social Services Order 1968(b), and of all other powers enabling them in that behalf, hereby make the following regulations after consultation with such organisations as appear to them to be representative of interests substantially affected by the regulations and after reference to the Food Hygiene Advisory Council under section 82 of the Act (in so far as the regulations are made in exercise of the powers conferred by the said section 7):—

Citation, commencement and interpretation

1.—(1) These regulations may be cited as the Soft Drinks (Amendment) Regulations 1976, and shall come into operation on 26th March 1976.

(2) The Interpretation Act 1889(c) shall apply to the interpretation of these regulations as it applies to the interpretation of an Act of Parliament.

Amendment of the principal regulations

2. The Soft Drinks Regulations 1964(d), as amended(e), shall be further amended—

(*a*) by substituting for paragraph (3) of regulation 5 thereof the following paragraph:—

"(3) Subject to the following provisions of this regulation, any soft drink intended for consumption after dilution which is of a description included in Part II of Schedule 2 or Part II of Schedule 3 to these regulations shall as respects the fruit juice or potable fruit content, as the case may be, and the quantities of added sugar and permitted artificial sweetener therein either conform to the requirements as to composition set out in relation thereto in the relevant Part II or be of such composition that after dilution in accordance

---

(a) 4 & 5 Eliz. 2. c. 16. (b) S.I. 1968/1699 (1968 III, p. 4585).
(c) 1889 c. 63. (d) S.I. 1964/760 (1964 II, p. 1605).
(e) The relevant amending instruments are S.I. 1969/1818, 1972/1510 (1969 III, p. 5644; 1972 III, p. 4441).

with the instructions referred to in regulation 7A of these regulations it conforms to the requirements as to composition set out in Part I of Schedule 2 or Part I of Schedule 3 to these regulations in relation to the corresponding soft drink intended for consumption without dilution.";

(*b*) by inserting after regulation 7 thereof the following regulation:—

"**7A.** Subject to the provisions of these regulations, no person shall sell, consign or deliver in a container any soft drink intended for consumption after dilution, which is of a description included in Part II of Schedule 2 or Part II of Schedule 3 to these regulations and does not conform to the requirements as to composition set out in relation thereto in the relevant Part II as respects the fruit juice or potable fruit content, as the case may be, and the quantities of added sugar and permitted artificial sweetener therein, unless that container bears a label on which there appear clear and precise instructions as to the manner in which the drink is to be diluted and the instructions expressly provide for a dilution ratio of not less than four parts of water to one part of the drink.";

(*c*) by substituting for regulation 14 thereof the following regulation:—

"**14.** All letters, words and instructions required by virtue of regulations 7, 7A, 8(2), 9, 10 and 11 hereof to appear on a label on a container or required by virtue of regulation 12 hereof to appear on a vending machine shall conform to the appropriate requirements set out in Schedule 4 to these regulations.";

(*d*) by deleting regulation 14A thereof;

(*e*) by substituting in paragraph 1 of Schedule 4 thereto for the words "every letter and word" the words "all letters, words and instructions" and by inserting in that paragraph immediately after the figure "7," the figure and letter "7A,".

In Witness whereof the Official Seal of the Minister of Agriculture, Fisheries and Food is hereunto affixed on 24th February 1976.

(L.S.)

Frederick Peart,
Minister of Agriculture, Fisheries and Food.

Barbara Castle,
Secretary of State for Social Services.

26th February 1976.

EXPLANATORY NOTE

(This Note is not part of the Regulations.)

These amending Regulations, which come into operation on 26th March 1976, further amend the Soft Drinks Regulations 1964—

(*a*) by providing that a soft drink intended for consumption after dilution which is of a specified description may as respects the fruit juice or potable fruit content and the quantities of added sugar and permitted artificial sweetener therein be of such composition that after dilution in accordance with the instructions referred to below it conforms to the requirements as to composition for the corresponding soft drink intended for consumption without dilution (regulation 2(*a*));

(*b*) by requiring containers of soft drinks intended for consumption after dilution which do not conform to the existing compositional requirements for those drinks to be labelled with clear and precise instructions as to the manner of dilution and as to the dilution ratio which must be not less than four parts water to one part of the particular drink (regulation 2(*b*)).

These Regulations also make consequential amendments (regulation 2(*c*) and (*e*)) and delete regulation 14A of the principal regulations, as amended, which is now spent.

STATUTORY INSTRUMENTS

1976 No. 299 (C. 8)

CRIMINAL PROCEDURE, ENGLAND AND WALES

The Criminal Justice Act 1972 (Commencement No. 5) Order 1976

Made - - - *25th February* 1976

In exercise of the powers conferred on me by section 66(6) of the Criminal Justice Act 1972(a), I hereby make the following Order:—

1. This Order may be cited as the Criminal Justice Act 1972 (Commencement No. 5) Order 1976.

2. Section 34 of the Criminal Justice Act 1972 shall come into force on 1st April 1976.

Roy Jenkins,
One of Her Majesty's Principal
Secretaries of State.

Home Office,
Whitehall.
25th February 1976.

EXPLANATORY NOTE

(This Note is not part of the Order.)

This Order brings into force on 1st April 1976 section 34 of the Criminal Justice Act 1972 which enables a constable who has power to arrest a person for various drunkenness offences to take him to any place approved for the purposes of the section by the Secretary of State as a medical treatment centre for alcoholics.

(a) 1972 c. 71.

STATUTORY INSTRUMENTS

1976 No. 300

ACQUISITION OF LAND

The Compulsory Purchase of Land Regulations 1976

Made - - - -	*26th February* 1976
Laid before Parliament	*11th March* 1976
Coming into Operation	*6th April* 1976

The Secretary of State for the Environment, in exercise of powers conferred by paragraphs 2, 3, 6, 13 and 18 of Schedule 1 to the Acquisition of Land (Authorisation Procedure) Act 1946(a), sections 30 and 104 of, and paragraphs 1, 2 and 4 of Schedule 3 to, the Town and Country Planning Act 1968(b), and section 125(2) of the Local Government Act 1972(c), and now vested in him(d), and of all other powers enabling him in that behalf, hereby makes the following regulations:—

Application, commencement and citation

1. These regulations apply to England and Wales, come into operation on 6th April 1976 and may be cited as the Compulsory Purchase of Land Regulations 1976.

Interpretation

2.—(1) In these regulations—

"the Acquisition of Land Act" means the Acquisition of Land (Authorisation Procedure) Act 1946; and

"the Planning Act" means the Town and Country Planning Act 1971(e).

(2) In these regulations, any reference to a numbered form is a reference to the form bearing that number in the Schedule hereto, or a form substantially to the like effect.

(3) In these regulations, unless the context otherwise requires, references to any enactment shall be construed as references to that enactment as amended, extended or applied by or under any other enactment.

(4) The Interpretation Act 1889(f) shall apply for the interpretation of these regulations as it applies for the interpretation of an Act of Parliament.

Prescribed forms in connection with compulsory purchase

3. The prescribed forms for the undermentioned paragraphs of Schedule 1 to the Acquisition of Land Act (which sets out the procedure for authorising compulsory purchases) shall be as follows:—

(*a*) for the purposes of paragraph 2, the form of compulsory purchase order shall be form 1, or if the order provides for the vesting of land given in exchange pursuant to paragraph 11, form 2;

(a) 1946 c. 49. (b) 1968 c. 72. (c) 1972 c. 70.
(d) S.I. 1951/142, 1900, 1970/1681 (1951 I, pp. 1348, 1347; 1970 III, p. 5551).
(e) 1971 c. 78. (f) 1889 c. 63.

(*b*) for the purposes of paragraph 3(1)(*a*), the form of newspaper notice concerning a compulsory purchase order shall be form 3;

(*c*) subject to the provisions of regulation 4 of these regulations, for the purposes of paragraph 3(1)(*b*) and (*c*), the form of notice to owners, lessees and occupiers of land comprised in a compulsory purchase order shall be form 4, or if the order is made on behalf of a parish (or in Wales community) council, form 5, or if the order is made under section 15 of the Community Land Act 1975**(a)** and contains a certificate under paragraph 1(2) of Schedule 4 to that Act, form 6;

(*d*) for the purposes of paragraph 6, the form of notice of confirmation of a compulsory purchase order shall be form 7; but in relation to an order made by a Minister, that form shall have effect with the substitution for references to the confirmation of an order submitted of references to the making of the order;

(*e*) for the purposes of paragraph 13, the form of newspaper notice stating that a certificate has been given under Part III of Schedule 1 to the Acquisition of Land Act shall be form 8.

Additional provisions with respect to listed buildings

4. Where a compulsory purchase order is made under section 114 of the Planning Act (which empowers the compulsory acquisition of listed buildings in need of repair), there shall be included in form 4, at the end of paragraph 2, the additional paragraphs set out after the notes on that form, as follows:—

(*a*) the additional paragraph numbered 3 shall be included in every case;

(*b*) the additional paragraph numbered 4 shall be included in any case where the notice is required by section 117(3) of the Planning Act (which provides for minimum compensation in the case of a building deliberately left derelict) to include a statement that the authority or Minister has included a direction for minimum compensation;

(*c*) the additional paragraph numbered 5 shall be included in every case;

and the remaining paragraphs shall be re-numbered as necessary.

Prescribed forms in connection with general vesting declaration

5. The prescribed forms for the undermentioned paragraphs of Schedule 3 to the Town and Country Planning Act 1968 (which sets out the procedure for executing general vesting declarations for land compulsory acquired) shall be as follows:—

(*a*) for the purposes of paragraph 1, the form of general vesting declaration shall be form 9;

(*b*) for the purposes of paragraph 2(1), the form of statement of the effect of paragraphs 1 to 8 shall be Part I of form 10 and the form for the giving of information to the authority shall be Part II of form 10;

(*c*) for the purposes of paragraph 4, the form of notice specifying the land and stating the effect of a general vesting declaration shall be form 11.

(a) 1975 c. 77.

Prescribed form for the purposes of section 125(2) *of the Local Government Act 1972.*

6. The prescribed form for the purposes of section 125(2) of the Local Government Act 1972 of notice of a proposed inquiry into a proposal to acquire land compulsorily on behalf of a parish or community council shall be form 12.

Manner of publication of notice under section 125(2) *of the Local Government Act 1972*

7. The notice under section 125(2) of the Local Government Act 1972 of a proposed inquiry by a district council in relation to the compulsory acquisition of land on behalf of a parish or community council under sub-section (1) of that section, to be published in the parish or community, shall be published:—

(*a*) by affixation in a conspicuous place on or near the land and in one or more places where public notices are usually posted in the locality; and

(*b*) by publication in one or more local newspapers circulating in the locality in which the land is situated.

Revocations

8. The Compulsory Purchase of Land Regulations 1972(a) and the Compulsory Purchase of Land Regulations 1974(b) are hereby revoked; but this revocation shall not affect the validity of any order, notice, advertisement, declaration or other document made, executed, published or issued before the commencement of these regulations in a form or in a manner prescribed by any of the revoked regulations.

SCHEDULE

Contents

Form 1   Compulsory purchase order.

Form 2   Compulsory purchase order providing for the vesting of exchange land.

Form 3   Newspaper notice concerning a compulsory purchase order.

Form 4   Notice to owners, lessees and occupiers of land comprised in a compulsory purchase order.

Form 5   Notice to owners, lessees and occupiers of land comprised in a compulsory purchase order on behalf of a parish or community council.

Form 6   Notice to owners, lessees and occupiers, and in Wales local authorities, of land comprised in a compulsory purchase order made under section 15 of the Community Land Act 1975 and containing a certificate under paragraph 1(2) of Schedule 4 to that Act.

Form 7   Notice of confirmation of a compulsory purchase order.

Form 8   Newspaper notice of the giving of a certificate under Part III of Schedule 1 to the Acquisition of Land (Authorisation Procedure) Act 1946.

Form 9   General vesting declaration.

Form 10   Statement concerning general vesting declaration.

Form 11   Notice stating effect of general vesting declaration.

Form 12   Notice of proposed inquiry for purposes of section 125(2) of the Local Government Act 1972.

(a) S.I. 1972/1313 (1972 II, p. 3979).   (b) S.I. 1974/423 (1974 I, p. 1371).

FORM 1   *Regulation 3(a)*

COMPULSORY PURCHASE ORDER

The   Act   (a)

and the Acquisition of Land (Authorisation Procedure) Act 1946

[The   Act(s)   ]

The   hereby make the following order:—

1. Subject to the provisions of this order, the said   are, under
section   of the   Act   , hereby
authorised to purchase compulsorily [on behalf of the parish council of   ]
for the purpose of   (b) the land which is described
in the schedule hereto and is delineated and shown
(c) on the map prepared in duplicate, sealed with the common seal of the said
                            and marked "Map referred to in the
Compulsory Purchase Order 19   ". One duplicate of the map is deposited in the
offices of the said   and the other is deposited in the offices of the
                    (d).

[2. (e) Section 27 of the Compulsory Purchase Act 1965 shall not apply in relation
to the purchase of land authorised by this order.]

[3. (f) In relation to the foregoing purchase section 77 of the Railways Clauses
Consolidation Act 1845 [and sections 78 to 85 of that Act excluding any amendment
thereof by section 15 of the Mines (Working Facilities and Support) Act 1923] [is]
[are] hereby incorporated with the enactment under which the said purchase is
authorised, subject to the modifications that (g)   ].

[4. (j) It is hereby certified that there are no material interests comprised in this order
other than outstanding material interests in development land. "Material interest",
"outstanding material interest" and "development land" have the same meanings as
in the Community Land Act 1975].

5. This order may be cited as the   Compulsory
Purchase Order 19   .

Schedule

Number on map	Extent, description and situation of the land (k)	Owners or reputed owners	Lessees or reputed lessees	Occupiers (other than tenants for a month or less)
(1)	(2)	(3)	(4)	(5)

(l)

[(m) The order includes land falling within special categories to which Part III of
Schedule 1 to the Acquisition of Land (Authorisation Procedure) Act 1946
applies, namely—

      Number on map   *Description*   ]

Date (n)

For notes see after Form 2.

1z

Regulation 3(*a*)   FORM 2

COMPULSORY PURCHASE ORDER

(Providing for the vesting of exchange land)

The   Act   (*a*)

and the Acquisition of Land (Authorisation Procedure) Act 1946

[The   Act(s)   ]
The   hereby make the following order:—

1. Subject to the provisions of this order, the said
are, under section   of the   Act   ,
hereby authorised to purchase compulsorily [on behalf of the parish council of
        ] for the purpose of   (*b*) the land which is
described in schedule 1 hereto and is delineated and shown
(*c*) on the map prepared in duplicate, sealed with the common seal of the said
                and marked "Map referred to in the
Compulsory Purchase Order 19   ". One duplicate of the map is deposited in the
offices of the said   and the other is deposited in the
offices of the   (*d*).

[2. (*e*) Section 27 of the Compulsory Purchase Act 1965 shall not apply in relation
to the purchase of land authorised by this order.]

[3. (*f*) In relation to the foregoing purchase section 77 of the Railways Clauses
Consolidation Act 1845 [and sections 78 to 85 of that Act excluding any amendment
thereof by section 15 of the Mines (Working Facilities and Support) Act 1923] [is]
[are] hereby incorporated with the enactment under which the said purchase is
authorised, subject to the modifications that (*g*)   ].

4.—(1) In this article "the order land" means (*h*) [the land referred to in article 1
hereof] [the land described as   in schedule 1 hereto]
and "the exchange land" means the land which is described in schedule 2 hereto and is
delineated and shown   (*c*) on the said map.

(2) As from the date on which this order becomes operative or the date on which the
order land, or any of it, is vested in the said   (whichever is the
later), the exchange land shall vest in the persons in whom the order land was vested
immediately before that date, subject to the like rights, trusts and incidents as attached
thereto; and the order land shall thereupon be discharged from all rights, trusts and
incidents to which it was previously subject.

[5. (*j*) It is hereby certified that there are no material interests comprised in this order
other than outstanding material interests in development land. "Material interest",
"outstanding material interest" and "development land" have the same meanings as
in the Community Land Act 1975.]

6. This order may be cited as the   Compulsory Purchase
Order 19   .

Schedule 1

Land to be purchased

Number on map	Extent, description and situation of the land (*k*)	Owners or reputed owners	Lessees or reputed lessees	Occupiers (other than tenants for a month or less)
(1)	(2)	(3)	(4)	(5)

(*l*)

[(*m*) The order includes land falling within special categories to which Part III of Schedule 1 to the Acquisition of Land (Authorisation Procedure) Act 1946 applies, namely—

| *Number on map* | *Description* |]

Schedule 2
Exchange land

Date (*n*)

NOTES TO FORMS 1 AND 2

(*a*) Insert the title of the Act authorising compulsory purchase. If the purpose of acquisition as stated in article 1 of the order is contained in some other Act, the title of that Act (or a collective title) should be added as a sub-heading.

(*b*) Describe the purpose in precise terms. Where practicable the words of the relevant Act may be used, but where those words are in general terms covering a range of purposes, the particular purpose for which the land is required should be stated if possible.

(*c*) Describe the colouring or other method used to identify the land on the map. The boundaries of each parcel of land separately numbered in the schedule to the order should be clearly delineated. Also, the map itself should contain sufficient detail to enable the situation of the land to be readily identified and related to the description given in the schedule. Maps should normally be on a scale of 1/500 or 1/1250.

(*d*) Insert the name of the confirming authority.

(*e*) This article should be omitted in the case of an order under the Housing Act 1957 and is optional in other cases.

(*f*) This article may be omitted, or may be inserted with or without reference to sections 78 to 85.

(*g*) Insert any consequential modifications required—e.g. "references in the said [section] [sections] to the company shall be construed as references to the said . . . . . . and references to the [railway or] works shall be construed as references to the land authorised to be purchased and any buildings or works constructed or to be constructed thereon".

(*h*) Use the first alternative if the whole of the land referred to in article 1 falls within paragraph 11 of Schedule 1 to the Acquisition of Land (Authorisation Procedure) Act 1946. Otherwise, use the second alternative and specify the parcel number(s) of the land which does fall within paragraph 11.

(*j*) To be included, if appropriate, only where the order is made under section 15 of the Community Land Act 1975. The modifications of paragraph 4 of Schedule 1 to the Acquisition of Land Act made by paragraphs 2 and 3 of Schedule 4 to the 1975 Act, do not have effect unless the order contains this certificate.

(*k*) This column should contain sufficient detail to tell the reader approximately where the land is situated, without reference to the map.
   In describing the land regard should be had (where appropriate) to note (*m*) below.

(*l*) Column (1) need not be completed where the order relates only to one parcel of land. Where there are two or more parcels they should be numbered 1, 2 etc. on the map and referred to accordingly in column (1). In the case of any land in respect of which the confirming authority has dispensed with service on owners, lessees and occupiers under paragraph 19(4) of Schedule 1 to the Acquisition of Land Act, the appropriate columns should be endorsed "unknown".

(*m*) The compulsory acquisition of land—
   (i) which is the property of a local authority;
   (ii) which has been acquired by statutory undertakers for the purposes of their undertaking;
   (iii) forming part of a common, open space or fuel or field garden allotment;
   (iv) held inalienably by the National Trust; or
   (v) being, or being the site of, an ancient monument or other object of archaeological interest;
is subject to Part III of Schedule 1 to the Acquisition of Land Act and consequently may be subject to Special Parliamentary Procedure in certain circumstances, unless section 41 of the Community Land Act 1975 applies in the case of (i) and (ii).
   The column 'Description' need only refer to the special category into which the relevant parcel of land falls.

(*n*) The order should be made under seal, duly authenticated, and dated.

Regulation 3(*b*)   Form 3

NEWSPAPER NOTICE CONCERNING A COMPULSORY PURCHASE ORDER

COMPULSORY PURCHASE OF LAND IN   (*a*)

Notice is hereby given that the
have made the
Compulsory Purchase Order 19   under the   Act   (*b*)
They are about to submit this order to
for confirmation, and if confirmed, the order will authorise them to purchase
compulsorily the land described below for the purpose of   (*c*)

A copy of the order and of the accompanying map may be seen at all reasonable
hours at   (*d*)

Any objection to the order must be made in writing to   (*e*)
before   (*f*) and should state the title of the order and the
grounds of objection.

Description of Land
(*g*)

[Date and signature]

NOTES

(*a*) Insert the name of the area in which the land concerned is situated.

(*b*) Insert the title of the Act authorising compulsory purchase. The Acquisition of Land
(Authorisation Procedure) Act 1946 need not be mentioned.

(*c*) Insert the purpose as stated in the order.

(*d*) The place of deposit must be "within the locality". It should therefore be within
reasonably easy reach of persons living in the area affected.

(*e*) Insert name and address of the confirming authority.

(*f*) Insert a date at least 21 days from the date of first publication of the notice (i.e. 21 days
excluding the date of first publication).

(*g*) Insert description of all the land described in the order. This need not repeat the
schedule to the order, but must be in terms which enable the reader to appreciate what
land is included.

Regulation 3(*c*)   Form 4

NOTICE TO OWNERS, LESSEES AND OCCUPIERS OF LAND COMPRISED IN A COMPULSORY
PURCHASE ORDER

The   Act   (*a*)
and the Acquisition of Land (Authorisation Procedure) Act 1946

[The   Act(s)   ]
1. The   ,
in exercise of their powers under the above Acts, on
19   made the   Compulsory Purchase Order 19   ,
which is about to be submitted to the   for confirmation.
The order, if confirmed, will authorise the   to purchase
compulsorily, for the purpose of   (*b*), the land described below.

2. A copy of the order and of the map referred to therein have been deposited at
(*c*) and may be seen there at all reasonable hours.

3. If no objection is duly made by an owner, lessee or occupier (except a tenant for a month or less), or if all objections so made are withdrawn, or if the confirming authority is satisfied that every objection so made (*d*) [either] relates exclusively to matters of compensation which can be dealt with by the Lands Tribunal [or amounts in substance to an objection to the provisions of the development plan defining the proposed use of the land comprised in the order or any other land] [or amounts in substance to an objection to the Scheme/Order 19], the confirming authority may confirm the order with or without modifications.

4. In any other case where an objection has been made by an owner, lessee or occupier (except a tenant for a month or less), the confirming authority is required, before confirming the order, either to cause a public local inquiry to be held or to afford to the objector an opportunity of appearing before and being heard by a person appointed by the confirming authority for the purpose, and may then, after considering the objection and the report of the person who held the inquiry or hearing, confirm the order with or without modifications.

5. Any objection to the order must be made in writing to (*e*) before (*f*), and should state the title of the order and the grounds of objection.

Description of Land
(*g*)

[Date and signature]

NOTES

(*a*) The heading and any sub-heading should be the same as in the order.

(*b*) Insert the purpose as stated in the order.

(*c*) The place of deposit must be "within the locality". It should therefore be within reasonably easy reach of persons living in the area affected.

(*d*) The words in square brackets containing the reference to the development plan are required only where the order is made under sections 112 and 113 of the Town and Country Planning Act 1971. The words in square brackets containing the reference to the Scheme/Order 19 are required only when the order is made under highway land acquisition powers (as defined in section 47(2) of the Highways Act 1971) and the circumstances specified in section 54(1) of the Highways Act 1971 apply. In all other cases the bracketed words should be omitted.

(*e*) Insert name and address of confirming authority.

(*f*) Insert a date at least 21 days from the date of service of the notice (i.e. 21 days excluding the date of service).

(*g*) Insert description of all the land comprised in the order. This need not repeat the schedule to the order, but must be in terms from which persons interested can readily see how their land is affected.

Additional provisions in relation to compulsory purchase orders made under section 114 *of the Town and Country Planning Act* 1971

3. Under section 114 of the Town and Country Planning Act 1971, any person having an interest in a listed building which it is proposed to acquire compulsorily under that section may, within 28 days after the service of this notice, apply to the magistrates' court for an order staying further proceedings on the compulsory purchase order, and, if the court is satisfied that reasonable steps have been taken for properly preserving the building, the court must make an order accordingly.

4. The (*a*) have included in the order a direction for minimum compensation (the meaning of which is explained (*b*)). Under section 117 of the Town and Country Planning Act 1971, any person having an interest in the building may, within 28 days after the service of this notice, apply to the magistrates' court for an order that the direction be not included in the order as [confirmed] [made] (*c*); and if the court is satisfied that the building has not been deliberately allowed to fall into disrepair for the purpose of justifying its demolition and the development or re-development of the site or any adjoining site, the court must make the order applied for.

5. Subject to any action taken under the 1971 Act (which also provides for appeals against decisions of the court) the position with respect to this order is as set out below.

NOTES

(a) Insert the name of the acquiring authority. If the acquiring authority is a Minister, the paragraph should begin "The   has included in the draft order".

(b) Insert a reference to the place where the meaning of "direction for minimum compensation" is explained—e.g. "below" or "on the attached note". (This explanation is required by section 117(3) of the Town and Country Planning Act 1971 in any case where a direction is included in an order; and it should normally include the text of section 117(4)).

(c) Delete as appropriate.

Regulation 3(c)   FORM 5

NOTICE TO OWNERS, LESSEES AND OCCUPIERS OF LAND COMPRISED IN A COMPULSORY PURCHASE ORDER MADE ON BEHALF OF A PARISH OR COMMUNITY COUNCIL.

THE LOCAL GOVERNMENT ACT 1972

AND

THE ACQUISITION OF LAND (AUTHORISATION PROCEDURE) ACT 1946

[THE   ACT(S)   (a)]

1. The district council of   , in exercise of their powers under the above Acts, on   19   made the   Compulsory Purchase Order 19   , which is about to be submitted to the   (b) for confirmation. The order, if confirmed, will authorise the council to purchase compulsorily, on behalf of the [parish] [community] (c) council of   for the purpose of   (d), the land described below.

2. A copy of the order and the map referred to therein have been deposited at   (e) and may be seen there at all reasonable hours.

3. If no objection is duly made by any of the owners, lessees and occupiers of the land in question, or if all objections so made are withdrawn, or if the Secretary of State is satisfied that the objection relates exclusively to matters of compensation which can be dealt with by the Lands Tribunal and disregards the objection, the Secretary of State is required to confirm the order with or without modification if he is satisfied that the proper notices have been published and served.

4. In any other case, the Secretary of State is required, before confirming the order, either to cause a public local inquiry to be held or to afford to the objector an opportunity of appearing before and being heard by a person appointed by the Secretary of State for the purpose, and may then, after considering the objection and the report of the person who held the inquiry or hearing, confirm the order with or without modifications.

5. Any objection to the order must be made in writing to the   (f) before   (g), and should state the title of the order and the grounds of objection.

Description of Land (h)

[Date and signature]

NOTES

(a) Any sub-heading should be the same as the sub-heading in the order.

(b) Insert the name of the confirming authority.

(c) Delete whichever is inapplicable.

(d) Insert the purpose as stated in the order.

(e) The place of deposit must be "within the locality". It should therefore be within reasonably easy reach of persons living in the area affected.

(f) Insert name and address of the confirming authority.

(g) Insert a date at least 21 days from the date of service of the notice (i.e. 21 days excluding the date of service).

(h) Insert description of all the land comprised in the order. This need not repeat the schedule to the order, but must be in terms from which persons interested can readily see how their land is affected.

FORM 6 *Regulation* 3(*c*)

NOTICE TO OWNERS, LESSEES AND OCCUPIERS, AND IN WALES LOCAL AUTHORITIES, OF LAND COMPRISED IN A COMPULSORY PURCHASE ORDER MADE UNDER SECTION 15 OF THE COMMUNITY LAND ACT 1975 AND CONTAINING A CERTIFICATE UNDER PARAGRAPH 1(2) OF SCHEDULE 4 TO THAT ACT

The Community Land Act 1975, section 15,
and the Acquisition of Land (Authorisation Procedure) Act 1946

1. The
in exercise of their powers under the above Acts, on
19   made the   Compulsory Purchase Order 19   .
which is about to be submitted to the   for confirmation.
The order, if confirmed, will authorise the   to purchase
compulsorily, for the purpose of   (*a*), the land described below.

2. A copy of the order and of the map referred to therein have been deposited at
(*b*) and may be seen there at all reasonable hours.

3. If no objection is duly made by an owner, lessee or occupier (except a tenant for a month or less, [or by a local authority within whose area the land is situated (*c*),] or if all objections so made are withdrawn, or if the confirming authority is satisfied that every objection so made either relates exclusively to matters of compensation which can be dealt with by the Lands Tribunal or is made on the ground that the acquisition is unnecessary or inexpedient, the confirming authority may confirm the order with or without modifications.

4. In any other case where an objection has been made by an owner, lessee or occupier (except a tenant for a month or less), the confirming authority may, before confirming the order, either cause a public local inquiry to be held or afford to the objector an opportunity of appearing before and being heard by a person appointed by the confirming authority for the purpose. An inquiry or hearing must be held unless the confirming authority is satisfied

(*a*) that planning permission for relevant development (as defined in section 3 of the Community Land Act 1975) is in force in respect of the land comprised in the order, and that the planning permission was granted by the confirming authority after a public local inquiry; or

(*b*) where a local plan for the district in which the land is situated has been adopted or approved under Part II of the Town and Country Planning Act 1971, that the grant of planning permission for relevant development in respect of the land comprised in the order would be in accordance with the provisions of that plan; or

(*c*) where no such plan has been so adopted or approved, that the grant of planning permission for relevant development in respect of the land comprised in the order would be in accordance with the provisions of the development plan.

After considering the objection, and the report of the person who held the inquiry or hearing if there was one, the confirming authority may then confirm the order with or without modifications.

5. Any objection to the order must be made in writing to   (*d*)
before   (*e*), and should state the title of the order and the grounds
of objection.

Description of Land
(*f*)

[Date and signature]

NOTES

(a) Insert the purpose as stated in the order.

(b) The place of deposit must be "within the locality". It should therefore be within reasonably easy reach of persons living in the area affected.

(c) Insert if any of the land comprised in the order is in Wales.

(d) Insert name and address of confirming authority.

(e) Insert a date at least 21 days from the date of service of the notice (i.e. 21 days excluding the date of service).

(f) Insert description of all the land comprised in the order. This need not repeat the schedule to the order, but must be in terms from which persons interested can readily see how their land is affected.

Regulation 3(d) FORM 7

NOTICE OF CONFIRMATION OF A COMPULSORY PURCHASE ORDER

The Act (a)

and the Acquisition of Land (Authorisation Procedure) Act 1946

[The Act(s)]

1. Notice is hereby given that the , in exercise of [his] powers under the above Acts, on confirmed [with modifications] the Compulsory Purchase Order 19 submitted by the [on behalf of the parish council of]. [on behalf of the community council of].

2. The order as confirmed provides for the purchase for the purpose of (b) of the land described in [the] schedule [1] hereto. [By a direction given under section 132 of the Town and Country Planning Act 1971, consideration of the order, so far as it relates to the land described in schedule 2, has been postponed until]. [By a direction given under section 55 of the Highways Act 1971 consideration of the order, so far as it relates to the land described in schedule 2, has been postponed until .] [By a direction given under paragraph 4 of Schedule 4 to the Community Land Act 1975 consideration of the order, so far as it relates to the land described in schedule 2, has been postponed until](c).

3. A copy of the order as confirmed by the and of the map referred to therein have been deposited at (d) and may be seen there at all reasonable hours.

4. (e) The order as confirmed becomes operative on the date on which this notice is first published; but a person aggrieved by the order may, by application to the High Court within 6 weeks from that date, question its validity on the grounds (i) that the authorisation granted by the order is not empowered to be granted or (ii) that his interests have been substantially prejudiced by failure to comply with any statutory requirement relating to the order.

OR

4. The order as confirmed is subject to special parliamentary procedure and will become operative as provided by the Statutory Orders (Special Procedure) Act 1945. Unless the order is confirmed by Act of Parliament under section 6 of that Act, a person aggrieved by the order may, by application to the High Court within 6 weeks from the operative date, question its validity on the ground (i) that the authorisation granted by the order is not empowered to be granted or (ii) that his interests have been substantially prejudiced by failure to comply with any statutory requirement relating to the order.

Schedule [1]

Land comprised in the order as confirmed

[Schedule 2

Land in respect of which consideration has been postponed]

(f)

[Date and signature]

NOTES

(a) The heading and any sub-heading should be the same as in the order as confirmed.

(b) Insert the purpose as stated in the order.

(c) Omit the passages in square brackets where inappropriate.

(d) The place of deposit should be "within the locality". It should therefore be within reasonably easy reach of persons living in the area affected.

(e) Leave standing whichever alternative is appropriate.

(f) Where this form is to include a statement concerning general vesting declarations, (Form 10) the statement should be included at this point.

FORM 8   *Regulation 3(e)*

NOTICE OF THE GIVING OF A CERTIFICATE UNDER PART III OF SCHEDULE 1 TO THE ACQUISITION OF LAND (AUTHORISATION PROCEDURE) ACT 1946

The Acquisition of Land (Authorisation Procedure) Act 1946

1. The   Compulsory Purchase Order 19   , which has been [submitted by   to the   for confirmation] [prepared in draft by   ], includes the land described in the schedule hereto.

2. (a) This land was acquired by   for the purposes of their undertaking and the Secretary of State is satisfied that [it is used] [an interest is held in it] for the purposes of the carrying on of their undertaking.

OR

This land [is] [forms part of] [a common] [an open space] [a fuel or field garden allotment].

OR

This land [is] [forms part of] [is the site of] an ancient monument or other object of archaeological interest.

3. Notice is hereby given that the Secretary of State, in exercise of his powers under paragraph [10] [11] [12] of Part III of Schedule 1 to the above-mentioned Act, has certified (b).

4. A map showing the land to which the certificate relates [and the land proposed to be given in exchange] may be inspected at (c)   at all reasonable hours.

5. The certificate becomes operative on the date on which this notice is first published; but a person aggrieved by the certificate may, by application to the High Court within 6 weeks from that date, question its validity on the ground that his interests have been substantially prejudiced by failure to comply with any statutory requirement relating to the certificate.

Schedule
(d)

[Date and signature]

NOTES

(a) Delete as appropriate.

(b) Insert the terms of the certificate.

(c) The place of deposit should be "within the locality". It should therefore be within reasonably easy reach of persons living in the area affected.

(d) Insert description of the land to which the certificate relates.

Regulation 5(*a*)   FORM 9

GENERAL VESTING DECLARATION

This GENERAL VESTING DECLARATION is made the   day
of   19   by   (*a*) (hereinafter
called "the Authority").

WHEREAS:

(1) On   19   an order entitled the
                        was [made] [confirmed] by   (*b*)
under the powers conferred on [him] [them] by the
Act   (*c*) authorising the Authority to acquire certain land
specified in the schedule hereto.

(2) Notice of the [making] [confirmation] of the order was first published in accordance with [paragraph 6 of Schedule 1 to the Acquisition of Land (Authorisation
Procedure) Act 1946(*d*)] on   19 .

(3) (*e*) The said notice included a statement and a notification complying with
paragraph 2(1) of Schedule 3 to the Town and Country Planning Act 1968.

OR

(3) A subsequent notice given on   19   before the service of
any notice to treat in respect of any of the land described in the schedule hereto
included a statement and a notification complying with paragraph 2(1) of Schedule 3
to the Town and Country Planning Act 1968.

(4) (*e*) The said [subsequent] notice did not specify any period longer than two
months beginning with the date of the first publication thereof as the period before
the end of which this general vesting declaration could not be executed.

OR

(4) The said [subsequent] notice specified the period of   months beginning
with the date of the first publication thereof as the period before the end of which the
general vesting declaration could not be executed.

OR

(4) The consent in writing of every occupier of any of the land described in the
Schedule hereto was obtained for the execution on the date above mentioned of this
general vesting declaration.

NOW THIS DEED WITNESSETH that in exercise of the powers conferred on them
by section 30 of the Town and Country Planning Act 1968 (hereinafter called "the
Act") the Authority hereby declare as follows:

1. The land described in [Part I of (*f*)] the schedule hereto (being [the whole]
   [part] of the land authorised to be acquired by the order) and more particularly
   delineated on the plan annexed hereto together with the right to enter upon and
   take possession of the same shall vest in the Authority as from the end of the
   period of [insert period of 28 days or longer] from the date on which the service
   of notices required by paragraph 4 of Schedule 3 to the Act is completed.

2. For the purposes of paragraph 16(1) of Schedule 3 to the Act (which defines "long
   tenancy which is about to expire" in relation to a general vesting declaration as
   meaning a tenancy granted for an interest greater than a minor tenancy as
   therein defined but having at the date of the declaration a period still to run which
   is not more than the specified period, that is to say, such period, longer than one
   year, as may be specified in the declaration in relation to the land in which the
   tenancy subsists) the Authority hereby specify that [in relation to the land
   comprised in this declaration that period shall be   years and
   months] [in relation to each area of land specified in column 1 of Part II of the
   schedule hereto that period shall be the period stated with respect to that area
   in column 2 thereof].

                                        Schedule
(*g*)   Date

NOTES

(*a*) Insert the name of the acquiring authority.

(*b*) Insert the name of the confirming authority or, where the order was made by a Minister that Minister.

(*c*) Insert the title of the Act authorising compulsory purchase.

(*d*) Where the notice was published under a procedure prescribed by some enactment other than the Acquisition of Land (Authorisation Procedure) Act 1946, refer instead to the relevant provision of that enactment.

(*e*) Delete any alternative which does not apply.

(*f*) The schedule should be divided into Part I and Part II where Part II is required for the purpose of the final sentence of paragraph 2 of the declaration.

(*g*) The declaration should be made under seal, duly authenticated.

FORM 10   *Regulation 5(b)*

STATEMENT CONCERNING GENERAL VESTING DECLARATIONS (*a*)

Part I below contains a statement of the effect of paragraphs 1 to 8 of Schedule 3 to the Town and Country Planning Act 1968 and Part II contains a form for giving information.

PART I

Power to make general vesting declaration

1. The   (hereinafter called   *   )
(*b*) may acquire any of the land described in [the] schedule [1] [above] [below] [hereto] (*c*) by making a general vesting declaration under section 30 of the Town and Country Planning Act 1968 which has the effect, subject to paragraph 4 below, of vesting the land in the   (*b*) at the end of the period mentioned in paragraph 2 below. A declaration may not be made before the end of a period of two months from the first publication of a notice including this statement except with the consent of every occupier of the land affected.

Notices concerning general vesting declaration

2. As soon as may be after the   (*b*) make a general vesting declaration, they must serve notice of it on every occupier of any of the land specified in the declaration (except land where there is one of the tenancies described in paragraph 3) and on every person who gives them information relating to the land in pursuance of the invitation contained in any notice including this statement. When the service of notices of the general vesting declaration is completed, an intermediate period before vesting begins to run. This period, which must not be less than 28 days, will be specified in the declaration. At the end of this period the land described in the declaration will, subject to what is said in paragraph 4, vest in the   (*b*) together with the right to enter on the land and take possession of it. In addition every person on whom the   (*b*) could have served a notice to treat in respect of his interest in the land (other than a tenant under one of the tenancies described in paragraph 3) will be entitled to compensation for the acquisition of his interest in the land and to interest on the compensation from the date of vesting.

Application to certain tenancies

3. In the case of certain tenancies, the position stated above is subject to modifications. For the modifications to apply, the tenancy must be either a "minor tenancy", i.e. a tenancy for a year or a yearly tenancy or a tenancy for a lesser interest, or "a long tenancy which is about to expire". The latter expression means a tenancy granted for an interest greater than a minor tenancy but having at the date of the general vesting declaration a period still to run which is not more than the period specified in the declaration for this purpose (which must be more than a year). In calculating how long a tenancy has to run, where any option to renew or to terminate it is available to either party, it shall be assumed that the landlord will take every opportunity open to him to terminate the tenancy while the tenant will use every opportunity to retain or extend his interest.

Notice of entry

4. The   (*b*) may not exercise the right of entry referred to in paragraph 2 in respect of land subject to one of the tenancies described in paragraph 3 unless they first serve notice to treat in respect of the tenancy and then serve every occupier of the land with a notice of their intention to enter and take possession after the period (not less than 14 days) specified in the notice. The right of entry will be exercisable at the end of that period. The vesting of the land will be subject to the tenancy until the end of that period or until the tenancy comes to an end, whichever happens first.

[Schedule] (*c*)

PART II (*a*)
Form for giving information
The   Compulsory Purchase Order 19
To: (*b*)

[I] [We] being [a person] who, if a general vesting declaration were made under paragraph 1 of Schedule 3 to the Town and Country Planning Act 1968 in respect of all the land comprised in the compulsory purchase order cited above in respect of which notice to treat has not been given, would be entitled to claim compensation in respect of [all] [part of] that land, hereby give you the following information, pursuant to the provisions of paragraph 2(1) of the said Schedule.

1. Name and address of claimant(s) (i)......................................
   ....

2. Land in which an interest is held by claimant(s) (ii).......................
   ....

3. Nature of interest (iii)..
   Signed ....
   [on behalf of..].
   Date ....

  (i) In the case of a joint interest insert the names and addresses of all the claimants.

 (ii) The land should be described concisely.

(iii) If the interest is leasehold, the date of commencement and length of term should be given. If the land is subject to a mortgage or other incumbrance, details should be given, e.g. name of building society and roll number.

NOTES

(*a*) The acquiring authority are obliged by paragraph 2(1) of Schedule 3 to the Act to include in the notice of making or confirmation (Form 7) or a subsequent notice:—

  (i) a statement of the effect of paragraphs 1 to 8 of that Schedule in a prescribed form (i.e. this form); and

 (ii) a notification to the effect that every person who, if a general vesting declaration were made in respect of all the land comprised in the order in respect of which notice to treat has not been given, would be entitled to claim compensation in respect of any such land is invited to give information to the authority making the declaration in the prescribed form with respect to his name and address and the land in question.

The acquiring authority may find it convenient to include this notification immediately before the prescribed form in Part II which may then be introduced by such words as "The relevant prescribed form is set out below".

(*b*) Insert the name of the acquiring authority, and define them by an appropriate term. Thereafter rely on the definition wherever "(*b*)" appears in the text.

(*c*) If this notice is served separately from the notice of making or confirmation (Form 7), insert a description of the land in a schedule following paragraph 4. Otherwise delete square brackets and preceding words as appropriate.

FORM 11   *Regulation 5(c)*

NOTICE STATING EFFECT OF GENERAL VESTING DECLARATION

The   Compulsory Purchase Order 19

To:

of:

NOTICE IS HEREBY GIVEN that the   (hereinafter called
"the   ") (*a*) on   19   made a general vesting
declaration under section 30 of the Town and Country Planning Act 1968 (hereinafter
called "the Act") vesting the land described in the schedule to this notice (hereinafter
called "the said land") in themselves as from the end of the period of   days from
the date on which the service of the notices required by paragraph 4 of Schedule 3
to the Act is completed.

Paragraph 4 of Schedule 3 to the Act requires notices to be served on every occupier
of any of the land specified in the declaration (other than land in which there subsists
a "minor tenancy" or a "long tenancy which is about to expire"—these expressions
are defined in Appendix A to this notice) and on every other person who has given
information to the   (*a*) with respect to any of that
land in pursuance of the invitation published and served under paragraph 2(1) of
Schedule 3 to the Act.

The   (*a*) will in due course specify in a certificate the
date on which the service of the said notices is completed.

The effect of the general vesting declaration is as follows:—

On the date of vesting (as determined in accordance with the first paragraph of this
notice) the said land, together with the right to enter upon and take possession of it,
will vest in the   (*a*) as if the   (*a*)
had on that date exercised their powers to execute a deed poll under Part I of the
Compulsory Purchase Act 1965.

Also, on the date of vesting, the Acts providing for compensation will apply as if,
on the date on which the general vesting declaration was made (namely,
19   ), a notice to treat had been served on every person on whom the   (*a*)
could have served such a notice (other than any person entitled to an interest in the
land in respect of which such a notice had actually been served before the date of
vesting and any person entitled to a minor tenancy or a long tenancy which is about
to expire).

If the land includes any land in which there is a minor tenancy or a long tenancy
which is about to expire, the right of entry will not be exercisable in respect of that
land unless, after serving a notice to treat in respect of that tenancy, the
                    (*a*) have served on every occupier of any of the land in which the tenancy
subsists a notice stating that, at the end of a specified period (at least 14 days from the
date of the service of the notice, i.e. 14 days excluding the date of first publication)
they intend to enter upon and take possession of the land specified in the notice, and
that period has expired: the vesting of the land will then be subject to the tenancy
until that period expires, or the tenancy comes to an end, whichever happens first.

Schedule 3A to the Act (as enacted in Appendix A of Schedule 2 to the Land Commission (Dissolution) Act 1971) contains supplementary provisions as to general
vesting declarations. These provisions are set out in Appendix B to this notice.

A copy of the general vesting declaration to which this notice refers and of the
plan annexed to the declaration can be inspected at   (*b*) and may be
seen at all reasonable hours.

Schedule

[Description of the land vested in the   (a) by the general
vesting declaration].

Appendix A

[Here set out paragraph 16 of Schedule 3 to the Act]

Appendix B

[Here set out Schedule 3A to the Act]
[Date and signature]

(a) Insert the name of the authority, and define them by an appropriate term. Thereafter
rely on that definition wherever "(a)" appears in the text.

(b) Insert address of the authority's office, as appropriate.

Regulation 6   FORM 12

NOTICE OF PROPOSED INQUIRY FOR PURPOSES OF SECTION 125(2) OF THE
LOCAL GOVERNMENT ACT 1972

To (a)

[owner] [lessee] [occupier] of (b)

Take notice that the [parish] [community] (c) council of   have
represented to the district council of   that they are unable to purchase by agreement and on reasonable terms suitable land for (d)
being a purpose for which they are authorised to acquire land, and that they have
requested the district council to make an order for the compulsory purchase of the
land described in the schedule hereto for the said purpose.

A map showing the land concerned has been deposited at
and may be seen at all reasonable hours.

The district council have appointed   to hold a local inquiry
in the above matter.

The inquiry will be held at   on   19 ,
at   a.m./p.m., and you have the right to attend and be heard.

Schedule
(Insert description of land)

[Date and signature]

NOTES

(a) Insert name of owner, lessee or occupier.
(b) Insert description of land proposed to be acquired.
(c) Delete whichever is inapplicable.
(d) Insert purpose for which the land is proposed to be acquired.

John Silkin,
Signed by authority of the   Minister for Planning and Local Government,
Secretary of State   Department of the Environment.
26th February 1976.

EXPLANATORY NOTE

(This Note is not part of the Regulations.)

These Regulations consolidate with amendments the previous regulations which prescribe forms for use in connection with—

(*a*) the compulsory purchase of land under the procedure of the Acquisition of Land (Authorisation Procedure) Act 1946;

(*b*) general vesting declarations, following a compulsory purchase order, and

(*c*) compulsory purchase orders and inquiries where a District Council propose to purchase land on behalf of a Parish or Community Council.

The forms prescribed by these Regulations include—

(i) the compulsory purchase order itself. This now provides for a certificate in accordance with paragraph 1(2) of Schedule 4 to the Community Land Act 1975 that there are no material interests comprised in the order other than outstanding material interests in development land. The note (*j*) to forms 1 and 2 makes it clear that this certificate can only be included where the order is made under section 15 of the Act of 1975, and that the modifications of paragraph 4 of Schedule 1 to the Act of 1946 made by paragraphs 2 and 3 of Schedule 4 to the Act of 1975, do not have effect unless the order contains this certificate;

(ii) the preliminary notice i.e. the newspaper notice and the personal notice to owners, lessees and occupiers, describing the effect of the order and specifying how objections can be made. Form 4 has been amended to take account of the effect of the Local Government Act 1974 (c. 7) on section 117 of the Town and Country Planning Act 1971. Form 6 is a new form of notice for use where the order is made under section 15 of the Community Land Act 1975 and contains the certificate referred to in (i) above;

(iii) the notice of confirmation of the order. This now allows for a direction under paragraph 4 of Schedule 4 to the Community Land Act 1975 that consideration of the order has been postponed so far as part of the land is concerned.

(iv) the notice that a certificate has been given under Part III of Schedule 1 to the Act of 1946;

(v) the general vesting declaration itself;

(vi) the statement of the effect of the statutory provisions relating to a general vesting declaration. This has been amended to remove minor errors;

(vii) the notice that such a declaration has been made; and

(viii) the notice of a proposed inquiry for the purposes of section 125(2) of the Local Government Act 1972.

The other changes in the regulations and the forms are minor and drafting alterations.

1976 No. 301

TOWN AND COUNTRY PLANNING, ENGLAND AND WALES

The Town and Country Planning General Development (Amendment) Order 1976

Made	- - -	*26th February* 1976
Laid before Parliament		10*th March* 1976
Coming into Operation		6*th April* 1976

The Secretary of State for the Environment, in exercise of the powers conferred on him by sections 24, 27, 31, 37 and 287 of and Schedule 14 to the Town and Country Planning Act 1971(a) and of all other powers enabling him in that behalf, hereby makes the following order:—

1.—(1) This order may be cited as the Town and Country Planning General Development (Amendment) Order 1976, and the Town and Country Planning General Development Order 1973(b), the Town and Country Planning General Development (Amendment) Order 1973(c), the Town and Country Planning General Development (Amendment) Order 1974(d) and this order may be cited together as the Town and Country Planning General Development Orders 1973 to 1976.

(2) This order shall come into operation on 6th April 1976.

2. The Interpretation Act 1889(e) shall apply for the interpretation of this order as it applies for the interpretation of an Act of Parliament.

3. The Town and Country Planning General Development Order 1973 as amended(f) is hereby amended as follows:—

(*a*) In article 7, for paragraphs (2) and (3) there shall be substituted the following paragraphs:—

" (2) On receipt of—

(*a*) in the case of an application made under paragraph (1) or (2) of article 5, the form of application required by article 5(1) together with a certificate under section 27 of the Act; or

(*b*) in the case of an application made under article 5(3), sufficient information to enable the authority to identify the previous grant of planning permission, together with a certificate under section 27 of the Act; or

(*c*) in the case of an application made under article 6, the documents and information required by paragraph (1) or paragraph (2) of that article, as the case may be,

---

(a) 1971 c. 78.   (b) S.I. 1973/31 (1973 I, p. 207).
(c) S.I. 1973/273 (1973 I, p. 1022).   (d) S.I. 1974/418 (1974 I, p. 1318).
(e) 1889 c. 63.
(f) The relevant amending order is S.I. 1974/418 (1974 I, p. 1318).

the local planning authority (in Greater London) or the district planning authority (elsewhere than in Greater London) shall send to the applicant an acknowledgement thereof in the terms (or substantially in the terms) set out in Part I of Schedule 2 hereto.

(2A) In the case of an application which falls to be determined by the county planning authority the district planning authority shall as soon as may be notify the applicant that the application will be so determined and shall transmit to the county planning authority all relevant plans, drawings, particulars and documents submitted with or in support of the application and notify the county planning authority of all action taken by the district planning authority in relation to the application.

(2B) Where, after the sending of an acknowledgement as required by paragraph (2) of this article, the local planning authority, county planning authority or district planning authority (as the case may be) form the opinion that the application is invalid by reason of failure to comply with the requirements of article 5 or 6 or with any other statutory requirement they shall as soon as may be notify the applicant that his application is invalid.

(3) Where a valid application under article 5 or 6 has been received by a local planning authority, the period within which the authority shall give notice to the applicant of their decision or determination or of the reference of the application to the Secretary of State shall be eight weeks from the date when the form of application or application in writing, as the case may be, and any certificates required by the Act were lodged as required by paragraph (1) of this article, or (except where the applicant has already given notice of appeal to the Secretary of State) such extended period as may be agreed upon in writing between the applicant and (a) in Greater London, the local planning authority, (b) elsewhere, the district planning authority or, in the case of an application which falls to be determined by the county planning authority, either the district planning authority or the county planning authority.".

(b) In article 13, for paragraph (1) there shall be substituted the following paragraphs:—

"(1) Before permission is granted by a local planning authority for development in any of the following cases, whether unconditionally or subject to conditions, a local planning authority shall consult with the following authorities or persons, namely:—

(a) where it appears to the local planning authority that the development is likely to affect land in the area of any other local planning authority:—

(i) with the district planning authority in whose area the land affected is situate (except where that land is in Greater London or a National Park);

(ii) where the land affected is in Greater London, with the Common Council or council of the London borough, as the case may be, in whose area that land is situate;

(iii) where the land affected is in a National Park, with the county planning authority in whose area that land is situate;

(*b*) where it appears to the local planning authority that the development is likely to create or attract traffic which will result in a
material increase in the volume of traffic entering or leaving
a trunk road or using a level crossing over a railway, with the
Secretary of State at such office or address as he may appoint;

(*c*) where the development involves the formation, laying out or
alteration of any means of access to a highway (other than
a trunk road) and the local highway authority concerned are not
the authority making the decision, with the local highway
authority concerned;

(*d*) where the development consists of the erection of a building
(other than an alteration, extension or re-erection of an existing
building or the erection of a building of a temporary character)
in an area of coal working notified by the National Coal Board
to the local planning authority, with the National Coal Board;

(*e*) where the development is of land which is situate within three
kilometres from Windsor Castle, Windsor Great Park, or Windsor
Home Park, or which is within 800 metres from any other royal
palace or park, and might affect the amenities of that palace
or park, with the Secretary of State at such office or address
as he may appoint;

(*f*) where the development consists of or includes:—

(i) the carrying out of works or operations in the bed or
on the banks of a river or stream;

(ii) the carrying out of building or other operations or use
of land for the purpose of refining or storing mineral oils
and their derivatives;

(iii) the use of land for the deposit of any kind of refuse
or waste;

(iv) the carrying out of building or other operations (other
than the laying of sewers, the construction of pumphouses
in a line of sewers, the construction of septic tanks and cesspools
serving single dwellinghouses or single buildings in which
not more than ten people will normally reside, work or congre-
gate, and works ancillary thereto) or use of land for the retention, treatment or disposal of sewage, trade waste or sludge;

(v) the use of land as a cemetery,

with the water authority exercising functions in the area in which
the development is to take place;

(*g*) where the development is of land in an area of special interest
notified to the local planning authority by the Nature Conservancy
Council in accordance with section 23 of the National Parks and
Access to the Countryside Act 1949(**a**), with the Nature Conservancy Council (except where that Council dispense with this
requirement);

(**a**) 1949 c. 97.

(*h*) where the development is not development for agricultural purposes and is not in accordance with the provisions of a development plan and—

 (i) it would, in the opinion of the local planning authority, involve the loss of not less than 10 acres of land which is for the time being used (or was last used) for agricultural purposes; or

 (ii) it would, in the opinion of the local planning authority, involve the loss of less than 10 acres of land which is for the time being used (or was last used) for agricultural purposes, but the circumstances are such that the development of that land is likely to lead to further loss of agricultural land,

with the Minister of Agriculture, Fisheries and Food.

(1A) For the purposes of paragraph (1)(*h*) of this article, development is to be treated as not being in accordance with the provisions of a development plan if it would be inconsistent in any respect with the provisions of:—

 (i) a local plan adopted or approved in accordance with the provisions of section 14 of the Act; or

 (ii) a development plan approved under Part I of Schedule 5 to the Act, or any other enactment which is re-enacted in that Schedule, which is in force in the area in which the land is situated; or

 (iii) an old development plan within the meaning of paragraph 2 of Schedule 7 to the Act.".

(*c*) In article 18, for paragraph (2) there shall be substituted the following paragraph:—

"(2) An application for an established use certificate shall not be entertained by the local planning authority unless it is accompanied by one or other of the following certificates signed by or on behalf of the applicant, that is to say:—

 (*a*) a certificate stating that at the beginning of the period of twenty-one days ending with the date of the application, no person (other than the applicant) was the owner of any of the land to which the application relates;

 (*b*) a certificate stating that the applicant has given the requisite notice of the application to all the persons (other than the applicant) who, at the beginning of the period of twenty-one days ending with the date of the application, were owners of any of the land to which the application relates, and setting out the names of those persons, the addresses at which notice of the application was given to them respectively, and the date of service of each such notice;

 (*c*) a certificate stating that the applicant is unable to issue a certificate in accordance with either of the preceding sub-paragraphs, that he has given the requisite notice of the application to such one or more of the persons mentioned in the last preceding sub-paragraph as are specified in the certificate (setting out their names, the addresses at which notice of the application was given to them respectively and the date of the service of each such notice), that he has taken such steps as are reasonably open to him (specifying them) to ascertain the names and addresses of the remainder of those persons and that he has been unable to do so;

(*d*) a certificate stating that the applicant is unable to issue a certificate in accordance with sub-paragraph (*a*) of this paragraph, that he has taken such steps as are reasonably open to him (specifying them) to ascertain the names and addresses of the persons mentioned in sub-paragraph (*b*) of this paragraph and that he has been unable to do so.

For the purposes of this paragraph the persons who are to be treated as owners of the land to which the application for an established use certificate relates are:—

(i) a person who, in respect of any part of the land, is entitled to the freehold or a lease the unexpired term of which at the relevant time is not less than 7 years; and

(ii) any other person who is the occupier of any part of the said land.".

(*d*) In Schedule 2—

(1) for Part I there shall be substituted the following:—

"PART I

TOWN AND COUNTRY PLANNING ACT 1971

Notification to be sent to applicant on receipt of application

Your application dated   was received on (*a*)

*[Examination of the form of application and accompanying plans and documents to ascertain whether your application complies with the statutory requirements has not been completed.

If on further examination it is found that the application is invalid for failure to comply with such requirements (or for any other reason) a further communication will be sent to you as soon as possible.]

*[Your application relates to a county matter and [will be] [has been] passed to the county planning authority for determination.] [A further notification will be sent to you if it is decided in the light of further consideration that your application relates to a county matter and that it is necessary to pass the application to the county planning authority for determination.] [As the land which is the subject of the application lies within (*b*)... National Park, the application [will be] [has been] passed to the (*c*)... for determination.]

If by (*d*) ....* [you have not received notification that your application is invalid and] the authority dealing with your application have not given you notice of their decision (and you have not agreed with them in writing that the period within which their decision shall be given may be extended) you may appeal to the Secretary of State in accordance with sections 36 and 37 of the Town and Country Planning Act 1971 by notice sent within six months from that date (unless the application has already been referred by this authority to the [Secretary of State for the Environment] [Secretary of State for Wales]). Appeals must be made on a form which is obtainable from the [Department of the Environment] [Welsh Office.]

* Delete where inappropriate.
  (*a*) insert date when relevant document(s) referred to in article 7(2) were received.
  (*b*) insert name of National Park.
  (*c*) insert name of county council or planning board.
  (*d*) insert date eight weeks from date of receipt of application (as given at (*a*))."

(2) In Part II, in paragraph (1), the words " Caxton House, Tothill Street, London SW1H 9LZ " and the words " Summit House, Windsor Place, Cardiff CF1 3BX " shall be deleted.

(e) For Schedules 4 and 5 there shall be substituted the new Schedules 4 and 5 set out in the Schedule to this Order.

(f) In Schedule 6, in Part I, the words "Caxton House, Tothill Street, London SW1H 9LZ" and the words "Summit House, Windsor Place, Cardiff CF1 3BX" shall be deleted.

SCHEDULE

"SCHEDULE 4

PART I

TOWN AND COUNTRY PLANNING ACT 1971
Certificate under section 27

I hereby certify that:—   Certificate A*

1. No person other than the $\frac{\text{*applicant}}{\text{appellant}}$ was an owner (a) of any part of the land to which the $\frac{\text{*application}}{\text{appeal}}$ relates at the beginning of the period of 20 days before the date of the accompanying $\frac{\text{*application}}{\text{appeal}}$;

(a) "owner" means a person having a free-hold interest or a leasehold interest the unexpired term of which was not less than 7 years.

or:—

I hereby certify that:—   Certificate B*

$\frac{\text{I have}}{}$

1. $\frac{\text{*The applicant has}}{\text{The appellant has}}$ given the requisite notice to all the persons other than

$\frac{\text{myself}}{\text{*the applicant}}$ who, 20 days before the date of the accompanying $\frac{\text{*application}}{\text{appeal}}$,

the appellant were owners† of any part of the land to which the $\frac{\text{*application}}{\text{appeal}}$ relates, viz.—

†See Note (a) to Certificate A

Name of owner	Address	Date of service of notice

or:—

I hereby certify that:—   Certificate C*

$\frac{\text{I am}}{}$

1. (i) $\frac{\text{*The applicant is}}{\text{The appellant is}}$ unable to issue a certificate in accordance with either paragraph (a) or paragraph (b) of section 27(1) of the Act in respect of the accompanying $\frac{\text{*application}}{\text{appeal}}$ dated (a) ....

(a) Insert date of application or appeal.

(ii) $\frac{\text{*The applicant has}}{\text{The appellant has}}$ given the requisite notice to the following persons

$\frac{\text{myself}}{\text{*the applicant}}$ other than $\frac{\text{*the applicant}}{\text{the appellant}}$ who, 20 days before the date of the $\frac{\text{*application}}{\text{appeal}}$, were

owners† of any part of the land to which the $\frac{\text{*application}}{\text{appeal}}$ relates, viz.—

†See Note (a) to Certificate A.

Name of owner	Address	Date of service of notice

$$\underline{\text{I have}}$$

(iii) *The applicant has taken the steps listed below, being steps reasonably

The appellant has

open to $\dfrac{\text{*me}}{\text{him}}$, to ascertain the names and addresses of the other owners of the

land or part thereof and $\dfrac{\text{*have}}{\text{has}}$ been unable to do so:

(b) Insert
description of
steps taken.

(b) ....

....

(c) Insert
name of local
newspaper
circulating in
the locality in
which the land
is situated.

....

(iv) Notice of the $\dfrac{\text{*application}}{\text{appeal}}$ as set out below has been published in the

(d) Insert
date of
publication
(which must
not be earlier
than 20 days
before the
application or
appeal).

(c) ....

....

on (d)..

Certificate D*

Copy of notice as published

or :—

I hereby certify that :—

$$\underline{\text{I am}}$$

1. (i) *The applicant is unable to issue a certificate in accordance with

The appellant is

section 27(1)(a) of the Act in respect of the accompanying $\dfrac{\text{*application}}{\text{appeal}}$ dated

(a) Insert
date of
application or
appeal.

(a) ....

and $\dfrac{\text{*have}}{\text{has}}$ taken the steps listed below, being steps reasonably open to $\dfrac{\text{*me}}{\text{him}}$, to

ascertain the names and addresses of all the persons, other than $\dfrac{\text{*myself}}{\text{himself}}$, who,

†See Note (a)
to Certificate A 20 days before the date of the $\dfrac{\text{*application}}{\text{appeal}}$, were owners† of any part of the land

to which the $\dfrac{\text{*application}}{\text{appeal}}$ relates and $\dfrac{\text{*have}}{\text{has}}$ been unable to do so:

(b) Insert
description of
steps taken.

(b) ....

....

(c) Insert
name of local
newspaper
circulating
in the locality
in which the
land is
situated.

(ii) Notice of the $\dfrac{\text{*application}}{\text{appeal}}$ as set out below has been published in the

(c) ....

....

(d) Insert
date of
publication
(which must
not be earlier
than 20 days
before the
application or
appeal).

on (d)..

Copy of notice as published

*2. None of the land to which the $\dfrac{\text{*application}}{\text{appeal}}$ relates constitutes or forms

part of an agricultural holding;

[Whichever is
appropriate of
these alterna-
tives should
form part of
any certificate
A, B, C or
D above.]

or :—

$$\underline{\text{I have}}$$

*2. *The applicant has given the requisite notice to every person other than

The appellant has

$\dfrac{\text{*myself}}{\text{himself}}$ who, 20 days before the date of the $\dfrac{\text{*application}}{\text{appeal}}$, was a tenant

of any agricultural holding any part of which was comprised in the land to which

the $\dfrac{\text{*application}}{\text{appeal}}$ relates, viz.:—

Name of tenant (e)   Address   Date of service of notice

> (e) If you are the sole agricultural tenant enter "None".

Signed ....

*On behalf of ....

Date ....

* Delete where inappropriate.

PART II

TOWN AND COUNTRY PLANNING ACT 1971

Notice under section 27 of application for planning permission

Proposed development at (a)..

TAKE NOTICE that application is being made to the (b)..

..............................Council by (c).. for planning

permission to (d) ....

If you should wish to make representations about the application, you should make them in writing not later than (e).. to the Council at (f) ....

Signed ....

*On behalf of ....

Date ....

* Delete where inappropriate.

> [Notice for service on individuals]
> (a) Insert address or location of proposed development.
> (b) Insert name of Council.
> (c) Insert name of applicant.
> (d) Insert description of proposed development.
> (e) Insert date not less than 20 days later than the date on which the notice is served.
> (f) Insert address of Council.

TOWN AND COUNTRY PLANNING ACT 1971

Notice under section 27 of application for planning permission

Proposed development at (a) ....

NOTICE is hereby given that application is being made to the (b)..

..............................Council by (c).. for planning

permission to (d) ....

Any owner of the land (namely a freeholder or a person entitled to an unexpired term of at least seven years under a lease) who wishes to make representations to the above-mentioned Council about the application should make them in writing not later than (e)..to the Council at (f)..

Signed ....

*On behalf of ....

Date ....

* Delete where inappropriate.

> [Notice for publication in local newspaper]
> (a) Insert address or location of proposed development.
> (b) Insert name of Council.
> (c) Insert name of applicant.
> (d) Insert description of proposed development.
> (e) Insert date not less than 20 days later than the date on which the notice is published.
> (f) Insert address of Council.

PART III

TOWN AND COUNTRY PLANNING ACT 1971

Notice under sections 27 *and* 36 *of appeal*

[Notice for
service on
individuals]

(a) Insert
address or
location of
proposed
development.

Proposed development at (a)..

(b) Insert
name of
appellant.

TAKE NOTICE that an appeal is being made to the [Secretary of State for
the Environment] [Secretary of State for Wales] by (b)..

(c) Insert
name of
Council.

   *(i) against the decision of the (c)...Council

   *(ii) on the failure of the (c)..Council
      to give notice of a decision

(d) Insert
description of
proposed
development

on an application to (d) ....

....

If you should wish to make representations to the Secretary of State about

(e) Insert
date not less
than 20 days
later than the
date on which
the notice is
served.

the appeal you should make them not later than (e) ....
to the Secretary [Department of the Environment] [Welsh Office] at.............................

                    Signed ....

                    *On behalf of ....

                    Date ....

   * Delete where inappropriate.

[Notice for
publication in
local news-
paper].

TOWN AND COUNTRY PLANNING ACT 1971

Notice under sections 27 *and* 36 *of appeal*

(a) Insert
address or
location of
proposed
development.

Proposed development at (a) ....

(b) Insert
name of
appellant.

NOTICE is hereby given that an appeal is being made to the [Secretary of
State for the Environment] [Secretary of State for Wales] by (b) ....

....

(c) Insert
name of
Council.

   *(i) against the decision of the (c)...Council

   *(ii) on the failure of the (c) ....Council
      to give notice of a decision

(d) Insert
description of
proposed
development.

on an application to (d) ....

....

Any owner of the land (namely, a freeholder or a person entitled to an
unexpired term of at least seven years under a lease) who wishes to make
representations to the Secretary of State about the appeal should make them

(e) Insert
date not less
than 20 days
later than the
date on which
the notice is
published.

in writing not later than (e) .... to the Secretary
[Department of the Environment] [Welsh Office] at ....

                    Signed ....

                    *On behalf of ....

                    Date ....

   * Delete where inappropriate.

SCHEDULE 5

PART I

TOWN AND COUNTRY PLANNING ACT 1971

TOWN AND COUNTRY PLANNING GENERAL DEVELOPMENT ORDER 1973

Certificate under article 18(2) in relation to an application for an established use certificate

I hereby certify that:—

Certificate A*

1. No person other than the $\frac{\text{*applicant}}{\text{appellant}}$ was an owner (a) of any part of the land to which the $\frac{\text{*application}}{\text{appeal}}$ relates at the beginning of the period of 20 days before the date of the accompanying $\frac{\text{*application}}{\text{appeal}}$;

(a) "owner" means—
  (i) a person having a freehold interest or a leasehold interest the unexpired term of which was not less than 7 years; or
  (ii) an occupier of any part of the land.

or:—

I hereby certify that:—

Certificate B*

1. $\frac{\text{*The applicant has}}{\frac{\text{I have}}{\text{The appellant has}}}$ given the requisite notice to all the persons other than $\frac{\text{*the applicant}}{\frac{\text{myself}}{\text{the appellant}}}$ who, 20 days before the date of the accompanying $\frac{\text{*application}}{\text{appeal}}$, were owners† of any part of the land to which the $\frac{\text{*application}}{\text{appeal}}$ relates, viz.—

(†) See Note (a) to Certificate A.

Name of owner   Address   Date of service of notice

or:—

I hereby certify that:—

Certificate C*

1. (i) $\frac{\text{*The applicant is}}{\frac{\text{I am}}{\text{The appellant is}}}$ unable to issue a certificate in accordance with either sub-paragraph (a) or sub-paragraph (b) of article 18(2) of the Town and Country Planning General Development Order 1973 in respect of the accompanying $\frac{\text{*application}}{\text{appeal}}$ dated (a) ....

(a) Insert date of application or appeal.

(ii) $\frac{\text{*The applicant has}}{\frac{\text{I have}}{\text{The appellant has}}}$ given the notice required by the said article 18 to the following persons other than $\frac{\text{*the applicant}}{\frac{\text{myself}}{\text{the appellant}}}$ who, 20 days before the date of the $\frac{\text{*application}}{\text{appeal}}$, were owners (†) of any part of the land to which the $\frac{\text{*application}}{\text{appeal}}$ relates, viz.—

(†) See Note (a) to Certificate A.

Name of owner (†)   Address   Date of service of notice

(iii) *The applicant has taken the steps listed below, being steps reasonably
$\overline{\text{I have}}$ / $\overline{\text{The appellant has}}$

open to $\dfrac{*me}{him}$, to ascertain the names and addresses of the other owners

of the land, or part thereof, and $\dfrac{*have}{has}$ been unable to do so:

(b) Insert description of steps taken.

(b) ....

....

(c) Insert name of local newspaper circulating in the locality in which the land is situated.

(iv) Notice of the $\dfrac{*application}{appeal}$ as set out below has been published in the

(c) ....

(d) Insert date of publication (which must not be earlier than 20 days before the application or appeal).

on (d) ....

Copy of notice as published

or:—

Certificate D*   I hereby certify that:—

1. (i) *The applicant is unable to issue a certificate in accordance with
$\overline{\text{I am}}$ / $\overline{\text{The appellant is}}$
sub-paragraph (a) of article 18(2) of the Town and Country Planning General

Development Order 1973 in respect of the accompanying $\dfrac{*application}{appeal}$ dated

(a) Insert date of application or appeal.

(a) ....

and $\dfrac{*have}{has}$ taken the steps listed below, being steps reasonably open to $\dfrac{*me}{him}$,

to ascertain the names and addresses of all the persons other than $\dfrac{*myself}{himself}$

† See Note (a) to Certificate A.

who, 20 days before the date of the $\dfrac{*application}{appeal}$, were owners (†) of any part

(b) Insert description of steps taken.

of the land and $\dfrac{*have}{has}$ been unable to do so:

(c) Insert name of local newspaper circulating in the locality in which the land is situated.

(b) ....

....

(ii) Notice of the $\dfrac{*application}{appeal}$ as set out below has been published in the

(d) Insert date of publication (which must not be earlier than 20 days before the application or appeal).

(c) ....

....

on (d) ....

Copy of notice as published

[Whichever is appropriate of these alternatives should form part of any certificate A, B, C or D above.]

*2. None of the land to which the $\dfrac{*application}{appeal}$ relates constitutes or forms

part of an agricultural holding;

or:—

I have

*2. *The applicant has given the requisite notice to every person other than
The appellant has

*myself / himself who, 20 days before the date of the *application / appeal, was a tenant of any agricultural holding any part of which was comprised in the land to which the *application / appeal relates, viz.—

Name of tenant *(e)*   Address   Date of service of notice

Signed ....

*On behalf of ....

Date ....

* Delete where inappropriate.

(e) If you are the sole agricultural tenant, enter "None".

Part II

Town and Country Planning Act 1971
Town and Country Planning General Development Order 1973
Notice under article 18 of application for established use certificate

[Notice for service on individuals]

TAKE NOTICE that application is being made to the

(a) ....Council by

(b) ....

for an established use certificate relating to the use of land at *(c)*..................

....

for the purposes of *(d)*...

If you should wish to make representations about the application, you should make them in writing not later than *(e)*.............................

to the Council at *(f)*..

....

Signed ....

*On behalf of ....

Date ....

* Delete where inappropriate.

(a) Insert name of Council.

(b) Insert name of applicant.

(c) Insert address or location of land.

(d) Insert use claimed to be established.

(e) Insert date not less than 20 days later than the date on which the notice is served.

(f) Insert address of Council.

Town and Country Planning Act 1971
Town and Country Planning General Development Order 1973
Notice under article 18 of application for established use certificate

[Notice for publication in local newspaper]

NOTICE is hereby given that application is being made to the *(a)*...................

.... Council by

(b) ....

for an established use certificate relating to the use of land at *(c)*..................

....

for the purpose of *(d)*...

(a) Insert name of Council.

(b) Insert name of applicant.

(c) Insert address or location of land.

(d) Insert use claimed to be established.

Any person who, in respect of the land or part thereof, is an owner (i.e. is a freeholder or a person entitled to an unexpired term of at least 7 years under a lease) or an occupier and who wishes to make representations to the above-mentioned Council about the application should make them in writing not

(e) Insert date not less than 20 days later than the date on which the notice is published.

(f) Insert address of Council.

later than (e) ....

to the Council at (f)...

....

Signed ....

*On behalf of ....

Date ....

* Delete where inappropriate.

PART III

TOWN AND COUNTRY PLANNING ACT 1971

TOWN AND COUNTRY PLANNING GENERAL DEVELOPMENT ORDER 1973

Notice under article 18 of appeal against refusal of an established use certificate

[Notice for service on individuals]

TAKE NOTICE that an appeal is being made to the [Secretary of State for the Environment] [Secretary of State for Wales] by (a) ....

(a) Insert name of appellant.

(b) Insert name of Council.

*(i) against the decision of the (b)...Council

*(ii) on the failure of the (b)...Council
to give notice of a decision

on an application for an established use certificate relating to the use of

(c) Insert address or location of land.

(c) ....

....

(d) Insert use claimed to be established.

for the purpose of (d) ....

(e) Insert date not less than 20 days later than the date on which the notice is served.

If you should wish to make representations to the Secretary of State about the appeal you should make them in writing not later than (e)...................

.... to the Secretary [Department of the Environment] [Welsh Office]

at ....

Signed ....

*On behalf of ....

Date ....

* Delete where inappropriate.

TOWN AND COUNTRY PLANNING ACT 1971

TOWN AND COUNTRY PLANNING GENERAL DEVELOPMENT ORDER 1973

Notice under article 18 of appeal against refusal of an established use certificate

[Notice for publication in local newspaper]

NOTICE is hereby given that an appeal is being made to the [Secretary of State for the Environment] [Secretary of State for Wales] by (a) ....

(a) Insert name of appellant.

(b) Insert name of Council.

* (i) against the decision of the (b)...Council

*(ii) on the failure of the (b)...Council

to give notice of a decision on an application for an established use certificate relating to the use of (*c*)..

....

for the purpose of (*d*).. .

(*c*) Insert description and address or location of land.

Any person who, in respect of the land or part thereof, is an owner (i.e. is a freeholder or a person entitled to an unexpired term of at least 7 years under a lease) or is an occupier and who wishes to make representations to the Secretary of State about the appeal should make them in writing not later than (*e*) ....

to the Secretary [Department of the Environment] [Welsh Office] at ....

....

(*d*) Insert use claimed to be established.

(*e*) Insert date not less than 20 days later than the date on which the notice is published.

Signed ....

` *On behalf of ....

Date ....

* Delete where inappropriate."

26th February 1976.

Anthony Crosland,
Secretary of State for the
Environment.

EXPLANATORY NOTE
(This Note is not part of the Order.)

This Order amends the Town and Country Planning General Development Order 1973 (as amended by the Town and Country Planning General Development (Amendment) Order 1973 and the Town and Country Planning General Development (Amendment) Order 1974) as follows:—

(a) Paragraphs (2) and (3) of article 7(3) (which require a local planning authority to acknowledge receipt of planning applications and prescribe the period within which the authority must notify the applicant of their decision) have been replaced by new paragraphs containing provisions to secure that notice of the decision is given within 8 weeks from the date when the application was actually received by the district planning authority (in Greater London, by the London borough council or the Common Council), regardless of the date when the authority acknowledged receipt, and that the 8-week period does not apply to applications which are found to be invalid for failure to comply with the statutory requirements (or any other reason);

(b) an additional requirement has been included in article 13(1) (consultations before grant of planning permission), under which a local planning authority must consult the Minister of Agriculture, Fisheries and Food before granting permission for development which is for non-agricultural purposes, which constitutes a departure from a development plan (as defined) and which is to be carried out on agricultural land, if the development is likely to result in the loss of 10 acres or more of land used for agricultural purposes;

(c) the prescribed form of notification to an applicant of receipt of his planning application (Part I of Schedule 2) has been amended to take account of the changes referred to in paragraph (a) above;

(d) the prescribed forms set out in Schedule 4 (forms of certificate that notice of a planning application has been given to owners of the land to which it relates, and forms of the relevant notices) have been altered in consequence of the amendments made to section 27 of the Act of 1971 by the Community Land Act 1975 (1975 c. 77): formerly, an applicant who was the freeholder or tenant of the whole of the application site was not required to notify other persons with an interest in the land, but now, by virtue of the amended section 27 and of the prescribed forms, an applicant must give notice of his application to all the persons (other than himself) who have a freehold interest in the land or are entitled to a lease with an unexpired term of 7 years;

(e) article 18 and Schedule 5 (which set out requirements in relation to applications for established use certificates) have been amended to secure that the prescribed forms relating to notification of persons with an interest in the land correspond to the new prescribed forms relating to applications for planning permission;

(f) some minor drafting amendments and corrections have been made.

1976 No. 302

MERCHANT SHIPPING
The Merchant Shipping (Radar) Rules 1976

Made - - - -	*26th February* 1976
Laid before Parliament	*8th March* 1976
Coming into Operation	*1st April* 1976

The Secretary of State, after consulting with the organisations referred to in section 85(3) of the Merchant Shipping Act 1970(a), in exercise of powers conferred by sections 1 and 6 of the Merchant Shipping (Safety Convention) Act 1949(b) as having effect by virtue of section 85(1) of, and Schedule 1 to, the said Act of 1970, and by section 2 of the Merchant Shipping Act 1964(c), and now vested in him (d) and of all other powers enabling him in that behalf, hereby makes the following Rules:

Citation, commencement and interpretation

1.—(1) These Rules may be cited as the Merchant Shipping (Radar) Rules 1976 and shall come into operation on 1st April 1976.

(2) The Interpretation Act 1889(e) shall apply for the interpretation of these Rules as it applies for the interpretation of an Act of Parliament.

(3) In these Rules, unless the context otherwise requires, the following expressions shall have the meanings respectively assigned to them, that is to say:

"radar installation" means a radio navigational aid (other than a direction-finder) required to be provided under Rule 3 below;

"maintenance" means any activity intended to keep a radar installation in satisfactory working condition and includes tests, measurements, replacements, adjustments and repair.

Application

2. These Rules apply to ships of 1600 gross registered tons and more which are registered in the United Kingdom.

Provision of radar

3.—(1) Every ship to which these Rules apply shall be provided with a radar installation which shall comply with:

(*a*) the Marine Radar Performance Specification 1957 or

(*b*) the Marine Radar Performance Specification 1968

issued by the Department of Trade:

Provided that a radar installation which is already provided in such a ship shall not be required to comply with such specifications before the expiry of one year from the date on which these Rules come into operation.

(a) 1970 c. 36.   **(b)** 1949 c. 43.   **(c)** 1964 c. 47.
(d) *See* S.I. 1965/145 and S.I. 1970/1537 (1965 I, p. 438; 1970 III, p. 5293).
(e) 1889 c. 63.

(2) Every such ship shall be provided with adequate means for readily determining any significant diminution in performance of the radar installation:

Provided that such equipment shall not be required to be provided before the expiry of four years from the date on which these Rules come into operation.

(3) Where a radar installation includes facilities for inter-switching different units of equipment, at least one arrangement of units when used together shall comply with all the requirements of these Rules.

Interference with other installations

4.—(1) At no time while the ship is at sea shall any interference or mechanical noise produced by the radar installation be such as to prevent the effective reception of radio signals.

(2) Units of the radar installation shall not, where practicable, be installed closer to the ship's standard and steering compasses than the appropriate "safe distance" marked on the unit. The "safe distance" means the minimum distance from the compasses specified on the unit, at which it should be installed.

Provision of electrical energy

5.—(1) There shall be provided in every ship to which these Rules apply, at all times while the ship is at sea and at all reasonable times when it is in port, a supply of electrical energy suitable and sufficient for the operation of the radar installation or for the purpose of testing and charging any batteries which are a source of electrical energy for the radar installation.

(2) The supply of electrical energy shall not exceed the limits set out below and adequate means shall be provided for disconnecting the supply of electrical energy:

AC   Variation from nominal voltage of $\pm\, 10\%$
         Variation from nominal frequency of $\pm\, 6\%$

DC   Variation from nominal voltage:
         110/220 Volt $+\, 10\% - 20\%$
         24/32 Volt $+\, 25\% - 10\%$

Charging of batteries

6.—(1) If batteries are provided as a source of electrical energy for any part of the radar installation, adequate means shall be provided on board every ship to which these Rules apply for the charging of such batteries from the ship's main source of electrical energy.

(2) When any battery provided for a radar installation is not in use, it shall be capable of being fully charged within a period of not more than 16 hours by the means of charging required by paragraph (1) of this Rule.

(3) When any battery is float charged whilst in use, the voltage used for charging the battery shall be within the limits set out in Rule 5(2) above.

Siting of radar installation

7.—(1) The provisions of this Rule apply only to a radar installation installed one year or later after the coming into operation of these Rules.

(2) The radar installation shall, where practicable, be mounted sufficiently rigidly to prevent the performance and reliability of the installation being adversely affected by vibration.

(3) The aerial unit of the radar installation shall be sited so that the best overall performance is achieved in relation to:

(a) the avoidance of shadow sectors;

(b) the avoidance of false echoes caused by reflections from the ship's structure; and

(c) the effect of aerial height on the amplitude and extent of sea-clutter.

(4) The radar display shall be sited on the bridge from which the ship is normally navigated. The site shall be such that:

(a) an observer, when viewing the display, faces forward and is readily able to maintain visual lookout;

(b) there is sufficient space for two observers to view the display simultaneously, with any fitted display visor removed if necessary.

(5) For the purposes of this Rule, "sufficiently rigidly" means that the radar installation will not, whilst in service, normally be subject to greater vibration than that specified in the Marine Radar Performance Specification 1968 issued by the Department of Trade.

Serviceability of radar installation

8.—(1) The radar installation shall be in a satisfactory working condition whenever the ship goes to sea:

Provided that this paragraph shall not apply when a ship is going to sea from a place at which prompt maintenance is not available or practicable without unduly delaying the ship.

(2) The radar installation shall be in a satisfactory working condition at all times when the ship is at sea, unless there is a defect in the installation and maintenance is not practicable.

Alignment of heading marker

9. The radar heading marker (or stern marker if fitted) shall be accurately aligned with the ship's fore-and-aft line as soon as practicable after the radar installation has been installed in the ship. The marker shall be re-aligned as soon as practicable whenever a relative bearing taken by radar is not substantially the same as that obtained visually.

Measurement of shadow sectors

10. The angular width and bearing of any shadow sector displayed by the radar installation shall be determined and kept up to date following any changes likely to affect shadow sectors.

Servicing and operating information

11. Adequate information and instructions as to the use and maintenance of the radar installation shall be provided and shall be available at all times for use by any person operating, testing or servicing the radar installation.

Spares and tools

12. For each radar installation there shall be supplied such special tools and equipment as are necessary for shipboard maintenance and such spares as are likely to be required for the duration of the intended voyage.

Stanley Clinton Davis,
Parliamentary Under-Secretary of State,
Department of Trade.

26th February 1976.

EXPLANATORY NOTE
(This Note is not part of the Rules.)

These Rules introduce requirements for the provision of a radar installation in ships of 1600 gross registered tons and above registered in the United Kingdom. Provision is also made in respect of the siting and serviceability of the radar installation.

STATUTORY INSTRUMENTS

1976 No. 304

SEA FISHERIES

BOATS AND METHODS OF FISHING

The Fishing Vessels (Acquisition and Improvement) (Grants) Scheme 1976

Made - - -	*29th January* 1976
Laid before Parliament	*10th February* 1976
Coming into Operation	*27th February* 1976

The Minister of Agriculture, Fisheries and Food, the Secretary of State for Scotland and the Secretary of State for Wales (being the Secretaries of State concerned with the sea fishing industry in Scotland and Wales respectively) in exercise of the powers conferred on them by sections 44 and 45 of the Sea Fish Industry Act 1970(a) and of all other powers enabling them in that behalf, with the approval of the Treasury and after consultation with the White Fish Authority and the Herring Industry Board, hereby make the following scheme:—

Citation, extent and commencement

1. This scheme, which may be cited as the Fishing Vessels (Acquisition and Improvement) (Grants) Scheme 1976, shall apply to Great Britain and shall come into operation on the day after it has been approved by resolution of each House of Parliament.

Interpretation

2.—(1) In this scheme, unless the context otherwise requires—

"the appropriate authority" means—

(*a*) in relation to a grant in respect of expenditure incurred in the acquisition of a vessel intended to be engaged in catching or processing white fish or in respect of expenditure incurred in an improvement of or for a vessel so engaged or intended to be so engaged, the White Fish Authority, and

(*b*) in relation to a grant in respect of expenditure incurred in the acquisition of a vessel intended to be engaged in catching or processing herring or in respect of expenditure incurred in an improvement of or for a vessel so engaged or intended to be so engaged, the Herring Industry Board;

(a) 1970 c. 11.

"the control period" has the meaning assigned to it by paragraph 15(2) of this scheme;

"improvement" has the meaning assigned to it by paragraph 3(1)(*b*) of this scheme;

"the Ministers" means the Minister of Agriculture, Fisheries and Food and the Secretaries of State concerned with the sea fishing industry in Scotland and Wales respectively;

"processing", in relation to fish, includes preserving or preparing fish, or producing any substance or article from fish, by any method for human or animal consumption;

"products", in relation to fish, means anything produced by processing the fish;

"a relevant activity" means any one of the following activities, that is to say, catching or processing white fish or herring;

"relevant equipment" means equipment or apparatus of any description constructed or adapted for the purposes of catching or processing white fish or herring;

"white fish" means fish of any kind found in the sea except herring, salmon and migratory trout.

(2) The Interpretation Act 1889(**a**) shall apply for the interpretation of this scheme as it applies for the interpretation of an Act of Parliament.

Application for grant

3.—(1) Subject to the provisions of this scheme, a person engaged or proposing to be engaged in the white fish industry or herring industry in Great Britain by carrying on the business of operating one or more vessels registered in Great Britain (of whatever size and in whatever way propelled) for a relevant activity may apply to the appropriate authority for a grant in respect of expenditure incurred—

(*a*) in the acquisition of a new vessel, registered or intended to be registered in Great Britain, to be engaged in a relevant activity, including equipment required for the operation of the vessel which is sold with the vessel; or

(*b*) in the acquisition, installation, modification, renewal or replacement of any part of a vessel registered or intended to be registered in Great Britain, engaged or to be engaged in a relevant activity, or of an engine or of any part of an engine of or for such a vessel, or of any relevant equipment required for, or installed or used on, such a vessel (such acquisition, installation, modification, renewal or replacement being hereinafter referred to as an "improvement"):

Provided that no grant shall be made under sub-paragraph (*b*) of this paragraph in respect of—

(i) expenditure incurred in the acquisition or installation of any second-hand part of a vessel, engine, part of an engine or relevant equipment; or

(ii) expenditure incurred in relation to an improvement in so far as, in the opinion of the appropriate authority, such expenditure can be regarded as laid out on the routine repair or maintenance of the vessel or of its engine or of any relevant equipment required for the vessel or installed or used there on.

(**a**) 1889 c. 63.

(2) Applications for grants under this scheme shall be made in writing in such form as the appropriate authority may from time to time require, and shall be delivered to the appropriate authority at such address as they may at any time or in any particular case direct.

4. Applications for grants under this scheme may be made only by British subjects resident in Great Britain or corporations incorporated by or under the law of any part of Great Britain.

5. Applicants for grants under this scheme in respect of the acquisition of a vessel shall be required to satisfy the appropriate authority with regard to the prospect of their being able to operate the fishing vessel successfully and that they have the ability to manage, and sufficient financial resources for the purposes of, the business in which the fishing vessel will be employed.

6. The appropriate authority may require applicants to make a full statement of their financial position, including their assets, debts and obligations, and to make available for inspection by the appropriate authority, or their duly authorised agents, such books of account and other records and documents as the appropriate authority may reasonably require.

7. Where expenditure is shared by two or more persons, applications for grants under this scheme may be made in respect of either the full expenditure or part of the expenditure incurred and may be made by individual applicants or by two or more applicants jointly.

8.—(1) No grant shall be paid under this scheme unless—

    (*a*) the application for the payment of the grant has been approved by the appropriate authority before 1st January 1977, and

    (*b*) the conditions set out in paragraphs 10 and 11 of this scheme have been complied with.

(2) In considering whether or not to approve an application for the payment of a grant under this scheme, the appropriate authority—

    (*a*) shall have regard to the needs and interests of the white fish industry or herring industry (as appropriate to the application) or to that section thereof to which the application relates, but

    (*b*) shall not approve the application so far as it relates to any proportion or item of the proposed expenditure which in their opinion is unnecessary or unwarranted having regard to the benefit likely to be derived from the expenditure in respect of which the application is made.

9.—(1) The amount of grant which may be paid under this scheme shall be 25 per cent. of the expenditure approved by the appropriate authority.

(2) No grant shall be paid in respect of expenditure incurred in the acquisition of a vessel, or part of a vessel, constructed elsewhere than in the United Kingdom, unless the Ministers are satisfied that the expenditure was incurred at a cost which compares fairly with the cost at which the construction of the vessel, or part of the vessel, could have been carried out in the United Kingdom.

(3) For the purposes of this paragraph any expenditure which is incurred in the acquisition of an engine or part of an engine or any relevant equipment, incorporated into a vessel at the time of its construction elsewhere than in the United Kingdom, shall be deemed to be expenditure incurred in the acquisition of such vessel.

Conditions for payment of grants

10.—(1) The plans and specifications of the vessel in respect of the acquisition of which or of the improvement in respect of which an application for a grant is made, the tender for expenditure to be incurred and the form of contract to be entered into between the applicant and the builder, supplier or other contractor shall respectively be approved by the appropriate authority before the contract is made:

Provided that in a case where the applicant himself intends to undertake the whole or a part of any work in relation to the expenditure on which a grant may be payable the appropriate authority, instead of approving the tender for expenditure and form of contract as aforesaid shall, before such work is begun, give their approval to the undertaking both as regards the manner in which it is to be carried out and the kind, quantity and cost of the equipment or materials to be supplied in the course thereof.

(2) The vessel in respect of the acquisition of which an application for a grant is made shall be constructed and equipped, and the improvement in respect of which an application for a grant is made shall be carried out, to the satisfaction of the appropriate authority and in accordance with the plans and specifications approved as aforesaid.

(3) The vessel in respect of or in connection with which an application for a grant is made shall conform to any standards laid down under the Merchant Shipping Acts 1894 to 1970 and shall be constructed or adapted so as to make such provision for the accommodation of officers and crew as, in the opinion of the appropriate authority, conforms to the best modern practice after making due allowance for the age and kind of vessel concerned, for sleeping and messing accommodation, sanitary accommodation, medical or first-aid facilities, store rooms, catering facilities and other accommodation.

11. Any person authorised in writing by the appropriate authority shall have the right to inspect the vessel in respect of or in connection with which a grant has been or is to be made under this scheme at any time either during its construction and on its completion or during the carrying out of the improvement and on the completion of the improvement, as the case may be, and thereafter at all reasonable times within the control period.

12. No grant shall be payable under this scheme in respect of an improvement unless the appropriate authority are satisfied that the expenditure in relation to which it will be payable is likely to result in an increase in the efficiency or economy of the operation of the vessel in respect of or in connection with which the application is made as regards one or more of the following matters, that is to say,

(*a*) the catching of fish,

(*b*) the handling, processing or storage of fish,

(*c*) the working conditions of the officers or crew,

(*d*) the condition of fish or the products of fish at the time of landing, and

(*e*) the safety and seaworthiness of the vessel,

regard being had to the technical and economic standards prevailing in the fishing industry at the time of the consideration of the application by the appropriate authority and to the results of any experiments and research which have relation to the subject of the particular expenditure.

13. No payment of or on account of a grant shall be made until the sum to be found by the applicant has been paid towards the expenditure in respect of which the application is made and thereafter payment of or on account of the grant may be made by the appropriate authority direct to the applicant, or on the applicant's behalf to the builder, supplier or other contractor in one sum or by such instalments and at such times as may be required in conformity with the contract, on the receipt of certificates or such further or other evidence that payment is due as may be required by the appropriate authority.

14. If any person makes a false statement or furnishes false information in respect of any of the matters required to be disclosed in connection with an application for payment of a grant under this scheme or if any of the conditions relating to the payment of grants under this scheme are not complied with by an applicant, any payment of or on account of a grant to that applicant may at any time be refused, and any such payment already made in relation to that application may be recovered by the appropriate authority.

15.—(1) Any person whose application for a grant under this scheme is approved by the appropriate authority may be required to give such undertakings as the appropriate authority may consider appropriate to the case, and in particular (but without prejudice to the generality of the foregoing) shall be required in any case—

(*a*) during the control period, and as may be appropriate to the case, either to employ the vessel in respect of or in connection with which the application was made (hereinafter in this paragraph referred to as "the vessel") or to take all reasonable steps to ensure its employment in the diligent and vigorous prosecution of the catching or processing of white fish or herring to the satisfaction of the appropriate authority;

(*b*) to insure the vessel and keep it insured against all marine risks and war risks during the control period in a sum approved by the appropriate authority, which shall be at least sufficient to ensure that in the event of the total loss of the vessel there will be made available sufficient moneys to meet the repayment of the grant or any part thereof which might be repayable at the date of the loss;

(*c*) to keep and make available for inspection by the appropriate authority at all reasonable times during the control period any books, records or other documents necessary to enable the appropriate authority to satisfy themselves that any conditions of the grant have been complied with;

(*d*) if there occurs within the control period—

(i) the total loss of the vessel arising out of any insured risk, to repay to the appropriate authority the whole of the grant or, if the loss occurs more than three years from the commencement of the control period, a proportion of the grant to be calculated by multiplying the total amount of the grant by the fraction which represents the relationship which the unexpired part of the control period bears to the full control period;

(ii) a breach of any undertaking or condition subject to which the grant was made, or a disposition by way of mortgage, transfer of registration, charter for any purpose other than the employment of the vessel in a relevant activity based on a port in Great Britain, sale or otherwise of the vessel or of any part thereof or of its engine or of any part thereof or of any equipment or apparatus used on or in connection therewith, or of any part of a vessel, engine, part of an engine or relevant equipment which is the subject of the improvement in respect of which the grant or any part of it was made, to repay to the appropriate authority, if in their discretion they shall so require, the whole of the grant, or such lesser sum as they shall deem appropriate:

Provided that repayment under sub-paragraph (1)(*d*)(ii) of this paragraph shall not be required in excess of the amount which would have been repayable at the same date had the provisions of sub-paragraph (1)(*d*)(i) of this paragraph been applicable to the case:

Provided also that sub-paragraph (1)(*d*)(ii) of this paragraph shall not have effect in relation to a disposition by way of mortgage created for the raising of money applied towards the cost of construction or improvement of the vessel, being a mortgage in favour of the appropriate authority or one approved by them before it was made.

(2) For the purposes of paragraphs 11 and 15(1) of this scheme "the control period" means—

    (*a*) in the case of a grant paid in respect of any improvement, a period of five years commencing with the date on which the improvement was completed to the satisfaction of the appropriate authority, and

    (*b*) in the case of any other grant paid in respect of or in connection with a vessel, a period of 10 years commencing with the date on which the vessel was first registered in Great Britain.

In Witness whereof the Official Seal of the Minister of Agriculture, Fisheries and Food is hereunto affixed on 22nd January 1976.

(L.S.)

Frederick Peart,
Minister of Agriculture,
Fisheries and Food.

William Ross,
Secretary of State for Scotland.

26th January 1976.

John Morris,
Secretary of State for Wales.

27th January 1976.

James A. Dunn,
J. Dormand,
Two of the Lords Commissioners
of Her Majesty's Treasury.

Approved on 29th January 1976.

EXPLANATORY NOTE

(This Note is not part of the Scheme.)

This Scheme enables grants to be made by the White Fish Authority and the Herring Industry Board towards expenditure incurred in the acquisition or improvement of vessels engaged or to be engaged in catching or processing white fish or herring.

No grant may be paid under this scheme unless the relevant application is approved before 1st January 1977. The rate of grant for all vessels is 25 per cent. of the approved expenditure.

The Scheme was approved by a resolution of the House of Commons on 26th February 1976 and a resolution of the House of Lords on 26th February 1976 and comes into operation on 27th February 1976.

STATUTORY INSTRUMENTS

1976 No. 305

SEA FISHERIES

LANDING AND SALE OF SEA FISH
The Immature Crabs and Lobsters Order 1976

Made - - - -	26th February 1976
Laid before Parliament	5th March 1976
Coming into Operation	15th March 1976

The Minister of Agriculture, Fisheries and Food and the Secretary of State concerned with the sea fishing industry in Scotland, in exercise of the powers conferred upon them by section 1 of the Sea Fish (Conservation) Act 1967(a) as amended by section 16 of the Sea Fisheries Act 1968(b) and of all other powers enabling them in that behalf, hereby make the following Order:—

1. This Order may be cited as the Immature Crabs and Lobsters Order 1976 and shall come into operation on 15th March 1976.

2. The Interpretation Act 1889(c) shall apply to the interpretation of this Order as it applies to the interpretation of an Act of Parliament, and as if this Order and the Order hereby revoked were Acts of Parliament.

3. The Sea-Fishing Industry (Crabs and Lobsters) Order 1966(d) is hereby revoked.

4. For the purposes of section 1(1) of the Sea Fish (Conservation) Act 1967 (which prohibits in Great Britain the landing, sale, exposure or offering for sale or the possession for the purpose of sale of any sea fish of any description, being a fish of a smaller size than such size as may be prescribed in relation to sea fish of that description) the following sizes are hereby prescribed:—

(a) in relation to crabs of the species Cancer pagarus, a width of 115 millimetres across the broadest part of the back;

(b) in relation to lobsters, a carapace length of 80 millimetres, being the length measured from the rear of either eye socket to the rear end of the body shell along a line parallel to the centre line of the body shell.

5. There shall not be carried in any foreign fishing boat in waters adjacent to the United Kingdom and within the fishery limits of the British Islands

---

(a) 1967 c. 84. (b) 1968 c. 77. (c) 1889 c. 63.
(d) S.I. 1966/737 (1966 II. p. 1713).

any crab or lobster which is of less than the minimum size prescribed in relation thereto by article 4 of this Order.

In witness whereof the Official Seal of the Minister of Agriculture, Fisheries and Food is hereunto affixed on 24th February 1976.

(L.S.)

Frederick Peart,
Minister of Agriculture, Fisheries and Food.

William Ross,
26th February 1976.   Secretary of State for Scotland.

EXPLANATORY NOTE

(This Note is not part of the Order.)

This Order supersedes the Sea-Fishing Industry (Crabs and Lobsters) Order 1966. The principal changes made are the introduction of metric sizes, a new system of measurement for lobsters and the prohibition of the carrying of immature crabs and lobsters in foreign fishing boats within the fishery limits of the British Islands (as defined in section 1 of the Fishery Limits Act 1964).

STATUTORY INSTRUMENTS

1976 No. 306

POLICE

The Police Pensions (Amendment) Regulations 1976

Made - - - -   *27th February* 1976

Laid before Parliament   *10th March* 1976

Coming into Operation   *1st April* 1976

In exercise of the powers conferred on me by section 1 of the Police Pensions Act 1948(a), as extended and amended by section 43 of the Reserve and Auxiliary Forces (Protection of Civil Interests) Act 1951(b), section 5(3) of the Overseas Service Act 1958(c) and Schedule 2 thereto, section 1(1) of the Police Pensions Act 1961(d), sections 40, 43(4), 45(4) and 63 of the Police Act 1964(e) and Schedules 6 and 9 thereto, sections 35 and 38(4) of the Police (Scotland) Act 1967(f), section 4(5) of the Police Act 1969(g) and sections 12, 15 and 29(1) of the Superannuation Act 1972(h) and Schedule 6 thereto, and after consultation with the Police Council for the United Kingdom, I hereby, with the consent of the Minister for the Civil Service (i), make the following Regulations:—

PART I

CITATION, OPERATION ETC.

1. These Regulations may be cited as the Police Pensions (Amendment) Regulations 1976.

2. These Regulations shall come into operation on 1st April 1976 and shall have effect—

(a) for the purposes of Part II thereof, as from 24th January 1975;

(b) for the purposes of Part III thereof, as from 1st April 1975;

(c) for the purposes of Part IV thereof, as from 1st August 1975.

3. In these Regulations references to the principal Regulations are references to the Police Pensions Regulations 1973(j), as amended (k).

(a) 1948 c. 24.   (b) 1951 c. 65.
(c) 1958 c. 14.   (d) 1961 c. 35.
(e) 1964 c. 48.   (f) 1967 c. 77.
(g) 1969 c. 63.   (h) 1972 c. 11.
(i) Formerly the Treasury, *see* S.I. 1968/1656 (1968 III, p. 4485).
(j) S.I. 1973/428 (1973 I, p. 1401).
(k) The amending instruments are not relevant to the subject matter of these Regulations.

PART II

PROVISIONS HAVING EFFECT AS FROM 24TH JANUARY 1975

4. After Regulation 11 of the principal Regulations (aggregate pension contributions) there shall be inserted the following Regulation:—

"Reckoning of service etc. for purposes of awards

11A.—(1) Subject to paragraph (2), for the purpose of calculating an award payable to or in respect of a member of a police force by reference to any period in years (including a period of pensionable or other service)—

(*a*) that period shall be reckoned in completed years and a fraction of a year;

(*b*) a part of a year shall be taken to be that fraction of a year whereof the denominator is 365 and the numerator the number of completed days in that part and, accordingly, a part of a year which includes 29th February in a leap year and comprises 365 days shall be treated as a whole year.

(2) Paragraph (1)(*b*) shall not apply where the member ceased to serve as such before 24th January 1975 and, in such case, Schedule 11 shall have effect for the purposes mentioned in paragraph (1).".

5. For paragraph 1 of Part I of Schedule 2 to the principal Regulations (policeman's ordinary pension) there shall be substituted the following provision:—

"1. Subject as hereinafter in this Schedule provided, the pension shall be of an amount equal to 30 sixtieths of the policeman's average pensionable pay with the addition, subject to a maximum of 40 sixtieths, of an amount equal to 2 sixtieths of that pay multiplied by the period in years by which his pensionable service exceeds 25 years.".

6. For paragraphs 2, 3 and 4 of Part II of Schedule 2 to the principal Regulations (policeman's ill-health pension) there shall be substituted the following provisions:—

"2. Where the policeman has less than 5 years' pensionable service, the amount of the pension shall not be less than a sixtieth of his average pensionable pay and, subject as aforesaid, shall be of an amount equal to a sixtieth of that pay multiplied by the period in years of his pensionable service.

3. Where the policeman has 5 or more years', but not more than 10 years' pensionable service, subject to paragraph 5, the pension shall be of an amount equal to 2 sixtieths of that pay multiplied by the period in years of his pensionable service.

4. Where the policeman has more than 10 years' pensionable service, the pension shall be not less than 20 sixtieths of his average pensionable pay and, subject as aforesaid and to paragraph 5, shall be equal to 7 sixtieths of that pay with the addition—

(*a*) of an amount equal to a sixtieth of that pay multiplied by the period in years of his pensionable service up to 20 years, and

(*b*) of an amount equal to 2 sixtieths of that pay multiplied by the period in years by which his pensionable service exceeds 20 years.".

7. For Part III of Schedule 2 to the principal Regulations (policeman's short service pension) there shall be substituted the following Part:—

Regulation 21   "Part III

POLICEMAN'S SHORT SERVICE PENSION

Subject as hereafter in this Schedule provided, the pension shall be of an amount which is the aggregate of—

  (a) an amount equal to a sixtieth of the policeman's average pensionable pay multiplied by the period in years of his pensionable service up to 20 years, and

  (b) an amount equal to 2 sixtieths of that pay multiplied by the period in years by which his pensionable service exceeds 20 years.".

8. In paragraph 2(a) of Part IV of Schedule 2 to the principal Regulations (policeman's ill-health or short service gratuity) for the words "the number of his completed years of pensionable service;" there shall be substituted the words "the period in years of his pensionable service;".

9.—(1) In paragraph 2 of Part VI of Schedule 2 to the principal Regulations (policeman's deferred pension) for the words following "calculated" there shall be substituted the words "in years".

(2) For paragraph 3 of the said Part VI there shall be substituted the following paragraph:—

"3. The hypothetical pension referred to in paragraph 2 is a pension of an amount which is the aggregate of—

  (a) an amount equal to a sixtieth of his average pensionable pay multiplied by the period in years of his hypothetical service up to 20 years, and

  (b) an amount equal to 2 sixtieths of that pay multiplied by the period in years by which his hypothetical service exceeds 20 years.".

10. In paragraph 1(4) of Part VII of Schedule 2 to the principal Regulations (reduction of pension at insured pensionable age) for the words "highest whole number of years in the aggregate period during" there shall be substituted the words "period of service in years in respect of".

11.—(1) For paragraph 4(a) of Part II of Schedule 3 to the principal Regulations (transitional modifications of Part I) there shall be substituted the following provision:—

"(a) an amount which is the aggregate of—

  (i) an amount equal to a sixtieth of the husband's average pensionable pay multiplied by the period in years of his pensionable service up to 20 years, and

  (ii) an amount equal to 2 sixtieths of that pay multiplied by the period in years by which his pensionable service exceeds 20 years;".

(2) For paragraph 5(1) of the said Part II there shall be substituted the following provision:—

"(1) In this paragraph the following expressions have the meanings hereby respectively assigned to them, that is to say:—

"relevant period" means the period (if any) in years by which the policeman's pre-1972 pensionable service falls short of 20 years;

"relevant pensionable service" means a policeman's pensionable service reduced by his pre-1972 pensionable service and expressed in years;

"weighted relevant pensionable service" means a policeman's relevant pensionable service, so much of such service as exceeds the relevant period being counted twice.".

(3) In paragraph 5(2)(*b*) of the said Part II for the words "a half year for each completed year of" there shall be substituted the words "a half of his".

(4) In paragraph 6 of the said Part II the words "completed years of" shall be omitted in each of the four places where they occur and for the word "exceed" there shall be substituted the word "exceeds".

12. In paragraph 2(2) of Part IV of Schedule 3 to the principal Regulations (widow's accrued pension) the words following "reckonable by him" shall be omitted.

13.—(1) For paragraph 4(2)(*a*) of Part I of Schedule 4 to the principal Regulations (child's ordinary allowance) there shall be substituted the following provision:—

"(*a*) an amount which is the aggregate of—
   (i) an amount equal to a sixtieth of the father's average pensionable pay multiplied by the period in years of his pensionable service up to 20 years, and
   (ii) an amount equal to 2 sixtieths of that pay multiplied by the period in years by which his pensionable service exceeds 20 years;".

(2) In paragraph 4(3) of the said Part I the words "completed years of" shall be omitted in each of the three places where they occur and for the word "exceed" there shall be substituted the word "exceeds".

14. In paragraph 3(2) of Part III of Schedule 4 to the principal Regulations (child's accrued allowance) the words "each period being reckoned in completed years up to 20 years and in completed half years in so far as it exceeds 20 years" shall be omitted.

15. After Schedule 10 to the principal Regulations (limits in respect of awards to or in respect of servicemen) there shall be added the Schedule set out in Appendix 1 to these Regulations.

Part III

Provisions Having Effect as from 1st April 1975

16.—(1) For paragraph (1) of Regulation 24 of the principal Regulations (commutation) there shall be substituted the following provision:—

"(1) A regular policeman may, in accordance with this Regulation, commute for a lump sum a portion of any pension, other than an injury pension, to which he is or may become entitled, provided, in the case of an ordinary pension, that—

(*a*) he retires or retired either when entitled to reckon at least 30 years' pensionable service or in the circumstances mentioned in sub-paragraph (*a*), (*b*), (*d*) or (*e*) of Regulation 21(1), or

(*b*) he retires or retired otherwise than as aforesaid but on or after 1st April 1975.".

(2) In paragraph (3) of the said Regulation 24 for the words following "but for the provisions of" there shall be substituted the words "paragraph (7)(*b*) and of Regulation 25 as (subject to the limitations contained in paragraphs (3A) and (8) and in Regulation 26) he may specify.".

(3) After paragraph (3) of the said Regulation 24 there shall be inserted the following provision:—

"(3A) A regular policeman who retires or retired as mentioned in paragraph (1)(*b*) shall not commute such a portion of his ordinary pension that the lump sum calculated by reference thereto in accordance with paragraph (6) (disregarding any reduction in accordance with the proviso thereto) exceeds the aggregate of—

(*a*) an amount equal to 90 eightieths of the average pensionable pay by reference to which his pension is calculated, and

(*b*) an amount equal to 6 eightieths of that pay multiplied by the period in years by which his pensionable service exceeds 25 years.".

(4) At the end of paragraph (4) of the said Regulation 24 there shall be added the following provision:—

"Provided that a person who retired with an ordinary pension as mentioned in paragraph (1)(*b*) before 1st December 1975 may give such notice at any time before 1st June 1976.".

(5) For paragraph (8) of the said Regulation 24 there shall be substituted the following provision:—

"(8) Where a person wishes to surrender and commute for a lump sum a portion of a pension which falls to be reduced under paragraph (7)(*b*), the portion which, under paragraphs (3) and (3A), he may commute shall be reduced by the amount of the said reduction.".

PART IV

PROVISION HAVING EFFECT AS FROM 1ST AUGUST 1975

17. After Regulation 101 of the principal Regulations (chief constables who joined or were transferred to a county force) there shall be inserted the Regulation set out in Appendix 2 to these Regulations.

Roy Jenkins,
One of Her Majesty's Principal
Secretaries of State.

26th February 1976.

Consent of the Minister for the Civil Service given under his Official Seal on 27th February 1976.

(L.S.)

K. H. McNeill,
Authorised by the Minister for
the Civil Service.

APPENDIX 1

<small>SCHEDULE INSERTED AFTER SCHEDULE 10</small>
<small>TO THE PRINCIPAL REGULATIONS</small>

Regulation 11A(2)　　　　　**SCHEDULE 11**

<small>RECKONING OF SERVICE ETC. FOR PURPOSES OF AWARDS TO OR IN RESPECT
OF POLICEMEN WHO CEASED TO SERVE BEFORE 24TH JANUARY 1975</small>

1. This Schedule shall apply for the purposes of the calculation of an award payable to or in respect of a member of a police force who ceased to serve as such before 24th January 1975.

2.—(1) This paragraph shall apply for the purposes of paragraph 1 of Part I of Schedule 2.

(2) For the purposes mentioned in sub-paragraph (1) the period in years by which a period exceeds 25 years shall be computed in completed half-years and, accordingly—

　　(a) a part of a year less than a half shall be ignored, and

　　(b) a part of a year exceeding a half shall be treated as a half.

3.—(1) This paragraph shall apply—

　　(a) for the purposes of—
　　　　paragraphs 2 and 3 of Part II of Schedule 2,
　　　　Part IV of Schedule 2,
　　　　paragraph 1(4) of Part VII of Schedule 2,
　　　　paragraph 6 of Part II of Schedule 3;

　　(b) subject to paragraph 4, for the purposes of—
　　　　paragraph 4 of Part II of Schedule 2,
　　　　Part III of Schedule 2,
　　　　Part VI of Schedule 2,
　　　　paragraph 4 of Part II of Schedule 3,
　　　　paragraph 4 of Part I of Schedule 4;

　　(c) subject to paragraphs 5 and 6, for the purposes of paragraph 5 of Part II of Schedule 3;

　　(d) subject to paragraph 7, for the purposes of—
　　　　paragraph 2 of Part IV of Schedule 3,
　　　　paragraph 3 of Part III of Schedule 4.

(2) Save as otherwise provided in paragraphs 4, 5, 6 and 7, for the purposes mentioned in sub-paragraph (1) a period shall be computed in completed years and, accordingly, a part of a year shall be ignored.

4.—(1) This paragraph shall apply for the purposes mentioned in paragraph 3(1)(b).

(2) For the purposes so mentioned the period in years by which a period exceeds 20 years shall be computed in completed half years as mentioned in paragraph 2(2).

5.—(1) This paragraph shall apply for the purposes of the definition of the expression "weighted relevant pensionable service" in paragraph 5(1) of Part II of Schedule 3.

(2) For the purposes aforesaid the period in years by which a period exceeds the relevant period (as defined in paragraph 5(1) of the said Part II) shall be computed in completed half-years as mentioned in paragraph 2(2).

6.—(1) This paragraph shall apply for the purposes of paragraph 5(2)(b) of Part II of Schedule 3.

(2) For the purposes aforesaid a half of a person's pre-1972 pensionable service shall be computed in completed half years as mentioned in paragraph 2(2).

7.—(1) This paragraph shall apply for the purposes mentioned in paragraph 3(1)(*d*).

(2) For the purposes aforesaid, in so far as a period exceeds 20 years it shall be computed in completed half-years as provided in paragraph 2(2).

APPENDIX 2

REGULATION INSERTED AFTER REGULATION 101
OF THE PRINCIPAL REGULATIONS

Certain regular policemen with service on or after 1st August 1975

101A.—(1) This Regulation shall apply in the case of a regular policeman of a rank above that of superintendent who has served as such during a period beginning on or after 1st August 1975 ("the relevant period").

(2) Notwithstanding anything in these Regulations, an award to or in respect of a regular policeman to whom this Regulation applies shall not be less than it would have been had the pay to which he was entitled as a member of a police force, in respect of the relevant period, fallen to be calculated in accordance with the scale of pay in force immediately before 1st August 1975 for a member of that force holding the rank, or the rank and office, held by him during the relevant period:

Provided that where the award is an ordinary pension which falls to be reduced in accordance with paragraph 6 of Part VIII of Schedule 2, the reduction shall be calculated without regard to this paragraph.

EXPLANATORY NOTE

(This Note is not part of the Regulations.)

These Regulations amend the Police Pensions Regulations 1973 with effect, as provided in Regulation 2, from the dates mentioned below (retrospection is authorised by sections 12 and 15 of the Superannuation Act 1972).

Part II of the present Regulations relates to the calculation of awards by reference to periods of pensionable service and other periods. Under the Regulations of 1973 only completed years, or in certain cases completed half-years, are taken into account. Part II provides that any fraction of a year shall be taken into account except that the existing position is preserved in the case of persons who ceased to be members of a police force before 24th January 1975, from which date Part II has effect.

Part III relates to the commutation of a portion of a pension for a lump sum. Under the Regulations of 1973 a member of a police force cannot commute an ordinary pension (save in specified circumstances) unless he has 30 years' pensionable service. Part III provides with effect from 1st April 1975 that a member with less than this service may commute an ordinary pension subject, however, to a new restriction on the portion which may be commuted.

Part IV, with effect from 1st August 1975 (the date of commencement of the Remuneration, Charges and Grants Act 1975 (c. 57)), provides that an award under the Regulations of 1973 to or in respect of a member of a police force of a rank above that of superintendent, with service on or after that date, shall not be less than it would have been had his scale of pay in respect of that service been the scale in force immediately before that date.

STATUTORY INSTRUMENTS

1976 No. 307

WATER, ENGLAND AND WALES

The Anglian and Thames Water Authorities (Alteration of Boundaries) Order 1976

Made - - -	*26th February* 1976
Laid before Parliament	*11th March* 1976
Coming into Operation	*1st April* 1976

The Secretary of State for the Environment and the Minister of Agriculture, Fisheries and Food, in exercise of the powers conferred on them by sections 2(5) to (7), 8(3) and 36(2) of, and paragraphs 1, 14 and 15 of Schedule 2 to, the Water Act 1973(a), and of all other powers enabling them in that behalf, on recommendations made to them by the Anglian Water Authority and the Thames Water Authority in pursuance of the said section 8(3), and after consultation with such persons and representative bodies as they considered it appropriate to consult, hereby make the following order:—

Citation and commencement

1. This order may be cited as the Anglian and Thames Water Authorities (Alteration of Boundaries) Order 1976 and shall come into operation on 1st April 1976.

Interpretation

2.—(1) The Interpretation Act 1889(b) shall apply for the interpretation of this order as it applies for the interpretation of an Act of Parliament.

(2) In this order, unless the context otherwise requires—

"the Act" means the Water Act 1973;

"the Anglian Authority" means the Anglian Water Authority, and "the Thames Authority" means the Thames Water Authority;

"the authorities" means the Anglian Authority and the Thames Authority;

"the day of transfer" means 1st April 1976;

"the map" means the map, prepared in duplicate, signed by an Under Secretary in the Department of the Environment and an Under Secretary in the Ministry of Agriculture, Fisheries and Food, and marked "Map referred to in the Anglian and Thames Water Authorities (Alteration of Boundaries) Order 1976", of which one duplicate has been deposited and is available for inspection at the offices of the Secretary of State for the Environment and the other at the offices of the Minister of Agriculture, Fisheries and Food;

(a) 1973 c. 37.　　　　　　　　　(b) 1889 c. 63.

"the relevant constitution order" means—

    (*a*) in relation to the Anglian Authority, the Anglian Water Authority Constitution Order 1973(**a**),

    (*b*) in relation to the Thames Authority, the Thames Water Authority Constitution Order 1973(**b**), as amended(**c**);

"the transferred area" has the meaning given in article 3;

"the transferred undertaking" has the meaning given in article 4(3);

"water supply area", in relation to a water authority, means the area within which, by virtue of the relevant constitution order, it is the duty of the authority to supply water under Part II of the Act.

(3) Any reference in this order to a numbered article shall be construed as a reference to the article bearing that number in this order.

Alteration of boundaries of water supply areas

3. The water supply area of the Thames Authority shall be altered so as to include the area shown hatched black and bounded externally by a black line on the map (in this order referred to as "the transferred area"), and the water supply area of the Anglian Authority shall be altered so as to exclude that area; and the boundary between the water supply area of the Thames Authority and the water supply area of the Anglian Authority shall be altered accordingly between the points marked "A" and "B" on the map.

Transfer of water undertaking

4.—(1) Subject to the provisions of this order, on the day of transfer the transferred undertaking shall by virtue of this order be transferred to and vest in the Thames Authority.

(2) The authorities may agree between them in any particular case that, for the purposes of this order—

    (*a*) any property which, but for this sub-paragraph, would form part of the transferred undertaking, shall be treated as not forming part thereof;

    (*b*) any property held by the Anglian Authority partly for the purposes of the transferred undertaking which, but for this sub-paragraph, would not form part of the transferred undertaking, shall be treated as forming part thereof.

(3) In this article "the transferred undertaking" means that part of the water undertaking of the Anglian Authority which immediately before the day of transfer exists within, or is wholly or mainly related to, the transferred area, and includes—

    (*a*) all land, buildings, works, equipment and other real and personal property, assets and rights vested in, or held or enjoyed by, the Anglian Authority for, or in relation to, that part of that water undertaking immediately before the day of transfer, and all liabilities and obligations to which they were then subject in relation to that part of that undertaking;

(**a**) S.I. 1973/1359 (1973 II, p. 4170).   (**b**) S.I. 1973/1360 (1973 II, p. 4178).
(**c**) The amending order is not relevant to the subject matter of this order.

(b) the benefits of all contracts (other than contracts for the employment of officers or servants) in force immediately before the day of transfer in respect of that part of that undertaking, subject to any obligations thereunder;

(c) the rights and benefits under any licence under the Water Resources Act 1963(a) in force immediately before the day of transfer, being a licence to abstract water or to obstruct or impede the flow of an inland water which has effect in relation to that part of that undertaking, subject to any obligations thereunder;

(d) all registers, books of account, maps, specifications, engineering reports and other documents relating solely to that part of that undertaking;

but excludes—

(i) any funds, money or securities for money of the Anglian Authority, whether invested or in hand (other than consumers' deposits and any money or securities in money representing the unexpended balance of any sum borrowed by the Anglian Authority for the purposes of the said part of the said undertaking);

(ii) any liabilities or obligations in respect of any sum borrowed by the Anglian Authority for the purposes of their water undertaking;

(iii) any right of the Anglian Authority to receive payments under the Rural Water Supplies and Sewerage Acts 1944 to 1971(b), or any payments of a similar nature under any other enactment in respect of expenditure incurred in connection with their water undertaking.

Transfer of officers

5. The Thames Authority shall take over and employ, as from the day of transfer or as from such other date as they may agree in any particular case with the person concerned, every person who immediately before the day of transfer is an officer or servant of the Anglian Authority and—

(i) is employed wholly or mainly in connection with the transferred undertaking, or

(ii) not being so employed, but being wholly or mainly employed at a place of work in the transferred area, notifies the Thames Authority in writing within the period of three months beginning on the day of transfer that he wishes to enter their employment,

on terms and conditions not less favourable than those on which he is employed by the Anglian Authority immediately before the day of transfer.

Saving of agreements, etc.

6.—(1) Subject to the provisions of this order, all sales, conveyances, grants, assurances, deeds, contracts (other than contracts the benefits of which, and the liabilities under which, are not transferred by this order), bonds, agreements, notices and demands affecting the transferred undertaking and in force immediately before the day of transfer, shall, on and after that day, be as binding and of as full force and effect in every respect and may be enforced as fully and effectually against, or in favour of, the Thames Authority as if, instead of the Anglian Authority, the Thames Authority had been a party thereto or bound thereby or entitled to the benefits thereof.

(a) 1963 c. 38.   (b) 1944 c. 26; 1955 c. 13; 1971 c. 49.

(2) Where necessary for the purposes of this article, any revenues and out-goings shall be apportioned between the authorities.

(3) Any question which may arise under this article shall be determined by an arbitrator to be appointed either by agreement between the authorities or, in default of agreement, by the President of the Chartered Institute of Public Finance and Accountancy.

Repayment of loan charges

7.—(1) Subject to the provisions of this article, the Thames Authority shall pay to the Anglian Authority in the year commencing on the day of transfer and in each year thereafter any amounts which, in pursuance of arrangements in force immediately before the day of transfer for the redemption of loans (whether by depreciation charge or repayment of principal) and the payment of interest thereon, would, but for this order, have fallen on or after that day to be debited in the final revenue account of the Anglian Authority for that year in respect of money borrowed for purposes of the transferred undertaking.

(2) The Thames Authority shall not be liable to pay so much of any amount as aforesaid as is attributable to any period before the day of transfer, and any such amount shall be calculated as if the amount due in respect of redemption of loans and payment of interest accrued from day to day.

(3) In calculating the amounts which would have fallen to be debited in respect of any loan, regard shall be had to—

(i) the income earned by any sinking fund established for the redemption of that loan; and

(ii) any sum received by the Anglian Authority under the Rural Water Supplies and Sewerage Acts 1944 to 1971, or any payments of a similar nature made under any other enactment towards the financing of the liabilities in respect of which that loan was raised.

(4) Any sum payable under paragraph (1) above shall, unless otherwise agreed, be paid by half-yearly instalments.

(5) Any question which may arise as to the amounts payable by the Thames Authority under paragraph (1) above shall be determined by an arbitrator to be appointed either by agreement between the authorities or, in default of agreement, by the President of the Chartered Institute of Public Finance and Accountancy.

(6) Without prejudice to the right of the Thames Authority to charge any payment under paragraph (1) above to revenue account, any payment made by the Thames Authority under that paragraph in respect of the liability for the redemption of a loan shall be deemed to be a capital payment, and any other such payment (other than a payment in respect of debt management expenses) shall be deemed to be an annual payment.

(7) The Thames Authority may agree with the lender and with the Anglian Authority for the transfer to the Thames Authority of the liability with respect to any outstanding loan made to the Anglian Authority in respect of the transferred undertaking, and where any liability so transferred is in respect of a loan secured by a mortgage, the mortgage (unless otherwise agreed) shall take effect in all respects as a mortgage created by the Thames Authority of their revenues to secure the loan and the interest thereon.

Recovery and apportionment of debts

8.—(1) Subject to the provisions of this article, the Anglian Authority shall be entitled to and may recover all rates, rents, charges, profits and sums of money and shall discharge and pay all debts and liabilities in respect of the transferred undertaking which accrue due or become payable before the day of transfer and, subject to the provisions of this order, the Thames Authority shall be entitled to and may recover all such revenues and shall discharge or pay all such outgoings which accrue due or become payable on or after that day.

(2) Except so far as may be otherwise agreed between the authorities, so much of any amount recovered or paid by the Anglian Authority by virtue of this article as is attributable to any period beginning on or after the day of transfer shall (as the case may require) be paid by them to, or be repaid to them by, the Thames Authority; and so much of any amount so recovered or paid by the Thames Authority as is attributable to the period before the day of transfer shall (as the case may require) be paid by them to, or be repaid to them by, the Anglian Authority.

(3) Where necessary for the purposes of this article, any revenues and outgoings shall be apportioned between the authorities.

(4) Any question which may arise under this article shall be determined by an arbitrator to be appointed either by agreement between the authorities or, in default of agreement, by the President of the Chartered Institute of Public Finance and Accountancy.

Local statutory provisions and byelaws

9.—(1) Any local statutory provision which immediately before the day of transfer applies to the transferred area shall have effect, so far as relates to the supply of water in the transferred area and to things done or falling to be done in the exercise of functions relating to such supply of water, as if for any reference to the Anglian Authority (being an express reference to that authority or a reference thereto substituted for a reference to some other body by virtue of any enactment) there were substituted a reference to the Thames Authority.

(2) Any byelaws made by the Anglian Authority (or having effect as if so made) which relate to the supply of water, and which immediately before the day of transfer are in force in the transferred area, shall have effect on and after that day in relation to that area as if they had been made by the Thames Authority.

Collection of water rates and charges

10.—(1) Where, in pursuance of an order to which this article applies, the Anglian Authority have, before the day of transfer, issued a notice to any local authority requiring them to collect and recover on behalf of the Anglian Authority amounts payable to that authority in respect of the supply of water to premises in the transferred area during the year commencing on the day of transfer, that notice shall have effect on and after the day of transfer as if it had been issued by and in favour of the Thames Authority and the provisions of the said order shall have effect accordingly.

(2) This article applies to any order made by the Secretary of State in exercise of powers conferred upon him by section 254 of the Local Government Act 1972(a) as applied by section 34(1) of, and Schedule 6 to, the Water Act 1973 and as extended by paragraph 5(2) of the said Schedule 6, whereby water authorities are empowered to require local authorities to calculate, collect and recover on their behalf amounts payable in respect of water supplied by the water authorities.

(a) 1972 c. 70.

Continuance of actions

11. Any action, arbitration or other proceeding or any cause of action, arbitration or other proceeding, pending or existing on the day of transfer by, or against, or in favour of, the Anglian Authority in respect of the transferred undertaking shall not be prejudicially affected by reason of this order and may be continued, prosecuted and enforced by, or against, or in favour of, the Thames Authority.

Amendment of constitution orders

12. The relevant constitution orders relating to the authorities shall be amended as follows:—

(*a*) at the end of article 5 (water supply area) of the Anglian Water Authority Constitution Order 1973, and

(*b*) at the end of article 5 (water supply area) of the Thames Water Authority Constitution Order 1973—

there shall be added the words "as altered by article 3 of the Anglian and Thames Water Authorities (Alteration of Boundaries) Order 1976".

Anthony Crosland,
Secretary of State for the Environment.

26th February 1976.

In Witness whereof the Official Seal of the Minister of Agriculture, Fisheries and Food is hereunto affixed on 26th February 1976.

(L.S.)

Frederick Peart,
Minister of Agriculture, Fisheries and Food.

EXPLANATORY NOTE

(This Note is not part of the Order.)

When the Anglian Water Authority was established on 1st August 1973 by the Anglian Water Authority Constitution Order 1973, made under sections 2 and 3 of the Water Act 1973, the area within which it was to be the authority's duty to supply water was defined as comprising the limits of supply of 24 statutory water undertakers, including the Bucks Water Board. This Order transfers the southern part of the former Board's area to the water supply area of the Thames Water Authority and alters the water supply boundary between that authority and the Anglian Water Authority. (The transferred area and altered boundary are shown on the map forming part of this Note.)

The Order provides for related transfers of property, rights and liabilities between the two authorities, and makes transitional, incidental, supplementary and consequential provision concerning other matters, including the transfer of employees (article 5), the repayment of loan charges (article 7), local statutory provisions and byelaws (article 9) and the collection of water rates and charges (article 10).

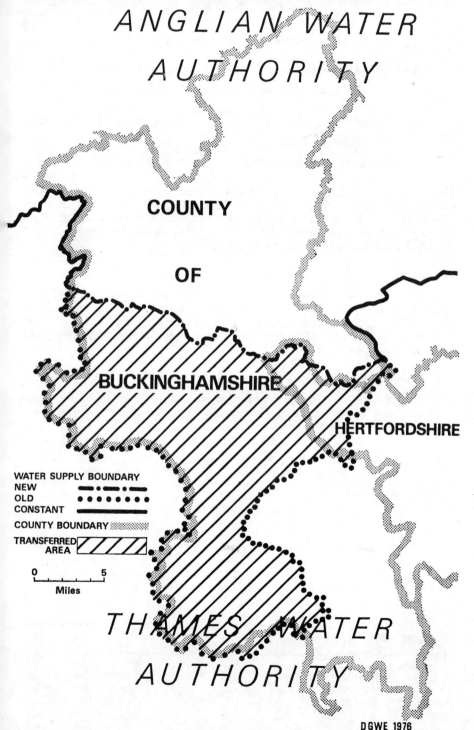

STATUTORY INSTRUMENTS

1976 No. 308

SOCIAL SECURITY

The Child Interim Benefit (Determination of Questions) Amendment Regulations 1976

Made - - - -	*1st March* 1976
Laid before Parliament	*9th March* 1976
Coming into Operation	*30th March* 1976

The Secretary of State for Social Services, in exercise of the powers conferred upon her by section 16(7) of the Child Benefit Act 1975(a), and of all other powers enabling her in that behalf, and after consultation with the Council on Tribunals as required by section 10(1) of the Tribunals and Inquiries Act 1971 (b), hereby makes the following regulations:—

Citation, interpretation and commencement

1. These regulations, which may be cited as the Child Interim Benefit (Determination of Questions) Amendment Regulations 1976, shall be read as one with the Child Interim Benefit (Determination of Questions) Regulations 1975(c) (hereinafter referred to as "the principal regulations"), and shall come into operation on 30th March 1976.

Amendment of regulation 11 of the principal regulations

2. In regulation 11 of the principal regulations (procedure on appeal from a decision of a tribunal), paragraphs (4) and (6) are hereby revoked and for paragraph (1) there shall be substituted the following paragraph:—

"11.—(1) The provisions of regulations 7(1) and (2) and 8(1) and (3) (procedure and right to representation at hearings before a tribunal) shall apply in relation to hearings before the Referee and for this purpose references in those provisions to the chairman of a tribunal and to a tribunal shall be construed as references to the Referee and the reference in regulation 8(1) to regulation 5 as a reference to regulation 10.".

Barbara Castle,
Secretary of State for Social Services.

1st March 1976.

(a) 1975 c. 61.   (b) 1971 c. 62.
(c) S.I. 1975/1925 (1975 III, p. 7146).

EXPLANATORY NOTE

(This Note is not part of the Regulations.)

These Regulations make a technical drafting amendment to regulation 11 of the Child Interim Benefit (Determination of Questions) Regulations 1975 (which relates to procedure on an appeal from a decision of a tribunal to the Referee) to resolve an ambiguity in the original version of that regulation.

1976 No. 309

RATING AND VALUATION

The Valuation (Post Office Telecommunication Services) (Northern Ireland) Order 1976

Made - - -	*26th February* 1976
Laid before Parliament	*9th March* 1976
Coming into Operation	*1st April* 1976

In pursuance of section 54 of the Post Office Act 1969 **(a)**, as amended by paragraph 7 of Schedule 1 to the Local Government Reorganisation (Consequential Provisions) (Northern Ireland) Order 1973 **(b)**, and after such consultation as is required by that section, I hereby make the following Order:—

Citation, commencement and extent

1.—(1) This Order may be cited as the Valuation (Post Office Telecommunication Services) (Northern Ireland) Order 1976 and shall come into operation on 1st April 1976.

(2) This Order extends to Northern Ireland only.

Interpretation

2.—(1) In this Order:—

"the Commissioner" means the Commissioner of Valuation for Northern Ireland;

"rate year" means the year for which apportionment of the net annual value of Post Office hereditaments is being determined;

"the valuation list" means the valuation list prepared under Article 45 of the Rates (Northern Ireland) Order 1972 **(c)** and coming into force on 1st April 1976;

"year" (except in Article 3) means a period of 12 months beginning with 1st April.

(2) The Interpretation Act 1889 **(d)** shall apply for the interpretation of this Order as it applies for the interpretation of an Act of Parliament.

Effect of Order

3. The provisions of this Order shall have effect with regard to the period commencing with the date of the coming into operation of this Order and expiring with 31st March in the relevant year (within the meaning of section 54 of the said Act of 1969) next after the year ending 31st December 1976, for the purposes of the valuation list.

(a) 1969 c. 48.
(c) S.I. 1972/1633 (N.I. 16).

(b) S.I. 1973/2095 (1973 III, p. 7247).
(d) 1889 c. 63.

Aggregate amount of net annual value

4. The aggregate amount of the net annual value of the following hereditaments occupied by the Post Office for the purposes of the telecommunication services namely posts, wires, underground cables and ducts, telephone kiosks and other equipment not within a building, shall for the year ending 31st March 1977 be £310,000 (subject to Article 7), but the aggregate amount in respect of each subsequent year shall be re-determined in accordance with Article 5 below.

Re-determination of net annual value

5.—(1) For the year ending 31st March 1978 and subsequent years the aggregate amount of the net annual value determined in Article 4 above shall be re-determined by the Commissioner in accordance with the following formula (subject to Article 7):—

$$C \times \frac{E}{212,000}$$

C   being the aggregate amount of the net annual value determined by Article 4 above, and

E   being the number of exchange connections on 31st March in the year penultimate to the rate year.

(2) Where the aggregate amount of the re-determined net annual value is not a multiple of £5,000 it shall be rounded to the nearest such multiple; and for the purpose of this paragraph a sum which is not a multiple of £5,000 but is a multiple of £2,500 shall be treated as if it were nearer to the multiple of £5,000 next above it than to the multiple of £5,000 next below it.

(3) In this Article "number of exchange connections" means the aggregate of the number of exclusive exchange telephone and telex lines and the number of telephone and telex subscribers sharing party lines of the Post Office in Northern Ireland and which the Post Office for the purpose of computing the re-determination required by paragraph (1) above certify to be the correct figure for the purposes of the expression E; but where the aggregate number of exchange telephone and telex connections is not a multiple of 1,000 it shall be sufficient for the Post Office to certify the aggregate number rounded to the nearest such multiple, and for this purpose a number which is a multiple of 500 but not of 1,000 shall be treated as nearer to the multiple of 1,000 next above it than to the multiple of 1,000 next below it.

(4) It shall be the duty of the Post Office, before 30th September in the year preceding the rate year, to transmit to the Commissioner the certificate required by paragraph (3) above.

Apportionment of net annual value

6.—(1) The Commissioner shall, in accordance with the following provisions of this Article, calculate the apportionment of the aggregate amount of the net annual value determined in accordance with Articles 4 and 5(1) among the districts of district councils and shall, as soon as may be after the beginning of the rate year, alter the valuation list in accordance with Article 50(1)(a)(iii) of the Rates (Northern Ireland) Order 1972.

(2) Subject to Article 7 and paragraph (3) of this Article the aggregate amount of the net annual value determined in accordance with Articles 4 and 5(1) shall for the year ending 31st March 1977 and subsequent years be apportioned among the districts of district councils in accordance with the following formula:—

$$\left(\frac{R}{4} \times \frac{A1}{A2}\right) \quad + \quad \left(\frac{R}{4} \times \frac{ND1}{ND2}\right) \quad + \quad \left(\frac{R}{2} \times \frac{H1}{H2}\right)$$

R being the aggregate amount of the net annual value determined in accordance with Articles 4 and 5(1) of this Order;

A1 being the acreage of the district in respect of which the apportionment is being made as at 1st April in the rate year;

A2 being the total acreage of all districts in Northern Ireland as at 1st April in the rate year;

ND1 being the non-domestic net annual value of the district in respect of which the apportionment is being made;

ND2 being the aggregate of the non-domestic net annual values of all districts in Northern Ireland;

H1 being the number of domestic hereditaments in the district in respect of which the apportionment is being made;

H2 being the aggregate of the number of domestic hereditaments in all districts in Northern Ireland.

(3) In this Article—

(a) "total net annual value" in relation to the district of a district council means (except for the year ending 31st March 1977) the aggregate of the net annual value of every hereditament in the district as assessed in the valuation list on 1st April in the year preceding the rate year excluding any hereditament there appearing occupied by the Northern Ireland Electricity Service or gas undertakings or by the Crown and any hereditament referred to in Article 4 above and occupied by the Post Office for the purposes of the telecommunication services; and for the year ending 31st March 1977 means the aggregate of the net annual value of every hereditament in the district as assessed in the valuation list on 31st December 1975 excluding such hereditaments as aforesaid;

(b) "non-domestic net annual value" in relation to the district of a district council means (except for the year ending 31st March 1977) the total net annual value excluding the net annual value of domestic hereditaments as assessed in the valuation list on 1st April in the year preceding the rate year; and for the year ending 31st March 1977 means the total net annual value excluding the net annual value of domestic hereditaments as assessed in the valuation list on 31st December 1975;

(c) "domestic hereditament" means a hereditament used wholly for the purposes of a private dwelling;

(2) Subject to Article 7 and paragraph (3) of this Article the aggregate amount of the net annual value determined in accordance with Articles 4 and 5(1) shall for the year ending 31st March 1977 and subsequent years be apportioned among the districts of district councils in accordance with the following formula:—

$$\left(\frac{R}{4} \times \frac{A1}{A2}\right) \quad + \quad \left(\frac{R}{4} \times \frac{ND1}{ND2}\right) \quad + \quad \left(\frac{R}{2} \times \frac{H1}{H2}\right)$$

R being the aggregate amount of the net annual value determined in accordance with Articles 4 and 5(1) of this Order;

A1 being the acreage of the district in respect of which the apportionment is being made as at 1st April in the rate year;

A2 being the total acreage of all districts in Northern Ireland as at 1st April in the rate year;

ND1 being the non-domestic net annual value of the district in respect of which the apportionment is being made;

ND2 being the aggregate of the non-domestic net annual values of all districts in Northern Ireland;

H1 being the number of domestic hereditaments in the district in respect of which the apportionment is being made;

H2 being the aggregate of the number of domestic hereditaments in all districts in Northern Ireland.

(3) In this Article—

(a) "total net annual value" in relation to the district of a district council means (except for the year ending 31st March 1977) the aggregate of the net annual value of every hereditament in the district as assessed in the valuation list on 1st April in the year preceding the rate year excluding any hereditament there appearing occupied by the Northern Ireland Electricity Service or gas undertakings or by the Crown and any hereditament referred to in Article 4 above and occupied by the Post Office for the purposes of the telecommunication services; and for the year ending 31st March 1977 means the aggregate of the net annual value of every hereditament in the district as assessed in the valuation list on 31st December 1975 excluding such hereditaments as aforesaid;

(b) "non-domestic net annual value" in relation to the district of a district council means (except for the year ending 31st March 1977) the total net annual value excluding the net annual value of domestic hereditaments as assessed in the valuation list on 1st April in the year preceding the rate year; and for the year ending 31st March 1977 means the total net annual value excluding the net annual value of domestic hereditaments as assessed in the valuation list on 31st December 1975;

(c) "domestic hereditament" means a hereditament used wholly for the purposes of a private dwelling;

(d) "number of domestic hereditaments" means the number of all those domestic hereditaments the net annual value of which is excluded from the non-domestic net annual value.

Special provision for Craigavon Borough Council district

7. The amount of net annual value apportioned to Craigavon Borough Council district in accordance with Article 6 shall be increased by £1,350 (net annual value of the hereditament occupied by the Post Office for television relay services).

Merlyn Rees,

One of Her Majesty's Principal Secretaries of State.

Northern Ireland Office.

26th February 1976.

EXPLANATORY NOTE
(This Note is not part of the Order.)

This Order determines for Northern Ireland the aggregate amount of the net annual value of certain Post Office hereditaments, (namely property (not in a building) used for telecommunication services, including television relay services in Craigavon Borough Council district), for the year ending 31st March 1977 and subsequent years, and provides for apportionment of that amount among local government districts. It also provides for re-determination of the amount with respect to the year ending 31st March 1978 and subsequent years.

STATUTORY INSTRUMENTS

1976 No. 314 (L. 5)

COUNTY COURTS

PROCEDURE

The County Court (Amendment) Rules 1976

Made - - - -	*27th February* 1976
Coming into Operation	*1st April* 1976

1.—(1) These Rules may be cited as the County Court (Amendment) Rules 1976.

(2) In these Rules an Order and Rule referred to by number means the Order and Rule so numbered in the County Court Rules 1936(a), as amended (b), and a form referred to by number means the form so numbered in Appendix A to those Rules.

(3) The Interpretation Act 1889(c) shall apply for the interpretation of these Rules as it applies for the interpretation of an Act of Parliament.

2.—(1) In Order 6, Rule 10, the paragraph beginning "In relation to" shall be revoked.

(2) Order 7, Rule 1(1A), Order 9, Rule 9(4), Order 24, Rule 3, and Order 25, Rule 7B, shall be revoked.

3. For Order 45A there shall be substituted the following Order:—

"ORDER 45A

FAMILY PROVISION ON DEATH

1. In this Order—

    "the Act of 1973" means the Matrimonial Causes Act 1973;

    "the Act of 1975" means the Inheritance (Provision for Family and Dependants) Act 1975;

    "the deceased" means, in the case of an application under section 36 of the Act of 1973, the deceased party to the agreement to which the application relates and, in the case of an application under section 1 of the Act of 1975, the person to whose estate the application relates.

Interpretation

1973 c. 18

1975 c. 63

2.—(1) An application under section 1 of the Act of 1975, or section 36 of the Act of 1973, shall be made by originating application in Form 370 or 370A, whichever is appropriate.

Mode of application

Form 370, 370A

(a) S.R. & O. 1936/626 (1936 I, p.282).
(b) The relevant amending instruments are S.I. 1967/276, 1970/204, 1201, 1871, 1971/2127, 1974/636 (1967 I, p. 990; 1970 I, p.911; II, p. 3984; III, p. 6154; 1971 III, p. 6276; 1974 I, p. 2527).
(c) 1889 c. 63.

(2) The application shall be filed—

    (*a*) in the court for the district in which the deceased resided at the date of his death, or

    (*b*) if the deceased did not then reside in England or Wales, in the court for the district in which the respondent or one of the respondents resides or carries on business or the estate or part of the estate is situate, or

    (*c*) if neither of the foregoing sub-paragraphs is applicable, in the court for the district in which the applicant resides or carries on business.

(3) The applicant shall file with his originating application—

    (*a*) an official copy of the grant of representation to the deceased's estate and of every testamentary document admitted to proof, and

    (*b*) in the case of an application under section 36 of the Act of 1973, a copy of the agreement to which the application relates.

Parties   3.—(1) Without prejudice to its powers under Orders 5 and 15, the court may, at any stage of the proceedings, direct that any person be added or struck out as a party to the application.

(2) Order 5, Rules 10 and 26, shall apply to an application under section 1 of the Act of 1975 or section 36 of the Act of 1973 as they apply to the proceedings mentioned in those Rules.

Answer   4.—(1) Every respondent shall, within 21 days after service of the originating application on him, inclusive of the day of service, file in the court office an answer, together with a copy thereof for every other party to the proceedings, which shall contain a statement of the respondent's case.

(2) The answer filed by a personal representative pursuant to paragraph (1) shall state to the best of his ability—

    (*a*) full particulars of the value of the deceased's net estate, as defined by section 25(1) of the Act of 1975;

    (*b*) the persons or classes of persons beneficially interested in the estate, giving the names and (in the case of those who are not already parties) the addresses of all living beneficiaries, and the value of their interests so far as ascertained;

    (*c*) if such be the case, that any living beneficiary (naming him) is a minor or a mental patient; and

    (*d*) in the case of an application under section 1 of the Act of 1975, any facts known to the personal representative which might affect the exercise of the court's powers under that Act.

(3) The registrar shall send to every other party to the proceedings a copy of any answer filed pursuant to paragraph (1).

Interim order   5. An application for an interim order under section 5 of the Act of 1975 may be made on notice in accordance with Order 13, Rule 1.

Subsequent application   6. Where an order has been made on an application under section 1 of the Act of 1975, any subsequent application, whether made by a party to the proceedings or by any other person, shall be made in those proceedings in accordance with Order 13, Rule 1.

7. Any application under section 1 of the Act of 1975 or section 36 of Hearing the Act of 1973 may, with the leave of the judge or the consent of the parties, be heard and determined by the registrar and may, if the court thinks fit, be dealt with in chambers.

8.—(1) On the hearing of an application under section 1 of the Endorse- Act of 1975, the personal representative shall produce to the court the ment of grant of representation to the deceased's estate and, if an order is made memoran-
dum on under the Act, the grant shall remain in the custody of the court until a grant memorandum of the order has been endorsed on, or permanently annexed to, the grant in accordance with section 19(3) of the Act of 1975.

(2) Immediately after any such order has been drawn up and filed the registrar shall send a sealed copy thereof, together with the grant of representation, to the principal registry of the Family Division.

9.—(1) The court in which an application under section 36 of the Transfer Act of 1973 or section 1 of the Act of 1975 is pending may order the transfer to the of the application to the High Court where the transfer appears to the High
Court court to be desirable.

(2) In considering whether an application should be transferred under paragraph (1) from a county court to the High Court, the court shall have regard to all relevant considerations, including the nature and value of the property involved, the relative expense of proceeding in the High Court and the county court and the limit for the time being of the jurisdiction of county courts under section 22 of the Act of 1975.

(3) Any order of transfer shall state whether it is desired that the proceedings be assigned to the Chancery Division or to the Family Division of the High Court."

4. Order 47 shall be amended as follows:—

(1) After Rule 1 there shall be inserted the following Rule:—

"**2.**—(1) Where in any proceedings any costs of a litigant in Litigant person are ordered to be paid by any other party or in any other in person way, then, subject to the following paragraphs of this Rule, there may be allowed to the litigant in person such costs as would have been allowed if the work and disbursements to which the costs relate had been done or made by a solicitor on his behalf and the provisions of these Rules shall apply with the necessary modifications to the costs of a litigant in person as they apply to solicitors' charges and disbursements.

(2) Nothing in Rule 36 of this Order or Appendix D shall apply where the plaintiff is a litigant in person.

(3) In relation to the costs of a litigant in person, Rule 37(2) of this Order shall have effect—

(a) where the costs are on scale 1, 2 or 3, as if for the words "may, if the solicitor for the party in whose favour the award was made so desires" there were substituted the words "shall, unless the court otherwise orders", and

(b) where the costs are on scale 4, as if the words "the solicitor for" were omitted.

(4) Where the costs of a litigant in person are taxed or assessed without taxation—

(*a*) he shall not be allowed more than £2 an hour in respect of the time reasonably spent by him on doing any work to which the costs relate if in the opinion of the court he has not suffered any pecuniary loss in doing the work, and

(*b*) the amount allowed in respect of any work done by the litigant in person shall not in any case exceed two-thirds of the sum which in the opinion of the court would have been allowed in respect of that work if the litigant had been represented by a solicitor.

(5) Where the costs of a litigant in person are assessed under Appendix E, or where on the taxation of the costs of a litigant in person he is allowed a charge for attending court to conduct his own case, then, notwithstanding anything in Rule 29 of this Order, he shall not be entitled to a witness allowance in addition.

(6) Nothing in this Rule shall apply to a solicitor to whom Rule 26 is applicable."

(2) In Rule 26 before the word "solicitor", where it first appears, there shall be inserted the word "practising".

(3) In Rule 37(3) for the word "registrar" there shall be substituted the word "court" and for the word "he" there shall be substituted the word "it".

5. Order 49, Rule 4, shall be revoked.

6. The following form shall be substituted for Form 370:—

"370

ORIGINATING APPLICATION FOR REASONABLE FINANCIAL PROVISION UNDER
SECTION 1 OF INHERITANCE (PROVISION FOR FAMILY AND DEPENDANTS)
ACT 1975

Order 45A,   [*General Title—Form* 1]
Rule 2(1)
        1. I,   of
        , apply to the Court for an order under section 1 of the
Inheritance (Provision for Family and Dependants) Act 1975 for reasonable
financial provision to be made for me out of the estate of
who died on the   day of   19   being domiciled
in England and Wales and resident at   .

2. I am the wife [*or* husband] of the deceased [*or state in what other way the applicant claims to be entitled to make the application*].

3. A grant of probate [*or* letters of administration] in regard to the estate of the deceased was first taken out on the   day of
                19   and the personal representative[s] is[are]
                                        of
[and   of   ].

4. To the best of my knowledge and belief the value of the deceased's net estate does not exceed £5,000.

5. The disposition of the deceased's estate effected by his will [*or* by the law relating to intestacy] [*or* by the combination of his will and the

law relating to intestacy] was such as to make no provision for me [*or* to make the following provision for me, namely
].

6. To the best of my knowledge and belief the persons or classes of persons interested in the estate and the nature of their interests are as follows:—

7. The following are particulars of my present and foreseeable financial resources and financial needs [*give details and add any other information which the applicant desires to place before the Court on the matters to which the Court is required to have regard under section 3 of the Act*].

8. [*Insert where appropriate*] I request the Court's permission to make this application notwithstanding that the period of six months has expired from the date on which representation in regard to the estate of the deceased was first taken out, and the grounds of my request are as follows:—

9. I ask for reasonable financial provision to be made for me out of the deceased's estate by way of an order for [*state nature of order applied for*].

10. The names and addresses of the respondents on whom this application is intended to be served are—

11. My address for service is :—

Dated this   day of   19 .

Applicant

To the Respondent
Within 21 days after service of this application on you, inclusive of the day of service, you must file in the court office an answer, together with a copy for every other party to the proceedings, containing a statement of your case and, if you are a personal representative of the deceased—

    (*a*) full particulars of the value of the deceased's net estate;

    (*b*) the persons or classes of persons beneficially interested in the estate (including the names and addresses of all living beneficiaries and whether any of them is a minor or a mental patient); and

    (*c*) any facts known to you which might affect the exercise of the Court's powers under the Act."

7. Form 370A shall be amended as follows:—

(1) For paragraph 10 there shall be substituted the following paragraph:—

"10. There have been no proceedings in any court against the deceased's estate under the Inheritance (Provision for Family and Dependants) Act 1975 or any Act repealed by that Act [except [*state the nature of the proceedings and the date and effect of any decree or order*]]."

(2) After the words "*Conclusion as in Form* 370" there shall be added the words "*omitting paragraph* (*c*)".

8. Nothing in Rules 3, 6 and 7 of these rules shall apply to proceedings relating to the estate of a person who died before 1st April 1976 and nothing in Rule 4 shall apply to any work done or disbursement made before that date.

We, the undersigned members of the Rule Committee appointed by the Lord Chancellor under section 102 of the County Courts Act 1959(**a**), having by virtue of the powers vested in us in this behalf made the foregoing Rules, do hereby certify the same under our hands and submit them to the Lord Chancellor accordingly.

> *Conolly H. Gage.*
> *H. S. Ruttle.*
> *David Pennant.*
> *W. Granville Wingate.*
> *T. Richard Nevin.*
> *E. A. Everett.*
> *A. A. Hibbert.*
> *Arnold Russell Vick.*
> *E. Somerset Jones.*
> *D. A. Marshall.*
> *Emyr O. Parry.*

I allow these Rules, which shall come into operation on 1st April 1976.

Dated 27th February 1976.

> *Elwyn-Jones,* C.

(**a**) 1959 c. 22.

EXPLANATORY NOTE

(This Note is not part of the Rules.)

These Rules amend the County Court Rules 1936 in consequence of two recent Acts. Order 45A is re-written so as to deal with proceedings under the Inheritance (Provision for Family and Dependants) Act 1975 (Rules 3, 6 and 7); and provision is made for the costs recoverable by a litigant in person under the Litigants in Person (Costs and Expenses) Act 1975 (Rule 4).

Minor amendments are also made so as to revoke the Rules which require claims and judgments, and warrants and orders for their enforcement, to be expressed in decimal currency (Rules 2 and 5).

STATUTORY INSTRUMENTS

1976 No. 315

LOCAL GOVERNMENT, ENGLAND AND WALES

The Local Authorities etc. (Miscellaneous Provision) Order 1976

Made - - -	*1st March* 1976
Laid before Parliament	*10th March* 1976
Coming into Operation	*31st March* 1976

The Secretary of State for the Environment and the Secretary of State for Wales, in exercise of the powers conferred upon them by sections 254(1)(*a*) and (2)(*a*) and (*c*), 255 and 266(2) of the Local Government Act 1972(**a**), section 84(1)(*a*) and (2)(*c*) of the London Government Act 1963(**b**) and section 34(1) of the Water Act 1973(**c**) and of all other powers enabling them in that behalf, hereby make the following order:—

Title and commencement

1. This order may be cited as the Local Authorities etc. (Miscellaneous Provision) Order 1976 and shall come into operation on 31st March 1976.

Territorial extent of exercise of powers

2. Subject to articles 5(1) and (2) and 9(1) and (2), this order is made by the Secretary of State for the Environment in relation to England and by the Secretary of State for Wales in relation to Wales.

Interpretation

3.—(1) The Interpretation Act 1889(**d**) shall apply for the interpretation of this order as it applies for the interpretation of an Act of Parliament.

(2) In this order—

    (*a*) references to any enactment shall be construed as references to that enactment as amended, extended or applied by or under any other enactment;

    (*b*) references to any instrument shall be construed as references to that instrument as amended, extended or applied by any other instrument, including this order.

(3) Any reference in this order to a numbered article shall, unless the reference is to an article of a specified order, be construed as a reference to the article bearing that number in this order.

(4) Any reference in any article of this order to a numbered paragraph shall, unless the reference is to a paragraph of a specified article, be construed as a reference to the paragraph bearing that number in the first-mentioned article.

(**a**) 1972 c. 70.   (**b**) 1963 c. 33.
(**c**) 1973 c. 37.   (**d**) 1889 c. 63.

Miscellaneous amendments of public general and other Acts

4.—(1) In the Act for inclosing lands in the borough and parish of Tewkesbury and for vesting the after or latter math of a meadow called Severn Ham in trustees, enacted on 30th June 1808(**a**), in section XXXIV (Trustees), for "the Bailiffs, principal Burgesses, High Steward, Recorder, Justices, Town Clerk, Coroner, and Chamberlain of the Borough of Tewkesbury in the County of Gloucester, and their Successors for the Time being" there shall be substituted "the Town Councillors of Tewkesbury".

(2) In the New Forest Act 1949(**b**), in section 1 (constitution of verderers), for "one by the authority which is the local planning authority for the purposes of the Town and Country Planning Act, 1947," there shall be substituted "one by the county planning authority".

(3) In the Highways Act 1959(**c**), in section 185 (certain highways and canals not to be chargeable with private street works expenses), for subsection (2) there shall be substituted—

"(2) This section shall not apply to a street existing at the date when the Private Street Works Act 1892 or the code of 1892, as the case may be, first became applicable in the area in which the street is situated.".

(4) In the Land Compensation Act 1961(**d**), in section 39(1), in the definition of "authority possessing compulsory purchase powers"—

after "parish council" there shall be inserted ", community council"; and

after "on whose behalf a" there shall be inserted "district council or".

Miscellaneous amendments of instruments

5.—(1) In the Local Authorities (England) (Property etc.) Order 1973(**e**), in article 39 (general provision as to disputes) as amended by article 4(15) of the Local Authorities etc. (England) (Property etc.: Further Provision) Order 1974(**f**) and article 4(2) of the Local Authorities (Miscellaneous Provision) Order 1975(**g**), in paragraph (2), "before 1st April 1976" shall be omitted.

Where notice that a question exists has been given under the said paragraph (2) as amended by this paragraph, the question shall be determined by agreement between the authorities concerned or failing such agreement by the decision of a person (or three persons) agreed on by such authorities or in default of agreement appointed by the Secretary of State for the Environment. Section 31 of the Arbitration Act 1950(**h**) shall have effect for the purposes of the determination of the question by any such person or persons as if such determination were an arbitration under any other Act within the meaning of that section.

This paragraph is made by the Secretary of State for the Environment.

(2) In the Local Authorities (Wales) (Property etc.) Order 1973(**i**), in article 38 (general provision as to disputes) as amended by article 4(11) of the Local Authorities etc. (Wales) (Property etc.: Further Provision) Order 1974(**j**) and article 4(3) of the Local Authorities (Miscellaneous Provision) Order 1975, in paragraph (2), "before 1st April 1976" shall be omitted.

Where notice that a question exists has been given under the said paragraph (2) as amended by this paragraph, the question shall be determined by agreement between the authorities concerned or failing such agreement by the decision

---

(**a**) 1808 c. cliii.
(**b**) 1949 c. 69.
(**c**) 1959 c. 25.
(**d**) 1961 c. 33.
(**e**) S.I. 1973/1861 (1973 III, p. 6401).
(**f**) S.I. 1974/406 (1974 I, p. 1276).
(**g**) S.I. 1975/244 (1975 I, p. 616).
(**h**) 1950 c. 27.
(**i**) S.I. 1973/1863 (1973 III, p. 6452).
(**j**) S.I. 1974/404 (1974 I, p. 1264).

of a person (or three persons) agreed on by such authorities or in default of agreement appointed by the Secretary of State for Wales. Section 31 of the Arbitration Act 1950 shall have effect for the purposes of the determination of the question by any such person or persons as if such determination were an arbitration under any other Act within the meaning of that section.

This paragraph is made by the Secretary of State for Wales.

(3) In the Local Authorities etc. (Staff Transfer and Protection) Order 1974(a), in article 14 (secondary transfers) as amended by article 4(4) of the Local Authorities etc. (Miscellaneous Provision) (No. 5) Order 1974(b) and article 6(2) of the Local Authorities etc. (Miscellaneous Provision) (No. 2) Order 1975(c), for "before 1st April 1976" there shall be substituted "before 1st October 1976".

Sodbury Commons

6. In the provisional order for the regulation of Sodbury Commons issued by the Board of Agriculture in 1902(d), in Part II, and in the award made thereunder on 1st April 1908, in paragraph 1 (both of which provisions provide for conservators), for "one by the Rural District Council of Chipping Sodbury three by the parish meeting of the parish of Chipping Sodbury three by the parish meeting of the parish of Old Sodbury and two by the parish meeting of the parish of Little Sodbury" there shall be substituted "one by the District Council of Northavon, six by the Parish Meeting of Sodbury and two by the Parish Meeting of Little Sodbury". In the said award, in paragraph 3, "Rural", where secondly occurring, shall be omitted, and in paragraph 4, for "The Rural District Council of Chipping Sodbury and the Parish Meetings of Chipping Sodbury Old Sodbury and Little Sodbury" there shall be substituted "The District Council of Northavon and the Parish Meetings of Sodbury and Little Sodbury".

Franchise and prescriptive rights

7. The power to maintain the Waltham Abbey market exercisable immediately before 1st April 1974 by the urban district council of Waltham Holy Cross shall be exercisable by the Town Council of Waltham Abbey, and the said Town Council shall have the same powers in relation to the said market as were exercisable immediately before 1st April 1974 by the said urban district council.

Temporary use of labour

8. The Borough Council of Bolton may until 31st March 1977 enter into agreements with any local authority for the construction of buildings or works wholly or substantially so in the area of the former county borough of Bolton which will engage the services of officers of the said Borough Council, including the holders of any offices or employments under it.

Property, liabilities, contracts etc., notices and proceedings

9.—(1) Paragraph (3), in so far as it relates to Part I of the Schedule to this order, and paragraph (4), are made by the Secretary of State for the Environment.

(2) Paragraph (3), in so far as it relates to Part II of the Schedule to this order, and paragraph (5), are made by the Secretary of State for Wales.

(a) S.I. 1974/483 (1974 I, p. 1709).   (b) S.I. 1974/2044 (1974 III, p. 7981).
(c) S.I. 1975/944 (1975 II, p. 3286).   (d) Confirmed by 1902 c. cxcix.

(3) Any property described in column (2) of Part I or II of the Schedule to this order of an authority named in column (1) and all liabilities attaching to the said authority in respect of any such property shall by virtue of this order be transferred to and vest in or attach to the authority specified in respect of such property in column (3), and—

(i) all contracts, deeds, bonds, agreements and other instruments subsisting in favour of, or against, and all notices in force which were given (or have effect as if they had been given) by, or to, the authority named in the said column (1) in respect of such property or liabilities shall be of full force and effect in favour of, or against, the authority specified in column (3); and

(ii) any action or proceeding or any cause of action or proceeding, pending or existing immediately before the coming into operation of this order, by, or against, the authority named in the said column (1) in respect of such property or liabilities shall not be prejudicially affected by reason of this article, and may be continued, prosecuted and enforced by, or against, the authority specified in column (3).

(4) Articles 11, 17, 23, 28, 29, 32, 33, 34(2), 35, 38 and 39 of the Local Authorities (England) (Property etc.) Order 1973 and articles 7 and 8 of the Local Authorities etc. (England) (Property etc.: Further Provision) Order 1974 shall apply as if paragraph (3) and Part I of the Schedule to this order were contained in the said order of 1973.

(5) Articles 11, 17, 23, 27, 28, 31, 32, 33(2), 34, 37 and 38 of the Local Authorities (Wales) (Property etc.) Order 1973 and articles 6 and 8 of the Local Authorities etc. (Wales) (Property etc.: Further Provision) Order 1974 shall apply as if paragraph (3) and Part II of the Schedule to this order were contained in the said order of 1973.

(6) The North of England Open-Air Museum shall be held by the County Council of Durham for the joint use and benefit of themselves and the County Councils of Cleveland, Northumberland and Tyne and Wear.

SCHEDULE Article 9

TRANSFER OF PARTICULAR PROPERTIES

PART I

(1) Transferor Authority	(2) Property	(3) Transferee Authority
The County Council of Kent	Cramptons Road Depot, Sevenoaks amounting to 2.042 acres	The District Council of Sevenoaks
do	Part of 113–115 Brook, Chatham, amounting to 240 square metres	The Southern Water Authority
The County Council of West Yorkshire	Any interest of the transferor authority in the cleansing depot, offices and adjoining land on the easterly side of Hammerton Street Bradford together with the dwelling house number 171 Hammerton Street	The City Council of Bradford
The City Council of Bradford	Any interest of the transferor authority in the refuse disposal plant and adjoining land on the westerly side of Birksland Street, Bradford	The County Council of West Yorkshire

(1) Transferor Authority	(2) Property	(3) Transferee Authority
The Borough Council of Derby	New Normanton Infants School, Blackmore Street, together with the Caretaker's Bungalow	The County Council of Derbyshire
do	Coleridge House Residential Home, Caxton Street, Derby	do
do	Redwood Junior and Infants School together with playing field, corner of Redwood Road and Sinfin Lane, Sinfin	do
do	Sinfin Community School and playing fields, Arleston Road and Farmhouse Road, Sinfin	do
The Borough Council of Medway	Part of 117–119 Brook, Chatham, amounting to 145 square metres	The County Council of Kent
The Borough Council of Northampton	That part of the Old People's Home/Elderly persons flatlets complex at Briar Hill, Northampton comprising the Old People's Home	The County Council of Northamptonshire
do	9 Witham Walk, Kings Heath, Northampton	do
do	23 Sandringham Road, Northampton	do
do	69 Chestnut Road, Northampton	do
The District Council of North Kesteven	Messuages, dwelling houses, cottages or tenements together with outbuildings, premises, yards, gardens and appurtenances thereto adjoining and belonging, known as 1, 2, 3, 4, 5, 6, 7, 9, 10 and 11 Nags Head Passage and No. 1 Station Road, and 417 square yards of land at the rear of Nos. 13 and 14 Nags Head Passage, Sleaford	The Town Council of Sleaford
do	5 acres 3 roods of land at No. 7 Sleaford, known as Woodside Playing field	do
do	14.168 acres of land at OS Nos. 64, 65 and 66 Sleaford, known as the Boston Road Recreation Ground	do
do	0.95 acre of land at OS No. 30 Sleaford, together with twenty-eight and two-thirds square yards of land adjoining No. 59 Meadow Field, Sleaford, known as Meadowfield Playing Field	do
do	2.25 acres of land at OS No. 150 Sleaford, known as Quarrington Playing Field	do
do	Parcel of land at the corner of Boston Road and Southgate, Sleaford, known as Monument Gardens, together with the public conveniences erected thereon	do
do	54 square yards of land in Church Lane Passage, Sleaford, together with the public conveniences erected thereon	do

(1) Transferor Authority	(2) Property	(3) Transferee Authority
The District Council of North Kesteven	2.384 acres of land at Eastgate, Sleaford, known as Eastgate Car Park, together with ten lock-up garages and the public conveniences erected thereon	The Town Council of Sleaford
The District Council of Sedgefield	Shildon Civic Hall, Main Street, Shildon	The Town Council of Shildon
do	Rest House, Redworth Road, Shildon	do
do	Burke Street Offices and Council Chamber, Shildon (excluding depot and single storey office block)	do
do	Recreation Ground off Central Parade, Shildon including Sports Ground at Surtees Avenue	do
do	Recreation Area off Princes Street, Shildon	do
do	Play Area, Jubilee Fields, Shildon	do
do	Play Area, Double Row, Eldon	do
do	St John's (Closed) Churchyard, Shildon	do
do	Land at Middleton Road, Shildon, 5.19 acres approximately	do
do	St Paul's (Closed) Churchyard	The Town Council of Spennymoor
do	Holy Innocents (Closed) Churchyard	do
do	Playing Field, Kirk Merrington (including Summerson's Building)	do
do	Recreation Ground, Wood Street, Middlestone Moor	do
do	Playground Byers Green (North of Rectory)	do
do	Victoria Jubilee Park (excluding Horticultural Nursery and Depot)	do
do	Brewery Football Field	do
do	Tudhoe Cricket Field	do
do	Playing Field, The Garth, Clyde Terrace	do
do	Open Space, Cow Plantation including Valley Burn east of Stream	do
do	Village Hall, Byers Green	do
do	Youth Centre and Play Area, Middlestone Moor (excluding site of Memorial Homes)	do
do	The Dene (between Dene Side and Ox Close Crescent)	do

(1) Transferor Authority	(2) Property	(3) Transferee Authority
The District Council of Sedgefield	Open Space and Play Area, Mount Pleasant (Salvin Street to Upper Church Street)	The Town Council of Spennymoor
do	Play Area, Oval Park, Spennymoor	do
do	Play Area (hard paved), Parkside, Greenways (Ex Yuill's)	do
The District Council of South Bedfordshire	Mill Road Open Space, Leighton Buzzard, bounded by Mill Road, Chapel Path, an area of land of varying width and Barrow Path, except land to a depth of 15 ft	The Town Council of Leighton Linslade
The Borough Council of Southend	Site bounded by West Street, North Road and Howards Chase and comprising the properties formerly described as 43 to 75 (odd numbers) West Street, 182 and 184 North Road and 1 to 10 West Cottages	The County Council of Essex
The District Council of Suffolk Coastal	The Moot Hall	The Town Council of Aldeburgh
do	The sea front greens adjoining the Moot Hall (stretching from the car park to Moot Green House) with the Model Yacht Pond and War Memorial	do
do	The Kings Field Playing Field and play-ground and cottages attached together with the public shelter situate thereon	do
do	The Tennis Courts, Bowling Green and Pavilion at Park Road	do
do	The Town Marshes	do
The District Council of West Dorset	Municipal Buildings, High East Street including the Corn Exchange, women's and men's public conveniences adjoining but excluding Municipal offices, North Square	The Town Council of Dorchester
do	19 North Square	do
do	Borough Gardens	do
do	The Walks (South Walk (including War Memorial), Chestnut Walk, Salisbury Walk, Colliton Walk (including Thomas Hardy Statue), Short Walk (including the Roman Wall), West Walk and Bowling Alley Walk)	do
do	Salisbury Field	do
do	Maumbury Rings	do
do	Weymouth Avenue Recreation Grounds	do
do	The Kings Road, Syward Close, Bridport Road, Mellstock Avenue and Poundbury Crescent playing fields	do

(1) Transferor Authority	(2) Property	(3) Transferee Authority
The District Council of West Dorset	Amenity space on the north side of Celtic Crescent, Castle Park	The Town Council of Dorchester
do	Land opposite Frome Terrace	do
The Town Council of Aldeburgh	Aldeburgh Cemetery	The District Council of Suffolk Coastal
do	All town and village greens except the sea front greens adjoining the Moot Hall	do
do	All public shelters (except that at the Kings Field Playing Field), public clocks and bicycle parking places	do
The Town Council of Denby Dale	Allotment site at Bilham Road, Clayton West, Skelmanthorpe	The Borough Council of Kirklees
do	Allotment site at Cumberworth Road, Skelmanthorpe	do
The Town Council of Meltham	Land at Meltham Hall Estate comprising field nos 843 and 555 containing 2.538 and 0.819 acres respectively	do
do	Cottages known as 142 and 175 Huddersfield Road, Meltham	do

PART II

(1) Transferor Authority	(2) Property	(3) Transferee Authority
The City Council of Swansea	Glanmor School, Glanmor Road, Uplands, Swansea	The County Council of West Glamorgan
do	Old Guildhall, Somerset Place, Swansea	do
do	Cambrian Yard, Cambrian Place, Swansea	do
The Borough Council of Ynys Môn—Isle of Anglesey	All those allotments gardens fronting Plas Road, Holyhead in the community of Holyhead Rural containing an area of 4.564 acres or thereabouts comprising enclosure number 1123 on Anglesey Ordnance Sheet X1.2 (1924 Edition)	The Town Council of Holyhead
do	Holyhead Town Hall	do
do	All that piece or parcel of land situate in Newry Street, Holyhead together with the messuage or dwelling house erected thereon or on some part thereof and known as Epworth, 25 Newry Street, Holyhead	do
do	Land situate at Kingsland, Holyhead, containing an area of 22,014 square metres used and occupied as children's playing fields	do

(1) Transferor Authority	(2) Property	(3) Transferee Authority
The Borough Council of Ynys Môn–Isle of Anglesey	Land situate adjacent to Llanfawr Road, Holyhead, containing an area of 9,429 square metres used and occupied as children's playing fields	The Town Council of Holyhead
do	Cemetery known as Mynwent Menai, Holyhead Road, Menai Bridge and containing an area of one acre or thereabouts together with rights of access thereto	The Town Council of Menai Bridge
do	Porth y Wrach Gardens and Slipway situate at Porth y Wrach, Menai Bridge	do
do	The area of woodland known as Coed Cyrnol situate off Holyhead Road, Menai Bridge	do
do	Bowling Green, situate at Beach Road, Menai Bridge (but excluding the part thereof on which public conveniences have been erected)	do
do	Pleasure grounds situate at Beach Road, Menai Bridge, containing an area of half of an acre or thereabouts	do
do	The pedestrian way known as the Belgian Promenade situate at the foreshore between the suspension bridge and Church Island, Menai Bridge	do
do	The natural rock area known as Boncan Fawr, off Cambria Road, Menai Bridge	do
do	Parc Playing Field containing an area of 1,955 square yards or thereabouts adjacent to Well Street and Quay Street, Amlwch Port, Amlwch	The Town Council of Amlwch
do	All that land situate at Machine Street, Amlwch Port, Amlwch being the site of the Cadet Hut and containing an area of 5,520 square yards or thereabouts	do
The Community Council of Dyffryn Clydach	All those pieces or parcels of land situate at Longford, Neath containing 5.474 acres or thereabouts and known as Longford Playing Fields, excluding the Memorial Hall and the land it stands upon	The Borough Council of Neath
do	All that piece or parcel of land abutting onto a footpath leading from Longford Lane, The Highlands, Neath Abbey and containing 0.07 acre or thereabouts and known as the Highlands Children's Playground	do
do	All that piece or parcel of land situate on the eastern side of Lon Glynfelin, Longford near Neath and containing 1,898 square yards or thereabouts and known as Lon Glynfelin Children's Playground	do

26th February 1976.

Anthony Crosland,
Secretary of State for the Environment.

1st March 1976.

John Morris,
Secretary of State for Wales.

EXPLANATORY NOTE
(This Note is not part of the Order.)

This Order makes further provision incidental, consequential, transitional and supplementary to the Local Government Act 1972 and the Water Act 1973, relating to—

(*a*) the amendment of certain Acts and instruments;

(*b*) the Waltham Abbey market;

(*c*) agreements by the Bolton Borough Council which will engage its direct labour force; and

(*d*) the transfer of certain property etc.

STATUTORY INSTRUMENTS

1976 No. 316

ROAD TRAFFIC

The Motor Vehicles (Type Approval) (Amendment) Regulations 1976

Made - - - -	*27th February* 1976
Laid before Parliament	*10th March* 1976
Coming into Operation	*31st March* 1976

The Secretary of State for the Environment, as the designated Minister under the European Communities (Designation) Order 1972(a), in exercise of his powers under section 2 of the European Communities Act 1972(b) and of all other enabling powers, hereby makes the following Regulations:—

1. These Regulations may be cited as the Motor Vehicles (Type Approval) (Amendment) Regulations 1976 and shall come into operation on 31st March 1976.

2. The Interpretation Act 1889(c) shall apply for the interpretation of these Regulations as it applies for the interpretation of an Act of Parliament and as if for the purposes of section 38 of that Act these Regulations were an Act of Parliament and the Regulations revoked by Regulation 3 were Acts of Parliament thereby repealed.

3. The Motor Vehicles (Type Approval) (Amendment) Regulations 1974(d), Regulation 9 of the Motor Vehicles (Type Approval) (Amendment) (No. 2) Regulations 1974(e), and the Motor Vehicles (Type Approval) (Amendment) Regulations 1975(f) are hereby revoked.

4. The Motor Vehicles (Type Approval) Regulations 1973(g) as amended **(h)** shall be further amended so as to have effect as though for Schedule 2 there were substituted the Schedule to these Regulations.

John Gilbert,

Signed by authority of
the Secretary of State.

Minister for Transport,
Department of the Environment.

27th February 1976.

(a) S.I. 1972/1811 (1972 III, p. 5216).　　(b) 1972 c. 68.
(c) 1889 c. 63.　　(d) S.I. 1974/65 (1974 I, p. 210).
(e) S.I. 1974/763 (1974 I, p. 2924).　　(f) S.I. 1975/642 (1975 I, p. 2320).
(g) S.I. 1973/1199 (1973 II, p. 3610).
(h) The only relevant amending instrument is S.I. 1974/763.

THE SCHEDULE

"

SCHEDULE 2 (See Regulations 3(1) and 5(1))

PART I

The Community Directives relating to the design, construction, equipment and marking of vehicles or vehicle components.

1 Item Number	2 Community Directive			3 Subject Matter
	(a) Reference Number	(b) Date	(c) Official Journal Reference	
1	70/157/EEC	6th February 1970	O.J. L42, 23.2.1970, p. 16 (S.E. 1970 (I), p. 111)	The permissible sound level and the exhaust system of motor vehicles.
	as amended by 73/350/ EEC	7th November 1973	O.J. L321, 22.11.73, p. 33.	
2	70/220/EEC	20th March 1970	O.J. L76, 6.4.1970, p. 25 (S.E. 1970 (I), p. 171)	Measures to be taken against air pollution by gases from positive ignition engines of motor vehicles.
	as amended by 74/290/ EEC	28th May 1974	O.J. L159, 15.6.1974, p. 61.	
3	70/221/EEC	20th March 1970	O.J. L76, 6.4.1970, p. 23 (S.E. 1970 (I), p. 192)	Liquid fuel tanks and rear protective devices for motor vehicles and their trailers.
4	70/222/EEC	20th March 1970	O.J. L76, 6.4.1970, p. 25 (S.E. 1970 (I), p. 194)	The mounting and fixing of rear registration plates on motor vehicles and their trailers.
5	70/311/EEC	8th June 1970	O.J. L133, 18.6.1970, p. 10 (S.E. 1970 (II), p. 375)	The steering equipment for motor vehicles and their trailers.
6	70/387/EEC	27th July 1970	O.J. L176, 10.8.1970, p. 5 (S.E. 1970 (II), p. 564)	The doors of motor vehicles and their trailers.
7	70/388/EEC	27th July 1970	O.J. L176, 10.8.1970, p. 12 (S.E. 1970 (II), p. 571)	Audible warning devices for motor vehicles.
8	71/127/EEC	1st March 1971	O.J. L68, 22.3.1971, p. 1 (S.E. 1971 (I), p. 136)	The rear-view mirrors of motor vehicles.
9	71/320/EEC	26th July 1971	O.J. L202, 6.9.1971, p. 37 (S.E. 1971 (III), p. 746)	The braking devices of certain categories of motor vehicles and their trailers.
	as amended by 74/132/EEC	11th February 1974	O.J. L74, 19.3.1974, p. 7.	
	and as amended by 75/524/EEC	25th July 1975	O.J. L236, 8.9.1975, p. 3.	

| 1 | 2 Community Directive | | | 3 |
Item Number	(a) Reference Number	(b) Date	(c) Official Journal Reference	Subject Matter
10	72/245/EEC	20th June 1972	O.J. L152, 6.7.1972, p. 15 (S.E. 1972 (II), p. 637)	The suppression of radio interference produced by spark-ignition engines fitted to motor vehicles.
11	72/306/EEC	2nd August 1972	O.J. L190, 20.8.1972, p. 1 (S.E. 1972 (III), p. 889)	The emission of pollutants from diesel engines for use in vehicles.
12	74/60/EEC	17th December 1973	O.J. L38, 11.2.1974, p. 2	The interior fittings of motor vehicles (interior parts of the passenger compartment other than the interior rear-view mirrors, layout of the controls, the roof or sliding roof, the back rest and rear part of the seats).
13	74/61/EEC	17th December 1973	O.J. L38, 11.2.1974, p. 22	Devices to prevent the unauthorised use of motor vehicles.
14	74/297/EEC	4th June 1974	O.J. L165, 20.6.1974, p. 16	The interior fittings of motor vehicles (the behaviour of the steering mechanism in the event of an impact).
15	74/408/EEC	22nd July 1974	O.J. L221, 12.8.1974, p. 1	The interior fittings of motor vehicles (strength of seats and of their anchorages).
16	74/483/EEC	17th September 1974	O.J. L266, 2.10.1974, p. 4	The external projections of motor vehicles.

PART II

The Council Regulations on the harmonisation of certain social legislation relating to road transport.

Community Reference No.	Date of Regulation	Official Journal Reference	Subject Matter
(EEC) No. 1463/70	20th July 1970	O.J. L164, 27.7.1970, p. 1 (S.E. 1970 (II), p. 482)	The introduction of recording equipment in road transport.

"

EXPLANATORY NOTE

(This Note is not part of the Regulations.)

1. These Regulations further amend the Motor Vehicles (Type Approval) Regulations 1973.

2. These further amendments—

(1) provide a new Schedule 2 which

(*a*) includes in the type approval requirements as to the braking devices of certain categories of motor vehicles and their trailers the amendments contained in the Commission Directives of 11th February 1974 and 25th July 1975 which are specified in Part I of this Schedule, and

(*b*) corrects minor errors, and

(*c*) otherwise reproduces, in a different form, the contents of the Schedule to be replaced; and

(2) revoke Regulations which made amendments now contained in the new Schedule.

STATUTORY INSTRUMENTS

1976 No. 317

ROAD TRAFFIC

The Motor Vehicles (Construction and Use) (Amendment) Regulations 1976

Made - - - -	*27th February* 1976
Laid before Parliament	*10th March* 1976
Coming into Operation	*31st March* 1976

The Secretary of State for the Environment, in exercise of his powers under sections 40(1) and (3) of the Road Traffic Act 1972(a) and of all other enabling powers, and after consultation with representative organisations in accordance with the provisions of section 199(2) of that Act, hereby makes the following Regulations:—

1. These Regulations shall come into operation on 31st March 1976, and may be cited as the Motor Vehicles (Construction and Use) (Amendment) Regulations 1976.

2. The Motor Vehicles (Construction and Use) Regulations 1973(b), as amended (c), shall be further amended so as to have effect in accordance with the following provisions of these Regulations.

3. In Regulation 3 (Interpretation), in paragraph (1), in the meaning given to the expression "close-coupled", for the words "840 millimetres" there shall be substituted the words "1 metre".

4. In Regulation 4A, in the table, after the entry relating to Council Directive 71/320/EEC of 26th July 1971 there shall be inserted the following items:—

"Council Directive 71/320/EEC of 26th July 1971(d) (relating to the braking devices of certain categories of motor vehicles and their trailers) as amended by Commission Directive 74/132/EEC of 11th February 1974(e)   1st October 1974   13, 14, 47, 50, 54, 59, 66 and 70.

(a) 1972 c. 20.   (b) S.I. 1973/24 (1973 I, p. 93).
(c) The only relevant amending Instruments are S.I. 1973/1347, 1974/64, 765, 1975/641 (1973 II, p. 4133; 1974 I, pp. 208, 2932; 1975 I, p. 2316).
(d) O.J. L202, 6.9.1971, p. 37 (S.E. 1971 (III), p. 746).
(e) O.J. L74, 19.3.1974, p. 7.

Council Directive 71/320/EEC of 26th July 1971 (relating to the braking devices of certain categories of motor vehicles and their trailers) as amended by Commission Directive 74/132/EEC of 11th February 1974 and by Commission Directive 75/524/EEC of 25th July 1975(a)

1st January 1976

13, 14, 47, 50, 54, 59, 66 and 70.

"

5. In Regulation 27 (Audible warning instrument), at the end of paragraph (5), there shall be inserted the following sub-paragraph:—

"(h) motor vehicles owned by the Secretary of State for Defence and used by the Royal Air Force Mountain Rescue Service for the purposes of rescue operations in connection with crashed aircraft or any other emergencies.".

6. In Regulation 70 (Brakes),—

(a) in paragraph (2), for the words "paragraph (3)" there shall be substituted the words "paragraphs (2A) and (3)";

(b) after paragraph (2) there shall be inserted the following paragraph:—

"(2A) Where a motor vehicle to which Regulation 4A applies by virtue of its conforming to the requirements of Council Directive 71/320/EEC of 26th July 1971 (which relates to the braking devices of certain categories of motor vehicles and their trailers) or, where appropriate, to the requirements of that Directive as amended by the amending Directives specified in Regulation 4A, is drawing a trailer to which that Regulation does not apply, paragraph (2)(b) of this Regulation shall apply to the trailer as if the words "or of any part (other than as aforesaid) of the braking system with which the trailer is equipped" were omitted."; and

(c) in paragraph (3), for the words "Paragraphs (1) and (2)" there shall be substituted the words "Paragraphs (1), (2) and (2A)".

7. After Regulation 70 there shall be inserted the following Regulation:—

"70A.—(1) Where a trailer to which Regulation 4A applies by virtue of its conforming to the requirements of Council Directive 71/320/EEC of 26th July 1971 (which relates to the braking devices of certain categories of motor vehicles and their trailers) or, where appropriate, to the requirements of that Directive as amended by the amending Directives specified in Regulation 4A, is drawn by a motor vehicle to which that Regulation does not apply, then the braking system of the drawing vehicle shall be so constructed that in the event of a failure of any part (other than a fixed member or a brake shoe anchor pin) of the service braking system with which the drawing vehicle is equipped (excluding the means of operation of a split braking system) brakes shall still be capable of being applied to at least two wheels of the trailer or, in the case of a two-wheeled trailer, to one wheel by the driver using the secondary braking system of the drawing vehicle.

(2) In this Regulation "service braking system" means the braking system which was designed and constructed to have the highest braking efficiency of any braking system with which the drawing vehicle is equipped and "secondary braking system" means a braking system applied by a second independent means of operation or by one of the independent sections comprised in a split braking system.".

(a) O.J. L236, 8.9.1975, p. 3.

8. In Regulation 80 (Laden weight of trailer), for paragraph (4) there shall be substituted the following paragraph:—

"(4) The total laden weight of a trailer—

(a) manufactured before 27th February 1977 and having no other brakes than a parking brake and brakes which automatically come into operation on the overrun of the trailer shall not exceed 3560 kilograms,

(b) manufactured on or after 27th February 1977 and fitted with brakes which automatically come into operation on the overrun of the trailer, whether or not it is fitted with any other brake, shall not exceed 3500 kilograms.".

9. In Regulation 86 (Total weights for certain closely spaced axles, etc.), in paragraph (3), for the words "that Schedule" there shall be substituted the words "the said Part IV".

10. In Regulation 88 (Distribution of weight), in sub-paragraph (c), for the words "18290 kilograms" there shall be substituted the words "18300 kilograms".

11. In Regulation 89 (Additional weight restrictions),—

(a) In paragraph (4), for sub-paragraphs (a), (b), and (c) there shall be substituted the following sub-paragraphs:—

"(a) neither the maximum gross weight shown in its plate nor the maximum gross weight in Great Britain shown in its plate shall be exceeded;

(b) neither the maximum axle weight for each axle shown in its plate nor the maximum axle weight in Great Britain for each axle shown in its plate shall be exceeded:

Provided that this sub-paragraph shall not apply in the case of any axle being one of two or more axles to which the following sub-paragraph applies;

(c) where any two or more axles are fitted with a compensating arrangement in accordance with Regulation 11, neither the sum of the maximum axle weights for those axles so fitted shown in its plate nor the sum of the maximum weights in Great Britain for those axles so fitted shown in its plate shall be exceeded;";

(b) In paragraph (6), for sub-paragraphs (a), (b), and (c) there shall be substituted the following sub-paragraphs:—

"(a) neither the maximum gross weight shown in its plate nor the maximum gross weight in Great Britain shown in its plate shall be exceeded;

(b) neither the maximum axle weight for each axle shown in its plate nor the maximum axle weight in Great Britain for each axle shown in its plate shall be exceeded:

Provided that this sub-paragraph shall not apply in the case of any axle being one of two or more axles to which the following sub-paragraph applies;

(*c*) where any two or more axles are fitted with a compensating arrangement in accordance with Regulation 11, neither the sum of the maximum axle weights for those axles so fitted shown in its plate nor the sum of the maximum axle weights in Great Britain for those axles so fitted shown in its plate shall be exceeded.".

12. In Regulation 90 (Maintenance and use of vehicles so as not to be a danger),—

(*a*) in the headnote the word "etc." shall be inserted after the word "danger";

(*b*) for paragraph (2) there shall be substituted the following paragraph:—

"(2) The load carried by a motor vehicle or trailer shall at all times be so secured, if necessary by physical restraint other than its own weight, and be in such a position, that neither danger nor nuisance is likely to be caused to any person or property by reason of the load or any part thereof falling or being blown from the vehicle or by reason of any other movement of the load or any part thereof in relation to the vehicle."; and

(*c*) in paragraph (3), after the words "cause danger" there shall be inserted the words "or nuisance".

13. In Regulation 100,—

(*a*) in paragraph (2), the words "the unladen weight of which does not exceed 1525 kilograms" shall be omitted;

(*b*) in paragraph (4), the words "the unladen weight of which does not exceed 1525 kilograms" shall be omitted; and

(*c*) in paragraph (5), after the words "For the purposes of this Regulation" there shall be added the words " "axle" includes all the axles of whatever type and number which are fitted to a vehicle".

14. In Regulation 131, in paragraph (4), in sub-paragraph (*a*), for the words "in the case at (ii) above the overall length of the vehicle" there shall be substituted the words "in the case at (ii) above the overall length of the vehicles".

15. In Schedule 2 (Particulars to be shown on plate for motor vehicles), in the heading, for the figure "88" there shall be substituted the figure "89".

16. In Schedule 7 (Permissible maximum weights),—

(*a*) in Part II, under the heading "column 1", in sub-paragraph (i) to paragraph (*b*), for the words "8385 kilograms" there shall be substituted the words "8390 kilograms";

(*b*) in Part IV, in the table of maximum weights for two closely spaced axles, in column 2, for the figures "15250", "16260", "18290" and "19310", there shall be substituted the figures "15260", "16270", "18300" and "19320" respectively; and in column 3 for the figures "18290", "19310" and "20330" there shall be substituted the figures "18300", "19320" and "20340" respectively; and

(*c*) in Part VI, in sub-paragraph (i) of the second paragraph, for the words "8385 kilograms" there shall be substituted the words "8390 kilograms".

17. In Schedule 8 (Vehicles carrying wide or long loads),—

(*a*) in paragraph 1 of Part I, for the words "The conditions referred to in Regulation 128 and in paragraphs (2), (4), (6), (7) and (9) of Regulation 131" there shall be substituted the words "The conditions referred to in paragraph (2) of Regulation 128, and in paragraphs (2), (4), (5), (6), (7) and (9) of Regulation 131"; and

(*b*) in paragraph 2 of Part I, for the words "The conditions referred to in Regulation 128 and in paragraphs (2), (4), (5), (6) and (9) of Regulation 131" there shall be substituted the words "The conditions referred to in paragraph (2) of Regulation 128 and in paragraphs (2), (4), (5), (6) and (9) of Regulation 131".

Signed by authority of
the Secretary of State.

John Gilbert,
Minister for Transport,
Department of the Environment.

27th February 1976.

EXPLANATORY NOTE

(*This Note is not part of the Regulations.*)

These Regulations amend the Motor Vehicles (Construction and Use) Regulations 1973 so as:—

(1) to amend the definition of "close-coupled" in relation to the wheels of a trailer so that the distance between the centres of their areas of contact with the road surface does not exceed 1 metre (approximately 39 inches) (Regulation 3);

(2) to exempt from the requirements of Regulations 13, 14, 47, 50, 54, 59, 66 and 70 (which relate to the braking devices of certain categories of motor vehicles and their trailers) certain vehicles in respect of which a type approval certificate or a certificate of conformity has been issued under the Motor Vehicles (Type Approval) Regulations 1973 by virtue of the vehicle conforming to the requirements of certain Council Directives (Regulation 4);

(3) to add motor vehicles used by the Royal Air Force Mountain Rescue Service to the list of vehicles which may be fitted with a gong, bell, siren or two-tone horn (Regulation 5);

(4) to provide for the braking of trailers where

(*a*) a motor vehicle to which Regulation 4A applies is drawing a trailer to which that Regulation does not apply (Regulation 6), and

(*b*) a motor vehicle to which Regulation 4A does not apply is drawing a trailer to which that Regulation does apply (Regulation 7);

(5) to restrict the laden weight of any trailer manufactured on or after 27th February 1977 fitted with brakes which come into operation on the overrun of the trailer to 3500 kilograms (approximately 3 tons 9 cwts), irrespective of any other brakes with which it may be fitted (Regulation 8);

(6) to remove inconsistencies resulting from rounding up in the course of metrication in cases where the Regulations specify the weight limits for combinations of closely spaced axles (Regulations 10 and 16(*b*));

(7) to facilitate the enforcement of certain weight restrictions (Regulation (11);

(8) to prevent loads being insecurely carried (Regulation 12);

(9) to make clear the meaning of the word "axle" for the purpose of Regulation 100 (Regulation 13(*c*));

(10) to extend the requirements as to tyres of different types to goods vehicles the unladen weight of which exceeds 1525 kilograms (approximately 30 cwts) (Regulation 13(*a*) and (*b*));

(11) to correct minor errors (Regulations 9, 14, 15 and 17); and

(12) to round up to the nearest 10 kilograms (approximately 22 lbs) certain maximum weights in accordance with the general policy in metricating these Regulations (Regulation 16(*a*) and (*c*)).

STATUTORY INSTRUMENTS

1976 No. 321 (C. 9)

TERMS AND CONDITIONS OF EMPLOYMENT

The Employment Protection Act 1975 (Commencement No. 3) Order 1976

Made -   -   -   -   2nd March 1976

The Lord Chancellor, in exercise of the powers conferred on him by section 129(2) and (5) of the Employment Protection Act 1975(a), hereby makes the following Order:—

Citation

1. This Order may be cited as the Employment Protection Act 1975 (Commencement No. 3) Order 1976.

Interpretation

2. The Interpretation Act 1889(b) shall apply to the interpretation of this Order as it applies to the interpretation of an Act of Parliament.

Employment Appeal Tribunal

3. Sections 87 and 88 of the Employment Protection Act 1975 and Schedule 6 to that Act shall come into operation on 30th March 1976.

Transitional Provisions

4. Where an appeal is transferred to the Employment Appeal Tribunal by virtue of paragraph 9 or 10 of Schedule 17 to the Employment Protection Act 1975 the Employment Appeal Tribunal shall have the same power to award costs in respect of that appeal as the High Court or the Court of Session, as the case may be, would have had if the appeal had not been so transferred.

Savings

5. Nothing in this Order or in the Employment Protection Act 1975 shall operate to transfer an appeal to the Employment Appeal Tribunal if the High Court or the Court of Session has, before 30th March 1976, entered upon the consideration of that appeal.

Dated 2nd March 1976.

Elwyn-Jones, C.

(a) 1975 c. 71.   (b) 1889 c. 63.

EXPLANATORY NOTE

(This Note is not part of the Order.)

This Order brings into operation the provisions of the Employment Protection Act 1975 which establish the Employment Appeal Tribunal.

STATUTORY INSTRUMENTS

1976 No. 322

TERMS AND CONDITIONS OF EMPLOYMENT

The Employment Appeal Tribunal Rules 1976

Made - - - -	*2nd March* 1976
Laid before Parliament	*10th March* 1976
Coming into Operation	*30th March* 1976

ARRANGEMENT OF RULES

The Lord Chancellor, in exercise of the powers conferred on him by paragraph 15 of Schedule 6 to the Employment Protection Act 1975(a) and after consultation with the Lord President of the Court of Session, hereby makes the following Rules:—

Citation and commencement

1. These Rules may be cited as the Employment Appeal Tribunal Rules 1976 and shall come into operation on 30th March 1976.

Interpretation

2.—(1) The Interpretation Act 1889(b) shall apply to the interpretation of these Rules as it applies to the interpretation of an Act of Parliament.

(2) In these Rules, unless the context otherwise requires—

"the Act" means the Employment Protection Act 1975 and a section or Schedule referred to by number means the section or Schedule so numbered in the Act;

"the Appeal Tribunal" means the Employment Appeal Tribunal established under section 87 and includes the President, a judge, a member or the Registrar acting on behalf of the Tribunal;

"judge" means a judge of the Appeal Tribunal nominated under section 87(2)(a) or (b) and includes a judge nominated under paragraph 5 or 6 of Schedule 6 to act temporarily in the place of a judge of the Tribunal;

"member" means a member of the Appeal Tribunal appointed under section 87(2)(c) and includes a member appointed under paragraph 7 of Schedule 6 to act temporarily in the place of a member appointed under that section;

"the President" means the judge appointed under section 87(4) to be President of the Appeal Tribunal and includes a judge nominated under paragraph 4 of Schedule 6 to act temporarily in his place;

"the Registrar" means the person appointed to be Registrar of the Appeal Tribunal and includes any officer of the Tribunal authorised by the President to act on behalf of the Registrar;

"the Secretary of Industrial Tribunals" means the person acting for the time being as the Secretary of the Central Office of the Industrial Tribunals (England and Wales) or, as may be appropriate, of the Central Office of the Industrial Tribunals (Scotland);

"the Certification Officer" means the person appointed to be the Certification Officer under section 7(1);

"taxing officer" means any officer of the Appeal Tribunal authorised by the President to assess costs and expenses.

Institution of appeal

3.—(1) Every appeal under section 88 to the Appeal Tribunal shall be instituted by serving on the Tribunal, within 42 days of the date on which the document recording the decision or order appealed from was sent to the appellant, a notice of appeal in, or substantially in accordance with, Form 1 or 2 in the Schedule to these Rules, together with a copy of the said decision or order.

(a) 1975 c. 71.   (b) 1889 c. 63.

(2) Where it appears to the Registrar that the grounds of appeal stated in the notice do not give the Appeal Tribunal jurisdiction to entertain the appeal, he shall notify the appellant accordingly, informing him of the reasons for his opinion and, subject to paragraph (3) of this rule, no further action shall be taken on the appeal unless the President or a judge otherwise directs.

(3) Where notification has been given under paragraph (2) of this rule, the appellant may serve a fresh notice of appeal within the time remaining under paragraph (1) or within 28 days from the date on which the Registrar's notification was sent to him, whichever is the longer period.

Service of notice of appeal

4. On receipt of notice under rule 3, the Registrar shall seal the notice with the Appeal Tribunal's seal and shall serve a sealed copy on the appellant and on—

(a) every person who, in accordance with rule 5, is a respondent to the appeal; and

(b) the Secretary of Industrial Tribunals in the case of an appeal from an industrial tribunal; or

(c) the Certification Officer in the case of an appeal from him to which he is not a respondent; or

(d) the Secretary of State in the case of an appeal under the Redundancy Payments Act 1965**(a)** to which he is not a respondent.

Respondents to appeals

5. The respondents to an appeal shall be—

(a) in the case of an appeal from an industrial tribunal or from a decision of the Certification Officer under section 3 of the Trade Union Act 1913**(b)**, or section 4 of the Trade Union (Amalgamations, etc.) Act 1964**(c)**, the parties (other than the appellant) to the proceedings before the industrial tribunal or the Certification Officer;

(b) in the case of an appeal against a decision of the Certification Officer under section 4 or 5 of the Trade Union Act 1913, section 8 of the Trade Union and Labour Relations Act 1974**(d)** or section 8 of the Act, that Officer.

Respondent's answer and notice of cross-appeal

6.—(1) The Registrar shall, as soon as practicable, notify every respondent of the date appointed by the Appeal Tribunal by which any answer under this rule must be delivered.

(2) A respondent who wishes to resist an appeal shall, within the time appointed under paragraph (1) of this rule, deliver to the Appeal Tribunal an answer in writing in, or substantially in accordance with, Form 3 in the Schedule to these Rules, setting out the grounds on which he relies, so, however, that it shall be sufficient for a respondent to an appeal referred to in rule 5(a) who wishes to rely on any ground which is the same as a ground relied on by the industrial tribunal or the Certification Officer for making the decision or order appealed from to state that fact in his answer.

(a) 1965 c. 62. (b) 2 & 3 Geo. 5. c. 30.
(c) 1964 c. 24. (d) 1974 c. 52.

(3) A respondent who wishes to cross-appeal may do so by including in his answer a statement of the grounds of his cross-appeal, and in that event an appellant who wishes to resist the cross-appeal shall, within a time to be appointed by the Appeal Tribunal, deliver to the Tribunal a reply in writing setting out the grounds on which he relies.

(4) The Registrar shall serve a copy of every answer and reply to a cross-appeal on every party other than the party by whom it was delivered.

(5) Where the respondent does not wish to resist an appeal, the parties may deliver to the Appeal Tribunal an agreed draft of an order allowing the appeal and the Tribunal may, if it thinks it right to do so, make an order allowing the appeal in the terms agreed.

Disposal of appeal

7.—(1) The Registrar shall, as soon as practicable, give notice of the arrangements made by the Appeal Tribunal for hearing the appeal to—

(a) every party to the proceedings; and

(b) the Secretary of Industrial Tribunals in the case of an appeal from an industrial tribunal; or

(c) the Certification Officer in the case of an appeal from him to which he is not a respondent; or

(d) the Secretary of State in the case of an appeal under the Redundancy Payments Act 1965 to which he is not a respondent.

(2) Any such notice shall state the date appointed by the Appeal Tribunal by which any interlocutory application must be made.

Joinder of parties

8. The Appeal Tribunal may, on the application of any person or of its own motion, direct that any person not already a party to the proceedings be added as a party, or that any party to proceedings shall cease to be a party, and in either case may give such consequential directions as it considers necessary.

Interlocutory applications

9.—(1) An interlocutory application may be made to the Appeal Tribunal by giving notice in writing specifying the direction or order sought.

(2) On receipt of a notice under paragraph (1) of this rule, the Registrar shall serve a copy on every other party to the proceedings who appears to him to be concerned in the matter to which the notice relates and shall notify the applicant and every such party of the arrangements made by the Appeal Tribunal for disposing of the application.

Disposal of interlocutory applications

10. Except where the President or a judge, whether generally or in any particular case, otherwise directs, every interlocutory application shall be considered by a judge who may—

(a) dispose of it himself; or

(b) refer it in whole or in part to the Appeal Tribunal as required to be constituted by paragraph 14 of Schedule 6; or

(c) refer it in whole or in part to the Registrar.

Appeals from Registrar

11.—(1) Where an application is disposed of by the Registrar in pursuance of rule 10, any party aggrieved by his decision may appeal to a judge and in that case the judge may determine the appeal himself or refer it in whole or in part to the Appeal Tribunal as required to be constituted by paragraph 14 of Schedule 6.

(2) Notice of appeal under paragraph (1) of this rule may be given to the Appeal Tribunal, either orally or in writing, within three days of the decision appealed from and the Registrar shall notify every other party who appears to him to be concerned in the appeal and shall inform every such party and the appellant of the arrangements made by the Appeal Tribunal for disposing of the appeal.

Hearing of interlocutory applications

12. The Appeal Tribunal may sit either in private or in public for the hearing of any interlocutory application.

Appointment for directions

13.—(1) Where it appears to the Appeal Tribunal that the future conduct of any proceedings would thereby be facilitated, the Tribunal may (either of its own motion or on application) at any stage of the proceedings appoint a date for the giving of directions as to their future conduct and thereupon the following provisions of this rule shall apply.

(2) The Registrar shall give to every party to the proceedings notice of the date appointed under paragraph (1) of this rule and any party applying for directions shall, if practicable, before that date give to the Appeal Tribunal particulars of any directions for which he asks.

(3) The Registrar shall take such steps as may be practicable to inform every party of any directions applied for by any other party.

(4) On the date appointed under paragraph (1) of this rule, the Appeal Tribunal shall consider every application for directions made by any party and any written representations relating to the application submitted to the Tribunal and shall give such directions as it thinks fit for the purpose of securing the just, expeditious and economical disposal of the proceedings, including, where appropriate, directions in pursuance of rule 23, for the purpose of ensuring that the parties are enabled to avail themselves of opportunities for conciliation.

(5) Without prejudice to the generality of paragraph (4) of this rule, the Appeal Tribunal may give such directions as it thinks fit as to—

 (*a*) the amendment of any notice, answer or other document;

 (*b*) the admission of any facts or documents;

 (*c*) the admission in evidence of any documents;

 (*d*) the mode in which evidence is to be given at the hearing;

 (*e*) the consolidation of the proceedings with any other proceedings pending before the Tribunal;

 (*f*) the place and date of the hearing.

(6) An application for further directions or for the variation of any directions already given may be made in accordance with rule 9.

Appeal Tribunal's power to give directions

14. The Appeal Tribunal may of its own motion, at any stage of any proceedings, give any party directions as to any steps to be taken by him in relation to the proceedings.

Default by parties

15. If a respondent to any proceedings fails to deliver an answer within the time appointed under these Rules, or if any party fails to comply with an order or direction of the Appeal Tribunal, the Tribunal may order that he be debarred from taking any further part in the proceedings, or may make such other order as it thinks just.

Attendance of witnesses and production of documents

16.—(1) The Appeal Tribunal may, on the application of any party, order any person to attend before the Tribunal as a witness or to produce any document.

(2) No person to whom an order is directed under paragraph (1) of this rule shall be treated as having failed to obey that order unless at the time at which the order was served on him there was tendered to him a sufficient sum of money to cover his costs of attending before the Appeal Tribunal.

Oaths

17. The Appeal Tribunal may, either of its own motion or on application, require any evidence to be given on oath.

Oral hearings

18.—(1) Subject to paragraph (2) of this rule, an oral hearing at which any proceedings before the Appeal Tribunal are finally disposed of shall take place in public before such members of the Tribunal as (subject to paragraph 14 of Schedule 6) the President may nominate for the purpose.

(2) The Appeal Tribunal may sit in private to hear evidence which in the opinion of the Tribunal—

(a) relates to matters of such a nature that it would be against the interests of national security to allow the evidence to be given in public; or

(b) is likely to consist (wholly or in part) of information which—

(i) the person giving the evidence could not disclose without contravening a prohibition imposed by or under an enactment; or

(ii) has been communicated to that person in confidence or which he has otherwise obtained in consequence of the confidence reposed in him by another person; or

(iii) is information the disclosure of which would cause substantial injury to an undertaking of the person giving the evidence or any undertaking in which he works for reasons other than its effect on any negotiations with respect to any of the matters mentioned in section 29(1) of the Trade Union and Labour Relations Act 1974.

Drawing up, reasons for, and enforcement of orders

19.—(1) Every order of the Appeal Tribunal shall be drawn up by the Registrar and a copy. sealed with the seal of the Tribunal, shall be served by the Registrar on every party to the proceedings to which it relates and—

(*a*) in the case of an order disposing of an appeal from an industrial tribunal, on the Secretary of Industrial Tribunals; or

(*b*) in the case of an order disposing of an appeal from the Certification Officer to which he is not a respondent on that Officer.

(2) The Appeal Tribunal shall, on the application of any party made within 14 days after the making of an order finally disposing of any proceedings, give its reasons in writing for the order unless it was made after the delivery of a reasoned judgment.

(3) Subject to any order made by the Court of Appeal or Court of Session and to any directions given by the Appeal Tribunal, an appeal from the Tribunal shall not suspend the enforcement of any order made by it.

Review of decisions and correction of errors

20.—(1) The Appeal Tribunal may, either of its own motion or on application, review any order made by it and may, on such review, revoke or vary that order on the grounds that—

(*a*) the order was wrongly made as the result of an error on the part of the Tribunal or its staff;

(*b*) a party did not receive proper notice of the proceedings leading to the order; or

(*c*) the interests of justice require such review.

(2) An application under paragraph (1) above shall be made within 14 days of the date of the order.

(3) A clerical mistake in any order arising from an accidental slip or omission may at any time be corrected by, or on the authority of, a judge or member.

Costs

21.—(1) Where it appears to the Appeal Tribunal that any proceedings were unnecessary, improper or vexatious or that there has been unreasonable delay or other unreasonable conduct in bringing or conducting the proceedings, the Tribunal may order the party at fault to pay to any other party the whole or such part as it thinks fit of the costs or expenses incurred by that other party in connection with the proceedings.

(2) Where an order is made under paragraph (1) of this rule, the Appeal Tribunal may assess the sum to be paid, or may direct that it be assessed by the taxing officer, from whose decision an appeal shall lie to a judge.

(3) Rules 11 and 12 shall apply to an appeal under paragraph (2) of this rule as they apply to an appeal from the Registrar.

Service of documents

22.—(1) Any notice or other document required or authorised by these Rules to be served on, or delivered to, any person may be sent to him by post to his address for service or, where no address for service has been given, to his registered office, principal place of business, head or main office or last known address, as the case may be, and any notice or other document required or authorised to be served on, or delivered to, the Appeal Tribunal may be sent by post or delivered to the Registrar—

(a) in the case of a notice instituting proceedings, at the central office or any other office of the Tribunal; or

(b) in any other case, at the office of the Tribunal in which the proceedings in question are being dealt with in accordance with rule 25(2).

(2) Any notice or other document required or authorised to be served on, or delivered to, an unincorporated body may be sent to its secretary, manager or other similar officer.

(3) Every document served by post shall be assumed, in the absence of evidence to the contrary, to have been delivered in the normal course of post.

(4) The Appeal Tribunal may inform itself in such manner as it thinks fit of the posting of any document by an officer of the Tribunal.

(5) The Appeal Tribunal may direct that service of any document be dispensed with or be effected otherwise than in the manner prescribed by these Rules.

Conciliation

23. Where at any stage of any proceedings it appears to the Appeal Tribunal that there is a reasonable prospect of agreement being reached between the parties, the Tribunal may take such steps as it thinks fit to enable the parties to avail themselves of any opportunities for conciliation, whether by adjourning any proceedings or otherwise.

Time

24.—(1) The time prescribed by these Rules or by order of the Appeal Tribunal for doing any act may be extended (whether it has already expired or not) or abridged, and the date appointed for any purpose may be altered, by order of the Tribunal.

(2) Where the last day for the doing of any act falls on a day on which the appropriate office of the Tribunal is closed and by reason thereof the act cannot be done on that day, it may be done on the next day on which that office is open.

Tribunal offices and allocation of business

25.—(1) The central office and any other office of the Appeal Tribunal shall be open at such times as the President may direct.

(2) Any proceedings before the Tribunal may be dealt with at the central office or at such other office as the President may direct.

Non-compliance with, and waiver of, rules

26.—(1) Failure to comply with any requirements of these Rules shall not invalidate any proceedings unless the Appeal Tribunal otherwise directs.

(2) The Tribunal may, if it considers that to do so would lead to the more expeditious or economical disposal of any proceedings or would otherwise be desirable in the interests of justice, dispense with the taking of any step required or authorised by these Rules, or may direct that any such step be taken in some manner other than that prescribed by these Rules.

Dated 2nd March 1976.

Elwyn-Jones, C.

SCHEDULE

Rule 3

FORM 1

Notice of Appeal from Decision of Industrial Tribunal

1. The appellant is (*name and address of appellant*).

2. Any communication relating to this appeal may be sent to the appellant at (*appellant's address for service, including telephone number if any*).

3. The appellant appeals from
(*here give particulars of the decision of the industrial tribunal from which the appeal is brought*)

on the following question of law:
(*here set out the question of law on which the appeal is brought*).

4. The parties to the proceedings before the industrial tribunal, other than the appellant, were (*names and addresses of other parties to the proceedings resulting in decision appealed from*).

5. The appellant's grounds of appeal are:
(*here state the grounds of appeal*).

6. A copy of the industrial tribunal's decision is attached to this notice.

Date   Signed

Rule 3

FORM 2

Notice of Appeal from Decision of Certification Officer

1. The appellant is (*name and address of appellant*).

2. Any communication relating to this appeal may be sent to the appellant at (*appellant's address for service, including telephone number if any*).

3. The appellant appeals from:
(*here give particulars of the order or decision of the Certification Officer from which the appeal is brought*).

4. The appellant's grounds of appeal are:
(*here state the grounds of appeal*).

5. A copy of the Certification Officer's decision is attached to this notice.

Date   Signed

FORM 3

Respondent's Answer

1. The respondent is (*name and address of respondent*).

2. Any communication relating to this appeal may be sent to the respondent at (*respondent's address for service, including telephone number if any*).

3. The respondent intends to resist the appeal of (*here give name of appellant*). The grounds on which the respondent will rely are [the gounds relied upon by the industrial tribunal/Certification Officer for making the decision or order appealed from] [and] [the following grounds]:
(*here set out any grounds which differ from those relied upon by the industrial tribunal or Certification Officer, as the case may be*).

4. The respondent cross-appeals from:
(*here give particulars of the decision appealed from*).

5. The respondent's grounds of appeal are:
(*here state the grounds of appeal*).

Date   Signed

EXPLANATORY NOTE

(*This Note is not part of the Rules.*)

These Rules prescribe the procedure relating to the institution, hearing and disposal of an appeal in the Employment Appeal Tribunal established by the Employment Protection Act 1975 to hear appeals from industrial tribunals in England, Wales and Scotland, and from the Certification Officer appointed under section 7(1) of the Act. The schedule to the Rules prescribes the forms of notices of appeal and of a respondent's answer and cross-appeal.

STATUTORY INSTRUMENTS

1976 No. 323

ROAD TRAFFIC

The Motor Vehicles (Authorisation of Special Types) (Amendment) Order 1976

Made - - - - *2nd February* 1976

Coming into Operation   *31st March* 1976

The Secretary of State for the Environment, in exercise of his powers under section 42 of the Road Traffic Act 1972(a) and of all other enabling powers, hereby makes the following Order:—

1. This Order may be cited as the Motor Vehicles (Authorisation of Special Types) (Amendment) Order 1976 and shall come into operation on 31st March 1976.

2. The Motor Vehicles (Authorisation of Special Types) General Order 1973(b) as amended (c) shall have effect in accordance with the following provisions of this Order.

3. In Article 9, in paragraph (*a*), for the words "115 and 131" there shall be substituted the words "115, 131 and 136".

4. In Article 16—

    (i) in paragraph (*m*), the words "the overall width exceeds 2·44 metres on a road on which a tramcar is operated and to the use of a vehicle of which" and the word "other" shall be omitted; and

    (ii) in paragraph (*n*), the words "if its overall width exceeds 2·44 metres, before using it on a road on which a tramcar is operated or, if its overall width exceeds 2·9 metres," shall be omitted.

5. In Article 17, in sub-paragraph (*b*) of paragraph (2), for the words "125 and 129 to 133 (inclusive)" there shall be substituted the words "125, 129 to 133 (inclusive) and 136".

6. In Article 20—

    (i) in paragraph (*a*), for the words "in paragraph (*p*)" there shall be substituted the words "in paragraphs (*p*) and (*q*)"; and

---

(a) 1972 c. 20.   (b) S.I. 1973/1101 (1973 II, p. 3343).
(c) There is no relevant amending Order.

(ii) after paragraph (*p*) there shall be added the following paragraph—

"(*q*) where an abnormal indivisible load consists of engineering plant from which one or more constituent parts have been detached, such abnormal indivisible load and such constituent parts may be carried:

Provided that—

(i) no dimension of such constituent parts protrudes beyond any dimension of the vehicle or combination of vehicles on which such abnormal indivisible load and such constituent parts are being carried to an extent greater than such abnormal indivisible load would protrude if it were being carried without such constituent parts;

(ii) such abnormal indivisible load and such constituent parts are loaded at the same place and have the same destination; and

(iii) the sum of the weights transmitted to the road surface by all the wheels of the vehicle or vehicles carrying such abnormal indivisible load and such constituent parts does not exceed 76,200 kilograms.".

7. In Article 21, in paragraph (*f*), for the words "119 and 120" there shall be substituted the words "119, 120 and 136".

8. In Article 27, for sub-paragraph (*a*) of paragraph (1), there shall be substituted the following sub-paragraph—

"(*a*) the overall width of a vehicle the use of which on roads is authorised by Article 20 or 21 of this Order or of the vehicle together with the width of any lateral projection or projections of its load exceeds 2·9 metres, or".

Signed by authority of
the Secretary of State.
2nd February 1976.

Hugh Ellis-Rees,
An Under Secretary in the
Department of the Environment.

EXPLANATORY NOTE

(This Note is not part of the Order.)

This Order makes further amendments to the Motor Vehicles (Authorisation of Special Types) General Order 1973.

These amendments—

(i) bring within the provisions as to a vehicle carrying or drawing an abnormal indivisible load such a load consisting of partly dismantled engineering plant together with the parts which have been dismantled from it (Article 6);

(ii) bring certain special types of vehicle within the restrictions as to the number of trailers which may be drawn (Articles 3, 5 and 7); and

(iii) remove certain variations in the widths of loads the transport of which requires prior notice to be given to the police (Articles 4 and 8).

STATUTORY INSTRUMENTS

1976 No. 324

SUGAR

The Sugar Beet (Research and Education) Order 1976

Made - - - -	*1st March* 1976
Laid before Parliament	*10th March* 1976
Coming into Operation	*1st April* 1976

The Minister of Agriculture, Fisheries and Food in exercise of the powers conferred upon him by section 18(1) and (2) of the Sugar Act 1956(a), and of all other powers enabling him in that behalf, after consultation with the British Sugar Corporation Limited and with such bodies as in his opinion are substantially representative of growers of home-grown beet and having prepared a programme for carrying out research and education in matters affecting the growing of home-grown beet, hereby makes the following order:—

1.—(1) This order, which applies in England and Wales only, may be cited as the Sugar Beet (Research and Education) Order 1976, and shall come into operation on 1st April 1976.

(2) The Interpretation Act 1889(b) shall apply to the interpretation of this order as it applies to the interpretation of an Act of Parliament.

2. The programme of research and education set out in the Schedule to this order together with the expenditure estimated to be incurred in carrying it out shall be the programme for the year beginning on 1st April 1976.

3. The contributions from the British Sugar Corporation Limited (hereinafter referred to as "the Corporation") and every grower of home-grown beet who delivers beet to the Corporation during the year beginning on 1st April 1976, towards defraying the expenditure to be incurred in carrying out the aforesaid programme shall be assessed as follows:—

(a) in the case of any grower of home-grown beet, the contribution shall be at the rate of 6.25p for every tonne of home-grown beet sold by him for delivery to the Corporation in that year;

(b) in the case of the Corporation the contribution shall be at the rate of 6.25p for every tonne of home-grown beet purchased by them for delivery in that year.

4.—(1) All contracts made between the Corporation and any grower for the sale of home-grown beet for delivery to the Corporation during the year beginning on 1st April 1976 shall provide that the total amount of the grower's contribution assessed in accordance with the foregoing provisions of this order shall be payable by the grower to the Corporation out of any sums standing to the credit of that grower in account with the Corporation and be deducted by the Corporation from the amount payable to the grower.

(a) 1956 c. 48. (b) 1889 c. 63.

(2) The Corporation shall pay the proceeds, together with the amount of the contribution from the Corporation assessed in accordance with sub-paragraph (b) of Article 3 of this order, to the Minister of Agriculture, Fisheries and Food by 30th April 1977.

5. The amount of any contribution which has not been paid to the Minister of Agriculture, Fisheries and Food by the date when it is due shall become a debt due to that Minister.

In Witness whereof the Official Seal of the Minister of Agriculture, Fisheries and Food is hereunto affixed on 1st March 1976.

(L.S.)

Frederick Peart,
Minister of Agriculture, Fisheries and Food.

SCHEDULE

Projects of research and education in matters affecting the growing of home-grown beet to be carried out by the persons or bodies described in relation thereto and estimates of expenditure to be incurred in carrying them out.

	£	£
A. RESEARCH		
1. Plant Breeding: Plant Breeding Institute, Cambridge	139,468	
2. Variety Trials: National Institute of Agricultural Botany, Cambridge	18,520	
3. Disease Investigations, Fertiliser and Seed Production Experiments: Broom's Barn Experimental Station ..	242,353	
4. Crop Husbandry: Norfolk Agricultural Station ..	36,688	
5. Machinery Experiments: National Institute of Agricultural Engineering	17,868	
6. Agronomy: School of Agriculture, University of Nottingham	10,540	
7. Physiology: Rothamsted Experimental Station ..	18,450	
		483,887
B. EDUCATION		
8. British Sugar Corporation Ltd.— Publicity:		
(a) British Sugar Beet Review	19,600	
(b) Films	1,080	
(c) Virus Yellows	2,700	
		23,380
Demonstrations:		
(d) Cultivation	71,132	
(e) Spring Demonstration ..	8,100	
(f) Autumn Demonstration	8,100	
		87,332
Audit Fee ..		432
C. GENERAL		
9. Travelling and Subsistence Expenses of Members and Officers of the Sugar Beet Research and Education Committee and its sub-committees		800
10. Administrative Charges:		
(a) Ministry of Agriculture, Fisheries and Food	3,949	
(b) Exchequer and Audit Department ..	335	
		4,284
11. Institut International de Recherches Betteravières:		
(a) Subscriptions ..	6,000	
(b) Expenses and Visits ..	5,400	
		11,400
12. Other Items		
(a) Visits Abroad..	450	
(b) Contingencies..	1,500	
		1,950
Total ..		£613,465

EXPLANATORY NOTE
(This Note is not part of the Order.)

This Order, which applies in England and Wales only, provides for the assessment and collection of contributions for the year beginning on 1st April 1976 from the British Sugar Corporation Limited and from growers of home-grown beet towards the programme of research and education set out in the schedule to the order. The contributions are increased from 5p per ton to 6.25p per tonne.

STATUTORY INSTRUMENTS

1976   No. 328

SOCIAL SECURITY

The Social Security (Unemployment, Sickness and Invalidity Benefit) Amendment Regulations 1976

Made	-	-	-	*2nd March* 1976
Laid before Parliament				*10th March* 1976
Coming into Operation				*31st March* 1976

The Secretary of State for Social Services, in exercise of the powers conferred upon her by section 17(2)(*a*) of the Social Security Act 1975(**a**) and of all other powers enabling her in that behalf, hereby makes the following regulations which provide only that a day in respect of which there is payable a particular description of any payment to which section 112 of the Employment Protection Act 1975(**b**) applies shall not be treated as a day of unemployment for the purposes of entitlement to unemployment benefit:—

Citation, interpretation and commencement

1. These regulations, which may be cited as the Social Security (Unemployment, Sickness and Invalidity Benefit) Amendment Regulations 1976, shall be read as one with the Social Security (Unemployment, Sickness and Invalidity Benefit) Regulations 1975(**c**) (hereinafter referred to as "the principal regulations") and shall come into operation on 31st March 1976.

Amendment of Regulation 7 of the principal regulations

2. Regulation 7 of the principal regulations (days not to be treated as days of unemployment or incapacity for work) shall be amended by the insertion, after sub-paragraph (*k*) of paragraph (1) of that regulation, of the following sub-paragraph:—

"(*l*) a day shall not be treated as a day of unemployment in relation to any person if it is a day in respect of which there is payable to that person—

(i) a guarantee payment under section 22 of the Employment Protection Act 1975 or under a collective agreement or a wages order having regard to which the appropriate Minister has made an exemption order under section 28 of that Act, or a guarantee payment under a collective agreement or under a wages order referred to in the said section 28 where that person has an obligation in connection with such agreement or order to place his services at the disposal of an employer on that day; or

(ii) remuneration under section 29 of the Employment Protection Act 1975 while he is suspended from work on medical grounds; or

---

(a) 1975 c. 14.   (b) 1975 c. 71.   (c) S.I. 1975/564 (1975 I, p. 2062).

(iii) an amount specified by an industrial tribunal, on making an order under section 71 or 78 of the Employment Protection Act 1975 for reinstatement or re-engagement, as payable to that person or an amount awarded to that person under section 72 or 80 of that Act as compensation for unfair dismissal or for non-compliance with an order under section 78 (7) or (8) of that Act, where either of those amounts includes a sum representing remuneration which the industrial tribunal considers he might reasonably be expected to have had for that day but for the dismissal, so however that this provision shall not apply to any day which does not fall within the period of one year from the date of registration of the order by the industrial tribunal; or

(iv) an amount specified by an industrial tribunal, on making an order under section 78 or 80 of the Employment Protection Act 1975 for interim relief pending determination of a claim for unfair dismissal, as payable to that person by way of pay in respect of a pay period which includes that day; or

(v) remuneration under a protective award made under section 101 of the Employment Protection Act 1975 or an amount ordered to be paid under section 103 of that Act.".

Barbara Castle,
Secretary of State for Social Services.

2nd March 1976.

EXPLANATORY NOTE

(This Note is not part of the Regulations.)

These Regulations amend the Social Security (Unemployment, Sickness and Invalidity Benefit) Regulations 1975 so as to provide that a day, in respect of which there is payable to a person certain payments to which section 112 of the Employment Protection Act 1975 applies, shall not be treated as a day of unemployment for the purposes of entitlement to unemployment benefit and, as this provision is the only one made by these Regulations, by virtue of the said section 112, they are not required to be, and have not been, referred to the National Insurance Advisory Committee.

STATUTORY INSTRUMENTS

1976 No. 329

TRANSPORT

The National Freight Corporation (Commencing Capital Debt) Order 1976

Made - - - -	*1st March* 1976
Laid before the House of Commons	*8th March* 1976
Coming into Operation	*29th March* 1976

The Secretary of State for the Environment, with the approval of the Treasury, hereby makes this Order in exercise of the powers conferred by paragraphs 1 and 4 of Schedule 2 to the Transport Act 1968 **(a)** and now vested in him **(b)** and of all other enabling powers:—

1. This Order shall come into operation on 29th March 1976 and may be cited as the National Freight Corporation (Commencing Capital Debt) Order 1976.

2. The amount of the commencing capital debt of the National Freight Corporation due to the Secretary of State, shall be £98,096,733.

John Gilbert,

Minister for Transport,
Department of the Environment.

Signed by authority of
the Secretary of State,
27th February 1976.

We approve the making of this Order.

Donald R. Coleman,

James A. Dunn,

1st March 1976.

Two of the Lords Commissioners
of Her Majesty's Treasury.

(a) 1968 c. 73.   (b) SI 1970/1681 (1970 III, p.5551).

EXPLANATORY NOTE

(This Note is not part of the Order.)

This Order fixes the commencing capital debt of the National Freight Corporation at £98,096,733. The sum represents the assets taken over by the National Freight Corporation from the Transport Holding Company and the British Railways Board under sections 4, 5 and 53 of the Transport Act 1968.

STATUTORY INSTRUMENTS

1976 No. 330 (C.10)

COMMUNITY LAND

The Community Land Act 1975 (First Appointed Day) (England and Wales) Order 1976

Made -   -   -   -   *1st March* 1976

The Secretary of State for the Environment, in relation to England, and the Secretary of State for Wales, in relation to Wales, in exercise of the powers conferred on them by sections 7(1) and (2) and 53(2) of the Community Land Act 1975(a), and of all other powers enabling them in that behalf, hereby order as follows:—

1. This order may be cited as the Community Land Act 1975 (First Appointed Day) (England and Wales) Order 1976.

2. The Interpretation Act 1889(b) shall apply for the interpretation of this order as it applies for the interpretation of an Act of Parliament.

3. In England and Wales the first appointed day for the purposes of the Community Land Act 1975 shall be 6th April 1976.

John Silkin,
Signed by authority of   Minister for Planning and Local Government,
the Secretary of State,   Department of the Environment.
25th February 1976.

John Morris,
1st March 1976.   Secretary of State for Wales.

(a) 1975 c. 77.   (b) 1889 c. 63.

EXPLANATORY NOTE

(This Note is not part of the Order.)

This Order appoints 6th April 1976 as the first appointed day in England and Wales for the purposes of the Community Land Act 1975. The main provisions where this expression appears are listed in Part I of Schedule 2 to the Act as follows:

Provision of Act	Subject Matter
Section 15	Powers of acquisition and appropriation
Section 17	General duties of authorities
Sections 19 and 20	Planning permission for relevant development
Sections 23 and 24	Disposal notification areas
Section 48	Reserve powers

Section 7(2) of the Act requires that the first appointed day should not be earlier than the first date when a draft of regulations under section 3 of the Act excepting one or more classes of development from relevant development has been approved by resolution of each House of Parliament. Such a draft was approved by a resolution of the House of Commons on 2nd February 1976 and by a resolution of the House of Lords on 17th February 1976.

STATUTORY INSTRUMENTS

1976 No. 331

COMMUNITY LAND

The Community Land (Excepted Development) Regulations 1976

Laid before Parliament in draft

Made - - - - *1st March* 1976

Coming into Operation *6th April* 1976

The Secretary of State for the Environment, in relation to England, the Secretary of State for Scotland, in relation to Scotland, and the Secretary of State for Wales, in relation to Wales, in exercise of the powers conferred on them by sections 3(2) and 53(2) of the Community Land Act 1975(a), and of all other powers enabling them in that behalf, hereby make the following regulations in the terms of a draft which has been laid before and approved by a resolution of each House of Parliament:—

Citation and commencement

1. These regulations may be cited as the Community Land (Excepted Development) Regulations 1976 and shall come into operation on 6th April 1976.

Interpretation

2.—(1) In these regulations, unless the context otherwise requires—

"the Act" means the Community Land Act 1975;

"builder or developer of residential or industrial property" means any person carrying on a business which—

    (*a*) consists wholly or mainly of the carrying out of building operations or of building and engineering operations and includes the building of dwelling-houses or industrial buildings, or

    (*b*) consists wholly or mainly of building, or arranging for the building of, dwelling-houses or industrial buildings, and of selling, feuing or letting them;

"building" includes part of a building;

(a) 1975 c. 77.

"industrial building" has in relation to England and Wales the meaning assigned to it by section 66 of the Act of 1971 and in relation to Scotland the meaning assigned to it by section 64 of the Scottish Act of 1972;

"industrial undertaker" in relation to England and Wales means any person carrying on any such process or research as is mentioned in section 66(1) of the Act of 1971 and in relation to Scotland means any person carrying on any such process or research as is mentioned in section 64(1) of the Scottish Act of 1972.

(2) Any expression not referred to in paragraph (1) above which is used in these regulations and which is also used in the Act shall, unless the context otherwise requires, have the same meaning as it has in the Act.

(3) In these regulations any reference to the time when planning permission is or was granted, in the case of planning permission granted on an appeal, is a reference to the time of the decision appealed against or, in the case of planning permission granted on an appeal in the circumstances mentioned in section 37 of the Act of 1971 or section 34 of the Scottish Act of 1972, a reference to the time when in accordance with that section notification of the decision is or was deemed to have been received.

(4) For the purposes of these regulations a material interest in land shall be treated as owned by any person at any time if, at that time, that person has or had entered into a binding contract for its acquisition.

(5) For the purposes of these regulations if at any time a company is

(a) a member of a group of companies for any of the purposes of the Income and Corporation Taxes Act 1970(a), and

(b) a builder or developer of residential or industrial property or, as the case may be, an industrial undertaker,

then all the companies who are (at that time) members of that group of companies shall, at that time, be deemed to be builders or developers of industrial or residential property or, as the case may be, industrial undertakers.

(6) For the purposes of these regulations the amount of the gross floor space in or to be comprised in a building shall be ascertained by external measurement of that space whether or not the building is to be bounded (wholly or partly) by external walls.

(7) References in these regulations to any enactment shall, except where the context otherwise requires, be construed as references to that enactment as amended or extended by or under any other enactment.

(8) The Interpretation Act 1889(b) shall apply for the interpretation of these regulations as it applies for the interpretation of an Act of Parliament.

Excepted Development

3. The classes of development described in the Schedule to these Regulations are prescribed for the purposes of section 3(2)(c) of the Act so that development of such classes is excepted from the definition of "relevant development" contained in section 3(2) of the Act.

(a) 1970 c. 10.   (b) 1889 c. 63.

SCHEDULE

PART I

EXCEPTED DEVELOPMENT

Class 1

Any development the carrying out of which is authorised by planning permission granted on or before 12th September 1974.

Class 2

Development consisting wholly or mainly of the building of dwelling-houses or industrial buildings on any land so long as—

(*a*) during the whole of the period beginning with 12th September 1974 and ending with the relevant time, the freehold of that land has been owned by a builder or developer of residential or industrial property (but not necessarily the same builder or developer of residential or industrial property throughout), and

(*b*) notice in the appropriate form as set out in Part II of this Schedule (or in a form substantially to the like effect) was given to any one of the authorities whose areas include the land by a builder or developer of residential or industrial property who, at the time of giving such notice, owned the freehold of the land described in that notice, and the notice was received by that authority not later than 5th October 1976, or where application is made before that date for planning permission to carry out the development not later than whichever of the following dates is appropriate (if it is earlier than 5th October 1976)—

(i) if it appears from a certificate under section 27 of the Act of 1971 or section 24 of the Scottish Act of 1972 that notices have been served or published under either of those sections, the date of expiration of a period of 21 days beginning with the date appearing from the certificate to be the latest of the dates of service of notices as mentioned in the certificate, or with the date of publication of a notice as therein mentioned, whichever is the later, or

(ii) if it appears from the certificate mentioned in (i) above that no such notices as therein mentioned have been served or published, the date of the application.

Class 3

The erection of any number of industrial buildings on any land so long as during the whole of the period beginning with 12th September 1974 and ending with the relevant time, a material interest in that land has been owned by an industrial undertaker (but not necessarily the same industrial undertaker throughout).

Class 4

The erection of one or more industrial buildings so long as the gross floor space or the aggregate of the gross floor space to be comprised in that building or those buildings does not exceed 1,500 sq. metres.

Class 5

The erection of one or more buildings other than any industrial building so long as the gross floor space or the aggregate of the gross floor space to be comprised in that building or those buildings does not exceed 1,000 sq. metres.

Class 6

The erection on any land of one or more buildings to be used for agriculture.

Class 7

The rebuilding or the enlargement, improvement or other alteration of any building which was in existence at the relevant time, or of any building which was in existence in the period of 10 years immediately preceding the relevant time but was destroyed or demolished before that time, so long as the gross floor space to be comprised in the building as proposed to be rebuilt, enlarged, improved or altered under this class does not exceed by more than 10 per cent the gross floor space comprised in the building before rebuilding, enlargement, improvement or alteration.

For the purposes of this class—

(*a*) the erection, on land within the curtilage of a building, of an additional building to be used in connection with that building, shall be treated as the enlargement of that building, and

(*b*) where any two or more buildings comprised in the same curtilage are used as one unit for the purposes of any institution or undertaking, the reference in this class to the gross floor space comprised in the building shall be construed as a reference to the aggregate of the gross floor space comprised in those buildings.

Class 8

Any development on any land the freehold in which is owned by the Scottish Development Agency or the Welsh Development Agency.

Class 9

Any development on any land which is operational land of statutory undertakers or would be such land if it were used or held by statutory undertakers for the purposes of the development.

Class 10

Any development for which planning permission would be granted by a general development order for the time being in force but for a condition imposed in any planning permission granted or deemed to be granted otherwise than by such an order, and which is carried out so as to comply with any condition or limitation subject to which planning permission would be so granted.

Class 11

Any development so long as—

(*a*) it does not include the erection of a building, and

(*b*) it is not wholly or mainly connected with and ancillary to the use of one or more buildings not in existence at the relevant time and whose erection would constitute relevant development.

Class 12

Any development consisting of development in any two or more of classes 1-11 inclusive so long as it does not include any development solely in class 4 or class 5.

Class 13

Any development consisting of development in any two or more of classes 1-11 inclusive so long as it does not include any development solely in class 7.

PART II

FORM OF NOTICE (LAND IN ENGLAND AND WALES)

COMMUNITY LAND ACT 1975

NOTICE BY BUILDER OR DEVELOPER OF OWNERSHIP OF LAND ON 12TH SEPTEMBER 1974

To: (insert name and address of authority)

On 12th September 1974 the land described in the Schedule to this notice and delineated on the plan attached hereto was in the freehold ownership of the builder or developer of residential or industrial property named in the Schedule and is now in our freehold ownership.

Signed

on behalf of (insert name and address of the builder or developer of residential or industrial property)

Date

Schedule

1. Description of land.

2. Name and address of builder or developer of residential or industrial property who were freehold owners of the land on 12th September 1974.

Note: Land is treated as being in the freehold ownership of any person at any time if, at that time, that person has entered into a binding contract for the acquisition of the freehold.

FORM OF NOTICE (LAND IN SCOTLAND)

COMMUNITY LAND ACT 1975

NOTICE BY BUILDER OR DEVELOPER OF OWNERSHIP OF LAND IN SCOTLAND ON 12TH SEPTEMBER 1974

To: (insert name and address of authority)

On 12th September 1974 the land described in the Schedule to this notice and delineated on the plan attached hereto was in the ownership of the builder or developer of residential or industrial property named in the Schedule and is now in our ownership.

Signed

on behalf of (insert name and address of builder or developer of residential or industrial property)

Date

Schedule

1. Description of land.

2. Name and address of builder or developer of residential or industrial property who was owner of the land on 12th September 1974.

Note: Land is treated as being in the ownership of any person at any time if, at that time, that person has entered into a binding contract for the acquisition of the land.

Signed by authority of
the Secretary of State.
25th February 1976.

John Silkin,
Minister for Planning and Local Government,
Department of the Environment.

26th February 1976.

William Ross,
Secretary of State for Scotland.

1st March 1976.

John Morris,
Secretary of State for Wales.

EXPLANATORY NOTE

(This Note is not part of the Regulations.)

Various provisions of the Community Land Act 1975 (eg. sections 17-24, Schedules 6, 7 and 8, and the definition of "development land" in section 3(1)) depend for their effect on the meaning of "relevant development".

Section 3(2) of the Act defines "relevant development" as meaning any development except

(*a*) development of any class specified in Schedule 1 to the Act,

(*b*) development consisting exclusively of the building of a single dwelling-house, and

(*c*) development of such class or classes as may be prescribed by regulations.

These Regulations prescribe the classes of development which are excepted from the definition of "relevant development" in section 3 of the Act.

STATUTORY INSTRUMENTS

1976 No. 332

OFFSHORE INSTALLATIONS

The Continental Shelf (Protection of Installations) Order 1976

Made - - - -	1*st March* 1976
Laid before Parliament	5*th March* 1976
Coming into Operation	25*th March* 1976

The Secretary of State, in exercise of powers conferred by sections 2(1) and (3) of the Continental Shelf Act 1964**(a)** (hereinafter referred to as "the Act") and now vested in him**(b)**, hereby orders as follows:—

1.—(1) This Order may be cited as the Continental Shelf (Protection of Installations) Order 1976 and shall come into operation on 25th March 1976.

(2) The Interpretation Act 1889**(c)** shall apply to the interpretation of this Order as it applies to the interpretation of an Act of Parliament and as if this Order and the Orders hereby revoked were Acts of Parliament.

(3) The Continental Shelf (Protection of Installations) Orders specified in Schedule 1 hereto are hereby revoked.

2.—(1) Subject to paragraph (2) of this Article, ships are prohibited from entering, without the consent of the Secretary of State, those areas (hereinafter referred to as "safety zones") specified in Schedule 2 hereto (being parts of areas designated by Orders in Council made under section 1(7) of the Act).

(2) Nothing in paragraph (1) of this Article shall apply to prohibit a ship from entering a safety zone:

(*a*) in connection with the laying, inspection, testing, repair, alteration, renewal or removal of any submarine cable or pipe-line in or near that safety zone;

(*b*) to provide services for, to transport persons or goods to or from, or under the authority of a government department to inspect, an installation in that safety zone;

(*c*) if it is a ship belonging to a general lighthouse authority and it enters to perform duties relating to the safety of navigation;

(*d*) when carrying out movements with a view to saving or attempting to save life or property;

(a) 1964 c. 29.
(b) S.I. 1969/1498, 1970/1537 (1969 III, p. 4797; 1970 III, p. 5293).
(c) 1889 c. 63.

(*e*) owing to stress of weather; or

(*f*) when in distress.

John Smith,
Minister of State,
1st March 1976. Department of Energy.

SCHEDULE 1

CONTINENTAL SHELF (PROTECTION OF INSTALLATIONS) ORDERS REVOKED

The Continental Shelf (Protection of Installations) (No. 6) Order 1973 S.I. 1973/284

The Continental Shelf (Protection of Installations) (No. 7) Order 1975 S.I. 1975/511

The Continental Shelf (Protection of Installations) (No. 8) Order 1975 S.I. 1975/981

The Continental Shelf (Protection of Installations) (No. 9) Order 1975 S.I. 1975/1080

SCHEDULE 2

SAFETY ZONES

The areas being within a radius of 500 metres of each of the points having the following co-ordinates of latitude and longitude according to European Datum (1950) set out respectively in columns 2 and 3 of the table below so far as they comprise part of any designated area.

TABLE

European Datum (1950)

	Latitude North	Longitude East
1.	53 42′ 12″	01° 09′ 00″
2.	53 43′ 09″	01° 07′ 09″
3.	53 42′ 23″	01° 07′ 17″
4.	52 59′ 58″	01° 50′ 52″
5.	53 05′ 23″	02° 07′ 48″
6.	53 03′ 18″	02° 13′ 58″
7.	53 01′ 03″	01° 47′ 45″
8.	53 01′ 41″	02° 15′ 23″
9.	53 03′ 08″	02° 17′ 05″
10.	53 21′ 50″	02° 34′ 07″
11.	53 04′ 35″	02° 11′ 05″
12.	53 45′ 13″	01° 04′ 52″
13.	53 04′ 52″	02° 10′ 55″
14.	53 05′ 48″	02° 09′ 46″
15.	53 19′ 38″	02° 37′ 55″
16.	53 32′ 04″	02° 15′ 27″
17.	53 00′ 34″	02° 11′ 10″
18.	53 16′ 50″	02° 41′ 30″
19.	53 01′ 03″	02° 20′ 23″
20.	53 03′ 39″	02° 12′ 39″
21.	53 19′ 23″	02° 34′ 29″
22.	53 03′ 10″	01° 41′ 15″
23.	53° 26′ 50″	02° 19′ 59″
24.	53 23′ 31″	02° 31′ 28″
25.	53° 02′ 26″	02° 18′ 54″
26.	53° 25′ 26″	02° 22′ 36″
27.	53° 26′ 31″	02° 23′ 42″
28.	57 43′ 56″	00° 58′ 21″
29.	53° 49′ 30″	00° 28′ 17″
30.	53° 29′ 50″	02° 19′ 32″
31.	57° 43′ 38″	00° 50′ 50″
32.	53° 26′ 01″	02° 09′ 18″
33.	56° 24′ 01″	02° 03′ 48″
34.	56° 22′ 52″	02° 03′ 42″
35.	53° 26′ 53″	02° 15′ 21″
36.	56° 10′ 41″	02° 46′ 52″
37.	57° 44′ 58″	00° 54′ 54″
38.	58° 28′ 01″	00° 15′ 36″
39.	59° 32′ 44″	01° 32′ 16″
40.	57° 43′ 21″	00° 54′ 12″
41.	56° 10′ 27″	02° 49′ 02″
42.	53° 05′ 52″	01° 45′ 56″
43.	59° 52′ 42″	02° 03′ 54″
44.	59° 52′ 54″	02° 03′ 21″
45.	59° 52′ 31″	02° 03′ 42″
46.	61° 03′ 21″	01° 42′ 47″
47.	61° 03′ 55″	01° 46′ 10″
48.	57° 27′ 02″	01° 23′ 16″

EXPLANATORY NOTE

(This Note is not part of the Order.)

This Order specifies as safety zones certain areas (being areas within any designated area and within a radius of 500 metres of offshore installations) and prohibits ships from entering such zones except with the permission of the Secretary of State or in the circumstances provided for in Article 2(2).

This Order replaces all previous Orders, in force immediately before the making of this Order, made under section 2(1) of the Continental Shelf Act 1964 and specifies in paragraphs 39 to 48 of Schedule 2, ten additional safety zones.

STATUTORY INSTRUMENTS

1976 No. 333 (S. 24)

LEGAL AID AND ADVICE, SCOTLAND

The Legal Aid (Scotland) (General) Amendment Regulations 1976

Made - - -	*2nd March* 1976
Laid before Parliament	*10th March* 1976
Coming into Operation	*30th March* 1976

In exercise of the powers conferred on me by section 15 of the Legal Aid (Scotland) Act 1967 (**a**) and of all other powers enabling me in that behalf, and with the concurrence of the Treasury, I hereby make the following regulations:—

1.—(1) These regulations may be cited as the Legal Aid (Scotland) (General) Amendment Regulations 1976 and shall come into operation on 30th March 1976.

(2) The Interpretation Act 1889 (**b**) shall apply for the interpretation of these regulations as it applies for the interpretation of an Act of Parliament.

(3) In these regulations a regulation referred to by number means a regulation so numbered in the Legal Aid (Scotland) (General) Regulations 1960 (**c**), as amended (**d**).

2. In the Arrangement of Regulations at the beginning of the Legal Aid (Scotland) (General) Regulations 1960, as amended, in place of "4A. Applications for legal aid in connection with proceedings before the National Industrial Relations Court" there shall be substituted "4A. Applications for legal aid in connection with proceedings before the Employment Appeal Tribunal."

3. The following regulation shall be substituted for regulation 3 (2):—

"(2) For the purpose of subsection (4) of section 3 of the Act the expression 'property' shall be taken not to include any moneys payable under an order made by the Employment Appeal Tribunal established under section 87 of the Employment Protection Act 1975 (**e**)."

4. The following regulation shall be substituted for regulation 4A:—

"*Applications for legal aid in connection with proceedings before the Employment Appeal Tribunal.*

(**a**) 1967 c. 43.   (**b**) 1889 c. 63.   (**c**) S.I. 1960/2195 (1960 II, p. 1817).

(**d**) The relevant amending instrument is S.I. 1973/2125 (1973 III, p. 7313).

(**e**) 1975 c. 71.

4A.—(1) In this regulation the expression 'the Employment Appeal Tribunal' means the Employment Appeal Tribunal established under section 87 of the Employment Protection Act 1975 and the expression 'the Registrar of the tribunal' means the person appointed to be Registrar of the Employment Appeal Tribunal and includes any officer of the Employment Appeal Tribunal authorised to act on behalf of the Registrar.

(2) Except in so far as otherwise provided by this regulation, these regulations shall apply to applications for legal aid in connection with proceedings in the Employment Appeal Tribunal in like manner as they apply to applications for legal aid in connection with proceedings in any other court.

(3) (a) Where it appears to the appropriate committee that an application for legal aid relates to proceedings which are likely to be conducted in England and Wales they shall transmit the application forthwith to the Law Society in England and Wales and shall notify the applicant and his solicitor that they have done so.

(b) Where it appears to the appropriate committee doubtful whether the proceedings to which an application for a certificate relates will be conducted in Scotland or in England and Wales, they shall request the Registrar of the tribunal to determine that question and that determination shall be binding upon the committee.

(4) Where a certificate has been issued and there is a change of circumstances regarding the conduct of proceedings in that, by direction of the Employment Appeal Tribunal, they will be wholly or partly conducted in England and Wales, the assisted person's certificate shall remain in force and he may continue to be represented for the proceedings in England and Wales by the solicitor and counsel, if any, who represented him in Scotland; and any counsel subsequently appointed to represent him may be selected from the appropriate list of counsel willing to act for assisted persons which is maintained by the Society.

(5) Where on the coming into force of these regulations a certificate has been granted in respect of an appeal to the Court of Session from a decision of an industrial tribunal and that appeal has been transferred to the Employment Appeal Tribunal in pursuance of any order made by virtue of paragraph 9 of Schedule 17 of the Employment Protection Act 1975, the certificate shall be deemed to have been granted in respect of an appeal to the Employment Appeal Tribunal."

5. For regulation **8** (2) there shall be substituted the following:—
"(2) Where a legal aid certificate is suspended or discharged by a Committee acting under the powers given to them by these regulations or by paragraphs (5) or (6) of article 16 of the Legal Aid (Scotland) Scheme 1958, or by paragraphs (5) or (6) of article 8 of the Legal Aid (Scotland) (House of Lords) Scheme 1960, or by paragraphs (5) or (6) of article 9 of the Legal Aid (Scottish Land Court) Scheme 1971 or by paragraphs (5) or (6) of article 9 of the Legal Aid (Lands Tribunal for Scotland) Scheme 1971 or paragraphs (5) or (6) of article 9 of the Legal Aid (Scotland) (Restrictive Practices Court) Scheme 1973 or paragraphs (5) or (6) of article 9 of the Legal Aid (Scotland) (Employment Appeal Tribunal) Scheme 1976 or under a direction given by a court under Rule 5 of the Act of Sederunt (Legal Aid Rules) 1958 **(a)**, as amended **(b)**, or

---

(a) S.I. 1958/1872 (1958 I, p. 389).   (b) S.I. 1971/174 (1971 I, p. 530).

otherwise, the assisted person shall remain liable to pay to the Society so much of his contribution as is required to defray the expenses incurred up to the date of suspension or discharge: Provided that where a certificate is discharged under paragraph (6) of article 16 of the Legal Aid (Scotland) Scheme 1958 or paragraph (6) of article 8 of the Legal Aid (Scotland) (House of Lords) Scheme 1960 or paragraph (6) of article 9 of the Legal Aid (Scottish Land Court) Scheme 1971 or paragraph (6) of article 9 of the Legal Aid (Lands Tribunal for Scotland) Scheme 1971 or paragraph (6) of article 9 of the Legal Aid (Scotland) (Restrictive Practices Court) Scheme 1973 or paragraph (6) of article 9 of the Legal Aid (Scotland) (Employment Appeal Tribunal) Scheme 1976 or the direction of a court requiring discharge of a certificate is given under sub-paragraph (c) of paragraph (1) of the said rule 5 or where, in any other case, a court so directs, the Society shall have the right to recover from the person by whom the certificate was held any sum over and above the amount of his contribution which may be required to meet the sums paid or payable by the Society on his account in respect of the proceedings to which the discharged certificate related".

6. For regulation **10**(5) there shall be substituted the following:—

"(5) Where, at any stage in proceedings, a party who is an assisted person ceases to receive legal aid, he shall be deemed to be an assisted person for the purpose of any award of expenses made against him only to the extent that those expenses were incurred before he ceased to receive legal aid: Provided that where an assisted person's legal aid certificate is discharged under paragraph (6) of article 16 of the Legal Aid (Scotland) Scheme 1958 or paragraph (6) of article 8 of the Legal Aid (Scotland) (House of Lords) Scheme 1960 or paragraph (6) of article 9 of the Legal Aid (Scottish Land Court) Scheme 1971 or paragraph (6) of article 9 of the Legal Aid (Lands Tribunal for Scotland) Scheme 1971 or paragraph (6) of article 9 of the Legal Aid (Scotland) (Restrictive Practices Court) Scheme 1973 or paragraph (6) of article 9 of the Legal Aid (Scotland) (Employment Appeal Tribunal) Scheme 1976 or the direction of a court requiring discharge of his certificate is given under sub-paragraph (c) of pargaraph (1) of rule 5 of the Act of Sederunt (Legal Aid Rules) 1958, the provisions of paragraph (e) of subsection (6) of section 2 of the Legal Aid (Scotland) Act 1967 shall not apply to him".

William Ross,

One of Her Majesty's Principal Secretaries of State.

New St. Andrew's House,
Edinburgh.
2nd March 1976.

We concur.

J. Dormand,

M. Cocks,

Two of the Lords Commissioners of Her Majesty's Treasury.

2nd March 1976.

EXPLANATORY NOTE

(This Note is not part of the Regulations.)

These Regulations apply the Legal Aid (Scotland) (General) Regulations 1960 to proceedings in the Employment Appeal Tribunal; and make provision for legal aid applications made in Scotland to be transferred to England and Wales if proceedings are to be conducted there, for legal aid certificates granted in Scotland to remain in force in the event of proceedings being transferred to England and Wales, and for transitional matters.

STATUTORY INSTRUMENTS

1976 No. 334

NATIONAL HEALTH SERVICE, ENGLAND AND WALES

The National Health Service (Family Practitioner Committees: Membership and Procedure) Amendment Regulations 1976

Made - - - -	*2nd March* 1976
Laid before Parliament	*11th March* 1976
Coming into Operation	*31st March* 1976

The Secretary of State for Social Services, as respects England, and the Secretary of State for Wales, as respects Wales, in exercise of powers conferred upon them by section 6(4) of, and paragraph 12 of Schedule 1 to, the National Health Service Reorganisation Act 1973(a) and of all other powers enabling them in that behalf, hereby make the following regulations:—

Citation, commencement and interpretation

1.—(1) These regulations may be cited as the National Health Service (Family Practitioner Committees: Membership and Procedure) Amendment Regulations 1976 and shall come into operation on 31st March 1976.

(2) The rules for the construction of Acts of Parliament contained in the Interpretation Act 1889(b) shall apply for the purposes of the interpretation of these regulations as they apply for the purposes of the interpretation of an Act of Parliament.

Amendment of regulations

2. The National Health Service (Family Practitioner Committees: Membership and Procedure) Regulations 1973(c) shall be amended as follows:—

(*a*) for regulation 3(1) there shall be substituted the following:—

"*Term of office of members appointed by an authority or by a local representative body*

3.—(1) Subject to the provisions of these regulations the term of office of members appointed by an Authority or by a local representative body shall be four years expiring on 31st July in any year.".

(*b*) for regulation 3(2) there shall be substituted the following:—

"(2) Where a Committee is established in England before 1st April 1977 those original members who were appointed by the relevant Authority or by any local representative body shall hold office for a period ending on 31st July 1977 and one half of the members appointed by the relevant Authority or by each local representative body whose appointments take effect from 1st August 1977 shall be

---

(a) 1973 c. 32.   (b) 1889 c. 63.
(c) S.I. 1973/2012 (1973 III, p. 6927).

appointed for a period ending on 31st July 1979 and the remainder of such members shall be appointed for a period ending on 31st July 1981.".

(c) for regulation 3(3) there shall be substituted the following:—

"(3) Where a Committee is established in Wales before 1st April 1974 one half of the original members appointed by the relevant Authority or by each local representative body shall hold office for a period ending on 31st July 1976 and the remainder of such members shall hold office for a period ending on 31st July 1978.".

(d) for regulation 3(4) there shall be substituted the following:—

"(4) Where a Committee is established in Wales after 31st March 1974 and in England after 31st March 1977 one half of the original members appointed by the relevant Authority or by each local representative body shall hold office for such a period, not exceeding two years and four months expiring on 31st July in any year as the relevant Authority shall, in the case of such Committee, determine (and such determination may be made after the date of appointment) and the remainder of such members shall be appointed for a period two years greater than the period of office of the first half of such original members.".

(e) for regulation 5(1) there shall be substituted the following:—

"*Variation of membership of Committees*

5.—(1) Where the Secretary of State has by Order provided that paragraph 6 of Schedule 1 to the Act of 1973 should apply with such modifications as are specified in the Order to a Committee established in accordance with that paragraph or where he makes an Order revoking or varying such Order as aforesaid, he may terminate the appointment of any member of the Committee as established before the date of coming into operation of the Order, and the term of office of any original member appointed in accordance with provisions taking effect upon that date shall be for such a period, not exceeding four years and four months expiring on 31st July in any year as the relevant Authority shall, in each case, determine.".

1st March 1976.
Barbara Castle,
Secretary of State for Social Services.

Signed by authority of the Secretary of State for Wales,

2nd March 1976.
Barry Jones,
Parliamentary Under-Secretary, Welsh Office.

EXPLANATORY NOTE
(*This Note is not part of the Regulations.*)

These Regulations amend the National Health Service (Family Practitioner Committees: Membership and Procedure) Regulations 1973 by altering the date of terminations of office of certain members of Family Practitioner Committees from 31st March to 31st July and by adjusting appropriately the terms of office of the original members.

STATUTORY INSTRUMENTS

1976 No. 337 (L. 6)

SUPREME COURT OF JUDICATURE, ENGLAND

PROCEDURE

The Rules of the Supreme Court (Amendment) 1976

Made - - - -	*27th February* 1976
Laid before Parliament	*10th March* 1976
Coming into Operation	*1st April* 1976

We, the Rule Committee of the Supreme Court, being the authority having for the time being power under section 99(4) of the Supreme Court of Judicature (Consolidation) Act 1925(a) to make, amend or revoke rules regulating the practice and procedure of the Supreme Court of Judicature, hereby exercise those powers and all other powers enabling us in that behalf as follows:—

1.—(1) These Rules may be cited as the Rules of the Supreme Court (Amendment) 1976 and shall come into operation on 1st April 1976.

(2) In these Rules an Order referred to by number means the Order so numbered in the Rules of the Supreme Court 1965(b), as amended(c), and Appendix A means Appendix A to those Rules.

(3) The Interpretation Act 1889(d) shall apply to the interpretation of these Rules as it applies to the interpretation of an Act of Parliament.

2. Order 1, rule 4(3), shall be revoked.

3. Order 11, rule 6(1), shall be amended as follows:—

(1) For sub-paragraphs (*b*) and (*c*) there shall be substituted the following sub-paragraphs:—
"(*b*) any independent Commonwealth country;
(*c*) any colony or protectorate".

(2) Sub-paragraph (*d*) shall be omitted and sub-paragraph (*e*) re-lettered as sub-paragraph (*d*).

4. Order 18, rule 6(3A), shall be revoked.

5. In Order 32, rule 8, for the words "second class clerk" there shall be substituted the words "executive officer".

(a) 1925 c. 49. (b) S.I. 1965/1776 (1965 III, p. 4995).
(c) The relevant amending instruments are S.I. 1967/829, 1970/1208, 1971/1269, 1972/1898 (1967 II, p. 2476; 1970 II, p. 4001; 1971 II, p. 3634; 1972 III, p. 5523).
(d) 1889 c. 63.

6. Order 39, rule 3(4), shall be amended as follows:—

(1) The words from "Unless" to "English" shall be omitted.

(2) For the words "that country" where they first appear there shall be substituted the words "the country in which the examination is to be taken".

(3) At the end there shall be added the words "unless—

(a) the senior master has given a general direction in relation to that country that no translation need be provided, or

(b) the official language or one of the official languages of that country is English.".

7. In Order 41, rule 5(1), after "4(2)" there shall be inserted the words "to Order 86, rule 2(1)".

8. Order 42, rule 1(4), and Order 45, rule 1(5), shall be revoked.

9. In Order 49, rule 2, the word "and" shall be omitted at the end of paragraph (a) and inserted at the end of paragraph (b) and after that paragraph there shall be added the following paragraph:—

"(c) stating, where the garnishee is a bank having more than one place of business, the name and address of the branch at which the judgment debtor's account is believed to be held or, if it be the case, that this information is not known to the deponent."

10. Order 56, rule 5(2), shall be amended as follows:—

(1) For the words "section 14 of the Matrimonial Proceedings and Property Act 1970" there shall be substituted the words "section 35 of the Matrimonial Causes Act 1973(**a**)".

(2) In sub-paragraph (b) after "1950" the word "or" shall be omitted and for the words "or confirmed by such a court under the last-mentioned Act" there shall be substituted the words "or the Maintenance Orders (Reciprocal Enforcement) Act 1972(**b**) or confirmed by such a court under either of the two last-mentioned Acts".

(3) For sub-paragraph (c) there shall be substituted the following sub-paragraph:—

"(c) an order for periodical or other payments made, or having effect as if made, under Part II of the Matrimonial Causes Act 1973 and registered in a magistrates' court under the Maintenance Orders Act 1958(**c**)".

11. Order 59 shall be amended as follows:—

(1) After rule 12 there shall be inserted the following rule:—

"*Non-disclosure of payment into court*

12A.—(1) Where—

(a) any question on an appeal in an action for a debt, damages or salvage relates to liability for the debt, damages or salvage or to the amount thereof, and

---

(a) 1973 c. 18.   (b) 1972 c. 18.   (c) 1958 c. 39.

(*b*) money was paid into court under Order 22, rule 1, in the proceedings in the court below before judgment,

neither the fact of the payment nor the amount thereof shall be stated in
the notice of appeal or the respondent's notice or in any supplementary
notice or be communicated to the Court of Appeal until all such questions
have been decided.

This rule shall not apply in the case of an appeal as to costs only or an
appeal in an action to which a defence of tender before action was pleaded.

(2) For the purpose of complying with this rule the appellant must
cause to be omitted from the copies of the documents lodged by him under
rules 9(*d*) and (f) every part thereof which states, or fiom which it can
be inferred, that money was paid into court in the proceedings in that court
before judgment.".

(2) In rule 19(5) after the words "a stay of" there shall be inserted the
words "execution or of", and after "the judge of that court" there
shall be inserted "or the Court of Appeal".

12. Order 62 shall be amended as follows:—

(1) In rule 9—

 (*a*) in paragraph (2) after "28" there shall be inserted "28A";
 (*b*) at the end of paragraph (4) there shall be added the words "but
  where the person entitled to such a gross sum is a litigant in
  person, rule 28A shall apply with the necessary modifications to
  the assessment of the gross sum as it applies to the taxation of the
  costs of a litigant in person".

(2) In rules 12(7) and 13, for the words "principal clerk" and "clerk",
wherever they appear, there shall be substituted the words "senior
executive officer".

(3) In rule 25 before the words "bill of costs", wherever they appear in
paragraphs (1) and (2), there shall be inserted the word "solicitor's".

(4) In rule 27 the word "solicitor's" shall be omitted and for the word
"solicitor" there shall be substituted the words "party whose bill
it is".

(5) After rule 28 there shall be inserted the following rule:—

"*Costs of a litigant in person*

 28A.—(1) On a taxation of the costs of a litigant in person there
may, subject to the provisions of this rule, be allowed such costs as
would have been allowed if the work and disbursements to which
the costs relate had been done or made by a solicitor on the litigant's
behalf.

 (2) The amount allowed in respect of any item shall be such
sum as the taxing officer thinks fit not exceeding, except in the case of
a disbursement, two-thirds of the sum which in the opinion of the
taxing officer would have been allowed in respect of that item if the
litigant had been represented by a solicitor.

 (3) Where in the opinion of the taxing officer the litigant has not
suffered any pecuniary loss in doing any work to which the costs
relate, he shall not be allowed in respect of the time reasonably
spent by him on the work more than £2 an hour.

(4) A litigant who is allowed costs in respect of attending court to conduct his own case shall not be entitled to a witness allowance in addition.

(5) Nothing in Order 6, rule 2(1)(*b*), or rule 32(4) of this Order or Appendix 3 shall apply to the costs of a litigant in person.

(6) For the purposes of this rule a litigant in person does not include a litigant who is a practising solicitor.".

13. In Part X of Appendix 2 to Order 62—

(*a*) in paragraph 1(1) after the words "subject to" there shall be inserted the words "rule 28A and to";

(*b*) in paragraph 7(2) the words "the solicitor for" shall be omitted.

14. Order 70 shall be amended as follows:—

(1) For rule 1 there shall be substituted the following rule:—

"Interpretation and exercise of jurisdiction

1.—(1) In this Order "the Act of 1975" means the Evidence (Proceedings in Other Jurisdictions) Act 1975(**a**) and expressions used in this Order which are used in that Act shall have the same meaning as in that Act.

(2) The power of the High Court to make an order under section 2 of the Act of 1975 may be exercised by a master of the Queen's Bench Division.".

(2) In rule 2—

(*a*) in paragraph (1) for the words from "Foreign Tribunals Evidence Act 1856" to "Evidence by Commission Act 1859" there shall be substituted the words "Act of 1975" and the words from "by a person" to "tribunal in question" shall be omitted;

(*b*) for paragraph (2) there shall be substituted the following paragraph:—

"(2) There shall be exhibited to the affidavit the request in pursuance of which the application is made, and if the request is not in the English language, a translation thereof in that language.";

(*c*) paragraph (3) shall be omitted.

(3) In rule 3—

(*a*) for the words "Where a letter" to "country be obtained" there shall be substituted the words "Where a request";

(*b*) for the words "pending before the" in paragraph (*a*) there shall be substituted the words "pending or contemplated before the foreign".

(*c*) for the words "Foreign Tribunals Evidence Act 1856" there shall be substituted the words "Act of 1975".

(4) In rule 4(2) after the words "Subject to" there shall be inserted the words "rule 6 and to".

(5) In paragraph (*a*) of rule 5 for the words from "the letter of request" to "the examination" there shall be substituted the words "the request", and in paragraph (*b*) for "letter of request, certificate or other document" there shall be substituted "request".

(**a**) 1975 c. 34.

(6)   After rule 5 there shall be added the following rule:—

"Claim to privilege

6.—(1) The provisions of this rule shall have effect where a claim by a witness to be exempt from giving any evidence on the ground specified in section 3(1)(*b*) of the Act of 1975 is not supported or conceded as mentioned in sub-section (2) of that section.

(2) The examiner may, if he thinks fit, require the witness to give the evidence to which the claim relates and, if the examiner does not do so the Court may do so, on the *ex parte* application of the person who obtained the order under section 2.

(3) If such evidence is taken—

(*a*) it must be contained in a document separate from the remainder of the deposition of the witness;

(*b*) the examiner shall send to the senior master with the deposition a statement signed by the examiner setting out the claim and the ground on which it was made;

(*c*) on receipt of the statement the senior master shall, notwithstanding anything in rule 5, retain the document containing the part of the witness's evidence to which the claim relates and shall send the statement and a request to determine the claim to the foreign court or tribunal with the documents mentioned in rule 5;

(*d*) if the claim is rejected by the foreign court or tribunal, the senior master shall send to that court or tribunal the document containing that part of the witness's evidence to which the claim relates, but if the claim is upheld he shall send the document to the witness, and shall in either case notify the witness and the person who obtained the order under section 2 of the court or tribunal's determination.".

15. In Order 76 after rule 15 there shall be added the following rule:—

"Probate counterclaim in other proceedings

16.—(1) In this rule "probate counterclaim" means a counterclaim in any action other than a probate action by which the defendant claims any such relief as is mentioned in rule 1(2).

(2) Subject to the following paragraphs, this Order shall apply with the necessary modifications to a probate counterclaim as it applies to a probate action.

(3) A probate counterclaim must contain a statement of the nature of the interest of the defendant and of the plaintiff in the estate of the deceased to which the counterclaim relates.

(4) Before it is served a probate counterclaim must be indorsed with a memorandum signed by a master of the Chancery Division showing that the counterclaim has been produced to him for examination and that three copies of it have been lodged with him.

(5) Unless an application under Order 15, rule 5(2), is made within seven days after the service of a probate counterclaim for the counterclaim to be

struck out and the application is granted, the Court shall, if necessary of its own motion, order the transfer of the action to the Chancery Division (if it is not already assigned to that Division) and to the Royal Courts of Justice (if it is not already proceeding there).".

16. For paragraph (1) of Order 86, rule 2, there shall be substituted the following paragraph:—

"(1) An application under rule 1 shall be made by summons supported by an affidavit verifying the facts on which the cause of action is based and stating that in the deponent's belief there is no defence to the action.

Unless the Court otherwise directs, an affidavit for the purposes of this paragraph may contain statements of information or belief with the sources and grounds thereof.".

17. Order 88, rule 3, shall be amended as follows:—

(a) In the heading the words "*in district registry*" shall be omitted.

(b) The following paragraph shall be added at the end:—

"(3) The writ or originating summons by which a mortgage action is begun shall be indorsed with or contain a statement showing—

(a) where the mortgaged property is situated, and

(b) if the plaintiff claims possession of the mortgaged property and it is situated outside Greater London, whether the property consists of or includes a dwelling house and, if so, whether the net annual value for rating of the property exceeds £1,000.".

18. In Order 94, after rule 10, there shall be inserted the following rule:—

"*Consumer Credit Act* 1974: *appeal from Secretary of State*

10A.—(1) A person who is dissatisfied in point of law with a decision of the Secretary of State for Prices and Consumer Protection on an appeal under section 41 of the Consumer Credit Act 1974(a) from a determination of the Director General of Fair Trading and had a right to appeal to the Secretary of State, whether or not he exercised that right, may appeal to the High Court.

(2) The persons to be served with notice of the originating motion by which such an appeal is brought are the Secretary of State and, where the appeal is by a licensee under a group licence against compulsory variation, suspension or revocation of that licence, the original applicant, if any; but the Court may in any case direct that the notice be served on any other person.

(3) The Court hearing the appeal may remit the matter to the Secretary of State to the extent necessary to enable him to provide the Court with such further information in connection with the matter as the Court may direct.

(4) If the Court is of the opinion that the decision appealed against was erroneous in point of law, it shall not set aside or vary that decision but shall remit the matter to the Secretary of State with the opinion of the Court for hearing and determination by him.

(5) Order 55, rule 7(5), shall not apply in relation to the appeal.".

(a) 1974 c. 39.

19.—(1) For Order 99 there shall be substituted the following Order:—

"ORDER 99

INHERITANCE (PROVISION FOR FAMILY AND DEPENDANTS)

ACT 1975

Interpretation

1. In this Order "the Act" means the Inheritance (Provision for Family and Dependants) Act 1975(a) and a section referred to by number means the section so numbered in that Act.

Assignment to Chancery or Family Division

2. Proceedings in the High Court under the Act may be assigned to the Chancery Division or to the Family Division.

Application for financial provision

3.—(1) Any originating summons by which an application under section 1 is made may be issued out of the Central Office, the principal registry of the Family Division or any district registry.

(2) No appearance need be entered to the summons.

(3) There shall be lodged with the Court an affidavit by the applicant in support of the summons, exhibiting an official copy of the grant of representation to the deceased's estate and of every testamentary document admitted to proof, and a copy of the affidavit shall be served on every defendant with the summons.

Powers of Court as to parties

4.—(1) Without prejudice to its powers under Order 15, the Court may at any stage of proceedings under the Act direct that any person be added as a party to the proceedings or that notice of the proceedings be served on any person.

(2) Order 15, rule 13, shall apply to proceedings under the Act as it applies to the proceedings mentioned in paragraph (1) of that rule.

Affidavit in answer

5.—(1) A defendant to an application under section 1 who is a personal representative of the deceased shall and any other defendant may, within 21 days after service of the summons on him, inclusive of the day of service, lodge with the Court an affidavit in answer to the application.

(2) The affidavit lodged by a personal representative pursuant to paragraph (1) shall state to the best of the deponent's ability—

   (a) full particulars of the value of the deceased's net estate, as defined by section 25(1);

   (b) the person or classes of persons beneficially interested in the estate, giving the names and (in the case of those who are not already parties) the addresses of all living beneficiaries, and the value of their interests so far as ascertained;

   (c) if such be the case, that any living beneficiary (naming him) is a minor or a patient within the meaning of Order 80, rule 1; and

   (d) any facts known to the deponent which might affect the exercise of the Court's powers under the Act.

(a) 1975 c. 63.

(3) Every defendant who lodges an affidavit shall at the same time serve a copy on the plaintiff and on every other defendant who is not represented by the same solicitor.

Separate representation

6. Where an application under section 1 is made jointly by two or more applicants and the originating summons is accordingly issued by one solicitor on behalf of all of them, they may, if they have conflicting interests, appear on any hearing of the summons by separate solicitors or counsel or in person; and where at any stage of the proceedings it appears to the Court that one of the applicants is not but ought to be separately represented, the Court may adjourn the proceedings until he is.

Endorsement of memorandum on grant

7. On the hearing of an application under section 1 the personal representative shall produce to the Court the grant of representation to the deceased's estate and, if an order is made under the Act, the grant shall remain in the custody of the Court until a memorandum of the order has been endorsed on or permanently annexed to the grant in accordance with section 19(3).

Disposal of proceedings in chambers

8. Any proceedings under the Act may, if the Court so directs, be disposed of in chambers and Order 32, rule 14(1), shall apply in relation to proceedings in the Family Division as if for the words from the beginning to "the purpose" there were substituted the words "A registrar of the Family Division shall".

Subsequent applications in proceedings under section 1

9. Where an order has been made on an application under section 1, any subsequent application under the Act, whether made by a party to the proceedings or by any other person, shall be made by summons in those proceedings.

Drawing up and service of orders

10. The provisions of the Matrimonial Causes Rules relating to the drawing up and service of orders shall apply to proceedings in the Family Division under this Order as if they were proceedings under those Rules.

Transfer to county court

11.—(1) Where an application to which section 22(1) relates is within the jurisdiction of a county court, the Court may, if the parties consent or it appears to the Court to be desirable, order the transfer of the application to such county court as appears to the Court to be most convenient to the parties.

(2) An order under paragraph (1) may be made by the Court of its own motion or on the application of any party, but before making an order of its own motion otherwise than by consent the Court shall give the parties an opportunity of being heard on the question of transfer and for that purpose the master or registrar may give the parties notice of a date, time and place at which the question will be considered.".

(2) In the title of Order 99 in the Arrangement of Orders at the beginning of the Rules of the Supreme Court 1965 for "The Inheritance (Family Provision) Act 1938" there shall be substituted "The Inheritance (Provision for Family and Dependants) Act 1975".

20. Order 110 shall be revoked and the reference to that Order in the Arrangement of Orders at the beginning of the Rules of the Supreme Court 1965 shall be omitted.

21. In Appendix A, Form 10 shall be amended as follows:—

(1) After the word "o'clock" there shall be inserted the words "[*or, if no application has yet been made for a day to be fixed*, on a day to be fixed]".

(2) The following paragraph shall be added at the end:—

"[*In the case of an application under section* 1 *of the Inheritance (Provision for Family and Dependants) Act* 1975. A defendant who is a personal representative must, within 21 days after service of this summons on him, inclusive of the day of service, lodge with the court an affidavit in answer, stating the particulars required by Order 99, rule 5, of the Rules of the Supreme Court.]".

22. In Appendix A, in Form 72, immediately above the words "Dated the
     day of   19   " there shall be inserted the following paragraph:—

"[*Add where appropriate* The name and address of the branch of the garnishee bank at which the debtor's account is believed to be held is
                                        ]."

23. In Appendix A, for Form 93 there shall be substituted the following form:—

" No. 93

Order under the Evidence (Proceedings in Other Jurisdictions) Act 1975
(O. 70, r. 1)

In the High Court of Justice

Queen's Bench Division

[*Name of Master*], master in chambers

In the matter of the Evidence (Proceedings in Other Jurisdictions) Act 1975

and

In the matter of a civil [*or* commercial *or* criminal] proceeding now pending [*or* contemplated] before [*description of court or tribunal*] entitled as follows:—

[*give title of proceedings in foreign court or tribunal or state in proceedings contemplated between   plaintiff and defendant*].

Upon reading the affidavit of   filed the   day of   19   and the request exhibited thereto and it appearing that proceedings are pending [*or* contemplated] in the [*description of foreign court or tribunal*] in [*name of country*] and that such court wishes to obtain the testimony of [*name of witness*].

It is ordered that the said witness   do attend before [*name and address of examiner*] who is hereby appointed examiner herein, at [*place appointed for examination*] on   day the   day of   19   at   o'clock, or such other day and time as the said examiner may appoint, and do there submit to be examined [*upon oath or affirmation*] touching the testimony so required as aforesaid and do then and there produce [*description of documents, if any, to be produced*].

It is also ordered that the said examiner do take down or cause to be taken down in writing the evidence of the said witness according to the rules and practice of Her Majesty's High Court of Justice pertaining to the examination and cross-examination of witnesses [*or as may be otherwise directed*], and do request the said witness [*or* each and every witness] to sign his deposition in the said examiner's presence and do sign the depositions taken in pursuance of this order, and when so completed do send them, together with this order and the request, to the [*Senior Master, Royal Courts of Justice, Strand, London WC2A 2LL*] for transmission to the court desiring the evidence of the said witness.".

24. Nothing in rules 12(1), (3) to (5) and 13 shall apply to any work done or disbursement made before 1st April 1976, and nothing in rules 19 and 21(2) shall apply to proceedings relating to the estate of a person who died before that date.

Dated 27th February 1976.

Elwyn-Jones, C.
Widgery, C. J.
Denning, M. R.
George Baker, P.
R. E. Megarry, V-C.
Eustace Roskill, L. J.
Ralph Cusack, J.
E. W. Eveleigh, J.
John Blofeld.
Christopher McCall.
H. Montgomery-Campbell.
R. K. Denby.

EXPLANATORY NOTE

(*This Note is not part of the Rules.*)

These Rules amend the Rules of the Supreme Court in consequence of a number of recent Acts. Changes are made in Orders 39 and 70 to take account of the replacement of the Foreign Tribunals Evidence Act 1856 (c. 113) and the Evidence by Commission Act 1859 (22 Vic c. 20) by the Evidence (Proceedings in Other Jurisdictions) Act 1975 (rules 6, 14 and 23). Provision is made for the costs recoverable by a litigant in person under the Litigants in Person (Costs and Expenses) Act 1975 (rules 12(1), (3) to (5) and 13). Order 99 is re-written so as to deal with proceedings under the Inheritance (Provision for Family and Dependants) Act 1975 and enable them to be brought in either the Chancery Division or the Family Division (rules 19 and 21). Provision is made for an appeal to the High Court from a decision of the Secretary of State on an application for a consumer credit licence under the Consumer Credit Act 1974 (rule 18). Order 110 is revoked in consequence of the repeal of the Limitation Act 1963 (c. 47) by the Limitation Act 1975 (c. 54) (rule 20).

Minor amendments are also made so as—

    (*a*) to revoke the rules which require claims and judgments and writs and orders for their enforcement to be expressed in decimal currency (rules 2, 4 and 8);

(*b*) to bring up to date the designation of Commonwealth countries for the purpose of service of process (rule 3);

(*c*) to substitute general Civil Service grades for old departmental grades mentioned in the Rules (rules 5 and 12(2));

(*d*) to enable a deponent to an affidavit in support of an application for summary judgment in a specific performance action to swear to the facts from his information or belief (rules 7 and 16);

(*e*) to require the applicant for a garnishee order against a bank to state in his supporting affidavit the name and address of the branch at which the judgment debtor's account is believed to be held (rules 9 and 22);

(*f*) to assign appeals against the enforcement of orders registered in magistrates' courts under the Maintenance Orders (Reciprocal Enforcement) Act 1972 to the Family Division (rule 10);

(*g*) to prevent a payment into court being disclosed to the Court of Appeal until all questions of liability and quantum have been decided (rule 11(1));

(*h*) to clarify the rules relating to stay of execution on an appeal from a county court to the Court of Appeal (rule 11(2));

(*i*) to provide for a counterclaim for probate in a non-probate action (rule 15);

(*j*) to require the originating process in a mortgage action to contain information as to the address of the property and its rateable value (rule 17).

S.O.
HMSO
£26.50
for 2